P9-DTS-129

PSYCHOLOGISTS' DESK REFERENCE

Psychologists' Desk Reference

Second Edition

Editors

Gerald P. Koocher

John C. Norcross

Sam S. Hill III

2005

OXFORD
UNIVERSITY PRESS

Oxford New York

Auckland Bangkok Buenos Aires Cape Town Chennai
Dar es Salaam Delhi Hong Kong Istanbul Karachi Kolkata
Kuala Lumpur Madrid Melbourne Mexico City Mumbai Nairobi
São Paulo Shanghai Taipei Tokyo Toronto

Published by Oxford University Press, Inc.
198 Madison Avenue, New York, New York 10016

www.oup.com

Library of Congress Cataloging-in-Publication Data
Psychologists' desk reference / editors, Gerald P. Koocher,
John C. Norcross, Sam S. Hill, III.—2nd ed.
p. cm.
Includes bibliographical references and index.
ISBN 0-19-516606-X
1. Clinical psychology—Handbooks, manuals, etc. I. Koocher, Gerald P.
II. Norcross, John C., 1957– III. Hill, Sam S.
RC467.2.P78 2004
616.89—dc22 2004046937

1 3 5 7 9 8 6 4 2

Printed in the United States of America
on acid-free paper

We dedicate this volume to
Robin C. Koocher
Nancy A. Caldwell
and
Betty Ann Pratt Hill

PREFACE

The *Psychologists' Desk Reference* is intended as an authoritative and indispensable companion of mental health practitioners of all theoretical orientations and professional disciplines. This volume compiles, organizes, and presents key guides and essential information that clinicians, from practicum students to seasoned practitioners, want on their desks. It contains diagnostic codes, test information, report checklists, practice guidelines, treatment principles, ethics refreshers, legal regulations, special-population materials, professional resources, practice management tips, and related data that all clinicians need at their fingertips.

When asked what the *Psychologists' Desk Reference* includes, we reply, "Everything essential but the tissue box." When asked who should purchase it, we reply, "Every clinician."

This new edition features:

- Thoroughly revised chapters by the field's leaders
- 29 new chapters, now totaling 140
- Elimination of 14 chapters that readers deemed dated or of too-limited utility
- Sections reorganized into smaller and more specific chunks, making topics easier to find
- A listing of valuable Internet sites in many chapters
- Increased emphasis on evidence-based practices (broadly defined)
- An accompanying Web site containing hyperlinks, graphics, PowerPoint presentations, illustrations, tables, primary sources, extensive bibliographies, and much more

A brief history of the *Psychologists' Desk Reference* places our objectives and the revised contents into proper perspective. In 1994, we sent letters to directors of psychology training programs requesting their thoughts on the contents of such a desk reference. In 1995, we surveyed members of the American Psychological Association's (APA) Division of Clinical Psychology. Over 500 practicing psychologists responded to the question, "All clinicians seem to have a file in which they place useful checklists, guidelines, and summaries. If you had such a collection at your desk, what topics would you want in it?" In addition to providing hundreds of nominations and a healthy consensus on the contents, the vast majority agreed that a *Psychologists' Desk Reference* would be both a very practical and a very popular manual for the practicing clinician. In 1996 and 1997, we inventoried the desk contents of several colleagues and interviewed dozens of practitioners regarding their preferences for a functional desk reference. In sum, the project began with an ambitious idea, was sharpened by program directors' responses, was strengthened by nominations of clinical psychologists across the nation, and was shaped by field observation and collegial feedback.

This second edition continues the years of sequential research and development. The final page of the first edition of the *Psychologists' Desk Reference* cordially invited readers to inform us of what they would like to be included in future editions. Many excellent ideas were offered in response. Published reviews of the first edition and five reviewers secured by Oxford University Press further helped to sharpen our focus. And if imitation is indeed the sincerest form of flattery, then we are flattered that the *Psychologists' Desk Reference* has spawned several imitators; not nearly as good as this volume, but imitators nonetheless.

The positive reception to the first edition convinced us to vigorously maintain our original emphasis on a compact and user-friendly resource. In the words of one reviewer, "The coverage is broad but not superficial; it is comprehensive yet focused." As a consequence, all 140 contributions are concisely written, designed as summaries or thumbnail guides. We chose only authors who possessed special expertise in particular subject areas and who manifested an ability to synthesize the material in 10 manuscript pages or less. The text is a combination of narrative text, numbered or bulleted points, tables, and checklists. The chapter titles are succinct and descriptive; subtitles were largely abandoned. The references accompanying each contribution are not intended as an exhaustive listing but, rather, as documentation of key sources and recommendations for additional reading.

The format of the *Psychologists' Desk Reference* contributes to its ease of use. These entail:

- A detailed table of contents
- A coherent organization into 11 parts, in which the chapters are arranged both chronologically (according to how a treatment or a consultation would proceed) and topically
- Running heads that identify the part number and title on the left-hand page and the chapter number and title on the right-hand page
- Cross-references within contributions to related chapters in the book
- A comprehensive index at the end of the book

We also present a computer icon in the text—in the table of contents and again at the ends of individual chapters (typically next to the "References" heading)—to indicate that additional relevant material is available on the *Psychologists' Desk Reference* Web site. This material may include detailed strategies, forms, figures, practice guidelines, or items useful in making presentations on topics germane to the material in the particular chapter noted. The Web site can be accessed at www.oup.com/us/psychdeskref, and the in-text icon appears as follows: 💻

This volume is the culmination of lengthy labors and multitudinous contributions; in the best sense of the term, it has been a "group effort." Although we are, of course, ultimately responsible for the book, we genuinely hope that the second edition of the *Psychologists' Desk Reference* does justice to all those who have assisted us.

From its inception, Joan Bossert, editor extraordinaire at Oxford University Press, nurtured the book. In selecting the contents, directors of training programs, members of APA's Division of Clinical Psychology, dozens of colleagues, and the editorial board of Oxford Textbooks in Clinical Psychology provided invaluable assistance. We appreciate the affirming evaluations and constructive suggestions of the reviewers of the previous edition, as we do the nine colleagues who recommended new chapters that appear in this edition. More than 150 authors participated generously and adhered to a challenging writing format. These authors represent, in the words of another reviewer, "a veritable *Who's Who* in psychology." Not to be outdone, our spouses and children endured our absences and preoccupations with grace. Finally, we acknowledge each other for the collaborative spirit and the interpersonal pleasures of coediting this volume. Both the process and the product have improved over the years.

Gerald P. Koocher, Ph.D.
Chestnut Hill, Massachusetts

John C. Norcross, Ph.D.
Clarks Summit, Pennsylvania

Sam S. Hill III, Psy.D.
Corpus Christi, Texas

CONTENTS

Contributors xvii

PART I: ASSESSMENT AND DIAGNOSIS

1 Lifetime Prevalence of Mental Disorders in the General Population 3
CHRISTIE P. KARPIAK & JOHN C. NORCROSS

2 Mental Status Examination 7
ROBERT W. BAKER & PAULA T. TRZEPACZ

3 Improving Diagnostic and Clinical Interviewing 13
RHONDA S. KARG & ARTHUR N. WIENS

4 The Multimodal Life History Inventory 16
ARNOLD A. LAZARUS & CLIFFORD N. LAZARUS

5 Increasing the Accuracy of Clinical Judgment (and Thereby Treatment Effectiveness) 23
DAVID FAUST

6 Developmental Neuropsychological Assessment 28
JANE HOLMES BERNSTEIN, BETSY KAMMERER, PENNY A. PRATHER, & CELIANE REY-CASSERLY

7 Adult Neuropsychological Assessment 33
AARON P. NELSON & MARGARET O'CONNOR

8 Assessment and Intervention for Executive Dysfunction 38
ROBERT M. ROTH, PETER K. ISQUITH, & GERARD A. GIOIA

9 Child and Adolescent Diagnosis With *DSM-IV* 41
STUART M. GOLDMAN

10 Formulating Diagnostic Impressions With Ethnic and Racial Minority Children Using the *DSM-IV-TR* 45
RONN JOHNSON

11 Medical Evaluation of Children With Behavioral or Developmental Disorders 50
JAMES L. LUKEFAHR

12 Interviewing Parents 55
CAROLYN S. SCHROEDER & BETTY N. GORDON

13 Attention-Deficit/Hyperactivity Disorder Through the Life Span 60
ROBERT J. RESNICK

14 Assessment of Suicidal Risk 63
KENNETH S. POPE & MELBA J. T. VASQUEZ

15 Assessment of Malingering on Psychological Measures 67
RICHARD ROGERS

16 Identification and Assessment of Alcohol Abuse 71
LINDA CARTER SOBELL & MARK B. SOBELL

17 Measures of Acculturation 77
JUAN CARLOS GONZALEZ

18 *DSM-IV-TR* Classification System 80
AMERICAN PSYCHIATRIC ASSOCIATION

19 A Practical Guide for the Use of the Global Assessment of Functioning (GAF) Scale of the *DSM-IV-TR* 91
AMERICAN PSYCHIATRIC ASSOCIATION

20 Assessment of Character Strengths 93
CHRISTOPHER PETERSON, NANSOOK PARK, & MARTIN E. P. SELIGMAN

PART II: PSYCHOLOGICAL TESTING

21 50 Widely Used Psychological Tests 101
THOMAS P. HOGAN

22 Sources of Information About Psychological Tests 105
THOMAS P. HOGAN

23 Publishers of Psychological and Psychoeducational Tests 108
THOMAS P. HOGAN

24 Types of Test Scores and Their Percentile Equivalents 111
THOMAS P. HOGAN

25 Assessing the Quality of a Psychological Testing Report 117
GERALD P. KOOCHER

26 Child Behavior Observations 119
JANICE WARE

27 Measures of Children's Psychological Development 124
SAM S. HILL III

28 Assessing MMPI-2 Profile Validity 128
JAMES N. BUTCHER

29 Clinical Scales of the MMPI-2 132
JOHN R. GRAHAM

30 Supplementary Scales of the MMPI-2 137
ROGER L. GREENE

31 Characteristics of High and Low Scores on the MMPI-2 Clinical Scales 141
JOHN R. GRAHAM

32 Empirical Interpretation of the MMPI-2 Codetypes 149
JAMES N. BUTCHER

33 Millon Clinical Multiaxial Inventory (MCMI-III) 153
THEODORE MILLON & SETH D. GROSSMAN

34 Millon Adolescent Clinical Inventory (MACI) 159
THEODORE MILLON & SETH D. GROSSMAN

35 Thumbnail Guide to the Rorschach Method 166
BARRY A. RITZLER

36 Rorschach Assessment: Questions and Reservations 169
HOWARD N. GARB, JAMES M. WOOD, & SCOTT O. LILIENFELD

37 Rorschach Assessment: Scientific Status and Clinical Utility 173
IRVING B. WEINER

PART III: INDIVIDUAL PSYCHOTHERAPY AND TREATMENT

38 Patients' Rights in Psychotherapy 181
DOROTHY W. CANTOR

39 Compendium of Empirically Supported Therapies 183
DIANNE L. CHAMBLESS

40 Compendium of Psychotherapy Treatment Manuals 192
MICHAEL J. LAMBERT, TAIGE BYBEE, RYAN HOUSTON, MATTHEW BISHOP, A. DANIELLE SANDERS, RON WILKINSON, & SARA RICE

41 Compendium of Empirically Supported Therapy Relationships 202
JOHN C. NORCROSS & CLARA E. HILL

42 Enhancing Adherence 208
M. ROBIN DIMATTEO

43 Methods to Reduce and Counter Resistance in Psychotherapy 212
ALBERT ELLIS

44 Repairing Ruptures in the Therapeutic Alliance 216
JEREMY D. SAFRAN

45 Systematic Assessment and Treatment Matching 220
OLIVER B. WILLIAMS, LARRY E. BEUTLER, & KATHRYN YANICK

46 Stages of Change: Prescriptive Guidelines 226
JAMES O. PROCHASKA, JOHN C. NORCROSS, & CARLO C. DICLEMENTE

47 Psychotherapy Treatment Plan Writing 232
ARTHUR E. JONGSMA, JR.

48 Key Principles in the Assessment of Psychotherapy Outcome 236
MICHAEL J. LAMBERT, BRUCE W. JASPER, & JOANNE WHITE

49 Treatment and Management of the Suicidal Patient 240
BRUCE BONGAR & GLENN R. SULLIVAN

50 Crisis Intervention 245
KENNETH FRANCE

51 Impact of Disasters 249
ERIC M. VERNBERG & R. ENRIQUE VARELA

52 Principles in the Treatment of Borderline Personality Disorder 255
JOHN F. CLARKIN & PAMELA A. FOELSCH

53 Psychotherapy With Reluctant and Involuntary Clients 257
STANLEY L. BRODSKY

54 Treatment Matching in Substance Abuse 263
CARLO C. DICLEMENTE

55 Motivational Interviewing 267
WILLIAM R. MILLER & THERESA B. MOYERS

56 Anxiety/Anger Management Training 271
RICHARD M. SUINN

57 Psychological Interventions in Adult Disease Management 274
CAROL D. GOODHEART

58 Assessing and Treating Normative Male Alexithymia 278
RONALD F. LEVANT

59 Assessing and Treating Male Sexual Dysfunction 282
JOSEPH LOPICCOLO & LYNN M. VAN MALE

60 Assessing and Treating Female Sexual Dysfunction 286
JOSEPH LOPICCOLO & LYNN M. VAN MALE

61 Assessing and Reducing Risk of Infection With the Human Immunodeficiency Virus 291
MICHAEL P. CAREY

62 Guidelines for Treating Women in Psychotherapy 295
LAURA S. BROWN & FELICIA A. MUELLER

63 Assessment and Treatment of Lesbians, Gay Men, and Bisexuals 299
ROBIN A. BUHRKE & DOUGLAS C. HALDEMAN

64 Psychotherapy With Older Adults 305
MARGARET GATZ & BOB G. KNIGHT

65 Refusal Skills Training 308
ROBERT H. WOODY & JENNIFER K. H. WOODY

66 Sexual Feelings, Actions, and Dilemmas in Psychotherapy 313
KENNETH S. POPE

67 Six Steps to Improve Psychotherapy Homework Compliance 319
MICHAEL A. TOMPKINS

68 Stimulus Control Instructions for the Treatment of Insomnia 325
RICHARD R. BOOTZIN

69 Parent Management Training for Childhood Behavior Disorders 327
LAURA J. SCHOENFIELD & SHEILA M. EYBERG

70 Hypnosis and Relaxation Scripting 332
DOUGLAS FLEMONS

71 Working With the Religiously Committed Client 338
P. SCOTT RICHARDS & KARI A. O'GRADY

72 Psychotherapy With Cognitively Impaired Adults 342
KATHLEEN B. KORTTE, FELICIA HILL-BRIGGS, & STEPHEN T. WEGENER

73 Early Termination and Referral of Clients in Psychotherapy 346
MANFERD D. KOCH

74 Guidelines for Relapse Prevention 350
KATIE WITKIEWITZ & G. ALAN MARLATT

75 Guidelines for Terminating Psychotherapy 354
OREN M. SHEFET & REBECCA C. CURTIS

PART IV: COUPLES, FAMILY, AND GROUP TREATMENT

76 Choice of Treatment Format 363
JOHN F. CLARKIN

77 Genograms in Assessment and Therapy 366
SUELI S. PETRY & MONICA MCGOLDRICK

78 Guidelines for Conducting Couple and Family Therapy 373
JAY L. LEBOW

79 Treating High-Conflict Couples 378
SUSAN HEITLER

80 Treatment of Marital Infidelity 384
DON-DAVID LUSTERMAN

81 Group Psychotherapy: An Interpersonal Approach 388
VICTOR J. YALOM

82 Psychoeducational Group Treatment 393
GARY M. BURLINGAME & NATHANAEL W. RIDGE

PART V: CHILD AND ADOLESCENT TREATMENT

83 Principles of Treatment With the Behaviorally Disordered Child 401
ESTHER J. CALZADA, ARWA AAMIRY, & SHEILA M. EYBERG

84 Psychological Interventions in Childhood Chronic Illness 406
ROBERT J. THOMPSON, JR. & KATHRYN E. GUSTAFSON

85 Methods to Engage the Reluctant Adolescent 410
ALICE K. RUBENSTEIN

86 The APSAC Study Guides 416
JEANNIE BAKER & SAM S. HILL III

87 Interviewing Children When Sexual Abuse Is Suspected 423
KAREN J. SAYWITZ & JOYCE S. DORADO

88 Treatment of Child Sexual Abuse 430
KATHRYN KUEHNLE

PART VI: BIOLOGY AND PHARMACOTHERAPY

89 Normal Medical Laboratory Values and Measurement Conversions 439
GERALD P. KOOCHER & SAMUEL Z. GOLDHABER

90 Use of Height and Weight Assessment Tools 445
NANCIE H. HERBOLD & SARI EDELSTEIN

91 Medical Conditions That May Present as Psychological Disorders 447
WILLIAM J. REED

92 Adult Psychopharmacology 1: Common Usage 454
JOSEPH K. BELANOFF, CHARLES DEBATTISTA, & ALAN F. SCHATZBERG

93 Adult Psychopharmacology 2: Side Effects and Warnings 460
ELAINE ORABONA MANTELL

94 Pediatric Psychopharmacology 466
TIMOTHY E. WILENS, THOMAS J. SPENCER, & JOSEPH BIEDERMAN

95 Dietary Supplements and Psychological Functioning 476
SARI EDELSTEIN & NANCIE H. HERBOLD

96 Common Drugs of Abuse 481
CHRISTOPHER J. CORREIA & JAMES G. MURPHY

PART VII: SELF-HELP RESOURCES

97 Top Internet Sites for Psychologists and Their Clients 491
JOHN M. GROHOL

98 Highly Rated Self-Help Books and Autobiographies 494
JOHN C. NORCROSS & JENNIFER A. SIMANSKY

99 Popular Films Portraying Mental Disorders 497
DANNY WEDDING

100 Facilitating Client Involvement in Self-Help Groups 502
ELENA KLAW & KEITH HUMPHREYS

101 National Self-Help Groups and Organizations 506
DENNIS E. REIDY & JOHN C. NORCROSS

102 Known and Unproven Herbal Treatments for Psychological Disorders 517
PAULA J. BIEDENHARN

PART VIII: ETHICAL AND LEGAL ISSUES

103 Ethical Principles of Psychologists and Code of Conduct (2002) 525
AMERICAN PSYCHOLOGICAL ASSOCIATION

104 Privacy, Confidentiality, and Privilege 545
GERALD P. KOOCHER

105 Involuntary Psychiatric Hospitalization (Civil Commitment): Adult and Child 548
STUART A. ANFANG & PAUL S. APPELBAUM

106 Physical Restraint and Seclusion: Regulations and Standards 553
THOMAS P. GRAF

107 Basic Principles for Dealing With Legal Liability Risk Situations 558
GERALD P. KOOCHER

108 Defending Against Legal Complaints 560
ROBERT H. WOODY

109 Dealing With Licensing Board and Ethics Complaints 566
GERALD P. KOOCHER & PATRICIA KEITH-SPIEGEL

110 Dealing With Subpoenas 570
GERALD P. KOOCHER

111 Glossary of Legal Terms of Special Interest in Mental Health Practice 572
GERALD P. KOOCHER

112 Fifteen Hints on Money Matters and Related Ethical Issues 577
GERALD P. KOOCHER & SAM S. HILL III

113 How to Confront an Unethical Colleague 579
PATRICIA KEITH-SPIEGEL

114 Confidentiality and the Duty to Protect 584
TIFFANY CHENNEVILLE

PART IX: FORENSIC MATTERS

115 Forensic Evaluations and Testimony 591
STANLEY L. BRODSKY

116 Forensic Evaluation Outline 593
DAVID L. SHAPIRO

117 Forensic Referrals Checklist 595
GEOFFREY R. MCKEE

118 Expert Testimony in Depositions 599
GEOFFREY R. MCKEE

119 Forensic Assessment Instruments 603
RANDY BORUM

120 Evaluation of Competency to Stand Trial 607
PAUL D. LIPSITT

121 A Model for Clinical Decision Making With Dangerous Patients 612
LEON VANDECREEK

122 Principles for Conducting a Comprehensive Child Custody Evaluation 615
BARRY BRICKLIN

123 Recognizing, Assisting, and Reporting the Impaired Psychologist 620
GARY R. SCHOENER

124 Essential Features of Professional Liability Insurance 625
BRUCE E. BENNETT

PART X: PRACTICE MANAGEMENT

125 Sample Psychotherapist-Patient Contract 635
ERIC A. HARRIS & BRUCE E. BENNETT

126 Fundamentals of the HIPAA Privacy Rule 640
JASON M. BENNETT

127 Basic Elements of Consent 645
GERALD P. KOOCHER

128 Basic Elements of Release Forms 647
GERALD P. KOOCHER

129 Prototype Mental Health Records 649
GERALD P. KOOCHER

130 Utilization Review Checklist 652
GERALD P. KOOCHER

131 Contracting With Managed Care Organizations 653
STUART L. KOMAN & ERIC A. HARRIS

132 Billing Issues 657
GERALD P. KOOCHER

133 Psychologists' Fees and Incomes 662
JOHN C. NORCROSS

134 Establishing a Consultation Agreement 666
LEN SPERRY

135 Computerized Billing and Office Management Programs 670
EDWARD L. ZUCKERMAN

PART XI: PROFESSIONAL RESOURCES

136 Therapist Self-Care Checklist 677
JOHN C. NORCROSS & JAMES D. GUY, JR.

137 Conducting Effective Clinical Supervision 682
NICHOLAS LADANY

138 Guide to Interacting With the Media 686
LILLI FRIEDLAND & FLORENCE W. KASLOW

139 Common Clinical Abbreviations and Symbols 691
JOHN C. NORCROSS

140 Major Professional Associations 697
JOHN C. NORCROSS

Index 701

What Do You Want in the Next Edition? 735

CONTRIBUTORS

Gerald P. Koocher, Ph.D., is Professor and Dean of the School for Health Studies at Simmons College in Boston. He also serves as a lecturer on the faculties of Boston College and Harvard Medical School. A diplomate of the American Board of Professional Psychology in clinical, clinical child and adolescent health, family, and forensic psychology, Dr. Koocher is former editor of the *Journal of Pediatric Psychology* and *The Clinical Psychologist*. He serves on the editorial boards of several scholarly journals and currently edits the journal *Ethics & Behavior*. A past president of the Massachusetts and New England Psychological Associations as well as three divisions of the American Psychological Association (APA), he is currently a member of the Board of Directors and Treasurer of the APA. Dr. Koocher is the author or coauthor of more than 160 articles and chapters, in addition to nine books. His text (with Patricia Keith-Spiegel) *Ethics in Psychology: Professional Standards and Cases* is the best-selling textbook in its field. He has won research grant support from federal and foundation sources totaling more than $3 million. Gerry lives in Chestnut Hill, Massachusetts, with his wife, daughter, and an assortment of vociferous psittacines.

John C. Norcross, Ph.D., is professor of psychology at the University of Scranton, editor of *In Session: Journal of Clinical Psychology*, and a clinical psychologist in part-time independent practice. Author of more than 150 scholarly publications, Dr. Norcross has cowritten or edited 12 books, most recently *Psychotherapy Relationships That Work* (Oxford University Press), *Authoritative Guide to Self-Help Resources in Mental Health*, the fifth edition of *Systems of Psychotherapy: A Transtheoretical Analysis*, and the *Insider's Guide to Graduate Programs in Clinical and Counseling Psychology*. He is president of the International Society of Clinical Psychology, past president of the APA Division of Psychotherapy, Council Representative of the APA, and a director of the National Register of Health Service Providers in Psychology. Dr. Norcross has also received numerous awards, including the Pennsylvania Professor of the Year from the Carnegie Foundation, the Rosalee Weiss Award from the American Psychological Foundation, and election to the National Academies of Practice. John lives in northeastern Pennsylvania with his wife, two children, and deranged cat.

Sam S. Hill III, Psy.D., is associate professor of psychology at Texas A&M University–Corpus Christi and a clinical psychologist in part-time practice of pediatric psychology at the Driscoll Children's Hospital in Corpus Christi, where he is associate director of medical education for psychology. Dr. Hill conducts and reviews research on the psychological aspects of pediatric cancer and other chronic illnesses. He is an analytic candidate of the Interregional Society of Jungian Analysts. He is director of the Division for the Psychological Study of Diverse Populations of the Texas Psychological Association, and is a former chair of the Multicultural Affairs Committee of the APA's Division of Psychotherapy. Sam lives in Corpus Christi with his wife and their best friends Schatzie, Gus, and Pippin—the family dachshunds.

Arwa Aamiry, Ph.D.
Pediatric Child Clinical Psychologist
Faculty of Arts and Sciences, American University of Beirut, Lebanon

Stuart A. Anfang, M.D.
Western Massachusetts Area Medical Director, Massachusetts Department of Mental Health
Assistant Professor of Psychiatry, University of Massachusetts Medical School, Worcester, MA

Paul S. Appelbaum, M.D.
A. F. Zeleznik Distinguished Professor of Psychiatry and Chair, Department of Psychiatry, University of Massachusetts Medical School, Worcester, MA

Jeannie Baker, M.A.
Licensed Psychological Associate, Licensed Specialist in School Psychology, Driscoll Children's Hospital, Corpus Christi, TX

Robert W. Baker, M.D.
Associate Director, U.S. Neurosciences, Eli Lilly and Company
Clinical Associate Professor of Psychiatry and Pharmacology, University of Mississippi Medical School, Jackson, MS

Joseph K. Belanoff, M.D.
Chief Executive Officer, Corcept Therapeutics, Menlo Park, CA

Bruce E. Bennett, Ph.D.
Chief Executive Officer, American Psychological Association Insurance Trust, Washington, DC

Jason M. Bennett, J.D.
American Psychological Association Insurance Trust, Washington, DC

Jane Holmes Bernstein, Ph.D.
Director, Neuropsychology Program, Children's Hospital, Boston, MA
Associate Clinical Professor, Harvard Medical School, Boston, MA

Larry E. Beutler, Ph.D., ABPP
William McInnes, SJ, Distinguished Professor of Psychology, Pacific Graduate School of Psychology, Palo Alto, CA
Consulting Professor of Psychiatry, Stanford University School of Medicine, Stanford, CA

Paula J. Biedenharn, Ph.D.
Department of Psychology, Texas A&M University, Corpus Christi, TX

Joseph Biederman, M.D.
Professor of Psychiatry, Harvard Medical School, Boston, MA
Chief of Pediatric Psychopharmacology, Massachusetts General Hospital, Boston, MA

Matthew Bishop, B.S.
Department of Psychology, Brigham Young University, Provo, UT

Bruce Bongar, Ph.D., ABPP, FAPM
Pacific Graduate School of Psychology–Stanford Psy.D. Consortium, Palo Alto, CA
Department of Psychiatry and Behavioral Services, Stanford University School of Medicine, Stanford, CA

Richard R. Bootzin, Ph.D.
Professor of Psychology, Department of Psychology, University of Arizona
Director, Insomnia Clinic, University of Arizona Sleep Disorders Center

Randy Borum, Psy.D.
Associate Professor, Department of Mental Health Law and Policy, University of South Florida, Tampa, FL

Barry Bricklin, Ph.D.
President, Bricklin Associates, Wayne, PA
Adjunct Associate Professor, Widener University, Chester, PA

Stanley L. Brodsky, Ph.D.
Professor, Department of Psychology, University of Alabama, Tuscaloosa, AL

Laura S. Brown, Ph.D., ABPP
Professor, Washington School of Professional Psychology at Argosy University, Seattle, WA

Robin A. Buhrke, Ph.D.
Staff Psychologist, Counseling and Psychological Services, and Assistant Clinical Professor in Psychiatry and Behavioral Sciences, Duke University, Durham, NC

Gary M. Burlingame, Ph.D.
Professor of Psychology, Brigham Young University, Provo, UT

James N. Butcher, Ph.D.
Professor of Psychology, University of Minnesota, Minneapolis, MN

Taige Bybee, B.S.
Department of Psychology, Brigham Young University, Provo, UT

Esther J. Calzada, Ph.D.
Assistant Professor of Psychiatry, Child Study Center, New York University School of Medicine, New York, NY

Dorothy W. Cantor, Psy.D.
Independent practice, Westfield, NJ

Michael P. Carey, Ph.D.
Professor or Psychology and Director, Center for Health and Behavior, Syracuse University, Syracuse, NY
Adjunct Professor of Medicine, Upstate Medical University (Syracuse) and University of Rochester School of Medicine and Dentistry

Dianne L. Chambless, Ph.D.
Merriam Term Professor of Psychology, Department of Psychology, University of Pennsylvania, Philadelphia, PA

Tiffany Chenneville, Ph.D.
Pinellas County Schools, St. Petersburg, FL
Independent practice, St. Petersburg, FL

John F. Clarkin, Ph.D.
Professor of Clinical Psychology in Psychiatry, Weill Medical College of Cornell University and New York Presbyterian Hospital, New York, NY

Christopher J. Correia, Ph.D.
Assistant Professor of Psychology, Auburn University, Auburn, AL

Rebecca C. Curtis, Ph.D.
Professor, Gordon F. Derner Institute, Adelphi University, Garden City, NY
William Alanson White Institute of Psychiatry, Psychology, and Psychoanalysis, New York, NY

Charles DeBattista, M.D.
Associate Professor of Psychiatry, Stanford University, Stanford, CA

Carlo C. DiClemente, Ph.D.
Professor and Chair, Department of Psychology, University of Maryland, Baltimore County, Baltimore, MD

M. Robin DiMatteo, Ph.D.
Professor of Psychology, University of California, Riverside, CA

Joyce S. Dorado, Ph.D.
Co-Director of Clinical Training, Department of Psychiatry, University of California, San Francisco/San Francisco General Hospital, San Francisco, CA

Sari Edelstein, Ph.D., R.D.
Registered Dietitian and Assistant Professor of Nutrition, Simmons College, Boston, MA

Albert Ellis, Ph.D.
President, Albert Ellis Institute, New York, NY

Sheila M. Eyberg, Ph.D., ABPP
Professor of Clinical and Health Psychology, University of Florida, Gainesville, FL

David Faust, Ph.D.
Professor of Psychology, University of Rhode Island, Kingston, RI

Douglas Flemons, Ph.D.
Professor of Family Therapy and Director of the Brief Therapy Institute, Nova Southeastern University, Fort Lauderdale, FL

Pamela A. Foelsch, Ph.D.
Weill Medical College of Cornell University, White Plains, NY
Adjunct Assistant Professor, Smith College School of Social Work, Northampton, MA

Kenneth France, Ph.D.
Professor of Psychology, Shippensburg University, Shippensburg, PA
Lead Online Mentor, New Hope Crisis Counseling Center

Lilli Friedland, Ph.D., ABPP
President, Executive Advisors, Los Angeles, CA

Howard N. Garb, Ph.D.
Chief, Psychology Research Service, Wilford Hall Medical Center, Lackland Air Force Base, San Antonio, TX

Margaret Gatz, Ph.D.
Professor of Psychology, University of Southern California, Los Angeles, CA

Gerard A. Gioia, Ph.D.
Pediatric Neurology Program, Children's National Medical Center, Washington, DC
Associate Professor, Departments of Pediatrics and Psychiatry, George Washington University School of Medicine, Washington, DC

Samuel Z. Goldhaber, M.D.
Staff Cardiologist, Brigham and Women's Hospital, Boston, MA
Associate Professor of Medicine, Harvard Medical School, Boston, MA

Stuart M. Goldman, M.D.
Director, Affective Disorders Clinic, Children's Hospital, Boston, MA
Assistant Professor of Psychiatry, Harvard Medical School, Boston, MA

Juan Carlos Gonzalez, Ph.D.
Children's Psychiatric Center, Miami, FL

Carol D. Goodheart, Ed.D.
Independent practice, Princeton, NJ

Betty N. Gordon, Ph.D.
Associate Professor Emerita, University of North Carolina at Chapel Hill, Chapel Hill, NC

Thomas P. Graf, Ph.D
Driscoll Children's Hospital, Corpus Christi, TX

John R. Graham, Ph.D.
Professor of Psychology, Kent State University, Kent, OH

Roger L. Greene, Ph.D.
Professor of Psychology, Pacific Graduate School of Psychology, Palo Alto, CA

John M. Grohol, Psy.D.
International Society for Mental Health Online, PsychCentral.com

Seth D. Grossman, Psy.D.
Institute for Advanced Studies on Personology and Psychopathology, Coral Gables, FL

James D. Guy, Jr., Ph.D.
Headington Institute, Pasadena, CA

Kathryn E. Gustafson, Ph.D.
Assistant Professor of Medical Psychology, Duke University, Durham, NC

Douglas C. Haldeman, Ph.D.
University of Washington, Seattle, WA
Independent practice, Seattle, WA

Eric A. Harris, J.D., Ed.D.
Risk Management Consultant, American Psychological Association Insurance Trust, Washington, DC
Legal Counsel, Massachusetts Psychological Association, Wellesley, MA

Susan Heitler, Ph.D.
Independent practice, Denver, CO

Nancie H. Herbold, Ed.D., R.D., L.D.N.
Registered Dietitian and Ruby Winslow Linn Professor of Nutrition, Simmons College, Boston, MA

Clara E. Hill, Ph.D.
Professor of Psychology, University of Maryland, College Park, MD

Felicia Hill-Briggs, Ph.D.
Department of Physical Medicine and Rehabilitation, Johns Hopkins University School of Medicine, Baltimore, MD

Thomas P. Hogan, Ph.D.
Professor of Psychology, University of Scranton, Scranton, PA

Ryan Houston, B.S.
Department of Psychology, Brigham Young University, Provo, UT

Keith Humphreys, Ph.D.
Associate Professor of Psychiatry, Stanford University, Stanford, CA
Director, Veterans Affairs Program Evaluation and Resource Center, Menlo Park, CA

Peter K. Isquith, Ph.D.
Pediatric Neuropsychology, Department of Psychiatry, Dartmouth Medical School

Bruce W. Jasper, B.S.
Department of Psychology, Brigham Young University, Provo, UT

Ronn Johnson, Ph.D.
Child and Adolescent Services Research Center, Children's Hospital, San Diego, CA

Arthur E. Jongsma, Jr., Ph.D.
Psychological Consultants, Grand Rapids, MI

Betsy Kammerer, Ph.D.
Children's Hospital, Boston, MA
Harvard Medical School, Boston, MA

Rhonda S. Karg, Ph.D.
Research Triangle Institute, Research Triangle Park, NC

Christie P. Karpiak, Ph.D.
Department of Psychology, University of Scranton, Scranton, PA

Florence W. Kaslow, Ph.D., ABPP
Director, Florida Couples and Family Institute, West Palm Beach, FL
Visiting Professor of Medical Psychology, Duke University Medical School, Durham, NC

Patricia Keith-Spiegel, Ph.D.
Professor of Psychology Emerita, Ball State University, Muncie, IN
Visiting Professor of Psychology, Harvard Medical School, Boston, MA

Elena Klaw, Ph.D.
Department of Psychology, San José State University, San Jose, CA

Bob G. Knight, Ph.D.
Merle H. Bensinger Professor of Gerontology, Professor of Psychology and Director of Clinical Training, University of Southern California, Los Angeles, CA

Manferd D. Koch, Ph.D.
Department of Psychology, Texas A&M University, Corpus Christi, TX

Stuart L. Koman, Ph.D.
Koman Associates, Winchester, MA

Kathleen B. Kortte, Ph.D.
Neuropsychology Service, National Rehabilitation Hospital, Washington, DC

Kathryn Kuehnle, Ph.D.
Assistant Professor, University of South Florida, Florida Mental Health Institute Department of Mental Health Law and Policy, Tampa, FL
Independent practice, Tampa, FL

Nicholas Ladany, Ph.D.
Department of Psychology, Lehigh University, Bethlehem, PA

Michael J. Lambert, Ph.D.
Professor of Psychology, Brigham Young University, Provo, UT

Arnold A. Lazarus, Ph.D., ABPP
Professor Emeritus of Psychology, Rutgers University
President, Center for Multimodal Psychological Services, Princeton, NJ

Clifford N. Lazarus, Ph.D.
Director, Comprehensive Psychological Services, Princeton, NJ

Jay L. Lebow, Ph.D., ABPP
Family Institute at Northwestern and Adjunct Associate Professor, Northwestern University, Evanston, IL

Ronald F. Levant, Ed.D., ABPP
Dean, Center for Psychological Studies, Nova Southeastern University, Fort Lauderdale, FL

Scott O. Lilienfeld, Ph.D.
Associate Professor, Department of Psychology, Emory University, Atlanta, GA

Paul D. Lipsitt, LL.B., Ph.D.
Student Health Service, Boston University, Boston, MA

Joseph LoPiccolo, Ph.D.
Professor of Psychology, University of Missouri, Columbia, MO
Director of Psychological Services, Sexual Medicine Center of Missouri, Columbia, MO

James L. Lukefahr, M.D.
Professor of Pediatrics, University of Texas Medical Branch, Galveston, TX

Don-David Lusterman, Ph.D., ABPP
Independent practice, Baldwin, NY

Elaine Orabona Mantell, Ph.D.
Prescribing Psychologist, Lt. Colonel, United States Air Force

G. Alan Marlatt, Ph.D.
Addictive Behaviors Research Center, University of Washington, Seattle, WA

Monica McGoldrick, M.S.W.
The Multicultural Family Institute, Highland Park, NJ

Geoffrey R. McKee, Ph.D., ABPP
University of South Carolina School of Medicine, Columbia, SC

William R. Miller, Ph.D.
Center on Alcoholism, Substance Abuse, and Addictions, University of New Mexico, Albuquerque, NM

Theodore Millon, Ph.D., D.Sc.
Institute for Advanced Studies on Personology and Psychopathology, Coral Gables, FL

Theresa B. Moyers, Ph.D.
Center on Alcoholism, Substance Abuse, and Addictions, University of New Mexico, Albuquerque, NM

Felicia A. Mueller, B.A.
Washington School of Professional Psychology at Argosy University, Seattle, WA

James G. Murphy, M.S.
Brown Center for Alcohol and Addiction Studies, Auburn University, Auburn, AL

Aaron P. Nelson, Ph.D., ABPP
Chief of Neuropsychology, Brigham and Women's Hospital, Boston, MA
Instructor in Psychology, Harvard Medical School, Boston, MA

Margaret O'Connor, Ph.D.
Division of Behavioral Neurology, Beth Israel Deaconess Medical Center, Boston, MA
Harvard Medical School, Boston, MA

Kari A. O'Grady, B.S.
Department of Psychology, Brigham Young University, Provo, UT

Nansook Park, Ph.D.
Department of Psychology, University of Rhode Island, Kingston, RI

Christopher Peterson, Ph.D.
Professor of Psychology, University of Michigan, Ann Arbor, MI

Sueli S. Petry, M.A., Ed.S.
The Multicultural Family Institute, Highland Park, NJ
Seton Hall University, South Orange, NJ

Kenneth S. Pope, Ph.D., ABPP
Independent practice, Norwalk, CT

Penny A. Prather, Ph.D.
Educational Enhancement Center, Newton Center, MA
Harvard Medical School, Boston, MA

James O. Prochaska, Ph.D.
Professor of Psychology, University of Rhode Island, Kingston, RI

William J. Reed, M.D., F.A.A.P
Associate Professor of Pediatrics, Texas A&M College of Medicine, Corpus Christi, TX
Clinical Assistant Professor of Pediatrics, University of Texas Medical Branch
Adjunct Professor of Psychology, Texas A&M University, Corpus Christi, TX

Dennis E. Reidy, B.S.
Department of Psychology, University of Scranton, Scranton, PA

Robert J. Resnick, Ph.D., ABPP
Professor of Psychology, Randolph-Macon College, Ashland, VA

Celiane Rey-Casserly, Ph.D., ABPP
Children's Hospital, Boston, MA
Harvard Medical School, Boston, MA

Sara Rice, B.S.
Department of Psychology, Brigham Young University, Provo, UT

P. Scott Richards, Ph.D.
Professor of Counseling Psychology, Brigham Young University, Provo, UT

Nathanael W. Ridge, B.S.
Department of Psychology, Brigham Young University, Provo, UT

Barry A. Ritzler, Ph.D., ABPP
Long Island University and Rorschach Workshops, Inc., Brooklyn, NY

Richard Rogers, Ph.D., ABPP
Professor of Psychology, University of North Texas, Denton, TX

Robert M. Roth, Ph.D.
Neuropsychology and Neuroimaging Program, Dartmouth Medical School, Hanover, NH

Alice K. Rubenstein, Ed.D.
Monroe Psychotherapy and Consultation Center, Pittsford, NY

Jeremy D. Safran, Ph.D.
Professor, Department of Psychology, New School University, New York, NY

A. Danielle Sanders, B.S.
Department of Psychology, Brigham Young University, Provo, UT

Karen J. Saywitz, Ph.D.
Professor, UCLA School of Medicine, Division of Child and Adolescent Psychiatry, Los Angeles, CA

Alan F. Schatzberg, M.D.
Kenneth T. Norris, Jr., Professor and Chairman, Department of Psychiatry and Behavioral Sciences, Stanford University Medical School, Stanford, CA

Gary R. Schoener, B.A.
Walk-in Counseling Center, Minneapolis, MN

Laura J. Schoenfield, B.A.
Department of Clinical and Health Psychology, University of Florida, Gainesville, FL

Carolyn S. Schroeder, Ph.D.
Adjunct Professor, Clinical Child Psychology Program, University of Kansas, Lawrence, KS

Martin E. P. Seligman, Ph.D.
Fox Professor of Psychology and Director, Positive Psychology Center, University of Pennsylvania, Philadelphia, PA

David L. Shapiro, Ph.D.
Nova Southeastern University, Fort Lauderdale, FL

Oren M. Shefet, M.A.
The Derner Institute of Advanced Psychological Studies, Adelphi University, Garden City, NY

Jennifer A. Simansky, B.S.
University of Scranton, Scranton, PA

Linda Carter Sobell, Ph.D., ABPP
Professor, Center for Psychological Studies, Nova Southeastern University, Fort Lauderdale, FL

Mark B. Sobell, Ph.D., ABPP
Professor, Center for Psychological Studies, Nova Southeastern University, Fort Lauderdale, FL

Thomas J. Spencer, M.D.
Assistant Director, Pediatric Psychopharmacology, Massachusetts General Hospital, Boston, MA
Assistant Professor, Harvard Medical School, Boston, MA

Len Sperry, M.D., Ph.D, ABPP
Clinical Professor of Psychiatry and Behavioral Medicine, Medical College of Wisconsin, Milwaukee, WI

Richard M. Suinn, Ph.D., ABPP
Professor of Psychology Emeritus, Colorado State University, Fort Collins, CO

Glenn R. Sullivan, M.S.
Pacific Graduate School of Psychology, Palo Alto, CA

Robert J. Thompson, Jr., Ph.D.
Dean of Trinity College and Professor of Psychology: Social and Health Sciences, Duke University, Durham, NC

Michael A. Tompkins, Ph.D.
Director of Training, San Francisco Bay Area Center for Cognitive Therapy, Oakland, CA
Associate Clinical Professor, Department of Psychology, University of California, Berkeley, CA

Paula T. Trzepacz, M.D.
Medical Director, U.S. Neurosciences, Eli Lilly and Company
Clinical Professor of Psychiatry, University of Mississippi Medical School, Jackson, MS

Leon VandeCreek, Ph.D., ABPP
School of Professional Psychology, Wright State University, Dayton, OH

Lynn M. Van Male, M.A.
Doctoral Candidate, Department of Psychology, University of Missouri, Columbia, MO

R. Enrique Varela, Ph.D.
Assistant Professor of Psychology, Tulane University, New Orleans, LA

Melba J. T. Vasquez, Ph.D., ABPP
Independent practice, Austin, TX

Eric M. Vernberg, Ph.D.
Professor of Psychology, University of Kansas, Lawrence, KS

Janice Ware, Ph.D.
Associate Director, Developmental Medicine Center, Children's Hospital, Boston, MA
Assistant Professor of Psychology, Harvard Medical School, Boston, MA

Danny Wedding, Ph.D., MPH
Missouri Institute of Mental Health, St. Louis, MO
University of Missouri–Columbia School of Medicine, Columbia, MO

Stephen T. Wegener, Ph.D., ABPP
Department of Physical Medicine and Rehabilitation, Johns Hopkins University School of Medicine, Baltimore, MD

Irving B. Weiner, Ph.D.
Professor of Psychology, University of South Florida, Tampa, FL

Joanne White, B.S.
Department of Psychology, Brigham Young University, Provo, UT

Arthur N. Wiens, Ph.D., ABPP
Professor Emeritus of Medical Psychology, Oregon Health Sciences University, Portland, OR

Timothy E. Wilens, M.D.
Director of Substance Abuse Services, Massachusetts General Hospital, Pediatric Psychopharmacology, Boston, MA
Associate Professor, Harvard Medical School, Boston, MA

Ron Wilkinson, J.D.
Brigham Young University, Provo, UT

Oliver B. Williams, Ph.D.
Center for Behavioral HealthCare Technologies, Inc., Oxnard, CA

Katie Witkiewitz, Ph.D.
Addictive Behaviors Research Center, University of Washington, Seattle, WA

James M. Wood, Ph.D.
Associate Professor of Psychology, University of Texas at El Paso, El Paso, TX

Jennifer K. H. Woody, M.S.
Omaha, NE

Robert H. Woody, J.D., Sc.D., Ph.D., ABPP
University of Nebraska, Omaha, NE
Private practice of law, Omaha, NE

Victor J. Yalom, Ph.D.
President, Psychotherapy.net
Independent practice, San Francisco, CA

Kathryn Yanick, B.A., A.D.R.N.
Pacific Graduate School of Psychology, Palo Alto, CA

Edward L. Zuckerman, Ph.D.
Independent practice, Armbrust, PA

PART I
Assessment and Diagnosis

1 LIFETIME PREVALENCE OF MENTAL DISORDERS IN THE GENERAL POPULATION

Christie P. Karpiak & John C. Norcross

The following table summarizes the approximate lifetime prevalence rates of mental disorders in the general population. These rates will obviously vary as a result of the different sample compositions, diagnostic criteria, and assessment methods employed in each study.

TABLE 1. Lifetime Prevalence of Mental Disorders in the General Population

Disorder	National Comorbidity Study (NCS)	*Diagnostic and Statistical Manual of Mental Disorders*, rev. 4th ed. (*DSM-IV-TR*)	Epidemiological Catchment Area (ECA)	International Consortium in Psychiatric Epidemiology (ICPE)
Adjustment disorders		2.0–8.0%		
Agoraphobia without panic disorder	5.3% overall 3.5% of men 7.0% of women			2.1–3.4% overall 0.8–1.9% of men 3.0–4.9% of women
Alcohol abuse	9.4% overall 12.5% of men 6.4% of women			
Alcohol dependence	14.1% overall 20.1% of men 8.2% of women	15.0%	13.8% overall 23.8% of men 4.6% of women	
Alzheimer's		0.6% of men age 65 0.8% of women age 65 11.0% of men age 85 14.0% of women age 85 21.0% of men age 90 25.0% of women age 90		

(continued)

TABLE 1. Lifetime Prevalence of Mental Disorders in the General Population *(continued)*

Disorder	National Comorbidity Study (NCS)	*Diagnostic and Statistical Manual of Mental Disorders,* rev. 4th ed. (*DSM-IV-TR*)	Epidemiological Catchment Area (ECA)	International Consortium in Psychiatric Epidemiology (ICPE)
Amphetamine dependence/abuse		1.5%		
Anorexia nervosa		0.05% of men 0.5% of women		
Antisocial personality disorder	3.5% overall 5.8% of men 1.2% of women	3.0% of men 1.0% of women	2.6% overall 4.5% of men 0.08% of women	
Anxiety disorder, any type[a]				5.6–25.0% overall[a] 5.6% in Mexico; 7.4% in Turkey; 9.8% in Germany; 17.4% in Brazil; 20.1% in the Netherlands; 21.3% in Canada; 25.0% in the United States
Attention-deficit/hyperactivity disorder		3.0–7.0%		
Autism		0.02–0.2%		
Avoidant personality disorder		0.5–1.0%		
Bipolar I disorder		0.4–1.6%		1.0–1.8%
Bipolar II disorder		0.5%		
Borderline personality disorder		2.0%		
Bulimia nervosa		0.1–0.3% of men 1.0–3.0% of women		0.2–0.3% of men 1.1–2.4% of women
Conduct disorder		<1.0–>10.0%		
Cyclothymic disorder		0.4–1.0%		
Delirium		0.4% age 18 and older 1.1% age 55 and older		
Delusional disorder		0.05–0.1%		
Dementia		1.4–1.6% age 65–69 16.0–25.0% over age 85		
Dissociative fugue		0.2%		
Dissociative identity disorder		Subject of controversy		
Drug abuse	4.4% overall 5.4% of men 3.5% of women			
Drug dependence	7.5% overall 9.2% of men 5.9% of women		6.2% overall 7.7% of men 4.8% of women	
Dysthymic disorder	6.4% overall 4.8% of men 8.0% of women	6.0%	3.3% overall 2.2% of men 4.1% of women	4.3–6.3%
Encopresis		1.0% of 5-year-olds		
Enuresis		5.0–10.0% 5-year-olds 3.0–5.0% 10-year-olds 1.0% age 15 and older		
Gender identity disorder		0.003% of men 0.001% of women[b]		
Generalized anxiety disorder	5.1% overall 3.6% of men 6.6% of women	5.0%	5.8% overall 4.5% of men 6.8% of women	1.9–5.3% overall 1.4–3.5% of men 2.4–7.3% of women

TABLE 1. Lifetime Prevalence of Mental Disorders in the General Population (*continued*)

Disorder	National Comorbidity Study (NCS)	*Diagnostic and Statistical Manual of Mental Disorders*, rev. 4th ed. (*DSM-IV-TR*)	Epidemiological Catchment Area (ECA)	International Consortium in Psychiatric Epidemiology (ICPE)
Histrionic personality disorder		2.0–3.0%		
Learning disorders		2.0–10.0% 5.0% of students in public schools 4.0% reading disorder 1.0% mathematics disorder		
Major depressive disorder	17.1% overall 12.7% of men 21.3% of women	5.0–12.0% of men 10.0–25.0% of women	6.4% overall 3.6% of men 8.7% of women	15.4–16.8% overall 10.9–13.5% of men 19.2–20.1% of women
Manic episode	1.6% overall 1.6% of men 1.7% of women		0.8% overall 0.7% of men 0.9% of women	
Mental retardation		1.0%		
Mood disorder, any type[c]				7.3–19.4% overall[c] 7.3% in Turkey; 9.2% in Mexico; 10.2% in Canada; 15.5% in Brazil; 17.1% in Germany; 18.9% in the Netherlands; 19.4% in the United States
Narcissistic personality disorder		<1.0%		
Narcolepsy		0.02–0.16%		
Nonaffective psychosis (also see schizophrenia)[b]	0.7% overall 0.6% of men 0.8% of women			0.4–1.9% overall 0.4–1.7% of men 0.3–2.0% of women
Obsessive-compulsive disorder		2.5% adults 1.0–2.3% children and adolescents	2.6% overall 2.0% of men 3.0% of women	
Obsessive-compulsive personality disorder		1.0%		
Oppositional defiant disorder		2.0–16.0%		
Panic disorder	3.5% overall 2.0% of men 5.0% of women	1.0–3.5%	1.6% overall 1.0% of men 2.1% of women	1.6–3.8% overall 0.7–1.9% of men 2.3–5.7% of women
Paranoid personality disorder		0.5–2.5%		
Pathological gambling		0.4–3.4% adults in the United States, up to 7.0% adults international, 2.8–8.0% adolescents and students		
Phobia (general)			14.3% overall 10.0% of men 17.4% of women	
Posttraumatic stress disorder		8.0%		
Schizophrenia (also see nonaffective psychosis)[d]		0.5–1.5%	1.5% overall 1.2% of men 1.7% of women	

(*continued*)

TABLE 1. Lifetime Prevalence of Mental Disorders in the General Population (*continued*)

Disorder	National Comorbidity Study (NCS)	*Diagnostic and Statistical Manual of Mental Disorders*, rev. 4th ed. (*DSM-IV-TR*)	Epidemiological Catchment Area (ECA)	International Consortium in Psychiatric Epidemiology (ICPE)
Schizotypal personality disorder		3.0%		
Selective mutism		<1.0%		
Separation anxiety disorder		4.0% children and adolescents		
Sleep terror disorder		unknown		
Episodes		1.0–6.0% children <1.0% adults		
Sleepwalking disorder		1.0–5.0% of children		
Episodes		10.0–30.0% of children 1.0–7.0% adults		
Social phobia	13.3% overall 11.1% of men 15.5% of women	3.0–13.0%		3.5–7.8% overall 2.9–5.9% of men 3.5–9.7% of women
Somatization disorder		0.2–2.0% of women <0.2% of men	0.1% overall 0.02% of men 0.23% of women	
Specific/simple phobia	11.3% overall 6.7% of men 15.7% of women	7.2–11.3%		4.8–10.1% overall 2.2–6.6% of men 6.7–13.6% of women
Stuttering		1.0% children 0.8% adolescents		
Substance abuse/dependence, any type[e]				0.0–28.2% overall[e] 0.0% in Turkey; 9.6% in Mexico; 16.1% in Brazil; 18.7% in the Netherlands; 19.7% in Canada; 21.5% in Germany; 28.2% in the United States
Tourette's disorder		0.05–0.3% children 0.01–0.02% adults		
Trichotillomania		0.6%		

[a]Any anxiety disorder = panic disorder, agoraphobia, simple phobia, social phobia, and/or generalized anxiety disorder.
[b]Information obtained from a survey conducted in smaller European countries.
[c]Any mood disorder = depression, dysthymia, and/or mania.
[d]Includes schizophrenia, schizophreniform disorder, schizoaffective disorder, delusional disorder, and atypical psychosis.
[e]Any substance = alcohol and/or drug abuse or dependence.

Four data sources are presented: the National Comorbidity Study (NCS; Kessler et al., 1994); the text revision of the fourth edition of the *Diagnostic and Statistical Manual of Mental Disorders* (*DSM-IV-TR*; American Psychiatric Association, 2000); the NIMH Epidemiological Catchment Area (ECA) study (Robins & Reiger, 1991); and the World Health Organization International Consortium in Psychiatric Epidemiology (ICPE; World Health Organization, 2000). The NCS reports prevalence rates of mental disorders from a national probability sample of noninstitutionalized civilians across the 48 continental United States and uses *DSM-III-R* diagnostic criteria. The *DSM-IV-TR* extracts its prevalence rates from various epidemiological and clinical studies reported in the literature. The ECA bases its prevalence rates on structured interviews of more than 20,000 adults in five cities across the United States and uses *DSM-III* criteria.

The first three data sources are largely based on the population of the United States of America; in contrast, the fourth data source is international in scope. The ICPE studies employ a version of the WHO Composite International Diagnostic Interview, a structured diagnostic that encompasses criteria from both the *International Classification of Diseases* (*ICD*) and the *DSM*. The international prevalence estimates in the table are based on published data from participating countries, with between two and seven countries contributing to the reported prevalence ranges. The WHO efforts to generate cross-national information on mental disorders are ongoing, with data currently being gathered from general populations in more than 20 countries.

References, Readings, & Internet Sites 

American Psychiatric Association. (2000). *Diagnostic and statistical manual of mental disorders* (4th ed., rev.). Washington, DC: Author.

Andrade, L., Walters, E. E., Gentil, V., & Laurenti, R. (2002). Prevalence of ICD-10 mental disorders in a catchment area in the city of São Paulo, Brazil. *Social Psychiatry and Psychiatric Epidemiology, 37,* 316–325.

Bijl, R. V., Ravelli, A., & van Zessen, G. (1998). Prevalence of psychiatric disorder in the general population: Results of the Netherlands Mental Health Survey and Incidence Study (NEMESIS). *Social Psychiatry and Psychiatric Epidemiology, 33,* 587–595.

International Consortium in Psychiatric Epidemiology. (n.d.). Home page. Retrieved 2004 from http://www.hcp.med.harvard.edu/icpe

Kessler, R. C., Andrade, L. H., Bijl, R. V., Offord, D. R., Demler, O. V., & Stein, D. J. (2002). The effects of co-morbidity on the onset and persistence of generalized anxiety disorder in the ICPE surveys. *Psychological Medicine, 32,* 1213–1225.

Kessler, R. C., McGonagle, K. A., Zhao, S., Nelson, C. B., Hughes, M., Eshleman, S., et al. (1994). Lifetime and 12-month prevalence of DSM-III-R psychiatric disorders in the United States: Results from the National Comorbidity Study. *Archives of General Psychiatry, 51,* 8–19.

National Institute of Mental Health (NIMH). (n.d.). Statistics. Retrieved 2004 from http://www.nimh.nih.gov/stats.cfm

Reiger, D. A., Myers, J. K., Kramer, M., Robins, L. N., Blazer, D. G., Hough, R. L., et al. (1984). The NIMH Epidemiologic Catchment Area program. *Archives of General Psychiatry, 41,* 934–941.

Robins, L. N., Helzer, J. E., Weissman, M. M., Orvaschel, H., Gruenberg, E., Burke, J. D., Jr., et al. (1984). Lifetime prevalences of specific psychiatric disorders in three sites. *Archives of General Psychiatry, 41,* 949–958.

Robins, L. N., & Reiger, D. A. (Eds.). (1991). *Psychiatric disorders in America: The Epidemiological Catchment Area Study.* New York: Free Press.

World Health Organization. (n.d.). Mental health links page. Retrieved 2004 from http://www.who.int/health_topics/mental_health/en

World Health Organization (WHO) International Consortium of Psychiatric Epidemiology. (2000). Cross-national comparisons of the prevalences and correlates of mental disorders. *Bulletin of the World Health Organization, 78,* 413–426.

Related Topic

Chapter 18, "*DMS-IV-TR* Classification System"

2 MENTAL STATUS EXAMINATION

Robert W. Baker & Paula T. Trzepacz

In conjunction with history taking, mental status examination (MSE) provides the database for psychiatric assessment and differential diagnosis. It comprises the observed and objective portion of the evaluation, along with results of laboratory and radiological testing. Although the MSE is part of a thorough physical examination, it is usually more comprehensive when performed by a psychiatrist than when performed by other physicians. Except for the cognitive and language portions of the MSE, which usually are administered in a structured fashion, much of the MSE is semistructured, and information is obtained throughout an interview.

The following material describes a standard format for documenting the MSE, along with some advice for its performance. During assessments for follow-up, only particular portions of the MSE may be emphasized. This outline for the MSE has six sections and is derived from our textbook, *The Psychiatric Mental Status Examination*.

APPEARANCE, ATTITUDE, AND ACTIVITY

Appearance is ascertained by direct observation of physical characteristics. The following items should be considered:

- *Level of consciousness:* Normally patients are attentive and respond to stimuli; when this is not the case, the examiner may try to rouse the patient, such as by speaking loudly or shaking the patient's arm. "Hyperarousal" or "hypervigilance" is sometimes seen, such as in mania or stimulant intoxication. A decreased level of consciousness can be described in rough order of increasing severity with the following terms: drowsy, lethargic, obtunded, stuporous, comatose.
- *Apparent age* is judged by vigor, mode of dress, mannerisms, and condition of hair and skin.
- *Position/posture* records where the patient is (e.g., in bed, on a chair, or on the floor) and pertinent abnormalities, such as the "waxy flexibility" of catatonia or the use of leather restraints.
- *Attire/grooming* is reported in nonjudgmental, descriptive terms, such as casually dressed, neat, clean, meticulously groomed, unshaven, disheveled, clothing torn, mismatched socks.
- *Abnormal physical traits* are noted, such as skin lesions or tattoos, body odor, sweating, amputations, and Down's syndrome facies.
- *Eye contact* can be described as "good" or "poor" or is described quantitatively (e.g., "made normal eye contact about half of the time").

Attitude describes the patient's approach to the interview:

- Degree and type of *cooperativeness:* Useful terms are cooperative/uncooperative, friendly, open, hostile, guarded, suspicious, or regressed.
- *Resistance,* if any, is noted here, such as "He refused to answer any questions about his family." Resistance may be nonverbal, such as avoiding eye contact, muteness, or fist shaking.

Activity describes physical movement. Five aspects to consider are as follows:

- *Voluntary movement* and its intensity: Increased movement is described directly ("He was pacing/fidgety/restless") or is labeled "psychomotor agitation." Decreased movement is localized (e.g., paresis or masked facies) or general, known as bradykinesia or (especially if mentation also is slowed or delayed) psychomotor retardation.
- *Involuntary movements* are observed at rest, during motion, and, if relevant, with provocative maneuvers, such as having the patient stand with eyes closed and arms outstretched. Tremors are regular or rhythmic. Resting tremor improves during action, whereas intention tremor is worst during the most demanding phase of an action. Chorea is sudden and irregular, while athetoid movements are irregular and writhing. Dystonias are sustained, like a muscle spasm.
- *Automatic movements* may appear spontaneously during partial seizures. Common examples are chewing, lip smacking, or clumsy limb movements. Movements may

be more complex, such as walking or pulling at buttons, but purposeful action is not characteristic of automatism. Typically the patient has decreased alertness during automatic movement; if repetitive, automatisms usually are stereotyped, that is, the same movement is repeated.

- *Tics* are sudden, stereotyped, brief, abrupt, and sometimes (temporarily) consciously mitigated or suppressed. They may increase if topic matter is stressful. Most noticeable are facial tics, but other body areas can be affected, and tics can be verbal utterances, such as in Tourette's disorder.
- *Compulsions* may be reported by the patient or observed by the examiner. Screen by asking about repeated or undesired activities. Patients should recognize that the behavior is unreasonable, but they may become anxious if the action is resisted. Common compulsions include hand washing or checking (locks, stove, wallet, etc.).

MOOD AND AFFECT

Mood is a person's predominant feeling state at a given time. It is judged primarily by self-report but also by observation throughout the interview. Individuals with "alexithymia" have diminished awareness and inability to describe their mood state; nonverbal expression is inhibited. Listed below are six categories of mood states that are used to describe the predominant mood:

- *Normal:* calm, euthymic, pleasant, unremarkable
- *Angry:* belligerent, frustrated, hostile, irritable, sullen
- *Euphoric:* cheerful, elated, happy
- *Apathetic:* bland, dull
- *Dysphoric:* despondent, distraught, hopeless, overwhelmed, sad
- *Apprehensive:* anxious, fearful, frightened, panicky, tense, worried

Affect describes external manifestations of a person's emotional state. Unlike mood, description of affect is entirely objective, and affect is usually variable over the course of an interview, whereas mood usually is sustained for relatively longer periods. The following parameters of affect can be recorded:

- *Type* of affect: Types of affect seen during the interview are reported, using the same list of terms outlined for mood above.
- *Intensity* of affect: When increased, affect is described as "heightened" or "exaggerated"; reduced is "blunted"; no emotional expression is "flat" (flat affect has no intensity, range, or mobility).
- *Reactivity* of affect is assessed in the response to emotional cues from the examiner. Normally the examiner should see reaction to very subtle cues, such as smiling or commiserating.
- *Range* of affect is measured in the variety of emotions expressed during an interview. Inability to express both happy and negative feelings is "restricted" affective range.
- *Appropriateness* or congruence of affect is monitored by comparing emotional expression to the subject matter. For example, the examiner should expect a frightened appearance when anyone is describing being pursued or poisoned by the CIA.
- *Mobility* is the changeability of affect. Rapidly changing affect, especially if precipitous and unprovoked, is "labile" or "volatile." Slowness in change of affective expression can be called "constricted" or "phlegmatic" affect; unchanging affect is "fixed" or "immobile."

SPEECH AND LANGUAGE

Careful examination can differentiate types of aphasia (demonstrated in Figure 4.2 and Table 4.2 of Trzepacz and Baker, 1993) or other language disorders. Major psychiatric disorders (e.g., mania) can affect speech or language. Eight speech and language parameters should be considered:

- *Fluency* is the initiation and flow of speech in conversation; its description is based on the smoothness of the speech rather than its communicativeness. Fluency is assessed in spontaneous speech, its initiation and maintenance, pauses between words, use of connectors, and grammatical correctness. Abnormalities include nonfluent aphasia, scanning, stuttering, and cluttering.

- *Comprehension:* Spoken and written comprehension is tested by increasingly complex commands (such as "open your mouth" and "touch your right ear with your left hand"). Deafness, paresis, or apraxia may falsely suggest impaired comprehension.
- *Repetition:* Tested by asking the patient to repeat words and phrases.
- *Naming:* Assessed by confronting with an object or picture and asking the patient for the name. Other approaches include requesting the patient to generate a list of words starting with a given letter or testing in nonvisual modalities (e.g., naming a small object by touch alone).
- *Writing:* Assessed by giving dictation and also by requesting spontaneous composition.
- *Reading:* Assessed by requesting patient to read aloud (visual impairment should be excluded).
- *Prosody:* Assessed by monitoring intonation, rate, rhythm, and musicality of speech and relationship of intonation to content of speech. With deficient prosody, speech is monotonous. Prosody underlies much of the emotional expressiveness of speech, such as sarcasm (consider the different ways to say "you're *really* smart"). Abnormally fast or slow speech is recorded here. Irrespective of rate, speech that is persistently difficult to interrupt is "pressured."
- *Quality of speech:* Assessed in pitch, volume, articulation, and amount. Articulation is tested with phrases like "no ifs, ands, or buts." Dysarthrias reduce clarity. Manics often speak loudly, and depressed individuals may speak softly, with prolonged latency and reduced spontaneity.

THOUGHT PROCESS, THOUGHT CONTENT, AND PERCEPTION

Thought process (or "form") is assessed in spontaneous communication and in answers to questions throughout the interview. This part of the MSE is objective in that it is based on observation only, but it requires significant reflection and judgment by the clinician, such as "How clear was the communication?"; "Was I frequently confused by the patient?"; "Did he jump from subject to subject, or keep returning to one subject?"; "Did words or ideas keep coming 'out of the blue'?" The following two elements should be included in the MSE report:

- *Connectedness* of thought is how logically or smoothly statements and ideas flow from each other and how relevant answers are to questions. Decreased connectedness is described (in terms for increasing severity) as tangentiality, loosening of associations, or word salad. Circumstantiality is talking around a subject. Flight of ideas is quick and frequent tangentiality.
- *Peculiar thought processes:* neologisms, perseveration, clanging, or blocking.

Thought content also is described. Spontaneous speech is important, especially in identifying predominant themes, but it is helpful to specifically inquire about the following:

- *Delusions* may be clear-cut and spontaneously divulged or may appear only on questioning. For example, when persecutory psychosis is suspected, gentle probes such as "How safe do you feel?"; "How are people treating you?"; or "Do strangers seem to be noticing you?" may be revealing. Reality testing similarly can be assessed: "How certain are you of that?"; "What do you think is the reason for that?"; or "Do you think it could have been a coincidence?" Behavioral impact determines the severity or dangerousness of delusions. The type of delusion is recorded, such as persecutory, grandiose, referential, somatic, religious, or nihilistic.
- *Overvalued ideas* are illogical or objectively false beliefs, but compared with delusions they are held less tenaciously or with better recognition that they may be wrong.
- *Obsessions* are undesired and unpleasant ("ego-dystonic"); at times difficult to distinguish from delusions, obsessions are recog-

nized by the patient as unreasonable or unwarranted. Ask about any ideas or thoughts that keep repeating; specifically query for common obsessions like losing control, doing something dangerous or embarrassing, or being contaminated by germs.

- *Rumination* is persistent mulling over of an unpleasant thought or theme.
- *Preoccupation* is an unduly prominent recurrent topic that is not a delusion or an obsession.
- *Suicidal ideation* may be expressed spontaneously; if not, probe directly by asking about thoughts of death and indirectly by discussing future plans. Questions about suicidality include "Have you thought about dying?"; "Would you be better off/happier/more comfortable dead?"; "Would you like to die?"; "Have you thought about killing yourself?"; "Are you going to kill yourself?" Other potentially relevant information includes intent, past suicidality, steps taken to settle affairs, means for suicide, alternatives to suicide, barriers to suicide, and so on.
- *Other violent ideas:* Self-harm ideation may be less severe than suicidality, such as laceration, mutilation, or intentional neglect. Ideation of violence to others can be of varying urgency and intensity (e.g., "I'd like to punch him" versus "I'd like to shoot him"). Some important issues are identification of a specific intended victim, availability of a weapon, and barriers to violent action.
- *Phobias:* Agoraphobia, social phobia, and relevant simple phobias are recorded here if the patient manifests such symptoms while being observed by the examiner.

Perceptual Abnormalities

- *Hallucinations* may be of any sensory modality, but auditory hallucinations are most characteristic of primary psychiatric illness. Helpful inquiries include asking whether people are talking about the patient, the patient hears voices without seeing anyone, or there has been communication from God or spirits. Auditory hallucinations may be behaviorally evident if the patient appears to talk to the unseen. Voices that talk to each other or make running commentary on the patient's behavior are particularly severe, but perhaps most important is the impact of hallucinations on behavior (e.g., obeying "command" hallucinations that require violence). Hallucinations of a visual, olfactory, tactile, or gustatory nature further raise suspicion of an identifiable organic etiology.
- *Other perceptual abnormalities* include illusions, derealization, depersonalization, déjà vu, and so on.

COGNITION

This section of the MSE describes higher cortical functions, such as the ability to use intellect, reason, attentiveness, logic, and memory. It is an important part of most screening exams and many follow-up exams, especially when neuropsychiatric dysfunction is likely. Some examination may be indirect, such as evaluating memory by discussion of past conversations, names of medicines, or last week's football game. Cognitive functions can be categorized into a number of main areas. Definitions vary, however, for different types of declarative memory. MSE usually does not include testing of procedural memory. Testing each of the following areas is a reasonable screen for cognitive impairment.

- *Orientation:* Orientation to time, place, and person usually are assessed.
- *Attention and concentration:* Attentiveness or distractibility can be monitored in the interview itself or formally tested. Digit span is a measure of attention. Tests of concentration include backward recitation of months or weekdays, spelling backward, or serial subtraction.
- *Registration:* The capacity to immediately repeat a very short list of information, such as three to five words.
- *Short-term memory:* Memory over the course of a few minutes. It can be saturated and is not permanent. A common approach is testing recollection of three unrelated items after two to three minutes. More detailed

approaches include story recall, word list learning tasks, or testing other modalities such as visual memory.

- *Long-term memory:* More permanent memory stores that cannot be saturated. May be recent, such as days or weeks ago, or remote, such as years or decades ago. "Episodic" memory is personal and time tagged; a corroborative source is needed to exclude confabulation. "Semantic" memory tests general information, such as names of recent presidents.
- *Visuoconstructional ability:* Visuospatial abilities are necessary for everyday functions like driving or preparing a meal. Drawing or copying figures, such as a cube, intersecting pentagons, a clock, or a map of the state or country, or making a puzzle can test this function.
- *Executive functions:* These are higher level cognitive functions that include abstracting ability. Abstraction can be assessed in the interview through general conversation or by formal testing. For example, cognitively concrete individuals may respond literally to questions such as "What brought you to the hospital?" Formal testing includes identifying similarities between pairs of objects (e.g., table/chair, orange/apple, painting/poem) or meanings of well-known proverbs.

INSIGHT AND JUDGMENT

Insight is awareness of internal and external realities. For the MSE, assess the patient's recognition of illness, how it impacts other people, and the role of treatment.

Assessment of *judgment* considers the ability to weigh different aspects of an issue. The examiner can discuss important past choices (marriage, work, retirement, big purchases) and recent choices (e.g., how did the patient come to clinical attention?) to demonstrate the degree of judgment used by the patient in decision making. Traditional tests for judgment (e.g., "What would you do if you found a stamped, unmailed envelope on the street?") are relatively insensitive.

Insight and judgment are impacted by *defense mechanisms*. These are less frequently cited in mental status reports than in the past, but, if included, they belong here. One categorization of defense mechanisms is mature types—altruism, humor, sublimation, suppression; neurotic types—repression, displacement, dissociation, reaction formation, intellectualization; immature types—splitting, externalization, idealization, projection, acting out; psychotic types—denial, distortion.

References & Readings 

American Psychiatric Association. (1994). *Diagnostic and statistical manual of mental disorders* (4th ed.). Washington, DC: Author.

Campbell, R. J. (1989). *Psychiatric dictionary* (6th ed.). New York: Oxford University Press.

Cutting, J. (1990). *The right cerebral hemisphere and psychiatric disorders.* New York: Oxford University Press.

Kaplan, H. I., & Sadock, B. J. (1995). Psychiatric report, and typical signs and symptoms of psychiatric illness. In H. I. Kaplan & B. J. Sadock (Eds.), *Comprehensive textbook of psychiatry* (6th ed., pp. 531–544). Baltimore: Williams & Wilkins.

Strauss, G. D. (1995). The psychiatric interview, history, and mental status examination. In H. I. Kaplan & B. J. Sadock (Eds.), *Comprehensive textbook of psychiatry* (6th ed., pp. 521–531). Baltimore: Williams & Wilkins.

Trzepacz, P. T., & Baker, R. W. (1993). *The psychiatric mental status examination.* New York: Oxford University Press.

Vaillant, G. E. (1977). *Adaptation to life: How the best and brightest come of age.* Boston: Little, Brown.

Related Topics

Chapter 3, "Improving Diagnostic and Clinical Interviewing"

Chapter 5, "Increasing the Accuracy of Clinical Judgment (and Thereby Treatment Effectiveness)"

3 IMPROVING DIAGNOSTIC AND CLINICAL INTERVIEWING

Rhonda S. Karg & Arthur N. Wiens

First and foremost, the purpose of a clinical interview is to give clients the opportunity to present their unique perspectives on the reasons they have sought help. From the standpoint of the interviewer, the purposes of a clinical interview are to gather information about the client and his or her problems, to establish a relationship with the client that will facilitate assessment and treatment, and to support and direct the client in his or her search for relief. Toward these goals, the following list describes empirically supported and clinically tested guidelines to improve the efficacy and efficiency of interviews.

1. *Prepare for the interview:* Before the initial meeting, carefully review the referral request and other available data. Clients become understandably annoyed by being asked for information contained in the record and frequently feel slighted by interviewers who did not take the time to review their files. In a similar vein, interview preparation should involve becoming well-informed regarding the problem areas presented by the client, such as substance use, attention-deficit/hyperactivity disorder, or depression (Wiens & Tindall, 1995).

2. *Determine the purpose of the interview:* Before proceeding with an interview, the clinician should have a clear understanding of what he or she desires to accomplish in the interview. Ask yourself: What are the objectives of this interview? For example, is the purpose to make a diagnosis, to plan treatment, to initiate psychotherapy, or all three? In other cases, the interview will accomplish more detailed objectives. For example, should the client be considered incompetent? Should this patient be released from the hospital?

3. *Convey the purpose and parameters of the interview:* Present the rationale for the interview and describe what information you expect the client (or other informant) to provide. The intent is to give the interviewee a "set" or an expectation of what will occur during the interview and why this time is important. Describe the amount of available time, the type of questions you will ask, the limits of privileged information, and to whom the interview findings may be reported. Monumental misunderstandings can occur when clinician and client are not "on the same page."

4. *Use a collaborative interview style:* Put two minds to work and explore problems *with* the client. A collaborative interview style not only helps build rapport but also sets the tone for *working together* during the course of treatment. By sharing the responsibilities of their assessment and treatment, clients gain a sense of control, and are thereby more likely to adhere to recommendations and are less likely to complain if their progress is bumpy.

5. *Hear what the interviewee has to say:* Clients often express their appreciation that someone was willing to hear them. Give clients (or other informants) sufficient time to talk and tell their story in their own ways and words. Listen profoundly; devote 100% of yourself to the interview, hearing not only what the individual is saying (content) but also what meaning lies beneath the words (process and emotion). Truly listening to interviewees is vital to developing rapport and encourages the expression of valid diagnostic information.

6. *Use structured interviews:* By ensuring coverage of critical areas of functioning and by standardizing the diagnostic assessment, structured interviews enhance diagnostic reliability and validity (Rogers, 2001; Wiens, 1990). Examples of these include the Structured Clinical Interview for the *Diagnostic and Statistical Manual of Mental Disorders,* or *DSM-IV* (SCID-I and SCID-II; First, Spitzer, Gibbon, & Williams, 1996), the Schedule for Affective Disorders and Schizophrenia (SADS; Endicott & Spitzer, 1978), the Clinician-Administered PTSD Scale (CAPS; Blake et al., 1995), and the Composite International Diagnostic Interview (CIDI) (World Health Organization, 1997).

7. *Administer screening instruments:* To increase efficiency and improve the accuracy of the clinical interview, administer psychometrically sound screening instruments immediately prior to the structured interview. Two of our favorites are the Psychiatric Diagnostic Screening Questionnaire (Zimmerman & Mattia, 1999) and the SCID Screen Patient Questionnaire (First et al., 1996).

8. *Complement the interview with other assessment methods:* Clinicians who rely exclusively on the clinical interview are prone to miss important information. The comprehensiveness and validity of an interview are enhanced by the use of psychological testing, behavioral or situational observations, and family or social reports. In fact, research consistently demonstrates that objective psychological testing (especially actuarially driven) should be used in practically all diagnostic interviews (e.g., Dawes, Faust, & Meehl, 1989; Meyer et al., 2001).

9. *Ensure that the interviewee comprehends the questions:* Clients are often unfamiliar with psychiatric nomenclature and the constructs underlying the symptoms. Thus, take pains to ensure that the interviewee comprehends the content of the questions. Speak in terms interviewees can understand. Assess their understanding by soliciting examples of the symptoms they endorse and by providing examples of the symptoms they deny. Rephrasing questions using more concrete or lay terms will often help interviewees grasp the underlying constructs.

10. *Include a comprehensive analysis of the problem behaviors:* Begin the functional analysis of behavior by probing for the three dimensions of problematic behavior: frequency (how often?), duration (how long?), and intensity (how severe?). Thoroughly examine the contexts in which the problem behaviors developed and in what contexts they are most likely to manifest themselves. For example, what was happening in the life of the person just prior to the onset of symptoms? What internal and external events appear to trigger or exacerbate the symptoms? What appears to strengthen or weaken the problem behaviors? Giving serious consideration to environmental or situational determinants can assist us in making a multiaxial diagnosis (particularly Axis IV, Psychosocial and Environmental Problems) and might reduce the chance of committing the fundamental attribution error.

11. *Integrate the use of behavioral referents:* Anchoring verbal assessments with behavioral referents will supply greater reliability and validity to individualized assessments. Employing this strategy will also help teach clients to describe and conceptualize their problems in concrete, behavioral terms (versus vague, general terms, like "I have a drinking problem"). Ask questions such as "Can you give me an example of what you mean when you say 'drinking problem'?" or "On a scale of 0–100, with 0 being 'no desire to use alcohol' and 100 being 'the strongest desire to use alcohol I have ever experienced just prior to using,' how would you rate your current craving to drink?"

12. *Differentiate between skill and motivation:* Traditional interviews frequently confuse a person's skill and motivation. Ask: Is this behavior within the person's behavioral repertoire? In other words, does he or she have the skills to perform the behavior in question? Or is it a motivational deficit: Is he or she sufficiently motivated? What consequences are maintaining his or her behavior? While interrelated, the two have differing diagnostic and treatment implications and thus should be clearly delineated.

13. *Consider base rates of behaviors:* Base rates should guide, in part, the prediction of behaviors and the establishment of diagnostic decisions (Finn & Kamphuis, 1995). A corollary is to consider base rates when conducting the clinical interview. Acquire some knowledge of the frequencies of psychiatric symptoms and disorders in the population from which the client is drawn. For example, what is the base rate of committing suicide among older Caucasian males? Consult the extant literature on prevalence rates of psychiatric disorders across client characteristics, paying particular attention to those relevant to your professional setting.

14. *Avoid common biases:* Although formulating hypotheses is an integral component of interviews, one must guard against biases that might result in skewing information and in making incorrect decisions. As described by Meehl (1977), examples of such biases include a tendency to perceive people very unlike ourselves as being sick (the "sick-sick fallacy"), denying the diagnostic significance of an event because it has also happened to us (the "me-too fallacy"), and the idea that understanding clients' behaviors strip them of their significance (the "understanding-it-makes-it-normal fallacy").

15. *Employ debiasing strategies:* Our natural tendency is to search for supporting evidence for our expectations. To help combat this bias, employ a disconfirmation strategy, hunting for information that will disprove initial impressions. What in this protocol disputes the evidence for, say, schizophrenia? Another debiasing strategy is to make yourself think about alternatives after you have generated an initial impression (Arkes, 1981). If we find ourselves unable to generate alternatives, it is time to seek consultation with colleagues. Again, we suggest using base rates and other objective means to help avoid biases and expectations.

16. *Delay reaching decisions while the interview is being conducted:* Research has generally shown that the most accurate clinical decision makers tend to arrive at their conclusions later than do less accurate clinicians (e.g., Elstein, Shulman, & Sprafka, 1978). The clinical implication of these findings is to reserve your diagnostic judgments until after the interview has been completed so that you are less susceptible to prematurely terminating data collection.

17. *Provide a proper termination:* Anticipate the termination of the interview and prepare the client accordingly. Point out when time is running short (usually 5 to 10 minutes prior to ending the interview). One can combine this forewarning with a brief recapitulation, followed by eliciting the client's reactions to the interview and asking if there is any additional topic he or she would like to discuss before ending. Communicate your diagnostic impressions and your treatment recommendations, if applicable. End the interview with a concluding statement expressing your appreciation and your interest.

References, Readings, & Internet Sites 

Arkes, H. R. (1981). Impediments to accurate clinical judgment and possible ways to minimize their impact. *Journal of Consulting and Clinical Psychology, 49,* 323–330.

Blake, D. D., Weathers, F. W., Nagy, L. M., Kaloupek, D. G., Gusman, F. D., Charney, D. S., & Keane, T. M. (1995). The development of a clinician-administered PTSD scale. *Journal of Traumatic Stress, 8,* 75–90.

Cormier, W. H., & Cormier, L. S. (1998). *Interviewing strategies for helpers* (4th ed.). Pacific Grove, CA: Brooks/Cole.

Dawes, R. M., Faust, D., & Meehl, P. E. (1989). Clinical versus actuarial judgment. *Science, 243,* 1668–1674.

Elstein, A. S., Shulman, A. S., & Sprafka, S. A. (1978). *Medical problem solving: An analysis of clinical reasoning.* Cambridge, MA: Harvard University Press.

Endicott, J., & Spitzer, R. L. (1978). A diagnostic interview: The Schedule for Affective Disorders and Schizophrenia. *Archives of General Psychiatry, 35,* 837–844.

Finn, S. E., & Kamphuis, J. H. (1995). What a clinician needs to know about base rates. In J. N. Butcher (Ed.), *Clinical personality assessment* (pp. 224–235). New York: Oxford University Press.

First, M. B., Spitzer, R. L, Gibbon, M., & Williams, J. B. W. (1996). *Structured Clinical Interview for DSM-IV Axis I Disorders, Clinician Version (SCID-CV).* Washington, DC: American Psychiatric Press.

Meehl, P. E. (1977). Why I do not attend case conferences. In P. E. Meehl (Ed.), *Psychodiagnosis: Selected papers* (pp. 225–302). New York: Norton.

Meyer, G. J., Finn, S. E., Eyde, L. D., Kay, G. G., Moreland, K. L., Dies, R. R., Eisman, E. J., Kubiszyn, T. W., & Read, G. M. (2001). Psychological testing and psychological assessment: A review of evidence and issues. *American Psychologist, 56,* 128–165.

Morrison, J. R. (1995). *The first interview: Revised for the DSM-IV.* New York: Guilford Press.

Rogers, R. (2001). *Handbook of diagnostic and structured interviewing.* New York: Guilford Press.

Structured Clinical Interview for DSM-IV. (2001). SCID resource page. Retrieved 2004 from http://cpmcnet.columbia.edu/dept/scid/

Wiens, A. N. (1990). Structured clinical interviews for adults. In G. Goldstein & M. Hersen (Eds.), *Comprehensive textbook of psychiatry* (6th ed., pp. 521–531). Baltimore: Williams & Wilkins.

Wiens, A. N., & Brazil, P. J. (2000). Structured clinical interviews for adults. In G. Goldstein & M. Hersen (Eds.), *Handbook of psychological assessment* (pp. 108–125). New York: Pergamon.

Wiens, A. N. & Tindall, A. G. (1995). Interviewing. In L. Heiden & M. Hersen (Eds.), *Introduction to clinical psychology* (pp. 173–190). New York: Plenum.

World Health Organization. (1997). *Composite International Diagnostic Interview (CIDI), Version 2.1.* Geneva, Switzerland: Author.

Zimmerman, M., & Mattia, J. L. (2001). A self-report scale to help make psychiatric diagnoses: The Psychiatric Diagnostic Screening Questionnaire. *Archives of General Psychiatry, 58,* 787–794.

Related Topics

Chapter 2, "Mental Status Examination"
Chapter 4, "The Multimodal Life History Inventory"
Chapter 18, "*DSM-IV-TR* Classification System"

4 THE MULTIMODAL LIFE HISTORY INVENTORY

Arnold A. Lazarus & Clifford N. Lazarus

Arnold Lazarus in Wolpe and Lazarus (1966) wrote: "Anamnestic interviews may be considerably shortened with literate individuals by asking them to complete, at their leisure, a Life History Questionnaire. . . . Using the completed questionnaire as a guide, patient and therapist may quite rapidly obtain a comprehensive picture of the patient's past experiences and current status" (p. 26). One of the first Life History Questionnaires that Arnold Lazarus compiled appeared in Wolpe and Lazarus (1966, pp. 165–169). Five years later, the initial Life History Questionnaire had been revised and considerably amplified and was published in 1971 (Lazarus, 1971, pp. 239–251). A new version, one that had benefited from further field testing, appeared in 1981 (Lazarus, 1981, pp. 239–251). Prepared in collaboration with Clifford N. Lazarus, the most recent version, now referred to as the Multimodal Life History Inventory, appeared in 1997 (Lazarus, 1997, pp. 127–142). This 15-page inventory is copyrighted and sold by Research Press, 2612 North Mattis Avenue, Champaign, IL 61821.

The use of the Multimodal Life History Inventory facilitates treatment by

- Encouraging clients to focus on specific problems, their sources, and attempted solutions;
- Providing focal antecedents, presenting problems, and relevant historical data; and
- Generating a valuable perspective regarding a client's style and treatment expectations.

Basically, the inventory provides a therapeutic "road map" that aids in clinical decision making by helping patients, and hence therapists, identify a wide range of potentially salient problems within all the major spheres of biopsychosocial functioning. Typically, the Multimodal Life History Inventory is handed to patients at the end of the initial interview, and they are asked to fill it out and bring it with them to their second session. Seriously disturbed (e.g., deluded, deeply depressed, highly agitated) clients will obviously not be expected to comply, but most psychiatric patients who are reasonably literate will find the exercise useful for speeding up routine history taking, thus readily providing the therapist with significant data to generate a viable treatment plan. For individuals who cannot or will not complete it, the inventory may be used as a guide during the sessions to obtain a thorough overview of the client's background—early development, family interactions, and educational, sexual, occupational, and other experiences.

Clients are advised not to try to complete the inventory in a single sitting, but to space it out over several days. When the completed form is received, the therapist peruses it in his or her own time, making notations and queries that are discussed during the next and perhaps subsequent sessions. Items that have been omitted also become grist for the mill.

We tend to read through the brief section "Expectations Regarding Therapy" before anything else because it gives clues to the patient's expectations, as well as the type of therapeutic style and cadence to which he or she may best respond. For example, a client who sees therapy as an opportunity to ventilate and to be heard by a good listener will require a different treatment trajectory than one who expects to be coached and reeducated. We also zero in on the 15 questions at the end of the section titled "Thoughts" that appear as a 5-point rating scale on the inventory. This section immediately alerts the therapist to dysfunctional thoughts and irrational ideas the client may harbor.

We instruct clients to omit their names, addresses, or any other identifying information if this will lead them to answer the inventory more honestly and completely.

We now present the items that constitute the inventory. The actual forms, of course, are laid out differently, with adequate space for different answers and room for clients to elaborate should they so desire.

Multimodal Life History Inventory

The purpose of this inventory is to obtain a comprehensive picture of your background. In psychotherapy, records are necessary since they permit a more thorough dealing with one's problems. By completing these questions as fully and as accurately as you can, you will facilitate your therapeutic program. You are requested to answer these routine questions in your own time instead of using up your actual consulting time (please feel free to use extra sheets if you need additional answer space).

It is understandable that you might be concerned about what happens to the information about you because much or all of this information is highly personal. Case records are strictly confidential.

(*continued*)

General Information

Name:
Address:
Telephone numbers: Day, Evening
Age:
Occupation:
Sex:
Date of birth:
Place of birth:
Religion:
Height:
Weight:
Does your weight fluctuate?
If yes, by how much?
Do you have a family physician?
Name of family physician:
Telephone number:
By whom were you referred?
Marital status:
Remarried? How many times?
With whom do you live?
What sort of work are you doing now?
Does your present work satisfy you?
If no, please explain:
What kind of jobs have you held in the past?
Have you been in therapy before or received any professional assistance for your problems?
Have you ever been hospitalized for psychological/psychiatric problems? If yes, when and where?
Have you ever attempted suicide?
Does any member of your family suffer from an "emotional" or "mental" disorder?
Has any relative attempted or committed suicide?

Personal and Social History

Father:
Name:
Age:
Occupation:
Health:
If deceased, give his age at time of death:
How old were you at the time?
Cause of death:
Mother:
Name:
Age:
Occupation:
Health:
If deceased, give her age at time of death:
How old were you at the time?
Cause of death:
Siblings:
Age(s) of brother(s):
Age(s) of sister(s):
Any significant details about siblings:
If you were not brought up by your parents, who raised you and between what years?
Give a description of your father's (or father substitute's) personality and his attitude toward you (past and present):
Give a description of your mother's (or mother substitute's) personality and her attitude toward you (past and present):
In what ways were you disciplined or punished by your parents?
Give an impression of your home atmosphere (i.e., the home in which you grew up). Mention state of compatibility between parents and between children.
Were you able to confide in your parents?
Basically, did you feel loved and respected by your parents?
If you have a stepparent, give your age when your parent remarried:
Has anyone (parents, relatives, friends) ever interfered in your marriage, occupation, etc.?
Scholastic strengths:
Scholastic weaknesses:
What was the last grade completed (or highest degree)?
Check any of the following that applied during your childhood/adolescence: Happy childhood; Unhappy childhood; Emotional/behavior problems; Legal trouble; Death in family; Medical problems; Ignored; Not enough friends; Sexually abused; School problems; Severely bullied or teased; Financial problems; Eating disorder; Strong religious convictions; Drug use; Used alcohol; Severely punished

Description of Presenting Problems

State in your own words the nature of your main problems:
Please estimate the severity of your problem(s):
Mildly upsetting; Moderately upsetting; Very severe; Extremely severe; Totally incapacitating
When did your problems begin?
What seems to worsen your problems?
What have you tried that has been helpful?
How satisfied are you with your life as a whole these days?
Not satisfied 1 2 3 4 5 6 7 Very satisfied
How would you rate your overall level of tension during the past month?
Relaxed 1 2 3 4 5 6 7 Tense

Expectations Regarding Therapy

In a few words, what do you think therapy is all about?
How long do you think your therapy should last?
What personal qualities do you think the ideal therapist should possess?

Modality Analysis of Current Problems

The following section is designed to help you describe your current problems in greater detail and to identify problems that might otherwise go unnoticed. This will enable us to design a comprehensive treatment program and tailor it to your specific needs. The following section is organized according to the seven modalities of Behaviors, Feelings, Physical sensations, Images, Thoughts, Interpersonal relationships, and Biological factors.

Behaviors

Check any of the following behaviors that often apply to you:
Overeat; Loss of control; Phobic avoidance; Crying; Take drugs; Suicidal attempts; Spend too much money; Outbursts of temper; Unassertive; Compulsions; Can't keep a job; Odd behavior; Smoke; Insomnia; Drink too much; Withdrawal; Take too many risks; Work too hard; Nervous tics; Lazy; Procrastination; Concentration difficulties; Eating problems; Impulsive reactions; Sleep disturbance; Aggressive behavior; Others:
What are some special talents or skills that you feel proud of?
What would you like to start doing?
What would you like to stop doing?
How is your free time spent?
What kind of hobbies or leisure activities do you enjoy or find relaxing?
Do you have trouble relaxing or enjoying weekends and vacations? If yes, please explain:
If you could have any two wishes, what would they be?

Feelings

Check any of the following feelings that often apply to you:
Angry; Fearful; Happy; Hopeful; Bored; Optimistic; Annoyed; Panicky; Conflicted; Helpless; Restless; Tense; Sad; Energetic; Shameful; Relaxed; Lonely; De-

(*continued*)

pressed; Envious; Regretful; Jealous; Contented; Anxious; Guilty; Hopeless; Unhappy; Excited; Others:
List your five main fears:
What are some positive feelings you have experienced recently?
When are you most likely to lose control of your feelings?
Describe any situations that make you feel calm or relaxed:

Physical sensations

Check any of the following physical sensations that often apply to you:
Abdominal pain; Bowel disturbances; Hear things; Pain or burning with urination; Tingling; Watery eyes; Menstrual difficulties; Numbness; Flushes; Headaches; Stomach trouble; Nausea; Dizziness; Tics; Skin problems; Palpitations; Fatigue; Dry mouth; Muscle spasms; Twitches; Burning or itching skin; Tension; Back pain; Chest pains; Sexual disturbances; Tremors; Rapid heartbeat; Unable to relax; Fainting spells; Don't like to be touched; Blackouts; Excessive sweating; Visual disturbances; Hearing problems; Others:
What sensations are pleasant for you? Unpleasant for you?

Images

Check any of the following that apply to you. I picture myself:
Being happy; Being talked about; Being trapped; Being hurt; Being aggressive; Being laughed at; Not coping; Being helpless; Being promiscuous; Succeeding; Hurting others; Losing control; Being in charge; Being followed; Failing; Others:
I have:
Pleasant sexual images; Seduction images; Unpleasant childhood images; Images of being loved; Negative body image; Unpleasant sexual images; Lonely images; Others:
Describe a very pleasant image, mental picture, or fantasy:
Describe a very unpleasant image, mental picture, or fantasy:
Describe your image of a completely "safe place":
Describe any persistent or disturbing images that interfere with your daily functioning:
How often do you have nightmares?

Thoughts

Check each of the following that you might use to describe yourself:
Intelligent; Confident; A nobody; Inadequate; Useless; Confused; Worthwhile; Evil; Ambitious; Sensitive; Crazy; Worthless; Ugly; Stupid; Can't make decisions; Morally degenerate; Naive; Suicidal ideas; Loyal; Considerate; Trustworthy; Deviant; Full of regrets; Unattractive; Honest; Incompetent; Concentration difficulties; Memory problems; Attractive; Persevering; Deviant; Good sense of humor; Horrible thoughts; Hardworking; Unlovable; Conflicted; Undesirable; Lazy; Untrustworthy; Dishonest; Others:
What do you consider to be your craziest thought or idea?

Are you bothered by thoughts that occur over and over again? If yes, what are these thoughts?

What worries do you have that may negatively affect your mood or behavior?

On each of the following items, please circle the number that most accurately reflects your opinions:

[On the actual inventory, this appears as a scale ranging from "1," Strongly Disagree, to a "5," Strongly Agree.] I should not make mistakes; I should be good at everything I do; When I do not know something, I should pretend that I do; I should not disclose personal information; I am a victim of circumstances; My life is controlled by outside forces; Other people are happier than I am; It is very important to please other people; Play it safe, don't take any risks; I don't deserve to be happy; If I ignore my problems, they will disappear; It is my responsibility to make other people happy; I should strive for perfection; Basically, there are two ways of doing things—the right way and the wrong way; I should never be upset.

Interpersonal relationships

Do you make friends easily? Do you keep them?

Did you date much during high school? College?

Were you ever bullied or severely teased?

Describe any relationship that gives you: Joy; Grief

Rate the degree to which you generally feel relaxed and comfortable in social situations: Very relaxed 1 2 3 4 5 6 7 Very anxious

Do you have one or more friends with whom you feel comfortable sharing your most private thoughts?

Marriage (or a committed relationship):

How long did you know your spouse before your engagement?

How long were you engaged before you got married?

How long have you been married?

What is your spouse's age? His/her occupation?

Describe your spouse's personality:

What do you like most about your spouse?

What do you like least about your spouse?

What factors detract from your marital satisfaction?

How satisfied are you with your marriage?

How do you get along with your partner's friends and family?

How many children do you have?

Please give their names and ages:

Do any of your children present special problems? If yes, please describe:

Any significant details about a previous marriage(s)? Sexual relationships?

Describe your parents' attitude toward sex. Was sex discussed in your home?

When and how did you derive your knowledge of sex?

When did you first become aware of your own sexual impulses?

Have you ever experienced any anxiety or guilt arising out of sex or masturbation?

Relevant details regarding your first or subsequent sexual experiences?

Is your present sex life satisfactory? If no, please explain:

Provide information about any significant homosexual reactions or relationships:

Are there any problems in your relationships with people at work? If yes, please describe:

(*continued*)

Please complete the following:

One of the ways people hurt me is; I could shock you by; My spouse (or boyfriend/girlfriend) would describe me as; My best friend thinks I am; People who dislike me:

Are you currently troubled by any past rejections or loss of a love relationship?

Biological factors

Do you have any current concerns about your physical health?

List any medications you are currently taking:

Do you eat three well-balanced meals each day?

Do you get regular physical exercise? If yes, what type and how often?

Please list any significant medical problems that apply to you or to members of your family:

Please describe any surgery you have had (give dates):

Please describe any physical handicap(s) you have:

Menstrual history

Age at first period:

Were you informed? Did it come as a shock?

Are you regular? Duration: Do you have pain?

Do your periods affect your moods? Date of last period:

Check any of the following that apply to you:

Muscle weakness; Tranquilizers; Diuretics; Diet pills; Marijuana; Hormones; Sleeping pills; Aspirin; Cocaine; Painkillers; Narcotics; Stimulants; Hallucinogens (e.g., LSD); Laxatives; Cigarettes; Tobacco (specify); Coffee; Alcohol; Birth control pills; Vitamins; Undereat; Overeat; Eat junk foods; Diarrhea; Constipation; Gas; Indigestion; Nausea; Vomiting; Heartburn; Dizziness; Palpitations; Fatigue; Allergies; High blood pressure; Chest pain; Shortness of breath; Insomnia; Sleep too much; Fitful sleep; Early morning awakening; Earaches; Headaches; Backaches; Bruise or bleed easily; Weight problems; Others:

STRUCTURAL PROFILE

[On the actual inventory, clients are asked to rate the following items on a 7-point scale.]

Behaviors: Some people may be described as "doers"—they are action oriented; they like to busy themselves, get things done, take on various projects. How much of a doer are you?

Feelings: Some people are very emotional and may or may not express it. How emotional are you? How deeply do you feel things? How passionate are you?

Physical sensations: Some people attach a lot of value to sensory experiences, such as sex, food, music, art, and other "sensory delights." Others are very much aware of minor aches, pains, and discomforts. How "tuned in" to your sensations are you?

Mental images: How much fantasy or daydreaming do you engage in? This is separate from thinking or planning. This is "thinking in pictures," visualizing real or imagined experiences, letting your mind roam. How much are you into imagery?

Thoughts: Some people are very analytical and like to plan things. They like to reason things through. How much of a "thinker" and "planner" are you?

Interpersonal relationships: How important are other people to you? This is your self-rating as a social being. How important are close friendships to you, the tendency to gravitate toward people, the desire for intimacy? The opposite of this is being a "loner."

Biological factors: Are you healthy and health conscious? Do you avoid bad habits like smoking, too much alcohol, drinking a lot of coffee, overeating, and so on? Do you exercise regularly, get enough sleep, avoid junk foods, and generally take care of your body?

Please describe any significant childhood (or other) memories and experiences you think your therapist should be aware of.

References & Readings 

Lazarus, A. A. (1971). *Behavior therapy and beyond.* New York: McGraw-Hill.

Lazarus, A. A. (1981). *The practice of multimodal therapy.* New York: McGraw-Hill.

Lazarus, A. A. (1997). *Brief but comprehensive psychotherapy.* New York: Springer.

Lazarus, A. A. (2002). The Multimodal Assessment Therapy approach. In F. Kaslow (Series Ed.) & J. L. Lebow (Ed.), *Comprehensive handbook of psychotherapy: Vol. 4, Integrative/eclectic* (pp. 241–254). New York: Wiley.

Wolpe, J., & Lazarus, A. A. (1966). *Behavior therapy techniques.* Oxford: Pergamon Press.

Related Topics

Chapter 2, "Mental Status Examination"

Chapter 3, "Improving Diagnostic and Clinical Interviewing"

Chapter 5, "Increasing the Accuracy of Clinical Judgment (and Thereby Treatment Effectiveness)"

Chapter 77, "Genograms in Assessment and Therapy"

5 INCREASING THE ACCURACY OF CLINICAL JUDGMENT (AND THEREBY TREATMENT EFFECTIVENESS)

David Faust

Increased predictive accuracy improves clinical practice. This is not only because patients may seek guidance about the likelihood of various outcomes (e.g., "Am I in a relationship with a future?") but also because intervention usually presumes prediction. Our interventions are guided by our expectations (predictions) of their effects and effectiveness. After all, we would not say, "Let's try this, although I don't have the slightest idea how well it's going to work, and who cares anyway, because what's going to happen next is of no concern," but rather, "I think what's most likely to help is . . ." Similarly, therapeutic interpretation is guided by predicted impact or what is expected to benefit the patient.

There is much useful knowledge and methodology for increasing predictive accuracy, although, unfortunately, this information usually is not provided in the training of mental health professionals (see Dawes, 1988; Faust, 1984; Meehl, 1973). A few of the more important principles are conveyed in the "rules of thumb" that follow.

GO WITH THE MORE FREQUENT EVENT

Principle

Assume the evidence points about equally toward two alternatives and that the potential disadvantages of misidentifying both conditions or outcomes are about the same. Under such circumstances, you should guess that the more frequent of the two conditions is present. To the extent the frequency of the two conditions or outcomes varies, such a strategy will enhance predictive accuracy. In fact, not uncommonly, the frequency of an event (i.e., the base rate) is the single most predictive variable or useful piece of information.

Illustration

To illustrate, suppose that Alzheimer's disease occurs about 10 times more often than Pick's disease and that the manifestations of these disorders, at least initially, are often very similar. If one guesses Alzheimer's disease every time, one will be correct about 9 in 10 times. For example, if, across a series of 100 cases, there are 91 cases of Alzheimer's disease and 9 cases of Pick's disease, and if one guesses Alzheimer's every time, one will achieve a 91% accuracy rate.

Elaboration

This guide, as narrowly stated above, assumes that evidence points about equally in the direction of two conditions and that there are roughly equal costs and benefits for both types of correct and incorrect judgments (i.e., correctly identifying Condition A versus missing Condition A; correctly identifying Condition B versus missing Condition B). Of course, such relatively clean examples are not that common, and often there is an imbalance across one or both of these dimensions. This does not negate the underlying principle, that is, that frequency data or base rates are often among the most important guides to decision making, but it does call for adjustments.

Suppose, for example, that a set of signs indicate posttraumatic stress disorder (PTSD) versus major depression (MD) at a 2:1 ratio, but that in the setting of application MD occurs four times more often than PTSD. Under such circumstances, most individuals with the sign will still have MD. One can think of this as the 4:1 ratio (or base rate) in favor of MD more than offsetting the 2:1 ratio (the sign) in favor of PTSD. It is simply a matter of one indicator pointing to MD and the other to PTSD, with the former indicator being a more powerful or accurate one. However, there is a partial offset of the 4:1 ratio, and the base rate will not be as strong an indicator of MD as it would be were the sign neutral or not indicative of the alternative diagnosis. The point is that deviations from clean examples change the operating characteristics, although not the underlying principles, and call for certain steps to determine, for example, shifts in the relative probabilities of alternative outcomes.

These adjustments can be difficult to make impressionistically, especially as the differences among alternatives become less extreme. Fortunately, exact determinations can be made using relatively simple formalisms (see Meehl & Rosen, 1973). Steps can also be taken to deal with gaps in information about frequencies or base rates and to consider utilities or the costs and benefits of different types of correct and incorrect decisions (see Faust & Nurcombe, 1989).

Summary of the First Principle

In summary, the frequency of a condition or event is often among the most useful, if not the single best, predictor of that event or outcome. The extreme case illustrates this point: If something never occurs or always occurs, knowing this alone would lead to 100% predictive accuracy. Indeed, as events become more or less frequent, or more or less frequent than one another, greater and greater predictive accuracy can be achieved by playing the base rates, that is, by guessing that the event that is less frequent will not occur or that the event that is more frequent will occur. Under such circumstances, the rate of accurate decisions can increase 10-fold or more by utilizing base rates versus contrary diagnostic or predictive signs or indicators, even those that, in conditions of equal frequency, perform reasonably well.

INCLUDING A BAD PREDICTOR IS USUALLY MUCH WORSE THAN EXCLUDING A GOOD PREDICTOR

Principle

For technical reasons to be described, mistakenly including a weak or invalid variable in the predictive mix usually does considerably more harm than mistakenly overlooking or disregarding a good predictor. Therefore, in most situations, especially when other predictors of known value are available, if in doubt, exclude rather than include; in other words, avoid incorporating additional variables into the decision process.

Explanation of Principle

Clinicians are commonly advised to integrate most or all the data, a strategy that flows from mistaken beliefs about validity and is almost sure to *decrease* overall accuracy. The misconception is that validity is cumulative, and hence the more (data or predictors) the better. It is not uncommon, for example, for authors to call for the integration of dozens, if not hundreds, of test scores and data points. Were validity strictly cumulative, then, if one could identify 15 predictors that each accounted for 10% of the variance, their combination would account for 150% of the variance! This does not hold because predictors are often redundant or overlap with each other. Consequently, they are not carving out unique pieces of the predictive pie but are re-covering the same ground. To illustrate, if we are trying to obtain a proper physical description of a person and measure the person's weight first in pounds and then in kilograms, the second measurement really adds nothing new. We have only measured the same dimension twice. Similarly, two depression inventories may both measure roughly the same thing.

Starting with the first predictor (and for purposes of this discussion bypassing the issue of reliability), additional predictors are valuable to the extent they are *both* valid and nonredundant. In many domains in clinical psychology, once one combines about three to five of the most valid and independent variables, adding a new variable often does little or nothing to increase predictive accuracy, even if it has a very respectable level of validity (owing to its redundancy). However, combining or integrating a weaker or invalid variable cannot help matters and will often decrease judgmental accuracy.

Suppose, for example, that sexual abuse has not occurred and that the three best predictors of possible abuse are negative. Three other variables, which, unfortunately and unbeknownst to the clinician, are really weak or poor predictors, indicate otherwise. Obviously, a correct conclusion might be overturned, and in the long run, the inclusion of weak or invalid variables will have a detrimental overall effect.

Further Elaboration

Precisely determining alterations in predictive accuracy as variables are combined in different ways or are added or subtracted is very difficult to do via observation or experientially. For example, even an astute observer is rather unlikely to get it just right when subjectively "calculating" the figure for shared variance or redundancy across two variables. Proper development of decision procedures through formal research includes analysis of predictive accuracy, level of redundancy, and the impact of adding new variables to the predictive mix. This is clearly a situation in which human ingenuity, via the development of scientific and analytic methods, has gone a long way toward solving tasks that place unrealistic demands on the unaided human mind, much like the telescope has extended human senses.

Also contrary to common belief, the exact weighting of variables is often of much lesser importance than selecting which variables to use and which to exclude. Indeed, in many situations, weighting the relevant variables equally results in the same, or about the same, predictive accuracy as optimal weighting, and the "optimal" weights derived in one situation are often relatively unstable across other situations anyway, reducing their potential advantages (Dawes, 1979; Dawes & Corrigan, 1974; Dawes, Faust, & Meehl, 1989). All these considerations lead to the same prescription: Identify (preferably through well-conducted research) the limited set of variables that are most valid and nonredundant and then be conservative, that is, worry much more about adding questionable variables to the mix than overlooking additional valid variables.

TO REDUCE RISK OF A BAD OUTCOME, START WITH THE *LEAST* LIKELY EVENT IN THE CHAIN OR SET

Principle and Explanation

When a set of events *all* must occur for something bad to happen, the greatest proportionate reduction in risk occurs when one lowers the probability of the *least* likely link. Consider the following example. Suppose two things, Event A and Event B, must take place for a bad outcome to occur. Suppose that the probability of Event A is .20 and of Event B is .90, making the probability of the outcome .20 × .90 = .18. Now suppose for practical reasons that you can intervene with either A or B but not both, perhaps because of limited time or resources. Suppose further that you can decrease the probability of either of the variables by .10.

In attempting to reduce risk, intuition usually leads one to focus first on the segment of the chain that appears most likely to occur. For example, if we are trying to avoid a suicide attempt, we might direct most of our efforts toward the most probable event (e.g., access to a means). However, it is instructive to examine the consequences of this strategy using the hypothetical figures stated above. If I reduce Event B by .10, or from .90 to .80, the result is .20 × .80 = .16, or a minimal reduction in risk. In contrast, if I decrease A by .10, or from .20 to .10, the result is .10 × .90 = .09; that is, I have cut the risk in half.

The results or proportionate impact can be even more dramatic as the probability of the least likely event decreases below that stated in the hypothetical, especially when these probabilities start out rather low. For example, assume that the probability of A is now .06 and that B is still at .90, and that we could reduce either A or B by .05. Before intervention, we start at .06 × .90 = .054. If we reduce B by .05, the result is .06 × .85 = .051; but if we reduce A by .05, the result is .01 × .90 = .009. By intervening in the right place, rather than achieving a very minor decrease in risk, we have reduced it almost sixfold, or from about 1 in 18 to about 1 in 100. The obverse also holds and tends to align more closely with intuition; that is, when one wants a positive outcome to occur, all other things being equal, bolster the least likely link in the chain.

Cautionary Note

It is of utmost importance to recognize that this principle of risk reduction assumes that all events in the set must occur for the event to occur. (Technically, it is better to use the term *set* rather than *chain* because no particular sequence needs to be assumed.) Also, as with base rates, the conditions stated here (i.e., all other things being equal) often will not hold, and adjustments will have to be made (e.g., What if I can reduce A, the less frequent event, by .10 and B by .20?). However, the mathematics are usually simple because one need only multiply the probabilities of each relevant variable by the others (i.e., A × B × C, etc.). The main point is that the tendency to focus time and effort on the most likely event is often misdirected and opposite to the more effective approach.

BEFORE DECIDING, GENERATE REASONS TO DECIDE OTHERWISE

Principle and Explanation

The simple exercise of generating reasons to decide otherwise or of actively considering or bringing to mind contrary evidence tends to counter a number of problematic judgment tendencies. For one, once individuals formulate hypotheses or tentative conclusions, they tend to look for possible confirming evidence more so than contrary evidence, or, given a certain mental set, supportive evidence may be more salient or noticeable. This may skew the evidence that is gathered or considered in favor of supportive evidence, resulting in premature termination of data collection, erroneous conclusions, and overconfidence. Active attempts to recognize and consider contrary evidence tend to rebalance the scales.

Further Explanation

Given the variability of human behavior over time and place, as well as error in our measuring devices, a plausible but false, or mainly false, conclusion will often still find considerable supportive evidence. For example, if one concludes that the patient has more than expectable levels of interpersonal conflict, when the patient actually is a little better than average on this score, thorough probing of his or her history ought to uncover many instances in which interpersonal conflicts occurred. If alternative or contrary evidence becomes more salient, the false initial impression may be overturned.

Confidence that is unduly inflated by the tendency to focus on one side of the coin, or evidence consistent with one's conclusions, can lead to many secondary, damaging judgment practices. For example, when one is more confident than is justified, there is a tendency (a) to make overly extreme or risky predictions ("I know he won't commit murder when on parole"); (b) to fail to gather important sources of information (because one feels one already knows); and (c) to not learn or implement the many useful methods that scientific research and work in decision making, such as those discussed in this chapter, have uncovered.

References & Readings

Arkes, H. R. (1981). Impediments to accurate clinical judgment and possible ways to minimize their impact. *Journal of Consulting and Clinical Psychology, 49,* 323–330.

Dawes, R. M. (1979). The robust beauty of improper linear models in decision making. *American Psychologist, 34,* 571–582.

Dawes, R. M. (1988). *Rational choice in an uncertain world.* New York: Harcourt Brace Jovanovich.

Dawes, R. M., & Corrigan, B. (1974). Linear models in decision making. *Psychological Bulletin, 81,* 95–106.

Dawes, R. M., Faust, D., & Meehl, P. E. (1989). Clinical versus actuarial judgment. *Science, 243,* 1668–1674.

Faust, D. (1984). *The limits of scientific reasoning.* Minneapolis: University of Minnesota Press.

Faust, D., & Nurcombe, B. (1989). Improving the accuracy of clinical judgment. *Psychiatry, 52,* 197–208.

Meehl, P. E. (1973). *Psychodiagnosis: Selected papers.* Minneapolis: University of Minnesota Press.

Meehl, P. E., & Rosen, A. (1973). Antecedent probability and the efficiency of psychometric signs, patterns, and cutting scores. In P. E. Meehl, *Psychodiagnosis: Selected papers* (pp. 32–62). Minneapolis: University of Minnesota Press.

Slovic, P., Fischhoff, B., & Lichtenstein, S. (1982). Facts versus fears: Understanding perceived risk. In D. Kahneman, P. Slovic, & A. Tversky (Eds.), *Judgment under uncertainty: Heuristics and biases* (pp. 463–489). New York: Cambridge University Press.

Related Topics

Chapter 3, "Improving Diagnostic and Clinical Interviewing"

Chapter 48, "Key Principles in the Assessment of Psychotherapy Outcome"

6 DEVELOPMENTAL NEUROPSYCHOLOGICAL ASSESSMENT

Jane Holmes Bernstein, Betsy Kammerer, Penny A. Prather, & Celiane Rey-Casserly

FUNDAMENTAL ASSUMPTIONS OF NEUROPSYCHOLOGICAL (NP) ASSESSMENT OF CHILDREN

- Clinical assessment in neuropsychology, as in psychology, involves extracting diagnostic meaning from an individual's history, from direct and indirect observations of behavior, and from performance on targeted tests.
- NP assessment requires analysis of both neurological and psychological (behavioral) variables. Observed behavior is a function of the interaction of the brain with the environment.
- NP assessment is situated within a wider social context, requiring sensitivity to issues of culture, language, and diversity.
- The goal of NP assessment is optimal adaptation in all aspects of "real life"—by promoting the child's psychosocial and intellectual development.
- The practice of neuropsychology is based on knowledge of the brain as a necessary, but not sufficient, substrate for behavior relationships. Its goal is to explicate brain-behavior relationships. Neuropsychology is not defined by a set of tests, no matter how extensive or well organized the cognitive domains tapped by the tests.
- The practice of neuropsychology requires formal and rigorous training of the clinician.
- Children are not small adults. Comprehensive assessment models for children must incorporate development in their analysis of behavior. Models of relatively static, modular adult behavioral function should be applied to children with extreme caution.

ASSUMPTIONS OF DEVELOPMENTAL ANALYSIS

- Development implies a dynamic interaction between an organism and its environment. The principles at the core of a developmental NP analysis of behavior are those of the developmental sciences: structure, context, process, and experience.
- In the developing child the contribution of "brain" to observed behavior cannot be meaningfully assessed without reference to the child's developmental course, maturational status, immediate environmental demands, and wider sociocultural context.
- Knowledge of normal development and its variation is a prerequisite for all developmental analysis.
- A disturbance of the brain at any point in time is necessarily incorporated into the subsequent developmental course. Both neurological and behavioral development will proceed in a different fashion around the new brain organization.
- A brain insult will have differential impact on behavioral outcome as a function of the developmental status of the disrupted brain system at the time of the insult.
- The behaviors or "symptoms" that prompt

referral occur in the context of the expected competencies of the child at a given developmental stage. Thus, the same underlying neuropsychological problem will be manifest in different ways at different points in development.

INDICATIONS FOR NP ASSESSMENT

- In contrast to adults, children undergo frequent psychological and/or educational testing. "Overtesting" is thus of serious concern. Referral questions should be carefully reviewed. NP consultation, rather than comprehensive NP assessment, should be considered where appropriate.
- NP assessment should be considered when a child unexpectedly fails to meet environmental demands in either academic or psychosocial contexts, and/or when psychological, psychiatric, psychoeducational, or multidisciplinary assessment does not provide an adequate explanation for presenting behavior or sufficient information to guide intervention planning.
- NP assessment is indicated (a) when behavioral change is seen in the context of known or suspected neurological disorders; known or suspected systemic disorders with impact on the central nervous system (CNS); treatment regimens with potentially deleterious impact on CNS status; degenerative, metabolic, or specific genetic disorders; and disorders associated with structural CNS abnormalities; (b) to clarify the relationship of behavioral change to specific medical/neurological/psychiatric diagnoses or to specific neural substrates; (c) to provide a baseline profile to monitor recovery, effects of treatment, and/or the impact of developmental change on behavioral function; (d) to provide ongoing monitoring of neurobehavioral status in the context of developmental change, recovery, and/or treatment—particularly in the case of specific injury and/or medical or surgical intervention (e.g., epilepsy surgery, medication trials or changes, radiation therapy) and in the context of the use of medications; and (e) for clinical research in neurological, psychiatric, and psychological populations.
- NP assessment provides important information to aid in the better understanding and management of behavioral consequences of childhood disorders—such as (but not limited to) the role of executive functions in spina bifida, prematurity, or attentional disorders; the prediction of behavioral late effects in treated brain tumor and leukemias; the impact of seizure activity and/or medications in epilepsy; the contribution of language-processing variables to reading disorders; the interplay of social and cognitive factors in the outcome of traumatic brain injury; the potential brain substrates for deficits in processing socially relevant information; or the elucidation of NP deficits associated with psychiatric disorders (such as schizophrenia or obsessive-compulsive disorder).
- NP services are provided in the form of (a) comprehensive individual assessments (outpatient); (b) consultation—to educational, psychiatric, social work, medicine, and rehabilitation professionals—including review of records, analysis of behavioral data, interpretation of neurological data in the behavioral arena, application of neurologically relevant information to everyday settings (home, school), and assistance in diagnostic formulation and intervention strategies; (c) inpatient assessment or consultation to localize function (seizures), monitor behavioral change in the intraoperative setting, and document behavioral functioning in psychiatric patients; and (d) forensic evaluation to provide a comprehensive description of developmental status, cognitive functioning, academic achievement, and psychosocial adjustment and to address future risks/needs in forensic situations.

DIAGNOSTIC STRATEGY

- Diagnosis in neuropsychology is not a function of test performance. It is the result of a formal assessment strategy that is ideally formulated as an experiment with an *N* of 1, theoretically driven, with hypotheses that are systematically tested and with a design and methodology that include appropriate controls for variability and bias.

- The diagnostic strategy not only should address the referral questions but also should be framed within the biopsychosocial context of the child's life. It should incorporate adaptive competence, emotional well-being, and functional processing style, as well as cognitive and academic abilities.
- The diagnostic strategy must integrate the "vertical" dimension of development with the "horizontal" dimension of the child's current neurobehavioral repertoire.
- Relevant diagnostic data are derived from the individual's history, direct and indirect observations of behavior, and performance on psychological tests.
- The diagnostic formulation is the basis for referencing the child's profile to categories of neurological, psychological, and/or educational disorders.
- Diagnostic categories can be framed in terms of neuropsychological or neurodevelopmental variables, specific psychological (cognitive, perceptual, information processing) factors, primary academic deficits, and/or specific nosological schemes (e.g., *DSM-IV*).
- The diagnostic formulation is the basis for determination of *risk* (prediction of future response to expectable challenges, both psychosocial and intellectual) and for the design and implementation of the *comprehensive, individualized management strategy* that addresses the pattern of risks faced by *this* child in *this* family with *this* history, *this* profile of skills, and *these* goals (both short- and long-term).

BEHAVIORAL DOMAINS

- In NP assessment, behavioral domains rather than test performance are the units of analysis.
- Behavioral domains tapped can be organized in a number of ways—and labeled differently by clinicians with differing theoretical perspectives. What they have in common, however, is that they are sufficiently wide-ranging to address both the behavioral repertoire of the individual being assessed and the referral question(s).
- Domains include regulatory and goal-directed *executive capacities* (arousal, attention, memory, learning, mood, affect, emotion, reasoning, planning, decision making, monitoring, initiating, sustaining, inhibiting, and shifting abilities); *skills and knowledge bases* (sensory and perceptual processing in [primarily] visual and auditory modalities, motor capacities, communicative competence, social cognition, linguistic processing, speech functions, spatial cognition); and *achievement* (academic skills, adaptive functioning, social comportment, societal adjustment).

SOURCES OF DATA

- The history is typically obtained from interviews of the child, parent(s)/guardian(s), teacher(s), psychologist, and physician; from medical/educational records; and from questionnaires. The goal of the history is to determine the *child's heritage* (genetic, medical, socioeconomic, cultural, educational) derived from the family history and to assess the *child's ability to take advantage of this heritage* (the child's developmental, medical, psychological, and educational history). The interviews also provide important information on the attributions given by others as to the nature and source of the child's presenting difficulties.
- Observational data are derived from examination of the child's appearance and behavior, from information obtained from questionnaires and interviews completed with people familiar with the child in nonclinical contexts, from direct observation of the child-parent interaction during the clinical interview, from analysis of the examiner-child dyad, and from observation of the child's behavior and problem-solving style under specific performance demands (including both specific tests and the activities of the natural environment).
- Tests provide *psychometric* data relating level of performance to that of age peers; *behavioral* data on behaviors elicited under different problem-solving demands and problem-

solving strategies for reaching solutions; and *task analysis* data such as information regarding complexity of task demands, allocation of resources, systemic relationships in task/situation.

THE USE OF PSYCHOLOGICAL TESTS

- Psychological tests are designed to tap specific aspects of behavioral function. They are constructed according to sound psychometric principles, administered rigorously, and scored according to standard guidelines. Their normative data should be up to date, reliable, valid, and appropriate in terms of age and/or cultural or language group for the population under study.
- NP assessment protocols require a core of population-based standardized psychological test instruments. These typically include a measure of general mental/cognitive abilities, appropriate to the child's age and general competency, which serves to "anchor" the clinician by referencing this child's performance to that of other children of the same age. It also provides a context of general ability against which specific neuropsychologically relevant skills and weaknesses can be evaluated. Additional tests are then selected to address the full range of behavioral domains and to provide more detailed analysis of specific psychological processes. These may have population-based or research-based norms. The latter typically have less extensive normative bases but can target specific skills more precisely.
- Tests provide samples of observed behavior under structured conditions; they complement, but do not substitute for, observations (direct or elicited) of the child in the natural environment.
- Test performance varies in response to contextual variables, including the nature of the test setting, rapport with the clinician, age of the child, test format/materials, and test construction/scoring criteria. No test can be rendered so "objective" that the interaction between child and examiner is eliminated as an important source of diagnostic information.
- No test measures just one thing. All behavior, including test responses, is the result of a complex interaction of executive, cognitive, and perceptual variables, motor and sensory capacities, and emotional factors.
- Psychological tests have limitations with respect to NP assessment. They can provide interchild rating and cognitive profiling. Used alone, they cannot model the neural substrate or explicate childhood neuropathology.

COMMUNICATION OF FINDINGS

- Communication of findings is undertaken by means of a written report and an informing session. These are complementary: The informing session provides a forum for discussion of the findings and their meaning, as well as an opportunity for parents to discuss and reframe their understanding of the child. The report provides details of the assessment process, the scores derived from standardized measures, the diagnostic formulation, and the management and recommendations.
- The goal of the report and informing session is to educate the child, parents/guardians, and teachers/other professionals about the nature of children's neurobehavioral development in general; to explain how brain-behavior relationships in children are examined in the evaluation; to "normalize" this child's NP performance by situating it in the larger context of neurobehavioral development; to relate observed behaviors to the specific medical/neurological condition (where relevant); and to demonstrate the relationship of the diagnostic formulation to the management plan proposed.
- The written report should present a clear statement of the referral question(s); summarize relevant history, observations, and test findings organized so that the weight of the findings is clear; integrate the findings into a clear diagnostic statement (not a list of what the child "can" and "cannot" do); discuss the relationship of the diagnostic formulation to the child's real-world function-

ing; address the referral question specifically; reference the findings to the medical/neurological condition where relevant (noting specifically when data are, or are not, consistent with a known disorder and locus); identify areas of concern (risks) based on or referenced to the diagnostic statement; and outline the management plan and recommendations to maximize the child's functioning in the real-world contexts of family, school, and society at large.

THE MANAGEMENT PLAN

- A management plan has two important components: *education* and *recommendations*.
- The goal of the educational component is to inform the child, parents/guardians, and other involved professionals about neurobehavioral development in children; to relate this child's performance to that of other children (with and without a similar diagnosis); and to provide detailed information about this child's individual style, expectable risks (both short- and long-term), and educational and psychosocial/emotional needs. The clinician will also address issues of medical and psychological health, as well as development and achievement in academic/vocational and psychosocial spheres.
- Recommendations should respond to the specific risks that the child faces now and in the future; be tailored to different contexts as necessary; provide general guidelines for maximizing behavioral adjustment in both social and academic settings; foster specific cognitive, social, and academic skills; and address psychosocial development and emotional well-being. Recommendations include specific interventions involving accommodations, compensatory strategies, remedial instruction, rehabilitation programming, and/or assistive technologies, as well as referral for additional services/evaluation from medical, psychological, physical, and/or educational-vocational specialists as indicated.

References & Readings

Baron, I. S. (2003). *Neuropsychological evaluation of the child.* New York: Oxford University Press.

Bernstein, J. H. (2000). Developmental neuropsychological assessment. In K. O. Yeates, M. D. Ris, & H. G. Taylor (Eds.), *Pediatric neuropsychology: Research, theory, and practice* (pp. 401–422). New York: Guilford Press.

Rey-Casserly, C. (1999). *Neuropsychological assessment of preschool children.* In E. V. Nuttall, I. Romero, & J. Kalesnik (Eds.), *Assessing and screening preschoolers* (2nd ed.). Boston: Allyn and Bacon.

Reynolds, C. R., & Fletcher-Janzen, E. (1997). *Handbook of clinical child neuropsychology* (2nd ed.). New York: Plenum Press.

Rourke, B. P., van der Vlugt, H., & Rourke, S. B. (2002). *Practice of child-clinical neuropsychology.* Lisse, The Netherlands: Swets & Zeitlinger.

Taylor, H. G. (1988). Neuropsychological testing: Relevance for assessing children's learning disabilities. *Journal of Consulting & Clinical Psychology, 56*(6), 795–800.

Yeates, K. O., Ris, M. D., & Taylor, H. G. (2000). *Pediatric neuropsychology: Research, theory, and practice.* New York: Guilford Press.

Related Topics

Chapter 7, "Adult Neuropsychological Assessment"
Chapter 8, "Assessment and Intervention for Executive Dysfunction"
Chapter 11, "Medical Evaluation of Children With Behavioral or Developmental Disorders"
Chapter 12, "Interviewing Parents"
Chapter 13, "Attention-Deficit/Hyperactivity Disorder Through the Life Span"
Chapter 27, "Measures of Children's Psychological Development"

7 ADULT NEUROPSYCHOLOGICAL ASSESSMENT

Aaron P. Nelson & Margaret O'Connor

GENERAL CONSIDERATIONS

Fundamental Assumptions of Clinical Neuropsychological Assessment

1. It is possible to make valid inferences regarding the integrity of the brain through the observation of behavior. Such inferences require a firm grasp of brain-behavior relationships and characteristic neurobehavioral syndromes.
2. Observable behavior is frequently the most sensitive manifestation of brain pathology.
3. Observable behavior, including "test behavior," is a reflection of the interaction between the domains of person and environment; variables from each domain must be assessed in order to arrive at an understanding of the clinical significance of a given behavior.
4. A neuropsychological test is simply one means of eliciting a sample of behavior, under standardized conditions, which is then to be observed and analyzed.
5. Test performance and "real-life" behavior are imperfectly correlated. Proceed with caution in using test data to predict behavior.
6. Most behaviors are multifactorial and depend on a complex interplay of cognitive, perceptual, emotional, and environmental factors.
7. Most neuropsychological tests are multifactorial and depend on a confluence of cognitive and perceptual functions for their performance.
8. As with any psychological intervention, the neuropsychological evaluation should proceed in a sensitive manner and with explicit communications regarding the use of clinical information.
9. A dynamic developmental life span perspective is critical in the evaluation of each patient.
10. All behavior should be viewed within a sociocultural context.

Uses of Neuropsychological Assessment

1. Neuropsychological assessment is indicated for questions of differential diagnosis and prognosis.
2. Neuropsychological assessment should be considered in the setting of a deterioration in neuropsychological status or when there is a history of neurological disease, injury, or developmental abnormality affecting cerebral functions.
3. Neuropsychological assessment is used to clarify the significance of known or suspected pathology for "real-life" functioning in day-to-day activities, relationships, education, and work.
4. Neuropsychological assessment provides information relevant to management, rehabilitation, and treatment planning for identified cognitive problems.
5. Baseline (pretreatment) status and measurement of treatment response (medication, neurosurgery, behavioral intervention,

electroconvulsive therapy) can be monitored with serial neuropsychological testing.
6. Neuropsychological consultation is frequently critical in determination of legal/forensic issues, including need for guardianship, neuropsychological damages, criminal responsibility, and competence to stand trial.
7. Neuropsychological research investigations enhance the understanding of brain-behavior relationships and neurobehavioral syndromes. These studies are of tremendous value to the understanding of neurological disease and normal brain function.

Approach to Neuropsychological Evaluation

1. Evaluation should be individually tailored to each patient.
2. Test data are viewed from both qualitative and quantitative perspectives.
3. Assessment proceeds in a hypothesis testing manner. Tests are selected to answer specific questions, some of which emerge during the evaluation process.
4. Standardized tests can be modified to test limits and produce richer qualitative data.
5. Task performance is analyzed to determine component processes, with the goal of identification of dissociations between such processes.

CLINICAL METHOD

Referral Question

The chief complaint and presenting problems are reviewed to produce a clear description of their onset and course, as well as information regarding the medical and social context in which the problem(s) emerged. The patient's overall understanding of his or her current circumstances and the reason for the consultation are sought.

History

Information is obtained from a variety of sources, including the patient's self-report, observations of family members or close friends, medical records, and prior evaluations from academic or work situations. Information is obtained regarding the following:

1. Developmental background, including circumstances of gestation, birth/delivery, acquisition of developmental milestones, and early socialization skills
2. Social development, including major autobiographical events and relationships (a three-generational genogram is highly useful in gaining relevant family information)
3. Past medical history, including illnesses, injuries, surgeries, medications, hospitalizations, substance abuse, and relevant familial medical history
4. Psychiatric history, including hospitalizations, medications, and outpatient treatment
5. Educational background, including early school experiences and academic performance during high school, college, postgraduate study, and other educational and technical training
6. Vocational history, including work performance, work satisfaction, and relationships with supervisors and coworkers
7. Recreational interests and hobbies

Behavioral Observation

Physical appearance is inspected, including symmetry of gross anatomic features, facial expression, manner of dress, and attention to personal hygiene. The patient is asked specific questions regarding unusual sensory or motor symptoms. Affect and mood are assessed with respect to range and modulation of felt/expressed emotions and their congruence with concurrent ideation and the contemporaneous situation. Interpersonal comportment is assessed in the context of the interview. Does the patient's behavior reflect a normal awareness of self and other in interaction? The patient's motivation and compliance with examination requests, instructions, and test procedures are observed with respect to the validity of test findings.

Domains of Neuropsychological Function

A sufficiently broad range of neuropsychological functions is evaluated using tests and other assessment techniques.

1. *General intellectual ability:* Intelligence encompasses a broad array of capacities, many of which are not directly assessed in the traditional clinical setting. The estimate of general intellectual ability is based on both formal assessment methods and a survey of demographic factors and life accomplishments. Particular care must be exercised in the evaluation of patients from varying educational and sociocultural backgrounds. In cases of known or suspected impairment, premorbid ability is surmised from performance on measures presumed less sensitive to cerebral dysfunction (i.e., vocabulary), so-called best performance methods, educational/professional accomplishment, avocational interests and pursuits, and demographic variables. The level of general ability provides a reference point from which to view performance on other measures.
2. *Sensation and perception:* It is important to establish to what degree primary sensation and perception are intact prior to initiation of testing. Significant impairment of sensory function (auditory, visual, kinesthetic) is usually obvious and points to a need for specialized assessment procedures. Unusual or abnormal gustatory and olfactory experiences should be sought through direct questioning. Simple auditory function can be assessed by finger-rub stimuli to each ear. Vision is examined with tests of acuity, tracking, scanning, depth perception, color perception, and attention/neglect for visual field quadrants. Kinesthetic perception is assessed with tests of graphesthesia and stereognosis. Double simultaneous stimulation can be used in auditory, visual, and kinesthetic modalities to determine whether hemiextinction occurs.
3. *Motor functions:* Naturalistic observations of the patient's gait and upper and lower extremity coordination are an important part of the motor examination. Hand preference should be assessed through either direct inquiry or a formal handedness questionnaire. Motor speed, dexterity, and programming are tested with timed tasks, some of which involve repetition of a specific motor act (e.g., finger tapping, peg placement) and others of which involve more complex movements (e.g., finger sequencing, sequential hand positions). Manual grasp strength can be assessed with a hand dynamometer. Various forms of verbally guided movement or praxis are examined.
4. *Attention/concentration:* The capacity to selectively maintain and shift attentional focus forms the basis of all cognitive activity. Evaluation of attention includes observations of a broad array of interrelated behaviors. General level of arousal or alertness is determined through clinical observation. An appraisal is made of the extent to which environmental or diurnal factors modify arousal. Attentional functions are assessed in both auditory/acoustic and visual modalities. Attention span is measured by determining the number of unrelated "bits" of information that can be held on line at a given moment in time. Sustained attention is assessed with tests that require the patient to maintain focused attention over longer periods. Selective attention is measured with tasks requiring the patient to shift focus from one event to another. Resistance to interference is assessed with tasks requiring the patient to inhibit overlearned responses or other distractions that could undermine a desired response.
5. *Learning and memory:* The assessment of memory function is perhaps the most complex endeavor of the neuropsychological examination. Memory is assessed with respect to time of initial exposure (anterograde vs. retrograde), modality of presentation (acoustic vs. visual), material (linguistic vs. figural), and locus of reference (personal vs. nonpersonal). The evaluation of memory should include measures that allow the neuropsychologist to parse out the component processes (encoding, consolidation, retrieval) entailed in the acquisition and later recall of information. To this end, measures are used

to assess performance with respect to length of interval between exposure and demand for recall (none vs. short vs. long delay) and extent of facilitation required to demonstrate retention (free recall vs. recognition). The assessment of retrograde memory function poses a special problem insofar as it is difficult to know with certainty what information was contained at one time in the remote memory of a particular patient. Although a number of formal tests can be used for this purpose, we also assess this aspect through asking for personal information that presumably is or had been well known at one time by the patient (e.g., names of family members, places of prior employment).

6. *Language:* Language is the medium through which much of the neuropsychological examination is accomplished. Language function is assessed both opportunistically, as during the interview, and via formal test instruments. Conversational speech is observed with respect to fluency, articulation, and prosody. The patient's capacity to respond to interview questions and test instructions provides an informal index of receptive language ability or comprehension. Visual confrontation naming is carefully assessed so that word-finding problems and paraphasic errors may be elicited. Repetition is measured with phrases of varying length and phonemic complexity. Auditory comprehension is evaluated by asking the patient questions that vary in length and grammatical complexity. Reading measures include identification of individual letters, common words, irregularly spelled words, and nonwords, as well as measures of reading speed and comprehension. Spelling can be assessed in both visual and auditory modalities. A narrative handwriting sample can be obtained by instructing the patient to describe a standard stimulus scene.
7. *Visuospatial functions:* After basic visuoperceptual status is established, the assessment of visuospatial function commences with the evaluation of the spatial distribution of visual attention. Visual neglect is examined by way of tasks entailing scanning across all quadrants of visual space. Left/right orientation can be assessed by having the patient point to specific body parts on himself or herself or the examiner. Topographic orientation can be tested in most patients by instructing them to indicate well-known locales on a blank map. Graphic reproduction of designs and assembly of patterns using sticks, blocks, or other media are used to assess visual organization and constructional abilities.
8. *Executive functions:* Executive functions comprise the capacity of the patient to produce cognitive behavior in a planned, organized, and situationally responsive manner. The assessment of executive functions is accomplished in an ongoing fashion through observation of the patient's approach to all types of tests and via his or her comportment within the consultation. Although few tests assess these functions directly or specifically, the clinician looks for evidence of flexibility versus perseveration, initiation versus abulia, self-awareness versus obliviousness, planfulness versus impulsivity, and capacity to assume an abstract attitude versus concreteness.
9. *Psychological factors and emotion:* Standardized measures of mood, personality, and psychopathology can be used to explore the role of these issues in the patient's presentation and diagnosis. It is important to note, however, that neurological and other medical conditions can skew performance on certain personality tests; hence, interpretation must take this into account through the use of "correction" methods where available and in exercising caution in drawing diagnostic conclusions.

Diagnostic Formulation

Data from the history, observation, and testing of the patient are analyzed collectively to produce a concise understanding of the patient's symptoms and neuropsychological diagnosis. A configuration of abilities and limitations is developed and used both diagnostically and as a framework for the elucidation of goals for treatment. When possible, the diagnostic formulation should identify the neuropathological factors giving rise to the patient's clinical presentation, including underlying anatomy and disease process.

Recommendations and Feedback

Consultation concludes with feedback, in which findings and recommendations are reviewed with relevant individuals (e.g., referring physician, patient, family, treatment team members). A variety of treatment plans may be advised, including pharmacological intervention, psychiatric consultation, psychotherapy, vocational guidance, and cognitive-behavioral remediation. Recommendations should be pragmatic and individually tailored to each patient's specific needs. Strategies for optimizing performance in personal, educational, and occupational spheres are identified and discussed in lay language that the patient and family member can comprehend. Where possible, specific behaviorally based suggestions are made for remediation of identified problems. Further clinical evaluations and other neurodiagnostic procedures are suggested when appropriate in order to provide more information relevant to differential diagnosis, response to treatment, and functional status over time. Appropriate neuropsychological follow-up is also arranged.

References & Readings

Feinberg, T., & Farrah, M. (Eds.) (1997). *Behavioral neurology and neuropsychology*. New York: McGraw-Hill.

Heilman, K., & Valenstein, E. (Eds.) (1993). *Clinical neuropsychology* (3rd ed.). New York: Oxford University Press.

Kaplan, E. (1983). Process and achievement revisited. In S. Wapner & B. Kaplan (Eds.), *Toward a holistic developmental psychology* (pp. 143–156). Hillsdale, NJ: Erlbaum.

Kaplan, E. (1988). A process approach to neuropsychological assessment. In T. Boll & B. Bryant (Eds.), *Clinical neuropsychology and brain function: Research, measurement, and practice*. Washington, DC: American Psychological Association.

Kolb, B., & Wishaw, I. Q. (Eds.) (1990). *Fundamentals of human neuropsychology* (3rd ed.). New York: Freeman.

Lezak, M. (1995). *Neuropsychological assessment* (3rd ed.). New York: Oxford University Press.

Mesulam, M. M. (Ed.) (1985). *Principles of behavioral neurology*. Philadelphia: F. A. Davis.

Spreen, O., & Strauss, E. (1991). *A compendium of neuropsychological tests: Administration, norms, and commentary*. New York: Oxford University Press.

Walsh, K. W. (1987). *Neuropsychology: A clinical approach* (2nd ed.). Edinburgh: Churchill Livingstone.

Walsh, K. W. (1992). Some gnomes worth knowing. *Clinical Neuropsychologist, 6*, 119–133.

Related Topics

Chapter 8, "Assessment and Intervention for Executive Dysfunction"

Chapter 13, "Attention-Deficit/Hyperactivity Disorder Through the Life Span"

8 ASSESSMENT AND INTERVENTION FOR EXECUTIVE DYSFUNCTION

Robert M. Roth, Peter K. Isquith, & Gerard A. Gioia

Executive functions are interrelated control processes involved in the selection, initiation, execution, and monitoring of cognitive functioning, as well as aspects of motor and sensory functioning. They are self-regulatory functions that organize and direct cognitive activity, emotional responses, and overt behaviors. Neisser (1967) described executive functions as the orchestration of basic cognitive processes during goal-oriented problem-solving, differentiating "basic" cognitive functions from "executive" cognitive control functions. In this metaphor, the executive serves as the conductor of the orchestra by making intentional decisions regarding the final output of the music and recruiting the necessary components in reaching the intended goal (Goldberg, 2002). The "instruments" are the domain-specific functions, such as language, visual/nonverbal reasoning, and memory.

The specific cognitive processes subsumed under the "executive" umbrella include:

- *Inhibit:* Ability to not act on an impulse, stop one's own activity at the proper time, and suppress distracting information from interfering with ongoing mental or behavioral activity
- *Shift:* Move flexibly from one situation, activity, or aspect of a problem to another as the situation demands
- *Emotional control:* Control one's emotional response as appropriate to the situation or stressor; maintain an optimal level of arousal
- *Initiate:* Begin a task or activity
- *Working memory:* Hold information actively in mind over time
- *Sustain:* Stay with or stick to an activity for an age-appropriate amount of time
- *Plan:* Anticipate future events, set goals, and develop appropriate steps ahead of time
- *Organize:* Establish or maintain order in information, an activity or place; carry out tasks in a systematic manner
- *Self-monitor:* Check on one's own actions during, or shortly after, finishing a task to assure appropriate attainment of goal; awareness of one's cognitive, physical, and emotional abilities or state
- *Problem solving:* Ability to think abstractly and form or develop concepts necessary to achieve a goal

Individuals with executive dysfunction can exhibit a broad range of problems such as acting inappropriately due to difficulty inhibiting impulses, quickly losing track of what they are thinking or doing, making poor financial or other personal decisions, or having considerable difficulty getting started on tasks. Difficulties with executive functions are often manifested in more than one specific cognitive domain, such that inhibitory control deficits can be expressed as verbal disinhibition, behavioral impulsivity, attentional distractibility, emotional reactivity, or social inappropriateness.

Historically, executive functions have been closely associated with the integrity of the frontal lobes of the brain. Much of the evidence supporting a role for the frontal lobes in executive functions has come from studies of patients with acquired focal damage to this region (Luria, 1966; Stuss & Levine, 2002).

More recently, studies using advanced brain imaging techniques such as positron emission tomography (PET) and functional magnetic resonance imaging (fMRI) have shown that the frontal lobes play an intimate role in executive functions (Cabeza & Nyberg, 2000). However, neuroimaging studies have also clearly shown that executive functions are not subserved by the frontal lobes alone, but rather by distributed neural circuitry that includes other cortical regions such as the temporal and parietal lobes, subcortical structures such as the hippocampus and basal ganglia, and the cerebellum. Furthermore, studies of patients with acquired focal lesions in nonfrontal brain regions such as the basal ganglia have provided further support for a distributed circuitry model of executive functions. Damage to any given component of this circuitry may result in executive dysfunction.

Executive functions are mediated by a number of neurochemicals, particularly dopamine, serotonin, and norepinephrine (Robbins, 2000). Roles for other neurochemicals such as glutamate, acetylcholine, and GABA are being increasingly investigated. Disruption of one or more of these neurochemical systems may in part account for executive dysfunction in conditions where there is no obvious structural brain damage.

The following list includes some of the more common disorders with executive deficits:

- Attention-deficit/hyperactivity disorder (ADHD)
- Autism spectrum disorders
- Tourette's syndrome (TS)
- Learning disabilities
- Traumatic brain injury
- Epilepsy
- Brain tumors
- Multiple sclerosis and other disorders affecting white matter connectivity
- Parkinson's disease, Huntington's disease, and other movement disorders
- Alzheimer's disease and other dementias
- Psychiatric disorders such as schizophrenia, major depressive disorder, obsessive-compulsive disorder (OCD), and bipolar disorder
- Alcoholism and substance abuse disorders

The precise nature of the executive dysfunction observed in such conditions varies. For example, some disorders have been commonly, but not exclusively, associated with deficits in inhibitory control (e.g., ADHD-combined type, OCD, TS), while others appear to involve prominent deficits in working memory (e.g., ADHD-inattentive type, schizophrenia, multiple sclerosis).

ASSESSMENT OF EXECUTIVE DYSFUNCTION

Numerous measures have been designed to assess subdomains of executive function (Rabbitt, 1997). Some of the most commonly employed performance measures are the Wisconsin Card Sorting Test, the Stroop Task, Verbal Fluency tests, Tower tasks (e.g., Tower of London, Tower of Hanoi), and Trail Making tests (Lezak, 1995; Spreen & Strauss, 1998). Establishing that an individual has executive dysfunction usually includes not only such psychometric tests but also a clinical interview and behavioral observations, at times supplemented by reports from informants familiar with the individual. Confirming that executive dysfunction is present also requires that problems in the basic cognitive, sensory, and motor functions be ruled out as accounting for the appearance of executive dysfunction. These include basic attention, language, visuospatial skills, sensory inputs (e.g., hearing, vision), peripheral motor function, and learning and memory.

Assessment of executive function is thus complicated. It is difficult to tease apart deficits in executive from domain-specific functions, given that most neuropsychological tests are multifactorial in nature. Highly structured testing may be providing the organization, guidance, and cuing necessary for optimal performance on tests of executive function, which would generally not be available in naturalistic settings. Many tests of executive functions are susceptible to practice effects. That is, once a person figures out how to successfully complete the test, he or she often performs much better on repeat testing or on similar tests. This is consistent with evidence that executive dysfunction is more readily observed when patients are faced with novel tasks or stimuli, rather than familiar or routine tasks.

Despite these limitations, performance tests of executive function can be useful in discriminating between clinical and normal samples, and exhibit good sensitivity but not necessarily high specificity for specific disorders (Gioia, Isquith, & Guy, 2001; Grant & Adams, 1996; Pennington & Ozonoff, 1996). Increased attention has been devoted to developing instruments with greater ecological validity, including:

- Performance tests that require patients to complete "real-world" type tasks in the laboratory, such as the Test of Everyday Attention (TEA), Test of Everyday Attention for Children (TEA-Ch), and the Behavioural Assessment of the Dysexecutive Syndrome (BADS)
- Structured clinician rating scales such as the Frontal Behavioral Inventory
- Patient and/or informant completed questionnaires such as the Behavior Rating Inventory of Executive Function (BRIEF), Dysexecutive Questionnaire (DEX), and Frontal Systems Behavioral Scale (FrSBe)

INTERVENTION FOR EXECUTIVE DYSFUNCTION

An understanding of the executive components of an individual's functioning can lead to targeted pharmacological, behavioral, cognitive, or other therapeutic interventions. Such strategies may be specifically targeted toward one area of executive functions, such as antecedent management for children with inhibitory control deficits, or may be more programmatic, such as the comprehensive cognitive rehabilitation programs.

An executive system intervention focus is possible in most daily activities involving more than one step for completion, including classroom, therapy, social/recreational, and activities of daily living at home (Ylvisaker & Feeney, 1998). For example, any of these activities can include:

- *Goal-setting:* An initial decision about or choice of a goal to pursue (What do I need to accomplish?)
- *Self-awareness of strengths/weaknesses:* Recognition of one's stronger and weaker abilities, and a decision about how easy or difficult it will be to accomplish the goal (How easy or difficult is this task/goal? Have I done this type of task before?)
- *Organization/planning:* Development of an organized plan (What materials do we need? Who will do what? In what order do we need to do these things? How long will it take?)
- *Flexibility/strategy use:* As complications or obstructions arise, planned (e.g., staff members ensure that problems arise) or unplanned coaching of the students in flexible problem solving/strategic thinking (When/if a problem arises, what other ways should I think about to reach the goal? Should I ask for assistance?)
- *Monitoring:* A review of the goal, plan, and accomplishments at the end (How did I do?)
- *Summarizing:* What worked and what didn't; what was easy and what was difficult and why

For individuals just starting to learn executive control behaviors, young children, or individuals with extreme executive dysfunction, the focus of intervention often needs to be more externalized or environmental, such as organizing and structuring the external environment for them, and cuing strategies and behavioral routines. They often need help to know when and how to apply the appropriate problem-solving behavioral routine. Direct rewards and positive incentives are often necessary to motivate the individual to attend to and practice new behavioral routines. Once behavioral routines have become established, positive cuing becomes the crucial factor; cuing can then be faded, as a function of the individual's increasing autonomy.

References, Readings, & Internet Sites 

Cabeza, R., & Nyberg, L. (2000). Imaging cognition II: An empirical review of 275 PET and fMRI studies. *Journal of Cognitive Neuroscience, 12,* 1–47.

Gioia, G. A., Isquith, P. K., & Guy, S. C. (2001). Assessment of executive function in children with neurological impairments. In R. Simeonsson & S. Rosenthal (Eds.), *Psychological and developmental assessment* (pp. 317–356). New York: Guilford Press.

Goldberg, E. (2002). *The executive brain: Frontal lobes and the civilized mind*. New York: Oxford University Press.

Grant, I., & Adams, K. M. (Eds.). (1996). *Neuropsychological assessment of neuropsychiatric disorders* (2nd ed.). New York: Oxford University Press.

Krasnegor, N. A., Lyon, G. R., & Goldman-Rakic, P. S. (1997). *Development of the prefrontal cortex: Evolution, neurobiology, and behavior*. Baltimore: Paul H. Brookes.

Lezak, M. D. (1995). *Neuropsychological assessment* (3rd ed.). New York: Oxford University Press.

Luria, A. R. (1966). *Higher cortical functions in man*. New York: Basic Books.

National Academy of Neuropsychology. (n.d.). Home page. Retrieved 2004 from http://www.nanonline.org

Neisser, U. (1967). *Cognitive psychology*. New York: Appleton-Century-Crofts.

Neuropsychology Central. (n.d.). Home page. Retrieved 2004 from http://www.neuropsychology central.com

Pennington, B. F., & Ozonoff, S. (1996). Executive functions and developmental psychopathology. *Journal of Child Psychology and Psychiatry and Allied Disciplines, 37*, 51–87.

Rabbitt, P. (Ed.). (1997). *Methodology of frontal and executive function*. Hove, UK: Psychology Press.

Robbins, T. W. (2000). Chemical neuromodulation of frontal-executive functions in humans and other animals. *Experimental Brain Research, 133*, 130–138.

Sohlberg, M. M., & Mateer, C. A. (2001). *Cognitive rehabilitation: An integrative neuropsychological approach*. New York: Guilford Press

Spreen, O., & Strauss, E. (1998). *A compendium of neuropsychological tests* (2nd ed.). New York: Oxford University Press.

Stuss, D. T., & Levine, B. (2002). Adult clinical neuropsychology: Lessons from studies of the frontal lobes. *Annual Review of Psychology, 53*, 401–433.

Ylvisaker, M., & Feeney, T. J. (1998). *Collaborative brain injury intervention: Positive everyday routines*. San Diego: Singular.

Related Topics

Chapter 6, "Developmental Neuropsychological Assessment"

Chapter 7, "Adult Neuropsychological Assessment"

9 CHILD AND ADOLESCENT DIAGNOSIS WITH *DSM-IV*

Stuart M. Goldman

The fourth edition of the *Diagnostic and Statistical Manual of Mental Disorders* (*DSM-IV*) follows the approach to diagnosis established by *DSM-III* and *DSM-III-R* of an atheoretical, descriptive assessment based primarily on history. It provides a five-axis system of evaluation, each of which covers a different realm of information.

- Axis I refers to the majority of the primary psychiatric disorders.
- Axis II refers to personality disorders and mental retardation.
- Axis III covers general medical conditions.
- Axis IV provides a scale of psychosocial stressors from 1 (none) to 6 (catastrophic).
- Axis V details, utilizing the Global Assessment Scale of Functioning, the patient's level of functioning on a scale of 1 (worst) to 100 (best).

This multiaxial, multidimensional system enhances the clinician's capacity for assessment, planning, and prognosis. In addition to its clinical utility, it was designed to be interrater reliable, compatible with *ICD-9CM*, and consistent with and suitable for research studies.

In practice, most clinicians want a practical and succinct approach to arrive at a working *DSM-IV* diagnosis. It must include both childhood and general diagnosis, since almost all diagnoses are applicable to a child or adolescent population. To this end, we have developed an easy-to-use schema utilizing four questions to arrive rapidly at a working diagnosis, which then must be confirmed against the full *DSM* criteria.

1. Where is the problem primarily located?

If it is within the child (such as attention-deficit/hyperactivity disorder [ADHD]), continue with the next set of questions.

If it is not within the child, is it between the parent and the child? *V-codes.*

In the parent? Consider *adjustment disorders* for the child and a *primary diagnosis* for the parent.

Between the child and the school? Consider a *systems-based etiology* and intervention.

2. Is the problem reactive to an identifiable stressor or event?

No: Move on to Question 3.

Yes: The child has either an *adjustment disorder* or *posttraumatic stress disorder (PTSD).*

Did the event include actual or threatened serious injury or death with intense affects?

No: Move on to *adjustment disorder.*

Yes: What has been the duration (Question 4)?

Less than 1 month? *Acute stress disorder.*

More than 1 month? Is there reexperiencing, avoidance, or numbing and increased arousal? Yes: *PTSD* (all three must be present).

No: *Adjustment disorder,* which is modified by the affected area (Question 3) to include disturbance of mood (anxiety, depression), conduct, or mixed.

3. What basic area or areas are affected?

As one gathers history, are the primary symptoms behavioral, mood, body parts or functions, disconnection, multiple/pan, or externally induced? This refers to the predominant areas of concern as one is undertaking the diagnostic evaluation. Each area, when answered in the affirmative, leads to a short decision tree culminating in *DSM-IV* diagnosis. There may be more than one area of significant concern, leading to several diagnoses. When there are concerns in almost every area, the multiple/pan category should be considered first.

Behavioral disorders are characterized by either an inability or an unwillingness to behave and/or follow social or societal rules.

Does the child appear to deliberately misbehave?

Yes: Does he or she break societal rules (things that would lead to arrest in adults)? Likely *conduct disorder.*

Yes: Breaks mostly social rules (hard, unpleasant to manage or get along with)? Likely *oppositional defiant disorder.*

No: Is the child inattentive, hyperactive, or impulsive? Likely *ADHD.*

If the child is hyperactive, inattentive, impulsive, and deliberately misbehaves, likely both *ADHD* and either *oppositional defiant* or *conduct disorder.*

Mood disorders are characterized by a predominance of unpleasant or inappropriate moods and may include anxiety, depression, mania, irritability, or some combination. They must be sufficiently intense to cause some dysfunction. Each leads to a symptom-focused decision tree.

Which affect is primarily involved?

Anxiety?

Is the child anxious in almost all ways? *Generalized anxiety disorder.*

If specific, is it fear of being away from family/home? *Separation anxiety disorder.*

Fear or difficulty being in places? *Agoraphobia.*

Fear with multiple incapacitating somatic symptoms? *Panic attacks.*

Anxiety with unremitting worries or persistent useless behaviors? *Obsessive-compulsive disorder.*

Fear of a certain circumscribed thing? *Simple phobia* reflecting the specific item.

Depression (may present as sadness, irritability)?

Is this a clinically significant depression with dysphoria, isolation, boredom, or irritability?

No: Return to other categories.

Yes: What is the duration of symptoms?

Greater than 1 year, with disruption of functioning? Likely *dysthymic disorder.*

Greater than 2 weeks, with major somatic symptoms (sleep, weight, concentration) and/or suicidal elements (ideation, plan, attempts)? Likely *major depressive disorder.*

Elements of both? *Dysthymic and major depressive disorder.*

Have there been periods of elation, increased activity, racing thoughts, out-of-control actions, decreased sleep, hypersexuality, or extreme irritability?

No: *Unipolar major depression.*

Yes: Mild? Likely *cyclothymia.* Severe? *Manic-depressive disorder.*

Body part or function disorders are characterized by specific troubles in carrying out a daily bodily function or by complaints about a specific body part or parts.

Is there a body part or function that the clinical difficulties center upon?

No: Return to schema.

Yes: Name the part or dysfunction, and the disorder follows.

Does the trouble center on eating?

Too little: *Anorexia nervosa.*

Too much: *Bulimia nervosa.*

Not food: *Pica.*

Regurgitation: *Rumination disorder.*

Bowel or bladder problems (specify if never controlled [primary] versus regression [secondary])?

Bladder: *Enuresis.*

Bowel: *Encoporesis.*

Unwanted movements or sounds?

Less than a year? *Transient tic disorder.*

More than a year?

Muscles: *Motor tic.*

Sounds: *Vocal tic.*

Both: *Tourette's syndrome.*

Sleep problems?

Dramatic awakening with morning memories? *Nightmares.*

Dramatic awakening without morning memories? Likely *night terrors.*

Genitalia, gender complaints?

With complaints or confusion about physical parts, roles, and so on: *Gender identity dx.*

Complaints about other body parts?

One part not working: *Conversion disorder.*

Many things (13) not working: *Somatoform disorder.*

Parts working but very worried: *Hypochondriasis.*

Language trouble?

Input: *Receptive language.*

Output: *Expressive.*

Both: *Mixed.*

Decreased output but normal capability: *Selective mutism.*

Learning trouble?

Specific area? *Reading, writing, math.*

General cognition?

Mild to profound retardation on Axis II.

Disconnection disorders appear around a discontinuity in sense of self or in functioning that is not deliberate on the part of the patient. They are relatively uncommon and should raise the suspicion of abuse or maltreatment.

Many selves? *Dissociative identity disorder.*

Travel? (How did I get here? Where am I?) *Fugue disorder.*

Forgetting? *Amnestic disorder.*

Unreal? *Depersonalization disorder.*

Multiple or pan disorders present with major disruptions in all spheres of the patient's functioning, including school, home, peers, and self. Generally patients' impairments are quite obvious, even if their diagnosis is not.

Has the child's ability to interact with others been the major area of concern since early childhood?

No: Continue below.

Yes: Is language capacity mostly spared, even if collaborative communication is not?

No: Likely *autism* (must consider other diagnoses, such as major language disorders).

Yes: Probably *Asperger's syndrome.*

Has the child been related but developed major dysfunctioning with odd or bizarre behaviors?

No: Continue below.

Yes: There is bizarre or odd behavior, but there is minimal affective component. Probably *childhood schizophrenia.*

Yes: Is there a major ongoing component of depression or of elation, increased activity, or irritability?

Yes: Depression? Probably *major depressive disorder* (likely with psychotic features).

Yes: Elation, activity, and so on, or a combination of depression and elation? *Manic-depressive disorder.*

Does the child have marked shifts in his or her level of functioning dependent upon the context?

No: Return to earlier on the decision tree.

Yes: Possibly *borderline character of childhood* Axis II (trouble with relationships, rage, identity concerns/confusion, self-destructive, all in a shifting framework of functioning).

Externally induced disorders are caused by an external substance such as alcohol, marijuana, tobacco, or cocaine. Each of these disorders is diagnosed by a significant involvement with the substance in question and then named accordingly. Although they are far more common in adolescents, they are seen in younger children as well. They are commonly seen as comorbid disorders with a wide range of other psychiatric diagnoses.

Is there substantial involvement with a substance?

Yes: Give the child a *substance disorder* (naming the substance in question).

4. Are the symptoms in question longstanding and ego-syntonic? If yes, then consider the relevant Axis II diagnosis, except for antisocial personality disorder.

SUMMARY

The schema just described is designed to help clinicians in a time- and energy-sensitive manner to focus their diagnostic efforts and come to a probable *DSM-IV* diagnosis. Each diagnosis should be confirmed by applying the full *DSM-IV* criteria. The diagnosis must then be placed in the context of a multidimensional formulation to ensure that an optimal treatment plan is implemented.

References & Readings

American Psychiatric Association. (1994). *Diagnostic and statistical manual of mental disorders* (4th ed.). Washington, DC: Author.

Beitman, B., & Goldfried, M. (1989). The movement toward integration of the psychotherapies. *American Journal of Psychiatry, 146,* 138–147.

Goodman, A. (1991). Organic unity theory: The mind-body revisited. *American Journal of Psychiatry, 148*, 553–563.

Sperry, L., Gudeman, J. E., Blackwell, B., & Faulkner, L. R. (1992). *Psychiatric case formulations.* Washington, DC: American Psychiatric Association.

Weiner, J. M. (1997). Diagnostic classification in *DSM-IV*. In J. Weiner (Ed.), *Textbook of child and adolescent psychiatry*. Washington, DC: American Psychiatric Association.

Related Topic

Chapter 10, "Formulating Diagnostic Impressions With Ethnic and Racial Minority Children Using the *DSM-IV-TR*"

10 FORMULATING DIAGNOSTIC IMPRESSIONS WITH ETHNIC AND RACIAL MINORITY CHILDREN USING THE *DSM-IV-TR*

Ronn Johnson

The *Diagnostic and Statistical Manual of Mental Disorders* (text rev., or *DSM-IV-TR*; American Psychiatric Association, 2000) is a primary clinical reference assessment tool used in the psychodiagnostic process with children. It includes information critical for rendering diagnostic impressions across ethnoracial groups. Yet, while the inclusion of cultural factors within the *DSM-IV-TR* is a noteworthy development in psychiatric nosology, it represents a somewhat turbulent milestone. For example, there is more of an extensive coverage of culture within the *DSM-IV-TR* than was the case in previous editions of the *Diagnostic and Statistical Manual*. In many respects, the *DSM-IV-TR* reinforces the need to assess ethnoracial factors while in the diagnostic process. In this case, the *DSM-IV-TR* seemed to follow the cross-cultural momentum that was seemingly endorsed by the American Psychological Association (APA). The APA emphasized the relevance of culture by developing a set of guidelines for psychological practice with culturally diverse populations. One example included addressing the cultural issues within the *Ethical Principles of Psychologists and Code of Conduct* (APA, 2002). Attention to cultural issues is also a guiding principle in determining APA accreditation for all clinical, counseling, and school psychology training programs. In spite of such professional attention, there are persistent concerns about how culture is being integrated within the diagnostic classification of mental illness.

The *DSM*'s cultural infusion occurs in a disjointed, uneven manner. It could be argued by some that it is beyond the scope of the *DSM-IV-TR* to completely establish the role of culture within the diagnostic process. Despite the lengthy debates that could occur in this area, it is important to recognize and examine three central issues related to the use of the *DSM-IV-TR* with ethnic minority children.

1. Culture must be viewed as a relevant factor when developing diagnostic impressions related to the mental illness in children. However, the *DSM-IV-TR* does not provide enough guidance in how to cogently integrate cultural influences with specific diagnostic questions.
2. The huge variance in the cultural competencies of clinicians working with ethnic-racial minority children is also often reflected in their diagnostic skills. While it is obvious that ethnoracial factors are important for clinical work, only within the past decade have they emerged as a consistent topic within mainstream training programs.
3. Since cultural factors influence the way ethnic minority children present themselves (e.g., patterns of cultural characteristics associated with behavior or shared meanings), it is the objective of this chapter to introduce some of the cultural elements that are often relevant to the diagnosis of ethnic minority children.

The goal of this chapter is to provide a starting place for clinicians as they perform diagnostic work using the *DSM-IV-TR* with ethnic minority children. Because all ethnic groups cannot be considered here individually, some ethnoracial African American and Hispanic children are used as illustrative examples, but it is hoped that the guidelines presented here can serve as a conceptual diagnostic framework when working with any ethnic minority children. It is important to recognize that cultural factors associated with African American and Hispanic children are different from those presented by children of other ethnic minority groups, and that the examples provided here do not exhaust the content base necessary for working effectively with African American and Hispanic children.

- By definition, "culture" generally refers to the meanings held by members of a particular group. This includes their worldview, beliefs, ethics, values, norms of conduct, and so forth. These meanings must be accounted for when formulating a diagnostic impression with ethnic minority children or the diagnosis will be invalid (Johnson, 1993).
- The clinician is the largest source of error in the reliability and validity of *DSM-IV-TR* diagnosis with ethnic minority children. Three factors associated with that error are discussed below.
- The clinician must competently assess the child's level of acculturation and the child's transition distress from the home culture to another cultural experience. "Transition distress" refers to a child's reluctance or struggle to successfully move from one activity or setting to another. To do so, the clinician must (minimally) establish credibility (Sue & Sue, 1990) with the child as well as with the adult caretakers and must conduct an appropriate interview addressing these issues.
- The clinician must accept the client's language, socioeconomic status, and attitude toward mental health treatment as irrelevant to any psychopathology diagnosis that is to be established.
- The clinician must remain supremely aware of his or her impact on the interviewee. There is some indication that less obvious and unintentional discrimination by a clinician can affect the assessment data presented by ethnic minority patients.
- The use of assessment tools to measure acculturation should be considered.
- The clinician must collect a culturally relevant history that includes an assessment of the child's racial identity. An informed examination of all the cultural influences on the child's identity may not be readily observable by the clinician, and some issues of racial identity development may contribute to the child's negative reaction to the clinician. One preferred method of determining a child's racial identity development involves studying the various racial identity models (e.g., Cross, 1991; Ponterotto, 1988). Unfortunately, this approach relies too heavily on the competencies that the clinician brings into the diagnostic process.

- The more mainstream the clinician's own cultural identification, the more likely is the clinician to overlook certain salient cultural frameworks. In this case, cultural sensitivity is not synonymous with cross-cultural competency. Cross-cultural training and requisite supervision are highly recommended for the clinician involved with an ethnic minority child.
- Finally, the clinician's knowledge of ethnoracial oppression and rejection may offer a critical insight into the patient's response to the diagnostic process. For example, African Americans have historically been the targets of undesirable attributes or stereotypes (e.g., low intelligence, sexual prowess, criminal behaviors). African Americans also carry into the diagnostic process significant experiences of exploitation, discrimination, and generally bad treatment within the mental health service system. Consequently, many children are taught by adult caretakers to be wary of their disclosures to mainstream clinicians. That is, part of the cultural will passed on from generation to generation is aimed at insulating and protecting children from what is often perceived as service-related hostility.

It is only logical to presume these children's cultural expectations and experiences may cloud a clinician's ability to develop a more accurate diagnostic impression, so knowledge of those expectations and experiences is critical. One way a mainstream clinician may start to learn more about ethnoracial oppression and rejection could involve reading history and devoting part of the clinical interview to discussion of racism experiences. Consultation with more culturally competent clinicians is also recommended.

TREATMENT PLANNING

In a cautionary statement, the *DSM* warns clinicians that the manual is not intended to encompass all mental health conditions. Unfortunately, there is no such warning that information available in the *DSM-IV-TR* may be irrelevant for the development of treatment plans for ethnic minority children. Historically, the *DSM* has been ripe for ethnocentric criticisms. Many of its diagnostic criteria have limited cross-cultural utility, and diagnosis with the *DSM-IV-TR* is too dependent on clinicians who often are not adequately cross-culturally trained. In addition, the tools or methods typically used to arrive at a *DSM* diagnostic impression for ethnic minority children are inappropriate (Berry, Poortinga, Segall, & Dasen, 1992).

Johnson (1993) points out the restricted clinical utility of certain diagnostic categories with these children (e.g., conduct disorder, oppositional disorder, and posttraumatic stress disorder). For example, there is an undesirable tendency for the *DSM-IV-TR* to be overly inclusive (i.e., yield increased false-positive diagnoses). This characteristic is likely to have a more damaging effect on ethnic minority children. For example, under conduct disorder the psychologist is strongly encouraged to consider a child's "reaction to the immediate social context." Despite this *DSM-IV-TR* warning, some ethnic minority children displaying externalizing behaviors related to poverty or exposure to violence may be inappropriately labeled as having a conduct disorder. Anderson (1991) demonstrates that stress is underdiagnosed in some of these ethnoracial populations.

The most common mental disorders of childhood and adolescence listed in the *DSM-IV-TR* include adjustment disorders, behavior disorders, attention-deficit/hyperactivity disorder, oppositional defiant disorder, conduct disorder, depressive disorders, anxiety disorders, substance-related disorders, and eating disorders.

One of the strengths of the *DSM-IV-TR* is the fact that it is empirically based. It was developed in conjunction with the World Health Organization's publication of the 10th edition of the *International Classification of Diseases* (*ICD-10*). It is at least minimally sensitive to culturally relevant issues and represents a considerable improvement over the *DSM-III-R* in terms of cultural factors. Cultural considerations are now mentioned in a significant manner, in contrast to the scant allusion made to culture in the introductory sections of the *DSM-III-R*. In the *DSM-IV-TR*, the criteria for many disorders are accompanied by descriptive sections on culture, age, and gender, reflecting an understanding of mental disorders in a context broader than their symptoms. Extending this thinking, the clinician can take the following steps to use the *DSM-IV-TR* more effectively with ethnic minority children:

1. Clinicians should become as familiar as possible with the sections that specifically address childhood diagnostic issues. The *DSM-IV-TR*'s classification of disorders usually diagnosed in infancy, childhood, and adolescence is based on empirical findings and is developmentally relevant. For example, mental retardation, attention-deficit/hyperactivity disorder to stereotypic movement disorder, and other childhood-onset disorders may occur within the context of poverty, racial trauma, generational differences, immigration stress, and acculturation (Johnson, 1993), though they are not caused by cultural factors.
2. Clinicians must recognize that cultural conditions can have an impact on the presentation of these disorders. For example, an African American foster child was diagnosed as having oppositional defiant disorder, but it was never disclosed that he had experienced several episodes on a school bus in which he was racially taunted by other riders.
3. Understanding of acculturation problems is a key when an ethnic minority child comes to the attention of the psychologist. Acculturation reflects the extent to which ethnic minority children completely release, modify, and retain aspects of both their home environment and the mainstream culture (Locke, 1992). Acculturation may occur in at least two ways. External acculturation may be assessed through behavioral patterns (e.g., dress, language use). Internal acculturation involves the extent to which children articulate their experiences according to the home culture versus the more mainstream culture. There may in fact be no reportable difference. In this case, the child may feel less compelled to display a prescribed set of behaviors just to accommodate to the mainstream. On the other hand, some children feel a need to display different sets of behavior due to some discomfort or other reasons. Diagnostically, the way the child presents under either of these conditions influences the clinical picture as assessed by the psychologist.
4. The clinician should also recognize that diagnostically relevant behaviors might be cloaked by the stage of racial identity development. This may be important with biracial children who can have a more dichotomous racial identity. Some empirical evidence suggests that biracial children move through racial identity development in different ways than children from more racially homogeneous backgrounds.
5. The *DSM-IV-TR*'s 11 appendixes should be utilized fully. While Appendix I's outline for cultural formulation and glossary of culture-bound syndromes examination appears to be most relevant to the issues being addressed here, each appendix has the potential to influence the effective use of the *DSM-IV-TR* with ethnic minority children. These appendixes require the clinician to take a proactive stance in using culture as a factor in the diagnostic process.

For example, Appendix A presents decision trees for six diagnostic categories. The decision tree framework allows the culturally skilled clinician to inject culturally relevant questions at appropriate decision points before arriving at a diagnosis. One of the question points for clarifying an anxiety diagnosis, for instance, regards anxiety concerning attachment figures with the onset in childhood. Some Hispanic girls are brought up to rely on and value a close-knit family. In their case, it is culturally appropriate to experience some distress when placed in situations away from the immediate family (e.g., distant sleepover or leaving home to attend college). The culturally informed clinician will question whether the distress represents a true anxiety disorder or more simply a culturally appropriate response to separation.

Appendix I describes cultural influences on

pathology and defines culturally based syndromes. It also presents cultural issues salient to diagnosis (e.g., cultural identity, cultural explanations of the individual's illness) and encourages the clinician to generate narrative summaries for these same categories. The brevity of this section might erroneously lead some clinicians to believe there is little to know regarding cultural issues, but the intent of this appendix is clearly the opposite. It makes passing mention of indigenous clinicians' capability of formulating their own diagnostic systems for some of the more commonly occurring North American idioms of distress (e.g., anorexia nervosa, dissociative disorders). Johnson (1993) has shown that some single-entity disorders (e.g., posttraumatic stress disorder) may be sorted into several subcategories, such as racial trauma or racial encounter distress disorder. Other extensions of Appendix I include consideration of certain ethnoracial factors such as cultural will in assigning a global adaptive functioning rating on Axis V.

The *DSM-IV-TR*'s attempt to be culturally appropriate makes it reasonably responsive to practical clinical issues while allowing room for culturally competent practice (Tucker, 2002). This article was guided by an assumption that cultural patterns affect the presentation of psychopathology and the diagnostic process. A culturally relevant diagnosis is at the heart of effective therapeutic interventions and outcome assessment. Communication between clinicians is enhanced when practitioners can share treatment information that includes cultural nuances.

A culturally competent clinician must identify clearly the subtle interactions between the child, the clinician, and the *DSM-IV-TR* in order to yield the most useful clinical assessment. Quintana, Castilllo, and Zamarripa (2000) offer cultural and linguistic competencies an assessing clinician should possess in this regard. It is also worth noting that some practitioners have misgivings or serious doubts about the presumptions within the *DSM-IV-TR*. Others might argue the need to extend the *DSM-IV-TR* axes to include identification of cultural and gender factors. Here, the clinician is challenged to more fully understand the behavior of children from diverse backgrounds.

References & Readings 

American Psychiatric Association. (1987). *Diagnostic and statistical manual of mental disorders* (3rd ed., rev.). Washington, DC: Author.

American Psychiatric Association. (1994). *Diagnostic and statistical manual of mental disorders* (4th ed.). Washington, DC: Author.

American Psychiatric Association. (2000). *Diagnostic and statistical manual of mental disorders* (4th ed., rev.). Washington, DC: Author.

American Psychological Association. (2002). *Ethical principles of psychologists and code of conduct.* Washington, DC: Author.

Anderson, L. P. (1991). Acculturative stress: A theory of relevance to black Americans. *Clinical Psychology Review, 11,* 685–702.

Berry, J. W., Poortinga, Y. H., Segall, M. H., & Dasen, P. R. (1992). *Cross-cultural psychology: Research and applications.* Cambridge, UK: Cambridge University Press.

Cross, W. E. (1991). *Shades of black: Diversity in African-American identity.* Philadelphia: Temple University Press.

Hardiman, R. (1982). *White identity development: A process oriented model for describing the racial conscious of white Americans.* Unpublished doctoral dissertation, University of Massachusetts, Amherst.

Helms, J. E. (1984). Toward a theoretical explanation of the effects of race on counseling: A black 137 and white model. *Counseling Psychologist, 12,* 153–165.

Johnson, R. (1993). Clinical issues in the use of the *DSM-III* with African American children: A diagnostic paradigm. *Journal of Black Psychology, 19,* 447–460.

Locke, D. C. (1992). *Increasing multicultural understanding: A comprehensive model.* Newbury Park, CA: Sage.

Ponterotto, J. G. (1988). Racial consciousness development among white counselor trainees: A stage model. *Journal of Multicultural Counseling and Development, 16,* 146–156.

Quintana, S. M., Castillo, E. M., & Zamarripa, M. X. (2000). Assessment of ethnic and linguistic minority children. In S. Shapiro & T. R. Kratchochwill (Eds.), *Behavioral assessment in schools: Theory, research and clinical foundations* (2nd ed., pp. 435–463). New York: Guilford Press.

Sue, D. W., & Sue, D. (1990). *Counseling the culturally different: Theory and practice* (2nd ed.). New York: Wiley.

Tucker, C. M. (2002). Expanding pediatric psychology beyond hospital walls to meet the health needs of ethnic minority children. *Journal of Pediatric Psychology, 27,* 315–323.

World Health Organization. (1992). *International classification of diseases and related health problems* (10th ed.). Geneva: Author.

Related Topics

Chapter 9, "Child and Adolescent Diagnosis With *DSM-IV*"

Chapter 18, "*DSM-IV-TR* Classification System"

11 MEDICAL EVALUATION OF CHILDREN WITH BEHAVIORAL OR DEVELOPMENTAL DISORDERS

James L. Lukefahr

This chapter is designed to familiarize the psychologist with the diagnostic medical evaluation of children with disordered development or behavior. The three components of a comprehensive medical evaluation (*history, physical examination,* and *laboratory evaluation*) will be described, with emphasis on those considerations pertinent to children with behavioral or developmental disorders.

MEDICAL HISTORY

Birth History

- *Prenatal factors: Prematurity* (birth prior to 37 weeks of gestation) and *low birth weight* are risk factors for developmental and cognitive delays, as well as for some behavior disorders, such as attention-deficit/hyperactivity disorder (ADHD). *Intrauterine growth retardation* (IUGR), also referred to as *small for gestational age,* refers to conditions that impair fetal growth, so that birth size is disproportionately small for the gestational age. IUGR is a particularly important risk factor because its presence indicates significant toxic, nutritional, or infectious insult to the developing fetus. A partial list of causes of IUGR is shown in Table 1.

For example, congenital infection with *cytomegalovirus* (CMV) affects 1% of U.S. newborns (about 40,000 infants every year). Although most of these newborns are asymptomatic, 6% have severe disease evident at birth with IUGR, psychomotor retardation, microcephaly, and multiple organ involvement. Another 14% of CMV-infected infants do not have obvious disease at birth but are later found to have sensorineural hearing loss (making CMV infection the

TABLE 1. Common Causes of Intrauterine Growth Retardation

Fetal
Chromosomal disorders (e.g., Down syndrome [trisomy 21], trisomies 18 or 13)
Chronic fetal infection (e.g., human immunodeficiency virus [HIV], cytomegalovirus [CMV], syphilis)
Severe congenital anomalies or syndrome complexes
Radiation injury
Multiple gestation
Placental
Decreased placental size
Placental infection or tumor
Twin-to-twin transfusion
Maternal
Hypertension or preeclampsia
Renal disease
Hypoxemia (chronic lung or cardiac disease)
Malnutrition or anemia
Drugs (e.g., tobacco, alcohol, cocaine, narcotics)

most common noninherited cause of deafness).

- *Perinatal factors: Complications during labor and delivery* appear to cause developmental and learning disabilities less often than previously believed. However, very premature infants and infants with severe perinatal complications remain at risk if they sustain episodes of hypoxemia or intracerebral hemorrhage. Advances in neonatal intensive care have diminished the impact of *respiratory distress syndrome* (or *hyaline membrane disease*) on later development for most premature infants.

  Neonatal jaundice (*hyperbilirubinemia*) is an extremely common condition, reported to affect as many as 60% of all infants. Developmental sequelae appear to occur only in those infants who experience extremely high serum bilirubin levels or (more often) when the jaundice is a result of a severe perinatal illness.

Complete Past Medical History

- *Chronic severe illnesses:* Children with chronic illnesses such as diabetes mellitus, seizure disorders, and asthma often have concurrent behavioral and developmental problems. For example, children with severe *congenital heart disease* often experience developmental delays due to the cerebral effects of chronic hypoxemia. Similarly, severe *chronic renal disease* may also cause cognitive or developmental compromise as a result of growth failure and high levels of circulating toxic metabolic products. Children with *cancer* may have cognitive impairments due to either the malignancy itself or the toxic effects of the cancer treatment. Severe *seizure disorders* are often associated with brain lesions or malformation syndromes with developmental and cognitive implications.

  Children with chronic illnesses frequently experience concurrent behavioral problems. For example, small children with severe asthma may experience separational difficulties as a result of parental overprotection. Adolescents with diabetes or epilepsy often rebel against their dependency on medical treatment regimens and refuse to comply with prescribed therapy—frequently resulting in serious complications.
- *Other chronic conditions:* The United States and other developed countries are experiencing an epidemic of obesity affecting children as well as adults. Severely overweight children manifest a variety of physical, psychosocial, and economic dysfunctions. Familial and community factors typically exert strong influences in the development of obesity in children and greatly complicate therapy.
- *Recurrent illnesses:* Children with recurrent otitis media during the first few years of life may sustain speech and language delays due to prolonged periods of decreased hearing. Frequent episodes of asthma may affect physical and social development by inhibiting normal childhood activities.
- *Family history:* The clinician should inquire about heritable conditions known to occur within the family. Examples of congenital familial conditions with developmental consequences include *tuberous sclerosis,* which is often associated with severe seizures and mental retardation, and *fragile X syndrome,*

the most common cause of mental retardation in boys. Acquired conditions can also have familial occurrence patterns. *Thyroid disease, collagen-vascular disease* (e.g., systemic lupus or juvenile rheumatoid arthritis), and *inflammatory bowel disease* (e.g., Crohn's disease) commonly cluster within families. These may first present with changes in behavior or school performance, or with chronic pain that initially may appear to be functional in nature.

- *Body mass index (BMI)*: This is the most widely accepted parameter for detecting and monitoring childhood obesity. Standardized growth charts for calculating and plotting BMI for age are now available and are also included on the accompanying Web site.
- *Social history:* Physicians recognize the importance of psychosocial factors in disease states and are accustomed to exploring these concerns with parents of young children. Direct discussion of psychosocial issues with older children and adolescents during a single medical encounter is often more difficult. A brief structured interview technique, commonly utilized with adolescents, is the *HEADSSS interview*, summarized in Table 2.

PHYSICAL EXAMINATION

Growth Parameters

Many chronic developmental and somatic disorders are accompanied by disordered physical growth, and physicians routinely maintain *standardized growth charts* for their child patients. These growth charts allow comparison of children's length or height, weight, and head circumference to national norms for those growth parameters and are reproduced on the accompanying Web site. A child with any growth parameter less than the 5th percentile for age (or greater than the 95th percentile) should undergo thorough medical evaluation. *Head circumference* is particularly important in evaluating developmentally delayed children, since this growth parameter is closely correlated with brain growth.

In recent years there has been increased recognition of a hereditary or familial component in the development of several behavioral disorders. The role of heredity has been most strongly established in schizophrenia, bipolar disorder, and ADHD. Other conditions in which heredity may play a role include obsessive-compulsive disorder and the autistic disorders.

TABLE 2. The HEADSSS Psychosocial Interview Technique

H	Home environment (e.g., relations with parents and siblings)
E	Education/employment (e.g., school performance)
A	Activities (e.g., sports participation, after-school activity, peer relations)
D	Drug, alcohol, or tobacco use
S	Sexuality (e.g., is the patient sexually active; does he/she use condoms or contraception)
S	Suicide risk or symptoms of depression or other mental disorder
S	"Savagery" (e.g., violence or abuse in home environment or in neighborhood)

General Physical Examination

- *Vital signs:* Temperature, pulse, blood pressure, and respiratory rate.
- *Head:* Malformations of the skull, external ears, and other structures (often the most visible signs of major malformation syndromes). Microcephaly, small palpebral fissures, and short, flat upper lips are the classic physical findings of *fetal alcohol syndrome*.
- *Eyes, ears, nose, and throat:* Abnormalities of the iris, pupil, lens, or retina; middle-ear fluid or tympanic membrane abnormality; malformations of the nose and throat (such as cleft or high arched palate).
- *Neck:* Enlargement of the thyroid gland (goiter) or lymph nodes.
- *Chest:* Malformations of the chest wall; heart murmur or other evidence of cardiac malformation; lung abnormalities.
- *Abdomen:* Enlarged liver, spleen, or kidneys (associated with congenital infection or metabolic disorders); abnormal masses; cachexia or obesity.
- *Back:* Evidence of spina bifida or scoliosis.

- *Genitalia and anus:* Malformations of sexual organs or perineum; testicular enlargement (common in fragile X syndrome).
- *Extremities:* Signs of limb malformation; decreased or asymmetrical muscle mass.
- *Skin:* Pigmentation abnormalities, such as the café au lait spots of neurofibromatosis, ash-leaf spots of tuberous sclerosis, hyperpigmentation of incontinentia pigmenti, and *acanthosis nigricans* associated with type II diabetes.
- *Neurological examination:* Neurological examination is a critical element in the evaluation of children with behavioral or developmental disorders. It includes cranial nerve function, tendon reflexes, muscle tone, muscle strength, cerebellar function (such as stereognosis and proprioception), gait abnormalities, and presence of persistent or abnormal infantile reflexes (such as the startle and glabellar reflexes).

Vision and Hearing Testing

Accurate assessment of visual and auditory function should be performed in all children with behavioral or developmental disorders. Several technologies, such as auditory and visual brain stem evoked potentials, are now available that allow such testing even in newborns or children with severe communication impairment.

LABORATORY TESTS AND IMAGING PROCEDURES

Table 3 provides a partial listing of laboratory tests commonly obtained during evaluation of children with developmental or behavioral disorders. Developmental disorders presenting in early infancy are usually more severe and often warrant extensive evaluation for metabolic disorders or congenital infection. Studies

TABLE 3. Selected Laboratory Tests and Their Indications in Evaluating Behavioral or Developmental Disorders

Laboratory Test	Indication
Alpha-fetoprotein, serum	Abnormal in maternal serum or fetal amniotic fluid in Down syndrome and neural tube defects
Amino or organic acids, serum or urine	Elevated in some congenital metabolic diseases
Ammonia, blood	Elevated in some congenital metabolic diseases
Antinuclear antibody (ANA), serum	Elevated in collagen-vascular diseases (e.g., systemic lupus erythematosus)
Bilirubin, serum	Elevated in neonatal jaundice and in liver disease
Chromosome evaluation (karyotype)	Abnormal in many major malformation syndromes (e.g., Down syndrome, trisomy 18)
Creatinine, serum	Elevated in chronic renal diseases
DNA testing	Detection of fragile X syndrome and numerous other hereditary conditions
Electrolytes, serum	Abnormal in some congenital metabolic diseases
Erythrocyte sedimentation rate (ESR), blood	Elevated in chronic inflammatory diseases, such as systemic lupus erythematosus and Crohn's disease
Gamma-glutamyltransferase (GGT), serum	Elevated in chronic liver disease
Glucose, blood or serum	Abnormal in diabetes mellitus and in some inborn errors of metabolism
Glycosylated hemoglobin (hemoglobin A1C), serum	Elevated in diabetes mellitus with undertreatment or poor compliance with treatment
Hemoglobin electrophoresis, blood	Detects abnormal hemoglobin types, such as in sickle-cell disease
Lead, blood	Elevated in chronic lead exposure
Thyroid function tests (thyroxine, triiodothyronine, thyroid-stimulating hormone, T4, T3, TSH), serum	Used to detect abnormal thyroid function
Transaminases (AST, ALT, SGOT, SGPT), serum	Elevated in acute or chronic liver disease
Urea nitrogen (BUN), serum	Elevated in acute or chronic renal disease

aimed at detecting infectious agents that may cause fetal injury and subsequent developmental delay include *urine for CMV culture* and *serum antibody titers* for congenital infection by organisms such as toxoplasmosis and syphilis. *Skull and extremity X rays* are often obtained to detect metabolic or infectious damage to skeletal structures. *Computed tomography* (CT) or *magnetic resonance imaging* (MRI) of the brain may be ordered to identify congenital malformations. *Chromosome determination* (karyotype) is ordered if a major malformation syndrome (e.g., Down syndrome or Turner syndrome) is suspected. Specific *DNA testing* for a variety of disorders with developmental or behavioral implications is now available. These include fragile X syndrome, Huntington's disease, and Duchenne's muscular dystrophy, with DNA tests for other conditions being announced regularly.

Laboratory evaluation of behavior disorders and learning disabilities presenting later in childhood is usually not as extensive. In the typical case, where a child has a long and relatively stable symptomatology with a diagnosis such as reading disability or ADHD, laboratory evaluation is usually not helpful. However, a child who was previously thriving and over a short time begins to do poorly in school is more likely to have a treatable medical condition. *Electroencephalography* (EEG) should be performed if a child's abnormal behaviors show a discrete episodic pattern that may represent seizure activity. Otherwise, the EEG is not routinely indicated for the evaluation of learning and behavior problems. *Thyroid function tests* may be indicated, particularly in girls with recent changes in cognitive performance or if there is a family history of thyroid disease.

References & Readings 

Behrman, R. E., Kliegman, R. M., & Jenson, H. B. (Eds.). (2000). *Nelson textbook of pediatrics* (16th ed.). Philadelphia: W. B. Saunders.

Brodsky, M., & Lombroso, P. J. (1998). Molecular mechanisms of developmental disorders. *Development and psychopathology, 10*(1), 1–20.

Burke, W. (2002). Genetic testing. *New England Journal of Medicine, 347*(23), 1867–1875.

Jones, K. L. (1997). *Smith's recognizable patterns of human malformation* (5th ed.). Philadelphia: W. B. Saunders.

Kimm, S. Y. S., & Obarzanek, E. (2002). Childhood obesity: A new pandemic of the new millennium. *Pediatrics, 110*(5), 1003–1007.

Kuban, K. C. K., & Leviton, A. (1994). Cerebral palsy. *New England Journal of Medicine, 330*(3), 188–195.

Parker, S., & Zuckerman, B. S. (Eds.). (1995). *Behavioral and developmental pediatrics: A handbook for primary care.* Philadelphia: Lippincott Williams & Wilkins

Pass, R. F. (2002). Cytomegalovirus infection. *Pediatrics in Review, 23*(5), 163–170.

Rapin, I. (1997). Autism. *New England Journal of Medicine, 337*(2), 97–104.

Roberts, M. C. (Ed.). (1995). *Handbook of pediatric psychology* (2nd ed.). New York: Guilford Press.

Schwartz, I. D. (2000). Failure to thrive: An old nemesis in the new millennium. *Pediatrics in Review, 21*(8), 257–264.

Related Topics

Chapter 9, "Child and Adolescent Diagnosis With *DSM-IV*"

Chapter 89, "Normal Medical Laboratory Values and Measurement Conversions"

12 INTERVIEWING PARENTS

Carolyn S. Schroeder & Betty N. Gordon

Parents are usually the primary referral source when a child is brought to the attention of a mental health professional. They have a unique knowledge and understanding of the child and thus are an integral part of the assessment and treatment process. During the initial interview with the parent(s), the information-gathering process begins, essential preliminary clinical decisions are made, and the parents become engaged in a collaborative working relationship with the therapist. A successful parent interview will ultimately determine treatment goals and their priority and will ensure that parents will cooperate in carrying out these goals.

Parent interviews can be structured or unstructured. Both methods have advantages and disadvantages. Structured interviews involve a prearranged set of questions to be asked in sequential order that usually focus on gathering information about a specific *DSM* disorder. Although providing a more standardized format, structured interviews generally give more global information about the existence of a disorder rather than specific details about a particular child, family, or peer group that are needed for planning an intervention program. An unstructured interview, on the other hand, allows the clinician more freedom to explore the nature and context of a particular problem, as well as the opportunity to investigate potential contributing factors, such as stimuli that may elicit the problem behaviors. Moreover, this type of interview allows the clinician to begin to delineate acceptable behavioral alternatives, as well as other potential problem areas for the child or family. Unstructured interviews, however, assume that the interviewer has the necessary knowledge about the nature of the specific presenting problem to guide the content and process of the interview. Some other problems with unstructured interviews include collecting information selectively, a lack of a systematic way to combine different types of information, and a tendency to make a judgment or diagnosis based on what is familiar to the clinician (McClellan & Werry, 2000).

Given the limited psychometric support for structured interviews and the uniqueness of each child, family, and environment, we think the unstructured interview has more advantages than disadvantages over the structured interview format. Thus, this discussion will focus on unstructured parent interviews. The reader is referred to McClellan and Werry (2000) for a description and critique of structured parent interviews.

One format for gathering and organizing information using an unstructured interview is called the Comprehensive Assessment-to-Intervention System (CAIS; Schroeder & Gordon, 2002). The CAIS focuses on the specifics of the behavior of concern and the characteristics of the child, family, and environment that potentially influence the behavior. It helps the interviewer decide which questions need to be asked and ensures that essential information is gathered quickly and efficiently (Schroeder & Gordon, 2002).

SETTING THE STAGE

Prior to interviewing parents, it is helpful to have them complete a general questionnaire about the child and family (see Schroeder & Gordon, 2002, for an example), as well as a rating scale that screens for problem behavior and compares the child's behavior to a normative sample. Examples of useful behavior rating scales are the Child Behavior Checklist (Achenbach, 1991, 1992), the Parenting Stress Index (Abidin, 1995), the Eyberg Child Behavior Inventory (Eyberg & Pincus, 1999), and the Behavior Assessment System for Children (Reynolds & Kamphaus, 1992). Each parent should be asked to complete the selected behavior rating scale; if they are separated or divorced, each should be asked to complete a general parent questionnaire. The information gained from the completed questionnaires permits the clinician to generate preliminary hypotheses about the nature and causes of the problem, as well as to plan for and focus the parent interview.

It is important to include both parents in the initial interview if they both are actively involved in the child's life. If they are unable or unwilling to participate in a joint interview, an attempt should be made to interview them separately, even if this is done by telephone. Each parent brings his or her own perspective on the problem and also will provide the clinician with information about his or her willingness to support the child's treatment. We routinely include preschool children in the initial parent interview, with age-appropriate toys and activities provided to keep the child occupied. Although some clinicians may find this difficult, we have discovered that the information being discussed is rarely new to the child. Moreover, the opportunity to observe the child and the parent-child interaction firsthand far outweighs any disadvantages. If necessary, later interviews can be conducted with the parents alone, to go over more sensitive information or to receive information or provide information to the parents without the distraction of a particularly disruptive child. Parents of school-age children are typically interviewed alone, before the child is seen; parents of adolescents are first seen with the adolescent present or absent, depending on the nature of the problem.

Interviewing parents is an interactive process that sets the tone for future intervention efforts. To promote collaboration, it is important for the interviewer to create an atmosphere that puts the parents at ease in discussing their child's problems and gives them some sense of optimism that the child's or family's life can improve as a result of professional help. Characteristics of a good interviewer can contribute to a positive tone. These include warmth, empathy, a sensitive and nonjudgmental approach that respects others' feelings and cultures, and an ability to keep the interview moving along in a smooth, purposeful fashion (Kanfer, Eyberg, & Krahn, 1992). The ability to listen also is an essential skill. Listening helps parents focus on the problem, and reflecting or paraphrasing lets the parents know that they have been heard. Recognizing the parents' distress as they discuss areas of concern encourages them to share their fears and beliefs about the problem(s).

It is helpful to begin the interview by briefly summarizing what is already known about the situation and explaining the purpose of the interview (i.e., to get a better understanding of their concerns in order to help determine what, if any, intervention is necessary). This gives parents some initial information on what is expected of them, as well as on what they can expect from the interviewer. Further, it helps them start talking about their concerns. Whereas it is important to get a thorough understanding of the nature and context of the problematic behavior, it is not possible or advisable to assess everything in the child's or family's background. Background information is important, but the goal is to be selective in pursuing a particular topic. It should also be remembered that working with children almost always involves an ongoing relationship with the parents; if a relevant area is missed initially, it is very likely to be discussed in future meetings. Problems with parent interviews include inaccurate recall, conflicting perceptions of the child between parents, and a tendency to describe the child in unrealistically positive and precocious terms (Kanfer et al., 1992). Parents also may describe their child's behavior in excessively negative terms when they are under personal stress (e.g., marital discord, depression). Focusing on the current situation—that is, current behavior, current child management techniques, and current family strengths and weaknesses—can help increase the reliability of parental reports.

COMPREHENSIVE ASSESSMENT-TO-INTERVENTION SYSTEM

The following is a logical and systematic guide to assuring that information in important areas is gathered. The information does not have to be obtained in any particular order, and although it may be gathered during the parent interview, a variety of other sources and methods could be used (e.g., parent or teacher questionnaires, psychometric testing, observation of parent-child interaction). The CAIS is very useful for complex cases, but it also provides a framework to assist the clinician in quickly gathering essential information for brief assessment cases.

Clarifying the Referral Question

Although the need to clarify the referral question seems obvious, its importance cannot be overemphasized. After the parent has described the problem, the clinician should be certain that he or she and the parent are thinking about the same problem. This can be done by simply reflecting what the parent has said: "It sounds like you are concerned about your child refusing to go to school, as well as the different ways you and your husband are handling the situation." This gives the parent the opportunity to restate his or her concerns until there is a mutual understanding of the concerns that are to be addressed.

Determining the Social Context

A child is referred because someone is concerned. This does not necessarily mean that the child needs treatment or that the child's behavior is the problem. The clinician should ask: Who is concerned about the child? Why is this person concerned? Why is this person concerned now as opposed to some other time? The parents' affect in describing the problems is also significant. Are they overwhelmed, anxious, depressed, or nonchalant? Two mothers, for example, describe their 3-year-old daughters as being anxious and fearful. One mother is calm, in control of herself, and using good judgment in attempting to deal with the problem. The other mother, however, is extremely upset, fearful, and unable to view the problem objectively. Each of these parents presents a different focus for the assessment/intervention process.

The family's sociocultural characteristics can play an important role in the planning and implementation of a treatment program (García Coll & Meyer, 1993). Questions such as the following can help the clinician get a better understanding of the parent's perspective: What do you think has caused your child's problem? Why do you think it started when it did? How does the problem affect you or your child? How severe do you feel your child's problem is? Do you expect it will have a short- or long-term course? What kind of treatment do you think your child should receive? Who can help with the treatment? What are the most important results that you hope your child will receive from treatment? What is your greatest fear about your child (García Coll & Meyer, 1993)? Asking the parents about their expectations, hopes, and fears in coming to a mental health professional helps in both gathering and interpreting the material, especially if the clinician's recommendations are contrary to the parents' expectations or confirm their worst fears. This information also can help the clinician develop a treatment program that is sensitive to sociocultural influences.

Assessing General Areas

Information about the characteristics of the child and the family is important in putting problems or concerns in perspective and determining the resources the family has or will need to carry out a successful intervention plan. Asking parents to briefly describe a typical day for their child (when he or she gets up; the morning, daily, and evening routines; when he or she goes to bed, etc.) usually gives a great deal of information about how the family and child functions, their stresses and limitations, and, in general, the context in which they live. The following general areas are important to assess:

- *Developmental status:* Knowledge of the child's developmental status (physical/motor, cognitive, language, social, personality/emotional, psychosexual) allows the clinician to evaluate the child's behavior in comparison with that of other children of the same age or developmental level. Behavior that may be considered a significant problem at one stage in development or at one age may be quite normal at another. The job of the clinician is to judge whether the behavior of concern is less or more than one would expect of any child at that age and in that environment. A 3-year-old who wets the bed, for example, may be considered "normal" for that age, whereas a 10-year-old who wets the bed is viewed as having a significant problem. Behavior also changes over the course of development, and some problem behaviors change in the appropriate or desired direction without intervention. Thus, the time at which a behavior occurs in a child's life is as important as the behavior itself. Furthermore, knowledge of early development is important when assessing children in the preschool years, since this is a critical time for identification of and intervention in developmental problems.

- *Characteristics of parents and extended family:* Although it is difficult to identify causal mechanisms in the development of childhood disorders, and equally difficult to delineate the specific factors contributing to or mediating outcome, the child development and child clinical literature does provide evidence for certain parent characteristics and parenting practices that facilitate development, as well as those that make the child more vulnerable (Schroeder & Gordon, 2002). Moreover, these factors affect how parents view their children. It is generally accepted, for example, that low parental tolerance, high expectations for child behavior, marital stress, and family problems influenced parents' perception of their child's behavior. Similarly, Wahler's (1980) work shows that a mother's perception of her child's behavior is highly correlated with the type of environmental interactions (positive or coercive) she has just experienced. Thus, the perspective of the referring person must be taken into account. The referring person may lack information about child development in general, may have emotional problems, or may be experiencing stress, all of which can distort his or her perception of the child's behavior. In addition, parenting styles, techniques, and models; marital status; and the presence of psychopathology in parents and other family members are especially important areas to assess, as are sibling relationships and the availability and use of social support.
- *Environment:* Recent stressful life events, socioeconomic status, and subculture norms and values can provide important information about the problems the child is experiencing and the intervention strategies that may be most helpful. The child's environment provides the setting conditions for the behavior and in some cases may be a more appropriate focus for intervention than the behavior itself. The setting conditions can include very specific antecedents to the behavior (repeated commands, teasing, criticism, or hunger), socioeconomic status, or major events such as parental divorce, a death in the family, a chronic illness, or an impending move.
- *Consequences of the behavior:* Information in this area includes the ways in which the parents are currently handling the behavior problem; the techniques that have been tried in the past and the "payoff" for the child; the impact of the problem behavior on the child, parents, and environment; and the prognosis with and without treatment. Lack of careful assessment of these factors usually leads to parents' responding to suggestions by saying, "Yes, but we've tried that and it doesn't work."
- *Medical/health status:* This area should include information on the family's history of medical/genetic problems, chronic illnesses of the child, current health and medications, prenatal history, and early development. Much of this information can be gathered in a general parent questionnaire with specific areas of concern followed up in the interview.

Assessing Specific Areas

In addition to the general areas already mentioned, it is important to gather information on the specific behaviors or concerns, including (a) the persistence of the behavior (how long has it been going on?); (b) changes in behavior (is it getting worse?); (c) severity (is the behavior very intense or dangerous or low-level but "annoying"?); (d) frequency (has the behavior occurred only once or twice or many times?); (e) situation specificity (does the behavior occur only at home or in a variety of settings?); and (f) the type of problem (is the problem a discrete behavior or a set of diffuse problems?).

Determining the Effects of the Problem

It is important to note who is suffering from the referral problem(s). It may be that the child's behavior is bothering one parent but not the other or is annoying to the teacher but is not a problem for the parents. In other cases, although the behavior may be interfering with some aspect of the child's development, it may not be seen as a problem to the parents or other adults and without intervention may lead to a poor outcome for the child. For example, a learning disability may not be seen as a problem for the parents, but the child is likely to suffer negative consequences in school and in future opportunities.

Determining Areas for Intervention

After assessing each of these areas, the clinician should have a good idea about the nature of the problem and should know what additional information is needed to conceptualize the problem. It should be possible at this time to formulate plans for further assessment and/or intervention strategies. Although it is not possible to answer every question and/or to intervene effectively in every situation, intervention strategies follow naturally from the assessment, if the child's development and behavior and the emotional, physical, and sociocultural context in which he or she lives have been examined systematically. For example, interventions in the *developmental area* could include (a) teaching new responses; (b) providing appropriate stimulation; or (c) increasing or decreasing specific behaviors. In the *parental area*, one could (a) teach new parenting techniques; (b) focus on the emotional atmosphere in the home or school; (c) treat (or refer for treatment) marital problems or parent psychopathology; or (d) change parental expectations, attitudes, or beliefs. *Environmental* interventions might involve (a) changing the specific cues that elicit inappropriate behavior or prevent appropriate behavior from occurring; (b) focusing on the emotional atmosphere in the home by helping parents build support networks and deal with the stresses of daily life; (c) helping the child/family cope with life events such as a death; or (d) changing the physical environment where the problem behavior most often occurs. Focusing intervention on the *consequences of the behavior* might involve (a) changing the responses of the parents; (b) changing the responses of other significant adults such as teachers; or (c) changing the behavior of the child by focusing on a more appropriate payoff for the child (e.g., providing reinforcers). Intervening in the *medical/health* area may involve (a) referral for treatment of the cause of the problem (e.g., persistent ear infections) or (b) treating the effect of the problem (e.g., teaching relaxation skills to a child with cerebral palsy).

CLOSING THE INTERVIEW

Time should be allowed at the end of the initial parent interview to summarize and integrate the information gathered. This lets the parents know that their concerns have been accurately heard and gives them feedback on the clinician's initial conceptualization of the problem. An explanation should be given for any additional information that is needed (e.g., school visit, behavioral rating scales, psychometric testing of the child, child interviews, further interviews with the parents, observations of parent-child interactions, medical evaluation) and how this information will be gathered. If possible, potential treatment strategies should be discussed, as well as the estimated length of time and cost for that treatment. While it might not be possible to give all this information without further assessment, it is important that the parents have some understanding of the clinician's thoughts regarding treatment and a sense of hope that something can be done to help them and their child. Early in the interview, the clinician should have asked about the parents' expectations, and at the end of the interview, their expectations can be discussed in relation to the gathered information. A collaborative relationship with parents is developed by sharing information with them and allowing them choices in how to proceed. Asking the parents what they think (or feel) about what they have heard and engaging them in the process of setting treatment goals encourage them to be part of this process and maximize the chances that they will support the child's treatment.

References & Readings

Abidin, R. R. (1995). *Parenting Stress Index manual* (3rd ed.). Odessa, FL: Psychological Assessment Resources.

Achenbach, T. M. (1991). *Manual for the Child Behavior Checklist/4-18 and 1991 Profile.* Burlington: University of Vermont, Department of Psychiatry.

Achenbach, T. M. (1992). *Manual for the Child Behavior Checklist/2-3 and 1992 Profile.* Burlington: University of Vermont, Department of Psychiatry.

Eyberg, S. M., & Pincus, D. (1999). *The Eyberg Child Behavior Inventory and Sutter-Eyberg Student Behavior Inventory: Professional manual.* Odessa, FL: Psychological Assessment Resources.

García Coll, C. T., & Meyer, E. C. (1993). The sociocultural context of infant development. In C. H. Zeanah, Jr. (Ed.), *Handbook of infant mental health* (pp. 56–70). New York: Guilford Press.

Kanfer, F., Eyberg, S. M., & Kahn, G. L. (1992). Interviewing strategies in child assessment. In C. E. Walker & M. C. Roberts (Eds.), *Handbook of clinical child psychology* (2nd ed., pp. 49–62). New York: Wiley Interscience.

Reynolds, C. R., & Kamphaus, R. W. (1992). *Behavioral Assessment System for Children (BASC).* Circle Pines, MN: American Guidance Services.

Schroeder, C. S., & Gordon, B. N. (2002). *Assessment and treatment of childhood problems: A clinician's guide* (2nd ed.). New York: Guilford Press.

Wahler, R. G. (1980). The insular mother: Her problems in parent-child treatment. *Journal of Applied Behavior Analysis, 13,* 207–219.

Related Topics

Chapter 9, "Child and Adolescent Diagnosis With *DSM-IV*"

Chapter 11, "Medical Evaluation of Children With Behavioral or Developmental Disorders"

13 ATTENTION-DEFICIT/ HYPERACTIVITY DISORDER THROUGH THE LIFE SPAN

Robert J. Resnick

Attention-deficit/hyperactivity disorder (ADHD) is the most frequent reason children access health care. On average there are two children with ADHD in every classroom. This disorder is not outgrown in adolescence, and up to 70% of children so diagnosed will have discernible symptoms into adulthood. It is estimated that 3–5% of children and 10–20 million adults have symptoms of ADHD. Boys outnumber girls by about 4 to 1, and they may present in different ways: boys tend to be more externalizing and aggressive, whereas girls tend to be more internalizing, showing more difficulties with emotion and much less assertiveness along with oversocializing and being overly talkative. ADHD is not caused by poor parenting, diet, excess sugar, or inadequate schools, but all of these may exacerbate the ADHD behaviors.

According to the *DSM-IV* (1994), the two primary symptom clusters are inattention and impulsivity and hyperactivity. The diagnostic rubrics are attention-deficit/hyperactivity disorder: predominantly inattentive type (note there is no hyperactivity of significance); attention-deficit/hyperactivity disorder: predominantly hyperactive-impulsive type; attention-deficit/hyperactivity disorder: combined type (incorporating both clusters); and attention-deficit/hyperactivity disorder: not otherwise specified, for individuals who exhibit symptoms of ADHD but do not meet full criteria. For adolescents and adults who currently have symptoms but no longer meet full criteria, the notation "in partial remission" should be added. Onset of symptoms occurs before age 7, lasts at least 6 months, and is observed in more than one setting (e.g., home, school, church, work, neighborhood, day care). Symptoms must be at an age-inappropriate level, with significant impairment in social, occupational, or academic functioning.

Appropriate "rule outs" need to be considered because they can present as ADHD. In children and adolescents, mood disorders, anxiety, autism and other developmental disorders, intellectual retardation, learning disabilities, hearing loss, and poor vision can mask as ADHD. Similarly, seizure disorders (especially brief but frequent seizures known as "absence" and petit mal) need to be considered as well. Because of the nature of the symptoms, conduct disorders and oppositional defiant disorders are common comorbid conditions. Similarly, many children will carry a dual diagnosis of ADHD and learning disabilities; some will be learning disabled because of the ADHD, and in others the learning disability is a parallel process. The former type of learning disability shows much more improvement with treatment of the ADHD than the latter.

With adults, depressive disorders as well as bipolar disorders can present as ADHD. Anxiety disorders, schizophrenia, borderline and schizotypal personality disorders, intellectual retardation, and learning disabilities may also mask as ADHD. It would be unusual for an adult to have had a seizure undiagnosed since childhood. Academic and vocational underachievement, multiple marriages, and problems in social relationships should raise the question of ADHD. Disorganization, procrastination, problems handling everyday stress, moodiness, and hair-trigger temper, usually with quick offset, all can be related to ADHD. In both adolescents and adults, alcohol and substance abuse are not unusual cofindings.

THE EVALUATION

- *History:* A rigorous psychological, developmental, and social history must be taken. Include employment and educational history for adults.
- *School records:* A complete copy of school records, including report cards, achievement tests, teacher/school commentaries, and special services/special education testing along with individualized educational plans (IEPs), should be obtained. These provide an invaluable view of the person over time in school. For older children, look for a downward spiral of grades, especially starting in third or fourth grade.
- *Teacher ratings:* Teacher rating scales are helpful at baseline and treatment points. They are commercially available.
- *Parent ratings:* Parents should fill out ratings separately because they, like teachers, frequently have different thresholds of tolerance for the child's behavior.
- *Computerized assessments:* These measure inattention, distractibility, and impulsivity. Continuous performance tests (CPTs) are the most common and are commercially available

(e.g., Conner's Continuous Performance Test).
- *Mental status exam:* Observe the person for ADHD symptoms and behaviors while ruling out other diagnoses by appropriate questioning/observation.
- In adults, information from spouse/significant other is most helpful.

TREATMENT

School-Age Children

- Thorough explanation to parents and child of the nature of ADHD, including etiology, treatment, and outcome. Significant understanding of ADHD by family and child is imperative.
- School-based behavioral strategies to ensure homework, class work, and school participation are at an acceptable level. Strategies are also aimed at increasing compliance (on task) and decreasing inappropriate and frequently aggressive behaviors. Referral to the school system for special education screening and evaluation may be necessary so that the ADHD child can be identified as qualifying for special education services. Academic tutoring may also be necessary.
- Home-based behavioral interventions similar to the end points in school (i.e., ensuring completion and turning in of all schoolwork); additional intervention around household chores, siblings, and play/recreation. The goal again is to increase compliance with rules in the household and community. Parental skills training may be necessary.
- Stimulant medication is most often, and appropriately, used in conjunction with the above strategies. Other pharmacological agents can be used as well (i.e., antidepressants).
- Individual therapy around issues of ADHD and/or comorbid features. Therapy may be intermittent over the course of time.
- Connect family to local, state, and national parents' support group, such as Children and Adults with Attention Deficit Disorder (CHADD) at www.chadd.org, Attention Deficit Disorders Association (ADDA) at www.add.org, and *Additude* magazine at www.additudemag.com.
- Bibliotherapy for child and parents. Connect them to ADD Warehouse (800-233-9273) for free catalog.

Adults

- Thorough explanation of the life course of the ADHD to adult and significant other.
- Cognitive and behavioral interventions at home and at work to decrease disorganization, inattention, and distractibility.
- Use of prompts such as *Voice It*, a personal audio-reminder, and/or organizers such as the *Franklin Planner.*
- Focused trial on stimulant medication or other pharmacological agents.
- Individual psychotherapy as needed for issues around ADHD and/or other comorbid conditions.
- Marital/couples psychotherapy focusing on the relationship and ways of coping with ADHD within that relationship.
- Bibliotherapy to augment understanding, intervention skills, and interpersonal relationships (e.g., Katie Kelly and Peggy Ramundo's *You Mean I'm Not Lazy, Stupid or Crazy?!* and Lynn Weiss's *Attention Deficit Disorders in Adulthood: Practical Help for Sufferers and Their Spouses*). Connect the person to the ADD Warehouse for a catalog.
- Provide information about CHADD and/or ADDA.

A number of federal statutes have a bearing on treatment of ADHD and therefore on the outcome. A school-age population with ADHD can be affected by Section 504 of the Rehabilitation Act of 1973 and the Individuals With Disabilities Education Act of 1990 (IDEA), which was reauthorized in 1997. Both can require specific interventions when a school-age person has been identified as having ADHD. A person at any age with ADHD may have legal standing under the Americans with Disabilities Act (ADA) of 1990 if education or employment as a "major life activity" is "substantially limited."

References & Readings

Abikoff, H. (2001). Tailored psychosocial treatment for AD/HD: The search for a good fit. *Journal of Clinical Psychology, 30,* 122–125.

American Psychiatric Association. (1994). *Diagnostic and statistical manual of mental disorders* (4th ed.). Washington, DC: Author.

Barkley, R. (1995). *Taking charge of ADHD: The complete authoritative guide for parents.* New York: Guilford Press.

Barkley, R. A. (1998). *Attention-deficit/hyperactivity disorder: A handbook for diagnosis and treatment* (2nd ed.). New York: Guilford Press.

Connors, C. K., March, J. S., Frances, A., Wells, K. C., & Ross, R. (2001). Treatment of attention deficit/hyperactivity disorder: Expert consensus guidelines. *Journal of Attention Disorders, 4,* 7–128.

Gaub, M., & Carlson, C. L. (1997). Gender differences in ADHD: A meta-analysis and critical review. *Journal of Child and Adolescent Psychiatry, 36,* 1036–1045.

Gingerich, K. J., Turncock, P., Litfin, J. K., & Rosen, L. A. (1998). Diversity and attention deficit hyperactivity disorder. *Journal of Clinical Psychology, 54,* 425–436.

Ingersoll, B., & Goldstein, S. (1993). *Attention deficit disorder and learning disabilities.* New York: Doubleday.

Resnick, R. J. (2000). *The hidden disorder: A clinician's guide to attention deficit hyperactivity disorder in adults.* Washington, DC: American Psychological Association.

Root, R. W., & Resnick, R. J. (2003). An update on the diagnosis and treatment of attention deficit hyperactivity disorder in children. *Professional Psychology: Theory and Practice, 14,* 34–41.

Spencer, T., Biederman, J., Wilens, T., Harding, M., O'Donnell, D., & Griffin, B. (1996). Pharmacotherapy of attention-deficit hyperactivity disorder across the life cycle. *Journal of the American Academy of Child and Adolescent Psychiatry, 35,* 409–432.

Related Topics

Chapter 6, "Developmental Neuropsychological Assessment"

Chapter 7, "Adult Neuropsychological Assessment"

14 ASSESSMENT OF SUICIDAL RISK

Kenneth S. Pope & Melba J. T. Vasquez

Evaluating suicidal risk is one of the most challenging aspects of clinical work, in part because it is literally a life-or-death matter. False positives and false negatives are frequent because of such issues as suicide's low base rate (Pope, Butcher, & Seelen, 2000). The following list, adapted from Pope and Vasquez (1998), notes some factors that are widely accepted as significantly associated with suicide attempts. Awareness of such factors as they emerge from the research and clinical literature may be helpful in assessing suicidal risk.

Among the essential qualifications are the following. First, space limitations allow mentioning these factors only in a very general way. There may be many exceptions to the trends outlined here, and various factors may interact with one another. The purpose is solely to call attention to some areas that clinicians should be aware of in assessing risk. Second, this list is merely a snapshot of some current trends. Emerging research continues to correct false assumptions and refine our understandings, as well as reflect changes. For example, there are indications of an increase in the suicide rate for women, bringing it closer to that for men. Third, this list is by no means comprehensive. It provides examples only of some of the kinds of factors statistically associated with suicide attempts or completed suicides. Fourth, this list is meant to increase awareness of factors empirically associated with suicidal risk, but it should never be used in an unthinking, mechanical manner. Awareness of such factors can serve as an important aspect of—but never a substitute for—a careful, informed, comprehensive evaluation of suicidal risk.

1. *Direct verbal warning:* A direct statement of intention to commit suicide often precedes a suicide attempt. Such statements deserve careful attention and adequately comprehensive exploration. It is crucial to resist the temptation to reflexively dismiss such warnings as "a hysterical bid for attention," "a borderline manipulation," "a clear expression of negative transference," "an attempt to provoke the therapist," or "yet another grab for power in the interpersonal struggle with the therapist." It is possible that the statement may reflect issues other than an actual increase in suicidal risk, but such a working hypothesis should be set forth only after a respectful, careful, open-minded evaluation.
2. *Plan:* The presence of a plan frequently reflects an increased suicidal risk. The more specific, detailed, lethal, and feasible the plan, the more likely it may be that the person will attempt suicide.
3. *Past attempts:* The research suggests that most completed suicides have been preceded by a prior attempt. Schneidman (1976) found that the clients with the greatest suicidal rate were those who had entered into treatment with a history of at least one attempt.
4. *Indirect statements and behavioral signs:* People planning to end their lives may communicate their intent indirectly through their words and actions—for example, talking about "going away," speculating on what death would be like, giving away their most valued possessions, wondering aloud what it might be like to attend their own funeral, or acquiring lethal instruments.
5. *Depression:* As might be expected, the research suggests that the suicide rate for those with clinical depression is much higher—perhaps as much as 20 times greater—than the suicide rate for the general population.
6. *Hopelessness:* The sense of hopelessness appears to be closely associated with suicidal intent (see, e.g., Kazdin, 1983; Petrie & Chamberlain, 1983; Wetzel, 1976; however, see also Nimeus, Traskman-Bendz, & Alsen, 1997).
7. *Intoxication:* The research suggests that many suicides are associated with alcohol as a contributing factor; an even greater number may be associated with the presence of alcohol (without clear indication of its contribution to the suicidal process and lethal outcome).
8. *Special clinical populations:* Some clinical populations such as clients who have been sexually involved with a prior therapist (Pope, 1994), who have AIDS (Pope & Morin, 1990), or who have been victims of torture (Pope & Garcia-Peltoniemi, 1991) may be at increased risk for suicide.
9. *Sex:* The suicide rate for men tends to be about three times that for women. For youths, the rate is closer to 5:1 (see, e.g., Safer, 1997). The rate of suicide attempts for women is about three times that for men.
10. *Age:* The risk for suicide tends to increase over the adult life cycle. Attempts by older people are much more likely to be lethal. The ratio of attempts to completed suicides for those up to age 65 is about 7:1 but is 2:1 for those over 65. Assessing suicidal risk differs according to whether the client is an adult or minor. Safer's review of the literature found that the "frequent practice of

combining adult and adolescent suicide and suicide behavior findings can result in misleading conclusions" (1997, p. 61).

11. *Race:* Generally in the United States, Whites tend to have one of the highest suicide rates. Gibbs (1997) highlights the apparent cultural paradox: "African-American suicide rates have traditionally been lower than White rates despite a legacy of racial discrimination, persistent poverty, social isolation, and lack of community resources" (p. 68). EchoHawk (1997) observed that the Native-American suicide rate is "greater than that of any other ethnic group in the U.S., especially in the age range of 15–24 years" (p. 60).
12. *Religion:* Suicide rates among Protestants tend to be higher than those among Jews and Catholics.
13. *Living alone:* The research suggests that suicidal risk tends to be reduced if someone is not living alone; it is reduced more if he or she is living with a spouse and even further if there are children.
14. *Bereavement:* Brunch, Barraclough, Nelson, and Sainsbury (1971) found that 50 of those in their sample who had committed suicide had lost their mothers within the last three years (compared with a 20% rate among controls matched for age, sex, marital status, and geographic location). Furthermore, 22 of the suicides, compared with only 9 of the controls, had experienced the loss of their father within the past five years. Krupnick's (1984) review of studies revealed a link between childhood bereavement and suicide attempts in adult life, perhaps doubling the risk for depressives who had lost a parent compared with depressives who had not experienced the death of a parent. Klerman and Clayton (1984; see also Beutler, 1985) found that suicide rates are higher among the widowed than the married (especially among elderly men) and that, among women, the suicide rate is not as high for widows as for the divorced or separated.
15. *Unemployment:* Unemployment tends to increase the risk for suicide.
16. *Health status:* The research suggests that illness and somatic complaints tend to be associated with increased suicidal risk, as are disturbances in patterns of sleeping and eating. Clinicians who are helping people with AIDS, for example, need to be sensitive to this risk (Pope & Morin, 1990).
17. *Impulsivity:* Those with poor impulse control are at increased risk for taking their own lives (see, e.g., Patsiokas, Clum, & Luscumb, 1979).
18. *Rigid thinking:* Suicidal individuals often display a rigid, all-or-none way of thinking (see, e.g., Neuringer, 1964). A typical statement might be: "If I don't find work within the next week, then the only real alternative is suicide."
19. *Stressful events:* Excessive numbers of undesirable events with negative outcomes have been associated with increased suicidal risk (Cohen-Sandler, Berman, & King, 1982; Isherwood, Adam, & Hornblow, 1982). Bagley, Bolitho, and Bertrand (1997), in a study of 1,025 adolescent women in grades 7–12, wrote that "15 percent of . . . women who experienced frequent, unwanted sexual touching had 'often' made suicidal gestures or attempts in the previous 6 months, compared with 2 percent of . . . women with no experience of sexual assault" (p. 341; see also McCauley et al., 1997). Some types of recent events may place clients at extremely high risk. For example, Ellis, Atkeson, and Calhoun (1982) found that 52 of their sample of multiple-incident victims of sexual assault had attempted suicide.
20. *Release from hospitalization:* Some clinicians use voluntary or involuntary hospitalization to address severe suicidal risk. However, even when it has been determined that a person may safely leave the hospital setting, suicidal risk cannot be ignored. Research suggests that suicidal risk may increase—sometimes sharply—when a person leaves the hospital, for example, for a family visit, during a weekend pass, or at discharge.

References & Readings 

Bagley, C., Bolitho, F., & Bertrand, L. (1997). Sexual assault in school, mental health, and suicidal behaviors in adolescent women in Canada. *Adolescence, 32,* 341–366.

Beutler, L. E. (1985). Loss and anticipated death: Risk factors in depression. In H. H. Goldman & S. E. Goldston (Eds.), *Preventing stress-related psychiatric disorders* (pp. 177–194). Rockville, MD: National Institute of Mental Health.

Brunch, J., Barraclough, B., Nelson, M., & Sainsbury, P. (1971). Suicide following death of parents. *Social Psychiatry, 6,* 193–199.

Cohen-Sandler, R., Berman, A. L., & King, R. A. (1982). Life stress and symptomatology: Determinants of suicidal behavior in children. *Journal of the American Academy of Child Psychiatry, 21,* 178–186.

EchoHawk, M. (1997). Suicide: The scourge of Native American people. *Suicide & Life-Threatening Behavior, 27,* 60–67.

Ellis, E. M., Atkeson, B. M., & Calhoun, K. S. (1982). An examination of differences between multiple- and single-incident victims of multiple sexual assault. *Journal of Abnormal Psychology, 91,* 221–224.

Gibbs, J. T. (1997). African-American suicide: A cultural paradox. *Suicide & Life-Threatening Behavior, 27,* 68–79.

Isherwood, J., Adam, K. S., & Hornblow, A. R. (1982). Life event stress, psychosocial factors, suicide attempt, and auto-accident proclivity. *Journal of Psychosomatic Research, 26,* 371–383.

Kazdin, A. E. (1983). Hopelessness, depression, and suicidal intent among psychiatrically disturbed inpatient children. *Journal of Consulting and Clinical Psychology, 51,* 504–510.

Klerman, G. L., & Clayton, E. (1984). Epidemiologic perspectives on the health consequences of bereavement. In M. Osterweis, G. Solomon, & M. Green (Eds.), *Bereavement: Reactions, consequences, and care* (pp. 15–44). Washington, DC: National Academy Press.

Krupnick, J. L. (1984). Bereavement during childhood and adolescence. In M. Osterweis, E. Solomon, & M. Green (Eds.), *Bereavement: Reactions, consequences, and care* (pp. 99–141). Washington, DC: National Academy Press.

McCauley, J., Kern, D. E., Kolodner, K., Dill, L., et al. (1997). Clinical characteristics of women with a history of child abuse: Unhealed wounds. *Journal of the American Medical Association, 277,* 1367–1368.

Neuringer, C. (1964). Rigid thinking in suicidal individuals. *Journal of Consulting Psychology, 28,* 54–58.

Nimeus, A., Traskman-Bendz, L., & Alsen, M. (1997). Hopelessness and suicidal behavior. *Journal of Affective Disorders, 42,* 137–144.

Patsiokas, A. T, Clum, G. A., & Luscumb, R. L. (1979). Cognitive characteristics of suicidal attempters. *Journal of Consulting and Clinical Psychology, 47,* 478–484.

Petrie, K., & Chamberlain, K. (1983). Hopelessness and social desirability as moderator variables in predicting suicidal behavior. *Journal of Consulting and Clinical Psychology, 51,* 485–487.

Pope, K. S. (1994). *Sexual involvement with therapists: Patient assessment, subsequent therapy, forensics.* Washington, DC: American Psychological Association.

Pope, K. S., Butcher, J. N., & Seelen, J. (2000). *The MMP1, MMPI-2, and MMPI-A in court: A practical guide for expert witnesses and attorneys* (2nd ed.). Washington, DC: American Psychological Association.

Pope, K. S., & Garcia-Peltoniemi, R. E. (1991). Responding to victims of torture: Clinical issues, professional responsibilities, and useful resources. *Professional Psychology: Research and Practice, 22,* 269–276. http://kspope.com.

Pope, K. S., & Morin, S. E. (1990). AIDS and HIV infection update: New research, ethical responsibilities, evolving legal frameworks, and published resources. *Independent Practitioner, 10,* 43–53.

Pope, K. S., & Vasquez, M. J. T. (1998). *Ethics in psychotherapy and counseling* (2nd ed.) San Francisco: Jossey-Bass.

Safer, D. J. (1997). Adolescent/adult differences in suicidal behavior and outcome. *Annals of Clinical Psychiatry, 9,* 61–66.

Schneidman, E. (1976). *Suicidology: Contemporary developments.* New York: Grune and Stratton.

Wetzel, R. (1976). Hopelessness, depression, and suicide intent. *Archives of General Psychiatry, 33,* 1069–1073.

Related Topic

Chapter 49, "Treatment and Management of the Suicidal Patient"

15 ASSESSMENT OF MALINGERING ON PSYCHOLOGICAL MEASURES

Richard Rogers

Psychologists vary considerably in their understanding of malingering and their sophistication at its detection. As a prelude to this synopsis, the standard definition of malingering is the deliberate fabrication or gross exaggeration of psychological or physical symptoms for some external goal (American Psychiatric Association, 2000). Critical decision points include (a) the deliberateness of the presentation (e.g., somatoform disorder vs. malingering), (b) the magnitude of the dissimulation (e.g., minor embellishment vs. gross exaggeration), and (c) the identification of the goal and its primary source (e.g., internal vs. external). Rogers (1997) provides a comprehensive resource for addressing these issues.

The focus of this synopsis is twofold. First, I address common misconceptions about malingering that are likely to influence professional practice. Second, I distill the empirical literature relative to the clinical detection of malingering. This distillation is necessarily selective and concentrates on the more robust clinical indicators for feigned mental disorders and cognitive impairment.

COMMON MISCONCEPTIONS

- *Because malingering is very infrequent, it should not be a cause of diagnostic concern.* Survey data strongly question the premise of this fallacy. Two extensive surveys of clinical practice yielded almost identical estimates that accounted for an appreciable percentage of assessment cases (7.4% and 7.8%). Even if the premise were true, psychologists should not equate infrequency with inconsequentiality. As an analogue, suicide attempts are very rare in certain clinical populations but no responsible psychologist would argue against their examination.
- *Because malingering is a global response style, it is easy to detect.* This premise is easily assailable. Psychological practice with veteran populations, for example, provides ample evidence of how some malingerers become very targeted in their feigned posttraumatic stress disorder (PTSD). The implicit message of this misconception is that malingering is relatively easy to detect because of its obviousness. At least with feigned cognitive deficits, the available literature (for a review, see Rogers, Harrell, & Liff, 1993) suggests that many simulators remain undetected, unless specific measures of malingering are employed.
- *If psychologists pay attention to* Diagnostic and Statistical Manual of Mental Disorders (DSM-IV-TR) *indices, they are likely to be effective at identifying malingerers.* This viewpoint disregards the nature of *DSM-IV-TR* indices. Unlike inclusion criteria found with most disorders, these indices are intended merely to raise the index of suspicion. Moreover, the only available data suggest that the use of these indices may result in a false-positive rate in the range of 80%. In ad-

dition, the *DSM-IV-TR* emphasis on criminality (i.e., medicolegal evaluation and antisocial personality disorder) is largely unwarranted (see Rogers, 1990) and may lead to misclassifications in both forensic (false-positives) and nonforensic (false-negatives) cases.

- *Inconsistencies are the hallmark of malingerers.* Although inconsistencies are found among many malingerers, the equating of inconsistencies with malingering is a grievous error. For example, research on the MMPI-2 has demonstrated convincingly that inconsistent profiles may result from psychosis, inability to attend, and inadequate comprehension (Greene, 1997). Data from structured interviewing (Structured Interview of Reported Symptoms [SIRS]; Rogers, Bagby, & Dickens, 1992) further illustrates this point. Although malingerers tend to be inconsistent in their symptom presentation, a substantial minority of the clinical population is also inconsistent. Depending on the prevalence rate for malingering in a particular setting, an inconsistent presentation may have a greater likelihood of being a genuinely disordered patient than a malingerer.
- *Mental illness and malingering are mutually exclusive.* Most psychologists are not likely to embrace openly this false dichotomy. However, many clinical evaluations appear to be concluded once malingering is determined. I also suspect that the establishment of a bona fide disorder reduces the scrutiny given to the genuineness of other presented symptoms. Unquestionably, neither malingering nor mental illness offers any natural immunity to the other.
- *Deceptive persons are likely to be malingerers.* The mislogic that "if you lie, you will malinger" is readily apparent. While malingerers are deceptive persons, the obverse is not necessarily true. The sustained effort involved in successful feigning, the stigmatization of mental disorders, and the often severe penalties for detection are likely to militate against widespread malingering. Moreover, Ford, King, and Hollender (1988) cogently describe the numerous genuine disorders for which deception is commonplace. Finally, much deception in clinical practice (e.g., underreporting of substance abuse) is the polar opposite of malingering in the denial and minimization of mental disorders.

ASSESSMENT OF FEIGNED MENTAL DISORDERS

The assessment of feigned psychopathology involves the use of well-validated measures in a multimethod evaluation. Although a number of brief self-report measures have been recently published, these measures lack the discriminability and extensive cross-validation for their use in the determination of malingering (see Smith, 1997); however, they may serve a useful screening function. The two best established measures are the MMPI-2 and the SIRS. Each will be summarized separately.

Meta-analysis of the MMPI (Berry, Baer, & Harris, 1991) and the MMPI-2 (Rogers, Sewell, Martin, & Vitacco, 2003; Rogers, Sewell, & Salekin, 1994) underscore (a) its general usefulness in the evaluation of feigning and (b) the marked variability in optimum cutting scores. For example, Rogers et al. (2003) found cut scores for F that ranged from 9 to 30. The following guidelines are proposed:

1. Is the profile consistent? A random or inconsistent profile likely will be indistinguishable from a feigned profile on fake-bad indicators. One benchmark is to exclude profiles with VRIN > 14.
2. Are the standard validity indicators extremely elevated? Psychologists should have greater confidence in scores that exceed all or nearly all studies in a meta-analysis. As a benchmark of malingering, is F > 30? Please note that persons with schizophrenia or PTSD are likely to have marked elevations on F and Fb.
3. Are specialized indicators markedly elevated? The best overall indicator of feigned mental disorders is a Fp raw score > 9. A second useful indicator is Ds raw score > 35.
4. Caution should be exercised in applying these results to minority populations. For instance, nonclinical populations (African Americans and Hispanic Americans) score higher on F

than their Anglo-American counterparts. Likewise, Spanish-language and audiotaped versions have not been validated.

The SIRS is a structured interview that has been extensively validated with clinical, community, and correctional samples. Unlike the numerous cutting scores generated for multiscale inventories, the SIRS has employed standard cutting scores throughout its development and validation. Its results combine data from both simulation and known-groups comparisons. Guidelines (see Rogers, 1997; Rogers et al., 1992) for its use are straightforward:

- *Any SIRS scale in the definite feigning range:* Any extreme elevations on the primary scales designate feigning and have a negligible false-positive rate (1.0%).
- *Three or more scales in the probable feigning range:* The most robust measure of feigning is the combination of markedly elevated primary scales; again, the false positive rate appears to be very small (<3.0%).
- *Total SIRS score (all scores except Repeated Inquiries):* In indeterminant cases, a summation of endorsed items represents a supplementary criterion; Rogers et al. (1992) found no false-positives.

Further research is needed on the use of the SIRS with adolescents and persons with neuropsychological impairment. As clearly articulated in the test manual (Rogers et al., 1992), the SIRS is designed to assess the feigning of psychopathology and mental disorders; entirely different strategies are needed with persons faking cognitive impairment.

ASSESSMENT OF FEIGNED COGNITIVE IMPAIRMENT

Unlike simulated mental disorders, feigned cognitive impairment does not require the complex generation believable symptoms and associated features with concomitant data on the onset and course of the simulated disorder. Rather, persons that malinger intellectual or neuropsychological impairment must simply put forward a suboptimal effort with an appearance of sincerity. Because of the disparateness between types of malingering, different strategies are recommended for its detection. As an important caution, the MMPI-2 is frequently recommended in neuropsychological consults where malingering is suspected; however, it is unlikely to be effective in detecting markedly suboptimal performances on cognitive tasks. Nonetheless, the MMPI-2 may be useful in those cases of global malingering when feigning encompasses both psychopathology and cognitive functioning.

Rogers et al. (1993) summarized detection strategies for feigned cognitive impairment. Importantly, most strategies are useful in screening for feigned impairment, but not for making the actual determination. The detection strategies include the following:

1. *Floor effect:* Some malingerers fail on exceptionally simple questions that even very impaired persons are able to answer correctly. For example, "Who is older, a mother or her child?" The most common use of the floor-effect strategy is found in the presentation of Rey's 15-Item Memory Test that has only modest sensitivity.
2. *Performance curve:* Many malingerers do not take into account item difficulty. While they fail more difficult than easy items, the decline based on item difficulty is generally more gradual than found with genuine patients. Frederick (1997) has successfully applied this strategy to the Validity Indicator Profile (VIP). It has also been successfully applied to Ravens Progressive Matrices.
3. *Symptom validity testing (SVT):* Pankratz (1988) championed this method for the detection of feigned sensory or memory deficits through the presentation of a large number of trials. Based on probability, some malingering cases can be identified based on performance worse than chance. The best validated measure for this purpose is the Portland Digit Recognition Test (PDRT; Binder, 1993). More recent efforts to establish performance below expectations (called "forced choice testing"); it lacks the certitude of SVT's below-chance results.

4. *Magnitude of error:* Some malingerers are theorized to make very atypical mistakes, either in terms of gross errors or near misses, akin to the Ganser syndrome. Martin, Franzen, and Orey (1998) demonstrated the efficacy of this approach.
5. *Psychological sequelae:* An important issue is the effectiveness of persons feigning cognitive impairment at describing both decrements to their daily functioning and psychological symptoms that are likely to arise from their purported impairment. Recent research would suggest that untrained persons are likely to recognize symptoms associated with post-concussion syndrome and mild brain injury. What remains to be investigated is whether such persons can accurately depict psychological sequelae (e.g., depression and anxiety) that frequently follow such injuries.
6. *Inconsistent or atypical presentations:* Many clinicians believe that variable performance or an atypical pattern of test scores signify malingering. Many factors argue against any facile conclusions: (a) no cutting scores are established for making this determination; (b) patients with neuropsychological impairment often have variable performances; and (c) personality changes, as a result of brain injury, are likely to affect performance.

In closing, determinations of malingering are complex, multimethod evaluations. Conclusions should never be based on a single symptom, scale, or measure. When data are inconclusive but suggestive of feigning, the response style may be described as "inconsistent" or "unreliable." To misclassify a genuine patient as a malingerer may have devastating consequences to that individual's future treatment, financial well-being, and legal status. To misclassify a malingerer as a genuine patient may have grave consequences for other concerned parties (e.g., insurance companies, employers, or criminal justice system). Psychologists shoulder a heavy responsibility to minimize both types of misclassification in their assessment of malingering. They must base their findings on a comprehensive evaluation that utilizes specific measures well-validated for malingering and related response styles.

References & Readings

American Psychiatric Association. (2000). *Diagnostic and statistical manual of mental disorders* (4th ed., rev.). Washington, DC: Author.

Berry, D. T. R., Baer, R. A., & Harris, M. J. (1991). Detection of malingering on the MMPI: A meta-analysis. *Clinical Psychology Review, 11,* 585–598.

Berry, D. T. R., Wetter, M. W., & Baer, R. A. (1995). Assessment of malingering. In J. N. Butcher (Ed.), *Clinical personality assessment: Practical approaches* (pp. 236–248). New York: Oxford University Press.

Binder, L. M. (1993). Assessment of malingering after mild head trauma with the Portland Digit Recognition Test. *Journal of Clinical and Experimental Neuropsychology, 15,* 170–183.

Frederick, R. I. (1997). *The Validity Indicator Profile.* Minneapolis: National Computer Systems.

Greene, R. L. (1997). Assessment of malingering and defensiveness by multiscale personality inventories. In R. Rogers (Ed.), *Clinical assessment of malingering and deception* (2nd ed., pp. 169–207). New York: Guilford Press.

Martin, R. C., Franzen, M. D., & Orey, S. (1998). Magnitude of error as a strategy to detect feigned memory impairment. *The Clinical Neuropsychologist, 12,* 84–91.

Pankratz, L. (1988). Malingering on intellectual and neuropsychological measures. In R. Rogers (Ed.), *Clinical assessment of malingering and deception* (pp. 169–192). New York: Guilford Press.

Rogers, R. (1990). Models of feigned mental illness. *Professional Psychology, 21,* 182–188.

Rogers, R. (Ed.). (1997). *Clinical assessment of malingering and deception* (2nd ed.). New York: Guilford Press.

Rogers, R., Bagby, R. M., & Dickens, S. E. (1992). *Structured Interview of Reported Symptoms (SIRS) and professional manual.* Odessa, FL: Psychological Assessment Resources, Inc.

Rogers, R., Harrell, E. H., & Liff, C. D. (1993). Feigning neuropsychological impairment: A critical review of methodological and clinical considerations. *Clinical Psychology Review, 13,* 255–274.

Rogers, R., Sewell, K. W., & Goldstein, A. (1994). Explanatory models of malingering: A prototypical analysis. *Law and Human Behavior, 18,* 543–552.

Rogers, R., Sewell, K. W., Martin, M. A., & Vitacco, M. J. (2003). Detection of feigned mental disorders: A meta-analysis of the MMPI-2 and malingering. *Assessment, 10,* 160–177.

Rogers, R., Sewell, K. W., & Salekin, R. (1994). A meta-analysis of malingering on the MMPI-2. *Assessment, 1,* 227–237.

Schretlen, D. J. (1988). The use of psychological tests to identify malingered symptoms of mental disorder. *Clinical Psychology Review, 8,* 457–476.

Smith, G. (1997). Assessment of malingering with self-report instruments. In R. Rogers (Ed.), *Clinical assessment of malingering and deception* (2nd ed., pp. 351–370). New York: Guilford Press.

Related Topic

Chapter 28, "Assessing MMPI-2 Profile Validity"

16 IDENTIFICATION AND ASSESSMENT OF ALCOHOL ABUSE

Linda Carter Sobell & Mark B. Sobell

A well-formulated assessment is fundamental to successful treatment planning. The following brief overview is intended to help health care practitioners better identify, assess, and treat individuals with alcohol problems, both those with only primary alcohol problems, as well as those with comorbid disorders.

1. *Setting clients at ease:* Because there is a social stigma related to having an alcohol problem, making the first call to a treatment program can be highly stressful. Similarly, arriving for the first appointment can provoke considerable anxiety. Individuals who are thinking of changing their drinking have probably made a decision to seek treatment only after careful consideration and with some degree of ambivalence. For these reasons, it is very important for anyone working with individuals with alcohol problems to set clients at ease by establishing rapport and being empathetic and supportive. Because clients are often asked to complete several assessment instruments, it is important to gain their cooperation by explaining the nature of each instrument, why it is being used, and what feedback, if any, they might expect from the instrument. Early discussion of how long treatment will take and what treatment will entail will also help establish a good therapeutic relationship that will gain the client's trust and cooperation. One way to help ensure that accurate information is gathered is to assure clients that what is discussed in treatment is confidential and to explain the conditions under which confidentiality would have to be broken.

2. *Choosing assessment instruments/measures:* When choosing an assessment instrument, health care practitioners should consider the following questions: (a) What purpose will it serve (e.g., screening, diagnosis, triage, treatment planning, goal setting, monitoring, evaluating treatment)? (b) Is it clinically useful (i.e., Will it help develop a better course of treatment?)? (c) Is it user-friendly for clients (e.g., easy to complete, relevant)? (d) How long does it take to administer and score, and over what time interval can information be collected (e.g., one month, one year)? (e) What costs are involved, if any?

3. *Value of an assessment:* Good assessments have several clinical benefits: (a) They can serve as the basis for treatment planning and goal setting (e.g., determining intensity of treatment; focusing on motivation or action; matching clients to treatments; identifying high-risk triggers for use); (b) they can help in formulating diagnoses; (c) the results can be used to give clients feedback or advice about their past drinking and related behaviors; such advice can enhance or strengthen motivation for change (Miller & Rollnick, 2002; Sobell et al., 2002); and (d) because assessments are dynamic and ongoing throughout treatment, they can determine whether treatment is working (e.g., self-monitoring of alcohol use during treatment), and, if not, what the next step should be to modify the course of treatment (i.e., stepped care; Sobell & Sobell, 2000b).

4. *Alcohol problem severity:* When evaluating a client's use of alcohol, it is important to assess problem severity because such information is relevant to goal setting and treatment planning (Sobell & Sobell, 1993). Problem severity can be viewed as lying on a continuum ranging from mild (e.g., problem drinkers) to severe (e.g., chronic alcohol abuse). Table 1 lists a good measure (AUDIT) that can be used to evaluate problem severity.

5. *Alcohol abusers' self-reports are generally accurate:* Health care practitioners must rely on their clients' self-reports for a considerable amount of assessment and treatment planning information. Contrary to folklore, several studies have shown that alcohol abusers' self-reports are generally accurate if they are interviewed when (a) alcohol-free, (b) given assurances of confidentiality, and (c) in a clinical or research setting (Babor, Sterling, Anton, & Del Boca, 2000; Sobell, Sobell, Connors, & Agrawal, 2003). When individuals with alcohol problems have been drinking, however, their self-reports may not be accurate. In this regard, a portable breath alcohol tester can be used to determine whether a person is under the influence of alcohol (Sobell, Tonneato, & Sobell, 1994), and if so, the assessment should be rescheduled.

6. *Key measures in assessing alcohol use and abuse:* There is no shortage of instruments, scales, and questionnaires for assessing individuals with alcohol problems (for a review and sample copies of instruments, see Allen & Wilson, 2003). For health care practitioners the key question is "What will I learn from the instrument/measure that I will not otherwise know from a routine clinical interview?" To assist health care practitioners in assessing a person's alcohol use and related problems, a listing of one or two key measures in each of several areas and a brief description of the measure is presented in Table 1. These measures were selected because they are user-friendly, require minimal time and resources, are psychometrically sound, and, whenever possible, provide meaningful feedback to clients.

7. *Motivational interviewing:* Interviewing style is very important for obtaining accurate information about an individual's alcohol use (Miller & Rollnick, 2002). The way questions are asked can also affect a client's answers. Motivational interviewing is an interviewing style designed to minimize resistance, a helpful strategy when interviewing clients who are ambivalent about changing. There are several important considerations when conducting assessments with individuals who might have alcohol problems.

- *Empathy:* Empathy helps health care practitioners gain the acceptance and trust of clients and is associated with decreased client resistance and improved outcomes. A key way of expressing empathy is *reflective listening,* in which the practitioner forms a reasonable guess about what the client has said and shares it with the client. Reflective listening helps minimize resistance.
- *Periodic summary:* Frequent summarizing throughout the interview allows health care practitioners to synthesize the information gathered and solicit a client's feedback about the accuracy of the therapist's understanding.

TABLE 1. Key Measures for Assessing Alcohol Use and Related Problems

Area	Measure and Brief Description
Adverse consequences of use/problem severity	*Alcohol Use Disorders Identification Test (AUDIT):* 10-item, self-administered questionnaire addressing past and recent alcohol consumption and alcohol-related problems; identifies high-risk drinkers as well as those experiencing consequences. It is available in several languages, including Spanish.[a,b,c]
Alcohol use	*Timeline Followback (TLFB; for alcohol use before treatment):* Using memory aids, individuals are asked to recall their estimated daily drinking for intervals ranging from 30 to 360 days; the TLFB can be used in treatment as an advice-feedback tool to analyze clients' drinking and to increase their motivation to change. It is available in Spanish.[a,b,c,d,e,f]
	Self-Monitoring (SM; for alcohol use during treatment): Requires clients to record aspects of their alcohol use or urges (e.g., amount, frequency, mood, consequences); SM has several clinical advantages including identifying situations that pose a high-risk of excessive drinking and providing feedback about changes in drinking. Available in Spanish.[a,b,c,e,f]
Drug use other than alcohol	*Drug Use History Questionnaire (DUHQ):* Captures lifetime and recent information (e.g., years used, route of administration, year last used, frequency of use) about the use of different drugs.[c,f,g]
	Drug Abuse Screening Test (DAST-10): 10-item, self-administered measure of drug-use consequences in past 12 months; assesses severity of drug problems. Available in Spanish.[c,f,h]
Cigarette use	*Time to the First Cigarette:* A Single question—"How many minutes upon waking until the first cigarette is smoked?"—is strongly predictive of nicotine dependence.[c,i]
Cognitive functioning	*Trails A and B:* A brief, sensitive, nonspecific, age-adjusted screening test for assessing probable signs of organic brain dysfunction that may be related to severe alcohol problems.[c,j]
	Mini Mental Status Exam: A standardized 8-item questionnaire for assessing current cognitive functioning.[j]
High-risk triggers for use	*Brief Situational Confidence Questionnaire (BSCQ):* An 8-item variant of the SCQ,[k] the BSCQ assesses situational self-efficacy, in other words, how confident people are at the present time that they would be able to resist the urge to drink heavily in 8 major relapse situational categories (BSCQ can also assess drug use situations).[a,b,f,l]
Motivation/readiness to change	*Decisional Balance Exercise:* A Brief exercise that asks clients to evaluate their perceptions of the costs and benefits of continuing to drink problematically versus changing; it is intended to make more salient the costs and benefits of changing and to identify obstacles to change.[f,m,n]
	Readiness to Change Ruler: A simple method for determining clients' readiness to change by asking where they are on a scale of 1 to 10 (0 = not ready to change to 10 = very ready to change). Depending on clients' readiness to change, discussions may take different directions (e.g., for clients who are unsure, with ratings from 4 to 7, explore the pros and cons of treatment). As clients continue their treatment, the ruler can be used periodically to see how motivation changes over treatment.[m,o,p]
Pyschiatric comorbidity	*Symptom Checklist 90-R (SCL-90-R):* 90-item self-report questionnaire that reflects psychiatric symptoms that occurred in the past week; items are rated on 5-point scales of discomfort; the SCL-90-R takes about 15 minutes to complete and has been widely used as an outcome measure in psychotherapy; three global scores of distress can be derived as well as scores for nine primary symptom dimensions (e.g., somatization, depression, anxiety, anger, paranoid ideation, psychoticism); this instrument reflects patterns of psychological distress currently being experienced by clients.[q,r]

Note: Information and reviews about and/or copies of the measures/instruments can be found in the footnoted publication after each measure.

[a]Allen & Wilson, 2003.
[b]http://www.niaaa.nih.gov/publications/guide.htm.
[c]Sobell, Sobell, & Toneatto, 1994.
[d]Sobell & Sobell, 2000a.
[e]Sobell, Sobell, Connors, & Agrawal, 2003.
[f]http://ww.nova.edu/~gsc.
[g]Sobell, Kwan, & Sobell, 1995.
[h]Skinner, 1982.
[i]Heatherton, Kozlowski, Frecker, & Robinson, 1989.
[j]Lezak, 1995.
[k]Annis & Davis, 1989.
[l]Breslin, Sobell, Sobell, & Agrawal, 2000.
[m]Substance Abuse and Mental Health Administration, 1999.
[n]Sobell et al., 1996.
[o]Rollnick, 1998.
[p]Rollnick, Mason, & Butler, 1999.
[q]Seidner & Kilpatrick, 1988.
[r]Derogatis, 1983.

- *Flexibility:* When a health care practitioner senses that a client finds the interview threatening, is ambivalent, or is reluctant to discuss issues, it is important to "roll with resistance" by using reflective listening rather than confronting the resistance directly. It is also important to emphasize to clients that it is their choice whether a matter will be discussed.
- *Avoid confrontation:* Confrontation and arguments should be avoided whenever possible because confrontational strategies can be counterproductive. Miller, Benefield, and Tonigan (1993), for example, found that alcohol abusers randomly assigned to confrontational counseling had higher levels of resistance, drank more during treatment, and had poorer outcomes than clients assigned to motivational counseling.
- *Avoid labeling:* Clients are generally reluctant to be labeled as "alcoholic." This especially applies to individuals whose problems are not severe (i.e., problem and heavy drinkers). Labeling should be avoided because it has no clinical advantages and because it has been associated with alcohol abusers' delaying or avoiding entry into treatment (Sobell & Sobell, 2000b). Asking about an individual's alcohol use in the past year and any concerns he or she may have is more likely to get a client to engage in an open dialogue about drinking than asking, "How many years have you had an alcohol problem?" or "How long have you been an alcoholic?"
- *Terminology:* Explaining the meaning of key terms to clients is an important part of the interviewing process. Health care practitioners need to know how to properly ask questions in relation to the following terms: blackouts, delirium tremens (DTs), morning drinking, and cirrhosis. All these terms reflect the severity of the disorder, but their meaning can be easily misunderstood (reviewed in Sobell et al., 1994). For example, DTs, which must include actual delirium, are often confused with minor withdrawal symptoms (e.g., psychomotor agitation). Similarly, the term *morning drinking,* which refers to drinking upon waking to avoid withdrawal symptoms, is different than drinking before noon while on a fishing trip. Morning drinking and DTs are significant because they are associated with severe dependence on alcohol.

8. *Measures complementary to self-reports:* There has been a tendency to view biochemical measures such as liver function and urinalysis and collateral (e.g., friends or family) reports as superior to a client's report of his or her drinking (Sobell & Sobell, 1990). However, several major comparative evaluations have revealed problems with biochemical measures and collateral reports (reviewed in Babor et al., 2002; Maisto & Connors, 1992; Sobell et al., 1994). Consequently, at the present time, biological markers and collateral reports should be seen as complementing rather than replacing self-reports of alcohol use.

9. *Psychiatric comorbidity:* Psychiatric comorbidity among alcohol abusers has been well documented (Modesto-Lowe & Kranzler, 1999; Schuckit, 1996). Because of the high prevalence of psychiatric comorbidity among alcohol abusers (rates range from 7% to 75%), diagnostic formulations involve a two-step process: document the extent and nature of the alcohol problem and establish whether other psychiatric disorders are present; if so, determine whether the alcohol use disorder is primary or secondary. Because of the lack of empirical guidelines about how to treat alcohol abusers who have other clinical disorders (Drake & Mueser, 2000; Smyth, 1996), decisions about treating alcohol and psychiatric problems simultaneously or sequentially need to be made on a case-by-case basis.

10. *Comorbidity of other drug problems, including nicotine:* For alcohol abusers who use or abuse other drugs, including nicotine, it is important to gather a profile of their psychoactive substance use (e.g., see DUHQ in Table 1). Also, drug use patterns may change over the course of treatment (e.g., decreased alcohol use, increased smoking; decreased alcohol use, increased cannabis use). Three issues are important when assessing alcohol abusers who use other drugs: (a) pharmacological synergism (i.e., a multiplicative effect of similarly acting drugs taken concurrently); (b) cross-tolerance (i.e., decreased effect of a drug due to previous or current heavy use of pharmacologically similar drugs); and (c) cigarette use (80–90% of alcohol abusers report having at some time smoked cigarettes; Sobell, Sobell, & Agrawal, 2002). Finally, because it appears that continued smoking may serve as a trigger for relapse for some alcohol abusers attempting to change their drinking (Sobell et al., 2002), the smoking behavior of alcohol abusers should be a part of the assessment and treatment planning process.

11. *Motivation for change:* An important assessment issue is the need to evaluate a client's motivation for and commitment to change. Motivation can be conceptualized as a state of readiness to change that may fluctuate over time and can be influenced by several variables, including the therapist's behavior and treatment procedures. For a thorough description of motivational interviewing, see Miller and Rollnick (2002). Table 1 lists a measure (Readiness to Change Ruler) that can be used to assess readiness for change and an exercise (Decisional Balance) that can be used to enhance or strengthen motivation for change. The most important issue regarding motivation is that treatment of clients who are assessed as weakly committed to changing their drinking should initially focus on increasing their motivation rather than on methods for achieving change. Use of a motivational interviewing style can be helpful for increasing clients' motivation (Miller & Rollnick, 2002; Resnicow, Dilorio, Soet, Borrelli, & Ernst, 2002; Sobell & Sobell, 2000b).

12. *Base conclusions on a convergence of information:* While alcohol abusers' self-reports are generally accurate if gathered under the conditions noted earlier, a small proportion of reports will be inaccurate. To deal with this potential problem, it is advisable to obtain information from several sources when possible (e.g., psychological tests, family, friends, probation officers, medical records, biochemical tests). Basing conclusions on a convergence of information should result in increased confidence in that information (Sobell & Sobell, 1990).

SUMMARY

A careful and ongoing assessment is an important part of the treatment process for individuals with alcohol problems. Accurate evaluation of alcohol problems and other concurrent disorders is integral to the assessment process, and a good assessment is critical to the development of meaningful treatment plans. Assessment instruments and procedures should be user-friendly and relevant to treatment planning and goal setting. Various interviewing strategies can be used to enhance the accuracy of information obtained from clients and to increase clients' motivation for change.

References & Readings 

Allen, J. P., & Wilson, V. (2003). *Assessing alcohol problems* (2nd ed.; NIH Publication no. 03-3745). Rockville, MD: National Institute on Alcohol Abuse and Alcoholism.

Annis, H. M., & Davis, C. S. (1989). Relapse prevention. In R. K. Hester & W. R. Miller (Eds.), *Handbook of alcoholism treatment approaches: Alternative approaches* (pp. 170–182). New York: Pergamon Press.

Babor, T. F., Steinberg, K., Anton, R., & Del Boca, F. (2000). Talk is cheap: Measuring drinking outcomes in clinical trials. *Journal of Studies on Alcohol, 61*(1), 55–63.

Breslin, F. C., Sobell, L. C., Sobell, M. B., & Agrawal, S. (2000). A comparison of a brief and long version of the Situational Confidence Questionnaire. *Behaviour Research and Therapy, 38*(12), 1211–1220.

Derogatis, L. R. (1983). *SCL-90 Revised Version Manual-1.* Baltimore, MD: Johns Hopkins University School of Medicine.

Drake, R. E., & Mueser, K. T. (2000). Psychosocial approaches to dual diagnosis. *Schizophrenia Bulletin, 26*(1), 105–118.

Heatherton, T. F., Kozlowski, L. T., Frecker, R. C., & Robinson, J. (1989). Measuring the heaviness of smoking: Using self-reported time to the first cigarette of the day and number of cigarettes smoked per day. *British Journal of Addiction, 84,* 791–800.

Lezak, M. D. (1995). *Neuropsychological assessment* (3rd ed.). New York: Oxford University Press.

Maisto, S. A., & Connors, G. J. (1992). Using subject and collateral reports to measure alcohol consumption. In R. Z. Litten & J. Allen (Eds.), *Measuring alcohol consumption: Psychosocial and biological methods* (pp. 73–96). Towota, NJ: Humana Press.

Miller, W. R., & Rollnick, S. (2002). *Motivational interviewing: Preparing people to change* (2nd ed.). New York: Guilford.

Modesto-Lowe, V., & Kranzler, H. R. (1999). Diagnosis and treatment of alcohol-dependent patients with comorbid psychiatric disorders. *Alcohol Health & Research World, 23*(2), 144–149.

Resnicow, K., Dilorio, C., Soet, J. E., Borrelli, B., Hecht, J., & Ernst, D. (2002). Motivational interviewing in health promotion: It sounds like something is changing. *Health Psychology, 21*(5), 444–451.

Rollnick, S. (1998). Readiness, importance, and confidence. In W. R. Miller & N. Heather (Eds.), *Treating addictive behaviors* (2nd ed., pp. 49–60). New York: Plenum.

Schuckit, M. A. (1996). Alcohol, anxiety, and depressive disorders. *Alcohol Health & Research World, 20*(2), 81–85.

Seidner, A. L., & Kilpatrick, D. G. (1988). Derogatis symptom checklist 90-R. In M. Hersen & A. S. Bellack (Eds.), *Dictionary of behavioral assessment techniques* (pp. 174–175). New York: Pergamon Press.

Skinner, H. A. (1982). The Drug Abuse Screening Test. *Addictive Behaviors, 7*, 363–371.

Smyth, N. J. (1996). Motivating persons with dual disorders: A stage approach. *Families in Society: The Journal of Contemporary Human Services, 77*, 605–614.

Sobell, L. C., Cunningham, J. A., Sobell, M. B., Agrawal, S., Gavin, D. R., Leo, G. I., et al. (1996). Fostering self-change among problem drinkers: A proactive community intervention. *Addictive Behaviors, 21*(6), 817–833.

Sobell, L. C., Kwan, E., & Sobell, M. B. (1995). Reliability of a Drug History Questionnaire (DHQ). *Addictive Behaviors, 20*(2), 233–241.

Sobell, L. C., & Sobell, M. B. (1990). Self-report issues in alcohol abuse: State of the art and future directions. *Behavioral Assessment, 12*, 91–106.

Sobell, L. C., & Sobell, M. B. (2000a). Alcohol Timeline Followback (TLFB). In American Psychiatric Association (Ed.), *Handbook of psychiatric measures* (pp. 477–479). Washington, DC: American Psychiatric Association.

Sobell, L. C., Sobell, M. B., Connors, G., & Agrawal, S. (2003). Is there one self-report drinking measure that is best for all seasons? *Alcoholism: Clinical and Experimental Research, 27*, 1661–1666.

Sobell, L. C., Sobell, M. B., Leo, G. I., Agrawal, S., Johnson-Young, L., & Cunningham, J. A. (2002). Promoting self-change with alcohol abusers: A community-level mail intervention based on natural recovery studies. *Alcoholism: Clinical and Experimental Research, 26*, 936–948.

Sobell, L. C., Toneatto, T., & Sobell, M. B. (1994). Behavioral assessment and treatment planning for alcohol, tobacco, and other drug problems: Current status with an emphasis on clinical applications. *Behavior Therapy, 25*, 533–580.

Sobell, M. B., & Sobell, L. C. (1993). *Problem drinkers: Guided self-change treatment*. New York: Guilford Press.

Sobell, M. B., & Sobell, L. C. (2000b). Stepped care as a heuristic approach to the treatment of alcohol problems. *Journal of Consulting and Clinical Psychology, 68*(4), 573–579.

Substance Abuse and Mental Health Administration. (1999). *Enhancing motivation for change in substance abuse treatment (Treatment Improvement Protocol Series)*. Rockville, MD: U.S. Department of Health and Human Services.

Related Topics

Chapter 54, "Treatment Matching in Substance Abuse"

Chapter 55, "Motivational Interviewing"

17 MEASURES OF ACCULTURATION

Juan Carlos Gonzalez

The importance of cultural awareness and respect in the provision of psychological services to individuals from other countries or subcultures has been clearly outlined in the *APA Guidelines for Providers of Psychological Services to Ethnic, Linguistic, and Culturally Diverse Populations* (American Psychological Association, 1990). Acculturation is highlighted in these guidelines as one of the factors that all psychologists should be familiar with when working with individuals from nonmajority groups. The ability to differentiate between psychopathology and the effects of acculturative stress is essential for psychologists who assess and treat individuals from different cultures.

DEFINITION

Acculturation is the stressful and complex process that individuals undergo in adjusting to a new culture. A useful structure of four distinct acculturation styles is commonly used to help categorize and understand an individual's response to this difficult adaptational process (Berry, 1984):

- *Assimilation:* Embracing the characteristics of the majority culture while rejecting the characteristics of the culture of origin.
- *Integration:* Embracing the majority culture while maintaining a strong culture-of-origin identity.
- *Rejection:* Maintaining own culture while rejecting both assimilation and integration.
- *Deculturation:* Eventual rejection of both the majority culture and the culture of origin.

NEGATIVE EFFECTS OF ACCULTURATIVE STRESS

The process of acculturation has been hypothesized to lead to a deterioration in physical, social, and emotional well-being (Berry, Kim, Minde, & Mok, 1987). Elevations in anxiety, depression, identity confusion, and somatic complaints have been associated with elevated levels of acculturative stress (Williams & Berry, 1991). Psychologists assess the individual's acculturation experience in order to ascertain how this stressful process may contribute to the presenting symptomatology. In general, individuals who are able to find a balance between the majority culture and their own tend to exhibit fewer negative consequences (Berry et al., 1987; Pawliuk et al., 1996; Szapocznik, Kurtines, & Fernandez, 1980). However, multiple variables (i.e., race, education, language proficiency, reason for immigration, premorbid adjustment, similarity between culture of origin, and new culture) often serve to ameliorate or exacerbate the effects of acculturation.

BRIEF LINGUISTIC MEASURES OF ACCULTURATION

Psychologists practicing in clinical settings may find brief linguistic measures of acculturation particularly useful for determining an individual's general level of acculturation. The proponents of these circumscribed measures have argued persuasively that language usage and proficiency may serve as accurate estimates of overall acculturation (Epstein, Botvin, Dusenbury, Diaz, & Kerner, 1996; Marin & Marin, 1991; Marin, Sabogal, Marin, Otero-Sabogal,

& Perez-Stable, 1987). When using these measures, it is also important to keep in mind that lack of English proficiency may exacerbate acculturative stress by limiting employment options and other important economic and social domains (Westermeyer & Her, 1996). Although research regarding these brief strategies has focused primarily on Hispanic adolescents, it is likely that the general findings may apply to other groups. In general, individuals from non-English-speaking groups who report using their native language in all or most interpersonal settings are less likely to be significantly assimilated or integrated into the majority culture. The following multiple-choice questions may be useful in helping to determine linguistic acculturation (suggested answer choices adapted from Epstein et al., 1996, are only English, mostly English, English and my native language, mostly my native language, only my native language):

- What language do you usually use with your (parents, children, spouse, friends)?
- In what language do you (think, dream, describe emotional experiences)?
- In what language do you (listen to the radio, watch TV, read)?

SELF-REPORT OF ACCULTURATION AND ACCULTURATIVE STRESS

Another useful strategy in clinical settings is to simply ask about the individual's perception of his or her own degree of acculturation and the stressors associated with this adaptational process. Allow the individual to educate you about his or her culture of origin, as well as goals, wishes, and fears concerning the new environment.

- What has the process of adapting to a new environment (i.e., language, diet, culture, rules, expectations) been like for the individual?
- What is the individual's perception of the benefits and risks of embracing the majority culture?
- How does the individual define his or her own cultural, linguistic, and/or ethnic identity in relation to the majority culture?

STANDARDIZED MEASURES OF ACCULTURATION

Most measures of acculturation have been designed by researchers studying the acculturation process. The following encompasses a small sampling of the measures available for assessing acculturation in various nonmajority groups. These measures are available directly from the authors.

- The *Acculturation Rating Scale for Mexican Americans-II* (ARSMA-II; Cuellar, Arnold, & Maldonado, 1995) is a behavioral measure designed to yield five levels of acculturation (from a very Mexican orientation to very assimilated or Anglicized). It also has two subscales that measure the individual's orientation toward Anglo culture and toward Mexican culture.
- The *African American Acculturation Scale* (AAAS; Landrine & Klonoff, 1994) is designed to assess eight dimensions: traditional family structure, preference for things African American, traditional food preferences, interracial attitudes/cultural mistrust, religious beliefs, traditional health beliefs, traditional child-rearing practices, and superstitions.
- The *Bicultural Involvement Scale* (Szapocznik, Kurtines, & Fernandez, 1980) is designed to assess general cultural involvement (i.e., comfort with majority language, preference for recreational activities). This scale was originally used with Cuban-Americans, but it may easily be adapted for use with other groups (Pawliuk et al., 1996).
- The *Brief Acculturation Scale for Hispanics* (Norris, Ford, & Bova, 1996) is a four-item linguistic measure of acculturation for Hispanics.
- The *Minority-Majority Relations Survey* (Sodowsky, Lai, & Plake, 1991) is a 38-item questionnaire designed to assess the atti-

tudes of Hispanics and Asians along three subscales: perceived prejudice, language usage, and acculturation.

- The *Suinn-Lew Asian Self-Identity Acculturation Scale* (Suinn, Ahuna, & Khoo, 1992) is a 21-item questionnaire that focuses on attitudes, identity, language, friendships, behaviors, and geographic background. It is used to rate individuals along an acculturation continuum (low acculturation to high acculturation) and in terms of being "Asian-identified" or "Western-identified."

ADDITIONAL RESOURCES

Those interested in a comprehensive review of theoretical and applied developments in the measurement of acculturation—particularly for African Americans, Asian Americans, American Indians, and Hispanics—will find the text *Acculturation: Advances in Theory, Measurement, and Applied Research* (Chun, Organista, & Marin, 2002) to be an up-to-date and invaluable resource.

Further information regarding the process of acculturation for various nonmajority groups can be found in the *Gale Encyclopedia of Multicultural America* (Vecoli & Galens, 1995). Additional measures of acculturation may be found by using the frequently updated ERIC/AE Test Locator service on the Internet (http://ericae.net/testcol.htm), as well as by consulting the psychological research literature.

References, Readings, & Internet Sites 

American Psychological Association. (1990). *APA guidelines for providers of psychological services to ethnic, linguistic, and culturally diverse populations.* Washington, DC: Author. http://www.apa.org/pi/guide.html

Berry, J. W. (1984). Multicultural policy in Canada: A sociopsychological analysis. *Canadian Journal of Behavioral Sciences, 16*(4), 353–370.

Berry, J. W., Kim, U., Minde, T., & Mok, M. (1987). Comparative studies of acculturative stress. *International Migration Review, 21,* 491–511.

Chun, K. M., Organista, P. B., & Marin, G. (Eds.). (2002). *Acculturation: Advances in theory, measurement, and applied research.* Washington, DC: American Psychological Association.

Cuellar, I., Arnold, B., & Maldonado, R. (1995). Acculturation Rating Scale for Mexican Americans-II: A revision of the original ARSMA scale. *Hispanic Journal of Behavioral Sciences, 17,* 275–304.

Epstein, J. A., Botvin, G. J., Dusenbury, L., Diaz, T., & Kerner, J. (1996). Validation of an acculturation measure for Hispanic adolescents. *Psychological Reports, 76,* 1075–1079.

Landrine, H., & Knonoff, E. A. (1994). The African American Acculturation Scale: Development, reliability, and validity. *Journal of Black Psychology, 20,* 104–127.

Marin, G., & Marin, B. V. (1991). *Research with Hispanic populations* (Applied Social Research Methods Series, Vol. 23). Newbury Park, CA: Sage.

Marin, G., Sabogal, R., Marin, B. V., Otero-Sabogal, R., & Perez-Stable, E. J. (1987). Development of a short acculturation scale for Hispanics. *Hispanic Journal of Behavioral Sciences, 9,* 183–205.

Norris, A. E., Ford, K., & Bova, C. A. (1996). Psychometrics of a brief acculturation scale for Hispanics in a probability sample of urban Hispanic adolescents and young adults. *Hispanic Journal of Behavioral Sciences, 18,* 29–38.

Pawliuk, N., Grizenko, N., Chan-Yip, A., Gantous, P., Mathew, J., & Nguyen, D. (1996). Acculturation style and psychological functioning in children of immigrants. *American Journal of Orthopsychiatry, 66,* 111–121.

Sodowsky, G. R., Lai, E. W., & Plake, B. S. (1991). Moderating effects of sociocultural variables on acculturation attitudes of Hispanics and Asian Americans. *Journal of Counseling and Development, 70,* 194–204.

Suinn, R., Ahuna, C., & Khoo, G. (1992). The Suinn-Lew Asian Self-Identity Acculturation Scale: Concurrent and factorial validation. *Educational and Psychological Measurement, 52,* 1041–1046.

Szapocznik, J., Kurtines, W. M., & Fernandez, T. (1980). Bicultural involvement and adjustment in Hispanic-American youths. *International Journal of Intercultural Relations, 4,* 353–365.

Vecoli, R. J., & Galens, J. (Eds.). (1995). *Gale encyclopedia of multicultural America* (2 vols.). Detroit: St. James Press.

Westermeyer, J., & Her, C. (1996). English fluency and social adjustment among Hmong refugees in Minnesota. *Journal of Nervous and Mental Disease, 184*(2), 130–132.

Williams, C. L., & Berry, J. W. (1991). Primary prevention of acculturative stress among refugees: Application of psychological theory and practice. *American Psychologist, 46,* 632–641.

Related Topic

Chapter 10, "Formulating Diagnostic Inpressions With Ethnic and Racial Minority Children Using the *DSM-IV-TR*"

18 *DSM-IV-TR* CLASSIFICATION SYSTEM

American Psychiatric Association

Since the last edition of the *Psychologists' Desk Reference,* there have been two revisions of the *Diagnostic and Statistical Manual* composed by the American Psychiatric Association. Those changes have been noted below, and all the codes are produced here for the reader's convenience and with permission from the *Diagnostic and Statistical Manual of Mental Disorders* (4th ed., rev.; copyright 2000 American Psychiatric Association).

The following notes are offered for the convenience of the user in navigating the *DSM* and for a better understanding of the taxonomy.

- NOS = Not Otherwise Specified
- An *x* appearing in a diagnostic code indicates that a specific code number is required.
- An ellipsis (. . .) is used in the names of certain disorders to indicate that the name of a specific mental disorder or general medical condition should be inserted when recording the name (e.g., 293.0 Delirium Due to Hypothyroidism).
- If criteria are currently met, one of the following severity specifiers may be noted after the diagnosis:
  - Mild
  - Moderate
  - Severe
- If criteria are no longer met, one of the following specifiers may be noted:
  - In Partial Remission
  - In Full Remission
  - Prior History

DSM-IV-TR CLASSIFICATION

Disorders Usually First Diagnosed in Infancy, Childhood, or Adolescence

Mental Retardation

Note: These are coded on Axis II.

317	Mild Mental Retardation
318.0	Moderate Mental Retardation
318.1	Severe Mental Retardation
318.2	Profound Mental Retardation
319	Mental Retardation, Severity Unspecified

Learning Disorders

- 315.00 Reading Disorder
- 315.1 Mathematics Disorder
- 315.2 Disorder of Written Expression
- 315.9 Learning Disorder NOS

Motor Skills Disorder

- 315.4 Developmental Coordination Disorder

Communication Disorders

- 315.31 Expressive Language Disorder
- 315.32 Mixed Receptive-Expressive Language Disorder
- 15.39 Phonological Disorder
- 307.0 Stuttering
- 307.9 Communication Disorder NOS

Pervasive Developmental Disorders

- 299.00 Autistic Disorder
- 299.80 Rett's Disorder
- 299.10 Childhood Disintegrative Disorder
- 299.80 Pervasive Developmental Disorder NOS

Feeding and Eating Disorders of Infancy or Early Childhood

- 307.52 Pica
- 307.53 Rumination Disorder
- 307.59 Feeding Disorder of Infancy or Early Childhood

Tic Disorders

- 307.23 Tourette's Disorder
- 307.22 Chronic Motor or Vocal Tic Disorder
- 307.21 Transient Tic Disorder (*specify if:* Single Episode/Recurrent)
- 307.20 Tic Disorder NOS

Elimination Disorders

- ——.— Encopresis
- 787.6 With Constipation and Overflow Incontinence
- 307.7 Without Constipation and Overflow Incontinence
- 307.6 Enuresis (Not Due to a General Medical Condition) (*Specify type:* Nocturnal Only/Diurnal Only/Nocturnal and Diurnal)

Other Disorders of Infancy, Childhood, or Adolescence

- 309.21 Separation Anxiety Disorder
- 313.23 Selective Mutism

Reactive Attachment Disorder of Infancy or Early Childhood *(Specify:* Inhibited Type/Disinhibited Type)

- 307.3 Stereotypic Movement Disorder *(Specify if:* With Self-Injurious Behavior)
- 313.9 Disorder of Infancy, Childhood, or Adolescence NOS

Delirium, Dementia, and Amnestic and Other Cognitive Disorders

Delirium

- 293.0 Delirium Due to . . . [*Indicate the General Medical Condition*]
- ——.— Substance Intoxication Delirium (*Refer to Substance-Related Disorders for substance-specific codes)*
- ——.— Substance Withdrawal Delirium (*Refer to Substance-Related Disorders for substance-specific codes)*
- ——.— Delirium Due to Multiple Etiologies (*Code each of the specific etiologies)*
- 780.09 Delirium NOS

Dementia

- 294.xx* Dementia of the Alzheimer's Type, With Early Onset (*Also code 331.0 Alzheimer's disease on Axis III*)
- .10 Without Behavioral Disturbance
- .11 With Behavioral Disturbance
- 294.xx* Dementia of the Alzheimer's Type, With Late Onset (*Also code 331.0 Alzheimer's disease on Axis III*)
- .10 Without Behavioral Disturbance
- .11 With Behavioral Disturbance
- 290.xx Vascular Dementia
- .40 Uncomplicated
- .41 With Delirium

.42 With Delusions
.43 With Depressed Mood

(*Specify if:* With Behavioral Disturbance)

Code presence or absence of a behavioral disturbance in the fifth digit for Dementia Due to a General Medical Condition:

0 = Without Behavioral Disturbance
1 = With Behavioral Disturbance

294.1x* Dementia Due to HIV Disease (*Also code 042 HIV on Axis III*)
294.1x* Dementia Due to Head Trauma (*Also code 854.00 on Axis III)*
294.1x* Dementia Due to Parkinson's Disease (*Also code 332.0 Parkinson's disease on Axis III*)
294.1x* Dementia Due to Huntington's Disease (*Also code 333.4 Huntington's disease on Axis III*)
294.1x* Dementia Due to Pick's Disease (*Also code 331.1 Pick's disease on Axis III*)
294.1x* Dementia Due to Creutzfeld-Jakob Disease (*Also code 046.1 Creutzfeld-Jakob disease on Axis III*)
294.1x* Dementia Due to . . . [*Indicate the General Medical Condition not listed above*] (*Code the general medical condition on Axis III*)
——— Substance-Induced Persisting Dementia (*Refer to Substance-Related Disorders for substance specific codes*)
——— Dementia Due to Multiple Etiologies (*Code each of the specific etiologies)*
294.8 Dementia NOS

Amnestic Disorders
294.0 Amnestic Disorder Due to . . . [*Indicate the General Medical Condition*] (*Specify if:* Transient/Chronic)
——— Substance-Induced Persisting Amnestic Disorder (*Refer to Substance-Related Disorders for substance-specific codes*)
294.9 Amnestic Disorder NOS

Other Cognitive Disorders
294.9 Cognitive Disorder NOS

Mental Disorders Due to a General Medical Condition Not Elsewhere Classified

293.89 Catatonic Disorder Due to . . . [*Indicate the General Medical Condition*]
310.1 Personality Change Due to . . . [*Indicate the General Medical Condition*]
Specify type: Labile Type/Disinhibited Type/Aggressive Type/Apathetic Type/Paranoid Type/Other Type/Combined Type/Unspecified Type
293.9 Mental Disorder NOS Due to . . . [*Indicate the General Medical Condition*]

Substance-Related Disorders

The following specifiers apply to Substance Dependence as noted:
[a]With Physiological Dependence/Without Physiological Dependence
[b]Early Full Remission/Early Partial Remission/Sustained Full Remission/Sustained Partial Remission
[c]In a Controlled Environment
[d]On Agonist Therapy
The following specifiers apply to Substance-Induced Disorders as noted:
[I]With Onset During Intoxication
[W]With Onset During Withdrawal

Alcohol-Related Disorders
Alcohol Use Disorders
303.90 Alcohol Dependence[a,b,c]
305.00 Alcohol Abuse

Alcohol-Induced Disorders
303.00 Alcohol Intoxication
291.81 Alcohol Withdrawal (*Specify if:* With Perceptual Disturbances)
291.0 Alcohol Intoxication Delirium
291.0 Alcohol Withdrawal Delirium
291.2 Alcohol-Induced Persisting Dementia
291.1 Alcohol-Induced Persisting Amnestic Disorder

291.x Alcohol-Induced Psychotic Disorder
.5 With Delusions[I,W]
.3 With Hallucinations[I,W]
291.89 Alcohol-Induced Mood Disorder[I,W]
291.89 Alcohol-Induced Anxiety Disorder[I,W]
291.89 Alcohol-Induced Sexual Dysfunction[I,W]
291.89 Alcohol-Induced Sleep Disorder[I,W]
291.0 Alcohol-Related Disorder NOS

Amphetamine (or Amphetamine-Like)-Related Disorders

Amphetamine Use Disorders
304.40 Amphetamine Dependence[a,b,c]
305.70 Amphetamine Abuse

Amphetamine-Induced Disorders
292.89 Amphetamine Intoxication (*Specify if:* With Perceptual Disturbances)
292.0 Amphetamine Withdrawal
292.81 Amphetamine Intoxication Delirium
292.xx Amphetamine-Induced Psychotic Disorder
.11 With Delusions[I]
.12 With Hallucinations[I]
292.84 Amphetamine-Induced Mood Disorder[I,W]
292.89 Amphetamine-Induced Anxiety Disorder[I]
292.89 Amphetamine-Induced Sexual Dysfunction[I]
292.89 Amphetamine-Induced Sleep Disorder[I,W]
292.0 Amphetamine-Related Disorder NOS

Caffeine-Related Disorders

Caffeine-Induced Disorders
305.90 Caffeine Intoxication
292.89 Caffeine-Induced Anxiety Disorder[I]
292.89 Caffeine-Induced Sleep Disorder[I]
292.9 Caffeine-Related Disorder NOS

Cannabis-Related Disorders

Cannabis Use Disorders
304.30 Cannabis Dependence
304.20 Cannabis Abuse

Cannabis-Induced Disorders
292.89 Cannabis Intoxication (*Specify if:* With Perceptual Disturbances)
292.81 Cannabis Intoxication Delirium
292.xx Cannabis-Induced Psychotic Disorder
.11 With Delusions[I]
.12 With Hallucinations[I]
292.89 Cannabis-Induced Anxiety Disorder[I]
292.89 Cannabis-Related Disorder NOS

Cocaine-Related Disorders

Cocaine Use Disorders
304.20 Cocaine Dependence
304.60 Cocaine Abuse

Cocaine-Induced Disorders
292.89 Cocaine Intoxication (*Specify if:* With Perceptual Disturbances)
292.0 Cocaine Withdrawal
292.81 Cocaine Intoxication Delirium
292.xx Cocaine-Induced Psychotic Disorder
.11 With Delusions[I]
.12 With Hallucinations[I]
292.84 Cocaine-Induced Mood Disorder[I,W]
292.89 Cocaine-Induced Anxiety Disorder[I,W]
292.89 Cocaine-Induced Sexual Dysfunction[I]
292.89 Cocaine-Induced Sleep Disorder[I,W]
292.9 Cocaine-Related Disorder NOS

Hallucinogen-Related Disorders

Hallucinogen Use Disorders
304.50 Hallucinogen Dependence[b,c]
305.30 Hallucinogen Abuse

Hallucinogen-Induced Disorders
292.89 Hallucinogen Intoxication
292.89 Hallucinogen Persisting Perception Disorder (Flashbacks)
292.81 Hallucinogen Intoxication Delirium

292.xx Hallucinogen-Induced Psychotic Disorder
.11 With Delusions[I]
.12 With Hallucinations[I]
292.84 Hallucinogen-Induced Mood Disorder[I]
292.89 Hallucinogen-Induced Anxiety Disorder[I]
292.9 Hallucinogen-Related Disorder NOS

Inhalant-Related Disorders

Inhalant Use Disorders
304.60 Inhalant Dependence[b,c]
305.90 Inhalant Abuse

Inhalant-Induced Disorders
292.89 Inhalant Intoxication
292.81 Inhalant Intoxication Delirium
292.82 Inhalant-Induced Persisting Dementia
292.xx Inhalant-Induced Psychotic Disorder
.11 With Delusions[I]
.12 With Hallucinations[I]
292.84 Inhalant-Induced Mood Disorder[I]
292.89 Inhalant-Induced Anxiety Disorder[I]
292.9 Inhalant-Related Disorder NOS

Nicotine-Related Disorders

Nicotine Use Disorders
305.1 Nicotine Dependence

Nicotine-Induced Disorders[a,b]
292.00 Nicotine Withdrawal
292.9 Nicotine-Related Disorder NOS

Opioid-Related Disorders

Opioid Use Disorders
304.00 Opioid Dependence
305.50 Opioid Abuse

Opioid-Induced Disorders
292.89 Opioid Intoxication (*Specify if:* With Perceptual Disturbances)
292.0 Opioid Withdrawal
292.81 Opioid Intoxication Delirium
292.xx Opioid-Induced Psychotic Disorder
.11 With Delusions[I]
.12 With Hallucinations[I]
292.84 Opioid-Induced Mood Disorder[I]
292.89 Opioid-Induced Sexual Dysfunction[I]
292.89 Opioid-Induced Sleep Disorder[I,W]
292.9 Opioid-Related Disorder NOS

Phencyclidine (or Phencyclidine-Like)-Related Disorders

Phencyclidine Use Disorders
304.60 Phencyclidine Dependence[b,c]
305.90 Phencyclidine Abuse

Phencyclidine-Induced Disorders
292.89 Phencyclidine Intoxication (*Specify if:* With Perceptual Disturbances)
292.81 Phencyclidine Intoxication Delirium
292.xx Phencyclidine-Induced Psychotic Disorder
.11 With Delusions[I]
.12 With Hallucinations[I]
292.84 Induced Mood Disorder[I]
292.89 Induced Anxiety Disorder[I]
292.9 Phencyclidine-Related Disorder NOS

Sedative-, Hypnotic-, or Anxiolytic-Related Disorders

Sedative, Hypnotic, or Anxiolytic Use Disorders
304.10 Sedative, Hypnotic, or Anxiolytic Dependence
305.40 Sedative, Hypnotic, or Anxiolytic Abuse

Sedative, Hypnotic, or Anxiolytic-Induced Disorders
292.89 Sedative, Hypnotic, or Anxiolytic Intoxication
292.0 Sedative, Hypnotic, or Anxiolytic Withdrawal (*Specify if:* With Perceptual Disturbances)
292.81 Sedative, Hypnotic, or Anxiolytic Intoxication Delirium
292.81 Sedative, Hypnotic, or Anxiolytic Withdrawal Delirium
292.82 Sedative, Hypnotic, or Anxiolytic-Induced Persisting Dementia
292.83 Sedative, Hypnotic, or Anxiolytic-

Induced Persisting Amnestic Disorder
292.xx Induced Psychotic Disorder
.11 With Delusions[I]
.12 With Hallucinations[I]
292.84 Sedative, Hypnotic, or Anxiolytic-Induced Mood Disorder[I,W]
292.89 Sedative, Hypnotic, or Anxiolytic-Induced Anxiety Disorder[I,W]
292.89 Sedative, Hypnotic, or Anxiolytic-Induced Sexual Dysfunction[I]
292.89 Sedative, Hypnotic, or Anxiolytic-Induced Sleep Disorder[I,W]
292.9 Sedative, Hypnotic, or Anxiolytic-Related Disorder NOS

Polysubstance-Related Disorder
304.80 Polysubstance Dependence[a,b,c,d]

Other (or Unknown) Substance-Related Disorders

Other (or Unknown) Substance Use Disorders

304.90 Other (or Unknown) Substance Dependence[a,b,c,d]
305.90 Other (or Unknown) Substance Abuse

Other (or Unknown) Substance-Induced Disorders
292.89 Other (or Unknown) Substance Intoxication (*Specify if:* With Perceptual Disturbances)
292.0 Other (or Unknown) Substance Withdrawal
292.81 Other (or Unknown) Substance-Induced Delirium
292.82 Other (or Unknown) Substance-Induced Persisting Dementia
292.82 Other (or Unknown) Substance-Induced Persisting Amnestic Disorder
292.xx Other (or Unknown) Substance-Induced Psychotic Disorder
292.11 With Delusions[I,W]
292.12 With Hallucinations[I,W]
292.84 Other (or Unknown) Substance-Induced Mood Disorder[I,W]
292.89 Other (or Unknown) Substance-Induced Anxiety Disorder[I,W]
292.89 Other (or Unknown) Substance-Induced Sexual Dysfunction[I]
292.89 Other (or Unknown) Substance-Induced Sleep Disorder[I,W]
292.9 Other (or Unknown) Substance-Related Disorder NOS

Schizophrenia and Other Psychotic Disorders

295.xx Schizophrenia
The following Classification of Longitudinal Course applies to all subtypes of Schizophrenia:

Episodic
With Interepisode Residual Symptoms (*Specify if:* With Prominent Negative Symptoms)/Episodic
With No Interepisode Residual Symptoms
Continuous (*Specify if:* With Prominent Negative Symptoms)
Single Episode in Partial Remission (*Specify if:* With Prominent Negative Symptoms)/
Single Episode in Full Remission
Other or Unspecified Pattern

.30 Paranoid Type
.10 Disorganized Type
.20 Catatonic Type
.90 Undifferentiated Type
.60 Residual Type
295.40 Schizophreniform Disorder (*Specify if:* Without Good Prognostic Features/With "Good Prognostic Features)
295.70 Schizoaffective Disorder (*Specify type:* Bipolar type/Depressive Type)
297.1 Delusional Disorder (*Specify type:* Erotomanic Type/Grandiose Type/Jealous Type/Persecutory Type/Somatic Type/Mixed Type/Unspecified Type)
298.8 Brief Psychotic Disorder (*Specify if:* With Marked Stressor(s)/Without Marked Stressor(s)/With Postpartum Onset)
298.3 Shared Psychotic Disorder

293.xx Psychotic Disorder Due to . . . *[Indicate the General Medical Condition]*
.81 With Delusions
.82 With Hallucinations
——.— Substance-Induced Psychotic Disorder (*Refer to Substance-Related Disorders for substance-specific codes; specify if:* With Onset During Intoxication/With Onset During Withdrawal)
298.9 Psychotic Disorder NOS

Mood Disorders

Code current state of Major Depressive Disorder or Bipolar I Disorder in fifth digit:
1 = Mild
2 = Moderate
3 = Severe Without Psychotic Features
4 = Severe With Psychotic Features (*Specify:* Mood-Congruent Psychotic Features/Mood-Incongruent Psychotic Features)
5 = In Partial Remission
6 = In Full Remission
0 = Unspecified

The following specifiers apply (for current or most recent episode) to Mood Disorders as noted:
[a]Severity/Psychotic/Remission Specifiers
[b]Chronic
[c]With Catatonic Features
[d]With Melancholic Features
[e]With Atypical Features
[f]With Postpartum Onset

The following specifiers apply to Mood Disorders as noted:
[g]With or Without Full Interepisode Recovery
[h]With Seasonal Pattern
[i]With Rapid Cycling

Depressive Disorders

296.xx Major Depressive Disorder
.2x Single Episode[a,b,c,d,e,f]
.3x Recurrent[a,b,c,d,e,f,g,h]
300.4 Dysthymic Disorder (*Specify if:* Early Onset/Late Onset; *Specify:* With Atypical Features)
311. Depressive Disorder NOS

Bipolar Disorders

296.xx Bipolar I Disorder
.0x Single Manic Episode[a,c,f] (*Specify if:* Mixed)
.40 Most Recent Episode Hypomanic[g,h,i]
.4x Most Recent Episode Manic[a,c,f,g,h,i]
.6x Most Recent Episode Mixed[a,c,f,g,h,i]
.5x Most Recent Episode Depressed[a,b,c,d,e,f,g,h,i]
.7 Most Recent Episode Unspecified[g,h,i]
296.89 Bipolar II Disorder[a,b,c,d,e,f,g,h,I] (*Specify current or most recent episode:* Hypomanic/Depressed)
301.13 Cyclothymic Disorder
296.80 Bipolar Disorder NOS
293.83 Mood Disorder Due to . . . [*Indicate the General Medical Condition*] (*Specify type:* With Depressive Features/With Major Depressive-Like Episode/With Manic Features/With Mixed Features. *Specify if:* With Onset During Intoxication/With Onset During Withdrawal)
296.90 Mood Disorder NOS

Anxiety Disorders

300.01 Panic Disorder Without Agoraphobia
300.21 Panic Disorder With Agoraphobia
300.22 Agoraphobia Without History of Panic Disorder
300.29 Specific Phobia (*Specify type*: Animal Type/Natural Environment Type/Blood-Injection-Injury Type/Other Type)
300.23 Social Phobia (*Specify if*: Generalized)
300.3 Obsessive-Compulsive Disorder (*Specify if*: With Poor Insight)
309.81 Post Traumatic Stress Disorder (*Specify if*: Acute/Chronic. *Specify if*: With Delayed Onset)
308.3 Acute Stress Disorder
300.02 Generalized Anxiety Disorder
293.84 Anxiety Disorder Due to . . . [*Indicate the General Medical Condition*] (*Specify if*: With General

Anxiety/With Panic Attacks/With Obsessive Compulsive Symptoms)

——— Substance-Induced Anxiety Disorder (*Refer to* Substance Related Disorders for substance-specific codes; *specify if*: With Generalized Anxiety/With Panic Attacks/With Obsessive Compulsive Symptoms/With Phobic Symptoms. *Specify if*: With Onset During Intoxication/With Onset During Withdrawal)

300.00 Anxiety Disorder NOS

Somatoform Disorders

300.81 Somatization Disorder
300.82 Undifferentiated Somatoform Disorder
300.11 Conversion Disorder (*Specify type*: With Motor Symptom or Deficit/With Sensory Symptom or Deficit/With Seizures or Convulsions/With Mixed Presentation)
307.xx Pain Disorder
.80 Associated With Psychological Factors and a General Medical Condition (*Specify if* Acute/Chronic)
300.7 Hypochondriasis (*Specify if*: With Poor Insight)
300.7 Body Dysmorphic Disorder

Factitious Disorders

300.xx Factitious Disorder
.16 With Predominantly Psychological Signs and Symptoms
.19 With Predominantly Physical Signs and Symptoms
.19 With Combined Psychological and Physical Signs and Symptoms
300.19 Factitious Disorder NOS

Dissociative Disorders

300.12 Dissociative Amnesia
300.13 Dissociative Fugue
300.14 Dissociative Identity Disorder
300.6 Depersonalization Disorder
300.15 Dissociative Disorder NOS

Sexual and Gender Identity Disorders

Sexual Dysfunctions

The following specifiers apply to all primary Sexual Dysfunctions:
Lifelong Type/Acquired Type
Generalized Type/Situational Type
Due to Psychological Factors/Due to Combined Factors

Sexual Desire Disorders
302.71 Hypoactive Sexual Desire Disorder
302.79 Sexual Aversion Disorder

Sexual Arousal Disorders
307.72 Female Sexual Arousal Disorder
307.72 Male Erectile Disorder

Orgasmic Disorder
302.73 Female Orgasmic Disorder
302.74 Male Orgasmic Disorder
302.75 Premature Ejaculation

Sexual Pain Disorders
302.76 Dyspareunia (Not Due to a General Medical Condition)
302.51 Vaginismus (Not Due to a General Medical Condition)

Sexual Dysfunction Due to General Medical Condition
625.8 Female Hypoactive Sexual Desire Disorder Due to . . . [*Indicate the General Medical Condition*]
608.89 Male Hypoactive Sexual Desire Disorder Due to . . . [*Indicate the General Medical Condition*]
607.84 Male Erectile Disorder Due to . . . [*Indicate the General Medical Condition*]
625.0 Female Dyspareunia Due to . . . [*Indicate the General Medical Condition*]

608.89 Male Dyspareunia Due to . . . [*Indicate the General Medical Condition*]
302.70 Sexual Dysfunction NOS
625.8 Other Female Sexual Dysfunction Due to . . . [*Indicate the General Medical Condition*]
608.89 Other Male Sexual Dysfunction Due to . . . [*Indicate the General Medical Condition*]
——— Substance-Induced Sexual Dysfunction NOS (*Refer to Substance-Related Disorders for substance-specific codes; specify if:* With Impaired Desire/With Impaired Arousal/With Impaired Orgasm/With Sexual Pain. *Specify if:* With Onset During Intoxication)
302.70 Sexual Dysfunction NOS

Paraphilias

302.4 Exhibitionism
302.81 Fetishism
302.89 Frotteurism
302.2 Pedophilia (*Specify if:* Sexually Attracted to Males/Sexually Attracted to Females/Sexually Attracted to Both. *Specify if:* Limited to Incest. *Specify Type:* Exclusive Type/Nonexclusive Type)
302.83 Sexual Masochism
302.84 Sexual Sadism
302.3 Transvestic Fetishism
302.82 Voyeurism
302.9 Paraphilia NOS

Gender Identity Disorders

302.xx Gender Identity Disorder
.6 in Children
.85 in Adolescents or Adults (*Specify if:* Sexually Attracted to Males/Sexually Attracted to Females/Sexually Attracted to Both/Sexually Attracted to Neither)
302.6 Gender Identity Disorder NOS
302.9 Sexual Disorder NOS

Eating Disorders

307.1 Anorexia Nervosa (*Specify if:* Restricting Type; Binge-Eating/Purging Type)
307.51 Bulimia Nervosa (*Specify type:* Purging Type/Non-Purging Type)
307.50 Eating Disorder NOS

Sleep Disorders

Primary Sleep Disorders
Dyssomnias

307.42 Primary Insomnia
307.44 Primary Hypersomnia (*Specify if:* Recurrent)
347 Narcolepsy
780.59 Breathing-Related Sleep Disorder
307.45 Circadian Rhythm Sleep Disorder (*Specify type:* Delayed Sleep Phase Type/Jet Lag Type/Shift Work Type/Unspecified Type)
307.47 Dyssomnia NOS

Parasomnias

307.47 Nightmare Disorder
307.46 Sleep Terror Disorder
307.46 Sleepwalking Disorder
307.47 Parasomnia NOS

Sleep Disorders Related to Another Mental Disorder

307.42 Insomnia Related to . . . [*Indicate the Axis I or Axis II Disorder*]
307.44 Hypersomnia Related to . . . [*Indicate the Axis I or Axis II Disorder*]

Other Sleep Disorders

780.xx Sleep Disorder Due to . . . [*Indicate the General Medical Condition*]
.52 Insomnia Type
.54 Hypersomnia Type
.59 Parasomnia Type
.59 Mixed Type
——— Substance-Induced Sleep Disorder (*Refer to Substance-Related Disorders for substance-specific*

codes; specify type: Insomnia Type/Hypersomnia Type/Mixed Type. *Specify if:* With Onset During Intoxication/With Onset During Withdrawal)

Impulse-Control Disorders Not Elsewhere Classified

312.34 Intermittent Explosive Disorder
312.32 Kleptomania
312.33 Pyromania
312.31 Pathological Gambling
312.39 Trichotillomania
312.30 Impulse Control Disorder NOS

Adjustment Disorders

309.xx Adjustment Disorder
.0 With Depressed Mood
.24 With Anxiety
.28 With Mixed Anxiety and Depressed Mood
.3 With Disturbance of Conduct
.4 With Mixed Disturbance of Emotions and Conduct
.9 Unspecified
Specify if Acute/Chronic

Personality Disorders

Note: These are coded on Axis II.
301.0 Paranoid Personality Disorder
301.20 Schizoid Personality Disorder
301.22 Schizotypal Personality Disorder
301.7 Antisocial Personality Disorder
301.83 Borderline Personality Disorder
301.50 Histrionic Personality Disorder
301.81 Narcissistic Personality Disorder
301.82 Avoidant Personality Disorder
301.6 Dependent Personality Disorder
301.4 Obsessive-Compulsive Disorder
301.9 Personality Disorder NOS

Other Conditions That May Be a Focus of Clinical Attention

Psychological Factors Affecting Medical Condition

316 . . . (*Specified Psychological Factor*) *Affecting . . .* [*Indicate the General Medical Condition*]. *Choose name based on nature of factors:*
Mental Disorder Affecting Medical Condition
Psychological Symptoms Affecting Medical Condition
Personality Traits or Coping Style Affecting Medical Condition
Maladaptive Health Behaviors Affecting Medical Condition
Stress-Related Physiological Response Affecting Medical Condition
Other or Unspecified Psychological Factors Affecting Medical Condition

Medication-Induced Movement Disorders

332.1 Neuroleptic-Induced Parkinsonism
333.92 Neuroleptic Malignant Syndrome
333.7 Neuroleptic-Induced Acute Dystonia
333.99 Neuroleptic-Induced Acute Akathisia
333.82 Neuroleptic-Induced Tardive Dyskinesia
333.1 Medication-Induced Postural Tremor
333.90 Medication-Induced Movement Disorder NOS

Other Medication-Induced Disorder
995.2 Adverse Effects of Medication NOS

Relational Problems

V61.9 Relational Problem Related to a Mental Disorder or General Medical Condition

V61.20 Parent-Child Relational Problem
V61.10 Partner Relational Problem
V61.8 Sibling Relational Problem
V62.81 Relational Problem NOS

Problems Related to Abuse or Neglect

V61.21 Physical Abuse of Child (*Code 995.54 if focus of attention is on victim*)
V61.21 Sexual Abuse of Child (*Code 995.53 if focus of attention is on victim*)
V61.21 Neglect of Child (*Code 995.52 if focus of attention is on victim*)
——— Physical Abuse of Adult
V61.12 (if by partner)
V62.83 (if by person other than partner) (*Code 995.81 if focus of attention is on victim*)
——— Sexual Abuse of Adult
V61.12 (if by partner)
V62.83 (if by person other than partner) (*Code 995.83 if focus of attention is on victim*)

Additional Conditions That May Be a Focus of Clinical Attention

V15.81 Noncompliance With Treatment
V65.2 Malingering
V71.01 Adult Antisocial Behavior
V62.89 Borderline Intellectual Functioning
Note: This is coded on Axis II
780.9 Age-Related Cognitive Decline
V62.82 Bereavement
V62.3 Academic Problem
V62.2 Occupational Problem
V62.89 Religious or Spiritual Problem
V62.4 Acculturation Problem
V62.89 Phase of Life Problem

Additional Codes

300.9 Unspecified Mental Disorder (nonpsychotic)
V71.09 No Diagnosis or Conditions on Axis I
799.9 Diagnosis or Condition Deferred on Axis I
V71.09 No Diagnosis on Axis II

Diagnosis Deferred on Axis II

MULTIAXIAL SYSTEM

Axis I Clinical Disorders and Other Conditions That May Be a Focus of Clinical Attention
Axis II Personality Disorders and Mental Retardation
Axis III General Medical Conditions
Axis IV Psychosocial and Environmental Problems
Axis V Global Assessment of Functioning

Source: Reprinted with permission from the *Diagnostic and Statistical Manual of Mental Disorders, Fourth Edition, Text Revision,* copyright 2004 American Psychiatric Association.

Reference and Internet Site

American Psychiatric Association. (2000). *The diagnostic and statistical manual of mental disorders* (4th ed., rev.). Washington, DC: Author. http://www.appi.org

Related Topics

Chapter 9, "Child and Adolescent Diagnosis With *DSM-IV*"
Chapter 19, "A Practical Guide for the Use of the Global Assessment of Functioning (GAF) Scale of the *DSM-IV-TR*"

19 A PRACTICAL GUIDE FOR THE USE OF THE GLOBAL ASSESSMENT OF FUNCTIONING (GAF) SCALE OF THE *DSM-IV-TR*

American Psychiatric Association

One of the criticisms of the *Diagnostic and Statistical Manual of Mental Disorders* is that it fails to provide an adequate range of description to encompass the whole range of human psychology. While a wider range of description is an admirable goal, it may one that will have to wait a long time, if ever, for someone to accomplish. The authors of the *DSM* series have attempted to make the best of the task at hand by designing a multiaxial system that will reflect as many of the individual qualities of the patient while retaining its meaningful generalizability. To this end, Axis V of the *DSM* was provided to allow clinicians to state their impressions of a patient's overall level of functioning. The *Manual* provides the following paraphrased instruction and warnings.

- The reporting of the patient's general overall condition should not include impairment in functioning due to factors other than psychological in nature, such as one's physical or environmental limitations.
- The scale presents 10 ranges of functioning and the clinician is asked to pick a single value that best reflects the patient's adaptive functioning.
- Each of the 10 ranges has two aspects—symptoms severity and functioning. The GAF score should be in the decile that reflects either of these aspects.

To achieve the best use of this scale, the authors provide a four-step process for assigning a GAF:

1. Starting at the top level, evaluate each range by asking, "Is *either* the individual's symptom severity *or* level of functioning worse than what is indicated in the range description?"
2. Keep moving down the scale until the range that best matches the individual's symptom severity *or* the level of functioning is reached, *whichever is worse.*
3. Look at the next lower range as a double-check against having stopped prematurely. This range should be too severe on *both* symptom severity *and* level of functioning. If it is, the appropriate range has been reached (continue with Step 4). If not, go back to Step 2 and continue moving down the scale.
4. To determine the specific GAF rating within the selected 10-point range, consider whether the individual is functioning at the higher or lower end of the 10-point range.

GLOBAL ASSESSMENT OF FUNCTIONING (GAF) SCALE

Code

Note: Use intermediate codes when appropriate (e.g., 45, 68, 72).

100 Superior functioning in a wide range of activities, life's problems never seem to get out of hand, is sought out by others because of his or her many positive qualities. No symptoms.

90 Absent or minimal symptoms (e.g., mild anxiety before an exam), good functioning in all areas, interested and involved in a wide range of activities, socially effective, generally satisfied with life, no more than everyday problems or concerns (e.g., an occasional argument with family members).

80 If symptoms are present, they are transient and expectable reactions to psychosocial stressors (e.g., difficulty concentrating after family argument), no more than slight impairment in social, occupational, or school functioning (e.g., temporarily falling behind in schoolwork).

70 Some mild symptoms (e.g., depressed mood and mild insomnia) *or* some difficulty in social, occupational, or school functioning (e.g., occasional truancy or theft within the household), but generally functioning pretty well, has some meaningful interpersonal relationships.

60 Moderate symptoms (e.g., flat affect and circumstantial speech, occasional panic attacks) *or* moderate difficulty in social, occupational, or school functioning (e.g., few friends, conflicts with peers and coworkers).

50 Serious symptoms (e.g., suicidal ideation, severe obsessional rituals, frequent shoplifting) *or* any serious impairment in social, occupational, or school functioning (e.g., no friends, unable to keep a job).

40 Some impairment in reality testing or communication (e.g., speech is at times illogical, obscure, or irrelevant) *or* major impairment in several areas, such as work or school, family relations, judgment, thinking, or mood (e.g., depressed man avoids friends, neglects family, and is unable to work; child frequently beats up younger children, is defiant at home, and is failing at school).

30 Behavior is considerably influenced by delusions or hallucinations *or* serious impairment in communication or judgment (e.g., sometimes incoherent, acts grossly inappropriately, suicidal preoccupation) *or* inability to function in almost all areas (stays in bed all day; no job, home, or friends).

20 Some danger of hurting self or others (e.g., suicide attempts without clear expectation of death; frequently violent; manic excitement) *or* occasionally fails to maintain minimal personal hygiene (e.g., smears feces) *or* gross impairment in communication (e.g., largely incoherent or mute).

10 Persistent danger of severely hurting self or others (e.g., recurrent violence)

1 *or* serious suicidal act with clear expectation of death.

0 Inadequate information.

Sources: The rating of overall psychological functioning on a scale of 1–100 was operationalized by Luborsky in the Health-Sickness Rating Scale (L. Luborsky, "Clinicians' Judgments of Mental Health," *Archives of General Psychiatry* 7 [1962]: 407–417). Spitzer and colleagues developed a revision of the Health-Sickness Rating Scale called the Global Assessment Scale (GAS) (J. Endicott, R. L. Spitzer, J. L. Fleiss, & J. Cohen, "The Global Assessment Scale: A Procedure for Measuring Overall Severity of Psychiatric Disturbance," *Archives of General Psychiatry* 33 [1976]: 766–771). A modified version of the FAS was included in *DSM II-R* as the "Global Assessment of Functioning (GAF) Scale." Text for the GAF is reprinted with permission from the *Diagnostic and Statistical Manual of Mental Disorders, Fourth Edition, Text Revision,* copyright 2000 American Psychiatric Association.

Reference and Internet Site

American Psychiatric Association. (2000). *The diagnostic and statistical manual of mental disorders* (4th ed., rev.). Arlington, VA: American Psychiatric Association. http://www.appi.org

Related Topics

Chapter 10, "Formulating Diagnostic Impressions With Ethnic and Racial Minority Children Using the *DSM-IV-TR*"
Chapter 18, "*DSM-IV-TR* Classification System"

20 ASSESSMENT OF CHARACTER STRENGTHS

Christopher Peterson, Nansook Park, & Martin E. P. Seligman

The new field of positive psychology calls for as much focus on strength as on weakness, as much interest in building the best things in life as in repairing the worst, and as much concern with fulfilling the lives of healthy people as healing the wounds of the distressed (Seligman & Csikszentmihalyi, 2000). The past concern of psychology with human problems is, of course, understandable and will not be abandoned anytime in the foreseeable future, but psychologists interested in promoting human potential need to pose different questions from their predecessors who assumed a disease model. Critical tools for positive psychologists include a vocabulary for speaking about the good life and assessment strategies for investigating its components.

For the past several years, we have focused our attention on positive traits—strengths of character such as curiosity, kindness, and hope. What are the most important of these, and how can they be measured as individual differences? Our project—the VIA (Values in Action) Classification of Strengths—means to complete what the *Diagnostic and Statistical Manual* (*DSM*) of the American Psychiatric Association (1987) has begun by focusing on what is right about people and specifically about the strengths of character that make the good life possible (Peterson & Seligman, 2004).

Two points frame our discussion of the VIA Classification. First, we are not the first psychologists to grapple with character strengths and how to assess them. We refer the reader to Jahoda's (1958) prescient treatise on positive mental health, which made the case for understanding psychological well-being in its own right, not simply as the absence of disorder or distress. We also refer the reader to other attempts to measure character strengths with self-report inventories: for example, Greenberger, Josselson, Knerr, and Knerr's (1975) measures of psychosocial maturity; Ryff and Singer's (1996) dimensions of psychological well-being; and Cawley, Martin, and Johnson's (2000) virtues approach to personality assessment.

Second, we believe that attention to character strengths is as productive for clinical psychologists interested in troubled individuals as it is for positive psychologists interested in the untroubled (Seligman & Peterson, 2003). There are hints in the research literature that certain strengths of character—for example, hope, love, and perspective—can buffer the deleterious effects of stress and trauma, containing or precluding disorders in their wake. And even if disorder occurs, character strengths often coexist with symptoms of disorder and provide a sturdy foundation on which to base interventions (cf. social work from a strengths perspective; Saleebey, 1992). Furthermore, our own research suggests that individuals who recover from psychological or physical problems may in the process forge certain character strengths such as appreciation of beauty or gratitude. Highlighting these as possible outcomes of successful therapy might destigmatize the seeking of treatment and sustain client motivation. Finally, we call on clinical psychologists not only to treat disorder but also to help a client "deal with it" in the course of treatment. Emphasizing to individuals that they have strengths of character in addition to symptoms might lead them to keep on with their lives, regardless of the outcome of therapy. We find the examples of Abraham Lincoln and Winston Churchill instructive in this regard—profoundly depressed men and great leaders. How would they (and the world) have fared in the contemporary mental health system?

THE VIA CLASSIFICATION

There are various ways to approach character. A *DSM*-like approach would talk about it as unitary and categorical—one either has character or not. Or one could think about character in terms of underlying processes like autonomy or reality orientation. One might wed it to an a priori theory. One could view character as only a social construction, revealing of the observer's values but not of who or what is observed. But in all of these respects, the VIA Classification has taken a different approach. Its stance is in the spirit of personality psychology, and specifically modern trait theory, recognizing individual differences that are stable and general but also shaped by the individual's setting and thus capable of change.

The initial step in our project was to unpack the notion of character—to start with the assumption that character is plural—and we did so by specifying the separate strengths and virtues, then devising ways to assess these as individual differences. We recognize the components of good character as existing at different levels of abstraction. Virtues are the core characteristics valued by moral philosophers and religious thinkers: wisdom, courage, humanity, justice, temperance, and transcendence. These six broad categories of virtue emerge consistently from historical surveys. We speculate that these are universal, perhaps grounded in biology through an evolutionary process that selected for these predispositions toward moral excellence as means of solving the important tasks necessary for survival of the species.

Character strengths are the psychological ingredients—processes or mechanisms—that define the virtues. Said another way, they are distinguishable routes to displaying one or another of the virtues. For example, the virtue of wisdom can be achieved through such strengths as curiosity, love of learning, open-mindedness, creativity, and what we call perspective—having a "big picture" on life. These strengths are similar in that they all involve the acquisition and use of knowledge, but they are also distinct. Again, we regard these strengths as ubiquitously recognized and valued, although a given individual will rarely if ever display all of them.

We generated the entries for the VIA Classification by reviewing pertinent literatures that addressed good character—from psychiatry, youth development, character education, religion, ethics, philosophy, organizational studies, and psychology. From the many candidate strengths identified, we winnowed the list by combining redundancies and applying the criteria in Table 1. (This table and all others cited in this chapter may be found not only here, but also on the accompanying Web site.) What resulted were 24 positive traits organized under the six broad virtues (see Table 2).

ASSESSING THE VIA STRENGTHS

What distinguishes the VIA Classification from many previous attempts to articulate

TABLE 1. Criteria for the VIA Classification Character Strengths

1. *A strength needs to be manifest in the range of an individual's behavior—thoughts, feelings, and/or actions—in such a way that it can be assessed.*
2. *A strength contributes to various fulfillments that comprise the good life, for the self and for others.* Although strengths and virtues determine how an individual copes with adversity, our focus is on how they fulfill an individual. In keeping with the broad premise of positive psychology, strengths allow the individual to achieve more than the absence of distress and disorder. They "break through the zero point" of psychology's traditional concern with disease, disorder, and failure to address quality of life outcomes.
3. *Although strengths can and do produce desirable outcomes, each strength is morally valued in its own right, even in the absence of obvious beneficial outcomes.* To say that a strength is morally valued is an important qualification, because there exist individual differences that are widely valued and contribute to fulfillment but still fall outside of our classification. Consider intelligence or athletic prowess. Talents and abilities can be squandered, but strengths and virtues cannot.
4. *The display of a strength by one person does not diminish other people in the vicinity but rather elevates them.* Onlookers are impressed, inspired, and encouraged by their observation of virtuous action.
5. *The larger society provides institutions and associated rituals for cultivating strengths and virtues.* These can be thought of as simulations: trial runs that allow children and adolescents to display and develop a valued characteristic in a safe (as-if) context in which guidance is explicit.
6. *Yet another criterion for a character strength is the existence of consensually recognized paragons of virtue.*
7. *A final criterion is that the strength is arguably unidimensional and not able to be decomposed into other strengths in the classification.* For example, the character strength of "tolerance" meets most of the other criteria enumerated but is a complex blend of open-mindedness and fairness. The character strength of "responsibility" seems to result from perseverance and teamwork. And so on.

good character is its simultaneous concern with assessment. Sophisticated social scientists sometimes respond with suspicion when they hear our goal, reminding us of the pitfalls of self-report and the validity threat posed by "social desirability" (Crowne & Marlowe, 1964). We do not dismiss these considerations out of hand, but their premise is worth examining. We seem to be quite willing, as researchers and practitioners, to trust what individuals say about their problems. With notable exceptions, like substance abuse and eating disorders, the preferred way to measure psychological disorder relies on self-report, in the form of either symptom questionnaires or structured interviews. So why not ascertain wellness in the same way?

Suppose that people really do possess moral virtues. Most philosophers emphasize that virtuous activity involves choosing virtue in light of a justifiable life plan (Yearley, 1990). In more psychological language, this characterization means that people can reflect on their own virtues and talk about them to others. They may, of course, be misled and/or misleading, but virtues are not the sort of entities that in principle are outside the realm of self-commentary. Furthermore, character strengths are not "contaminated" by a response set of social desirability; they are socially desirable, especially when reported with fidelity.

We mention again the previous research that measured character strengths with self-report questionnaire batteries. In no case did a single methods factor order the data. Rather, different clusters of strengths always emerged. External correlates were sensible. These conclusions converge with what we have learned to date from our own attempts to measure the VIA strengths among young people and adults with self-report questionnaires.

We have developed two general strategies for assessing character strengths: self-report inventories and structured interviews. Thumbnail sketches are found in Table 3 and details in Peterson and Seligman (2004).

Our measure development is ongoing, but we can offer some general observations. First, given our interest in identifying ubiquitous strengths of character, not all possible strengths of interest to a psychologist are assessed by our measures. If there is a reason to ascertain a client's achievement or autonomy, then the psychologist should ask about such strengths.

Second, our interest as researchers has been

TABLE 2. VIA Classification of Character Strengths

1. *Wisdom and knowledge—cognitive strengths that entail the acquisition and use of knowledge*

Creativity: Thinking of novel and productive ways to do things; includes artistic achievement but is not limited to it

Curiosity: Taking an interest in all of ongoing experience; finding all subjects and topics fascinating; exploring and discovering

Judgment/critical thinking: Thinking things through and examinng them from all sides; *not* jumping to conclusions; being able to change one's mind in light of evidence; weighing all evidence fairly

Love of learning: Mastering new skills, topics, and bodies of knowledge, whether on one's own or formally. Obviously related to the strength of curiosity but goes beyond it to describe the tendency to add *systematically* to what one knows

Perspective: Being able to provide wise counsel to others; having ways of looking at the world that make sense to the self and to other people

2. *Courage—emotional strengths that involve the exercise of will to accomplish goals in the face of opposition, external or internal*

Bravery: *Not* shrinking from threat, challenge, difficulty, or pain; speaking up for what is right even if there is opposition; acting on convictions even if unpopular; includes physical bravery but is not limited to it

Industry/perseverance: Finishing what one starts; persisting in a course of action in spite of obstacles; "getting it out the door"; taking pleasure in completing tasks

Authenticity: Speaking the truth but more broadly presenting oneself in a genuine way; being without pretense; taking responsibility for one's feelings and actions

Zest: Approaching life with excitement and energy; *not* doing things halfway or halfheartedly; living life as an adventure; feeling alive and activated

3. *Humanity—interpersonal strengths that involve "tending" and "befriending" others*

Kindness: Doing favors and good deeds for others; helping them; taking care of them

Love/intimacy: Valuing close relationships with others, in particular those in which sharing and caring are reciprocated; being close to people

Social intelligence: Being aware of the motives and feelings of other people and the self; knowing what to do to fit in to different social situations; knowing what makes other people tick

4. *Justice—civic strengths that underlie healthy community life*

Citizenship/teamwork: Working well as a member of a group or team; being loyal to the group; doing one's share

Fairness: Treating all people the same according to notions of fairness and justice; *not* letting personal feelings bias decisions about others; giving everyone a fair chance

Leadership: Encouraging a group of which one is a member to get things done and at the same time good relations within the group; organizing group activities and seeing that they happen

5. *Temperance—strengths that protect against excess*

Forgiveness/mercy: Forgiving those who have done wrong; giving people a second chance; *not* being vengeful

Modesty/humility: Letting one's accomplishments speak for themselves; *not* seeking the spotlight; *not* regarding one's self as more special than one is

Prudence: Being careful about one's choices; *not* taking undue risks; *not* saying or doing things that might later be regretted

Self-control/self-regulation: Regulating what one feels and does; being disciplined; controlling one's appetites and emotions

6. *Transcendence—strengths that forge connections to the larger universe and provide meaning*

Awe/appreciation of beauty and excellence: Noticing and appreciating beauty, excellence, and/or skilled performance in all domains of life, from nature to art to mathematics to science to everyday experience

Gratitude: Being aware of and thankful for the good things that happen; taking time to express thanks

Hope: Expecting the best in the future and working to achieve it; believing that a good future is something that can be brought about

Playfulness: Liking to laugh and tease; bringing smiles to other people; seeing the light side; making (not necessarily telling) jokes

Spirituality: Having coherent beliefs about the higher purpose and meaning of the universe; knowing where one fits within the larger scheme; having beliefs about the meaning of life that shape conduct and provide comfort

TABLE 3. VIA Strengths Assessment Strategies

The 240-item *VIA Inventory of Strengths (VIA-IS)* is intended for use by adults. It is a face-valid self-report questionnaire that uses 5-point Likert-style items to measure the degree to which respondents endorse each of the strengths of character in the VIA Classification. It takes 30 minutes to complete. All scales have satisfactory alphas (>.70) and substantial test-retest correlations (>.70). The VIA-IS has been validated against self- and other-nomination of character strengths and correlates with measures of subjective well-being and happiness.

The 182-item *VIA Inventory of Strength for Youth (VIA-Youth)* is intended for use by young people (ages 10–17). It is a face-valid self-report questionnaire that uses 5-point Likert-style items to measure the degree to which respondents endorse each of the 24 strengths of character in the VIA Classification. It takes 45 minutes to complete. All scales have satisfactory alphas (>.70). The VIA-Youth has been validated against self- and other-nomination of character strengths and correlates with measures of subjective well-being, happiness, and school grades.

The 9-item *VIA-Rising-to-the-Occasion Iventory (VIA-RTO)* is intended to measure the character strengths in the VIA Classification that are arguably *phasic* (rising and falling depending on specifiable circumstances—e.g., the experience of fear for the display of bravery; the occurrence of wrongdoing for the display of forgiveness) as opposed to *tonic* (showing themselves steadily in most situations—e.g., kindness, zest, playfulness). It takes less than 10 minutes to complete and has been used to date only with adults. Respondents are asked how frequently they have found themselves in a strength-relevant setting and then to answer an open-ended question about how they typically respond in that setting; the question spelled out the essence of the strength without explicitly labeling it. These responses are not analyzed but are intended to discourage answers off the top of one's head to the next question, which explicitly asks the respondent to use a 5-point Likert-style scale to describe the degree to which these situated responses reflect the strength of character on focus. VIA-RTO responses converge strongly (all *r*s between 40 and .60) with other-nominations of character strengths (so long as the informant has had the opportunity to observe the individual in the strength-relevant setting).

The *VIA Structured Interview (VIA-SI)* adopts the logic and format of the VIA-RTO to an individual interview format. It takes about 25 minutes to complete and has been used to date only with adults. The interviewer asks respondents how they "usually" act in a given setting vis-à-vis the character strength on focus—in the case of phasic strengths, the setting is detailed, and in the case of tonic strengths, it is presented as "everyday life." If people describe displaying the strength the majority of the time, follow-up questions ask: (i) how they "name" the strength; (ii) if the strength however named is "really" who they are; and (iii) whether friends and family members would agree that the strength is "really" who they are. To count as an individual's signature strength, it must be displayed the majority of the time in relevant settings, be named as the intended strength (or a synonym) as opposed to another strength, be "owned" by the individual, and be recognized by others as highly characteristic of the individual. Our studies to date show that adults usually have between two and five signature strengths.

comparing and contrasting VIA scores across individuals, but we believe that these measures also have utility—theoretical and practical—when scored ipsatively and used to judge an individual's strengths in relation to one another. We have speculated that most individuals have "signature strengths," the use of which at work, love, and play provide a route to the psychologically fulfilling life (Seligman, 2002). The effects of naming these strengths for an individual and encouraging their use deserve study.

Third, our adult inventory (the VIA-IS) is available online at no cost to respondents; it takes 30 minutes to complete and provides immediate feedback about an individual's signature strengths. These can be printed out or written down and should provide ample grist for the psychotherapeutic mill.

Note: We acknowledge the encouragement and support of the Manuel D. and Rhoda Mayerson Foundation in creating the Values in Action Institute, a nonprofit organization dedicated to the development of a scientific knowledge base of human strengths.

References, Readings, & Internet Sites 

American Psychiatric Association. (1987). *Diagnostic and statistical manual of mental disorders* (3rd ed., rev.). Washington, DC: Author.

Authentic Happiness. (n.d.). Home page (contains links to the VIA-IS and other positive psychology measures; requires registration). Retrieved 2004 from www.authentichappiness.org

Cawley, M. J., Martin, J. E., & Johnson, J. A. (2000). A virtues approach to personality. *Personality and Individual Differences, 28,* 997–1013.

Crowne, D. P., & Marlowe, D. (1964). *The approval motive: Studies in evaluative dependence.* New York: Wiley.

Greenberger, E., Josselson, R., Knerr, C., & Knerr, B. (1975). The measurement and structure of psychosocial maturity. *Journal of Youth and Adolescence, 4,* 127–143.

Jahoda, M. (1958). *Current concepts of positive mental health.* New York: Basic Books.

Peterson, C., & Seligman, M. E. P. (2004). *The Values in Action (VIA) classification of strengths.* Washington, DC: American Psychological Association.

Positive Psychology Center. (n.d.). Home page (contains links to information about the VIA Classification). Retrieved 2004 from www.positive psychology.org.

Ryff, C. D., & Singer, B. (1996). Psychological wellbeing: Meaning, measurement, and implications for psychotherapy research. *Psychotherapy and Psychosomatics, 65,* 14–23.

Saleebey, D. (Ed.). (1992). *The strengths perspective in social work practice.* New York: Longman.

Seligman, M. E. P. (2002). *Authentic happiness.* New York: Free Press.

Seligman, M. E. P., & Csikszentmihalyi, M. (2000). Positive psychology: An introduction. *American Psychologist, 55,* 5–14.

Seligman, M. E. P., & Peterson, C. (2003). Positive clinical psychology. In L. G. Aspinwall & U. M. Staudinger (Eds.), *A psychology of human strengths: Fundamental questions and future directions for a positive psychology* (pp. 305–317). Washington, DC: American Psychological Association.

Yearley, L. H. (1990). *Mencius and Aquinas: Theories of virtue and conceptions of courage.* Albany, NY: State University of New York Press.

Related Topic

Chapter 5, "Increasing the Accuracy of Clinical Judgment (and Thereby Treatment Effectiveness)"

PART II
Psychological Testing

21 50 WIDELY USED PSYCHOLOGICAL TESTS

Thomas P. Hogan

Table 1 lists 50 of the most widely used psychological tests. The table shows ranked usage of the tests for five groups of psychologists as reported in several different studies.

TABLE 1. 50 Widely Used Psychological Tests With Usage Rankings for Five Groups of Psychologists

	Psychologists				
Test	Clinical	Counseling	Forensic	Neuro	School
Aphasia Screening Test	23	—	27	17	—
Beck Depression Inventory	10	—	13	11	—
Bender Visual Motor Gestalt Test	5	8	7	25	8.5
Benton Revised Visual Retention Test	52	—	42	32	—
Boston Naming Test	42	—	18	8	—
California Verbal Learning Test	36	—	29	14	—
Category Test	31	—	8	9	—
Child Behavior Checklist	22	—	—	43	10
Children's Apperception Test	16	—	—	60	—
Conners' Parent and Teacher Rating Scales	18	—	—	39	13
Development Test of Visual-Motor Integration	31	—	—	49	5
FAS Word Fluency Test	37	—	—	5	—
Finger Tapping Test	29	—	6[a]	6	—
Grooved Pegboard Test	44	—	15	15	—
Halstead-Reitan Neuropsychological Test Battery	23	—	—[b]	7	—
Hand Dynamometer (Grip Strength)	44	—	20	20	—
Hooper Visual Organization Test	59	—	19	19	—
House-Tree-Person Projective Technique	8	11	—	31	4

(continued)

TABLE 1. 50 Widely Used Psychological Tests With Usage Rankings for Five Groups of Psychologists (*continued*)

Test	Psychologists				
	Clinical	Counseling	Forensic	Neuro	School
Human Figure Drawings	13	—	26	41	4.5
Kaufman Assessment Battery for Children	33	—	—	53	15.5
Kinetic Family Drawing	25	—	—	62	6
Luria-Nebraska Neuropsychological Battery	40	—	33	37	—
Memory Assessment Scales	44	—	—	45	—
Millon Adolescent Clinical Inventory	16	—	—	56	—
Millon Clinical Multiaxial Inventory	10	11	34	24	—
Minnesota Multiphasic Personality Inventory	2	1	2	1	—
Peabody Individual Achievement Test	52	—	—	45	4
Peabody Picture Vocabulary Test	20	—	—	28	10
Rey Complex Figure Test	25	—	21	12	—
Roberts Apperception Test for Children	25	—	—	63	—
Rorschach Inkblot Test	4	12	23	18	—
Rotter Incomplete Sentences Blank	14	—	—	51	—
Sentence Completion Test(s)	15	5	10	42	—
Shipley Institute of Living Test	48	—	—	39	—
Sixteen Personality Factor Questionnaire	38	7	—	64	—
Stanford-Binet Intelligence Scale	29	—	—	53	14
Strong Interest Inventory	38	1.5	—	72	—
Stroop Neuropsychological Screening Test	33	—	22	22	—
Symptom Checklist-90-R	44	—	44	49	—
Tactile Performance Test	78	—	11[c]	33	—
Test of Visual Motor Integration	25	—	—	35	—
Thematic Apperception Test	6	6	39	26	11
Trail Making Test	12	—	4[d]	4	—
Vineland Adaptive Behavior Scales	18	—	—	44	8.5
Wechsler Adult Intelligence Scale	1	3	1	2	4.5
Wechsler Intelligence Scale for Children	3	5	—	16	1
Wechsler Memory Scale	9	—	3	3	—
Wide Range Achievement Test	7	8.5	12	9	5.5
Wisconsin Card Sorting Test	33	—	9	12	—
Woodcock-Johnson Test[e]	21	—	—	38	7

[a]Includes finger oscillation.
[b]Halstead-Reitan was not listed in original source, but the source included several components of the Halstead-Reitan as separate entries.
[c]Listed as Tactual Performance Test.
[d]Trails A and B reported separately in original source, with ranks of 4 and 5.
[e]Includes Woodcock-Johnson Psychoeducational Battery as well as the more recent WJ Test of Cognitive Abilities and Test of Achievement.

Constructing a single list of widely used tests and rankings for psychologists is a daunting, even risky challenge. At a surface level, the numerous surveys of test usage are highly similar. Most surveys present a laundry list of better-known tests for the respondent to check with space for write-in candidates. Most surveys cover all major categories of tests—for example, intelligence, objective personality, projectives, and so on. However, lurking beneath the surface similarities are substantial methodological differences militating against direct comparisons among the surveys. For example, one survey may lump together all the "Wechsler scales" while other surveys list the WAIS, WISC, and WPPSI separately. Some surveys treat the Bender-Gestalt as a projective test, while others treat it as a visual-motor test. Some surveys list "interviews" and "observations" as tests; others do not. Some surveys simply require checking whether a test is used, while others request a rating of uses per month.

For all of these and related reasons, it is difficult to construct a single list with multiple rankings. Nevertheless, we have done so. We encourage readers to consult the original sources for methodological details.

Sources for the rankings were limited to relatively recent reports. Data for clinical psychologists came from a survey by Camara, Nathan, and Puente (1998), who collected self-reports of the frequency of test usage from 933 clinical psychologists (62% response rate) in independent practice, specializing in mental health services. Data for neuropsychologists also came from Camara et al. (1998), specifically from 566 neuropsychologists (47% response rate) who were members of the National Association of Neuropsychologists.

Camara et al. (1998) served as the base for the tests listed in Table 1 because they provided the most extensive list of tests. We retained in the list all tests appearing with higher ranks for at least three groups, and eliminated the two lowest ranking remaining tests to bring the list to exactly 50. As a result, a few tests that were highly ranked in the other sources but were not captured in the original pool of tests from Camara et al. (1998) do not appear in Table 1. A few of these special cases of exclusion are noted below in connection with specific sources for their respective subgroups.

Rankings for counseling psychologists came from a combination of three reports. Bubenzer, Zimpfer, and Mahrle (1990) listed the 18 most frequent tests in responses from 743 (response rate 50%) members of the American Association of Counseling and Development (since renamed American Counseling Association). Frauenhofer, Ross, Gfeller, Searight, and Piotrowski (1998) provided ranks for 14 tests used by 166 professional counselors drawn from licensing directories in four states. Watkins, Campbell, and McGregor (1988) identified the 10 most frequently used tests for a sample of 630 (63% response rate) members of the APA Division of Counseling Psychology. To prepare the counseling column in Table 1, we determined the average rank for test usage from these three studies provided that a test appeared in at least two of them. Other tests highly ranked only among counseling psychologists but not listed in Table 1 were several career interest surveys and objective personality tests.

For the forensic column in Table 1, we used the results of Lees-Haley, Smith, Williams, and Dunn (1995). They employed a methodology quite different from the self-reports used in other studies summarized here. They identified tests actually used in a sample of 100 forensic cases in litigation for personal injury. Other tests highly ranked only for forensic usage but not listed in Table 1 were additional sensory and perceptual tests.

Data for school psychologists came from two sources. First, Hutton, Dubes, and Muir (1992) obtained responses from a random sample of 389 (39% response rate) members of the National Association of School Psychologists. We took their percent usage data, thus allowing development of a single ranking across the nine reporting categories in their study. When constructing the single set of rankings for Hutton et al., we excluded group-administered achievement tests (e.g., Stanford Achievement Test), three of which were among the most widely used tests in this source. Second, Wilson and Reschly (1996) used a random sample of 251 (80% response rate) members of the National Association of School Psychologists. Like Hutton et al., they ranked tests within broad categories. We used their mean ratings of usage per to construct a single ranking across categories. We combined the rankings from the two studies, showing in Table 1 the average ranking regardless of whether the rank appeared in just one or in both studies. Other tests highly ranked only among school psychologists but not listed in Table 1 were several behavior rating inventories.

Although most studies of test usage employ a self-report methodology, there are alternative methods for defining frequency of test usage. In *Tests in Print V* (*TIP V*), Murphy, Impara, and Plake (1999) provided a good example of an alternative approach. They gave a citation count for published references to tests appearing in the *Thirteenth Mental Measurements Yearbook*.

Information for all of the tests in Table 1

may be obtained from the Educational Testing Service (2003) Test Collection Web site.

Finally, we should note that in terms of total test usage, the widely used group administered tests (achievement batteries and mental ability tests) far exceed the usage for tests in Table 1. Although psychologists frequently receive and interpret information from these tests, psychologists rarely, if ever, administer them directly. Hence, we have not included them in the table.

References, Readings, & Internet Sites

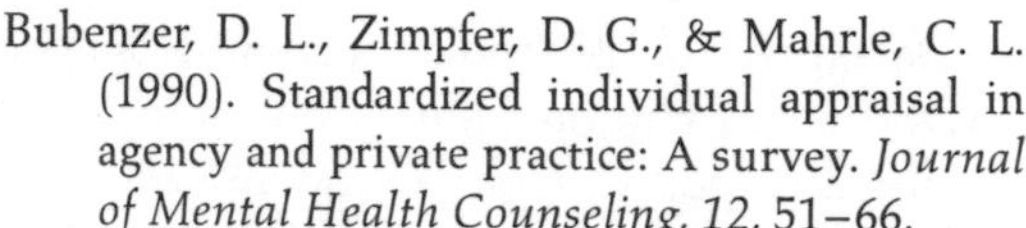

Bubenzer, D. L., Zimpfer, D. G., & Mahrle, C. L. (1990). Standardized individual appraisal in agency and private practice: A survey. *Journal of Mental Health Counseling, 12,* 51–66.

Camara, W., Nathan, J., & Puente, A. (1998). *Psychological test usage in professional psychology: Report to the APA practice and science directorates.* Washington, DC: American Psychological Association.

Camara, W., Nathan, J., & Puente, A. (2000). Psychological test usage: Implications for professional practice. *Professional Psychology: Research and Practice, 31,* 141–154.

Cashel, M. L. (2002). Child and adolescent psychological assessment: Current clinical practices and the impact of managed care. *Professional Psychology: Research and Practice, 33,* 446–453.

Educational Testing Service. (2003). Test collection. Retrieved February 11, 2003, from http://www.ets.org/testcoll/

Frauenhoffer, D., Ross, M. J., Gfeller, J., Searight, H. R., & Piotrowski, C. (1998). Psychological test usage among licensed mental health practitioners: A multidisciplinary survey. *Journal of Psychological Practice, 4,* 28–33.

Hutton, J. B., Dubes, R., & Muir, S. (1992). Assessment practices of school psychologists: Ten years later. *School Psychology Review, 21,* 271–284.

Lees-Haley, P. R., Smith, H. H., Williams, C. W., & Dunn, J. T. (1995). Forensic neuropsychological test usage: An empirical study. *Archives of Clinical Neuropsychology, 11,* 45–51.

Murphy, L. L., Impara, J. C., & Plake, B. S. (1999). *Tests in Print V.* Lincoln: University of Nebraska.

Murphy, L. L., Plake, B. S., Impara, J. C., & Spies, R. A. (2002). *Tests in Print VI.* Lincoln: University of Nebraska.

Piotrowski, C. (1999). Assessment practices in the era of managed care: Current status and future directions. *Journal of Clinical Psychology, 55,* 787–796.

Watkins, C. E., Campbell, V. L., & McGregor, P. (1988). Counseling psychologists' uses of and opinions about psychological tests: A contemporary perspective. *The Counseling Psychologist, 16,* 476–486.

Wilson, M. S., & Reschly, D. J. (1996). Assessment in school psychology training and practice. *School Psychology Review, 25,* 9–23.

Related Topics

Chapter 22, "Sources of Information About Psychological Tests"

Chapter 23, "Publishers of Psychological and Psychoeducational Tests"

22 SOURCES OF INFORMATION ABOUT PSYCHOLOGICAL TESTS

Thomas P. Hogan

Tests are essential in the work of many psychologists. New tests and revisions of older tests now appear at an astonishing rate. It is impossible to be familiar with all of them or even a significant fraction of them. Hence, it is important to be competent in acquiring information about the many tests that one may encounter. We present here an overview of six major sources of information about psychological and psychoeducational tests.

ELECTRONIC LISTINGS

Here are three exceptionally useful tools for obtaining information about tests through the World Wide Web:

1. ETS Test Collection at www.ets.org/testcoll
2. Buros Institute at www.unl.edu/buros
3. ERIC/AE Test Locator at www.ericae.net

The Educational Testing Service (ETS) Test Collection contains information on over 20,000 tests. The source provides descriptive information about a test, such as author, publisher, scores, and number of items. The database can be searched by test title, author, or keyword descriptor (e.g., "anxiety"). The Buros site, home for the Buros Institute of Mental Measurements, provides searches for test publishers, test reviews, and several other sources of information. Some reviews can be downloaded directly from the site for a fee. The ERIC/AE site previously provided a service similar to the ETS Test Collection site, but now simply cross-links to the ETS site. The ERIC/AE site also provides a Test Review Locator, identifying reviews available in *Test Critiques* and the *Mental Measurements Yearbooks* (both described below).

SYSTEMATIC REVIEWS

Two published sources provide professional reviews of tests: the *Mental Measurements Yearbooks* and *Test Critiques*. Both limit themselves to commercially available tests published in English. Both are updated every few years, providing reviews of new or revised tests. These two sources are the only ones that give thorough, professional reviews of a wide variety of tests.

The *Fifteenth Mental Measurements Yearbook* (Plake, Impara, & Spies, 2003) is the most recent in the classic series of reviews sometimes referred to as *MMY*, or "Buros," after Oscar K. Buros, who compiled and published the first volume in 1938. The *MMY* series is now prepared by the Buros Institute of Mental Measurements (Buros Institute of Mental Measurements, University of Nebraska–Lincoln, 21 Teachers College Hall, Lincoln, NE 68588-0348; 402-472-6203) and published by the University of Nebraska Press. Historically, new editions of *MMY* appeared every three to five years, but new editions are now projected to appear every 18 to 20 months, thus precluding the need for the inter-edition supplements. Each new yearbook contains references to reviews in earlier yearbooks.

Subsets of *MMY* reviews have been published as separate volumes from time to time. These publications, for tests in such categories as intelligence, personality, and reading, contain nothing more than what is available in the main *MMY* volumes and in the *TIP* series (see below). *MMY* reviews for the most recent volumes are also available on CD-ROM from SilverPlatter (SilverPlatter Information, 100 Ridge Drive, Norwood, MA 02062-5043; 718-769-2599 or 800-343-0064); this source is available online in many academic libraries. As noted earlier, individual reviews may be downloaded (for a fee) from the Buros Web site.

The second source of systematic reviews is *Test Critiques* (*TC*; Keyser, 2004). This series is now available in 11 volumes, the first having been issued in 1984. Each volume of *TC* covers about 100 tests. In comparison with *MMY*, *TC* limits itself to more widely used tests and the reviews are somewhat longer, although covering the same basic points. Like *MMY*, each new *TC* volume contains a systematic listing of reviews contained in earlier volumes. *Test Critiques* is published by Pro-Ed (8700 Shoal Creek Boulevard, Austin, TX, 78757-6897; 800-897-3202).

COMPREHENSIVE LISTINGS

Several sources give comprehensive, hard-copy listings of tests. Generally, these sources provide basic information about the tests (e.g., target ages, publishers, types of scores) but refrain from giving evaluative comments. These sources are most helpful for two purposes. First, if one needs to know what tests are available for a particular purpose, these listings will provide an initial pool of possibilities for more detailed review. Second, if one knows the name of a test but nothing else about it, information in these listings will provide a brief description of the test and its source. Currently, there is much overlap between these comprehensive listings in hard copy and the electronic lists described earlier.

The venerable series known as *Tests in Print* is now in its sixth edition: *Tests in Print-VI* (Murphy, Plake, Impara, & Spies, 2002). Usually referred to as *TIP-VI*, the current edition contains entries for several thousand tests. *TIP* attempts to include all tests that are commercially available in English. Earlier editions appeared in 1961, 1974, 1983, and 1999. The Buros Institute (see above for contact information) prepares *TIP*.

Tests: A Comprehensive Reference for Assessments in Psychology, Education, and Business, 5th edition (Maddox, 2003), is a continuing series, first appearing in 1983, by the same publisher as *Test Critiques*. This source presents, for the three areas identified in the title, lists of tests from 219 publishers. Each entry includes the age/grade range for the test, purpose, format and timing, type of scoring, publisher, cost, and a brief description of the test structure and content. (See *Test Critiques* above for contact information.)

The ETS Test Collection referenced earlier under Electronic Listings also provides *Tests in Microfiche*, a microfiche collection of unpublished instruments and *Test Bibliographies* on selected topics. For further information on all these derivatives consult www.ets.org/testcoll, e-mail Library@ets.org, or phone 609-734-5689.

The *Directory of Unpublished Experimental Mental Measures* (Goldman & Mitchell, 2003) is a multivolume effort published by the American Psychological Association. As suggested by the title, the work concentrates exclusively on tests that are not available from regular publishers but appear in journal articles. The volumes include information (name, purpose, source, format, timing, etc.) for over 1,000 tests in a wide variety of areas.

SPECIAL-PURPOSE COLLECTIONS

Several books provide collections of tests and/or test reviews within a relatively narrow band of interest. The following list is illustrative of the books in this category. Fischer and Corcoran (1994) provide a collection of simple, paper-and-pencil measures of clinically relevant constructs. There are two volumes, one concentrating on measures for families, children, and couples; the other on measures for adults. Robinson, Shaver, and Wrightsman (1991) provide an excellent collection of more than 100 measures of attitudes, broadly conceived to include such areas as self-concept, locus of control, values, and life satisfaction. The work includes both published and unpublished measures; for unpublished measures, generally the entire test is included in the entry. Shaw and Wright (1967) is another excellent, albeit dated collection of attitudinal measures, mostly of the unpublished variety in such areas as social institutions, significant others, and social practices. Byrne (1996) provides a collection of self-concept measures organized by age level. All of these references provide basic descriptive information about the measures included, plus at least some evaluative commentary on matters such as reliability and validity.

Health and Psychosocial Instruments (HaPI) is a database of instruments produced by Behavioral Measurement Database Services, PO Box 110287, Pittsburgh, PA 15232-0787, 412-687-6850. HaPI is available on CD-ROM.

PUBLISHERS' CATALOGS

All the major test publishers produce catalogs listing their products. The publisher's catalog is the best source of information about the most recent editions of a test, including variations such as large-print editions, foreign language versions; costs of materials and scoring; types of scoring services; and ancillary materials. Publishers typically issue catalogs annually or semi-annually. Publishers' representatives, either in the field or in the home office, are also an important source of information, especially about new products and services. A call to a publisher's representative can often save hours of searching for information about a price or scoring service. For contact information for major test publishers, see chapter 23. Contact information is also available in the Test Locator service described above.

OTHER TEST USERS

Finally, a valuable but often overlooked source of information about tests is other users of tests. Experienced colleagues can be especially helpful in identifying the tests widely used in a particular field and the peculiarities of certain tests. In effect, colleagues can provide brief, informal versions of the lengthier reviews one would find in the formal sources cited in this article.

References, Readings, & Internet Sites 

Buros Institute of Mental Measurements. (2003). Center for Testing home page. Retrieved January 6, 2003, from http://www.unl.edu/buros/

Byrne, B. M. (1996). *Measuring self-concepts across the lifespan.* Washington, DC: American Psychological Association.

Educational Testing Service. (2003). Test collection. Retrieved January 6, 2003, from http://www.ets.org/testcoll/

ERIC Clearinghouse on Assessment and Evaluation. (2003). Home page. Retrieved January 6, 2003, from http://ERICAE.net/

Fischer, J., & Corcoran, K. (1994). *Measures for clinical practice: A sourcebook* (2nd ed., Vols. 1–2). New York: Free Press.

Goldman, B. A., & Mitchell, D. F. (2003). *Directory of unpublished experimental mental measures* (Vol. 8). Washington, DC: American Psychological Association.

Keyser, D. J. (Ed.). (2004). *Test critiques* (Vol. 11). Austin, TX: Pro-Ed.

Maddox, T. (2003). *Tests: A comprehensive reference for assessments in psychology, education, and business* (5th ed.). Austin, TX: Pro-Ed.

Murphy, L. L., Plake, B. S., Impara, J. C., & Spies, R. A. (Eds.). (2002). *Tests in Print VI.* Lincoln: University of Nebraska Press.

Plake, B. S., Impara, J. C., & Spies, R. A. (Eds.). (2003). *The fifteenth mental measurements yearbook.* Lincoln: University of Nebraska Press.

Robinson, J. P., Shaver, P. R., & Wrightsman, L. S. (Eds.). (1991). *Measures of personality and social psychological attitudes.* San Diego, CA: Academic Press.

Shaw, M. E., & Wright, J. M. (1967). *Scales for the measurement of attitudes.* New York: McGraw-Hill.

Related Topics

Chapter 21, "50 Widely Used Psychological Tests"
Chapter 23, "Publishers of Psychological and Psychoeducational Tests"

23 PUBLISHERS OF PSYCHOLOGICAL AND PSYCHOEDUCATIONAL TESTS

Thomas P. Hogan

The following is a list of major test publishers in the United States and some of their popular tests. For more complete lists of test publishers or to determine the publisher of a specific test, use one of these Web sites:

- ETS Test Collection at www.ets.org/testcoll
- Buros Institute at www.unl.edu/buros
- ERIC/AE Test Locator at www.ericae.net/testcoll.htm

American College Testing Program (ACT)
PO Box 168
2201 North Dodge Street
Iowa City, IA 52243-0168
Phone: 800-645-1992
www.act.org
Publishes the ACT Assessment, Career Planning Survey, EXPLORE, and PLAN

American Guidance Service
4201 Woodland Road
Circle Pines, MN 55014-1796
Phone: 800-328-2560
www.ags.net
Publishes the Behavior Assessment System for Children (BASC), Kaufman Assessment Battery for Children (K-ABC), several other Kaufman tests, Peabody Individual Achievement Test (PIAT), Peabody Picture Vocabulary Test (PPVT), Vineland Adaptive Behavior Scales, and Woodcock Reading Mastery Tests

Association of State and Provincial Psychology Boards (formerly American Association of State Psychology Boards)
7177 Halcyon Summit Drive
Montgomery, AL 36117
Phone: 800-448-4069
www.asppb.org
Publishes the Examination for Professional Practice in Psychology

The College Board
45 Columbus Avenue
New York, NY 10023-6992
Phone: 212-713-8000
www.collegeboard.com
Publishes the Graduate Record Examination, SAT I and II, Test of English as a Second Language (some tests are sponsored jointly with Educational Testing Service)

Consulting Psychologists Press
3803 East Bayshore Road
Palo Alto, CA 94303
Phone: 800-624-1765
www.cpp-db.com
Publishes the Adjective Checklist, California Psychological Inventory (CPI), Myers-Briggs Type Indicator, Self-Directed Search, and the Strong Interest Inventory

CTB/McGraw-Hill
20 Ryan Ranch Road
Monterey, CA 93940

Phone: 800-538-9547
www.ctb.com
Publishes the California Achievement Test (Terra Nova), Comprehensive Test of Basic Skills, and Test of Cognitive Skills

Educational & Industrial Testing Service (EdITS)
PO Box 7234
San Diego, CA 92167
Phone: 800-416-1666
www.edits.net
Publishes the Personal Orientation Dimensions (POD), Comrey Personality Scales (CPS), Eysenck Personality Inventory (EPI), and Profile of Mood States (POMS)

Educational Testing Service
Rosedale Road
Princeton, NJ 08541
Phone: 609-921-9000
www.ets.org
Publishes the Advanced Placement Examinations and College Level Examination Program (some tests are sponsored jointly with the College Board)

Harcourt Educational Measurement
555 Academic Court
San Antonio, TX 78204-2498
Phone: 800-211-8378
www.hemweb.com
Publishes the Metropolitan Achievement Tests, Naglieri Nonverbal Ability Test, Otis-Lennon School Ability Tests, Stanford Achievement Tests, and the Stanford Diagnostic Tests

Harvard University Press
79 Garden Street
Cambridge, MA 02138
Phone: 800-405-1619
www.hup.harvard.edu
Publishes the Thematic Apperception Test

Institute for Personality and Ability Testing (IPAT)
PO Box 1188
Champaign, IL 61824-1188
Phone: 800-225-IPAT
www.ipat.com
Publishes the IPAT Anxiety Scale, IPAT Depression Scale, and 16 Personality Factor Inventory (16PF)

Lafayette Instrument Company
3700 Sagamore Parkway North
Lafayette, IN 47903
Phone: 800-428-7545
www.lafayetteinstrument.com
Publishes the Purdue Pegboard and a variety of biofeedback and physiological recording equipment

Mind Garden
1690 Woodside Road, Suite 202
Redwood City, CA 94061
Phone: 650-261-3500
www.mindgarden.com
Publishes the Coopersmith Self-Esteem Inventories, Moos' Family Environment Scale, Classroom Environment Scale, and Group Environment Scale, and State Trait Anxiety Inventory (STAI)

Multi-Health Systems (MHS)
908 Niagara Falls Boulevard
North Tonawanda, NY 14120-2060
Phone: 800-456-3003
www.mhs.com
Publishes the Children's Depression Inventory (CDI) and Conners' Rating Scales

National Career Assessment Services
601 Visions Parkway
PO Box 277
Adel, IA 50003
Phone: 800-314-8972
www.ncasi.com
Publishes the Kuder Occupational Interest Survey (KOIS) and Kuder Career Planning System (KCPS)

NCS Pearson
11000 Prairie Lakes Drive
Eden Prairie, MN 55344
Phone: 800-627-7271
www.ncspearson.com

Publishes the Millon Clinical Multiaxial Inventory (MCMI) and several other Millon inventories; distributes the Minnesota Multiphasic Personality Inventory (MMPI)

PRO-ED
8700 Shoal Creek Boulevard
Austin, TX 78757-6897
Phone: 800-897-3202
www.proedinc.com
Publishes the Detroit Tests of Learning Aptitude, Draw A Person: Screening Procedure for Emotional Disturbance (DAP: SPED), Test of Visual Motor Integration (TVMI), and Test of Nonverbal Intelligence (TONI)

Psychological Assessment Resources (PAR)
PO Box 998
Odessa, FL 33556
Phone: 800-331-8378
www.parinc.com
Publishes the Beery Developmental Test of Visual-Motor Integration, Eating Disorder Inventory (EDI), NEO Personality Inventory (NEO PI), NEO Five Factor Inventory (NEO FFI), and Rogers Criminal Responsibility Assessment Scales

The Psychological Corporation
555 Academic Court
San Antonio, TX 78204-2498
Phone: 800-211-8378
www.hbtpc.com
Publishes the Bayley Scales of Infant Development, Beck Depression Inventory (BDI), McCarthy Scales of Children's Abilities, Miller Analogies Test, and the Wechsler scales (WAIS, WISC, WPPSI, WASI, WMS, WIAT, WTAR)

Riverside Publishing
425 Spring Lake Drive
Itasca, IL 60143-2079
Phone: 800-323-9540
www.riverpub.com
Publishes the Cognitive Abilities Test, Das Naglieri Cognitive Assessment System, Gates-MacGinitie Reading Tests, Iowa Tests of Basic Skills, Stanford-Binet Intelligence Scale, and the Woodcock-Johnson Tests of Achievement and Cognitive Abilities

Sigma Assessment Systems
PO Box 610984
Port Huron, MI 48061-0984
Phone: 800-265-1285
www.sigmaassessmentsystems.com
Publishes the Personality Research Form (PRF) and Jackson Personality Inventory

Slosson Educational Publications
538 Buffalo Road
East Aurora, NY 14052-0280
Phone: 888-SLOSSON (756-7766)
www.slosson.com
Publishes the Slosson Intelligence Test and the Slosson Oral Reading Test

Stoelting Company
620 Wheat Lane
Wood Dale, Illinois 60191
Phone: 630-860-9700
www.stoeltingco.com
Publishes the Gray Oral Reading Tests, Kohs Block Design Test, Knox's Cube Test, Leiter International Performance Scale, and a variety of biofeedback and physiological recording equipment

University of Minnesota Press
111 Third Avenue South, Suite 290
Minneapolis, MN 55455
Phone: 800-388-3863
www.upress.umn.edu
Publishes the Minnesota Multiphasic Personality Inventory (MMPI) and Minnesota Multiphasic Personality Inventory–Adolescent (MMPI-A)

Western Psychological Services
12031 Wilshire Boulevard
Los Angeles, CA 90025-1251
Phone: 800-648-8857
www.wpspublish.com
Publishes the Bender Visual Motor Gestalt Test for Children, Hamilton Depression Scale, Luria Nebraska Neuropsychological Battery, Personality Inventory for Children (PIC), and Piers-Harris Children's Self-Concept Scale; distributes the Bender Visual Motor Gestalt Test (adult version)

Wide Range
PO Box 3410
Wilmington, DE 19804
Phone: 800-221-9728
www.widerange.com
Publishes the Wide Range Achievement Test (WRAT)

See accompanying Web site for additional materials.

Related Topics

Chapter 21, "50 Widely Used Psychological Tests"
Chapter 22, "Sources of Information About Psychological Tests"

24 TYPES OF TEST SCORES AND THEIR PERCENTILE EQUIVALENTS

Thomas P. Hogan

This chapter defines the converted or normed scores commonly used with psychological and educational tests and presents their percentile equivalents. In addition, Figure 1 and Table 1 show the relationships among many of these normed scores. Figure 1 illustrates the equivalence of the various scores that are based on the normal curve. The figure has insufficient resolution for making conversions among the scores for practical or clinical purposes. However, Table 1 allows for such conversions. The table is constructed with percentile ranks as the reference columns on the left and right. The body of the table shows conversions to several types of scores, each of which is defined below. Slightly different values might be entered for any particular percentile depending on how one rounds the entries or reads up or down for points covering multiple scores. This is particularly true at the extremes of the distribution.

Figure 1 and Table 1 treat the equivalence of different score modes, not the equivalence of different standardization groups. Scores from tests standardized on different groups cannot be equated simply by using the equivalencies illustrated here. It should also be noted that some tests may have independently determined norms for two different score modes (e.g., in standard scores and in percentiles); if the norms are independently determined, they will not correspond exactly with the equivalencies given here.

STANDARD SCORES

Standard scores constitute one of the most frequently used types of norms. Standard scores convert raw scores into a system with an arbitrarily chosen mean and standard deviation. Although the standard score mean and standard deviation are "arbitrarily" chosen, they are selected to yield round numbers such as 50 and 10 or 500 and 100.

Standard scores may be either linear or nonlinear transformations of the raw scores. It will usually not be apparent from a table of standard score norms whether they are linear or nonlinear; the test manual (or publisher) must be consulted for this purpose. Nonlinear transforma-

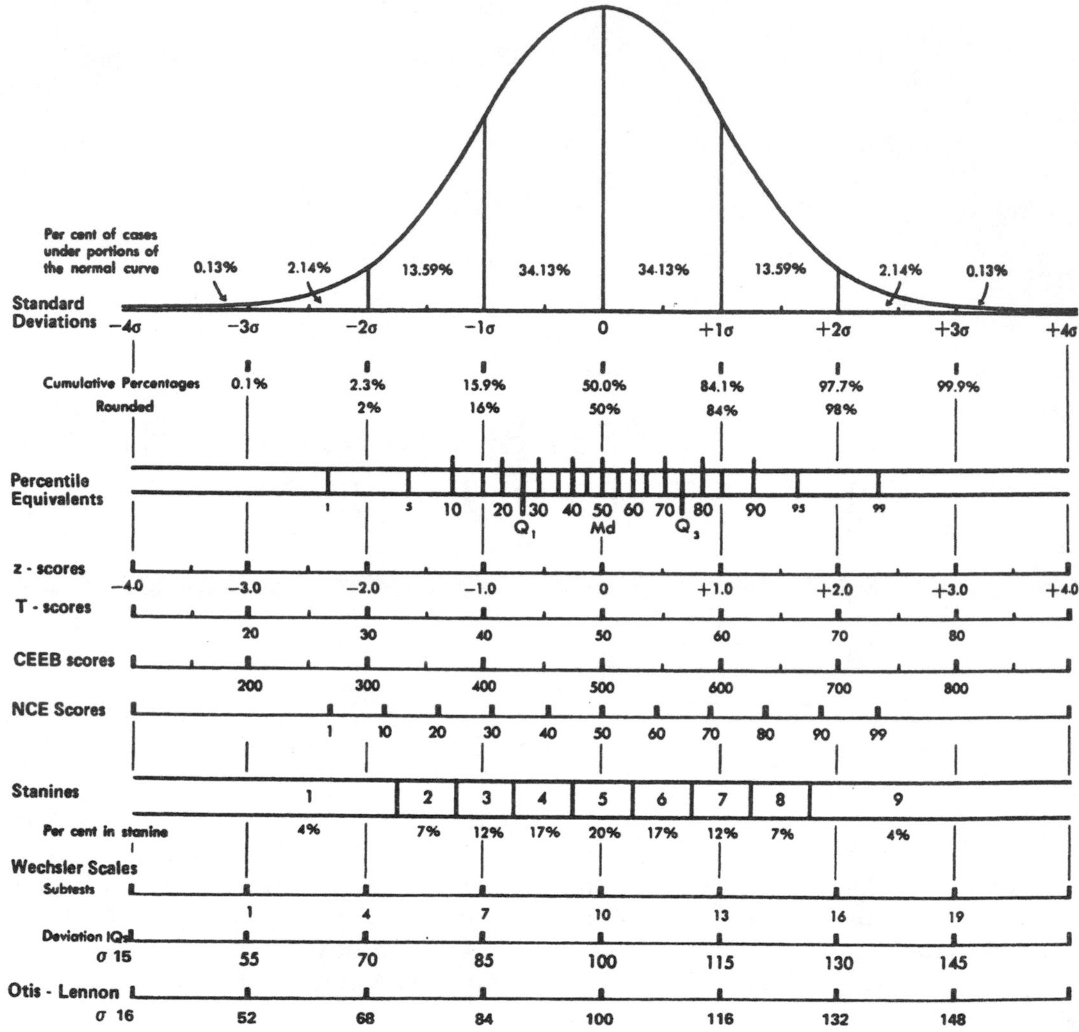

FIGURE 1. Equivalences of Several Standard Scores in the Normal Distribution (reprinted by permission of the Psychological Corporation from Seashore, n.d.)

tions are used either to yield normal distributions or to approximate an equal interval scale (as in Thurstone scaling). When used for this latter purpose, particularly in connection with multilevel tests, the standard scores are sometimes called *scaled scores*, and they usually do not have a readily interpretable framework.

COMMON STANDARD SCORE SYSTEMS

The following are commonly used standard score systems. In these descriptions, M = mean and SD = standard deviation.

IQs: The "IQ" scores on most contemporary intelligence tests are standard scores with $M = 100$ and SD = either 15 or 16, based on age groupings in the standardization sample.

T scores: T scores (sometimes called McCall's T scores) are standard scores with $M = 50$ and $SD = 10$. *T* scores are frequently used with personality tests, such as the MMPI-2 and NEO PI-R.

Wechsler subtests: Wechsler subtests use standard scores with $M = 10$ and $SD = 3$.

SAT, GRE scores: The SAT I (formerly, Scholastic Assessment Test) Verbal and Mathematics Tests; the Graduate Record Examination (GRE) Verbal, Quantitative, and Analytical

TABLE 1. Percentile Equivalents of Several Standard Score Systems

Percentile	Stanine	NCE	IQ (15)	IQ (16)	W Sub	T Score	SAT	Z Score	Percentile
99	9	99	133	135	17	73	730	2.33	99
98	9	93	130	132	16	70	700	2.05	98
97	9	90	129	130		69	690	1.88	97
96	9	87	127	128		68	680	1.75	96
95	8	85	125	126	15	66	660	1.65	95
94	8	83	123	125				1.56	94
93	8	81	122	124		65	650	1.48	93
92	8	80	121	123		64	640	1.40	92
91	8	78	120	122				1.34	91
90	8	77	119	121	14	63	630	1.28	90
89	8	76		120				1.23	89
88	7	75	118	119		62	620	1.18	88
87	7	74	117	118				1.13	87
86	7	73	116	117		61	610	1.08	86
85	7	72						1.04	85
84	7	71	115	116	13	60	600	.99	84
83	7	70						.95	83
82	7	69	114			59	590	.92	82
81	7	68	113	114				.88	81
80	7	68						.84	80
79	7	67	112	113		58	580	.81	79
78	7	66						.77	78
77	7	66	111	112				.74	77
76	6	65				57	570	.71	76
75	6	64	110	111	12			.67	75
74	6	64						.64	74
73	6	63	109	110		56	560	.61	73
72	6	62						.58	72
71	6	62		109				.55	71
70	6	61	108					.52	70
69	6	60		108		55	550	.50	69
68	6	60	107					.47	68
67	6	59		107				.44	67
66	6	59	106			54	540	.41	66
65	6	58		106				.38	65
64	6	58						.36	64
63	6	57	105		11			.33	63
62	6	56		105		53	530	.31	62
61	6	56	104					.28	61
60	6	55		104				.25	60
59	5	55						.23	59
58	5	54	103			52	520	.20	58
57	5	54		103				.18	57
56	5	53						.15	56
55	5	53	102	102				.13	55
54	5	52				51	510	.10	54
53	5	52	101					.08	53
52	5	51		101				.05	52
51	5	50						.02	51
50	5	50	100	100	10	50	500	.00	50
49	5	50						–.02	49
48	5	49		99				–.05	48
47	5	48	99					–.08	47
46	5	48				49	490	–.10	46
45	547	98	98					–.13	45
44	5	47						–.15	44

(continued)

TABLE 1. Percentile Equivalents of Several Standard Score Systems (*continued*)

Percentile	Stanine	NCE	IQ (15)	IQ (16)	W Sub	T Score	SAT	Z Score	Percentile
43	5	46		97				–.18	43
42	5	46	97			48	480	–.20	42
41	5	45						–.23	41
40	5	45		96				–.25	40
39	4	44	96					–.28	39
38	4	44		95		47	470	–.31	38
37	4	43	95		9			–.33	37
36	4	42						–.36	36
35	4	42		94				–.38	35
34	4	41	94			46	460	–.41	34
33	4	41		93				–.44	33
32	4	40	93					–.47	32
31	4	40		92		45	450	–.50	31
30	4	39	92					–.52	30
29	4	38		91				–.55	29
28	4	38						–.58	28
27	4	37	91	90		44	440	–.61	27
26	4	36						–.64	26
25	4	36	90	89	8			–.67	25
24	4	35				43	430	–.71	24
23	4	34	89	88				–.74	23
22	3	34						–.77	22
21	3	33	88	87		42	420	–.81	21
20	3	32						–.84	20
19	3	32	87	86				–.88	19
18	3	31	86			41	410	–.92	18
17	3	30		85				–.95	17
16	3	29	85	84	7	40	400	–.99	16
15	3	28						–1.04	15
14	3	27	84	83		39	390	–1.08	14
13	3	26	83	82				–1.13	13
12	3	25	82	81		38	380	–1.18	12
11	3	24		80				–1.23	11
10	2	23	81	79	6	37	370	–1.28	10
9	2	22	80	78				–1.34	9
8	2	20	79	77		36	360	–1.40	8
7	2	19	78	76		35	650	–1.48	7
6	2	17	77	75				–1.56	6
5	2	15	76	74	5	34	340	–1.65	5
4	2	13	74	72		32	320	–1.75	4
3	1	10	72	70		31	310	–1.88	3
2	1	7	70	68	4	29	290	–2.05	2
1	1	1	67	65	3	27	270	–2.33	1

Note: IQ (15) is for IQ tests with $M = 100$ and $SD = 15$, such as Wechsler Verbal, Performance, and Total Scores. IQ (16) is for IQ tests with $M = 100$ and $SD = 16$, such as Stanford-Binet (4th ed.) and Otis-Lennon School Ability Test. W Sub is for Wechsler subtests and Stanford-Binet (5th ed.) subtests, where $M = 10$ and $SD = 3$. SAT covers any of the several tests that use $M = 500$ and $SD = 100$; these scores are usually reported to two significant digits (i.e., with the farthest right digit always 0), and that is how they are presented here.

Tests; the GRE Subject Tests; and the Graduate Management Admissions Tests (GMAT) all use standard score systems with $M = 500$ and $SD = 100$. In determining total scores for these tests (e.g., SAT Total), means are additive but *SDs* are not. Hence, the mean for SAT Total (Verbal + Mathematics) is 1,000, but the *SD* is not 200; it is less than 200, since the two tests being added are not perfectly correlated.

Stanford-Binet, fifth edition (SB5): The fifth edition of the Stanford-Binet Intelligence Scale (2003) features two important changes from previous editions in terms of score scales. First, the *SD* for IQs is 15 (*M* is still 100), rather than 16, thus bringing the SB IQ scale into alignment with the Wechsler scales. Second, subtest scores for SB5 use *M* = 10 and *SD* = 3, as for the Wechsler subtests, rather than the previously used *M* = 50 and *SD* = 8. It must be emphasized that this convergence in numerical values between SB5 and Wechsler scales does not mean their scores are directly comparable, because the two tests have different normative bases.

Other tests: The ACT (American College Test) uses a score scale ranging from 1 to 36, with *M* = 16 for high school students and *M* = 19 for college-bound students and *SD* = 5. The LSAT (Law School Admission Test) has *M* = 150 and *SD* = 10.

Stanines: Stanines (a contraction of "standard-nine") are standard scores with *M* = 5 and *SD* = 2 (approximately), thus dividing the distribution into nine intervals (1–9), with stanines 2–8 spanning equal distances (each stanine covers ½ *SD*) on the base of the normal curve. Stanines are usually determined from their percentile equivalents, thus normalizing the resulting distribution. Stanines are frequently used with achievement tests and group-administered ability tests but are not used much outside these types of tests.

Stens: Stens (a contraction of "standard-ten") are standard scores that span the normal curve with 10 units and with *M* = 5.5 and *SD* = 2; each sten covers ½ *SD*.

Z scores: Z scores are standard scores with *M* = 0.0 and *SD* = 1.0. These scores are used frequently in statistical work but virtually never for practical reporting of test results.

Normal curve equivalents: Normal curve equivalents (NCEs) are a type of standard score designed to match the percentile scale at points 1, 50, and 99. Thus an NCE of 1 equals a percentile of 1, an NCE of 50 equals a percentile of 50, and an NCE of 99 equals a percentile of 99. The NCE scale divides the base of the normal curve into equal units between percentiles of 1 and 99. Using these criteria, NCEs work out to have *M* = 50 and *SD* = 21.06. NCEs were designed for use in federally funded programs in elementary and secondary schools and are used almost exclusively in that context.

PERCENTILES AND PERCENTILE RANKS

Percentiles and percentile ranks are among the most commonly used normed scores for all types of tests. A *percentile* is a point in the distribution at or below which the given percentage of cases falls. A *percentile rank* is the position of a particular score in the distribution expressed as a ranking in a group of 100. There is a fine, technical distinction between percentiles and percentile ranks, but the terms are often used interchangeably without harm.

Quartiles, quintiles, and deciles are offshoots of the percentile system, dividing the distribution of scores into quarters, fifths, and tenths, respectively. Unfortunately, there is no uniformity in designating the top and bottom portions of each of these divisions. For example, the "second" quartile may be either the second from the bottom (25th–49th percentiles) or the second from the top (50th–74th percentiles). Hence, special care is needed on this point when communicating results in any of these systems.

AGE/GRADE EQUIVALENTS

Age and grade equivalents are normed scores, but they are very different in important respects from standard scores and percentiles. Hence, they cannot be represented conveniently in Figure 1 or in Table 1.

An *age equivalent* score converts a raw score into an age—usually years and months—corresponding to the typical (usually median) raw score attained by a specified group. The specified group is ordinarily defined within a fairly narrow age range (e.g., in 3-month intervals in the standardization group).

Age equivalents are used almost exclusively with tests of mental ability, in which case they are referred to as *mental ages*. However, they are also used with anthropometric measurements (e.g., height and weight) for infants and children.

Grade equivalents convert raw scores into a grade in school that is typical for the students at that grade level. "Typical" is usually defined as the median performance of students at a grade level. The grade equivalent (GE) is ordinarily given in school year and 10th of a year, in which the 10ths correspond roughly to the months specified below. Exact definitions of 10ths may vary by half months from one test series to another. Levels above grade 12.9 are sometimes given a nonnumerical descriptor such as PHS for "post–high school."

Sept.	Oct.	Nov.	Dec.	Jan.
.0	.1	.2	.3	.4

Feb.	Mar.	Apr.	May	June
.5	.6	.7	.8	.9

One of the peculiarities of age and grade equivalents is that their standard deviations are not equal across different age and grade levels. It is this feature that prevents them from being charted in Figure 1. Generally the standard deviations increase with successively higher age or grade levels.

OTHER SCORES

Proficiency levels: Recent trends in educational assessment require the reporting of scores in proficiency levels. The most common designations are advanced, proficient, basic, and below basic. Cutoffs between levels are determined judgmentally, usually by panels of educators and laypersons and are not comparable from one application (e.g., test area or state) to another.

Theta: An increasing number of tests utilize item response theory (IRT) for test development. The most immediate output from such a test is a theta score, representing position on the underlying trait. Theta scores usually range from approximately −6.00 to +6.00. For ordinary use, theta is converted into one of the familiar normed scores described earlier. Rudner (1998) provides a useful, on-line demonstration of theta scores operating in a computer adaptive test.

References, Readings, & Internet Sites

Anastasi, A. & Urbina, S. (1997). *Psychological testing* (7th ed.). Upper Saddle River, NJ: Prentice Hall.

ERIC Clearinghouse. (1999). Assessment and Evaluation on the Internet. Retrieved January 7, 2003, from http://ERICAE.NET/nintbrod.htm

Hogan, T. P. (2003). *Psychological testing: A practical introduction*. New York: Wiley.

Mitchell, B. C. (n.d.). *Test Service Notebook 13: A glossary of measurement terms*. San Antonio, TX: Psychological Corporation.

Rudner, L. M. (1998). *An on-line, interactive, computer adaptive testing tutorial*. Retrieved January 7, 2003, from http://ERICAE.NET/scripts/cat/catdemo.htm

Seashore, H. G. (n.d.). *Test Service Notebook 148: Methods of expressing test scores*. San Antonio, TX: Psychological Corporation.

Related Topics

Chapter 21, "50 Widely Used Psychological Tests"
Chapter 22, "Sources of Information About Psychological Tests"

25 ASSESSING THE QUALITY OF A PSYCHOLOGICAL TESTING REPORT

Gerald P. Koocher

This summary describes key points that should be addressed in conducting any psychological assessment for which a report is prepared. The quality of the assessment report can be evaluated by assessing the thoroughness and accuracy with which each of these 10 points is addressed.

REFERRAL QUESTIONS AND CONTEXT

- Does the report explain the reason the client was referred for testing and state the assessment questions to be addressed?
- Does the report note that the client or legal guardian was informed about the purpose of and agreed to the assessment?
- Is the relevant psychological ecology of the client mentioned (e.g., recently divorced, facing criminal charges, candidate for employment)?
- If the evaluation is being undertaken at the request of a third party (e.g., a court, an employer, or a school), does the examiner note that the client was informed of the limits of confidentiality and whether a release was obtained?

CURRENT STATUS/BEHAVIORAL OBSERVATIONS

- What was the client's behavior like during the interview, especially with respect to any aspects that might relate to the referral questions or the validity of the testing (e.g., mood, ability to form rapport, concentration, mannerisms, medication side effects, language problems, cooperation, phenotype, or physical handicaps)?
- Were any deviations from standard testing administration or procedures necessary?

LISTING OF INSTRUMENTS USED

- Is a complete list (without jargon or abbreviations) of the tests administered presented, including the dates administered?
- Does the report explain the nature of any unusual instruments or test procedures used?
- If more than one set of norms or test forms exists for any given instrument, does the psychologist indicate which forms or norms were used?

RELIABILITY AND VALIDITY

- Does the psychologist comment specifically on whether or not the test results in the present circumstances are to be regarded as reasonably accurate (e.g., the test administration was valid and the client fully cooperative)?
- If there are mediating factors, are these discussed in terms of reliability and validity implications?
- Are the tests used valid for assessing the aspects of the client's abilities in question? This should be a special focus of attention if the instrument used is nonstandard or is being used in a nonstandard manner.

DATA PRESENTATION

- Are scores presented and explained for each of the tests used? (If an integrated narrative or description is presented, does this address all the aspects assessed, such as intellectual functioning, personality structure, etc.?)
- Are the meanings of the test results explained in terms of the referral questions asked?
- Are examples or illustrations included if relevant?
- Are technical terms and jargon avoided?
- Does the report note whether the pattern of scores (e.g., variability in measuring similar attributes across instruments) is a consistent or heterogeneous one?
- For IQ testing, arc subtest scatter and discrepancy scores mentioned?
- For personality testing, does the psychologist discuss self-esteem, interpersonal relations, emotional reactivity, defensive style, and areas of focal concern?

SUMMARY

- If a summary is presented, does it err by surprising the reader with material not mentioned earlier in the report?
- Is it overly redundant?

RECOMMENDATIONS

- If recommendations are made, is it evident why or how these flow from the test results mentioned and discussed earlier?
- Do the recommendations mention all relevant points raised as initial referral questions?

DIAGNOSIS

- If a diagnosis is requested or if differential diagnosis was a referral question, does the report specifically address this point?

IS THE REPORT AUTHENTICATED?

- Is the report signed by the individual who conducted the evaluation?
- Are the credentials/title of the person noted (e.g., Mary Smith, Ph.D., Staff Psychologist, or John Doe, M.S., Psychology Intern)?
- If the examiner is unlicensed or a trainee, is the report cosigned by a qualified licensed supervisor?

FEEDBACK

- Is a copy of the report sent to the person who made the referral?
- Is some mechanism operational for providing feedback to the client, consistent with the context of testing and original agreement with the client?

References, Readings, & Internet Sites 

American Psychological Association. (1993). Record keeping guidelines. *American Psychologist, 48,* 308–310.

American Psychological Association, American Educational Research Association, & National Council on Measurement in Education. (1998). *Standards for educational and psychological testing.* Washington, DC: American Psychological Association.

American Psychological Association, American Educational Research Association, & National Council on Measurement in Education. (1999). *Standards for educational and psychological testing.* Washington, DC: American Educational Research Association.

American Psychological Association, Testing and Assessment. (n.d.). Resource site. Retrieved 2004 from http://www.apa.org/science/testing

Bersoff, D. N., & Hofer, P. J. (1995). Legal issues in computerized psychological testing. In D. N. Bersoff (Ed.), *Ethical conflicts in psychology* (pp. 291–294). Washington, DC: American Psychological Association.

Eyde, L. D., Robertson, G. J., Krug, S. E., Moreland, K. L., Robertson, A. G., Shewan, C. M., et al. (1993). *Responsible test use: Case studies for assessing human behavior.* Washington, DC: American Psychological Association.

Koocher, G. P, & Keith-Spiegel, P. C. (1998). *Ethics in psychology: Professional standards and cases* (2nd ed.). New York: Oxford University Press.
Koocher, G. P., & Rey-Casserly, C. M. (2002). Ethical issues in psychological assessment. In J. R. Graham & J. A. Naglieri (Eds.), *Handbook of Assessment Psychology*. New York: John Wiley.
Matarazzo, J. D. (1990). Psychological assessment versus psychological testing: Validation from Bitnet to the school, clinic, and courtroom. *American Psychologist, 45*, 999–1016.
Moreland, K. L., Eyde, L. D., Robertson, C. J., Primoff, E. S., & Most, R. B. (1995). Assessment of test user qualifications: A research-based measurement procedure. *American Psychologist, 50*, 14–23.
University of Nebraska, Buros Center for Testing. (n.d.). Home page. Retrieved 2004 from http://www.unl.edu/buros
Wetter, M. W., & Corrigan, S. K. (1995). Providing information to clients about psychological tests: A survey of attorneys' and law students' attitudes. *Professional Psychology: Research and Practice, 26*, 474–477.

Related Topic

Chapter 129, "Prototype Mental Health Records"

26 CHILD BEHAVIOR OBSERVATIONS

Janice Ware

WHY USE DIRECT OBSERVATION?

Direct observation of child behavior is probably the most accurate means of assessing behavior, despite the many limitations of the available techniques. Direct observational data are multipurpose. In addition to their most frequent use for treatment planning, they also provide an important mechanism for evaluating treatment outcomes and are used as a base for developing theoretical understanding of childhood problems. Methods range from brief, informal single-session observations to highly structured techniques requiring extensive examiner training and considerable time input. Observations should serve not as a stand-alone tool but as an important component of a multimethod assessment. Direct observation is particularly effective when used as a complement to parent and/or self-report. Factors influencing the choice of an appropriate observational technique include (a) the stage of the evaluation process, (b) the nature of the behaviors of interest, (c) the setting in which the behavior occurs, and (d) the resources required to implement the observations.

WHAT METHODOLOGICAL CONCERNS EXIST?

The psychometric properties of specific observation strategies reflect a wide range of variability. Many of the most frequently used tools offer the least stable properties, including problems of objectivity, reliability, validity, reactivity, observer bias, and drift.

A vast number of semistructured and structured direct observation tools are available. The published tools that systematize observations range from broad-based observations of overall child functioning to quantification of specific child behaviors in specific patient populations. Currently, there is a strong movement to develop population-specific techniques that are sensitive to the developmental characteristics of children.

WHAT TECHNIQUES ARE AVAILABLE FOR DIRECT OBSERVATION?

Observation sites include naturalistic settings and simulated settings, such as role-playing. Frequency/rate, duration, latency, intensity, topography, and locus are aspects of behavior that can be systematically measured regardless of the setting. Data are collected using either continuous or sampling techniques. Observation codes that measure various aspects of child noncompliance and adult response to the behaviors are used extensively.

The worth of these tools depends largely on the quality of the data documenting adult antecedent and consequent behavior to the child's oppositional patterns. O'Neill, Horner, Albin, Storey, and Sprague (1990) have expanded these observational strategies to include codes for documenting severely maladaptive behavioral patterns of individuals with developmental disabilities.

Home visit observations offer the unique opportunity to investigate the multiplicity of ecological influences contributing to a developmental problem. Typical observed influences include the family's living conditions, the level of parental attachment, the degree of structure present in the home, the presence of appropriate play materials, and the degree of family cohesion. Tools for assessing these factors range from highly structured coding tools to the taking of clinical notes. Regardless of the level of structure involved in the home observation, the actual writing and note taking are best deferred until after the visit in order not to detract from the spontaneity of the visit.

The most commonly used tool for home observation is the Home Observation for Measurement of the Environment Inventory (HOME; Caldwell & Bradley, 1978). HOME uses standardized norms and a simple dyadic coding system to identify at-risk family settings. HOME is frequently criticized because of its high correlation with family socioeconomic status and its reliance on maternal report to supplement direct observations. Despite its shortcomings, HOME has made important contributions by systematically focusing the attention of the observer on characteristics of the home environment that are known to be important influences on developmental outcome.

TECHNOLOGICAL ADVANCES

Innovative techniques ranging from the use of fiber-optic televideo network systems (known as *televideo* or *teleassessment*) to the more readily available use of audio/videotape equipment are increasingly incorporated as standard procedure in child assessment. The use of video and TV provides additional opportunities to collect developmental observations when it is not possible or desirable for an examiner to be present. Comparisons of coding from live and videotaped situations indicate that little information is lost. Observational studies that have been found to be effective in minimizing psychometric concerns use behavior sampling techniques such as intermittently activated tape recorders or time-lapse video procedures.

Teleassessment is now successfully incorporated into many developmental and psychiatric assessment centers and is especially useful for sites serving remote locations. Research reveals high levels of patient and provider satisfaction with the technique. This technique has been particularly successful in settings where multidisciplinary assessment is desirable but prohibitive because of the cost involved in transporting a team of professionals to a remote location. Typical uses of televideo include multidisciplinary neurodevelopmental evaluation of high-risk infants and provision of child and adolescent psychiatric interviews in areas underserved by specialty providers.

Review of audio/videotape segments provides an opportunity for the therapist to help the patient and the family reconcile differing perceptions of the problem behaviors. This can be a practical time- and cost-effective technique because of the wide availability of portable home video equipment. It also can minimize the need for costly home and school visits. Parental reluctance to use videotaped material as a part of the clinical assessment may be due to unfamiliarity with the potential benefits of the procedure.

Parents will want to know what confidentiality procedures have been put in place to safeguard their child. Parental concerns about confidentiality and potential misuse of the tapes can be markedly diminished by identifying the parents at the outset of the audio/videotaping discussion as the "keepers" of the tape. Informed consent procedures, including obtaining written permission for taping, must be closely followed prior to the first taping session. Increasingly, school systems require written parental permission from the parents of each child present in the classroom when the videotaping takes place, regardless of whether or not their child is targeted for observation.

FREQUENTLY USED OBSERVATION TOOLS FOR COMMONLY REFERRED CHILDHOOD PROBLEMS

Attachment Behavior

No standard, widely used clinical tool exists for assessing the attachment of the young child to his or her primary caregiver. Although the descriptive categories of disordered attachment generated through Main and Ainsworth's Strange Situation Procedure (SSP; Ainsworth, Blehar, Waters, & Wall, 1978) are frequently applied in clinical settings (e.g., the "secure," "avoidant," "resistant," or "disorganized" child), the SSP is a research rather than a clinical tool normed on children aged 12–18+ months. Caution should be used in attempting to apply SSP findings to situations where child behavior is observed under either clinical or naturalistic conditions. Nevertheless, the SSP procedure has served as a foundation for several clinical assessment tools, such as the work of Gaensbauer and Harmon (1981) that assesses infant social and emotional functioning in structured settings, including attachment behavior.

Many unstructured informal observational variations of the SSP have evolved to evaluate the young child's attachment to a primary caregiver. These paradigms focus on observing child proximity seeking to the attachment figure and reciprocal attachment figure–child emotional responsivity following a separation.

Clinical observations of attachment parameters can be further enhanced by use of the nosological categories of attachment disorder outlined by Lieberman and Pawl (1988). This system can be used to describe disorders diagnosed in children between the ages of 1 and 4–5 years.

Attention-Deficit Disorder

The cost of obtaining direct observations for children with attention problems most often precludes the inclusion of this valuable technique into standardized assessment batteries. Observations of children with attentional problems are used to confirm the diagnosis and treatment plan and to evaluate stimulant medication effects. The most widely published observation system for assessing attention-deficit disorder (ADD) is that developed by Routh and his colleagues (Routh & Schroeder, 1976). Many modifications to this system have been made by subsequent authors, including a clinic analogue system (Barkley, 1997).

Stimulant medications are well-known elicitors of different effects for different domains of development. For example, a symptom trade-off may occur, such as achieving optimal academic performance at the cost of increasing impulsivity. Thus, observational techniques documenting stimulant medication effects must be multidimensional.

Well-regarded tools for evaluating child behavior in the classroom include specifics of the target child's behavior, as well as critical information on classroom environmental factors unlikely to be available through parent or teacher report. These tools record behaviors such as being off task or out of seat, attentional shifts, and amount of motor activity. The same tool used for gathering baseline attentional data should be readministered to monitor medication effects, including the critical variable of dosage increments. Observer bias can be minimized through the use of crossover designs that alternate placebo with treatment over the course of several weeks such that the observer is unaware of the child's status at the time of the observation.

An interesting and alternative strategy for assessing attentional problems in preschoolers is the Goodman Lock Box, a play-based observational coding system for use in clinical settings (Goodman, 1981). In addition to attention, the Lock Box assesses other aspects of preschool children's mental organization, such as sequencing skills and perceptual-motor and visuospatial capacities.

Autism and Mental Retardation

Autism and mental retardation are two of the most frequently diagnosed developmental disorders. They are particularly complex to diagnose and treat because of the high degree of behavioral inconsistencies that interfere with the ability to use standardized assessment tools (Schopler, Reichler, & Renner, 1988). Consequently, differential diagnosis relies heavily on the adequacy of the behavioral observations, coupled with caregiver reports of typical behavior. Comorbidity between the two conditions also increases the importance of careful observations of specific behaviors so that the diagnoses can be discriminated and/or confirmed as coexisting. Similar observation strategies and tools are used for both disorders.

Parent-Child Interactions

Behavioral observations of parent-child interactions during infancy assess the parent's capacities across different situations to provide an emotional scaffolding for the child. The most widely used tools for assessing the parent-child dyad are the tests embedded within the Nursing Childhood Assessment Tool (NCAST; Barnard, 1979). The paradigm on which the NCAST scales are based assumes that parent-child interaction is reciprocal and, therefore, that distinct parent and child contributions to the interaction can be discriminated.

The NCAST Teaching Scale observes and rates parent and child responses to parental efforts to "teach" a common play task of childhood such as block building. The task is taught under semistructured circumstances. The NCAST Feeding Scale offers a variation of this task and is an observation of parent-child interactions during an actual child feeding situation.

Strengths of the NCAST system are its ability to capture the contingent and reciprocal nature of the interaction using both the infant and the parent's behavior as data. The NCAST system is difficult for some programs to incorporate because it requires specialized training by a certified instructor.

Play Assessments

Developmental aspects of childhood behavior such as interaction inhibition often make standardized assessments nearly impossible, rendering play observations an important medium for gathering critical information. The systematic observation of play can provide a useful, unobtrusive means to understand and interpret child behavior. Play observations are typically nonthreatening to parent and child alike, often offering an enjoyable means for parents to learn about their children.

The majority of structured, clinical play-based assessments address representational and cognitive capacities rather than the broader range of developmental tasks, including social and emotional development. However, inferences based on observed affective displays, ability to socially reference others during the play episode, general interest in social relatedness, joint attention capacities, and mastery motivation are often drawn from structured and unstructured play tasks.

For children with disabilities, play provides a wealth of otherwise unobtainable information. Populations that lend themselves to developmental play observations include children with general cognitive delay and children with sensory and language disabilities and behavior problems seen in autism, elective mutism, and conduct disorders.

There are a tremendous number of play observation tools (Schaefer, Gitlin, & Sandgrund, 1991). Advantages and disadvantages of the various play observation tools should be carefully considered (Cohen, Stern, & Balaban, 1983).

References & Readings

Ainsworth, M. S., Blehar, M. D., Waters, E., & Wall, S. (1978). *Patterns of attachment: A psychological study of the Strange Situation.* Hillsdale, NJ: Erlbaum.

Barkley, R. A. (1997). *Defiant children: A clinician's manual for assessment and parent training* (2nd ed.). New York: Guilford Press.

Barnard, K. E. (1979). *Instructor's learning resource manual.* Seattle: NCAST Publications, University of Washington.

Caldwell, B. M., & Bradley, R. H. (1978). *Manual for the home observation of the environment.* Little Rock: University of Arkansas Press.

Cohen, D., Stern, V., & Balaban, N. (1983). *Observing and recording the behavior of young children.* New York: Teachers College Press.

Gaensbauer, T. G., & Harmon, R. J. (1981). Clinical assessment in infancy utilizing structured playroom situations. *Journal of the American Academy of Child Psychiatry, 20,* 264–280.

Goodman, J. F. (1981). The Lock Box: A measure of psychomotor competence and organized behavior in retarded and normal preschoolers. *Journal of Consulting and Clinical Psychology, 49,* 369–378.

Lieberman, A. F., & Pawl, J. H. (1988). Clinical applications of attachment theory. In J. Belsky and T. Nezworski (Eds.), *Clinical implications of attachment* (pp. 88–93). Hillsdale, NJ: Erlbaum.

Linder, T. W. (1996). *Transdisciplinary play-based assessment: A functional approach to working with young children.* Baltimore: Paul H. Brooks.

Mash, E. J., & Terdal, L. G. (1988). *Behavioral assessment of childhood disorders* (2nd ed.). New York: Guilford Press.

O'Neill, R. E., Horner, R. H., Albin, R. W., Storey, K., & Sprague, J. R. (1990). *Functional analysis of problem behavior: A practical assessment guide.* Sycamore, IL: Sycamore.

Routh, D. K., & Schroeder, C. S. (1976). Standardized playroom measures as indices of hyperactivity. *Journal of Abnormal Child Psychology, 4,* 199–207.

Schaefer, C. E., Gitlin, K., & Sandgrund, A. (Eds.). (1991). *Play diagnosis and assessment.* New York: Wiley.

Schopler, E., Reichler, R. J., & Renner, B. R. (1988). *The childhood autism rating scale.* Los Angeles: Western Psychological Services.

Related Topics

Chapter 12, "Interviewing Parents"

Chapter 27, "Measures of Children's Psychological Development"

27 MEASURES OF CHILDREN'S PSYCHOLOGICAL DEVELOPMENT

Sam S. Hill III

This chapter is essentially an updated entry of that submitted by Karen Levine in the first edition (Koocher, Norcross, & Hill, 1998). It contains an annotated listing of measures of children's intellectual ability and emotional development.

MEASURES OF INFANT DEVELOPMENT

There are an ever increasing number of standardized tests that can be administered to infants. In the past, assessment of infants was more an art than a science. Infant behavior and cooperation are extremely variable from minute to minute, so results must be interpreted with great caution. Infant testing can be useful in recognizing infants with developmental delays and to assist in the determination of eligibility for services. Infant assessment can also lead to early detection autism and other developmental disorders. Early intervention in many cases can be significant in the long-term effectiveness of treatment. The reader should know infant tests for normally developing children do not correlate with later measures of intelligence until 1.5 to 2 years of age (Bayley, 1969). Hence, infant testing is extremely valuable as a route to intervention but not as a predictor of later IQ.

Brazelton Neonatal Behavioral Scale (NBAS)

- Used primarily with premature infants or full-term newborns
- Requires substantial training and experience with infants to administer
- Improvements over time correlate with later Bayley Scales (Lester, 1984)

Infant assessment has moved away from individually administered standardized tests and toward a multidisciplinary approach. This interdisciplinary perspective is one in which each domain of child development stands on its own merits and offers findings that are coordinated in a practical developmental/treatment plan for the individual infant. The emphasis here is on the practical. Each specialty coordinates and contributes to the child's development and progress measured in terms of the stated goals of the clinician working with the family. A typical infant/development assessment team is made up of:

- Medicine
- Education
- Occupational therapy
- Physical therapy
- Psychology
- Speech and language
- Nutrition
- Audiology
- Social work

This approach allows members of each discipline to employ the best practice in their field.

PRESCHOOL INTELLIGENCE TESTS

Preschool-age children are referred for psychological testing for four reasons: kindergarten readiness, language delays, global developmental delays, and executive control difficulties. Preschool instruments usually assess the child's abilities across several domains including: expressive and receptive language; visual-spatial processing; fine motor skills; visual-motor integration; memory; general knowledge; and preacademic skills (e.g., knowledge of letters and numbers). By preschool age, many children are able to attend and follow directions sufficiently to obtain useful test results across a broad set of learning skills, while other children, especially children with communication, attentional, and developmental problems, cannot. A child's performance and skills at this age are also highly dependent on familial environment and history. Some preschool children have had little exposure to the educational process of school. Careful psychological assessment of preschool children can be helpful in determining specific types of problems, as well as executive functioning problems.

Stanford-Binet Intelligence Scale–Fifth Edition

- New norms for children 2 years of age through adults 90+, scales vary substantially at different ages
- New but wide use by psychologists is anticipated given the use of the fourth edition
- Yields full-scale IQ
- Less demand for strong attention in young children than the fourth edition
- Improved low-end items for better evaluation of young children and children with low cognitive functioning
- Administration in Spanish provided

Wechsler Preschool and Primary Scale of Intelligence–III

- Normed for children ages 2 years 6 months to 7 years 3 months
- Scale has been divided into two age bands, 2–6 to 3–11 and 4–0 to 7–3
- Well normed
- Widely used by psychologists in educational systems and hospitals
- Highly correlated with WPPSI-R and to WISC-R
- Scores tend to be 8 points lower on the WPPSI

McCarthy Scales of Children's Abilities–Second Edition

- Normed for children 2 years 6 months to 8 years 6 months
- Well normed
- "Fun"; good for young children and children who are difficult to test
- Children with significant speech and language delays score erroneously lower than on WPPSI Performance Scales (Morgan, Dawson, & Kerby, 1992)

If children are easy to test with normal language and over age 6, the WPPSI-R is preferable.

Kaufman Assessment Battery for Children–II

- Normed for children 3 to 18 years
- "Fun"; good for young children and children who are difficult to test
- Well standardized
- Offers standard scores, age equivalent scores, and percentile ranks
- Several subtests containing unique and appealing types of tasks can be useful for assessing abilities in difficult-to-test children (e.g., Face Recognition; Magic Window)

The original version was criticized for an artificially high "floor" effect. The tests' authors feel they have answered those questions in the second edition.

SCHOOL-AGE INTELLIGENCE TESTS

Wechsler Intelligence Scale for Children–IV

- For children ages 6 to 16 years
- The most widely used IQ test for school-age children
- Very well normed
- Can detect substantial but not all subtle learning disabilities
- Involves a significant amount of cultural knowledge and experience
- May be more challenging for poor and diverse children due to language of administration

Woodcock-Johnson Psycho-Educational Battery III

- Well normed for ages 2 years and above
- Measures general intellectual ability, scholastic aptitude, oral language, and academic achievement
- The achievement test has 12 subtests in the normal administration and an additional 10 subtests in the extended version
- Eight new cognitive subtests, five new cognitive clusters, two additional clusters when the cognitive and achievement batteries are used together
- Useful for identification of learning problems and formulating individual education plans

SCHOOL-AGE TESTS OF SPECIFIC ABILITIES

Wide Range Assessment of Memory and Learning–II (WRAML-2)

- Normed for children 5 to 17 years
- Useful supplement to any of the major tests of cognitive ability
- Includes three verbal scales, three memory scales, and three learning scales
- Especially useful when memory of visual processing problems is suspected

Bender Visual Motor Gestalt Test–Second Edition

- Brief shape-copying paper-and-pencil test
- Useful in about the 4 to 85+ year range
- Assesses visual-spatial and visual-motor integration skills

Rey-Osterrieth Complex Figures Test

- Complex shape-copying task
- Useful in assessing visual-spatial, organizational, and learning style
- Often used as part of a neuropsychological battery
- Multiple administration and scoring systems exist, with a great deal of research on each

Peabody Picture Vocabulary Test–Revised

- Normed for children aged 2 years 6 months through 90+
- Test of receptive vocabulary
- Requires ability to sustain attention
- Can be adapted to be used with eye gaze instead of pointing
- Correlates with verbal IQ
- Useful as a screening instrument
- Does not identify language-processing or language-formation problems

TESTS FOR SPECIAL POPULATIONS

Individuals from cultures different from those of the norming sample should be tested with caution. Whenever possible, these individuals should be tested by a psychologist from the same culture as the child and using instruments normed on that culture. Omitting testing and conducting interviews and observations are the best options when this sort of validity question arises. When testing is necessary for the child's best interests, test results should be interpreted cautiously and combined with the observations of reliable observers.

Some individuals with developmental disabilities cannot be validly assessed using standardized measures. Specific assessment measures have been designed for some populations. These measures contain items that do not rely on systems that are impacted by the specific disability, and they also generally are normed on people with the same disability. However, these tests are generally normed on smaller groups and are less frequently revised. Hence, when a more traditional test is felt to yield valid information, it is preferable. The following are some tests for special populations.

The Hiskey-Nebraska Test of Learning Aptitude

- Normed for children ages 3 to 16 years
- Separate norms for hearing impaired
- For children with hearing impairment
- Contains many traditional subtests in visual form (e.g., number recall with plastic numerals), easing interpretation

Pictoral Test of Intelligence–Second Edition

- Normed for children ages 3 to 8 years
- Useful for young children who have significant motor and/or language deficits, including many children with spastic quadriplegic cerebral palsy
- Children respond to questions by pointing or by eye gaze
- Measures a variety of processing, memory, and achievement domains

Merrill-Palmer Scale of Mental Tests

- Normed for children ages 2 years 6 months to 11 years
- Uses an array of interesting and appealing visual materials, most of which are self explanatory
- Nonverbal items useful for children with little language and/or children who are difficult to test
- Most useful as a qualitative rather than a quantitative IQ instrument
- Developed in 1948 and never revised

Leiter International Performance Scale–Revised (Leiter-R)

- Normed for children 2 years to 20 years 11 months
- Assess cognitive function in children and adolescents. The battery includes measures of nonverbal intelligence, fluid reasoning, and visualization
- Examines visual-spatial memory and attention
- Based on increasingly complex one-to-one matching (e.g., by shape, color, genus)
- Useful for nonverbal children or children who speak a language other than that of the examiner
- Can also be adapted for children with little motor ability through use of eye gaze
- 1997 revision of the 1979 test

TESTS OF ADAPTIVE FUNCTIONING

It can often be helpful to obtain information about a child's level of independent functioning in areas such as self-care, motor development, communication development, community functioning, and social functioning. While this information is helpful in assessing any child, it can be particularly valuable when assessing children for whom traditional tests are not valid or when mental retardation is suspected.

Vineland Adaptive Behavior Scale–Third Edition

- Interview form, classroom edition, and expanded edition
- Classroom edition, ages 3 years to 12 years and 11 months
- A comprehensive and thorough interview measure of social, self-care, motor, and community functioning
- Parent and teacher versions, as well as Spanish-parent and teacher versions

AAMD Adaptive Behavior Scale

- Provides assessor with domain, factor, and comparison scores

- Designed to measure a person's independence and social skills

References & Readings

Barkley, R. A. (1990). *Attention deficit hyperactivity disorder: A handbook for diagnosis and treatment.* New York: Guilford Press.

Bayley, N. (1969). *Manual for the Bayley Scales of infant development.* New York: Psychological Corporation.

Lester, B. M. (1984). Data analysis and prediction. In T. B. Brazelton (Ed.), *Neonatal Behavioral Assessment Scale* (pp. 85–96). Philadelphia: Lippincott.

Morgan, R. L., Dawson, B., & Kerby, D. (1992). The performance of preschoolers with speech/language disorders on the McCarthy Scales of Children's Abilities. *Psychology in the Schools, 20,* 11–17.

Sattler, J. M. (2001). *Assessment of children: Cognitive applications* (4th ed.). San Diego, CA: Jerome M. Sattler.

Sattler, J. M. (2002). *Assessment of children: Behavioral and clinical applications* (4th ed.). San Diego, CA: Jerome M. Sattler.

Woodrich, D. L. (1997). *Children's psychological testing: A guide for nonpsychologists* (3rd ed.). Baltimore: Brooks.

Related Topics

Chapter 22, "Sources of Information About Psychological Tests"

Chapter 23, "Publishers of Psychological and Psychoeducational Tests"

28 ASSESSING MMPI-2 PROFILE VALIDITY

James N. Butcher

The most important step in the Minnesota Multiphasic Personality Inventory-2 (MMPI-2) profile interpretation is the initial one of determining whether the profile contains valid, useful, and relevant information about the client's personality and clinical problems. A number of indices are available on the MMPI-2 to aid the clinician in determining whether the client's item responses provide key personality information or are simply reflecting response sets or deceptive motivational patterns to fend off the assessor as to the client's true feelings and motivations. This brief introduction to assessing MMPI-2 profile validity will provide the following: a summary of each of the useful response indices contained on the MMPI-2, a strategy for evaluating the validity indices, and key references for the information presented.

RESPONSE INDICES

Cannot Say Score

This index is not a scale but simply the number of omitted items in the record and is used as an index of cooperativeness. If the item omissions are at the end of the booklet (beyond item 370), the validity and clinical scales may be interpreted, but the supplemental and MMPI-2 content scales should not be interpreted. The content of omitted items often provides interesting information about the client's problems. If the individual has omitted more than 10 items, the MMPI-2 scales should be evaluated to determine the percentage of omitted items that appear on a particular scale. For example, a large number of items could appear on a particular scale, thereby reducing its value as a personality measure. If the person has omitted more than 30 items, the response record is probably insufficient for interpretation, particularly if the omissions fall within the first 370 items.

The L Scale

The L scale is a measure of cooperativeness and willingness to endorse faults or problems. Individuals who score high on this scale (T > 60) are presenting an overly favorable picture of themselves. If the L score is greater than 65, the individual is claiming virtue not found among people in general. The L scale is particularly valuable in situations like personnel screening or forensic cases because many individuals being assessed in these settings try to put their best foot forward and present themselves as "better" adjusted than they really are.

The K Scale

The K scale was developed as a measure of test defensiveness and as a correction for the tendency to deny problems. The profiles of persons who are defensive on the MMPI-2 are adjusted to offset their reluctance to endorse problems by correcting for the defensiveness. Five MMPI scales are corrected by adding a determined amount of the K score to the scale scores of Hs, Pd, Pt, Sc, and Ma. The K scale appeared to operate for MMPI-2 normative subjects much as it did for the original MMPI subjects. Consequently, the K weights originally derived by Meehl were maintained in the MMPI-2. In the MMPI-2, both K corrected and non-K corrected profiles can be obtained for psychologists interested in using non-K corrected scores.

The S Scale or Superlative Self-Description Scale

The S scale is an empirical measure developed by contrasting individuals who took the MMPI-2 in an employment selection situation from the normative sample. Applicants are usually defensive when they are assessed in an employment screening context. Even well-educated individuals who are applying for a highly desirable job tend to approach the MMPI-2 items with a cognitive set to convince the assessment psychologist that they have a sound mind, high responsibility, strong moral values, and great capacity to work effectively with others. In their efforts to perform well on personality evaluation, applicants tend to deny psychological symptoms, aggressively disclaim moral flaws, and assert that they are responsible people who get along extremely well with others and have the ability to compromise in interpersonal situations for the good of safety. In addition, they report being responsible and optimistic about the future, and they assert that they have a degree of good adjustment that most normals do not. In sum, they present themselves in a superlative manner, claiming to be superior in terms of their mental health and morality. The five subscales contained on the S scale are described as follows: Beliefs in Human Goodness, Serenity, Contentment with Life, Patience/Denial of Irritability and Anger, and Denial of Moral Flaws.

The F Scale

The F scale is an infrequency scale that is sensitive to extreme or exaggerated problem endorsement. The items on this scale are very rare or bizarre symptoms. Individuals who endorse a lot of these items tend to exaggerate symptoms on the MMPI-2. High F responding is frequently obtained by individuals with a set to convince professionals that they need to have psychological services. This motivational pattern is also found among individuals with a need to claim problems in order to influence the court in forensic cases. High-ranging F scores can raise several possible interpretations: The profile could be invalid because the client became confused or disoriented or got mixed up in responding. The F scale is also elevated in random response records. High F scores are also found among clients who are malingering or producing exaggerated responding in order to falsely claim mental illness.

The $F_{(B)}$ Scale

The $F_{(B)}$ scale, or Back F scale, was developed for the revised version of the MMPI to detect possible deviant responding to items located toward the end of the item pool. Some subjects may modify their approach to the items partway through the item pool and answer in a random or unselective manner. Since the items on the F scale occur earlier in the test, before item number 370, the F scale will not detect deviant response patterns occurring later in the booklet. The 40-item $F_{(B)}$ scale was developed following the same method as for the original F scale, that is, by including items that had low endorsement percentages in the normal population. Suggested interpretations of the $F_{(B)}$ scale include the following considerations: If the F scale is above T = 90, no additional interpretation of $F_{(B)}$ is indicated, since the clinical and validity scales are invalid by F scale criteria; if the T score of the F scale is valid, that is, below a T = 89, and the $F_{(B)}$ is below T= 70, then a valid response approach is indicated throughout the booklet and no additional interpretation is needed; or if the T score of the F scale is valid, that is, below a T = 89, and the $F_{(B)}$ is above a T = 90 (that is, if the original F scale is valid and the individual has dissimulated on the later part of the booklet), then an interpretation of $F_{(B)}$ is needed. In this case, interpretation of the clinical and validity scales is possible; however, interpretation of scales such as the content scales, which require valid response to the later appearing items, needs to be deferred.

The $F_{(P)}$ Scale

The Psychopathology Infrequency Scale $F_{(P)}$ was developed by Arbisi and Ben-Porath (1995) to assess infrequent responding in psychiatric settings. This scale is valuable in appraising the tendency for some people to exaggerate mental health symptoms in the context of patients with genuine psychological disorder. A high score on $F_{(P)}$, for example, above a T score of 80, indicates that the individual is endorsing more bizarre item content than even inpatient psychiatric cases endorse.

TRIN and VRIN

Two inconsistency scales for determining profile validity have been included in the MMPI-2. These scales are based on the analysis of the individual's response to the items in a consistent or inconsistent manner. The first scale, True Response Inconsistency (TRIN), is made up of 20 pairs of items in which a combination of 2 true or 2 false responses is semantically inconsistent—for example, a pair of items that contain content that cannot logically be answered in the same direction if the subject is responding consistently to the content.

TRIN can aid in the interpretation of scores on L and K, since the former is made up entirely of items that are keyed false and the latter is made up of items all but one of which is keyed false. Thus, an individual who inconsistently responds "false" to MMPI-2 pairs of items that contain opposite content will have elevated scores on scales L and K that do not reflect intentional misrepresentation or defensiveness. An individual whose TRIN score indicates inconsistent "true" responding will have deflated scores on L and K that do not reflect a particularly honest response pattern or lack of ego resources.

The Variable Response Inconsistency (VRIN) scale may be used to help interpret a high score on F. VRIN is made up of 49 pairs of (true-false; false-true; true-true; false-false) patterns. The scale is scored by summing the number of inconsistent responses. A high F in conjunction with a low to moderate VRIN score rules out the possibility that the F score reflects random responding.

Two Obsolete Traditional Measures

Two measures, popular with the original MMPI, are not recommended for interpreting in MMPI-2: the F-K index (though sensitive to dissimulation) and the so-called subtle-obvious items. First, the F-K index does not appear to provide much additional information beyond what is provided by the F scale alone. The F-K index, in which F is higher than K, tends to be superfluous and does not add any interpretive power beyond F alone. The F-K index in which K is greater than F (sometimes suggested as a measure to assess "fake good" profiles) has not worked out well in practice and is not recommended for clinical use because too many valid and interpretable protocols are rejected by this index.

Second, the subtle-obvious items are essentially chance items. They are not related to the criteria for the scales (Weed, Ben-Porath, & Butcher, 1990) and do not provide an index of invalidity. The subtle scales have been eliminated from official MMPI-2 scoring services and are not recommended for use in clinical decisions.

VALIDITY ASSESSMENT GUIDELINES

The following guidelines or strategies are recommended for determining the interpretability of profiles:

Clues to non–content-oriented responding

- High Cannot Say's (≥ 10)
  Noncompliance
- Preponderance of T or F
  Careless or devious omissions
- VRIN greater than 80
  Inconsistency
- TRIN greater than 80
  "Yea-saying" or "Nay-saying" (depending on whether the score is TRIN [T] or TRIN [F])

Indicants of defensive self-presentation

1. Overly positive self-presentation, leading to a somewhat attenuated record, if any, of these conditions, is present.
   - Cannot Say between 5 and 29
   - L over 60 but less than 65
   - K over 60 but less than 69
   - S over 65
2. Likely invalid MMPI-2 because of test defensiveness if any of the following conditions are present:
   - Cannot Say greater than 30
   - L greater than 66
   - K greater than 70
   - S greater than 70

Indicators of exaggerated responding and malingering of symptoms

1. Excessive symptom claiming
   - F (infrequency) greater than 90
   - $F_{(B)}$ greater than 90
   - $F_{(P)}$ greater than 80
2. Possibly exaggerated-invalid range
   - F greater than 100
   - $F_{(B)}$ greater than 10
   - $F_{(P)}$ greater than 90
3. Likely malingering
   - F greater than 109, with VRIN less than or equal to 79
   - $F_{(B)}$ greater than 109, with VRIN less than or equal to 79
   - VRIN less than 79, with VRIN less than or equal to 79
   - $F_{(P)}$ greater than 100, with VRIN less than or equal to 79

References & Readings

Arbisi, P., & Ben-Porath, Y. S. (1995). An MMPI-2 infrequency scale for use with psychopathological populations: The Infrequency-Psychopathology Scale, $F_{(P)}$. *Psychological Assessment, 7,* 424–431.

Baer, R. A., Wetter, M. W., & Berry, D. T. (1992). Detection of underreporting of psychopathology on the MMPI: A meta-analysis. *Clinical Psychology Review, 12,* 509–525.

Baer, R. A., Wetter, M. W., Nichols, D., Greene, R., & Berry, D. T. (1995). Sensitivity of MMPI-2 validity scales to underreporting of symptoms. *Psychological Assessment, 7,* 419–423.

Berry, D. T., Baer, R. A., & Harris, M. J. (1991). Detection of malingering on the MMPI: A meta-analysis. *Clinical Psychology Review, 11,* 585–591.

Berry, D. T., Wetter, M. W., Baer, R. A., Larsen, L., Clark, C., & Monroe, K. (1992). MMPI-2 random responding indices: Validation using a self-report methodology. *Psychological Assessment: A Journal of Consulting and Clinical Psychology, 4,* 340–345.

Berry, D. T., Wetter, M. W., Baer, R. A., Widiger, T. A., Sumpter, J. C., Reynolds, S. K., et al. (1991). Detection of random responding on the MMPI-2: Utility of F, Back F, and VRIN scales. *Psychological Assessment: A Journal of Consulting and Clinical Psychology, 3*, 418–423.

Berry, D. T. R., Wetter, M. W., Baer, R., Youngjohn, J. R., Gass, C., Lamb, D. G., et al. (1995). Overreporting of closed-head injury symptoms on the MMPI-2. *Psychological Assessment, 7*, 517–523.

Butcher, J. N., & Han, K. (1995). Development of an MMPI-2 scale to assess the presentation of self in a superlative manner: The S Scale. In J. N. Butcher & C. D. Spielberger (Eds.), *Advances in personality assessment* (Vol. 10, pp. 25–50). Hillsdale, NJ: LEA Press.

Graham, J. R., Watts, D., & Timbrook, R. (1991). Detecting fake-good and fake-bad MMPI-2 profiles. *Journal of Personality Assessment, 57*, 264–277.

Lim, J., & Butcher, J. N. (1996). Detection of faking on the MMPI-2: Differentiation between faking-bad, denial, and claiming extreme virtue. *Journal of Personality Assessment, 67*, 1–26.

Schretlen, D. (1988). The use of psychological tests to identify malingered symptoms of mental disorder. *Clinical Psychology Review, 8*, 451–476.

Timbrook, R. E., Graham, J. R., Keiller, S. W., & Watts, D. (1993). Comparison of the Wiener-Harmon subtle-obvious scales and the standard validity scales in detecting valid and invalid MMPI-2 profiles. *Psychological Assessment, 5*, 53–61.

Weed, N., Ben-Porath, Y. S., & Butcher, J. N. (1990). Failure of the Weiner-Harmon MMPI subtle scales as predictors of psychopathology and as validity indicators. *Psychological Assessment, 2*, 281–283.

Wetter, M. W., Baer, R. A., Berry, D. T., Robison, L. H., & Sumpter, J. (1993). MMPI-2 profiles of motivated fakers given specific symptom information. *Psychological Assessment, 5*, 317–323.

Wetter, W., Baer, R. A., Berry, D. T., Smith, G. T., & Larsen, L. (1992). Sensitivity of MMPI-2 validity scales to random responding and malingering. *Psychological Assessment, 4*, 369–374.

Related Topics

Chapter 29, "Clinical Scales of the MMPI-2"
Chapter 31, "Characteristics of High and Low Scores on the MMPI-2 Clinical Scales"
Chapter 32, "Empirical Interpretation of the MMPI-2 Codetypes"

29 CLINICAL SCALES OF THE MMPI-2

John R. Graham

This chapter summarizes each Minnesota Multiphasic Personality Inventory-2 (MMPI-2) clinical scale in terms of the dimensions assessed by the scale. Descriptive material on persons who have particularly high or low scale scores is given in chapter 28. Summary information is based on previously reported data for the clinical scales of the original MMPI and consideration of data concerning extra-test correlates of the MMPI-2 clinical scales, which are basically the same as in the original MMPI. A few items were deleted from the original test as outdated or because the content was deemed objectionable (e.g., content having to do with religious beliefs or bowel and bladder function). Other items were modified slightly to modernize them, eliminate sexist references, or improve readability.

SCALE 1 (HYPOCHONDRIASIS)

- Scale 1 originally was developed to identify patients manifesting symptoms associated with hypochondriasis. The syndrome is characterized by preoccupation with the body and concomitant fears of illness and disease. Although such fears usually are not delusional in nature, they tend to be quite persistent. One item was deleted because of objectionable content, reducing Scale 1 from 33 items in the original MMPI to 32 items in the MMPI-2.
- Scale 1 seems to be the most homogeneous and unidimensional in the MMPI-2. All the items deal with somatic concerns or with general physical competence. Factor analysis indicates that much of the variance in Scale 1 is accounted for by a single factor, characterized by the denial of good health and reporting a variety of somatic symptoms. Patients with bona fide physical problems typically show somewhat elevated T scores on Scale 1 (approximately 60). Elderly individuals tend to produce Scale 1 scores that are slightly more elevated than those of adults in general, probably reflecting the declining health typically associated with aging.

SCALE 2 (DEPRESSION)

- Scale 2 originally was developed to assess symptomatic depression. The primary characteristics of depression are poor morale, lack of hope in the future, and a general dissatisfaction with one's life situation. Of the 60 items originally in Scale 2, a total of 57 were retained in the MMPI-2. Many of the items in the scale deal with aspects of depression such as denial of happiness and personal worth, psychomotor retardation, withdrawal, and lack of interest in one's surroundings. Other items in the scale cover a variety of symptoms and behaviors, including somatic complaints, worry or tension, denial of hostile impulses, and difficulty in controlling one's own thought processes.
- Scale 2 is an excellent index of people's discomfort and dissatisfaction with their life situations. Whereas highly elevated scores on this scale suggest clinical depression, more moderate scores tend to be indicative of a general attitude or lifestyle characterized by poor morale and lack of involvement.
- Scale 2 scores are related to age, with elderly persons typically scoring approximately 5–10 T-score points higher than the mean for the total MMPI-2 normative sample. Some individuals who have recently been hospitalized or incarcerated tend to show moderate elevations on Scale 2 that reflect dissatisfaction with current circumstances rather than clinical depression.

SCALE 3 (HYSTERIA)

- This scale was developed to identify patients who were utilizing hysterical reactions to stress situations. The hysterical syndrome is characterized by involuntary psychogenic loss or disorder of function.
- All 60 items in the original version of Scale 3 were retained in MMPI-2. Some of the items deal with a general denial of physical health and a variety of rather specific somatic complaints, including heart or chest pain, nausea and vomiting, fitful sleep, and headaches. Another group of items involves a general denial of psychological or emotional problems and of discomfort in social situations. Although these two clusters of items are reasonably independent in normal people, those utilizing hysterical defenses seem to score high on both clusters.
- Scale 3 scores are related to intellectual ability, with brighter persons scoring higher. In addition, high raw scores are much more common among women than among men in both normal and psychiatric populations.
- It is important to take into account the level of scores on Scale 3. Whereas marked elevations ($T > 80$) suggest a pathological condi-

tion characterized by classical hysterical symptoms, moderate levels are associated with characteristics that are consistent with hysterical disorders but do not include the classical hysterical symptoms. As with Scale 1, patients with bona fide medical problems for whom there is no indication of psychological components to the conditions tend to obtain T scores of about 60 on this scale.

SCALE 4 (PSYCHOPATHIC DEVIATE)

- Scale 4 was developed to identify patients diagnosed as having a psychopathic personality, asocial or amoral type. Whereas persons in the original criterion group were characterized in their everyday behavior by such delinquent acts as lying, stealing, sexual promiscuity, excessive drinking, and the like, no major criminal types were included. All 50 of the items in the original scale were maintained in MMPI-2. The items cover a wide array of topics, including absence of satisfaction in life, family problems, delinquency, sexual problems, and difficulties with authorities. Interestingly, the keyed responses include both admissions of social maladjustment and assertions of social poise and confidence.
- Scores on Scale 4 tend to be related to age, with younger people scoring slightly higher than older people. In the MMPI-2 normative samples, Whites and Asian Americans scored somewhat lower on Scale 4 (5–10 T-score points) than did African Americans, Native Americans, and Hispanics.
- One way of conceptualizing what Scale 4 assesses is to think of it as a measure of rebelliousness, with higher scores indicating rebellion and lower scores indicating acceptance of authority and the status quo. The highest scorers on the scale rebel by acting out in antisocial and criminal ways; moderately high scorers may be rebellious but may express the rebellion in more socially acceptable ways; and low scorers may be overly conventional and accepting of authority.

SCALE 5 (MASCULINITY-FEMININITY)

- Scale 5 originally was developed by Hathaway and McKinley to identify homosexual invert males. The test authors identified only a very small number of items that differentiated homosexual from heterosexual men. Thus, items were added to the scale if they differentiated between men and women in the standardization sample. Items from an earlier interest test were also added to the scale. Although Hathaway and McKinley considered this scale preliminary, it has come to be used routinely in its original form.
- The test authors attempted, without success, to develop a corresponding scale for identifying "sexual inversion" in women. As a result, Scale 5 has been used for both men and women. Fifty-two of the items are keyed in the same direction for both genders, whereas 4 items, all dealing with frankly sexual content, are keyed in opposite directions for men and women. After obtaining raw scores, T-score conversions are reversed for the sexes so that a high raw score for men automatically is transformed by means of the profile sheet itself into a high T score, whereas a high raw score for women is transformed into a low T score. The result is that high T scores for both genders are indicative of deviation from one's own gender.
- In the MMPI-2, 56 of the 60 items in the original Scale 5 were maintained. Although a few of the items in Scale 5 have clear sexual content, most items are not sexual in nature, instead covering a diversity of topics, including work and recreational interests, worries and fears, excessive sensitivity, and family relationships.
- Although MMPI Scale 5 scores were strongly related to the individual's amount of formal education, the relationship is much more modest in the MMPI-2. More highly educated men tend to obtain slightly higher Scale 5 T scores than do less educated men. More highly educated women tend to obtain slightly lower Scale 5 T scores than do less educated women. These differences probably

reflect the broader interest patterns of more educated men and women and are not large enough to necessitate different Scale 5 interpretations for persons with differing levels of education.

SCALE 6 (PARANOIA)

- Scale 6 originally was developed to identify patients who were judged to have paranoid symptoms such as ideas of reference, feelings of persecution, grandiose self-concepts, suspiciousness, excessive sensitivity, and rigid opinions and attitudes. Although the scale was considered preliminary because of problems in cross-validation, it was retained because it produced relatively few false positives. Persons who score high on this scale usually have paranoid symptoms. However, some patients with clearly paranoid symptoms are able to achieve average scores on Scale 6.
- All 40 of the items in the original scale were maintained in the MMPI-2. Although some of the items in the scale deal with frankly psychotic behaviors (e.g., excessive suspiciousness, ideas of reference, delusions of persecution, grandiosity), many items cover such diverse topics as sensitivity, cynicism, asocial behavior, excessive moral virtue, and complaints about other people. It is possible to obtain a T score greater than 65 on this scale without endorsing any of the clearly psychotic items.

SCALE 7 (PSYCHASTHENIA)

- Scale 7 originally was developed to measure the general symptomatic pattern labeled *psychasthenia*. Although this diagnostic label is not used commonly today, it was popular when the scale was developed. Among currently popular diagnostic categories, the obsessive-compulsive disorder probably is closest to the original meaning of the psychasthenia label. Such persons have thinking characterized by excessive doubts, compulsions, obsessions, and unreasonable fears. This symptom pattern was much more common among outpatients than among hospitalized patients, so the number of cases available for scale construction was small.
- All 48 items in the original scale were maintained in the MMPI-2. They cover a variety of symptoms and behaviors. Many of the items deal with uncontrollable or obsessive thoughts, feelings of fear and/or anxiety, and doubts about one's own ability. Unhappiness, physical complaints, and difficulties in concentration also are represented in the scale.

SCALE 8 (SCHIZOPHRENIA)

- Scale 8 was developed to identify patients diagnosed as schizophrenic. This category included a heterogeneous group of disorders characterized by disturbances of thinking, mood, and behavior. Misinterpretations of reality, delusions, and hallucinations may be present. Ambivalent or constricted emotional responsiveness is common. Behavior may be withdrawn, aggressive, or bizarre.
- All 78 of the items in the original scale were maintained in the MMPI-2. Some of the items deal with such frankly psychotic symptoms as bizarre mentation, peculiarities of perception, delusions of persecution, and hallucinations. Other topics covered include social alienation, poor family relationships, sexual concerns, difficulties in impulse control and concentration, and fears, worries, and dissatisfactions.
- Scores on Scale 8 are related to age and race. College students often obtain T scores in a range of 50–60, perhaps reflecting the developmental turmoil associated with that period in life. In some studies, African Americans, Native Americans, and Hispanics in the MMPI-2 normative sample have scored higher than whites. The elevated scores for members of ethnic minority groups do not necessarily suggest greater psychopathology. They may simply be indicative of the feelings of alienation and social estrangement sometimes experienced by minority group members.

- Some elevations of Scale 8 can be accounted for by persons who are reporting a large number of unusual experiences, feelings, and perceptions related to the use of prescription and nonprescription drugs, especially amphetamines. Also, some persons with disorders such as epilepsy, stroke, or closed-head injury endorse sensory and cognitive items, leading to high scores on Scale 8.

SCALE 9 (HYPOMANIA)

- Scale 9 originally was developed to identify psychiatric patients manifesting hypomanic symptoms. Hypomania is characterized by elevated mood, accelerated speech and motor activity, irritability, flight of ideas, and brief periods of depression.
- All 46 items in the original scale were maintained in the MMPI-2. Some of the items deal specifically with features of hypomanic disturbance (e.g., activity level, excitability, irritability, grandiosity). Other items cover topics such as family relationships, moral values and attitudes, and physical or bodily concerns. No single dimension accounts for much of the variance in scores, and most of the sources of variance represented in the scale are not duplicated in other clinical scales.
- Scores on Scale 9 are related to age and race. Younger people (e.g., college students) typically obtain scores in a T-score range of 50–60. For elderly people, Scale 9 T scores below 50 are common. African Americans, Native Americans, and Hispanics in the MMPI-2 normative samples scored somewhat higher (5–10 T-score points) than Whites.
- Scale 9 can be viewed as a measure of psychological and physical energy, with high scorers having excessive energy. When Scale 9 scores are high, one expects that characteristics suggested by other aspects of the profile will be acted out. For example, high scores on Scale 4 suggest asocial or antisocial tendencies. If Scale 9 is elevated along with Scale 4, these tendencies are more likely to be expressed overtly in behavior.

SCALE 0 (SOCIAL INTROVERSION)

- Scale 0 was designed to assess a person's tendency to withdraw from social contacts and responsibilities. Items were selected by contrasting high and low scorers on the Social Introversion-Extroversion Scale of the Minnesota T-S-E Inventory. Only women were used to develop the scale, but its use has been extended to men as well.
- All but 1 of the 70 items in the original scale remain in the MMPI-2. The items are of two general types: one group deals with social participation, whereas the other group deals with general neurotic maladjustment and self-depreciation. High scores can be obtained by endorsing either kind of item or both.
- Scores on Scale 0 are quite stable over extended periods.

References & Readings

Ben-Porath, Y. S., Graham, J. R., Hall, G. N., Hirschman, R. D., & Zaragoza, M. S. (Eds.). (1995). *Forensic applications of the MMPI-2*. Thousand Oaks, CA: Sage.

Butcher, J. N., Graham, J. R., Ben-Porath, Y. S., Tellegen, A., Dahlstrom, W. G., & Kaemmer, B. (2001). *Minnesota Multiphasic Personality Inventory-2 (MMPI-2): Manual for administration, scoring, and interpretation*. Minneapolis: University of Minnesota Press.

Butcher, J. N., & Williams, C. L. (2000). *Essentials of MMPI-2 and MMPI-A interpretation*. Minneapolis: University of Minnesota Press.

Graham, J. R. (1990). MMPI-2: *Assessing personality and psychopathology* (3rd ed.). New York: Oxford University Press.

Graham, J. R., Ben-Porath, Y. S., & McNulty, J. L. (1999). *MMPI-2 correlates for outpatient community mental health settings*. Minneapolis: University of Minnesota Press.

Greene, R. (2000). *The MMPI-2: An interpretive manual* (2nd ed.). Boston: Allyn and Bacon.

Related Topics

Chapter 28, "Assessing MMPI-2 Profile Validity"

Chapter 31, "Characteristics of High and Low Scores on the MMPI-2 Clinical Scales"

Chapter 32, "Empirical Interpretation of the MMPI-2 Codetypes"

30 SUPPLEMENTARY SCALES OF THE MMPI-2

Roger L. Greene

This overview of the MMPI-2 supplementary scales will be organized into four groupings of scales: generalized emotional distress scales (Welsh Anxiety [A], College Maladjustment [Mt], and Post Traumatic Stress Disorder–Keane [PK]); control/inhibition and dyscontrol/dysinhibition scales (Welsh Repression [R], Hostility [Ho], and MacAndrew Alcoholism–Revised [MAC-R]); alcohol/drug scales (MacAndrew Alcoholism–Revised [MAC-R], Addiction Admission [AAS], Addiction Potential [APS], and Common Alcohol Logistic–Revised [CAL-R]); and the Personality Psychopathology Five scales (PSY-5: Harkness, McNulty, & Ben-Porath, 1995) that recently were added to the National Computer Systems Extended Score Report for the MMPI-2. Given the limited amount of space, the less frequently used supplementary scales covering general personality dimensions (Dominance [Do], Over-Controlled Hostility [O-H]; Social Responsibility [Re]) and gender role scales (Gender Role–Feminine [GF] and Gender Role–Masculine [GM]) will not be discussed. Information on all of these supplementary scales can be found in Friedman, Lewak, Nichols, and Webb (2001); Graham (2000); and Greene (2000). Clinicians should keep in mind that a general style for individuals to maximize or minimize their reported symptoms will have a significant impact on the elevation, or lack thereof, for all of the MMPI-2 supplementary scales, as well as the standard validity and clinical scales and content scales. It will be assumed in discussing the supplementary scales below that individuals have endorsed the items in an accurate manner.

GENERALIZED EMOTIONAL DISTRESS SCALES

Factor-analytic studies of the MMPI-2 clinical scales have consistently identified two factors that are variously labeled and interpreted. The first factor is generally acknowledged to be a measure of generalized emotional distress and negative affectivity, and Welsh developed his Anxiety (A) scale to measure this factor. There are 10 to 20 other scales in the MMPI-2 that measure this factor of generalized emotional distress and negative affectivity, all of which have high positive correlations with the A scale: the clinical Scales 7 (Pt: .95) and 8 (Sc: 90); the content scales Work Interference (WRK: .94), Depression (DEP: .92), Anxiety (ANX: .90), Obsessions (OBS: .89), and Low Self-Esteem (LSE: .87); and the supplementary scales Post Traumatic Stress Disorder–Keane (PK: .93), College Maladjustment (Mt: .93), and Marital Distress Scale (MDS: .79). There also are a number of MMPI-2 scales that have high negative correlations with the A scale and as such are simply inverted measures of generalized distress: Ego Strength (Es: –.83) and K (Correction: –.79). All of these scales can be characterized as generalized measures of emotional distress with little or no specificity despite the name of the scale and there are little empirical data to support any distinctions among them.

CONTROL/INHIBITION AND DYSCONTROL/DYSINHIBITION SCALES

The second factor identified in these factor-analytic studies of the MMPI-2 clinical scales is a measure of control and inhibition, and Welsh developed his Repression (R) scale to measure this factor. The major content area of the R scale is the denial, suppression, constriction, and inhibition of all kinds of interests either positive or negative—that is, these individuals like to keep their behavior within very narrow limits. There are 5 to 10 other scales in the MMPI-2 that measure this factor of control and inhibition, but the pattern of correlations with the R scale is much more variable and smaller than found with the A scale: the clinical Scale 9 (Ma: .45), the content scale Antisocial Practices (ASP: .36), the supplementary scales MacAndrew Alcoholism–Revised (MAC-R: .52) and Social Responsibility (Re: .38), and the PSY-5 scales Aggression (AGGR: .53) and Disconstraint (DISC: .46). The specific correlates of the second factor will be a function of the scale that is used to define it, but it is evident that this group of MMPI-2 scales is characterized by significant dyscontrol or dysinhibition associated with acting out or externalization of psychopathology.

Conjoint interpretations of the first two factors of the MMPI-2 (generalized emotional distress and control/inhibition) provide a succinct approach for how individuals are coping with the behaviors and symptoms that led them to treatment (see Greene, 2000, Table 6.5, p. 225). The A scale provides a quick estimate of how much generalized emotional distress the individual is experiencing, and the R scale indicates whether the individual is trying to inhibit or control the expression of this distress. It is particularly noteworthy in a clinical setting when the A scale is not elevated (T < 50) because it signifies that the individual is not experiencing any distress about the behaviors and symptoms that led, usually someone else to refer, them to treatment. Similarly low scores (T < 45) on the R scale suggest that the individual has no coping skills or abilities to control or inhibit the overt expression of their distress. When one of these two scales is elevated significantly and the other scale is unusually low, clinicians should give serious consideration to the hypothesis that the individual is maximizing (A > 75; R < 45) or minimizing (A < 45; R > 60) his or her report of psychopathology. It is particularly pathognomonic when both the A and R scales are low (T < 50), a pattern that is seen in chronic, ego syntonic psychopathology.

ALCOHOL AND DRUG SCALES

The alcohol and drug scales on the MMPI-2 can be easily subdivided into rationally derived, or direct, measures (Addiction Admission [AAS] and Common Alcohol Logistic–Revised [CAL-R]) and empirically derived, or indirect measures (MacAndrew Alcoholism–Revised [MAC-R] and Addiction Potential [APS]). These four alcohol and drug scales contain 111 different items, 96 of which are found on only one of the four scales. These different methodologies yielded very different item groupings on these four scales that can be seen in the low positive intercorrelations among them: MAC-R with AAS .48, APS .29, and CAL-R .32; and AAS with APS .34; CAL-R .46. Consequently, the manifestations of alcohol and drug abuse will differ in specific individuals depending upon which scale is elevated.The MAC-R scale is best conceptualized as a general personality dimension. Individuals who produced elevated scores (raw scores > 24 to 26) on the MAC-R scale are described as being impulsive, risk-taking, and sensation-seeking, and they frequently have a propensity to abuse alcohol and/or stimulating drugs. They are uninhibited, sociable individuals who appear to use repression and religion in an attempt to control their rebellious, delinquent impulses. They also are described as having a high energy level, having shallow interpersonal relationships, and being generally psychologically maladjusted. Low scorers (raw scores < 18 to 20) are described as being risk-avoiding, introverted, and depressive, and they abuse sedative-hypnotics and alcohol if they abuse substances. Once the MAC-R scale is understood as a general personality dimension for risk-taking versus risk-avoiding, the fact that mean scores vary drastically by codetype makes sense. For example, in men, the mean raw score on the MAC-R scale in a 4-9/9-4 (risk-taking) codetype is 26.5 and in a 2-0/0-2 (risk-avoiding) codetype is 17.1 (see Greene, 2000, Appendix D), a difference of over two standard deviations.There are a number of issues that must be kept in mind when interpreting the MAC-R scale: men score about 2 raw-score points higher than women across most samples, which indicates that different cutting scores are necessary by gender; there is not a single, optimal cutting score with raw scores anywhere from 24 to 29 being used in different studies; clinicians need to be very cautious in using the MAC-R scale in nonwhite ethnic groups, if it is used at all; classification accuracy decreases when clinicians are trying to discriminate between substance abusers and nonsubstance-abusing psychiatric patients, which is a frequent differential diagnosis; and classification accuracy may be unacceptably low in medical samples.

The Addiction Potential Scale (APS) consists of 39 items that differentiated among groups of male and female substance-abuse patients, normal individuals, and psychiatric patients. Individuals with elevated (T > 64) scores on the APS scale are generally distressed and upset, as well as angry and resentful. They also are concerned about what others think of them, a concern that is not evident in individuals who elevate the MAC-R scale. The APS scale appears to be more accurate at discriminating between substance-abuse patients and psychiatric patients than is the MAC-R scale. The APS scale also tends to be less gender biased than the MAC-R scale and to be less codetype sensitive. For example, in men, the mean T score on APS in a 4-9/9-4 codetype is 56.2 and in a 2-0/0-2 codetype is 49.0 (see Greene, 2000, Appendix D), a difference slightly over one-half of a standard deviation.The Addiction Admission Scale (AAS) consists of 13 items directly related to the use of alcohol and drugs. Clinicians should review the clinical history and background of any individual who elevates the AAS scale (T > 59) because of the explicit nature of the items and the fact that three or more of these items have been endorsed in the deviant direction to produce this elevation. The AAS scale typically performs better at identifying individuals who are abusing substances than less direct measures such as the APS and MAC-R scales, even though the items are face-valid, allowing individuals not to report the substance abuse if they desire to do so. Weed, Butcher, and Ben-Porath (1995) have provided a thorough review of all MMPI-2 measures of substance abuse.

Davis, Offord, Colligan, and Morse developed the Common Alcohol Logistic (CAL) scale because of their concern that existing MMPI alcohol scales lacked adequate positive predictive power given the low base rate or prevalence of alcohol-related problems in general medical settings. Gottesman and Prescott (1989) raised similar concerns about the MAC-R scale in psychiatric patients. The 33 items for the CAL scale were identified and the item weights were assigned by using logistic regression in large samples of alcoholic patients, medical patients, and normal individuals. Malinchoc, Offord, Colligan, and Morse (1994) revised the CAL scale for the MMPI-2 by dropping the six items on the CAL scale that were not retained on the MMPI-2. They recomputed the item weights using logistic regression on similar groups of patients and the resulting 27 items became the CAL-R scale that is appropriate for use with either the MMPI or MMPI-2. They did not use the MMPI-2 item pool in this revision so it remains to be seen whether any of the new MMPI-2 items, particularly the items asking about alcohol and drug abuse, would have been selected for inclusion on the scale. The CAL-R scale appears to be particularly useful to identify substance abuse in medical settings, no doubt reflecting the context in which the scale was developed.

Although the focus of this section is on alcohol and drug scales, it is important to note that there are a number of specific MMPI-2 items related to alcohol and drug use (264, 489, 511, 544) that warrant further inquiry any time they are endorsed in the deviant direction. Most of these items are phrased in the past tense so the clinician cannot assume without inquiry whether the alcohol and drug use is a current or past event.

PERSONALITY PSYCHOPATHOLOGY FIVE (PSY-5) SCALES

Harkness and McNulty created a five-factor model called the Personality Psychopathology Five (PSY-5) to aid in the description of normal personality and to complement the diagnosis of personality disorders. Using replicated rational selection, Harkness and McNulty identified five factors within 60 descriptors of normal and abnormal human behavior: Aggressiveness (AGGR), Psychoticism (PSYC), Disconstraint (DISC), Negative Emotionality/Neuroticism (NEGE), and Introversion/ Low Positive Emotionality (INTR) (cf. Harkness, McNulty, Ben-Porath, & Graham, 2002). The AGGR scale assesses offensive aggression and possibly the enjoyment of dominating, frightening, and controlling others, and the lack of regard for social rules and conventions. The PSYC scale assesses the cognitive ability of the individual to model the external, objective world in an accurate manner. Persons who are low on the PSYC construct can realize that their model is not working and accommodate or revise the model to fit their environment. Although the PSYC scale has its largest correlations with Scales F, 8 (Sc), and Bizarre Mentation (BIZ), it appears to be measuring a general distress factor, much like the NEGE scale. The DISC scale assesses a dimension from rule following versus rule breaking and criminality. The DISC scale is not correlated to most of the other MMPI-2 scales and, thus, would appear to have the potential to contribute additional information when interpreting the MMPI-2. The largest correlations of the DISC scale are with Scales 9 (Ma), the MacAndrew Alcoholism–Revised (MAC-R), and Antisocial Practices (ASP). The NEGE scale assesses a broad affective disposition to experience negative emotions focusing on anxiety and nervousness. The NEGE scale is another of the numerous markers for the first factor of general distress and negative emotionality on the MMPI-2. The INTR construct assesses a broad disposition to experience negative affects and to avoid social experiences. Although the INTR scale generally has its largest correlations with MMPI-2 markers for the first factor, the INTR scale is a measure of anhedonia that is suggestive of rather serious psychopathology. Such an interpretation of the INTR scale is particularly likely when the NEGE scale is not elevated significantly.

The PSY-5 scales are another potential source of information for the clinician in interpreting the MMPI-2 profile. Research that demonstrates their usefulness in patients with personality disorder diagnoses is needed. Until such information is available clinicians are cautioned to interpret them very conservatively.

SUMMARY

The MMPI-2 supplementary scales should be scored and interpreted routinely as a valuable source of additional information that is not readily available in the standard validity and clinical scales or the content scales. For example, the conjoint interpretation of the A and R scales provides a quick insight into how individuals are experiencing and coping with their psychopathology that brought them to treatment. In addition, the information on alcohol and drug use can only be inferred indirectly from the MMPI-2 clinical and content scales, while this information is available both directly and indirectly in the supplementary scales. The information provided by the supplementary scales is invaluable in the treatment-planning process.

References & Readings

Friedman, A. F., Lewak, R., Nichols, D. S., & Webb, J. T. (2001). *Psychological assessment with the MMPI-2*. Mahwah, NJ: Erlbaum.

Gottesman, I. I., & Prescott, C. A. (1989). Abuses of the MacAndrew MMPI alcoholism scale: A critical review. *Clinical Psychology Review, 9*, 223–242.

Graham, J. R. (2000). *MMPI-2: Assessing personality and psychopathology* (3rd ed.). New York: Oxford University Press.

Greene, R. L. (2000). *The MMPI-2: An interpretive manual* (2nd ed.). Boston: Allyn & Bacon.

Harness, A. R., McNulty, J. L., Ben-Porath, Y. S., & Graham, J. R. (2002). *MMPI-2 Personality Psychopathology Five (PSY-5) scales: Gaining an overview for case conceptualization and treat-*

ment planning. Minneapolis: University of Minnesota Press.

Malinchoc, M., Offord, K. P., Colligan, R. C., & Morse, R. M. (1994). The Common Alcohol Logistic–Revised scale (CAL-R): A revised alcoholism scale for the MMPI and MMPI-2. *Journal of Clinical Psychology, 50*, 436–445.

Weed, N. C., Butcher, J. N., & Ben-Porath, Y. S. (1995). MMPI-2 measures of substance abuse. In J. N. Butcher & C. D. Spielberger (Eds.), *Advances in personality assessment* (Vol. 10, pp. 121–145). Hillsdale, NJ: Erlbaum.

Related Topics

Chapter 29, "Clinical Scales of the MMPI-2"
Chapter 31, "Characteristics of High and Low Scores on the MMPI-2 Clinical Scales"
Chapter 32, "Empirical Interpretation of the MMPI-2 Codetypes"

31 CHARACTERISTICS OF HIGH AND LOW SCORES ON THE MMPI-2 CLINICAL SCALES

John R. Graham

These descriptions of high and low scores on each clinical scale of the Minnesota Multiphasic Personality Inventory-2 (MMPI-2) are based on examination of previously reported data for the original MMPI and data concerning the MMPI-2.

DEFINITIONS

- The definition of a high score on a clinical scale has varied considerably in the literature and from one scale to another. Some consider MMPI-2 T scores above 65 as "high." Others have defined high scores as the upper quartile in a distribution or have described several T-score levels on each scale. Another approach identifies the highest scale in the profile (high point) as significant irrespective of its T-score value. The most usual practice is to consider T scores above 65 as high scores.
- Low scores also have been defined in different ways, sometimes as T scores below 40 and other times as scores in the lowest quartile of a distribution. This latter approach has led to scores well above the mean being considered as low scores. In contrast with high scores, limited information is available in the literature concerning the meaning of low scores. The most usual practice is to consider T scores below 40 as low scores.

GENERAL PRINCIPLES

- Some data support the notion that low scores on a particular scale indicate the absence of problems and symptoms characteristic of high scorers on that scale. Other data have suggested that low scores on some scales are associated with general problems and negative characteristics. Still other data have been interpreted as indicating that both high and low scores on some scales indicate similar problems and negative characteristics.

- It is clear that low scores on some MMPI-2 scales may convey important information but not as important as high scores. In nonclinical settings, low scores are associated with fewer than average symptoms and problems and above-average adjustment. There is little basis for interpreting low scores on the clinical scales as indicating problems and negative characteristics in nonclinical samples.
- Based on the empirical data concerning the meaning of low scores on the MMPI and MMPI-2, a very conservative approach to interpretation of low scores on the MMPI-2 clinical scales is recommended. In nonclinical settings (e.g., personnel selection), low scores in a valid protocol should be interpreted as indicating more positive adjustment than high or average scores. However, if the validity scales indicate that the test was completed in a defensive manner, low scores should not be interpreted at all. In clinical settings, it is recommended that low scores on the clinical scales not be interpreted. The exceptions are Scales 5 and 0, for which some limited inferences can be made about low scorers (see below).
- In general, T scores greater than 65 are considered high, although inferences about persons with scores at different levels are presented for some scales. Note that the T-score levels presented are somewhat arbitrary and that clinical judgment is critical in deciding which inferences should be applied to scores at or near the cutoff scores described. Not every inference presented will apply to every person who has a T score at that level.
- In general, greater confidence should be placed in inferences based on more extreme scores, with all inferences treated as hypotheses to be considered in the context of other available information about the person.

INTERPRETATION OF HIGH SCORES ON SCALE 1

- For persons with extremely high scores on Scale 1 (T > 80), dramatic and sometimes bizarre somatic concerns should be suspected. If Scale 3 also is elevated, the possibility of a conversion disorder should be considered. If Scale 8 is very elevated along with Scale 1, somatic delusions may be present.
- Persons with more moderate elevations on Scale 1 (T = 60–80) tend to have generally vague, nonspecific complaints. When specific symptoms are elicited, they tend to be epigastric in nature. Chronic weakness, lack of energy, and sleep disturbance also tend to be characteristic of high scorers. Medical patients with bona fide physical problems generally obtain T scores of about 60 on this scale. When medical patients produce T scores much above 60, one should suspect a strong psychological component to the illness. Moderately high scores on Scale 1 tend to be associated with diagnoses such as somatoform disorders, somatoform pain disorders, anxiety disorders, and depressive disorders. Acting-out behavior is rare among high Scale 1 scorers.
- High Scale 1 scorers (T > 60) in both psychiatric and nonpsychiatric samples tend to be characterized by a rather distinctive set of personality attributes. They are likely to be selfish, self-centered, and narcissistic. Their outlook toward life tends to be pessimistic, defeatist, and cynical. They are generally dissatisfied and unhappy and are likely to make those around them miserable. They complain a great deal and communicate in a whiny manner. They are demanding of others and are very critical of what others do, although they are likely to express hostility in rather indirect ways. High scorers on Scale 1 often are described as dull, unenthusiastic, unambitious, and lacking ease in oral expression.
- High scorers generally do not exhibit much manifest anxiety, and in general they do not show signs of major incapacity. Rather, they appear to be functioning at a reduced level of efficiency. Problems are much more likely to be long-standing than situational or transient.
- Extremely high and moderately high scorers typically see themselves as physically ill, and they seek medical explanations and treatment for their symptoms. They tend to lack

insight concerning the causes of their somatic symptoms, and they resist psychological interpretations. These tendencies, coupled with their generally cynical outlook, suggest that these individuals are not very good candidates for psychotherapy or counseling. They tend to be highly critical of their psychotherapists and to terminate therapy if the therapist is perceived as suggesting psychological reasons for their symptoms or as not giving them enough support and attention.

INTERPRETATION OF HIGH SCORES ON SCALE 2

- High scorers on Scale 2 (particularly if the T scores exceed 70) often display depressive symptoms. They may report feeling depressed, blue, unhappy, or dysphoric. They tend to be quite pessimistic about the future in general and more specifically about the likelihood of overcoming their problems and making a better adjustment. They often talk about committing suicide. Self-depreciation and guilt feelings are common. Behavioral manifestations may include lack of energy, refusal to speak, crying, and psychomotor retardation. Patients with such high scores often receive depressive diagnoses.
- Other symptoms of high scorers include physical complaints, bad dreams, weakness, fatigue or loss of energy, agitation, tension, and fearfulness. They also are described as irritable, high-strung, and prone to worry and fretting. They may have a sense of dread that something bad is about to happen to them.
- High scorers also show a marked lack of self-confidence. They report feelings of uselessness and inability to function in a variety of situations. They act helpless and give up easily when faced with stress. They see themselves as having failed to achieve adequately in school and at their jobs.
- High scorers tend to be described as introverted, shy, retiring, timid, seclusive, and secretive. A lifestyle characterized by withdrawal and lack of intimate involvement with other people is common. These individuals also tend to be aloof and to maintain psychological distance from other people. They may feel that others do not care about them, and their feelings are easily hurt. They often have a severely restricted range of interests and may withdraw from activities in which they previously participated. They are very cautious and conventional in their activities, and they are not very creative in problem solving.
- High scorers may have great difficulty in making even simple decisions and may feel overwhelmed when faced with major life decisions such as vocational choice or marriage. They tend to be very overcontrolled and to deny their own impulses. They are likely to avoid unpleasantness and tend to make concessions in order to avoid confrontations.
- Because high Scale 2 scores are suggestive of great personal distress, they suggest a good prognosis for psychotherapy or counseling. There is some evidence, however, that high scorers may tend to terminate treatment prematurely when the immediate crisis passes.

INTERPRETATION OF HIGH SCORES ON SCALE 3

- Marked elevations on Scale 3 ($T > 80$) suggest persons who react to stress and avoid responsibility by developing physical symptoms. The symptoms usually do not fit the pattern of known organic disorders, often including, in some combination, headaches, stomach discomfort, chest pains, weakness, and tachycardia. Nevertheless, such persons may be symptom free most of the time, but when they are under stress, symptoms may appear suddenly and are likely to disappear just as abruptly after the stress subsides.
- Except for the physical symptoms, high scorers may tend to be relatively free of other symptoms. Although they sometimes describe themselves as prone to worry, lacking energy and feeling worn out, and having sleep disturbances, they are not likely to report severe anxiety, tension, or depression. Hallucinations, delusions, and suspiciousness are rare. The most frequent diagnoses for high Scale 3 scorers among psychiatric pa-

tients are conversion disorder and psychogenic pain disorder.

- A salient feature of the day-to-day functioning of high scorers is a marked lack of insight concerning the possible underlying causes of their symptoms. In addition, they show little insight concerning their own motives and feelings.
- High scorers are often described as extremely immature psychologically and at times even childish or infantile. They are self-centered, narcissistic, and egocentric, and they expect a great deal of attention and affection from others. They often use indirect and devious means to get the attention and affection they crave. When others do not respond appropriately, they may become hostile and resentful, but these feelings are likely to be denied and not expressed openly or directly.
- High Scale 3 scorers tend to be emotionally involved, friendly, talkative, enthusiastic, and alert. Although affectional and attention needs drive them into social interactions, their relationships tend to be superficial and immature. They are involved with people primarily because of what they can get from them, rather than out of sincere interest.
- Because of their needs for acceptance and affection, high scorers may initially be quite enthusiastic about counseling and psychotherapy. However, they may view themselves as having medical problems and want to be treated medically. They are slow to gain insight into underlying causes of their behavior, and they resist psychological interpretations. If therapists insist on examining psychological causes of symptoms, premature termination of therapy is likely. High Scale 3 scorers may be willing to talk about problems in their lives as long as they are not conceptualized as causing or contributing to their symptoms. These individuals often respond well to direct advice and suggestion.
- When high Scale 3 scorers become involved in therapy, they discuss worry about failure in school or work, marital unhappiness, lack of acceptance by their social groups, and problems with authority figures.

INTERPRETATION OF HIGH SCORES ON SCALE 4

- Extremely high scores (T > 75) on Scale 4 tend to be associated with difficulty incorporating the values and standards of society. Such high scorers are likely to engage in a variety of asocial, antisocial, and even criminal behaviors. These behaviors may include lying, cheating, stealing, sexual acting out, and excessive use of alcohol and/or other drugs.
- High scorers on Scale 4 tend to be rebellious toward authority figures and often are in conflict with authorities. They often have stormy relationships with families, and family members tend to blame others for their difficulties. Underachievement in school, poor work history, and marital problems are also characteristic of high scorers.
- High scorers are highly impulsive persons who strive for immediate gratification. They often do not plan their behavior, and they act without considering the consequences. They are very impatient and have limited frustration tolerance. Their behavior may involve poor judgment and considerable risk taking. They tend not to profit from experiences and may find themselves in the same difficulties repeatedly.
- High scorers on Scale 4 are described by others as immature and childish. They are narcissistic, self-centered, selfish, and egocentric, and their behavior often is ostentatious and exhibitionistic. They are insensitive to the needs and feelings of other people and are interested in others in terms of how they can be used. Although they tend to be seen as likable and generally create good first impressions, their relationships often are shallow and superficial. This may be due in part to rejection on the part of the people they mistreat, but it also seems to reflect their inability to form warm attachments with others.
- High scorers often describe significant family problems. They may see their home environments as unpleasant and family members as unloving and unsupportive.
- In addition, high Scale 4 scorers typically are extroverted and outgoing. They are talkative,

active, adventurous, energetic, and spontaneous. They are viewed by others as intelligent and self-confident. Although they have a wide range of interests and may become involved in many activities, they lack definite goals and clear direction.

- High scorers tend to be hostile and aggressive. They are resentful, rebellious, antagonistic, and refractory. Their attitude is characterized by sarcasm and cynicism. Often there does not appear to be any guilt associated with the aggressive behavior. Whereas high scorers may feign guilt and remorse when their behaviors get them into trouble, such responses typically are short-lived, disappearing when the immediate crisis passes.
- Although high scorers typically are not seen as being overwhelmed by emotional turmoil, at times they may admit feeling sad, fearful, or worried about the future. They may experience absence of deep emotional response, which may produce feelings of emptiness and boredom. Among psychiatric patients, high scorers tend to receive personality disorder diagnoses, with antisocial personality disorder or passive-aggressive personality disorder occurring most frequently.
- Because of their verbal facility, outgoing manner, and apparent intellectual resources, high scorers on Scale 4 are often perceived as good candidates for psychotherapy or counseling. Unfortunately, the prognosis for change is poor. Although these individuals may agree to treatment to avoid something more unpleasant (e.g., jail or divorce), they generally are unable to accept responsibility for their own problems and tend to terminate treatment as soon as possible. In therapy they often intellectualize excessively and blame others for their difficulties.

INTERPRETATION OF SCORES ON SCALE 5

- High scores (T > 60) for men on Scale 5 indicate a lack of stereotypical masculine interests. These individuals tend to have aesthetic and artistic interests and are likely to participate in housekeeping and child-rearing activities to a greater extent than most men.
- High scores on Scale 5 are uncommon among women. When encountered, they generally indicate rejection of traditional female roles. Women with high Scale 5 scores are interested in sports, hobbies, and other activities that tend to be stereotypically more masculine than feminine, and they often are described as competitive and assertive.
- Men who score low on Scale 5 are presenting themselves as extremely masculine. They have stereotypically masculine preferences in work, hobbies, and other activities.
- Women who score low on Scale 5 have many stereotypically feminine interests. They are likely to derive satisfaction from their roles as spouses and mothers. They may be traditionally feminine or may have adopted a more androgynous lifestyle.

INTERPRETATION OF HIGH SCORES ON SCALE 6

- Persons whose Scale 6 T scores are above 70, especially when Scale 6 also is the highest scale in the profile, may exhibit frankly psychotic behavior. Their thinking may be disturbed, including delusions of persecution or grandeur. Ideas of reference also are common. These individuals may feel mistreated and picked on; they may be angry and resentful; and they may harbor grudges. Projection is a common defense mechanism. Among psychiatric patients, diagnoses of schizophrenia or paranoid disorders are most frequent.
- When Scale 6 T scores range from 60 to 70, blatant psychotic symptoms are not as common. However, persons with scores within this range are characterized by a variety of traits and behaviors suggesting a paranoid orientation. They tend to be excessively sensitive and overly responsive to the opinions of others. They believe they are getting a raw deal out of life and tend to rationalize and blame others for their difficulties. Also, they are suspicious and guarded and commonly exhibit hostility, resentment, and an argumentative manner. They tend to be very moralistic and rigid in their opinions and at-

titudes. Rationality is likely to be greatly overemphasized.

- Prognosis for psychotherapy is poor because these people do not like to talk about emotional problems and are likely to rationalize most of the time. They have great difficulty in establishing rapport with therapists. In therapy, they are likely to reveal hostility and resentment toward family members.

INTERPRETATION OF HIGH SCORES ON SCALE 7

- Scale 7 is a good index of psychological turmoil and discomfort, with higher scorers experiencing greater turmoil. High scorers tend to be very anxious, tense, and agitated. They worry a great deal, even over small problems, and are fearful and apprehensive. They are high-strung and jumpy, report difficulties in concentrating, and often receive anxiety disorder diagnoses.
- High scorers tend to be highly introspective and sometimes report fears that they are losing their minds. Obsessive thinking, compulsive and ritualistic behavior, and ruminations, often centering around feelings of insecurity and inferiority, are common among very high scorers. These persons lack self-confidence; are self-critical, self-conscious, and self-degrading; and are plagued by self-doubts. They tend to be very rigid and moralistic and to have high standards of behavior and performance for themselves and others. They are likely to be quite perfectionistic and conscientious, experiencing guilt feelings about not living up to their own standards or depression about falling short of goals.
- In general, high scorers are neat, orderly, organized, and meticulous. They are persistent and reliable but lack ingenuity and originality in their approach to problems. They are seen by others as dull and formal and as having great difficulty in making decisions. In addition, they are likely to distort the importance of problems and to be overreactive in stressful situations.
- High scorers tend to be shy and do not interact well socially. They are described as hard to get to know, and they worry a great deal about popularity and social acceptance. Other people see them as sentimental, peaceable, softhearted, trustful, sensitive, and kind. Other adjectives used to describe them include dependent, unassertive, and immature.
- Some high scorers on Scale 7 express physical complaints centering around the heart or the gastrointestinal or genitourinary system. Complaints of fatigue, exhaustion, insomnia, and bad dreams are common.
- Although high scorers may be motivated to seek therapy because they feel so uncomfortable and miserable, they are not very responsive to brief psychotherapy or counseling. In spite of some insight into their problems, they tend to rationalize and intellectualize a great deal. They often are resistant to interpretations and may express much hostility toward the therapist. However, they tend to remain in therapy longer than most patients and may show slow but steady progress. Problems presented in therapy may include difficulties with authority figures, poor work or study habits, or concern about homosexual impulses.

INTERPRETATION OF HIGH SCORES ON SCALE 8

- Although one should be cautious about assigning a diagnosis of schizophrenia on the basis of only the score on Scale 8, T scores in a range of 75–90 suggest the possibility of a psychotic disorder. Confusion, disorganization, and disorientation may be present. Unusual thoughts or attitudes, perhaps even delusional in nature, hallucinations, and extremely poor judgment may be evident.
- Extreme scores (T > 90) usually are not produced by psychotic individuals; they more likely indicate an individual in acute psychological turmoil or a less disturbed person who is endorsing many deviant items as a cry for help. However, some recently hospitalized psychiatric patients obtain high scores on Scale 8, accurately reflecting severe psychopathology.

- High scores on Scale 8 may suggest a schizoid lifestyle. Such people tend to feel isolated, alienated, misunderstood, and unaccepted by their peers. They are withdrawn, reclusive, secretive, and inaccessible and may avoid dealing with people and with new situations. They are described by others as shy, aloof, and uninvolved.
- High scorers experience a great deal of apprehension and generalized anxiety, and they often report having bad dreams. They may feel sad or blue. They may feel very resentful, hostile, and aggressive, but they are unable to express such feelings. A typical response to stress is withdrawal into daydreams and fantasies, and some high scorers may have a difficult time separating reality and fantasy.
- High scorers may be plagued by self-doubts. They feel inferior, incompetent, and dissatisfied. They give up easily when confronted with problem situations. Sexual preoccupation and sex role confusion are common. The behavior of such persons often is characterized by others as nonconforming, unusual, unconventional, and eccentric. Physical complaints may be present, and these usually are vague and long-standing.
- High scorers may at times be stubborn, moody, and opinionated. At other times they are seen as generous, peaceable, and sentimental. Other adjectives used to describe high scorers include immature, impulsive, adventurous, sharp-witted, conscientious, and high-strung. Although they may have a wide range of interests and may be creative and imaginative in approaching problems, their goals generally are abstract and vague. They seem to lack basic information required for problem solving.
- It is important to consider the possibility that high Scale-8 scores are reflecting the reporting of unusual symptoms associated with substance abuse or with medical disorders such as epilepsy, stroke, or closed head injury.
- The prognosis for psychotherapy is not good because of the long-standing nature of high scorers' problems and their reluctance to relate in a meaningful way to the therapist. However, high scorers tend to stay in therapy longer than most patients and eventually may come to trust the therapist. Medical consultation to evaluate the appropriateness of medication may be indicated.

INTERPRETATION OF HIGH SCORES ON SCALE 9

- Extreme elevations (T > 80) on Scale 9 may suggest a bipolar (manic) disorder. Patients with such scores are likely to show excessive, purposeless activity and accelerated speech; they may have hallucinations and/or delusions of grandeur; and they are emotionally labile. Some confusion may be present, and flight of ideas is common.
- Persons with more moderate elevations are not likely to exhibit frank psychotic symptoms but have a tendency toward overactivity and unrealistic self-appraisal. They are energetic and talkative, and they prefer action to thought. They have a wide range of interests and are likely to have many projects going at once. However, they do not use energy wisely and often do not see projects through to completion. They may be creative, enterprising, and ingenious, but they have little interest in routine or details. Such persons become bored and restless easily and have low frustration tolerance. They have great difficulty inhibiting impulsivity, and periodic episodes of irritability, hostility, and aggressive outbursts are common. Unrealistic and unqualified optimism is also characteristic of high scorers. They seem to think that nothing is impossible, and they have grandiose aspirations. They also have an exaggerated appraisal of their own self-worth and self-importance and are not able to see their own limitations. High scorers have a greater than average likelihood of using nonprescription drugs and getting into trouble with the law.
- High scorers are very outgoing, sociable, and gregarious. They enjoy other people and generally create good first impressions. They impress others as being friendly, pleasant, enthusiastic, poised, and self-confident. They often try to dominate other people. Their relationships are usually quite superficial, and

as others get to know them better, they become aware of their manipulations, deceptions, and unreliability.

- In spite of an outward picture of confidence and poise, high scorers are likely to harbor feelings of dissatisfaction about what they are getting out of life. They may feel upset, tense, nervous, anxious, and agitated, and they describe themselves as prone to worry. Periodic episodes of depression may occur.
- In psychotherapy, high scorers often report negative feelings toward domineering parents, difficulties in school or at work, and a variety of delinquent behaviors. They resist interpretations, are irregular in their attendance, and are likely to terminate therapy prematurely. They engage in a great deal of intellectualization and may repeat problems in a stereotyped manner. They do not become dependent on the therapist, who may be a target for hostility and aggression.

INTERPRETATION OF SCORES ON SCALE 0

- The most salient characteristic of high scorers on Scale 0 is social introversion. These persons are very insecure and uncomfortable in social situations, tending to be shy, reserved, timid, and retiring. They feel more comfortable when alone or with a few close friends, and they do not participate in many social activities. They may be especially uncomfortable around members of the opposite sex.
- High scorers lack self-confidence and tend to be self-effacing. They are hard to get to know and may be described by others as cold and distant. They are sensitive to what others think of them and are likely to be troubled by their lack of involvement with other people. They are overcontrolled and are unlikely to display feelings directly. They are submissive, compliant, and overly accepting of authority.
- High scorers are also described as serious and having a slow personal tempo. Although they are reliable and dependable, their approach to problems tends to be cautious, conventional, and unoriginal. They give up easily and are somewhat rigid and inflexible in their attitudes and opinions. They also have great difficulty in making even minor decisions. They seem to enjoy their work and get pleasure from personal achievement.
- High scorers tend to worry, to be irritable, and to feel anxious. They are described by others as moody. Guilt feelings and episodes of depression may occur. Such persons lack energy and do not have many interests.
- Low scorers on Scale 0 tend to be sociable and extroverted. They are outgoing, gregarious, friendly, and talkative. They have a strong need to be around other people, and they mix well socially. They are seen by others as verbally fluent, expressive, active, energetic, and vigorous. They are interested in power, status, and recognition, and they tend to seek out competitive situations.
- Low scores on Scale 0 are indicative of persons who are sociable, extroverted, outgoing, gregarious, friendly, and talkative; who have a strong need to be around other people; who mix well; and who are seen as expressive and verbally fluent.
- Scores on Scale 0 are quite stable, even over very long periods of time.

References & Readings 

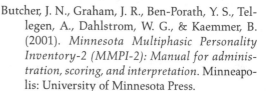

Butcher, J. N., Graham, J. R., Ben-Porath, Y. S., Tellegen, A., Dahlstrom, W. G., & Kaemmer, B. (2001). *Minnesota Multiphasic Personality Inventory-2 (MMPI-2): Manual for administration, scoring, and interpretation*. Minneapolis: University of Minnesota Press.

Butcher, J. N., & Williams, C. L. (2000). *Essentials of MMPI-2 and MMPI-A interpretation*. Minneapolis: University of Minnesota Press.

Graham, J. R. (2000). *MMPI-2: Assessing personality and psychopathology* (3rd ed.). New York: Oxford University Press.

Graham, J. R., Ben-Porath, Y. S., & McNulty, J. L. (1997). Empirical correlates of low scores on MMPI-2 scales in an out-patient mental health setting. *Psychological Assessment, 9*, 386–391.

Graham, J. R., Ben-Porath, Y. S., & McNulty, J. L. (1999). *MMPI-2 correlates for outpatient community mental health settings*. Minneapolis: University of Minnesota Press.

Graham J. R., & McCord, G. (1985). Interpretation of moderately elevated MMPI scores for normal subjects. *Journal of Personality Assessment, 49*, 477–484.

Greene, R. (2000). *The MMPI-2: An interpretive manual* (2nd ed.). Boston: Allyn and Bacon.

Keiller, S. W., & Graham, J. R. (1993). The meaning of low scores on MMPI-2 clinical scales of normal subjects. *Journal of Personality Assessment, 61*, 211–223.

Related Topics

Chapter 28, "Assessing MMPI-2 Profile Validity"
Chapter 29, "Clinical Scales of the MMPI-2"
Chapter 32, "Empirical Interpretation of the MMPI-2 Codetypes"

32 EMPIRICAL INTERPRETATION OF THE MMPI-2 CODETYPES

James N. Butcher

The Minnesota Multiphasic Personality Inventory (MMPI) is the most widely researched and extensively used objective instrument in clinical assessment (Butcher & Rouse, 1996; Lubin, Larsen, & Matarazzo, 1984). Following its initial publication in 1940, the MMPI came to be employed across a wide variety of clinical, academic, military, industrial, and forensic settings. The initial test developers, Hathaway and McKinley, followed an empirical scale construction strategy by finding items that separated groups of individuals with known psychiatric problems, such as anxiety or depression, from "normals" (Hathaway & McKinley, 1940).

The original MMPI underwent a substantial revision and redevelopment during the 1980s, and the MMPI-2 was published for use with adults in 1989 and for adolescents (the MMPI-A) in 1992. The modern versions of the instrument were standardized on contemporary, representative samples of individuals in the United States. The resulting instruments, with their expanded range of scales, have demonstrated strong psychometric properties similar to those of their predecessor (Butcher & Williams, 1992) and have now replaced the original MMPI for assessment in mental health settings.

Although portions of the test remained the same, several changes were made during the revision, such as the omission of items with objectionable content and rewording of items that were out of date. The traditional validity and clinical scales were retained for the revised versions in order to maintain continuity with the original MMPI—that is, L (Lie), F (Infrequency), K (Defensiveness), 1 (Hypochondriasis), 2 (Depression), 3 (Hysteria), 4 (Psychopathic Deviate), 5 (Masculinity/Femininity), 6 (Paranoia), 7 (Psychasthenia), 8 (Schizophrenia), 9 (Mania), and 0 (Social Introversion). In addition, a number of new validity measures were developed for the revised forms (i.e., True Response Inconsistency [TRIN] and Variable Response Inconsistency [VRIN]). In addition to the traditional clinical scales, an important new set of scales, the MMPI-2 (Butcher, Graham, Williams, & Ben-Porath, 1990) and MMPI-A content scales, was published (Williams, Butcher, Ben-Porath, & Graham,

1992). These scales were derived according to a rational-empirical scale construction strategy to provide several measures of specific clinical problems.

Since the MMPI-2 revision, there have been numerous studies to examine whether the extensive literature on the use of the original MMPI can be generalized to the revised instruments (Archer, Griffin, & Aiduk, 1995). The psychometric properties of the MMPI-2 and MMPI-A scales have been found to be comparable to those of the clinical scales for the original MMPI. Test-retest coefficients were of a similar magnitude (Butcher, Dahlstrom, Graham, Tellegen, & Kaemmer, 1989). Results from validity studies on the MMPI-2 and MMPI-A to date have been very promising (Ben-Porath, Butcher, & Graham, 1991; Williams & Butcher, 1989a, 1989b).

The extensive objective information available for each of the MMPI-2 patterns makes interpretation of the test relatively straightforward. Empirical scale interpretation with the MMPI-2 works as follows: An individual taking the MMPI-2 answers a series of true-false questions, which are scored according to objective rules. The scores are assigned T-score values on different scales (e.g., Scale 1 = Hypochondriasis; Scale 2 = Depression); profiles are then drawn to allow for easy comparison to normals. When a new case is obtained with profiles that resemble known patient groups, that is, that match a particular prototype, the empirical descriptors (referred to as *scale correlates*) are generated to provide an indication of that individual's psychological adjustment problems. That is, when a particular pattern is obtained by an individual, the interpreter simply refers to the established behaviors and personality factors established for it. These established behavior patterns can be *automatically* applied whenever the scores are obtained.

The scale scores have been extensively researched, and a number of resources, known as codebooks or "cookbooks," have accumulated to provide a rich catalog of personality descriptors that have been empirically shown to be associated with various scale patterns. This objective strategy makes it possible for individual test protocols to be effectively interpreted by electronic computer (Butcher, 1995). Automated interpretation, that is, interpreting MMPI profiles using actuarial tables, was initially shown by Meehl (1954) to be a more powerful strategy than clinical interpretation. He convincingly demonstrated that clinical predictions based on automatic combination of actuarial data for MMPI codetypes were more accurate than those based on "clinical" or intuitive interpretation strategies.

A number of empirical studies followed Meehl's recommendations for developing an actuarial "cookbook" as an aid to stringent test interpretation. The empirical research on MMPI profile patterns that followed during the 1960s and 1970s has established a broad interpretive base for many of the common MMPI codetypes found in clinical settings (Gilberstadt & Duker, 1965; Marks, Seeman, & Haller, 1974). Meehl's compelling argument on the strength of the actuarial method and the empirical demonstration that such mechanically generated predictions were highly accurate influenced a number of investigators to develop "actuarial tables" for personality description using MMPI scales and profile codes.

A codetype is defined by the highest elevated scale or groupings of clinical scales in the profile and their rank order in terms of elevation. Most of the empirical research on MMPI codetypes has included only the basic clinical scales Hs, D, Hy, Pd, Pa, Pt, Sc, and Ma. Research-based behavioral descriptions associated with codetypes can be confidently applied to individuals whose profiles match the codetype. The *Single-Point Code*, or "profile spike," occurs when a single clinical scale is elevated in the critical range, that is, above a T score of 65. The *Two-Point Codetype*, one of the most frequently researched profile codes, occurs when two clinical scales, such as D and Pt, are elevated above a T = 65. This codetype would be defined as a two-point code of 2-7/7-2. The *Three-Point Code*, prominent in several research populations, occurs when three clinical scales are elevated in the profile. For example, clinical elevations on scales D, Pd, and Pt produce a three-point code of 2-4-7, a profile type often found in drug and alcohol treatment programs. A few *Four-Point Codes* have been researched, for example, the 1-2-3-4 codetype in medical settings.

Two general rules are followed to determine whether a particular profile pattern meets the requirements of a reliable codetype: First, the profile should be clearly defined; that is, if the profile code is at least five points greater than the next scale in the profile, the codetype is likely to be the same on MMPI or on MMPI-2 norms and likely to be a good prototypal match. In general, Graham, Smith, and Schwartz (1986) recommend exercising caution in applying traditional MMPI behavioral correlates for a given codetype if the MMPI profile does not possess clear codetype definition or a clear elevation above the next scale in the profile. Graham, Timbrook, Ben-Porath, and Butcher (1991) demonstrated that MMPI-2 codes were quite congruent with MMPI profile codes when codetype definition was maintained. Over 90% of the profiles with a five-point profile code definition will have the same codetype on MMPI-2 as with the original MMPI. Second, when there has been sufficient research on the behavioral descriptions for the code (e.g., 2-7-8 codetype), there would likely be a sufficient empirical base to provide reliable information about the client. If a codetype is an infrequent one (with a relatively small database such as with the 2-9/9-2 profile code), then a scale-by-scale interpretation strategy should be followed. With the MMPI-2, as with the original MMPI, empirical descriptors are sparse for some codetypes. Not enough codetypes have been empirically studied and described across a broad range of settings to classify the range of profiles that clinicians can obtain.

How likely are MMPI-2 profile codes to remain stable over time, for example, if the client is retested at a later date? First, as a general rule, MMPI scales tend to have high test-retest stability. Test-retest correlations for various groups have been reported to range from moderate to high, depending on the population studied and the retest interval. Even test-retest correlations over very long intervals, for example, over 30 years (Leon, Gillum, Gillum, & Gouze, 1979), are quite high, with some scales (i.e., Si) showing correlations as high as .73.

Several studies of MMPI profile stability have been conducted. Graham et al. (1986) reported that the percentages of people with the same high-point, low-point, and two-point code showed only modest congruence on retest. They noted, however, that codetypes with more extreme scores, and those that were well defined by a substantial point separation between scale scores in the codetype from those not included in the code, tended to be similar at retest. The greatest codetype agreement at retest was obtained for profiles having a 10-point T-score spread between the codetype. However, high congruence was obtained at retest if the codetype was even 5 points higher than the next scale in the profile.

ILLUSTRATION OF THE 2-7/7-2 PROFILE CODE

The 2-7/7-2 profile code is defined by having two scales (Scale 2, or Depression, and Scale 7, or Psychasthenia) elevated above a T score of 65 and appearing as the highest two clinical scales in the profile. The following summary would likely be found to apply with the client producing the 2-7/7-2 code:

Symptomatic Pattern

Individuals with this profile code appear anxious, tense, nervous, and depressed. They report feeling unhappy and sad and tend to worry to excess. They feel vulnerable to real and imagined threat and typically anticipate problems before they occur—often overreacting to minor stress as though it is a major catastrophe. They usually report somatic symptoms such as fatigue, exhaustion, tiredness, weight loss, slow personal tempo, slowed speech, and retarded thought processes. They tend to brood and ruminate a great deal.

These persons may have high expectations for themselves and others and show a strong need for achievement and recognition for accomplishments. They may feel guilty when their goals are not met. These individuals typically have perfectionistic attitudes and a conscientious life history. They may be excessively religious or extremely moralistic.

Personality Characteristics

Individuals with this pattern appear docile and passive-dependent in relationships. They report problems in being assertive. They usually show a capacity for forming deep, emotional ties and tend to lean on people to an excessive degree. They tend to solicit nurturance from others. Feelings of inadequacy, insecurity, and inferiority are long term issues. They tend to be intropunitive in dealing with feelings of aggression.

Predictions and Dispositions
Individuals with this profile code are usually diagnosed as depressive, obsessive-compulsive, or anxiety disordered. They are usually motivated for psychotherapy and tend to remain in therapy longer than other patients. They tend to be somewhat pessimistic about overcoming problems and are indecisive and rigid in their thinking. This negative mind set is likely to interfere with their problem-solving ability. However, they usually improve in treatment. (Butcher & Williams, 1992)

The empirically based MMPI-2 correlates have considerable robustness when applied to new samples—even across other languages and cultural groups. The MMPI-2, if adapted carefully to new cultures, can provide important information on psychopathology about patients in diverse clinical settings. The MMPI-2 appears to work similarly in a wide variety of countries. The original MMPI was widely translated, with over 140 translations in 46 countries (Butcher & Pancheri, 1976), and the MMPI-2 has undergone a number of foreign-language translations since it was published in 1989. Butcher (1996) conducted an extensive cross-national MMPI-2 research program detailing the clinical and research use of the MMPI-2 across a large number of countries.

The MMPI-2 empirical descriptors apply well across international boundaries even when applied by an electronic computer. A recent study by Butcher et al. (1998) found that patients from several countries were described with a high degree of accuracy by computer-based reports generated from U.S. norms and descriptors derived from American based research. This research provided support for the generalization validity of MMPI-2 correlates in cross-cultural contexts.

References & Readings

Archer, R. P., Griffin, R., & Aiduk, R. (1995). Clinical correlates for ten common code types. *Journal of Personality Assessment, 65*, 391–408.

Ben-Porath, Y. S., Butcher, J. N., & Graham, J. R. (1991). Contribution of the MMPI-2 scales to the differential diagnosis of schizophrenia and major depression. *Psychological Assessment: A Journal of Consulting and Clinical Psychology, 3*, 634–640.

Butcher, J. N. (1995). Clinical use of computer-based personality test reports. In J. N. Butcher (Ed.), *Clinical personality assessment: Practical approaches*. New York: Oxford University Press.

Butcher, J. N. (Ed.). (1996). *International adaptations of the MMPI-2: Research and clinical applications*. Minneapolis: University of Minnesota Press.

Butcher, J. N., Berah, E., Ellertsen, B., Miach, P., Lim, J., Nezami, E., et al. (1998). Objective personality assessment: Computer-based MMPI-2 interpretation in international clinical settings. In C. Belar (Ed.), *Comprehensive clinical psychology: Sociocultural and individual differences*. New York: Elsevier.

Butcher, J. N., Dahlstrom, W. G., Graham, J. R., Tellegen, A., & Kaemmer, B. (1989). *Minnesota Multiphasic Personality Inventory-2 (MMPI-2): Manual for administration and scoring*. Minneapolis: University of Minnesota Press.

Butcher, J. N., Graham, J. R., Williams, C. L., & Ben-Porath, Y. S. (1990). *Development and use of the MMPI-2 content scales*. Minneapolis: University of Minnesota Press.

Butcher, J. N., & Pancheri, P. (1976). *Handbook of cross-national MMPI research*. Minneapolis: University of Minnesota Press.

Butcher, J. N., & Rouse, S. V. (1996). Personality: Individual differences and clinical assessment. *Annual Review of Psychology, 47*, 87–111.

Butcher, J. N., & Williams, C. L. (1992). *Essentials of MMPI-2 and MMPI-A interpretation*. Minneapolis: University of Minnesota Press.

Butcher, J. N., Williams, C. L., Graham, J. R., Archer, R. P., Tellegen, A., & Ben-Porath, Y. (1992). *MMPI-A (Minnesota Multiphasic Personality Inventory-Adolescent): Manual for administration, scoring, and interpretation*. Minneapolis: University of Minnesota Press.

Gilberstadt, H., & Duker, J. (1965). *A handbook for clinical and actuarial MMPI interpretation*. Philadelphia: Saunders.

Graham, J. R., Smith, R., & Schwartz, G. (1986). Stability of MMPI configurations for psychiatric inpatients. *Journal of Consulting and Clinical Psychology, 54*, 375–380.

Graham, J. R., Timbrook, R., Ben-Porath, Y. S., &

Butcher, J. N. (1991). Code-type congruence between MMPI and MMPI-2: Separating fact from artifact. *Journal of Personality Assessment, 57,* 205–215.

Hathaway, S. R., & McKinley, J. C. (1940). A multiphasic personality schedule (Minnesota) I: Construction of the schedule. *Journal of Psychology, 10,* 249–254.

Leon, G., Gillum, B., Gillum, R., & Gouze, M. (1979). Personality stability and change over a thirty-year period: Middle age to old age. *Journal of Consulting and Clinical Psychology, 47,* 517–524.

Lubin, B., Larsen, R. M., & Matarazzo, J. (1984). Patterns of psychological test usage in the United States, 1935–1982. *American Psychologist, 39,* 451–454.

Marks, P. A., Seeman, W., & Haller, D. L. (1974). *The actuarial use of the MMPI with adolescents and adults.* Baltimore: Williams and Wilkins.

Meehl, P. E. (1954). *Clinical versus statistical prediction: A theoretical analysis and a review of the evidence.* Minneapolis: University of Minnesota Press.

Williams, C. L., & Butcher, J. N. (1989a). An MMPI study of adolescents: I. Empirical validity of the standard scales. *Psychological Assessment: A Journal of Consulting and Clinical Psychology, 1,* 251–259.

Williams, C. L., & Butcher, J. N. (1989b). An MMPI study of adolescents: II. Verification and limitations of code type classification. *Psychological Assessment: A Journal of Consulting and Clinical Psychology, 1,* 260–265.

Williams, C. L., Butcher, J. N., Ben-Porath, Y. S., & Graham, J. R. (1992). *MMPI-A content scales: Assessing psychopathology in adolescents.* Minneapolis: University of Minnesota Press.

Related Topics

Chapter 28, "Assessing MMPI-2 Profile Validity"
Chapter 29, "Clinical Scales of the MMPI-2"
Chapter 31, "Characteristics of High and Low Scores on the MMPI-2 Clinical Scales"

33 MILLON CLINICAL MULTIAXIAL INVENTORY (MCMI-III)

Theodore Millon & Seth D. Grossman

Diagnostic instruments are most useful when developed on the basis of a comprehensive theory of psychopathology and coordinated with a recognized diagnostic system. Both the Millon Clinical Multiaxial Inventory's (MCMI) Personality Disorder (Axis II) and Clinical Syndrome (Axis I) categories meet these criteria. In the MCMI-III, further parallelism has been achieved by rephrasing major criteria of the fourth-edition *Diagnostic and Statistical Manual of Mental Disorders* (*DSM-IV*) constructs and validating these items in the self-report mode. Accordingly, the diagnostic efficiency of the MCMI-III (Millon, 1997; Millon, Millon, & Davis, 1994) shows an incremental increase over that of the MCMI-II (Davis, Wenger, & Guzman, 1997). Few diagnostic instruments currently available are as fully consonant as the MCMI-III with the nosological format and conceptual terminology of the *DSM-IV*.

DESCRIPTION

The inventory itself consists of 24 clinical scales (presented as a profile in Table 1) and 3

TABLE 1. Sample Profile Illustrating the Structure and Scales of the MCMI-III

Category		Score Raw	Score BR	Profile of BR Scores (0 60 75 85 115)	Diagnostic Scales
Modifying indices	X	135	79		Disclosure
	Y	18	84		Desirability
	Z	7	56		Debasement
Clinical personality patterns	1	7	63		Schizoid
	2A	6	69		Avoidant
	2B	3	55		Depressive
	3	7	60		Dependent
	4	22	68		Histrionic
	5	27	103		Narcissistic
	6A	20	88		Antisocial
	6B	21	85		Aggressive (sadistic)
	7	10	34		Compulsive
	8A	17	80		Negativistic
	8B	1	15		Masochistic
Severe personality pathology	S	2	37		Schizotypal
	C	11	69		Borderline
	P	9	63		Paranoid
Clinical syndromes	A	3	57		Anxiety disorder
	H	2	57		Somatoform disorder
	N	6	59		Bipolar manic disorder
	D	3	57		Dysthymic disorder
	B	17	99		Alcohol dependence
	T	12	70		Drug dependence
	R	2	27		Posttraumatic stress
Severe syndromes	SS	2	27		Thought disorder
	CC	1	17		Major depression
	PP	3	60		Delusion disorder

"modifier" scales. The purpose of these first three indices, Disclosure, Desirability, and Debasement (X, Y, and Z), is to identify distorting tendencies in clients' responses. The next two sections constitute the basic personality disorder scales, reflecting Axis II of the *DSM*. The first section (1–8B) appraises the moderately severe personality pathologies, ranging from the Schizoid to the Self-Defeating (masochistic) scales; the second section (scales S, C, and P) represents more severe personality pathologies: the Schizotypal, Borderline, and Paranoid. The following two sections cover several of the more prevalent Axis I disorders, ranging from the moderate clinical syndromes (scales A to T) to those of greater severity (scales SS, CC, and PP). The division between personality and clinical disorder scales parallels the multiaxial model and has important interpretive implications.

Development of the Millon inventories has been informed by several post-MMPI psychometric developments. When the MCMI was initially constructed, all item selections were based on target diagnostic groups contrasted with representative, but undifferentiated, psychiatric patients (rather than normals), thus increasing differential diagnostic efficiency. Item selection and scale development for both older and more recent forms progressed through three sequential validation stages (Loevinger, 1957): theoretical-substantive, internal-structural, and external-criterion. Such an approach builds validity into the instrument from the beginning, upholding standards of developers committed to diverse construction and validation methods (Hase & Goldberg, 1967). The resulting scales are theoretically, statistically, and empirically valid. Because each item must survive each stage of refinement, the chance that any item will prove "rationally surprising," "structurally unsound," or "empirically indiscriminant" is greatly diminished. The final MCMI-III items are weighted either 2 points or 1 point, depending on the extent to which they fulfill this tripartite logic: centrality to their respective constructs, relation to other items on the same scale, and external validity. As might be expected, the likelihood of instrument generalizability is greatly increased by such an approach to instrument construction.

Actuarial base rate transformations were used as the final measure of pathology. These not only provide a basis for selecting optimal differential diagnostic cutting lines but also help ensure that the frequencies of MCMI-generated diagnoses and profile patterns are comparable to representative clinical prevalence rates. Although the use of base rate scores has been one of the most widely misunderstood aspects of the MCMI, their utility is easily understood intuitively when contrasted with the more familiar T score. On the MMPI, for example, T scores of 65 and above indicate pathology, with roughly equal numbers of patients scoring above this threshold. Clinical experience, however, shows the number of depressed patients, for example, to be greater than the number of patients with a thought disorder. Base rate scores are constructed to reflect these clinical realities, to yield more depressives than delusional patients, more borderlines and antisocials than schizoids, and so on, rather than to assume their numbers to be equal. In the construction of the MCMI, target prevalence rates were set according to reviews of epidemiological data, estimates derived from clinicians who participated in the development project, and the senior author's own expert judgment. Thus, if it was deemed that 8% of patients are most likely to resemble the schizoid prototype, then the lookup table for this personality was constructed so schizoid was the highest personality elevation for 8% of the patients in the normative sample.

A discussion of base rate scores often leads to considerations of local versus global base rates, that is, the fact that the prevalence rates for different disorders vary somewhat by clinical setting. When this is raised in criticism of the concept, it is usually intended to support the continued use of T scores. However, as noted earlier, the base rate scores of the MCMI are intended to remedy the global base rate assumptions made in the use of T scores. Thus, while the prevalence rates of some disorders in particular clinical settings may differ from the base rates assumed by the MCMI and in the use of T scores, the MCMI's base rate scores at least do not implicitly assume the prevalence rates of all disorders to be equal. More frequently, the distinction between local and global prevalence rates is made in support of the base rate concept by clinicians who realize its importance in improving diagnostic efficiency, that is, positive and negative predictive power, sensitivity, and specificity. These clinicians, far from reverting back to T scores, often wish to optimize the base rate scores for their particular setting.

USES, SETTINGS, AND LIMITATIONS

The primary purpose of the MCMI is to provide information to clinicians—psychologists, counselors, psychiatrists, and social workers—who must make assessments and treatment decisions about persons with emotional and interpersonal difficulties. Because of the simplicity of administration and the availability of hand-scoring and rapid computer-scoring and interpretive procedures, the MCMI can be used on a routine basis in outpatient clinics, community agencies, mental health centers, college counseling programs, general and mental hospitals, correctional institutions (for which there is a special interpretive report), forensic settings, and courts, as well as in general independent practice offices. Individual scale-cutting lines can be used to make decisions concerning personality disorders or clinical syndrome diagnoses. Similarly, elevation levels among subsets of scales can furnish grounds for judgments about impairment, severity, and chronicity of pathology. More comprehensive and dynamic interpretations of relationships among symptomatology, coping behavior, interpersonal style, and personality structure may be derived from an examination of the configural pattern of the clinical scales.

The MCMI-III, however, is not a general personality instrument to be used for "normal" populations. To administer the MCMI to a wider range of problems or class of participants, such as those found in business and industry, or to use it to identify neurological lesions or for the assessment of general personality traits among college students is to apply the instrument to settings and samples for which it is neither intended nor appropriate.

The MCMI is frequently used in research. Upwards of 650 publications to date have included or focused primarily on the MCMI, with some 60 or so new references currently published annually (a list of these references can be obtained from National Computer Systems, attention: Christine Herdes). A series of special grants for conducting research using the MCMI-III is currently available from National Computer Systems. Those interested should also request *Doing Publishable Research With the MCMI* (Hsu & Maruish, 1993) for helpful suggestions.

ADMINISTRATION AND SCORING

A principal goal in constructing the MCMI was to keep the total number of items small enough to encourage use in diverse diagnostic and treatment settings yet large enough to permit the assessment of a wide range of clinically relevant behaviors. At 175 items, the final form is much shorter than comparable instruments. Potentially objectionable items have been screened out, with terminology geared to an eighth-grade reading level. Most clients can complete the MCMI in 20–30 minutes, thereby minimizing client resistance and fatigue.

Administration follows a procedure similar to that of most self-report inventories. Test directions, a patient information chart, an identification grid, and special coding sections for clinicians are printed on the front page. No special conditions or instructions are required to achieve reliable results beyond those printed on the test booklet itself. Answer choices (true and false) are printed next to each of the 175 item statements. This increases the accuracy of patient markings and allows the clinician to scan individual item responses.

INTERPRETATION

Clinicians interpreting the MCMI should bear in mind that the richness and accuracy of all self-report measures are enhanced when their findings are viewed in the context of other clinical sources and data, such as demographic background, biographical history, and other clinical features. The personality and clinical features characterizing each of the separate scales should be reviewed before analyzing profile configurations. Configural interpretation is a deductive synthesis achieved by refining, blending, and integrating the separate characteristics tapped by each scale. The accuracy of such interpretations depends on the meaning and significance of the individual scales composing the profile. Such an interpretive procedure seeks to break the pattern of labeling patients and fitting them into Procrustean categories. Information concerning sex, age, socioeconomic class, mental status observations, and interviews should all be used to provide a perspective for assessing the MCMI profile.

A basic separation should be made in the initial phase of interpretation between those scales pertaining to the basic clinical personality pattern (1–8B), those pointing to the presence of severe Axis II personality pathology (S, C, and P), those signifying moderate Axis I clinical syndromes (A–R), and those indicating a severe clinical state (SS, CC, and PP). Each section of the profile reflects different and important dimensions of the clinical picture. Therefore, the clinician should begin by dividing the profile into a series of subsections, focusing first on the significance of scale elevations and profile patterns within each section. Once this is completed, the clinician can proceed with the step of integrating each subsection.

The theoretical framework and clinical characterizations associated with each personality style are available in *Modern Psychopathology* (Millon, 1969/1983), *Toward a New Personology: An Evolutionary Model* (Millon, 1990), and *Disorders of Personality: DSM-IV and Beyond* (Millon & Davis, 1996). Several synopses of the various personality styles that serve as useful aids to interpretation are included in these works. In each of these, the characteristics of personality have been usefully organized in

TABLE 2. Domain Descriptors for the Narcissistic Personality

Behavioral Level

(F) Expressively Haughty (e.g., acts in an arrogant, supercilious, pompous, and disdainful manner, flouting conventional rules of shared social living, viewing them as naive or inapplicable to self; reveals a careless disregard for personal integrity and a self-important indifference to the rights of others)

(F) Interpersonally Exploitive (e.g., feels entitled, is unempathic, and expects special favors without assuming reciprocal responsibilities; shamelessly takes others for granted and uses them to enhance self and indulge desires)

Phenomenological Level

(F) Cognitively Expansive (e.g., has an undisciplined imagination and exhibits a preoccupation with immature and self-glorifying fantasies of success, beauty, or love; is minimally constrained by objective reality, takes liberties with facts, and often lies to redeem self-illusions)

(S) Admirable Self-Image (e.g., believes self to be meritorious, special, if not unique, deserving of great admiration, and acting in a grandiose or self-assured manner, often without commensurate achievements; has a sense of high self-worth, despite being seen by others as egotistic, inconsiderate, and arrogant)

(S) Contrived Objects (e.g., internalized representations are composed far more than usual of illusory and changing memories of past relationships; unacceptable drives and conflicts are readily refashioned as the need arises, as are others often stimulated and pretentious)

Intrapsychic Level

(F) Rationalization Mechanism (e.g., is self-deceptive and facile in devising plausible reasons to justify self-centered and socially inconsiderate behaviors; offers alibis to place oneself in the best possible light, despite evident shortcomings or failures)

(S) Spurious Organization (e.g., morphologic structures underlying coping and defensive strategies tend to be flimsy and transparent, appear more substantial and dynamically orchestrated than they are in fact, regulating impulses only marginally, channeling needs with minimal restraint, and creating an inner world in which conflicts are dismissed; failures are quickly redeemed and self-pride is effortlessly reasserted)

Biophysical Level

(S) Insouciant Mood (e.g., manifests a general air of nonchalance, imperturbability, and feigned tranquility; appears coolly unimpressionable or buoyantly optimistic, except when narcissistic confidence is shaken, at which time either rage, shame, or emptiness is briefly displayed)

a manner similar to distinctions drawn in the biological realm, that is, by dividing them into *structural* and *functional* attributes. Functional characteristics represent dynamic processes that transpire within the intrapsychic world and between the individual's self and psychosocial environment. They represent "expressive modes of regulatory action." Structural attributes represent a deeply embedded and relatively enduring template of imprinted memories, attitudes, needs, fears, conflicts, and so on, which guide experience and transform the nature of perceived events. These domains are further differentiated according to their respective data level, either biophysical, intrapsychic, phenomenological, or behavioral, reflecting the four historical approaches that characterize the study of psychopathology, namely, the biological, the psychoanalytic, the cognitive, and the behavioral.

Table 2 presents domain descriptors for the Narcissistic personality. A more complete set of descriptors is available in the above sources and in the MCMI-III manual. A series of content scales has recently been derived on the basis of theoretical and factional studies (Grossman, 2003). For example, the Schizoid scale turns out to be composed of three broad factors, namely "social isolation," "cognitive vagueness," and "emotional flatness." The Negativistic or Passive-Aggressive scale also is made up of three content sub-scales namely "contradictory feelings," "resentful discontent," and "problematic outlook." Another example, the Borderline scale, is composed of content scales that are described as "affective instability," "identity difficulties," and "desperate impulsivity." Similarly, the three content scales comprising the Schizotypal personality are labeled "social awkwardness," "paranoid-like ideation," and "dysfunctional cognition." All MCMI personality scales are included in these recent clinical and factional studies; they will be included as facets in future Interpretive Reports. In addition, *Disorders of Personality* presents new adult subtypes for each of the various personality disorders. These descriptions form more specific prototypes against which real patients can be compared.

In addition to undertaking interpretation's on one's own, the Microtest Q program (available from National Computer Systems, attention: Christine Herdes) is available for generating rapid and convenient MCMI narratives. These integrate both the personological and symptomatic features of the patient; the final report is arranged in a style similar to those prepared by clinical psychologists. As the report is generated, data are drawn from both scale score elevations and profile configurations and are based on both actuarial research findings and the MCMI's theoretical schema (Millon, 1969/1983, 1986a, 1986b, 1990; Millon et al., 1994; Millon & Davis, 1996), as well as the *DSM-IV.* Following current psychodiagnostic thinking, the Interpretive Report focuses on a multiaxial framework of assessment and summarizes findings along its several axes: clinical syndrome, personality disorder, psychosocial stressors, and therapeutic implications. The latter section has been greatly expanded specifically for the MCMI-III. These reports prove highly accurate in about 55–65% of cases; are appraised as both useful and generally valid, but with partial misjudgments, in about another 25–30% of cases; and seem off target or appreciably in error about 10–15% of the time. These positive figures are in the quantitative range of 5–6 times greater than are random diagnostic assignments or chance (Millon, 1987). Note, however, that the report is intended to serve as a rich source of clinical hypotheses. What is selected, rejected, emphasized, or de-emphasized in the final analysis depends on the individual case and the user's experience and judgment. As noted by Wetzler and Marlowe (1992), "The test is only as good as its user" (p. 428). A more basic Profile Report is also available.

The MCMI's diagnostic scale cutoffs and profile interpretations are oriented to the majority of patients who take the inventory, that is, to those displaying psychic disturbances in the midranges of severity rather than those whose difficulties are either close to "normal" (e.g., workers' compensation litigants, spouses of patients) or of marked clinical severity (e.g., acute psychotics, chronic schizophrenics). Accordingly, narrative analyses of patients experiencing ordinary life difficulties or minor adjustment disorders will tend to be construed as more troubled than they are; conversely, analyses of the most serious pathologies will often be construed as less severe than they are.

CONCLUSION

Within the limitations of the self-report mode and the inherent restrictions of psychometric technology, all steps were taken to maximize the MCMI-III's concordance with its generative theory and the official *DSM* classification system. Pragmatic and philosophical compromises were made where valued objectives could not be simultaneously achieved—instrument brevity versus item independence, representative national patient norms versus local base rate specificity, theoretical criterion considerations versus empirical data. As was the case with its forebears, the MCMI-III is not cast in stone. It is and will remain an evolving assessment instrument, upgraded and refined to reflect substantive advances in knowledge, be it from theory, research, or clinical experience.

References & Readings

Butcher, J. N. (Ed.) (1972). *Objective personality assessment.* New York: Academic Press.

Choca, J. P., Shanley, L. A., & Van Denburg, E. (1992). *Interpretive guide to the Millon Clinical Multiaxial Inventory.* Washington, DC: American Psychological Association.

Davis, R. D., & Millon, T. (1993). Putting Humpty Dumpty back together again: The MCMI in personality assessment. In L. Beutler (Ed.), *Integrative personality assessment* (pp. 240–279). New York: Guilford Press.

Davis, R. D., Wenger, A., & Guzman, A. (1997). Diagnostic efficiency of the MCMI-III. In T. Millon (Ed.), *The Millon inventories.* New York: Guilford Press.

Grossman, S. D. (2003). *Theoretically and factorially derived content scales for the MCMI-III.*

Unpublished doctoral dissertation, Carlos Albezo University, Miami, FL.
Hase, H. D., & Goldberg, L. R. (1967). Comparative validity of different strategies of constructing personality inventory scales. *Psychological Bulletin, 67*, 231–248.
Hsu, F., & Maruish, M. (1993). *Doing publishable research with the MCMI.* Minneapolis, MN: National Computer Systems.
Loevinger, J. (1957). Objective tests as instruments of psychological theory. *Psychological Reports, 3*, 635–694.
McCann, J. T., & Dyer, F. J. (1996). *Forensic assessment with the Millon inventories.* New York: Guilford Press.
Millon, T. (1983). *Modern psychopathology: A biosocial approach to maladaptive learning and functioning.* Prospect Heights, IL: Waveland Press. (Original work published 1969.)
Millon, T. (1986a). Personality prototypes and their diagnostic criteria. In T. Millon & G. Klerman (Eds.), *Contemporary directions in psychopathology: Toward the DSM-IV.* New York: Guilford Press.
Millon, T. (1986b). A theoretical derivation of pathological personalities. In T. Millon & G. Klerman (Eds.), *Contemporary directions in psychopathology: Toward the DSM-IV.* New York: Guilford Press.
Millon, T. (1987). *Millon Clinical Multiaxial Inventory-II manual.* Minneapolis, MN: National Computer Systems.
Millon, T. (1990). *Toward a new personology: An evolutionary model.* New York: Wiley-Interscience.
Millon, T. (Ed.). (1997). *The Millon inventories: Contemporary clinical and personality assessment.* New York: Guilford Press.
Millon, T., (with Davis, R. D.). (1996). *Disorders of personality: DSM-IV and beyond.* New York: Wiley-Interscience.
Millon, T., Millon, C., & Davis, R. D. (1994). *Millon Clinical Multiaxial Inventory-III manual.* Minneapolis, MN: National Computer Systems.
Rosen, A. (1962). Development of the MMPI scales based on a reference group of psychiatric patients. *Psychological Monographs, 76*, 527.
Wetzler, S., & Marlowe, D. (1992). What they don't tell you in the test manual: A response to Millon. *Journal of Counseling and Development, 70*, 427–428.

Related Topic

Chapter 34, "Millon Adolescent Clinical Inventory (MACI)"

34 MILLON ADOLESCENT CLINICAL INVENTORY (MACI)

Theodore Millon & Seth D. Grossman

The Millon Adolescent Clinical Inventory (MACI; Millon, Millon, & Davis, 1993) is an expansion of the earlier Millon Adolescent Personality Inventory (MAPI; Millon, Green, & Meagher, 1982). It is a 160-item, 31-scale, self-report inventory designed specifically for assessing clinically troubled adolescent personalities, their typical areas of concern, and Axis I clinical syndromes. Table 1 lists the MACI scales and reports scale changes from the MAPI to the MACI. The MACI and its forerunners were developed in consultation with psychiatrists, psychologists, and other mental health professionals who work with adolescents, and they reflect issues most relevant to understanding adolescents' behavior and concerns. The MACI was developed primarily for use in clinical, residential, and correctional settings. The Expressed

TABLE 1. A Comparison of MACI and MAPI Scales

MACI	MAPI
Personality Scales	
1. Introversive (schizoid)	1. Introversive (schizoid)
2A. Inhibited (avoidant)	2. Inhibited (avoidant)
2B. Doleful (depressive)	
3. Cooperative (dependent)	3. Cooperative (dependent)
4. Sociable (histrionic)	4. Sociable (histrionic)
5. Confident (narcissistic)	5. Confident (narcissistic)
6A. Unruly (antisocial)	6. Unruly (antisocial)
6B. Forceful (sadistic)	
7. Respectful (compulsive)	7. Respectful (compulsive)
8A. Negative (negativistic)	
8B. Sensitive (self-defeating)	8. Sensitive (self-defeating)
9. Borderline tendency	
Expressed Concerns	
A. Identify diffusion	A. Self-concept
B. Self-devaluation	B. Personal esteem
C. Body disapproval	C. Body comfort
D. Sexual discomfort	D. Sexual acceptance
E. Peer insecurity	E. Peer security
F. Social insensitivity	F. Social tolerance
G. Family discord	G. Family rapport
H. Childhood abuse	
	H. Academic confidence
Clinical Indices and Behavioral Correlates	
AA. Eating dysfunctions	
BB. Substance abuse proneness	
CC. Delinquent predisposition	TT. Societal conformity
DD. Impulsive propensity	SS. Impulsive control
EE. Anxious feelings	
FF. Depressive affect	
GG. Suicidal tendency	
	UU. Scholastic achievement
	WW. Attendance consistency

Concerns scales of the MACI assess teenagers' attitudes regarding significant developmental problems, while the Personality Patterns and Clinical Syndromes scales reflect significant areas of pathological feelings, thoughts, and behavior that require professional attention.

HISTORICAL DEVELOPMENT

The original Millon Adolescent Inventory (MAI) was developed in 1974. The MAI served as the forerunner to the MAPI, first published and distributed by National Computer Systems (NCS) in 1982. The MAI and the MAPI were identical in item content but differed in their norms and intended purposes. The MAPI was subsequently divided into two forms. The MAPI-Clinical was designed to aid mental health workers in assessing adolescent difficulties among youngsters who were in a diagnostic or treatment setting at the time of testing; the MAPI-Guidance was designed for school settings, primarily to help counselors better understand adolescent personalities and to identify students who might benefit from further psychological evaluations.

The decision to develop a purely clinical reference group with appropriate, comparison norms served as the impetus for development of the MACI. The MAPI-C, useful as it was for diagnostic assessment, was not sufficiently broad-based to encompass the full range of clinical populations. There was also clearly a need to strengthen its psychometric features, make it more consonant with developments in its guiding theory, and fortify its coordination with the descriptive characteristics in the most recent *Diagnostic and Statistical Manual of Mental Disorders* (*DSM*) classifications. Like the other Millon inventories, the MACI's personality and clinical scales are grounded on a comprehensive theory (Millon, 1969, 1981, 1986a, 1986b, 1990, 1997), significantly increasing the instrument's clinical utility. Item selection and scale development progressed through three validation stages: theoretical-substantive, internal-structural, and external-criterion. This approach created an instrument that meets the standards of developers who are committed to diverse construction and validation methods (Hase & Goldberg, 1967). Each item had to pass satisfactorily through all three stages of development to be retained in the inventory.

ADMINISTRATION AND SCORING

The MACI was constructed specifically with an adolescent population in mind. Questions are presented in language teenagers use, with content that deals with their concerns and experiences. Both reading level and vocabulary were set to allow for ready comprehension by the vast majority of adolescents. The final 160-item inventory, geared to a sixth-grade reading level, can be completed by most adolescents in approximately 20 minutes. The brevity and clarity of the instrument facilitate quick administration with a minimum of youngster resistance. Norms were established employing samples of 13- to 19-year-olds in clinical settings (its use with other normative age-groups is inappropriate and may lead to erroneous diagnostic judgments). The presence of overwhelming anxiety, a confusional state, drug intoxication, or sedation may also significantly alter test results. If the instrument is administered under such circumstances, the client should be retested at a later date.

The MACI is available in two paper-and-pencil formats, one for hand scoring and one for computer scoring. Hand-scoring materials include a reusable test booklet and a separate answer sheet. For computer scoring, there is a combination test booklet and answer sheet and an on-line format. Audiocassette recordings of the MACI are available for use with both English- and Spanish-speaking clients. While mail-in scoring is available through NCS, on-site computer scoring is the fastest and most convenient scoring option. Both options allow the user to select either a Profile Report or an Interpretive Report based on the examinee's scores.

Instructions for completing the MACI are printed on the test and are largely self-explanatory. No special conditions or instructions beyond those printed on the test are required. Accordingly, administration can be readily and routinely handled by properly trained assistants in clinic settings. The brevity of the test and the minimal facilities required make it convenient for use in settings where time, space, and privacy are limited. However, the MACI should not be mailed to clients or sent home with them for completion.

The MACI, like all the Millon inventories, employs actuarial base rate or prevalence data to establish scale cutting lines. These not only provide a basis for selecting optimal differential diagnostic cutting lines but also help ensure that the frequencies of MCMI-generated diagnoses and profile patterns are comparable to representative clinical prevalence rates. While the use of base rate scores has been one of the most widely misunderstood aspects of the MCMI, their utility is easily and intuitively understood when contrasted with the more familiar T score. On the MMPI, for example, T scores of 65 and above indicate pathology, with roughly equal numbers of patients scoring above this threshold. Clinical experience, however, shows the number of depressed patients, for example, to be greater than the number of patients with a thought disorder. Base rate scores are constructed to reflect these clinical realities, yielding more depressives than delusional patients, more borderlines and antisocials than schizoids, and so on, rather than assuming their numbers to be equal. In the construction of the MACI, target prevalence rates were set according to reviews of epidemiological data, estimates derived from clinicians who participated in the development project, and the senior author's own expert judgment. Thus, if it was deemed that 8% of patients are most likely to resemble the introversive prototype, then the lookup table for this personality was constructed so schizoid was the highest personality elevation for 8% of the patients in the normative sample.

A discussion of base rate scores often leads to considerations of local versus global base rates, that is, the fact that the prevalence rates for different disorders vary somewhat by clinical setting. When this is raised in criticism of the concept, it is usually intended to support the continued use of T scores. However, as noted earlier, the base rate scores of the MACI are intended to remedy the global base rate assumptions made in the use of T scores. Thus, while the prevalence rates of some disorders in particular clinical settings may differ from the base rates assumed by the MACI and in the use of T scores, the MACI's base rate scores at least do not implicitly assume the prevalence rates of all disorders to be equal. More frequently, the distinction between local and global prevalence rates is made in support of the base rate concept by clinicians who realize its importance in improving diagnostic efficiency: positive and negative predictive power, sensitivity, and specificity. These clinicians, far from reverting back to T scores, often wish to optimize the base rate scores for their particular setting.

SCALE DESCRIPTIONS

The major personality patterns, expressed psychosocial concerns, and clinical syndromes typical of adolescents have been organized into the following formal scales.

Personality Patterns

Twelve personality patterns are included, based on the senior author's theoretical schema (Millon, 1969, 1981, 1986a, 1986b, 1990, 1997) and similar material in the fourth edition of the *DSM* (*DSM-IV*).

- *Introversive* (Scale 1): High scorers keep to themselves, appearing rather quiet, unemotional, apathetic, listless, distant, and asocial. Affectionate needs and feelings are minimal. Not only do they not get emotionally involved, they simply do not often feel strongly about things, lacking the capacity to experience both joy and sadness in any depth. They do not avoid others, but they are indifferent about the presence of others and the possibilities inherent in relationships.
- *Inhibited* (Scale 2A): High scorers are quite shy and ill at ease with others. Although they would like to be close to others, they have learned that it is better to keep their distance, and they do not readily trust friendship. Although they often feel lonely, they avoid close interpersonal contact, fearing rejection, and they closet feelings that are often very strong.
- *Doleful* (Scale 2B): High scorers characteristically exhibit a dejected and gloomy mood, perhaps since childhood. Their outlook on life is sad, brooding, and pessimistic. Most are prone to guilty and remorseful feelings, viewing themselves as inadequate or even worthless.
- *Submissive* (Scale 3): High scorers tend to be softhearted, sentimental, and kindly in relationships with others. They are extremely reluctant to assert themselves, however, and avoid taking initiative or assuming a leadership role. They are not only inclined to be quite dependent but also exhibit clinging behavior and a fear of separation. They typically play down their own achievements and underestimate their abilities.
- *Dramatizing* (Scale 4): High scorers tend to be talkative, charming, and frequently exhibitionistic or emotionally expressive. They tend to have intense but brief relationships with others. These adolescents look for interesting experiences and new forms of excitement. They often find themselves becoming bored with routine and long-standing relationships.
- *Egotistic* (Scale 5): High scorers tend to be quite confident of their abilities and are often seen by others as self-centered and narcissistic. They rarely doubt their own self-worth, and they act in a self-assured manner. These individuals tend to take others for granted, are often arrogant and exploitative, and do not share or concern themselves with the needs of others.

- *Unruly* (Scale 6A): High scorers tend to act out in an antisocial manner, often resisting efforts to make them adhere to socially acceptable standards of behavior. These adolescents may display a pervasively rebellious attitude that could bring them into conflict with parents and school or legal authorities.
- *Forceful* (Scale 6B): High scorers are strong-willed and tough-minded, tending to dominate and abuse others. They frequently question the rights of others and prefer to control most situations. They are often blunt and unkind, tending to be impatient with the problems or weaknesses of others.
- *Conforming* (Scale 7): High scorers are very serious-minded, efficient, respectful, and rule-conscious individuals who try to do the "right" and "proper" things. They tend to keep their emotions under check and to be overcontrolled and tense. They prefer to live their lives in a very orderly and well-planned fashion, avoiding unpredictable and unexpected situations.
- *Oppositional* (Scale 8A): High scorers tend to be discontented, sullen, passive-aggressive, and unpredictable. They may be outgoing and pleasant one moment but hostile and irritable the next. Often they are confused and contrite about their moodiness but are unable to control these swings for long.
- *Self-demeaning* (Scale 8B): High scorers tend to be their own worst enemies, acting in self-defeating ways, at times seeming content to suffer. Many undermine the efforts of others to help them. Often they deny themselves pleasure and sabotage their own efforts to achieve success.
- *Borderline tendency* (Scale 9): High scorers exhibit severe personality dysfunctions, displaying more pathological variants of the preceding personality traits and features. They may also exhibit marked affective instabilities, erratic interpersonal relationships, behavioral capriciousness, impulsive hostility, fear of abandonment, and self-destructive actions.

Expressed Concerns

The following eight scales focus on areas of life that troubled adolescents often find problematic. The intensity of the problem is reflected in the elevation of the scale score.

- *Identity diffusion* (Scale A): High scorers are confused about who they are, what they want from life, and what they would like to become. Free-floating and unfocused about future goals and values, they are unclear and directionless about the course of their future development.
- *Self-devaluation* (Scale B): Although high scorers have a sense of who they are, they are very dissatisfied with that self-image. They speak openly about feelings of low self-esteem, find little to admire in themselves, and fear that they will fall far short of what they aspire to be.
- *Body disapproval* (Scale C): High scorers are discontent with what they perceive to be shortcomings or deviance in their physical maturation or morphology. They may also express dissatisfaction with their level of physical attractiveness and social appeal.
- *Sexual discomfort* (Scale D): High scorers find sexual thoughts and feelings confusing or disagreeable. They are troubled by their impulses and often fear the expression of their sexuality. They may be preoccupied with or in conflict over the roles their sexuality requires.
- *Peer insecurity* (Scale E): High scorers report dismay and sadness concerning perceived peer rejection. Wanting the approval of peers but unsuccessful in attaining it, many are likely to withdraw and become even more isolated.
- *Social insensitivity* (Scale F): High scorers are cool and indifferent to the welfare of others. Willing to override the rights of others to achieve personal ends, they lack empathy and show little interest in building warm personal ties.
- *Family discord* (Scale G): High scorers report that their families are tense and full of conflict. They note few sources of support and possess a general feeling of estrangement from parents. Depending on the individual's personality, these difficulties may reflect either parental rejection or adolescent rebellion.
- *Childhood abuse* (Scale H): High scorers report shame or disgust about having been subjected to verbal, physical, or sexual abuse from parents, siblings, relatives, or family friends.

Clinical Syndromes

The final seven scales of the MACI involve areas of direct clinical significance that call for intervention on the part of a therapist. These diagnostic categories represent difficulties that are found in a significant proportion of adolescents who are seen by mental health professionals.

- *Eating dysfunctions* (Scale AA): High scorers exhibit distinct tendencies toward anorexia nervosa or bulimia nervosa. Though already below normal weight, they fear "getting fat." They may engage in uncontrolled eating, followed by self-induced vomiting or the misuse of laxatives or diuretics.
- *Substance-abuse proneness* (Scale BB): High scorers exhibit a pattern of alcohol or drug abuse that has led to significant impairment of performance and behavior. Some spend inordinate amounts of time obtaining their substances, behave in an unacceptable social manner, and continue substance use despite cognizance of its long-term harmful effect on their life.
- *Delinquent predisposition* (Scale CC): High scorers behave in ways or involve themselves in situations in which the rights of others are likely to be violated. In doing so, any number of societal norms or rules may be broken, including threats, use of weapons, deception and lying, stealing, and other antisocial behaviors.
- *Impulsive propensity* (Scale DD): High scorers have poor control over sexual and aggressive impulses and are likely to act out their feelings with minimal provocation. Easily excited over minor matters, these adolescents may discharge their urges in sudden, impetuous, and often foolhardy ways.
- *Anxious feelings* (Scale EE): High scorers have a sense of foreboding, an apprehensiveness about all sorts of matters. Uneasy, disquieted, fretful, and nervous, they are often on pins and needles as they fearfully await the coming of unknown torments or calamitous events.
- *Depressive affect* (Scale FF): High scorers show a decreased level of activity, clearly distinct from that which has been characteristic of them in the past. They exhibit a notable decrease in effectiveness, feelings of guilt and fatigue, a tendency to be despairing about the future, social withdrawal, loss of confidence, and diminished feelings of adequacy and attractiveness.
- *Suicidal tendency* (Scale GG): High scorers admit to suicidal thoughts and plans. They express feelings of worthlessness and purposelessness and a sense that others would be better off without them. High scores call for professional attention and alertness on the part of family members.

CLINICAL INTERPRETATION AND COMPUTER-GENERATED REPORTS

Configural interpretation of the MACI is essentially similar to that of the MCMI-III (see chapter 33), proceeding from single-scale to configural syntheses, with appropriate integration of auxiliary data. Considerable interpretive material related to personality disorders, and on Millon's evolutionary theory, is presented in various writings, most notably *Modern Psychopathology* (Millon, 1969), *Toward a New Personology: An Evolutionary Model* (Millon, 1990), and *Disorders of Personality: The DSM-IV and Beyond* (Millon & Davis, 1996).

The MACI automated interpretive reports are substantially more detailed than those of the MAPI. They are based on clinically derived configurations and statistical clusters as synthesized by the underlying theory. MACI results can be furnished either in profile form or as an automated interpretive report. The profile provides limited information and assumes knowledge of the relevant clinical literature. The more comprehensive and detailed interpretive report is considered a professional-to-professional consultation. Its function is to serve as one component in the evaluation of the adolescent, and it should be viewed by the clinician as a series of probabilistic rather than definitive judgments. Although this information is appropriate for use in developing a therapeutic program, sharing the report with adolescents or their families is discouraged. Careful rephrasing of text interpretations may be undertaken with appropriate clients, using sound clinical judgment to assure a constructive outcome.

An actuarial system, particularly one that is supplemented by a systematic clinical theory, should yield reports as good as those prepared by human interpreters. Moreover, a computer database is far more substantial in scope and variety than are the disorders seen by the average clinician. Diagnosticians must resort to highly tenuous speculations when they encounter novel profile configurations. In contrast, a computer database is well supplied with comparable cases to be drawn upon for interpretive reference. In a few seconds, the computer can match a profile with comparable configurations and generate an appropriate narrative report. From a purely practical viewpoint, automated reports provide a significant savings of professional time and effort.

Computer-generated MACI interpretive reports include (a) a cover page, a summary page providing the raw and BR scores for each scale and a score profile, test validity information, and the personality code; (b) an initial paragraph noting the appropriate context, limitations, and restrictions of the use, a demographic summary, and a judgment as to the probable validity and reliability of test data given the adolescent's response tendencies and biases; (c) a series of paragraphs describing the major features of the teenager's personality patterns, the manner in which difficulties are manifested, and the probable course of relationships with therapists; (d) a series of descriptive statements characterizing the primary areas of concern as expressed by the youngster; (e) an interpretive summary of the nature and character of the highest Clinical Syndromes scales in order of their magnitude; (f) a section called "Noteworthy Responses," which indicates problem areas that call for closer inspection and further evaluation; (g) a summary section of "Diagnostic Hypotheses" related to the *DSM-IV*, arranged in a multiaxial format; and (h) a series of paragraphs pointing out the treatment implications of the preceding information.

References & Readings

Hase, H. D., & Goldberg, L. R. (1967). Comparative validity of different strategies of constructing personality inventory scales. *Psychological Bulletin, 67,* 231–248.

McCann, J. T. (1999). *Assessing adolescents with the MACI: Using the Millon Adolescent Clinical Inventory*. New York: Wiley.

Millon, T. (1969). *Modern psychopathology*. Philadelphia: Saunders.

Millon, T. (1981). *Disorders of personality: DSM-III, Axis II*. New York: Wiley.

Millon, T. (1986a). Personality prototypes and their diagnostic criteria. In T. Millon & G. Klerman (Eds.), *Contemporary directions in psychopathology: Toward the DSM-IV*. New York: Guilford Press.

Millon, T. (1986b). A theoretical derivation of pathological personalities. In T. Millon & G. Klerman (Eds.), *Contemporary directions in psychopathology: Toward the DSM-IV*. New York: Guilford Press.

Millon, T. (1990). *Toward a new personology: An evolutionary model*. New York: Wiley-Interscience.

Millon, T. (Ed.). (1997). *The Millon inventories: Contemporary clinical and personality assessment*. New York: Guilford Press.

Millon, T., & Davis, R. D. (1996). *Disorders of personality: The DSM-IV and beyond*. New York: Wiley-Interscience.

Millon, T., Green, C. J., & Meagher, R. B., Jr. (1982). *Millon Adolescent Personality Inventory manual*. Minneapolis, MN: National Computer Systems.

Millon, T., Millon, C., and Davis, R. D. (1993). *Millon Adolescent Clinical Inventory manual*. Minneapolis, MN: National Computer Systems.

Related Topics

Chapter 9, "Child and Adolescent Diagnosis With *DSM-IV*"

Chapter 33, "Millon Clinical Multiaxial Inventory (MCMI-III)"

35 THUMBNAIL GUIDE TO THE RORSCHACH METHOD

Barry A. Ritzler

MATERIALS

The Rorschach Method stimulus materials consist of 10 drawings based on inkblots designed by Hermann Rorschach when he developed the method in the early 1920s (Rorschach, 1921). All 10 cards should be administered in numerical order (I–X). A notepad is necessary for verbatim note taking, with two sections on the same page for First Viewing responses and Inquiry (see "Administration Procedures"). A scoring summary sheet and a location chart (a page with miniature copies of the 10 cards) also should be used.

FREQUENTLY USED SYSTEMS

Four somewhat different systems are used with noticeable frequency by psychologists in the United States:

- The *Rorschach Comprehensive System* (Exner, 2003): First published in 1974, this system was derived from empirical analysis of the Rorschach to establish acceptable levels of reliability and validity. The Comprehensive System incorporates coding variables from several other systems and has become the most frequently used Rorschach system in the United States (Piotrowski & Keller, 1992).
- The *Beck System* (Beck, Beck, Levitt, & Molish, 1961): Prior to the development of the Comprehensive System, this was one of the two most frequently used systems.
- The *Klopfer System* (Klopfer & Kelley, 1942): This was the other most frequently used system before the Comprehensive System.
- The *Rapaport System* (Rapaport, Gill, & Schafer, 1946): Though less frequently used than the Beck and Klopfer Systems, the Rapaport System tends to be favored by psychoanalytically oriented psychologists because of its conceptual ties to the theory.

The Rorschach is used throughout the world, and numerous systems exist in other countries but have not been introduced in the United States. The International Rorschach Society (Weiner, 1994) is an organization that brings together Rorschach psychologists from many different countries for the exchange of views on different approaches to the Rorschach Method.

ADMINISTRATION PROCEDURES

Although administration procedures differ somewhat between the frequently used systems, some basic principles apply to all systems. For instance, the key to administration is to minimize the influence of the examiner. The Method should be introduced with a minimum of explanation. It usually is sufficient to indicate that the Method is a common procedure used by psychologists to assess personality. No more specific information about the Method should be conveyed before administration.

The initial instructions are very simple. For example, the Comprehensive System (Exner, 2003) simply asks the initial question "What might this be?" as the subject is handed the first card.

For most systems, all 10 cards are presented consecutively for a First Viewing, which affords the subject an opportunity to respond to each card with little intervention by the examiner, who primarily is occupied taking verbatim notes. After the initial responses to all 10 cards are recorded, the blots are presented again for an Inquiry period in which the examiner attempts to gain more information about the responses by making concise, nonleading inquiries. The subject's responses to these inquiries also are recorded verbatim. The only exception to this procedure is the Rapaport System (Rapaport et al., 1946), which administers the Inquiry immediately after the First Viewing response is obtained for each card and before the next card is presented. It was Rapaport's intention to obtain Inquiry information while the process of the First Viewing response was fresh in the subject's mind. The other systems are concerned that immediate Inquiry will bias the subject's responses on subsequent cards.

The purpose of the Inquiry is to determine where each response is located on the card and what stimulus qualities of the card influenced (or determined) the subject's responses (e.g., shape, color, or shading). The Inquiry also is used to clarify ambiguities in the subject's communication of the response.

Detailed administration manuals exist for each system and should be consulted for more specific instruction in proper administration.

CODING (SCORING)

The Rorschach Method should not be used without the application of one of the accepted coding systems. Without coding, the psychologist cannot take advantage of the substantial empirical validation and systematic methods of interpretation that exist for the Method. Rorschach interpretation without coding risks an overly subjective assessment biased by the psychologist's idiosyncratic associations to the form and content of the subject's responses. Most Rorschach experts consider interpretation without coding to be a misuse of the Method (Allison, Blatt, & Zimet, 1968; Exner, 2003).

INTERPRETATION

Interpretation of personality functioning using the Rorschach Method is based on tallies and variables calculated from the coding of all responses and the content of the responses. For all frequently used systems, the calculated variables yield interpretive hypotheses supported by empirical research. Content analysis complements and broadens the understanding of the subject's personality, but it should not be done without integration with interpretive hypotheses obtained from the Method's quantitative variables.

Although the Rorschach Method yields much useful information, it should seldom, if ever, be used by itself for personality assessment. Integration must be made with other valid personality information from testing, behavioral observations, facts of the subject's life history and current living situation, and objectively reported symptoms.

TRAINING

The Society for Personality Assessment's Standards for Training (Society for Personality Assessment, 1995) sets the minimum standard for training in the Rorschach and other assessment methods at two semesters of graduate school coursework followed by practicum, internship, and postdoctoral training in the methods. Surveys indicate that most American Psychological Association (APA–approved graduate programs in applied psychology teach the Rorschach Method (e.g., Ritzler & Alter, 1986) but that the majority of such programs offer only one semester of instruction, so that the student must often seek supplementary training. However, since the Rorschach is a frequently used clinical method (Piotrowski & Keller, 1992), it is not difficult to find internships that offer training in the Method. Also, opportunities exist for postdoctoral training in the Method through postdoctoral fellowships and/or widely advertised workshops presented by qualified instructors. Such training beyond the graduate school level is essential for development of expertise in the Rorschach Method.

APPLICATIONS

The Rorschach Method has proved useful in the following settings and situations, among others:

- Treatment planning for inpatients and outpatients in public and private settings
- School assessments, particularly for classroom behavioral and learning problems
- Forensic applications such as the assessment of competence and criminal insanity, parole evaluations, custody determinations, assessment of psychological trauma and injury, and sentencing consultation
- Research methodology (see especially Exner, 1995)
- Assessment of the personality consequences of brain dysfunction (in conjunction with neuropsychological assessment)
- Vocational assessment for such purposes as employee selection and placement, evaluation of individual vocational problems, and consultation for workplace relationship problems

SOURCES OF INFORMATION REGARDING THE RORSCHACH METHOD

Psychologists can follow current developments in the Rorschach Method by consulting the following publications:

- *Journal for Personality Assessment* (journal published by the Society for Personality Assessment)
- *Psychological Assessment* (journal published by the American Psychological Association)
- *Assessment* (journal published by Psychological Assessment Resources)
- *Rorschachiana* (yearbook published by the International Rorschach Society)

References & Readings

Allison, J., Blatt, S., & Zimet, C. (1968). *The interpretation of psychological tests*. New York: Harper and Row.

Beck, S., Beck, A., Levitt, E., & Molish, B. (1961). *Rorschach's test I: Basic processes* (3rd ed.). New York: Grune and Stratton.

Exner, J. (2003). *The Rorschach: A comprehensive system*. New York: Wiley.

Exner, J. (Ed.). (1995). *Issues and methods in Rorschach research*. Mahwah, NJ: Erlbaum.

Klopfer, B., & Kelley, D. (1942). *The Rorschach technique*. Yonkers, NY: World Book.

Piotrowski, C., & Keller, J. (1992). Psychological testing in applied settings: A literature review from 1982–1992. *Journal of Training and Practice in Professional Psychology, 6,* 74–82.

Rapaport, D., Gill, M., & Schafer, R. (1946). *Diagnostic psychological testing* (Vols. 1 & 2). Chicago: Yearbook Publishers.

Ritzler, B., & Alter, B. (1986). Rorschach teaching in APA approved clinical graduate programs: A ten-year update. *Journal of Personality Assessment, 50,* 44–49.

Rorschach, H. (1921). *Psychodiagnostik*. Bern: Bircher; trans., Bern: Hans Huber Verlag, 1942.

Society for Personality Assessment (1995). *Membership directory*. Mahwah, NJ: Erlbaum.

Weiner, I. (1994). Speaking Rorschach: Building bridges of understanding. *Rorschachiana, 19,* 1–6.

Related Topics

Chapter 36, "Rorschach Assessment: Questions and Reservations"

Chapter 37, "Rorschach Assessment: Scientific Status and Clinical Utility"

36 RORSCHACH ASSESSMENT
Questions and Reservations

Howard N. Garb, James M. Wood, & Scott O. Lilienfeld

The Rorschach has become increasingly controversial, in part because its use can lead psychologists to make judgments that are harmful. Since 1999, the controversy has been reviewed in numerous peer-reviewed journals (e.g., *Assessment, Journal of Personality Assessment, Psychological Assessment*) and the popular press.

The goal of this chapter is to help psychologists use the Rorschach in a scientifically and ethically responsible manner. We will propose and discuss three clinical guidelines (Garb, Wood, Lilienfeld, and Nezworski, 2002):

1. *Exercise caution when using the Comprehensive System (CS) norms. Their use is related to the overperception of psychopathology. In many instances, it may be best not to use them.*

The most popular system for administering, scoring, and interpreting the Rorschach is Exner's (2001) Comprehensive System (CS). Exner administered the Rorschach to children and adults in the community, then tabulated sets of norms to summarize the results. When assessing clients, psychologists typically compare their scores with these norms.

Researchers have recently uncovered errors in the CS normative samples. Although Exner had long described the 1993 adult normative sample as being composed of 700 distinct protocols, it was actually made up of 479 distinct protocols with the scores for 221 protocols mistakenly counted twice (Exner, 2001, p. 172). Furthermore, the 2001 sample is composed of protocols that were scored using some rules that are now outdated. After administering and scoring the test, Exner revised his scoring system but did not rescore the protocols using all of the new rules (Hibbard, 2003, p. 261).

Perhaps the most serious problem with the Rorschach is that the use of the CS norms can lead psychologists to overperceive psychopathology. Because these norms are in error, relatively normal individuals often appear to be psychologically disturbed. Thus, psychologists interpreting Rorschach results may erroneously conclude that the individuals they have assessed have significant psychopathology. This can have harmful consequences. For instance, individuals in clinical settings may be falsely identified as being psychologically disturbed.

Results on the adequacy of the CS norms have been hotly contested. Here we summarize the results from (a) two recent studies conducted in the United States (Hamel, Shaffer, & Erdberg, 2000; Shaffer, Erdberg, & Haroian, 1999); (b) a comprehensive review of the literature (Wood, Nezworski, Garb, & Lilienfeld, 2001b); and (c) analyses of data pooled from nine international studies (Meyer, 2001; Wood, Nezworski, Garb, & Lilienfeld, 2001a). In addition, we will evaluate criticisms of this body of research (e.g., Weiner, Spielberger, & Abeles, 2003).

In the first study (Shaffer et al., 1999), researchers administered the WAIS-R, MMPI-2, and Rorschach to 123 nonpatient adults. They excluded adults who had a history of psychiatric hospitalization, psychological treatment in the past two years, psychological testing in the past year, a major medical illness in the past six months, or a felony conviction. Participants obtained WAIS-R and MMPI-2 results that were similar to the normative data for these instruments, indicating that their level of psychological functioning was about average. However, Rorschach results were markedly different from the CS norms. In fact, if one used the CS norms to interpret the Rorschach results, one would conclude that many of these relatively normal adults appear to suffer from a serious thought disorder.

In a second study (Hamel et al., 2000), investigators administered the Rorschach to 100 schoolchildren. They excluded children if they had a history of (a) being evaluated or treated for an emotional or behavioral disorder or (b) antisocial behavior or academic difficulties. The children were healthier than average, as measured by the Conners Parent Rating Scale-93 (Conners, 1989). Hamel and associates (2000, p. 291) concluded that if one used the CS norms to interpret the Rorschach results for these children, one would infer that "their distortion of reality and faulty reasoning approach psychosis." A prominent Rorschach proponent, Gregory Meyer, speculated in the *Los Angeles Times* that the Rorschach was not properly administered in this study, although he provided no evidence for this claim (Mestel, 2003).

Wood and colleagues (2001b) searched for studies in which nonpatient adults had been administered the Rorschach using the CS. In these studies, the Rorschach was used to distinguish a clinical group (e.g., individuals with antisocial personality disorder) from nonpatient adults (e.g., undergraduate students). Wood et al. examined results for 14 scores that are critical for CS interpretation—for example, EB style (purportedly a measure of inefficient problem solving) and WSumC (purportedly a measure of emotional control). The results from this literature review also indicate that the use of the CS norms is likely to lead to the overperception of psychopathology.

The importance of the Wood et al. (2001b) findings has been minimized by some Rorschach proponents. For example, Meyer (2001) claimed that "Exner's 1993 nonpatient reference sample consists of people with no history of mental health treatment and some positive evidence of healthy functioning. . . . Although Wood et al. referred to their 32 samples as 'nonpatients,' at least 5 explicitly included current or former psychiatric patients" (p. 390). Weiner and his associates (2003) repeated these same points: "These criticisms are unfounded. Contrary to the claim that no one in the CS nonpatient sample had a history of mental health treatment, 15% to 20% of the respondents in this sample had been in counseling or had received psychiatric treatment" (John Exner, personal communication, February 6, 2001). Similarly, it is not true that five of the Wood et al. samples included current or former psychiatric patients. In the five studies cited by Meyer (2001) and by Weiner et al. (2003), there is no evidence that any of the participants had ever had a psychiatric hospitalization. Some of the participants in four of the samples had received psychotherapy, but some of the individuals included in the CS normative sample had similarly received counseling.

Results have also been reported for nine international samples that contained a total of 2,125 nonclinical participants. Meyer (2001) analyzed the results for 69 CS Rorschach scores and found that these samples were about four-tenths of a standard deviation more impaired than the CS normative sample. Using the data from the same samples, Wood, Nezworski, Garb, and Lilienfeld (2001a) analyzed the results for the 14 CS scores examined in their literature review (Wood et al., 2001b). They found that the international samples were about seven-tenths of a standard deviation more impaired than the CS normative sample. These findings also indicate that the use of the CS norms can lead to the overperception of psychopathology.

In conclusion, researchers have discovered serious problems with the CS norms. Relatively normal individuals in the community will appear disturbed when their Rorschach protocols are interpreted using the CS norms. Thus, psychologists should exercise caution when using the CS norms, and in many instances it may be appropriate not to use them at all.

2. *Interpretations should be based on scores that are valid for their intended purposes. Scores should be validated in well-designed studies, findings should be consistent, and positive results should be replicated by independent investigators.*

There is general agreement that some Rorschach scores are valid for their intended purposes. Even investigators who are critical of the Rorschach generally agree that the Rorschach can be helpful for some tasks—for example, for detecting thought disorder and conditions characterized by thought disorder (Lilienfeld, Wood, & Garb, 2000; Wood, Nezworski, & Garb, 2003).

There is also general agreement that many variables have not been adequately validated. As noted by Meyer and Archer (2001, p. 496), "Yet many variables given fairly substantial interpretive emphasis have received little or no attention. . . . These include the Coping Deficit Index, Obsessive Style Index, Hypervigilance Index, active-to-passive movement ratio, D-score, food content, anatomy and X-ray content, Intellectualization Index, and Isolation Index." The best-validated CS scale, the Schizophrenia Index, has recently been replaced by the Perceptual Thinking Index (Exner, 2001), a measure that has not yet been well validated.

Some of the most persuasive evidence for the Rorschach derives from meta-analyses. In global meta-analyses, results for a range of CS and non-CS scores are pooled and average effect size estimates are calculated. Positive results have been obtained, indicating that at least some Rorschach indicators are empirically supported. However, the results have not always been accurately reported. For example, according to Weiner and Kuehnle (1998, p. 440), "Parker et al. [Parker, Hanson, & Hunsley, 1988] used the effect sizes reported in 411 studies to derive population estimates of convergent validity of 0.41 for the Rorschach and 0.46 for the MMPI." This statement is misleading because the convergent validity coefficient of .41 for the Rorschach is based on the results from only five studies (Parker et al., 1988, p. 370, Table 1). Even more important, global meta-analyses do not tell us which scores are valid for which tasks. As observed by Meyer and Archer (2001, p. 491): "Global meta-analyses are inherently limited because they provide diffuse information. They do not cumulatively organize evidence for specific test scales and thus fail to provide fine-grained and clinically useful information about the value of a scale in relation to specific criteria. This is a genuine limitation of global meta-analyses, and it is impossible to circumvent this shortcoming.

In focused meta-analyses, results for a single scale are pooled. Results have supported the validity of several scores, such as the Rorschach Oral Dependency Scale" (Bornstein, 1996).

To evaluate the validity of Rorschach scores, we used the following criteria: (1) studies must be methodologically sound, (2) significant findings must be replicated by independent investigators, and (3) results must be consistent across studies (Lilienfeld et al., 2000). Rorschach scores have received at least provisional empirical support for a number of tasks (Wood et al., 2003) including: (a) the assessment of psychotic conditions and thought disorder, (b) the estimation of intelligence, (c) the prediction of treatment outcome, (d) the assessment of objective behaviors related to dependency, (e) the assessment of anxious and hostile behaviors, and (f) the differentiation of what used to be called "organic" and "functional" brain disorders. However, many of the scores that have been supported are not part of the CS, and they lack adequate norms and involve elaborate scoring procedures that many psychologists may find impractical.

The overwhelming majority of Rorschach scores do not satisfy the above three criteria. Psychologists should limit their use of the Rorschach to the small number of indices that have been empirically supported.

3. *How one uses the Rorschach should depend on whether one is testifying in court as an expert witness, evaluating a client in clinical practice, or using the test as an aid for exploration in psychotherapy.*

Psychologists should be extremely cautious when using the Rorschach, especially when testifying in court or writing test reports. Using the Rorschach to generate exploratory hypotheses for psychotherapy can be more easily defended. Even here, however, clinicians must be cautious. Whether testifying in court, writing a test report, or exploring issues with a client in psychotherapy, psychologists should avoid interpreting Rorschach protocols "by the book" because problems exist with the CS norms and because most CS scores have scant empirical support.

Note: For a history of the Rorschach and an account of how psychologists have sought to transcend their prescientific past, see Wood, Nezworski, Lilienfeld, and Garb (2003).

References & Readings 

Bornstein, R. F. (1996). Construct validity of the Rorschach Oral Dependency Scale: 1967–1995, *Psychological Assessment, 8,* 200–205.

Conners, K. (1989). *Manual for Conners' rating scales.* North Tonawanda, NY: Multi-Health Systems.

Exner, J. E. (2001). *A Rorschach workbook for the Comprehensive System* (5th ed.). Asheville, NC: Rorschach Workshops.

Garb, H. N., Wood, J. M., Lilienfeld, S. O., & Nezworski, M. T. (2002). Effective use of projective techniques in clinical practice: Let the data help with selection and interpretation. *Professional Psychology: Research and Practice, 33,* 454–463.

Hamel, M., Shaffer, T. W., & Erdberg, P. (2000). A study of nonpatient preadolescent Rorschach protocols. *Journal of Personality Assessment, 75,* 280–294.

Hibbard, S. (2003). A critique of Lilienfeld et al.'s (2000) "The Scientific Status of Projective Techniques." *Journal of Personality Assessment, 80,* 260–271.

Lilienfeld, S. O., Wood, J. M., & Garb, H. N. (2000). The scientific status of projective techniques. *Psychological Science in the Public Interest, 1,* 27–66.

Mestel, R. (2003, May 19). Rorschach tested. Blot out the famous method? *Los Angeles Times,* F-1.

Meyer, G. J. (2001). Evidence to correct misperceptions about Rorschach norms. *Clinical Psychology: Science and Practice, 8,* 389–396.

Meyer, G. J., & Archer, R. P. (2001). The hard science of Rorschach research: What do we know and where do we go? *Psychological Assessment, 13,* 486–502.

Parker, K. C. H., Hanson, R. K., & Hunsley, J. (1988). MMPI, Rorschach, and WAIS: A Meta-analytic comparison of reliability, stability, and validity. *Psychological Bulletin, 103,* 367–373.

Shaffer, T. W., Erdberg, P., & Haroian, J. (1999). Current nonpatient data for the Rorschach, WAIS-R, and MMPI-2. *Journal of Personality Assessment, 73,* 305–316.

Weiner, I. B., & Kuehnle, K. (1998). Projective assessment of children and adolescents. In A. S. Bellack & M. Hersen (Series Eds.) & C. R. Reynolds (Vol. Ed.), *Comprehensive clinical psychology: Vol. 4. Assessment* (pp. 431–458). Oxford, UK: Elsevier.

Weiner, I. B., Spielberger, C. D., & Abeles, N. (2003). Once more around the park: Correcting misinformation about Rorschach assessment. *The Clinical Psychologist, 56,* 8–9.

Wood, J. M., Nezworski, M. T., & Garb, H. N. (2003). What's right with the Rorschach? *Scientific Review of Mental Health Practice, 2,* 142–146.

Wood, J. M., Nezworski, M. T., Garb, H. N., & Lilienfeld, S. O. (2001a). The misperception of psychopathology: Problems with the norms of the Comprehensive System for the Rorschach. *Clinical Psychology: Science and Practice, 8,* 350–373.

Wood, J. M., Nezworski, M. T., Garb, H. N., & Lilienfeld, S. O. (2001b). Problems with the norms of the Comprehensive System for the Rorschach: Methodological and conceptual considerations. *Clinical Psychology: Science and Practice, 8,* 397–402.

Wood, J. M., Nezworski, M. T., Lilienfeld, S. O., & Garb, H. N. (2003). *What's wrong with the Rorschach? Science confronts the controversial inkblot test.* San Francisco: Jossey-Bass.

Related Topics

Chapter 35, "Thumbnail Guide to the Rorschach Method"

Chapter 37, "Rorschach Assessment: Scientific Status and Clinical Utility"

37 RORSCHACH ASSESSMENT
Scientific Status and Clinical Utility

Irving B. Weiner

The Rorschach Inkblot Method is a psychometrically sound, performance-based instrument for measuring personality functioning. Rorschach assessment provides dependable information about the manner in which people focus their attention, perceive people and events, think about their experience, express feelings, manage stress, view themselves, and relate to other people. Rorschach responses also provide clues to underlying needs, attitudes, conflicts, and concerns that are likely to influence a person's behavior, sometimes without the person's conscious awareness (Weiner, 2003). Information about personality characteristics identified by the RIM often facilitates decision making in clinical, forensic, and organizational settings.

The purposes of this brief chapter are to review empirical evidence demonstrating the psychometric soundness of the Rorschach and to describe the utility of the instrument in clinical practice.

SCIENTIFIC STATUS

Contemporary research demonstrates that Rorschach assessment is a scientifically sound procedure with good intercoder agreement, substantial retest reliability, adequate validity when used properly for its intended purposes, and a broad and useful normative reference base. These research findings are based primarily on Exner's (2003) Comprehensive System (CS), which is a standardized procedure for Rorschach coding and administration and is by far the most widely applied and studied Rorschach system.

Intercoder Agreement

Intercoder agreement for CS Rorschach variables has consistently proved good in numerous studies, whether measured by percentage agreement or by kappa and intraclass correlation coefficients (ICC) that take account of chance agreement. Two recent studies exemplify these findings. Meyer and colleagues (2002), examining four different samples and 219 protocols containing 4,761 responses, found a median ICC of .93 for intercoder agreement across 138 regularly occurring Rorschach variables, with 134 of these variables falling in the excellent range for chance-corrected agreement. Viglione and Taylor (2003), examining coder concurrence for 84 protocols with 1,732 responses, found a median ICC of .92 for 68 variables considered to be of central interpretive significance in the CS.

Some critics of the Rorschach have nevertheless noted that codes were originally included in the CS solely on the basis of the percentage of intercoder agreement (80% or more) and that there is no "field" study of intercoder agreement (i.e., whether individuals in practice code reliably) (Lilienfeld, Wood, & Garb, 2000). The contemporary kappa and ICC findings render the first of these arguments moot. The second argument is specious because (1) field studies of coder agreement are not ordinarily considered necessary to demonstrate the psychometric adequacy of an assessment instrument (what is known, for example, about field agreement in scoring 0, 1, or 2 points on Wechsler Comprehension items?), and (2) if people in the field are coding Rorschach responses inaccurately and thus unreliably, the fault lies with them, for not being adequately informed or careful, not with the instrument. Rorschach critics have not published or adduced any original research showing poor intercoder agreement for CS variables.

Reliability

Retest studies with both children and adults over intervals ranging from 7 days to 3 years have demonstrated substantial reliability for Rorschach summary scores and indices that are conceptualized as relating to trait characteristics, which include almost all of the CS variables. In adults, the short- and long-term stability of most CS variables exceeds .75, and 19 core variables with major interpretive significance have shown 1-year or 3-year retest correlations of .85 or higher.

The only Rorschach summary scores that show low retest correlations are based on a small number of variables and combinations of these variables that are conceptualized as measuring situational state characteristics. Children show stability coefficients similar to those of adults when retested over brief intervals. Over a 2-year retest interval, young people initially fluctuate considerably in their Rorschach scores but then show steadily increasing long-term consistency as they grow older, which is consistent with the gradual consolidation of personality characteristics during the developmental years (Exner, 2003, chap. 11).

Rorschach critics have argued that the reliability of the Rorschach is yet to be demonstrated because only a portion of the CS variables have been included in reports of retest studies (Lilienfeld et al., 2000). This argument is specious on two accounts. First, most of the retest correlations identified as "missing" pertain either to composite variables for which reliable data are available for their component parts or to variables that do not occur with sufficient frequency to allow for meaningful statistical treatment. Second, some variables are more critical to the interpretive process than others, and, as just noted, the critical interpretive variables in the CS tend to show particularly high retest correlations. Viglione and Hilsenroth (2001) have published an extensive summary of the Rorschach retest data that encompasses, either individually or within some combination, virtually all of the CS structural variables.

The retest correlations for all regularly occurring Rorschach variables having interpretive significance for trait dimensions of personality compare favorably with the reliability data for other frequently used and highly regarded assessment instruments, including the Wechsler Scales and the Minnesota Multiphasic Personality Inventory (MMPI). Rorschach critics have not published or adduced any original research showing poor reliability for these regularly occurring Rorschach indices of trait variables.

The retest and reference data for children contain some compelling evidence of construct validity for Rorschach variables. The increasing 2-year stability of Rorschach findings as children age is one case in point. The *Egocentricity Index,* conceptualized as a measure of self-focusing or self-centeredness in the Piagetian sense, shows an almost perfect linear decrease in young people from age 5 to 16, which is consistent with theory and data in developmental psychology. Similarly, the ratio of *Form-Color* to *Color-Form* responses, conceptualized as relating respectively to relatively reserved (mature) and relatively intense (immature) affective expression, shifts gradually from a *Color-Form* to a *Form-Color* preference during the childhood and adolescent years, which is consistent with what is known about emotional maturation in young people (Exner, 2003, chap. 12).

Validity

In the most thorough study of Rorschach validity available in the literature, Hiller, Rosenthal, Bornstein, Berry, and Brunell-Neuleib (1999) conducted a meta-analysis based on a random sample of Rorschach and MMPI research studies published from 1977 to 1997 in which there was at lest one external (nontest) variable and in which some reasonable basis had been posited for expecting associations between variables. Their analysis of 2,276 Rorschach protocols and 5,007 MMPI protocols produced the following results:

1. The average effect sizes in these studies indicated almost identical validity for the Rorschach and the MMPI. The unweighted mean validity coefficients were .29 for Rorschach variables and .30 for MMPI variables.
2. According to Hiller et al. (1999), the validity for both the Rorschach and the MMPI "is about as good as can be expected for personality tests" (p. 291), and the average effect sizes warrant examiner confidence in using both measures for their intended purposes.
3. The MMPI correlated more highly than the Rorschach with psychiatric diagnosis and self-reports (average effect sizes of .37 and .18, respectively). On the other hand, Rorschach variables showed higher effect sizes than MMPI variables in predicting behavioral outcomes, such as whether patients continue in or drop out of treatment (mean validity coefficients of .37 and .20, respectively). These differences found by Hiller et al. probably reflect method variance between these two instruments, with the self-report format of the MMPI resembling the basis on which psychiatric diagnoses are made, and the performance-based Rorschach being more sensitive to persistent behavioral dispositions.

In addition to providing theoretically consistent information about developmental progression in nonpatient children age 5 to 16, the CS reference include 600 nonpatient adults and adult samples of 535 psychiatric outpatients, 279 patients hospitalized with major depressive disorder, and 328 patients hospitalized with a first admission for schizophrenia. These four groups can be expected, on average, to constitute a continuum of increasingly severe psychological disturbance. Consistent with expectation, posited Rorschach indices of impaired reality testing (*X-%*) and disordered thinking (*WSum6*) increase in linear fashion across these groups, thus supporting them as measures of disturbance. The mean *X-%* ranges from .07 in nonpatients to .16 in outpatients, .20 in depressed inpatients, and .37 in schizophrenic inpatients. The mean *WSum6* for these four groups, respectively, are 4.48, 9.36, 18.36, and 42.17 (Exner, 2003, chap. 12). Viglione and Hilsenroth (2001) and Weiner (2001) provide overviews of a vast body of specific research studies demonstrating the validity of Rorschach assessment.

Rorschach critics have nevertheless argued that validity data for the Rorschach are not sufficient to warrant its use. In view of the Hiller et al. (1999) findings, this argument would imply that practicing psychologists should not use the MMPI either, or most other currently available personality assessment instruments, for that matter. The critics have contended that the Hiller et al. meta-analysis is flawed, which seems unlikely given the care with which it was conducted and the methodological sophistication of those who conducted it (see Rosenthal, Hiller, Bornstein, Berry, & Brunell-Neulieb, 2001). Critics have pointed out that the Rorschach does not correlate well with the MMPI, while ignoring not only method differences between the instruments, but also research showing that RIM and MMPI correlate quite well when people respond to both instruments in either an open or guarded manner, as opposed to being forthcoming on one and defensive on either or both (Meyer, 1997) They have noted that the Rorschach does not correlate well with psychiatric diagnosis, while not acknowledging that it is neither designed nor intended to do.

Normative Reference Base

As already indicated, the Rorschach Comprehensive System includes normative reference data on nonpatient adults (n = 600), children age 5 to 16 (1,390), and several patient groups. Because the adult nonpatient data were collected mainly between 1974 and 1986, there has been concern that they may be outdated and in need of revision. Exner (2003, chap. 12) has accordingly undertaken a new normative study in which, as in his original work, well-functioning nonpatient adults are being examined in different parts of the country by experienced examiners. As of this writing, data have been tabulated for 350 persons in the new normative sample. With some minor exceptions having minimal interpretive significance, the new reference data are strikingly similar to the older data and have thus far not called for any noteworthy modifications in interpretive strategy.

Rorschach critics have alleged that the CS overpathologizes by identifying people as psychologically disturbed when they are not (Wood, Nezworski, Garb, & Lilienfeld, 2001). This allegation is based in part on a normative study conducted in northern California that showed some differences from the CS reference data in frequency of pathological indicators. However, the critics have ignored methodological shortcomings of this study that have been pointed out in the literature, including a small (n = 123) and demographically unrepresentative sample and the use of inexperienced examiners to collect the data (Meyer, 2001).

The allegation of overpathologizing is additionally based on control sample data, collected from 32 diverse studies, that also differ from CS nonpatient data. However, the samples in these studies do not qualify as representative samples of nonpatient adults. The critics fail to mention that 16 of these 32 samples constituted college students or elderly persons, who commonly produce atypical test responses when serving as volunteer participants in research studies. Five of the samples included current or former psychiatric patients, and 11 others were recruited without any mental health screening. Finally of note, participants in some of these samples were given the Rorschach under unusual conditions, such as being instructed to remain motionless during the testing (Meyer, 2001).

As for the new CS normative study in process, the existence of which has yet to be acknowledged by Rorschach critics, the 350 nonpatient adults examined so far have shown no indication of overpathologizing. With reference to four key CS indices of psychological disorder, the Perceptual Thinking Index is elevated (PTI > 3) in just 1 (0%) of these 350 nonpatients; the Depression Index is elevated (DEPI > 4) in just 38 (11%); the Coping Deficit Index is elevated (CDI > 3) in just 25 (7%); and the D-Score is less than zero in just 17% and less than −1 in just 5%.

CLINICAL UTILITY

Rorschach assessment facilitates decision making in clinical practice by identifying personality characteristics that have implications for differential diagnosis and treatment planning. Although the Rorschach is not a diagnostic test and should not be used as the sole basis for diagnosing psychological disorder, Rorschach variables can reveal aspects of maladaptive functioning that are associated with particular conditions. As cases in point, Rorschach indices of disordered thinking (elevated *WSum6*) and impaired reality testing (poor form quality) assist in identifying schizophrenia; indices of dysphoric mood (achromatic color and color-shading blends) and pessimistic thinking (morbid contents) assist in identifying depression; and indices of subjectively felt distress (D and AdjD scores) assist in identifying anxiety disorders.

Along with helping to clarify the diagnostic status of persons seen clinically, Rorschach findings contribute to treatment planning by identifying personality characteristics that have implications for the types of intervention that are likely to prove effective, the kinds of problems or concerns that should be treatment targets, and the nature of possible obstacles to progress in therapy that can be anticipated (Weiner, 1999).

In forensic settings, Rorschach indications of psychosis, depression, and anxiety disorders often have a bearing on legal determinations relating to a person's competence to proceed, sanity at the time of an alleged offense, and the extent of psychic trauma in personal injury cases. In family-law cases involving questions of custody and visitation rights, Rorschach information concerning the personality strengths and limitations of parents and the special needs of their children frequently assist judges in arriving at their decisions.

Some Rorschach critics have alleged that the RIM does not meet current standards for admission into evidence in the courtroom (Grove

& Barden, 1999). Logical reasoning and empirical fact, as summarized by Ritzler, Erard, and Pettigrew (2002), prove them mistaken in this regard.

Finally with respect to organizational settings, the RIM can be used with good effect in the selection and evaluation of personnel. Personnel decisions are typically based in part on personality characteristics considered relevant to whether a person should be hired to fill a particular job, promoted to a position of responsibility, or considered fit to return to a previously held position. Rorschach findings concerning these characteristics accordingly facilitate these decisions.

References, Readings, & Internet Sites 

Exner, J. E., Jr. (2003). *The Rorschach: A comprehensive system. Vol. 1. Basic foundations and principles of interpretation* (4th ed.). Hoboken, NJ: Wiley.

Grove, W. M., & Barden, R. C. (1999). Protecting the integrity of the legal system: The admissibility of testimony from mental health experts under Daubert/Kumho analysis. *Psychology, Public Policy, and the Law, 5,* 224–242.

Hiller, J. B., Rosenthal, R., Bornstein, R. F, Berry, D. T. R., & Brunell-Neuleib, S. (1999). A comparative meta-analysis of Rorschach and MMPI validity. *Psychological Assessment, 11,* 278–296.

International Rorschach Society. (n.d.). Home page. Retrieved 2004 from http://www.rorschach.com

Lilienfeld, S. O., Wood, J. M., & Garb, H., N. (2000). The scientific status of projective techniques. *Psychological Science in the Public Interest, 1,* 27–66.

Meyer, G. J. (1997). On the integration of personality assessment methods: The Rorschach and MMPI. *Journal of Personality Assessment, 68,* 297–330.

Meyer, G. J. (2001). Evidence to correct misperceptions about Rorschach norms. *Clinical Psychology: Science and Practice, 8,* 389–396.

Meyer, G. J., Hilsenroth, M. J., Baxter, D., Exner, J. E., Jr., Fowler, J. C., Pers, C. C., et al. (2002). An examination of interrater reliability for scoring the Rorschach in eight data sets. *Journal of Personality Assessment, 78,* 219–274.

Ritzler, B., Erard, R., & Pettigrew, G. (2002). Protecting the integrity of Rorschach expert witnesses: A reply to Grove and Barden (1999) re: The admissibility of testimony under Daubert/Kumho analysis. *Psychology, Public Policy, and the Law, 8,* 201–215.

Rosenthal, R., Hiller, J. B., Bornstien, R. F, Berry D. T. R., & Brunell-Neuleib, S. (2001). Meta-analytic methods, the Rorschach, and the MMPI. *Psychological Assessment, 13,* 449–451.

Society for Personality Assessment. (n.d.). Home page. Retrieved 2004 from http://www.personality.org

Viglione, D. J., & Hilsenroth, M. J. (2001). The Rorschach: Facts, fictions, and future. *Psychological Assessment, 13,* 452–471.

Viglione, D. J., & Taylor, N. (2003). Empirical support for interrater reliability of Rorschach Comprehensive System coding. *Journal of Clinical Psychology, 59,* 111–121.

Weiner, I. B. (1999). Rorschach Inkblot Method. In M. Maruish (Ed.), *The use of psychological testing in treatment planning and outcome evaluation* (2nd ed., pp. 1123–1156). Mahwah, NJ: Erlbaum.

Weiner, I. B. (2001). Advancing the science of psychological assessment: The Rorschach Inkblot Method as exemplar. *Psychological Assessment, 13,* 423–432.

Weiner, I. B. (2003). *Principles of Rorschach interpretation* (2nd ed.). Mahwah, NJ: Erlbaum.

Wood, J. M., Nezworski, M. T., Garb, H. N., & Lilienfeld, S. O. (2001). The misperception of psychopathology: Problems with the norms of the Comprehensive System of the Rorschach. *Clinical Psychology, 8,* 350–373.

Related Topics

Chapter 35, "Thumbnail Guide to the Rorschach Method"

Chapter 36, "Rorschach Assessment: Questions and Reservations"

PART III

Individual Psychotherapy and Treatment

38 PATIENTS' RIGHTS IN PSYCHOTHERAPY

Dorothy W. Cantor

Patients who enter psychotherapy have rights that psychologists are responsible for honoring and rights for which third-party payers and other entities are responsible. It is the obligation of treating psychologists to respect the rights of patients and, to the limits of their ability, to assist patients to press third-party payers and other entities to do likewise.

1. *Confidentiality:* Confidentiality is the cornerstone of the psychotherapy process. Therefore, patients have the right to be guaranteed the protection of the confidentiality of their relationship with a psychologist, except when laws or ethics dictate otherwise.

- Patients should not be required to disclose confidential information, other than diagnosis, prognosis, type of treatment, time and length of treatment, and cost.
- Patients should make only time-limited disclosure with full written informed consent.
- Any entity receiving information about a patient should maintain clinical information in confidence with the same rigor and subject to the same violation as the direct provider of care.
- Information technology should be used for transmission, storage, or data management *only* with methodologies that remove individual identifying information and assure the protection of the patients' privacy. Information should not be transferred, sold, or otherwise utilized.

2. *Respectful treatment:* Patients have the right to courtesy, respect, dignity, responsiveness, and timely attention to their needs.

3. *Respect for boundaries:* Patients have the right to expect their therapists to honor the boundaries between them and not to intrude in areas that go beyond the therapeutic relationship.

- Psychologists do not engage in sexual intimacies with current patients or with former patients for at least 2 years after treatment has ended.

- Psychologists do not accept persons with whom they have engaged in sexual intimacies as therapy patients.
- Psychologists do not exploit patients. They refrain from entering into or promising another relationship—personal, scientific, professional, financial, or otherwise—with a patient.

4. *Respect for individual differences:* Patients have the right to quality treatment, without regard to race, color, religion, national origin, gender, age, sexual orientation, or disabilities.

- Patients have the right to expect their therapists to have competency in dealing with their individual differences.
- Patients can expect their therapists to respect their values, attitudes, and opinions, even when they differ from their own.

5. *Knowledge of the psychologist's professional expertise:* Patients have the right to receive full information about the psychologist's knowledge, skills, preparation, experience, and credentials. They also have the right to be informed about their options for treatment interventions.

6. *Choice:* Patients have the right to choose their therapists, according to their own preferences and without pressure from third-party payers to select from a limited panel.

7. *Informed consent to therapy:* Patients have the right to informed consent. The language of that consent must be comprehensible. The patient should be informed of significant information concerning the treatment or assessment being entered into.

8. *Determination of treatment:* Patients have the right to have recommendations about their treatment made by the treating psychologist in conjunction with them or their family, as appropriate. Treatment decisions should not be made by third-party payers. The patient has the right to make final decisions regarding treatment.

- Patients have the right to continuity of care and to not be abandoned by their therapist.
- Patients can expect a psychologist to terminate a professional relationship when it becomes reasonably clear that the patient no longer needs the service, is not benefiting, or is being harmed by continued service.
- Patients can expect that prior to termination, whatever the reason, there will be a discussion of their needs and views and suggestions for alternative services and that reasonable steps will be taken to facilitate transfer to another therapist, if appropriate.

9. *Parity:* Patients have the right to receive benefits for mental health and substance abuse treatment on the same basis as for any other illnesses, with the same provisions, copayments, lifetime benefits, and catastrophic coverage in both insurance and self-funded/self-insured health plans.

10. *Right to know:* Patients have the right to full disclosure regarding terms of their health insurance coverage.

- *Benefits:* Patients have the right to be provided information from the purchasing entity (such as employer, union, or public purchaser) and the insurance/third-party payer describing the nature and extent of their mental health and substance abuse treatment benefits. This information should include details on procedures to obtain access to services, on utilization management procedures, and on appeal rights. The information should be presented clearly in writing with language that the individual can understand.
- *Contractual limitations:* Patients have the right to be informed by the psychologist of any arrangements, restrictions, and/or covenants established between the third-party payer and the psychologist that could interfere with or influence treatment recommendations. Patients have the right to be informed of the nature of information that may be disclosed for the purposes of paying benefits.
- *Appeals and grievances:* Patients have the right to receive information about the methods they can use to submit complaints or grievances regarding provision of care by the psychologist to the licensing

board and to the professional association. Patients also have the right to be provided information about the procedures they can use to appeal benefit utilization decisions to the third-party payer system, to the employer or purchasing entity, and to external regulatory entities.

11. *Treatment review:* To assure that treatment review processes are fair and valid, patients have the right to be guaranteed that any review of their mental health and substance abuse treatment shall involve a professional having the training, credentials, and licensure required to provide the treatment in the jurisdiction in which it will be provided. The reviewer should have no financial interest in the decision and is subject to the section on confidentiality.

12. *Accountability:* Patients have the right to have both the psychologist treating them *and* the third-party payer be accountable to them.

- Psychologists may be held accountable and liable to individuals for any injury caused by gross incompetence or negligence on the part of the professional. The psychologist has the obligation to advocate for and document necessity of care and to advise the patient of options if payment authorization is denied.
- Payers and other third parties may be held accountable and liable to patients for any injury caused by gross incompetence or negligence or by their clinically unjustified decisions.

13. *Benefit usage:* Patients are entitled to the entire scope of the benefits within the benefit plan that will address their clinical needs.

14. *Nondiscrimination:* Patients who use their mental health and substance abuse benefits shall not be penalized when seeking other health insurance or disability, life, or any other insurance benefits.

References & Readings 

American Psychological Association. (1992). Ethical principles of psychologists and code of conduct. *American Psychologist, 47,* 1597–1611.

Mental Health Bill of Rights Project. (1997). Principles for the provision of mental health and substance abuse treatment services. *Independent Practitioner, 17*(2), 57–58.

Related Topics

Chapter 125, "Sample Psychotherapist-Patient Contract"

Chapter 127, "Basic Elements of Consent"

Chapter 131, "Contracting With Managed Care Organizations"

39 COMPENDIUM OF EMPIRICALLY SUPPORTED THERAPIES

Dianne L. Chambless

Beginning in 1993, the Division (now Society) of Clinical Psychology of the American Psychological Association has sponsored an endeavor to identify empirically supported psychological interventions and to publicize their existence to clinical psychologists, training programs, and consumers (Task Force, 1995). The goals are to serve the public and the profession by (1) helping psychologists and training programs readily identify promising treatments upon which their training efforts might, in part, be focused; (2) aiding psychologists in practice by providing data to support their choice of psychological interventions and the efficacy of their treatment in order to make their services available and to obtain reimbursement for them; and, more recently, (3) providing information for the public about evidence-based psychotherapies. This effort is akin to movements within American psychiatry and medicine in Britain (Sackett, Richardson, Rosenberg, & Haynes, 1997) to foster evidence-based practice by educating clinicians about the research base for practice. Within clinical psychology, this work may be seen as a logical extension of the Boulder model of scientist-practitioner training.

A succession of task forces appointed by presidents of the Division of Clinical Psychology have constructed and elaborated lists of empirically supported treatments (ESTs, also called *empirically validated therapies*) for adults and children. Other professional groups have joined in this effort. These lists are necessarily incomplete: Not all treatments have yet been reviewed, and new evidence for treatments emerges monthly.

A number of factors need to be taken into account in using these lists. First, the task forces have concentrated on specific treatments for specific psychological problems. That psychotherapy in general is beneficial for the average adult psychotherapy client is well known. The lists of ESTs represent an attempt to provide more focused information. Second, the task forces have followed a number of decision rules in determining what is sufficient evidence for listing a treatment. Decisions are largely based upon randomized controlled studies that passed muster for methodological soundness, and the preponderance of the data across studies must have been positive (Chambless & Hollon, 1998). Third, broad generic labels (e.g., cognitive-behavior therapy) may be misleading. Readers should check the original sources to determine the precise treatment procedures used in studies providing efficacy evidence. Finally, the absence of a treatment from the tables does not mean it is ineffective. It may or may not be. No listing may simply reflect a dearth of data.

In their 2001 review, Chambless and Ollendick compiled the work of eight major efforts to identify ESTs conducted in the United States or Great Britain. In Tables 1 and 2, the groups are

TABLE 1. Empirically Supported Therapies for Adults: Summary Across Work Groups

	Well-Established/ Efficacious and Specific Category I	Probably Efficacious/ Efficacious or Possibly Efficacious Category II	Experimental/ Promising Category III
Anxiety and Stress			
Agoraphobia/Panic Disorder with Agoraphobia			
CBT	A, E? F	E?	
Couples communication training as adjunct to exposure		A, D	
Exposure	A, D, E? F	E?	
Partner-assisted CBT		D, F	
Blood Injury Phobia			
Applied tension		F	E
Exposure			E
Generalized Anxiety Disorder			
Applied relaxation	F	A, D, E	
CBT	A, D, E? F	E?	

TABLE 1. *(continued)*

	Well-Established/ Efficacious and Specific Category I	Probably Efficacious/ Efficacious or Possibly Efficacious Category II	Experimental/ Promising Category III
Geriatric Anxiety			
CBT			F
Relaxation		F	
Obsessive-Compulsive Disorder			
Exposure and response prevention	A, D, E?, F	E?	
Cognitive therapy		A, D	E
RET and exposure			E
Family-assisted ERP and relaxation		D	
Relapse prevention		A	
Panic Disorder			
Applied relaxation	F	A, D, E	
CBT	A, D, E? F	E?	
Emotion-focused therapy			F
Exposure	E?	D, E?	
Post-Traumatic Stress Disorder			
EMDR		A (civilian only), D	
Exposure	F	A, D	
Stress inoculation	F	A, D	
Stress inoculation combined with CT and exposure	E?	E? F	
Structured psycho-dynamic treatment			E
Public Speaking Anxiety			
Systematic desensitization		A	
Social Anxiety/Phobia			
CBT	E? F	A, D, E?	
Exposure	E?	A, D, E? F	
Systematic desensitization		A	
Specific Phobia			
Exposure	A, E? F	E?	
Systematic desensitization		A	
Stress			
Stress inoculation	A		
Chemical Abuse and Dependence			
Alcohol Abuse and Dependence			
Community reinforcement	E? F?	A, D, E? F?	
Cue exposure		A, D	
Cue exposure therapy and urge coping skills		D	
Motivational interviewing	E?	E?	
BMT and disulfiram	E? F?	A, D, E? F?	
Social skills training with inpatient treatment	E? F?	A, D, E? F?	
Benzodiazepine Withdrawal for Panic Disorder			
CBT		A	
Cocaine Abuse			
Behavior therapy		A	
CBT relapse prevention		A, D	
Opiate Dependence			
Behavior therapy (reinforcement)		D	
Brief dynamic therapy		A, D	
Cognitive therapy		A, D	

(continued)

TABLE 1. Empirically Supported Therapies for Adults: Summary Across Work Groups (*continued*)

	Well-Established/ Efficacious and Specific Category I	Probably Efficacious/ Efficacious or Possibly Efficacious Category II	Experimental/ Promising Category III
Depression			
Bipolar Disorder			
CBT for medication adherence		F	
Family therapy			F
Psychoeducation		F	
Geriatric Depression			
Behavior therapy	E? F	E? G	
Brief dynamic therapy	E? F	E? G	
CBT	E? F	A, E? G	
Interpersonal therapy		F	
Problem-solving therapy		F, G	
Psychoeducation	F		
Reminiscence therapy	F (mild-moderate)	A, G	
Major Depression			
Behavior therapy	A, F	D	
BMT (for MDD conjoint with marital distress)	F	D	
Brief dynamic therapy		A	E
CBT	A, D, E? F	E?	
Interpersonal therapy	A, E? F	D, E?	
Self-control therapy		A, F	
Social problem solving		A, D	
Health Problems			
Anorexia			
Behavioral family systems therapy		F	
Behavior therapy	E?	E?	
Cognitive therapy	E?	E?	
Family therapy		F Patients < 19 years old	
Binge-Eating Disorder			
Comprehensive behavioral weight loss program		F	
CBT	F	A	
Interpersonal therapy		A, F	
Bulimia			
CBT	A, E? F	D, E?	
Interpersonal therapy	E?	A, D, E? F	
Chemotherapy Side Effects (for Cancer Patients)			
Progressive muscle relaxation with or without guided imagery		D	
Chronic Pain (Heterogeneous)			
CBT with physical therapy		A, D, H	
EMG biofeedback		A	
Operant behavior therapy		A, D	
Chronic Pain (Back)			
CBT	H	A, D	
Operant behavior therapy		D	
Headache			
Behavior therapy	A		
Idiopathic Pain			
CBT		H	

TABLE 1. *(continued)*

	Well-Established/ Efficacious and Specific Category I	Probably Efficacious/ Efficacious or Possibly Efficacious Category II	Experimental/ Promising Category III
Irritable Bowel Syndrome			
Cognitive therapy		A, D	
Hypnotherapy		D	
Multicomponent CBT		A, D	
Migraine			
EMG biofeedback and relaxation		D	
Thermal biofeedback and relaxation training		A, D	
Obesity			
Hypnosis with CBT		A	
Raynaud's			
Thermal biofeedback		A	
Rheumatic Disease Pain			
Multicomponent CBT	A, D, H		
Sickle Cell Disease Pain			
Multicomponent cognitive therapy		A	
Smoking Cessation			
Group CBT		D	
Multicomponent CBT with relapse prevention	A, D		
Scheduled reduced smoking with multicomponent behavior therapy		A, D	
Somatoform Pain Disorders			
CBT		F	
Marital Discord			
BMT	A, D		
CBT		D	
Cognitive therapy		D	
Emotion-focused couples therapy		A (no more than moderately distressed), D	
Insight-oriented marital therapy		A, D	
Systematic therapy		D	
Sexual Dysfunction[a]			
Erectile Dysfunction			
Behavior therapy aimed at reducing sexual anxiety and improving communication	E?	E?	
CBT aimed at reducing sexual anxiety and improving communication	E?	E?	
Female Hypoactive Sexual Desire			
Hurlbert's combined therapy		A, D	
Zimmer's combined sex and marital therapy		A, D	
Female Orgasmic Disorder/Dysfunction			
BMT with Masters and Johnson's therapy		D	
Masters and Johnson's sex therapy		A, D	
Sexual skills training		D	
Premature Ejaculation			
Behavior therapy			E
Vaginismus			
Exposure-based behavior therapy	E?	E?	

(continued)

TABLE 1. Empirically Supported Therapies for Adults: Summary Across Work Groups (*continued*)

	Well-Established/ Efficacious and Specific Category I	Probably Efficacious/ Efficacious or Possibly Efficacious Category II	Experimental/ Promising Category III
Other			
Avoidant Personality Disorder			
Exposure		F	
Social skills training	E?	E? F	
Borderline Personality Disorder			
Dialectical behavior therapy	E?	A, E? F	
Body Dysmorphic Disorder			
CBT		F	
Dementia			
Behavioral interventions applied at environmental level for behavior problems	G		
Memory and cognitive training for slowing cognitive decline		G	
Reality orientation		G	E
Geriatric Caregivers			
Psychoeducation		G	
Psychosocial interventions	E?	E?	
Hypochondriasis			
CBT			F
Paraphilias/Sex Offenders			
Behavior therapy		A	
CBT			F
Schizophrenia			
Assertive case management			F
Behavior therapy and social learning/token economy programs	F		
Clinical case management			F
Cognitive therapy (for delusions)			E, F
Behavorial family therapy	D, E? F	A, E?	
Family systems therapy		D	
Social learning programs	F		
Social skills training	F	A, D	
Supportive group therapy		F	
Supportive long-term family therapy	D		
Training in Community Living program	F		
Severely Mentally Ill			
Supported employment		A, F	
Sleep Disorders			
Behavior therapy			F
CBT (for geriatric sleep disorders)		G	
Unwanted Habits			
Habit reversal and control techniques		A	

Source: From "Empirically Supported Psychological Interventions: Controversies and Evidence," Chambless and Ollendick, 2001. Reprinted, with permission, from the *Annual Review of Psychology,* Volume 52, © 2001 by Annual Reviews (www.annualreviews.org).

? = unclear from authors' description whether the treatment belongs in Category I or II; CBT = cognitive behavior therapy; BMT = behavioral marital therapy; ERP = exposure plus ritual prevention; CT = cognitive therapy; EMG = electromyographic; EMDR = eye movement desensitization and reprocessing.

[a]Group F's review of sexual dysfunction did not describe the treatments clearly enough to categorize them here.

Workgroups: A = Task Force, Chambless et al., 1998; B = Special Section of *Journal of Pediatric Psychology* (Spirito, 1999); C = Special Section of *Journal of Clinical Child Psychology* (Lonigan & Elbert, 1998); D = Special Section of *Journal of Consulting and Clinical Psycology* (Kendall & Chambless, 1998); E = *What Works for Whom?* (Roth & Fonagy, 1996); F = *A Guide to Treatments That Work* (Nathan & Gorman, 1998); G = Gatz et al., 1998; H = Wilson & Gil, 1996.

TABLE 2. Empirically Supported Therapies for Children and Adolescents: Summary Across Work Groups

	Well-Established/ Efficacious and Specific Category I	Probably Efficacious/ Efficacious or Possibly Efficacious Category II	Experimental/ Promising Category III
ADHD			
Behavioral parent training	C		
Behavior modification in classroom	C		F
Long-term multimodal therapy			E
Anxiety Disorders (Separation Anxiety, Avoidant Disorder, Overanxious Disorder)			
CBT		A, C	E
CBT and family AMT		A, C	
Pyschodynamic psychotherapy			E
Chronic Pain (Musculoskeletal Disorders)			
CBT			B
Conduct Disorder and Oppositional Defiant Disorder			
Anger control training with stress inoculation (adolescents)		C	
Anger coping therapy (children)		C	
Assertiveness training		C	
CBT	E?	E?	
Cognitive problem-solving skills	F		
Delinquency prevention program		C	
Functional family therapy	F		
Multisystemic therapy	F		
Parent-child interaction therapy		C	
Living with Children (children)		C	
Parent training based on *Living with Children* (children)	A, E? F	C, E?	
Parent training based on *Living with Children* (adolescents)	C, F		
Problem-solving skills training		C	
Rational emotive therapy		C	
Time-out plus signal seat treatment		C	
Videotape-modeling parent training	C		
Depression			
Coping with Depression course with skills training (adolescents)		C	
CBT (children)		C	
Disruptive Disorders			
Structural family therapies			E
Distress Due to Medical Procedures (mainly for cancer)			
CBT	B		
Encopresis			
Behavior modification	E?	A, E?	
Enuresis			
Behavior modification	A, E?	E?	
Obesity			
Behavior therapy		A	
Obsessive-Compulsive Disorder			
Exposure and response prevention			E
Phobias			
CBT		C	
Filmed modeling		C	
Imaginal desensitization		C	
In vivo desensitization		C	
Live modeling		C	
Participant modeling	C		
Rapid exposure (school phobia)	E?	E?	
Reinforced practice	C	A	

(continued)

TABLE 2. Empirically Supported Therapies for Children and Adolescents: Summary Across Work Groups (*continued*)

	Well-Established/ Efficacious and Specific Category I	Probably Efficacious/ Efficacious or Possibly Efficacious Category II	Experimental/ Promising Category III
Psychophysiological Disorder			
Family therapy	E?	E?	
Psychodynamic psychotherapy			E
Pervasive Developmental Disorders, Undesirable Behavior In			
Contingency management	E?	E?	
Recurrent Abdominal Pain			
CBT		D, F	
Recurrent Headache			
Biofeedback with self-hypnosis			B
Relaxation/self-hypnosis	B		
Thermal biofeedback		B	

Source: From "Empirically Supported Psychological Interventions: Controversies and Evidence," Chambless and Ollendick, 2001. Reprinted, with permission, from the *Annual Review of Psychology*, Volume 52, © 2001, by Annual Reviews (www.annualreviews.org).
ATM = anxiety management training. See footnote in Table 1 for definition of other abbreviatons.

identified by letters: A for the original Division 12 task force (Chambless et al., 1998); B for a special section of *Journal of Pediatric Psychology* (Spirito, 1999); C for a special issue of *Journal of Clinical Child Psychology* (Lonigan & Elbert, 1998); D for a special section of *Journal of Consulting and Clinical Psychology* (Kendall & Chambless, 1998); E for Roth and Fonagy's (1996) review for the British National Health Service; F for a separate Division 12 effort, Nathan and Gorman's (1998) *A Guide to Treatments That Work;* G for Gatz et al.'s (1998) review of treatments for the elderly; and H for Wilson and Gil's (1996) review of treatments for pain.

For purposes of comparison, treatments are grouped into three rough categories indicating level of support, with Category I being the highest. These take into account the number of studies available and their experimental rigor. Category I refers to well established or efficacious and specific treatments; Category II to probably efficacious, efficacious, or possibly efficacious treatments; and Category III to treatments that show promise pending further investigation (see Chambless & Ollendick, 2001, for additional details). These categories do not map precisely on those used by the different work groups because of differences among the groups in the evidence base required for various EST classifications, and because Nathan and Gorman did not establish categories. In addition, because Roth and Fonagy did not distinguish between Category I and II treatments, their ESTs are listed in the tables under both these categories with a question mark. Finally, not all work groups listed promising (Category III) treatments; those doing so were groups B, E, and F.

Table 1 lists ESTs for adults, including geriatric clients, and Table 2 lists ESTs for children. Some treatments were reviewed by only one (or some subset) of the work groups. However, when more than one group evaluated a given treatment, the agreement across groups was remarkable, given the differences among reviewers in theoretical orientation and work-group membership. Thus, it appears that psychological interventions can be reliably evaluated, but this does not speak to the question of whether treatments should be so evaluated.

The EST projects have been lauded and condemned (Chambless & Ollendick, 2001). Those who favor it appear to be those who believe that training in specific psychological interventions is meaningful—that is, that there are important differences among approaches to psychotherapy and among approaches for different disorders. Those who believe that individual difference variables (e.g., characteristics of the client, the therapist, or the particular therapeutic relationship) are of the utmost importance in treatment outcome find EST lists less useful, as do those who believe that psychologists are not yet able to define clients' problems or even our interventions in terms meaningful enough to allow fruitful matching of treatments to target problems. Indeed, there is still debate about the relative importance of symptom relief (the major, although not the sole, focus of EST evidence) versus less well specified goals like personal growth, and whether the most important changes clients make in experiential and psychodynamic therapies can be reliably and validly assessed.

Reactions to the EST lists also probably differ as a function of viewing the identification of evidence-based treatments as a support or a threat to clinical practice. A review of Tables 1 and 2 will readily demonstrate that most, although not all, of the treatments identified to date are behavioral or cognitive-behavioral in nature, reflecting the greater research activity of psychotherapy outcome researchers of that orientation. Some practitioners of other orientations have expressed fear that their access to third-party payments will be reduced because they do not practice treatments on the list. Other clinicians have found that they can draw on the list to promote the efficacy and desirability of their treatment plans. To some degree, this particular controversy also centers on the best ways to react to the escalating demands for more efficient use of health care dollars.

Finally, the EST movement seems to displease psychologists to the degree that they see identifying manualized efficacious treatments as threats to their autonomy and creativity. To the degree that one believes psychotherapy is based upon artistry rather than science, an emphasis on ESTs may be viewed as a restriction. Other psychologists see no reason that manual-based treatments cannot be combined and altered into a configuration best for a particular client.

However controversial, the EST movement has gained sufficient credence that some didactic instruction and clinical supervision in empirically supported therapies is now specified in the *Guidelines and Principles for Accreditation of Programs in Professional Psychology* (American Psychological Association, 1996) for both internships and doctoral training programs. Thus, future generations of students should have exposure to one or more evidence-based treatments. Training for those in practice is likely to be more difficult, in that the various EST task forces have concluded that practitioners wishing to learn a new EST sharply different from treatments in their current repertory need supervised clinical work to acquire sufficient skill for ethical practice. Better vehicles for continuing education than the current 3-hour to 3-day workshops need to be developed.

References, Readings, & Internet Sites 

American Psychological Association. (1996). *Guidelines and principles for accreditation of programs in professional psychology*. Washington, DC: Author.

Chambless, D. L., Baker, M., Baucom, D. H., Beutler, L. E., Calhoun, K. S., Crits-Christoph, P., et al. (1998). Update on empirically validated therapies, II. *The Clinical Psychologist, 51*(1), 3–16. http://pantheon.yale.edu/~tat22/empirically_supported_treatments.htm

Chambless, D. L., & Hollon, S. D. (1998). Defining empirically supported therapies. *Journal of Consulting and Clinical Psychology, 66*, 7–18.

Chambless, D. L., & Ollendick, T. H. (2001). Empirically supported psychological interventions: Controversies and evidence. In S. T. Fiske, D. L. Schacter, & C. Zahn-Waxler (Eds.), *Annual Review of Psychology* (Vol. 52, pp. 685–716). Palo Alto, CA: Annual Reviews.

Dissemination Subcommittee of the Committee on Science and Practice. (n.d.). *A guide to beneficial psychotherapy.* Retrieved May 30, 2003, from Division 12, American Psychological Association's Web site: http://www.apa.org/divisions/div12/rev_est/index.html

EST Document Archive. (n.d.). *Task force on psychological interventions document repository.* Retrieved May 21, 2003, from Society for a Science of Clinical Psychology's Web site: http://pantheon.yale.edu/~tat22/empirically_supported_treatments.htm. Also available as *Empirically supported treatment documents.* Retrieved May 30, 2003 from Division 12, American Psychological Association's Web site: http://www.apa.org/divisions/div12/journals.html

Gatz, M., Fiske, A., Fox, L. S., Kaskie, B., Kasl-Godley, J. E., McCallum, T. J., et al. (1998). Empirically validated psychological treatments for older adults. *Journal of Mental Health and Aging, 4,* 9–46.

Kendall, P. C., & Chambless, D. L. (1998). Empirically supported psychological therapies. *Journal of Consulting and Clinical Psychology, 66,* 3–167.

Lonigan, C. J., & Elbert, J. C. (1998). Special issue: Empirically supported psychosocial interventions for children. *Journal of Clinical Child Psychology, 27,* 138–226.

Nathan, P. E., & Gorman, J. M. (Eds.). (1998). *A guide to treatments that work.* New York: Oxford University Press.

Roth, A. D., & Fonagy, P. (1996). *What works for whom? A critical review of psychotherapy research.* New York: Guilford Press.

Sackett, D. L., Richardson, W. S., Rosenberg, W., & Haynes, R. B. (1997). *Evidence-based medicine.* New York: Churchill Livingstone.

Spirito, A. (Ed.). (1999). Empirically supported treatments in pediatric psychology. *Journal of Pediatric Psychology, 24,* 87–174.

Task Force on Promotion and Dissemination of Psychological Procedures. (1995). Training in and dissemination of empirically-validated psychological treatments: Report and recommendations. *The Clinical Psychologist, 48*(1), 3–23.

Wilson, J. J., & Gil, K. M. (1996). The efficacy of psychological and pharmacological interventions for the treatment of chronic disease-related and non-disease-related pain. *Clinical Psychology Review, 16,* 573–597.

Related Topics

Chapter 40, "Compendium of Psychotherapy Treatment Manuals"

Chapter 41, "Compendium of Empirically Supported Therapy Relationships"

40 COMPENDIUM OF PSYCHOTHERAPY TREATMENT MANUALS

Michael J. Lambert, Taige Bybee, Ryan Houston, Matthew Bishop, A. Danielle Sanders, Ron Wilkinson, & Sara Rice

The earliest treatment manuals were developed in the 1960s. Manuals were originally created to provide specific definitions of treatment parameters for psychotherapy research (Strupp, 1992). By utilizing manuals in clinical trials, researchers can reduce variability among therapists by assuring their adherence to the different treatments under investigation (Crits-Christoph et al., 1991; Luborsky & Barber, 1993). Manuals have also been used to train and guide novice therapists (Moras, 1993) and have now become a means of delivering empirically supported treatments (Addis, 1997).

In clinical practice, the manuals have several

advantages. Manuals provide a succinct theoretical framework for treatment, concrete descriptions of therapeutic techniques, and case examples of appropriate applications (Addis, 1997). The increased precision in detailing treatment techniques has generated much enthusiasm among professionals and third-party providers (Strupp & Anderson, 1997).

However, others have expressed concerns over the use of treatment manuals in clinical practice. Among these concerns are questions regarding treatment efficacy and therapist adherence in clinical practice as opposed to controlled research settings (Addis, 1997), the engenderment of therapist rigidity and inflexibility (Lambert & Ogles, 1988), the neglect of nonspecific and relationship factors (Norcross, 2002), and the inadequacy of manuals for integrative approaches (Goldfried, 1993).

It is in light of the possible advantages afforded by treatment manuals and with consideration of concerns regarding them that we present the following inventory of current treatment manuals. Substantial reviews have taken place emphasizing empirically supported treatments (ESTs; Chambless & Ollendick, 2001) for particular disorders or problems. Not all of the treatment manuals listed here have received extensive empirical support, but they have been included for breadth of coverage and clinical interest.

The manuals shown in Table 1 are grouped

TABLE 1. Treatment Manuals

Author/Year	Title	Theoretical Orientation	Patient Population	Therapy Modality	Strengths
Anxiety Disorders					
Barlow & Cerny (1988)	*Psychological Treatment of Panic*	CBT	Panic disorder	Individual	1, 2, 3, 4
Beck, Emery, & Greenberg (1985)	*Anxiety Disorders and Phobias: A Cognitive Perspective*	Cognitive	Phobias	Individual	1, 2, 3
Bouman & Emmelkamp (1996)[a]	"Panic Disorder and Agoraphobia"	CBT	Agoraphobia	Individual	1, 2, 3
Brown, O'Leary, & Barlow (2001)[b]	"Generalized Anxiety Disorder"	Cognitive	GAD	Individual	1, 2, 3, 4
Clark & Salkovskis (1996)	*Treatment Manual for Focused Cognitive Therapy for Panic Disorder*	Cognitive	Panic disorder	Individual	1, 2, 4
Craske & Barlow (2001)[b]	"Panic Disorder and Agoraphobia"	CBT	Panic disorder and agoraphobia	Individual, group	1, 2, 3, 4, 6
Dugas (2002)[c]	"Generalized Anxiety Disorder"	Behavioral	GAD	Individual	3, 4
Falsetti & Resnick (2001)	*Posttraumatic Stress Disorder*	Cognitive	PTSD	Individual	1, 4
Foa & Franklin (2001)[b]	"Obsessive-Compulsive Disorder"	CBT	OCD	Individual	1, 2, 3, 4
Gaston (1995)	*Dynamic Therapy for Posttraumatic Disorder*	Dynamic	Trauma	Individual	1, 2, 3
Harris (1998)	*Trauma Recovery and Empowerment: A Clinician's Guide for Working with Women in Groups*	Dynamic	Trauma recovery, PTSD (mostly women)	Group	1, 2, 3, 4, 6
Kozak & Foa (1996)[a]	"Obsessive-Compulsive Disorder"	Behavioral	OCD	Individual	1, 2, 3
Resick & Calhoun (2001)[b]	"Posttraumatic Stress Disorder"	CBT	Rape victims w/ PTSD	Individual	1, 2, 3, 4
Scholing, Emmelkamp, & Van Oppen (1996)[a]	"Cognitive-Behavioral Treatment of Social Phobia"	CBT	Social phobia	Individual	1, 2, 3, 4

(*continued*)

TABLE 1. Treatment Manuals (*continued*)

Author/Year	Title	Theoretical Orientation	Patient Population	Therapy Modality	Strengths
Smucker & Dancu (1999)	"Cognitive-Behavioral Treatment for Adult Survivors of Childhood Trauma: Imagery, Rescripting, and Reprocessing"	CBT	PTSD, adult survivors of trauma	Individual	1, 2, 3, 4
Turk, Heimberg, & Hope (2001)[b]	"Social Anxiety Disorder"	CBT	Avoidant personality disorder, social anxiety	Group	1, 2, 3, 4
Turner & Beidel (1988)	*Treating Obsessive-Compulsive Disorder*	Behavioral	OCD	Individual	1, 2, ,3, 4
White (2000)	*Treating Anxiety and Stress: A Group Psycho-Educational Approach Using Brief CBT*	CBT	Anxiety disorders	Group	1, 2, 3, 4
Affective Disorders					
Beck, Rush, Shaw, & Emery (1979)	*Cognitive Therapy of Depression*	Cognitive	Depression	Individual,	1, 2, 3, 4, 5
Becker, Heimberg, & Bellack (1987)	*Social Skills Training Treatment for Depression*	Behavioral	Depression	Individual, group	1, 2, 3
Dick, Gallagher-Thompson, & Thompson (1996)	*Cognitive-Behavioral Therapy*	CBT	Depressed older adults	Individual,	4
Eells (1995)[d]	"Relational Therapy for Grief Disorders"	Dynamic	Adjustment difficulties	Individual	1, 2, 3, 4
Freeman & Reinecke (1993)	*Cognitive Therapy of Suicidal Behavior: A Manual for Treatment*	Cognitive	Suicide	Individual	1, 2, 3, 6
Gillies (2001)[b]	"Interpersonal Psychotherapy for Depression and Other Disorders"	Interpersonal	Depression: postpartum, adolescents, HIV-seropositive, late-life	Individual	1, 2, 4
Klerman, Weissman, Rounsaville, & Chevron (1984)	*Interpersonal Psychotherapy of Depression*	Interpersonal	Depression	Individual	1, 2, 3, 4, 5
Lewinsohn, Antonuccio, Steinmetz, & Teri (1984)	*The Coping With Depression Course: A Psychoeducational Intervention for Unipolar Depression*	Behavioral	Depression	Group	1, 2, 3, 4
Luborsky, Mark, Hole, Popp, Goldsmith, & Cacciola (1995)[d]	"Supportive-Expressive Dynamic Psychotherapy of Depression: A Time-Limited Version"	Dynamic	Depression	Individual	1, 2, 3
Miklowitz (2001)[b]	"Bipolar Disorder"	Family focused treatment	Bipolar disorder, families of those with bipolar disorder	Individual, family, couple	1, 2, 3, 4
Otto & Reilly-Harrington (2002)[e]	"Cognitive-Behavioral Therapy for the Management of Bipolar Disorder"	CBT	Bipolar disorder	Individual	2, 4
Rosselló & Bernal (1996)	*Adapting Cognitive-Behavioral and Interpersonal Treatments for Depressed Puerto Rican Adolescents*	CBT, interpersonal	Depressed Puerto Rican adolescents	Individual	1, 2, 4, 6
Swartz, Markowitz, & Frank (2002)[e]	"Interpersonal Psychotherapy for Unipolar and Bipolar Disorders"	Interpersonal	Bipolar disorder, depression	Individual	1, 2, 4
Thase (1996)[a]	"Cognitive Behavior Therapy Manual for Treatment of Depressed Inpatients"	CBT	Depressed inpatients	Individual	1, 2, 3, 4

TABLE 1. *(continued)*

Author/Year	Title	Theoretical Orientation	Patient Population	Therapy Modality	Strengths
Yost, Beutler, Corbishley, & Allender (1986)	*Group Cognitive Therapy: A Treatment Approach for Depressed Older Adults*	Cognitive	Depression	Group	1, 2, 3, 4
Young, Weinberger, & Beck (2001)[b]	"Cognitive Therapy for Depression"	Cognitive	Depression	Individual	1, 2, 3, 4
Childhood Adolescent Disorders					
Anastopoulos (1998)[f]	"A Training Program for Parents of Children with Attention-Deficit/Hyperactivity Disorder"	Parent training	Childhood ADHD	Parent(s)	1, 2, 3, 4
Barkley (1998)	*Attention-Deficit Hyperactivity Disorder: A Handbook of Diagnosis and Treatment*	CBT	ADHD	Individual, family	1, 2, 3, 4
Bratton (1998)[f]	"Training Parents to Facilitate Their Child's Adjustment to Divorce Using Filial/Family Play Therapy Approach"	Parent training	Adjustment disorders, children of divorce	Parent(s)	1, 2, 3, 4
Camino (2000)	*Treating Sexually Abused Boys*	Empowerment	Sexually abused boys	Group, individual	2, 3, 4
Eisen, Engler, & Geyer (1998)[f]	"Parent Training for Separation Anxiety Disorder"	Parent training	Separation anxiety disorder	Parent(s)	1, 2, 3, 4
Everett & Everett (1999)	*Family Therapy for ADHD: Treating Children, Adolescents, and Adults*	Family systems	ADHD	Family	3, 4
Fouse & Wheeler (1997)	*A Treasure Chest of Behavioral Strategies for Individuals with Autism*	Behavioral, systems	Autistic children	Individual, group	1, 2, 3, 4
Franklin, Rynn, March, & Foa (2002)[c]	"Obsessive-Compulsive Disorder"	Behavioral	OCD	Individual/systems	1, 2, 3
Landreth (1991)	*Play Therapy: The Art of the Relationship*	Dynamic	Children	Individual, group	1, 2, 3, 4
March & Mulle (1996)[g]	"Banishing OCD: Cognitive-Behavioral Psychotherapy for Obsessive-Compulsive Disorders"	CBT	OCD	Individual	1, 3, 4
O'Connor (2000)	*The Play Therapy Primer*	Ecosystemic	Children	Individual, group	1, 2, 3, 4
Reynolds (2002)[c]	"Childhood Depression"	Behavioral	Depression	Individual	3, 4
Roach & Gross (2002)[c]	"Conduct Disorder"	Behavioral	Conduct disorder	Individual	3, 4
Rotherman-Borus, Goldstein, & Elkavich (2002)[e]	"Treatment of Suicidality: A Family Intervention for Adolescent Suicide Attempters"	CBT	Outpatient families of suicidal adolescents	Family	3, 4
Sells (1998)	*Treating the Tough Adolescent: A Family-Based, Step-by-Step Guide*	Family systems	Conduct disorder, oppositional defiant disorder	Family	1, 2, 3, 4
Weiss & Wolchik (1998)[f]	"New Beginnings: An Empirically-Based Intervention Program for Divorced Mothers to Help Their Children Adjust to Divorce"	Group parent training	Adjustment disorders, children of divorce	Group	1, 2, 3, 4
Wolfson (1998)[f]	"Working with Parents on Developing Efficacious Sleep/Wake Habits for Infants and Young Children"	Parent training	Infant/childhood sleep disorders	Parent(s)	1, 2, 3, 4

(continued)

TABLE 1. Treatment Manuals (*continued*)

Author/Year	Title	Theoretical Orientation	Patient Population	Therapy Modality	Strengths
Dissociative Identity Disorders					
Kluft (1995)[d]	"Psychodynamic Psychotherapy of Multiple Personality Disorder and Allied Forms of Dissociative Disorder Not Otherwise Specified"	Dynamic	Dissociative disorder	Individual	1, 2, 3
Eating Disorders and Weight Management Treatments					
Cash & Grant (1996)[a]	"Cognitive-Behavioral Treatment of Body-Image Disturbances"	CBT	Eating disorders, body dysmorphic disorder	Individual	1, 2, 3, 4
Sansone & Johnson (1995)[d]	"Treating the Eating Disorder Patient with Borderline Personality Disorder: Theory and Technique"	Dynamic	Eating/borderline	Individual	1, 2, 3
Williamson, Champagne, Jackman, & Varnado (1996)[a]	"Lifestyle-Change: A Program for Long-Term Weight Management"	Behavioral	Obesity	Group (closed)	2, 3, 4
Wilson & Pike (2001)[b]	"Eating Disorders"	CBT	Bulimia nervosa, anorexia nervosa	Individual	2, 3, 4
Forensic					
Bricklin (1995)	*The Custody Evaluation Handbook: Research-Based Solutions & Applications*	Assessment	Divorce	Psychological testing	2, 3
Ellis (2000)	*Rationale and Goals of the Custody Evaluation*	Assessment	Divorce	Psychological testing	1, 2, 4
Ferguson & Mittenberg (1996)[a]	"Cognitive-Behavioral Treatments of Postconcussion Syndrome: A Therapist's Manual"	CBT	Brain trauma	Individual	1, 2, 3, 4
Marshall & Eccles (1996)[a]	"Cognitive-Behavioral Treatments of Sex Offenders"	CBT	Sex offenders	Group	1, 2, 3
Ward, Hudson, & Keenan (2001)	*The Assessment and Treatment of Sexual Offenders Against Children*	CBT	Sex offenders/ pedophiles & ebephiles	Group	2, 3, 4
Impulse Control Disorders					
Ciarrocchi (2002)	Counseling Problem Gamblers: A Self-Regulation Manual for Individual and Family Therapy	Eclectic/ pragmatic	Adult pathological gamblers	Individual, group, family, couple	1, 2, 3, 4
Larkin & Zayfert (1996)[a]	"Anger Management Training with Essential Hypertensive Patients"	Behavioral	Anger management	Group	1, 2, 3,4
Stanley & Mouton (1996)[a]	"Trichotillomania Treatment Manual"	Behavioral	Trichotillomania	Individual	1, 2, 3, 4
Outpatient Treatments					
Chethik & Morton (2000)	*Techniques for Child Therapy: Psychodynamic Strategies*	Dynamic	Outpatient children	Individual	1, 2, 3, 4
Daldrup, Beutler, Engle, & Greenberg (1988)	*Focused Expressive Psychotherapy*	Experiential	Outpatient	Individual	1, 2, 3, 4
De Domenico (2000)	*Sand Tray World Play: A Comprehensive Guide to the Use of the Sand Tray in Psychotherapeutic and Transformational Settings*	Dynamic, experiential	Outpatient children, adolescents, & adults	Individual, group, family	1, 2, 3, 4

TABLE 1. *(continued)*

Author/Year	Title	Theoretical Orientation	Patient Population	Therapy Modality	Strengths
Gumaer (1984)	*Counseling and Therapy for Children*	Various	Outpatient children	Individual, group, family	1, 2, 3, 4
Hayes, Strosahl, & Wilson (1999)	*Acceptance and Commitment Therapy: An Experiential Approach to Behavior Change*	Behavioral, experiential	Outpatient	Individual	1, 2, 3, 4
Hersen (2002)[c]	"Clinical Behavior Therapy: Adults & Children"	Behavioral	Outpatient	Individual	1, 2, 3, 4
Hibbs & Jensen (1996)[g]	"Psychosocial Treatments for Child & Adolescent Disorders: Empirically Based Strategies for Clinical Practice"	Various	Outpatient (child & adolescent)	Individual	1, 2, 3, 4
Padesky & Greenberger (1995)	*Clinician's Guide to Mind Over Mood*	Cognitive	Outpatient	Individual	1, 2, 4, 6
Strupp & Binder (1984)	*Psychotherapy in a New Key*	Dynamic	Outpatient	Individual	1, 2, 3, 4
Wright & Wright (1987)	*Clinical Practice of Hypnotherapy*	Hypnotherapy	Outpatient	Individual	1, 2
Partner Relational Problems					
Epstein & Baucom (2002)	*Enhanced Cognitive-Behavorial Therapy for Couples: A Contextual Approach*	CBT	Distressed couples	Couples	1, 2, 3
Greenberg & Johnson (1988)	*Emotionally Focused Therapy for Couples*	Experiential	Distressed couples	Couples	1, 2, 3, 4
Jacobson & Gurman (Ed.) (1995)	*Clinical Handbook of Couple Therapy*	Various	Distressed couples	Couples	1, 2, 3, 4
Wheeler, Christensen, & Jacobson (2001)[b]	"Couple Distress"	Integrative, behavioral	Distressed couples	Couples	1, 2, 3, 4
Young & Long (1998)	*Counseling and Therapy for Couples*	Integrative	Infidelity, divorce	Couples	1, 4, 6
Personality Disorders					
Beck & Freeman (1990)	*Cognitive Therapy of Personality*	Cognitive	Personality disorders	Individual	1, 2, 3
Benjamin (2002)	*Interpersonal Diagnosis and Treatment of Personality Disorders*	Interpersonal	Personality disorders	Individual	1, 2, 3, 4
Linehan, Cochran, & Kehrer (2001)[b]	"Dialectical Behavior Therapy for Borderline Personality Disorder"	CBT, dialectical behavior therapy	Borderline personality disorder (including those in substance abuse treatment settings)	Individual	1, 2, 3, 4
Piper, Rosie, Joyce, & Azim (1996)	*Time-Limited Day Treatment for Personality Disorders: Integration of Research and Practice in a Group Program*	Eclectic	Personality disorders	Group	1, 2, 3, 4
Sperry (1999)	*Cognitive Behavior Therapy of DSM-IV Personality Disorders: Highly Effective Interventions for the Most Common Personality Disorders*	CBT	Avoidant, borderline, dependent, narcissisic, OCPD, histrionic	Individual	1, 2, 3, 4
Whitehurst, Ridolfi, & Gunderson (2002)[e]	"Multiple Family Group Treatment for Borderline Personality Disorder"	Psychoeducational	Borderlines	Family, educational groups	1, 2, 3, 4

(continued)

TABLE 1. Treatment Manuals (*continued*)

Author/Year	Title	Theoretical Orientation	Patient Population	Therapy Modality	Strengths
Schizophrenia					
Herz, Marvin, Marder, & Stephen (2002)	*Schizophrenia: Comprehensive Treatment and Management*	Medical model	Schizophrenia	Individual, family	1, 2, 3, 4
Hogarty (2002)	*Personal Therapy for Schizophrenia and Related Disorders: A Guide to Individualized Treatment*	Systems	Schizophrenia	Individual, group	1, 2, 3, 4
McFarlane (2002)	*Multifamily Groups in Treatment of Severe Psychiatric Disorders*	Systems	Schizophrenia	Group	1, 2, 3, 4
Pratt & Mueser (2002)[e]	"Social Skills Training for Schizophrenia"	Social skills training	Schizophrenia (inpatient & outpatient)	Group	1, 2, 3, 4 (template for Group)
Wong & Liberman (1996)[a]	"Biobehavioral Treatment and Rehabilitation for Persons with Schizophrenia"	Biobehavioral	Schizophrenia	Individual, group	1, 2, 3
Sexual Disorders					
Bach, Wincze, & Barlow (2001)[b]	"Sexual Dysfunction"	CBT/systems	Desire disorders, arousal disorders, orgasmic disorders, pain disorders	Couple, individual	1, 2, 3, 4
Jehu (1979)	*Sexual Dysfunction: A Behavioral Approach to Causation, Assessment, and Treatment*	Behavioral	Sexual dysfunction	Individual, couple	1, 2, 3
McConaghy (1996)[a]	"Treatment of Sexual Dysfunctions"	CBT	Sexual dysfunction	Individual, couple	1, 2, 3
Sleep Disorders					
Van Brunt, Riedel, & Lichstein (1996)[a]	"Insomnia"	Behavioral, pharmacotherapy	Sleep disturbance	Individual	1, 2, 3
Somatic Disorders					
Martin (1993)	*Psychological Management of Chronic Headaches*	CBT	Headaches	Individual	1, 2, 3, 4
Warwick & Salkovskis (2001)	*Cognitive-Behavioral Treatment of Hypochondriasis*	CBT	Hypochondriasis	Individual	1, 2, 3, 4
Substance Abuse Disorders					
Budney & Higgens (1998)	*A Community Reinforcement Approach: Treating Cocaine Addiction*	Behavioral, relational	Cocaine dependence	Individual	1, 2, 3, 4
Carroll (1998)	*A Cognitive-Behavioral Approach: Treating Cocaine Addiction*	CBT	Cocaine	Individual	1, 2, 3, 4
Daley, Mercer, & Carpenter (1997)	*Drug Counseling for Cocaine Addiction: The Collaborative Cocaine Treatment Study Model*	Behavioral	Inpatient/outpatient cocaine addict	Group	1, 2, 3, 4
Handmaker & Walters (2002)[e]	"Motivational Interviewing for Initiating Change in Problem Drinking and Drug Use"	Client-centered	Inpatient/outpatient	Individual	1, 2, 3
Higgins, Budney, & Sigmon (2001)[b]	"Cocaine Dependence"	Community	Cocaine addict	Individual	1, 2, 3
Luborsky, Woody, Hole, & Velleco (1995)[d]	"Supportive-Expressive Dynamic Psychotherapy for Treatment of Opiate Drug Dependence"	Dynamic	Opiate dependence	Individual	1, 2, 3, 4

TABLE 1. *(continued)*

Author/Year	Title	Theoretical Orientation	Patient Population	Therapy Modality	Strengths
McCrady (2001)[b]	"Alcohol Disorders"	Relapse prevention	Alcoholics and spouses	Individual, couple	1, 2, 3, 4
Mercer & Woody (1998)	*An Individual Drug Counseling Approach to Treat Cocaine Addiction: The Collaborative Cocaine Treatment Study Model*	Behavioral	Outpatient cocaine addict	Individual	1, 2, 3, 4
Meyers, Dominguez, & Smith (1996)[a]	"Community Reinforcement Training with Concerned Others"	Behavioral	Families of alcoholics	Individual/ family	1, 2, 3, 4
Paolantonio (1990)	*Relapse Prevention Training Manual*	CBT	Drug and alcohol relapse	Group	1, 2, 4
Stasiewicz & Bradizza (2002)[c]	"Alcohol Abuse"	Behavioral	Alcohol disorders	Individual	3, 4
Wakefield, Williams, Yost, & Patterson (1996)	*Alcohol Disorders*	CBT	Alcoholics and spouses	Couple	1, 2, 3, 4

[a]Contained in *Sourcebook of Psychological Treatment Manuals for Adult Disorders.*
[b]Contained in *Clinical Handbook of Psychological Disorders: A Step-by-Step Treatment Manual.*
[c]Contained in *Clinical Behavior Therapy: Adults and Children.*
[d]Contained in *Dynamic Therapies for Psychiatric Disorders (Axis I).*
[e]Contained in *Treating Chronic and Severe Mental Disorders: A Handbook of Empirically Supported Interventions.*
[f]Contained in *Handbook of Parent Training: Parents as Co-Therapists for Children's Behavior Problems.*
[g]Contained in *Psychosocial Treatments for Child and Adolescent Disorders: Empirically Based Strategies for Clinical Practice.*

into patient problem or diagnostic category and listed in alphabetical order by author. The theoretical orientation, patient population, and therapy modality are given for each manual.

We rated the contents of each manual in the "Strengths" column according to six criteria:

1. A presentation of the main principles behind the techniques of the form of psychotherapy
2. Concrete examples of each technical principle/treatment intervention
3. Description of etiology and/or assessment approaches
4. Specifically delineated description of treatment program (e.g., session-by-session, step-by-step, phases)
5. Scales to guide independent judges in evaluating samples of sessions to determine the degree of conformity to the manual
6. Gives attention to cultural concerns that otherwise might interfere with treatment.

Three of these criteria were adapted from the work of Luborsky and Barber (1993), who stated that a true manual must present the main principles behind techniques, provide concrete examples of each technique, and include means of evaluating therapist adherence. Two other criteria are a specific description of the treatment program and a description of etiology or assessment approaches. We also evaluated the manuals on the basis of cultural sensitivity/appropriateness for various populations. In general, there is a paucity of manuals that provide information on session-by-session therapist activities. The Barlow (2001) text provides the best model for presenting and formatting manuals and is therefore recommended for emulation.

The interested clinician can obtain manuals by visiting the publishers' Internet sites, several of which include: John Wiley & Sons, www.wiley.com; Guilford Press, www.guilford.com; Basic Books, www.basicbooks.com; American Psychological Association, www.apa.org/books/; and Oxford University Press, www.oup.com. Unpublished manuals will need to be requested from the manual's author. New manuals appear at a rapid rate, and it is likely that this list fails to include a number of important manual-based treatments. We invite interested readers to inform us of published manuals that have come to their attention.

References & Readings 

Addis, M. E. (1997). Evaluating the treatment manuals as a means of disseminating empirically validated psychotherapies. *Clinical Psychology: Science and Practice, 4*, 1–11.

Barber, J. P., & Crits-Christoph, P. (Eds.). (2000). *Dynamic therapies for psychiatric disorders (Axis I)*. New York: Basic Books.

Barkley, R. A., (1998). *Attention-deficit hyperactivity disorder: A handbook for diagnosis and treatment.* New York: Guilford Press.

Barlow, D. H. (Ed.). (2001). *Clinical handbook of psychological disorders: A step-by-step treatment manual* (3rd ed.). New York: Guilford Press.

Barlow, D. H., & Cerny, J. A. (1988). *Psychological treatment of panic.* New York: Guilford Press.

Beck, A. T., Emery, G., & Greenberg, R. L. (2000). *Anxiety disorders and phobias: A cognitive perspective.* New York: Guilford Press.

Beck, A. T., & Freeman, A. (1990). *Cognitive therapy of personality disorders.* New York: Guilford Press.

Beck, A. T., Rush, A. J., Shaw, B. E., & Emery, G. (1979). *Cognitive therapy of depression.* New York: Guilford Press.

Becker, R. E., Heimberg, R. G., & Bellack, A. S. (1987). *Social skills training treatment for depression.* New York: Pergamon.

Benjamin, L. S. (2002). *Interpersonal diagnosis and treatment of personality disorders.* New York: Guilford Press.

Breismeister, J. M., & Schaefer, C. E. (Eds.). (1998). *Handbook of parent training: Parents as cotherapists for children's behavior problems* (2nd ed.). New York: Wiley.

Bricklin, B. (1995). *The custody evaluation handbook: Research-based solutions and applications.* New York: Brunner/Mazel.

Budney, A. J., & Higgens, S. T. (1998). *A community reinforcement approach: Treating cocaine addiction.* Washington, DC: National Institute on Drug Abuse (NIDA).

Camino, L. (2000). *Treating sexually abused boys: A practical guide for therapists & counselors.* San Francisco: Jossey-Bass.

Carroll, K. M. (1998). *A cognitive-behavioral approach: Treating cocaine addiction.* Washington, DC: National Institute on Drug Abuse.

Chambless, D. L., & Ollendick, T. H. (2001). Empirically supported psychological interventions: Controversies and evidence. *Annual Review Psychology, 52*, 685–716.

Chethik, M. (2000). *Techniques for child therapy: Psychodynamic strategies.* New York: Guilford Press.

Ciarrocchi, J. W. (2002). *Counseling for the problem gambler: A self-regulation manual for individual and family therapy.* San Diego: Academic Press.

Clark, D. M., & Salkovskis, P. M. (1996). *Treatment manual of focused cognitive therapy.* Unpublished manuscript, Oxford University, UK.

Crits-Christoph, P., Baranackie, K., Kurcias, J. S., Beck, A. T., Carroll, K, Perry, K., et al. (1991). Meta-analysis of therapist effects in psychotherapy outcome studies. *Psychotherapy Research, 1*, 81–91.

Daldrup, R. J., Beutler, L. E., Engle, D., & Greenberg, L. S. (1998). *Focused expressive psychotherapy: Freeing the overcontrolled patient.* New York: Guilford Press.

Daley, D. C., Mercer, D. E., & Carpenter, G. (1998). *Drug counseling for cocaine addition: The collaborative cocaine treatment study model.* Washington, DC: National Institute on Drug Abuse.

De Dominico, G. S. (2000). *Sand tray world play: A comprehensive guide to the use of the sand tray in psychotherapeutic and transformational settings.* Oakland, CA: Vision Quest Images.

Dick, L. P., Gallagher-Thompson, D., & Thompson, L. W. (1996). Cognitive-behavioral therapy. In R. T. Woods (Ed.), *Handbook of the clinical psychology of ageing* (pp. 509–544). New York: Wiley.

Ellis, E. M. (2000). *Divorce wars.* Washington, DC: American Psychological Association.

Epstein, N. B., & Baucom, D. H. (2002). *Enhanced cognitive-behavioral therapy for couples: A contextual approach.* Washington, DC: American Psychological Association.

Everett, C. A., & Everett, S. V. (1999). *Family therapy for ADHD: Treating children, adolescents, and adults.* New York: Guilford Press.

Falsetti, S. A., & Resnick, H. S. (2001). Posttraumatic stress disorder. In W. J. Lyddon & J. V. Jones, Jr. (Eds.), *Empirically supported cognitive therapies: Current and future applications* (pp. 182–199). New York: Springer.

Fouse, B., & Wheeler, M. (1997). *A treasure chest of behavioral strategies for individuals with autism.* Arlington, TX: Future Horizons.

Freeman, A., & Reinecke, M. A. (1993). *Cognitive therapy of suicidal behavior a manual for treatment.* New York: Springer.

Goldfried, M. R. (1993). Commentary on how the field of psychopathology can facilitate psychotherapy integration. *Journal of Psychotherapy Integrations, 3,* 353–360.

Greenberg, L. S., & Johnson, S. M. (1998). *Emotionally focused therapy for couples.* New York: Guilford Press.

Gumaer, J. (1984). *Counseling and therapy for children.* New York: Free Press.

Harris, M. (1998). *Trauma recovery and empowerment: A clinician's guide for working with women in groups.* New York: Free Press.

Hayes, S. C., Strosahl, K. D., & Wilson, K. G. (1999). *Acceptance and commitment therapy: An experiential approach to behavior change.* New York: Guilford Press.

Hersen, M. (Ed.). (2002). *Clinical behavior therapy: Adults and children.* New York: Wiley.

Herz, M., & Marder, S. (2002). *Schizophrenia: Comprehensive treatment and management.* New York: Lippincott, Williams & Wilkins.

Hibbs, E. D., & Jensen, P. S. (Eds.). (1996). *Psychosocial treatments for child and adolescent disorders: Empirically based strategies for clinical practice.* Washington, DC: American Psychological Association.

Hofmann, S. G., & Tompson, M. C. (Eds.). (2002). *Treating chronic and severe mental disorders: A handbook of empirically supported interventions.* New York: Guilford Press.

Hogarty, G. E. (2002). *Personal therapy for schizophrenia and related disorders: A guide to individualized treatment.* New York: Guilford Press.

Jacobson, N. S., & Gurman, A. S. (Eds.). (1995). *Clinical handbook of couple therapy.* New York: Guilford Press.

Jehu, D. (1979). *Sexual dysfunction: A behavioural approach to causation, assessment, and treatment.* New York: Wiley.

Klerman, G. L., Weissman, M. M., Rounasaville, B. J., & Chevron, E. S. (1984). *Interpersonal psychotherapy of depression.* New York: Basic Books.

Lambert, M. J. (2004). *Bergin & Garfield's Handbook of psychotherapy and behavior change* (5th ed.). New York: Wiley.

Lambert, M. J., & Ogles, B. M. (1988). Treatment manuals: Problems and promise. *Journal of Integrative and Eclectic Psychotherapy, 7,* 187–205.

Landreth, G. L. (1991). *Play therapy: The art of the relationship.* Muncie, IN: Accelerated Development.

Lewinsohn, P. M., Antonuccio, D. O., Steinmetz, J. L., & Teri, L. (1984). *The coping with depression course: A psychoeducational intervention for unipolar depression.* Eugene, OR: Castalia.

Luborsky, L., & Barber, J. P. (1993). Benefits of adherence to psychotherapy manuals and where to get them. In N. E. Miller, L. Luborsky, J. P. Barber, & J. P. Docherty (Eds.), *Psychodynamic treatment research* (pp. 211–226). New York: Basic Books.

Martin, P. R. (1993). *Psychological management of chronic headaches.* New York: Guilford Press.

McFarlane, W. R. (2002). *Multifamily groups in the treatment of severe psychiatric disorders.* New York: Guilford Press.

Mercer, D. E., & Woody, G. E. (1998). *An individual drug counseling approach to treat cocaine addiction: The collaborative cocaine treatment study model.* Washington, DC: National Institute on Drug Abuse.

Moras, K. (1993). The use of treatment manuals to train psychotherapists: Observations and recommendations. *Psychotherapy, 30,* 581–586.

Norcross, J. C. (Ed.). (2002). *Psychotherapy relationships that work.* New York: Oxford University Press.

O'Connor, K. J. (2000). *The play therapy primer.* New York: Wiley.

Padesky, C. A., & Greenberger, D. (1995). *The clinician's guide to mind over mood.* New York: Guilford Press.

Paolantonio, P. (1990). *Relapse prevention training manual.* Unpublished manuscript, spectrum, Inc., Westboro, MA.

Piper, W. E., Rosie, J. S., Joyce, A. S., & Azim, H. F. A. (1996). *Time-limited day treatment for personality disorders: Integration of research and practice in a group program.* Washington, DC: American Psychological Association.

Sells, S. P. (1998). *Treating the tough adolescent: A family-based, step-by-step guide.* New York: Guilford Press.

Smucker, M. R., & Dancu, C. V. (1999). *Cognitive-behavioral treatment for adult survivors of childhood trauma: Imagery rescripting and reprocessing.* Northvale, NJ: Jason Aronson.

Sperry, L. (1999). *Cognitive behavior therapy of DSM-IV personality disorders: Highly effective interventions for the most common personality disorders.* Ann Arbor, MI: Edwards Brothers.

Stamps, R. F., & Barach, P. M. (2001). *The therapist's internet handbook: More than 1300 web sites and resources for mental health professionals.* New York: Norton.

Strupp, H. H. (1992). The future of psychodynamic psychotherapy. *Psychotherapy, 29*, 21–27.

Strupp, H. H., & Anderson, T. (1997). On the limitations of therapy manuals. *Clinical Psychology: Science and Practice, 4*, 76–82.

Strupp, H. H., & Binder, J. L. (1984). *Psychotherapy in a new key: A guide to time-limited dynamic psychotherapy.* New York: Basic Books.

Turner, S. M., & Beidel, D. C (1988). *Treating obsessive-compulsive disorder.* New York: Pergamon.

Van Hasselt, V. B, & Hersen, M. (1996). *Sourcebook of psychological treatment manuals for adult disorders.* New York: Plenum.

Wakefield, P. J., Williams, R. E., Yost, E. B., & Patterson, K. M. (1996). *Couple therapy for alcoholism: A cognitive-behavioral treatment manual.* New York: Guilford Press.

Ward, T., Hudson, S. M., & Keenan, T. R. (2001). The assessment and treatment of sexual offenders against children. In C. R. Hollin (Ed.), *Handbook of offender assessment and treatment* (pp. 349–361). New York: Wiley.

Warwick, H. M. C., & Salkovskis, P. M. (2001). Cognitive-behavioral treatment of hypochondriasis. In V. Starcevic & D. R. Lipsitt (Eds.), *Hypochondriasis: Modern perspectives on an ancient malady* (pp. 314–328). Oxford: Oxford University Press.

White, J. (2000). *Treating anxiety and stress: A group psycho-educational approach using brief CBT.* New York: Wiley

Wright, M. E., & Wright, B. A. (1987). *Clinical practice of hypnotherapy.* New York: Guilford Press.

Yost, E. B, Beutler, L. E., Corbishley, M. A., & Allender, J. R. (1986). *Group cognitive therapy: A treatment approach for depressed older adults.* Elmsford, NY: Pergamon.

Young, M. E., & Long, L. L. (1998). *Counseling and therapy for couples.* Pacific Grove, CA: Brooks/Cole.

Related Topics

Chapter 39, "Compendium of Empirically Supported Therapies"

Chapter 41, "Compendium of Empirically Supported Therapy Relationships"

41 COMPENDIUM OF EMPIRICALLY SUPPORTED THERAPY RELATIONSHIPS

John C. Norcross & Clara E. Hill

Recent years have witnessed the controversial promulgation of practice guidelines and evidence-based treatments in mental health. Foremost among these initiatives in psychology was the APA Society of Clinical Psychology's Task Force efforts to identify empirically supported treatments (ESTs) for adults and to publicize these treatments to fellow psychologists and training programs. A succession of APA Division 12 Task Forces (now a standing committee) constructed and elaborated a list of empirically supported, manualized psychological interventions for specific disorders based on randomized controlled studies (Chambless, chap. 39, this volume; Chambless & Hollon, 1998; Task Force on Promotion and Dissemination of Psychological Procedures, 1995). Subsequently, ESTs were applied to both older adults and children (e.g., Gatz et al., 1998; Lonigan, Elbert, & Johnson, 1998).

In Great Britain, a Guidelines Development Committee of the British Psychological Society authored a Department of Health (2001) document titled *Treatment Choice in Psychological Therapies and Counselling: Evidence-Based Practice Guidelines*. In psychiatry, the American Psychiatric Association has published at least 10 practice guidelines on disorders ranging from schizophrenia to anorexia to nicotine dependence.

These and other efforts to promulgate evidence-based psychotherapies have been noble in intent and timely in distribution. At the same time, they neglect the therapy relationship, an interpersonal quality that makes substantial and consistent contributions to the psychotherapy outcome independent of the specific type of treatment. The therapy relationship accounts for as much of the treatment outcome as does the specific treatment method (Lambert, 2003; Wampold, 2001). Efforts to promulgate practice guidelines or evidence-based lists of effective psychotherapy without including the therapy relationship are thus seriously incomplete and potentially misleading.

Within this context, an APA Division of Psychotherapy Task Force was established to identify, operationalize, and disseminate information on empirically supported therapy relationships. We aimed to identify empirically supported (therapy) relationships rather than empirically supported treatments–or ESRs rather than ESTs. Specifically, the dual aims of the Division 29 Task Force were (1) to identify elements of effective therapy relationships, and (2) to identify effective methods of tailoring therapy to the individual patient on the basis of his/her (nondiagnostic) characteristics.

The Task Force generated a list of empirically supported relationship elements and a list of means for customizing therapy to the individual client. For each list, we judged whether the element was *demonstrably effective*, *promising and probably effective*, or *insufficient research to judge*. The evidentiary criteria for making these judgments were the number of supportive studies, the consistency of the research results, the magnitude of the positive relationship between the element and outcome, the directness of the link between the element and outcome, the experimental rigor of the studies, and the external validity of the research base.

The research reviews and clinical practices were compiled in *Psychotherapy Relationships That Work* (Norcross, 2002) and summarized in a special issue of *Psychotherapy* (Norcross, 2001). The following synopses are drawn from those documents.

GENERAL ELEMENTS OF THE THERAPY RELATIONSHIP

As noted, the first aim of the Task Force was to identify those relationship elements or behaviors, primarily provided by the psychotherapist, that are effective in general. For each of these relationship elements we provide a brief definition, a summary of the research linking the element to therapy effectiveness, and a few clinical implications.

Demonstrably Effective

- *Therapeutic alliance*. The "alliance" refers to the quality and strength of the collaborative relationship between client and therapist, typically measured as agreement on the therapeutic goals, consensus on treatment tasks, and a relationship bond. Across 89 studies, the effect size (ES) of the relation between the therapeutic alliance and therapy outcome was .21, a modest but very robust association. The alliance is harder to establish with clients who are more disturbed, delinquent, homeless, drug abusing, fearful, anxious, dismissive, and preoccupied. On the therapist side, a stronger alliance is fostered by communication skills, empathy, openness, and a paucity of hostile interactions.
- *Cohesion in group therapy*. "Cohesion" refers to the forces that cause members to remain in the group, a sticking-togetherness. Approximately 80% of the studies support positive relationships between cohesion (mostly mem-

ber-to-member) and therapy outcome. Methods to increase cohesion include pre-group preparation, addressing early discomfort using structure, encouraging member-to-member interaction, and actively modeling and setting norms (but not being overly directive). In addition, both feedback and establishing a good emotional climate contribute to cohesion.

- *Empathy*. Carl Rogers's definition, which has guided most of the research, is that empathy is the therapist's sensitive ability and willingness to understand the client's thoughts, feelings, and struggles from the client's point of view—in other words, entering the private, perceptual world of the other. A meta-analysis of 47 studies (encompassing 190 tests of the empathy-outcome association) revealed an ES of .32. Furthermore, a causal link between empathy and outcome has been demonstrated, with suggestions that empathy is linked to outcome because it serves a positive relationship function, is a corrective emotional experience, promotes exploration and meaning creation, and supports clients' active self-healing efforts.
- *Goal consensus and collaboration*. The former term refers to therapist-patient agreement on treatment goals and expectation; the latter is the mutual involvement of the participants in the helping relationship. 68% of the studies found a positive association between goal consensus and outcome, and 88% of the studies reported the same for collaboration and outcome. It is not concretely clear from the research how to build goal consensus or collaboration, but clinical experience suggests that clinicians should begin to develop consensus at intake, verbally attend to patient problems, address topics of importance to patients, resonate to patient attributions of blame regarding their problems, and frequently discuss or reevaluate goals.

Promising and Probably Effective

- *Positive regard*. This therapist quality is characterized as warm acceptance of the client's experience without conditions, a prizing, an affirmation, a deep nonpossessive caring. The early research reviews were very supportive of the association between positive regard and therapy outcome, with 80% of the studies in the positive direction. More recent and rigorous reviews report 49% to 56% of the findings in the positive direction, with no negative associations between positive regard and outcome. When treatment outcome and therapist positive regard were both rated by clients, the percentage of positive findings jumped to 88%. Clinically, results indicate that therapists cannot be content with feeling good about their patients, but instead should ensure that their positive feelings are communicated to them.
- *Congruence/genuineness*. The two facets here are the therapist's personal integration in the relationship (freely and deeply him/herself) and the therapist's capacity to communicate his or her personhood to the client as appropriate. Across 20 studies (and 77 separate results), 34% found a positive relation between therapist congruence and treatment outcome, and 66% found nonsignificant associations. The percentage of positive studies increased to 68% when congruence was tested in concert with empathy and positive regard, supporting the notion that the facilitative conditions work together and cannot be easily separated. Therapist congruence can be improved with self-confidence, good mood, increased involvement or activity, responsiveness, smoothness of speaking exchanges, and high levels of client self-exploration/experiencing.
- *Feedback*. "Feedback" is defined as descriptive and evaluative information provided to clients from therapists about the client's behavior or the effects of that behavior. Across 11 studies empirically investigating the feedback-outcome connection, 73% were positive and 27% were nonsignificant. To enhance the effects of feedback, therapists can increase their credibility (which makes acceptance of feedback more positive), give positive feedback (especially early to establish the relationship), and precede or sandwich negative feedback with positive comments.
- *Repair of alliance ruptures*. A rupture in the therapeutic alliance is a tension or breakdown in the collaborative relationship. The

small body of research indicates that the frequency and severity of ruptures are increased by strong adherence to a treatment manual and an excessive number of transference interpretations. By contrast, the research suggests that repairs of ruptures can be facilitated by the therapist responding nondefensively, attending directly to the alliance, and adjusting his or her behavior.

- *Self-disclosure.* Therapist "self-disclosure" is defined as therapist statements that reveal something personal about the therapist. Analogue research suggests that nonclients generally have positive perceptions of therapist self-disclosure. In actual therapy, disclosures were perceived as helpful in terms of immediate outcomes, although the effect on the ultimate outcome of therapy is unclear. The research suggests that therapists should disclose infrequently and, when they disclose, do so to validate reality, normalize experiences, strengthen the alliance, or offer alternative ways to think or act. By contrast, therapists should generally avoid self-disclosures that are for their own needs, remove the focus from the client, or blur the treatment boundaries.
- *Management of countertransference.* Although defined in various ways, "countertransference" refers to reactions in which the unresolved conflicts of the psychotherapist, usually but not always unconscious, are implicated. The limited research supports the interrelated conclusions that therapist acting out countertransference hinders psychotherapy, whereas effectively managing countertransference aids the process and probably the outcome of therapy. In terms of managing countertransference, five central therapist skills have been implicated: self-insight, self-integration, anxiety management, empathy, and conceptualizing ability.
- *Quality of relational interpretations.* In the clinical literature, "interpretations" are interventions that bring material to consciousness that was previously out of awareness; in the research literature, interpretations are behaviorally coded as making connections, going beyond what the client has overtly recognized, and pointing out themes or patterns in the patient's behavior. The research correlating frequency of interpretations and outcome has yielded mixed findings; however, it appears that high rates of transference interpretations lead to poorer outcomes, especially for clients with low quality-of-object relations. By contrast, other research has highlighted the importance of the quality of interpretations: better outcomes are achieved when the therapist addresses central aspects of client interpersonal dynamics. The clinical implications are to avoid high levels of transference interpretations, particularly for interpersonally challenged clients, and to focus interpretations on the central interpersonal themes for each patient.

CUSTOMIZING THE THERAPY RELATIONSHIP TO INDIVIDUAL PATIENTS

Emerging research indicates that adapting the therapy relationship to specific patient needs and characteristics (in addition to diagnosis) enhances the effectiveness of treatment. Accordingly, the second aim of the Task Force was to identify those patient behaviors or qualities that served as reliable markers for customizing the therapy relationship.

Demonstrably Effective as a Means of Customizing Therapy

- *Resistance.* "Resistance" refers to being easily provoked by external demands. Research confirms that high patient resistance is consistently associated with poorer therapy outcomes (in 82% of studies). But matching therapist directiveness to client level of resistance improves therapy efficiency and outcome (80% of studies). Specifically, clients presenting with high resistance benefited more from self-control methods, minimal therapist directiveness, and paradoxical interventions. By contrast, clients with low resistance benefited more from therapist directiveness and explicit guidance. The clinical implication is to match the therapist's level of directiveness to the patient's level of resistance.

- *Functional impairment.* This complex dimension reflects the severity of the patient's subjective distress, as well as areas of reduced behavioral functioning. Most of the available studies (76%) found a significant inverse relation between level of impairment and treatment outcome. These results indicate that patients who manifest impairment in two or more areas of functioning (family, social, intimate, occupational) are more likely to benefit from treatment that is lengthier, that is more intense, and that includes psychoactive medication. Furthermore, patients who have little support from other people will more likely benefit from a lengthier psychotherapy that explicitly targets the creation of social support in the natural environment.

Promising and Probably Effective as a Means of Customizing Therapy

- *Coping style.* Although defined differently across theoretical orientations, "coping style" broadly refers to habitual and enduring patterns of behavior that characterize the individual when confronting new or problematic situations. In the research, attention has been devoted primarily to the externalizing (impulsive, action or task-oriented, stimulation seeking, extroverted) and internalizing coping styles (self-critical, reticent, inhibited, introverted). 79% of the studies investigating this dimension demonstrated differential effects of the type of treatment as a function of patient coping style. Hence, interpersonal and insight-oriented therapies are more effective among internalizing patients, whereas symptom-focused and skill-building therapies are more effective among externalizing patients.
- *Stages of change.* People progress through a series of stages—precontemplation, contemplation, preparation, action, and maintenance—in both psychotherapy and self-change. A meta-analysis of 47 studies found ESs of .70 and .80 for the use of different change processes in the stages; specifically, cognitive-affective processes are used most frequently by clients in the precontemplation and contemplation stages, and behavioral processes are used most frequently by those in the action and maintenance stages. The therapist's optimal stance also varies depending on the patient's stage of change: a nurturing parent with patients in the precontemplation stage; a Socratic teacher with patients in the contemplation stage; an experienced coach with patients in the action stage; and a consultant during the maintenance stage. The clinical implications are to assess the patient's stage of change, match the therapeutic relationship and the treatment method to that stage, and systematically adjust tactics as the patient moves through the stages.
- *Anaclitic/sociotropic and introjective/autonomous styles.* In the psychoanalytic tradition, there are two broad personality configurations: a relatedness or anaclitic style that involves the capacity for satisfying interpersonal relationships, and a self-definitional or introjective style that involves the development of an integrated identity. Similar distinctions are made in cognitive therapy between sociotropic and autonomous styles. A small but growing body of research indicates that these two personality styles are differentially related to psychotherapy outcome. Specifically, anaclitic/sociotropic patients benefit more from therapies that offer more personal interaction and closer relatedness, whereas introjective/autonomous patients tend to do better in therapies emphasizing separation and autonomy. The identification of the patient's personality organization may enable therapists to adapt the degree of interpersonal closeness to the individual patient.
- *Expectations.* "Expectancy" refers to client expectations of therapeutic gain as well as of psychotherapy procedures, the therapist's role, and the length of treatment. Of 24 studies on clients' outcome expectations, 12 found a positive relation between expectations and outcome, 7 found mixed results, and 7 found no relationship. Of 37 studies on clients' role expectation, 21 found positive relationships with outcome, 12 found mixed support, and 8 found no association with outcome. The re-

search literature encourages therapists to explicitly assess and discuss client expectations, address overt skepticism, arouse positive expectations, and activate the client's belief that he or she is being helped.
- *Assimilation of problematic experiences.* The assimilation model suggests that, in successful psychotherapy, clients follow a regular developmental sequence of working through problematic experiences. The sequence is summarized in eight stages, from the patient being warded off/dissociated from the problem at the one end, to integration/mastery of the problem at the other end. A series of intensive case studies and two hypothesis-testing studies indicated that clients in the mid- to late stages of assimilation prosper more from directive, cognitive-behavioral therapy. Furthermore, the research suggests that as the client changes, the therapist should change responsively, reflecting the evolving feelings, goals, and behaviors that represent therapeutic progress.

Insufficient Research

The state of the current research was insufficient for the Task Force to make a clear judgment on whether customizing the therapy relationship to the following patient characteristics improves treatment outcomes:

- Attachment style
- Gender
- Ethnicity
- Religion and spirituality
- Preferences
- Personality disorders

PRACTICE RECOMMENDATIONS

The Task Force reports (Norcross, 2001, 2002) close with a series of recommendations, divided into general, practice, training, research, and policy recommendations. The general recommendations encourage readers to interpret the findings in the context of the limitations of the Task Force's work (as explicated in the reports) and remind readers that the current conclusions represent initial steps in aggregating and codifying available research. Here, we conclude with the practice recommendations.

1. Practitioners are encouraged to make the creation and cultivation of a therapy relationship characterized by the elements found to be demonstrably and probably effective in this report a primary aim in the treatment of patients.
2. Practitioners are encouraged to adapt the therapy relationship to specific patient characteristics in the ways shown in the report to enhance therapeutic outcome.
3. Practitioners are encouraged to routinely monitor patients' responses to the therapy relationship and ongoing treatment. Such monitoring leads to increased opportunities to repair alliance ruptures, to improve the relationship, to modify technical strategies, and to avoid premature termination. Concurrent use of empirically supported relationships *and* empirically supported treatments tailored to the patient's disorder and characteristics is likely to generate the best outcomes.

References, Readings, & Internet Sites 

APA Division of Psychotherapy. (n.d.). Home page (includes a link to the Task Force on Empirically Supported Psychotherapy Relationships). Retrieved 2004 from http://www.cwru.edu/affil/div29/div29.htm

Chambless, D. L., & Hollon, S. D. (1998). Defining empirically supported therapies. *Journal of Consulting and Clinical Psychology, 64,* 497–504.

Department of Health. (2001). *Treatment choice in psychological therapies and counselling.* London: Department of Health Publications.

Gatz, M., Fiske, A., Fox, L. S., Kaskie, B., Kaasl-Godley, J. E., McCallum, T. J., et al. (1998). Empirically validated psychological treatments for older adults. *Journal of Mental Health and Aging, 4,* 9–46.

Gelso, C. J., & Hayes, J. A. (1998). *The psychotherapy research: Theory, research, and practice.* New York: Wiley.

Hill, C. E., & O'Brien, K. M. (1999). *Helping skills: Facilitating exploration, insight, and action.* Washington, DC: American Psychological Association.

Lambert, M. (1993). The effectiveness of psychotherapy. In M. J. Lambert (Ed.), *Handbook of psychotherapy and behavior change* (5th ed., pp. 27–46). New York: Wiley.

Lonigan, C. J., Elbert, J. C., & Johnson, S. B. (1998). Empirically supported psychosocial interventions for children: An overview. *Journal of Clinical Child Psychology, 27,* 138–142.

Nathan, P. E., & Gorman, J. M. (Eds.). (2002). *A guide to treatments that work* (2nd ed.). New York: Oxford University Press.

Norcross, J. C. (Ed.). (2001). Empirically supported therapy relationships: Summary Report of the Division 29 Task Force. *Psychotherapy, 38*(4).

Norcross, J. C. (Ed.). (2002). *Psychotherapy relationships that work: Therapist contributions and responsiveness to patient needs.* New York: Oxford University Press.

Orlinsky, D. E., Grawe, K., & Parks, B. K. (1994). Process to outcome in psychotherapy—noch einmal. In A. E. Bergin & S. L. Garfield (Eds.), *Handbook of psychotherapy and behavior change* (4th ed., pp. 245–267). New York: Wiley.

Stiles, W. B., Honos-Webb, L., & Surko, M. (1998). Responsiveness in psychotherapy. *Clinical Psychology: Science and Practice, 5,* 439–458.

Task Force on Promotion and Dissemination of Psychological Procedures. (1995). Training in and dissemination of empirically validated psychological treatments: Report and recommendations. *The Clinical Psychologist, 48*(1), 3–23.

Wampold, B. E. (2001). *The great psychotherapy debate: Models, methods, and findings.* Mahwah, NJ: Erlbaum.

Related Topics

Chapter 39, "Compendium of Empirically Supported Therapies"

Chapter 40, "Compendium of Psychotherapy Treatment Manuals"

42 ENHANCING ADHERENCE

M. Robin DiMatteo

Adherence (also called *compliance*) refers to the success of a patient in implementing the recommendations of a health care professional for the prevention or management of health conditions. More simply, adherence refers to "cooperation with therapy." Health professionals are often frustrated by noncompliance, such as when clients fail to take their medication as prescribed, or test their blood glucose levels sporadically, or make misguided health care choices based on the recommendations of friends or television commercials instead of the advice of their providers. Consumers may forget or misunderstand the regimen, fail to put in the necessary effort, or ignore it altogether because they do not believe it is worth the trouble. Or, they may be quite committed to trying the regimen, but find it too difficult and beyond their resources.

Research on adherence began in 1948 with a study by psychologist Mary Crumpton Hardy, who followed Chicago-area children whose parents were given recommendations for their health care. This work was published in the *Journal of the American Medical Association,* and since then there have been nearly 12,000 citations on adherence and compliance in the medical and psychological literatures. About 1,000 of these are empirical studies, which constitute a sizable research literature. Adherence to treatment has been studied primarily in medical treatment (e.g., following regimens for the care of diabetes, cancer), psychiatric care (e.g., taking medication for schizophrenia), and psychological care (e.g., cognitive behavior therapy for anxiety). There are important commonalities in these literatures—factors that are important regardless of the treatment regimen—and the clinical implications of these findings are delineated below.

This literature demonstrates quite clearly that adherence to treatment significantly improves treatment outcomes. Failure to follow the treatments recommended by health professionals can result in reductions in patients' quality of life, confusion in the clinical picture, misleading information for subsequent care decisions, professional and patient frustration, and erosion of the therapeutic relationship.

PRACTICE GUIDELINES

1. *Assess adherence.* The first step in enhancing adherence involves assessing it correctly, an endeavor that can be surprisingly challenging. For example, determining whether a patient has been using cognitive therapy techniques or has taken the antidepressant medication prescribed requires trust and open communication about the challenges of behavior change. Clients may be reluctant to admit that they have failed to do what was recommended.

2. *Adopt an open and collaborative relationship.* A therapeutic relationship that fosters adherence is built with a patient through active listening, nonjudgment, and empathy. These are typically conveyed through supportive verbal messages and nonverbal cues of facial expressions, body orientation and attention, and vocal tone. A therapeutic relationship that allows both honest discussion about adherence difficulties and a commitment to working together to overcome them has the greatest chance of success. Although patients are usually not eager to tell their health professionals they have not followed a treatment directive, in the context of a supportive and trusting relationship, and in response to straightforward questions, patients will usually admit adherence difficulties. Researchers and clinicians often use other means as well—counting remaining pills, weighing the contents of canisters such as inhalers, and asking family members—but direct communication with patients about their adherence challenges remains the best way to determine what patients are doing.

3. *Do not equate adherence with outcome.* It is critically important not to confuse health outcomes with adherence. If the clinical picture is confusing and the patient is not having a predicted response, it is certainly possible that nonadherence is the reason, but it is also possible that the treatment is not working. It must be remembered that adherence is a behavior to be assessed. The success of the treatment depends on correct diagnosis and on the appropriateness and efficacy of the treatment regimen.

4. *Understand the prevalence.* The prevalence of nonadherence depends on the patient's disorder and on the complexity of the treatment regimen. Across hundreds of studies, adherence rates on average range from 20% to 40%, with the highest level of adherence occurring when the disease is considered very serious and adherence is essential to survival (e.g., HIV disease, cancer), and when the intervention has immediate and obvious effects (e.g., reduction in pain/distress in arthritis and gastrointestinal disorders). Adherence tends to be considerably lower for the treatment of such conditions as diabetes, where care can be complex and limiting and patients do not necessarily feel better when they adhere. In pharmacotherapy for psychiatric disorders, adherence to medication tends to be lower in the context of difficult side effects or the absence of obvious benefits, and higher when medications make people feel better.

5. *Address patients' views of effectiveness.* It is not the case that objectively more effective treatments yield better patient adherence; it is the patient's subjective assessment of the effectiveness of treatment that influences his or her adherence. Sometimes the more effective treatments are more difficult, and health professionals may be remiss in communicating the expected treatment efficacy to patients. Nonadherence may not make sense to the health professional, but it often makes sense to the health care consumer. Sometimes noncompliance is viewed by the patient as a perfectly rational choice because he or she remains unconvinced that the regimen is worthy of the time and trouble it demands. Patients will usually follow only treatments they believe in.

6. *Understand the practical reasons for nonadherence.* Health care delivery may be a small part of a patient's real life. What makes sense to "commit to" in the office may be quite difficult to implement at home, where competing demands of work and family jeopardize adherence.

- Resources may be limited and patients usually allocate them as best they can. The regimen that is tailored as much as possible to fit into the patient's life has the best chance of being followed.
- Sometimes the client has no idea what the health professional is talking about (but nods his or her head in agreement anyway). Patients can do only what they understand. Sometimes, unfortunately, television advertisements and neighbors' opinions make more sense to the client than those of the provider. Providers must convey their expertise and competence in the context of a supportive and trusting relationship; patients are likely to follow recommendations only from providers they trust, and who are viewed as credible.
- Patients will only follow regimens for which they have the necessary resources. There are many practical challenges to patient adherence that need to be addressed and overcome in all health care visits, whether they involve complex self-care routines for serious medical conditions, the control of thoughts and behaviors using psychological modalities, the management of psychiatric conditions with medication, or the achievement of vigor and longevity through healthy lifestyle choices.

7. *Use clear and written communication.* Misunderstanding and forgetting are common in the office visit. As many as 50% of patients cannot accurately report what their health professionals have told them. Therefore, clear communication, checking what patients understand, and reinforcement of the care message are essential. Written instructions can be useful, but only if they have been explained carefully and patient understanding has been ascertained.

8. *Encourage patient involvement.* Encouraging patients to be actively involved in their care, to voice concerns, and to state preferences for their care outcomes enhances their sense of control and meaning in the face of illness, conveys respect, and fosters healing. For example, a client who is encouraged to use meditation for stress must have the opportunity to discuss with the therapist various options for its implementation and to chart a plan for evaluating its effects.

9. *Incorporate cultural beliefs.* Many patients have their own personally or culturally based explanations for their illness, which, if understood by the health professional, can be used to help the patient follow the treatment regimen. Adherence depends upon patients' beliefs in their susceptibility to a serious health threat and their belief that a treatment is effective and offers enough benefits given its costs in time, money, and difficulty.

10. *Build in social support.* Many studies show that there is a profound impact of practical and emotional support on helping patients to adhere. Marital status and living with another are not nearly as important as having available supportive and helpful others. Family cohesiveness strongly supports adherence whereas family conflict can seriously jeopardize it. Determine what practical and emotional support is available to the patient, and screen for any family conflict that can derail the patient's attempts to adhere to the treatment regimen.

11. *Screen for depression.* Depression in patients is strongly linked to nonadherence to medical treatments. The risk of nonadherence is 27% higher in depressed than in nondepressed patients. Screening for depression in medical patients is essential so that something can be done to help activate their inner healing resources. Depressed patients are at increased risk of nonadherence because of the hopelessness, interference in constructive thinking and planning, and withdrawal from social support that can accompany depression. Patients receiving psychological or pharmacological treatment for depression may need particular attention and supportive care to adhere.

12. *Attend to risk factors for nonadherence.* In addition to depression, certain patient factors predispose patients toward nonadherence. Compared with the positive role of family support and the negative effects of mood disorders, demographic factors are not strong predictors of adherence. Some demographic factors do have a moderate effect on adherence, however, and should be noted by clinicians. There is a trend for adolescents to be less adherent than younger pediatric patients, and a trend for lower adherence among individuals in middle age (probably because of competing demands) and advanced older age (probably because of cognitive deficits). The relationship between education and adherence is stronger in the care of chronic illness than acute illness, likely due to the necessity for complex self-care for chronic illness.

In summary, adherence is unlikely to be fostered by trying to convince patients that they have a serious condition, that treatment is good for them, or that the health professional knows best and should be obeyed. Rather, building partnerships with patients, learning and respecting their perspectives on the illness, understanding their expectations for health care outcomes, and relating to them in an empathic and compassionate manner enhance patient adherence. Relationships with patients are a critical component of professional job satisfaction, an important factor in preventing job stress, and a critical predictor of patient adherence to treatment.

References, Readings, & Internet Sites 

Bowen, D. J., Helmes, A., & Lease, E. (2001). Predicting compliance: How are we doing? In L. E. Burke & I. S. Ockene (Eds.), *Compliance in healthcare and research* (pp. 25–41). Armonk, NY: Futura.

Brownell, K. D., & Cohen, L. R. (1995). Adherence to dietary regimens: 1. An overview of research. *Behavioral Medicine, 20,* 149–154.

DiMatteo, M. R. (2000). Practitioner-family-patient communication in pediatric adherence: Implications for research and clinical practice. In D. Drotar (Ed.), *Promoting adherence to medical treatment in childhood chronic illness: Concepts, methods, and interventions* (pp. 237–258). Mahwah, NJ: Erlbaum.

DiMatteo, M. R., Giordani, P. J., Lepper, H. S., & Croghan, T. W. (2002). Patient adherence and medical treatment outcomes: A meta-analysis. *Medical Care, 40,* 794–811.

DiMatteo, M. R., Lepper, H. S., & Croghan, T. W. (2000). Depression is a risk factor for noncompliance with medical treatment: A meta-analysis of the effects of anxiety and depression on patient adherence. *Archives of Internal Medicine, 160,* 2101–2107.

Dunbar-Jacob, J., & Schlenk, E. (2001). Patient adherence to treatment regimen. In A. Baum, T. A. Revenson, & J. E. Singler (Eds.), *Handbook of health psychology* (pp. 571–580). Mahwah, NJ: Erlbaum.

DiMatteo, M. R. (1999). The role of communication and physician-patient collaboration: Enhancing adherence with psychiatric medication. In J. Guimon, W. Fischer, & N. Sartorius (Eds.), *The image of madness* (pp. 222–230). Basel: Karger.

Epstein, L. (1984). The direct effects of compliance on health outcome. *Health Psychology, 3,* 385–393.

Epstein, L. H., & Cluss, P. A. (1982). A behavioral medicine perspective on adherence to long-term medical regimens. *Journal of Consulting and Clinical Psychology, 50,* 950–971.

Hardy, M. C. (1948). Follow-up of medical recommendations. *Journal of the American Medical Association, 136,* 20–27.

International Association of Physicians in AIDS Care. (n.d.). Information on Adherence in HIV/AIDS care. Retrieved 2004 from http://www.thebody.com/iapac/adherence.html

Norman, P., Abraham, C., & Conner, M. (Eds.). (2000). *Understanding and changing health behaviour: From health beliefs to self-regulation* (pp. 126–138). Amsterdam: Harwood.

RAND Organization. (n.d.). Medical outcome studies site. Retrieved 2004 from http://www.rand.org/health.surveys/core

Rosenthal, R., & DiMatteo, M. R. (2001). Meta-analysis: Recent developments in quantitative methods for literature reviews. *Annual Review of Psychology, 52,* 59–82.

Uchino, B, N., Cacioppo, J. T., & Kiecolt-Glaser, J. K. (1996). The relationship between social support and physiological processes: A review with emphasis on underlying mechanisms and implications for health. *Psychological Bulletin, 119,* 488–531.

Ziegelstein, R. C., Fauerbach, J. A., Stevens, S. S., Romanelli, J., Richter, D. P., & Bush, D. E. (2000). Patients with depression are less likely to follow recommendations to reduce cardiac risk during recovery from a myocardial infarction. *Archives of Internal Medicine, 160,* 1818–1823.

Zygmunt, A., Olfson, M., Boyer, C. A., & Mechanic, D. (2002). Interventions to improve medication adherence in schizophrenia. *American Journal of Psychiatry, 159,* 1653–1664.

Related Topics

Chapter 43, "Methods to Reduce and Counter Resistance in Psychotherapy"

Chapter 44, "Repairing Ruptures in the Therapeutic Alliance"

43 METHODS TO REDUCE AND COUNTER RESISTANCE IN PSYCHOTHERAPY

Albert Ellis

Resistant clients, like nonresistant ones, are unique individuals in their own right. But you, too, as a struggling psychotherapist, may have many different ways in which you interpret your clients' resistance. I basically follow rational emotive behavior therapy (REBT), a pioneering form of cognitive behavior therapy (CBT), that I created when I found that many of my clients resisted other forms of treatment that mainly used cognitive *or* emotional *or* behavioral methods. I went out of my way to stress cognitive techniques in REBT, but I also heavily emphasized a number of emotive-evocative and behavioral methods. I still do so—especially with my stubbornly resistant clients. But I use them flexibly and include some general methods that I describe below.

REBT and CBT easily show patients how they are choosing to upset themselves, but giving them this kind of insight has to be accompanied by their working very hard and persistently to get better and stay better (Ellis, 2001a, 2001b; Walen, DiGiuseppe, & Dryden, 1992). Because of their low frustration tolerance and their feelings of inadequacy, patients often do not complete the required therapeutic work; and their therapists, as well, are frequently lax in this respect. Of the many methods of REBT, CBT, and other therapies that you can use to help your resistant clients to uncharacteristically work at resisting their resisting, here are 16 that I have found to be the best.

1. *Investigate the real possibility that your clients' resisting may be mainly your own problem: your carelessness or insecurity.* Do you like a client too much or too little, thereby creating transference problems? Are you cavalierly taking things too easily and failing to see and work at overcoming resistances? Are you too needy of your clients' approval and afraid to be assertive and firm enough with them? Look intently at these and other likely lapses, not to damn yourself if you find them but to try to correct them. Give yourself unconditional self-acceptance

(USA) in spite of your failings while—as I shall show later—giving your clients unconditional other-acceptance (UOA) in spite of their self-defeating resistances and other failings (Ellis, 2002).

2. *If you think that your clients are mainly responsible for their own resistance, look for possible reasons for their sabotaging their therapy.* Do they have low frustration tolerance and think that you should magically change them? Do their feelings of worthlessness make them convinced that they are not able to change? Do their favorable or unfavorable feelings toward you—transference feelings—interfere with their hearing your views objectively and using your teachings to change themselves? Are they angry with their relatives who demand that they change, and are they therefore sabotaging their own efforts to do so? Since your clients are seeing you upset about their performances and their relationships, are they also disturbed about their therapy? Hypothesize and explore (Hanna, 2001). If you find them blocking themselves, tactfully but firmly reveal the blocks and see if you can get clients to unblock themselves.

3. *REBT, along with Acceptance and Commitment Therapy (ACT) and several other therapies, holds that even highly cooperative clients have to be strongly committed to therapy and work hard at change* (Ellis, 2001a, 2001b, 2002; Hayes, Strosahl, & Wilson, 1999). Did you clearly explain the importance of commitment to your clients when they started therapy? Did they agree with this goal? If not, raise this issue with your resistant clients now. Keep raising it! Also: are you really committed to doing the hard work of therapy, too?

4. *Clarify your and your clients' main therapeutic goals* (Cowan & Presbury, 2000; Walen et al., 1992). You may both differ somewhat in what you are seeking to do in therapy. But too much? See if the differences lead to resistances. If so, consider changing some of your own goals and no longer foist them on your unwilling clients; and consider persuading your clients to change some of their goals. If neither of these plans work, think about recommending another therapist to your clients who is more sympathetic with their goals and values.

5. *Experiment with different methods than the ones you steadily use* (Ellis, 2002). Preferably have a good many methods in your own therapeutic system, and do not rigidly swear by them. I find that if I authoritatively push my favorite techniques with clients, they often gain confidence in me and in these methods. But I watch for overselling my techniques because, when the oversold methods do not work, my clients lose confidence in me as a therapist. So, I often show clients the value of experimenting because what works for one may be ineffective for another. When I see that clients put themselves down for failing to successfully use one of my favorite methods, I explain that no matter how good it may be for many people it may not be for them, so they'd better experiment with it and see for themselves. Experimentation leads to good science; and it also leads to good therapy (Hanna, 2001).

6. *Encourage your client's special therapeutic inventiveness* (McMullin, 2000). While showing my own resistant (and nonresistant) clients how to try the techniques I suggest, I also recommend that they add their own special variations on these methods and creatively discover uniquely good methods for themselves. They can try my suggestion partially or completely, strongly or lightly, tentatively or permanently. They can also add to or subtract from them. I show them that when I do therapy, I learn from my own experiences—and also from theirs. So by being innovative, they may help me to become a better therapist!

7. *Consider using self-help materials that fit in with your form of therapy* (Ellis, 2002; McMullin, 2000). In my own case, I helped myself, long before I became a therapist, by using self-help materials to work on my anxieties. Because these worked so well for me, I naturally favor them for my clients. Resistant clients, I find, can often find self-help procedures helpful because, if they scan a number of methods, they can selectively choose to follow a few that work nicely in their own cases. Since they usually pick methods that they like to perform and that they believe will be effective for them, they have little resistance in carrying them out and often find some that really work. So don't just prescribe some of your favorite self-help methods, but give your clients leeway to pick a few of them out of many that they may try.

8. *Resistant clients are often more threatened than other clients and defensively ward off discussing "dangerous" topics, such as sex, anger, and defensiveness itself.* But you can also be afraid of what will happen if you force clients to discuss "dangerous" issues (Hanna, 2001; Navajits, 2001). You, for example, may fear that raising uncomfortable topics will antagonize, your clients and—horror of horrors!—lose them. I do my best to watch for signs of my own queasiness, for if I am anxious, I may help my clients to skirt what they think are dangerous issues. I also show myself that making my clients uncomfortable has its advantages as well as disadvantages. So I give myself little time to avoid discussing ticklish problems. This doesn't always work, and I do lose some clients by jumping into risky areas. But I make myself take the lesser evil of losing a client than the greater evil of unhelpfully drawing out our sessions and never discovering if my "dangerous" confrontation will work. For the clients, the danger of my not bringing up topics often results in letting them interminably go comfortably on with their resisting.

9. *Bite the bullet and openly discuss the clients' resistance with them.* A good many therapists recommend openly discussing such resistance with these clients: (a) their unawareness that they are resisting; (b) their hypotheses about why they are doing so; (c) your own feelings about their resisting; and (d) what both of you think had better be done to alleviate their (and your) resisting. Again, this kind of open discussion, which you will have to initiate, may—or may not—work like a charm. If it does, great! If it doesn't, you may still discover that your client has a severe personality disorder that practically no kind of therapy will effectively resolve; that you and the client are seriously mismatched; that your kind of therapy, though effective with most of your clients, won't work with this one; and that other important reasons exist for the client's resistance. Good knowledge—and you well might never come up with it without your forcing an uncomfortable discussion on the client.

10. *You can try forceful and emotional teaching* (McMullin, 2000). I have found that when clients want to improve but actually do not work to get better, they usually have two important irrational beliefs. The first is "I'd better change; but it's too difficult for me to change and I'm a total failure for not being able to do so." And second, "It's quite hard for me to change and it should not, must not be that hard! It's too hard and my therapist must make it much easier!" Clients will frequently agree that they have these self-destructive beliefs, but they still tightly hold on to them and don't work to give them up. Therefore, as their therapist, you have to not only help them see these beliefs but also induce them to strongly and emotionally fight them. This means that you often have to convince yourself that clients strongly hold such beliefs and that you had better vigorously work at getting them to surrender them. Both of you had better use force and persistence!

11. *You can encourage clients to record and listen to their therapy sessions.* Some of them will then regularly do so and give themselves the opportunity to hear what you are teaching uninterruptedly, and perhaps to see how they are wasting their time by avoiding important issues. They may also see that expressing themselves volubly may be indeed enjoyable but may have little to do with their changing themselves.

12. *Integrate your psychotherapy with other kinds of treatments.* You may be quite convinced that your kind of therapy is by far the best for any clients. Maybe! But when it isn't working, at least try some parts of other procedures that you think might work with a particular resistant client. If they work, you will learn something; and if they don't work, you will have more evidence that your methods are really as good as you think they are.

13. *Clients often have emotional problems about their emotional problems: secondary symptoms.* They blame themselves so much for being anxious or depressed that they create additional anxiety or depression. Or they "awfulize" so much about their original symptoms that they refuse to face them and are defensive about them. Assume that some of your resistant clients may have secondary disturbances, question them to see how they react to their primary disturbances, then especially show them how to stop denigrating themselves for having and awfulizing about having their original disturbances. Once you help them unconditionally accept while distinctly disliking their primary problems (such as panic) the problem itself may significantly decrease.

14. *When direct homework assignments do not work, consider using paradoxical assignments.* For example, clients with social anxiety may not risk in vivo desensization of approaching other people because rejection is seen as "demeaning" or "horrible." If, paradoxically, they accept the assignment of, say, making sure that they are rejected by several people, they view their "risks" differently and if they get rejected, may not view rejection as self-demeaning and horrible.

15. *You can use metaphors, poetry, and dramatic presentations when direct therapeutic teaching does not work* (Leahy, 2001). Although most clients probably listen better to your simple and direct communication, resistors may not do so. Therefore, you can sometimes reach them better with dramatic or humorous stores, poems, plays, metaphors, and other indirect ways of presentation. I would not advise that you give up using direct methods of arguing with clients' irrational beliefs and only use metaphorics. But if you add them to your direct communication, they may get the attention of some of your resistant clients.

16. *Resistant clients, more than others, often have extreme self-destructive philosophies and cling to them rigidly*. They have uncoping dogmas rather than coping self-statements. I have found that if I strongly and persistently show them the advantages of their using powerful coping statements, they may finally reduce their profound negativism and see themselves, other people, and the world in a much less pessimistic light. I do my best to teach them three basic constructive philosophies that largely overcome their negativism: (a) unconditional self-acceptance (USA): to honestly evaluate their *behaviors* as "good" when they work and as "bad" when they don't work— but never to overgeneralize and evaluate *themselves* as "good" or as "bad"; (b) unconditional other-acceptance (UOA): to think critically of other people's thoughts, feelings, and actions but refrain from damning other *people*, no matter how badly they *behave*; (c) unconditional life-acceptance (ULA): to dislike and even hate world conditions, but when you can't change them, accept life and the world in spite of these conditions and enjoy yourself as much as you can. I do my best to show my resistant clients that if I can convince them to work at achieving these three basic self-helping philosophies, this strategy will not be a cure-all for their problems but will help them be considerably less disturbed in the face of life's ubiquitous hassles and problems.

References, Readings, & Internet Sites 

Albert Ellis Institute. (n.d.). Home page. Retrieved 2004 from http://www.rebt.org/

Cowan, E. W., & Presbury, J. H. (2000). Meeting client resistance with reverence. *Journal of Counseling and Development, 78,* 411–419.

Ellis, A. (2001a). *Feeling better, getting better, staying better*. Atascadero, CA: Impact Publishers.

Ellis, A. (2001b). *Overcoming destructive beliefs, feelings, and behaviors*. Amherst, NY: Prometheus Books.

Ellis, A. (2002). *Overcoming resistance: A rational emotive behavior therapy integrated approach.* New York: Springer.

Hanna, F. J. (2001). *Therapy with difficult clients.* Washington, DC: American Psychological Association.

Hayes, S. C., Strosahl, K., & Wilson, K. G. (1999). *Acceptance and commitment therapy.* New York: Guilford Press.

Leahy, R. L. (2001). *Overcoming resistance in cognitive therapy.* New York: Guilford Press.

McMullin, R. E. (2000). *The new handbook of cognitive therapy*. New York: Norton.

Navajits, L. M. (2001). Helping "difficult" patients. *Psychotherapy Research, 11,* 131–152.

Walen, S., DiGiuseppe, R., & Dryden, W. (1992). *A practitioner's guide to rational-emotive therapy.* New York: Oxford University Press.

Related Topics

Chapter 42, "Enhancing Adherence"

Chapter 44, "Repairing Ruptures in the Therapeutic Alliance"

44 REPAIRING RUPTURES IN THE THERAPEUTIC ALLIANCE

Jeremy D. Safran

Although promising psychotherapies have been identified for a range of psychological disorders, substantial numbers of patients fail to benefit from these treatments. To begin with, dropout rates are relatively high. The NIMH Treatment of Depression Collaborative Research Program (TDCRP) had attrition rates of 33% for cognitive therapy and 23% for interpersonal therapy (Elkin, 1994). Estimates of patient attrition rates average about 47% and range as high as 67% (Sledge, Moras, Hartley, & Levine, 1990; Wierzbicki & Pekarik, 1993).

The evidence also indicates that there is still considerable room for improvement outcomes. In a meta-analysis of well-designed studies investigating treatments for major depression, generalized anxiety disorder, and panic disorder, only 63% of panic disorder patients, 52% of generalized anxiety disorder patients, and 54% of the depressed patients who completed treatment were considered improved at termination (Westin & Morrison, 2001). In a study of 2,405 community mental health center patients, 66% of treated patients could be considered improved, 26% unchanged, and 8% worse (Asay, Lambert, Christensen, and Beutler, 1984).

It is also important to remember that these studies used relatively lenient criteria for improvement, and they failed to assess maintenance at follow-up. The TDCRP found that at an 18-month follow-up interval, using relatively stringent (but clinically meaningful) criteria for recovery, only 30% of patients receiving cognitive therapy and 26% of patients receiving interpersonal therapy were considered improved. In a recent meta-analysis, 38% of depressed patients who completed treatment remained improved at follow-up intervals of 12 to 18 months. For panic disorder patients, the percentage remaining improved was 54% (Westin & Morrison, 2001).

Given the large body of evidence that a considerable proportion of patients fail to remain in or benefit from psychotherapy, it is critical to identify those who are at risk for treatment dropout or poor outcome and to develop ways of improving the likelihood that they will complete the treatment and benefit from it.

A strong or improving therapeutic alliance contributes to a positive treatment outcome, regardless of treatment modality (Martin, Garske, & Davis, 2000). Similarly, there is ample evidence that weakened alliances are correlated with unilateral termination (Samstag, Batchelder, Muran, & Winston, 1998). Another related finding is that poor outcome cases show greater negative interpersonal process (e.g., hostile and complex interactions) than good outcome cases (e.g., Henry, Schacht, & Strupp, 1986). These findings suggest that the process of recognizing and addressing alliance ruptures, and negative therapeutic process can be important for many patients who are at risk for treatment failure.

CLINICAL PRINCIPLES

Research evidence suggests common principles in resolving alliance ruptures (Foreman & Marmar, 1985; Rhodes, Hill, Thompson, & Elliot, 1994; Safran & Muran, 2000; Safran, Muran, Samstag, & Stevens, 2002). These are as follows:

1. Therapists should be aware that patients often have negative feelings about the therapy or the therapeutic relationship, which they are reluctant to broach for fear of the therapist's reactions. It is thus important for therapists to be attuned to subtle indications of ruptures in the alliance and to take the initiative in exploring what is transpiring in the relationship when they suspect that a rupture has occurred.
2. Patients profit from expressing negative feelings about the therapy to the therapist should they emerge or to assert their perspective on what is going on when it differs from the therapist's.
3. When this take place, it is important for therapists to attempt to respond in an open and nondefensive fashion, and to accept responsibility for their contribution to the interaction.
4. There is some evidence to suggest that the process of exploring patient fears and expectations that make it difficult for them to assert their negative feelings about treatment may contribute to the process of resolving the alliance rupture.

THERAPEUTIC META-COMMUNICATION

In addition to these principles, the literature suggests the value of skillful therapeutic meta-communication as a tool for resolving alliance ruptures (see Safran & Muran, 2000). Alliance ruptures take place when both patient and therapist unwittingly contribute to a maladaptive interpersonal cycle that is being enacted by the two of them. Meta-communication consists of treating this cycle as the focus of collaborative exploration.

Some of the key features of meta-communication in this context are that (a) there is an intensive focus on the here and now of the therapeutic relationship, (b) there is an ongoing collaborative exploration of both patients' and therapists' contributions to the interaction, (c) there is an emphasis on the in-depth exploration of the nuances of patients' experience in context of the therapeutic relationship (and a cautiousness about inferring generalized relational patterns), (d) the relational meaning of interventions (i.e., the idiosyncratic way in which each patient construes the therapist's intervention) is as important as the content of the intervention, and (e) intensive use is made of therapist self-disclosure and collaborative exploration of what is taking place in the therapeutic relationship for purposes of coming to understand and unhook from the cycle.

The therapist's task when engaging in this type of exploration is to identify his or her own feelings and use them as a point of departure for collaborative exploration. Different forms of exploration are possible. The therapist may provide patients with feedback about their impact on him or her. For example, "I feel cautious with you . . . as if I'm walking on eggshells" or "I feel like it's difficult to really make contact with you. On one hand, the things you're talking about really seem important. But on the other, there's a subtle level at which it's difficult for me to really feel you," or "I feel judged by you." Such feedback can help the patient begin to see his or her own contribution to the rupture. It can also pave the way for the exploration of the patient's inner experience. For example, the therapist can add, "Does this feedback make any sense to you? Do you have any awareness of judging me?" This can help the patient begin to articulate a critical attitude that he or she has not been fully aware of, thus allowing the therapist to begin working through the alliance rupture with the patient. It is often useful for therapists to pinpoint specific instances of patients' eliciting actions. For example, "I feel dismissed or closed out by you, and I think it may be related to the way in which you tend not to pause and reflect in a way that suggests you're really considering what I'm saying."

Below are described specific principles for enhancing the skillful use of therapeutic meta-communication:

1. *Explore with skillful tentativeness and emphasize one's own subjectivity.* Therapists should communicate observations in a tentative and exploratory fashion. The message at both explicit and implicit levels should be one of inviting patients to engage in a collaborative attempt to understand what is taking place, rather than conveying information with objective status. It is also important for therapists to emphasize the subjectivity of their perceptions since this encourages patients to use therapists' observations as a stimulus for self-exploration rather than to react to them either positively or negatively as authoritative statements.

2. *Do not assume a parallel with other relationships.* Therapists should be wary of prematurely attempting to establish a link between the configuration enacted in the therapeutic relationship and other relationships in the patient's life. Attempts to make links of this type (while useful in some contexts) can be experienced by patients as blaming and can also serve a defensive function for therapists. Instead the focus should be on exploring patients' internal experience and actions in a nuanced fashion, as they emerge in the here and now.

3. *Ground all formulations in awareness of one's own feelings and accept responsibility for one's own contributions.* All observations should attempt to take into account what the therapist is feeling. Failure to do so increases the risk of a distorted understanding that is influenced by factors that are out of awareness. It is critical for therapists to take responsibility for their own contributions to the interaction. We are always contributing to the interaction in ways that are not fully in awareness, and an important task consists of clarifying the nature of this contribution in an ongoing fashion.

In some situations, the process of explicitly acknowledging responsibility for one's contributions to patients can be a particularly potent intervention. First, this process can help patients become aware of unconscious or semiconscious feelings that they have difficulty articulating. For example, acknowledging that one has been critical can help patients to articulate their feelings of hurt and resentment. Second, by validating the patient's perceptions of the therapist's actions, the therapist can reduce his or her need for defensiveness.

4. *Start where you are.* Collaborative exploration of the therapeutic relationship should take into account feelings, intuitions, and observations that are emerging for the therapist at the moment. What was true one session may not be true the next, and what was true one moment may change the next. Two therapists will react differently to the same patient, and each therapist must begin by making use of his or her own unique experience. For example, while a third-party observer may be able to adopt an empathic response toward an aggressive patient, the therapist who is embedded in the interaction with that patient may have difficulty doing so. Therapists cannot conceptually manipulate themselves into an empathic stance they don't feel. They must begin by fully accepting and working with their own feelings and subjective reactions.

5. *Focus on the concrete, specific, and here and now of the therapeutic relationship.* Whenever possible, questions, observations, and comments should focus on concrete instances in the here and now rather than on generalizations. This promotes experiential awareness rather than abstract, intellectualized speculation. For example, "I experience you as pulling away from me right now. Do you have any awareness of doing this?"

6. *Track patients' responsiveness to all interventions.* Therapists should carefully monitor the impact of their interventions. Do they seem to facilitate the process or perpetuate the rupture? If therapists sense that an intervention has not been facilitative, they should explore the way it has been experienced by the patient. For example, "How did it feel when I said that to you?" or "I'm not sure know what's going on for you right now. I'm wondering if you might have felt criticized by what I said?" Exploring the patient's construal of an intervention that has failed can play a critical role in refining therapists' understanding of both the configuration that is being enacted and the patient's inner world. This helps therapists to refine their interventions in a way that ultimately will lead to the resolution of the alliance rupture.

7. *Collaborative exploration of the therapeutic relationship and unhooking take place at the same time.* It is not necessary for therapists to have a clear formulation prior to metacommunicating. In fact, the process of thinking out loud about the interaction often helps therapists to remove from the configuration that is being enacted by putting into words subtle perceptions that might otherwise remain implicit. Moreover, the process of telling patients about an aspect of one's experience that one is in conflict over can free therapists to see the situation more clearly.

8. *Remember that attempts to explore what is taking place in the relationship can function as new cycles of an ongoing enactment.* For example, the therapist articulates a growing intuition that the patient is withdrawing and says, "It feels to me like I'm trying to pull teeth." In response the patient withdraws further and an intensification of an existing vicious cycle ensues in which the therapist escalates his attempts to break through and the patient becomes more defensive. It is critical to track the quality of patients' responsiveness to all interventions and to explore their experience of interventions that have not been facilitative. Does the intervention deepen the patient's self-exploration or lead to defensiveness or compliance? The process of exploring the ways in which patients experience interventions that are not facilitative helps to refine the understanding of the cycle that is being enacted.

References & Readings 

Asay, T. P., Lambert, M. J., Christensen, E. R., & Beutler, L. E. (1984). *A meta-analysis of mental health treatment outcome.* Unpublished manuscript, Brigham Young University, Department of Psychology.

Elkin, I. (1994). The NIMH treatment of depression collaborative research program: Where we began and where we are. In A. E. Bergin & S. L. Garfield (Eds.), *Handbook of psychotherapy and behavior change* (4th ed., pp. 114–139). New York: Wiley.

Foreman, S. A., & Marmar, C. R. (1985). Therapist actions that address initially poor therapeutic alliances in psychotherapy. *American Journal of Psychiatry, 142,* 922–926.

Henry, W. P., Schact, T. E., & Strupp, H. H. (1986). Structural analysis of social behavior: Application to a study of interpersonal process in differential psychotherapeutic outcome. *Journal of Consulting and Clinical Psychology, 54,* 27–31.

Lambert, M. J., & Bergin, A. E. (1994). The effectiveness of psychotherapy. In A. E. Bergin & S. L. Garfield (Eds.), *Handbook of psychotherapy and behavior change* (4th ed., pp. 143–189). New York: Wiley.

Martin, D. J., Garske, J. P., & Davis, M. K. (2000). Relation of the therapeutic alliance with outcome and other variables: A meta-analytic review. *Journal of Consulting and Clinical Psychology, 68,* 438–450.

Rhodes, R. H., Hill, C. E., Thompson, B. J., & Elliot, R. (1994). Client retrospective recall of resolved and unresolved misunderstanding events. *Journal of Counseling Psychology, 41,* 473–483.

Safran, J. D., & Muran, J. C. (2000). *Negotiating the therapeutic alliance: A relational treatment guide.* New York: Guilford Press.

Safran, J. D., Muran, J. C., Samstag, L. W., & Stevens, C. (2002). Repairing the alliance ruptures. In J. C. Norcross (Ed.), *Psychotherapy relationships that work* (pp. 235–254). New York: Oxford University Press.

Samstag, L. W., Batchelder, S. T., Muran, J. C., & Winston, A. (1998). Early identification of treatment failures in short-term psychotherapy: An assessment of therapeutic alliance and interpersonal behavior. *Journal of Psychotherapy Practice and Research, 7,* 126–143.

Seligman, M. E. P. (1995). The effectiveness of psychotherapy—The *Consumer Reports* study. *American Psychologist, 50,* 965–974.

Sledge, W. H., Moras, K., Hartley, D., & Levine, M. (1990). Effect of time-limited psychotherapy on patient drop-out rates. *American Journal of Psychiatry, 147,* 1341–1347.

Westin, D., & Morrison, K. (2001). A multidimensional meta-analysis of treatments for depression, panic, and generalized anxiety disorder: An empirical examination of the status of empirically supported therapies. *Journal of Consulting and Clinical Psychology, 69,* 875–899.

Wierzbicki, M., & Pekaric, G. (1993). A meta-analyis of psychotherapy dropout. *Professional Psychology: Research and Practice, 24,* 190–195.

Related Topics

Chapter 42, "Enhancing Adherence"

Chapter 43, "Methods to Reduce and Counter Resistance in Psychotherapy"

45 SYSTEMATIC ASSESSMENT AND TREATMENT MATCHING

Oliver B. Williams, Larry E. Beutler, & Kathryn Yanick

This synopsis of Systematic Treatment Selection (STS; Beutler, Clarkin, & Bongar, 2000) presents two major components: (1) questionnaire responses that identify patient predictors and indicators, and (2) the translation of these variables to making treatment decisions. The first section presents items used to assess five basic domains of patient functioning. Once these domains have been assessed, treatment selection decisions can be addressed logically and algorithmically. The second section is divided into two parts: assigning the level of patient care and determination of optimal treatment approaches. Level-of-care decisions are based on a determination of patient functionality, safety, treatment setting, and the potential for medical consultation (mode). In contrast, the selection of optimal treatment approaches relies on a combination of indicators based on patient personality and interpersonal styles, all of which facilitate matching the patient to treatment.

SYSTEMATIC ASSESSMENT

There are five basic domains, each representing a general patient characteristic that can be rapidly assessed to match treatments. These five domains are the patient's (1) severity and functionality; (2) personal and problem complexity; (3) distress; (4) level of resistance (sometimes called "reactance"); and (5) coping style. Findings from a large body of research show that these patient characteristics can be measured reliably by a clinician during the course of an intake session, or by a clinician viewing a videotape of the intake session (e.g., Beutler et al., 2000). The items presented here to assess these dimensions do not constitute comprehensive and psychometrically pure scales. They are representative and clear items that can estimate patient characteristics that can be used for treatment selection; they should be seen as guides to help the clinician, rather than as standardized tests.

These assessment dimensions, and the treatment decisions that they portend, are derived from 18 research-informed principles on evidence-based treatment matching (Beutler & Clarkin, 1990). The interested clinician can obtain a demonstration of a more complete process of relating patient characteristics to treatment decisions at the Web site www.systematictreatmentselection.com. A more detailed discussion of the STS model and the internet-deployed system, respectively, is in Beutler and Harwood (2000) and Harwood and Williams (2003). And information about stand-alone or network versions of the computer program Systematic Treatment Selection for Windows may be obtained from New Standards (1080 Montreal Avenue, Suite 300, St. Paul, MN 55116; 800-755-6299).

Severity/Functionality

The safety of the patient and of those around her/him are central to determining the optimal level of care. Additionally, the patient's ability to conduct tasks necessary to physical and social living determine functionality, which is also central to level of care. The factors of severity and functionality prescribe the treatment setting and environment, or the amount of restriction imposed upon the patient necessary to maintain his or her safety and/or the safety of others.

Answer the following questions, assigning a score of 1 (yes) or 0 (no):

S1. Has the patient just recently suffered severe loss due to prolonged use of alcohol and/or other drugs?
S2. Is the patient disoriented in time, place, or person?
S3. Within the past year, has this patient ever been explosive, charged with criminal conduct, threatened harm to another, or destroyed property in a fit of anger or retribution?
S4. Does the patient currently demonstrate extremely violent behavior?
S5. Is the patient grossly disabled, or unable to care for herself/himself?

Add items S1–S5. Call this score *Severity.*

Patient/Problem Complexity

The depth, history, and thematic nature of the patient's profile provide important predictors of the prognosis and probable length of treatment. Situational problems suggest a more acute symptom architecture where brief and targeted psychotherapeutic procedures are indicated. More complex profiles are reflected in longstanding and thematic complaints that recur in almost all facets of the patient's life. A yes response to each of the following questions suggests greater complexity and chronicity. The total number of yes responses roughly identifies the level of problem complexity.

C1. Has there been more than one similar episode of the presenting problem, or of major depression?
C2. Does this patient merit more than one Axis I diagnosis?
C3. Does the patient have recurrent and distressful thoughts and feelings about his/her nuclear family (mother, father, close relatives)?
C4. Can the patient also be diagnosed with an Axis II disorder?

Add items C1–C4. This score is *Complexity*.

Distress

We conceptualize distress as three contributing factors: the comfort level as the patient reports it; how the clinician perceives the patient's distress level; and the patient's self-esteem, where low self-esteem is indicative of psychological distress. These distress factors are independent of diagnoses and are manifested as "psychological pain." Relief of such pain can motivate the patient to become involved in treatment and to initiate change. Answer the following questions to guide your estimate of patient distress.

The patient . . .

D1. Would probably frequently report, "I often feel nervous, anxious, or restless even when things are going OK"
D2. Overreacts to disappointments and discouragement
D3. Feels guilty, unworthy, or self-disliked most of the time
D4. Is very uncertain about the future
D5. Feels unhappy or sad
D6. Has many symptoms of emotional distress (e.g., agitation, dysphoria, confusion, guilt)

Total the number of yes responses. Call this sum *Distress.*

Level of Resistance

Resistance—or what may be, in extreme form, oppositional behavior—connotes an individual's relative sluggishness or alacrity to accept the therapist's direction. Resistance can be conceptualized as a kind of "psychological inertia." Analogously, the more inertia a patient has, the more effort is required to move him or her to change course and direction. Consider the following questions about the patient.

The patient . . .

R1. Is not likely to accept and follow the directions of those in authority

R2. Has trouble being a follower
R3. Is prone to criticize others
R4. Is controlling in relationships
R5. Is distrustful and suspicious of others' motives
R6. Often breaks "the rules"
R7. Is passive-aggressive

Add the number of yes responses, and call the total *Resistance*.

Coping Style

The patient's coping style is defined as the usual manner in which she or he manages anxiety and stress. Anxiety can be exhibited through outward expression into one's physical and social environment, called *externalization*. It can also be focused inwardly by containment of feelings and thoughts, called *internalization*. Individuals are not uniformly at one pole or the other, but rather are best defined as having both internalizing (self-reflective) and externalizing (impulsive) qualities, of which one dominates.

Externalizing Answer the following questions and call the total number of yes responses *Externalization*.

The patient . . .

E1. Is socially gregarious and outgoing
E2. Has used alcohol/drugs excessively at one time
E3. Gets frustrated easily
E4. Often gets into trouble because of his/her behavior
E5. Gets bored easily
E6. Has an inflated sense of importance

Internalizing Answer the following questions and call the total number of yes responses *Internalization*.

The patient . . .

I1. Is more likely to feel hurt than angry
I2. Worries or ruminates a lot
I3. Feels more than passing guilt, remorse, or shame about minor things
I4. Is more interested in ideas than taking action
I5. Is timid
I6. Likes to be alone

TREATMENT MATCHING

Treatment decisions are complex and, accordingly, are developed from weighing and integrating a number of patient and treatment dimensions. Balancing multiple factors in clinical practice usually is done through an idiosyncratic process that relies heavily on one's personal and clinical experience. Even expert clinicians are limited in the number of patient and environmental dimensions they can conceptually manage and effectively integrate in treatment planning.

This section presents a suggested method of weighing variables identified in the assessment and a systematic means of combining them to make decisions about the level of care and treatment approach for a particular patient. More specific recommendations than those presented here are possible, but they require more psychometrically rigorous assessments and more complex weightings. A computer-based version of this process produces complex algorithms in order to select appropriate therapists, identify particular treatments that fit the patient, and select specific techniques that are likely to be effective.

Level of Care

Severity = 0: Intensive or more than supportive treatment does not appear warranted for this patient at this time. Optional treatment settings could include the site of difficulty, office treatment, the home, or any combination of these environments during of treatment. The clinician may want to consider how the present environment optimally affects and facilitates treatment outcome.

S1 is Yes or S2 is Yes or S3 is Yes and S5 is No: Treatment is indicated for this patient. The level of problem severity suggests that the patient will be manageable as an outpatient.

S1 and S5 are Yes: The patient may require protective controls against harming himself/herself. Acute hospitalization should be considered while the patient becomes stabilized on a treatment regimen.

Total Severity ≥ 3: Serious consideration must be given to providing a protective environment along with medical management and consultation.

Severity = 1 and Axis I Count < 4 And Complexity = 1: The patient presents problems of mild to moderate severity. Most of the symptomatic presentations probably can be expected to be resolved within six months of regular treatment. If the problems prove to be complicated by personality disorder or multiple problems, a reconsideration of this projection will be indicated.

Severity > 1 and C3 = Yes and Complexity ≥ 2: This patient presents with chronic and difficult problems. These difficulties are likely to be resolved slowly. While one may expect some increased optimism and some dissipation of some symptoms within a period of less than six months, substantial change may require both long-term care and periods in which the frequency of visits and varieties of care are increased.

S2 is Yes and S5 is Yes: The patient is prone to aggressive acts and these may involve risk to other people. Protections against these acts are indicated. At least short-term hospitalization or legal management may be indicated.

Treatment Approaches

(Complexity = 1 or 2) and Distress ≥ 3: Both chronicity and acuteness are indicated, where acuteness has exacerbated long-standing problems. The first goal should be narrow focus and symptom removal; the second goal should be long-term behavioral management.

There are indications that this patient's problems reflect persistent and long-term conflicts. Thus, the long-term goals of treatment should not be limited to symptom removal. This patient is likely to have conflicts and recurrent dysfunctional behaviors in interpersonal relationships that prevent the long-term resolution of symptoms. An understanding of the patient's intrapersonal dynamics and interpersonal problems is necessary in addressing these problems. It often helps to define (1) the dominant interpersonal needs or desires that motivate the initiation of interpersonal relationships, (2) the avoided and feared responses that are expected to come from others as the patient tries to meet these needs or achieve these wants, and (3) the acts of the patient to attempt a compromise between personal desires and feared consequences.

Distress ≥ 3 and Complexity = 0: Indicators suggest focus and outcome objectives should be on symptom removal. There is little indication of a persistent and continuing problem beyond situational disturbance. Since this patient's presenting problems are relatively situational, this should not pose a major difficulty for the treatment. Good and even lasting outcomes have been noted with procedures that are designed to induce rapid symptom change. Indeed, insight-oriented treatments are often more time-consuming than warranted by the problems presented by patients such as this.

It may be possible to restrict the goals of treatment to symptom removal. If so, treatment can be expected to produce some diminution of the major symptoms of depression and anxiety within 20 to 30 sessions or weeks. If there are more focal symptoms being presented, such as sleep, sexual, or impulse-control problems, they may require a somewhat longer period of time. Treatment should be addressed to symptom removal, to the reduction of subjective distress, and to the increase in objective life adjustment. Cognitive control strategies, contingency programs for symptomatic control, and response prevention interventions should be considered.

Complexity ≥ 2 and Distress > 3: Complexity suggests chronic and long-standing symptoms. Treatment objectives should be on long-term behavioral management. Thus, the long-term goals of treatment should not be constrained to symptom removal.

This patient is likely to have conflicts and recurrent dysfunctional behaviors in interpersonal relationships that prevent the long-term resolution of symptoms. An understanding of the patient's intrapersonal dynamics and interpersonal problems is necessary in addressing these problems. It often helps to define (1) the dominant interpersonal needs or desires that motivate the initiation of interpersonal relationships, (2) the avoided and feared responses that are expected to come from others as the patient tries to meet these needs or achieve these wants, and (3) the acts of the patient to attempt a compromise between personal desires and feared consequences.

Distress < 3 and Complexity < 2: Given the low level of personal distress, a question must be raised as to why this person is seeking treatment at this time. Careful consideration must be given to the need and advisability of treatment, external (environmental and situational) factors that may be motivating it, and especially to the possible gains that may determine a referral for treatment at the present time.

C3 = Yes and Complexity > 1: Family therapy appears to be indicated. This therapy should focus on conflicts in the patient's current family. The role of other symptoms and problems may either be ancillary or primary in the family problems, but the significance of family disruption nonetheless warrants direct attention.

Externalization > 3 and Reactance > 3 and S2 is Yes: The patient exhibits possible explosive outbursts. Thus, caution is advised and treatment should include behavioral protections such as the initiation of nonviolence contracts, monitoring of impulsivity, and ongoing assessment of escalating emotional intensity. Training in emotional recognition, identification of risk environments, and cognitive management skills are indicated.

(Severity > 0 and Severity < 3) and Distress > 3 and Externalization > Internalization: The patient appears to be in sufficient distress to provide motivation for ongoing psychotherapy. Nonetheless, treatment progress is often slow with such individuals. They tend to work inconsistently in treatment, even withdrawing from treatment prematurely when their distress lessens. They have difficulty seeing their own contribution to their problems, they tend to blame others and to attribute their difficulties to forces that are outside of their personal control. Treatment would do well to reinforce assumptions of personal responsibility. Sometimes, group therapies have been useful in providing a level of confrontation that encourages the assumption of personal responsibility for initiating change.

Externalization > 3 and Reactance > 3: Behaviorally focused and cognitive change therapies may be particularly helpful for this patient. However, because the patient tends to be more resistant to direction than usual, modifications of the treatments may be necessary. Such modifications may employ self-help manuals and efforts to make homework assignments more flexible than usual.

Severity = 1 and Distress > 2 and Internalization > Externalization: Treatment is indicated for this patient, and the level of problem severity suggests that the patient will be manageable as an outpatient. Moreover, the patient appears to be in sufficient distress to provide motivation for ongoing psychotherapy. Such individuals tend to work quite well in psychotherapy relationships, especially if they have a history of being able to form social attachments. Their motivation for treatment is typically to reduce stress, however, and rapid change of symptoms may reduce their motivation.

Severity = 0 and Distress ≥ 3 and Externalization > Internalization: While the patient has little impairment functionally, the level of internal distress indicates the desirability of treatment. This distress level is sufficient to provide motivation for treatment and indicates that engagement in an outpatient treatment is possible. Engaging such patients in the process of therapy is difficult because they often have difficulty assessing their role in causing or maintaining their problems. A focus on problematic behaviors and cognitions with short-term, measurable objectives is more likely to be effective than insight oriented treatments.

Severity = 0 and Distress ≥ 3 and Internalization > Externalization: While the patient has little functional impairment, the level of internal distress indicates the desirability of treatment. This distress level is sufficient to provide motivation for treatment and indicates that engagement in an outpatient treatment is possible. The patient is self-reflective, suggesting that insight is possible and even desirable as a treatment goal. Insight into unwanted feelings may prove to be advantageous.

Severity = 0 and Distress < 3 and Externalization > Internalization: This patient apparently has minimal impairment of functioning. Coupled with the low level of personal distress, this raises a question as to why this person is seeking treatment at this time. Careful consideration must be given to the need and advisability of treatment, and especially to the motivations that are determining a referral for treatment at the present time. Engaging such patients in the process of therapy is difficult because they often have difficulty assessing their role in causing or maintaining their problems. A focus on problematic behaviors and cognitions with short-term, measurable objectives is more likely to be effective than insight oriented treatments.

Severity = 0 and Distress < 3 and Internalization > Externalization: This patient also apparently has minimal impairment of functioning. Coupled with the low level of personal distress, this raises a question as to why this person is seeking treatment at this time. Careful consideration must be given to the need and advisability of treatment, and especially of the motivations that are determining a referral for treatment at the present time. However, the patient is self-reflective, suggesting that insight is possible and even desirable as a treatment goal. Insight into both hidden motives and into unwanted feelings may prove to be advantageous.

Severity > 2: This patient may require a very structured and concrete approach to treatment including pretreatment preparation, clearly established goals, and an outline of in-treatment and outside of treatment expectations.

References, Readings, & Internet Sites

Beutler, L. E. (1979). Toward specific psychological therapies for specific conditions. *Journal of Consulting and Clinical Psychology, 47,* 882–897.

Beutler, L. E. (2001). Comparisons among quality assurance systems: From outcome assessment to clinical utility. *Journal of Consulting and Clinical Psychology, 69,* 197–204.

Beutler, L. E., & Clarkin, J. (1990). *Systematic treatment selection: Toward targeted therapeutic interventions.* New York: Brunner/Mazel.

Beutler, L. E., Clarkin, J. F., & Bongar, B. (2000). *Systematic guidelines for treating the depressed patient.* New York: Oxford University Press.

Beutler, L. E. & Harwood, T. M. (2000). *Prescriptive psychotherapy: A practical guide to Systematic Treatment Selection.* New York: Oxford University Press.

Beutler, L. E., & Williams, O. B. (1995). Computer applications for the selection of optimal psychosocial therapeutic interventions. *Behavioral Healthcare Tomorrow, 4,* 66–68.

Beutler, L. E., & Williams, O. B. (2002). www.systematictreatmentselection.com [Internet-deployed interactive system]. Oxnard, CA: Center for Behavioral HealthCare Technologies.

Harwood, T. M., & Williams, O. B. (2003). Identifying treatment relevant assessment: The STS. In L. E. Beutler & G. Groth-Marnat (Eds.), *Integrative assessment of adult personality* (2nd rev. ed., pp. 65–81). New York: Guilford Press.

Related Topics

Chapter 39, "Compendium of Empirically Supported Therapies"

Chapter 40, "Compendium of Psychotherapy Treatment Manuals"

Chapter 46, "Stages of Change: Prescriptive Guidelines"

46 STAGES OF CHANGE
Prescriptive Guidelines

James O. Prochaska, John C. Norcross,
& Carlo C. DiClemente

Over the past 25 years our research has focused on the structure of change that underlies both self-mediated and treatment-facilitated modification of problem behavior (for summaries, see DiClemente, 2003a; DiClemente, 2003b; Prochaska, DiClemente, & Norcross, 1992; Prochaska, Norcross, & DiClemente, 1995). From an integrative or transtheoretical perspective, this chapter summarizes prescriptive and proscriptive guidelines for psychosocial interventions based on the client's stage of change.

DEFINITIONS OF STAGES

The following are brief descriptions of each of the five stages. Each stage represents a period of time, as well as a set of tasks needed for movement to the next stage. Although the time an individual spends in each stage may vary, the tasks to be accomplished are assumed to be invariant.

1. *Precontemplation* is the stage at which there is no intention to change behavior in the foreseeable future. Most individuals in this stage are unaware or underaware of their problems. Families, friends, neighbors, or employees, however, are often well aware that the precontemplators have problems. When precontemplators present for psychotherapy, they often do so because of pressure from others. Usually they feel coerced into changing by spouses who threaten to leave, employers who threaten to dismiss them, parents who threaten to disown them, or courts who threaten to punish them.

There are multiple ways to measure the stages of change. In our studies employing the discrete categorization measurement of stages of change, we ask if the individual is seriously intending to change the problem behavior in the near future, typically within the next six months. If not, he or she is classified as a precontemplator. Even precontemplators can wish to change, but this is quite different from intending or seriously considering change. Items that are used to identify precontemplation on the continuous stage of change measure include: "As far as I'm concerned, I don't have any problems that need changing" and "I guess I have faults, but there's nothing that I really need to change." Resistance to recognizing or modifying a problem is the hallmark of precontemplation.

2. *Contemplation* is the stage in which people are aware that a problem exists and are seriously thinking about overcoming it, but they have not yet made a commitment to take action. People can remain stuck in the contemplation stage for long periods. In one study of self-changers we followed a group of 200 smokers in the contemplation stage for two years. The modal response of this group was to remain in the contemplation stage for the entire two years of the project without ever moving to significant action (Prochaska & DiClemente, 1983).

Contemplators struggle with their positive evaluations of their dysfunctional behavior and the amount of effort, energy, and loss it will cost to overcome it. On discrete measures, individuals who state that they are seriously considering changing their behavior in the next six months are classified as contemplators. On the continuous measure, these individuals endorse such items as "I have a problem and I really think I should work on it" and "I've been thinking that I might want to change something about myself." Serious consideration of problem resolution is the central element of contemplation.

3. *Preparation* is a stage that combines intention and behavioral criteria. Individuals in this stage are intending to take action in the next month and have unsuccessfully taken action in the past year. As a group, individuals who are prepared for action report small behavioral changes, such as smoking five fewer cigarettes or delaying their first cigarette of the day for 30 minutes longer than precontemplators or contemplators. Although they have reduced their problem behaviors, individuals in the preparation stage have not yet reached a criterion for effective action, such as abstinence from smoking or alcohol abuse. They are intending, however, to take such action in the very near future. On the continuous measure, they score high on both the contemplation and action scales.

4. *Action* is the stage in which individuals modify their behavior, experiences, and/or environment in order to overcome their problems. Action involves the most overt behavioral changes and requires considerable commitment of time and energy. Behavioral changes in the action stage tend to be most visible and externally recognized. Individuals are classified in the action stage if they have successfully altered the dysfunctional behavior for a period from one day to six months. On the continuous measure, individuals in the action stage endorse statements like "I am really working hard to change" and "Anyone can talk about changing; I am actually doing something about it." They score high on the action scale and lower on the other scales. Modification of the target behavior to an acceptable criterion and concerted overt efforts to change are the hallmarks of action.

5. *Maintenance* is the stage in which people work to prevent relapse and consolidate the gains attained during action. For addictive behaviors, this stage extends from six months to an indeterminate period past the initial action. For some behaviors, maintenance can be considered to last a lifetime. Being able to remain free of the addictive behavior and to consistently engage in a new incompatible behavior for more than six months are the criteria for the maintenance stage. On the continuous measure, representative maintenance items are "I may need a boost right now to help me maintain the changes I've already made" and "I'm here to prevent myself from having a relapse of my problem." Stabilizing behavior change and avoiding relapse are the hallmarks of maintenance.

As is now well known, most people taking action to modify dysfunctional behavior do not successfully maintain their gains on their first attempt. With New Year's resolutions, for example, the successful self-changers typically report three to five years of consecutive pledges before maintaining the behavioral goal for at least six months (Norcross, Mrykalo, & Blagys, 2002). Relapse is the rule rather than the exception across virtually all behavioral disorders.

Accordingly, change is not a linear progression through the stages; rather, most clients move through the stages of change in a *spiral pattern*. People progress from contemplation to preparation to action to maintenance, but most individuals will relapse. During relapse, individuals regress to an earlier stage. Some relapsers feel like failures—embarrassed, ashamed, and guilty. These individuals become demoralized and resist thinking about behavior change. As a result, they return to the precontemplation stage and can remain there for various periods of time. Approximately 15% of relapsers in our self-change research regress to the precontemplation stage. Fortunately, most—85% or so—move back to the contemplation stage and eventually back into preparation and action.

PRESCRIPTIVE GUIDELINES

1. *Assess the client's stage of change:* Probably the most obvious and direct implication is the need to assess the stage of a client's readiness for change and to tailor interventions accordingly. Stages of change can be ascertained by multiple means, of which three self-report methods will be described here.

A first and most efficient method is to ask the patient a simple series of questions to identify his or her stage—for example, "Do you think behavior X is a problem for you now?" (if yes, then contemplation, preparation, or action stage; if no, then maintenance or precontemplation stage) and "When do you intend to change behavior X?" (if some day or not soon, then contemplation stage; if in the next month, then preparation; if now, then the action stage). A second method is to assess the stage from a series of mutually exclusive questions, and a third is a continuous measure that yields separate scales for precontemplation, contemplation, action, and maintenance (McConnaughy, DiClemente, Prochaska, & Velicer, 1989; McConnaughy, Prochaska, & Velicer, 1983).

2. *Beware treating all patients as though they are in action:* Professionals frequently design excellent action-oriented treatment and self-help programs, but then are disappointed when only a small percentage of people register or when large numbers drop out of the program after registering. The vast majority of people are not in the action stage. Aggregating across studies and populations, we estimate that 10% to 15% are prepared for action, approximately 30% to 40% are in the contemplation stage, and 50% to 60% in the precontemplation stage. Thus, professionals approaching patients and settings only with action-oriented programs are likely to underserve or misserve the majority of their target population.

3. *Assist clients in moving one stage at a time:* If clients progress from one stage to the next during the first month of treatment, they can double their chances of taking action in the next six months. Among smokers, for example, of the precontemplators who were still in precontemplation at one-month follow-up, only 3% took action by six months. For the precontemplators who progressed to contemplation at one month, 7% took action by six months. Similarly, of the contemplators who remained in contemplation at one month, only 20% took action by six months. At one month, 41% of the contemplators who progressed to the preparation stage attempted to quit by six months. These data indicate that treatments designed to help people progress just one stage in a month may be able to double the chances of participants taking action on their own in the near future.

4. *Recognize that clients in the action stage are far more likely to achieve better and quicker outcomes:* The amount of progress clients make during treatment tends to be a function of their pretreatment stage of change. For example, an intensive action- and maintenance-oriented smoking cessation program for cardiac patients achieved success for 22% of precontemplators, 43% of contemplators, and 76% of those in action or prepared for action at the start of the study were not smoking six months later (Ockene, Ockene, & Kristellar, 1988). This repeated finding has direct implications for selecting and prioritizing treatment goals.

5. *Facilitate the insight-action crossover:* Patients in successful treatment evidence steady progression on the stages of change. Patients entering therapy are typically in the contemplation or preparation stage. In the midst of treatment, patients typically cross over from contemplation into action. Patients who remain in treatment progress from being prepared for action to taking action over time. That is, they shift from thinking about their problems to doing things to overcome them. Lowered precontemplation scores also indicate that, as engagement in therapy increases, patients reduce their defensiveness and resistance. The progression from contemplation to action is postulated to be essential for beneficial outcome regardless of whether the treatment is action-oriented or insight-oriented.

6. *Anticipate recycling:* Most self-changers and psychotherapy patients will recycle several times through the stages before achieving long-term maintenance. Accordingly, intervention programs and personnel expecting people to progress linearly through the stages are likely to gather disappointing results. Be prepared to include relapse prevention in treatment, anticipate the probability of recycling patients, and try to minimize therapist guilt and patient shame over recycling.

7. *Conceptualize change mechanisms as processes, not as specific techniques:* Literally hundreds of specific psychotherapeutic techniques have been advanced; however, a small and finite set of change processes or strategies underlie these multitudinous techniques.

Change processes are covert and overt activities that individuals engage in when they attempt to modify problem behaviors. Each process is a broad category encompassing multiple techniques, methods, and interventions traditionally associated with disparate theoretical orientations. These change processes can be used within therapy sessions, between therapy sessions, or without therapy sessions.

The processes of change represent an intermediate level of abstraction between metatheoretical assumptions and specific techniques spawned by those theories. While there are 400-plus ostensibly different psychotherapies, we have been able to identify only 12 different processes of change based on principal components analysis.

Table 1 presents the eight processes receiving the most theoretical and empirical support in our work, along with their definitions and representative examples of specific interventions. A common and finite set of change processes has been repeatedly identified across diverse disorders.

8. *Do the right things (processes) at the right time (stages):* Twenty-five years of research in behavioral medicine, self-change, and psychotherapy converge in showing that different processes of change are differentially effective in certain stages of change; a meta-analysis of 47 studies (Rosen, 2000) found effect sizes of .70 and .80 for the use of different change processes in the stages. In general terms, change processes traditionally associated with the experiential, cognitive, and psychoanalytic persuasions are most useful during the earlier precontemplation and contemplation stages. Change processes traditionally associated with the existential and behavioral traditions, by contrast, are most useful during action and maintenance.

In the transtheoretical model, particular change processes will be optimally applied at each stage of change. During the precontemplation stage, individuals use the change processes significantly less than people in any of the other stages. Precontemplators process less information about their problems, devote less time and energy to reevaluating themselves, and experience fewer emotional reactions to the negative aspects of their problems. In therapy, these are the most resistant or the least active clients.

TABLE 1. Titles, Definitions, and Representative Interventions of Eight Processes of Change

Process	Definition: Interventions
1. Consciousness raising	Increasing information about self and problem: observations; confrontations; interpretations; bibliotherapy
2. Self-reevaluation	Assessing how one feels and thinks about oneself with respect to a problem: value clarification; imagery; corrective emotional experience
3. Emotional arousal (or dramatic relief)	Experiencing and expressing feelings about one's problems and solutions: psychodrama; grieving losses; role playing
4. Social liberation	Increasing alternatives for nonproblem behaviors available in society: advocating for rights of repressed; empowering; policy interventions
5. Self-liberation	Choosing and committing to act or belief in ability to change: decision-making therapy; New Year's resolutions; logotherapy techniques; commitment-enchancing technques
6. Counterconditioning	Substituting alternatives for anxiety related behaviors: relaxation; desensitization; assertion; cognitive restructuring
7. Stimulus control	Avoiding or countering stimuli that elicit problem behaviors: restructuring one's environment (e.g., removing alcohol or fattening foods); avoiding high-risk cues; fading techniques
8. Contingency management	Rewarding oneself or being rewarded by others for making changes: contingency contracts; overt and covert reinforcement; self-reward

Source: Adapted from Prochaska, DiClemente, & Norcross, 1992.

Individuals in the contemplation stage are most open to consciousness-raising techniques, such as observations, confrontations, and interpretations, and are much more likely to use bibliotherapy and other educational techniques. Contemplators also profitably employ emotional arousal, which raises emotions and leads to a lowering of negative affect when the person changes. As individuals became more conscious of themselves and the nature of their problems, they are more likely to reevaluate their values, problems, and themselves both affectively and cognitively.

Both movement from precontemplation to contemplation and movement through the contemplation stage entail increased use of cognitive, affective, and evaluative processes of change. Some of these changes continue during the preparation stage. In addition, individuals in preparation begin to take small steps toward action.

During the action stage, people use higher levels of self-liberation or willpower. They increasingly believe that they have the autonomy to change their lives in key ways. Successful action also entails effective use of behavioral processes, such as counterconditioning and stimulus control, in order to modify the conditional stimuli that frequently prompt relapse. Contingency management also comes into frequent use here.

Successful maintenance builds on each of the processes that came before. Specific preparation for maintenance entails an assessment of the conditions under which a person would be likely to relapse and development of alternative responses for coping with such conditions without resorting to self-defeating defenses and pathological responses. Continuing to apply counterconditioning, stimulus control, and contingency management is most effective when based on the conviction that maintaining change supports a sense of self that is highly valued by oneself and significant others.

9. *Prescribe stage-matched "relationships of choice" as well as "treatments of choice":* Psychotherapists seek to customize or tailor their interpersonal stance to different patients. One way to conceptualize the matter, paralleling the notion of "treatments of choice" in terms of techniques, is how clinicians determine therapeutic "relationships of choice" in terms of interpersonal stances (Norcross, 2002).

The research and clinical consensus on the therapist's stance at different stages can be characterized as follows (Prochaska & Norcross, 2002). With precontemplators often the role is like that of a nurturing parent joining with the resistant youngster who is both drawn to and repelled by the prospects of becoming more independent. With contemplators, the therapist role is akin to a Socratic teacher who encourages clients to achieve their own insights and ideas into their condition. With clients who are in the preparation stage, the stance is more like that of an experienced coach who has been through many crucial matches and can provide a fine game plan or can review the person's own action plan. With clients who are progressing into action and maintenance, the psychotherapist becomes more of a consultant who is available to provide expert advice and support when action is not progressing as smoothly as expected.

10. *Avoid mismatching stages and processes:* A person's stage of change provides proscriptive as well as prescriptive information on treatments of choice. Action-oriented therapies may be quite effective with individuals who are in the preparation or action stages. These same programs may be ineffective or detrimental, however, with individuals in the precontemplation or contemplation stages.

We have observed two frequent mismatches. First, some therapists and self-changers rely primarily on change processes most indicated for the contemplation stage—consciousness raising, self-reevaluation—while they are moving into the action stage. They try to modify behaviors by becoming more aware, a common criticism of classical psychoanalysis: insight alone does not necessarily bring about behavior change. Second, other therapists and self-changers rely primarily on change processes most indicated for the action stage—contingency management, stimulus control, counterconditioning—without the requisite awareness, decision making, and readiness provided in the contemplation and preparation stages. They try to modify behavior without awareness, a common criticism of radical behaviorism: overt action without insight is likely to lead to temporary change.

11. *Think complementarily:* Competing systems of psychotherapy have promulgated purportedly rival processes of change. However, ostensibly contradictory processes become complementary when embedded in the stages of change. While some psychotherapists insist that such theoretical integration is philosophically impossible, our research has consistently documented that ordinary people in their natural environments and psychotherapists in their consultation rooms can be remarkably effective in synthesizing powerful change processes across the stages of change.

References, Readings, & Internet Sites

Cancer Prevention Research Center (home of the transtheoretical model). (n.d.). Home page. Retrieved 2004 from http://www.uri.edu/research/cprc/

DiClemente, C. C. (2003a). *Addiction and change.* New York: Guilford Press.

DiClemente, C. C. (2003b). Motivational interviewing and the stages of change. In W. R. Miller & S. Rollnick (Eds.), *Motivational interviewing* (2nd ed.). New York: Guilford Press.

DiClemente, C. C., Prochaska, J. O., Fairhurst, S. K., Velicer, W. F., Velasquez, M. M., & Rossi, J. S. (1991). The process of smoking cessation: An analysis of precontemplation, contemplation and preparation stages of change. *Journal of Consulting and Clinical Psychology, 59,* 295–304.

McConnaughy, E. A., DiClemente, C. C., Prochaska, J. O., & Velicer, W. F. (1989). Stages of change in psychotherapy: A follow-up report. *Psychotherapy, 26,* 494–503.

McConnaughy, E. A., Prochaska, J. O., & Velicer, W. F. (1983). Stages of change in psychotherapy: Measurement and sample profiles. *Psychotherapy, 20,* 368–375.

Norcross, J. C. (Ed.). (2002). *Psychotherapy relationships that work: Therapist contributions and responsiveness to patient needs.* New York: Oxford University Press.

Norcross, J. C., Mrykalo, M. S., & Blagys, M. D. (2002). *Auld lang syne:* Success predictors, change processes, and self-reported outcomes of New Year's resolvers and nonresolvers. *Journal of Clinical Psychology, 58,* 397–405.

Ockene, J., Ockene, I., & Kristellar, J. (1988). *The coronary artery smoking intervention study.* Worcester: National Heart Lung Blood Institute.

Prochaska, J. O., & DiClemente, C. C. (1983). Stages and processes of self-change in smoking: Toward an integrative model of change. *Journal of Consulting and Clinical Psychology, 5,* 390–395.

Prochaska, J. O., DiClemente, C. C., & Norcross, J. C. (1992). In search of how people change: Applications to addictive behaviors. *American Psychologist, 47,* 1102–1114.

Prochaska, J. O., & Norcross, J. C. (2002). *Systems of psychotherapy: A transtheoretical analysis* (5th ed.). Pacific Grove, CA: Brooks/Cole.

Prochaska, J. O., Norcross, J. C., & DiClemente, C. C. (1995). *Changing for good.* New York: Avon.

Prochaska, J. O., Velicer, W. F., Fava, J. L., Ruggiero, L., Laforge, R. G., Rossi, J. S., et al. (2001). Counselor and stimulus control enhancements of a stage-matched expert system intervention for smokers in a managed care setting. *Preventive Medicine, 32,* 23–32.

Rosen, C. S. (2000). Is the sequencing of change processes by stage consistent across health problems? A meta-analysis. *Health Psychology, 19,* 593–604.

Valasquez, M. M., Maurer, G., Crouch, C., & DiClemente, C. C. (2001). *Group treatment for substance abuse: A stages-of-change therapy manual.* New York: Guilford Press.

Related Topic

Chapter 45, "Systematic Assessment and Treatment Matching"

47 PSYCHOTHERAPY TREATMENT PLAN WRITING

Arthur E. Jongsma, Jr.

HISTORICAL BACKGROUND

Over the past 30 years, formalized treatment planning has gradually become a vital aspect of the entire health care delivery system, whether it is treatment related to physical health, mental health, child welfare, or substance abuse. What started in the medical sector in the 1960s spread into the mental health sector in the 1970s as clinics, psychiatric hospitals, agencies, and others began to seek accreditation from bodies such as the Joint Commission on Accreditation of Healthcare Organizations (JCAHO) to qualify for third-party reimbursements. To achieve accreditation, most treatment providers had to develop or strengthen their documentation skills in the area of treatment planning. Previously, most mental health and substance abuse treatment providers had, at best, a rudimentary plan that looked similar for most of the individuals they treated. As a result, patients often were uncertain as to what they were trying to attain in psychiatric treatment. Goals were vague, objectives were nonexistent, and interventions were applied equally to all patients. Outcome criteria were not measurable, and neither the patient nor the treatment provider knew exactly when treatment was completed.

Treatment planning has gained even greater importance since the coming of managed care in the 1980s. Managed care systems insist that clinicians move rapidly from assessment of the problem to the formulation and implementation of the treatment plan. The purpose of managed care organizations' emphasis on early treatment planning is to move the patient to focus on progressing toward change as soon as possible. Treatment plans must be specific as to the problems and interventions, individualized to meet the patient's needs and goals, and measurable in terms of setting milestones that can be used to chart the patient's progress. Pressure from third-party payers, accrediting agencies, and other outside parties has therefore increased the need for clinicians to produce effective, high-quality treatment plans in a short time frame. However, the pressure on clinicians from these outside sources to produce individualized treatment plans has brought with it several concomitant rewards.

TREATMENT PLAN UTILITY

Detailed, written treatment plans can benefit not only the patient, therapist, treatment team, insurance community, and treatment agency but also the overall psychotherapy profession. The patient is served by a written plan because it stipulates the issues that are the focus of the treatment process. It is very easy for both provider and patient to lose sight of what the issues were that brought the patient into therapy. The treatment plan is a guide that structures what the therapeutic contract is meant to focus on. Although issues can change as therapy progresses, the treatment plan must be viewed as a dynamic document that can and must be updated to reflect any major change of problem, definition, goal, objective, or intervention.

Patients and therapists benefit as a result of the treatment plan forcing both to think about therapy outcomes. Behaviorally stated, measurable objectives clearly focus the treatment endeavor. Patients no longer have to wonder what therapy is trying to accomplish. Clear objectives also allow the patient to channel effort into specific changes that will lead to the long-term goal of problem resolution. Therapy is no longer a vague contract to just talk honestly and openly about emotions and thoughts until the patient feels better. Both patient and therapist are concentrating on specifically stated objectives using specific interventions.

Providers are aided by treatment plans because they force them to think analytically and critically about therapeutic interventions that are best suited for objective attainment for specific patients. Therapists were traditionally trained to "follow the patient," but now a formalized plan is the guide to the treatment process. The therapist must give advance attention to the technique, approach, assignment, or cathartic target that will form the basis for interventions.

Clinicians benefit from clear documentation of treatment that becomes a part of the permanent record because it provides added protection against a disgruntled patient's litigation. Malpractice suits are increasing in frequency, and insurance premiums are soaring. The first line of defense against allegations is a complete clinical record that includes detail regarding the treatment process. A written, individualized, formal treatment plan that is the guideline for the therapeutic process, has been reviewed and signed by the patient, and is coupled with problem-oriented progress notes is a powerful defense against exaggerated or false claims.

A well-crafted, problem-focused treatment plan that clearly stipulates intervention strategies facilitates and guides the treatment process that must be carried out by all team members in an inpatient, residential, or intensive outpatient setting. Good communication between team members is critical about what approach is being implemented and who is responsible for each intervention. Team meetings to discuss patient treatment used to be the only communication approach, and often therapeutic conclusions or assignments were not recorded. Now a thorough treatment plan stipulates in writing the details of objectives and the varied interventions (pharmacological, milieu, group therapy, didactic, recreational, individual therapy, etc.) and who will implement them.

Every treatment agency or institution is constantly looking for ways to increase the quality and uniformity of the documentation in the clinical record. A standardized, written treatment plan with problem definitions, goals, objectives, and interventions in every patient's file enhances that uniformity of documentation. This uniformity eases the task of record reviewers inside and outside the agency. Outside reviewers, such as the JCAHO, insist on documentation that clearly outlines assessment, treatment, progress, and discharge status.

The demand for accountability from third-party payers and HMOs is partly satisfied by a written treatment plan and complete progress notes. More and more managed care systems are demanding a structured therapeutic contract that has measurable objectives and explicit interventions. Clinicians cannot avoid this move toward being accountable to those outside the treatment process.

The psychotherapy profession stands to benefit from the use of more precise, measurable objectives to evaluate success in mental health treatment. Outcome data can be more easily collected regarding interventions that are effective in achieving specific objectives. Comparisons between different treatment strategies involving various objectives and interventions will be possible by clinicians and researchers. Treatment planning computer software has been published that assists in creating a treatment plan but also tracks patients' progress, analyzing and graphing outcome data (Jongsma, Peterson, & McInnis, 1997).

HOW TO DEVELOP A TREATMENT PLAN

The process of developing a treatment plan involves a logical series of steps that build on each other much as one would construct a house.

The foundation of any effective treatment plan is the data gathered in a thorough biopsychosocial assessment. When the patient presents for treatment, the clinician must sensitively listen to and understand the patient's struggles in terms of family of origin issues, current stressors, emotional status, social network, physical health, coping skills, interpersonal conflicts, self-esteem, and so on. Assessment data may be gathered from a social history, physical exam, clinical interview, psychological testing, behavioral observations, or contact with a patient's significant others. The integration of all this information by the clinician or members of the multidisciplinary treatment team is a critical first step in arriving at an understanding of the patient and the focus of the patient's struggle. From this clinical formulation should evolve a list of problems that form the structure around which a treatment plan is created. An accurate and complete assessment of the nature of the patient's problems will provide focus in developing a specific treatment plan (Scholing, Emmelkamp, & Van Oppen, 1996). The development of the treatment plan from the integrated biopsychosocial assessment data is a six-step process.

Step One: Problem Selection

The problem list is like the structural beams that support the framework of a house under construction. Although the patient may discuss a variety of issues during the assessment, the clinician must ferret out the most significant problems on which to focus the treatment process. Usually a primary problem will surface, and additional secondary problems will also be evident. Some other problems may have to be set aside as not urgent enough to require treatment at this time. An effective treatment plan can deal with only a few selected problems or treatment will lose its direction.

As the problems to be selected become clear to the clinician or the treatment team, it is important to include opinions from the patient about his or her prioritization of issues for which he or she seeks help. A patient's motivation to participate in and cooperate with an eventual treatment process will depend somewhat on the degree to which treatment addresses his or her greatest needs.

Step Two: Problem Definition

The problem definition is similar to the specifications of what the structural beams are made of. Each individual patient presents with unique behavioral manifestations of the problem. Therefore, each problem that is selected for treatment focus requires a specific definition of how it is evidenced in this particular patient. The symptom pattern should be associated with diagnostic criteria and codes such as those found in *DSM-IV* or the *ICD-9*.

Step Three: Goal Development

The goals represent the rendering of what the finished house will look like. Setting broad goals for the resolution of the target problem is the next step in the treatment plan development process. These statements need not be crafted in measurable terms but can be global, long-term goals that indicate a desired positive outcome to the treatment procedures. One goal statement for each problem is all that is required in a treatment plan.

Step Four: Objective Construction

The objectives are like the building materials (the bricks, mortar, studs, and drywall) of the house under construction—the elements necessary to achieve the final product. In contrast to long-term goals, objectives must be stated in behaviorally measurable language. It must be clear when the patient has achieved the established objectives; therefore, vague, subjective objectives are not acceptable. Review agencies (e.g., JCAHO), HMOs, and managed care organizations insist that psychological treatment outcome be more measurable, so objectives must be crafted to meet this demand for accountability. The clinician must exercise professional judgment regarding which objectives are most appropriate for a given patient.

Each objective should be developed as a step toward attaining the broad treatment goal. In essence, objectives can be thought of as a series of steps that, when completed, will result in the achievement of the long-term goal. There should be at least two objectives for each problem, but the therapist should construct as many as necessary for goal achievement. New objectives should be added to the plan as the individual's treatment progresses. When all the necessary objectives have been achieved, the patient should have resolved the target problem successfully and achieved the treatment goal. Additional accountability is required as reviewers demand that target attainment dates be assigned to each objective. This is an attempt to shorten and focus the counseling process because the emphasis is on brief symptom resolution rather than personality change or personal growth.

Step Five: Intervention Creation

Interventions represent the creative skills of the architect—the tools of the trade—that guide the building process. Interventions are the actions of the clinician to help the patient complete the objectives. The clinician may choose from cognitive, dynamic, behavioral, pharmacological, family treatment, or solution-focused brief therapeutic interventions. There should be at least one intervention for every objective. New interventions should be added as the original interventions have been implemented but the patient has not yet accomplished the objective. Addition of new interventions and objectives to promote treatment success is especially appropriate given the recent trend toward a patient's progression through various levels of a continuum of care in mental health and substance abuse programs. The clinical skills of the provider are tested as therapeutic intervention strategies must be created to assist the patient in achieving the objectives. Treatment planning books are available that provide a menu of concise suggestions for behavioral definitions of problems, long-term goals, short-term objectives, as well as therapeutic interventions (Jongsma & Peterson, 1995; Jongsma, Peterson, & McInnis, 1996). Treatment plan resources that are more general and theoretically based are also available (e.g., Gabbard, 1995). The therapeutic approach of the clinician will influence what type of intervention statements are written.

Assigning interventions to a specific provider is most relevant if the patient is being treated by a team in an inpatient, residential, or intensive outpatient setting. Within these settings, personnel other than the primary clinician may be responsible for implementing a specific intervention. Review agencies require that stipulation of the provider's name be attached to every intervention if the patient is being treated by a multidisciplinary team.

Step Six: Diagnosis Determination

The determination of an appropriate diagnosis is based on an evaluation of the patient's complete clinical presentation. The clinician must compare the behavioral, cognitive, emotional, and interpersonal symptoms that the patient presents to the criteria for diagnosis of a mental illness condition as described in the *DSM-IV.* The issue of differential diagnosis is admittedly a difficult one that research has shown to have rather low interrater reliability. Psychologists have also been trained to think more in terms of maladaptive behavior than in terms of disease labels. In spite of these factors, diagnosis is a reality that exists in the world of mental health care, and it is a necessity for third-party reimbursement. (However, recently, managed care agencies have become more interested in behavioral indices that are exhibited by the patient than in the actual diagnosis.) It is the clinician's thorough knowledge of *DSM-IV* criteria and a complete understanding of the patient assessment data that contribute to the most reliable, valid diagnosis. An accurate assessment of behavioral indicators will also contribute to more effective treatment planning.

One final but important aspect of an effective treatment plan is that it must be designed to deal with each individual patient specifically. Treatment plans, like quality homes, are not to be mass-produced with the same plan applied to all patients, even if they have similar problems. The individual's strengths and weaknesses, unique stressors, social network, family circumstances, and symptom pattern must be considered in developing a treatment strategy (Axelrod, Spreat, Berry, & Moyer, 1993). A treatment plan that takes into account the uniqueness of the patient's dynamics, traits, and circumstances will stand a greater chance of producing a satisfactory, measurable outcome in a shorter time frame.

Note: This chapter was adapted from Introduction, in A. E. Jongsma & L. M. Peterson, *The Complete Psychotherapy Treatment Planner* (New York: Wiley, 1995), pp. 1–7. Reprinted with permission.

References & Readings

Axelrod, S., Spreat, S., Berry, B., & Moyer, L. (1993). A decision-making model for selecting the optimal treatment procedure. In R. Van Houten and S. Axelrod (Eds.), *Behavior analysis and treatment: Applied clinical psychology* (pp. 183–202). New York: Plenum Press.

Gabbard, G. O. (1995). *Treatment of psychiatric disorders* (2nd ed., Vols. 1 & 2). Washington, DC: American Psychiatric Press.

Jongsma, A. E., Jr., & Peterson, L. M. (1995). *The complete psychotherapy treatment planner.* New York: Wiley.

Jongsma, A. E., Jr., Peterson, L. M., & McInnis, W. P. (1996). *The child and adolescent psychotherapy treatment planner.* New York: Wiley.

Jongsma, A. E., Jr., Peterson, L. M., & McInnis, W. P. (1997). TheraScribe 3.0: The computerized assistant to psychotherapy treatment planning (Version 3.0) [Computer software]. New York: Wiley.

Scholing, A., Emmelkamp, P. M., & Van Oppen, P. (1996). Cognitive-behavioral treatment of social phobia. In V. B. Van Hasselt & M. Hersen (Eds.), *Sourcebook of psychological treatment manuals for adult disorders* (pp. 123–177). New York: Plenum Press.

Related Topics

Chapter 46, "Stages of Change: Prescriptive Guidelines

Chapter 76, "Choice of Treatment Format"

Chapter 130, "Utilization Review Checklist"

48 KEY PRINCIPLES IN THE ASSESSMENT OF PSYCHOTHERAPY OUTCOME

Michael J. Lambert, Bruce W. Jasper, & Joanne White

Psychotherapists have a scientific and ethical responsibility to learn whether they are providing helpful services to their clients. Effective outcome assessment can let clinicians know whether individual clients are deteriorating, remaining unchanged, or recovering and can improve the effectiveness of treatment. Although more and more therapists are employing outcome measures in their practices, most clinicians do not yet objectively assess psychotherapy outcome in routine practice (Hatfield & Ogles, in press).

The recent movement toward measuring the effects of therapy on individual clients (so-called patient-focused research) provides a strategy for clinicians who want to enhance client outcomes. This strategy involves using session-by-session outcome to inform individual therapy in real time. When outcome assessment is used in real time it can enhance the treatment of the persons who complete the outcome measure.

This chapter summarizes the key principles involved in (1) selecting potentially useful measures and (2) using outcome data to enhance routine practice.

SELECTING POTENTIALLY USEFUL MEASURES

The following principles of selecting measures attempt to strike a balance between what is practical for the everyday clinician and what is scientifically necessary in order to obtain useful outcome data.

1. *Select a brief measure (5-10 minutes) that can be easily administered and scored by clerical staff or computer:* Practical concerns in routine practice demand that outcome assessment be painless and resource effective (e.g., money, time, and energy). Most clinicians who are assessing client outcome are using brief self-report measures. Outcome measures have been developed that can be completed by the client, a parent/guardian/spouse, the therapist, or an independent judge. However, because it is usually feasible to obtain only one perspective, in the case of an adult, a self-report measure is ideal and in the case of a child/adolescent a parent-report measure is recommended. Additionally, it should be kept in mind that instruments and methods useful for diagnostic purposes and treatment planning are unsuitable for the purpose of measuring patient change (Vermeersch, Lambert, & Burlingame, 2000). Symptom-focused measures are most likely to reflect improvement and are therefore highly recommended. Literally hundreds of measures are available for use. We recommend the Brief Symptom Inventory (available at http://assessments/tests/bsi.htm), a shortened version of the Symptom Checklist-90-R that focuses on a wide variety of symptoms. The Short Form-36 Health Survey (http://www.sf-36.com) is also a promising measure for adults. The Outcome Questionnaire-45 (http://www.oqfamily.com) is growing in popularity. It measures symptoms, interpersonal functioning, social role performance, and quality of life, and has been shown to be sensitive to treatment effects. For children, the Ohio Youth Problems, Functioning, and Satisfaction Scales (http://oak.cats.ohiou.edu/ogles) or the Youth Outcome Questionnaire (http://www.oqfamily.com/) appear to be especially promising because they are relatively short, sensitive to change, and available in parent-, self-, and other-report formats.
2. *Use caution if you tailor the change criteria to the individual in therapy:* Tailoring change criteria with individualized goals for a particular patient has been advocated because it is likely to provide evidence for efficacy. The use of individualized change measures enables the therapist to assess change from an idiographic and multifaceted perspective, which is consistent with the wide range of problems presented by an individual (e.g., Persons, 1991). However, such change criteria are often poorly defined, subjective in nature, and have little credibility. The amount of change reflected by such measures is often overly dependent on the therapist's judgments. On the other hand, in difficult-to-treat individuals, idiographic change criteria may be a necessary addition to standardized outcome measures. Such individuals abound in residential, geriatric, severely mentally ill, or neuropsychologically impaired populations that may be atypically responsive or appear to be nonresponsive on standard measures.
3. *Make sure the measure covers broad, yet crucial, content areas:* The three broad areas to be assessed are the subjective state of the client (intrapersonal functioning, including

behavior, affect, and cognition), the state of the client's intimate relationships (interpersonal functioning), and the state of the individual's participation in the community (social role performance). Both symptomatic change and functioning are important, if not essential, targets for outcome assessment. A compendium of suitable measures has been edited by Maruish (2004).

4. *Select measures that can detect clinically meaningful change:* Methods have been developed to set standards for clinically meaningful client change (Jacobson & Truax, 1991). The clinical significance methodology provides for the calculation of two specific statistical indexes: a cutoff point between normal and dysfunctional samples and an evaluation of the reliability of the change score. These indexes provide specific cut scores for interpreting the importance of observed scores and some existing measures provide such guidelines. When they are not available, however, the clinician can consult the work of Jacobson for the formulas for establishing a cutoff score, as well as a reliable change index.

USING OUTCOME DATA TO ENHANCE ROUTINE PRACTICE

Once an outcome measure is selected, it is best to have it completed prior to treatment (even an intake interview can provide relief to the client and such relief is important to record). It is also important to gather data on a session-by-session basis; this ensures that there will be at least one measure of change, provided that the client has a second appointment. Since many patients improve rapidly, and most attend few sessions, delaying the second assessment is likely to result in underestimating treatment benefits or failing to gather any outcome data.

The initial assessment can be used to (1) determine the client's incoming symptom severity and forming an opinion about expected length of treatment, (2) highlight possible target symptoms seen at the individual item level, and (3) identify particular strengths that might be capitalized on. For example, the measure(s) you select will have several "critical" items that you may want to routinely examine (e.g., "I have thoughts of ending my life"; "I have people around me that I can turn to for support").

The most important aspect of tracking change after the initial assessment is assessing whether client scores tend to increase, stay the same, or decrease in relation to the intake score. Research demonstrates that early positive response to treatment foretells final success, while negative change foretells final failure (Haas, Hill, Lambert, & Morrell, 2002). In any case, until the client's functioning is within the normal range, some kind of treatment is needed. Many clinicians find it helpful to graphically display client data across time or sessions in order to better visualize score changes and general trends. If a client's scores worsen after beginning treatment, then the clinician can consider the causes and possibly modify treatment (e.g., more frequent sessions, medication referral, change in treatment focus). On the other hand, if the client's scores indicate improvement and a return to normal functioning, the focus of treatment could shift to preparing the client for termination and maintenance. The specific details of what to do in the individual cases vary and are up to the treating clinician and the client.

One might ask how much a client's score needs to change in order to be considered meaningful. Although clinicians can try to rely on personal methods of detecting significant change, standardized methods are available to better serve clinicians and clients. As already noted, these methods operationalize meaningful change so clinicians can know how much a client's score must change in order to be considered clinically significant. If a client's score changes by at least the amount of the Reliable Change Index (RCI; individually calculated for the particular instrument being used), then the client is considered to have reliably changed, becoming symptomatically worse or better. However, reliable change by itself cannot be equated with recovery. For example, a client's score may change in the amount of the RCI and still be in the dysfunctional range. If, however, a client's score (1) moves from the dysfunctional range to the functional range and (2) the amount of change is equal to or greater than the RCI, then the client is considered to have made clinically significant improvement, sometimes labeled recovery. Ogles, Lambert, and Fields (2002) have listed cutoff scores and Reliable Change Indices (RCIs) for some of the most commonly used measures, such as the SCL-90R, BDI, and CBCL.

Another way to use session-by-session data to enhance treatment outcome is to compare a client's treatment response to a typical or expected treatment response. By comparing a client's symptom course to the average symptom course among others that have the same initial assessment score, you can know if they are progressing as "expected." Although this technique is more specific than relying on RCIs and cutoff scores, it is not yet readily available for most outcome measures. Nevertheless, such data help to inform clinicians if the client is responding faster or slower than similar clients. Psychotherapy research investigating this method is promising and will probably become widely available for use in routine practice. The interested reader can consult other sources (Lambert et al., 2002; Ogles et al., 2002; Whipple et al., 2003). This research demonstrates that feedback to therapists about potential treatment failure (based on client deviations from expected treatment response) improves outcomes and reduces deterioration for the 20% of clients who are at risk for treatment failure (Lambert et al., 2003). It is our hope that clinicians will continue to improve the quality of their work through systematic assessment of outcomes.

References, Readings, & Internet Sites

Albert Einstein College of Medicine. (n.d.). Testing resources. Retrieved 2004 from http://library.aecom.yu.edu/resources/psychtest

American Psychological Association. (n.d.). Science directorate Web site. Retrieved 2004 from http://www.apa.org/science/faq-findtest.html

Haas, E., Hill, R., Lambert, M. J., & Morrell, B. (2002). Do early responders to psychotherapy maintain treatment gains? *Journal of Clinical Psychology, 58,* 1157–1172.

Hatfield, D. R., & Ogles, B. M. (in press). The current climate of outcome measures used by psychologists in clinical practice. *Professional Psychology: Research and Practice.*

Jacobson, N. S., & Truax, P. (1991). Clinical significance: A statistical approach to defining meaningful change in psychotherapy research. *Journal of Consulting & Clinical Psychology, 59,* 12–19.

Lambert, M. J., Whipple, J. L., Bishop, M. J., Vermeersch, D. A., Gray, G. V., & Finch, A. E. (2002). Comparison of empirically-derived methods for identifying patients at risk for treatment failure. *Clinical Psychology and Psychotherapy, 9,* 149–164.

Lambert, M. J., Whipple, J. L., Hawkins, E. L., Vermeersch, D. A., Nielsen, S. L., & Smart, D. W. (2003). Is it time for clinicians to routinely track patient outcome?: A meta-analysis. *Clinical Psychology: Science and Practice, 10,* 288–301.

Maruish, M. E. (2004). *The use of psychological testing for treatment planning and outcomes assessment* (3rd ed.). Mahwah, NJ: Erlbaum.

Ogles, B. M., Lambert, M. J., & Fields, S. A. (2002). *Essentials of outcome assessment.* New York: Wiley.

Persons, J. B. (1991). Psychotherapy outcome studies do not accurately represent current models of psychotherapy: A proposed remedy. *American Psychologist, 46,* 99–106.

Vermeersch, D. A., Lambert, M. J., & Burlingame, G. M. (2000). Outcome questionnaire: Item sensitivity to change. *Journal of Personality Assessment, 74,* 242–261.

Whipple, J. L., Lambert, M. J., Vermeersch, D. A., Smart, D. W., Nielsen, S. L., & Hawkins, E. J. (2003). Improving the effects of psychotherapy: The use of early identification of treatment failure and problem-solving strategies in routine practice. *Journal of Counseling Psychology, 50,* 59–68.

Related Topics

Chapter 39, "Compendium of Empirically Supported Therapies"

Chapter 40, "Compendium of Psychotherapy Treatment Manuals"

49 TREATMENT AND MANAGEMENT OF THE SUICIDAL PATIENT

Bruce Bongar & Glenn R. Sullivan

Suicide is the most frequently encountered of all mental health emergencies (Beutler, Clarkin, & Bongar, 2000; Schein, 1976), with a typical practicing psychologist treating an average of five suicidal patients per month (Greaney, 1995). Psychologists have a better than a one in five chance of losing a patient to suicide, and student therapists have a one in three chance of experiencing a patient suicide or suicide attempt during their training years (Stolberg, Glassmire, & Bongar, 1999). Psychotherapists consistently rank work with suicidal patients as the most stressful of all clinical endeavors (Deutsch, 1984).

Patient suicide must be considered a real occupational hazard for those clinicians involved in direct patient care (Bongar, Peruzzi, & Greaney, 1997). This hazard entails not only the threat of malpractice action but also an intense emotional toll on both the patient's family and the patient's psychologist. Psychologists respond to the loss of a patient to suicide as they do to the death of a family member (Chemtob, Hamada, Bauer, Torigoe, & Kinney, 1988).

A growing body of evidence suggests that the shift from fee-for-service to managed care has resulted in an erosion of standards of care for the management of suicidal patients. In some instances, this shift has resulted in adverse consequences for patients (Hall, Platt, & Hall, 1999). Hall et al. (1999) found that the criteria used by several managed-care organizations for approving the hospitalization of acutely suicidal patients were unrealistic and not based on accepted scientific standards. It is imperative that clinicians realize that they are legally, ethically, and professionally responsible for determining appropriate patient care. Clinicians must override managed-care decisions that inappropriately restrict patient services if it is necessary to prevent suicide.

GENERAL PRINCIPLES

The mental health professional's assessment and treatment efforts represent an opportunity to translate knowledge (albeit incomplete) of elevated risk factors into a plan of action (Bongar, 2002). The management plan for patients who are at an elevated risk for suicide should ameliorate those risk factors that are most foreseeably likely to result in suicide or self-harm (Brent, Kupfer, Bromet, & Dew, 1988). Several general principles that apply across broad diagnostic categories should guide the treatment of patients at elevated risk for suicide:

- The most basic principle is that, because most suicide victims take their own lives or harm themselves in the midst of a psychiatric episode, it is critical to understand that a proper diagnosis and careful management/treatment plan of the acute psychiatric disorder could dramatically alter the risk for suicide (Brent et al., 1988). The data on adult suicides indicate that more than 90% of these suicide victims were mentally ill before their deaths.
- Special precautions must be taken when assessing and treating patients who present with chronic suicidal ideation and behavior

(i.e., where the clinician takes repeated calculated risks in not hospitalizing). The clinician must weigh the short-term solution of hospitalization against the long-term solution of treating the chronic condition in an outpatient environment.

- Involve the patient's family and support network to maximize adherence to the treatment plan.
- Diagnose and treat any comorbid medical and psychiatric condition(s).
- Focus on the provision of hope, particularly to new-onset patients.
- Because the availability of firearms, especially handguns, plays such a prominent role as the "method of choice" for many completed suicides, the psychologist should assiduously assess the presence of, access to, and knowledge the patient has about this highly lethal means. This also necessitates carefully thinking through the patient's entire life environment and how the patient spends each day, so as to determine proactively the presence of any potentially lethal means (e.g., the hoarding of pills; access to poisons; or whether the patient has a means in mind, such as hanging, jumping from a particular building, or driving the car off the road). Furthermore, it is worth mentioning again that the psychologist must not hesitate to contact others in the life of the patient and enlist their support in the treatment plan.
- Continuously monitor indications for psychiatric hospitalization.
- Clinicians must assess their own technical proficiencies, as well as their emotional tolerance levels for the intense demands required in treating suicidal patients. The mental health professional who is called upon to treat the suicidal patient needs to have already evaluated the strengths and limitations of his or her own training, education, and experience in the treatment of specific patient populations in specific clinical settings. Welch (1989) noted that "the greatest threat to 'quality of care' comes not from those with limited training but from those with a limited recognition of the limitations of their own training" (p. 28).
- Meticulously document every aspect of the patient's care.
- Routinely involve other mental health professionals in evaluation and treatment planning; obtain a "biopsy of the standard of care" through consultation with a senior clinician (Appelbaum & Gutheil, 1991, p. 201).

All of our assessment and management activities also should include a specific evaluation of the patient's competency to participate in management and treatment decisions, especially the patient's ability to form a therapeutic alliance (Bongar, 2002). An essential element in strengthening this alliance is the use of informed consent—that is, patients have the right to participate actively in making decisions about their psychological/psychiatric care. Clinicians need to directly and continuously evaluate the quality of this special relationship—to understand that the quality of this collaborative alliance is inextricably part of any successful treatment/management plan (Bongar, Peterson, Harris, & Aissis, 1989).

RISK ASSESSMENT AND MANAGEMENT

There are common themes in complaints lodged against outpatient therapists, reflecting possible breaches in the duty of care and the practitioner's failure to act in a reasonable and prudent manner. Attention to these "failures" may therefore represent an opportunity to develop appropriate treatment and risk management strategies. The list below, adapted from Bongar, Maris, Berman, and Litman (1992), details the most common failure scenarios in outpatient care.

1. Failure to properly evaluate the need for psychopharmacological intervention, or unsuitable pharmacotherapy.
2. Failure to specify criteria for and to implement hospitalization.
3. Failure to maintain appropriate clinician-patient relationships (e.g., dual relationships and sexual improprieties).
4. Failures in supervision and consultation.
5. Failure to evaluate for suicide risk at intake.

6. Failure to evaluate suicide risk at management transitions.
7. Failure to secure records of prior treatment or inadequate history taking.
8. Failure to conduct a mental status exam.
9. Failure to diagnose.
10. Failure to establish a formal treatment plan.
11. Failure to safeguard the outpatient environment.
12. Failure to adequately document clinical judgments, rationales, and observations.

The consultation model operationalized by Bongar (2002) seeks to optimize clinical, legal, and ethical standards of care for suicidal patients. The model first emphasizes the importance of developing a strong therapeutic alliance, facilitated via informed consent procedures at treatment initiation. The informed consent procedure should begin an ongoing process of information-giving and collaboration with the client. By involving patients and their families, when appropriate, as "collaborative risk management partners" (Bongar, 2002, p. 232), cooperation with treatment is improved, the protective net is widened, responses to treatment are more closely monitored, and the quality and quantity of available data are improved.

Second, the model emphasizes the importance of routinely seeking professional consultations from colleagues, particularly ones who are senior clinicians and/or have forensic expertise. These consultants should be retained professionally and given sufficient information to provide reasonable advice, and their advice should be carefully recorded in the psychologist's records. This written record is necessary in order for the consultation to be legally recognized and unquestioned (Bongar, 2002).

Although the following list of discussion points is not exhaustive, it does suggest the sort of specific questions that could be discussed with a consultant when treating the suicidal patient. These include reviewing:

1. The overall management of the case, specific treatment issues, uncertainties in the assessment of elevated risk or in diagnosis. This can include a review of the mental status examination, history, information from significant others, the results of any psychological tests and data from risk estimators, suicide lethality scales, and so on; also, a review of the psychologist's formulation of the patient's *DSM-IV* diagnosis, together with any other specific psychotherapeutic formulations, clinical assessments, and evaluation of any special treatment and management issues (e.g., comorbidity of alcohol/substance abuse, physical illness).
2. Issues of managing the patient with chronically suicidal behavior, violent behavior, patient dependency, patient hostility and manipulation, toxic interpersonal matrices, lack of psychosocial supports, and the patient's competency to participate in treatment decisions, along with an assessment of the quality of the therapeutic alliance and the patient's particular response to the psychologist and to the course of treatment (e.g., intense negative or positive transference).
3. The psychologist's own feelings about the progress of treatment and feelings toward the patient (e.g., the psychologist's own feelings of fear, incompetency, anxiety, helplessness, or even anger) and any therapeutic reactions such as negative countertransference or therapist burnout.
4. The advisability of using medication or need for additional medical evaluation (e.g., any uncertainties as to organicity or neurological complications); also, a request for a reevaluation of any current medications that the patient is taking (e.g., effectiveness, compliance in taking medication, side effects, polypharmacy).
5. The indications and contraindications for hospitalization; a review of available community crisis intervention resources for the patient with few psychosocial supports; day treatment options; emergency and backup arrangements and resources; and, planning for the psychologist's absences.
6. Indications and contraindications for family and group treatment; indications and contraindications for other types of psychotherapy and somatic interventions; questions on the status of and progress in the integration of multiple therapeutic techniques.

7. The psychologist's assessment criteria for evaluating dangerousness and imminence (e.g., does the consultant agree with the clinician's assessment of the level of perturbation and lethality?); review of specifics of patient's feelings of despair, depression, hopelessness, impulsivity, cognitive constriction, and impulses toward cessation.
8. The issues of informed consent and confidentiality, and the adequacy of all current documentation on the case (e.g., intake notes, progress notes, utilization reviews, family meetings, supervisor notes, telephone contacts).
9. Whether the consultant agrees with the psychologist's current risk-benefit analysis and management plan in particular. Does the consultant agree that the dual issues of foreseeability and the need to take affirmative precautions have been adequately addressed? (Bongar, 2002, pp. 239–240).

SUMMARY GUIDELINES

We believe that the following steps constitute a set of standards that will ensure the highest level of professional treatment for the benefit of the patients under our care, suicidal patients in particular.

1. *Evaluation and assessment*. For each patient seen as part of a clinician's professional practice activities, there must be an initial evaluation and assessment, regular ongoing clinical evaluations and case reviews, consultation reports and supervision reports (where indicated), and a formal treatment plan. All of these activities need to demonstrate specifically a solid understanding of the significant factors used to assess elevated risk of suicide and how to manage such risk—with a documented understanding of the prognosis for the success (or possible paths to failure) of subsequent outpatient (or inpatient) treatment or case disposition.
2. *Documentation*. Clinicians must be aware of the vital importance of the written case record. In cases of malpractice, courts and juries often have been observed to operate on the simplistic principle that "if it isn't written down, it didn't happen" (no matter what the subsequent testimony or elaboration of the defendant maintains). Defensive clinical notes, written after the fact, may help somewhat in damage control, but there is no substitute for a timely, thoughtful, and complete chart record that demonstrates (through clear and well-written assessment, review, and treatment notes) a knowledge of the epidemiology, risk factors, and treatment literature for the suicidal patient. Such a case record should also include (where possible) a formal informed consent for treatment, formal assessment of competence, and a documentation of confidentiality considerations (e.g., that limits were explained at the start of any treatment).
3. *Information on previous treatment*. Clinicians must obtain, whenever possible, all previous treatment records, and consult with past psychotherapists. When appropriate, they should involve the family and significant others in the management or disposition plan.
4. *Consultation on present clinical circumstances*. Clinicians should routinely obtain consultation and/or supervision (or make referrals) on all cases where suicide risk is determined to be even moderate and after a patient suicide or serious suicide attempt. They also should obtain consultation and/or supervision on (or refer) cases that are outside their documented training, education, or experience, as well as when they are unsure of the best avenue for initiating or continuing treatment. The principle that two perspectives are better than one should guide the clinician in moments of clinical uncertainty.
5. *Sensitivity to medical issues*. Clinicians should be knowledgeable about the effects of psychotropic medication and make appropriate referrals for a medication evaluation. If the clinician decides that medication is not indicated in the present instance, he or she should thoroughly document the reasoning for this decision in the written case record. Where appropriate, the patient (and, when it is indicated, the patient's family or significant others) also should be included in this

decision-making process. Clinicians also need to know the possible organic etiologies for suicidality and seek immediate appropriate medical consultation for the patient when they detect any signs of an organic condition.

6. *Knowledge of community resources.* Clinicians who see suicidal patients should have access to the full armamentarium of resources for voluntary and involuntary hospital admissions, day treatment, 24-hour emergency backup, and crisis centers. This access can be direct or indirect (through an ongoing collaborative relationship with a psychologist or psychiatrist colleague).
7. *Consideration of the effect on self and others.* If a patient succeeds in committing suicide (or makes a serious suicide attempt), clinicians should be aware not only of their legal responsibilities (e.g., they must notify their insurance carrier in a timely fashion) but, more important, of the immediate clinical necessity of attending to both the needs of the bereaved survivors and to the clinician's own emotional needs. (The clinician must acknowledge that it is both normal and difficult to work through feelings about a patient's death or near-death and that he or she, having lost a patient to suicide, is also a suicide survivor.) The concern should be for the living. After consultation with a knowledgeable colleague and an attorney, immediate clinical outreach to the survivors is not only sensitive and concerned clinical care, but in helping the survivors to deal with the catastrophic aftermath via an effective clinical postvention effort, the clinician is also practicing effective risk management.
8. *Preventative preparation.* Most important, clinicians must be cognizant of the above standards and take affirmative steps to ensure that they have the requisite knowledge, training, experience, and clinical resources prior to accepting high-risk patients into their professional care. This requires that all of these mechanisms be in place before the onset of any suicidal crisis (Bongar, 2002, pp. 259–261).

Note: Portions of this chapter are adapted from Bruce Bongar, *The Suicidal Patient: Clinical and Legal Standards of Care,* 2nd edition (Washington, DC: American Psychological Association, 2002). Reprinted with permission.

References & Readings 

Appelbaum, P. S., & Gutheil, T. G. (1991). *Clinical handbook of psychiatry and the law* (2nd ed.). Baltimore: Williams & Williams.

Beutler, L. E., Clarkin, J. F., & Bongar, B. (2000). *Guidelines for the systematic treatment of the depressed patient.* New York: Oxford University Press.

Bongar, B. (2002). *The suicidal patient: Clinical and legal standards of care* (2nd ed.). Washington, DC: American Psychological Association.

Bongar, B., Maris, R. W., Berman, A. L., & Litman, R. E. (1992). Outpatient standards of care and the suicidal patient. *Suicide and Life Threatening Behaviors, 22,* 453–478.

Bongar, B., Peruzzi, N., & Greaney, S. (1997). Risk management with the suicidal patient. In P. Kleespies (Ed.), *Emergencies in mental health practice* (pp. 199–216). New York: Guilford Press.

Bongar, B., Peterson, L. G., Harris, E. A., & Aissis, J. (1989). Clinical and legal considerations in the management of suicidal patients: An integrative overview. *Journal of Integrative and Eclectic Psychotherapy, 8,* 53–67.

Brent, D. A., Kupfer, D. J., Bromet, E. J., & Dew, M. A. (1988). The assessment and treatment of patients at risk for suicide. In A. J. Frances & R. E. Hales (Eds.), *American Psychiatric Press Review of Psychiatry, Vol. 7* (pp. 353–385). Washington, DC: American Psychiatric Press.

Chemtob, C. M., Hamada, R. S., Bauer, G. B., Torigoe, R. Y., & Kinney, B. (1988). Patient suicide: Frequency and impact on psychologists. *Professional Psychology: Research and Practice, 19,* 416–420.

Deutsch, C. J. (1984). Self-report sources of stress among psychotherapists. *Professional Psychology: Research and Practice, 15,* 833–845.

Greaney, S. (1995). *Psychologists' behavior and attitudes when working with the non-hospitalized suicidal patient.* Unpublished doctoral dissertation, Pacific Graduate School of Psychology, Palo Alto, California.

Hall, R. C. W., Platt, D. E., & Hall, R. C. W. (1999). Suicide risk assessment: A review of risk factors for suicide in 100 patients who made severe suicide attempts: Evaluation of suicide risk in a time of managed care. *Psychosomatics, 40,* 18–27.

Maltsberger, J. T., & Goldblatt, M. J. (Eds.). (1996). *Essential papers on suicide.* New York: New York University Press.

Schein, H. M. (1976). Obstacles in the education of psychiatric residents. *Omega, 7,* 75–82.

Stolberg, R. R., Glassmire, D. M., & Bongar, B. (1999). *The effect of a patient suicide on student therapists.* Poster presented at the 107th Convention of the American Psychological Association, Boston, August.

Welch, B. (1989). A collaborative model proposed. *American Psychological Association Monitor, 20,* 28.

Related Topic

Chapter 14, "Assessment of Suicidal Risk"

50 CRISIS INTERVENTION

Kenneth France

1. *Clients who need crisis intervention:* A crisis exists when a person's usual coping methods fail to successfully handle current pressures and the individual feels overwhelmed by seemingly unresolvable difficulties. Finding oneself in crisis usually results in new coping efforts (Folkman, Lazarus, Dunkel-Schetter, DeLongis, & Gruen, 1986), which may include actions such as contacting a psychologist. A person reaching out in this way is desperate for an end to the stress and is likely to welcome the professional's crisis intervention assistance (Halpern, 1973, 1975). Together they work in a problem-solving alliance that draws on the client's knowledge and experience to forge the beginnings of an adaptive resolution. Empirical research has demonstrated that crisis intervention can result in client benefits such as decreased anxiety, depression, confusion, anger, and helplessness, as well as improved performance in career and family roles (Bunn & Clarke, 1979; Capone, Westie, Chitwood, Feigenbaum, & Good, 1979; Viney, Clarke, Bunn, & Benjamin, 1985; Koocher, Curtiss, Pollin, & Patton, 2001).

2. *Clients who need emergency mental health intervention:* An emergency is a life-threatening or other potentially catastrophic situation in which immediate action is necessary in order to rescue those at risk. Sometimes the situation involves a person who has struggled in crisis for so long that he or she is now withdrawing from the world either voluntarily (through contemplated suicide) or involuntarily (through personality disorganization). For psychologists, however, it is more common to encounter a patient who has a long history of emotional difficulties and who is again showing behaviors that have been problematic in the past. In either of these cases, the goal of an emergency mental health intervention is to arrange an appropriate disposition, which may involve the imposition of a solution (such as involuntary hospitalization and treatment).

3. *Choosing between crisis intervention and emergency mental health intervention:* Crisis intervention is appropriate if the person is in crisis and is able to participate in logical problem solving. Emergency mental health intervention is necessary when active guidance and assertive decision making by the psychologist are required to decrease imminent danger. Making the right choice between these two options is crucial. Individuals in crisis who are simply told what to do often fail to implement the suggestion. Consequently, emergency mental health intervention is inappropriate for most persons in crisis. Likewise, problem solving does not work with someone who is incapable of rational decision making. Thus, crisis intervention is doomed to failure with such individuals.

4. *Making the most of the time you have:* In a 50-minute session, you must make an early decision as to whether you should employ crisis intervention or emergency mental health intervention. If emergency mental health intervention is your choice, then the session's activities may involve the following: determining appropriate diagnoses; surveying previous treatment; exploring issues related to suicidal/homicidal danger, availability of support, and level of cooperation; and securing necessary authorizations from service gatekeepers. When you choose crisis intervention, there may be some exploration relating to danger and suicide lethality, but the majority of the time will be spent in collaborative problem solving.

5. *Characteristics of crises:* A crisis is precipitated by an identifiable event that overwhelms the person's ability to cope. We all encounter such distressing episodes, so crises are a normal part of being human. Because each of us has our own personal values and perspectives, what causes a crisis for one person may not bother another individual. There also can be pronounced differences among those who are in crisis. Some may fall into coping characterized by repression, denial, distortion, cognitive restriction, drug and alcohol abuse, or physical difficulties. Others may strive for accurate understanding, acceptance, gradual progress, and optimism. But one way or another, most crises are resolved within a matter of weeks. In the minority of instances in which that is not the case, the person eventually may be at risk for suicide or personality disorganization.

6. *The philosophy of crisis intervention:* The minimum goal in crisis intervention is restoration of the previous level of functioning. The optimal goal is for the crisis to become a learning experience that leaves the person better able to cope with future pressures. Positive outcomes are more likely when intervention is immediately available. Although the response from the psychologist is an active one, all efforts recognize and use the client's abilities. As a secondary prevention activity, crisis intervention catches the difficulties in their early stages, thereby decreasing the episode's duration and severity. Such progress is brought about by engaging the individual in a problem-solving process.

7. *Problem solving:* The central endeavor in crisis intervention is problem solving. Although there are many approaches to this activity, one strategy is to think of it as involving three phases: exploring thoughts and feelings, considering alternatives, and developing a plan (France, 2002). And while a variety of communication styles can be effective, the use of reflection, along with a judicious number of open-ended questions, tends to be beneficial. (Open questions usually begin with the word *what* or *how*. Reflection involves using new words to summarize central ideas and emotions communicated by the other person.)

8. *Exploring thoughts and feelings:* During this phase of problem solving, the task is for the client and the psychologist to develop a joint understanding of the issues confronting the person and the emotions associated with those topics. Specific events should be discussed in conjunction with the related feelings, so that a shared view develops as to how the crisis came about and what has been happening. As long as new material continues to emerge, the exploration phase should continue. It ends with agreement on three areas: the nature of the distressing circumstances, how the person is feeling about them, and what changes the individual desires.

9. *Considering alternatives:* Once there is an understanding of the issues, the interaction moves to deciding what to do about them. The goal of this phase is to identify and consider two or three solid options. One tactic for generating these possibilities is to explore three questions: What has the client already tried? What has the client thought about doing? And, right now as you are talking, what other ideas can the client generate? (Only after strongly pulling for options from the client would it be appropriate for the crisis intervener to make a suggestion.) When exploring in detail a promising possibility, have the client consider the likely positive and negative consequences associated with that option. This phase ends with agreement on an approach, or a combination of approaches, that can become the person's plan.

10. *Developing a plan:* The one absolute requirement of an initial crisis intervention contact is the development of a plan that has four characteristics. The plan is collaboratively created rather than dictated by the psychologist (Deci & Ryan, 1987); it focuses on current issues, and there are aspects of it that the client can begin working on the same day or the next day; it involves specific tasks that have been thought through; and it is likely, not just possible, that the individual will carry out those tasks. Once a negotiated, present-focused, concrete, and realistic plan has been developed, the client should review its major components. Clarify any misunderstandings or ambiguities that become apparent, and arrange a subsequent contact.

11. *Subsequent contact:* The initial activity of a subsequent contact is to review the client's efforts in implementing the plan. Successes should be highlighted, and difficulties should be identified. Negotiate necessary modifications in existing components of the plan, and engage in problem solving with regard to important issues that still need to be addressed.

12. *Suicide lethality assessment:* Both in crisis intervention and in emergency mental health intervention, it is appropriate to ask if the client has been thinking about suicide. An affirmative response to this question necessitates further exploration. If you believe there is an ongoing risk of suicide, you may want to examine the following five factors that have been shown to increase the probability of suicide: the existence of a plan for suicide that is specific, available, and deadly (or the person believes is deadly; Michel, 1987); feelings of hopelessness or depression (initial improvement during a clinical depression is an especially dangerous time); past suicide attempts by the client (although most people who die by suicide kill themselves on the first attempt) and past attempts or completed suicide by close relatives or friends; a recent upsurge in difficulties experienced by the client (Riskand, Long, Williams, & White, 2000); and significant object loss associated with the current crisis (Heikkinen, Aro, & Lonnqvist, 1993).

13. *Intervening with a suicidal person:* If the client has attempted suicide or is currently at risk, keep in mind the following five endeavors. Arrange an immediate medical evaluation for an individual who has just engaged in self-harm. Determine the appropriate intervention or combination of interventions: crisis intervention for a person in crisis who wants help, ongoing treatment for an individual with long-standing problems, and hospitalization for a client who is either ambivalent about wanting to be alive or certain about wanting to be dead. Decrease the availability of lethal means; for example, develop a plan for removing firearms from the person's residence. Engage the individual in problem solving that begins to move him or her toward adaptive ways of relieving the pain. For a client who remains suicidal, recognize the potential for homicide. (A study by Asnis, Kaplan, van Pragg, and Sanderson, 1994, focused on 403 psychiatric outpatients and found that of the 127 who had made a suicide attempt, 35% also had contemplated or attempted homicide.)

14. *Deciding whether to support outpatient therapy or hospitalization:* Bengelsdorf, Levy, Emerson, and Barile (1984) developed the Crisis Triage Rating Scale to assist clinicians in deciding whether a person needs outpatient or inpatient services. The evaluator assigns scores for dangerousness, support, and cooperation, then adds the numbers together. Bengelsdorf and his colleagues believe that a total score of 9 or lower suggests a need for hospitalization, whereas a score of 10 or higher tends to indicate outpatient services as being appropriate. The scale's scoring criteria are described below.

DANGEROUSNESS

1. Threats of suicidal or homicidal behavior, a recent dangerous attempt, or unpredictable violence
2. Threats of suicidal or homicidal behavior or a recent dangerous attempt, but sometimes views such ideas and actions as unacceptable, or past violence but no current problems
3. Ambivalence associated with life-threatening thoughts, a "suicide attempt" not intended to end in death, or impulse control that is inconsistent
4. Some ongoing or past life-threatening behavior or ideas but clearly wants to control such behavior and is able to do so
5. No life-threatening ideas or actions and no history of problems with impulse control

SUPPORT

1. Inadequate support from family members, friends, and community resources
2. Possible support but effect is likely to be small
3. Appropriate support possibly developed but with difficulty
4. Appropriate support possibly developed, but some components may not be reliable
5. Access to appropriate support

COOPERATION

1. Unwilling or unable to cooperate
2. Little appreciation or understanding of ongoing intervention efforts
3. Passively accepts intervention efforts
4. Ambivalence or limited motivation regarding intervention efforts
5. Actively requests outpatient services and wants to productively participate in therapy

References & Readings 

Asnis, G. M., Kaplan, M. L., van Praag, H. M., & Sanderson, W. C. (1994). Homicidal behaviors among psychiatric outpatients. *Hospital and Community Psychiatry, 45,* 127–132.

Bengelsdorf, H., Levy, L. E., Emerson, R. L., & Barile, F. A. (1984). A Crisis Triage Rating Scale: Brief dispositional assessment of patients at risk for hospitalization. *Journal of Nervous and Mental Disease, 172,* 424–430.

Bunn, T. A., & Clarke, A. M. (1979). Crisis intervention: An experimental study of the effects of a brief period of counselling on the anxiety of relatives of seriously injured or ill hospital patients. *British Journal of Medical Psychology, 52,* 191–195.

Capone, M. A., Westie, K. S., Chitwood, J. S., Feigenbaum, D., & Good, R. S. (1979). Crisis intervention: A functional model for hospitalized cancer patients. *American Journal of Orthopsychiatry, 49,* 598–607.

Deci, E. L., & Ryan, R. M. (1987). The support of autonomy and the control of behavior. *Journal of Personality and Social Psychology, 53,* 1024–1037.

Folkman, S., Lazarus, R. S., Dunkel-Schetter, C., DeLongis, A., & Gruen, R. J. (1986). Dynamics of a stressful encounter: Cognitive appraisal, coping, and encounter outcomes. *Journal of Personality and Social Psychology, 50,* 992–1003.

France, K. (2002). *Crisis intervention: A handbook of immediate person-to-person help* (4th ed.). Springfield, IL: Charles C Thomas.

Halpern, H. A. (1973). Crisis theory: A definitional study. *Community Mental Health Journal, 9,* 342–349.

Halpern, H. A. (1975). The Crisis Scale: A factor analysis and revision. *Community Mental Health Journal, 11,* 295–300.

Heikkinen, M., Aro, H., & Lonnqvist, J. (1993). Life events and social support in suicide. *Suicide and Life-Threatening Behavior, 23,* 343–358.

Koocher, G. P., Curtiss, E. K., Pollin, I. S., & Patton, K. E. (2001). Medical crisis counseling in a health maintenance organization: Preventive intervention. *Professional Psychology: Research and Practice, 32,* 52–58.

Michel, K. (1987). Suicide risk factors: A comparison of suicide attempters with suicide completers. *British Journal of Psychiatry, 150,* 78–82.

Riskind, J. H., Long, D. G., Williams, N. L., & White, J. C. (2000). Desperate acts for desperate times: Looming vulnerability and suicide. In T. Joiner & M. D. Rudd (Eds.), *Suicide science: Expanding the boundaries* (pp. 105–115). Boston: Kluwer Academic Publishers.

Viney, L. L., Clarke, A. M., Bunn, T. A., & Benjamin, Y. N. (1985). Crisis-intervention counseling: An evaluation of long- and short-term effects. *Journal of Counseling Psychology, 32,* 29–39.

Related Topics

Chapter 49, "Treatment and Management of the Suicidal Patient"
Chapter 51, "Impact of Disasters"
Chapter 121, "A Model for Clinical Decision Making With Dangerous Patients"

51 IMPACT OF DISASTERS

Eric M. Vernberg & R. Enrique Varela

This chapter describes important concepts and issues in evaluating the impact of disasters on individuals. Items are arranged chronologically in relation to the disaster events: predisaster planning, impact and short-term adaptation phases, and long-term adaptation phase.

PREDISASTER PLANNING

Almost every community in the United States has a local emergency management network in place, yet the emphasis on mental health aspects of disasters varies greatly. More widespread disasters require involvement of a state, regional, or national emergency management network. Participation in planning activities at one or more of these levels is a necessity for psychologists who want to be involved in the crisis management aspects of disaster mental health. Disasters, especially those receiving intense media coverage, often draw a tremendous number of offers of help from a broad range of mental health service providers. Understandably, emergency management personnel have difficulty processing such offers in the aftermath of a disaster and prefer to rely instead on relationships developed earlier.

Disaster Response Network

The American Psychological Association Disaster Response Network (DRN) was established in 1991 to organize psychologists within each state into a disaster response network with formal ties to the American Red Cross (ARC) and local emergency management services. The DRN offers short-term crisis intervention at disaster sites at the request of the ARC and is a useful resource for clinicians working with disaster survivors. To obtain information about the DRN in your state, contact the APA Practice Directorate at 202-336-5898.

The ARC offers a 2-day training program for psychologists who wish to provide emergency mental health services as part of a Red Cross disaster team. Contact your local ARC chapter or the DRN for a schedule of training opportunities.

In 2002, the National Child Traumatic Stress Network established a Terrorism and Disaster Branch (TDB) to promote the well-being of children and families by strengthening the nation's preparedness and response to terrorism and disaster. This organization focuses on increasing public awareness of the need to include resources and services specifically targeted for children and families after terrorism and disaster. The TDB offers consultation, informational support, and training on disaster mental health issues for children and families (www.NCTSNet.org).

IMPACT AND SHORT-TERM ADAPTATION PHASES

The *disaster impact phase* refers to the period when a disaster is occurring. Exposure to traumatic events of an overwhelming nature is a central characteristic of this phase, and mental health roles often involve acute crisis management. The *short-term adaptation phase* includes the period after the overwhelming disaster events end and the tasks of inventorying losses and developing a plan for recovery are accomplished. This phase generally requires 3–9 months to complete. Emergency services and intense media activity are generally withdrawn within this period.

Elements of Traumatic Exposure

The nature of exposure to trauma is an important indicator of risk for acute or chronic mental health sequelae of disasters. Indeed, most research finds a dose-response relationship between traumatic exposure and subsequent symptomatology. A useful typology distinguishes the following elements of traumatic exposure (Green, 1990; selected structured questions are included from the DIS/DS, Robins & Smith, 1993).

- *Threat to one's life or bodily integrity:* "At any time did you think you might die?"
- *Physical harm or injury to self:* "Did you have any illness or injuries as a result of the disaster?"
- *Receipt of intentional injury or harm:* "Do you think the disaster was just an act of God or nature, or do you think the people who were involved were in part to blame?"
- *Exposure to the grotesque:* "Sometimes people in disasters have to see or do things they find disgusting. Did this happen to you?"
- *Violent/sudden loss of a loved one:* "Were any of your family, friends, or companions injured or killed as a result of the disaster?"
- *Witnessing or learning of violence to a loved one:* "Did you see anyone get injured or killed?"
- *Exposure to toxins with long-term effects:* "Do you know of any health problems that could be caused by what happened to you in the disaster?"

Not all elements of traumatic exposure are equally likely to produce symptomatology. Additional important distinctions include the duration of exposure, the cause of the disaster (e.g., natural vs. human-made; accidental vs. deliberate or negligent), the proportion of the community affected, the degree of geographic dislocation, and the potential impact on the survivor's life (e.g., permanent disability, catastrophic economic loss, multiple deaths in family).

Context of Evaluation and Intervention

Hearing detailed descriptions of traumatic experiences may be troubling for family members or others who were not directly exposed. Detailed descriptions in group contexts should be solicited only among individuals who shared similar levels of traumatic exposure. Mixed groups of survivors and rescue workers (other than mental health personnel acting as facilitators) are not appropriate. Initial evaluation and intervention in community settings rather than clinical settings are preferable to minimize stigmatization and resistance to mental health services.

Psychological First Aid

Common initial reactions to overwhelming traumatic exposure include confusion, disorganization, and emotional numbness. Basic mental health roles during and shortly after the impact phase may be categorized as *psychological first aid* to connote the clear distinction from more traditional mental health interventions. Psychological first aid *does not* deal with chronic, long-term, or intrapsychic problems. Instead, the focus is on the here and now, enhancing current functioning, and providing sufficient environmental support to prevent further injury. Appropriate activities include the following:

- Providing direct, instrumental assistance with problem solving and practical needs; this may include active advocacy on behalf of survivors
- Providing factual information about the disaster, typical reactions, and resources for support and assistance
- Offering assistance in evaluating information and formulating responses
- Activating social support systems, including family and community networks and access to other survivors

Specific forms of psychological first aid include the following. *Debriefing and defusing* refer to sessions in which individuals or groups of survivors are encouraged to review the major elements of a traumatic experience soon after exposure. The goals of these interventions include emotional release, enhancing social support, reducing social isolation, translating iconic memories into language (to facilitate cognitive processing of the traumatic events), and providing education, information, and stress-management strategies. Debriefing and defusing sessions also offer opportunities to screen for severe impairment that may require additional evaluation and treatment (American Red Cross, 1991).

Although formal debriefing and defusing are widely practiced and strongly embraced by many disaster mental health workers, evidence for their efficacy in general or the superiority of one protocol over another remains sparse (Gist & Lubin, 1998).

Crisis reduction counseling is conducted with an individual or family and focuses on assessing psychological states, validating and normalizing thoughts and feelings, identifying and prioritizing current problems, and identifying sources of support (American Red Cross, 1991). Discussion is limited to issues related to the disaster recovery process.

Crisis intervention is carried out with an individual or family to mitigate extreme emotional distress in the immediate aftermath of a disaster or traumatic event. The goals are to assess the extent of current mental health impairment in relation to pretrauma functioning, to provide pragmatic emotional support, and to give information and advice to help regain emotional equilibrium. Depending on the psychological state, this may include information on the process of recovery from trauma, maladaptive versus adaptive coping strategies, resources and supports, and indicators of the need for further mental health assistance (American Red Cross, 1991).

Guidelines for Providing More Intensive Services

In the course of receiving psychological first aid, individuals should be provided with more extensive evaluations or treatments under the following conditions (American Red Cross, 1991):

- Preexisting serious mental disorder that is exacerbated by the disaster
- Extremely impaired functioning, including thought disturbances, dissociative episodes, extreme overarousal or mood lability, or inability to care for personal needs
- Acute risk of harm to self or others, including suicidality, homicidal ideation, extreme substance abuse, or inappropriate anger or abuse of others
- Evidence of a life-threatening health condition (e.g., heart problems, diabetes, high blood pressure) that is not currently being treated and appears to be causing problems

LONG-TERM ADAPTATION PHASE

Mental health issues related to long-term adaptation following disasters begin to fit more traditional approaches to clinical assessment and treatment. Still, several issues deserve special attention in assessing and treating disaster survivors in the months and years after traumatic exposure.

Common Mental Health Problems After Disasters

Anxiety, depression, and somatic complaints: The most consistent mental health problems found in studies of disaster survivors are symptoms of anxiety (including posttraumatic stress disorder), depression, and somatic symptoms.

Substance abuse: Although widely believed to be affected by disasters, increases in substance abuse problems among disaster survivors have been reported less consistently than the anxiety/depression/somatic complaint symptoms described above. The topic needs further study, as some studies have found increases in alcohol use (and other substances, such as tranquilizers) among disaster-exposed populations in the United States and others have not.

Aggression and anger: Problems with anger and aggression appear to be linked to disasters, although there is less evidence for this than for anxiety, depression, and somatic complaints. A number of studies have found anger and irritability to be higher in disaster-exposed populations than in nonexposed comparison groups, and there is some suggestion that these problems may be quite persistent over time. There is surprisingly little research documenting increases in actual aggression after disasters.

Factors Influencing Recovery

Social support: Social support is swiftly mobilized by most disasters but often is depleted and diminished long before recovery is accomplished (Kaniasty & Norris, 1997). This sense of declining support may contribute to distress. Assessment of access to needed support is essential in designing interventions for disaster survivors. Improving access to needed forms of social support is a major goal for mental health providers. Risk of poor access to social supports following disasters is especially high for marginalized members of communities (e.g., poorer, less educated individuals; geographically isolated individuals).

Ongoing disruptions: Many disasters cause serious disruptions for individuals long after the identified disaster event has ended. It is extremely important to inquire about ongoing stressful circumstances that follow many severe disasters. These include economic struggles, dislocation, rebuilding, employment disruption, changes in household composition, and increases in "daily hassles." When ongoing disruption is high, it is appropriate to continue the functions characteristic of psychological first aid long after the primary disaster event has ended.

Psychological resources: Several psychological resources have been linked to resilience following traumatic events of varying types. Religious faith and philosophical perspectives that in some way enable individuals to make sense of disaster experiences appear to be important resources following disasters. A second set of psychological resources includes at least average intelligence, good communication skills, and strong beliefs of self-efficacy.

Socioeconomic status: Education and financial status may influence recovery from disasters and even levels of exposure to traumatic experiences during disasters. Education may influence an individual's ability to cope with the demands for documentation and careful completion of applications for disaster assistance. Education is also linked to skills in seeking information regarding resources. Financial status exerts multiple possible influences on postdisaster functioning. In terms of increased exposure to traumatic experiences during disasters, housing built of less durable materials (e.g., mobile homes) or in less desirable locations (e.g., flood-prone land) is more likely to be damaged by disasters in the first place. This places poorer individuals, on average, at greater risk for loss of personal possessions and exposure to life-threatening circumstances. Following disasters, individuals with few financial resources (including personal property insurance) may find it virtually impossible to repair or replace lost belongings. Even for poorer families with some insurance, months of waiting may be required before claims are settled, placing extreme financial pressures on those with few financial reserves. Many lower-paying, lower-occupational-status jobs offer little in the way of paid personal leave or scheduling flexibility.

This may further complicate postdisaster recovery by making it difficult for individuals to find the time to pursue aid or repairs.

Age-Related Issues

Age is related to disaster response in numerous ways, and children and the elderly are typically viewed as "special populations" in the disaster literature. Children and some of the elderly are similar in their greater dependence on others to meet basic needs for food, clothing, and shelter. Impairment in individuals or systems that meet these dependency demands places both groups at risk for mental health disturbance, and possibly for physical danger.

Children and adolescents: Children of different ages have different types of difficulties related to disasters. *Infants and toddlers* are often very sensitive to disruptions in caretaking and may show increases in feeding problems, irritability, and sleep problems. These behavioral problems in turn place increased demands on caretakers, who may themselves be highly distressed by a disaster.

Preschool children are beginning to use language in relatively sophisticated ways but are very limited in their understanding of disaster-related events. This limited understanding often leads to fears that may seem unwarranted to older children and adults (e.g., extreme fears during thunderstorms that occur after a flood or tornado). These fears may lead to dramatic reactions to relatively harmless postdisaster events.

School-age children understand the physical environment much better than preschoolers but may be very preoccupied by the loss of possessions or pets or by memories of traumatic events. Elementary school–age children also are often able to recognize distress in their caretakers and may be quite worried about the safety and security of their families. Children of this age can do relatively little to help actively in the recovery process, which may increase feelings of isolation and helplessness. Children over 8 years old generally are competent reporters of psychiatric symptoms (especially internalizing symptoms) when given appropriate measures. Children typically report more postdisaster symptoms than others (e.g., parents, teachers) report for them. Relying solely on parent or teacher reports to identify postdisaster mental health problems in school-age children is almost certain to underestimate these problems.

Adolescents are more competent to help with recovery and are less dependent than younger children. At the same time, adolescents may engage in greater risk-taking behaviors after disasters. Adolescents also may have intense feelings of being cheated out of expected experiences (e.g., athletic and social events that are canceled or postponed) after disasters.

Young and middle-aged adults: There is some evidence of differences in disaster-related distress between young adults (18–40) and middle-aged adults (40–65), with the latter group typically faring worse. Middle-aged adults are more likely than other age cohorts to have responsibility for children and elderly parents during and after disasters, and this increased responsibility may contribute to psychological distress.

Older adults: Health status (including mental health) and competence to perform tasks of daily living are also important aspects in determining postdisaster needs of the elderly. Sensory changes accompanying aging are important to consider. Hearing and vision problems may make it more difficult for the elderly to obtain information regarding disaster relief efforts or to provide information to others. Noisy, crowded settings (such as disaster shelters or Disaster Assistance Centers) may be particularly problematic because it becomes increasingly difficult with age to filter out competing noises during conversations. Decreased sense of smell and taste tend to make the elderly prefer foods with more flavor, and elders may respond to bland food provided through disaster relief teams by adding salt (which aggravates hypertension) or reducing food intake (which may result in malnutrition). The relationship between cognitive functioning and physical health becomes increasingly strong during late adulthood, and declines in physical health due to poor nutrition or disruptions in medications may contribute to significant mental health problems, including confusion, disorientation, and depression. Similarly, loss of social support and disruptions in routines following disasters may produce poor health behaviors, leading to increased dysfunction. Sudden changes in living arrangements are difficult for older adults, especially those with cognitive, physical, or sensory impairments. Many elderly also attach a strong stigma to the use of mental health services, and substantial efforts may be required to make such service acceptable. Some older adults who are aware of their diminished capabilities may fear that they will be placed in nursing homes or other restrictive settings if their difficulties become known to relief workers. It is important to communicate that mental health workers are attempting to help the elderly live as independently as possible and that they may help garner the resources and support needed for this to occur.

References & Readings 

American Red Cross. (1991). *Disaster services regulations and procedures* (ARC Document 3050M). Washington, DC: Author.

Gist, R., & Lubin, B. (Eds.). (1998). *Response to disaster: Psychosocial, community, and ecological approaches.* Bristol, PA: Taylor and Francis.

Green, B. L. (1990). Defining trauma: Terminology and generic stressor dimensions. *Journal of Applied Social Psychology, 20,* 1632–1642.

Hobfoll, S. E., & de Vries, M. W. (Eds.) (1995). *Extreme stress and communities: Impact and intervention.* Dordrecht, The Netherlands: Kluwer Academic Publishers.

La Greca, A. M., Silverman, W. K., Vernberg, E. M., & Roberts, M. C. (Eds.). (2002). *Helping children cope with disasters and terrorism.* Washington, DC: American Psychological Association.

Norris, F. H., Friedman, M. J., & Watson, P. J. (2002). 60,000 disaster victims speak: Part II. Summary and implications of the disaster mental health research. *Psychiatry: Interpersonal and Biological Processes, 65,* 207–239.

Norris, F. H., Friedman, M. J., Watson, P. J., Byrne, C. M., Diaz, E., & Kaniasty, K. (2002). 60,000 disaster victims speak: Part 1. An empirical review of the empirical literature. *Psychiatry: Interpersonal and Biological Processes, 65,* 207–239.

Robins, L. N., & Smith, E. M. (1993). *Diagnostic interview schedule: Disaster supplement.* St. Louis, MO: Washington University School of Medicine, Department of Psychiatry.

Saylor, C. F. (Ed.). (1993). *Children and disasters.* New York: Plenum Press.

Ursano, R. J., McCaughey, B. G., & Fullerton, C. S. (Eds.). (1994). *Individual and community responses to trauma and disaster: The structure of human chaos.* Cambridge, UK: Cambridge University Press.

Related Topic

Chapter 50, "Crisis Intervention"

52 PRINCIPLES IN THE TREATMENT OF BORDERLINE PERSONALITY DISORDER

John F. Clarkin & Pamela A. Foelsch

Patients with borderline personality disorder (BPD) are characterized by identity diffusion, affective dyscontrol, impulsivity, and chaotic interpersonal relations. Often they exhibit repetitive self-mutilating or frank suicidal behaviors. These patients rarely present with BPD alone but manifest comorbid *Diagnostic and Statistical Manual of Mental Disorders* (*DSM-IV*) Axis II conditions, most frequently histrionic, narcissistic, and antisocial features or disorders, and common *DSM-IV* Axis I conditions of major depression, eating disorders, and substance abuse. This is a group of patients who have serious pathology, which is frightening to therapists because of the safety and legal implications, and they elicit intense countertransference feelings.

Based on the growing body of research and our own extensive experience, we present 10 important principles for the assessment and treatment of these patients.

1. Determine the specific criteria for BPD met by the individual patient. Since Axis II is polythetic in nature, patients may receive the diagnosis of BPD by meeting any 5, 6, 7, 8, or 9 *DSM-IV* criteria. This means that mathematically there are 256 ways of obtaining the diagnosis. Just on the BPD criteria themselves, the patients are quite heterogeneous. A factor analysis of the BPD criteria (Clarkin, Hull, & Hurt, 1993) suggests three factors: an identity diffusion factor, an affect disregulation factor including suicidal behavior, and an impulsive factor. Thus, BPD patients can be identity diffused patients primarily, or identity and impulsive, or affective with suicidal behavior. The prominence of the three factors is most important in setting and prioritizing treatment goals.
2. Carefully assess for comorbid Axis I and Axis II conditions. Only rarely does a patient meet criteria for BPD alone. The common comorbid Axis I conditions include affective disorder, eating disorders, and substance use and abuse. Common Axis II conditions include histrionic, narcissistic, and antisocial personality disorders/traits.
3. In the assessment, carefully explore two areas of pathology: (a) the manner in which the patient has used or abused prior treatments and (b) the interpersonal behaviors between patient, therapist, and significant others, particularly surrounding self-mutilating and suicidal behaviors. These prior behaviors must be considered in structuring the next treatment. For example, if the patient has destroyed a treatment by not talking during the regular session then telephoning the therapist on the weekend and insisting on crisis help, the likelihood of this happening in the new therapy will be discussed, along with how the therapist will structure the therapy.
4. Structure the treatment from the beginning with a clear contract delineating the patient's treatment role and responsibilities and the therapist's role and responsibilities. The need for a structured treatment contract is recognized in both psychodynamic and cognitive-behavioral orientations

(Linehan, 1993; Yeomans, Selzer, & Clarkin, 1992). It is especially around destruction of the patient (i.e., suicidal behavior) and destruction of the therapy (e.g., coming to sessions intoxicated, refusing to talk during sessions) that the roles and responsibilities of patient and therapist must be delineated. This verbal agreement provides both a structure within which the therapy can proceed and a treatment frame that the therapist can refer to later should difficulties arise.

5. Focus the treatment around goals identified early in process. These goals should be determined by the nature of the patient's pathology and the therapist's orientation. Two prominent treatment orientations are the cognitive-behavioral orientation (Linehan, 1993), which strives for reduction of therapy-interfering behaviors and for an increase in social skills, and the psychodynamic orientation (Clarkin, Yeomans, & Kernberg, 1999; Kernberg, Selzer, Koenigsberg, Carr, & Appelbaum, 1989), which focuses on the here-and-now transference with the goal of increasing identity as opposed to identity diffusion. One can also use a supportive orientation, which may be of assistance in achieving some equilibrium and maintenance of that status (Rockland, 1992). Still others (Horwitz et al., 1996) suggest tailoring the treatment with a balance of expressive and supportive techniques.
6. At times of crisis, especially those involving serious suicidal ideation and/or threats, hospitalization to control this behavior must be considered. The advantage of hospitalization in protecting the patient briefly from suicidal potential must be weighed against the possibility of rewarding suicidal threats with the comfort of around-the-clock attention, which may reinforce future suicidal ideation.
7. While individual treatment is often recommended for these patients, other treatment formats should be considered. One cognitive-behavioral approach uses a combination of individual treatment and group treatment for skills enhancement (Linehan, 1993). Others (Munroe-Blum, 1992) have used group treatment alone with these patients. Because there is insufficient research on the question of treatment format, the clinician must consider the specific goals and practicality in deciding on the individual case. Group treatment is more economical, but this advantage must be weighed against the high dropout rate of these patients, who strongly prefer individual treatment if given a choice.
8. Medication can be considered as an adjunct to a consistent therapeutic relationship (Koenigsberg, 1997). Medications can be of assistance with depressive symptoms and possibly with impulsive behaviors. Attention must be paid to the patient's tendency to seek medications as a "quick fix" or to undermine therapy. A strong working relationship between therapist and psychopharmacologist is essential.
9. The therapist should be alert to the clinical and legal standards of care when dealing with these patients, who are often suicidal. This includes information about legal perspectives, assessment of suicide risk, and risk management, such as documentation of clinical decisions and consultation with other professionals when appropriate (Bongar, 1991).
10. Borderline patients, especially those who are suicidal with comorbid narcissistic and antisocial traits are extremely difficult to treat. Their behavior in sessions is complicated by identity diffusion and intense affect, often of a hostile and aggressive nature. All these factors suggest that clinicians, even experienced ones, should seek consultation with colleagues about certain situations. Some therapists who treat borderline patients form a peer group with other professionals treating these patients.

References & Readings

Bongar, B. (1991). *The suicidal patient: Clinical and legal standards of care*. Washington, DC: American Psychological Association.

Clarkin, J. F., Hull, J. W., & Hurt, S. W. (1993). Factor structure of borderline personality disorder criteria. *Journal of Personality Disorders, 7,* 137–143.

Clarkin, J. F., & Lenzenweger, M. F. (1996). *Major theories of personality disorder*. New York: Guilford Press.
Clarkin, J. F., Marziali, E., & Munroe-Blum, H. (1992). *Borderline personality disorder: Clinical and empirical perspectives*. New York: Guilford Press.
Clarkin, J. F., Yeomans, F. E., & Kernberg, O. F. (1999). *Psychodynamic treatment of borderline personality organization*. New York: Wiley.
Horwitz, L., Gabbard, G. O., Allen, J., Frieswyk, S. H., Colson, D. B., Newsom, G. E., et al. (1996). *Borderline personality disorder: Tailoring the psychotherapy to the patient*. Washington, DC: American Psychiatric Press.
Kernberg, O. F. (1984). *Severe personality disorders: Psychotherapeutic strategies*. New Haven, CT: Yale University Press.
Kernberg, O. F. (1992). *Aggression in personality disorders and perversions*. New Haven, CT: Yale University Press.
Kernberg, O. F., Selzer, M. A., Koenigsberg, H. W., Carr, A. C., & Appelbaum, A. H. (1989). *Psychodynamic psychotherapy of borderline patients*. New York: Basic Books.
Koenigsberg, H. W. (1997). Integrating psychotherapy and pharmacotherapy in the treatment of borderline personality disorder. *In Session: Psychotherapy in Practice, 3*, 39–56.
Linehan, M. M. (1993). *Cognitive-behavioral treatment of borderline personality disorder*. New York: Guilford Press.
Meissner, W. W. (1984). *The borderline spectrum: Differential diagnosis and developmental issues*. New York: Jason Aronson.
Munroe-Blum, H. (1992). Group treatment of borderline personality disorder. In J. F. Clarkin, E. Marziali, & H. Munroe-Blum (Eds.), *Borderline personality disorder: Clinical and empirical perspectives* (pp. 288–299). New York: Guilford Press.
Rockland, L. H. (1992). *Supportive therapy for borderline patients: A psychodynamic approach*. New York: Guilford Press.
Stone, M. H. (1990). *The fate of borderline patients: Successful outcome and psychiatric practice*. New York: Guilford Press.
Yeomans, F. E., Selzer, M. A., & Clarkin, J. F. (1992). *Treating the borderline patient: A contract-based approach*. New York: Basic Books.

Related Topics

Chapter 46, "Stages of Change: Prescriptive Guidelines"
Chapter 49, "Treatment and Management of the Suicidal Patient"
Chapter 65, "Refusal Skills Training"
Chapter 76, "Choice of Treatment Format"

53 PSYCHOTHERAPY WITH RELUCTANT AND INVOLUNTARY CLIENTS

Stanley L. Brodsky

When therapists offer counseling from the same frame of reference for reluctant and involuntary clients as they do for eager, voluntary clients, they set up themselves and their clients for considerable frustration. Some reluctant clients will never fully participate in counseling; for them, quick termination of the treatment may be the decision of choice. For other clients, the reluctance becomes transformed into active participation and the treatment itself becomes a productive venture. The beginning points in approaching treatment of reluctant clients are awareness of therapist assumptions and of client roles and rights.

REACTIONS TO RELUCTANT CLIENTS

Therapists have a need to present themselves as expert and trustworthy in their therapeutic roles (Beutler, Machado, & Neufeldt, 1994). If therapists are frustrated by clients, these needs may rise to prominence, occasionally in exaggerated form. The resultant events are often confrontational demands by the therapists for clients to give up their reluctance or a facade by clients of conformity to the patient role.

Therapists enter their professions in part altruistically, to feel good about helping others (Guy, 1987). Reluctant clients are unappreciative and do not provide the customary positive feedback therapists want as part of their work. Many therapists take this lack of appreciation personally and feel threatened, incapable, and frustrated. In order to avoid becoming impaired in working with the client, they need to be able to address the threat and frustration as foreground personal issues.

THE MENTAL HEALTH–CRIME FALSE SYLLOGISM

Law violators are the most frequent category of reluctant client, often explicitly coerced to enter psychotherapy as a condition of probation or parole or as proof of progress toward being a desirable candidate for parole or privileges within prison. It is incorrectly concluded by many clinicians that being a serious offender is prima facie evidence of need for psychotherapy. This conclusion takes the form of the following implicit false syllogism (Davis & Brodsky, 1992):

> Most people are not offenders.
>
> Most people are not mentally ill.
>
> Therefore most offenders are mentally ill.

A fundamental rule emerges from this principle: Do not attempt to cure antisocial behavior per se through psychotherapy. Instead, treatment services should be offered without institutional pressures to offenders who request such services (Monahan, 1980).

THE RIGHT TO REFUSE TREATMENT

Every client's right to decline treatment as well as to choose treatment knowledgeably should be respected. The choice to refuse treatment, as fully as to participate in therapy, should be an informed one, particularly when there are institutional, occupational, or family consequences of not entering therapy. Clients should know precisely what choices they are declining. The therapist's responsibility is to ensure that the client understands the alternatives of what treatment is available, how long it lasts and how well it works, the nature of the therapeutic procedures, and the assumption of client self-determination in continuing therapy. Contracts with clients and outlines of information to be given to clients have been gathered in Bersoff (1995, pp. 305–334).

REFERRAL CLARIFICATION: WHY IS A CLIENT HERE?

Often agencies do not know exactly why they have referred a client. They know something is wrong and that the client needs help or an intervention but little more. Thus, the therapist should find out why a coercive referral has been made. The specific information needed includes the treatment aims, the referrer's anticipation of success, the time constraints, the legal or familial frames of reference, and the influences of the client's transient situation. These actions consist of clarifying and redefining the referral. Otherwise therapists become engaged in a vague plan of "just doing therapy."

LOW TRUST–HIGH CONTROL DILEMMAS

With voluntary clients, the customary therapeutic relationship is characterized by high trust and little effort to control the other's behaviors. With confined populations and clients pressured to enter therapy, mutual distrust of motives is often accompanied by the therapist having considerable control over client living conditions, privileges, and release (Harris & Watkins, 1987). The subsequent therapist fear of manipulation produces a role conflict between helping and "supervising." The normal trust and rapport between therapist and client become displaced by a concern over being used and by excessive control measures, which themselves are antagonistic to good treatment. The resolution of these dilemmas lies in explicit delineation of limits, as well as absolute separation of therapeutic roles from evaluative and organizational roles (Brodsky, 1973; Davis & Brodsky, 1992).

WHO IS THE CLIENT?

Therapists may be classified as falling on a continuum from system professional to system challenger, depending on the extent to which they accept the existing aims of the agency. Therapists need to define their stances and consider client versus agency responsibilities, coercion effects, and other values implicit in treatment activities. All psychotherapy has implicit values. The therapist needs to be especially sensitive to social values and imposing normative behaviors. This dilemma is best resolved by making explicit on an a priori basis the social values with which one is practicing.

Confidentiality is often the playing field on which these conflicts become tested. Confidentiality is not absolute. Explicit agreement from the beginning on confidentiality is important, with all parties being informed in writing and in advance about the level of confidentiality (Report of the Task Force on the Role of Psychology in the Criminal Justice System, 1980).

TREATING THE ABRASIVE CLIENT

Abrasive clients are individuals who have a special knack for irritating others. They know how to get under others' skin to annoy. They become adept at jabbing at the vulnerabilities of their therapists. Sometimes it is done with subtlety; therapists become aware of this process when they find themselves getting annoyed without apparent good reason. According to Wepman and Donovan (1984), abrasive individuals have both a high need for human intimacy and a fear of closeness. The need for intimacy brings them toward therapists emotionally, whereas their fear leads them to push therapists away. Clients who have criticized a therapist's clothing, family, office decor, facial expression, tone of voice, ethnicity, or personal appearance succeed when they are rejected. The treatment is to try to respond to the hurt and the desire for closeness: "The alliance must be made with the wounded, vulnerable aspects of the personality" (Wepman & Donovan, 1984, p. 17).

THERAPY AS AN AVERSIVE CONTINGENCY FOR INAPPROPRIATE BEHAVIOR

If the treatment itself is a negative experience for clients, it can be used as an aversive stimulus following undesirable behavior. In a discussion of behavioral treatment of delinquents, Levinson, Ingram, and Azcarate (1973) described just such an effective program with confined, severely antisocial youthful offenders. The youths were able to earn the right to discontinue mandatory group therapy by going 3 successive months without being sent to segregation. Once this program was introduced, misconduct reports among group members dropped 43% in a 6-month period after therapy. In other settings, such as family therapy, anecdotal reports have indicated that children's problem behaviors have diminished or disappeared with the promise that attendance in therapy would no longer be required.

ERRORS IN TECHNIQUE

When the criterion for success is reduced recidivism, nondirective and traditional psychodynamic therapies, as well as any approach with low-risk offenders, have little payoff (Gendreau, 1996). Therapy that is vaguely targeted and not intensive in nature seems to fail. With diagnosed psychopaths, these failures become even more compelling. Insight-oriented therapies and group therapies, in particular, are associated with higher rates of future crime (Hare, 1996). Therapy is best offered for specific behaviors that disrupt criminogenic social networks and to provide relapse prevention training.

Therapy also fails when therapists (a) passively accept problematic aspects of the client's behavior and attitudes, such as evasiveness and negativism; (b) fail to address deficiencies in the therapeutic relationship; or (c) present destructive or poorly timed interventions (Sachs, 1983). Effective therapists do not sit back and wait in the therapy office but instead are active. Timing, specificity of focus, and intense involvement in therapeutic work are crucial.

UTILIZING RESISTANCE

When clients actively resist involvement and change, therapists should not be in direct opposition. Instead, they should consider aiming at second-order change so that clients accept in an oppositional way the view therapists would originally have wanted. Thus, one can ask resistant clients, "Why should you change?" or instruct clients to "go slow." In the same spirit, one might tell a distrustful client to never trust the therapy fully. These procedures may be conceptualized as co-opting clients' cognitive space. Teyber's (1988) interpersonal process in psychotherapy addresses this approach by explicitly using what he calls "honoring the client's resistance."

LITIGIOUS CLIENTS

Therapists and clients alike can become influenced by fears of lawsuits. Clients who think about suing are poor candidates for therapeutic progress. Therapists fearful of lawsuits become legalistic, distant, overly cautious, and less effective. The therapist's role will be addressed here rather than that of the client. Most therapists' fears of litigation are excessive and irrational (Brodsky, 1988). The litigaphobic therapist becomes what he or she fears—a surrogate lawyer, second-guessing every action. The alternative is to assess realistically the base rate for such suits—statistically low—and to get consultation as necessary to manage such fears. A scale is available for assessing the extent of fear of litigation (Breslin, Taylor, & Brodsky, 1976).

OBJECTIVE SELF-AWARENESS

This phenomenon, described by Duval and Wicklund (1972), has powerful implications for reluctant clients. When clients are encouraged to listen in at staff meetings about their cases and discussions of their therapeutic progress, as well as to read documents written about them, they become, in effect, outside observers of themselves. As a result, they become motivated and fascinated. This principle can be used by sharing with clients the videotapes and audiotapes of sessions, ongoing therapy records, and especially the opportunity to hear discussions of their dynamics and progress (Brodsky & Myers, 1986).

LIFE SKILLS ENHANCEMENT

In enhancement of life skills, therapeutic efforts are offered as short courses that are closed ended and based on a published curriculum. Each unit of instruction attends to narrowly defined areas of functioning. The short courses have scheduled beginnings and endings, the use of pass or fail criteria, and the advance identification of specific treatment content. In this alternative to conventional open-ended therapies, topics that are addressed include conflict management, human sexuality, assertiveness training, and fairness awareness (Scapinello, 1992).

FOUR MORE PRACTICAL APPROACHES

1. *Keep the client for three sessions:* One third of therapy clients never return for a second appointment even after a definite time has been set. An additional 40% stop before the sixth session. In their research using the Vanderbilt Psychotherapy Process Scale, O'Malley, Suh, and Strupp (1983) found no relationship whatever between first-session events and eventual outcome. A strong relationship was found between third-session events and outcome. By that time, patients became involved, and that involvement made a difference. Thus, the therapist should set up contracts or trial therapy agreements for three or four sessions.
2. *Common foundations for therapy:* When conventional approaches to building rapport do not work, the therapist should consider adapting the "group conversation method" developed by DuBois and Li (1971). In this method, clients are asked to take turns describing sensory memories (such as smells and tastes from childhood), activities at school or home, or particular holidays. The questions include: How did you use to spend Halloween? What are your memories of worst teachers? Best teachers? Christmas smells? Where you grew up? Earliest religious memories? Otto (1973), who has called this network of positive formative experiences the Minerva experience, suggests the joint recollection of such experiences is a positive bonding.
3. *Time and therapy:* Our experiences are captured by conventions of time. Therapists become entrained by 50-minute hours and appointment books, and they believe that "good" clients should comply as well. As a beginning point with difficult clients, experiment with very short or long sessions. More broadly, however, try to understand the meaning of time in clients' lives. Responsibility and personal development are concepts seated in part in elements of time, such as continuity and comprehension of consequences (McGrath, 1988). How do the clients experience time passing? Five years from now, will they look back at the present with envy? With feelings of wasted living? Regret? One book compellingly develops this theme: Grudin's *Time and the Art of Living* (1982), which asserts that when time becomes a foreground issue, it can serve to help with problems in living and in therapy.
4. *Concrete changes:* Giving clients immediate and concrete self-coping methods yields good motivation to continue with therapy. For example, in the case of anxiety problems and panic attacks, cognitive therapies and teaching of diaphragmatic breathing and relaxation techniques lead to rapid improvement. Help with sleep problems has an especially strong impact, given that about 40% of the general population and 80% of institutionalized persons have sleeping difficulties. Clients welcome assistance in managing insomnia, difficulties falling asleep, and waking easily during the night.

SUMMARY

Therapists should not automatically assume that traditional therapies with voluntary and cooperative clients apply to reluctant and involuntary clients. Instead, referral questions, definitions of client, and confidentiality should be examined carefully. Milieu demands for control of client behavior can compromise therapeutic relationships, as can abrasive and resistant client behaviors. Therapists should consider utilizing client resistances, ensuring that therapy continues through at least three sessions, and adapting the length of therapy sessions to individual clients. With these clients, concrete and immediate changes are important, along with promoting objective self-awareness and using closed-ended short-term treatments.

References & Readings

Bersoff, D. N. (Ed.). (1995). *Ethical conflicts in psychology*. Washington, DC: American Psychological Association.

Beutler, L. E., Machado, P. P. P., & Neufeldt, S. A. (1994). Therapist variables. In A. E. Bergin & S. L. Garfield (Eds.), *Handbook of psychotherapy and behavior change* (4th ed., pp. 229–269). New York: Wiley.

Breslin, F. A., Taylor, K. R., & Brodsky, S. L. (1986). Development of a litigaphobia scale: Measurement of excessive fear of litigation. *Psychological Reports, 58,* 547–550.

Brodsky, S. L. (1973). *Psychologists in the criminal justice system.* Urbana: University of Illinois Press.

Brodsky, S. L. (1988). Fear of litigation in mental health professionals. *Criminal Justice and Behavior, 15,* 492–500.

Brodsky, S. L., & Myers, H. H. (1986). In vivo rotation: An alternative method of psychotherapy supervision. In F. W. Kaslow (Ed.), *Supervision and training: Models, dilemmas, and challenges* (pp. 95–104). New York: Haworth.

Davis, D. L., & Brodsky, S. L. (1992). Psychotherapy with the unwilling client. *Residential Treatment for Children and Youth, 9*(3), 15–27.

DuBois, R. D., & Li, M.-S. (1971). *Reducing social tension and conflict through the group conversation method.* New York: Association Press.

Duval, S., & Wicklund, R. A. (1972). *A theory of objective self-awareness.* New York: Academic Press.

Gendreau, P. (1996). Offender rehabilitation: What we know and what needs to be done. *Criminal Justice and Behavior, 23,* 144–161.

Grudin, R. (1982). *Time and the art of living.* New York: Ticknor and Fields.

Guy, J. D. (1987). *The personal life of the psychotherapist.* New York: Wiley.

Hare, R. D. (1996). Psychopathy: A clinical construct whose time has come. *Criminal Justice and Behavior, 23,* 25–54.

Harris, G. A., & Watkins, D. (1987). *Counseling the involuntary and reluctant client.* College Park, MD: American Correctional Association.

Levinson, R. B., Ingram, G. L., & Azcarate, E. (1973). Aversive group therapy: Sometimes good medicine tastes bad. In J. S. Stumphauzer (Ed.), *Behavior therapy with delinquents* (pp. 159–163). Springfield, IL: Thomas.

McGrath, J. E. (Ed.). (1988). *The social psychology of time.* Newbury Park, CA: Sage.

Monahan, J. (Ed.). (1980). *Who is the client? The ethics of psychological intervention in the criminal justice system.* Washington, DC: American Psychological Association.

O'Malley, S. S., Suh, C. S., & Strupp, H. H. (1983). The Vanderbilt Psychotherapy Process Scale: A report on the scale development and a process-outcome study. *Journal of Consulting and Clinical Psychology, 51,* 581–586.

Otto, H. A. (1973). *Ways of growth: Approaches to expanding awareness.* New York: Penguin.

Sachs, J. S. (1983). Negative factors in brief psychotherapy: An empirical assessment. *Journal of Consulting and Clinical Psychology, 51,* 557–564.

Scapinello, K. F. (1992). *Specialized services offered by the Psychology Department* (Programme Report No. PR92-2). Brampton: Ontario Correctional Institute.

Teyber, E. (1988). *Interpersonal process in psychotherapy: A guide to clinical training.* Boston: Dorsey.

Wepman, B. J., & Donovan, M. W. (1984). Abrasiveness: Descriptive and dynamic issues. *Psychotherapy Patient, 1,* 11–20.

Related Topics

Chapter 38, "Patients' Rights in Psychotherapy"
Chapter 121, "A Model for Clinical Decision Making With Dangerous Patients"
Chapter 125, "Sample Psychotherapist-Patient Contract"

54 TREATMENT MATCHING IN SUBSTANCE ABUSE

Carlo C. DiClemente

"Different strokes for different folks" certainly characterizes the treatment of substance abuse. Consider what substances of abuse encompass: (a) multiple classes of drugs (sedatives, stimulants, opiates); (b) different sources of drug availability (cocaine and crack; beer, wine, and hard liquor; cigarettes and smokeless tobacco); (c) varied routes of administration (oral, nasal, intravenous); and (d) a broad range of abusing individuals representing every social class, ethnicity, educational level, and profession.

The past few decades have witnessed substantial improvement in treating substance abusers and a more differentiated view of the critical differences and similarities across the various substances. Although interventions for alcohol, nicotine, and illegal drugs have been developed in parallel and not with a collaborative treatment development strategy, there is today an increasing level of communication and cross-fertilization. There is also a growing realization that substance abuse is a biobehavioral problem and that both pharmacological and psychosocial interventions are needed to adequately address the problem and promote effective change. Psychosocial treatments and treatment matching are the focus of this chapter.

TREATMENT APPROACHES

A variety of psychosocial treatments and treatment modalities have been applied to substance abuse problems (Onken & Blaine, 1990; McCrady & Epstein, 1999; Miller & Heather, 1998). Among the most popular are the following:

- *Group therapy,* whether dynamically oriented (Brown, 1995) or a skills-based/relapse-prevention approach (Marlatt & Gordon, 1985), has been the treatment of choice for drug abuse in most treatment settings, usually along with some case management and a referral to Alcoholics Anonymous, Narcotics Anonymous, Rational Recovery, or some other self-help support group.
- *Cognitive-behavioral treatment* includes a combination of treatment strategies to change habitual patterns of thoughts and behaviors. Counterconditioning techniques, including relaxation training and cue extinction; thought-stopping and countering techniques; skills training for affect management, assertiveness, and interpersonal interactions; efficacy-enhancing exercises; and relapse-prevention training, including recognizing cues and triggers, teaching drink and drug refusal skills, encouraging changes in the social environment, and coping with expectancies and triggers that promote relapse, are all standard components in the cognitive-behavioral treatment of substance abuse (Montt, Radden, Rohsenow, Cooney & Abrams, 2002; Rotgers, Keller, & Morgenstern, 2003).
- *Cognitive therapy* for substance abusers is a recent adaptation of the cognitive therapy approaches (Beck, Wright, Newman, & Liese, 1993) specifically to treat alcohol and drug abuse clients. These approaches typically focus on changing the beliefs, thoughts, and expectations that appear to underlie both the use of the substances and the difficulties in changing or quitting the substance abuse, including enduring withdrawal symptoms and craving.

- *Couples, family, and social network therapies:* Since the spouse and significant others play a role in abuse as either collaborators or critics, this approach focuses on the mutual interactions and how to change these interactions in order to facilitate change (McCrady & Epstein, 1999). These approaches have brought into the treatment spouses, friends, family members, colleagues, ministers, and so forth in order to support the substance abuser in the process of change.
- *Behavior-focused treatments* entail changing the reinforcements and contingencies associated with the substance use. They have been incorporated into what has been called a *community reinforcement approach,* which attempts to increase the positive reinforcers associated with work, social networks, and personal functioning in order to change the environment of the drug abuser (Rotgers, Keller, & Morgenstern, 2003). Token economies and offering rewards or punishments contingent on *not engaging* in the drug abuse have often been used quite effectively to achieve short-term change but have had difficulty maintaining that change after the contingencies are removed.
- *Motivational interventions:* Motivational interviewing strategies developed by Miller and Rollnick (2002) use motivation and decision-making to deal with the ambivalence and resistance often associated with changing an addictive behavior. However, confrontation is notably absent in this motivational approach. Instead, personal responsibility for the behavior change is emphasized, and the clinician offers feedback and advice in the context of an empathic, listening, and reflective style.
- *12-step approaches,* which are based on the principles of Alcoholics Anonymous and usually include attendance at AA or similar meetings, are very common in most community treatment programs. They have been incorporated into numerous comprehensive, medically oriented treatment approaches, including detox and inpatient programs.
- *Residential treatment* settings offer psychosocial rehabilitation based on either a 12-step or a more confrontive therapeutic community model. Often they employ psychological principles, including counterconditioning, reinforcement management, and relapse prevention.
- *Stage-based methods:* Since most substance abusers are not ready to change their behavior, action-oriented interventions have low levels of success. Viewing treatment as involving movement through a series of sequential steps and attempting to increase motivation prior to offering action-oriented interventions, like skills training and relapse prevention, is becoming a common approach among treatment providers (DiClemente, 2003; Prochaska, DiClemente, & Norcross, 1992).
- *Court-mandated treatment:* Many judges and probation officials are referring many clients as a condition of their probation for offenses that involve substance abuse. Mandated treatment increases the numbers of individuals who come to treatment but rarely produces internal motivation for change.
- *Relapse prevention and recycling treatments:* Relapse, or a return to the problematic behavior, is frequent with addictive behaviors. In fact, most clients experience multiple relapses and quitting attempts as they recycle through the process of change before achieving sustained change. Most treatment programs have a specific component devoted to relapse prevention that usually employs the cognitive-behavioral strategies (Marlatt & Gordon, 1985).

TREATMENT MATCHING

Over the past 30 years, psychologists have assumed that the extensive heterogeneity in substance abusers necessitated differentiation in treatment. Many hypothesized that clients with certain characteristics (e.g., antisocial personality, cognitive impairment, levels of cognitive complexity, severity of dependence) would respond differently to different types of treatments either to increase or to decrease the efficacy of that treatment approach. This matching hypothesis, which assumes a client attribute by treatment interaction (ATI), has been explored both in educational settings and in treatment programs. Although a number of individual studies have supported the matching hypothesis, they are typically small-*N* studies that often found matching post hoc.

In the largest single trial of psychosocial treatments of its kind, the National Institute on Alcohol Abuse and Alcoholism and a large group of senior addiction investigators examined the question of treatment matching through Project MATCH (Babor & DelBoca, 2003; Project MATCH Research Group, 1993, 1997). Do certain patient characteristics interact with certain types of treatments to produce differential outcomes? This randomized, clinical trial yielded several important findings:

1. Compliance of alcohol-dependent clients with all three of the individual treatments (cognitive-behavioral, 12-step facilitation, and motivational enhancement) was substantial, with patients receiving on average two thirds of the prescribed treatment dose over a 12-week period.
2. There were dramatic changes in drinking from pre- to posttreatment, with few differences in outcomes among the treatments. Although there was no treatment control comparison to definitively test for treatment effects, the changes in drinking were significant and were well sustained throughout the 12 months posttreatment and even extending out to 39 months posttreatment. Three years after treatment there continued to be dramatic differences from the pretreatment level of drinking.
3. There was only minimal support for the primary treatment matching hypotheses tested in this study, so that individuals could be assigned to any of these treatments with little difference in outcome.
4. There were two interesting treatment by characteristics interactions. Outpatients with higher levels of anger had better drinking outcomes when treated with a motivational enhancement approach rather than either cognitive-behavioral or 12-step approaches. Outpatients living in environments with more extensive drinking had better long-term drinking outcomes if they received a 12-step approach and attend AA.

Project MATCH studied a more static conceptualization of treatment matching, relying on the assumption that a single characteristic would interact with one type of treatment to produce better outcomes. If the process of change is a dynamic one represented by stages of change, a static model as a basis for matching would not be the most appropriate model, since the individual engaged in changing a behavior represents a moving target and not a static entity (DiClemente, 2003). Some data indicate that, when treatments are targeted at the stages change in a more dynamic type of matching, these interventions can be more effective. However, this requires complex individualization of the treatment process. Newer technologies, including computer-generated feedback, make it possible to create more individualized interventions that can target shifting client decisional considerations, current coping activities, levels of self-efficacy to abstain or refrain from the substance, and psychosocial risk factors. Early indications suggest that this more dynamic, process-oriented type of matching can aid the delivery and outcome of efforts to promote successful, sustained behavior change among substance abusers (DiClemente & Prochaska, 1998; Prochaska, DiClemente, Velicer, & Rossi, 1993).

PRACTICAL SUGGESTIONS FOR TREATMENT

Although there are only minimal data for specific treatment matching to client characteristics, current research does yield the following suggestions:

1. There is significant co-occurrence of alcohol and drug problems with many psychiatric syndromes. Screening for alcohol or drug abuse and dependence should be included in clinical intake procedures and both problems addressed.
2. Individuals currently experiencing serious withdrawal symptoms or those who have had indications of delirium tremens (alcohol)

or another drug-related organic brain syndrome need supervised detoxification from alcohol or drugs prior to psychosocial treatment.

3. Individuals with intact marriages and a spouse willing to attend treatment do better with some behavioral marital therapy.
4. Individuals with multiple psychosocial problems, including financial, social, housing, and occupational, do better when given access to multiple services or treatments addressing these problems in addition to the psychosocial treatment of the drinking or drug problems. Concurrent interventions, as in the community reinforcement approach or social network therapy, are recommended.
5. Brief interventions consisting of 30–60 minutes of discussion and advice appear to produce significant change in drinking and possibly drug use. At minimum, practitioners should offer some brief intervention of feedback and advice to everyone who screens positive for alcohol or drug abuse and dependence.
6. Intensity of treatment appears to have little relation to treatment outcome for a broad range of individuals with alcohol problems. Engagement and retention of individuals in treatment appear to be the most important dimensions. Offering choice and engaging the client in the treatment are important strategies with substance abusers.
7. Motivation to change the substance use is an important dimension to consider in designing treatments. Clients with low motivation need interventions that acknowledge the client's perspective and are proactive in keeping the client in treatment. Confrontation appears to increase defensiveness and denial.
8. There is a crucial role for behavioral and psychosocial interventions to be given in conjunction with pharmacological treatments such as nicotine replacement, naltrexone or other drugs used to reduce craving for opiates and alcohol, and disulfiram and other drugs used as antagonists for alcohol and other drugs (Volpicelli, Pettinati, McLellan, & O'Brien, 2001).
9. Matching patients high in anger with motivational approaches and those living in substance abuse infested environments with 12-step and self-help support systems make clinical sense and should be incorporated in treatment planning.

References, Readings, & Internet Sites 

Babor, T., & DelBoca, F. (Eds.). (2003). *Project MATCH: The book*. Cambridge University Press.

Beck, A. T., Wright, F. D., Newman, C. F., & Liese, B. S. (1993). *Cognitive therapy of substance abuse*. New York: Guilford Press.

Brown, T. (Ed.) (1995). *Treating alcoholism*. San Francisco: Jossey-Bass.

DiClemente, C. C. (2003). *Addiction and change: How addictions develop and addicted people change*. New York: Guilford Press.

DiClemente, C. C., & Prochaska, J. O. (1998). Toward a comprehensive, transtheoretical model of change. In Miller and Heather (Eds.), *Treating addictive behaviors* (2nd ed., pp. 3–24). New York: Plenum Press.

Marlatt, G. A., & Gordon, J. R. (Eds.). (1985). *Relapse prevention: Maintenance strategies in the treatment of addictive behaviors.* New York: Guilford Press.

McCrady, B. S., & Epstein, E. E. (Eds.). (1999). *Addictions: A comprehensive guidebook*. New York: Oxford University Press.

Miller, W. R., & Heather, N. (Eds.). (1998). *Treating addictive behaviors* (2nd ed.). New York: Plenum Press.

Miller, W. R., & Rollnick, S. (2002). *Motivational interviewing: Preparing people to change addictive behavior.* New York: Guilford Press.

Monti, P. M., Kadden, R. M., Rohsenow, D. J., Cooney, N. L., & Abrams, D. B. (2002). *Treating alcohol dependence* (2nd ed.). New York: Guilford Press.

National Institute of Alcohol Abuse. (n.d.). Home page. Retrieved 2004 from http://www.niaa.gov

National Institute of Drug Abuse. (n.d.). Home page. Retrieved 2004 from http://www.nida.gov

Onken, L. S., & Blaine, J. D. (Eds.). (1990). *Psychotherapy and counseling in the treatment of drug abuse* (NIDA Research Monograph 104, DHHS Publication No. ADM 90-1172). Washington, DC: Superintendent of Documents.

Prochaska, J. O., DiClemente, C. C., & Norcross, J. C. (1992). In search of how people change: Applications to addictive behaviors. *American Psychologist, 47,* 1102–1114.

Project MATCH Research Group. (1993). Project MATCH: Rationale and methods for a multisite clinical trial matching alcoholism patients to treatment. *Alcoholism: Clinical and Experimental Research, 17,* 1130–1145.

Project MATCH Research Group. (1997). Matching alcoholism treatments to client heterogeneity: Project MATCH posttreatment drinking outcomes. *Journal of Studies on Alcohol, 58,* 7–29.

Rotgers, F., Keller, D. S., & Morgenstern, J. (Eds.). (2003). *Treating substance abuse: Theory and technique*. New York: Guilford Press.

Substance Abuse and Mental Health Services Administration. (n.d.). Home page. Retrieved 2004 from http://www.samshsa.gov

University of Maryland, Baltimore County. (n.d.). Habits Lab home page. Retrieved 2004 from http://www.umbc.edu/psych/habits

Volpicelli, J. R., Pettinati, H. M., McLellan, A. T., & O'Brien, C. P. (2001). *Combining medication and psychosocial treatments for addictions: The BRENDA approach*. New York: Guilford Press.

Related Topics

Chapter 16, "Identification and Assessment of Alcohol Abuse"
Chapter 46, "Stages of Change: Prescriptive Guidelines"
Chapter 55, "Motivational Interviewing"
Chapter 74, "Guidelines for Relapse Prevention"
Chapter 96, "Common Drugs of Abuse"
Chapter 100, "Facilitating Client Involvement in Self-Help Groups"

55 MOTIVATIONAL INTERVIEWING

William R. Miller & Theresa B. Moyers

Psychotherapists are usually trained in how to work with people who want to change, but are less often prepared to help people want to change. People who seek treatment are often ambivalent about change: they want it, and they don't. Therapists sometimes dismiss clients who seem insufficiently motivated, inviting them to return when they are ready for change. Particularly in addressing addictive behaviors or criminal offenses, it has been common in the United States to use heavy-handed confrontational, punitive, or coercive strategies in order to provide extrinsic motivation for change. Faced with such pressure to change, the typical human response is resistance, which in turn decreases the likelihood of long-term behavior change (Brehm & Brehm, 1981; Miller, Benefield, & Tonigan, 1993).

Motivational interviewing (MI) was designed specifically to help psychotherapists work with clients who are less ready for change. Originally developed to address substance use disorders, MI is now used to enhance motivation for change in a wide array of health behaviors. It is defined as a client-centered, yet directive method for evoking intrinsic motivation to change (Miller & Rollnick, 2002). Ambivalence is understood as a normal stage in the process of change (Prochaska, DiClemente, & Norcross, 1992), and MI seeks to resolve ambivalence in the direction of commitment to change. For clients who perceive little or no need for change, the initial goal of MI is usually to develop discrepancy (ambivalence) that is then resolved toward change.

FOUR GUIDING PRINCIPLES

MI is not a technique so much as a method of psychotherapy. The underling spirit of MI is collaborative, evocative, and respectful of client autonomy (Miller & Rollnick, 2002). The collaborative aspect involves a companionable partnership of client and counselor, de-emphasizing power differentials. The therapist avoids an expert or authoritarian role, instead regarding clients as experts on themselves. Information and advice is provided when requested, but primary emphasis is on evoking the client's own intrinsic motivation for change and perspectives on how to achieve it. The clients' autonomy and ability to choose their own life course are emphasized.

Four principles guide the practice of MI, as follows:

1. *Express empathy*. MI is heavily rooted in a client-centered style of counseling, as formulated by Carl Rogers (1980) and his associates. Therapeutic empathy, acceptance, and respect are communicated through the use of reflective listening to attain accurate understanding of the client's own perspectives. Accurate empathy is a foundational skill, without which MI proficiency cannot be achieved.
2. *Develop discrepancy*. The MI therapist helps clients to recognize the discrepancy between their current behavior and their important goals or values. This is done primarily by having the client, rather than the therapist, give voice to the reasons for change. Clients literally talk themselves into changing.
3. *Roll with resistance*. "Resistance" is understood simply as clients voicing the status quo side of their ambivalence. The therapist avoids arguing, pushing against, or confronting such resistance, which only tends to entrench it. Instead, the therapist responds in ways that diffuse resistance and direct the client back toward intrinsic motivation for change.
4. *Support self-efficacy*. Finally, the therapist actively conveys the message that the client is capable of change. The client is the expert in solving the problem, and the therapist draws upon his or her own particular strengths and resources. The motivational interviewer is a consultant, offering options that clients may not have considered from a broad menu of change strategies, and particularly eliciting clients' own ideas.

TWO PHASES

It is helpful to think of MI as occurring in two phases. The first phase focuses on evoking intrinsic motivation by having the client give voice to change talk—in essence, arguments for change. Four types of change talk are distinguishable, memorable by the acronym DARN:

- *Desire*. Why and in what ways does the client want to change?
- *Ability*. Why and how would the client be able to change, should she choose to do so?
- *Reasons*. What are some reasons for change, from the client's perspective?
- *Need*. Why and in what ways is it important for the client to make a change?

Giving voice to such change talk moves the client along toward voicing commitment to change, which is the focus of the second phase of MI. Timing is important here. The therapist needs a sense for when the client is developing the intention to change, and at this point shifts toward evoking a specific plan for implementing change and commitment to carry it out. If the therapist shifts prematurely to phase two, resistance occurs and the therapist returns to phase one strategies for further evoking intrinsic motivation.

OARS AND THE DIRECTIVE ASPECT

Four specific skills are particularly emphasized for fostering client safety, acceptance, and change, represented by the acronym OARS:

1. *Open questions*. The psychotherapist asks open-ended questions intended to evoke change talk (desire, ability, reasons, need).

Relatedly, the therapist avoids asking questions the answer to which would be arguments for the status quo (e.g., "Why haven't you . . . ?" or "What keeps you from . . .?"). With a well-crafted open question, the answer is change talk.

2. *Affirmation.* The therapist emphasizes and affirms the client's strengths, efforts, abilities, and steps in the right direction.
3. *Reflective listening.* Again, the Rogerian skill of accurate empathy is crucial, manifest in skillful reflective listening that helps the client to continue exploring and experiencing the current dilemma.
4. *Summaries.* As the client offers arguments for change, the therapist provides periodic summaries in which change talk statements are drawn together. In essence, the therapist collects each change-talk theme like a flower, and then offers them back to the client in ever larger bouquets.

These four skills are used in a consciously directive manner to promote and reinforce change talk. The therapist first and foremost evokes clients' own motivations for change. Clients, of course, hear themselves voice these arguments for change. Next, they hear the therapist affirm and reflect their change talk, in essence emphasizing and reinforcing it. Then they hear their change statements yet again, collected into summaries.

In essence, MI involves the selective and strategic use of OARS with the goal that clients will talk themselves into change. The therapist asks particular open questions, selectively reflects change talk, affirms movement in the hoped-for direction, and selectively summarizes the clients' own motivations for change. It is here that MI evolves from Rogers's conception of client-centered therapy as nondirective by providing specific guidelines for strategically responding in a directive manner in order to evoke the client's own arguments for change. An analogy for MI is that of ballroom dancing: one moves smoothly with the partner, but is also leading in a particular direction.

THERAPEUTIC USES OF MOTIVATIONAL INTERVIEWING

There are at least three general therapeutic applications of MI. First, it has been used early in or as a prelude to treatment in order to enhance client motivation for change. Clinical trials indicate that an initial session at the beginning of treatment can enhance retention, adherence, and motivation for treatment. In substance-abuse randomized trials, these effects have been reflected in a doubling, on average, of abstinence rates following treatment. When added to other treatment approaches, MI appears to have a synergistic effect on outcomes.

Second, MI has been used as a stand-alone brief intervention. A single session of MI has been found to be effective in triggering significant change relative to no treatment or placement on a waiting list. If there is a waiting list, clients are likely to fare much better if given a single session of MI than if simply left to wait for treatment. MI has also been used for opportunistic interventions, where a problem is detected for which the person was not initially seeking help. For example, patients seeking health care can be screened for alcohol abuse, and MI can be used as a brief intervention within the context of primary health care.

Third, MI can be integrated into other treatments. The overall style of MI can be used by the therapist even when the specific focus on reducing ambivalence is no longer necessary. Maintaining the supportive-directive style of MI may help to minimize client resistance. Furthermore, it is not uncommon to encounter ambivalence and resistance later in treatment, as therapy progresses and new challenges are encountered. In this circumstance the therapist can augment the MI style with specific interventions to elicit and reinforce commitment language, thereby delivering the complete method as it is needed. As ambivalence resolves and resistance fades, the therapist can return to the intended therapeutic approach, dancing back and forth between the elements of MI and other methods. One of the best examples of combining MI with other methods is found in Motivational Enhancement Therapy (MET). Here, MI is combined with objective and personalized feedback in a structured, four-session intervention originally used in Project MATCH (Miller, Zweban, DiClemente, & Rychtarik, 1992).

EVIDENCE OF EFFICACY

More than 60 randomized clinical trials of MI have been published. The CD that accompanies this volume contains a PowerPoint file offering summaries of many of these studies. Space here permits only a summary of what is known about the efficacy of MI to date. Recent summaries of outcome research on MI (Burke, Arkowitz, & Dunn, 2002; Miller, in press) suggest that MI is useful at various points along the treatment continuum, although specific mechanisms of effectiveness have not yet been identified.

Client Motivation

First, there is evidence that MI does what it was intended to do: increase motivation for change. In one study, patients in an inpatient substance-abuse treatment center were randomly assigned to receive or not receive one MI session at intake. Ward staff unaware of group assignment reliably rated patients who had received a preparatory MI session as more cooperative, punctual, and working harder in treatment, and as more likely to remain sober. MI has been shown to yield higher rates of client change talk and commitment to change, and to promote advancement through one or more stages of change.

Retention and Adherence

There is published evidence that MI can increase retention in treatment, as well as behavioral adherence to specific change regimens. Studies have supported the effectiveness of MI in increasing attendance in outpatient substance-abuse treatment sessions for both adolescents and mandated adult offenders. Other trials have reported increased retention in methadone maintenance, cocaine detoxification, treatment for dual disorders, and aftercare attendance. Measures showing significant effects of MI in clinical trials include increased diabetic glucose self-monitoring, keeping of food diaries in a weight-loss program, and decreased salt intake in treatment for hypertension.

Outcomes

As intended, MI has also been shown to promote positive changes in health behaviors. Evaluations of MI in the treatment of abuse disorders have shown significant improvement on a broad range of outcome measures including total abstinence, frequency, and volume of alcohol use and alcohol problems. Reductions in illicit drug use have been reported for marijuana, stimulants, heroin, and polydrug abuse. Studies of other health behaviors have reported significant treatment effects of MI in dietary change, smoking cessation, use of water purification, and decreased incidence of unprotected sexual intercourse.

Amplification of Treatment Effects

As discussed above, MI has often been shown to enhance the efficacy of treatment programs to which it has been added. Significantly improved outcomes have been reported when MI has been added to cognitive-behavior therapy, disease-model treatment for alcoholism, diabetes management, cardiovascular rehabilitation, and dietary counseling. In the treatment of substance-use disorders, the magnitude of effect has been found in several studies to be a doubling of abstinence rates for the same treatment program with versus without an initial MI session.

References, Readings, & Internet Sites

Brehm, S. S., & Brehm, J. W. (1981). *Psychological reactance: A theory of freedom and control.* New York: Academic Press.

Burke, B. L., Arkowitz, H., & Dunn, C. (2002). The efficacy of motivational interviewing and its adaptations: What we know so far. In W. R. Miller & S. Rollnick, *Motivational interviewing: Preparing people for change* (2nd ed., pp. 217–250). New York: Guilford Press.

Holder, H. D., Cisler, R. A., Longabaugh, R., Stout, R. L., Treno, A. J., & Zweben, A. (2000). Alcoholism treatment and medical care costs from Project MATCH. *Addiction, 95,* 999–1013.

Miller, W. R. (1983). Motivational interviewing with problem drinkers. *Behavioural Psychotherapy, 11,* 147–172.

Miller, W. R. (2000). Rediscovering fire: Small interventions, large effects. *Psychology of Addictive Behaviors, 14,* 6–18.

Miller, W. R. (in press). Motivational interviewing in the service of health promotion. *American Journal of Health Promotion.*

Miller, W. R., Benefield, R. G., & Tonigan, J. S. (1993). *Journal of Consulting and Clinical Psychology, 61,* 445–461.

Miller, W. R., & Rollnick, S. (2002). *Motivational interviewing: Preparing people for change* (2nd ed.). New York: Guilford Press.

Miller, W. R., Zweban, A., DiClemente, C. C., & Rychtarik, R. (1992). Motivational enhancement therapy manual: A clinical research guide for therapists treating individuals with alcohol abuse and dependence. (Project MATCH Monograph Series: Volume 2). Rockville, MD: National Institute on Alcohol Abuse and Alcoholism.

Motivational Interviewing Network of Trainers. (n.d.). Resources for clinicians, researchers, and trainers. Retrieved 2004 from http://www.motivationalinterview.org

Prochaska, J. O., DiClemente, C. C., & Norcross, J. C. (1992). *American Psychologist, 47,* 1102–1114.

Rogers, C. R. (1980). *A way of being.* Boston: Houghton Mifflin.

Rollnick, S., Mason, P., & Butler, C. (1999). *Health behavior change: A guide for practitioners.* New York: Churchill Livingstone.

Rollnick, S., & Miller, W. R. (1995). What is motivational interviewing? *Behavioural and Cognitive Psychotherapy, 23,* 325–334.

Related Topics

Chapter 74, "Guidelines for Relapse Prevention"

Chapter 121, "A Model for Clinical Decision Making With Dangerous Patients"

56 ANXIETY/ANGER MANAGEMENT TRAINING

Richard M. Suinn

Anxiety and stress present major concerns for the general population. Primary care practitioners report that anxiety ranks next highest as the major reason patients see their physicians. Anxiety can be at the core of various disorders:

- Generalized anxiety disorder or phobic disorders
- The blocking of coping behaviors, healthy lifestyles, educational attainment, or successful performance
- Biomedical consequences

Anger is now being recognized as another crucial problem area. Severe angry episodes are experienced by as high as 20% of the population. Anger is the source of varied social and personal problems:

- Child or family abuse
- Physical or verbal assault
- Community property damage
- Disruption of work performance
- Interference with health and the immune system

Developed in the 1970s, Anxiety Management Training (AMT) was designed as a brief intervention for anxiety (Suinn, 1990, 1995). Since then, empirical results have proved its application for anger. It is a six- to eight-session structured procedure that trains patients in using relaxation to deactivate anxiety or angry emotional states.

APPLICATIONS: EMPIRICAL VALIDATION

Empirical results confirm the value of AMT for the following:

- Generalized anxiety disorder (Durhan et al., 1994
- Mathematics anxiety (Suinn & Richardson, 1971)
- Essential hypertension (Jorgensen, Houston, & Zurawski, 1981)
- Diabetes (Rose, Firestone, Heick, & Faught, 1983)
- Dysmenorrhea (Quillen & Denney, 1982)
- Depression (Cragan & Deffenbacher, 1984; Jannoun, Oppenheimer, & Gelder, 1982)
- Type A characteristics (Hart, 1984; Nakano, 1990)
- Anger (Deffenbacher, Filetti, Lynch, Dahlen, & Oetting, 2002; Suinn & Deffenbacher, 1988)
- Removing anxiety blocking patient's ability to respond to traditional psychotherapy (Van Hassel, Bloom, & Gonzales, 1982)

ADVANTAGES OF AMT

A major advantage of AMT is the fact that it is a brief therapy using a self-control approach that permits generalization. Moreover, because the procedure is structured, it is possible to determine progress at each session and to determine the need for additional or fewer sessions. The step-by-step characteristics of AMT also allow monitoring of gains from session to session. Such concrete information can be most useful for the practitioner who wishes to carefully monitor progress or for the researcher who wishes to study variables involved in change from each session.

HOW TO CONDUCT SESSIONS

Among the basic or core characteristics of the AMT method are the following:

- Guided imagery for anxiety or anger arousal
- Relaxation for deactivating the arousal
- Practice for self-control
- Homework for generalization

The guided imagery involves use of anxiety or anger imagery from the patient's experience to precipitate arousal. Anxiety or anger arousal is precipitated during the sessions in order to aid the client in the use of relaxation to reduce an actual experience of anxiety or anger. Thus, the client can first practice controlling his or her anxiety in the safe setting of the treatment environment, prior to being assigned homework in real-life applications. AMT covers six to eight sessions.

Session 1 involves relaxation training using the standard Jacobsen tension/relaxation method (1938) or biofeedback.

Session 2 involves identification of an anxiety (or anger scene for anger treatment), relaxation, and anxiety (or anger arousal) followed by relaxation. The anxiety (anger) scene involves a real experience that has been associated with a moderately high level of anxiety (anger). After the client is relaxed, anxiety (anger) arousal is initiated through the therapist's instruction to switch on this scene and use it to reexperience anxiety (anger). Instructions include description of both scene-setting and anxiety (anger)–arousal details to aid in arousal. After about 10–15 seconds of exposure, the scene is terminated and the therapist reintroduces the relaxation.

Session 3 follows the steps used in session 2, with the addition of self-initiated relaxation and attention to the client's personal signs associated with anxiety (anger). This might involve symptoms such as heightened respiration, clenched fists, catastrophic thoughts, and so on. After the client obtains arousal, the therapist instructs the client to pay attention to the anxiety (anger) symptoms. The following instructions are given: "Pay attention to how you experience anxiety [anger]; perhaps it is in body signs such as your hands or neck tensing, or your heart rate, or in some of your thoughts." Then relaxation is again retrieved, with the therapist taking responsibility for guiding the relaxation. This cycle of arousal, attention to anxiety (anger) signs, and retrieval of relaxation is continued to the end of the hour—a cycle of about three to five repetitions.

Session 4 adds two new major components. First, a high-intensity anxiety (or anger) scene is identified. During this session, this scene will be alternated with the moderate-level scene used in sessions 2 and 3. Second, the session requires the client to assume more responsibility for regaining self-control after anxiety (anger) arousal. Instead of the therapist terminating the anxiety (anger) scene and reinitiating the relaxation, the client decides when to end the anxiety (anger) scene and takes responsibility for relaxation retrieval.

Session 5 completes the fading out of therapist control and the completion of client self-control. At the start of the session, the client self-initiates relaxation, signaling its achievement. Although the therapist switches on the anxiety (anger) scene, all activities from this point are client controlled.

Sessions 6–8 repeat the session 5 format until self-control appears complete. New anxiety (anger) scenes may be employed as needed to increase generalization.

References & Readings

Cragan, M. K., & Deffenbacher, J. L. (1984). Anxiety management training and relaxation as self-control in the treatment of generalized anxiety in medical outpatients. *Journal of Counseling Psychology, 1,* 123–131.

Deffenbacher, J. (1994). Anger reduction: Issues, assessment, and intervention strategies. In A. Siegman & T. Smith (Eds.), *Anger, hostility, and the heart* (pp. 239–269). Hilsdale, NJ: Lawrence Erlbaum.

Deffenbacher, J., Filetti, L., Lynch, R., & Oetting, E. (2002). Cognitive-behavioral treatment of high anger drivers. *Behaviour Research and Therapy, 40,* 895–910.

Durhan, R., Murphy, T., Allan, T., Richard, K., Treliving, L. R., & Fenton, G. W. (1994). Cognitive therapy, analytic psychotherapy, and anxiety management training for generalized anxiety disorder. *British Journal of Psychiatry, 165,* 315–323.

Hart, K. (1984). Stress management training for Type A individuals. *Journal of Behavioral Medicine, 12,* 133–140.

Jacobsen, E. (1938). *Progressive relaxation.* Chicago: University of Chicago Press.

Jannoun, L., Oppenheimer, C., & Gelder, M. (1982). A self-help treatment program for anxiety state patients. *Behavior Therapy, 13,* 103–111.

Jorgensen, R., Houston, B., & Zurawski, R. (1981). Anxiety management training in the treatment of essential hypertension. *Behavior Research and Therapy, 19,* 467–474.

Nakano, K. (1990). Effects of two self-control procedures on modifying Type A behavior. *Journal of Clinical Psychology, 46,* 652–657.

Pantalon, M. V., & Motta, R. W. (1998). Effectiveness of anxiety management training in the treatment of posttraumatic stress disorder: A preliminary report. *Journal of Behavior Therapy and Experimental Psychiatry, 29,* 21–29.

Quillen, M. A., & Denney, D. R. (1982). Self-control of dysmenorrheic symptoms through pain management training. *Journal of Behavior Therapy and Experimental Psychiatry, 13,* 123–130.

Rose, M., Firestone, P., Heick, H., & Faught, A. (1983). The effects of anxiety management training on the control of juvenile diabetes mellitus. *Journal of Behavioral Medicine, 27,* 381–395.

Shoemaker, J. (1976). *Treatment for anxiety neurosis.* Unpublished doctoral dissertation, Colorado State University, Ft. Collins.

Suinn, R. (1990). *Anxiety management training: A behavior therapy.* New York: Plenum Press.

Suinn, R. (1995). Anxiety management training. In K. Craig & K. Dobson (Eds.), *Anxiety and depression in adults and children* (pp. 159–179). Thousand Oaks, CA: Sage.

Suinn, R., & Deffenbacher, J. (1988). Anxiety management training. *Counseling Psychologist, 16,* 31–49.

Suinn, R., & Richardson, F. (1971). Anxiety management training: A non-specific behavior therapy program for anxiety control. *Behavior Therapy, 2,* 498–512.

Van Hassel, J., Bloom, L. J., & Gonzales, A. C. (1982). Anxiety management training with schizophrenic outpatients. *Journal of Clinical Psychology, 38,* 280–285.

Related Topics

Chapter 79, "Treating High-Conflict Couples"

Chapter 121, "A Model for Clinical Decision Making With Dangerous Patients"

57 PSYCHOLOGICAL INTERVENTIONS IN ADULT DISEASE MANAGEMENT

Carol D. Goodheart

Chronic illnesses are now the primary cause of disability and death in the United States, a change from the acute conditions of the past. Over a 25-year span, the number of people with chronic conditions will increase by 35 million, from 99 million in 1995 to 134 million in 2020 (Institute for Health and Aging, 1996). The chronic illnesses form a spectrum of diseases; they may be life-threatening, progressive, manageable, unpredictable, or of known or unknown etiology. Such illnesses include cancer, cardiovascular disease, diabetes, asthma, arthritis, HIV disease, Alzheimer's disease, postviral syndromes, and gastrointestinal disorders, among many others.

Behavior, genetics, and the environment interact to produce or prevent disease. The Human Capital Initiative (1995) reports the state of the psychological research agenda on health and behavior, which fosters the understanding of basic processes necessary for the prevention and treatment of chronic illness. Once disease is present, symptomatology may be affected by behavior, cognition, emotion, and interpersonal dynamics. Overall, the application of psychological interventions to disease management results in improvements in mental health functioning and reductions in medical service use (Lechnyr, 1992; Pallak, Cummings, Dorken, & Henke, 1994; Schlesinger, Mumford, Glass, Patrick, & Sharfstein, 1983). The following summary highlights the key elements in the psychological treatment of adults with chronic illnesses.

There are many models of psychological intervention during illness, with variations according to theoretical orientation, population, setting, and emphasis. Among the diverse approaches, however, there are common themes for the clinician (Goodheart & Lansing, 1997).

1. *Obtain medical information:* Clinicians need not become medical experts, but they must obtain sufficient background to understand the choices, treatments, and experiences of the adult with a chronic condition. Collaboration with the patient's physician can provide information on the *o*utcome, *p*rocess, *e*tiology, and management *n*eeds of a particular disease (the acronym OPEN makes the list easy to remember). Other important medical resources are available through the Internet, medical reference libraries, federal and state government health agencies (on-line, mail, and facsimile transmissions), and specific disease organizations such as the American Cancer Society, the American Diabetes Association, and the American Heart Association. *The Merck Manual of Diagnosis and Therapy* (Beers & Berkow, 1999) provides a medical overview of most conditions a clinician will encounter and is searchable via the Internet (http://www.merck.com/pubs/mmanual/). Perhaps the most valuable and comprehensive source of on-line medical information is the National Institutes of Health home page for health information (http://www.health.nih.gov/). It is possible to search most health topics at this site and to gain access to MEDLINEplus, which is a health database maintained by NIH's National Library of Medicine, available in English and Spanish, and Healthfinder, a health resource maintained by the Department of Health and Human Services.

Links are provided for clinical studies, drug information, library references, special programs, and other health agencies.

2. *Assess response to illness and psychological status:* The adult's capacity to cope with illness is affected by premorbid personality organization, life stage roles and tasks, maturational development, internal resources such as temperament and intelligence, and external resources such as socioeconomic status, family support, and level of access to health care. These factors are evaluated through clinical interview and, in some situations, through specific standardized assessment measures/scales for depression, anxiety, somatization, hostility, or other relevant indices.

3. *Integrate theoretical orientation and illness:* Cross-fertilization between and among differing schools of psychological theory often occurs when clinicians work with chronically ill adults. Dynamic clinicians add behavioral and educational components; cognitive clinicians add inferred self- and relational components; family systems, feminist theory, humanistic, and eclectic clinicians add to the diversity. In general, clinicians tend to borrow from other clinicians' attitudes and techniques. Regardless of orientation, the focus on coping with illness is enhanced when clinicians understand the patient's global mastery-competence level and how the patient manages reality, affect, and anxiety, interpersonal relationships, and cognitive functions. Examples of three treatment approaches with theoretically different underpinnings are *Medical Family Therapy* (McDaniel, Hepworth, & Doherty, 1992), a family systems orientation; *Managing Chronic Illness: A Biopsychosocial Perspective* (Nicassio & Smith, 1995), a cognitive-behavioral orientation; and *Treating People With Chronic Disease: A Psychological Guide* (Goodheart & Lansing, 1997), a psychodynamic-pyschoeducational orientation. All three texts are based on a biopsychosocial model of understanding and intervention. All recommend an interdisciplinary collaborative approach to health care and are appropriate for community practice and medical settings. Another key reference guide is *Clinical Health Psychology in Medical Settings: A Practitioner's Guidebook* (Belar & Deardorff, 1995).

4. *Offer a menu of interventions:* The selection of interventions is based on the changing needs and capacities of the chronically ill adult and the knowledge and skills of the clinician. Interventions may be directed toward prevention of further illness (e.g., smoking cessation, weight control); toward screening for disease (e.g., decreasing the avoidance of warranted HIV testing or mammograms); or toward management of disease. Disease management interventions include the following:

- *Focused psychotherapy:* A time-limited approach to problem solving, based on biopsychosocial stressors and resources.
- *Decision making:* Helping adults arrive at the best decisions for their personal circumstances from among the medical choices they are given.
- *Medical symptom reduction:* Helping adults decrease pain, lessen side effects of treatments (e.g., anticipatory nausea associated with chemotherapy), or decrease frequency or intensity of acute episodes (e.g., incidents of asthma exacerbation).
- *Coping enhancement:* Helping adults to plan actively, elicit support, seek information, develop new habits, reduce anxiety, and facilitate mourning while preventing depression.
- *Treatment adherence:* Helping adults develop motivation and overcome obstacles to maintaining adherence to prescribed medical treatment regimens.
- *Stress and pain reduction:* Helping adults learn techniques of progressive relaxation, hypnosis, biofeedback, visualization, meditation, or focused breathing.
- *Interpersonal techniques:* Helping adults learn new or improved skills for communication, assertion, and conflict resolution with medical personnel, family, partners, employers, coworkers, friends.
- *Adaptation:* Helping adults make quality-of-life adjustments to an altered reality due to the losses of illness, effects of medications, aftereffects of medical treatments, or disability.
- *Crisis management:* Helping adults mobilize internal and external supportive re-

sources to regain control, for use when the patient is flooded with affect and overwhelmed by anxiety and when the patient's ability to cope on his or her own is compromised.

- *Anger management:* Helping adults control anger through the use of shame reduction, guided imagery, anger arousal combined with relaxation, and through improved self-efficacy in communication and problem solving.
- *Nonverbal psychotherapeutic techniques:* Helping adults express affect and experience through art therapy, sand play, or movement therapy. Rarely used alone, these visual, tactile, motile techniques are particularly useful in adults with learning disabilities, posttraumatic stress disorder, or a blocked, regressed, dissociated, or concrete state of functioning.
- *Family involvement:* Helping the caregivers, partners, and family members of adults with chronic illness by conjoint treatments and the development of coping and support structures within the home care system.
- *Support for self disease management:* Helping adults contribute to their own well-being through self-selected adjunctive activities (e.g., personal illness diaries, exercise and nutrition programs [within limits of medical recommendations], religious and spiritual participation, humorous tapes and books).
- *Referral:* Helping adults decrease their isolation and increase the support network available to them through disease support groups and community services.
- *Handling uncertainty and fear of death:* Helping adults with the anxiety and depression that often accompany disease progression. The primary technique for death anxiety is to listen fully, which may be difficult under severe and threatening circumstances. To listen fully means to listen without judgment, without withdrawal, without denial, and without interference to the patient's hopes. To listen fully is to be present, with the patient, in facing death.

It is not possible within the limits of this entry to detail the implementation of each intervention given. Even experienced clinicians may not be skilled in every type of intervention listed above. For example, most clinicians are trained in graduate school to offer crisis management, but few are trained to offer hypnosis for pain management. For further training in specific modalities, clinicians may turn to appropriate postdoctoral continuing education programs (e.g., the American Society for Clinical Hypnosis offers hypnosis training throughout the United States). There is now a practical self-assessment model available to help clinicians gauge their readiness to provide chronic illness consultation and services (Belar et al., 2001). This resource provides multiple avenues for further study to develop and enhance skills.

5. *Match the focus of intervention to the need:* No single intervention is sufficient if used exclusively. Individuals with chronic illness vary in their willingness or ability to make use of the strategies. Nevertheless, important overlapping areas of need that represent common impediments to functioning have been identified in chronically ill adults:

- Isolation, losses and dependency, fear of death, confines of illness, lack of familiarity with medical culture (Shapiro & Koocher, 1996)
- Separation, loss of key roles and autonomy and control, disruption of plans, assault on self-image and self-esteem, uncertain and unpredictable futures, distressing emotions (Turk & Salovey, 1995)
- Decreased self-esteem associated with body image changes, mourning associated with losses, negative affects associated with physical, psychological, and social discomfort (Goodheart & Lansing, 1997)

6. *Face the personal impact of working with chronically ill adults:* Clinicians have their own idiosyncratic responses to the presence of disease and to patients' characterological reactions to disease. Entering into a therapeutic relationship with a chronically ill adult carries special challenges. Like everyone else, clinicians have deeply held personal attitudes toward bodily needs, functions, disfigurements, and pains and toward caretaking and dependency. They have personal fears about debilitation, decline, and death. Working with ill patients often induces countertransference reactions in clinicians, which may be expressed as

- Anxiety (e.g., exposure to death, failure, vulnerability, or loss may stimulate anxiety)
- Affect (e.g., anger may be a marker of frustration with the toll of disease or with patients who complain more than the clinician thinks is necessary; disgust or distaste may be evoked by the graphic details of illness)
- Defensive reactions (e.g., withdrawal, denial, moralizing, minimizing, or rescuing may occur if clinicians' anxieties or negative affects are aroused sufficiently)

It is not always possible to resolve these issues in ideal ways, but it is realistic to identify and manage clinicians' personal responses that interfere with clinical care. Potential signs of difficulty include the following:

- Preoccupation with thoughts of the patient out of session
- Persistent intense feelings about the patient
- Depressive constellation of discouragement, fatigue, and pessimism
- Treatment impasse
- Feedback from patient, supervisor, colleagues, family, or friends regarding affects, anxieties, or reactions to the work

SUMMARY

Psychological interventions in adult chronic illness are becoming increasingly important as the number of people with chronic conditions grows. The research literature on interactions among behavior, biology, and disease provides the basis for increasingly targeted psychological intervention strategies. The overview framework for these strategies includes obtaining sufficient medical information, assessing response to illness and psychological status, integrating psychological theory and the illness, offering a varied selection of interventions, matching the focus of intervention to the need, and facing the personal impact of working with chronically ill adults.

References, Readings, & Internet Sites 

Belar, C. D., Brown, R. A., Hersch, L. E., Hornyak, L. M., Rozensky, R. H., Sheridan, E. P., et al. (2001). Self-assessment in clinical health psychology: A model for ethical expansion of practice. *Professional Psychology: Research and Practice, 32*(2), 135–141.

Belar, C. D., & Deardorff, W. W. (1995). *Clinical health psychology in medical settings: A practitioner's guidebook*. Washington, DC: American Psychological Association.

Beers, M., & Berkow, R. (Eds.) (1999). *The Merck manual of diagnosis and therapy*. Rahway, NJ: Merck. http://www.merck.com/pubs/mmanual/.

Goodheart, C., & Lansing, M. (1997). *Treating people with chronic disease: A psychological guide*. Washington, DC: American Psychological Association.

Human Capital Initiative. (1995). *Do the right thing: A research plan for healthy living*. Washington, DC: American Psychological Association.

Institute for Health and Aging, University of California, San Francisco. (1996). *Chronic care in America: A 21st century challenge*. Princeton, NJ: Robert Wood Johnson Foundation.

Lechnyr, R. (1992). Cost savings and effectiveness of mental health services. *Journal of the Oregon Psychological Association, 38*, 8–12.

McDaniel, S. H., Hepworth, J., & Doherty, W. J. (1992). *Medical family therapy*. New York: Basic Books.

National Institutes of Health. (2003). Health information. Retrieved 2004 from http://www.health.nih.gov/

Nicassio, P. M., & Smith, T. W. (Eds.). (1995). *Managing chronic illness: A biopsychosocial perspective*. Washington, DC: American Psychological Association.

Pallak, M. S., Cummings, N., Dorken, H., & Henke, C. J. (1994). Effects of mental health treatment on medical cost. *Mind/Body Medicine, 1*, 7–16.

Schlesinger, H. J., Mumford, E., Glass, G. V., Patrick, C., & Sharfstein, S. (1983). Mental health treatment and medical care utilization in a fee for service system: Outpatient mental health treatment following the onset of a chronic disease. *American Journal of Mental Health, 73,* 422–429.

Shapiro, D. E., & Koocher, G. P. (1996). Goals and practical considerations in outpatient medical crises intervention. *Professional Psychology: Research and Practice, 27,* 109–120.

Turk, D. C., & Salovey, P. (1995). Cognitive-behavioral treatment of illness behavior. In P. M. Nicassio & T. W. Smith (Eds.), *Managing chronic illness: A biopsychosocial perspective.* Washington, DC: American Psychological Association.

Related Topic

Chapter 84, "Psychological Interventions in Childhood Chronic Illness"

58 ASSESSING AND TREATING NORMATIVE MALE ALEXITHYMIA

Ronald F. Levant

Alexithymia literally means the inability to put emotions into words. The term is composed of a series of Greek roots: *a* ("without"), *lexus* ("words"), and *thymos* ("emotions")—"without words for emotions." This condition was originally described by Sifneos (1967) and Krystal (1982) to characterize the severe emotional constriction they encountered in their (primarily male) patients who were psychosomatic, drug-dependent, or affected by posttraumatic stress disorder (see also Sifneos, 1988). They were dealing with cases of severe alexithymia, which is at the far end of the continuum of this disorder. Through my work on this topic at the Boston University Fatherhood Project (Levant & Kelly, 1989) and in my subsequent research and clinical practice (Levant & Kopecky, 1995), I have found that alexithymia also occurs in mild to moderate forms and in these forms is very widespread among men. I have come to call this normative male alexithymia.

Simply put, as a result of the male role socialization ordeal, boys grow up to be men who are genuinely unaware of their emotions and sometimes even their bodily sensations. When men are required to give an account of their emotions and are unable to identify them directly, they tend to rely on their cognition to logically deduce what they should feel under the circumstances. They cannot do what is so easy, and almost automatic, for most women—to simply sense inward feelings and let the verbal description come to mind.

This widespread inability among men to identify emotions and put them into words has enormous consequences. It blocks men who suffer from it from utilizing the most effective means known for dealing with life's stresses and traumas—namely, identifying, thinking about, and discussing one's emotional responses to a stressor with a friend, family member, or therapist. Consequently, it predisposes such men to deal with stress in ways that make certain forms of pathology more likely, such as substance abuse, violent behavior, sexual compulsions, stress-related illnesses, and early death. It also makes it less likely that such men will be able to benefit from psychotherapy as traditionally practiced.

I hasten to point out that by characterizing men's traditional inability to put emotions into words as a mild form of alexithymia I do not mean to pathologize men. Rather, this aspect of traditional masculinity does not serve men well in today's world and is therefore dysfunctional, although it did serve a purpose in earlier historical eras.

Normative alexithymia, like the more severe forms, is a result of trauma—in this case, the trauma of the male role socialization process that is so normative that we do not think of it as trauma at all (Levant, 1995; Levant & Kopecky, 1995). In brief, the male role socialization ordeal, through the combined influences of mothers, fathers, and peer groups, suppresses and channels natural male emotionality to such an extent that boys grow up to be men who develop an action-oriented variant of empathy, cannot readily sense their feelings and put them into words, and tend to channel or transform their vulnerable feelings into anger and their caring feelings into sexuality.

My approach to helping men identify and process their emotions integrates cognitive-behavioral, psychoeducational, skills-training, and family systems components. The program is an active, problem-solving approach that relies on the use of homework assignments. I have found that many men find such an approach very congenial because it is congruent with aspects of the male code. In addition, men who are demoralized for one reason or another may find that it restores their sense of agency.

Helping men overcome normative alexithymia is useful at the beginning stages of therapy because it enables them to develop the skills of emotional self-awareness and emotional expressivity that will empower them to wrestle with deeper conflicts.

ASSESSMENT

During the first interview, in addition to taking a standard history, I also assess the man's ability to become aware of his emotions and put them into words. I typically use the following format.

1. To what extent is the patient aware of discrete emotions, as contrasted with either the neuroendocrinological and musculoskeletal components of emotions (e.g., tension in the forehead, tightness in the gut) or signs of stress (e.g., feeling "overloaded" or "zapped")? Some specific questions are, Do you have feelings that you can't quite identify? Is it easy for you to find the right words for your feelings? Are you often confused by what emotion you are feeling? Do you find yourself puzzled by sensations in your body? (Questions adapted from the Taylor Alexithymia Scale or TAS-20; Bagby, Taylor, & Parker, 1994.)
2. What emotions does the patient become aware of? Is he aware of his emotions in the vulnerable part of the spectrum—that is, emotions that make him feel vulnerable, such as worry, fear, anxiety, sadness, hurt, dejection, disappointment, rejection, or abandonment? A typical question is, When you are upset, do you know if you are sad, frightened, or angry? If he is not aware of his vulnerable emotions, are these emotions transformed into anger and expressed as anger, rage, or violence?
3. Is the patient aware of his emotions in the caring/connection part of the spectrum, such as concern, warmth, affection, appreciation, love, neediness/dependency, closeness, or attachment? Is he limited in his ability to express caring/connection emotions? Does he express them primarily through the channel of sexuality?
4. Is the patient aware of his emotions in the anger part of the spectrum? Does he become aware of an emotion—such as anger—only where it is very intense?
5. At what intensities does the patient experience his emotions? Some specific questions are, Would "cool, calm, and collected" describe you? When you are angry, is it easy for you to still be rational and not overreact? Does your heart race at the anticipation of an exciting event? Do sad movies deeply touch you? When you do something wrong, do you have strong feelings of shame and guilt? (Questions adapted from the Affect Intensity Measure or AIM; Larsen & Diener, 1987.)

TREATMENT

The treatment of alexithymia consists of five steps.

Step 1: Psychoeducation About Normative Alexithymia

In order for the patient to make sense of his experience and utilize the treatment techniques, he needs to know the limitations of his ability to know and express his emotions and how these limitations came about. An important part of this step is helping the patient develop his ability to tolerate certain emotions (such as fear or sadness) that he may regard as unmanly and therefore shameful (Krugman, 1995).

Step 2: Develop a Vocabulary for Emotions

Since men tend not to be aware of emotions, they usually do not have a very good vocabulary for emotions. This also follows from the research literature on the gender-differentiated development of language for emotions. The next step, then, is to help the man develop a vocabulary for the full spectrum of emotions, particularly the vulnerable and caring/connection emotions. I ask patients to record as many words for emotions as they can during the course of a week.

Step 3: Learn to Read the Emotions of Others

The third step involves learning to apply emotional words to feeling states. Since it is often less threatening to do this with other people, and since men can readily build on their action-empathy skills to learn emotional empathy, I recommend focusing on other people at this stage. I teach patients to read facial gestures, tone of voice, and other types of "body language" in other people. I encourage them to learn to identify the emotions of other people, in conversations, while observing other people or while watching movies. I instruct them to ask themselves questions during this process, such as, What is that person feeling? What does this feel like from that person's perspective?

Step 4: Keep an Emotional Response Log

The next step involves teaching the patient to apply emotional words to his own experience. To do this, I ask him to keep an emotional response log, noting when he experienced a feeling that he could identify or a bodily sensation or sign of stress that he became aware of and what circumstances led up to it. The instructions for keeping an emotional response log are as follows:

- Record the bodily sensation or sign of stress (or feelings, if you notice them) that you become aware of and when you first started to experience it.
- Describe the social or relational context within which the emotion was aroused: Who was doing what to whom? How did that affect you?
- Go through your emotional vocabulary list and pick out the words that seem to best describe the emotion that you were experiencing.

Step 5: Practice

The final step involves practice. Emotional self-awareness is a skill, and like any other skill, it requires practice to become an automatic part of one's functioning. In structured groups, I use role plays, videotaped for immediate feedback, to practice the skill. Men are taught to tune in to their feelings through watching and discussing immediate playbacks of role plays in which feelings were engendered. By pointing out the nonverbal cues and asking such questions as, What were your feelings when you grimaced in that last segment?, men learn how to access the ongoing flow of emotions within.

Although working on these matters in a group context with video feedback is obviously advantageous, one can also practice this skill without such arrangements. By systematically keeping an emotional response log and discussing the results in therapy, one can gradually improve the ability to recognize feelings and to put them into words.

Note: Portions of this article were adapted with permission from Levant, R. (1998). Desperately seeking language: Understanding, assessing and treating normative male alexithymia. In W. Pollack & R. Levant (Eds.), *New Psychotherapy for Men: A Case Approach* (pp. 35–56). New York: Wiley. This material is used by permission of John Wiley & Sons, Inc.

References & Readings

Bagby, R. M., Taylor, G. J., & Parker, J. D. A. (1994). The twenty-item Toronto Alexithymia Scale: II. Convergent, discriminant, and concurrent validity. *Journal of Psychosomatic Research, 38,* 33–40.

Krugman, S. (1995). Male development and the transformation of shame. In R. F. Levant & W. S. Pollack (Eds.), *A new psychology of men* (pp. 91–126). New York: Basic Books.

Krystal, H. (1979). Alexithymia and psychotherapy. *American Journal of Psychotherapy, 33,* 17–30.

Krystal, H. (1982). Alexithymia and the effectiveness of psychoanalytic treatment. *International Journal of Psychoanalytic Psychotherapy, 9,* 353–378.

Larsen, R. J., & Diener, E. (1987). Affect intensity as an individual difference characteristic: A review. *Journal of Research in Personality, 21,* 1–39.

Levant, R. F. (1995). Toward the reconstruction of masculinity. In R. F. Levant & W. S. Pollack (Eds.), *A new psychology of men* (pp. 229–251). New York: Basic Books.

Levant, R. F. (1996). The new psychology of men. *Professional Psychology, 27,* 259–265.

Levant, R. F. (1998). Desperately seeking language: Understanding, assessing, and treating normative male alexithymia. In W. S. Pollack & R. F. Levant (Eds.), *New psychotherapy for men: A case approach* (pp. 35–56). New York: Wiley.

Levant, R. F., & Kelly, J. (1989). *Between father and child.* New York: Viking.

Levant, R. F., & Kopecky, G. (1995). *Masculinity reconstructed.* New York: Dutton.

Pleck, J. H. (1995). The gender role strain paradigm: An update. In R. F. Levant & W. S. Pollack (Eds.), *A new psychology of men* (pp. 11–32). New York: Basic Books.

Sifneos, P. E. (1967). Clinical observations on some patients suffering from a variety of psychosomatic diseases. *Proceedings of the Seventh European Conference on Psychosomatic Research.* Basel, Switzerland: Kargel.

Sifneos, P. E. (1988). Alexithymia and its relationship to hemispheric specialization, affect, and creativity. *Psychiatric Clinics of North America, 11,* 287–292.

Taylor, G. J. (1994). The alexithymia construct: Conceptualization, validation, and relationship with basic dimensions of personality. *New Trends in Experimental and Clinical Psychiatry, 10,* 61–74.

Related Topics

Chapter 78, "Guidelines for Conducting Couple and Family Therapy"
Chapter 79, "Treating High-Conflict Couples"
Chapter 80, "Treatment of Marital Infidelity"

59 ASSESSING AND TREATING MALE SEXUAL DYSFUNCTION

Joseph LoPiccolo & Lynn M. Van Male

Assessing and treating sexual dysfunction in men is a challenging and multifaceted undertaking. In this overview we will present a brief summary of the theoretical concepts and principles underlying postmodern sex therapy for men, as well as summarize the major technologies available for treating erectile failure, premature ejaculation, and male orgasmic disorder.

POSTMODERN SEX THERAPY: A SUMMARY OF THEORETICAL CONCEPTS AND PRINCIPLES

Postmodern sex therapy is conceptualized as a blend of cognitive therapy, systems theory, and behavioral psychotherapy (LoPiccolo, 2002). This approach identifies five basic categories of causes of sexual dysfunction, which are applicable to both men and women:

- *Family of origin learning history*, including parental prohibitions against childhood masturbation and sex play, parental negativism about adolescent dating and premarital sexual experience, and unpleasant or traumatic sexual experiences in childhood and adolescence
- *Systemic issues in the couple's relationship*, including lack of attraction to partner, poor sexual skills of the partner, general marital unhappiness, fear of closeness or intimacy, lack of basic trust, differences between the couple in degree of "personal space" desired in the relationship, passive-aggressive solutions to a power imbalance, poor conflict resolution skills, and inability to blend feelings of love and sexual desire
- *Intrapsychic or cognitive issues*, including "performance anxiety," religious orthodoxy, gender identity conflicts, homosexual orientation or conflict, anhedonic or obsessive-compulsive personality, sexual phobias or aversions, fear of loss of control over sexual urges, masked sexual deviation, fears of having children, unresolved feelings about death or loss of a previous partner or spouse, underlying depression, aging concerns, and attempting sex in a context or situation that is not psychologically comfortable for the patient
- *Operant issues in the couple's day-to-day environment* or the reinforcing consequences of the dysfunction that come not from the relationship with the partner or from the patient's own psyche but from the external world
- *Physiological or medical issues*, including any of a number of illnesses and/or diseases that cause pain, chronic fatigue, restriction of movement, reduction of blood flow to the pelvis, or impairment in the neurological system that controls arousal and orgasm (e.g., diabetes, heart disease, spinal-cord injury, multiple sclerosis, pituitary/hypothalamic tumors, and end-state renal disorder); commonly prescribed medications (e.g., antihypertensive, antianxiety, antidepressant, and antipsychotic medications); chronic substance use/abuse (e.g., alcohol, marijuana, heroin, cocaine, and barbiturates); and hormonal imbalances (e.g., too much or too little prolactin, testosterone, estrogen). A comprehensive listing of sexual effects of medical conditions and medications with sexual side effects may be found in LoPiccolo (1993).

Although different practitioners may emphasize one of these five elements more than another, an examination of all factors is necessary to gain a complete understanding of the original causes and current maintainers of a sexual dysfunction. Failure to attend to the individual or couple dynamic relationship needs that are being served by the sexual dysfunction often creates a situation in which symptom removal can be disruptive, thus leading to "resistance" to therapeutic progress. We cannot overemphasize the importance of examining contextual factors prior to utilizing the specific sex therapy technologies enumerated later in this overview. (For further reading on postmodern sex therapy, see LoPiccolo, 2002.)

MECHANISMS OF CHANGE

Currently, sex therapy consists of a complex, multifaceted package of procedures. However, given that the postmodern view espouses considering the sexual problem in its full systemic context, treatment often focuses not only on the individual but also on the couple. We conceptualize couple sex therapy as involving nine major general principles:

- *Mutual responsibility:* Sexual dysfunctions are most often shared disorders. Thus, even if the nondysfunctional partner is not directly involved in causing or maintaining the dysfunction, both partners will need to change for therapy to help them in the solution of their problems.
- *Information and education:* In the present age of increased patient access to self-help books, magazine articles, and videos on sexuality, only rarely are people who enter sex therapy completely ignorant of the basic anatomy and physiology of the human sexual response. Nonetheless, even in cases where there are other complex causes and maintainers of the sexual dysfunction, it is always useful to include a specific informational and educational component to get maximally effective results. Zilbergeld (1999) provides an excellent source of such material.
- *Attitude changes:* For the specific technologies of sex therapy to be effective, positive attitude change and acceptance of sexuality as a normal, healthy part of being human often need to be addressed in treatment.
- *Elimination of performance anxiety:* Quite often patients in sex therapy experience anxiety as a result of "keeping score" and being goal-oriented or orgasm-focused. Since it is precisely this goal-directedness that interferes with arousal, the effect of focusing on pleasure and enjoying the sexual *process* automatically has the side effect of facilitating the goal of normal sexual functioning.
- *Increase of effective communication:* Sexually dysfunctional couples tend to be unable to tell each other what they like and dislike about sex. Postmodern sex therapy encourages open, clear, and effective communication about sexual techniques, preferences, responses, and the initiation and refusal of sexual activity.
- *Change of destructive sex roles and lifestyles:* Patients may need to be encouraged to examine issues such as rigidly adhering to a societally determined stereotypes about what men and women "should" want in sexual relationships, disengaging from in-laws who are a destructive influence on their relationship, withdrawing from their adult children's problems, or quitting a job that requires one of them to commute too far to and from work.
- *Change of disruptive marital systems and enhancement of the marital relationship:* Often it is not possible to directly intervene in the sexual problem without also directly intervening in the marital relationship. When the couple is having significant difficulties over finances, child rearing, or other issues, it is unrealistic to expect them to leave these issues outside the bedroom door when they begin to have a sexual session assigned by the therapist.
- *Physical and medical interventions:* As mentioned earlier, several major classes of medical diseases and chemical agents may interfere with sexual functioning. Thus, concurrent medical care is often necessary in the treatment of sexual dysfunction. In the event physiological antecedents to sexual dysfunc-

tion are not addressable, the patient's focus of treatment may not be on regaining full sexual functioning but rather on the appropriate adaptation to alternative erotic and intimate activities.

- *Prescription of direct changes in sexual behavior and teaching of effective sexual technique:* Although the eight types of procedures listed above are key elements in postmodern sex therapy, the truly distinctive element of sex therapy, as opposed to other psychotherapeutic approaches, is the prescription by the therapist of a series of specific sexual behaviors for the patients to perform in their own home. The particular behavioral prescriptions vary with the dysfunction and are summarized below.

Erectile Failure

Treatment of erectile failure consists of reducing performance anxiety and increasing stimulation (LoPiccolo, 2003). The following list summarizes the main steps in treating erectile failure.

- *Sensate focus:* Initially, attempts to have intercourse—and even to have an erection—are proscribed. Instead, during sensate focus, the couple learns the "tease technique," in which, if he gets an erection in response to her caressing, they stop until he loses it. This exercise teaches them that erections occur naturally in response to stimulation, as long as the couple does not focus on performance. More recently, increasing direct stimulation of the penis has been focused on in addition to reducing performance anxiety. Many men with erectile failure have either mild organic impairment or normal aging changes in erectile responsiveness, which make direct stimulation of the penis necessary for erection to occur. While this may seem obvious, many cases seen in current clinical practice involve unwillingness of the female partner—or sometimes the male himself—to engage in direct stimulation of the penis. In such cases, negative attitudes are explored, and the couple is helped to engage in normal "foreplay" stimulation of the penis.
- *"Stuffing" technique:* When the couple is ready to resume penile-vaginal intercourse, the man lies on his back and the woman kneels above him and uses her fingers to push his nonerect penis into her vagina. This procedure, known as the "stuffing technique," frees him from having to have a rigid penis to accomplish entry. The couple is instructed to achieve the woman's orgasms through manual or oral sex, again reducing pressure on the male to perform.
- *Intercourse:* When the couple has mastered sensate focus and "stuffing," they are ready to resume intercourse in their preferred position (e.g., female superior, male superior, side-by-side).

This set of procedures seems to work well in cases in which there is no major organic impairment of erection. Physical intervention is often indicated, however, for men with significant physical problems underlying or complicating their difficulty with erection. For these men, the following approaches may be suggested.

- *Penile prostheses:* One type of penile prosthesis consists of a semirigid rod made of rubber and wire, which, when surgically implanted, produces an artificial erection. It can be bent down so that the man can wear normal clothing but bent up to an erect position when the man wants to have intercourse. Another type of prosthesis consists of inflatable hollow cylinders inserted into the penis, a reservoir of fluid placed under the abdominal wall, and tubing connecting the penile cylinders and the reservoir to a pump inserted in the scrotum. When the man wants to have sex, he squeezes the pump, forcing fluid from the reservoir to the penile cylinders, which expand and produce an erection. These prostheses are expensive (between $5,000 and $15,000, depending on the type), but over 25,000 were installed in 1988 in the United States. In recent years, prostheses have become less commonly used as nonsurgical medical interventions (i.e., the vacuum erection device and penile injections) have become available.

- *Vacuum erection device (VED):* A hollow cylinder is placed over the penis and pushed against the body to create an airtight seal. The cylinder is connected to a hand pump, which pumps the air out of the cylinder and leaves the penis in a partial vacuum. The resultant pressure differential draws blood into the penis and produces an erection. The cylinder is removed, and a rubber constriction ring is placed around the base of the penis to maintain the erection. The VED is less expensive ($300–$600), but it interferes with the spontaneity of sex, since the man must take time to use it during lovemaking. The vacuum device is most often used for men whose erectile failure is caused by diabetes or neurological problems, and it seems to work well for these men (LoPiccolo, 1992).
- *Chemical vasodilators:* Another nonsurgical treatment for men with medically based erectile failure is injection of drugs that dilate the penile arteries. Drugs that were formerly used for this purpose tended to cause scarring in the penis over long periods of use and so were used more as a short-term "confidence booster" for men with situational erectile failure. However, the drugs that are now used do not seem to have this effect.
- The effectiveness of the oral medication Viagra has greatly reduced the usage of vacuum devices and penile injections. Viagra works in about 75% of cases, but sexual stimulation *plus* the medication is needed—Viagra alone does not produce erection, especially in older men.

Premature Ejaculation

Premature ejaculation is treated with almost a 100% success rate by direct behavioral retraining procedures (Masters & Johnson, 1970). The following summarizes the steps in this typically effective treatment.

- *"Stop-start" or "pause" procedure:* In this technique, the penis is manually stimulated until the man is fairly highly aroused. The couple then pauses until the man's arousal subsides, then the stimulation is resumed. This sequence is repeated several times before stimulation is carried through to ejaculation, so the man ultimately experiences much more total time of stimulation than he has ever experienced before and learns to have a higher threshold for ejaculation.
- *"Squeeze" procedure:* This technique is much like the "stop-start" procedure, except that when stimulation stops, the woman firmly squeezes the penis between her thumb and forefinger, at the place where the head of the penis joins the shaft. This squeeze seems to reduce arousal further.
- *Vaginal containment:* After a few weeks of training involving "stop-start" and "squeeze" procedures, the necessity of pausing diminishes. Then the couple may progress to putting the penis in the vagina, but without any thrusting movements. Again, if the man rapidly becomes highly aroused, the penis is withdrawn and the couple waits for arousal to drop off.
- *Active thrusting:* When good tolerance for inactive containment of the penis is achieved, the training procedure is repeated during active thrusting. Generally, 2 to 3 months of practice are sufficient to enable a man to enjoy prolonged intercourse without any need for pauses or squeezes.
- Medical practitioners now commonly treat premature ejaculation with SSRI antidepressants. While this is effective, the medication must be taken at full daily dosage constantly and does not work on an "as needed" basis. Therefore, psychotherapeutic treatment offers real advantages.

Male Orgasmic Disorder

Male orgasmic disorder is treated by reducing performance anxiety and ensuring adequate stimulation. The couple is instructed that during sex the penis is to be caressed manually (and, if acceptable to them, orally) until the man is aroused, but that stimulation is to stop whenever he feels he might be close to having an orgasm. This paradoxical instruction reduces goal-focused anxiety about performance and allows the man to enjoy the sexual pleasure provided by the caressing. An electric vibrator may be used to increase the intensity of stimulation. For men with neurological damage, therapy is likely to include some physiological treatment, possibly a drug that increases arousal of the sympathetic nervous system or stimulation of the anus with a vibrator to trigger the ejaculation reflex (LoPiccolo, 1996).

References & Readings

LoPiccolo, J. (1992). Post-modern sex therapy for erectile failure. In R. C. Rosen & S. R. Leiblum (Eds.), *Erectile failure: Diagnosis and treatment* (pp. 171–197). New York: Guilford Press.

LoPiccolo, J. (1996). Premature ejaculation and male orgasmic disorder. In G. O. Gabbard & S. D. Atkinson (Eds.), *Synopsis of treatments of psychiatric disorders* (pp. 797–804). Washington, DC: American Psychiatric Press.

LoPiccolo, J. (2002). Postmodern sex therapy. In F. W. Kaslow (Ed.), *Comprehensive handbook of psychotherapy* (Vol. 4, pp. 41–43). New York: John.

LoPiccolo, J. (2003). Male sexual dysfunction. In L. J. Haas (Ed.), *Handbook of psychology in primary care.* New York: Oxford University Press.

Masters, W. H., & Johnson, V. E. (1970). *Human sexual inadequacy*. Boston: Little, Brown.

O'Donohue, W., & Geer, J. H. (Eds.). (1993). *Handbook of sexual dysfunctions: Assessment and treatment*. Boston: Allyn and Bacon.

Wincze, J. P., & Carey, M. P. (1991). *Sexual dysfunction: A guide for assessment and treatment*. New York: Guilford Press.

Zilbergeld, B. (1999). *The new male sexuality*. New York: Bantam Books.

Related Topics

Chapter 58, "Assessing and Treating Normative Male Alexithymia"

Chapter 60, "Assessing and Treating Female Sexual Dysfunction"

Chapter 63, "Assessment and Treatment of Lesbians, Gay Men, and Bisexuals"

Chapter 78, "Guidelines for Conducting Couple and Family Therapy"

60 ASSESSING AND TREATING FEMALE SEXUAL DYSFUNCTION

Joseph LoPiccolo & Lynn M. Van Male

The assessment and treatment of sexual dysfunction in women are no less challenging and multifaceted than the assessment and treatment of sexual dysfunction in men. In addition to presenting a brief summary of the theoretical concepts and principles underlying postmodern sex therapy, this chapter reviews the major technologies available for treating female arousal and orgasm dysfunctions, vaginismus, dyspareunia, and low sexual desire and aversion to sex. (A detailed discussion of theoretical concepts and mechanisms of change is given in the overview of male sexual dysfunction in chapter 59.)

POSTMODERN SEX THERAPY: A SUMMARY OF THEORETICAL CONCEPTS AND PRINCIPLES

Postmodern sex therapy is an amalgamation of cognitive therapy, systems theory, and behavioral psychotherapy. The following five categories are theorized to account for the causes and maintainers of sexual dysfunction:

- Family of origin learning history
- Systemic issues in the couple's relationship
- Intrapsychic or cognitive issues
- Operant issues in the couple's day-to-day environment
- Physiological or medical issues

The degree to which each of these factors contributes to the development or maintenance of a sexual dysfunction varies case by case. However, a thorough examination of all five types of factors is necessary to gain a complete understanding of a sexual dysfunction. The sexual dysfunction often serves an important role in the individual or couple dynamic; thus attempts to remove it without attending to the need(s) it fulfills can meet with great resistance on the part of the individual or the couple. We cannot overemphasize the importance of examining contextual factors prior to utilizing the specific sex therapy technologies enumerated later in this overview. (For further reading on postmodern sex therapy, see LoPiccolo, 1985.)

MECHANISMS OF CHANGE

Currently, sex therapy consists of a complex, multifaceted package of procedures. However, given that the postmodern view espouses considering the sexual problem in its full systemic context, treatment often focuses not only on the individual but also on the couple. It is possible to conceptualize couple sex therapy as involving nine general principles:

- Mutual responsibility
- Information and education
- Attitude changes
- Elimination of performance anxiety
- Increase of effective communication
- Change of destructive sex roles and lifestyles
- Change of disruptive marital systems and enhancement of the marital relationship
- Physical and medical interventions
- Prescription of direct changes in sexual behavior and teaching of effective sexual technique

A Note on Sexual Victimization

Although sexual victimization is by no means the only route into the manifestation of sexual dysfunction, it is not uncommon for patients who have sexual dysfunction(s) to have a history of sexual trauma or childhood molestation. For such cases, it is vital to stress that the therapist's first objective is to address sexual victimization issues prior to treating any sexual dysfunction(s). For example, for an inorgasmic survivor of sexual trauma, some of the orgasm triggers mentioned below may serve as triggers for flashback rather than assisting in achieving orgasm. Thus, for patients with both a sexual dysfunction and a history of sexual trauma or childhood molestation, additional therapeutic procedures are indicated. These procedures are described in other works, such as Courtois (1988).

Female Arousal and Orgasm Dysfunctions

Global, Lifelong Inorgasmia Specific treatment techniques for female arousal and orgasm dysfunctions include self-exploration, body awareness, and directed masturbation training (Heiman & LoPiccolo, 1988). Masters and Johnson (1970) stressed the use of couple sensate-focus procedures for such cases, but later experience showed that it is more effective for the woman to learn to have orgasm by herself first and then share this knowledge with her partner. The directed masturbation program that has been most successful in our work has nine steps and a "pre-step":

- *Exploration of beliefs about sexuality:* Before the woman even begins the program steps, it is important for her to explore her beliefs and possible fears about becoming a fully sexual woman. What does she risk losing by becoming orgasmic?

- *Education:* In step 1 the woman uses diagrams and reading materials simply to learn about her body, her genitals, and the female sexual response.
- *Full-body exploration:* In step 2 she explores her whole body visually (with the aid of a mirror) and by touch.
- *Finding pleasure zones:* Step 3 consists of locating erotically sensitive areas on her entire body (lips, thighs, the curve of her waist, etc.), with a focus on her breasts and genitals, especially her clitoris.
- *Erotic self-pleasuring:* Actual stimulation (masturbation) of the areas identified in step 3 is the focus of step 4.
- *Enhanced erotic self-pleasuring:* Step 5 is erotic masturbation accompanied by sexual pictures, stories, and the woman's own fantasies. Women are encouraged to write their own erotic stories, as well as reading commercially published collections of women's sexual fantasies.
- *Masturbation aids, enactment, and "orgasm triggers":* Step 6 has three elements. First, if the woman has not yet experienced an orgasm, it is suggested that she begin to use an electric vibrator to increase the intensity of stimulation. Second, she will be instructed to act out or role-play a very exaggerated orgasm to overcome any fears about losing control or looking silly when she has a real orgasm. Finally, she will use "orgasm triggers," such as tilting her head back, holding her breath with diaphragm tensed as if trying to exhale, arching her feet and pointing her toes, contracting her pelvic muscles, tensing her leg muscles, and thrusting her pelvis.
- *Sensate focus and mutual masturbation:* Step 7 integrates Masters and Johnson's sensate focus procedure with the woman's individual progress. This training in communication and sexual skill teaches her to demonstrate for her partner how she prefers to be stimulated and how she can have an orgasm. Because most women find it easier to demonstrate how they like to be touched if they have the opportunity to observe how their partner prefers to be erotically stimulated, we suggest partners be the first to demonstrate self-stimulation to orgasm in order to help disinhibit clients.
- *Partner-assisted orgasm:* In step 8 her partner rests his hand on hers as she masturbates to orgasm. Once she is comfortable with this, she may guide his hand to teach him how she likes to be touched, and then the couple may move on until he is able to bring her to orgasm with manual, oral, or vibrator stimulation.
- *Intercourse:* In the last step, the woman and her partner practice intercourse in positions that permit one or the other of them to continue to stimulate her clitoris while the penis is in the vagina.

This training program has been found to be very effective: over 90% of women learn to have an orgasm during masturbation, about 80% during caressing by their partner, and about 30% during intercourse. Because it is a structured program, it works equally well in group therapy and even as a self-treatment, since the woman can go through the program without a therapist, using a self-help book (Heiman & LoPiccolo, 1988) and instructional videotape (LoPiccolo, 1980).

Situational Orgasmic Dysfunction In contrast to women with global, lifelong lack of orgasm, some women are able to have an orgasm in some way but not in a way that is satisfactory to them. Such types of situational orgasmic dysfunction include being able to reach orgasm only in solitary masturbation or only in some particular sexual activity, such as oral stimulation. Treatment for situational lack of orgasm includes a process of *gradual stimulus generalization.* This procedure is designed to help the woman expand the ways in which she reaches orgasm by the identification of numerous intermediate steps that will help her expand the situations in which she is able to achieve an orgasm.

For example, consider the case of a woman who can reach orgasm only when she is alone, through masturbating by pressing her thighs together, and cannot have orgasm in any way when her partner is present. The intermediate steps she and her therapist identify may include using thigh pressure but also putting her fingers on her clitoris, direct stimulation of her clitoris with her thighs spread apart, thigh pressure with her partner present, thigh pressure with her partner's fingers on her clitoris, her partner's direct stimulation of her clitoris without thigh pressure, and direct clitoral stimulation during intercourse (Zeiss, Rosen, & Zeiss, 1977). This approach is quite effective in helping women learn to have orgasm with a partner.

Sex therapists do not consider lack of orgasm during intercourse to be a problem, provided the woman enjoys intercourse and can have orgasm when her partner caresses her. For this reason, reassurance about their normality, not treatment, is indicated for women whose only concern is situational lack of orgasm during intercourse. Although sex therapists agree that lack of orgasm during intercourse is not a problem, popular books and magazines continue to suggest ways for women to achieve orgasm during intercourse. One such suggestion is the "high ride" position, in which the man positions his body upward on his partner until the top of her head is even with his shoulder area. This position bends the man's penis back until it is sliding along the woman's clitoris during intercourse. Although the "high ride" is supposed to lead to orgasm during intercourse, it does not seem to be effective and is also uncomfortable for many couples.

Vaginismus

Vaginismus refers to spastic contractions of the muscles around the vagina, which make it impossible for the penis to enter. The treatment for this dysfunction is shown in a video (LoPiccolo, 1981) and includes the following elements.

- *Deep muscle relaxation and breathing:* Vaginismic women are first taught how to relax the muscles of their bodies to promote somatic awareness prior to the focus of treatment being directed toward their presenting complaint. It is critical that the patient be allowed to progress at her own pace because "working hard" to make quick progress in the treatment of vaginismus is almost always countertherapeutic.
- *Voluntary control of the pubococcygeal muscle:* Vaginismic patients practice contracting and relaxing the pubococcygeal muscle, which is part of the pelvic floor and surrounds the vagina, until they have acquired voluntary control over their vaginal muscles.
- *Graduated dilator containment:* To assist in overcoming their fear of penetration, vaginismic women are taught to use a set of gradually larger dilators, which they insert in their own vagina at home and at their own pace, so that they are not frightened or traumatized. It is critical to emphasize that dilator insertion is done gently, *not* with a vigorous thrusting motion. Additionally, the woman should not progress to the next larger dilator until she is able to comfortably contain the previous, smaller one.
- *Partner participation in dilator insertion:* Later, when the woman can comfortably insert the largest dilator, she begins to guide her partner as he slowly and gently inserts the dilators. Again, it is important to stress that dilator insertion is *not* done forcefully or with repetitive thrusting motions.
- *Vaginal containment of the penis:* As her partner lies passively on his back, the woman kneels above him and gradually inserts his penis at a pace that is comfortable to her.
- *Intercourse:* Once the woman is able to comfortably contain her partner's penis, the couple may begin to add thrusting motions and to explore various intercourse positions that are enjoyable to both of them.

The therapist stresses the need for effective stimulation, so that the patient learns to associate penetration with vaginal lubrication, pleasure, and arousal instead of with fear or pain. Some therapists use muscle-relaxing drugs or hypnosis during dilation, but this does not seem to be a necessary part of the treatment. Therapy for vaginismus is highly successful: over 90% of the women treated become able to have pain-free intercourse.

Dyspareunia

Dyspareunia refers to pain that a woman experiences during intercourse. Most cases of dyspareunia involve some physiological abnormality, such as unrepaired damage following childbirth. However, some cases are exclusively psychogenic in origin. There are no specific treatment procedures for psychogenic dyspareunia. Since psychogenic dyspareunia is actually caused by lack of arousal, the general sex therapy procedures and the specific techniques for enhancing female arousal and orgasm are used (O'Donohue & Geer, 1993). When the pain is caused by scars or lesions, the couple can be taught positions for intercourse that do not put pressure on the traumatized sites. Since most cases of dyspareunia are caused by undiagnosed physical problems, an examination by a gynecologist who is expert in this area is essential (O'Donohue & Geer, 1993).

Low Sexual Desire and Aversion to Sex

Low sexual desire refers to a condition in which the patient is markedly lacking in sexual drive and interest. Although the judgment of just how low sexual desire must be to be dysfunctional is somewhat subjective and frequently societally determined, most patients who experience this dysfunction have virtually no sexual interest. Sexual aversion is not just a lack of interest in sex but an actual negative emotional reaction such as revulsion, fear, or disgust that occurs when sexual activity is attempted. Although the steps for addressing hyposexual desire are addressed in this overview, which focuses on female sexual dysfunctions, the same procedures have been applied with equal success to male patients.

Because of the many difficult psychological issues that are likely to underlie hypoactive sexual desire and sexual aversion, these dysfunctions typically require a longer and more complex program of treatment than others. Pridal and LoPiccolo (2000) have described a widely used four-element sequential treatment model for hypoactive drive and aversion.

- *Affectual awareness:* The first stage of therapy focuses on helping the client become aware of her negative emotions regarding sex. Therapy sessions during which the patient visualizes sexual scenes help uncover feelings of anxiety, fear, resentment, vulnerability, and so forth. Many patients claim that they have overcome negative ideas about sex, but such changes are likely to be superficial, leaving a negative affectual (emotional or gut-level) residue hidden under a bland umbrella feeling of lack of interest in sex. The purpose of the affectual awareness stage of therapy is to get under this umbrella and make the patient aware that she is not just naturally uninterested in sex but that something is blocking the normal biological sex drive.
- *Insight:* The second phase of therapy helps patients understand why they have the negative emotions identified in the affectual awareness phase. Negative messages from their religion, culture, family, and current and past relationships are explored. In a sense, this and the previous step are preparatory. The more active treatment follows.
- *Cognitive and emotional change:* In this phase, cognitive techniques are applied to the irrational thoughts and emotions that inhibit sexual desire. Patients generate "coping statements" that help them change their negative emotions and thoughts. Typical statements might be "If I allow myself to enjoy sex, it doesn't mean I'll lose control," and "When I was younger I learned to feel guilty about sex, but I'm a grown-up now, and I don't have to feel that way anymore."
- *Behavioral interventions:* It is at this stage that sensate focus, skill training, and other general sex therapy procedures are introduced. Sex drive is heightened in a number of ways: having patients keep a "desire diary" in which they record sexual thoughts and feelings, having them read books and view films with good erotic content, and encouraging them to develop their own sexual fantasies. All of these activities make sexual thoughts and cues more readily available to the patient. Nonsexual affection, consisting of simple hugs, squeezes, and pats, and pleasurable shared activities such as dancing and walking together are also encouraged to help

strengthen feelings of sensual enjoyment and sexual attraction.

This type of program seems to be fairly successful. In one study of the approach, frequency of sex increased from once a month to once a week for men who had experienced hypoactive sexual desire and from once every two weeks to more than once a week for female patients. Women who had experienced sexual aversion increased sexual intercourse from less than once every two weeks to more than once a week (Schover & LoPiccolo, 1982).

References & Readings

Courtois, C. A. (1988). *Healing the incest wound.* New York: Norton.

Heiman, J. R., & LoPiccolo, J. (1988). *Becoming orgasmic: A sexual and personal growth program for women.* New York: Simon and Schuster.

LoPiccolo, J. (1980). *Becoming orgasmic* [Videotape]. (Available from Focus International, 14 Oregon Drive, Huntington Station, NY 11746.)

LoPiccolo, J. (1981). *Treating vaginismus* [Videotape]. (Available from Focus International, 14 Oregon Drive, Huntington Station, NY 11746.)

LoPiccolo, J. (1985). Sex therapy: A postmodern model. In S. Lynn & J. P. Garske (Eds.), *Contemporary psychotherapies.* Pacific Grove, CA: Brooks/Cole.

Masters, W. H., & Johnson, V. E. (1970). *Human sexual inadequacy.* Boston: Little, Brown.

O'Donohue, W., & Geer, J. H. (Eds.). (1993). *Handbook of sexual dysfunctions: Assessment and treatment.* Boston: Allyn and Bacon.

Pridal, C. G., and LoPiccolo, J. (2000). Multielement treatment of desire disorders: Integration of cognitive, behavioral and systemic therapy. In S. R. Leiblum & R. C. Rosen, (Eds.), *Principles and Practice of Sex Therapy* (pp. 57–84). New York: Guilford.

Schover, L., & LoPiccolo, J. (1982). Treatment effectiveness for dysfunctions of sexual desire. *Journal of Sex and Marital Therapy, 8,* 179–197.

Zeiss, A. M., Rosen, G. M., & Zeiss, R. A. (1977). Orgasm during intercourse: A treatment strategy for women. *Journal of Consulting and Clinical Psychology, 45,* 891–895.

Related Topics

Chapter 59, "Assessing and Treating Male Sexual Dysfunction"

Chapter 62, "Guidelines for Treating Women in Psychotherapy"

Chapter 63, "Assessment and Treatment of Lesbians, Gay Men, and Bisexuals"

Chapter 78, "Guidelines for Conducting Couple and Family Therapy"

61 ASSESSING AND REDUCING RISK OF INFECTION WITH THE HUMAN IMMUNODEFICIENCY VIRUS

Michael P. Carey

Epidemiologic data from the Centers for Disease Control and Prevention confirm that the acquired immunodeficiency syndrome (AIDS) can affect anyone who comes into contact with the human immunodeficiency virus (HIV). Although AIDS was originally thought to be a disease that affected only gay men, recent data refute this notion. In the United States, rates of new infections among gay men have declined, whereas rates among heterosexual men and women have increased. HIV does not discriminate among persons on the basis of sexual orientation, gender, or race. In the United States, 800,000–900,000 persons are infected with HIV, and there have been more than 800,000 documented cases of AIDS; of the persons with AIDS, more than 468,000 have already died. AIDS is a leading cause of death among young adults in the United States; more deaths result from AIDS than from accidents, murders, suicides, cancer, or heart disease in this age-group.

Neither cure nor vaccine exists for HIV and AIDS; thus, behavioral avoidance of the virus provides the only protection against infection. Every psychologist is obliged to know the basics of HIV transmission and prevention, to evaluate clients for their risk of infection, and to provide risk reduction counseling when indicated. Because few psychologists have the time to become experts in infectious disease or sexual behavior, in this chapter I overview three areas necessary for ethical practice. First, I summarize the key information regarding HIV transmission. Second, I provide guidelines for the screening of HIV risk in a time-efficient manner; by asking a few simple questions, a psychologist will communicate concern for his or her clients' safety and, in some cases, help them to identify their risk of contracting a life-threatening disease. Third, I provide basic guidelines for counseling clients regarding risk reduction. Finally, I identify resources for further study and consultation.

HIV TRANSMISSION

The good news about HIV transmission is that HIV is a fluid-borne agent. What this means is that, unlike tuberculosis or other airborne infectious agents, HIV is not spread through sneezing, coughing, sharing eating utensils, or other forms of casual contact. For HIV transmission to occur, an infected person's blood, semen, vaginal secretions, or breast milk must enter the bloodstream of another person. The three most common routes of transmission are (a) *unprotected sexual intercourse* (anal, vaginal, or oral) with an infected partner; (b) *sharing unsterilized needles* (most commonly in the context of recreational drugs but also in tattooing, steroid use, and other needle uses) with an infected person; and (c) *maternal-child transmission* (e.g., infection through the placenta before birth and perhaps through breast-feeding after birth) when the mother is infected. Transmission can also occur through blood transfusions (when receiving but not when giving blood) and through a variety of accidental exposures (e.g., trauma situations, occupational needlesticks), but these routes are relatively rare.

ASSESSMENT OF RISK

Careful listening serves as the cornerstone of the assessment process. Some clients may freely offer their concerns about HIV-related risk as a reason for therapy. Despite the importance of sexual health, not all health professionals know how to listen when it comes to the sexual sphere. It is not uncommon for clients to report that they had tried previously to discuss sexual concerns with a health care professional but were met with avoidance, embarrassment, or apparent lack of interest; as a result, the clients did not pursue their concerns. Thus, the first guideline is to be open to clients' self-disclosures regarding sexual, drug use, and other risk behaviors and to be aware of subtle messages you might convey to discourage the disclosure of such material.

Even when a therapist is open to self-disclosure on such topics, many clients will be reluctant to independently raise their concerns regarding sexual or other risk behaviors. In these cases, the therapist will need to actively assess the client's risk in a sensitive and efficient manner. Assessment of risk should take place after a client and therapist have established a basic rapport and the therapist has assured the client of confidentiality. Specific risk assessment should always begin with an appropriate introduction for the client. During this time the reasons for asking questions about sexual and other socially sensitive behaviors should be provided. For example, one might say that a standard practice is to inquire about risk for HIV just as one routinely inquires about suicidal ideation, personal safety, and other important matters; thus, all clients get asked, and no client will feel singled out as being at unique risk. Although sensitivity is advised, it is also important to ask questions in a direct fashion, without apology or hesitancy (Kinsey, Pomeroy, & Martin, 1948). If the clinician appears embarrassed about or unsure of the appropriateness of the questions, a client may sense this and provide incomplete or ambiguous responses. After the introductory remarks, the client should be invited to ask any questions he or she might have.

When assessing sexual behavior, we have found it helpful to adopt certain assumptions in order to gather the most accurate information without wasting time and effort (Wincze & Carey, 2001). These assumptions reflect the preferred direction of error. Thus, for example, it is better to assume a low level of understanding on the part of the client so that information is conveyed in a clear, concrete manner. Other examples of useful assumptions include the notions that (a) clients will be embarrassed about and have difficulty discussing sexual matters; (b) clients will not understand medical terminology; and (c) clients will be misinformed about HIV and AIDS. As the clinician learns more about the client, these assumptions are adjusted.

Depending on the client and the context, it may be useful to sequence the inquiry from the least to the most threatening questions. Thus, questions about receipt of blood transfusions might precede questions regarding needle sharing or sexual behavior. Experience in the assessment of sexual behavior also suggests that it can be helpful to place the "burden of denial" on the client (Kinsey et al., 1948). That is, rather than ask whether a client has engaged in a particular activity, the clinician might ask the patient how many times he or she has engaged in it. Use of this strategy will depend on the nature of the relationship that has been established with the client.

Given these process considerations, the content of the risk screening follows the transmission categories identified earlier. We advise inquiring about each of the following domains and pursuing follow-up questions as appropriate.

1. "When were you last tested to determine if you are infected with HIV (the virus that causes AIDS)? What were the results of that test?" Knowledge of the date of the test is important for the determination of subsequent risk activity. Because of the "window period" (i.e., the amount of time between exposure to and infection with the virus and the development of antibodies detectable with serological tests), one should assess risk behavior going back at least 6 months prior to the most recent antibody test. If a client discloses that he or she is infected with HIV (i.e., is HIV-positive or HIV+), you will need to address the many health, relationship, and social issues associated with HIV disease. This is a complex set of clinical challenges that is beyond the scope of this chapter. Kalichman (1995) provides an excellent guide to mental health care for infected persons.
2. "Since your last HIV antibody test, have you received a blood transfusion (or treatment for a blood clotting problem)? If so, was it between 1977 and 1985?" Since 1985, donated blood has been tested for antibodies to HIV; thus, the risk of receiving HIV-infected blood during a transfusion in the United States is extremely low (1 in 60,000).
3. "Since your last HIV antibody test, with how many *men* have you had sex (oral, anal, or vaginal)? Did you always use condoms when having sex? If yes, did you use condoms during *every* penetrative contact, including oral sex? Did you always use *latex* condoms? Have any of your male partners had sex with other men?" Most experts agree that anal sex is more risky than vaginal sex, and that both are much more risky than oral sex. Experts disagree regarding the probability of HIV transmission through oral sex, although this vector of transmission has been demonstrated in a few epidemiologic studies. Experts agree that con-

doms protect against HIV only when used consistently and correctly with all partners. Because HIV is smaller than sperm cells, natural or lambskin condoms allow the virus to pass through and should not be used. Gay and bisexual men still account for the majority of infected persons in the United States, but infections among heterosexual women are on the increase.

4. "Since your last HIV antibody test, with how many *women* have you had sex (oral, anal, or vaginal)? Did you always use condoms or other barrier protection (e.g., dental dam) when having sex?" Transmission of HIV from an infected woman is less likely than from an infected male, but some risk is still involved.
5. "How many times have you shared or borrowed a needle, or used another person's works (cotton, corker, cooker), to prepare or inject drugs? Did you disinfect the needle prior to reusing it? If so, how did you do this?" Contaminated needles are responsible for the second-largest number of infections in the United States. Although needles can be properly disinfected (e.g., by flushing with a bleach solution two or more times), they are typically shared without cleaning or after improper cleaning.
6. "Have you ever had sex with a person who used injection drugs?" All else being equal, injection drug users (IDUs) are more likely to be infected with HIV than are non-IDUs.
7. "Have you ever had a sexual partner whom you knew or suspected was HIV infected or had AIDS? If so, did you always use condoms when you had sex?" Having a partner known to be infected with HIV introduces the greatest risk of infection.
8. "Are you at all concerned that you might have been infected with the virus?" This leaves the door open for people who may not have felt comfortable responding to the earlier questions.

RISK REDUCTION COUNSELING

Three levels of counseling may be appropriate. First, if a client reports that he or she has engaged in any high-risk activity (e.g., unprotected intercourse), it may be appropriate to encourage the client to seek testing for HIV. Early detection of infection can help clients to obtain preventive medical care, as well as psychosocial services. Knowledge of serostatus may enhance motivation for risk reduction practices in order to avoid infecting others. The recommendation to seek antibody testing is complex, involving legal, ethical, and political issues (e.g., confidentiality, possible discrimination, and duty to warn).

Clients who express concern despite apparent low risk may also be advised to consider testing. Clients who have been abstinent or those who strongly believe themselves to have been in a mutually monogamous sexual relationship with a HIV-negative partner and have never shared an injection drug needle can be reassured and counseled to maintain low risk.

Information about HIV-antibody testing is available from numerous sources, including American Red Cross chapters and local health departments. Two types of testing are available: with *confidential* testing, the results are recorded in the client's medical files and may be disclosed to those with legal access to records; with *anonymous* testing, a code number is given when blood is drawn, and this number must be presented by the client to receive the results. The client's name is not associated with test results. Many states offer anonymous and/or confidential tests without charge. Although sites that offer HIV testing are required to provide pretest and posttest counseling, therapists should be prepared to supplement such counseling, regardless of the outcome.

A second level of counseling involves simple education. If a client is misinformed about the basics of HIV and AIDS or has questions about transmission and prevention of HIV infection, most psychologists should be able to help immediately. If a client has been involved in risky sexual or drug-use practices, he or she should be advised promptly and specifically which behaviors enhance risk and what preventive action can be taken to reduce risk for infection. An at-risk client may require more than simple education, however.

The third level of intervention involves the

provision of intensive risk reduction counseling. Intervention programs have been developed that are well grounded in psychological theory and have been evaluated in clinical trials with many populations (Carey, 1999; Carey & Vanable, 2003). An excellent example of such a program is Kelly's (1995); his readable manual provides a step-by-step guide for implementing an empirically validated risk reduction program. Psychologists can also refer to the sources cited herein and can call local, state, and national hot lines to learn of additional resources (e.g., National AIDS Hotline at 800-342-AIDS; National AIDS Hotline TTY/TDD service at 800-243-7889; and National AIDS Information Clearinghouse at 800-458-5231).

References, Readings, & Internet Sites

AIDS Treatment News. (n.d.). AIDS.org resource page. Retrieved 2004 from http://www.aids.org

Carey, M. P. (1999). Prevention of HIV infection through changes in sexual behavior. *American Journal of Health Promotion, 14,* 104–111.

Carey, M. P., & Vanable, P. A. (2003). HIV/AIDS. In A. M. Nezu, C. M. Nezu, & P. A. Geller (Eds.), *Comprehensive handbook of psychology, Vol. 9: Health psychology* (pp. 219–244). New York: Wiley.

Centers for Disease Control (n.d.). HIV/AIDS Prevention division home page. Retrieved 2004 from http://www.cdc.gov/hiv

Joint United Nations Programme on HIV/AIDS. (n.d.). UNAIDS home page. Retrieved 2004 from http://www.unaids.org.

Kalichman, S. C. (1995). *Understanding AIDS: A guide for mental health professionals.* Washington, DC: American Psychological Association.

Kalichman, S. C., Carey, M. P., & Johnson, B. T. (1996). Prevention of sexually transmitted HIV infection: A meta-analytic review of the behavioral outcome literature. *Annals of Behavioral Medicine, 18,* 6–15.

Kelly, J. A. (1995). *Changing HIV risk behavior: Practical strategies.* New York: Guilford Press.

Kinsey, A. C., Pomeroy, W. B., & Martin, C. E. (1948). *Sexual behavior in the human male.* Philadelphia: Saunders.

Wincze, J. P., & Carey, M. P. (2001). *Sexual dysfunction: A guide for assessment and treatment* (2nd ed.). New York: Guilford.

Related Topics

Chapter 54, "Treatment Matching in Substance Abuse"

Chapter 55, "Motivational Interviewing"

Chapter 63, "Assessment and Treatment of Lesbians, Gay Men, and Bisexuals"

62 GUIDELINES FOR TREATING WOMEN IN PSYCHOTHERAPY

Laura S. Brown & Felicia A. Mueller

Women are a diverse and complex group, varying from one another on almost every dimension, including culture, ethnicity, sexual orientation, age, disability, and religious or spiritual affiliation (Brown, 1994). Women enter psychotherapy with any set of problems and distress, although certain diagnoses, such as major depression, eating disorders, and posttraumatic stress, are found at higher rates among women than among men, and others, such as the paraphilias, are found at markedly lower rates (Ballou & Brown, 2002). Women come into therapy as individuals, as members of heterosexual or same-sex couples, in their roles as parents, as caregivers of their own parents, as workers. How, then, can such a diverse and complex group be subsumed under one set of guidelines for psychotherapy?

The answer, of course, is that no one set of norms and rules will cover all bases for psychotherapy with every woman. Nonetheless, the therapist undertaking to work with women clients can find a rich body of information to consider when the client is a woman, be she a second-generation Asian-American lesbian police officer or a Euro-American heterosexual full-time homemaker.

Starting in the early 1970s, with the publication of a classic study by Broverman and colleagues (1970), which served as the impetus for the APA Task Force on Sex Bias and Sex Role Stereotyping in Psychotherapy, the profession of psychology began to be alerted to the pervasive presence of gender-based biases in psychotherapy with women. These biases were found to affect multiple aspects of training and practice in psychotherapy, and to adversely affect the quality of treatment received by women.

Several specific concerns were identified during this initial period, including:

- Androcentric biases in the construction of disorder and normalcy, with tendencies toward overrepresentation of feminine gendered behaviors in constructions of disorder.
- Lack of attention to the interaction between individual and social context in both diagnostic formulation and treatment planning.
- Sexist power dynamics in the psychotherapy relationship in which the therapist mirrored and transmitted nonconscious biases toward women clients.
- Inadequate scientific foundation for psychological practice with women, and overreliance on data derived solely from clinical, rather than population, samples.

A set of guidelines for psychotherapy with women was first published in 1986 (Fitzgerald & Nutt, 1986), revised and updated in 1996, and the latest revision was adopted by the APA Divisions on Women in Psychology and Counseling Psychology. Now titled *Guidelines for Psychological Practice With Girls and Women* (Nutt, Rice, & Enns, 2002), this latest draft is divided into three themes: diversity, social context, and power; professional responsibility; and best practices, A brief summary of this most recent document follows.

Guideline 1: Psychologists strive to recognize and validate that all girls and women are socialized into multiple social-group memberships and identities, and that girls and women have both shared and unique identities.

Guideline 2: Psychologists strive to recognize how the positions of oppression and privilege associated with each social group membership and identity affect girls and women.

Guideline 3: Psychologists strive to understand women's and girls' diverse experiences within the context of institutional and social relationships and how these factors are detrimental to or facilitate girls' and women's physical and mental health.

Guideline 4: Psychologists strive to be aware of how potentially oppressive biases, values, and actions are embedded in psychological theory, research, and practice, and they strive to create and use culturally sensitive, flexible, and affirming practices with girls and women.

Guideline 5: Psychologists strive to be aware of their socialization, social identities, values and attitudes, and positions of privilege and oppression that may affect their practice with diverse girls and women by engaging in continuous self-reflection, professional education, and consultation.

Guideline 6: Psychologists strive to create and implement strategies, applications and approaches that are most appropriate for girls and women.

Guideline 7: Psychologists strive to foster professional, educational, and therapeutic alliances and practices that empower girls and women and honor their strengths.

Guideline 8: Psychologists strive to provide appropriate nonbiased assessments and diagnoses that affirm rather than pathologize women's and girls' normal development.

Guideline 9: Psychologists strive to conceptualize girls' and women's issues in their sociopolitical context, attending to gender, cultural factors, and dynamics of power.

Guideline 10: Psychologists strive to become acquainted with and utilize relevant mental health, education, and community resources for girls and women.

Guideline 11: Psychologists strive to assume responsibility for challenging unhealthy power dynamics influencing girls and women at interpersonal, institutional, and systemic levels.

Practically speaking, these translate into specific behaviors:

- Psychologists need to remain aware of the emerging research on women, girls, and gender. This can be construed as insuring the competency necessary for ethical practice.
- Psychologists need to become acquainted with the range of women's diversity. Women clients from one cultural, social, or age group should not be assumed to be similar to or predictive of women clients from different groups. Psychologists who focus their practice on specific groups of women, such as women of color (Comas-Diaz & Greene, 1994), women with disabilities (Asch & Fine, 1988), lesbian or bisexual women (Falco, 1991; Firestein, 1996) or Jewish women (Siegel & Cole, 1991), to name a few such groups, need to become familiar with scholarship pertaining specifically to that group. Health psychologists working with women must acquaint themselves with information both on gender-specific women's health concerns such as reproductive and breast cancer or infertility and medical disorders occurring at higher rates in women. Child clinical psychologists need to attend to the gendered components of girls' development and the manners in which normative gendered issues can create risk factors for distress.
- In all instances, psychologists who themselves belong to a target group need to take care not to create false equivalencies of target experiences—for example, "I understand what it's like to be a woman with a disability because I'm a lesbian, even though I'm able-bodied."
- In psychological assessment, psychologists need to carefully read manuals to determine whether tests were constructed with a representative sample of diverse groups of women. Care should be taken in the use of computerized interpretations of standardized tests, since many of these interpretations contain sexist assumptions and fail to take context into account. Women survivors of violence have been shown to be especially at risk for misdiagnosis when cookbook approaches or blind interpretations of testing are used (Rosewater, 1985).
- When gender-role identification is assessed, the psychologist needs to learn whether it is being inappropriately conceptualized as a continuous variable running from masculinity to femininity or whether, consistent with scholarship, it is constructed as two separate continuous variables of masculinity and femininity. When a woman's fitness for parenting is being assessed, care must be taken that standards not be higher for her than for a male partner. Psychological evaluations in forensic matters where issues of gender harassment or discrimination are being raised must demonstrate familiarity with the research on women's test performance in those situations.
- Psychologists need to carefully attend to power dynamics in the therapy relationship (Brown, 1994; Mirkin, 1994; Worell & Remer, 1992) and to the development of therapeutic strategies that empower the female client. Models for gender-aware psychotherapy with women can be found in almost every major theoretical orientation, including psychodynamic, family systems, and cognitive behavioral. Feminist practice, an integrative, technically eclectic theory, offers a paradigm specifically constructed around issues of gender and power (Brown, 1994).

- Emphasize the development of an egalitarian relationship between therapist and client. Use a paradigm of collaboration, respect, and client-as-expert, so that the client's experience of being in therapy is empowering.
- Pay attention to social and political context. Women's and girls' lives, and the problems they bring into therapy, are affected by changes in law and social policy and by current social norms about femininity.
- Psychologists working with women and girls are most likely to be effective when they intentionally interweave knowledge of gender, as salient for the particular client, into treatment planning. Psychologists conducting therapy with women clients should become conversant on norms of women's psychological development (Jordan, Kaplan, Miller, Stiver, & Surrey, 1991), female sexuality, and women's experiences in relationships and the workplace.

Women and men therapists alike can work effectively with women when gender is taken explicitly into account from the very inception of the professional relationship. Even when clients do not themselves punctuate gender, a diagnostic formulation that integrates the realities of gender socialization and gendered experiences for women clients will lead to greater precision of understanding and to more empowerment of the client herself.

References, Readings, & Internet Sites 

APA Task Force in Intimate Partner Violence. (n.d.). Report. Retrieved 2004 from http://www.apa.org/pi/iparv.pdf

Asch, A., & Fine, M. (Eds.). (1988). *Women with disabilities.* Philadelphia: Temple University Press.

Ballou, M., & Brown, L. S. (Eds.). (2002). *Rethinking mental health and disorder: Feminist perspectives.* New York: Guilford Press.

Broverman, I. K., Broverman, D., Clarkson, F. E., Rosenkrantz, P., & Vogle, S. (1970). Sex role stereotypes and clinical judgments of mental health. *Journal of Consulting and Clinical Psychology, 34,* 1–7.

Brown, L. S. (1994). *Subversive dialogues: Theory in feminist therapy.* New York: Basic Books.

Comas-Diaz, L., & Greene, B. (Eds.). (1994). *Women of color: Integrating ethnic and gender identities in psychotherapy.* New York: Guilford Press.

Falco, K. (1991). *Psychotherapy with lesbian clients: Theory into practice.* New York: Brunner/Mazel.

Firestein, B. (Ed.). (1996). *Bisexuality: The psychology and politics of an invisible minority.* Thousand Oaks, CA: Sage.

Fitzgerald, L., & Nutt, R. (1986). The Division 17 Principles Concerning the Counseling/Psychotherapy of Women: Rationale and implementation. *Counseling Psychologist, 14,* 180–216.

Jordan, J., Kaplan, A., Miller, J. B., Stiver, I., & Surrey, J. (Eds.). (1991). *Women's growth in connection: Writings from the Stone Center.* New York: Guilford Press.

Mirkin, M. P. (Ed.). (1994). *Women in context: Toward a feminist reconstruction of psychotherapy.* New York: Guilford Press.

Nutt, R., Rice, J. K., & Enns, C. Z. (Eds.). (2002). *Guidelines for psychological practice with girls and women, 12/11/02 draft.* Washington, DC: American Psychological Association Society for Counseling Psychology and Society for the Psychology of Women.

Rosewater, L. B. (1985). Schizophrenic, borderline, or battered? In L. E. A. Walker & L. B. Rosewater (Eds.), *Handbook of feminist therapy: Women's issues in psychotherapy.* New York: Springer.

Siegel, R. J., & Cole, E. (Eds.). (1991). *Jewish women in therapy: Seen but not heard.* New York: Haworth.

Society for the Psychology of Women. (n.d.). Home page. Retrieved 2004 from http://www.apa.org/divisions/div35/

Worell, J. K., & Remer, P. (1992). *Feminist perspectives in therapy: An empowerment model for women.* New York: Wiley.

Related Topic

Chapter 66, "Sexual Feelings, Actions, and Dilemmas in Psychotherapy"

63 ASSESSMENT AND TREATMENT OF LESBIANS, GAY MEN, AND BISEXUALS

Robin A. Buhrke & Douglas C. Haldeman

Over 30 years have passed since psychology and psychiatry, in consideration of the scientific evidence, removed homosexuality from the list of mental disorders (Bayer, 1981). Since that time, the database supporting this decision has grown exponentially. We know that lesbian, gay, and bisexual individuals exist everywhere, do not always self-identify, and, because of socially instituted stigma, are more likely to be consumers of psychological services than heterosexuals (Garnets, Hancock, Cochran, Peplau, & Goodchilds, 1991). A study commissioned by the American Psychological Association's (APA's) Committee on Lesbian and Gay Concerns (Garnets et al., 1991) found that 90% of psychologists surveyed had treated a lesbian or gay individual, yet many reported a wide range of prejudicial and unfounded assumptions about lesbians and gay men. Given the lack of attention to this issue in most training programs, guidance for practitioners and trainers is necessary.

In this brief overview, guidelines on the assessment and treatment of lesbian, gay, and bisexual individuals are addressed. Assessment focuses on the construct of sexual orientation and how best to assist those struggling with sexual orientation–related concerns. Our discussion of treatment will focus on concerns that are common among lesbian, gay, and bisexual individuals.

ASSESSMENT GUIDELINES

The assessment of sexual orientation is made challenging by the fluid nature of the construct itself. Early work (e.g., Kinsey, Pomeroy, & Martin, 1948) defined sexual orientation as a continuum, as opposed to dichotomous. Subsequent models (e.g., Coleman, 1987) have included gender-based, social, and affectional variables in the construction of sexual orientation. Regardless of the model, sexual orientation is a complex phenomenon; for some, the behavioral aspects thereof may not be the most significant. That is, one can *identify* as lesbian, gay, or bisexual without ever having engaged in same-sex sexual behavior. Similarly, one can engage in same-sex sexual behavior and not identify as lesbian, gay, or bisexual. Sense of identity, internalized sociocultural expectations, importance of social/political affiliations, and fantasies are some of the variables that need to be examined in order to assist the patient in arriving at a cogent self-perception of sexual orientation. This makes the process of identifying as lesbian, gay, or bisexual laden with both practical and existential considerations.

Competence in serving lesbian, gay, and bisexual patients is measured by the ability to recognize and neutralize antigay bias and to refrain from assuming that normalcy implies heterosexuality. This may be accomplished by familiarizing oneself with the extant literature, as well as by developing a sense of "cultural literacy"—that is, an understanding of what the normative life experiences of lesbians, gay men, and bisexuals may entail. Ultimately, this implies a familiarity with normative developmental, familial, social, and vocational concerns faced by many lesbians, gay men, and bisexuals throughout the life span (D'Augelli & Patterson, 1994). Further, an appreciation for the added burdens of social stigma and the potential for discrimination and violence faced by many lesbians, gay men, and bisexuals is necessary to adequately understand the experiences of these groups. Finally, the clinician may benefit from an examination of personal values around same-gender sexual orientation.

Psychological research has firmly established that same-gender sexual orientation is not, in itself, a sign of poor psychological adjustment, psychopathology, or emotional disturbance (e.g., Gonsiorek, 1991; Reiss, 1980). Lesbians and gay men do not differ from heterosexual women and men on measures of psychological adjustment and self-esteem or in the capacity for decision making, vocational adjustment, or competence in family roles (as parent or spouse). Further, the development of a positive lesbian or gay identity is correlated with better psychological adjustment for lesbians and gay men. Self-identifying as lesbian or gay, accepting this as an aspect of identity, self-disclosing, and feeling accepted by others have been found to be strongly related to psychological adjustment (Bell & Weinberg, 1978; Murphy, 1989). Similarly, a more positive lesbian or gay male identity has been found to be correlated with significantly fewer symptoms of neurotic or social anxiety, higher ego strength, less depression, and higher self-esteem (Hammersmith & Weinberg, 1973; Savin-Williams, 1989). Generally, psychological adjustment appears to be highest among gay men and lesbian women who are committed to their lesbian, gay, or bisexual identity, reject the notion that homosexuality is an illness, are uninterested in changing their homosexuality, and have close and supportive associations with other gay people (Bell & Weinberg, 1978). Recent randomized survey research suggests that the level of emotional distress among lesbian, gay, and bisexual persons may be higher than among heterosexuals (Cochran & Mays, 2002). Still, this may likely be attributed to the harmful effects of internalized social stigma.

This is not meant to encourage clinicians to impose a "pro-gay" agenda, or any agenda at all, upon the confused or questioning patient. Rather, it is the clinician's responsibility to provide a safe, value-neutral environment for exploration, as well as accurate, scientific information about same-gender sexual orientation. The therapeutic task with many lesbian, gay, and bisexual patients is the neutralization of the toxic effects of internalized social opprobrium. This cannot be accomplished if the clinician is unaware of the scientific data regarding sexual orientation, is unacquainted with the lives of well-adjusted, high-functioning lesbians, gay men, and bisexuals, or attempts to work while harboring unexamined antigay prejudices.

Thus, a clinician who bases treatment on antiquated and scientifically unproven theories about the nature of same-gender sexual orientation can do little more than reinforce the societal stigma that causes many lesbian, gay, and bisexual individuals to seek help in the first place. This is particularly true with patients who seek to change their sexual orientation. Davison (1991) views "reparative" or "conversion" therapy as part of the inhospitable social context that causes many distressed lesbians and gay men to seek sexual orientation change. Conversion therapy programs are founded on unproven and biased theories and yield no support to the notion that sexual orientation can be changed, even if it were desirable to do so (Haldeman, 1994). Recent research in this area suggests that the potential negative consequences for the individual who "fails" conversion therapy can be serious (Shidlo & Schroeder, 2002). Such individuals need to be treated with additional consideration to the problems that may have been compounded by conversion treatments (Haldeman, 2002). No clinician should attempt to change an individual's sexual orientation, or instruct a homosexually oriented individual in heteroerotic activities, without carefully assessing the history and motives behind such a request and making certain that the patient is well aware of the damaging effects of internalized antigay prejudice and is acquainted with the normative life experiences of lesbians, gay men, and bisexuals.

What, then, should the clinician who is interested in conducting competent assessments with lesbians, gay men, and bisexuals take into consideration? Garnets et al. (1991) identify several themes that reflect exemplary practice:

1. Clinicians recognize that same-gender sexual orientation is not pathological.
2. Clinicians do not automatically attribute a patient's concerns to his or her sexual orientation and are able to recognize that negative attitudes about homosexuality, as well as experiences of rejection, harassment, and discrimination, can cause emotional distress.
3. Clinicians affirm that lesbians and gay men can and do lead productive and fulfilling lives and participate in healthy, long-term relationships, despite the lack of institutional support for them.

These themes, together with the literature on which they are based, form the foundation for APA's Guidelines for Psychotherapy with Lesbian, Gay, and Bisexual Clients (APA, 2002). These practice guidelines, which are aspirational in nature, are categorized along the following thematic lines: attitudes toward homosexuality and bisexuality, relationships and families, diversity issues, and education. Guidelines in the first category call upon the psychologist to be knowledgeable about sexual orientation, and to strive to understand how misinformation, internalized social prejudice, and trauma may affect a client's presentation. Psychologists are also encouraged to examine their own prejudices and beliefs about sexual orientation and their potential impact on treatment.

Psychologists are further encouraged to be knowledgeable about and respect the importance of lesbian, gay, and bisexual families, which may often include persons who are not legally or biologically related. Issues related to lesbian, gay, and bisexual individuals as parents are also considered. The diversity section calls upon psychologists to be aware that ethnic minority lesbian, gay, and bisexual individuals, bisexual people, and lesbian, gay, and bisexual persons with physical and/or sensory disabilities may face particular challenges due to multiple minority status. Finally, generational differences (lesbian, gay, and bisexual youth or elder individuals) may present unique challenges in the psychotherapy setting. Some of these issues are considered more fully in the following section.

TREATMENT CONSIDERATIONS

Most often, when lesbians, gay men, and bisexuals come to treatment, they do so to address the same types of issues that their heterosexual counterparts address: depression, anxiety, self-esteem, career concerns, relationship problems, and so on. There are a great deal more similarities between heterosexual patients and lesbian, gay, and bisexual patients than there are differences. However, there are important experiences that are unique for lesbians, gay men, and bisexuals, and these issues may arise in treatment.

A significant major issue facing lesbians, gay men, and bisexuals is that of "coming out." Coming out is the developmental process in which lesbians, gay men, and bisexuals become aware of their sexual orientation (Gonsiorek & Rudolph, 1991). This process occurs over a period of time, ranging anywhere from a few days to years, and may be extended for many bisexuals (Matteson, 1996). Many times, because of being raised in environments that are antigay or stigmatizing, early awareness of same-sex attractions may result in anxiety, shame, fear, and guilt. Patients who are questioning their sexual orientation may present to clinicians with confusion and sometimes even requests for help in ridding themselves of these unpleasant feelings. It is important for clinicians to help patients work through these feelings, identify environmental pressures that contribute to these feelings, and find resolution and affirmation, regardless of the outcome of their explorations.

Coming out also refers to disclosing one's sexual orientation to others. If clinicians are heterosexually biased—that is, if they assume that all patients are heterosexual—they may never know otherwise. If a clinician responds to a male patient's statements about his "partner" with questions about "her," a gay or bisexual man will be less likely to disclose that his partner is male. Keeping his sexual orientation hidden not only reinforces homophobic bias but also establishes a barrier between the patient and the clinician, which undermines the therapeutic process.

Because most lesbians, gay men, and bisexuals are invisible to the heterosexual majority, a number of consequences occur: There is a considerable underestimation of the numbers of lesbians, gay men, and bisexuals; we tend to stereotype based on those who are out and visible or those who come to treatment; and few role models exist for newly coming out lesbians, gay men, and bisexuals. This invisibility often creates marginalization and isolation, which clinicians can avoid perpetuating by educating themselves about normative lesbian, gay, or bisexual life experience and refraining from making heterosexist assumptions about patients' lives.

Marginalization and isolation are often magnified for lesbians, gay men, and bisexuals of color because of their multiple-minority status. An African American lesbian is often forced to choose between her sexual orientation and her ethnicity by overt or covert questions such as "Are you Black or are you gay?" It is important for the clinician to not perpetuate this splitting of patients' identities and to recognize each patient as an integrated whole. It is also important to recognize that these same patients may not feel at home in the lesbian, gay, and bisexual community because of being Black, while at the same time, because of being gay, they are not accepted in the Black community.

Family issues may raise particular problems for lesbians, gay men, and bisexuals. In many jurisdictions, lesbians, gay men, and bisexuals can lose custody of their children simply because of their sexual orientations. This places an incredible stress on parents in choosing between acknowledging their sexual orientations and risking their families. Without knowing clear boundaries of confidentiality, patients may be reluctant to disclose their sexual orientations to their clinicians for fear that that information may later be used against them in court cases. For lesbians, gay men, and bisexuals who have children, blending families can pose some unique problems—what and how to tell the children, how to deal with schools, and so on. For those who want children but don't have them, creating a family is more difficult, whether by natural or adoptive means.

Additionally, it is important to be sensitive to the potential for internalized reactions to prejudice, discrimination, and violence in lesbian, gay, and bisexual clients. In most jurisdictions, it is legal to deny housing, employment, and custody of children solely on the basis of sexual orientation. This reality places a high level of stress on many lesbians, gay men, and bisexuals. Falco (1996) presents eight stressors and strengths that are common among lesbian and bisexual women, which may be generalized to gay men as well. Clinicians should be mindful of the level of stress this lack of protection may place on many lesbians, gay men, and bisexuals.

- *Disclosure choices are continual:* Coming out or disclosing one's sexual orientation is not a onetime occurrence. It is a lifelong process, with decisions to be made about how much to tell and to whom with each new person met. And each decision to disclose has the potential to be met with antipathy and rejection.
- *Nondisclosure generalizes to other areas:* Most lesbians, gay men, and bisexuals do not disclose to everyone they meet. The process of hiding one aspect of oneself may generalize to other areas, and self-esteem may suffer as a result of interpreting "hidden" aspects as "bad."
- *Lack of support:* The absence of social support for and negative cultural attitudes about lesbians, gay men, and bisexuals can affect one's sense of self, as well as the stability of relationships. Bisexuals may be particularly prone to marginalization, since they are not often accepted in either the heterosexual or the lesbian and gay communities.
- *Absence of role models and cultural history:* Although lesbians, gay men, and bisexuals have a rich culture and history, most of it is invisible. As a result, many mistakenly believe that they are "the only one."
- *Internalized homophobia:* Some lesbians,

gay men, and bisexuals have internalized the negative messages about homosexuality from their culture, and they, too, believe that heterosexuality is preferred. This can create a great deal of conflict and anguish for the patient.

- *Identity development:* The process of establishing a lesbian, gay, or bisexual identity is complex and complicated. Although few individuals march through the stages of development in a lockstep manner, the models can be useful for clinicians in understanding their patients and in formulating appropriate interventions.
- *Androgyny and ego strength:* In order to recognize and accept their same-sex attractions, lesbians, gay men, and bisexuals must deviate from social norms. This calls for a certain amount of ego strength. Further, lesbians and gay men tend to have a greater capacity for both feminine and masculine traits, which is generally associated with better psychological health (Falco, 1991).
- *Gender socialization and its impact on relationships:* Same-sex relationships are, by their very nature, composed of two people with similar gender socialization histories. While this may serve as a source of commonality and connection, it can also create some difficulties. For example, as a result of their female socialization, both women in a lesbian or bisexual relationship may be sexually unaggressive and reluctant to initiate intimate contact.
- *Sexual identity as fluid:* For some individuals, sexual orientation may be experienced as variable over the lifespan. This may result in an identification that may or may not match the individual's sexual behavior or relationship choices. In any case, the individual retains the right to determine her or his own identity.

The life experiences of lesbian, gay, and bisexual individuals presenting for psychotherapy are tremendously varied. Competent clinical practice with these groups does not require one to be lesbian, gay, or bisexual. Rather, it is based on the ability to understand the lesbian, gay, or bisexual individual in his or her own frame of reference. This means approaching treatment with a nonstigmatizing view of sexual orientation and avoiding a heterocentric model for intervening. These basic principles enable the lesbian, gay, or bisexual individual to grow in a therapeutic environment free of the stigma that is so widespread in the sociocultural environment.

References & Readings 

Bayer, R. (1981). *Homosexuality and American psychiatry: The politics of diagnosis.* Princeton, NJ: Princeton University Press.

Bell, A. P., & Weinberg, M. S. (1978). *Homosexualities: A study of diversity among men and women.* Bloomington: Indiana University Press.

Cabaj, R. P., & Stein, T. S. (Eds.). (1996). *Textbook of homosexuality and mental health.* Washington, DC: American Psychiatric Association.

Cochran, S. (2001). Emerging issues on lesbians' and gay men's mental health: Does sexual orientation really matter? *American Psychologist, 56,* 931–947.

Coleman, E. (1987). The assessment of sexual orientation. *Journal of Homosexuality, 14,* 9–24.

D'Augelli, A. R., & Patterson, C. J. (1995). *Lesbian, gay, and bisexual identities over the lifespan.* New York: Oxford University Press.

Davison, G. (1991). Constructionism and morality in therapy for homosexuality. In J. Gonsiorek & J. Weinrich (Eds.), *Homosexuality: Research implications for public policy* (pp. 137–148). Newbury Park, CA: Sage.

Division 44 Committee on Lesbian, Gay and Bisexual Concerns Joint Task Force. (2000). Guidelines for psychotherapy with lesbian, gay and bisexual clients. *American Psychologist, 55,* 1440–1451.

Falco, K. L. (1991). *Psychotherapy with lesbian clients.* New York: Brunner/Mazel.

Falco, K. L. (1996). Psychotherapy with women who love women. In R. P. Cabaj & T. Stein (Eds.), *Textbook of homosexuality and mental health* (pp. 397–412). Washington, DC: American Psychiatric Association.

Garnets, L., Hancock, K., Cochran, S., Peplau, L., & Goodchilds, J. (1991). Issues in psychotherapy with lesbians and gay men: A survey of psychologists. *American Psychologist, 46,* 964–972.

Garnets, L. D., & Kimmel, D. C. (Eds.). (1993). *Psychological perspectives on lesbian and gay male experiences.* New York: Columbia University Press.

Gonsiorek, J. D. (1982). *Homosexuality and psychotherapy: A practitioner's handbook of affirmative models*. New York: Haworth.

Gonsiorek, J. (1991). The empirical basis for the demise of the illness model of homosexuality. In J. Gonsiorek & J. Weinrich (Eds.), *Homosexuality: Research issues for public policy* (pp. 115–136). Newbury Park, CA: Sage.

Gonsiorek, J. D., & Rudolph, J. R. (1991). Homosexual identity: Coming out and other developmental events. In J. D. Gonsiorek & J. D. Weinrich (Eds.), *Homosexuality: Research implications for public policy* (pp. 161–176). Newbury Park, CA: Sage.

Gonsiorek, J. D., & Weinrich, J. D. (Eds.). (1991). *Homosexuality: Research implications for public policy*. Newbury Park, CA: Sage.

Haldeman, D. C. (1994). The practice and ethics of sexual orientation conversion therapy. *Journal of Consulting and Clinical Psychology, 62*, 221–227.

Haldeman, D. (2002). Therapeutic antidotes: Helping gay and bisexual men recover from conversion therapies. *Journal of Lesbian and Gay Psychotherapy, 5*, 119–132.

Hammersmith, S. K., & Weinberg, M. S. (1973). Homosexual identity: Commitment, adjustments, and significant others. *Sociometry, 36*, 56–78.

Kinsey, A. C., Pomeroy, W. B., & Martin, C. E. (1948). *Sexual behavior in the human male*. Philadelphia: Saunders.

Matteson, D. R. (1996). Psychotherapy with bisexual individuals. In R. P. Cabaj & T. Stein (Eds.), *Textbook of homosexuality and mental health* (pp. 433–450). Washington, DC: American Psychiatric Association.

Murphy, B. (1989). Lesbian couples and their parents: The effects of perceived parental attitudes on the couple. *Journal of Counseling and Development, 68*, 46–51.

Reiss, B. F. (1980). Psychological tests in homosexuality. In J. Marmor (Ed.), *Homosexual behavior: A modern reappraisal* (pp. 296–311). New York: Basic Books.

Savin-Williams, R. C. (1989). Coming out to parents and self-esteem among gay and lesbian youth. *Journal of Homosexuality, 13*, 101–109.

Shidlo, A. & Schroeder, M. (2002). Changing sexual orientation: A consumers' report. *Professional Psychology, 33*(3), 249–259.

Weinberg, M. S., & Williams, C. J. (1974). *Male homosexuals: Their problems and adaptations*. New York: Oxford University Press.

Related Topics

Chapter 58, "Assessing and Treating Normative Male Alexithymia"

Chapter 62, "Guidelines for Treating Women in Psychotherapy"

64 PSYCHOTHERAPY WITH OLDER ADULTS

Margaret Gatz & Bob G. Knight

1. *Case formulation:* When seeing any older adult for treatment, an initial task of therapy is to create a picture of the older adult, including the individual's strengths and ways of functioning in the world, as well as the nature of the problem that has brought the person to treatment. This picture can be conceptualized in any of several ways: as building a model of the person, as describing the individual's characteristic defense mechanisms, or as identifying preferred coping styles.

2. *Cohort and culture:* In understanding an older adult client, it may be helpful to bring concepts from the study of cultural differences. The identity of an older adult will inevitably reflect the historical time during which she or he has matured. Working with a person who matured in a different time is similar in many ways to working with clients who matured in a different cultural context; the therapist must be careful about cohort- or culture-bound assumptions, word use, and values. Cohorts and cultures can also interact in the sense that earlier-born older adults may have a specific and strong sense of ethnic identity with regard to ethnicities that are no longer identified as separate or disadvantaged, for example, Irish or Italian.

3. *Epidemiology of disorder:* Other than the dementias, prevalence of psychological disorders is lower in older adults than in people of other ages. This statement flies in the face of stereotypes of old age as inevitably depressing or anxiety-provoking. In fact, most older adults seem to have developed sufficient psychological resilience that they do not develop new disorders in response to the transitions and life stressors that accompany aging. At the same time, depression and other disorders may be quite high in older adults with comorbid medical disorders, in both inpatient and outpatient medical care settings, and among those who are living in nursing homes. (Review chapters concerning the influence of physical disease and medication can be found in Carstensen, Edelstein, & Dornbrand, 1996).

4. *Age of onset:* Early in the assessment, a key question is to evaluate whether the current problem is a new situation altogether or whether it is a continuation, recurrence, or exacerbation of a previous problem. This consideration influences both inferences about etiology and choices about treatment.

5. *Differential diagnosis:* In older adults who are seen by the mental health care system, it is typical that multiple problems coexist; these may include emotional distress, cognitive impairment, chronic physical conditions, and changes in social network or environmental context. The classical differential diagnostic distinction is between depression and dementia; indeed, one frequent assessment question concerns the explanation for perceived changes in memory. A more encompassing way to consider differential diagnosis is through a decision tree: first, whether the pattern of functioning reflects normal aging versus some pathological process; second, what combination of emotional distress versus neuropathological changes (e.g., Alzheimer's disease, Parkinson's disease) is suggested; third, what aspects of the problem are reversible. Sometimes following a case over time is the most certain way of distinguishing among assessment hypotheses. (Review chapters about assessing dementia and depression as well as a directory of instruments and norms can be found in Storandt & VandenBos, 1994.)

6. *Assessment:* Psychological assessment is often complex in older adults and frequently requires a working knowledge of neuropsychological assessment, as well as the use of personality and emotional assessment techniques with appropriate age norms. Simple screening devices, such as mental status examinations and brief scales to measure depression and anxiety, can be helpful in day-to-day practice if their limitations are understood (See Lichtenberg, 1999, for a general resource about assessment.)

7. *Emergencies:* Often older adults seemingly wait to see a mental health professional until there is some emergency, whether financial or psychiatric or physical. In such instances, the therapist must first resolve the emergency and only then deal with the psychological circumstances (Scogin, 2000, covers these issues).

8. *Suicide:* Older adults, and especially older white males, are in the age group at highest risk for suicide (Conwell and Duberstein, 2001). This is due, in part, to the fact that the ratio of suicide attempts to suicide completions is much lower among older adults. Older adults with depression, substance abuse, and those with dementing illnesses who are aware of their cognitive impairment and depressed about it should be assessed for suicide risk. Older clients can, and do, make distinctions among not wanting to live, wanting to die, and wanting to kill themselves. While society debates the legality of rational suicide and assisted suicide, psychologists must be alert to those whose suicidal impulses are motivated by psychological distress (APA Working Group on Assisted Suicide and End-of-Life Decisions, 2000).

9. *Access:* The majority of older adults who meet diagnostic criteria for a mental disorder are not seen by any mental health professional. For this reason, the role of the psychologist includes home visits, medical hospital and nursing home consultation, outreach to senior centers, and cooperation with primary care physicians (Smyer, 1993).

10. *Family:* The family constitutes the primary social context of older adults. If an older adult is declining physically or cognitively, his or her health-related dependencies and needs for assistance have radiating effects on the family. Consequently, the family must be considered in the treatment plan, at the same time respecting the confidentiality of the patient (Qualls, 1996).

11. *End-of-life issues:* Grief work is an inevitable part of psychotherapy with older adults. Increasingly, too, psychologists are involving themselves in end-of-life care, including work at hospices and palliative care settings (Lawton, 2001).

12. *Spectrum of interventions:* As different theoretical approaches to psychotherapy have emerged, each has been applied to older adults—for example, psychoanalysis, behavior modification, community mental health consultation, and cognitive therapy. In addition, efforts have been made to use the knowledge base from research about developmental processes in later life in order to inform intervention. Research has shown that older adults respond well to a variety of forms of psychotherapy. Cognitive-behavioral, brief psychodynamic, and interpersonal therapies have shown utility in the treatment of depression, anxiety, and sleep disturbance; and 12-step programs have shown utility with older alcohol abusers. Cognitive training techniques, behavior modification strategies, and environmental modifications have relevance for improving functional abilities in cognitively impaired older adults. Finally, use of reminiscence or life review is common with older adults, both as an element of other therapies and as a separate, special technique. (The empirical evidence is summarized in Gatz et al., 1998. Overview chapters about implementing this array of treatments may be found in Zarit and Knight, 1996, while Karel, Ogland-Hand, and Gatz, 2002, focuses on depression.)

13. *Relationship issues:* From the beginning of psychotherapeutic work with older adults, therapists have noted the potential for differences in the therapeutic relationship when the client is older than the therapist. Older clients confront the therapist with aging issues in an "off time" way—that is, the therapist confronts reactions to aging, illness, disability, and death before these issues have arisen in the therapist's own life. Older clients may remind the therapist of older relatives and elicit countertransferential reactions related to parents, grandparents, and so forth (Knight, 1996). Therapists may share social stereotypes about the elderly and expect their older clients to be boring, unattractive, or asexual. Biases may also influence diagnosis; therapists are inclined to interpret the same symptoms as reflecting brain disorder in an older person but depression in a younger client.

14. *Interface with medical care system:* Older adults with significant mental health problems are most often seen by various nonspecialists, such as primary care physicians. Psychologists who see older adults must be prepared to work in interdisciplinary settings and to cooperate with other professionals (Zeiss & Steffen, 1996). Moreover, they must inform themselves about the reimbursement system and become advocates for making the system responsive to their clients (Koenig, George, & Schneider, 1994).

15. *When to refer to a specialist or to seek more training in clinical geropsychology:* When older clients have problems similar to younger clients and there is no reason to suspect a dementing illness, psychotherapy with older adults is very similar to therapy with younger adults. As assessment issues become more complex and more subtle, such as needing to disentangle multiple possible causes of symptoms, more specialized knowledge is needed. Practitioners working in an age-segregated environment (e.g., nursing homes) or becoming more specialized in treating older adults need more training in clinical geropsychology. Continuing education in clinical geropsychology can often be found through the American Psychological Association, sponsored by Section 2 (Clinical Geropsychology) of Division 12 (Clinical Psychology), or by Division 20 (Adult Development and Aging), by the Gerontological Society of America at its annual meeting, through state and local psychological associations, and through some universities and medical centers, especially those with Alzheimer's disease research centers.

References, Readings, & Internet Sites 

APA Working Group on Assisted Suicide and End-of-Life Decisions. (2000). *Report to the Board of Directors.* Retrieved 2004 from http://www.apa.org/pi/aseol/introduction.html

Carstensen, L. L., Edelstein, B. A., & Dornbrand, L. (Eds.). (1996). *The practical handbook of clinical gerontology.* Thousand Oaks, CA: Sage.

Conwell, Y., & Duberstein, P. R. (2001). Suicide in elders. *Annals of the New York Academy of Sciences, 932,* 132–150.

Gatz, M., Fiske, A., Fox, L. S., Kaskie, B., Kasl-Godley, J. E., McCallum, T. J., et al. (1998). Empirically-validated psychological treatments for older adults. *Journal of Mental Health and Aging, 4,* 9–46.

Karel, M. J., Ogland-Hand, S., & Gatz, M. (2002). *Assessing and treating late-life depression: A casebook and resource guide.* New York: Basic Books.

Knight, B. G. (1996). *Psychotherapy with older adults* (2nd ed.). Thousand Oaks, CA: Sage.

Koenig, H. G., George, L. K., & Schneider, R. (1994). Mental health care for older adults in the Year 2020: A dangerous and avoided topic. *Gerontologist, 34,* 674–679.

Lawton, M. P. (2001). Quality of life and the end of life. In J. E. Birren & K. W. Schaie (Eds.), *Handbook of the psychology of aging* (5th ed., pp. 592–616). San Diego: Academic Press.

Lichtenberg, P. A. (Ed.). (1999). *Handbook of assessment in clinical gerontology.* New York: Wiley.

Qualls, S. H. (1996). Family therapy with aging families. In S. H. Zarit & B. G. Knight (Eds.), *A guide to psychotherapy and aging* (pp. 121–137). Washington, DC: American Psychological Association.

Scogin, F. (2000). *The first session with seniors: A step-by-step guide.* San Francisco: Jossey-Bass.

Smyer, M. A. (Ed.). (1993). *Mental health and aging.* New York: Springer.

Storandt, M. A., & VandenBos, G. R. (Eds.). (1994). *Neuropsychological assessment of dementia and depression in older adults: A clinician's guide.* Washington, DC: American Psychological Association.

Zarit, S. H., & Knight, B. G. (Eds.). (1996). *A guide to psychotherapy and aging: Effective clinical interventions in a life-stage context.* Washington, DC: American Psychological Association.

Zeiss, A. M., & Steffen, A. M. (1996). Interdisciplinary health care teams: The basic unit of geriatric health care. In L. L. Carstensen, B. A. Edelstein, & L. Dornbrand, L. (Eds.), *The practical handbook of clinical gerontology* (pp. 423–450). Thousand Oaks, CA: Sage.

Related Topics

Chapter 2, "Mental Status Examination"

Chapter 7, "Adult Neuropsychological Assessment"

Chapter 57, "Psychological Interventions in Adult Disease Management"

Chapter 72, "Psychotherapy With Cognitively Impaired Adults"

65 REFUSAL SKILLS TRAINING

Robert H. Woody & Jennifer K. H. Woody

Regardless of service context (e.g., schools, clinics, hospitals, agencies, or private practices), psychologists need strategies and techniques for helping clients solve everyday or real-world problems. Moreover, the diminishing availability of mental health services for persons of all ages, particularly today's children and youth (with the behavioral problems and conduct disorders endemic to and seemingly epidemic in that age group), supports the need for evidenced-based interventions that have proven efficacy. Since most mental health services now occur in schools, educationally oriented professionals and clinical practitioners alike must be competent in brief strategies that are adaptable to a myriad of therapeutic objectives and compatible with the mission of schools.

This chapter presents a clear-cut approach that promotes behavior change in an efficacious manner, namely evidence-based Refusal Skills Training (RST). With a cognitive-behavioral basis, RST uses short-term interventions that focus on specific or targeted behavior problems (Shechtman, 2002; Woody, 2004) and capitalizes on social support (Demaray & Malecki, 2002). Further, RST is suited for use by educators or clinicians, and is compatible with the overall "educational" mission of schools.

FORMS AND EXAMPLES OF RST PROGRAMS

RST emphasizes two forms of influence: informational influence and normative influence. *Informational influence* is directed at the pressures or reinforcers experienced by the client in everyday life, such as advertisements of products and mass media depictions of behaviors that could reinforce unhealthy outcomes. This is clearly an educational approach, and it requires astute teaching methods and highly relevant informational materials. *Normative influence* is directed at the pressures or reinforcers that the client encounters, especially those emitted by other persons such as peers.

Generally, training programs rely on informational influence disseminated by a pamphlet or other material, perhaps supplemented with brief individual or group counseling. The normative influence is offered through behavioral rehearsal or modeling techniques (either in vivo or by videotape). A variety of studies indicate that electronic media, especially those involving video stimuli, can enhance learning (Herrmann & McWhirter, 1997). While there are innumerable variables to be considered, it would appear that normative influence may be the most effective for behavior change (Poler, Warzak, & Woody, 2003).

RST employs multiple interventions that may vary in the psychological processes that are emphasized. Goldstein, Reagles, and Amann (1990) suggest six types of interventions: cognitive, environmental, affective/interpersonal, therapeutic, school alternative, and social learning. While all of these approaches could be implemented proactively, the therapeutic and school alternative approaches are most often reactive (i.e., after the problem has occurred).

Cognitive interventions promote informational influence but can also involve normative influence. Using a variety of techniques and formats, the cognitive approach provides information that will presumably enable the client/student to make informed decisions (e.g., not to use drugs). Similarly, some strategies have sought cognitive change through aversive information, say, about detrimental substances or behaviors. Fear-arousing and punishment tactics have proved ineffective in altering high-risk behavior; moreover, Hansen et al. (1988) found that informational programs, such as explaining how a drug or alcoholic substance works or what it looks like, might actually arouse curiosity or promote experimentation. The latter result might occur especially if the information is presented in, say, a peer context and the positive message is subverted by adverse normative influence.

Environmental interventions are those that target the context in which the high-risk behavior takes place. For example, since the school is a critical site in a young person's life and has legal authority to restrict behavior, schools have implemented drug intervention strategies, such as strict policies, detection methods, and prevention/intervention organizations (Goldstein et al., 1990). This approach combines the possibility of informative and normative influence.

Affective/interpersonal interventions, which emphasize information and instruction, target the student's self-concept, self-acceptance, and decision-making processes. Again, research on these strategies, such as values clarification, has shown little assured effect on behavioral change (Goodstat & Sheppard, 1983). Although informative influence dominates, a group program or the descriptions in the information can draw upon normative influence.

Therapeutic interventions involve the student entering into individual or group counseling. The therapeutic focus is on the high-risk behavior or maladaptive behavior. Beyond any change that might occur from insight (e.g., improved definition of personal needs or development of coping abilities), the interpersonal relationships introduce normative influence. Certainly, counseling provided in a group context creates the possibility of powerful normative influence.

School alternative interventions, like the therapeutic approach, tend to be employed when a problem already exists. With the former, the student enters into individual or group counseling, with a focus on the high-risk behavior. With the latter, the student with an incorrigible behavior pattern is placed in an environment that includes treatment (e.g., an alternative school or group residence). The alternative approach, if managed properly, makes normative influence possible; if managed poorly, adverse modeling can occur.

Social learning interventions most closely parallel the normative influence approach. This strategy commonly incorporates observational learning, behavioral rehearsal, and reinforcement contingencies. The majority of social skill and refusal skill curricula fall under this rubric. Most often, these programs rely on providing information, developing social and self-regulatory skills, skill enhancement through guided practice and social support for behavioral change. A social learning approach can function in a preventive as well as a corrective manner. Further, behavioral rehearsal allows students to practice these skills in a socially valid context (e.g., with their peers, in a school setting).

EMPIRICAL RESEARCH ON RST PROGRAMS

Increasingly, research has demonstrated the effectiveness of RST that employs social learning/normative approaches (Goldstein, 1981, 1988; Katz, Robisch, & Telch, 1989; Reardon, Sussman, & Flay, 1989; Schinke & Blythe, 1982; Schinke & Gilchrist, 1984). Clearly, additional research is needed to evaluate the effectiveness of RST with lower-income and minority populations.

The research results for RST are, for the most part, efficacy studies. Despite an effort to carefully structure the intervention and the use of a particular educationally oriented program that can be defined, the research seldom, if ever, controls and measures the presence or absence (or degree of influence from) the interpersonal conditions that could facilitate learning and behavioral change for the client. Consequently, the effects of the interpersonal conditions remain unmeasured and likely contaminate the efficacy attributed to RST. In addition, the various RST programs contain unique contents, and "making comparison across programs is inherently difficult" (Herrmann & McWhirter, 1997, p. 177).

Since RST programs are finding ready reception in schools, the use of peers as models or leaders, either in vivo or by video recordings, is common. As would be expected, the results have been positive, such as enhancing the efforts of teachers or counselors (Perry, 1989).

From their review of the research, Herrmann and McWhirter (1997) conclude that RST (which they refer to as Refusal and Resistance Skills, or RRS) programs defy generalization: "In other words, neither general endorsements nor general criticisms of RRS programs are appropriate because a number of different mediating factors (including target behaviors and process variables) interact to determine the efficacy of different programs. Moreover, the quality of program delivery plays an important role in determining overall program effectiveness" (p. 184). They also believe that the research supports early intervention; caution that it remains unproved that refusal and resistance skills will actually be implemented behaviorally; and endorse a comprehensive prevention curriculum and use of peer facilitation.

Certainly, it is known that most therapeutic interventions, especially those based on promoting insight, do not modify maladaptive behavioral problems, such as tobacco smoking, substance abuse, and risky sexual activity. Therefore, there is nothing to lose and potentially much to gain from capitalizing on the proven informational and normative influences that can be included in behaviorally based RST programs. If supplemented with nurturance, empathy, and other facilitative conditions, RST programs, particularly in a peer-group context, most likely will lead to cognitive restructuring and behavioral shaping and become the intervention of choice for smoking, alcohol and substance abuse, delinquency, gang behavior, and risky sexual activity.

Promoting Maintenance

Possibly the most important criterion for the success of RST programs is maintenance. The question becomes: How can professionals ensure that a student who masters a skill within the therapeutic context will, in fact, use the skill in real-world experiences? Skill generalization should be addressed in any RST program. Transfer-enhancing procedures may include such strategies as overlearning, stimulus variability, and mediated generalization (e.g., self-recording, self-reinforcement). Maintenance-enhancing strategies incorporate the use of prompt fading, reinforcement fading/withdrawal, booster sessions, and natural reinforcers (Goldstein et al., 1990).

Clarifying the Intervention

Each RST program has an indiosyncratic theoretical basis, which means that even if the interventions appear to be the same or comparable, the underlying nuances may be quite different and, thus, the effects are like the proverbial "apples and oranges." For example, the majority of RST programs rely, to varying degrees, on learning theory, yet there is also use of interpersonal relationships (which may or may not actually adhere to a reinforcement paradigm). Analysis of the RST programs reveals both behavioral modification and cognitive restructuring techniques, as evidenced by "(1) an emphasis on the present and near future; (2) a problem-solving orientation that focuses on changing cognitions and/or overt behavior; and (3) attention to conscious rather than to unconscious determinants of behavior" (Robertson & Woody, 1997, p. 178). Thus, the practitioner should carefully delineate the change mechanisms for the purposes of practice improvement and clinical research.

GUIDELINES FOR PRACTICE

There is solid behavioral science for implementing RST programs, especially for prevention; other behavioral modification approaches may be as good as or better than RST for changing existing maladaptive behaviors. Before offering an RST program, the practitioner should, of course, be mindful of previous statements regarding promoting maintenance and clarifying the intervention. The following 10 guidelines provide a step-by-step approach.

1. Determine the characteristics of the clients/ students. While it is feasible to establish a

given RST program and then select clients/students who are seemingly compatible, it is preferable to first evaluate the pool of potential clients/students. Knowing the characteristics of possible recipients of RST services allows one to tailor the program to their needs.

2. Delineate and define the behavior that is to be targeted (e.g., tobacco smoking, substance abuse, or risky sexual activity), and establish reinforcement contingencies that rely on information and/or normative influence. These decisions should be stated in writing and critiqued by at least one other professional source.
3. Determine whether the format will be individual or group. Given the importance of peer interactions, generally a group format should be considered before deciding on an individual format. In keeping with research on group dynamics, five to eight students is appropriate to facilitate peer interactions.
4. If using a group format, structure for heterogeneity of skill proficiency. Clients/students with more proficient refusal skills provide supportive modeling and reinforcement for the group members with less proficient refusal skills.
5. Communication of information should be tailored to the developmental, emotional, and cognitive levels of the clients/students. Stated simply, the content and delivery style should be understandable to the clients/students.
6. Determine and adhere strictly to a behavior management plan. In accord with the behaviors that were delineated, introduce, monitor, and maintain rules. A behavior/rule contract signed by each client/student is advisable (e.g., required attendance, completing homework assignments). Relying on the behavior management plan allows individual and group behaviors to be reinforced systematically. At least initially, natural/tangible reinforcers are needed.
7. From the initial session and throughout, emphasis should be placed on establishing client/student rapport with the professional and motivation to benefit from the RST program. Empathic understanding and other facilitative conditions should preface any information that might be perceived as confrontive by the clients/students; these qualities should continue throughout the RST program. Each client/student should be comfortable with the professional and the other clients/students before being challenged by an RST task. The client/student who is insecure, shy, or easily threatened or who lacks expressive skills may merit special attention, within or outside the group.
8. Group dynamics should be monitored and managed. If a group format is used, special attention should be given to promoting cohesion. Care should be taken to avoid interpersonal conflicts that cannot be used therapeutically, as well as unnecessary dissonance and cleavage. Gamelike strategies may be useful for reinforcing critical dynamics in the group.
9. Techniques for maintaining the effects of the RST program outside the sessions should be applied. It is often helpful to use homework assignments, self-monitoring, journal writing, or booster sessions (in person or by telephone with, say, a designated "buddy" from the same program or with the professional). Family and social contacts should be enlisted to help the clients/students progress in real-life situations. The results of these external efforts or events should be discussed in the sessions.
10. When an RST program is completed, make a thoughtful evaluation of the successes and failures, individually and at the group level. By understanding the effects of an RST program, professionals will potentially design more effective future offerings.

References, Readings, & Internet Sites

Demaray, M. K., & Malecki, C. K. (2002). Critical levels of perceived social support associated with student adjustment. *School Psychology Quarterly, 17*, 213–241.

Goldstein, A. P. (1988). *The Prepare Curriculum:*

Teaching prosocial skill competencies. Champaign, IL: Research Press.

Goldstein, A. P., Reagles, K. W., & Amann, L. L. (1990). *Refusal skills: Preventing drug use in adolescents.* Champaign, IL: Research Press.

Goodstat, M., & Sheppard, M. (1983). Three approaches to alcohol education. *Journal of Studies on Alcohol, 44,* 362–380.

Hansen, W. B., Graham, J. W., Wolkenstein, B. H., Lundy, B. Z., Pearson, J., Flay, B. R., et al. (1988). Differential impact of three alcohol prevention curricula on hypothesized mediating variables. *Journal of Drug Education, 18,* 143–153.

Herrmann, D. S., & McWhirter, J. J. (1997). Refusal and resistance skills for children and adolescents: A selected review. *Journal of Counseling and Development, 75,* 177–187.

Katz, R. C., Robisch, C. M., & Telch, M. J. (1989). Acquisition of smoking refusal skills in junior high school students. *Addictive Behaviors, 14,* 201–204.

McQuillen, J. S., Higginbotham, D. C., & Cummings, M. C. (1984). Compliance-resisting behaviors: The effects of age, agent, and types of requests. In R. N. Bostrom (Ed.), *Communication yearbook 9* (pp. 747–762). Beverly Hills, CA: Sage.

No More Drugs. (n.d.). Home page. http://www.nodrugs.com

Perry, C. L. (1989). Prevention of alcohol use and abuse in adolescence: Teacher- vs. peer-led intervention. *Crisis, 10,* 52–61.

Poler, M., Warzak, W. J., & Woody, R. H. (2003). *Acceptability of refusal skills training modalities: A comparison of adolescents' and professionals' preferences.* Unpublished manuscript, University of Nebraska Medical Center.

Reardon, K. K., Sussman, S., & Flay, B. R. (1989). Are we marketing the right message: Can kids "just say no" to smoking? *Communication Monographs, 56,* 307–324.

Resource Center for Adolescent Pregnancy Prevention. (n.d.). Home page. http://www.etr.org/recapp

Robertson, M. H., & Woody, R. H. (1997). *Theories and methods for practice of clinical psychology.* Madison, CT: International Universities Press.

Schinke, S. P., & Blythe, B. (1982). Cognitive-behavioral prevention of children's smoking. *Child Behavior Therapy, 3,* 25–42.

Schinke, S. P., & Gilchrist, L. D. (1984). *Life skills counseling with adolescents.* Baltimore: University Park Press.

Shechtman, Z. (2002). Child group psychotherapy in the school at the threshold of a new millennium. *Journal of Counseling & Development, 80,* 293–299.

Utah Education Network. (n.d.). Resource sites. http://www.uen.org/utahlink and www.uen.org/lessonplan

Woody, R. H. (2004). *Group therapy: An integrative cognitive social-learning approach.* Sarasota, FL: Professional Resource Press.

Related Topics

Chapter 55, "Motivational Interviewing"

Chapter 66, "Sexual Feelings, Actions, and Dilemmas in Psychotherapy"

66 SEXUAL FEELINGS, ACTIONS, AND DILEMMAS IN PSYCHOTHERAPY

Kenneth S. Pope

A HISTORY OF THE PROHIBITION AGAINST THERAPIST-PATIENT SEX

The prohibition against engaging in sex with a patient is ancient, reaching back not only to the Hippocratic oath, which emerged in the 3rd or 4th century B.C., but also to the earlier codes of the Nigerian healing arts (Pope, 1994). The modern codes of clinical ethics contained no explicit mention of this topic until research began revealing that substantial numbers of therapists were violating the prohibition. Although the codes had not highlighted this particular form of patient exploitation by name, therapist-patient sex violated various sections of the codes prior to the 1970s (Hare-Mustin, 1974). The long history of prohibition against therapist-patient sexual involvement has also been recognized by the courts (see, e.g., the judge's statement in Roy v. Hartogs, 1976, p. 590).

SURVEY DATA, OFFENDERS, VICTIMS, AND GENDER PATTERNS

Despite the prohibition, a significant number of therapists report that they became sexually involved with at least one patient. When data from national studies published in peer-reviewed journals are pooled, 5,148 psychologists, psychiatrists, and social workers provide anonymous self-reports (Pope, 1994). According to these pooled data, about 4.4% of the therapists reported becoming sexually involved with a client. The gender differences are significant: 6.8% of the male therapists and 1.6% of the female therapists reported engaging in sex with a client.

Data from these studies, as well as others (e.g., anonymous surveys of patients, anonymous surveys of therapists working with patients who have been sexually involved with a prior therapist; records of disciplinary actions), suggest that therapist-patient sex is consistent with other forms of abuse such as rape and incest: the perpetrators are overwhelmingly (though not exclusively) male, and the victims are overwhelmingly (though not exclusively) female (Pope, 1994).

This significant gender difference has long been a focus of scholarship in the area of therapist-patient sex, but it is still not well understood. Holroyd and Brodsky's (1977) report of the first national study of therapist-patient sex concluded with a statement of major issues that had yet to be resolved: "Three professional issues remain to be addressed: (a) that male therapists are most often involved, (b) that female patients are most often the objects, and (c) that therapists who disregard the sexual boundary once are likely to repeat" (p. 849). Holroyd suggested that the significant gender differences reflected sex role stereotyping and bias: "Sexual contact between therapist and patient is perhaps the quintessence of sex-biased therapeutic practice" (Holroyd, 1983, p. 285).

Holroyd and Brodsky's (1977) landmark research was followed by a second national study focusing on not only therapist-patient but also professor-student sexual relationships (Pope, Levenson, & Schover, 1979), which found: "When sexual contact occurs in the context of psychology training or psychotherapy, the predominant pattern is quite clear and simple: An older higher status man becomes sexually active with a younger, subordinate woman. In each of the higher status professional roles (teacher, supervisor, administrator, therapist), a much higher percentage of men than women engage in sex with those students or clients for whom they have assumed professional responsibility. In the lower status role of student, a far greater proportion of women than men are sexually active with their teachers, administrators, and clinical supervisors" (Pope et al. 1979, p. 687).

COMMON SCENARIOS OF THERAPIST-PATIENT SEXUAL INVOLVEMENT

It is useful for therapists to be aware of the common scenarios in which therapists sexually exploit their patients. It is important to emphasize, however, that these are only general descriptions of some of the most common patterns, and many instances of therapist-patient sexual involvement will not fall into these 10 scenarios, which were discussed by Pope and Bouhoutsos (1986, p. 4):

1. *Role trading*: Therapist becomes the "patient," and the wants and needs of the therapist become the focus.
2. *Sex therapy:* Therapist fraudulently presents therapist-patient sex as valid treatment for sexual or related difficulties.
3. *As if . . . :* Therapist treats positive transference as if it were not the result of the therapeutic situation.
4. *Svengali:* Therapist creates and exploits an exaggerated dependence on the part of the patient.
5. *Drugs:* Therapist uses cocaine, alcohol, or other drugs as part of the seduction.
6. *Rape:* Therapist uses physical force, threats, and/or intimidation.
7. *True love:* Therapist uses rationalizations that attempt to discount the clinical, professional, and fiduciary nature of the professional relationship and its responsibilities.
8. *It just got out of hand:* Therapist fails to treat the emotional closeness that develops in therapy with sufficient attention, care, and respect.
9. *Time out:* Therapist fails to acknowledge and take account of the fact that the therapeutic relationship does not cease to exist between scheduled sessions or outside the therapist's office.
10. *Hold me:* Therapist exploits patient's desire for nonerotic physical contact and possible confusion between erotic and nonerotic contact.

WORKING WITH PATIENTS WHO HAVE BEEN SEXUALLY INVOLVED WITH A THERAPIST

National survey research suggests that most clinicians are likely to encounter at least one patient who has been sexually involved with a prior therapist (Pope & Vetter, 1991). Specialized treatment approaches, based on research, have been developed for this population (Pope, 1994). One of the first steps toward gaining competence in this area is recognition of the diverse and sometimes extremely intense reactions that a subsequent therapist can experience when encountering a patient who reports sexual involvement with a former therapist. The following list of common (but not universal) clinical reactions to victims of therapist-patient sexual involvement is adapted from Pope, Sonne, and Holroyd (1993, pp. 241–261):

1. *Disbelief and denial:* The tendency to reject reflexively—without adequate data gathering—allegations about therapist-patient sex (e.g., because the activities described seem outlandish and improbable).
2. *Minimization of harm:* The tendency to assume reflexively—without adequate data gathering—that harm did not occur or that, if it did, the consequences were minimally, if at all, harmful.
3. *Making the patient fit the textbook:* The tendency to assume reflexively—without adequate data gathering and examination—that the patient must inevitably fit a particular schema.

4. *Blaming the victim:* The tendency to attempt to make the patient responsible for enforcing the therapist's professional responsibility to refrain from engaging in sex with a patient, and holding the patient responsible for the therapist's offense.
5. *Sexual reaction to the victim:* The clinician's sexual attraction to or feelings about the patient. Such feelings are normal but must not become a source of distortion in the assessment process.
6. *Discomfort at the lack of privacy:* The clinician's (and sometimes patient's) emotional response to the possibility that under certain conditions (e.g., malpractice, licensing, or similar formal actions against the offending therapist; a formal review of assessment and other services by the insurance company providing coverage for the services) the raw data and the results of the assessment may not remain private.
7. *Difficulty "keeping the secret":* The clinician's possible discomfort (and other emotional reactions) when he or she has knowledge that an offender continues to practice and to victimize other patients but cannot, in light of confidentiality and/or other constraints, take steps to intervene.
8. *Intrusive advocacy:* The tendency to want to guide, direct, or determine a patient's decisions about what steps to take or what steps not to take in regard to a perpetrator.
9. *Vicarious helplessness:* The clinician's discomfort when a patient who has filed a formal complaint seems to encounter unjustifiable obstacles, indifference, lack of fair hearing, and other responses that seem to ignore or trivialize the complaint and fail to protect the public from offenders.
10. *Discomfort with strong feelings:* The clinician's discomfort when experiencing strong feelings (e.g., rage, neediness, or ambivalence) expressed by the patient and focused on the clinician.

Awareness of these reactions can prevent them from blocking the therapist from rendering effective services to the patient. The therapist can be alert to such reactions and can sort through them should they occur. In some instances, the therapist may seek consultation to help gain perspective and understanding.

SEXUAL ATTRACTION TO PATIENTS AND OTHER (SOMETIMES) UNCOMFORTABLE FEELINGS

Sexual attraction to patients seems to be a prevalent experience that evokes negative reactions. National survey research suggests that over 4 out of 5 psychologists (87%) and social workers (81%) report experiencing sexual attraction to at least one client (Bernsen, Tabachnick, & Pope, 1994; Pope, Keith-Spiegel, & Tabachnick, 1986). Yet simply experiencing the attraction (without necessarily even feeling tempted to act on it) causes most of the therapists who report such attraction (63% of the psychologists; 51% of the social workers) to feel guilty, anxious, or confused about the attraction.

That sexual attraction causes such discomfort among so many psychologists and social workers may be the reason that graduate training programs and internships tend to neglect training in this area. Only 9% of psychologists and 10% of social workers in these national studies reported that their formal training on the topic in graduate school and internships had been adequate. A majority of psychologists and social workers reported receiving no training about such attraction. This discomfort may also explain why scientific and professional books seem to neglect this topic:

> In light of the multitude of books in the areas of human sexuality, sexual dynamics, sex therapies, unethical therapist-patient sexual contact, management of the therapist's or patient's sexual behaviors, and so on, it is curious that sexual attraction to patients per se has not served as the primary focus of a wide range of texts. The professor, supervisor, or librarian seeking books that turn their primary attention to exploring the therapist's feelings in this regard would be hard pressed to assemble a selection from which to choose an appropriate course text. If someone unfamiliar with psychotherapy were to judge the prevalence and significance of therapists' sexual feelings on the basis of the books that focus exclu-

sively on that topic, he or she might conclude that the phenomenon is neither wide-spread nor important. (Pope, Sonne, & Holroyd, 1993, p. 23)

These and similar factors may form a vicious circle: Discomfort with sexual attraction may have fostered an absence of graduate training and relevant textbooks; in turn, an absence of programs providing training and relevant textbooks in this area may sustain or intensify discomfort with the topic. The avoidance of the topic may produce a real impact.

These studies reveal significant gender effects in reported rates of experiencing sexual attraction to a patient. About 95% of the male psychologists and 92% of the male social workers, compared with 76% of the female psychologists and 70% of the female social workers, reported experiencing sexual attraction to a patient. The research suggests that just as male therapists are significantly more likely to become sexually involved with their patients, male therapists are also more likely to experience sexual attraction to their patients.

These national surveys suggest that a sizable minority of therapists carry with them—in the physical absence of the client—sexualized images of the client and that a significantly greater percentage of male than female therapists experience such cognitions. About 27% of male psychologists and 30% of male social workers, compared with 14% of female psychologists and 13% of female social workers, reported engaging in sexual fantasies about a patient while engaging in sexual activity with another person (i.e., not the patient).

National survey research has found that 46% of psychologists reported engaging in sexual fantasizing (regardless of the occasion) about a patient on a rare basis and that an additional 26% reported more frequent fantasies of this kind (Pope, Tabachnick, & Keith-Spiegel, 1987), and 6% have reported telling sexual fantasies to their patients. Such data may be helpful in understanding not only how therapists experience and respond to sexual feelings but also how therapists and patients represent (e.g., remember, anticipate, think about, fantasize about) each other when they are apart and how this affects the therapeutic process and outcome.

Unfortunately, it is all too easy to consider such data intellectually but remain unaware of the ways in which the therapist's sexual feelings, anger, hatred, fear, and other responses affect clinical services. Specific, structured training exercises and other programs (e.g., Pope et al., 1993) may be helpful in graduate training programs, internships, continuing education workshops, and other settings to enable therapists to encounter such responses in a way that will enhance or at least not distort the effectiveness of clinical services.

WHEN THE THERAPIST IS UNSURE WHAT TO DO

What can the therapist do when he or she doesn't know what to do? One of the most important steps is to realize that the complexity of therapeutic work and the uniqueness of the human individual prevent any one-size-fits-all "answers" to what sexual feelings about patients mean or their implications for the therapy. Nor can one look to ethics codes for easy answers.

> Ethics codes cannot do our questioning, thinking, feeling, and responding for us. Such codes can never be a substitute for the active process by which the individual therapist or counselor struggles with the sometimes bewildering, always unique constellation of questions, responsibilities, contexts, and competing demands of helping another person. . . . Ethics must be practical. Clinicians confront an almost unimaginable diversity of situations, each with its own shifting questions, demands, and responsibilities. Every clinician is unique in important ways. Every client is unique in important ways. Ethics that are out of touch with the practical realities of clinical work, with the diversity and constantly changing nature of the therapeutic venture, are useless. (Pope & Vasquez, 1998, pp. xiii–xiv)

The book *Sexual Feelings in Psychotherapy* (Pope et al., 1993) suggests a 10-step approach to such daunting situations that places fundamental trust in the individual therapist, adequately trained and consulting with others, to draw his or her own conclusions. Almost without exception therapists learn at the outset the fundamental resources for helping themselves explore problematic situations. Depending on the situation, they may: introspect, study the available research and clinical literature, consult, seek supervision, and/or begin or resume personal therapy. But sometimes even after the most sustained exploration, the course is not clear. The therapist's best understanding of the situation suggests a course of action that seems productive yet questionable and perhaps potentially harmful. To refrain from a contemplated action may cut the therapist off from legitimately helpful spontaneity, creativity intuition, and the ability to respond effectively to the patient's needs. On the other hand, engaging in the contemplated action may lead to disaster. When reaching such an impasse therapists may find it useful to consider the potential intervention in light of the following 10 considerations (Pope et al., 1993):

1. *The fundamental prohibition:* Is the contemplated action consistent with the fundamental prohibition against therapist-patient sexual intimacy? Therapists must never violate this special trust. If the considered course of action includes any form of sexual involvement with a patient it must be rejected.
2. *The slippery slope:* The second consideration may demand deeper self-knowledge and self-exploration. Is the contemplated course of action likely to lead or to create a risk for sexual involvement with the patient? The contemplated action may seem unrelated to any question of sexual exploitation of a patient. Yet depending on the personality strengths and weaknesses of the therapist, the considered action may constitute a subtle first step on a slippery slope. In most cases the therapist alone can honestly address this consideration.
3. *Consistency of communication:* The third consideration invites the clinician to review the course of therapy from the start to the present: Has the therapist consistently and unambiguously communicated to the patient that sexual intimacies cannot and will not occur and is the contemplated action consistent with that communication? Does the contemplated action needlessly cloud the clarity of that communication? The therapist may be intensely tempted to act in ways that stir the patient's sexual interest or respond in a self-gratifying way to the patient's sexuality. Does the contemplated action represent however subtly a turning away from the legitimate goals of therapy?
4. *Clarification:* The fourth consideration invites therapists to ask if the contemplated action would be better postponed until sexual and related issues have been clarified. Assume, for example, that a therapist's theoretical orientation does not preclude physical contact with patients and that a patient has asked that each session conclude with a reassuring hug between therapist and patient. Such ritualized hugs could raise complex questions about their meaning for the patient about their impact on the relationship and about how they might influence the course and effectiveness of therapy. It may be important to clarify such issues with the patient before making a decision to conclude each session with a hug.
5. *The patient's welfare:* The fifth consideration is one of the most fundamental touchstones of all therapy: Is the contemplated action consistent with the patient's welfare? The therapist's feelings may become so intensely powerful that they may create a context in which the patient's clinical needs may blur or fade away altogether. The patient may express wants or feelings with great force. The legal context—with the litigiousness that seems so prevalent in current society—may threaten the therapist in a way that makes it difficult to keep a clear focus on the patient's welfare. Despite such competing factors and complexities, it is crucial to assess the degree to which any contemplated action is consistent with, is irrelevant to, or is contrary to the patient's welfare.
6. *Consent:* The sixth consideration is yet another fundamental touchstone of therapy: Is the contemplated action consistent with the basic informed consent of the patient?
7. *Adopting the patient's view:* The seventh consideration urges the therapist to em-

pathize imaginatively with the patient: How is the patient likely to understand and respond to the contemplated action? Therapy is one of many endeavors in which exclusive attention to theory, intention, and technique may distract from other sources of information, ideas, and guidance. Therapists-in-training may cling to theory, intention, and technique as a way of coping with the anxieties and overwhelming responsibilities of the therapeutic venture. Seasoned therapists may rely almost exclusively on theory, intention, and technique out of learned reflex, habit, and the sheer weariness that approaches burnout. There is always risk that the therapist will fall back on repetitive and reflexive responses that verge on stereotype. Without much thought or feeling, the anxious or tired therapist may, if analytically minded, answer a patient's question by asking why the patient asked the question; if holding a client-centered orientation, the therapist may simply reflect or restate what the client has just said; if gestalt-trained, the therapist may ask the client to say something to an empty chair; and so on. One way to help avoid responses that are driven more by anxiety, fatigue, or other similar factors is to consider carefully how the therapist would think, feel, and react if he or she were the patient. Regardless of the theoretical soundness, intended outcome, or technical sophistication of a contemplated intervention, how will it likely be experienced and understood by the patient? Can the therapist anticipate at all what the patient might feel and think? The therapist's attempts to try out, in his or her imagination, the contemplated action, and to view it from the perspective of the patient may help prevent, correct, or at least identify possible sources of misunderstanding, miscommunication, and failures of empathy (Pope et al., 1993, pp. 185–186).

8. *Competence:* The eighth consideration is one of competence: Is the therapist competent to carry out the contemplated intervention? Ensuring that a therapist's education, training, and supervised experience are adequate and appropriate for his or her work is a fundamental responsibility.
9. *Uncharacteristic behaviors:* The ninth consideration involves becoming alert to unusual actions: Does the contemplated action fall substantially outside the range of the therapist's usual behaviors? That an action is unusual does not, of course, mean that something is necessarily wrong with it. Creative therapists will occasionally try creative interventions, and it is unlikely that even the most conservative and tradition-bound therapist conducts therapy the same way all the time; however, possible actions that are considerably outside the therapist's general approaches likely warrant special consideration.
10. *Consultation:* The final consideration concerns secrecy: Is there a compelling reason for not discussing the contemplated action with a colleague consultant or supervisor? Therapists' reluctance to disclose an action to others is a "red flag" for a possibly inappropriate action. Therapists may consider any possible action in light of the following question: If they took this action would they be reluctant to let their professional colleagues know they had taken it? If the response is yes, the reasons for the reluctance warrant examination. If the response is no, it is worth considering whether one has adequately taken advantage of the opportunities to discuss the matter with a trusted colleague. If discussion with a colleague has not helped to clarify the issues, consultation with additional professionals, each of whom may provide different perspectives and suggestions, may be useful.

References, Readings, & Internet Sites 

Bernsen, A., Tabachnick, B. G., & Pope, K. S. (1994). National survey of social workers' sexual attraction to their clients: Results, implications, and comparison to psychologists. *Ethics and Behavior, 4,* 369–388.

Bouhoutsos, J. C., Holroyd, J., Lerman, H., Forer, B., & Greenberg, M. (1983). Sexual intimacy between psychotherapists and patients. *Professional Psychology: Research and Practice, 14,* 185–196.

Gartrell, N. K., Herman, J. L, Olarte, S., Feldstein, M., & Localio, R. (1986). Psychiatrist-patient sexual contact: Results of a national survey, I: Prevalence. *American Journal of Psychiatry, 143,* 1126–1131.

Hare-Mustin, R. T (1974). Ethical considerations in the use of sexual contact in psychotherapy. *Psychotherapy: Theory, Research, and Practice, 11,* 308–310.

Holroyd, J. (1983). Erotic contact as an instance of sex-biased therapy. In J. Murray & E. R. Abramson (Eds.), *Bias in psychotherapy* (pp. 285–308). New York: Praeger.

Holroyd, J., & Brodsky, A. (1977). Psychologists' attitudes and practices regarding erotic and nonerotic physical contact with clients. *American Psychologist, 32,* 843–849.

Pope, K. S. (1994). *Sexual involvement with therapists: Patient assessment, subsequent therapy, forensics.* Washington, DC: American Psychological Association.

Pope, K. S., & Bouhoutsos, J. C. (1986). *Sexual intimacies between therapists and patients.* New York: Praeger Greenwood.

Pope, K. S., Keith-Spiegel, P., & Tabachnick, B. G. (1986). Sexual attraction to patients: The human therapist and the (sometimes) inhuman training system. *American Psychologist, 41,* 147–158. http://kspope.com

Pope, K. S., Levenson, H., & Schover, L. R. (1979). Sexual intimacy in psychology training: Results and implications of a national survey. *American Psychologist, 34,* 682–689. http://kspope.com

Pope, K. S., Sonne, J. L., & Holroyd, J. (1993). *Sexual feelings in psychotherapy: Explorations for therapists and therapists-in-training.* Washington, DC: American Psychological Association.

Pope, K. S., Tabachnick, B. G., & Keith-Spiegel, R. (1987). Ethics of practice: The beliefs and behaviors of psychologists as therapists. *American Psychologist, 42,* 993–1006. http://kspope.com

Pope, K. S., & Vasquez, M. J. T. (1998). *Ethics in psychotherapy and counseling: A practical guide* (2nd ed.). San Francisco: Jossey-Bass.

Pope, K. S., & Vetter, V. A. (1991). Prior therapist-patient sexual involvement among patients seen by psychologists. *Psychotherapy, 28,* 429–438. http://kspope.com

Roy v. Hartogs, 381 N.Y.S. 2d 587 (1976); 85 Misc.2d 891.

Related Topics

Chapter 65, "Refusal Skills Training"
Chapter 113, "How to Confront an Unethical Colleague"
Chapter 123, "Recognizing, Assisting, and Reporting the Impaired Psychologist"

67 SIX STEPS TO IMPROVE PSYCHOTHERAPY HOMEWORK COMPLIANCE

Michael A. Tompkins

Clinicians' growing interest in briefer forms of psychotherapy has popularized the use of homework assignments (Kazantizis & Deane, 1999); however, most clinicians know that clients who are assigned homework do not always do it, nor do they always do it well (Hansen & Warner, 1994).

Improving homework compliance begins with

careful attention to how homework assignments are structured and implemented, as therapists have far more control over the nature of homework assignments than they do over a client's particular psychological variables that may also influence homework noncompliance (Tompkins, 2002). For this reason, it makes sense that therapists take as much care as possible when setting up homework assignments so that most clients, regardless of their particular psychological variables, can complete them. Similarly, it makes sense that therapists strive to maintain a manner with clients that (all things being equal) is likely to enhance clients' compliance with homework assignments. This article presents six steps to improve compliance with psychotherapy homework:

1. Make the homework doable.
2. Give a clear rationale for the homework assignment.
3. Make a homework backup plan.
4. Make a set of written homework instructions.
5. Practice the homework assignment in session.
6. Be curious, collaborative, and consistent when setting up and reviewing homework.

Make the homework assignment doable. Doable homework assignments are concrete, specific, and appropriate to the client's current skill level. Concrete and specific homework assignments are easier to carry out than vague assignments (Levy & Shelton, 1990; Shelton & Levy, 1981) and include details about when, where, with whom, for how long, and using what materials. A concrete and specific homework assignment might read, "Sit down at your desk at 9 a.m., Monday through Friday, and work on your dissertation for 10 minutes each day; use pencil and paper and disconnect the telephone before beginning to write; and, after you have written for 10 minutes, reward yourself by reading the sports section of the morning newspaper." In contrast, a vague homework assignment might read, "Work a little on your dissertation everyday."

A doable homework assignment also considers the client's level of functioning. A depressed client who spends the bulk of his day in bed is not likely to be able to hike all day Saturday with friends, even though he thinks he should be able to do this because he did it in the past. To assess whether a homework assignment is realistic given a client's current level of functioning, therapists can ask themselves two questions: (1) Is the client already doing the homework assignment (or some variation of the assignment) and how difficult is it? and (2) Has the client done the homework assignment (or some variation of it) in the past, how long ago was that, and how difficult was it then? Therapists can ask clients to rate the difficulty or discomfort of the task on a 10-point scale (where 10 is most difficult or uncomfortable). As a rule, it is best when beginning treatment to start with homework assignments that expect clients to do what they are already doing 30% of the time or more. For example, a client who sought treatment to become more assertive identified several types of people with whom she had trouble being assertive, ranked in order of the percentage of time she was assertive with that person. She and her therapist decided that at first she would focus on increasing her assertiveness with a coworker she liked and with whom she was able to be assertive 40% of the time.

Give a clear rationale for the homework assignment. Clients are more likely to complete a homework assignment if they understand how doing it will help them accomplish their treatment goals. If the client's goal is to become less depressed, then it must make sense to the client how a particular homework assignment will help him or her feel less depressed. A homework rationale can be quite simple: "We've agreed that when you're doing certain activities, like having lunch with a friend, you feel less depressed. How about if we schedule several activities like that this week?"

Therapists should not make a homework assignment if the client has not understood and accepted its rationale. Clients who reject a homework rationale may be less open to change (Addis & Jacobson, 2000); perhaps because they are hopeless about anything helping, they have clear beliefs about what will and will not help them solve their problems that the therapist has not explored, or they don't understand the reason for doing it. To check whether a client has accepted the homework rationale, therapists can ask, "Do you understand why I'm suggesting you schedule activities this week?" Or, "To what degree does the homework match your ideas about what needs to change to solve your problem? (on a scale of from 0 to 10, where 10 means the homework completely matches with your ideas about what needs to change)?"

Initially, the therapist provides the rationale for homework. However, over time and particularly when a homework assignment is repeated, the therapist can ask clients the reason for a homework assignment: "Grace, why do you think it might be a good idea for you to write down what you eat during the day and whether you binge or not?" Not only does this encourage clients to take greater responsibility for designing and implementing their homework assignments, but also it is a good check that the client understands the homework rationale.

Make a homework backup plan. Spend some time during the session anticipating potential homework obstacles and making a backup plan to handle them. For example, Josh, a depressed software engineer, agreed to call Philip, a friend, later in the day to invite him to go to for a jog. At the agreed-upon time, Josh dutifully called Philip, but when he heard a busy signal, he hung up the telephone and did not try again. Had Josh and his therapist planned how Josh would handle this situation if it arose (e.g., who would Josh call if he couldn't reach Philip), Josh might have completed his homework assignment.

There are a number of ways to uncover potential homework obstacles. Therapists can ask their clients directly: "Do you see any obstacles that would make it hard for you to carry out the assignment?" Therapists can ask clients if they have tried similar homework assignments in the past and, if so, how they turned out. What problems did they encounter? Watch for clients who hesitate or are uncertain: "I think that I can handle that if it happens," or who quickly dismiss the therapist's concerns: "No, there won't be any problem." Ask these clients how they would handle a typical homework problem and see whether the solution is appropriate and doable given the client's current level of functioning. Or ask clients to rate the likelihood (0 to 100%, where 100% is highly likely) that they will do the homework as agreed. Low numbers can alert therapists to potential homework obstacles. Therapists can then explore with clients why they believe they may not do the homework and alter the homework assignment or plan a different assignment altogether, such as monitoring the problem the client is not ready to tackle.

Therapists can use covert rehearsal (Beck, 1995) to identify obstacles to completing homework assignments. In covert rehearsal, the client is asked to imagine going through all the steps involved in completing the homework assignment, talking aloud to the therapist, who listens for potential obstacles. For example, Christine, a depressed childcare worker who also worked nights and weekends as a waitress, seldom found time to go out with friends or to do anything fun. She agreed to take a bubble bath as a pleasurable activity to improve her mood and decrease her stress level. During covert rehearsal, Christine imagined, out loud, each step of the process. As she imagined reaching for the bubble bath, she remembered that she had run out of bubble bath several weeks ago. Christine and her therapist then discussed how and when she would go to the grocery store to buy bubble bath and this task became her homework assignment. Had Christine not rehearsed her homework assignment beforehand, she might have thrown up her hands and gone to bed when she encountered the empty bubble-bath bottle.

Make a set of written homework instructions. Many clients will be able to remember the details of a homework assignment and follow through with what they have agreed to do. However, it is usually better to formalize these agreements with a set of written homework instructions (Shelton & Ackerman, 1974). Written homework instructions serve as a record of what the client has agreed to do, which can circumvent misunderstandings and disagreements that erode the therapeutic alliance. At the minimum, written homework instructions should describe exactly what the client will do (e.g., "Call Julio Thursday at 7 p.m. and invite him to the ballgame this Saturday"), and what they will do (e.g., "If Julio can't attend the ballgame, then call Bob, then George, then Frank") if they run into problems (Tompkins, 2004).

Practice the homework assignment in session. Although it is useful for clients to practice in session every homework before they try it on their own, there are times when in-session homework practice is particularly warranted: (1) when clients lack the necessary skill and knowledge; (2) when clients try a homework assignment for the first time; and (3) when clients are to perform a homework assignment in the presence of strong emotion.

In-session practice enables therapists to observe whether their clients can complete the homework as devised. Paul, a depressed and recently divorced civil engineer, wanted to start dating again and agreed to a homework assignment in which he would introduce himself to a woman at the company Christmas party. Paul assured the therapist he knew how to handle this kind of situation, but the therapist was not so confident. At the therapist's urging, however, Paul agreed to role-play the planned interaction. Paul began his introduction by staring at the floor while mumbling under his breath, "Hi, I don't suppose you're interested in talking to me." After feedback from his therapist, Peter agreed that further skills training was needed before he attempted this particular homework assignment.

In-session practice is advisable when clients are trying a newly learned skill or response for the first time. For example, the typical response of anxious clients is to avoid what makes them uncomfortable. Therapists can help these clients by modeling for them the new response (approach the feared object or situation) and coach them to practice this response in session. If a dog-phobic client agrees to touch a picture of a dog in a book three times during the coming week, it is best that the therapist show the client that he wants her to look at the picture the entire time while she presses the picture with the full palm of her hand and holds it there for 5 minutes.

In-session practice is particularly helpful when therapists anticipate that clients will have to perform homework assignments in the presence of intense negative affect, such as fear, anger, guilt, or shame. For example, Katherine, a depressed young human resource manager, sought help because she had a difficult relationship with her mother, who often arrived unannounced at her apartment and would look through her drawers and listen to the messages on her telephone answering machine. Katherine was quite anxious about dating or inviting men to her apartment for fear that her mother would appear at the door. As a step toward greater assertiveness with her mother, Katherine agreed to tell her that she couldn't speak to her right then when she called that evening, as was her routine. Katherine practiced the homework assignment while the therapist played the role of her mother. Katherine did well until her therapist began to whine and tell her that she was an ungrateful and spiteful daughter; when she heard this, Katherine burst into tears. The therapist stopped the role-play and praised Katherine for hanging in there as long she did and reviewed with her the rationale for the homework. The therapist and Katherine then developed a set of adaptive responses she was to read through to help her better tolerate her feelings of guilt. With more practice, Katherine was able to hold her ground in the role-plays with her therapist and in interactions with her mother.

Be curious, collaborative, and consistent when setting up and reviewing homework. Therapists are important reinforcers of client behavior and, as such, it is essential that they maintain a manner when speaking with their clients that increases the likelihood that homework will be tried and completed (Tompkins, 2003). Therapists can enhance homework compliance if they are: (1) curious, (2) collaborative, and (3) consistent.

Curiosity rather than firm certainty avoids assumptions that can lead to misunderstandings that derail attempts to set up or review homework. Clients always have more information about what contributed to an unsuccessful homework assignment than their therapists, and a curious stance recognizes and takes advantage of this fact. A curious stance encourages clients to become curious about the homework themselves, including the obstacles they encounter or may encounter and their role in homework noncompliance. Last, and perhaps most important, curious therapists shift the responsibility for solving homework compliance problems to clients. Over-responsible therapists suggest, "Try this next time," while curious therapists probe, "Tell me what you might try next time." Therapists should start any discussion of potential homework assignments by asking the client "Perhaps you have an idea for a homework assignment that would help you with this problem?"

Collaboration between therapist and client when designing and implementing homework offers several advantages. First, clients who have input into homework may perceive themselves as having greater control of the assignment itself. This may lessen their anxiety and thereby increase the likelihood that the assignment will be tried. Second, when the therapist and client successfully work through a misunderstanding or disagreement to set up homework, the therapeutic relationship is strengthened. Third, clients usually understand more fully than their therapists what is or is not a useful homework assignment and what difficulties may arise. Therapists who consult with their clients about potential obstacles to homework increase the likelihood that the homework will be completed. At times, clients may suggest a homework assignment that seems unrelated to the focus of the therapy or to the client's treatment goals. Rather than dismissing the assignment out of hand, therapists can explore the client's rationale for the assignment, perhaps soliciting the advantages and disadvantages of this homework assignment over another one the therapist suggests. Sometimes, after each contributes an idea for a homework assignment, it may be necessary for the client and therapist briefly to negotiate a mutually agreeable homework assignment. Successful negotiations such as this can strengthen the therapeutic alliance and thereby foster greater motivation to try this and future homework assignments.

Consistently reinforce all pro-homework behavior. When clients say, "I thought about what I learned from the homework on my drive here today," or, "Perhaps I could try a little tougher exposure assignment this week," nod, smile, and praise them. Similarly, avoid reinforcing homework noncompliance. Avoid saying, "That's okay," "No problem," No big deal," when it's not, or "Better luck next time," when luck had nothing to do with it. When clients complete homework assignments, congratulate them and chat for a few minutes (if they enjoy chatting) to reinforce homework compliance. Take care that the praise is appropriate to the effort and is not overblown or exaggerated. When clients fail to do homework, respond in a neutral but curious manner and focus on identifying problems that may have contributed to homework noncompliance. If the homework was not completed (or attempted), set aside the entire session to review why the homework was not done, once again, as someone who is curious and puzzled by this turn of events. Did we make the homework too difficult? Were the homework instructions unclear? Did some unanticipated problem arise?

When clients attempt the homework and some part of it was successful, focus on that part and praise their efforts: "Although we agreed that you would walk 5 minutes 3 times this week, you walked 5 minutes one day. Congratulations for walking 5 minutes that one day." Then, negotiate with the clients any modifications to their homework assignments so that they can do a bit more next time and reassign: "Now, let's take a look at how we can help you meet your goal of 5 minutes each day. What do you say?" However, if a client continues to fail to complete homework assignments, consider breaking future assignments into smaller doable pieces. In that way, the client can be reinforced for completing the entire homework assignment, even if it is smaller. Take care that clients do not interpret the therapist's efforts to shape approximations to the desired homework to mean that the therapists accept incomplete homework. The goal of rewarding small steps is to have clients always complete their homework consistently and as agreed upon.

The six steps presented here assume that therapists can improve homework compliance through careful attention to how they set up and review homework assignments. To that end, I encourage therapists to first consider whether they have done what they can do to improve homework compliance before assuming that clients fail to do homework because of their psychopathology. However, when clients consistently fail to complete the homework they have agreed to do, client factors come to the fore and therapists must manage homework noncompliance as they would manage any other client behavior that interferes with progress toward the client's treatment goals. In these instances, therapists will benefit from a case formulation that explains why a particular client at a particular point in therapy might fail to complete his or her homework, as well as the psychological, interpersonal, and behavioral problems for which the individual has sought treatment in the first place (Eells, 1997; Tompkins, 1999).

References & Readings

Addis, M. E., & Jacobson, N. S. (2000). A closer look at the treatment rationale and homework compliance in cognitive-behavioral therapy for depression. *Cognitive Therapy and Research, 24,* 313–326.

Beck, J. S. (1995). *Cognitive therapy: Basics and beyond.* New York: Guilford Press.

Eells, T. T. (Ed.). (1997). *Handbook of psychotherapy case formulation.* New York: Guilford Press.

Hansen, D. J., & Warner, J. E. (1994). Treatment adherence of maltreating families: A survey of professionals regarding prevalence and enhancement strategies. *Journal of Family Violence, 9,* 1–19.

Kazantizis, N., & Deane, F. P. (1999). Psychologists' use of homework assignments in clinical practice. *Professional Psychology: Research and Practice, 30,* 581–585.

Levy, R. L., & Shelton, J. L. (1990). Tasks in brief therapy. In R. A. Wells & V. J. Giannetti (Eds.), *Handbook of brief psychotherapies* (pp. 145–163). New York: Plenum.

Shelton, J. L., & Ackerman, J. M. (1974). *Homework in counseling and psychotherapy: Examples of systematic assignments for therapeutic use by mental health professionals.* Springfield, IL: Charles C. Thomas.

Shelton, J. L., & Levy, R. L. (1981). *Behavioral assignments and treatment compliance: A handbook of clinical strategies.* Champaign, IL: Research Press.

Tompkins, M. A. (1999). Using a case formulation to manage treatment nonresponse. *Journal of Cognitive Psychotherapy, 13,* 317–330.

Tompkins, M. A. (2002). Guidelines for enhancing homework compliance. *Journal of Clinical Psychology, 58,* 565–576.

Tompkins, M. A. (2003). Effective homework. In R. L. Leahy (Ed.), *Overcoming roadblocks in cognitive therapy* (pp. 49–66). New York: Guilford Press.

Tompkins, M. A. (2004). *Using homework in psychotherapy: Strategies, guidelines, and forms.* New York: Guilford Press.

Related Topics

Chapter 42, "Enhancing Adherence"

Chapter 43, "Methods to Reduce and Counter Resistance in Psychotherapy"

68 STIMULUS CONTROL INSTRUCTIONS FOR THE TREATMENT OF INSOMNIA

Richard R. Bootzin

Stimulus control instructions were derived from a learning analysis of sleep. They are a set of instructions designed to help the person with insomnia establish a consistent sleep-wake rhythm, strengthen the bed and bedroom as cues for sleep, and weaken them as cues for activities that might interfere with sleep.

STIMULUS CONTROL INSTRUCTIONS

The following rules constitute the stimulus control instructions (Bootzin, 1972; Bootzin & Nicassio, 1978):

1. Lie down intending to go to sleep only when you are sleepy.
2. Do not use your bed for anything except sleep—that is, do not read, watch television, eat, or worry in bed. Sexual activity is the only exception to this rule. On such occasions, the instructions are to be followed afterward when you intend to go to sleep.
3. If you find yourself unable to fall asleep, get up and go into another room. Stay up as long as you wish and then return to the bedroom to sleep. Although we do not want you to watch the clock, we want you to get out of bed if you do not fall asleep immediately. Remember the goal is to associate your bed with falling asleep *quickly*! If you are in bed more than about 10 minutes without falling asleep and have not gotten up, you are not following this instruction.
4. If you still cannot fall asleep, repeat Step 3. Do this as often as is necessary throughout the night.
5. Set your alarm and get up at the same time every morning irrespective of how much sleep you got during the night. This will help your body acquire a consistent sleep rhythm.
6. Do not nap during the day.

The focus of the instructions is primarily on sleep onset. For sleep maintenance problems, the instructions are to be followed after awakening when the patient has difficulty falling back to sleep. Although stimulus control instructions appear simple and straightforward, compliance is better if the instructions are discussed individually and a rationale is provided for each rule (Bootzin & Epstein, 2000; Bootzin, Epstein, & Wood, 1991).

- *Rule 1.* The goal of this rule is to help the patients become more sensitive to internal cues of sleepiness so that they will be more likely to fall asleep quickly when they go to bed.
- *Rule 2.* The goals here are to have activities that are associated with arousal occur elsewhere and to break up patterns that are associated with disturbed sleep. If bedtime is the only time patients have for thinking about the day's events and planning the next day, they should spend some quiet time doing that in another room before they go to bed. Many people who do not have insomnia read or listen to music in bed without problems. This is not the case for insomniacs, however. This instruction is used to help those who

have sleep problems establish new routines to facilitate sleep onset.

- *Rules 3 and 4*. In order to associate the bed with sleep and disassociate it from the frustration and arousal of not being able to sleep, the patients are instructed to get out of bed after about 10 minutes (20 minutes for those over 60 years old). This is also a means of coping with insomnia. By getting out of bed and engaging in other activities, patients are taking control of their problem. Consequently, the problem becomes more manageable and the patient is likely to experience less distress.
- *Rule 5*. Insomniacs often have irregular sleep rhythms because they try to make up for poor sleep by sleeping late or by napping the next day. Keeping consistent wake times helps patients develop consistent sleep rhythms. In addition, the set wake times mean that the patients will be somewhat sleep-deprived after a night of insomnia. This will make it more likely that they will fall asleep quickly the following night, strengthening the cues of the bed and bedroom for sleep. Often insomniacs will want to follow a different sleeping schedule on weekends or nights off than they do during the work-week. It is important to have as consistent a schedule as possible, seven nights a week. The goal is to produce variability of no more than one hour in the wake time on days off than on work or school days. However, it may be necessary to approach that goal gradually over a few weeks, using successive approximations, if the deviations are large as often seen in adolescents and college students.
- *Rule 6*. The goals of this rule are to keep insomniacs from disrupting their sleep patterns by irregular napping and to prevent them from losing the advantage of the sleep loss of the previous night for increasing the likelihood of faster sleep onset the following night. A nap that takes place seven days a week at the same time would be permissible. For those elderly insomniacs who feel that they need to nap, a daily late afternoon nap of 30 to 45 minutes or the use of 20 to 30 minutes of relaxation as a nap-substitute is recommended. In the elderly, late afternoon naps have the advantage of providing additional energy for evening activities.

Cognitive-behavioral treatments for insomnia, including stimulus control instructions, are primarily self-management treatments. The treatments are carried out by the patients at home. Consequently, compliance may be a problem. Most compliance problems can be solved by direct discussion with the patient. A common problem is the disturbance of the spouses' sleep when the insomniacs get out of bed. Discussions with the spouses are often helpful in ensuring full cooperation. During the winter in cold climates, some patients may be reluctant to leave the warmth of their beds. Suggestions for keeping warm robes near the beds and keeping an additional room warm throughout the night, along with encouragement to try to follow instructions, are usually effective in promoting compliance.

EFFECTIVENESS OF STIMULUS CONTROL INSTRUCTIONS

Stimulus Control Instructions has been evaluated either as a single-component treatment or as part of multicomponent interventions with adults of all ages. Reviews of outcome studies (Morin, Culbert, & Schwartz, 1994; Morin et al., 1999; Murtagh & Greenwood, 1995) have found that stimulus control instructions constitute one of the most effective, if not the most effective, single-component nonpharmacological therapy. In fact, in a practice parameters report on nonpharmacological treatments of insomnia published by the American Academy of Sleep Medicine (Chesson et al., 1999), stimulus control instructions is listed as the only treatment to achieve the category of "standard" treatment of care.

Multicomponent treatments are often found to be effective. The components employed, however, vary substantially from study to study. It is important to include treatment components, such as stimulus control instructions, that have empirical support within the multicomponent package.

References & Readings

Bootzin, R. R. (1972). A stimulus control treatment for insomnia. *American Psychological Association Proceedings,* 395–396.

Bootzin, R. R., & Epstein, D. R. (2000). Stimulus control instructions. In K. L. Lichstein & C. M. Morin (Eds.), *Treatment of late-life insomnia* (pp. 167–184). Thousand Oaks, CA: Sage.

Bootzin, R. R., Epstein, D., & Wood, J. M. (1991). Stimulus control instruction. In P. Hauri (Ed.), *Case studies in insomnia* (pp. 19–28). New York: Plenum.

Bootzin, R. R., Manber, R., Loewy, D. H., Kuo, T. F., & Franzen, P. L. (2001). Sleep disorders. In H. E. Adams & P. B. Sutker (Eds.), *Comprehensive handbook of psychopathology* (3rd ed., pp. 671–711). New York: Plenum.

Bootzin, R. R., & Nicassio, P. (1978). Behavioral treatments for insomnia. In M. Hersen, R. Eisler, & P. Miller (Eds.), *Progress in behavior modification* (Vol. 6, pp. 1–45). New York: Academic Press.

Chesson, A. L., Jr., Anderson, W. M., Littner, M., Davila, D., Hartse, K., Johnson, S., et al. (1999). Practice parameters for the nonpharmacologic treatment of chronic insomnia. *Sleep, 22,* 1128–1133.

Morin, C. M., Culbert, J. P., & Schwartz, S. M. (1994). Nonpharmacological interventions for insomnia: A meta-analysis of treatment efficacy. *American Journal of Psychiatry, 151,* 1172–1180.

Morin, C. M., Hauri, P. J., Espie, C. A., Spielman, A. J., Buysee, D. J., & Bootzin, R. R. (1999). Nonpharmacologic treatment of chronic insomnia: An American Academy of Sleep Medicine Review. *Sleep, 22,* 1134–1156.

Murtagh, D. R. R., & Greenwood, K. M. (1995). Identifying effective psychological treatments for insomnia: A meta-analysis. *Journal of Consulting and Clinical Psychology, 63,* 79–89.

Related Topic

Chapter 67, "Six Steps to Improve Psychotherapy Homework Compliance"

69 PARENT MANAGEMENT TRAINING FOR CHILDHOOD BEHAVIOR DISORDERS

Laura J. Schoenfield & Sheila M. Eyberg

Until recently, individual psychotherapy was the most common form of treatment for childhood behavior disorders. However, the trend toward evidence-based treatments has led to an increasing realization that the involvement of parents is crucial to the maintenance of treatment gains. Two reviews of treatments for disruptive behavior disorders found that parent management training (PMT) is well supported by empirical research as an effective treatment for this group of disorders (Brestan & Eyberg, 1998; Nock, 2003). In fact, Brestan and Eyberg found that the only well-established treatments for childhood disruptive behavior were PMT programs. These programs, designed to give parents skills to manage their children's behavior effectively, can decrease unwanted behaviors and increase prosocial behaviors while also increasing the warmth of the parent-child relationship. Parent training programs have been implemented for children with a range of disorders and have targeted specific populations of parents at risk for poor parenting as well.

Parent management training probably began with the work of Gerald Patterson, whose Living with Children program was the first well-established PMT program (see Patterson, 1976). This program, based on social learning theory, teaches parents to use positive reinforcers, such as stickers, snacks, or small toys, to increase positive behaviors while using timeout to decrease negative behaviors such as temper tantrums. Parents focus on one particular problem behavior at a time. First, they observe the behavior and count the number of times it occurs each day or week. Then, they continue to track the child's progress by charting the frequency of problem behaviors throughout treatment while giving stickers and small rewards when the child abstains from the negative behavior. At the same time, parents use time-out for each instance of the negative behavior. Parents are also instructed to identify behaviors that are incompatible with the problem behaviors, called *competing behaviors,* such as talking nicely instead of whining. Positive reinforcement is used to increase the frequency of competing behaviors. Patterson has emphasized the importance of consistency in discipline by punishing every occurrence of the negative behavior and rewarding every occurrence of the competing, positive behavior. As one problem behavior decreases, a new problem behavior can be targeted using the same principles of behavior change.

As treatment research has progressed, PMT has frequently been combined with other treatments, and new methods of treatment delivery of the core components of PMT have emerged as well. For example, programs may use modeling, role-playing, in vivo coaching, or videotaped demonstrations to teach parenting skills. The training may occur in individual, family, or group sessions including the parents alone or in sessions that include the child. Treatment may take place in the clinic, in a family's home, or in community facilities such as the school. PMT is often implemented in conjunction with other types of interventions, such as child social skills training, parent or child problem-solving skills training, teacher training, or medications.

Although PMT programs are designed primarily to treat the kinds of disruptive behaviors that characterize oppositional defiant disorder (ODD) or conduct disorder (CD), PMT is used to treat children with a range of disorders that have frequently co-occurring disruptive behavior, such as developmental delays and attention-deficit/hyperactivity disorder (ADHD). PMT programs for other disorders are similar to those for ODD and CD, typically with the addition of components specific to the primary diagnosis. For example, PMT programs for children with ADHD often include parent ADHD education or group discussion on topics such as realistic expectations, due to the persistence of characteristics such as impulsiveness, or safety issues such as child-proofing the home, due to the tendency of children with ADHD to be more clumsy and accident prone than other children at similar developmental levels (Pisterman et al., 1989). A recent review of the literature on treatments for children with ADHD found that the efficacy of particular PMT programs is well supported by research (Pelham, Wheeler, & Chronis, 1998).

LONG-TERM EFFECTIVENESS OF PARENT MANAGEMENT TRAINING

Disruptive behavior disorders are usually considered chronic conditions (Nock, 2003). For this reason, to be truly effective, treatments for these problems must show long-term maintenance of treatment gains. Unfortunately, a review of the literature found that most studies of treatment efficacy did not follow up participants for longer than one year (Eyberg, Edwards, Boggs, & Foote, 1998). The few longer-term studies suggested that only about 50% of children maintained treatment gains. Families for whom treatment does not last may have certain risk factors associated with poor maintenance, such as poverty or parental psychopathology. However, due to the small number of studies and methodological issues associated with follow-up studies, it is not possible to draw firm conclusions at this time.

Several strategies are used in PMT programs to increase the likelihood that treatment gains will continue after treatment has ended. These strategies are similar to those used in other treatments for many types of disorders. They include increasing parents' problem-solving skills so that they will be able to manage similar problems in the future, fading of treatment sessions, contact by phone or mail after treatment has ended, and booster sessions.

PARENTS AT RISK

PMT not only targets child and adolescent disorders, but also serves parents at risk for poor parenting skills who, in turn, have children at risk for behavior disorders. Studies of PMT with single parents, parents in poverty, and parents involved with child protection services have all demonstrated significant benefits for children. For example, recently separated mothers have reported improved discipline techniques and increased positive involvement with children after attending group PMT meetings (Forgatch & DeGarmo, 1999). Low-income parents of children in Head Start who received parent training focused on increasing parenting competence and involvement in Head Start reported a significant decrease in harsh and critical parenting styles and an increase in positive discipline (Webster-Stratton, 1998). Their children's behavior also improved after treatment, characterized by a decrease in noncompliance and negative affect that was maintained at one-year follow-up.

Abusive parents are often referred to PMT programs. In addition to teaching positive discipline skills, these programs typically teach methods of coping with negative child behavior, such as relaxation and anger-management training. A study of PMT for parents under supervision by child protection services found that at three-month follow-up, children whose parents received PMT had less frequent and less intense behavior problems and fewer adjustment problems associated with maltreatment (Wolfe, Edwards, Manion, & Koverola, 1988).

EXAMPLES OF PARENT MANAGEMENT TRAINING PROGRAMS

In this section we describe three evidence-based PMT programs. Each program incorporates basic PMT based on principles of social learning theory into a unique program of treatment for children with disruptive behavior.

Problem-Solving Skills Training and Parent Management Training

Kazdin (1996) developed a treatment program for disruptive children up to age 13 that combines individual PMT with problem-solving skills training (PSST) for children. The PMT component of Kazdin's treatment program is conducted in separate sessions with the child's parent. Through modeling and role-playing, the parent is taught to use effective commands and consistent consequences. The parent is also taught to establish a token economy in the home to reinforce the child's appropriate behavior. To deal with behavior problems the child presents in the classroom, the therapist sets up a system of reinforcement wherein the parent provides contingent consequences at home for behavior at school.

PSST provides a step-by-step guide for the child on how to approach difficult situations and choose the best solution. During the course of 20 sessions, the child learns to use the five steps of problem solving: identify the problem, create possible solutions, focus on and evaluate the solutions, choose a response, and evaluate the outcome. The therapist uses a token economy during therapy with the child as reinforcement for using the problem-solving steps appropriately. Parents are trained to help their children use the problem-solving steps correctly outside the therapy sessions.

By working individually with the child as well as the parent, Kazdin's combined PMT plus PSST program has the advantage of treating peer relation difficulties, which may be less easily targeted by PMT. In addition, although the program components are manualized, the format allows the possibility of adding sessions based on both the child's and parent's progress, which ensures flexibility in response to individual families.

The Incredible Years: Parents, Teachers, and Children Training Series

Developed by Webster-Stratton (2001), The Incredible Years is a multicomponent treatment for disruptive behavior in children ages 4 to 8. Although all components may be used separately, the combination of PMT, problem-solving and social skills training with the child, and teacher training addresses many areas where impairment may be present. Each component is conducted in group format and includes discussion of videotaped vignettes.

The original PMT component is a 12-week group treatment program for parents that includes vignettes designed to teach skills such as positive reinforcement, logical consequences, problem solving, and nonphysical discipline techniques. Discipline techniques include the use of time-out and ignoring. The group leaders use the videotaped scenes to stimulate group discussion and problem solving. Parents refine their skills by role-playing in the group and practicing at home.

The teacher component of The Incredible Years involves discussion of videotaped vignettes, in groups of 15 to 25 teachers, covering topics such as the importance of teacher attention, encouragement, and praise; motivating children through incentives; preventing problems proactively; decreasing inappropriate behavior; building positive relationships with students; and teaching social skills and problem-solving skills in the classroom. In addition to videotaped modeling, child sessions include fantasy play, use of puppets, and role play to help children deal with problems at school and with peers, such as being teased, lying, and feeling left out.

Three additional components are available if needed: *Advance* addresses potential areas of family dysfunction and includes parent coping skills, self-control, and marital conflict; *School Age* can be used as a prevention program for culturally diverse children up to age 10; and *Supporting Your Child's Education* focuses on academic readiness, educational activities at home, and creating connections between home and school. One of the benefits of The Incredible Years program is the cost-effectiveness of the group format used in all program components. In addition, the use of videotapes to present information, along with the detailed group leaders' manuals, makes the program easy to implement in many communities.

Parent-Child Interaction Therapy

Developed by Eyberg (Brinkmeyer & Eyberg, 2003) for the treatment of preschoolers with disruptive behavior and their parents, Parent-Child Interaction Therapy (PCIT) is based on developmental theory, emphasizing authoritative parenting and children's needs for both nurturance and firm limits. PCIT progresses through two distinct phases. The first phase, Child-Directed Interaction (CDI), resembles traditional play therapy and focuses on strengthening the parent-child attachment, increasing positive parenting, and improving child social skills. The second phase, Parent-Directed Interaction (PDI), resembles clinical behavior therapy and focuses on improving parents' expectations, ability to set limits, consistency and fairness in discipline, and reducing child noncompliance and other negative behaviors.

PCIT sessions are conducted once a week and are one hour in length. The principles and skills of each phase of treatment are first taught to the parents alone in a teaching session. In subsequent sessions, parents are coached in the skills as they play with their child. Families continue in treatment until the parents demonstrate mastery of the skills and the child's behavior comes to within normal limits. The average length of treatment is 13 sessions.

During the CDI, parents are taught to follow the child's lead by refraining from commands, questions, and criticism. They learn to use the nondirective *Pride* skills: *p*raising the child's behavior; *r*eflecting the child's statements; *i*mitating the child's play; *d*escribing the child's activities, and using *e*nthusiasm as they play with the child. The parents learn to change child behavior by directing the *Pride* skills to the child's appropriate play and ignoring the child's negative behaviors. The parents practice the skills at home in daily 5-minute play sessions called "special time." In the CDI coaching sessions, the therapist is able to observe the parent's progress firsthand and provide immediate feedback, encouraging and praising the parents' new skills and catching mistakes on-the-spot before they become habits. CDI coaching sessions continue until the parents meet criteria for skill mastery, as assessed by a 5-minute direct observation at the start of each session. It is through the CDI coaching that the therapist conveys important developmental expectations for child behavior and points out specific effects of the parent's behavior on the child. Coaching may also teach stress management or anger management skills to the parent as they interact with their child.

During the PDI, the parents learn to direct the child's behavior when necessary with effective commands and specific consequences for compliance (enthusiastic labeled praise and a return to CDI) and noncompliance (a time-out warning that begins an algorithm of parent responses to compliance or noncompliance at each step until the child complies). The use of time-out is introduced gradually, first in the treatment room where the therapist is able to coach the parent through all of the steps with the child before the parent uses it at home. Parents then practice the PDI skills in brief sessions after the CDI play sessions. Homework assignments proceed gradually to use of the PDI procedure throughout the day. In the last few sessions, parents are taught variations of the PDI procedure to deal with aggressive behavior and public misbehavior, as they approach mastery of the PCIT skills and assume increasing responsibility for applying the principles to new situations.

SUMMARY

Parent management training is a widely used treatment for child disruptive behavior disorders. Based on social learning theory, this approach to treatment has a strong evidence base supporting its effectiveness in changing both parent and child behaviors, and it is now considered the standard of care for disruptive behavior. Although variations in format and emphasis have been developed, and PMT has been combined in various ways with other treatments for disruptive children and related disorders of the child and family, the basic behavioral tenets of social learning theory have remained at its core. In this chapter, we have provided examples of three evidence-based PMT programs for disruptive behavior that illustrate the variation in parent training as well as the similarities in approach. Research provides promising early evidence of maintenance of change for a sizable percentage of children. Now the goal of PMT is to identify strategies that will engender enduring treatment gains for all children.

References, Readings, & Internet Sites

Brestan, E. V., & Eyberg, S. M. (1998). Effective psychosocial treatments of conduct-disordered children and adolescents: 29 years, 82 studies, and 5,272 kids. *Journal of Clinical Child Psychology, 27*, 180–189.

Brinkmeyer, M. Y., & Eyberg, S. M. (2003). Parent-child interaction therapy for oppositional children. In A. E. Kazdin & J. R. Weisz (Eds.), *Evidence-based psychotherapies for children and adolescents* (pp. 204–240). New York: Guilford Press.

Eyberg, S. M., Edwards, D., Boggs, S. R., & Foote, R. (1998). Maintaining the treatment effects of parent training: The role of booster sessions and other maintenance strategies. *Clinical Psychology: Science and Practice, 5*, 544–552.

Forgatch, M. S., & DeGarmo, D. S. (1999). Parenting through change: An effective prevention program for single mothers. *Journal of Consulting and Clinical Psychology, 67*, 711–724.

Kazdin, A. E. (1996). Problem solving and parent management in treating aggressive and antisocial behavior. In E. D. Hibbs & P. S. Jensen (Eds.), *Psychosocial treatments for child and adolescent disorders: Empirically based strategies for clinical practice* (pp. 377–408). Washington, DC: American Psychological Association.

Nock, M. K. (2003). Progress review of the psychosocial treatment of child conduct problems. *Clinical Psychology: Science and Practice, 10*, 1–28.

Patterson, G. R. (1976). *Living with children: New methods for parents and teachers*. Springfield, IL: Research Press.

Pelham, W. E., Wheeler, T., & Chronis, A. (1998). Empirically supported psychosocial treatments for attention deficit hyperactivity disorder. *Journal of Clinical Child Psychology, 27*, 190–205.

Pisterman, S., McGrath, P., Firestone, P., Goodman, J. T., Webster, I., & Mallory, R. (1989). Outcome of parent-mediated treatment of preschoolers with attention deficit disorder with hyperactivity. *Journal of Consulting and Clinical Psychology, 57*, 628–635.

Schaefer, C. E., & Briesmeister, J. M. (Eds.). (1998) *Handbook of parent training: Parents as co-therapists for children's behavior problems* (2nd ed.). New York: Wiley.

The Incredible Years. (2003). Home page. Retrieved 2004 from http://www.incredibleyears.com

Webster-Stratton, C. (1998). Preventing conduct problems in Head Start children: Strengthening parenting competencies. *Journal of Consulting and Clinical Psychology, 66*, 715–730.

Webster-Stratton, C. (2001). The Incredible Years: Parents, teachers, and children's training series. *Residential Treatment for Children and Youth, 18*, 31–45.

Wolfe, D. A., Edwards, B., Manion, I., & Koverola, C. (1988). Early intervention for parents at risk of child abuse and neglect: A preliminary investigation. *Journal of Consulting and Clinical Psychology, 56*, 40–47.

Related Topic

Chapter 12, "Interviewing Parents"

70 HYPNOSIS AND RELAXATION SCRIPTING

Douglas Flemons

As you've no doubt discovered during anxious or stressful times, purposefully trying to relax is like trying to fall asleep or trying to have fun—the expended effort undermines the intended goal. Any time your clients pit their conscious will against their racing thoughts or uptight bodies, attempting to compel themselves to unwind or let go, they initiate a battle they can only lose. Their thoughts refuse to slow down and their bodies stay tense, leaving them feeling frustrated and defeated.

Relaxation can't be dictated; it must be invited to develop, which is where hypnosis comes in. Bridging the chasm between mind and body, hypnosis offers your clients a wonderfully effective means to relax their efforts at relaxing, opening the possibility for nonvolitional change. In this chapter, I'll provide some guidelines and illustrations for how to incorporate it into your practice, but for that discussion to make sense, I first need to talk a bit about the differences between conscious awareness and hypnotic experience.

UNDERSTANDING HYPNOSIS

In the everyday process of consciously perceiving stuff, you typically distinguish yourself as an observer, separate from what you observe.

When the object of your perception lies outside of you, and particularly when it is somehow unpleasant—that annoying song blasting from the radio; the threatening clouds forming on the horizon; the odor emanating from the locker at the gym—you tend to experience a self-other split between you and it. But this same division between observer and observed also gets evoked when you're perceiving yourself, especially when you don't like what you're noticing—the damn itch on your legs; the cold nausea that's been gripping you as tonight's speech looms ever closer; the troubling memory that keeps popping up at inopportune times.

In everyday awareness, you often stay one step (or more) removed from your surroundings and your experience, as if there were an invisible wall erected between your "Observing-I" and the rest of the world, including the rest of you—your body, your thoughts, your emotions. This is the experiential source not only of alienation but also of the Cartesian mind-body split.

During hypnosis and related activities—meditation, prayer, reading, making love, playing sports, watching movies, playing or listening to music—the invisible wall disperses, allowing the insular separateness of your Observing-I to dissolve. This accounts for the nonvolitional character of hypnotic experience (Flemons, 2002). As your sense of self moves from outside to inside your experience, facilitating the emergence and merging of an embodied mind and mindful body, no insular Observing-I remains to claim ownership of, or responsibility for, the arm that's levitating, the numbness that's spreading, or the warm heaviness that's increasing. As a result, these and other hypnotic phenomena seem to "just happen." Such an environment is ideal for your clients to learn how to relax without trying.

INVITING HYPNOSIS, INVITING RELAXATION

Over the years, clients have told me stories of therapists they've had who, when it came time to do hypnosis, put on their glasses and read a scripted induction, read a few scripted "therapeutic" stories, and read some scripted directives. Good hypnotic technique requires something quite different. Rather than focusing on a bunch of words on a page, you must be focused on your clients—attuned to, and in sync with, their experience. Of course, if you're going to work this way, you have to know what to do with what you get from them. So, instead of giving you some scripts to read, I want to offer you some ideas and suggestions to think through and try out:

1. *Communicate your empathic understanding.* The best way to begin helping your clients change their relationship with themselves, facilitating a shift in their internal boundaries and the development of relaxation, is to help them change their relationship with you and their surroundings. Hypnosis doesn't begin when you start delivering an "induction"; it begins when your clients start trusting that you have a good handle on the intricacies of their experience. You help them relax into this trust by proving that you deserve it—by empathically communicating your understanding of the details and emotional nuances of their experience.

CLIENT: . . . and by then I'm so stressed out that when it comes time to go to sleep, all I can do is lay there and replay what happened during the day, over and over.

THERAPIST: It's bad enough that you have to go through it the first time during the day, but then to have to live through it again and again, instead of drifting off to sleep—I bet you just want to scream.

CLIENT: Exactly. I do.

You know that you're connecting well with your clients when they're agreeing with your empathic statements. This is the rapport you need to move forward.

2. *Use permissive words, inviting possibilities.* Imagine walking into a bank and having the manager say, in a commanding tone, "You will open an account right now and deposit your money into it. I will count backwards from 10 to 1, and as I do, you will find yourself signing your name on these forms, and you will give me all your money: 10, 9, 8, . . ." You'd head straight for the door, right? Well your clients are no different. What many therapists regard as resistance, I view as clients' healthy reluctance to go along with a course of action that doesn't fit for them (Flemons, 2002). My reluctance would certainly be heightened if a therapist were to start ordering me around:

THERAPIST: Now I want you to just relax as you look at me and listen to my voice. As I count backwards from 10 to 1, you will find yourself unable to look away from me, as if I were at the end of a dark tunnel and you could see nothing else. Soon that darkness will envelop you and your eyes will close all the way as you completely relax.

Yuk! Forget looking through a tunnel—I'd be looking at the therapist through the office window, shaking my head as I headed back to my car. Rather than issuing directives, you'll be much better off offering suggestions and possibilities, phrasing them with permissive words (O'Hanlon & Martin, 1992):

THERAPIST: I don't know if you'll be more comfortable closing your eyes or keeping them open. If they stay open for a while, they might want to rest somewhere as I talk. You can listen to what I'm saying or you can let your mind wander—either is fine. Certainly there's no need to pay attention, or to try to make something happen or to try to help me out.

3. *Utilize what the surroundings and your clients offer up.* Is your office too bright or warm or cold for you to do hypnosis? Are the seats too uncomfortable? Are the walls too thin to block out the sounds of traffic, voices, phones, and plumbing? Are your clients too uptight to let go? Are they too intent on maintaining control to experience hypnosis? It makes sense that you'd entertain such concerns, but if you approach hypnosis as an opportunity for utilization (Erickson, 1980), you can see each of these apparent roadblocks as possibilities for furthering hypnosis and relaxation.

THERAPIST: You can allow the sunshine streaming in through the window to shed light [utilizing the amount of light in the room to make a metaphorical statement about gaining understanding] on how you can feel so uptight, the temperature in the room helping you, perhaps, to warm you to the realization that warm light is light, that the lightness of warm air, the warmth of light air, takes it up, up, up [utilizing the too-warm room as part of a metaphorical expression ("to warm up to something") that suggests positive feelings, and to indirectly explore possibilities of developing sensations of lightness]. And I wonder just how high up, just how light, that feeling of being uptight can take you [utilizing being "uptight" as helpful in creating this movement up], like an updraft, perhaps accompanied by a developing sense, somewhere, probably not yet in your shoulders, maybe somewhere else already warming up to the possibility [again utilizing the temperature in the room] of sinking comfortably down, like water, aided by gravity, moving down through pipes [utilizing the sound of a toilet flushing], effortlessly moving along with nothing getting in the way.

No need to bother trying to help me out, as the cars and trucks out there, also rushing in their own way, speed by, and you can effortlessly follow the sound of their movement, rushing ahead of rush hour [utilizing the sound of traffic]. And what a rush it can be for it to slowly dawn on you, like the light of dawn [utilizing puns to change meanings], that the pace outside can be nicely complemented by the pace inside, that their zooming out can remind you how to more easily float in, like floating in the silence between each of the rings of the telephone. Such a relief that brief silence is [utilizing the incessant ringing of a telephone] more appreciated because of the lovely way it contrasts with the rings on either side of it, before and after it, and that voice out there answering, giving you the freedom to question [utilizing a voice answering the phone to move to the idea of questioning], going round and round, wondering what to make of hypnosis, knowing that you can question both before and after you experience it, wondering how your body is able to perfectly monitor and control your experience, just as it does when you're sleeping or otherwise occupied in some absorbing activity.

4. *Offer both-and suggestions.* If you think of contrasts—relaxed/tense; slow/fast; up/down—as exclusive opposites, you'll assume that obtaining the desirable side of any distinction requires the elimination of the other. But if you treat contrasts as compatible and mutually important, as I did in the example above, then one side of a contrast can coexist with, or be the conduit to, the other. Rather than lecturing my clients about this, I tell stories or vignettes that allow them to vicariously experience the ideas. For example, if a client's thoughts are racing, I might talk about how wolf packs work:

THERAPIST: Wolves protect themselves by continually patrolling the perimeter of their territory, but if all of the wolves in a pack were to patrol all the time, none of them would get any rest. So they take turns. Part of the pack keeps moving, always moving, along the edge of their territory, making sure everything is safe and secure, while the rest are able, in the center, to rest deeply, relaxing and sleeping. Why not allow part of you to continue patrolling the perimeter of your awareness, ensuring that everything is safe and secure, while the rest of you rests?

A both-and approach to offering suggestions helps you not presume that quiet, calm thoughts are a necessary precursor for hypnosis, and it helps clients not to have to try to slow down their thinking or breathing. Hypnosis makes it unnecessary for them to be at odds with themselves. Here are some more both-and contrasts I sometimes offer, allowing clients to experience something new without having to first not experience something else. Notice how the juxtaposition of stories creates a both-and relationship among my descriptions.

THERAPIST: Isn't it fascinating how you can be zipping along in a car at 80 mph and yet feel like you're going 20? How is it that something so fast can feel so slow? Your thoughts can race on ahead or along side or just behind me. I have a friend who, when we walk together, is always a half-step in front of me, and another, a former competitive ski racer, who always skis a half a breath in front of himself, staying on the leading edge of himself, effortlessly careening down the mountain, taking all the time he needs to ever . . . so slowly . . . carve . . . each screeching turn.

5. *Look for and bring forth small shifts, rather than dramatic transformations.* I grew up in Canada, where I gained a lot of experience liberating cars from snow banks. When a vehicle is stranded, you rock it forward and back, while the driver alternates between hitting the gas and engaging the clutch. The goal isn't instantaneous liberation but a process of every-increasing trajectories of change.

You'll enjoy greater success if you adopt the same attitude in helping clients. Instead of trying to get their shoulders to relax, help them discover that one of their fingers feels a little numb. A small change in sensation there can be the first step to an ever so slightly bigger change somewhere else.

6. *Offer interactive relaxation (via weird body conversations).* Many hypnotherapists offer their clients some form of progressive (sometimes called Jacobson) relaxation, which involves purposefully contracting and then releasing different muscle groups for 10 or 15 seconds at a time. Other clinicians combine this with deep breathing techniques, timing exhalations with the releasing of tension. Still others offer guided imagery, taking clients to a vividly described beach or an alpine meadow, or some other potentially relaxing setting, offering suggestions for enjoying the surroundings and relaxing into the experience.

Although these can all prove helpful, I, for the reasons I outlined earlier, invariably take a less directive path. I ask clients to find a place in their body that feels particularly tense, and I get them to describe the sensations there with as much detail as possible. I then have them go in search of a relaxed place—some part of them that is comfortable or numb or so relaxed that they haven't even noticed it for a while—and ask what they're able to describe about it, too. I then provide a rationale for why it would make sense for the two areas to get into a kind of developing "conversation," each one sharing some important information with the other. As we proceed, I frequently check in on what is changing and then fold that into what I say next (see below).

THERAPIST: Okay, so you feel the tension most in your shoulders, like a sharp, radiating ache.

CLIENT: Yes.

THERAPIST: And your right thigh feels warm and comfortable—almost asleep.

CLIENT: Pretty much, yeah.

THERAPIST: Great. You know, just as your lungs and heart work together to deliver oxygen to the cells throughout your body, they also coordinate with each other in the extraction and transportation of carbon dioxide from your body into the atmosphere. At a smaller level, the various cells of your immune system communicate with each other about intruders and, based on this shared information, they coordinate an appropriate response. So your body knows a lot about how to communicate within and between organs and systems, and it does this without your having to consciously understand how it happens.

So as you sit there and listen to me, why shouldn't your shoulders get into a body conversation with your right thigh? You can listen to me or think about whatever comes to mind, confident that your shoulders and your thigh can communicate in a way that you and I could never understand. But as your thigh keys into the sharp radiating tension there in your shoulders, it might learn something about how to allow sensations to radiate outward. If pain can radiate, why not comfort? I don't know how the muscles there in your thigh have figured out so brilliantly how to become so easily warm and loose, but your shoulders might as well get in on the secret. So let's let them get into a body conversation of sorts while you tell me what you're noticing.

7. *Practice extemporaneous collaboration.* Just as it is useful to encourage different parts of your clients' bodies to get into conversation with each other, so too it is vitally important for you to stay in touch with your clients as you help them develop their hypnotic ability. Watching their nonverbal responses to your suggestions will keep you partially apprised of what they are currently experiencing, but if you can get them to tell you in words, do it. Then, base your next suggestion on the information you've just received.

THERAPIST: What's happening now?

CLIENT: My right hand is warm and soft, but my shoulders are still tight.

THERAPIST: Great. Your right hand was first off the mark in adopting some important understanding from your thigh. And we didn't even know it was listening! So now I don't know if your thigh will continue to help your hand develop that sensation while it engages in contact with your shoulders or whether your hand will serve as an intermediary of some sort. Could be that your hand passes along the information to your shoulders, maybe directly, or maybe by way of some other body part.

Let's let things continue, and let's see if your shoulders get in on the action at this point, or if some other part will first.

8. *Teach self-hypnosis and self-reliance.* The hypnosis sessions you offer in your office may be all your clients require to change how they've been orienting to the stresses in their lives. Nevertheless, by teaching them how to do self-hypnosis, you will give them the skill to invite relaxation on their own (Sanders, 1993). I suggest to clients that since all hypnosis is, in a way, self-hypnosis, they, having already experienced it in my office, know almost everything they need to know in order to practice on their own.

THERAPIST: Find a comfortable place to sit or lie down at home, in your office, or wherever, and begin by noticing external and internal things or events that grab your attention—sounds and sights before and after you close your eyes; the sound and feel of your breathing; sensations on your skin; thoughts and feelings; smells or tastes; and so on. Devote one breath to each thing you notice, silently naming it in time with your exhalations: "The dog barking . . . birds chirping . . . jaw tense . . . the kids arguing downstairs . . . tight shoulders . . . the fan clicking . . . left hand heavy . . . " The more you practice, the easier it will be for you to invite yourself into hypnosis, not needing to try to make anything happen, not needing to try to relax.

If clients attempt to give themselves suggestions in the midst of self-hypnosis, they will reinvoke the split between the Observing-I (a.k.a. the Bossing-Around-I) and the rest of the self, and the hypnotic experience will end. To help them avoid this problem, I suggest, passing along an idea of Milton Erickson's: that they begin each self-hypnosis time by posing a question to themselves—for example, "I wonder how my body will relax?"—and then let that wondering hover around them as they proceed with noticing their experience.

9. *Trust yourself*. If you're just getting started with hypnosis, you might feel inclined, despite my earlier cautions, to use some of my examples as scripts for use with your clients. You'll be much better off studying them closely, exploring diverse examples of other hypnotic work, and then leaving them behind as you develop your own style.

10. *Get training*. Check with your state licensing board to find out whether you must obtain approved training in hypnosis prior to employing it in your practice. Even if there's no regulation to this effect in place, I highly recommend getting hands-on experience and supervision. Workshops are regularly offered by several professional organizations, including the American Society of Clinical Hypnosis, the Society for Clinical and Experimental Hypnosis, and the Milton H. Erickson Foundation (see References for Web site URLs), and some offer certification. Your state licensing board may also have a list of approved workshop providers in your area.

References, Readings, & Internet Sites

American Society for Clinical Hypnosis. (n.d.). Resources for research and teaching. Retrieved 2004 from http://www.hypnosis-research.org/hypnosis/index.html

American Society of Clinical Hypnosis. (n.d.). Home page. Retrieved 2004 from http://www.asch.net

Erickson, M. H. (1980). Further clinical techniques of hypnosis: Utilization techniques. In E. L. Rossi (Ed.), *The collected papers of Milton H. Erickson* (Vol. 1, pp. 177–205). New York: Irvington.

Flemons, D. (n.d.). *Of one mind*. New York: W. W. Norton.

Flemons, D. (n.d.). Web site: Theory and practice of hypnosis; hypnosis links. Retrieved 2004 from http://www.ofonemind.com

Milton H. Erickson Foundation. (n.d.). Home page. Retrieved 2004 from http://www.erickson foundation.org

O'Hanlon, W. H., & Martin, M. (1992). *Solution-oriented hypnosis: An Ericksonian approach*. New York: W. W. Norton.

Sanders, S. (1993). Clinical self-hypnosis: Transformation and subjectivity. In J. W. Rhue, S. J. Lynn, & I. Kirsch (Eds.), *Handbook of clinical hypnosis* (pp. 251–270). Washington, DC: American Psychological Association.

Society for Clinical and Experimental Hypnosis. (n.d.). Home page. Retrieved 2004 from http://www.sunsite.utk.edu/IJCEH/scehframe.htm

71 WORKING WITH THE RELIGIOUSLY COMMITTED CLIENT

P. Scott Richards & Kari A. O'Grady

The religious landscape of North America is breathtaking in its diversity and vibrancy. Members of all of the major world religions and countless smaller ones have found their homes in the United States or Canada. Over 80% of people in North America claim affiliation with Christianity (Berrett & Johnson, 1998), but there is great diversity within the Christian tradition. The *Yearbook of American and Canadian Churches* (Bedell, 1997) lists over 160 different religious denominations.

Although religious affiliation alone may reveal little about religious belief or commitment, there is evidence that large numbers of people believe in and are devoutly committed to their faith. Recent polls have found that over 95% of Americans profess belief in God, 64% are members of a church, and 62% said that religion can answer all or most of today's problems (Gallup Foundation, 2003). In light of these statistics, most psychotherapists will work with religiously committed clients from a variety of traditions during their careers. But if they are not adequately prepared, psychotherapists may find it particularly challenging to work sensitively and effectively with them (Shafranske & Malony, 1996).

There is evidence that many religiously committed people, including religious leaders, have an unfavorable view of the mainstream, secular mental health professions and a distrust of the process of psychotherapy. Worthington (1986) identified several possible concerns devout Christian clients may have about therapists: "Conservative Christians fear that a secular counselor will (a) ignore spiritual concerns, (b) treat spiritual beliefs and experiences as pathological or merely psychological, (c) fail to comprehend spiritual language and concepts, (d) assume that religious clients share nonreligious cultural norms (e.g., premarital cohabitation, premarital intercourse, divorce), (e) recommend therapeutic behaviors that clients consider immoral (e.g., experimentation with homosexuality), or (f) make assumptions, interpretations, and recommendations that discredit revelation as a valid epistemology" (p. 425). These fears are rooted in a public awareness of the reality that many psychologists during the past century have endorsed anti-religious, hedonistic, and atheistic values and practices that conflict with those of traditional religious communities (Bergin, 1980; Richards & Bergin, 1997).

Given their fears about psychotherapy, it is not surprising that members of many traditional religious communities, especially more devout members, appear to significantly underutilize mental health services (Richards & Bergin, 2000). Furthermore, there is some evidence that religious persons often seek professional therapy as a last resort, after first seeking assistance from family, friends, and their clergy. When they do seek psychotherapy, several studies have shown that devoutly religious persons often express a preference for working with therapists from their own faith, or at least with a religious therapist (Worthington, Kurusu, McCullough, & Sanders, 1996).

THERAPEUTIC GUIDELINES

- *Develop multicultural spiritual sensitivity.* The foundations of an ecumenical therapeutic stance are the attitudes and skills of effective multicultural therapists, but it goes beyond most contemporary multicultural approaches to include training and competency in working with religious and spiritual issues (Richards & Bergin, 1997, 2000). Therapists with good ecumenical skills are aware of their own religious and spiritual heritage and are sensitive to how they could impact their work with clients from different religious and spiritual traditions. They are capable of communicating interest, understanding, and respect to clients who have spiritual beliefs that are different from their own. They seek to learn more about the spiritual beliefs and cultures of clients with whom they work. They make efforts to establish trusting relationships with members and leaders in their clients' religious communities and seek to draw upon these sources of social support when it seems appropriate. They use spiritual resources and interventions that are in harmony with their clients' beliefs when it appears that this could help their clients cope and change.
- *Adopt a denominational therapeutic stance with some clients.* A denominational stance is one that is tailored for clients who are members of a specific religious denomination (Richards & Bergin, 1997, 2000). A denominational approach builds upon the foundation laid earlier in therapy by the therapist's ecumenical stance, but differs in that the therapist uses assessment methods and interventions that are tailored more specifically to the clients' unique denomination. Therapists should use a denominational approach only with clients who view them as able to deeply understand and respect their spiritual beliefs. Such an approach can give therapists added leverage to help clients because it can assist them in more fully addressing the fine nuances of a client's religious and spiritual issues, as well as tapping into the resources of the client's religious tradition.
- *Establish a spiritually safe environment.* We recommend that therapists explicitly let their clients know it is permissible to explore spiritual issues should they so desire. Therapists can do this in the written informed consent documents they give clients at the beginning of treatment and/or they can do so verbally during the course of therapy. Clients who fear that the therapist might view their spiritual beliefs as pathological could also be allayed in the informed consent document.
- *Respect other worldviews.* Therapists should deal with religious differences and value conflicts with clients in a respectful and tolerant manner. Differences in religious affiliation and disagreements about specific religious doctrines or moral behaviors can threaten the therapeutic alliance if they are disclosed prematurely or addressed inappropriately. When such value conflicts become salient during therapy, it is important for therapists to openly acknowledge their values, while also explicitly affirming clients' rights to differ from therapists without having their intelligence or morality questioned. Therapists should also openly discuss with clients whether the belief or value conflict is so threatening that referral is advisable.
- *Conduct a multisystemic assessment.* We recommend that when therapists first begin working with clients that they globally assess the following systems or dimensions of human functioning: physical, social, behavioral, intellectual, educational-occupational, psychological-emotional, and religious-spiritual (Richards & Bergin, 1997). Therapists can also include questions about clients' religious and spiritual backgrounds on an intake questionnaire.

During the initial global phase of the assessment process, we recommend that therapists collect only information that will help them understand whether their clients' religious background may be relevant to their presenting problems and treatment planning. Asking the following questions may help therapists make such a determination: (a) Is the client willing to discuss religious and spiritual issues during

treatment? If not, this must be respected, although the issue may be returned to if new information warrants it. (b) If so, what is the client's current religious-spiritual affiliation? How important is this affiliation to the client? How orthodox and devout is the client?
(c) Does the client believe his or her spiritual beliefs and lifestyle are contributing to his or her presenting problems and concerns in any way? (d) Does the client have any religious and spiritual concerns and needs? (e) Is the client willing to participate in spiritual interventions if it appears that they may be helpful? (f) Does the client perceive that his or her religious and spiritual beliefs and/or community are a potential source of strength and assistance?

- *Set appropriate spiritual therapy goals.* The purpose of psychotherapy is to help clients cope with and resolve their presenting problems and to promote their long-term well-being. Although not all religiously committed clients wish to explore religious issues or pursue spiritual goals, many do. There are several general spiritual goals that may be appropriate for therapy, depending on the clients' unique concerns: (a) help clients examine and better understand what impact their religious and spiritual beliefs may be having on their presenting problems and their lives in general; (b) help clients identify and use the religious or spiritual resources in their lives to assist them in their efforts to cope, heal, and change; (c) help clients examine and resolve religious and spiritual concerns that are pertinent to their disorders; (d) help clients examine how they feel about their spiritual well-being and, if they desire, help them determine how they can continue their quest for spiritual growth.
- *Refer as needed.* Therapists need not necessarily be religious or spiritually oriented themselves to pursue these goals (Lovinger, 1984). At the same time, therapists will feel uncomfortable working on spiritual issues because of lack of training or their personal views. In such circumstances, it would be appropriate and ethical for them to refer clients.
- *Appropriately use spiritual resources and interventions.* There is a growing body of evidence that religious and spiritual practices can both prevent problems and help promote coping and healing where problems have occurred (Benson, 1996; Koenig, McCullough, & Larson, 2001). In general, people who are religiously and spiritually devout, but not extremists, tend to enjoy better physical health and psychological adjustment, and lower rates of pathological social conduct than those who are not (Koenig et al., 2001; Richards & Bergin, 1997). Examples of spiritual interventions that may be used by psychotherapists include praying for clients, encouraging clients to pray, discussing theological concepts, making reference to scriptures, using spiritual relaxation and imagery techniques, encouraging repentance and forgiveness, helping clients live congruently with their spiritual values, self-disclosing spiritual beliefs or experiences, consulting with religious leaders, and recommending religious bibliotherapy (Richards & Bergin, 1997; Shafranske, 2000). Most of these spiritual interventions are actually practices that have been engaged in for centuries by religious believers.
- *Seek continuing education opportunities.* Psychotherapists can increase their competency to work with religiously committed clients from diverse backgrounds by: (a) reading books on the psychology and sociology of religion; (b) reading literature about religion and spirituality in mainstream mental health journals; (c) taking a workshop or class on religion and mental health and spiritual issues in psychotherapy; (d) reading books or taking a class on world religions; (f) acquiring specialized knowledge about religious traditions that they frequently encounter in therapy; (g) seeking supervision or consultation from colleagues when they first work with a client from a particular religious tradition; and (h) seeking supervision or consultation when they first begin using religious and spiritual interventions (Richards & Bergin, 1997, 2000).

References, Readings, & Internet Sites

Bedell, K. B. (Ed.). (1997). *Yearbook of American and Canadian Churches.* Nashville, TN: Abingdon Press.

Benson, H. (1996). *Timeless healing: The power and biology of belief.* New York: Scribner.

Bergin, A. E. (1980). Psychotherapy and religious values. *Journal of Consulting and Clinical Psychology, 48,* 75–105.

Berrett, D. B., & Johnson, T. M. (2002). Religion. *Britannica Book of the Year,* p. 303. Chicago Encyclopedia Britannica.

Gallup Foundation (2003). *Public gives organized religion its lowest rating: The Gallup Poll Tuesday briefing.* (January 7, 2003, pp. 1–2). Princeton, NJ: Gallup Organization.

Koenig, H. G., McCullough, M. E., & Larson, D. B. (2001). *Handbook of religion and health.* New York: Oxford University Press.

Lovinger, R. J. (1984). *Working with religious issues in therapy.* New York: Jason Aronson.

Melton, J. G. (1996). *Encyclopedia of American religions.* Detroit: Gale Research.

Miller, W. R. (1999). *Integrating spirituality into treatment: Resources for practitioners.* Washington, DC: American Psychological Association.

Richards, P. S., & Bergin, A. E. (1997). *A spiritual strategy for counseling and psychotherapy.* Washington, DC: American Psychological Association.

Richards, P. S., & Bergin, A. E. (Eds.). (2000). *Handbook of psychotherapy and religious diversity.* Washington, DC: American Psychological Association.

Shafranske, E. P. (2000). Religious involvement and professional practices of psychiatrists and other mental health professionals. *Psychiatric Annals, 30,* 525–532.

Shafranske, E. P., & Malony, H. N. (1996). Religion and the clinical practice of psychology: A case for inclusion. In E. P. Shafranske (Ed.), *Religion and the clinical practice of psychology* (pp. 561–586). Washington, DC: American Psychological Association.

Worthington, E. L., Jr. (1986). Religious counseling: A review of published empirical research. *Journal of Counseling and Development, 64,* 421–431.

Worthington, E. L., Jr., Kurusu, T. A., McCullough, M. E., & Sanders, S. J. (1996). Empirical research on religion and psychotherapeutic processes and outcomes: A ten-year review and research prospectus. *Psychological Bulletin, 119,* 448–487.

72 PSYCHOTHERAPY WITH COGNITIVELY IMPAIRED ADULTS

Kathleen B. Kortte, Felicia Hill-Briggs, & Stephen T. Wegener

Individuals with cognitive impairments may present for psychotherapy with a range of cognitive, behavioral, and emotional symptoms. The goal of psychotherapy is to assist them in adapting to the changes in their lives and themselves. The three primary diagnostic groups addressed in this overview are adult traumatic brain injury, stroke, and cognitive impairment and dementia in older adults. This chapter reviews the key issues influencing psychological functioning for these populations and suggests specific approaches and modifications to psychotherapy to accommodate for cognitive impairment.

TREATMENT POPULATIONS

A central feature of psychotherapy that cuts across diagnostic groups is the development of a therapeutic alliance (Prigatano, 1999; Sohlberg & Mateer, 2001). Because many patients with cognitive impairments are referred by family members, community agencies, or medical professionals, they may have a limited appreciation of the reason for psychotherapy. Initial goals focus on developing the collaborative relationship necessary to improve awareness of self and behavior. The therapeutic alliance and the individual's specific brain functioning provide the basis for tailoring psychotherapy.

Mild Adult Traumatic Brain Injury

Individuals who suffer a mild traumatic brain injury (mTBI) tend to experience headache, dizziness, fatigue, memory decrement, and attention problems. These symptoms typically subside approximately three to six months following a brief disruption in consciousness secondary to a head injury (Mittenberg, Canyock, Condit, & Patton, 2001). However, approximately 30% of these cases continue to experience these problems for longer periods of time, as well as symptoms of depression, anxiety, or preoccupation with these symptoms (Mittenberg et al., 2001). When this constellation of symptoms occurs and there is no objective evidence of marked impairment on neuropsychological evaluation, the resulting syndrome is known as post-concussion syndrome (PCS). Brief psychoeducational intervention provided early in the recovery process can have a significant effect on reducing subsequent development of PCS (Mittenberg et al., 2001). The focus of therapy with this diagnostic group includes education of what to expect following mTBI, review of the typical course of recovery and prognosis for complete recovery, and recommendations about gradual resumption of normal activities.

Moderate to Severe Adult Traumatic Brain Injury

The most enduring effects of traumatic brain injury are emotional, behavioral, and psychological ones (Ben-Yishey & Daniels-Zide, 2000). These effects can arise as a direct result of damage to the brain and/or within the personal and social context of the injury. Treatment following moderate to severe TBI is implemented generally within the context of the rehabilitation setting. Treatment goals are often oriented toward facilitating community reintegration and vocational rehabilitation, and therefore, interventions are collaborative and involve an interdisciplinary team (e.g., speech, occupational, and physical therapists; case managers; social workers; physicians), family and caregivers, and community agencies and resources (Frank & Elliot, 2000). Psychotherapy is focused on providing education about brain injury, improving self-monitoring skills, facilitating skills for impairment compensation, assisting the individual in integration of the changes associated with TBI, and managing psychiatric symptoms.

One of the most challenging aspects of working with TBI patients is their limited awareness of the changes in their functioning. One treatment goal is to facilitate understanding of changes in their behavior and, if they do not grasp the usefulness of psychotherapy, then they may resist treatment or only passively engage in it (Prigatano, 1999).

Structured group therapy, either alone or in combination with individual treatment, has particular advantages for addressing social and emotional aspects of neuropsychological impairment. This format provides opportunities for peer comparison of strengths and limitations, feedback for self-evaluation, sharing of compensatory strategies, and an improvement in feeling helpful to and accepted by others (Langer et al., 1999). Interventions focus on rebuilding basic social skills (e.g., eye contact, voice volume, listening, and body language) and providing practice for managing emotional reactions (social exercises, instruction, cuing, modeling, role-playing, and educational presentations).

Stroke

Research suggests that the prevalence of clinical depression following stroke ranges from 20% to 50% (Robinson, 1998). Supportive psychotherapy for disability, loss, depression, and anxiety is often provided during acute rehabilitation; however, there are very few studies of their effectiveness in this population (Frank & Elliot, 2000). Cognitive-behavioral interventions that focus on education, activity scheduling, and modifying unhelpful thoughts (e.g., Lincoln & Flannaghan, 2003) have demonstrated only limited effectiveness, and identification of how these approaches are adapted for use with varying levels of cognitive impairment is still needed. Intervention for caregiver burden is important both for caregiver coping and for survivor well-being (Frank & Elliot, 2000). Group approaches for families that focus on teaching active coping skills, providing education about stroke, and facilitating social support can be effective in increasing disease knowledge and use of coping strategies (van den Heuvel et al., 2002).

Cognitively Impaired Older Adults

The value of psychotherapy for maximizing the functioning and quality of life of older adults with cognitive impairment and dementia is increasingly recognized since cognitively impaired older adults are typically referred to psychotherapy by others. The therapy process involves communication and collaboration with the individuals and systems involved in the person's care. Both the cognitively impaired older adult and the caregiver(s) benefit from psychoeducational approaches to increase understanding of sequelae of neuropsychological impairment. Therapy addresses the agitation and behavioral disturbance that often presents with dementia. Here, the psychological intervention involves identifying triggers for disruptive verbal (e.g., screaming, cursing, temper outbursts) or physical (e.g., pacing, hitting, scratching) behaviors, gaining understanding of the meaning of the behaviors for the older person, developing environmental and behavioral approaches to decrease disturbance, and working with nursing-home staff or caregivers to implement the behavioral strategies (Lawton & Rubenstein, 2000).

The focus is on abilities rather than pointing out deficits. Cognitive-behavioral approaches to treat depression and anxiety have been the focus of the majority of research with demented individuals (e.g., Laidlaw, Thompson, Dick-Siskin, & Gallagher-Thompson, 2003). Cognitive psychotherapy goals are, first, to break down problems into basic components to reduce the person's feeling overwhelmed and, second, to teach cognitive strategies to facilitate adaptive ways of viewing the specific problem. Behavioral interventions are utilized with more moderately to severely demented persons; they focus on increasing positive activities and decreasing negative activities (Lawton & Rubenstein, 2000). Modified psychodynamic approaches with dementia patients focus on goals of providing an environment for emotional outlet, enhancement of self-esteem and role functioning, minimizing psychological and behavior problems, and increasing coping skills through modified therapy techniques including keeping notebooks and providing summaries, telling stories, or using pictures (Haussman, 1992).

Group treatments often utilized for persons with dementia who reside in long-term care situations provide emotional support through group interaction and may effectively reduce depression that stems from a lost sense of self (Brody & Semel, 1993). Reminiscence or life-review groups promote positive affect and reconnection with events of personal significance. Visual prompts (e.g., photographs of or clothing from a particular era) or auditory prompts (e.g., a popular song of an era) may be used to facilitate memory and discussion of the reminiscence topic.

MODIFICATION OF PSYCHOTHERAPY

Psychotherapy is useful following changes to brain functioning in assisting individuals in adapting to the changes in their functioning (Prigatano, 1999). However, the approach to psychotherapy must be modified. The typical structure of psychotherapy requires direct communication and discussion of presenting issues, therapeutic goals, and steps to achieving those goals. Such discussions require high-level cognitive processes.

For cognitively impaired individuals, cognitive remediation techniques are incorporated into the process to facilitate receptive and expressive communication, to help patients focus and learn during sessions, and to promote carryover of behavioral change and treatment goals to the home and community. Below are a series of specific strategies.

Communication

- Use short, simple sentences.
- Minimize the amount that is said at one time and in one session.
- Speak slowly and clearly.
- When repeating information, use the same words.
- Summarize key points throughout session.
- Allow the patient extra time to respond.

Environment

- Meet with the patient more frequently, but for shorter therapy sessions.
- Promote consistency by having a set meeting time and structure.
- Hold sessions at the individual's best time of day.
- Be receptive to between session contacts to assist individual in carrying over information.
- Plan for longer duration of treatment.
- Minimize distractions in therapy environment.

External Aids

- Write notes either by or for the individual.
- Employ diagrams, drawings, and checklists.
- Use rating or scaling techniques to anchor changes in subjective experiences.
- Have a session agenda.
- Audiotape or videotape sessions for later review.
- Use pictures, photos, and scrapbooks.

METATHERAPEUTIC ISSUES

Identifying personal biases and assumptions will help the psychotherapist avoid subscribing to a moral or medical model of disability. Such a model may bias the psychotherapist toward viewing persons with impairments as individuals with shameful conditions or innately disabled, causing the therapist to assume a paternalistic role (Olkin, 1999). An alternative and potentially more productive model is a social or minority perspective, in which the disability is viewed as occurring at the interface of the person and his or her environment. Adopting this model encourages the therapist to be aware of the strengths and abilities of the individual and to focus on the interpersonal and physical environment as key targets for intervention.

The psychotherapist must also guard against the bias that individuals with cognitive impairments will not benefit from psychotherapy or that behavior change is not possible because the impairment results from neurologic insult. Individuals with these deficits do benefit from psychotherapy to improve psychosocial function. Further, there is no evidence to suggest that nonspecific variables of psychotherapy—a confiding relationship, empathy, instillation of hope, increased perceived mastery—are any less important in achieving positive therapeutic outcomes. Due to the multiple physical and psychosocial impairments concomitant in persons with cognitive deficits, psychologists must develop a team of professionals with whom they work. Physician consultation for medication evaluation is common and effective for managing symptoms (Langer et al., 1999). While rehabilitation programs usually have established interdisciplinary teams, psychotherapists in the community would benefit from developing a network of consultants and resources. These resources may include relationships with independent living centers, vocational rehabilitation services, community services for the elderly, peer support groups, and advocacy groups, as well as rehabilitation personnel—physicians, speech-language therapists, and physical and occupational therapists. Finally, to effectively assist persons with disabilities, psychotherapists must have a working knowledge of the Americans with Disability Act (ADA) of 1990 (P.L.101-336) and the individual's rights under that law. These resources ensure access to necessary services and provide the framework for maximizing independence.

References, Readings, & Internet Sites

Alexopoulos, G. S., Raue, P., & Arean, P. (2003). Problem-solving therapy versus supportive therapy in geriatric major depression with executive dysfunction. *American Journal of Geriatric Psychiatry, 11,* 46–52.

Ben-Yishay, Y., & Daniels-Zide, E. (2000). Examined lives: Outcome after holistic rehabilitation. *Rehabilitation Psychology, 45,* 112–129.

Bowen, A., Chamberlain, M. A., Tennant, A., Neumann, V., & Conner, M. (1999). The persistence of mood disorder following traumatic brain injury: A 1-year follow-up. *Brain Injury, 13,* 547–553.

Brain Injury Association. (n.d.). Home page. Retrieved 2004 from http://www.biausa.org

Brody, C. M., &. Semel, V. G. (Eds.). (1993). *Strategies for therapy with the elderly: Living with hope and meaning.* New York: Springer.

Frank, R. G., & Elliot, T. R. (Eds.). (2000). *Handbook of rehabilitation psychology.* Washington, DC: American Psychological Association.

Hausman, C. (1992). Dynamic psychotherapy with elderly demented patients. In G. Jones & B. Miessen (Eds.), *Care-giving in dementia* (pp. 181–198). London: Tavistock/Routledge.

Laidlaw, K., Thompson, L. W., Dick-Siskin, L., & Gallagher-Thompson, D. (2003). *Cognitive behaviour therapy with older people.* New York: Wiley.

Langer, K. G., Laatsch, L., & Lewis, L. (Eds.). (1999). *Psychotherapeutic interventions for adults with brain injury or stroke: A clinician's treatment resource.* Madison, CT: International Universities Press.

Lawton, M. P., & Rubinstein, R. L. (Eds.). (2000). *Interventions in dementia care: Toward improving quality of life.* New York: Springer.

Lincoln, N. B., & Flannaghan, T. (2003). Cognitive behavioral psychotherapy for depression following stroke: A randomized controlled trial. *Stroke, 34,* 111–115.

Mittenberg, W., Canyock, E. M., Condit, D., & Patton, C. (2001). Treatment of post-concussion syndrome following mild head injury. *Journal of Clinical and Experimental Neuropsychology, 23,* 829–836.

National Stroke Association. (n.d.). Home page. Retrieved 2004 from http://www.stroke.org

Olkin, R. (1999). *What psychotherapists should know about disability.* New York: Guilford Press.

Prigatano, G. P. (1999). *Principles of neuropsychological rehabilitation.* New York: Oxford University Press.

Robinson, R. G. (1998). *The clinical neuropsychiatry of stroke*. New York: Cambridge University Press.

Sohlberg, M. M., & Mateer, C. A. (2001). *Cognitive rehabilitation: An integrative neuropsychological approach*. New York: Guilford Press.

Toseland, R. W. (1995). *Group work with the elderly and family caregivers*. New York: Springer.

Van den Heuvel, E. T. P., de Witte, L. P., Stewart, R. E., Schure, L. M., Sanderman, R., & Meyboom-de Jong, B. (2002). Long-term effects of a group support program and an individual support program for informal caregivers of stroke patients: Which caregivers benefit the most? *Patient Education and Counseling, 47*, 291–299.

Related Topics

Chapter 57, "Psychological Interventions in Adult Disease Management"

Chapter 64, "Psychotherapy With Older Adults"

Chapter 91, "Medical Conditions That May Present as Psychological Disorders"

73 EARLY TERMINATION AND REFERRAL OF CLIENTS IN PSYCHOTHERAPY

Manferd D. Koch

Early identification of a nontherapeutic client-therapist relationship is important in designing strategies for effective treatment intervention. Responsibility is placed on the therapist to construct a therapeutic environment where healthy change can occur. When a therapeutic impasse develops, clinicians are encouraged to undergo self-evaluation and make every attempt to facilitate progress by considering alternative treatment approaches, consulting with colleagues, and seeking formal supervision. Certain problems and populations require specific skills for effective intervention, and client-therapist mismatches may become inefficient or even countertherapeutic. Therapists are not expected to have the specific expertise necessary to treat all clinical populations; therefore, referral of the client to another practitioner may be indicated. Koocher (1995) suggests that therapists learn to identify clients with whom they cannot or should not work and refer them immediately and appropriately to avoid causing the client personal discomfort or stress. Therapists can identify specific ego deficits and environmental circumstances that predict premature psychotherapy termination, such as motivation frustration tolerance, countertransference issues, and life circumstances (Frayn, 1992). Psychologists are directed to terminate therapy when the client/patient is not likely to benefit or is harmed by continuing treatment (American Psychological Association, 2002). One or more of the following issues may be a potential reason to refer a client to another psychotherapist:

- *Competence to treat:* A cornerstone of American Psychological Association (APA) ethical principles is to maintain high standards of competence by providing services for which one is qualified or making appropriate referrals (2002). Historically, therapists have demonstrated competence through education, training, experience, research, licensure, and recognition by colleagues. Technical competencies may be demonstrated by adherence to a training manual for specific therapies, such as experiential therapy (Greenberg, Rice, & Elliot, 1993). General abilities like sensitivity and insightfulness are harder to demonstrate. The boundaries of a therapist's competence may be questioned in malpractice actions when the therapist has been found to have used nontraditional therapies, to have limited experience with a unique cultural population, to have had little training in working with addiction or suicide, or to have not restricted practice. Limited self-study may not be sufficient to demonstrate competence. Formal continuing education provided by professional organizations is essential given the knowledge explosion in psychology, where the half-life of professional competence may be 10 years.

- *Dual relationships:* In psychotherapy, dual relationships occur when the therapist, the person in power, enters into a significantly different relationship with the client. Whether sequential or concurrent, such relationships may unintentionally produce inappropriate influence over the client and impair the therapist's judgment by blurring and distorting professional boundaries. When in doubt, the therapist should consult with the client and colleagues concerning possible adverse consequences prior to the development of potential dual relationships, such as therapist and social friend, therapist and business partner, and therapist and supervisor or teacher (Bennett, Bryant, VandenBos, & Greenwood, 1990). Sexual relationships with clients in therapy are always judged to be exploitative, forbidden, and in several states a felony crime (APA, 2002). Nonerotic touching of clients in therapy is controversial and may be misinterpreted as sexual. Bartering for services and accepting gifts are questionable practices and should be avoided except when not clinically contra-indicated, and when the resulting arrangement is not exploitative (APA, 2002). Consultation of collleagues is recommended. Referral is essential when dual relationships are unavoidable and are deemed to be harmful or exploitative.
- *Countertherapeutic transference:* A client may develop unconscious feelings and behaviors toward a therapist based on significant relationships and conflicts originating early in the client's life. Such transference may eventually result in the client's having a positive infatuation toward the therapist or acting as if the therapist were infallible. Reliving previously repressed positive feelings in the form of a transference neurosis may have therapeutic value. However, the outcome of the therapy is dependent on the therapist's helping the client analyze and deal with maladaptive transference styles. In some cases, clients are so fearful of change that they refuse to abandon positive transference; consequently, the therapy should terminate, since continuation is not likely to produce significant change. In other instances, the client may quickly devalue the therapist and develop negative transference when the therapist cannot fulfill all of the client's needs. In other cases, transference is negative initially, and the client acts out feelings of mistrust, ambivalence, hostility, or aggression almost from the inception. The client who develops strong negative transference may be unconsciously motivated to act out hostile feelings in an escalating fashion and to passive-aggressively sabotage the therapy, even becoming suicidal and in rare instances homicidal. A client's verbal abuse and threats of physical harm can produce extreme anxiety and concerns about self-preservation for the therapist (Maier, 1993). Such actions on the part of the client and reactions from the therapist are countertherapeutic and potentially dangerous. These actions indicate that consultation with colleagues, referral to another therapist with different skills, or placement in a controlled facility is appropriate.
- *Unresolvable countertransference:* Subjective reactions of the therapist toward the

client are termed *countertransference*. As with transference, these feelings may be positive, such as being overly attracted and solicitous toward a client, or negative, as in disliking and acting in a rejecting fashion toward the client. Therapist reactions may be the consequence of the manner in which the client treats the therapist, unresolved issues on the part of the therapist, or a combination of both. Positive and negative reactions of the therapist are real and need to be recognized but not acted out toward the client. In some instances the therapist's feelings may contain important information that could exert a therapeutic effect when shared with the client. Therapists can use their reactions to help the client understand the impact the client has on relationships with significant others. It is a therapeutic skill to recognize one's personal countertransference attitudes, feelings, and biases and not act them out in the therapy. Eventually therapists will encounter people who make them feel angry or frustrated or whom they simply dislike. Every attempt should be made by the therapist to deal with countertransference issues, including consultation, supervision, and personal therapy. However, if these actions are not productive, referral is indicated, since strong unresolved positive or negative feelings and actions toward the client will inevitably result in dissolution of the therapeutic relationship (Kleinke, 1993).

- *Failure to form a therapeutic alliance:* To make progress in therapy, a client and therapist must form a working alliance with agreed-upon goals, rules, and responsibilities. A productive alliance involves bond-ing together and collaborating to accomplish the tasks of the therapy. Misalliance can be the consequence of the actions or failure to act on the part of either the client or the therapist. The therapist may contribute to the misalliance through poorly designed, planned, and executed interventions; inappropriate attitudes; and lack of self/other understanding and by allowing disruptive outside influences to enter the therapy. Clients may believe that benefit should be derived solely from efforts on the part of the therapist, without active client participation. Others resist entering into a closely bonded relationship, while the fear of change may keep some clients from forming an alliance. Therapist tolerance for maladaptive acts during therapy inadvertently encourages the continuation of problematic behaviors outside of therapy. Strupp (1980) found little evidence that therapists confronted clients' hostility and negativity. Often a poor therapy outcome was the consequence of a negative cycle of client hostility and therapist counterhostility, ultimately destroying the therapeutic alliance. If it becomes clear after observation and consultation that elements of the client-therapist interaction block productive work, transferring the client should be considered.
- *Resistance and therapeutic impasse:* Analysis of resistance has been a central element of analytic therapy. Because therapy can be painful and threatens current psychic structures, clients maintain their defenses, which control anxiety. Typically, resistance on the part of the client results from the fear that change will force one to give up a desired object, feeling, or behavior. The therapist should accept the existence of this process while at the same time helping the client identify what is threatening. Resistance may take the form of withholding information, attempts to manipulate the therapist, violating rules of the therapy, and even open hostility. Transference resistance is the consequence of dynamic issues between therapist and client, which typically are a repetition of earlier modes of interacting with significant others. Another form of resistance is the result of the client's belief that talk therapy will not be useful in problem solving, while others may experience therapist intervention as a loss of personal freedom. When resistance hinders the process of change, therapists should encourage the client to work through the dysfunctional resistance. Nevertheless, resistance may become so strong that it curtails effective treatment and results in a therapeutic impasse. Therapists may also impede the therapeutic process by engaging in counterresistance, which serves to preserve the therapist's psychological status quo. This re-

sults in therapist and client collusion to preserve and defend dysfunctional role interactions (Stearn, 1993). When these conditions occur, referral to another therapist with different skills is indicated.

- *Compassion fatigue:* It is essential that therapists maintain their own mental health when working with others. Therapists should be aware of signs of fatigue, distress, burnout, or other impairment within themselves (Bennett et al., 1990). *Compassion stress* and *compassion fatigue* are terms applied to the effects felt by mental health professionals who work repeatedly with highly traumatized people. Therapists are encouraged to recognize their shortcomings and special vulnerabilities to stress and fatigue and to develop strategies for prevention of compassion fatigue (Figley, 1995). Some categories of clients are more demanding, difficult to treat, and problematic than others. Clients with borderline personality disorder, severe depression, terminal illness, psychosis, or suicidal or homicidal tendencies or those who have recently lost a child may be emotionally taxing for the therapist. Professionals are wise to restrict their caseload to only a few of these difficult clients at any one time. After working extensively with emotionally draining clients, the mental health professional may experience signs of burnout, which result in increased mental and physical fatigue, irritability, distancing from clients, and impairment of competence to treat. Because it is essential that therapists maintain emotional integrity until their own mental well-being is restored, they should refer rather than treat additional demanding clients. Psychologists are advised to be aware of personal problems that interfere with professional performance and take measures to obtain consultation, or assistance and decide whether to limit, suspend or terminate their professional work (APA, 2002).

References & Readings 

American Psychological Association. (2002). Ethical principles of psychologists and code of conduct. *American Psychologist, 57,* 1060–1073.

Bennett, B. E., Bryant, B. K., VandenBos, G. R., & Greenwood, A. (1990). *Professional liability and risk management.* Washington, DC: American Psychological Association.

Figley, C. R. (1995). Compassion fatigue: Toward a new understanding of the cost of caring. In B. H. Stamm (Ed.), *Secondary traumatic stress: self-care issues for clinicians, researchers, and educators* (pp. 3–25). Lutherville, MD: Sidran.

Frayn, D. H. (1992). Assessment factors associated with premature psychotherapy termination. *American Journal of Psychotherapy, 46,* 250–261.

Greenberg, L. S., Rice, L. N., & Elliott, R. (1993). *Facilitating emotional change: The moment-by-moment process.* New York: Guilford Press.

Kleinke, C. L. (1993). *Common principles of psychotherapy.* Pacific Grove, CA: Brooks/Cole.

Koocher, G. P. (1995). Ethics in psychotherapy. In B. Bongar & L. E. Beutler (Eds.), *Comprehensive textbook of psychotherapy: Theory and practice* (pp. 456–473). New York: Oxford University Press.

Maier, G. J. (1993). Management approaches for the repetitively aggressive patient. In W. H. Sledge & A. Tasman (Eds.), *Clinical challenges in psychiatry* (pp. 181–213). Washington, DC: American Psychiatric Association.

Stearn, H. S. (1993). *Resolving counter-resistance in psychotherapy.* New York: Brunner/Mazel.

Strupp, H. H. (1980). Success and failure in time-limited psychotherapy: Further evidence. *Archives of General Psychiatry, 37,* 947–954.

Related Topics

Chapter 38, "Patients' Rights in Psychotherapy"
Chapter 76, "Choice of Treatment Format"

74 GUIDELINES FOR RELAPSE PREVENTION

Katie Witkiewitz & G. Alan Marlatt

Relapse is the modal outcome for alcohol and substance abuse treatment programs that promote abstinence goals. Treatment approaches have often focused on changing behavior (e.g., promoting abstention from all substances), but not necessarily on maintaining positive changes over time. Individuals often left treatment programs without specific knowledge about how to maintain treatment gains. This situation led to a "revolving door" phenomenon, whereby several treatment completers returned to treatment following a relapse. Clearly, during treatment more emphasis needs to be placed on the problem of relapse and skills for preventing its occurrence.

Relapse prevention (RP) is an intervention that focuses on the maintenance stage of change and the problem of relapse through an integration of behavioral skills training, cognitive interventions, and lifestyle change procedures (Marlatt & Gordon, 1985). Although initially developed for alcohol-use disorders, the principles and concepts of RP have been adapted to other addictive and nonaddictive disorders, including depression (Teasdale et al., 2000), eating disorders (Mitchell & Carr, 2000), erectile dysfunction (McCarthy, 2001), bipolar disorders (Lam et al., 2001), schizophrenia (Herz et al., 2000), and sexual offenses (Laws, 1995).

The effectiveness of RP has been reasonably well established across disorders. Irvin and colleagues (1999) conducted a meta-analysis on the efficacy of RP techniques in the improvement of substance abuse and psychosocial outcomes. Twenty-six studies representing a sample of 9,504 participants were included in the review, which focused on alcohol use, smoking, polysubstance use, and cocaine use. The overall treatment effects demonstrated that RP was a successful intervention for reducing substance use and improving psychosocial adjustment.

Carroll (1996) conducted a narrative review of controlled clinical trials evaluating RP in the treatment of smoking, alcohol, and other drug use. Across substances, RP was found to be generally effective compared with no treatment and as good as other active treatments. One interesting finding was that some RP treatment outcome studies identified sustained main effects for RP, suggesting that RP may provide continued improvement over a longer period of time (indicating a "delayed emergence effect"), whereas other treatments may be effective over only a shorter duration. This delayed emergence effect is consistent with the skills acquisition basis of the RP approach. As with learning any new skill, clients become more experienced in acquiring and performing the skill, leading to overall improvements in performance over time.

CLINICAL PRACTICE OF RP

Relapse prevention is a cognitive-behavioral self-management training program designed to enhance the maintenance of the behavior change process. Focusing on skills training, RP teaches clients how to (1) understand the relapse process; (2) identify high-risk situations for relapse; (3) learn how to cope with craving and urges to engage in the addictive behavior; (4) reduce the harm of relapse by minimizing the negative consequences and learning from the experience; and (5) achieve greater lifestyle balance. These five key themes, as well as suggestions on how to implement them in clinical practice, are described below.

Reframe Relapse as a Process

Begin by exploring the client's subjective associations with the term *relapse*. Relapse can be described as either an outcome—the dichotomous view that the person is either ill or well—or a process, encompassing any transgression in the cyclic process of behavior change (Brownell, Marlatt, Lichtenstein, & Wilson, 1986). Many clients view relapse in dichotomous terms ("I was either able to maintain abstinence or not"). Alternatively, we can teach clients to use the term *lapse* to describe the first episode of the behavior after the commitment to abstinence. A lapse is a single event, a reemergence of a previous habit, which may or may not lead to a complete relapse. When a slip is defined as a lapse, it implies that if a corrective action can be taken, the outcome can still be considered positive (called a *prolapse*). Small setbacks can be described as opportunities for new learning and the reevaluation of coping strategies in high-risk situations, rather than indications of personal failure or a lack of motivation (Marlatt, 1996).

Identify High-Risk Situations

The initial component in RP is the identification of a client's unique profile of high-risk situations for relapse and evaluating the client's ability to cope with these high-risk situations. A high-risk situation is one in which the individual's sense of perceived control is threatened. High-risk situations can include environmental influences, an interpersonal interaction, or intrapersonal factors (such as affective states, cognitions, and physiological states). The procedures available to identify high-risk situations differ based on the readiness of the client and whether or not the client is engaged in the target behavior at the time of the assessment.

1. *Self-monitoring:* Ask the client to keep a continuous, daily record of the target behavior (what time the behavior began and ended, amount consumed, amount of money spent, etc.), along with a brief description of additional situational factors (where, who was present, doing what); events that may have occurred prior to the target behavior (what was happening, how you were feeling); amount consumed (be specific); and consequences associated with use (what happened afterward, how you felt, what you were thinking). Self-monitoring can also be used as an assessment device, to monitor urges to use, along with records of coping responses and whether or not the urge was followed by engaging in substance use. Psychological reactivity to self-monitoring can serve as an intervention strategy, since the client's awareness of the target behavior increases as the assessment continues and can lead to reductions in the monitored behavior.
2. *Autobiographies:* Have clients provide a descriptive narrative of the history and development of their problem. Ask the client how and why he or she initiated or first became involved with the addictive behavior; how the patterns of engaging in the addictive behavior may have changed over time; and what people, places, and events are associated with the problematic behavior patterns.
3. *Assessment tools:* Numerous self-report measures and observational techniques have been developed to help clinicians and their clients identify and prioritize their individual high-risk situations. These include the Inventory of Drug-Taking Situations (Annis, 1985), the Inventory of Drinking Situations (Annis, 1982), and the Identifying High-Risk Situations Inventory (Daley, 1986). Once high-risk situations are identified, it is helpful to assess the client's degree of self-confidence in his or her ability to resist urges and maintain abstinence in those situations. The Situational Confidence Questionnaire (Annis & Graham, 1988) is a useful measure of an individual's perceived self-efficacy in specific high-risk situations.

Learn How to Cope With Urges to Use in High-Risk Situations

1. *Assess coping skills:* Any situation can be considered "high-risk" if the person is inca-

pable or unwilling to respond to that situation with an effective coping response. Therefore it is critical that the clinician focus on the assessment of a client's coping skills with regard to previous, or probable, high-risk situation.

2. *Teach effective coping behavior:* Following assessment, the clinician should teach the client how to respond to cues (that occur before or during a high-risk situation) by engaging in an alternative effective coping behavior. Coping skills can be behavioral (action or action), cognitive (planning, reminders of negative consequences, "urge surfing"), or a combination of cognitive and behavioral coping processes. The goal is to teach clients how to respond to early warning signs of relapse, such as the rationalization of making seemingly unimportant decisions that eventually lead to a lapse (e.g., maybe I should buy a bottle of vodka and keep it in the house, just in case guests drop by). RP combines practice in general problem-solving skills and specific coping responses. Skills training methods incorporate components of direct instruction, modeling and behavioral rehearsal and coaching, and therapist support and feedback. In those cases in which it is not practical to use new coping skills in real-life settings, the therapist can utilize imagery or role-plays to represent high-risk situations.
3. *Teach "urge-surfing":* Urge-surfing is a metaphor for coping with the conditioned response to stimuli associated with the addictive behavior (coping with reactivity to cue exposure). It is based on the analogy that urges are like ocean waves, in that they have a specific course of action, with a given latency of onset, intensity, and duration. Remind clients that urges will arise, subside, and pass away on their own. In this technique, the client is taught to label internal sensations and cognitive preoccupations as an urge, and to foster an attitude of detachment from that urge. The goal is to identify, accept, and "surf" the urge, keeping one's balance so as to not get wiped out by the temptation to give in.
4. *Develop a decisional matrix:* Clients who are on the verge of using may only selectively attend to the positive expectancies of use. Help clients develop a decisional matrix that summarizes both immediate and delayed negative consequences of engaging in the prohibited behavior. A reminder card (also referred to as an emergency card) is one way of listing both cognitive and behavioral techniques that can be used in the event a client has an urge to use.
5. *Train clients to be on the lookout for warning signs:* Clients can be taught to look for impending high-risk situations and to take preventive action at the earliest possible point. Depending on the situation and the client's self-efficacy, the recommended action might be to avoid the high-risk situation. However, not all high-risk situations can be identified in advance. Many situations arise suddenly without warning—for example, being with a supposed non-using friend who offers drugs. In this type of situation, the individual must rely on previously acquired coping responses. Emphasize that the earlier one intervenes in the chain of events leading up to a high-risk situation and possible relapse, the easier it will be to prevent the lapse from occurring.

Minimize the Negative Consequences of a Lapse by Learning From the Experience

1. *Explain the abstinence violation effect (AVE):* The client's attributional response to a slip can further increase the probability of a full-blown relapse. Clients who view relapse as inevitable following the occurrence of a lapse are setting themselves up for an even larger transgression of behavior. This abstinence violation effect results from two cognitive-affective elements: cognitive dissonance (conflict and guilt) and a personal attributional effect (blaming oneself as the cause of the uncontrollable relapse). Clients should be instructed that a slip does not have to result in a major relapse and that lapses provide an opportunity for corrective action. A lapse may turn out to be a valuable learning experience (prolapse) that raises consciousness and teaches the client informa-

tion about possible high-risk situations and sources of stress or lifestyle imbalance.

2. *Conduct relapse debriefings:* One way to learn from lapses is through the use of relapse debriefings. Explore all aspects of the chain of events leading up to the relapse (or a particular temptation or lapse), including details concerning the high-risk situation, alternative coping responses, and inappropriate and appropriate cognitions.

Achieve Lifestyle Balance

Intervene in the client's overall lifestyle to increase the capacity to deal with perceived hassles or responsibilities ("shoulds") and perceived pleasures or self-gratification ("wants"). A key goal for a lifestyle intervention is to provide alternative sources of reward and to replace the addictive behavior with other positive activities or positive addictions. A "positive addiction" is a behavior that may be experienced negatively at first, but is highly beneficial in the long-range effects and may become a lasting habit. Examples include aerobic exercise, relaxation training, or meditation.

References, Readings, & Internet Sites

Annis, H. M. (1982). *Inventory of Drinking Situations.* Toronto: Addiction Research Foundation.

Annis, H. M. (1985). *Inventory of Drug-Taking Situations.* Toronto: Addiction Research Foundation.

Annis, H. M., & Graham, J. M. (1988). *Situational Confidence Questionnaire (SCQ-39) user's guide.* Toronto: Addiction Research Foundation.

Brownell, K. D., Marlatt, G. A., Lichtenstein, E., & Wilson, G. T. (1986). Understanding and preventing relapse. *American Psychologist, 41,* 765–782.

Carroll, K. M. (1996). Relapse prevention as a psychosocial treatment: A review of controlled clinical trials. *Experimental and Clinical Psychopharmacology, 4,* 46–54.

Daley, D. (1986). *Relapse prevention workbook for recovering alcoholics and drug dependent persons.* Holmes Beach, FL: Learning Publications.

Herz, M. I., Lamberti, J. S., Mintz, J., Scott, R., O'Dell, S. P., McCartan, L., & Nix, G. (2000). A program for relapse prevention in schizophrenia: A controlled study. *Archives of General Psychiatry, 57,* 277–283.

Irvin, J. E., Bowers, C. A., Dunn, M. E., & Wang, M. C. (1999). Efficacy of relapse prevention: A meta-analytic review. *Journal of Consulting and Clinical Psychology, 67,* 563–570.

Lam, D. H., Bright, J., Jones, S., Hayward, P., Schuck, N., Chisholm, D., & Sham, P. (2000). Cognitive therapy for bipolar illness—A pilot study of relapse prevention. *Cognitive Therapy and Research, 24,* 503–520.

Larimer, M. E., Palmer, R. S., and Marlatt, G. A. (1999). Relapse prevention: An overview of Marlatt's cognitive-behavioral model. *Alcohol Research and Health, 23*(2), 151–160. Retrieved March 10, 2003, from the National Institute of Alcohol Abuse and Alcoholism publications Web site: http://www.niaaa.nih.gov/publications/arh23-2/151-160.pdf

Laws, D. R. (1995). Central elements in relapse prevention procedures with sex offenders. *Psychology, Crime and Law, 2,* 41–53.

Marlatt, G. A. (1996). Taxonomy of high-risk situations for alcohol relapse: Evolution and development of a cognitive-behavioral model of relapse. *Addiction, 91*(Suppl.), 37–50.

Marlatt, G. A., & Gordon, J. R. (1985). *Relapse prevention: Maintenance strategies in the treatment of addictive behaviors.* New York: Guilford Press.

Marlatt, G. A., Parks, G. A., and Witkiewitz, K. (2002, December). *Clinical Guidelines for Implementing Relapse Prevention Therapy.* Retrieved March 10, 2003, from the Behavioral Health Recovery Management Web site: http://www.bhrm.org/guidelines/RPT%20guideline.pdf

McCarthy, B. W. (2001). Relapse prevention strategies and techniques with erectile dysfunction. *Journal of Sex and Marital Therapy, 27,* 1–8.

Mitchell, K., & Carr, A. (2001). Anorexia and bulimia. In A. Carr (Ed.), *What works for children and adolescents? A critical review of psychological interventions with children* (pp. 233–257). London: Routledge.

Teasdale, J. D., Segal, Z. V., Williams, J. M. G., Ridgeway, V. A., Soulsby, J. M., & Lau, M. A. (2000). Prevention of relapse/recurrence in major depression by mindfulness-based cognitive therapy. *Journal of Consulting and Clinical Psychology, 68,* 615–623.

Walton, M. A., Blow, F. C., & Booth, B. M. (2001). Diversity in relapse prevention needs: Gender and race comparisons among substance abuse treatment patients. *American Journal of Drug and Alcohol Abuse, 27,* 225–240.

Related Topic

Chapter 55, "Motivational Interviewing"

75 GUIDELINES FOR TERMINATING PSYCHOTHERAPY

Oren M. Shefet & Rebecca C. Curtis

The end of the psychotherapy is a crucial part of the therapeutic endeavor. Mistakes made in this stage cannot usually be corrected in later sessions. Both the client and the therapist will evaluate the successes and failures of the treatment and consolidate achievements. Termination can also be viewed as a stage in therapy rather than as the end (Fox, 1993; Tyson, 1996).

TIMING: WHEN SHOULD THE THERAPY END?

The criteria for treatment termination are as numerous as the theoretical orientations. However, general guidelines have been provided in the literature.

1. *Avoid perfectionistic tendencies:* That is, avoid setting criteria that are too high. The patient who is leaving therapy does not have to be completely healthy, positive, efficient, or conflict free.
2. *Assess attainment of treatment goals:* Most therapies stress the importance of the goals set by the client (Goldfried, 2002). Termination, however, will often be when the momentum of the work and motivation for therapy have decreased (Greenberg, 2002). Major goals are usually the alleviation of symptoms and improvement in handling life problems on one's own. Psychodynamic orientations also aim for increased ability to tolerate emotions (Curtis, 2000) and resolution of transference issues (Weiner, 1998). The goal of a new living or working environment is also important with patients whose previous circumstances were major factors in their hospitalization or substance abuse.
3. *Avoid surprise:* If either the therapist or the client is surprised by termination, there can be a problem. Termination should usually come from the client's initiative, and a mutual agreement between the client and the therapist should be reached concerning its time and manner of execution. Clients often forget about termination dates and need reminders of the plan discussed. When the therapist must take time off or end treatment, it is preferable to let the client know in advance that this will be happening, even if the exact date is not known. Therapists may wish to avoid letting patients know about medical or other problems, but such avoidance is not in the patient's interest.
4. *Recognize treatment failure:* A therapist who reaches the conclusion that the client's problems cannot be helped in the existing therapy should also terminate and make a referral (Werner, 1982).
5. *Negotiate a termination date:* Clients often pick a date in which the therapy would have come to a halt even without the termination, such as the beginning of a vacation or a major holiday. This can be viewed as an attempt to avoid the feelings the termination creates. Therapists might point this out to clients and encourage them to pick a date without other meanings, a date that will stand on its own as the end of the therapy.

THE TERMINATION PROCESS

Setting a Termination Date

Setting and reminding the client of a proposed termination date has distinct advantages and disadvantages. Once a termination date has been agreed upon, the therapy may change. On the one hand, setting a date allows the client to prepare herself for the post-treatment period and engage in the separation process. Knowing that the end of the process is near may motivate the client to work harder. On the other hand, the client may be reluctant to be engaged in the work, due to sadness over abandonment or other feelings, and this may disrupt a psychotherapy that has been going quite well until that point.

Setting a termination date is difficult not only for the client, but also for the therapist (Curtis, 2002). Therapists may avoid discussing or initiating terminations for their own reasons, as previously mentioned, rather than their patients' interests. Therapists are advised to identify such a pattern in themselves (Fox, 1993; Weissman, Markowitz, & Klerman, 2000).

Time-Limited and Spaced Terminations

Announcing the end of the treatment and ending the treatment in the same session is usually not advised. Such a pace would not allow either the client or the therapist to deal with the difficult emotions the termination may bring about and prevent coming to terms with the treatment and its ending. This leads to the question of the time line between the termination announcement and the final session.

In timed-limited terminations, sessions occur with the same regularity as before, until the final session, when they stop. In spaced terminations, the session frequency is gradually lessened, with the final session perhaps a month or more after the one before it. Time-limited terminations imply to the client that the therapy is complete. The termination date that was set seems final, and the client continues to work on his reactions to this date in a manner not very different from other therapeutic work.

Spaced terminations, on the other hand, imply that this is a test. The therapist and the client enter a process of lessening the therapy, which can be hastened or slowed as needed. Upon each spaced session, they examine the effect of the further spacing on the client. The client and therapist may feel that the termination is an option, which may or may not come into being. The choice between the two options will depend upon the therapist's clinical orientation and the client's presumed ability to handle the emotions that a set termination date will raise.

The Client's Reaction

Clients vary in their reactions to termination. Some, especially in relatively short treatments, do not have a strong reaction. Therapists should beware of attempting to provoke and "uncover" feelings that do not exist. Some clients, however, while saying they feel little about the upcoming end, nevertheless experience a wide range of emotions, and ignoring those emotions is a mistake. In those cases, the therapist should encourage clients to discover their reactions, and may even raise suggestions concerning various emotions that clients might feel (Weissman et al., 2000). Deciding whether clients who "do not feel anything" are covering for strong emotional reactions or not requires great deal of clinical judgment.

Most clients, especially those who participate in long therapies, will experience strong emotions around termination. The pleasant emotions may include a sense of relief from the financial and time pressures surrounding psychotherapy, pride of accomplishment and "graduation" from a stage in life, and joy in a sense of agency and independence (Tyson, 1996). While not ignoring the negative emotions, the therapist should acknowledge these feelings and share in the client's pleasure.

A wide spectrum of negative emotions may arise. According to psychoanalytic theory, patients are likely to mourn the loss of the relationship (Fox, 1993; Garcia-Lawson & Lane, 1997; Tyson, 1996; Weissman et al., 2000). Kübler-Ross's stage theory of mourning can help the therapist understand the client's reactions (Fox, 1993). In the first stage—denial—patients may ignore the upcoming termination, deny their feelings about the termination, and make relatively few attempts to approach the subject. In the second stage—anger—patients may feel rage about "being abandoned" by the therapist. In this stage, they may accuse their therapists of being hostile and uncaring, and devalue them and the therapy they offered. Such a tactic, however, can decrease the client's ability to consolidate the gains achieved in the therapy and leave him or her with a sense of failure. A temptation exists to avoid the issue of termination in order to avoid the patient's discomfort or devaluation, and retain the image of oneself as a "good therapist." This temptation should be avoided.

In the third stage—bargaining—clients may attempt to find a way to prolong the therapy. They may try to renegotiate the therapeutic contract. Another common strategy is finding a new problem or symptom, or relapsing into symptoms that were resolved during the therapy. In the fourth stage—depression—the client will not attempt to work through his or her affective reactions, but rather obsess on them, perhaps with a growing sense of helplessness to change the coming end of the therapy. Only in the fifth stage—acceptance—will the client come to terms with the termination. This is perhaps one of the best stages of the therapy to work on separation/individuation.

One of the reasons for the severity of the mourning is that patients may mourn not just the current relationship but also important past relationships that ended in separation. Clients may cast the therapist in three roles that led to separation in their earlier experience: the all-powerful parent, the rejecting lover, or the ideal mentor (Tyson, 1996).

The first is the parent-infant interaction. In some cases, patients create a highly dependent relationship with the therapist, whom they construe as an omnipotent benevolent parental figure (Frank, 1999). In such cases, separation from the therapist revives anxieties that were experienced in very early childhood or infancy, leading to rage against the therapist combined with deep feelings of helplessness and loss. This need not be a detriment to the therapy because it can allow the client and therapist to work through those archaic fears before the termination of the therapy.

The second pattern of interaction is the feeling of a romantic rejection. Some clients develop strong romantic yearnings toward their therapists, and the termination signals to clients that their yearnings will remain unfulfilled. Like any rejected lover, the patient may feel jealous of the therapist's other clients, or of the therapist's family, colleagues, or friends. Those feelings of jealousy may also promote emotions of guilt and loss of self-esteem. Other patients may develop a fantasy that would allow them to retain some contact with the therapist, such as writing a book about the therapy or using the therapist as a future mentor. The therapist's task will be to help the client renounce his unrealistic ambitions and come to terms with this loss.

Some patients idealize their therapists and wish to emulate them. The process at termination may be similar to the one some adolescents experience as they begin to see the limitations of their parents and develop values that may differ from theirs. At termination it is useful if clients who have heretofore focused primarily on the positive qualities of the therapist see the therapist more realistically and value their own independence. Some clients plunge to an opposite extreme and devalue the therapy and therapist, while fearing a future that is relatively empty of important relationships. The therapist should aid in helping clients remain aware of positive and negative qualities in themselves and others simultaneously. This will help the client feel hopeful and empowered concerning future relationships, without overvaluing or devaluing the therapist.

A prevalent client reaction is to induce a preemptive strike. The client would himself attempt to terminate the therapy, fearing that the therapist will announce one. The positive side of this attempt is that the client turns himself into the active agent of the termination, and thus acquires a sense of control and agency. This premature termination, however, is often the result of avoidance of the complicated and painful emotions involved in the termination process, and may interfere with the termination tasks, such as the consolidation of the therapeutic gains. It is better to deal with the frustrations of the therapy and the therapy's end during the therapy itself, rather than leave the client to deal with those issues alone in the post-treatment stage

In some cases the reaction of the client, as expressed by eleventh-hour problems, relapse, or distress, will be extremely severe. In those cases, it is advised to reconsider the termination. The therapist should not fear to do so, even at the price of appearing inconsistent or unresolved (Tyson, 1996).

TERMINATION TASKS

The therapist should take several steps upon terminating the therapy:

1. *Work through the separation anxiety.* The therapist should be aware of the complex emotions induced by the termination and help the client work through them.
2. *Resolve any unrealistic views of the therapist.* In therapies that have centered on transference resolution as a therapeutic mechanism, steps should be taken to resolve any unrealistic perceptions. In the psychoanalytic tradition, this will be achieved by interpretation of the transference relationship (Tyson, 1996). Other authors, such as Weiner (1998) and Curtis (2002), advise therapists to gradually abandon the "blank-slate" position and allow their real personalities to enter the therapeutic relationship directly. Strengthening the real relationship will diminish any remaining tendency to idealize the therapist.
3. *Consolidate therapeutic gains.* The therapist should review with the client the problems that led her to the therapy and the new ways of coping that she learned to utilize. The therapist should point out specific instances in which the client used new ways to react to situations and gently point to recent incidences in which the client could have done so. In some therapies, creating a ritual to consolidate the gains may be helpful (Greenberg, 2002). In others, creating a narrative of the therapeutic change can also help the client retain the therapeutic gains.
4. *Empower the client.* Clients should feel a sense of empowerment and an ability to resolve their own problems. This can be done not just by reviewing the gains, but also by reviewing the client's contribution to the therapeutic process. Expressing confidence in the client's future may also help the client feel empowered and may even act as a self-fulfilling prophecy.
5. *Create a more egalitarian relationship.* A more egalitarian relationship can be done by increasing the personal revelations of the therapist and initiating direct discussions of the therapeutic process (Curtis, 2002; Fox, 1993; Greenberg, 2002). Another mechanism is to focus on the client's initiative and actions that led to the therapeutic change.
6. *Discuss future problems.* An important task of the termination stage is to discuss possible problems that may occur in the future, and various actions and coping skills the client may utilize to solve them.
7. *Address the possibility of relapse.* Clients should be aware of the possibility of relapse, especially with disorders such as depression. The client should learn to recognize early warning signs, that would allow her to seek help sooner rather than later. The client should be made aware that such a relapse is not a failure and that the therapist would be available to the client, if such a relapse, or another problem, occurs.
8. *Consider attribution of responsibility for therapeutic failure.* When psychotherapies end due to the client's lack of improvement, the therapist should explain to the client that it is the therapy that has failed the individual, rather than the individual that has failed the therapy. Moreover, the therapist should point to other therapies that may help the client, such as pharmacotherapy or different orientations, and encourage the client to continue in his or her search for a cure, in spite of the failure (Greenberg, 2002).
9. *Asking questions about the therapy.* It is useful to ask the client about the psychotherapy and to inquire what was helpful,

what was not helpful, and what the client felt led to the therapeutic gains. Such questions will allow the therapist to view the therapy through the client's eyes and perhaps alter therapeutic techniques with other clients.

10. *Address post-termination contacts.* It is helpful if therapists inquire of clients what sort of conversation they want and how they should be introduced should they encounter each other elsewhere in the future. Depending upon the type of termination and many other factors, the therapist may wish to tell the client to feel free to return in the future should another problem develop where the client thinks the therapist might be helpful.
11. *Express hope of hearing from the client.* Therapists may wish to tell clients that they would be pleased to hear from them at some point in the future. Hearing from clients after the therapy has ended allows therapists to find out more about the effects of the therapy and to listen to clients' views after some time has passed. Moreover, it is an extremely human wish to know what happened to a person whom one has known well, and there is no reason for denying this to the therapist (Curtis, 2002).

ASSESSING AND AVOIDING PREMATURE TERMINATIONS

Because of the serious consequences of premature termination, therapists should routinely assess at the outset of treatment those variables associated with clients' ending treatment prematurely. These include delays in the commencement of treatment, missing sessions, history of alcohol or drug abuse, self-destructiveness, unemployment, paranoid ideation, divorced marital status, lack of health insurance, closed-mindedness, problems in relationship formation, somatization, narcissism, paucity of a support system, seeing the therapist as not trustworthy and not expert, weak alliance with the therapist, low in contemplation of change, low in self-reevaluation, low in self-liberation, and clients who have not changed much in their lives before treatment.

SPECIAL CONSIDERATIONS FOR CHILD THERAPY

Most of the guidelines elaborated in this chapter apply also to child psychotherapy. Specific case examples of saying goodbye to children are provided by Schmukler (1991). Several matters deserve special consideration.

1. The client often is conceptualized not only as suffering from specific symptoms but also as lagging in development. An important criterion for termination is the resumption of development and the overcoming of the developmental gap. Viewed in this way, the termination is the beginning of a new stage in the child's life (Chazan, 1997).
2. Children who have suffered losses, such as parental loss due to death or divorce, are frequent clients. These children confront a relationship with an inevitable end—that is, entering a relationship with a caregiver who will also leave them. Therefore, the therapy as a whole is endangering a repetition of their loss, with the narcissistic injury and reduced self-esteem. In these cases, the therapy should be geared toward its end from the first session. Announcing the therapeutic termination a few weeks, or even months, before the termination date may not be sufficient with children who have already suffered caregiver separation traumas. The therapist is advised to encourage verbalizations of reactions toward termination even when the termination is not imminent (Bembry & Ericson, 1999).
3. Unlike adult treatment, which is dyadic, child treatment is usually a triangular relationship, involving the child, the therapist, and the child's caregivers. The latter, through their financial control and their emotional power on the child, are in a unique position to prematurely terminate the therapy. The risk of premature termination is especially strong in child therapies,

and the degree of threat can be a derivative of the parents' internalized hostility (Venable & Thompson, 1998), their wish to avoid the guilt implied by the fact that their child is in need of a therapy (Hailparn & Hailparn, 2000), or their own relationship with the therapist. A child therapist should try to assess the caregivers' commitment, attempt to involve them in the beginning stages of the therapy, assuage their guilt by praising their dedication and care for the child whom they bring to therapy, and remain aware of the effect of the therapy on the parents (Hailparn & Hailparn, 2000).

4. The wish to hear about the client's progress after the therapy has been completed is more prevalent and accepted in child therapies (Chazan, 1997). Further interventions can be suggested if the need arises.

References & Readings

Bembry, J. X., & Ericson, C. (1999). Therapeutic termination with the early adolescent who has experienced multiple losses. *Child & Adolescent Social Work Journal, 16,* 177–189.

Chazan, S. E. (1997). Ending child psychotherapy: Continuing the cycle of life. *Psychoanalytic Psychology, 14,* 221–238.

Curtis, R. (2002). Termination from a psychoanalytic perspective. *Journal of Psychotherapy Integration, 12,* 350–357.

Fox, R. (1993). *Elements of the helping process: A guide for clinicians.* New York: Haworth.

Frank, G. (1999). Termination revisited. *Psychoanalytic Psychology, 16,* 119–129.

Garcia-Lawson, K. A., & Lane, R. C. (1997). Thoughts on termination: Practical considerations. *Psychoanalytic Psychology, 14,* 239–257.

Goldfried, M. R. (2002). A cognitive-behavioral perspective on termination. *Journal of Psychotherapy Integration, 12,* 364–372.

Greenberg, L. S. (2002). Termination of experiential therapy. *Journal of Psychotherapy Integration, 12,* 358–363.

Hailparn, D. F., & Hailparn, M. (2000). Parent as saboteur in the therapeutic treatment of children. *Journal of Contemporary Psychotherapy, 30,* 341–351.

Schmukler, A. G. (Ed.). (1991). *Saying goodbye: A casebook of termination in child and adolescent analysis and therapy.* Hillsdale, NJ: Analytic Press.

Tyson, P. (1996). Termination of psychoanalysis and psychotherapy. In E. Neressian & R. G. Kopf (Eds.), *Textbook of psychoanalysis* (pp. 501–524). Washington, DC: American Psychiatric Press.

Venable, W. M., & Thompson, B. (1998). Caretaker psychological factors predicting premature termination of children's counseling. *Journal of Counseling & Development, 76,* 286–293.

Weiner, I. B. (1998). *Principles of psychotherapy* (2nd ed.). New York: Wiley.

Weissman, M. M., Markowitz, J. C., & Klerman, G. L. (2000). *Comprehensive guide to interpersonal psychotherapy.* New York: Basic Books.

Werner, H. D. (1982). *Cognitive therapy: A humanistic approach.* London: Collier Macmillan.

Related Topics

Chapter 73, "Early Termination and Referral of Clients in Psychotherapy"

Chapter 121, "A Model for Clinical Decision Making With Dangerous Patients"

PART IV

Couples, Family, and Group Treatment

76 CHOICE OF TREATMENT FORMAT

John F. Clarkin

The goal of psychological treatment is symptom relief, whether it be one or a constellation of symptoms or conflicts in interpersonal relationships. However, for the mental health professional operating on a clinical (i.e., single case) basis, making the initial probes required to determine a treatment plan necessitates focusing on patient symptoms and diagnosis, the natural course of those symptoms, the personality of the patient, and process and mediating goals of the therapy. The key treatment planning factors include the patient's diagnosis and related problem areas; mediating and final goals of treatment; patient enabling factors; and treatment choice points (treatment setting, format, technique, somatic treatments, and duration and frequency; Clarkin, Frances, & Perry, 1992). The focus of this chapter is to articulate the principles guiding the choice of treatment format (i.e., individual, couples/family, group), given the information of patient diagnosis and mediating and final goals of treatment. Table 1 summarizes several of these selection criteria.

Because the individual treatment format is familiar, private, relatively flexible, and built on the basic trust inherent in a dyadic relationship, it remains the most prevalent format of psychological treatment. Over the past 40 years, partly because the limitations of an individual format have become more widely appreciated and partly because the field has shifted toward interpersonal models, clinicians have increasingly used couples/family and group treatment formats.

There are clinical, cultural, and economic issues that guide the clinician in choosing among individual, couples/family, and group treatment formats: (a) patient problem/diagnosis; (b) problem demonstration, that is, in marital, family, or group display; (c) model of treatment intervention; (d) patient preference; and (e) efficiency of treatment.

TABLE 1. Selection Criteria for Format: Individual, Couples/Family, and Group

Individual	Couples/Family	Group
1. Adolescent who is striving for autonomy 2. Patient symptoms based on internal conflict that is expressed in environmental situations	1. Relationship problems are presented as such 2. Symptoms are predominantly within the couples/family situation 3. Family presents with current structured difficulties in its relationships 4. Adolescent acting-out behavior 5. Sexual dysfunction in a couple	1. Patient's problems are interpersonal, both outside and inside family situations. 2. Patient presents with problems that fit the focus of specialized groups (e.g., alcohol or drug abuse)

PATIENT PROBLEM/DIAGNOSIS

Many patient problems and diagnoses lend themselves to specific treatment formats. For example, a sexual dysfunction with one's spouse in the context of marital disputes and with no physical reasons for the dysfunction may lend itself to treatment in the couples format, where the contributions of both parties to the dysfunction can be identified and explored. Alternately, an adolescent acting-out problem can be explored in the family therapy context to address a possible interaction between adolescent impulsivity and parental skills in setting limits.

The Axis V diagnosis or GAF rating may be of particular importance in choosing a treatment format. Independently of the particular Axis I (and Axis II) diagnosis, the relative level of the GAF score may relate to the nature and process of differential treatment planning. In several contexts it has been suggested that relatively healthy individuals (those with GAF scores roughly between 100 and 70) are most likely to respond to most formats of therapeutic intervention and may even be the most likely to be able to cope with difficulties without intervention. At the other end of the spectrum, those patients with severe and chronic difficulties (with GAF scores of roughly 30 to 0) may improve relatively little from most interventions without the assistance of significant others. This would suggest a family format of treatment.

PROBLEM DEMONSTRATION

Where is the problem presented by the individual patient demonstrated? For example, is it a hostility problem in a 43-year-old male who has this problem with his wife but not in social and work situations? Or, alternately, is he hostile in multiple environments in his life? Thus, the environment in which the problem arises is a clue to the selection of the treatment format.

MEDIATING GOALS OF TREATMENT

The alleviation of a particular symptom complex is the typical final goal of treatment. However, the mediating goals of treatment—those intermediate goals that must be reached in order to achieve the final goals—are not always so obvious. They are dictated by the model of the diagnosis/problem area or successive steps to health. These mediating goals will depend on the particular diagnosis/problem area, the theoretical orientation of the assessor, and current understanding of the particular problem area in question. The nature and extent of these mediating goals provide the indications for the therapeutic formats, strategies/techniques, somatic treatments, and treatment durations. Therefore, in the evaluation and treatment planning, the clinician must be as precise as possible about the mediating goals of treatment.

These mediating goals of treatment go beyond the mere description of the symptoms and hypothesize causal relationships between the symptoms and other biological, intrapsychic, and environmental factors. There are many pathways to a common descriptive diagnosis of, for example, major depression (Beutler, Clarkin, & Bangar, 2000). Thus, treatment will depend not only on the descriptive diagnosis but also on the variables that contribute to this symptom state.

The phrase "mediating goals of treatment" refers to those essential subgoals that must be achieved for the treatment or combination of treatments to achieve their final goal. There are two types of mediating goals: (a) the goals of the treatment process itself and (b) the successive approximations to health that are expected to occur sequentially in the patient's/family's behavior. The former goals are related to the enabling factors that the patient brings to therapy; the latter are related to the model of the illness that is being treated and to the particular school of therapy and its understanding of the covariance of certain patient behaviors.

One can articulate mediating goals of treatment that are consistent with each of the treatment formats. Individual treatment is consistent with mediating goals of changes in the individual patient's cognitions and attitudes. Couples treatment is consistent with mediating goals of changes in the interaction between two partners. Family treatment is congruent with changes in parenting behavior toward a child or adolescent. Group treatment is consistent with goals in the change of social behavior in the individual.

PATIENT PREFERENCE

Most patients, as thinking individuals and problem solvers in their own right, have hypotheses about what caused their problems and what changes are necessary to alleviate them. Couples who call a therapist for conjoint treatment have a different conceptualization of the problem than a married individual who calls for individual treatment. The family that sends the adolescent to individual treatment is different from the family that together seeks assistance in dealing with the teenager's acting out. These patient preferences for a particular treatment format confront the clinician with a decision. The clinician should heed the ideas of the patient, at least initially, and whenever possible follow the treatment preferences of the patient and significant others.

TREATMENT EFFICIENCY

Psychologists increasingly function in a managed care world that emphasizes treatment efficiency. The most efficient treatment format is obviously group treatment, in which one (or two) professionals can treat some eight patients at one time. Therefore, a guiding issue is what treatment can be delivered as effectively in a group format as in other formats? In fact, there may be situations in which the group format is not only more efficient than the individual format but also more effective because of the mutual support and confrontation of fellow patients.

References & Readings

Beutler, L. E., & Clarkin, J. F. (1990). *Systematic treatment selection.* New York: Brunner/Mazel.

Beutler, L. E., Clarkin, J. F., & Bangar, B. (2000). *Guidelines for the systematic treatment of the depressed patient.* New York: Oxford University Press.

Clarkin, J. F., Frances, A., & Perry, S. (1992). Differential therapeutics: Macro and micro levels of treatment planning. In J. Norcross & M. Goldfried (Eds.), *Handbook of psychotherapy integration.* New York: Basic Books.

Feldman, L. B. (1992). *Integrating individual and family therapy.* New York: Brunner/Mazel.

Frances, A., Clarkin, J. F., & Perry, S. (1984). *Differential therapeutics: A guide to the art and science of treatment planning in psychiatry.* New York: Brunner/Mazel.

Perry, S., Frances, A., & Clarkin, J. F. (1990). *A DSM-III-R casebook of treatment selection.* New York: Brunner/Mazel.

Pinsof, W. M. (1995). *Integrative problem-centered therapy.* New York: Basic Books.

Related Topics

Chapter 39, "Compendium of Empirically Supported Therapies"

Chapter 45, "Systematic Assessment and Treatment Matching"

Chapter 47, "Psychotherapy Treatment Plan Writing"

77 GENOGRAMS IN ASSESSMENT AND THERAPY

Sueli S. Petry & Monica McGoldrick

The *genogram* is a practical, visual tool for assessment of family patterns and context, as well as a therapeutic intervention in itself. Genograms allow clinicians to quickly conceptualize the individual's context within the growing diversity of family forms and patterns in our society. Using the genogram to collect historical and contextual assessment information is a collaborative, client-centered therapeutic process. By its nature, the process involves the telling of stories and emphasizes respect for the client's perspective, while encouraging multiple views and possible outcomes. While the genogram has been used for decades, it is a tool in progress, and clinicians use it for assessment of functioning, relational patterns, ethnicity, spirituality, migration, class, and other socioeconomic factors (Carter & McGoldrick, 1999; Congress, 1994; Dunn & Dawes, 1999; Hardy & Laszloffy, 1995; McGoldrick, 1995, 1998; McGoldrick, Giordano, & Pearce, 1996; Walsh, 1999) and for therapeutic interventions such as the creative play therapy genogram (Gil, 2002, 2003).

Gathering genogram information should be seen as an integral part of a comprehensive, clinical assessment. There is no quantitative measurement scale by which the clinician can use a genogram in a cookbook fashion to make clinical predictions. Rather, the genogram is a subjective, interpretive tool that enables clinicians to generate tentative hypotheses for further evaluation in a family assessment. Typically, the genogram is constructed from information gathered during the first session and revised as new information becomes available. Thus, the initial assessment forms the basis for treatment. Of course, we cannot compartmentalize assessment and treatment. Each interaction with the family informs the assessment and thus influences the next intervention.

We include on the genogram the nuclear and extended family members, as well as significant nonblood "kin" who have ever lived with or played a major role in the family's life. We also note on the side of the genogram significant events and problems (Figure 1). Current behavior and problems of family members can be traced on the genogram from multiple perspectives. The index person (the IP, or person with the problem or symptom) may be viewed in the context of various subsystems, such as siblings, triangles, and reciprocal relationships, or in relation to the broader community, social institutions (schools, courts, etc.), and sociocultural context.

The genogram usually includes cultural and demographic information about at least three generations of family members, as well as nodal and critical events in the family's history, particularly as related to family changes (migration, loss, and the life cycle). When family members are questioned about the present situation in relation to the themes, myths, rules, and emotionally charged issues of previous generations, repetitive patterns become clear. Copies of both figures and more extensive illustrative genogram materials are included on the Web site accompanying this book.

THE FAMILY INFORMATION NET

The process of gathering family information can be thought of as casting out an information net in larger and larger circles to capture rele-

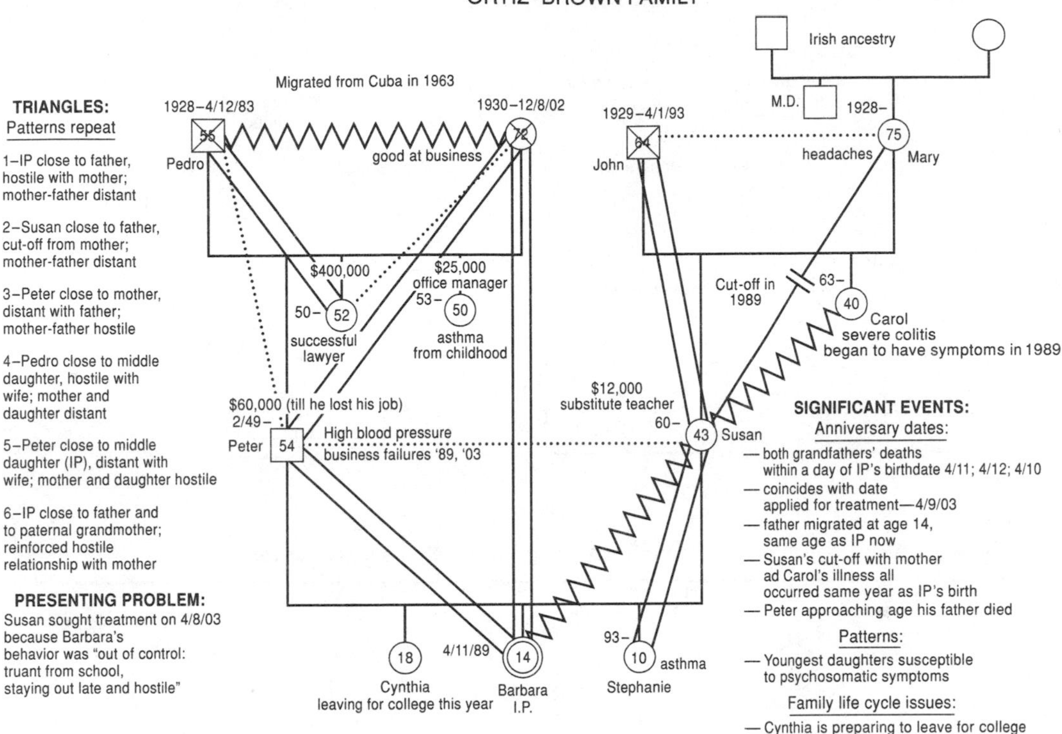

FIGURE 1 Ortiz-Brown Family Genogram

vant information about the family and its broader context. The net spreads out in a number of different directions:

- From the presenting problem to the larger context of the problem
- From the immediate household to the extended family and broader social systems
- From the present family situation to a chronology of historical family events
- From easy, nonthreatening queries to difficult, anxiety-provoking questions
- From obvious facts to judgments about functioning and relationships to hypothesized family patterns

The IP usually comes with specific problems, which are the clinician's starting point. At the outset, the IP is told that some basic information about the family is needed to fully understand the problem. Such information usually grows naturally out of exploring the presenting problem and its impact on the immediate household. The clinician asks the name, age, gender, and occupation of each person in the household in order to sketch the immediate family structure. Other revealing information is elicited through inquiring about the problem. This is also a good time to inquire about previous efforts to get help for the problem, including previous treatment, therapists, hospitalizations, and the current referring person.

Next the clinician spreads the information net into the current family situation. This line of questioning usually follows naturally from questions about the problem and who is involved:

- What has been happening recently in your family?
- Have there been any recent changes in the family (e.g., people coming or leaving, illnesses, job problems)?

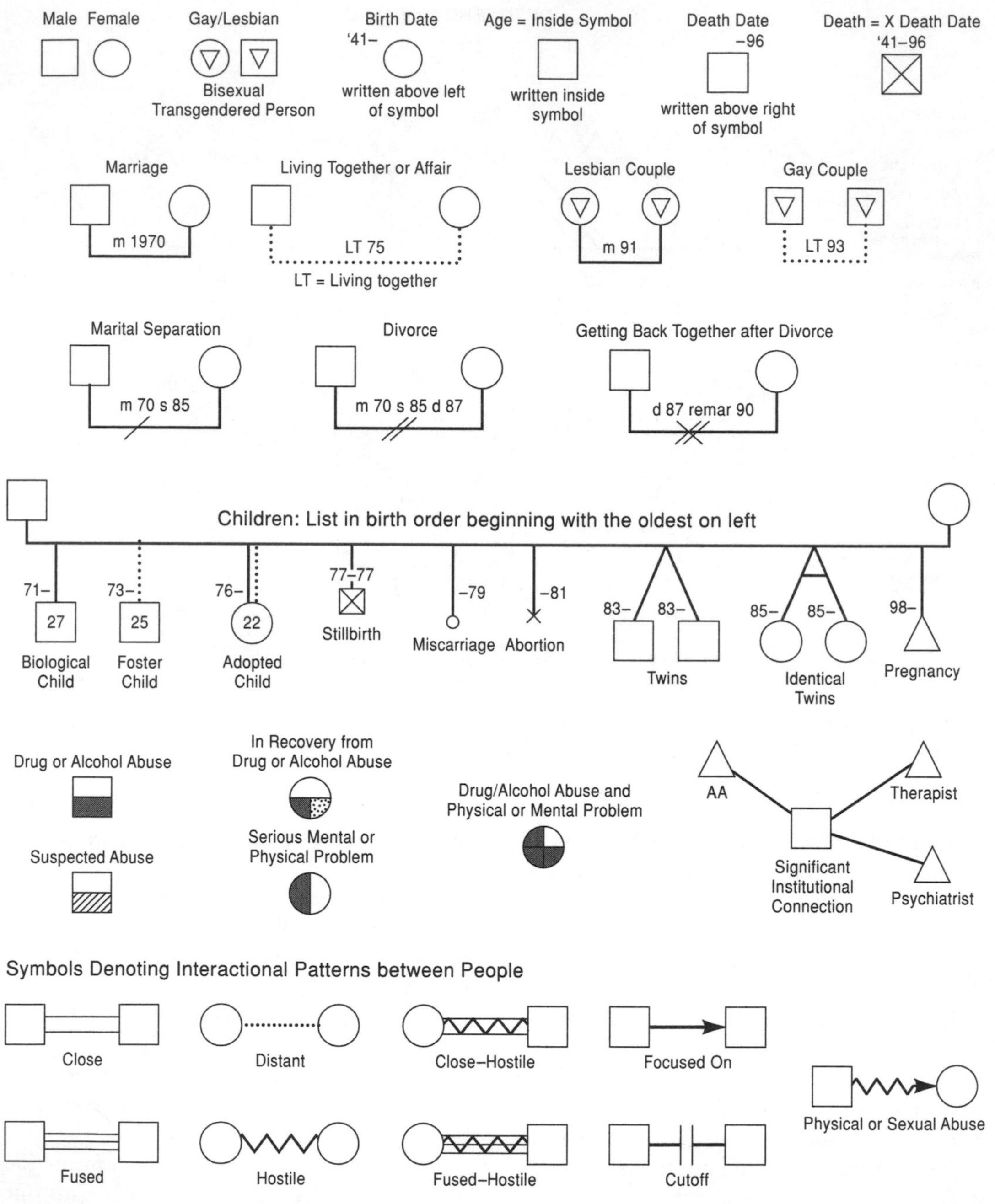

FIGURE 2 Standard Symbols of Genograms

It is important to inquire about recent life cycle transitions as well as anticipated changes in the family situation (especially exits and entrances of family members—births, marriages, divorces, deaths, or the departure of family members).

The clinician looks for an opportunity to explore the wider family context by asking about the extended family and cultural background of all the adults involved. The interviewer might move into this area by saying, "I would now like to ask you something about your background to help make sense of your present problem."

DEALING WITH A FAMILY'S RESISTANCE TO DOING A GENOGRAM

When family members react negatively to questions about the extended family or complain that such matters are irrelevant, it often makes sense to redirect the focus back to the immediate situation until the connections between the present situation and other family relationships or experiences can be established. Gentle persistence over time will usually result in obtaining the information and demonstrating its relevance to the family.

The clinician inquires about each side of the family separately, beginning, for example, with the mother's side:

- Let's begin with your mother's family. Your mother was which one of how many children?
- When and where was she born?
- Is she alive? If not, when did she die? What was the cause of her death?
- If alive, where is she now? What does she do? How is her health?
- When and how did your mother meet your father? When did they marry?
- Had she been married before? If so, when? Did she have children by that marriage?
- Did they separate or divorce or did the spouse die? If so, when was that?

And so on. In like fashion, questions are asked about the father. Then the clinician might ask about each parent's family of origin (i.e., father, mother, and siblings). The goal is to get information about at least three or four generations, including grandparents, parents, aunts, uncles, siblings, spouses, and children of the IP.

ETHNIC AND CULTURAL HISTORY

It is essential to learn something about the family's socioeconomic, political, and cultural background in order to place presenting problems and current relationships in context. When the questioning expands to the extended family, it is a good point to begin exploring issues of ethnicity, since the birthplace of the grandparents has now been established. Exploring ethnicity and migration history helps establish the cultural context in which the family is operating and offers the therapist an opportunity to validate family attitudes and behaviors determined by such influences. It is important to learn what the family's cultural traditions are about problems, health care, and healing, and where the current family members stand in relation to those traditional values. It is also important to consider the family's cultural expectations about relationships with health care professionals, since this will set the tone for their clinical responses.

Furthermore, class background between family members or between family members and the health care professional may create discomfort, which will need to be attended to in the meeting. Questions to ascertain class assumptions pertain not just to the family's current income but also to cultural background, education, and social status within their community. Once the clinician has a clear picture of the ethnic and cultural factors influencing a family (and, it is hoped, keeping his or her own biases in check), it is possible to raise delicate questions geared to helping families identify any behaviors that—while culturally sanctioned—may be keeping them stuck, such as traditional gender roles (see McGoldrick et al., 1996).

DIFFICULT QUESTIONS ABOUT INDIVIDUAL FUNCTIONING

Assessment of individual functioning may or may not involve much clinical judgment. Alcohol abuse, chronic unemployment, and severe symptomatology are facts that directly indicate poor functioning. However, many family members may function well in some areas but not in others or may cover up their dysfunction. Often, it takes careful questioning to reveal the true level of functioning. A family member with a severe illness may show remarkable adaptive strengths and another may show fragility with little apparent stress. Questions about individual functioning may be difficult or painful for family members to answer and must be approached with sensitivity and tact. The family members should be warned that questions may be difficult and they should let the clinician know if there is an issue they would rather not discuss. The clinician will need to judge the degree of pressure to apply if the family resists questions that may be essential to dealing with the presenting problem.

Clinicians need to exercise extreme caution about when to ask questions that could put a family member in danger. For example, if violence is suspected, a wife should never be asked about her husband's behavior in his presence, since the question assumes she is free to respond, which may not be the case. It is the clinician's responsibility to take care that the questions do not put a client in jeopardy.

SETTING PRIORITIES FOR ORGANIZING GENOGRAM INFORMATION

One of the most difficult aspects of genogram assessment remains setting priorities for inclusion of family information on a genogram. Clinicians cannot follow every lead the genogram interview suggests. Awareness of basic genogram patterns can help the clinician set such priorities. As a rule of thumb, the data are scanned for the following:

- Repetitive symptoms, relationship, or functioning patterns across the family and over the generations. Repeated triangles, coalitions, cut-offs, patterns of conflict, over- and under-functioning are central to genogram interpretation.
- Coincidences of dates. For example, the death of one family member or anniversary of this death occurring at the same time as symptom onset in another, or the age at symptom onset coinciding with the age of problem development in another family member.
- The impact of change and untimely life cycle transitions: particularly changes in functioning and relationships that correspond with critical family life events and untimely life cycle transitions—for example, births, marriages, or deaths that occur "off schedule."

Awareness of possible patterns makes the clinician more sensitive to what is missing. Such missing information about important family members or events and discrepancies in the information offered frequently reflects charged emotional issues in the family. The clinician should take careful note of the connections family members make or fail to make to various events.

MAPPING THE GENOGRAMS OF THOSE WHO GROW UP IN MULTIPLE SETTINGS

Many children grow up in multiple settings because their parents divorce, die, remarry, migrate, or have other special circumstances that require the child to live for a while or even permanently in a different setting. Genograms are an exceptionally useful tool to track children's experiences through the life cycle, taking into account the multiple family and other institutional contexts to which they have belonged (Carter & McGoldrick, 1999). The more clearly the clinician tracks the actuality of this history, however complex, the better able he or she is to validate the child's actual experience and multiple forms of belonging. Such a map can begin to make order out of the at times chaotic placement changes a child must go through when sudden transitions or shifts in placement are necessary because of illness, trauma, or other loss. It can also help validate for a child the realities of his or her birth and life connections that vary from traditional norms.

Sometimes the only feasible way to clarify where children were raised is to take chronological notes on each child in a family and then transform them into a series of genograms that show the family context each child has grown up in. When the "functional" family is different from the biological or legal family, as when children are raised by a grandparent or in an informal adoptive family, it is useful to create a separate genogram to show the functional structure (see Watts Jones, 1998). Where children have lived as part of several families—biological, foster, and adoptive—separate genograms may help to depict the child's multiple families over time.

PLAY GENOGRAMS FOR INDIVIDUAL CHILD AND FAMILY THERAPY

Gil (2002, 2003) developed the *play genogram* technique during her consultations at the Multicultural Family Institute in Highland Park, New Jersey, as a natural expansion of the assessment and therapeutic benefits of the genogram. The play genogram can be used with individual children, and with families, as an assessment tool and to facilitate therapeutic conversation. The basic genogram is drawn on a large sheet of easel paper. When working with individual children, clinicians invite the child to "choose a miniature that best shows your thoughts and feelings about everyone in the family, including yourself" and to place the miniature on the squares and circles on the easel paper. The clinician may give reluctant children examples of concrete and abstract choices to encourage the child to explore choices freely. When completed, the individual play genogram will have one miniature on each circle or square.

Some individuals may use more than one miniature to represent family members. This may reflect the complexity of a relationship or self-image. When working with children in foster care or other family situations where children have had multiple caretakers, it is helpful to construct a series of genograms on the same sheet of paper. Children may include friends, therapists, teachers, pets, or other important relationships, both past and present. This helps children to reference and prioritize their world and gives the clinician a complex, yet easily scanned assessment.

The directives for the family play genogram are the same as for individuals: clinicians help the family to construct a genogram of their immediate and extended family, then family members are asked to choose a miniature that best shows their thoughts and feelings about everyone in the family, including themselves. Clinicians observe the selection process for the type and level of interactions between family members. The interactions between family members will inform the clinician about the family's current relationship styles and patterns of relating. Encouraging family members to make their choices at the same time will yield a broader range of assessment information. Conflicts about specific miniatures are more likely to arise when the family is engaged in activity together, and as conflicts arise the clinician observes the family patterns of problem solving.

When everyone has made his or her choice, family members are encouraged to look at the family play genogram, and to make comments and ask questions. Clinicians should not ask family members to explain why they chose a particular object. It is more useful to facilitate an open dialogue in which family members volunteer a broad range of information. The first person to speak tends to set the tone for the type of information that will be provided. Thus, the clinician should ask expansive questions in order to promote a more extensive dialogue, for example, "Can you tell me more about that?" (For more details and examples, see accompanying Web site.)

After the initial play genograms, the clinician may request a second level of activity by asking family members to choose a miniature that best represents their relationships with other family members; this yields other valuable information. Clinicians ask permission to take a photograph of the individual or family play genogram. The family may take the photograph home with them to facilitate additional conversation, or clinicians can keep the pictures to recreate play genograms at a later time for a continuation of the therapeutic dialogue. The play genogram technique is just one of the many ways that the genogram facilitates therapy.

CONCLUSION

The genogram, which is a highly condensed map of a rich and complex family, is an awesome lesson to anyone who is unable to see beyond the cutoffs that may occur in a family (McGoldrick, Gerson, & Shellenberger, 1999). We believe that no relationship is to be disregarded or discounted. All our relationships inform the wholeness of who we are and where we come from; more important, they can give us the possibility of making constructive, conscious choices about who we will choose to be in the future.

One of the most powerful aspects of genograms is the way in which they can steer us to the rich ongoing possibilities of complex kin relationships, which continue throughout life to be sources of connection and life support. It is not just our shared history that matters but also the spiritual power of our history of survival, as well as our current connections that strengthen us and can enrich our future. All our relationships inform the wholeness of who we are and where we came from, and more important, can give us the possibility of making constructive and conscious choices about who we will choose to become.

GENOGRAM FORMAT

The following section provides fundamental instructions for completion of the relevant genogram elements as illustrated in the accompanying sample genograms.

A. *Symbols.* These describe basic family membership and structure (include on genogram significant others who lived with or cared for family members—place them on the side of the genogram with a notation about who they are).

B. *Family interaction patterns.* The relationship indicators are optional. The clinician may prefer to note them on a separate sheet. They are among the least precise information on the genogram, but may be key indicators of relationship patterns the clinician wants to remember.

C. *Medical history.* Since the genogram is meant to be an orienting map of the family, there is room to indicate only the most important factors. Thus, list only major or chronic illnesses and problems. Include dates in parentheses where feasible or applicable. Use *DSM-IV* categories or recognized abbreviations where available (e.g., cancer: CA, stroke: CVA).

D. *Other information.* Family information of special importance may also be noted on the genogram: (1) ethnic background and migration date; (2) religion or religious change; (3) education; (4) occupation or unemployment; (5) military service; (6) retirement; (7) trouble with the law; (8) physical or sexual abuse or incest; (9) obesity; (10) alcohol or drug abuse; (11) smoking; (12) dates when family members left home: LH '74; and (13) current location of family members. It is useful to have a space at the bottom of the genogram for notes or other key information. This would include critical events, changes in the family structure since the genogram was made, hypotheses, and other notations of major family issues or changes. These notations should always be dated, and should be kept to a minimum, since every extra piece of information on a genogram complicates it and therefore diminishes its readability.

References & Readings 

Carter, B., & McGoldrick, M. (Eds.). (1999). *The expanded family life cycle: Individual, family and social perspectives* (3rd ed.). Boston: Allyn & Bacon.

Congress, E. P. (1994, November). The use of culturagrams to assess and empower culturally diverse families. *Families in Society, 79,* 531–540.

Dunn, A. B., & Dawes, S. J. (1999). Spiritually-focused genograms: Keys to uncovering spiritual resources in African American families. *Journal of Multicultural Counseling & Development, 27*(4), 240–255.

Gil, E. (2002). *Family play therapy: Rationale and techniques.* [Videotape and accompanying text.] Fairfax, VA: Starbright Training Institute for Family and Child Play Therapy.

Gil, E. (2003). Play genograms. In C. F. Sori & L. L. Hecker (Eds.), *The therapist's notebook for children and adolescents: Homework, handouts, and activities for use in psychotherapy* (pp. 97–118). New York: Haworth Press.

Hardy, K. V., & Laszloffy, T. A. (1995). The cultural genogram: Key to training culturally competent family therapists. *Journal of Marital and Family Therapy, 21*(3), 227–237.

McGoldrick, M. (1995). *You can go home again: Reconnecting with your family*. New York: Norton.

McGoldrick, M. (Ed.). (1998). *Revisioning family therapy: Culture, class, race, and gender*. New York: Guilford Press.

McGoldrick, M., Gerson, R., & Shellenberger, S. (1999). *Genograms: Assessment and intervention* (2nd ed.). New York: Norton.

McGoldrick, M., Giordano, J., & Pearce, J. K. (Eds.) (1996). *Ethnicity and family therapy* (2nd ed.). New York: Guilford Press.

Walsh, F. (Ed.). (1999). *Spiritual resources in family therapy*. New York: Guilford Press.

Watts Jones, D. (1998). Towards an African-American genogram. *Family Process, 36*(4), 373–383.

Related Topic

Chapter 4, "The Multimodal Life History Inventory"

78 GUIDELINES FOR CONDUCTING COUPLE AND FAMILY THERAPY

Jay L. Lebow

The following guidelines stem from a review of the couple and family therapy literature; from research assessing couples, families, and couple and family therapy; and from clinical experience. The goal of this chapter is to suggest widely accepted generic guidelines for practice that transcend the numerous schools of couple and family therapy.

1. *Develop a systemic perspective:* A system consists of interacting components; in a family, these include such subsystems as couple, sibling, and individual. Individuals do not function in a vacuum but continually influence one another through feedback.
2. *Always consider context in attempting to understand couples and families:* Behavior that appears to make little sense often emerges as far more understandable when the surrounding conditions are understood. For example, a child's school phobia or a spouse's depression frequently becomes more intelligible when its meaning in the life of the family system is recognized.
3. *Understand multiple perspectives:* The therapist should attempt to grasp and communicate understanding of the respective viewpoints of various family members, which may vary considerably.
4. *Examine potential circular pathways of causality that may maintain problems:* The therapist should attempt to understand ways in which family members are influenced within circular pathways in which the behavior, thoughts, and feelings of one person promote those of another, which in turn promote those of the first person. Al-

though not all causal pathways are circular, and even among circular causal chains the participation of family members may not be coequal, such cycles frequently block problem resolution. For example, parents' angry and punitive behavior may both lead to and flow from the acting-out behavior of a child. Regardless of where the cycle begins, the punitive behavior by the parents leads to more acting out by the child, which, in turn, leads to more parental punitive behavior.

5. *Respect the diversity of family forms:* Families assume many forms, including single-parent, remarried, and gay and lesbian. The therapist should become knowledgeable about typical life across this range of forms and, along with the families, should develop therapeutic goals that honor the family's form and culture.
6. *Understand the special ethical considerations of couple and family therapy, particularly concerning confidentiality:* Couple and family therapists face special ethical dilemmas, such as deciding who is the client and who is entitled to confidentiality of communication. All individuals who attend conjoint sessions become clients and should retain the same rights. In couple and family therapy, confidentiality should be broken only with agreement of all participants, except in those circumstances in which legal duty to report or warn takes precedence. The therapist should articulate a clear position about confidentiality for confidences made outside of sessions, as well as for when participants vary across sessions. Therapists should understand state law about these and similar matters, as well as ethical guidelines.
7. *Begin assessment and intervention with the first phone call:* Couple and family therapies require more effort before the first session on the part of the therapist than do other therapies. Active efforts before the first session to engage family members who are clearly important to the problem or its solution substantially increase participation in therapy and thereby impact on treatment outcome.
8. *Determine and clarify who will be included in treatment:* There are a variety of methods in family therapy, ranging from some that include multiple generations to others that include only a few or even one member of the family. Who is and who is not part of the therapy always needs to be clearly designated and understood. In general, it is easier to include additional members of the family earlier in treatment, rather than later, by which time alliances are well set. Involving fathers as well as mothers (who tend more readily to make themselves available) in the treatment of children promotes better outcome.
9. *Begin with an emphasis on engagement and alliance building:* The therapist must build an alliance with each member of the family, with each subsystem, and with the family as a whole. Techniques such as eliciting input from each family member, joining with each around some aspect of the problem, and assimilating and adapting to the culture of the family help build such alliances. Pay particular attention to the alliance with those member(s) of the family who have most say in whether the therapy will continue. Alliance with the therapist appears to predict outcome regardless of the form of couple or family therapy.
10. *Assess through history gathering and observing interaction:* Assessment should have multiple foci, including the family system, its subsystems, and individuals. Assessment typically is *intermingled* with treatment, rather than a distinct phase. The intervention *strategy* should be grounded in the assessment.
11. *Understand that certain difficulties in family life are grossly underreported:* Family violence, sexual abuse, infidelity, alcoholism, and drug abuse, among other problems, are typically reported at much lower frequencies than they occur. Inquire about them in a standard noninvasive way.
12. *Understand each client's expectations and how well they are satisfied:* Family members bring a range of expectations about such issues as money, sex, and intimacy.

These expectations are manifested at several levels ranging from expectations about behavior to expectations about deeper levels of object relations. Relationship satisfaction is often more the product of unmet expectations than of particular problematic patterns. Help family members articulate and negotiate their expectations.

13. *Compile a genogram to understand how family of origin factors affect the system:* Elaborating on who is in the extended family, what the key experiences have been in the life of the family, and repetitive issues across the generations increases mutual understanding, promotes the working through of experiences, and potentially sets the stage for exploring individual and interactive patterns.
14. *Remember that couple and family therapy is usually brief:* Families typically are only willing to engage in therapies of under 10 sessions. Keep therapy accordingly focused.
15. *Promote better family relationships:* Relationships have a variety of positive effects beyond their intrinsic value in promoting better individual mental health, individual health, and child functioning.
16. *Promote solutions, a focus on coping, and a view of family health:* Families respond far better to a focus on creating solutions. Reframe behavior in a form that can be more positively understood. Stress the normal developmental aspects of what the couple or family is experiencing.
17. *Negotiate clear goals for treatment:* Family life presents endless possible goals, and participants often begin with varying agendas. Negotiating an agreed set of goals for therapy is an essential task early in treatment. Goals may be added or modified as therapy progresses.
18. *Establish control:* Therapists in couple and family therapy must intervene actively to move clients from habitual patterns. For example, the therapist must be able to interrupt habitual patterns of destructive arguing in couples.
19. *Develop a clear plan:* Couple and family therapy is innately complex and typically has multiple foci. A clear road map mitigates the dangers of losing focus. This road map may require revision as treatment progresses.
20. *Employ individual, biological, couple, family, and macrosystemic interventions in the context of the treatment:* Empirical support is strongest for approaches that combine intervention with the whole family with other intervention strategies. Treatment of severe mental illness almost invariably should include the use of medication; treatment of adolescent disorders focuses on school and peer systems; and treatment of depression should include "individual" intervention that addresses the depression.
21. *Teach empathy, communication, how to deliver reinforcement, and other skills when such skills are inadequately developed:* Many couples and family members lack the requisite skills to perform essential conjoint tasks. Instruction, modeling, in-session practice, and homework can help family members master these skills. Such instruction and practice can help premarital couples significantly reduce their risk of divorce and parents reduce the likelihood of child behavior problems.
22. *Suggest tasks that have a high likelihood of being carried out successfully:* Suggestions that are not followed are likely to increase client reactivity and resistance. For example, repeatedly proposing communication exercises to a family that is not ready to utilize them is likely to retard progress.
23. *Develop contracts between family members that are mutually satisfying:* Couples and families who are dissatisfied with their relationships typically have much lower rates of positive exchange and higher rates of coercion. Negotiating positive quid pro quo exchanges leads to more satisfying relationships.
24. *Promote clear family structure:* Flexible yet clear boundaries, stable yet not rigid patterns of alliance, and an age-appropriate distribution of power promote family health.
25. *Understand the personal narratives of fam-*

ily members and promote the development of a positive understanding of the narratives of other family members: The stories created by family members often carry with them the seeds of difficulties. Examining these narratives and helping create new ones that frame motives and behaviors in a more positive way promote more harmonious family life and problem resolution.

26. *Coach individuals to take responsibility for their own behavior:* Blame leads to endless cycles of misunderstanding and alienation. Helping clients assume an "I" stance about their own behavior helps break such cycles.
27. *Promote the expression of underlying softer affect that lies behind anger and criticism:* Individuals often express defensive reactions rather than feelings such as sadness or fear. Exploring such underlying feelings in a safe environment promotes understanding and empathic connection. For example, uncovering the sad affect that lies behind anger expressed toward a spouse in couple therapy can alter typical dysfunctional patterns of conflict.
28. *See couples with relationship distress conjointly:* Conjoint couples therapy is the only demonstrated effective form of treatment for couple relationship problems. Although spouses who are unhappy with their relationships frequently seek individual therapy, there is no evidence that this helps the couple relationship and some evidence that it has a deleterious effect.
29. *Focus a major part of treatment on conjoint couple therapy when there is coexisting relationship difficulty along with depression in an individual:* Individual treatment of depression does not appear to impact on the relationship problems, and the presence of relationship difficulties predicts poor prognosis over time for depression. Depressed individuals who do not have comorbid couple difficulties do not require couple therapy, although there is benefit from including conjoint sessions centered in psychoeducation about depression as part of the treatment.
30. *Recognize and target Gottman's four signs of severe relationship difficulty and imminent divorce—criticism, contempt, defensiveness, and stonewalling:* Clients presenting such patterns should be warned of their risk of divorce, and initial work should center directly on developing alternative patterns of relating. Couples are unlikely to benefit from treatment unless these signs change.
31. *In divorcing and remarried systems, promote good-enough communication to allow for coparenting:* Help families understand the typical stresses and coping strategies. Refer for mediation if substantial conflicts arise between coparents.
32. *Utilize psychoeducational interventions when dealing with severe mental illness:* Families in which there is severe individual dysfunction often fail to understand the origins of disorders and feel blamed when encountering therapists. An educative stance that teaches about the disorder and about typical family processes is enormously helpful in gaining cooperation and reducing symptoms and recidivism. Reducing expressed emotion (i.e., highly emotional critical affect) appears to have particularly great value in the context of severe mental illness. Treatment that increases emotional arousal and conflict in these families is contraindicated.
33. *In disorganized families, promote the creation of stabilizing rituals:* In particular, families with members with alcohol and substance use disorders fare much better when they maintain such rituals as a regular dinner hour.
34. *In family violence and abuse, protect safety first:* At times, couples and families present in situations where contact is dangerous. The ethical obligation must be first to safety and then to other goals of therapy.
35. *In child behavior problems, train parents to engage in predictable schedules of reinforcement to reward positive behaviors and extinguish problematic behaviors:* Reinforcement may focus on a single behavior or may utilize a point system to focus on a constellation of targets.

36. *In oppositional children and in adolescent conduct disorder and substance abuse, utilize family therapy as part of a multisystemic approach that also addresses other relevant systems, such as school, peer, and legal systems, as well as the individual child, or adolescent:* The relevant social system in these cases does not stop at the boundary of the family but extends into various other domains. Research suggests treatment is more effective when these parts of the social system are considered.
37. *Attend to tasks of termination, such as planning for the future, throughout the treatment:* Families often end treatment abruptly, despite the best efforts of therapists for planned termination. Addressing termination issues as the treatment unfolds lessens the negative effect of unplanned termination.
38. *Assess the impact of treatment on each individual, each subsystem, and the system as a whole, as well as on the presenting problem:* Outcome in family systems is complex, including many stakeholders and numerous foci, such as the presenting problem, individual functioning, and family functioning.
39. *Promote the maintenance of change:* All treatment effects appear to wane over time. Promote maintenance of change through follow-up sessions, tasks, and through the family's continuing homework, and self-monitoring of their processes after treatment.
40. *Be aware of the meanings of gender and culture in therapy:* The therapist's work should be informed by an understanding of the impact of gender and culture. Therapist gender and culture also affect treatment process, regardless of therapist behavior.
41. *Coordinate with other therapists, health providers, and agencies involved with a family:* Coordinating goals and intervention strategies often is a major factor in treatment success; inconsistent goals and methods frequently create obstacles to success.
42. *Utilize couple and family therapies to engage difficult-to-engage cases:* There is considerable evidence that many difficult-to-engage clients, such as alcoholics, substance abusers, and oppositional and delinquent adolescents are more easily engaged with couple and family therapy. Specifically, engaging another member of the family system who recognizes the problem first can dramatically increase the rates of engagement and retention of individuals with these difficulties in treatment.
43. *Consider the effects on the family system of any therapy you conduct:* Potent effects of psychotherapy extend beyond the individual. When seeing a couple, consider the effects on children and extended family. When seeing an individual, consider the effects on spouse, parents, children, and other members of the family.
44. *Expect treatment to have an impact:* Couple and family therapies have been demonstrated to be effective in 75% of cases and have been shown to have effect sizes much like those of individual therapy. Specifically, couple and family therapy has been demonstrated efficacious in helping alleviate couple relationship problems, depression in unhappily married women, schizophrenia, manic-depressive disorder, agoraphobia, panic disorder, adolescent substance abuse, adolescent delinquent behavior, childhood oppositional behavior and conduct disorder, childhood attention deficit disorder, alcohol and substance use disorders, eating disorder, and the psychological consequences of physical illness.

References, Readings, and Internet Sites

Alexander, J. F., Holtzworth-Munroe, A., & Jameson, P. (1994). The process and outcome of marital and family therapy: Research review and evaluation. In A. E. Bergen & S. L. Garfield (Eds.), *Handbook of psychotherapy and behavior change* (4th ed.). New York: Wiley.

American Association of Marriage and Family Therapists. (n.d.). Home page. Retrieved 2004 from http://www.aamft.org

American Family Therapy Academy. (n.d.). Web resources page. Retrieved 2004 from http://www.afta.org/resources.html

American Psychological Association Division of Family Psychology. (n.d.). Home page. Retrieved 2004 from http://www.apa.org/divisions/div43

Family Process. (n.d.) Home page. http://www.familyprocess.org

Goldner, V. (1985). Feminism in family therapy. *Family Process, 24,* 31–48.

Gottman, J. M., & Levenson, R. W. (1992). Marital processes predictive of later dissolution: Behavior, physiology, and health. *Journal of Personality and Social Psychology, 63,* 221–233.

Gurman, A. S., & Jacobson, N. S. (Eds.). (2002). *Clinical handbook of couple therapy* (3rd ed.) New York: Guilford Press.

Gurman, A. S., & Kniskern, D. P. (Eds.). (1981). *Handbook of family therapy.* New York: Brunner/Mazel.

Gurman, A. S., & Kniskern, D. P. (Eds.). (1991). *Handbook of family therapy* (Vol. 2). New York: Brunner/Mazel.

Gurman, A. S., Kniskern, D. P., & Pinsof, W. M. (1986). Research on marital and family therapies. In S. L. Garfield & A. E. Bergin (Eds.), *Handbook of psychotherapy and behavior change* (3rd ed., pp. 565–624). New York: Wiley.

Gurman, A. S., & Lebow, J. (2000). Family and couple therapy. In H. Sadock & R. Sadock *Comprehensive textbook of psychiatry* (Ed.), *VII.* New York: Williams & Wilkins.

Lebow, J. (2000). What does research tell us about couple and family therapies. *Journal of Clinical Psychology: In Session, 56,* 1083–1094.

Lebow, J., & Gurman, A. S. (1995). Research assessing couple and family therapy. *Annual Review of Psychology, 46,* 27–57.

Lebow, J., & Gurman, A. (1998). Family systems and family psychology. In E. Walker (Ed.). *Comprehensive clinical psychology, volume one: Foundations of clinical psychology.* New York: Pergamon.

Lebow, J. (Vol. Ed.), & Kaslow, F. W. (Series Ed.) *Comprehensive handbook of psychotherapy: Vol. 4.* Integrative/Eclectic. New York: Wiley.

MFT Source.com. (n.d.). Home page. Retrieved 2004 from http://www.mftsource.com

Mikesell, R. H., Lusterman, D. D., & McDaniel, S. H. (Eds.) (1995). *Integrating family therapy: Handbook of family psychology and systems therapy.* Washington, DC: American Psychological Association.

Pinsof, W. M., & Wynne, L. (Eds.) (1995). Special issue: The effectiveness of marital and family therapy. *Journal of Marital and Family Therapy, 21.*

Sprenkle, D. H. (Ed.). (2002). *Effectiveness research in marriage and family therapy.* Washington, DC: AAMFT Press.

Walsh, F. (Ed.). (2003). *Normal family processes* (3rd ed.). New York: Guilford Press.

Weeks, G., Sexton, T., & Robbins, M. (Eds.). (2004). *Handbook of family therapy.* New York: Brunner-Mazel.

Related Topics

Chapter 79, "Treating High-Conflict Couples"
Chapter 80, "Treatment of Marital Infidelity"

79 TREATING HIGH-CONFLICT COUPLES

Susan Heitler

1. *Arrange the therapy room for symmetry and interaction:* Place the three chairs in an equilateral triangle. Rollers on the therapist's chair are preferable so that the therapist can roll closer to the couple or to one or the other partner for interventions and then roll back when the couple's dialogue flows cooperatively. Do not seat the couple side by side on a sofa because this arrangement encourages the couple to talk to the therapist rather than to each other.

2. *Set up equipment for audiotaping the treatment sessions:* Explain that you will hand the audiotapes to the couple at the end of each session; the tapes are for them, not for you. Explain that listening to their session tapes as homework can accelerate and consolidate their learning.

Be certain that participants complete a consent-to-taping form (in their initial paperwork) before beginning any recording. Taping is contraindicated if court involvement or divorce proceedings are likely lest the tapes be used in a way that could be detrimental to either participant.

3. *Begin the therapy by welcoming the couple,* and by asking what each partner has come to therapy to accomplish. Alternatively, ask the partners to discuss with each other what they each have come to accomplish. This technique enables you to observe capacity for dialogue at the same time as you secure information about treatment goals.

4. *Obtain a threefold diagnostic picture:*

- A history of each individual's symptoms. Accelerate this assessment by having each partner fill out a symptom checklist before beginning treatment
- A laundry list of conflicts about which the couple fights
- An initial assessment of communication and conflict resolution skills and deficits

This threefold diagnostic workup organizes diagnostic information to correspond to the three main strands of treatment:

- Eliminate symptoms (excessive anger, depression, etc.)
- Resolve each conflict on the laundry list and, in the process of resolving the conflicts, gain understanding of the central problematic relationships of childhood and their reenactments in the marriage (Lewis, 1997)
- Build skills so the partners learn to resolve conflicts without angry fighting

5. *Define conflict levels, assessing ceilings and frequency.* If the symptom checklist or your interview questions indicate that anger outbursts have been occurring, obtain detailed reports of exactly what happens at these times, bearing in mind the tendency to minimize and deny rages, emotional abuse, and physical violence (Holtzworth-Munroe, Beatty, & Anglin, 1995). Early clarification of the dangerousness of a couple's conflict escalations is essential in order to know whether treating the couple in marital format will be safe or could lead to dangerous post-session fights, and to know whether immediate separation or safe house options need to be made available.

To obtain information about escalation levels, meet with each partner privately for a few minutes, and ask direct questions. Using explicit words like "shouts," "curses you," or "hits you" can make it easier for spouses to admit to what is actually happening. Ask each what is the worst their partner does when angry, and what they themselves do. Ask when the couple tends to fight, how frequently, and whether drugs or alcohol tend to be present.

Clarify how the anger in these fights is expressed verbally. Verbally expressed anger usually begins with blame and criticism, can escalate to deprecating or demanding words and tone of voice, and can further escalate to abusive levels with trumped up accusations, angry shouting, intimidating threats, and name-calling. In highest conflict levels of verbal abuse, a batterer berates his wife so she will feel bad about herself and be weakened with guilt and shame. In his verbal harangues the abuser builds a case to justify his anger, his urge to dominate and harm, and forthcoming violence.

Clarify next if anger escalates to physical aggression. Violence may include (in order of increasing escalation level):

- Threatening physical acts such as shaking a fist in front of the wife's face
- Throwing objects and breaking things
- Pushing
- Punching, slapping, choking
- Sexual aggression

- Use of weapons such as a heavy object or knife
- Killing, the culmination of violent escalations

While most high-conflict couples escalate to a standard ceiling of emotional agitation and then disengage, batterers tend to gradually escalate their levels. The violence of one day must be stepped up the next to effect the same emotional potency. Batterers' rhetoric becomes increasingly virulent over time, and their physical attacks become increasingly harmful. At some point even batterers do set a ceiling on escalation, but some do not set a ceiling until they reach the level of murder.

While the term "high conflict" usually refers to high and frequent levels of escalation, couples who do not escalate angrily can still lock into persistently adversarial stances. The treatment strategies in this chapter also pertain to these couples. Persistent conflict may be manifested in anxious tension (when conflicts hover but do not get directly addressed), depression (giving up instead of fighting), disengagement (for fear of fights), passive-aggressive patterns, or addictive or other obsessive-compulsive behavior (which distracts from conflicts).

6. *Note contraindications for couple therapy:*

- Unwillingness to agree that violence is out of bounds, at home and in the therapy session
- Poor impulse control or other signs that therapy may be unsafe
- Reprisals for talking openly about concerns in the sessions
- A paranoid-like blaming stance with a rigid set of beliefs about the other (a fixed ideational system), ego-syntonic controlling behavior, and projection
- Drug or alcohol abuse

If these symptoms can be addressed with individual treatment or medication, subsequent couple treatment may be productive. Also, individual therapy for the healthier partner can help him or her to cope more effectively with the spouse. Both partners' individual therapies may be best accomplished by the therapist handling the couple treatment, unless special expertise such as medications is necessary (Heitler, 2001). Two therapists tend to pull the system apart, and results in the couple therapist being uninformed about critical individual issues essential to the couple's progress. When one therapist conducts both the individual and the couple treatment components, however, confidentiality policies, such as whether information from individual sessions will be shared in the couple sessions, must be made explicit from the outset.

7. *Ensure safety:* Early in treatment teach disengagement/reengagement routines to prevent hurtful fights (see Table 1). Practice these routines in the session. Inquire intermittently about the couple's experiences with their exit routines to ensure their plan is fully effective.

8. *Initiate a collaborative set:* Create a shared perspective on the part of each spouse that they are mutually responsible for the problems in the relationship and that they both need to change themselves if the relationship is going to improve (Christensen et al., 1995). To help make a transition from conflict to cooperation, develop face-saving explanations for the conflicts:

- Define the last comfortable phase of marriage and then identify external or developmental stresses that may subsequently have overloaded the system (e.g., arrival of children, illness, financial setbacks).
- Explain the role of insufficient communication and conflict resolution skills.
- Identify conflict resolution models in each spouse's family of origin. Alleviate blaming of parents by looking compassionately at parents' family of origin histories.

9. *Set and fulfill agendas:* Just as in the initial session, you ask what each spouse wants to accomplish overall from therapy, begin each subsequent session by asking what each spouse wants to focus on in that session (e.g., skills, a difficult feeling or issue, an argument from the prior week).

Close sessions by summarizing progress on each agenda item. Connect side issues to the focal concerns. In general, in a 45- to 50-minute

TABLE 1. Time-Out Routines for Emotional Safety at Home

Initiate Time-outs When Either of You
- Feels too upset or negative to talk constructively.
- Senses that the other is getting too emotional to dialogue constructively.

To Initiate a Time-out
- Use a nonverbal signal, such as sports signals.
- Go to separate spaces immediately, without any further discussion.
- Self-soothe by doing something pleasant.
- Write in a journal if it feels helpful, but write primarily about yourself, not your partner.

To Reengage
- Wait until you both have regained normal humor.
- Reengage first in normal activity before you attempt to talk again about a difficult subject.
- If a difficult subject again provokes unconstructive discussion, save it for therapy.

Exit Rules
- No door slamming or parting comments.
- *Never* block the other from leaving or pursue the other when he or she needs to disengage.
- As soon as the going gets even a little bit hot, keep cool and exit. Prevention is preferable to destruction.

session, one main conflict can be brought to resolution and one main skill improved.

If violence is involved, immediate steps must be taken to remove guns from the home, to assure escape options, to address impacts of alcohol and drugs on safety, to teach ways of controlling anger, to ensure that both partners understand the high danger of even "minor" violence (e.g., a small push can cause a serious head injury), and to implement a temporary separation if violence risk is high. Firmly adopt the stance that no violent acts are acceptable (Holtzworth-Munroe et al., 1995).

10. *Intervene immediately if anger escalates in a session:* If the angry partner continues to escalate, stand between the two spouses and/or ask one spouse to step out for a few moments. Simplifying the situation by having one partner leave enables tempers to de-escalate and calm to return. If an angry spouse threatens to leave the session, agree, inviting him or her to return when he or she feels calmer. Thank him or her for demonstrating self-awareness and self-control.

After an angry outburst, reiterate the angry person's underlying concerns in a quiet voice so that dialogue resumes in a calm mode and the angry person knows he or she is being heard. Detoxify the incident by reframing the contents of the outburst in nonblaming language.

11. *Explain that ability to resolve conflicts sustains couple harmony; insufficient conflict resolution skills produce psychopathology.* Anger may serve as a means of coercion in couples that settle their differences by means of dominant-submissive, winner-loser strategies. Anger expresses frustration when stances have polarized and defensiveness has replaced listening. Anger energizes increased voice volume in order to be heard or to have one's viewpoint prevail. It also may serve to prevent discussion of hidden behavior (e.g., gambling, an affair, drugs).

Other poor conflict-resolution strategies also commonly occur in high-conflict couples. Anxiety arises when conflicts hover unaddressed. Depression is the by-product of dominant-submissive conflict resolution, that is, of submitting to the preferences or will of the other. Addictive and obsessive-compulsive disorders (including eating disorders and hypochondria) indicate attempts to escape from conflicts by means of distraction. These syndromes generally can be removed by readdressing conflicts with healthier dialogue and conflict resolution patterns.

12. *Teach about anger:* Explain that when we are angry, we may feel like we are "seeing red." Rather than attacking when we see red, as if we were bulls, we can interpret the red as a stop sign. Anger tells us to stop, look to identify the difficulty, listen to our and to our partner's concerns, and then choose a safe route for continuing. Angry feelings enable us to identify problems; angry actions, however, seldom effectively ameliorate problems.

13. *Resolve current disputes:* Guide conflicts through the three stages of conflict resolution:

- Express initial positions. Be sure that both spouses speak up *and* listen to each other.
- Explore underlying concerns. Be sure both spouses talk about their own thoughts and feelings, not about their partner's, and that both listen to absorb, not to criticize.
- Design a mutually satisfying plan of action, a solution set responsive to all the concerns of both spouses.

14. *Utilize the four Ss* that are essential in conflict resolution (Heitler, 1997):

- Specifics lead to resolution; generalities breed misunderstandings.
- Short segments mean that for conflicts to move toward resolution, participants need to speak a paragraph at a time, not multiple pages. For spouses who ramble or lecture, suggest a three-sentence rule.
- Symmetry of air time gives a sense of fairness and equal power.
- Summaries consolidate understanding and propel conflict resolution forward.

15. *Have spouses talk with each other, not through you:* High-conflict couples need to learn to talk with each other when they have differences. To redirect comments when the partners are speaking to you, suggest that the couple talk directly with each other. Look at the listener rather than the speaker, or using a hand or head gesture to indicate that the partners are to talk with each other, to further guide couples who resist talking directly to each other.

There are times, however, when it can be helpful to funnel the dialogue through you:

- To de-escalate tensions when anger is escalating
- To discuss a conflict in the early phases of treatment when the couple's skills are poor
- To accelerate the resolution of a specific conflict when time remaining in a session is short

16. *Identify core concerns:* Hot spots in a dialogue indicate strongly felt concerns. As you discuss conflicts, certain underlying concerns will surface repeatedly, raising strong feelings each time. Luborsky, Crits-Christoph, and Mellon (1986) call these transference issues—such as "I don't want to be controlled" or "People disappoint me by not doing what they should" —*core conflictual themes*. I call them *core concerns*. Identify these.

Note where spouses' core concerns dovetail, repeatedly reengaging the other's central concerns in what Wachtel (1993) calls vicious cycles. For instance, her thought "I can't seem to please him" and resultant depressive withdrawal may interact with his "I never get the affection I want" and angry complaining stance. Her depressive withdrawal triggers his anger; his angry complaints trigger her withdrawal. Establish new solutions for these concerns, replacing negative cycles with positive ones (e.g., she greets him warmly when he comes home from work; he expresses appreciation for her dinner).

17. *Access family of origin roots of core concerns:* Deeper concerns are less accessible to conscious thought and generally arise from historically earlier life experiences (Norcross, 1986). During explorations of the family of origin roots of current emotionally potent concerns, the spouse listens, holding his or her comments for the discussion afterwards.

18. *Allow only healthy communication:*

- Intervene immediately as soon as dialogue slips off the track of healthy, safe, and constructive dialogue. Do not allow blaming, criticizing or inadequate listening to pass un-remarked. Allow zero crossovers (you-statements), which occur with particular frequency in couples prone to anger. Rephrase inappropriate comments, or have the speaker restate the comment more constructively—translating "don't likes" to "would likes" and shifting you-statements to I-statements. Ask listeners who listen for what is wrong in what their partner says, "What was right or made sense about what you just heard?" (Heitler, 1997).

- Prevent poor skills by prompting spouses before they speak. For example, to prompt effective listening, suggest, "What makes sense to you in what your spouse just said?"
- If you did not succeed with prevention, rectify skill errors by inviting a redo.
- Alternatively, serve as translator, converting provocative comments into better form. For instance, after an accusatory "You don't do your part in keeping up the house," pull your chair next to the speaker and reiterate for him or her, "I feel like I'm doing more than my share."
- Repeat frequently simple iterations of basic communication rules, such as "You can talk about yourself or ask about the other; it's out of bounds to talk about the other." "What's right, what makes sense, what's useful in what your partner is saying?" Learning increases with repetition.

19. *Coach communication skills:* Design practice exercises to teach and consolidate essential skills such as:

- *Insightful self-expression:* Good spousal communication involves expressing one's own concerns and feelings instead of criticizing the other. Explain the difference between self-expression and "crossovers" (my term for crossing the boundary between self and other by talking about what you think the other is thinking or feeling or telling them what to do). Practice self-expressive when-you's ("When you left early, I felt rejected"). Emphasize that the subject of a when-you is the pronoun *I*.
- *Digestive listening:* Instead of listening like an adversary for what's wrong with what the other is saying, cooperative partners listen to learn, to sponge in what makes sense in what their partner says. "But . . . ," by contrast, indicates that the prior comments are being deleted, not digested.
- *Bilateral listening:* Two-sided listening to both self and other enables both partners' viewpoints to count. Bilateral listening contrasts with either-or thinking and the belief that if one person is right the other is wrong.

20. *Convert blame after upsets to apologies and learning:* Teach the couple to piece together the puzzle of what happened, with each spouse describing his or her own feelings, thoughts, actions, and mistakes. Attribute the problem to a "mis-" (e.g., a misunderstanding, mistake, miscommunication). Guide apologies, with each spouse owning his or her part in the difficulties. Conclude with each having learned something that will help to prevent future similar upsets (Heitler, 1997).

21. *Terminate therapy* when the symptoms have been ameliorated (i.e., anger is no longer contaminating the relationship), the conflicts have been resolved, and dialogue is consistently cooperative.

References, Readings, & Internet Sites

Christensen, A., Jacobson, N. S., & Babcock, J. (1995). Integrative behavioral couple therapy. In N. S. Jacobson & A. S . Gurman (Eds.), *Clinical handbook of couple therapy* (pp. 31–64). New York: Guilford Press.

Heitler, S. (1993). *From conflict to resolution*. New York: Norton.

Heitler, S. (1995). *The angry couple: Conflict-focused treatment*. New York: Newbridge.

Heitler, S. (1997). *The power of two*. Oakland, CA: New Harbinger.

Heitler, S. (2001). Combined individual/marital therapy: A conflict resolution framework and ethical considerations. *Journal of Psychotherapy Integration, 11*, 349–383.

Holtzworth-Munroe, A., Beatty, S. B., & Anglin, K. (1995). The assessment and treatment of marital violence: An introduction for the marital therapist. In N. S. Jacobson & A. S. Gurman (Eds.), *Clinical handbook of couple therapy* (pp. 317–339). New York: Guilford Press.

Intimate Partner Abuse and Relationship Violence. (n.d.). Home page. Retrieved 2004 from http://www.apa.org/pi/iparv.pdf

Lewis, J. M. (1997). *Marriage as a search for healing*. New York: Brunner/Mazel.

Luborsky, L., Crits-Christoph, P., & Mellon, J. (1986). Advent of objective measures of the transference concept. *Journal of Consulting and Clinical Psychology, 54*, 39–47.

Norcross, J. (1986). In J. O. Prochaska (Ed.), Integrative dimensions for psychotherapy. *International Journal of Eclectic Psychotherapy, 5*, 256–274.

TherapyHelp.com. (n.d.) Materials on psychotherapy with conflictual couples. Retrieved 2004 from http://www.therapyhelp.com

Wachtel, P. (1993). *Therapeutic communication*. New York: Guilford.

Related Topics

Chapter 78, "Guidelines for Conducting Couple and Family Therapy"

Chapter 80, "Treatment of Marital Infidelity"

80 TREATMENT OF MARITAL INFIDELITY

Don-David Lusterman

Estimates of extramarital sex (EMS) vary widely. Glass and Wright (1992) found that 44% of husbands and 25% of wives had at least one extramarital experience. They found a correlation between extramarital involvement (EMI) and low marital satisfaction. A full-probability study ($N = 1{,}200$) conducted annually over a 5-year period (Smith, 1993) reports a roughly 15% incidence, including 21% of men and 12% of women. All studies find that married men are more frequently involved than are married women. The discovery of EMI is traumatic for spouses and the couple's children, families, and friends. The following observations and guidelines are based on clinical experience and the research literature.

1. *Definition:* Infidelity is the breaking of trust. While often thought of as sexual misconduct, it may also include nonsexual but secret relationships. The most distinguishing characteristic of all types of infidelity is secrecy. Most discoverers report that deceit is the most traumatic element of discovery. Thus, if a couple agrees that extramarital sex is acceptable, no infidelity has occurred. A negative answer to the therapist's question "Could you discuss your actions comfortably with your mate?" helps the patient to understand the relationship between deceit and infidelity. A wife's discovery that her husband has been involved in a "computer romance" might be as shocking to her as the discovery that he had been involved in a sexual adventure. If a partner in a foursome becomes secretly involved with another member of the foursome, it becomes an infidelity. The violation of intimacy boundaries may be much more crucial than that of sexual boundaries; an intense and secretive platonic relationship may be more threatening than a sexual relationship.

2. *Types of marital infidelity:* Humphrey (1987) categorizes EMI by the following criteria:

- Time
- Degree of emotional involvement
- Sexual intercourse or abstinence

- Single or bilateral EMS
- Heterosexual or homosexual

An additional criterion is the number of EMI partners. Glass and Wright (1992) use three categories: *primarily sexual, primarily emotional,* and *combined-type.* Careful questioning of the involved partner using these sets of criteria helps the therapist to develop an understanding of the type and degree of involvement. Such questioning may reveal philandering. Philanderers are compulsively driven to have frequent and brief EMS. They avoid intimacy and are primarily interested in power over the other person (Pittman, 1989). They are best seen as suffering a personality disorder NOS, with narcissistic features, and they require individual treatment parallel with conjoint therapy.

3. *Discovery:* EMI is a systemic phenomenon, involving the discoverer and the discovered and, if it takes the form of an affair, the third party as well. Children, families of origin, and friends are also often affected. Partners in "good" marriages rate as most important "trust in each other that includes fidelity, integrity and feeling 'safe'" and "permanent commitment to the marriage" (Kaslow & Hammerschmidt, 1992). The discovery of infidelity shatters these assumptions, producing great trauma (Janoff-Bulman, 1992). The discoverer feels betrayed, and the discovered person is often ashamed and fearful of the discoverer's responses.

4. *The initial session:* The discoverer often exhibits a rapid succession of conflicting emotions and behaviors. At one moment he or she may be sobbing, at another, ready to strike at the offending mate. The discovered partner may be by turns apologetic, defensive, and angry. The discovered person may deny the infidelity despite copious proof. Admission is often accompanied by the demand that there be no further discussion about it. The therapist's first responsibility is to indicate that avoiding the topic, while it may provide some momentary relief for the discovered party, will in the end cause more problems. The therapeutic approach, while sensitive to the affective issues, must also include a psychoeducational aspect. Couples and individuals alike find that clear information brings a degree of relief and often helps to restore marital communication.

5. *Therapeutic ground rules:* The couple should be told that the purpose of the therapy is to help them change their relationship. With work, they will be moving toward a better marriage or a better divorce. In a better divorce, both accept mature responsibility for the failure of the marriage. This lays the groundwork for an amicable settlement that is in the best interests of their children, and it also permits them to leave the marriage with new insights about future relationships. A better marriage is characterized by open and honest communication about both positive and negative issues.

6. *Confidentiality:* Although it is crucial to establish a relationship with the couple, it is equally important that the therapist schedule a session to meet each member of the couple alone. (Not all authorities view confidentiality the same way; for other views, see Brown, 1991; Glass & Wright, 1995; and Pittman, 1989.) I believe that individual sessions enable the therapist to see whether there are issues that one or the other is not yet ready to reveal in conjoint sessions. Individual sessions also enable the therapist to know whether the affair or other extramarital and secret sexual activity is still going on. The therapist prepares the couple for individual sessions by assuring each partner that anything discussed in such meetings is confidential. While nothing will be divulged to the other partner, the information obtained will enable the therapist to organize a treatment plan. Making this contract with the couple provides the therapist with the freedom to decide whether subsequent sessions should be held with each individual, with the couple, or as some mix of individual and couples work. In some instances only one mate undertakes therapy when marital infidelity is involved. It may be the person who is suspicious of or has just discovered a mate's EMI or the person who is extramaritally involved and conflicted about it. A systemically oriented therapist will inform the person that it is probable that the mate will be included in the therapy at some point. It is very important to inform the involved person that at no time will conjoint therapy include the third party. The involved person who decides to confess the infidelity to the mate should be strongly cautioned not to do so in the therapist's office. This person may require coaching in order to develop an appropriate strategy for revealing the infidelity. Only after the person has acted on this responsibility should conjoint therapy be undertaken.

7. *Moratorium:* It is crucial that the therapist press the involved partner to declare a moratorium on the affair. Failing that, the involved person should be helped to disclose the affair to his or her partner. Until such time, the other partner should also be seen individually, so that both partners' perceptions of the marriage can be examined. Seeing the couple individually greatly increases their anxiety. This tension helps to break the impasse of denial and brings them back to therapy to work more directly on the marital or divorce issues.

8. *Trust-building:* Many discoverers consider themselves "victims." In such a case, it is wise for the therapist to begin by accepting this perceptual frame. Only when the discoverer feels fully supported is it possible to examine the predisposing factors that often play a role in infidelity.

9. *Sequelae of victimhood:* When the discoverer experiences himself or herself as the victim, the therapist must validate these feelings and provide the couple with information about the nature of trauma. Many discoverers report or evidence the following symptoms:

- Difficulty staying or falling asleep
- Irritability or outbursts of anger
- Difficulty concentrating
- Hypervigilance
- Exaggerated startle response
- Physiological reactivity upon exposure to events that symbolize or resemble an aspect of the traumatic event (e.g., being unable to watch a TV show or movie about infidelity)

The discoverer's responses are best reframed as a *normal,* nonpathological response to the shock of discovery (Glass & Wright, 1995; Lusterman, 1995). The therapist should make clear to both husband and wife that these intrusive recollections and obsessive searching for more details or for evidence that the infidelity continues (when the mate has denied it) are all part of a posttraumatic stress reaction as described in *DSM-IV* (American Psychiatric Association, 1994). Working together, the couple can alleviate and even overcome this trauma. The therapist should explain to the discovered mate that he or she can play a crucial role in helping the discoverer, who needs to express grief, shock, and anger directly to the mate and requires honest answers to his or her questions. This process is crucial to the restoration of trust. If the offending party blocks this process, recovery is slowed. Dealing with trauma is the first order of business. Several sessions may pass during which the therapist has the illusion that the couple is beyond the posttraumatic phase, only to discover that a fight has broken out between sessions because the discoverer, once again, *feels* that the mate is lying, withholding, and/or unable to empathize with the discoverer's pain. The mate's ability both to admit the deception and to express remorse is a necessary step in the restoration of communication. In its absence, the prognosis for good recovery from the trauma is poor.

There are situations in which an appropriate and timely reaction to infidelity does not occur:

- An affair happened during the courtship or early in marriage, and only came into the discoverer's awareness many years later.
- The affair happened during the courtship or early in the marriage, and the discoverer did not react at all at that time, or reacted only briefly.

The discoverer's long-delayed reaction usually takes on a strongly obsessive and very angry quality. Since it is so long "after the fact," the discovered partner is often unable to perceive any justification for the discoverer's intense reaction. It is the therapist's task to indicate that this is a genuine, delayed posttraumatic reaction and to validate the discoverer's reaction. Patients often accept the metaphor that the suppressed information has functioned as a time bomb in the marriage. Therapy will be most successful if the therapist treats the newly acknowledged infidelity as if it had just occurred.

10. *Jealousy:* It is an error to label normal reactive jealousy following the affair as if it were a personality problem. Treating it as such is a frequent cause of premature termination of therapy. In rare instances, the discoverer *is* obsessively jealous, despite honest reassurance. If careful examination reveals a history of pathological jealousy predating the marriage, this problem may require separate treatment for the pathologically jealous mate, in conjunction with the marital therapy. Pathological jealousy is best seen as an aspect of a paranoid personality disorder.

11. *Predisposing factors:* Once the couple has negotiated the hurdle of discovery, it is then possible to begin a review of the prediscovery phase of the marriage. During this process, the therapist helps the couple to move beyond the issue of perceived victimhood and on to an examination of factors within the marriage that may have contributed to the affair. Such factors generally include low self-disclosure and consequent poor problem solving (Lusterman, 1989). During this phase, the therapist must be alert to the recurrence of posttraumatic signs. These can be precipitated, for example, by the discovery of old evidence, hang-up telephone calls, or stalking by the third party. Each time there is such a recurrence, it is important to address the posttraumatic issues before returning to the review process. Once the predisposing factors have been examined, the couple is ready for traditional marital therapy, with a focus on honest communication.

12. *Termination:* Couples are ready for termination when they have examined the context and meaning of the infidelity and have resolved that they can either proceed to a healthier relationship or move toward divorce. A better marriage includes an improvement in mutual empathy and joint responsibility (Glass & Wright, 1995).

Because the discoverer remains vulnerable to a possible recurrence, it is important to discuss with both mates the importance of a detection mechanism. The offending mate is reminded that, should the discoverer need reassurance, it must be patiently given. The discoverer is asked to agree with the offending mate that if there is a recurrence, the next stage will be divorce.

13. *Bibliotherapy:* As part of a psychoeducational approach, suggested readings can be helpful. Janoff-Bulman (1992), Lusterman (1989), Pittman (1989), and Vaughan (1989) have been found to be of value. A number of Web sites also provide an opportunity to receive information and participate in a bulletin board.

References, Readings, & Internet Sites

American Psychiatric Association. (1994). *Diagnostic and statistical manual of mental disorders* (4th ed.). Washington, DC: Author.

AOL. Extramarital affairs forum: keyword: online psych; *Divorce and Separation Community*: keyword: better health; then, under "Community Connection," go to "Divorce and Separation"

Brown, E. (1991). *Patterns of infidelity and their treatment.* New York: Brunner/Mazel.

Glass, S., & Wright, T. (1992). Justifications for extramarital relationships: The association between attitudes, behavior, and gender. *Journal of Sex Research, 29,* 361–387.

Glass, S., & Wright, T. (1995). Reconstructing marriages after the trauma of infidelity. In K. Halford & H. Markman (Eds.), *Clinical handbook of marriage and couple interventions.* New York: Wiley.

Humphrey, F. (1987). Treating extramarital sexual relationships in sex and couples therapy. In G. Weeks & L. Hof (Eds.), *Integrating sex and marital therapy: A clinical guide.* New York: Brunner/Mazel.

Janoff-Bulman, R. (1992). *Shattered assumptions: Towards a new psychology of trauma.* New York: Free Press.

Kaslow, F., & Hammerschmidt, H. (1992). Long-term "good marriages": The seemingly essential ingredients. *Journal of Couples Therapy, 3*(2/3), 15–38.

Lusterman, D.-D. (1989, May/June). Marriage at the turning point. *Family Networker, 13,* 44–51.

Lusterman, D.-D. (1995). Treating marital infidelity. In R. Mikesell, D.-D. Lusterman, & S. McDaniel (Eds.), *Integrating family therapy: Handbook of family psychology and systems theory.* Washington, DC: American Psychological Association.

Pittman, D. J. (1989). *Private lies: Infidelity and the betrayal of intimacy.* New York: Norton.

Smith, T. (1993). *American sexual behavior: Trends,*

socio-demographic differences, and risk behavior (Version 1.2). Chicago: National Opinion Research Center, University of Chicago.

Vaughan, P. (1989). *The monogamy myth.* New York: Newmarket Press.

Vaughan, P. (n.d.). Home page (resource site: DearPeggy.com). Retrieved 2004 from http://www.vaughan-vaughan.com

Related Topics

Chapter 78, "Guidelines for Conducting Couple and Family Therapy"

Chapter 79, "Treating High-Conflict Couples"

81 GROUP PSYCHOTHERAPY

An Interpersonal Approach

Victor J. Yalom

Group psychotherapy is an extremely effective modality and potentially a more efficient use of professional resources than individual psychotherapy. Its efficacy has been demonstrated in treating a wide range of disorders, yet it continues to be underutilized or misused by clinicians who are not sufficiently trained in group techniques. The current pressures toward providing briefer, more cost-effective treatment provide a renewed opportunity for a broader utilization of group methods of treatment.

APPLICATIONS

Psychotherapy groups generally consist of between 6 and 10 clients and one or two therapists. Some formats, such as multifamily groups, may be much larger. Groups are run in almost every setting, from private practice to hospitals, and are applicable for almost every conceivable clinical population. For some populations, such as substance abusers or domestic violence offenders, groups are generally considered the preferred method of treatment.

THEORY

The interactional or interpersonal approach described here assumes that patients' presenting symptoms and underlying difficulties are to a large extent the result of maladaptive patterns of interpersonal relationships. A major therapeutic factor in group psychotherapy occurs in the form of interpersonal learning—that is, group members become more aware of and modify their maladaptive interpersonal behaviors and beliefs. Through the course of a successful group therapy, patients obtain direct and repeated feedback about the effects of their behavior on others—honest feedback, which they are unlikely to receive in a constructive and supportive manner anywhere else in their lives. Other important therapeutic factors in groups include the feeling of support and belonging, catharsis, the instillation of hope, and the experience of altruism in helping other members.

With the therapist's active promptings, members will increase their awareness and understanding of how their behaviors impact other group members: which behaviors elicit positive reactions, such as compassion, empathy, attraction, and a desire for increased emotional closeness, and which provoke negative reactions, such as anger, hurt, fear, and a general desire to withdraw. They then have the opportunity to "try out" new behaviors in the relative safety of the group, learning how to develop social relationships that are more fulfilling. Success begets success, and patients begin to internalize these experiences, altering some of their negative self-images. Finally, they apply these new social skills and internalized identities in their relationships outside the group.

A basic assumption underlying this process of change is that the group is a "social microcosm"—that is, that the types of relationships patients tend to form in their daily lives will eventually be re-created within the group itself. Thus the concept of transference from individual psychotherapy is broadened to include the "parataxic distortions," as coined by Harry Stack Sullivan, which occur in all relationships. Because of the variety and number of group members, the opportunity to work through the multiple transferences or distortions that develop is much richer than in individual therapy.

Because of this phenomenon, the most powerful and efficacious way to learn from these recapitulated relationships is to focus on them as they continuously recur during the course of therapy. This is referred to as the "here-and-now," because the focus is here (in the group) and now (interactions that occur during the therapy session). Accordingly, past events or relationships outside the group are used primarily as jumping-off points, which then guide the here-and-now work in the group rather than remaining the central focus.

For example, if a group member complains of repeated conflicts with his or her boss, it is usually of limited benefit to hear a lengthy recounting of these conflicts, since the patient's report is undoubtedly a skewed one, biased by the member's needs and distorted perceptions. Attempts to interpret or make suggestions about the work situation are often unproductive because the patient always has the upper hand, being privy to infinitely more information about the situation than the other group members or leader. Instead, the therapist draws attention to the manner in which the group member engages in, or avoids, conflict with other group members—with the assumption that in some way his or her troublesome relationship with the boss will be reenacted here. Because all the group members can witness his or her exchanges in the group, they are able to give feedback that is more accurate and compelling.

TASKS OF THE GROUP THERAPIST

Given the premise that interpersonal learning is maximized in a group that operates largely in the here-and-now, what must the therapist do for this to occur? First and foremost, the therapist must actively assist patients in translating their presenting complaints into interpersonal issues. For example, a patient who initially requests therapy because of a feeling of depression would be urged to explore the interpersonal context of his or her depression—for example, the depression might be triggered by feelings of rejection by a lover, with subsequent loneliness or humiliation. This initial reformulation of the problem must then be broadened so that it can be addressed in the group. With additional effort the therapist might help the patient restate the complaint as "I feel depressed when others don't give me the attention I want, and yet I am unable to state my needs directly." In this manner the complaint has been transformed into one that can be addressed in the here-and-now of the therapy group: the patient can explore how he or she experiences similar feelings of rejection by other group members and yet has difficulty in letting them know what he or she wants from them.

The other main task of the therapist is to help the group continuously attend to the interpersonal dynamics that occur within the group. This can be broken down into two subtasks. The first is to help plunge the group into the here-and-now, allowing the members to interact with each other as much as possible. The second is to help them reflect on these interactions and learn from them.

The therapist must, in a very active manner, help the group members to interact directly with each other and to share their observations and feelings about one another. During the initial session, it is common for the members to take turns talking about themselves, including their reasons for seeking therapy and the areas in which they would like to change. From this very first meeting, the astute therapist will look for every opportunity to direct the interactions toward the here-and-now. For example, if a patient states that he or she is feeling quite anxious, a few probing questions may reveal that the patient invariably compares himself or herself with others and usually concludes that they will look down on him or her because of lack of education and sophistication. The therapist can bring this general concern into the here-and-now by asking, "Of the people in this group, which ones have you imagined are having critical thoughts of you?"

Although the group members may initially resist the leap into the here-and-now, with time and reinforcement they will begin to engage with each other more spontaneously. This is not to suggest that the therapist can relax and expect the group to internalize these norms enough to be a self-correcting mechanism; members are far too preoccupied attending to the issues that brought them to the group. The leader must continuously attend to the group process and seize upon or create opportunities to steer the group into productive here-and-now exchanges. But, over time, productive working groups should require less guidance into the here and now if the therapist consistently reinforces this norm.

The experiential element of these interactions is crucial but by itself is insufficient. Experience, like catharsis, rarely by itself leads to personal change. It is necessary for the here-and-now experience to be linked with some mechanism that helps patients understand and learn from these interactions. In other words, the patients need to be able to look back and reflect upon the encounters they experience in the group.

To facilitate this, therapists must first have a clear understanding of group process. Process can be most easily defined in contradistinction to content: Whereas content consists of the actual words or topics discussed, process refers to the meaning that these conversations have in terms of the relationships between the group members. Thus, from a process orientation, the same utterance by a patient will have vastly different connotations depending on the manner in which it was delivered, the timing, and the context of the group discussion.

Therapists thus must find ways to help the group reflect back on its own process. Again this is an area where therapists must be very active, since group members themselves are unlikely to initiate this type of activity. Process comments can range from simple observations by the therapist of specific incidents (e.g., "I noticed that when you said that your fists were clenched") to more generalized interpretations (e.g., "You seem to instinctively challenge whatever the other men say in the group; I wonder if you feel the need to be competitive with them?"). Over the course of therapy, process comments serve to heighten patients' awareness of how their behavior appears to others in the group. Ultimately patients become aware of how they determine the quality of the interpersonal world they live in, and with this awareness comes the possibility for true behavior change, leading to more satisfying relationships.

COMMON ERRORS

One of the most common errors of novice group psychotherapists is to practice some form of individual psychotherapy in the group. In this scenario the therapist typically spends an inordinate amount of time focusing on some issue or problem that a group member is experiencing, attempting to solve or analyze that problem. This approach has several obvious drawbacks. The first is that it reinforces the therapist as the expert, disempowering other group members. The experience group members gain in being able to give and receive help from each other is in itself extremely therapeutic and should be cultivated as much as possible. The second drawback is that a prolonged exchange between the therapist and a group member leaves the other members on the sideline, uninvolved, and likely to become disinterested. Group therapists need to be alert to ensure that the unique ingredients of the psychotherapy group—that is, a number of individuals who are motivated to come together to help each other grow and gain relief from suffering under the direction of a skilled leader—are fully utilized. This is accomplished by keeping the group interactive, with members participating fully, taking risks, and giving each other feedback and support.

The other most vexing misuse, or underutilization, of the group format is a failure to work in the here-and-now. This is usually caused by therapists leading groups without proper training or supervision. Once therapists have observed and understood the power and energy that here-and-now interactions generate, they will be more likely to develop the skills necessary to use this approach. Another reason for avoiding the here-and-now is the fear that this will lead to excessive conflict. A successful course of group psychotherapy, as with individual psychotherapy, involves the experience and expression of a wide range of feelings: anger, disappointment, and hurt, as well as caring, support, and even joy. The skilled therapist facilitates the direct expression of conflict rather than going underground but also ensures that difficult feelings are aired in a safe, nonabusive manner. Only rarely does conflict dominate the interactions and threaten group cohesion; in fact, in most settings the therapist needs to be more active in facilitating the expression of conflict rather than in containing it.

OBSTACLES TO FORMING AND STARTING GROUPS

Getting groups up and running can be the most challenging aspect of conducting group psychotherapy. The solo private practitioner needs a large base of clients to put together an appropriate mix in a timely fashion; if the process of group formation is stretched out too long, some individuals may drop out before the group begins. On the other hand, starting a group with fewer than five members is likely to be problematic. With anticipated absences and unanticipated dropouts, some meetings will have as few as two or three clients. These meetings lack the richness of exchanges and overall dynamism experienced in larger group sessions. Furthermore, they are likely to engender in the members (and the leader) fears about group survival, which are unproductive and distract from the therapeutic goals.

Thus therapists need a steady referral base or an ability to effectively market their groups. Often it is easier to publicize groups targeted to specific populations, such as incest survivors, teens with eating disorders, or recovering alcoholics. Another possibility is for therapists to team up as coleaders, which allows them to draw patients from their combined practices, making it easier to fill groups and keep them filled as openings occur. This also has other advantages for the therapists, including complementing each other's clinical skills and combating the isolation of private practice.

Group practices, clinics, and managed care organizations offer their own set of hurdles to developing successful group psychotherapy programs. Although they have the advantage of having large numbers of patients necessary for conducting multiple groups, they pose challenges in appropriately and tactfully funneling these patients to the therapists leading these groups. It is quite common to encounter a great deal of resistance (conscious and unconscious) at every level of an organization—from intake workers to front-line therapists to administrators—to implementing a group program. Many clinicians still have limited knowledge and training regarding groups and view group psychotherapy suspiciously as a second-class form of treatment. Unfortunately, some large institutions that are successful in running large numbers of groups unwittingly encourage these beliefs by emphasizing to their staffs the necessity to accommodate large patient populations rather than the particular treatment benefits of groups.

To overcome this, each level of the organization must in essence be retrained to think "group" as one of the treatment options for each patient. Telephone intake workers should think in interpersonal terms as they ask about presenting symptoms and should inform callers of available group treatments. If a client appears to be a good candidate for a group, he or she should be referred directly to the group leader, who can do a more in-depth assessment. If the client is a good fit, then it is essential that the therapist spend some time preparing the client for the group to increase acceptance of the referral and decrease the likelihood of early dropout. Both intake workers and therapists need to fully understand how groups work so they can intelligently discuss how the group will address the particular concerns of each client. For example, a chronically shy individual may at first be quite reluctant to accept a referral for a social skills training group but might become more enthusiastic when it is explained how the therapist will assist in working directly on his or her shyness via interactions with other group members.

Needless to say, top administrators must fully support any attempt to increase group psychotherapy utilization, taking significant concrete steps to ensure the success of these efforts. Group psychotherapists should be given adequate training and supervision. Also, it is important that reimbursement or other institutional rewards encourage the use of group psychotherapy. For example, if therapists are required to provide a specified amount of direct services per week, a 90-minute group should be counted as more than 1½ hours because of the extra paperwork, phone calls, and effort involved in starting the group. Without institutional support, therapists are likely to be discouraged from leading groups.

ISSUE-FOCUSED GROUPS

Most groups being led today are formed for clients who possess shared symptoms, such as panic attacks, depression, or posttraumatic stress disorder, or have common life experiences, such as incest survivors or single parents. These homogeneous groups offer several advantages. They are often easier to form, and from a community mental health perspective, they help to destigmatize the symptoms, thus making group treatment more accessible to many who otherwise might not seek out psychiatric or psychological services. Once the group has been formed, the commonality, either of symptoms or of life experiences among the members, can increase the group's cohesion. Because these groups are often time-limited, a sense of cohesion is especially important, since it accelerates the development of safety and, hence, of risk taking.

However, the therapist should be aware of and strive to avoid potential pitfalls with homogeneous groups. There is a tendency among patients to focus on the commonalties of their symptoms and conditions rather than on their unique individual experiences. Thus they avoid taking responsibility for their current dilemmas and the areas they would like to change. The therapist must steer the group away from theoretical discourses about the nature of their symptoms, excessive advice giving, and personal historical accounts and instead address the ways in which their symptoms manifest in their day-to-day relationships. This is not to say that a psychoeducational approach is not useful but to suggest that ultimately the group leader should highlight the interpersonal components of the issues or symptoms under discussion and utilize the group format to work directly on those issues in the here-and-now.

References & Readings

Leszcz, M. (1992). The interpersonal approach to group psychotherapy. *International Journal of Group Psychotherapy, 42,* 37–62.

MacKenzie, R. K., & Grabovac, A. D. (2001). "Interpersonal Psychotherapy Group (IPT-G) for depression." *Journal of Psychotherapy Practice and Research, 10,* 46–51.

Marziali, E., & Munroe-Blum, H. (1994). *Interpersonal group psychotherapy for borderline personality disorder*. New York: Basic Books.

Ormont, L. (2003). *Group psychotherapy*. New York: Jason Aronson.

Roller, B. (1997). *The promise of group psychotherapy*. San Francisco: Jossey-Bass.

Rutan, J. S., & Stone, W. N. (1993). *Psychodynamic group psychotherapy* (2nd ed.). New York: Guilford.

Sadock, H., & Kaplan, B. (Eds.). (1993). *Comprehensive group psychotherapy* (3rd ed.). Baltimore: Williams and Wilkins.

Vinogradov, S., & Yalom, I. D. (1989). *Concise guide to group psychotherapy*. Washington DC: American Psychiatric Press.

Wilfley, D. E., MacKenzie, K. R., Ayers, V. E., Welch, R. R., & Weissman, M. M. (2000). *Interpersonal psychotherapy for groups*. New York: Basic Books.

Yalom, I. D. (1983). *Inpatient group psychotherapy*. New York: Basic Books.

Yalom, I. D. (1995). *The theory and practice of group psychotherapy* (4th ed.). New York: Basic Books.

Related Topics

Chapter 76, "Choice of Treatment Format"

Chapter 78, "Guidelines for Conducting Couple and Family Therapy"

82 PSYCHOEDUCATIONAL GROUP TREATMENT

Gary M. Burlingame & Nathanael W. Ridge

The ubiquity of the small-group treatments as a primary vehicle to deliver services in the clinical, counseling, educational, and medical settings is indisputable. Unfortunately, the plethora of available groups invariably leads to confusion in the consumer's mind regarding the differences between distinct types of small-group treatments. For instance, it is a rare health care consumer who can accurately distinguish between the goals, procedures, and functions of support, counseling, psychoeducational, and psychotherapy groups. Indeed, the professional literature inadvertently encourages confabulation of distinct types of small-group treatment when reviewers combine findings from studies using different types of group treatments to arrive at conclusions regarding the successful treatment of particular disorders (Burlingame, MacKenzie, & Strauss, 2003). Nonetheless, some guidance exists regarding the distinctive features of psychoeducational groups, or PEGs.

The Association of Specialists in Group Work (ASGW, 1991) identified PEGs as a separate type of group treatment, distinguishing it from psychotherapy, counseling, and activity groups. A cardinal feature of PEGs is the focus on developing members' cognitive, affective, or behavioral knowledge and skills through a structured and sequenced set of procedures and exercises. In particular, group psychoeducation separates itself from other types of group treatments by its primary focus on education.

APPLICATION AND EFFECTIVENESS

The wide range of extant PEG models is partially reflected by diversity in settings (e.g., inpatient, outpatient, primary care medicine, schools, etc.), populations (e.g., psychiatric, medically ill, normal, etc.), and professions that rely upon this group format. PEGs are found in traditional outpatient and inpatient mental health settings focusing on common psychiatric disorders such as anxiety and depression, as well as more intractable conditions including schizophrenia, substance-related, and bipolar disorders. A growing number of models are being developed to respond to survivors of natural and man-made disasters. PEGs played a significant role in the treatment of survivors and emergency personnel associated with the terrorist attacks on September 11, 2001, as well as with the increasing number of victims of community- and school-based violence in North America.

An equally impressive number of PEGs can be found in medical settings. Examples include groups composed of patients with terminal (e.g., oncology) or chronic (e.g., cardiology, pain) medical conditions that have dual needs for education regarding the disease and its treatment, as well as support for psychosocial sequelae associated such. Other medical applications include conditions that require patient compliance with changes in lifestyle and medication management (e.g., diabetes, HIV/AIDS). Such groups provide patients with needed information and an opportunity to discuss obstacles and difficulties with others who are facing similar transitions.

There is a dearth of independent reviews regarding the effectiveness of PEGs. Rather, evidence for their effectiveness is found in single studies or reviews of psychiatric or medical conditions that frequently rely upon this type of group treatment. While evidence exists for their effectiveness with specific populations (e.g., schizophrenia; cf. Burlingame et al., 2003), it should be emphasized that the outcomes measured with PEGs often relate to educational objectives and behavioral compliance instead of symptom reduction or remission.

DISTINCTIVE CHARACTERISTICS OF PEGS

The lack of integrated reviews focused on the effectiveness of PEGs in the literature may lead some to question whether they are a distinct type of group treatment. For instance, the diversity of foci across extant psychoeducational groups is illustrated when one considers the cognitive, affective, and behavioral skills emphasized in a cancer PEG run by a nurse at a medical setting versus the knowledge and skills emphasized in a PEG for eating-disordered patients led by a social worker in an outpatient clinic. One cannot help but wonder if these groups have anything in common. However, careful examination of diverse PEG protocols leads to three emergent components. More specifically, the typical PEG session contains a didactic presentation, an experiential exercise, and discussion. Herein lies the common characteristics and goals associated with PEGs.

1. *Specific learning goal and related objectives*. Patient education is the most important aim. Thus, PEGs have clearly defined educational goals. For instance, the typical goal of a symptom management PEG is to teach the patient about the probable etiology of the disease, symptoms, and practices that are likely to hinder or assist in recovery from or management of these symptoms (e.g., medication, lifestyle, behaviors). These three educational goals find further operational clarity in specific learning objectives associated with each. For instance, learning objectives clarify which symptoms, etiologies, and treatments will be presented to the group and organize the flow of material to be presented over the course of the PEG. At minimum, written goals, objectives, and material should be available for each PEG session.
2. *Incorporation of pedagogical methods that enhance patient learning*. Because patient education is paramount, PEG leaders are sensitive to different styles of learning and teaching methods. Leaders are advised to provide a framework where the "big picture" (learning goal) is initially presented and linked to session objectives establishing a gestalt for the entire PEG. Sensitivity to "how" members learn will lead to objectives being ordered hierarchically. For instance, Brown (1998) suggests a hierarchy where facts are initially presented followed by application, which then leads to an analysis and synthesis of knowledge. Periodic evaluation of knowledge acquisition is recom-

mended to provide both patient and leader with feedback on patient understanding and areas that lack clarity.

3. *Use of structured exercises to increase skill acquisition and experiential learning.* Active participation or experiential learning is a cardinal principle of long-term retention. PEGs incorporate this principle by involving members in experiential learning through structured exercises. These exercises can range from the completion of a simple self-report instrument that is tied to a learning objective (e.g., assessment of symptoms) to activities that require members to use a principle or practice a skill learned during the didactic phase of the group. Successful structured exercises must have a direct link to objectives in the didactic presentation.
4. *Personal analysis and synthesis through discussion.* A danger inherent in PEGs is that members will experience the group as an "academic" exercise having no personal meaning. One method that may counteract this tendency is to include structured exercises that require member involvement and disclosure. Such exercises can lead to spontaneous interaction regarding the topic under consideration, as members analyze and synthesize their didactic and personal experiences with one another. Material that has personal meaning leads to longer retention. Thus, PEG leaders are encouraged to plan for personal exchange and discussion between members in each session.
5. *Focus on careful patient selection.* Leaders should select members who are well matched to the educational goals of the group. The content and structured exercises used in the PEG should be calibrated with the educational level and motivation of the patient. For example, if a commercially available PEG manual is used, the content and homework within will often need to be modified to match the unique patient population. Other patient factors to consider include readiness and level of anxiety, both of which can interfere with the learning objectives of PEGs.
6. *Structural features.* PEGs are time-limited interventions ranging from 1 to 12 sessions that take place over a brief time period. Size also varies with membership spanning 5 to 100 members depending up the primary goal of the group. PEGs with a remedial focus (i.e., overcoming a specific deficit) are typically smaller (fewer than 15 members) while preventative groups represent the larger end of the spectrum. The amount of time focused on didactic, experiential, and discussion systematically varies by underlying theoretical orientation. Cognitive models devote more time to the didactic component while existential and process models put greater emphasis on the experiential and discussion components.

SHARED CHARACTERISTICS WITH OTHER TYPES OF GROUP TREATMENTS

PEGs are not immune to the dynamic and therapeutic properties that have been associated with group treatments over the past several decades. Indeed, some have persuasively argued for the importance of PEGs' maintaining the "therapeutic" quality found in traditional therapy groups by maintaining a focus on familiar group processes and dynamics. This is not surprising given the interactive, dynamic nature of groups. A few of the more salient considerations include the following.

Group Dynamics

Group dynamics has been described "as the ongoing process in the group; the shifting, changing, individual, and group-as-a-whole variables, including level of participation, resistance, communication patterns, relationships between members and between members and the leader, nonverbal behaviors, feeling tone, and feelings aroused and/or expressed" (Brown, 1998, p. 105). An understanding and appreciation of group dynamics can assist in developing a group environment that is conducive to learning. These principles may be especially important to the experiential and discussion components of PEGs. For instance, there is some evidence that groups pass through predictable stages of development, which, in turn, change the interactive climate and responsiveness of members. Knowledge of such may assist in selecting stage-appropriate activities and discussion topics.

Group Climate

There is ample evidence to suggest that the relationships that a member establishes in a group are related to the ultimate benefit obtained. Use of empirically grounded principles on how to manage group climate can assist PEG leaders in creating an environment most conducive to patient learning. In addition, short self-report measures of such (e.g., Group Climate Questionnaire; MacKenzie, 1983) when used periodically throughout the course of a group can provide invaluable information on patient perceptions.

Problem Members

Troublesome member roles emerge in group treatment, irrespective of the type or theoretical orientation guiding the group. For instance, problematic member roles range from the overparticipating to the underparticipating member, as well as those who engage in disruptive socializing conduct. Each can be detrimental to learning goals and will interrupt the group climate. For instance, overparticipating members might begin telling unrelated stories, use nonverbal distracting behaviors, or seek attention by any means necessary. It behooves the PEG leader to become familiar with the general group process literature to learn of interventions to counteract such behaviors.

Ethical Issues

A PEG leader should be aware of the ethical underpinnings behind group work. The public nature of treatment in a group imposes a unique ethical responsibility upon the leader. Examples are such principles as allowing freedom of exit, orienting and providing information to the client regarding the nature of the group, avoiding imposing the group leader's values, developing goals with member consultation, and considering the issues around a member's premature termination from group. The foremost issue in most members' minds is that of privacy. While PEGs have lower levels of member disclosure, clarity on this point is essential for the leader to address at the beginning of the group and periodically thereafter.

LEADER COMPETENCIES AND TRAINING

A successful PEG leader must master two dimensions of knowledge and skill. The first reflects competencies specific to conducting a psychoeducational group treatment. These are briefly outlined above and are more completely delineated by professional association standards (e.g., ASGW) and in recent texts (Brown, 1998; Coyne, Wilson, & Ward, 1997). The second reflects competencies associated with the subject matter of the PEG. For instance, leaders conducting PEGs that focus on prevention (e.g., HIV) or remediation (e.g., anger management) are expected to develop content mastery associated with a specific topic or psychiatric disorder. These skills often require specialized training.

While it appears that the use of small-group treatments is increasing in mental health delivery systems, an unsettling trend in training mental health professionals was recently reported. Specifically, mental health training programs (e.g., clinical psychology, social work, and psychiatry) appear to be decreasing the number of didactic and experiential courses on small-group treatment. More problematic is that while providers of mental health services (i.e., managed behavioral health companies) expect an increased use of PEGs in the future, the group courses found in mental health training programs typically do not focus on PEGs. This may leave the development of leader competencies to postgraduate training opportunities.

STEPS IN FORMING AND RUNNING A PEG: A PRACTICAL ILLUSTRATION

The literature suggests six steps to form and run a PEG: (1) state a purpose; (2) establish goals; (3) set objectives; (4) select content; (5) design experiential activities; and (6) evaluate. The following example illustrates how these were implemented in developing a PEG for severely and persistently mentally ill patients at a state hospital.

A task force at the hospital was formed to develop a psychoeducational group program for the three patient groups that constituted the bulk of the census: schizophrenia, bipolar disorder, and major depressive disorder. After reviewing the available literature, the task force's statement of purpose was to "provide instruction on management of symptoms associated with the three most frequently occurring disorders." Although separate goals were established for disorders, each was matched to the range of patient abilities considering factors such as cognitive impairment and length of stay. For example, a goal for each disorder was to develop an understanding of the symptoms, symptom triggers, and coping methods for symptom triggers. After establishing goals for the patients, the task force began setting learning objectives that would provide a "road map," or the best way for the members in the group to reach their goals. For instance, a learning objective associated with the aforementioned goal was for patients to identify their own symptoms, articulate the relationship between their symptoms and symptom triggers, and then identify personal methods to deal with symptom triggers. This learning objective actually represented a hierarchy of learning objectives that was laid out as a road map for the group. The PEG initially began with sessions devoted to facts (e.g., typical symptoms and symptom triggers associated with a particular disorder). Facts were followed by in-session application (e.g., identification of personal symptoms and triggers), which then led to an analysis and synthesis of knowledge (e.g., personal methods to deal with symptom triggers) that were presented in a group discussion. Prior to engaging the patients in this learning hierarchy, a road map was presented to the group that articulated the relationship between symptoms, triggers of symptoms, and the relationship between coping with symptom triggers and a prevention of a relapse. Placing learning objectives in a logical order facilitated patient comprehension and also allowed members to understand the importance and links between PEG sessions.

After establishing learning objectives, the task force operationalized each objective by selecting content to support the didactic component of each group session. Relevant literature was culled and material was selected that was engaging and matched the skills and abilities of the patient population at the hospital. After selecting content for the didactic component, exercises were designed that mapped the affective intensity of each with the stage of group treatment (i.e., early, middle, and ending stages of group). For instance, an activity around forming personal strategies to coping with symptom triggers is a common element in symptom management PEGs. However, level of affective intensity with respect to self-disclosure led to exercises with higher disclosure being scheduled for the middle stages of the group. Additionally, less intense content was scheduled for the beginning and ending stages of the group.

The final step for the task force was evaluation, which was approached from three perspectives: content mastery, application, and group climate. Content mastery was assessed using a pre/post measure of the symptom management content presented in the didactic phase of the group. Change on this measure enabled the members and leader to track the major learning objectives of the PEG. The success of the application phase was assessed by a self-report measure of how well the patients were coping with their target symptoms. Finally, a measure of group climate was taken at three times during the course of the group to provide a behavioral assessment of group properties and processes (e.g., engagement, conflict, and avoidance).

References & Readings

Association for Specialists in Group Work. (1991). Association for Specialists in Group Work: Professional standards for training of group workers. *Journal of Specialists in Group Work, 17*(1), 12–19.

Brown, N. W. (1998). *Psychoeducational groups*. New York: Brunner-Routledge.

Burlingame, G., Fuhriman, A., & Johnson, J. (2002). Cohesion in group psychotherapy. In J. C. Norcross (Ed.), *A guide to psychotherapy relationships that work* (pp. 71–88). New York: Oxford University Press.

Burlingame, G. M., MacKenzie, K. R., & Strauss, B. (2003). Small group treatment: Evidence for effectiveness and mechanisms of change. In M. J. Lambert (Ed.), *Handbook of psychotherapy and behavior change* (5th ed., pp. 647–696). New York: Wiley.

Coyne, R. K., Wilson, F. R., & Ward, D. E. (1997). *Comprehensive group work: What it means and how to teach it*. Alexandria, VA: American Counseling Association.

Fuhriman, A., & Burlingame, G. (2001). Group psychotherapy training and effectiveness. *International Journal of Group Psychotherapy, 51*(3), 399–416.

Furr, S. R. (2000). Structuring the group experience: A format for designing psychoeducational groups. *Journal for Specialists in Group Work, 25*(1), 29–49.

Jones, K. D., & Robinson, E. H., III. (2000). Psychoeducational groups: A model for choosing topics and exercises appropriate to group stage. *Journal for Specialists in Group Work, 25*(4), 356–365.

MacKenzie, K. R. (1983). The clinical application of group measure. In R. R. Dies & K. R. MacKenzie (Eds.), *Advances in group psychotherapy: Integrating research and practice* (pp. 159–170). New York: International Universities Press.

Murphy, M. F., & Moller, M. D. (1998). *My symptom management workbook: A wellness expedition*. Nine Mile Falls, WA: Psychiatric Rehabilitation Nurses, Inc.

Rindner, E. C. (2000). Group process-psychoeducation model for psychiatric clients and their families. *Journal of Psychosocial Nursing and Mental Health Issues, 38*(9), 34–41.

Related Topic

Chapter 81, "Group Psychotherapy: An Interpersonal Approach"

PART V
Child and Adolescent Treatment

83 PRINCIPLES OF TREATMENT WITH THE BEHAVIORALLY DISORDERED CHILD

Esther J. Calzada, Arwa Aamiry, & Sheila M. Eyberg

We provide a set of principles for effective psychosocial treatment of children and adolescents with conduct-disordered behavior to which psychologists may refer in preparation for treating these youngsters. The scope of this chapter is limited to children and adolescents between the ages of 2 and 16 years whose problems are related to disruptive behavior disorders, including attention-deficit/hyperactivity disorder, oppositional defiant disorder, and conduct disorder. The challenges to treatment presented by these children and their families are considerable. The following eight principles are designed to maximize treatment effectiveness.

ESTABLISHING AND MAINTAINING RAPPORT

To conduct effective psychotherapy with a disruptive child or adolescent, the psychologist must first establish a safe and comfortable atmosphere for the child in the therapeutic situation. Disruptive children may express their initial apprehensions through behaviors that reflect oppositionality or defiance of the unfamiliar situation in which they may not be voluntarily involved. Providing a structure for the child in the initial stages of therapy will reduce the child's anxiety and help to motivate him or her to participate. This can be accomplished, for example, by reading together *A Child's First Book About Play Therapy* (Nemiroff & Annunziata, 1990) for the 4- to 7-year-old child, which provides age-appropriate information about therapy. Older children also require age-appropriate information about the purpose and process of therapy, presented in a positive but noncoercive atmosphere of understanding and acceptance. To establish a therapeutic alliance, it is always necessary to convey respect for the child and to avoid judging (e.g., belittling, siding with third persons) or laughing at/minimizing problems.

Certain communication techniques help establish and maintain rapport. The use of paraphrasing, for example, through either reflective or summary statements, conveys genuine interest and concern for the child. Paraphrasing also increases the child's willingness to provide information and to consider it and enables the psychologist to verify understanding of that information. Phrasing questions in ways that avoid leading (e.g., closed-ended questions) or blaming (e.g., "why" questions) helps the child feel at ease and consequently increases his or her willingness to participate as well. With disruptive children, key strategies for managing behavior must also be used to keep therapy progressing productively, including, for example, not reinforcing an adolescent for unacceptable verbalizations that are part of the target problem constellation (such as lying, sassing) but conveying respect for both self and client in a matter-of-fact response.

CONSIDERING AGE AND DEVELOPMENTAL LEVEL OF CHILD

Children are constantly undergoing biological, cognitive, social, and affective changes. The span of childhood and adolescence is a disjointed period during which there are rapid shifts in what is deemed appropriate in children's thinking, feeling, and behaving. Thus many expressions of children in therapy are ones that would characterize maladjustment in older or younger children but have no clinical significance for their age-group. Psychologists who work with children must have strong academic grounding in child development but also must keep current with fads and trends by observing normal children at different ages with their peers and by examining children's media and other sources for developmental information.

It is important to keep in mind that a child's rate of development is often not consistent across developmental domains. Knowledge of the child's level of cognitive development is a critical domain in psychotherapy, for many potential therapeutic approaches are cognitive. Even psychologists are prey to assumptions about intellectual functioning based on a child's verbosity and attractiveness. In general, cognitive therapy components of treatment should be reserved for school-age children, although certain preschoolers with exceptional cognitive capacities will benefit from such approaches, just as certain school-age children will require a more concrete therapeutic approach. Cognitive tasks that involve long-term planning are generally reserved for adolescents at or above a 14-year level of cognitive functioning.

DETERMINING DEGREE OF PARENT INVOLVEMENT AND MOTIVATION

To a large extent, the motivation of the parents will determine whether the child remains in therapy. Parents who are not motivated to seek treatment for their child may skip appointments, arrive late, convey to the child that taking him or her to therapy is an inconvenience, or even sabotage therapy, for example, by criticizing the therapy or the therapist to the child. Through parent counseling that addresses the nature and causes of their child's disorder and the notion of a "no-fault disorder," the importance of their child's therapy, and the expected benefits for both the child and themselves, psychologists may increase a parent's motivation.

Among parents who are motivated to bring their child to therapy, there may be significant life stressors that make it difficult for them to do so. For example, it is not uncommon for a single working mother with several young children to feel overwhelmed by the practical issues of her child's therapy such as the financial responsibility, care of her other children, and transportation issues. Psychologists must address these issues before beginning treatment. By anticipating practical solutions to these common problems, psychologists prepare parents for possible obstacles and provide ways to overcome them.

The decision to involve parents in the child's treatment depends in large part on the degree to which the parents are involved in the child's life and the role their behavior plays in the maintenance of the child's symptoms. For most children and adolescents, it is important to involve their parents in treatment (McNeil, Hembree-Kigin, and Eyberg, 1996).

CONSIDERING PARENT PSYCHOPATHOLOGY

A child's psychological functioning is related to the psychological functioning of his or her own parents. Psychological dysfunction in a primary caregiver may contribute powerfully to maintenance of behavior problems in the child; conversely, children with disruptive behavior problems create stressful situations that may exacerbate the parent's dysfunction. Thus assessment of the parent and of the parent-child interaction must precede child treatment. To treat a child successfully, it may be necessary to provide or obtain treatment for the parent as well.

Parent psychopathology must also be considered as it relates to the assessment of the child. Parent interview and parent report measures are the most typical and easiest methods of assessing the child's problems for treatment. Yet parents with significant psychopathology may provide a distorted description and may exaggerate in either direction. Thus, additional sources of information are critical for determining and guiding the course of treatment. These may include teacher rating scales, simple behavior coding of targeted problem behaviors in the session, or use of other informants or methods relevant to the treatment goals.

USING ASSESSMENT TO GUIDE TREATMENT

A thorough understanding of the affective, behavioral, and cognitive functioning of the child is necessary for choosing and implementing a successful treatment. To evaluate the affective and behavioral domains of the child's problems, multiple assessment measures with established validity and reliability—including self-report inventories, ratings by others, and direct observation measures—should be used. Multiple measures provide a fuller understanding of the presenting problem(s) and allow the psychologist to draw on more than a single source of information.

Measures of intellectual functioning and academic achievement are necessary to determine the mode of treatment (e.g., parent training, individual treatment), the type of treatment (e.g., behavioral, insight-oriented), the communication strategies that may be beneficial (e.g., interpretation, instruction), as well as the multiple considerations in the preparation of the individual treatment activities and homework (e.g., What can the child read? How far apart can tangible incentives be used effectively? To what degree can the child understand metaphors?).

The initial assessment must also incorporate a description of the family's strengths and weaknesses in terms of affective, behavioral, and cognitive factors to provide an understanding of the context in which the child's problems exist. For example, factors such as strong parent-child bonding or borderline intellectual functioning of parents would have implications for the child's treatment plan. Exploring the physical, social, and cultural environment of the family is also important for determining the resources available to the child and the limitations imposed by them. All these individual child and family factors must be considered in selecting the most effective treatment.

MAINTAINING TREATMENT INTEGRITY

Integrity of treatment refers to the accuracy of application of the intended treatment. This would include adherence to the techniques that constitute theoretically driven therapies; to specific, session-by-session content and process elements of manualized treatment protocols; and to individual session outlines based on assessment information from the child and family in treatment. Treatment integrity is difficult to maintain with highly complex interventions or with children whose families have multiple social adversities and psychopathologies. Such problems are more common in the treatment of conduct-disordered children than in children with some other disorders, and psychologists must guard against unproductive sidetracking while still helping children and families cope with life events that impinge on the progress of therapy. The integrity of a treatment is protected by preparation of detailed session plans that include specific guidelines for others involved even minimally in the child's treatment, as well as circumspect implementation of the plans. Yeaton and Sechrest (1995) suggest that treatment integrity is best ensured by constant monitoring of the child's change.

PLANNING FOR GENERALIZATION OF TREATMENT

Generalization occurs when the outcome of treatment results in changes extraneous to the original targeted change. These effects should be sought across all settings important to the child's life and across all behaviors relevant to treatment goals. To obtain generalization, it is essential to identify target behaviors that occur in many situations and settings. For example, teaching a young noncompliant child to comply to adult requests will have greater consequence than teaching the child to feed the bird when reminded. Psychologists need to include generalization explicitly within the treatment plan by targeting behaviors most apt to be reinforced in dissimilar natural settings. Psychologists, too, must reinforce occurrences of prosocial behavior within the treatment session with defiant children. Another technique to intensify generalization is to use diverse stimulus and response exemplars that broaden the context in which the child learns new and adaptive behaviors; the more diversity, the greater the generalization (Stokes & Osnes, 1989).

EVALUATING TREATMENT PROGRESS AND OUTCOME

Although the most comprehensive assessment takes place at the beginning of treatment, ongoing assessment is necessary to guide the course of treatment. Frequent and regular assessment allows the psychologist to time strategic changes and to change strategies when progress is not maintained. Ongoing assessment also provides an objective basis on which to determine treatment termination. Monitoring measures must be ones that can be completed quickly and easily and typically are brief rating scales or behavioral frequency counts of target behaviors collected from parents and teachers or by the psychologist during the session.

At the time of termination, treatment outcome assessment allows the psychologist to evaluate the progress of the child and family in a comprehensive and quantified way by readministering measures used at the initial assessment. One criterion by which outcome can be measured is the restoration of the child to a level of functioning attained before the problem(s) developed. Another criterion might be the functioning of the child at a level typical of a normative, or peer-relevant, population. In some cases, the criterion might be the return of a child to school or to the home. In addition to the target goals of treatment, the psychologist should document the associated or generalized areas of change, as well as the areas in which problems remain.

Follow-up assessments serve to evaluate the long-term impact of treatment and provide important information to document the degree to which treatment effects last. For chronic conditions such as the disruptive behavior disorders, it is important to implement multiple strategies for maintenance (see Eyberg, Edwards, Boggs, & Foote, 1998, for a review). The knowledge that the psychologist will be checking in on the child or family after treatment ends often serves to enhance treatment maintenance. A follow-up assessment can also catch early relapse and occasion a booster session to reverse a turnaround. Psychologists should program specific strategies for maintenance into each treatment plan; discussion and planning for maintenance and follow-up with the child and family are always an important part of the treatment termination process.

SUMMARY

The principles of psychosocial treatment of children with disruptive behavior disorders outlined here address the treatment process from the initial assessment through follow-up and maintenance. The principles are applicable to psychosocial treatments broadly, regardless of theoretical orientation. They highlight the uniqueness of the individual child and family, as well as characteristics shared by disruptive children in the therapeutic process. By following these principles, therapists who treat the consequential problems of children with behavior disorders will have maximal efficacy and the highest likelihood of success.

References & Readings 

Bagner, D., & Eybert, S. M. (2003). Father involvement in treatment. In T. H. Ollendick & C. S. Schroeder (Eds.), *Encylopedia of clinical child and pediatric psychology*. New York: Plenum.

Eyberg, S. (1992). Assessing therapy outcome with preschool children: Progress and problems. *Journal of Clinical Child Psychology, 21*, 306–311.

Eyberg, S., Edwards, D., Boggs, S., & Foote, R. (1998). Maintaining the treatment effects of parent training: The role of booster sessions and other maintenance strategies. *Clinical Psychology: Science and Practice, 5*, 544–554.

Foote, R., Eyberg, S., & Schuhmann, E. (1998). Parent-child interaction approaches to the treatment of child conduct problems. In T. Ollendick & R. Prinz (Eds.), *Advances in clinical child psychology* (pp. 125–151). New York: Plenum Press.

Harwood, M., & Eyberg, S. M. (2003). Developmental issues in treatment. In T. H. Ollendick & C. S. Schroeder (Eds.), *Encyclopedia of clinical child and pediatric psychology*. New York: Kluwer.

Herschell, A., Calzada, E., Eyberg, S. M., & McNeil, C. B. (2002). Clinical issues in parent-child interaction therapy. *Cognitive and Behavioral Practice, 9*, 16–27.

Jacobson, N., & Truax, P. (1992). Clinical significance: A statistical approach to defining meaningful change in psychotherapy research. In A. Kazdin (Ed.), *Methodological issues and strategies in clinical research* (4th ed., pp. 631–648). Washington, DC: American Psychological Association.

Jensen, P., Hibbs, E., & Pilkonis, P. (1996). From ivory tower to clinical practice: Future directions for child and adolescent psychotherapy research. In E. Hibbs & P. Jensen (Eds.), *Psychosocial treatments for child and adolescent disorders: Empirically based strategies for clinical practice* (pp. 701–711). Washington, DC: American Psychological Association.

Neary, E. M., & Eyberg, S. M. (2002). Management of disruptive behavior in young children. *Infants and Young Children, 14*, 53–67.

Nemiroff, M. A., & Annunziata, J. (1990). *A child's first book about play therapy*. Washington, DC: American Psychological Association.

Querido, J., Eyberg, S. M., Kanfer, R., & Krahn, G. (2001). Process variables in the child clinical assessment interview. In C. E. Walker & M. C. Roberts (Eds.), *Handbook of clinical child psychology* (3rd ed.). New York: Wiley.

Reisman, J., & Ribordy, S. (1993). *Principles of psychotherapy with children* (2nd ed.). New York: Lexington Books.

Yeaton, W. H., & Sechrest, L. (1995). Critical dimensions in the choice and maintenance of successful treatments: Strength, integrity, and effectiveness. In A. Kazdin (Ed.), *Methodological issues and strategies in clinical research* (4th ed., pp. 137–156). Washington, DC: American Psychological Association.

Related Topic

Chapter 11, "Medical Evaluation of Children With Behavioral or Developmental Disorders"

84 PSYCHOLOGICAL INTERVENTIONS IN CHILDHOOD CHRONIC ILLNESS

Robert J. Thompson, Jr. & Kathryn E. Gustafson

Although specific childhood illnesses are rare, approximately 1 million children (i.e., 2%) have a severe chronic illness that may impair their daily functioning, and an additional 10 million have a less serious chronic illness. Because of advances in health care, children and their families are, in increasing numbers, coping with chronic illness over substantial periods of their lives, which has caused concern about quality of life in general and psychological adjustment in particular (Thompson & Gustafson, 1996).

It is estimated that children with chronic illness have a risk for psychological adjustment problems that is 1½–3 times as high as that of their healthy peers (Pless, 1984). These children seem to be particularly at risk for anxiety-based internalizing difficulties or a combination of internalizing difficulties and milder forms of externalizing problems such as oppositional disorders (Thompson & Gustafson, 1996). Parents and siblings are also at increased risk for adjustment problems. However, good adjustment is not only possible but the norm. Therefore, attention has been focused on delineating processes that account for this variability in adjustment and that may serve as salient intervention targets (Wallander & Thompson, 1995).

Systems-theory perspectives on human development focus on the progressive accommodations that occur throughout the life span between the developing organism and his or her changing environment. Chronic illness can disrupt normal processes of child development and family functioning, and it can be viewed as a potential stressor to which the individual and family systems endeavor to adapt. The goals of care are to diminish the impact of the illness and to prevent dysfunction (Perrin & MacLean, 1988). A major hypothesized mechanism of effect for the impact of chronic illness on children and their families is through disrupting normal processes of child development and family functioning (Perrin & MacLean, 1988).

Models of adaptation that incorporate biomedical, psychosocial, and developmental dimensions, such as the risk and resistance and transactional stress and coping models (Wallander & Thompson, 1995), suggest that the impact of chronic illness can be lessened and adaptation promoted through stress reduction, enhancement of support-eliciting social problem-solving skills, and effective parenting (Thompson & Gustafson, 1996). Additional intervention targets include enhancing adherence to medical regimens and pain management. The effectiveness of psychological interventions can be assessed in accordance with the criteria established by the Task Force on Prevention and Dissemination of Psychological Procedures for "well-established" and "probably efficacious" treatments, with a third category of "promising intervention" added to increase applicability to children with rare health problems (Spirito, 1999).

ENHANCING ADAPTATION

The focus of intervention efforts is on fostering positive adaptation by children and their families to the stresses associated with a chronic illness. One intervention target is stress reduction through multicomponent cognitive and behavioral treatment programs that address cognitive processes of appraisal of stress and methods of coping with stress. More specifically, a combination of emotion-focused and problem-focused coping skills is necessary to deal with the controllable and noncontrollable aspects of chronic illness and their treatments.

Enhancing social skills is another intervention target. In particular, perceived social support, especially classmate support, appears to serve as a protective factor in adaptation to chronic childhood illness. Social skills are necessary to elicit and maintain peer support. Intervention programs focus on developing social-cognitive problem-solving skills. Frequently these skills are developed in the context of school reentry programs designed to reintegrate the child into the school setting after the diagnosis of the chronic illness or a prolonged absence because of the illness and/or treatment regimen. This typically involves a three-pronged approach of enhancing the child's academic and social skills, modifying the school environment, and helping parents be effective advocates for the needs of their child (Thompson & Gustafson, 1996). To improve children's social skills and peer relationships, school reentry programs incorporate social skills training and social-cognitive problem-solving training. For example, one well-developed program has three modules (Varni, Katz, Colegrove, & Dolgin, 1993). The social-cognitive problem-solving module teaches children to identify the problems, explore possible solutions, and evaluate the outcome. The assertiveness-training module teaches children to express their thoughts, wishes, and concerns. The teasing module teaches children how to cope with verbal and physical teasing associated with changes in their physical appearance. The success of these multicomponent programs has been documented in children with cancer (Varni et al., 1993).

Intervention programs are beginning to target improved parenting as a method of fostering adaptation to chronic childhood illness. More specifically, systems theory perspectives suggest that adaptation can be enhanced by reducing parental stress and distress and developing parenting skills conducive to child cognitive and social development. Parenting intervention programs to foster developmentally conducive parent-child interactions are beginning to be designed to meet the illness-related tasks of specific chronic illnesses. The multifamily group intervention for children with diabetes (Satin, La Greca, Zigo, & Skyler, 1989) is an example. The family component consisted of three to five families meeting together for six weekly sessions during which discussion facilitators promoted independent problem-solving skills for managing diabetes. The intervention also included a 1-week simulation component in which parents followed a meal and exercise plan; accomplished blood testing, twice-daily injections of normal saline, and measurement four times daily of urinary glucose and ketones using simulated urine; and recorded results in a diabetes-monitoring diary. Improvements in metabolic functioning relative to controls at both the 3- and 6-month assessment periods occurred for the participants in this multifamily group, with and without the simulated experience component. Increasingly, interventions for children with chronic illness are being provided within a group context. Group treatment of patients, with/without collateral parent/family groups, that target coping and disease management have been found to meet criteria for "well-established" intervention for enhancing psychological adaptation and improving physical symptoms in children and adolescents with diabetes and children with asthma (Plante, Lobato, & Engel, 2001).

ADHERENCE

The estimated adherence rate for medical regimens for the pediatric population is 50% (Lemanek, Kamps, & Chung, 2001). Given the less than one-to-one correspondence between treatment and outcome and the movement to a family-centered, parent-professional, collaborative model of care, noncompliance is no longer viewed as an indicator of irresponsibility and can be a well-reasoned, adaptive choice. Correspondingly, adherence intervention efforts are now directed to providing knowledge, developing specific procedural skills, and tailoring a management plan to the specific needs and realities of the family situation.

Educational and behavioral strategies have been developed for improving adherence to therapeutic regimens. It is clear that knowledge of the therapeutic regimen is necessary but not sufficient for improving adherence. There are three types of behavioral strategies: *stimulus control techniques* include flavoring pills and tailoring the drug regimen to specific daily events; *self-control techniques* include self-regulation of dosage and self-monitoring of both symptoms and medications; *reinforcement techniques* include reinforcing symptom reduction, medication use, and health contacts and feedback on whether drug levels are in the therapeutic range. A review of psychological interventions for nonadherence to medical regimes in patients with asthma, juvenile rheumatoid arthritis (JRA) and type I diabetes found no interventions that met criteria for "well-established" treatment (Lemanek et al., 2001). However, interventions involving changes in clinic and regimen characteristics met criteria for "probably efficacious" and educational and behavioral intervention met criteria for "promising" for asthma; behavioral intervention met criteria for "probably efficacious" for JRA; and multicomponent and operant learning interventions and cognitive-behavioral interventions met criteria for "probably efficacious" and "promising," respectively, for diabetes (Lemanek et al., 2001). Future research needs to use health behavior change theories and findings regarding correlates of adherence to develop interventions that target improved health outcomes as well as adherence (Rapoff, 2001). Single-subject designs are particularly well suited for examination of individual treatment components (Lemanek et al., 2001) and assessment of adherence and disease outcome over time (Rapoff, 2001).

PAIN MANAGEMENT

Pain is a normative experience of everyday life and is also associated with illness and treatments. Pain involves a sensation component and a response component, which includes the psychological, emotional, and behavioral responses to the sensation. Pain management is one of the tasks associated with chronic illness (Thompson & Gustafson, 1996). Approaches to pain management can involve analgesics, cognitive-behavioral therapy, or a combination of both.

Children with illnesses typically confront two types of pain: pain associated with invasive medical procedures and recurrent pain that is a frequent symptom of a number of illnesses such as sickle-cell disease, hemophilia, juvenile rheumatoid arthritis, and recurrent abdominal pain. Cognitive-behavioral treatment approaches to managing chronic and recurrent pediatric pain have been characterized by techniques to regulate pain perception and techniques to modify pain behavior. The self-regulatory techniques for pain perception include muscle relaxation, deep breathing, and guided imagery and active coping strategies, including diverting attention and reinterpreting pain sensations (Varni, Walco, & Katz, 1989). Pain behavior regulation techniques focus on identifying and modifying socioenvironmental factors that influence pain expression. Cognitive-behavioral family interventions call attention to the role of caregivers in providing discriminative cues and in selectively reinforcing behavioral expressions of pain and self-management skills through attention (Sanders, Shepherd, Cleghorn, & Woolford, 1994). Cognitive-behavioral therapy meets criteria for "well-established" treatment for procedural pain (Powers, 1999), "probably efficacious" treatment for reducing symptoms of recurrent abdominal pain (Janicke & Finney, 1999), and "promising" intervention for reducing musculoskeletal pain (Walco, Sterling, Conte, & Engel, 1999). However, cognitive-behavioral interventions with children with cancer and sickle cell disease have not met efficacy criteria due to small sample sizes and absence of control groups and replicable treatments (Walco et al., 1999).

SUMMARY

Interventions based on social-learning theory are effective in relation to primary intervention targets. More specifically, cognitive-behavioral interventions improve stress management, enhance support-eliciting social problem-solving skills, enhance parental fostering of their children's cognitive and social development and management of children's behavior problems, and improve adherence and pain management skills. These cognitive-behavioral interventions have multiple components; are beginning to be incorporated within family systems approaches; and are being modified to fit the particular tasks and situations associated with specific chronic illnesses.

References & Readings 

Janicke, D. M., & Finney, J. W. (1999). Empirically supported treatments in pediatric psychology: Recurrent abdominal pain. *Journal of Pediatric Psychology, 24,* 115–128.

Lemanek, K. L., Kamps, J., & Chung N. B. (2001). Empirically supported treatments in pediatric psychology: Regimen adherence. *Journal of Pediatric Psychology, 26,* 253–276.

Perrin, J. M., & MacLean, W. E., Jr. (1988). Children with chronic illness: The prevention of dysfunction. *Pediatric Clinics of North America, 35,* 1325–1337.

Plante, W. A., Lobato, D., & Engel, R. (2001). Renew of group interventions for pediatric chronic conditions. *Journal of Pediatric Psychology, 26,* 435–453.

Pless, I. B. (1984). Clinical assessment: Physical and psychological functioning. *Pediatric Clinics of North America, 31,* 33–45.

Powers, S. (1999). Empirically supported treatments in pediatric psychology. *Journal of Pediatric Psychology, 24,* 131–146.

Rapoff, M. A. (2001). Commentary: Pushing the envelope: Furthering research on improving adherence to chronic pediatric regimens. *Journal of Pediatric Psychology, 26,* 277–278.

Sanders, M. R., Shepherd, R. W., Cleghorn, G., & Woolford, H. (1994). The treatment of recurrent abdominal pain in children: A controlled comparison of cognitive-behavioral family intervention and standard pediatric care. *Journal of Consulting and Clinical Psychology, 62,* 306–314.

Satin, W., La Greca, A. M., Zigo, M. A., & Skyler, J. S. (1989). Diabetes in adolescence: Effects of multifamily group interventions and parent simulation of diabetes. *Journal of Pediatric Psychology, 14,* 259–275.

Spirito, A. (1999). Introduction to special series on empirically supported treatments in pediatrics psychology. *Journal of Pediatric Psychology, 24,* 87–90.

Thompson, R. J., Jr., & Gustafson, K. E. (1996). *Adaptation to chronic childhood illness.* Washington, DC: American Psychological Association.

Varni, J. W., Katz, E. R., Colegrove, R., Jr., & Dolgin, M. (1993). The impact of social skills training on the adjustment of children with newly diagnosed cancer. *Journal of Pediatric Psychology, 18,* 751–767.

Varni, J. W., Walco, G. A., & Katz, E. R. (1989). A cognitive-behavioral approach to pain associated with pediatric chronic disease. *Journal of Pain and Symptom Management, 4,* 238–241.

Walco, G. A., Sterling, C. N., Conte, P. M., & Engel, R. G. (1999). Empirically supported treatments in pediatric psychology: Disease-related pain. *Journal of Pediatric Psychology, 24,* 155–167.

Wallander, J. L., & Thompson, R. J., Jr. (1995). Psychosocial adjustment of children with chronic physical conditions. In M. C. Roberts (Ed.), *Handbook of pediatric psychology* (2nd ed., pp. 124–141). New York: Guilford Press.

Related Topics

Chapter 11, "Medical Evaluation of Children With Behavioral or Developmental Disorders"

Chapter 57, "Psychological Interventions in Adult Disease Management"

85 METHODS TO ENGAGE THE RELUCTANT ADOLESCENT

Alice K. Rubenstein

ADOPT AN INTEGRATIVE FRAMEWORK

The majority of difficulties facing adolescents today are systemic, requiring an integrative approach in regard to both diagnosis and treatment. Although effective psychotherapeutic interventions draw from the more traditional therapies, treating adolescents requires system interventions with a focus on here-and-now problem solving. Adolescents who are reluctant to enter treatment often believe that we have nothing to offer them. They assume we will not understand them, that we will align with their parents and other authority figures against them, and that we have no clue about their lives. Therefore, from the moment of first interaction, it is critical to communicate your allegiance to the adolescent and to demonstrate that you have some understanding of their ecology.

AVOID TRADITIONAL MODELS

Traditional models, developed for working with children and adults, are frequently not appropriate. Adolescents are beyond the playroom, and most do not have the patience for the traditional "talk" therapies. Insight can come later. In treating reluctant adolescents, it is important to begin by focusing on *their* concerns in the present. As soon as possible, you must be able to get the reluctant adolescents to believe that you can help with something that matters to them.

BEGIN WITH THE FIRST CONTACT

The initial phone contact provides the opportunity to begin assessing the presenting problem(s) and ascertaining the adolescent's appropriateness for the therapist's skills and setting. Most often, initial contact is made by a parent and provides the opportunity to present the general parameters of treatment. Specific points to be covered include: The timing and content of feedback to the parents; the likely need for collateral contacts with the other systems and professionals who interact with the adolescent; the responsible parties for getting the adolescent to his/her appointments; payment and insurance coverage procedures; expectation of their support and involvement in the adolescent's treatment; and most important, the confidential nature of your sessions with the adolescent. While reluctant adolescents rarely initiate treatment, an adolescent who has been court-ordered to seek treatment might make the first contact. In those cases, it is most often both legally and financially necessary to gain parental permission for treatment.

SCHEDULE AN INITIAL MEETING WITH PARENTS

Parents are a critical resource for gathering diagnostic data. The decision to have an initial meeting with the parent(s) is based on a number of factors, including the age of the adolescent; the therapist's initial feel for the presenting problems; the parents' anxiety; and the therapist's style. Reluctant adolescents will often test a therapist's trustworthiness by seeing how he or she handles confidentiality. The adolescent's confidentiality is best ensured by having the initial meeting with the parents prior to the first session with the adolescent. Except in unusual circumstances, any additional meetings with parents should take place in the presence of the adolescent or, if this is not possible, with the adolescent's full knowledge and permission. In addition to being a chance to gather diagnostic information, the meeting with the parent(s) provides insight into parenting style and family dysfunction. It is helpful to have both parents attend this meeting, even in cases of separation or divorce. If a joint meeting is not possible, meet separately with each parent.

MAKE CONTACT WITH THE ADOLESCENT

In most cases, the parent(s) arrange the initial appointment for the adolescent. However, I recommend telephone confirmation directly with the adolescent. This direct contact not only communicates respect for the adolescent as a separate person but also provides data regarding the degree of the adolescent's resistance to treatment. While the majority of adolescents have been bribed, forced, or prodded into entering treatment, the reluctant adolescent poses the greatest challenge for the therapist. Often feeling coerced or forced to see a therapist, they feel controlled and intruded on. Many treatment-reluctant adolescents often have great difficulty owning and verbalizing their problems, and they do not see how talking to someone whom they have never met before and who knows nothing about them can help.

CONDUCT INDIVIDUAL AND SYSTEMS ASSESSMENTS

When a therapist is working with adolescents, two diagnostic assessments are being made simultaneously: the traditional individual assessment of the adolescent as "patient" and an assessment of the adolescent's systems. Assessment is interwoven with the ongoing process of listening, supporting, confronting, and reframing. Systems assessment is accomplished by exploring the adolescent's experience of all the systems in which he or she interacts—for example, family, school, community—as well as accessing as much direct information as possible from and about these systems. This includes an assessment of relevant stressors, such as parent-adolescent conflicts; peer group relationships; school achievement, including possible learning disabilities; daily stressors, including home and work responsibilities; and stressful life events, including geographic relocation, divorce, and deaths. It usually takes three sessions or more to establish the rapport necessary to identify the major contributors to the reluctant adolescent's dysfunctional affect and behavior. Understanding the adolescent in developmental and systemic contexts is key to engaging the reluctant adolescent.

EMPHASIZE THE FIRST SESSION

In their first few minutes of contact, adolescents usually determine whom they can and cannot trust. The first encounter with the treatment-reluctant adolescent must be handled carefully. If there is a parent in the waiting room, greet the adolescent first. Express appreciation directly to the adolescent for coming, especially since it was likely not his/her decision. Cover the limits and boundaries of confidentiality as soon as possible. Since in most instances you will have already met with the parent(s), share with the adolescent what you have been told about the "problem." Ask the adolescent if he or she agrees or disagrees with what you have been told. Inquire about what the adolescent thinks the problem is. Find out what he or she wants. Emphasize that you work for the *adolescent,* not for his/her parents, school, or the court. Be honest and don't be afraid to use humor.

REFER FOR PSYCHOLOGICAL TESTING

Standardized assessment methods are useful with this population, particularly if the therapist suspects intellectual, learning, or neurological problems. At the same time, it is important to move slowly and work with the reluctant adolescent to help him or her see how such an assessment can benefit *him or her*. Careful consideration must be given to who will conduct the testing, and the adolescent must be assured that all test results will be shared with him or her, preferably before they are shared with anyone else. No test results should be shared with a school or any agency without the adolescent's knowledge or permission, unless legally required. In light of the complexity of forming a therapeutic alliance with an adolescent, many clinicians refer diagnostic testing to an outside resource.

ASSURE CONFIDENTIALITY

Confidentiality is essential in establishing and maintaining the integrity of a viable working relationship with any adolescent, but it is especially critical with the treatment-reluctant adolescent. The guidelines for confidentiality should be established at the time of initial contact with the parents and discussed with the adolescent at the beginning of treatment. Assuring confidentiality is the first step in gaining trust and empowering the treatment-reluctant adolescent. Explaining to parents the therapeutic value of confidentiality not only helps them to support the treatment process but also provides for developmentally appropriate separation between the adolescent and his/her parents.

CLARIFY THE BOUNDARIES OF CONFIDENTIALITY

Confidentially requires that the therapist not repeat anything the adolescent says (except for the legally mandated exceptions). The adolescent needs assurance that the therapist will not withhold any contact the therapist has with the adolescent's parents. Treatment-reluctant adolescents will often watch for any behavior on the part of the therapist that can be considered a violation of confidentiality. If the adolescent suggests such a violation has occurred, the therapist should immediately inquire why he or she believes that confidentiality has been compromised. The therapist should then either clarify what did or did not happen and, in either case, express concern for the adolescent's understandable feelings of betrayal, as well as offer an apology if something was said that made the adolescent feel that trust had been compromised. What is most important is not to allow this confrontation to be used as a justification to stop treatment.

The confidentiality agreement requires that parents have assurance that the therapist is taking clinical responsibility for determining the boundaries of confidentiality. Both the adolescent and his/her parents should be informed that confidentiality will be waived if the therapist judges that the adolescent is in danger of harming him or herself. If this becomes necessary, it is best to tell the adolescent first. In keeping with the goal of empowerment, the adolescent should be encouraged to talk directly with his/her parents, possibly in a family session. In cases where there is suspected physical or sexual abuse, the adolescent must be informed that you are required by law to notify the appropriate agency.

INVOLVE PARENTS

In most cases, particularly with younger adolescents, therapeutic change necessitates parental involvement in the treatment process. At the same time, working with treatment-reluctant adolescents requires balancing parental involvement with patient confidentiality. It is often necessary to wait for many weeks—until there is a solid therapeutic alliance—before directly addressing the parents' role in the adolescent's dysfunctional behavior. Whenever possible, sessions with parents should take place when the adolescent is present. Having the adolescent directly involved in negotiations with his/her family system enhances developmentally appropriate empowerment. However, the treatment-reluctant adolescent may well refuse to be part of any such meeting, or the therapist's clinical judgment may suggest having separate meetings with parents before meeting with them together with the adolescent. If the adolescent does not attend the meeting, be sure to meet, call, or e-mail the adolescent as soon as possible after the meeting. What is most important is to assure the adolescent that the clinician has maintained his/her confidentiality during the meeting and share, as clinically indicated, what transpired at the meeting.

INVOLVE THE ADOLESCENT IN EXTERNAL CONTACTS

In all situations, it is essential to involve adolescents in decisions regarding contact with their parents, teachers, and other adults or agencies. A signed release should be secured from the parents *and* the adolescent before any collateral contacts are made. This is particularly important in regard to medical and legal issues. In terms of the parents, this is a legal necessity; with the adolescent it is a therapeutic one. Whenever possible, work directly with the adolescent in the preparation of any court-ordered written report.

HANDLE PARENTAL CONTACT WITH CARE

The therapist should take phone calls from parents regarding their adolescents. The therapist may listen, but should not offer any information that might compromise confidentiality. If there is a question about how the adolescent would feel about your sharing something with their parents, check with the adolescent first. You can call the parent(s) back. It is a lot more difficult to get the treatment-reluctant adolescent back if he or she believes you have violated his/her trust. The therapist is free to share with the adolescent all communications with the parents.

FIT THE THERAPIST AND OFFICE TO THE ADOLESCENT

If the adolescent is coming straight from school or work, then offer a snack or beverage. The therapist's attire should be casual, avoiding strong images of power and authority. Consider your office environment. Adolescents do not wish to be confronted with how learned we are. Shelves stacked with books and journals are often distancing. The physical environment should be comfortable and inviting.

CONSIDER MULTIPLE TREATMENT MODALITIES

Group therapy is often the treatment of choice for adolescents with dual or multiple diagnoses, particularly in cases of substance abuse, depression, and oppositional disorders. Group psychotherapy makes use of peer confrontation and support, while providing for connection and belonging. As increased autonomy emerges as a primary struggle during adolescence, family therapy can help to mediate parent-adolescent conflicts, as well as foster effective communication through the process of separation and individuation. Treatment-reluctant adolescents are surprised and affirmed when the therapist confronts the parents with the fact that their sons or daughters' problems are not *all* their fault. Resistance is lowered when the adolescent sees that the therapist does not see the parents as always being *right*. As with individual psychotherapy, confidentiality, collateral contacts, and parental involvement must be clearly defined.

CULTIVATE EMPOWERMENT

Psychotherapy with adolescents requires a special kind of advocacy. It is a delicate balance between helping adolescents empower themselves while providing support, confrontation, and direct intervention when needed. Focus on *what they need*, not why they were sent or ruminate about their helplessness. It is important to begin to set operational goals early on. Tangible things *they* want to be different. Help them to identify exchanges or trade-offs they can make with those in power—for example, a C average in exchange for being able to get a driving permit. It is often helpful to make a list. Their goals might include such things as a later curfew, increased spending money, having more friends, getting a job, doing better in school, eliminating substance abuse, reducing delinquent behaviors, surviving in a dysfunctional system. Identify ways *they* can try to reach *their* goals by brainstorming with them. The process involves teaching and modeling how they can take control of their own life. Be careful not to take responsibility for their reaching their goals. It is *their* job, and then the success is *theirs*.

AVOID SPLITTING WITH THE SYSTEMS

Almost every adolescent who appears for treatment is angry with one or more of the systems with which he or she interacts. While it is important for the therapist to be supportive of the adolescent's feelings, it is equally important not to pair with the adolescent against all of these systems and to engage in institutional splitting. Adolescents want and need the support and approval of these systems, even if they are dysfunctional. Whenever possible, the adolescent should be encouraged and helped to figure out ways to meet his/her own needs while, at the same time, find ways to work with the systems with which he or she must interact.

MONITOR COUNTERTRANSFERENCE CAREFULLY

It is critical for therapists to maintain a therapeutic boundary between themselves and their adolescent patients. Overidentification with the treatment-reluctant adolescent can damage the therapeutic relationship and interfere with productive change. Adolescents must learn how to navigate their own systems, regardless of the degree of dysfunction. Empowerment necessitates appropriate boundaries. Adolescents will not feel truly empowered unless they believe that *they* are primarily responsible for making positive changes in their lives.

INTERVENE OUTSIDE OF THE OFFICE

Since the world of the adolescent is significantly impacted by other systems, it is important to be willing to leave the office. This may include meetings with teachers, youth leaders, and probation officers. Always inform the adolescent that such a meeting has been requested or that you would like to have such a meeting. Empower adolescent patients to take an active role in effecting change by encouraging them to attend. If they refuse, review with them what you will say at the meeting. In seeking to engage the reluctant adolescent, the therapist may determine that it is therapeutically appropriate to meet with the adolescent outside the office setting for one or more sessions. In any of these situations, do whatever is necessary to ensure his/her trust and connection.

BE FLEXIBLE AND AVAILABLE

Unlike adults, adolescents require a great deal more flexibility and availability in the course of treatment. They often require far more phone contact, especially in a crisis. The therapist must establish a balance between keeping appropriate boundaries and becoming too rigid. It is helpful to let adolescents know if and how they can reach you between sessions. In addition, the course of treatment with adolescents is likely to be more variable than it is with adults. Particularly with the reluctant adolescent, it is important to balance regular contact with offering some choice of when the next session should take place. If possible, try to leave no more than ten days between the first three sessions.

MODEL AN APPROPRIATE TERMINATION

The psychotherapy relationship is critical in an adolescent's life, and thus termination has special ramifications and opportunities. Emphasize an open-ended arrangement and the ability to reinitiate contact. Underscore the ongoing process of solving life problems. Reinforce the adolescent's successes and his/her acquired skills. Remind adolescents of any initial reluctance and tell them again how much you appreciate their willingness to give you a chance to work with them. Let them know that you have learned things from them that will help in your work with other adolescents. Discuss your position on posttherapy contacts, such as writing, phone contact, graduations, holiday cards, and weddings. Encourage adolescents to discuss their feelings about termination. Within a therapeutic context, share your own feelings about the termination. Model a healthy and mature farewell.

References, Readings, & Internet Sites 

Benhke, S. H., & Warner, E. W. (2002, March). Confidentiality in the treatment of adolescents. *Monitor on Psychology,* 44–45.

Bratter, T. (1977). The psychotherapist as advocate: Extending the therapeutic alliance with adolescents. *Journal of Contemporary Psychotherapy, 8,* 119–126.

Cauce, A. M., Domenech-Rodriguez, M., Paradise, M., Cochran, B. N., Shea, J. M., Srebnick, D., & Baydar, N. (2002). Cultural and contextual influences in mental health help seeking: A focus on ethnic minority youth. *Journal of Consulting and Clinical Psychology, 70,* 44–55.

Holmbeck, G. N., & Kendall, P. C. (2002). Introduction to the special section on clinical adolescent psychology: Developmental psychopathology and treatment. *Journal of Consulting and Clinical Psychology, 70,* 3–5.

Kazdin, A. E. (1993). Adolescent mental health: Prevention and treatment programs. *American Psychologist, 48,* 127–141.

Lazarus, A. A. (1995). Can psychotherapists transcend the shackles of their training and superstitions. *Journal of Clinical Psychology, 46,* 351–358.

Mental Health Risk Factors for Adolescents. (n.d.). Resource page. Retrieved 2004 from http://www.education.indiana.edu/cas/adol/mental.html

Petersen, A., Compas, B., Brooks-Gunn, J., Stemmler, M., Ey, S., & Grant, K. (1993). Depression in adolescence. *American Psychologist, 48,* 155–168.

Rubenstein, A. (2003). (Ed.). Issue on adolescent psychotherapy. *In Session: Journal of Clinical Psychology, 59*(11).

Rubenstein, A., & Zager, K. (Eds.). (1995). Adolescent treatment: New frontiers and new dimensions. *Psychotherapy, 32,* 2–6.

Sommers-Flanagan, J., & Sommers-Flanagan, R. (1997). *Tough kids, cool counseling: User-friendly approaches with challenging youth.* Alexandria, VA: American Counseling Association.

Steinberg, L. (2002). Clinical adolescent psychology. What it is and what it needs to be. *Journal of Consulting and Clinical Psychology, 70,* 124–128.

Surviving Adolescence. (n.d.). Home page. Retrieved 2004 from http://www.rcpsych.ac.uk/info/help/adol/index.htm

Weisz, J. R., & Hawley, K. M. (2002). Developmental factors in the treatment of adolescents. *Journal of Consulting and Clinical Psychology, 70,* 21–43.

Weisz, J. R., Weiss, B., Alicke, M. D., & Klotz, M. L. (1987). Effectiveness of psychotherapy with children and adolescents: Meta-analytic findings for clinicians. *Journal of Consulting and Clinical Psychology, 55,* 542–549.

Young, I., Anderson, C., & Steinbrecher, A. (1995). Unmasking the phantom: Creative assessment of the adolescent. *Psychotherapy, 32,* 34–38.

Related Topics

Chapter 78, "Guidelines for Conducting Couple and Family Therapy"

Chapter 83, "Principles of Treatment With the Behaviorally Disordered Child"

Chapter 121, "A Model for Clinical Decision Making With Dangerous Patients"

86 THE APSAC STUDY GUIDES

Jeannie Baker & Sam S. Hill III

The American Professional Society on the Abuse of Children (APSAC) is the nation's largest interdisciplinary professional society for those working in the field of child abuse and neglect. APSAC's mission is to improve society's response to the abuse and neglect of its children by promoting effective interdisciplinary approaches to the identification, intervention, treatment, and prevention of child maltreatment.

APSAC currently has three study guides available:

- Volume 1. *Assessment of Sexual Offenders Against Children* (Quinsey and Lalumiere, 1996)
- Volume 2. *Evaluating Children Suspected of Having Been Sexually Abused* (Faller, 1996)
- Volume 3. *Medical Evaluation of Physically and Sexually Abused Children* (Jenny, 1996)

These study guides are intended to provide an outline of information in specific aspects of child maltreatment and to direct the professional to available research material.

They are summarized in the following pages.

APSAC STUDY GUIDE, VOLUME 1: *ASSESSMENT OF SEXUAL OFFENDERS AGAINST CHILDREN*

The APSAC Study Guide, Volume 1, *Assessment of Sexual Offenders Against Children* (Quinsey & Lalumiere, 1996), is written for health care professionals involved in assessment of child molesters. It is not intended to be a "how to" manual but, rather, an outline of the key elements that constitute the assessment of child molesters. This guide also provides direction to available research in this area.

Introduction

- Defining the sexual offender
- Understanding child molestation as a common, transcultural, and historical occurrence
- Key differences of forensic assessment versus nonforensic clinical assessments
- Theorizing an explanation for offender behavior

Characteristics of Sexual Offenders Against Children

- Differentiating characteristics peculiar to child molesters
- Level of social competence and social skills as a variable
- Studies of sexual offenders' cognitive beliefs and patterns
- Sexual preferences of child molesters as a function of sexual response patterns and sexual history
- Relationship between personality tests results and psychopathology
- Suggested differences in hormone and brain dysfunction in child molesters
- Taxonomic research
- Situational determinants as predictors

Implications for Practice

- Assessment utilizing the clinical interview, psychological testing, phallometric assessment, and polygraph tests

Appraising Risk

- Recidivism risk appraisal

Treatment Planning

- Determining treatability and treatment needs

Ethical Issues

- Determining the referral source and client
- Maintaining confidentiality amid reporting mandates
- Professional and legal guidelines

The Report

- Possible conflicts of interest
- Adequate and inadequate reports

Recommended Assessment Instruments

- Standard assessment battery to assess risk of recidivism, treatment needs, and supervision needs
- Battery also to include (when relevant) measures of personality, psychopathology, social skills, brain and hormonal dysfunction
- Free drawings by the child as evaluative measures of sexual abuse
- Interpretation caveats
- Lack of research on evaluation of very young children
- Significant reliance on nonabusing caregiver report
- Observation of alleged abuser-child interaction as an alternative
- Use of multiple, brief interview sessions

APSAC STUDY GUIDE, VOLUME 2:
EVALUATING CHILDREN SUSPECTED OF HAVING BEEN SEXUALLY ABUSED

The APSAC Study Guide, Volume 2, *Evaluating Children Suspected of Having Been Sexually Abused* (Faller, 1996), is written to familiarize the health care professional with the basics of (alleged) child sexual abuse assessment. The study guide also provides the reader with information necessary to evaluate current research, conduct a comprehensive evaluation, and defend his or her feelings.

Models for Evaluating Child Sexual Abuse

- The most widely used and accepted model for determining an allegation of sexual abuse is the Child Interview model
- Less widely used for evaluating sexual abuse allegations is the Parent-Child Interaction model
- The Comprehensive Evaluation model is best suited for assessment of allegations of intrafamilial sexual abuse, where complexity and multiple victims/offenders may be present

Interviewer Objectivity and Allegations of Sexual Abuse

- Gender, profession, and age differences
- Other factors affecting evaluation objectivity
- Research on false allegations by children

Number of Child Interviews

- Repetition of allegations to multiple professionals increases risk of contamination of disclosure, trauma to child
- Advantages and disadvantages of both too few and too many interviews by a single professional
- Individual differences among children in disclosing sexual victimization
- Situational and logistical factors affecting the interview

Documentation

- Advantages and disadvantages of videotaping
- Determining the specifics of videotaping procedure
- Necessity for informed consent of the child, including familiarization with equipment and professionals involved

- Assessment of child's overall functioning over and above the sexual abuse through audio/visual documentation

Standardized Tests

- Appropriateness of psychological testing for differentiating the sexually abused child
- Behavior checklists for accessing symptomology in the victim and as third-party report by caregiver
- Using projective tests to elicit information related to the victim's sexual experience

Questioning Techniques

- Avoiding the use of leading questions—i.e., yes or no questions or multiple choice, as well as coercive techniques; utilizing open-ended questions instead, primarily, or in combination with free narrative

Media for Interviewing Children

- Appropriateness of using anatomical dolls to elicit sexualized doll play
- Sexually abused children more likely to engage in sexual behavior with anatomical dolls than nonabused children.
- In general, no significant difference between uses of anatomical versus nonanatomical dolls as "props" to elicit responses from sexually abused children
- Preferability of having experienced professionals use anatomical dolls
- Seven primary functions of anatomical dolls
- Timing and scenarios of presentation of anatomical dolls
- Opinions vary as how to use anatomical dolls—in general, taking cues from the child and varying techniques circumstantially
- Anatomical drawings as a substitute for, or prelude to, anatomical dolls
- Anatomical drawings are not as controversial as anatomical dolls and can become a permanent part of the case record

Special Considerations for Cases Involving Very Young Children

- Chronological age versus developmental age
- Reliance upon caregiver report
- Observation of alleged abuser-child interaction as an alternative
- Need for multiple interviews
- Play themes

Children as Witnesses

- Abundance of analogue studies to assess the accuracy of sexual abuse experiences
- Ecological validity of child participation
- Ecological validity of questioning procedures
- Children's memory of events varies by age and context of experience
- Children are fairly resistant to suggestive questioning, but children less than 4 years of age are less resistant than their older peers
- Children more likely to make errors of omission than commission
- Use of positive reinforcement appears to affect the responses of younger children more than older children
- Children take what adults communicate to them seriously—that is, if an adult communicates certain facts about a situation of which a child has no direct knowledge, the child assumes the adult is telling the truth
- Young children can be programmed to believe they have had experiences which they have not

False Allegations

- Determining the difference between a false allegation and an unsubstantiated allegation
- Consensually arrived-at criteria are the most valid measure to identify false allegations
- False allegations generated by adults are more common than false allegations by children
- False accusations of sexual abuse by children are quite uncommon, but more likely to be made by older children, usually adolescents
- Very young children may make fictitious al-

legations, primarily to please the evaluator or in response to leading questions.
- Custody and/or visitation battles between parents occasionally result in false allegations
- Children also occasionally identify the wrong abuser—someone less feared or less loved

Criteria for Deciding Whether an Allegation Is Valid

- Review of various professionals' suggested guidelines for determining sexual abuse
- Child interview is central to any sexual abuse evaluation, especially documentation of affect consistent in the abuse description, details of the sexual abuse, and advanced sexual knowledge

Forming Conclusions

- Reaching conclusions regarding the truthfulness of the child
- Drawing conclusions about whether the child has been sexually abused
- Utilization of supporting evidence
- Inconclusive evaluations—using an extended evaluation
- Protection of the child when the evaluation is inconclusive

APSAC STUDY GUIDE, VOLUME 3: *MEDICAL EVALUATION OF PHYSICALLY AND SEXUALLY ABUSED CHILDREN*

The APSAC Study Guide, Volume 3, *Medical Evaluation of Physically and Sexually Abused Children* (Jenny, 1996), has been designed to familiarize the health care professional with the broad range of information contained in the medical literature about the physical and sexual abuse of children. It is not intended to be a textbook on child abuse, but rather to serve as a guide to the best information available and to help the professional locate that information. Also included in the study guide is a glossary of medical terms in laypersons' terms.

Child Physical Abuse: Epidemiology, Risk Factors, and Evaluation

- Necessity for a complete medical and psychosocial history and circumstances leading to the injury in question, including report by the child, where appropriate
- Environmental assessment of the abuse site, including interviews with neighbors and others present at the time of the alleged incident
- Exam should be performed as soon as child is stable and should include growth chart measurements and a detailed comprehensive head-to-toe physical, including genitalia and anus
- Siblings should also be interviewed and examined
- Skeletal X-rays, bone scans, CT scans, and MRIs are recommended, as well as blood work
- Findings should be thoroughly documented in the child's chart

Abdominal Trauma

- Small bowel injuries are uncommon. Diagnosis can be difficult and symptoms nonspecific.
- Stomach injuries are also less common, frequently presenting as peritonitis from gastric rupture.
- Liver injuries can be very difficult to diagnose, especially in the absence of history of trauma; urinalysis and blood tests are useful.
- Pancreatic injuries, especially pancreatitis, can be diagnosed by CT, ultrasound, or blood work.
- Urinary tract injuries are not commonly reported but can be life-threatening.
- Adrenal gland and cardiac injuries are uncommon but do occur.
- Suspected chest and abdominal trauma can be confirmed through computerized tomography (CT), ultrasound, or upper GI tract series.

Burns

- Burns, a common form of child abuse, are categorized by burn depth as it relates to the layer of skin affected.
- First-degree, or epidermal, burns affect the outermost skin layer, causing only redness.
- Second-degree, or partial thickness, burns involve both the epidermal and dermal layers; they can be superficial or deep.
- Third-degree, or full thickness, burns completely destroy the dermis.
- Depth of burn depends on temperature of water and length of time in water.
- Hot-liquid burns are often accidental, the result of a children pulling a pan of water or grease from a stove; these burns are especially damaging.
- Cigarettes, electric irons, hair dryers, and cigarette lighters result in pattern (contact) burns; like other burns their severity depends on temperature of object and length of exposure.
- Open flame, such as a gas stove, or flammable liquids cause flame burns, often accompanied by smoke inhalation.
- Heat stroke frequently occurs when neglectful caregivers leave children in parked cars; heat stroke results in cerebral edema and bleeding, liver and kidney failure, and circulatory collapse.
- Predictive factors associated with child abuse by burning include delay in seeking medical assistance and an injury not consistent with the report of injury cause.
- Psychological factors in children with abusive burn injuries include depression, language deficits, inappropriate affect, withdrawal, attention deficits, and tactile defensiveness.
- Social factors associated with abused burn victims include low SES, adolescent parents, premature birth, postnatal illness, physical or mental handicap.

Chest Injuries

- Chest injuries, other than rib fractures from squeezing or shaking an infant's thorax, are seldom noted as a consequence of child abuse.
- Lung, heart, and mediastinal injuries constitute the number of child physical abuse classified as chest injuries.

Injuries to the Face, Ears, Mouth, Throat, and Nose

- Orofacial trauma is routinely encountered in physically abused children.
- Facial contusions are the most common according to recent studies.
- Injuries to the lips, tongue, and teeth are frequent.
- Facial fractures are less common, but when present involve the nose, jawbone, temporal bone, and eye socket.
- Other frequent orofacial injuries occur to the palate, pharynx, larynx, nose, and ears.

Fractures

- Certain fractures occur more frequently as a result of abuse than by accident.
- Peritoneal elevation is not often seen in nonabused children.
- Long bone fractures reflect the type of force applied to the bone, either spiral fractures from rotational force, transverse fractures from translational forces, or compression fractures from axial loading.
- Metaphysical fractures are rarely seen as the result of an accidental injury; these fractures usually occur in children under the age of 2 as the result of child abuse.
- Nine other fracture types are moderately to highly particular to abused children; they include posterior rib, scapular, spinous process, sternal fractures; digital and complex skull, multiple fractures, and fractures of different ages; epiphyseal plate injuries; and vertebral body fractures and subluxations.
- Differential diagnosis is important in distinguishing between abuse and nonabuse fractures.
- Specific guidelines are available for imaging of suspected child abuse victims.
- Healing of fractures varies by injury site and between individual children.

Head Injuries

- The most lethal form of child abuse is head trauma; often fatal; if not fatal, children are left with permanent neurological illnesses such as seizures, cerebral palsy, blindness, or deafness.
- Infants are more vulnerable to head trauma because of a softer brain with immature neurons, and unmyelinated nerves; also, the presence of more cerebrospinal fluid and proportionately larger heads.
- Types of abusive head injuries include injuries to the scalp, hair loss, bleeding under the scalp, bleeding under the external periosteum of the skull, skull fractures, epidural and subdural hematomas, dural tears, brain tissue injury, and spinal cord injuries.

Retinal Hemorrhages and Other Eye Injuries

- Retinal hemorrhages are unusual in accidental head injuries.
- The chief sign of abusive head traumas, especially shaken baby syndrome, is retinal hemorrhage.
- Other eye injuries include traumatic retinoschisis, retinal detachment, retinal folds around the macula, bleeding into the optic nerve sheath, and traumatic avulsion of the nerve from the back of the eye.
- Retinal hemorrhage differential diagnosis is extensive; retinal hemorrhages from causes other than trauma are rare.

Injuries to the Skin

- Injuries to the skin are uncommon in children 9 months old and younger.
- Common skin trauma includes bruises, abrasions, and lacerations.
- Other skin lesions found on abused children include bite marks, masque ecchymotique, stun-gun injuries, tattoos or other symbolic lacerations, lesions caused by folk medicine practices, and constriction devices.

Child Sexual Abuse: Epidemiology, Risk Factors, and Evaluation

- Recent research indicates sexual abuse to be a common experience of children—.7 per 1,000 children.
- Many cases of child sexual abuse go unreported.
- Reports by adults of sexual abuse as children vary from 6% to 62% in women and 3% to 30% in men.
- Girls are more likely to be abused than boys and more likely to report abuse.
- Greatest risk is among children 8 to 10 years old. Also, those from socially isolated families, those with an absent parent or unavailable parents, children growing up in homes with a nonbiologically related father or father figure.
- Availability of evidence in sexual assault depends on type of assault, age of child, orifices assaulted, and post-assault activities of the victim.
- Immediate physical exam—within 72 hours of contact—is crucial.
- Behavioral reactions in sexually abused children are similar to PTSD.
- Sexual "acting out" behavior is frequently seen in sexually abused children.
- A coordinated comprehensive medical and psychosocial history is essential; when possible, a single interview with all professionals—i.e., physician, law enforcement, social worker, and prosecutor—present can minimize further trauma to the child.
- Children's responses to interviews vary by their level of cognitive development, emotional development, behavioral development, circumstances of the sexual abuse, and response of those individuals in the child's immediate sphere of contact.
- Physical examination documentation is important; equally important is enlisting the child's cooperation and participation; allowing the child to have control of certain elements of the exam, as well as advance knowledge of procedures, can reduce fearfulness.
- Photographs and/or drawings of injury sites are essential.

- "Re-traumatizing" a child during genital exam should be avoided; numerous techniques can be utilized to reduce discomfort and embarrassment to the child.
- Examining physician should be familiar with the differences between abnormal and normal anatomy, including nonsexual abuse trauma that can be easily mistaken for sexual abuse trauma.
- Sexual abuse trauma can be documented as acute, subacute, or chronic.
- Photoculposcope usage has both advantages and disadvantages; it is widely used to evaluate child sexual abuse; it allows for confirmation of findings and consistency of diagnosis; colposcopy results can be easily evaluated for second opinions, and effectively presented in court; the major disadvantage is cost.
- Detailed, comprehensive documentation, including observations of the victims affect and language skills, as well as remarks made by the child, will go a long way in assisting the medical professional in being an effective witness.

Forensic Examination of the Sexually Assaulted Child

- Forensic examinations should be conducted according to specific protocols.
- Protocols are provided by law enforcement agencies or particular medical facilities.
- Proper collection, handling, and storage of forensic specimens are crucial to court presentation.
- Medical records can be used as evidence in court; accuracy, legibility, and complete documentation will greatly assist the presentation.
- Direct quotes from the child should be used whenever possible.
- Photographs and/or drawings are also a key element in documentation.

Sexually Transmitted Diseases in Children

- Common nonvenereal pathogens not caused by sexually transmitted diseases (STDs) include vaginitis, vulvitis, and anal infections; pinworms and foreign bodies also account for genital and anal discomfort.
- STDs in children may differ from those in adults; most often STDs in children indicate sexual abuse.
- Common STDs include syphilis, gonorrhea, chlamydia, human papilloma virus (HPV), herpes, and trichomonas vaginalis.
- Guidelines for STD diagnostic tests are recommended by the Center for Disease Control.

Glossary of Medical Terms in Physical Abuse

- Medical terms frequently used in evaluating physical abuse are defined in easy-to-understand language.

APSAC Guidelines on Descriptive Terminology in Child Sexual Abuse Medical Evaluations

- Descriptive terminology used in medical evaluations of sexually abused children

References & Readings 

Faller, K. C. (1996). *Evaluating children suspected of having been sexually abused.* Thousand Oaks, CA: Sage.

Jenny, C. (1996). *Medical evaluation of physically and sexually abused children.* Thousand Oaks, CA: Sage.

Quinsey, V. L., & Lalumiere, L. L. (1996). *Assessment of sexual offenders against children.* Thousand Oaks, CA: Sage.

Related Topics

Chapter 87, "Interviewing Children When Sexual Abuse Is Suspected"

Chapter 88, "Treatment of Child Sexual Abuse"

87 INTERVIEWING CHILDREN WHEN SEXUAL ABUSE IS SUSPECTED

Karen J. Saywitz & Joyce S. Dorado

Mandated by law to report suspicions of child abuse, practitioners face a dilemma. There is rarely physical evidence or an adult witness to verify a child's report. Hence, professionals rely heavily on children's statements to determine protection, liability, and treatment. There is no legally sanctioned interview protocol free of trial ramifications. And despite the rapid expansion of scientific research, researchers have not produced a gold standard protocol that can be held out as the criterion by which all children should be interviewed. In fact, there is little expectation that a single protocol can emerge as useful for all ages, clinical conditions, levels of severity, family functioning, and agency needs, given the developmental and individual differences among children, the variations among circumstances from case to case, and the varied responsibilities of the agencies involved. There is, however, a good deal of consensus on many of the general guidelines for interviewing children. The discussion and outline that follow include interviewing suggestions that overlap substantially (not completely) with both clinical consensus and a large body of laboratory findings on child development. These suggestions will no doubt require revision as the knowledge base grows and public policies evolve.

QUESTIONS AND ANSWERS

What Are the Objectives of the Interview?

In the forensic context, interviewers' goals vary greatly. Interviews often are conducted to determine if the findings are consistent with the occurrence of abuse. At other times, interviews are conducted to plan treatment, custody arrangements, home and school placements, visitation, or family reunification. Sometimes the goal is formulating a traditional description of functioning and differential diagnosis. However, the need for questioning can also arise in the midst of therapy with an unanticipated need to assess imminent risk of danger. Before the interview begins, it behooves the interviewer to clarify the objectives for all parties and agencies involved. The objectives dictate many of the methodological choices the interviewer faces. Procedures that are legitimate for one purpose can have unintended ramifications when used for another.

What Is the Interviewer's Proper Role?

Interviewers must understand the limitations of the interview process as a means of proving that abuse occurred. Moreover, interviewers must be knowledgeable of relevant legal and ethical issues (see Myers, 1998). Interviewers must avoid dual relationships. When an interviewer is both the treating therapist and an evaluator who provides information to the court, competing demands often can undermine confidentiality and therapeutic alliance, creating ethical dilemmas. Many professional organizations recommend that in a given case, professionals take one role and refer out for the other. Interviewers must clearly define their unique role for themselves, the child, the family, and the court. They should carefully consider invitations to expand and alter their role midstream.

Interviewers should be careful to employ methods sufficient to provide the necessary substantiation for their conclusions. Psychological tests can provide useful information but do not provide proof of abuse or of a false allegation. Abuse is an event, not a diagnosis. A reliable and valid test to verify its occurrence does not exist.

What Do Behavioral Indicators Mean?

Often children are referred for an interview because of behavioral changes, for example, nightmares or imitations of adult sexual activity. Although many reactions to trauma can accompany the onset of maltreatment (e.g., nightmares, personality change, fearfulness, anxiety), these occur more frequently in a population of nonabused children who are distressed for other reasons. No single constellation of behaviors or symptoms is pathognomonic to child abuse, and many genuinely abused children, even those with sexually transmitted diseases, may show no measurable behavioral problems. Behavior changes indicate that further evaluation and investigation are necessary (Lamb, 1994). Their occurrence cannot be used to determine the existence of maltreatment, nor can their absence be used to conclude that a child was not maltreated.

The one indicator that is unique to a history of sexual abuse is age-inconsistent sexual behavior and knowledge. Studies suggest that sexually abused children demonstrate significantly higher rates of sexualized behavior than normative and clinical (nonabused) samples (Friedrich et al., 2001). Still, nonabused children do engage in sexualized behaviors, albeit at a lower rate. The available research on children's knowledge of sexuality suggests that preschoolers are rarely aware of adult activities like genital, oral, and anal penetration. However, there is no definitive way to know when a child's age-inconsistent knowledge is a function of victimization or of exposure to pornography, crowded living conditions, and so forth.

Are Children's Reports Reliable?

There appears to be interdisciplinary consensus that children are "able to provide reliable and accurate accounts of events they have witnessed or experienced. Furthermore, despite frequent claims that children are uniquely susceptible to external influence, it is clear that when children are encouraged to describe their experiences without manipulation by interviewers, their accounts can be extremely informative and accurate. Such interviewing is difficult, however, and is best conducted by well trained and experienced interviewers" (Lamb, 1994, p. 1024).

The most reliable information is obtained in response to open-ended questions that elicit free narratives. School-age children can provide such accounts, and follow-up questions can be used to elaborate, clarify, and justify information provided by the child. However, children under 5 years of age depend on context cues and adult questions to help trigger recall. They rarely provide more information than is asked for. Further information is forthcoming in response to specific questions that help focus children's attention on the topic at hand, trigger recall of detail, organize retrieval efforts, and overcome reluctance and anxiety. Unfortunately, if such questions are misleading, they have the potential to distort young children's reports. When specific questions are asked, they should be formulated in as nonsuggestive a manner as possible.

What Do Children Remember?

For both adults and children, central actions and events can be recalled for long periods of time, but peripheral details may be forgotten over long delays. Children may find it more difficult to remember in detail after long delays all that they were able to remember initially. However, without coaching or suggestive questions, their errors tend to be a matter of confusing details of similar experiences, especially when the event to be recalled is not very distinctive or personally meaningful. Infants and toddlers have surprising memories for personally experienced events over time; however, children who are nonverbal at the time of the event are unlikely to ever be able to give a narrative account of events that occurred prior to the acquisition of language (Fivush, 2002). Children often perceive different aspects of an event to be salient and memorable. They can remember details that go unnoticed by adults and fail to report information that adults find crucial. Even genuine accounts of abuse from young children will lack detail. This is especially true when acts of abuse are repeated over long periods of time. Accurate recounts may not include unique details placing individual incidents in spatiotemporal context. Lack of detail is to be expected and cannot be used as an indicator of reliability.

Younger children tend to report the actions that occurred. Older children begin to include descriptions of participants, timing, location, conversations, and affect states. Eventually, children develop the ability to ask themselves the questions necessary to spontaneously include the who, when, where, and how of an event. Older children are likely to notice, make sense of, and store more information of relevance. They have a greater vocabulary to describe a memory verbally. Researchers have begun to develop innovative techniques to help younger children report additional information not otherwise produced spontaneously (e.g., Dorado & Saywitz, 2001). With such techniques, more complete and detailed narratives allow follow-up questions to focus on expanding information provided by children rather than adult supposition, lowering the need for leading questions.

When Should Interviews Be Conducted?

In the laboratory, the most detailed and complete accounts are found when memory is fresh. Interviews should be conducted as soon as possible. In the field, however, practical, motivational, and emotional considerations affect the timing of interviews. Repeated interviewing in and of itself is not necessarily detrimental to the quality of children's recall (Fivush, 2002). However, when misleading questions are used in multiple interviews, they have the potential to distort young children's statements. Reducing the number of interviews is often advised. Yet disclosure of genuine abuse is sometimes a process that occurs over time rather than a singular event. When several interviews are necessary, returning to the same interviewer is optimal. It is stressful for children to start over repeatedly with unfamiliar adults.

Do Children Readily Disclose Abuse to Unfamiliar Interviewers?

Many children do report abuse when questioned carefully. Others are reluctant to discuss traumatic events with strangers. In one study, over half of the children with sexually transmitted diseases failed to disclose abuse in a clinical interview. Children typically cope with anxiety-provoking topics via avoidance. Avoiding reminders of traumatic events is one hallmark of posttraumatic stress disorder. The interviewer often has to contend with emotional reactions, including anxiety, depression, guilt, shame, ambivalence, as well as fears of the unknown, separation, retaliation, and humiliation. Taking the time to establish rapport and providing a supportive, yet unbiased, atmosphere may help offset the effects of these emotional factors.

Should Anatomically Detailed Dolls Be Used?

Over the last decade, the use of anatomically detailed dolls has declined considerably. There is little doubt that a child's manipulation of dolls is not a test of whether abuse occurred (Koocher et al., 1995). Still, sometimes dolls are used in a limited fashion, as demonstration aids after children make verbal statements suggesting abuse or as a body map to facilitate inquiry about injuries or anal/genital touch. However, studies of 2- to 3-year olds suggest dolls are contraindicated for this age range. Such young children have difficulty using dolls to represent themselves in demonstrations.

Research with older children is confusing because studies rarely distinguish between the impact of dolls alone and the impact of suggestive techniques used in conjunction with dolls. The combination of dolls, toy props, and highly suggestive questions can lead to distortion and error in young children's recall (Ceci, Crossman, Scullin, Gilstrap, & Huffman, 2002). There is some evidence that in the absence of suggestive, leading, highly specific questioning the recall of private parts touching by children over 5 years of age can be enhanced by anatomical models in comparison to unaided free recall or purely verbal interviews. However, there is insufficient research to know whether anatomical drawings of the fronts and backs of bodies would be equally beneficial and many issues related to forensic practice remain unresolved (Everson & Boat, 2002). The introduction of anatomically detailed dolls into a forensic interview and the interpretation of children's sexualized play with such dolls should be undertaken by those well versed in the literature.

What Factors Contribute to Children's Suggestibility?

Suggestibility is multiply determined. There is little evidence that suggestibility is a personality trait. Similarly, it is not merely a function of age, although both developmental and individual differences play a role. Very young children (3–4 years of age) are the most vulnerable to the effects of suggestive techniques. By 6–7 years of age, children's resistance to suggestion increases dramatically. By 10–11 years of age, there is another shift toward adult levels of suggestibility. Still, some 3-year-olds remain resistant in response to the most relentless interviewers, while some older children may acquiesce readily under certain conditions.

Several factors are responsible for children's vulnerability to suggestive interviewing techniques (Saywitz & Lyon, 2002). Young children store more information in memory than is reported spontaneously or in response to open-ended questions. If follow-up questions are misleading and suggestive, reports can be distorted. Preschoolers assume adults possess a superior knowledge base, and they are particularly deferential to adult's beliefs. Adults may convey biased views through the questions they ask. Additionally, preschoolers may confuse memories of the event with memories of false information embedded in adult questioning or coaching. This emphasizes the danger of telling, rather than asking, young children what occurred. Researchers have found several techniques increase error, including assisting children to visualize details or pretend after they have stated they cannot remember, presenting false physical evidence, and selective reinforcement (Ceci et al., 2002).

Although recent studies have shown disconcerting levels of suggestibility in children, these effects are primarily found in studies of very young children, under 5 years of age. These effects are most prevalent when using presumptive questions rather than mildly leading ones. Some of the coercive techniques studied may not be typical of actual interviews in the field. Nevertheless, children's suggestibility should be of central concern for the interviewer. Interviewers must minimize conditions that increase suggestibility and maximize conditions that promote resistance, as discussed below.

Can We Detect False Allegations?

Thus far, researchers have not produced reliable and valid tests to discriminate true from false cases of abuse. Although there is some ongoing research on checklists of credibility criteria, many criteria thought to be indicative of false cases can also appear in cases of genuine abuse. For example, consistency is often relied upon as an indicator of reliability. However, inconsistency across interviews is frequent, if not expected, among young children questioned by different adults, with different questions, in different settings, even when memories are largely accurate. In one study, children telling the truth about being touched were more inconsistent than children coached to lie about being touched.

INTERVIEW OUTLINE

Preparation and Gathering of Background Information

- Before questioning, coordinate with other agencies to reduce multiple interviews. Verifying information by contacting collaterals is often necessary. Reports may be reviewed from schools, law enforcement agencies, pediatric records, child protective services, and prior court hearings.

Documentation

- Questions and responses should be documented verbatim whenever possible. Never paraphrase children's statements; use their words.
- Documentation of the following is optimal: description of abusive acts and alleged offender, age of child at each incident, first and most recent incidents, location(s), enticements, threats, elements of secrecy, and evidence of motive to fabricate. Also, document indicia of reliability associated with the child's statement and behavior (e.g., age-appropriate use of terms, spontaneity, hurried speech, belief that disclosure leads to punishment).
- To conduct a forensically defensible interview, it is important to document precautions taken to avoid contamination, consultation with colleagues, rationales for special techniques, and alternate hypotheses pursued.

Setting the Context

- Interview children alone to avoid undue influence on children's statements, unless there is good reason indicating support persons are necessary. Support persons if present should not have an obvious stake in the outcome of the case and should sit behind the child and refrain from advising the child.
- Before questioning children about the alleged abuse, interviewers can discuss the limits on confidentiality. Also, children need an outline of the forthcoming interview and its unique task demands, as well as education about the flow of information through the investigative and judicial process.
- Interviewers may want to consult the growing literature on pre-interview instructions that can be given to children to enhance recall and minimize distortion (Saywitz & Lyon, 2002).

Guidelines for Talking to Children

- Interviewers must talk to children in language they can understand. The vocabulary and grammar of the question must match the child's stage of language development. Simplify language by using shorter sentences and words with fewer syllables.
- Interviewers must avoid asking questions that require skills children have not yet mastered. Such questions are fertile grounds for misinterpretation. A child who has not yet learned to count cannot be asked how many times something happened. If he or she is, the answer must be weighed accordingly within a developmental framework. Potentially problematic topics include conventional systems of measurement (e.g., weight in pounds, height in feet, timing in minutes/hours), ethnicity labels, kinship terms, and relational terms (e.g., first, always, never, before, ever).
- Interviewers must do everything in their power to minimize the potential for distortion of children's statements. Interviewers should avoid suggesting answers and should maintain an objective, neutral stance in regard to the veracity of the allegations. They should explore all possible alternative explanations.

Getting Started

- Take time to develop rapport in order to promote motivation, cooperation, openness, and honesty with unfamiliar adults in unfamiliar settings, especially when secrets, threats, embarrassments, and loyalties are involved. Convey that it is safe for children to tell what really happened without fear of adult rejection or detachment.
- Make it clear that the interview is a joint effort in which children are to tell as much as

possible in their own words. Model an expectation for independent verbalization (e.g., ask children to explain something unrelated to the event in question; refrain from filling in silence too quickly or asking detailed questions.). Model the format you plan to use later (Saywitz & Lyon, 2002).

- Explain the interviewer's purpose (e.g., "to be sure children stay safe and healthy, to help children with problems, or to help a judge make the best plan for the whole family").

Questioning Children about Child Abuse

- Provide children with an opportunity for an unbiased spontaneous statement (e.g, "Is there anything you want to tell me? . . . think I should know? Why did you come here today?"). Start with open-ended questions (What happened?).
- If open-ended questions are successful, invite children to elaborate on the information provided in their own words ("You said Nora was there, what did she do? What happened next?").
- Follow-up with "Wh" questions (Who? What? When? Where? How?).
- Reserve specific questions until open-ended ones fail. When they do, start by focusing children on general topics of relevance (e.g., "Tell me about school, . . . church . . . best/worst parts."
- Query information from the child first and from other sources last.
- For more information there are a number of interview formats derived from the experimental literature to consult, including the NICHD protocol (Sternberg, Lamb, Esplin, Orbach, & Hershkowitz, 2002), cognitive interview (Fisher, Brennan, & McCauley, 2002), and narrative elaboration procedure (Dorado & Saywitz, 2001; Saywitz & Snyder, 1996), as well as professional guidelines (e.g., American Academy of Child and Adolescent Psychiatry, 1997; American Professional Society on the Abuse of Children, 1997).

Introducing the Topic of Abuse

- One method involves an inventory of body parts from head to toe, asking for each part's name, function, and history of being touched or hurt by others in ways the child did not like.
- Ask children to list important people and events, and to describe household routines, sleeping arrangements, and rules for privacy.
- Use roundabout, indirect ways of eliciting relevant information without leading questions. Ask children who brought them to the interview and why (e.g., "My social worker because I can't be with my dad." "Why?" "Because of the way he touched me." Oh, what happened?"). Ask children to describe recent changes at home (e.g., "My uncle had to leave after my mom got mad at him." "What was she mad about." "What happened to me." "What happened?").
- Inquire about most and least favorite experiences, reasons the child gets upset, things that make him mad, concerns about privacy and safety, and how she copes with fear.
- Decisions about raising specific information not yet mentioned by the child are made on a case by case basis. Some questions may be justified when there is corroborating evidence to suggest a child may be in danger of further abuse and decisions of protection are paramount. The same questions may be controversial in cases where alleged perpetrators have no access to children and there is little evidence other than children's statements.

Precautions to Minimize Suggestion

- Avoid creating an accusatory atmosphere by referring to suspects in derogatory or accusatory terms (e.g., "Tell me the bad things that the bad man did to you." "He wasn't supposed to do that, that was bad").
- Avoid suggesting the interviewer is an infallible authority figure with "inside" knowledge of what happened gained from other sources (e.g., "Well, that's not what your mom said"). Suggest the child is the expert on the event in question, not the adults.

- Interviewers can be supportive of children's efforts (e.g., "Thanks for listening carefully") but should avoid reinforcing specific content that might shape children's responses. Don't allow preconceived notions to be reinforced while other leads are ignored or devalued.
- Respect children's denials (Camparo, Wagner, & Saywitz, 2001). Don't press children to imagine, visualize, or pretend about what might have happened (Ceci et al., 2002).
- Avoid suggestive questions that increase children's errors: Statements followed by requests for affirmation ("He hurt you, didn't he?"), insertions of negatives (e.g., "Didn't he hurt you?"), multiple choice, and suppositional questions. In the latter, information is embedded into the question without giving the child the opportunity to affirm or deny the presumption (e.g., "When John hurt you, was your mother home? Did he hit you with his hand or a club?").
- Turn yes-no questions into "Wh" questions when possible (e.g., "Did he hit you?" becomes "What did he do with his hands?").

Closure

- Children may need time to regain composure and ask their own questions. They can be praised for their effort and bravery but not for the content of their statements. Children need to know what will happen next to dispel misperceptions and reduce fears.

References & Readings 

American Academy of Child and Adolescent Psychiatry. *Practice parameters for the forensic evaluation of children and adolescents who may have been physically or sexually abused.* (1997). Washington, DC: Author.

American Professional Society on the Abuse of Children. *Psychosocial evaluation of suspected sexual abuse in children.* (2nd ed.). (1997). Chicago, IL: Author.

Camparo, L. B., Wagner, J. T., & Saywitz, K. J. (2001). Interviewing children about real and fictitious events: Revisiting the narrative elaboration procedure. *Law and Human Behavior, 25*(1), 63–80.

Ceci, S. J., Crossman, A. M., Scullin, M. H., Gilstrap, L., & Huffman, M. A. (2002). Children's suggestibility research: Implications for the courtroom and the forensic interview. In Westcott, G. M. Davies, & R. H. Bull (Eds.), *Children's testimony: A handbook of psychological research and forensic practice* (pp. 117–130). West Sussex, England: Wiley.

Dorado, J., & Saywitz, K. (2001). Interviewing preschoolers from low and middle income communities: A test of the Narrative Elaboration recall improvement technique. *Journal of Clinical Child Psychology, 30,* 566–578.

Everson, M. D., & Boat, B. W. (2002). The utility of anatomical dolls and drawings in child forensic interviews. In M. L. Eisen, J. A. Quas, & G. S. Goodman (Eds.), *Memory and suggestibility in the forensic interview* (pp. 383–408). Mahwah, NJ: Erlbaum.

Fisher, R. P., Brennan, K. H., & McCauley, M. R. (2002). The cognitive interview method to enhance eyewitness recall. In M. L. Eisen, J. A. Quas, & G. S. Goodman (Eds.), *Memory and suggestibility in the forensic interview* (pp. 265–286). Mahwah, NJ: Erlbaum.

Fivush, R. (2002). The development of autobiographical memory. In G. M. Westcott, F. Davies & R. H. Bull (Eds.), *Children's testimony: A handbook of psychological research and forensic practice* (pp. 55–68). West Sussex, England: John Wiley & Sons, Ltd.

Friedrich, W. N., Dittner, C. A., Action, R., Berliner, L., Butler, J., Damon, L., et al. (2001). Child sexual behavior inventory: Normative, psychiatric and sexual abuse comparisons. *Child Maltreatment, 6,* 37–49.

Koocher, G. P., Goodman, G. S., White, C. S., Friedrich, W. N., Sivan, A. B., & Reynolds, C. R. (1995). Psychological science and the use of anatomically detailed dolls in child sexual abuse assessments. *Psychological Bulletin, 118,* 199–122.

Lamb, M. E. (1994). The investigation of child sexual abuse: An interdisciplinary consensus statement. *Child Abuse and Neglect, 18,* 1021–1028.

Myers, J. E. B. (1998). *Legal issues in child abuse and neglect* (2nd ed.). Newbury Park, CA: Sage.

Saywitz, K. J., & Lyon, T. D. (2002). Coming to grips with children's suggestibility. In M. L. Eisen, J. A. Quas, & G. S. Goodman (Eds.), *Memory and suggestibility in the forensic interview,* (pp. 85–114). Mahwah, NJ: Erlbaum.

Sternberg, K. J., Lamb, M. E., Esplin, P. W., Orbach, Y., & Hershkowitz, I. (2002). Using a structured interview protocol to improve the quality of investigative interviews. In M. L. Eisen, J. A. Quas, & G. S. Goodman (Eds.), *Memory and suggestibility in the forensic interview* (pp. 409–436). Mahwah, NJ: Erlbaum.

Saywitz, K., & Snyder, L. (1996). Narrative elaboration: Test of a new procedure for interviewing children. *Journal of Consulting and Clinical Psychology, 64*, 1347–1357.

Related Topics

Chapter 12, "Interviewing Parents"
Chapter 88, "Treatment of Child Sexual Abuse"

88 TREATMENT OF CHILD SEXUAL ABUSE

Kathryn Kuehnle

Sexually abused children are a heterogeneous group. Child sexual abuse is not a discrete clinical syndrome; rather, it is a life event or a series of life events. There is no behavior, symptom, or cluster of symptoms that is characteristic of the majority of sexually abused children, nor does a child sexual-abuse syndrome exist. Sexually abused children exhibit a wide range of symptoms and behaviors, as well as an absence of symptoms in some cases (see Kendall-Tackett, Williams, & Finkelhor, 1993). Professionals cannot determine whether a child has or has not been sexually abused based on the presence or absence of a particular behavior or pattern of symptoms and, if a child is identified as having experienced sexual abuse, treatment planning must focus on addressing the child's unique and varied needs.

Research is robust in showing that child sexual abuse is a significant risk factor in children's development of mental health disorders and serious emotional and behavioral difficulties (Kilpatrick et al., 2003). Sexual behavior problems are found in approximately one third of sexually abused children (Friedrich, 1993). Symptoms of posttraumatic stress disorder, depression, fears, affect dysregulation (e.g., poorly controlled states of arousal), poor self-esteem, cognitive distortions (e.g., self-blame), social skills deficits, disruptive behavior, aggression, sexualized behaviors, and sexual anxiety are among the problems more frequently identified in sexually abused compared to non-abused children (Beitchman, Zucker, Hood, da Costa, & Akman, 1992). However, these symptoms are not specific to sexually abused children and are also observed in children experiencing other forms of maltreatment or traumatic events. Children who experience multiple forms of child maltreatment, such as sexual abuse and physical abuse and/or domestic violence, are at the greatest risk for long-term psychopathology (Shipman, Rossman, & West, 1999; see Family Research Laboratory and National Clearinghouse on Child Abuse and Neglect, in References).

Longitudinal studies show that some symptoms and behaviors displayed by sexually abused children can diminish without therapy. The majority of children show improvement in adjustment during the 12- to 24-month period following exposure of their abuse, particularly with respect to behaviors related to posttraumatic stress symptoms and fearfulness. Findings regarding spontaneous improvement of other symptoms and behaviors such as withdrawal, acting out, and depression are variable (Gomes-Swartz, Horowitz, Cardarelli, & Sauzier, 1990).

Research indicates that one quarter to one third of child sexual abuse victims may show no signs or symptoms that are related to the abuse (Kendall-Tackett et al., 1993). In comparison to symptomatic sexually abused children, asymptomatic children generally have more limited histories of abuse; the abuse to which they were subjected is less likely to have involved force, violence, or penetration; they are more likely to have been abused by someone who is not a father figure; and they typically live in more supportive and higher functioning families (Browne & Finkelhor, 1986). Although empirically derived findings are limited, some researchers propose the existence of subgroups of asymptomatic children to include those children who are resilient and dealing successfully with their abuse, those who suppress conflicts related to the abuse but remain distressed at another psychological level, and those who have a delayed onset of disturbance (Gomes-Schwartz et al., 1990).

MEDIATING FACTORS IN PSYCHOLOGICAL RECOVERY

Sexual-abuse events interact with a complex matrix of factors including the abuse characteristics, family dynamics, co-occurring forms of maltreatment, caretaker response to the abuse allegation, involvement in the legal system, and the premorbid personality of the victim (Friedrich, 1993). Mediating factors found to be important in the child victim's psychological recovery involve the child's cognitive processing of the event and the family's response to the abuse. Levels of distress in sexually abused children, psychological symptomatology, and speed of recovery are related to parental support and level of parent distress (Cohen & Mannarino, 1998a). Differences in how child victims make sense of and think about their abuse experience (e.g., attributions, optimism, and positive reframing) also mediate the consequences of the sexual-abuse experience. Parental response to the abuse, of course, can influence the child victim's cognitions. Family supportiveness may be a possible alternative explanation for some cases in which there is a positive treatment effect for a sexually abused child.

FORMING THE TREATMENT PLAN: SUBSTANTIVE ISSUES

The likelihood of effective outcomes is aided when interventions are matched to specific problems through appropriate assessment. In developing the treatment plan, the first step in the assessment process is to determine the level of risk for harm in the child's current environment and to create a safety plan for the child, if necessary. The second step requires an "abuse informed" assessment. This assessment requires the examiner to identify the direct effects of the abuse, as well as any pre-existing or co-occurring conditions and difficulties. The third step is to determine family system characteristics (Saunders & Meinig, 2000).

Treatment goals for sexually abused children must specify the therapeutic interventions and what aspects of these interventions (e.g., content of treatment) are specifically targeted to behavioral symptoms and/or pathological cognitions. While the content of treatment interventions should ideally be informed by science, research on this aspect of treatment is limited. For example, it is currently unknown if expression of abuse memories is beneficial for all children, if repression of abuse memories is beneficial for some children, and whether the pursuit of traumatic memories prior to the development of coping strategies and reinforcement of internal resources may be iatrogenic.

Prior to designing and implementing interventions with sexually abused children, the mental health professional must also consider the larger environmental context regarding culture, religious, and racial/ethnic groups to which the child and his/her family belong (Cohen, Deblinger, Mannarino, & de Arellano, 2001). Values and beliefs about issues such as sexuality, nudity, personal privacy, family roles, and help-seeking are all influenced by a family's cultural, religious, and racial/ethnic connections, and must be considered in treatment planning and intervention.

TREATMENT OF SPECIFIC SYMPTOMS

Several important conclusions are derived from research regarding treatment of specific symptoms and behavior problems, including that: (1) children show differential responses to treatment with some showing greater treatment effects than others; (2) the variables that distinguish sexually abused children who make significant improvement in treatment from children who make no improvement have not been identified; (3) sexual problems and externalizing behaviors (e.g., aggression, acting out) are less likely to improve with treatment compared to internalizing behaviors (e.g., depression, fearfulness); and (4) preschool children's externalizing symptoms may show greater positive treatment responses when the treatment intervention includes helping parents to manage the acting out behaviors.

MODALITIES OF TREATMENT

Preliminary findings regarding effectiveness of interventions with sexually abused children are, in many ways, consistent with the findings from the general literature on child psychotherapy indicating an absence of reliable, significant differences for treatment outcomes between group, individual, or play therapies (Finkelhor & Berliner, 1995). However, conjoint or combined (i.e., separate parent and separate child) treatment of the nonoffending parent has been identified as a critical element in the treatment of sexually abused children (Deblinger, Lippman, & Steer, 1996), which is likely since the nonoffending parent's emotional support has been found to be associated with the child's post-abuse functioning. For example, parents may experience adverse emotional responses to the sexual abuse of their child that may impede their ability to provide support. Conjoint treatment may decrease premature termination of treatment and facilitate generalization of the child's treatment gains. Parent treatment only and parent/child treatment combined are shown to be the most effective in decreasing externalizing behaviors, while child treatment only and parent/child treatment combined are the most effective in decreasing internalizing behaviors (Deblinger, Steer, & Lippman, 1999).

TREATMENT APPROACHES

There is a growing body of research testing the efficacy of mental health interventions with sexually abused children (Cohen, Berliner, & March, 2000; Cohen & Mannarino, 1998b; Deblinger et al., 1999). However, much of the social science literature focuses on treatments, developed by individual clinicians, that have not been empirically tested. In order to identify for practitioners effective and appropriate treatments, a criterion-based classification system was designed to categorize treatment approaches. Treatments were categorized as child, family, child-parent, and parent focused, and they were rated as follows: 1 = well-supported (i.e., research base) efficacious treatment; 2 = supported and probably efficacious; 3 = supported and acceptable treatment; 4 = promising and acceptable treatment; 5 = innovative or novel treatment; 6 = concerning treatment (see Saunders, Berliner, & Hanson, 2003; National Crime Victims Research and Treatment Center).

CHILD-FOCUSED INTERVENTIONS

The core child-focused treatment approaches include (1) cognitive behavioral therapy (CBT); (2) eye movement desensitization and reprocessing (EMDR); (3) play therapy; (4) pharmacotherapy (medication); and (5) psychodynamic psychotherapy. The strongest empirical support exists for behavioral and cognitive-behavioral interventions (Saunders et al., 2003). Using the criterion-based categorization referenced above, the majority of child-focused treatment approaches reviewed were classified with a level three rating. Trauma-Focused Cognitive Behavioral Therapy (Deblinger et al., 1999) was the only approach assigned a level one rating.

Many of the treatment studies using behavioral and cognitive-behavioral interventions with sexually abused children have relied on skills training, particularly coping skills, problem-solving skills, and communication skills. Sexually inappropriate behaviors, regardless of the reasons for these behaviors, more readily respond to behavioral interventions than to play therapy or psychodynamic treatment. A clear relationship between treatment duration and effectiveness has not been found with any of the various approaches.

A commonly employed technique for treating sexually abused children is "abuse-focused" therapy, which uses supportive and psychoeducational interventions. Abuse-focused therapy is not associated with any particular theoretical perspective, nor is it associated with any single therapeutic approach. It borrows from a wide variety of behavioral, cognitive, systemic, and reconstructive or dynamic therapies, and it is most effective with victims who will benefit from supportive and educational interventions, including: (1) the processing of their sexual abuse memories; (2) exposure to other victims (e.g., group therapy) to decrease feelings of stigmatization and isolation; (3) encouragement of expression of abuse-related feelings (e.g., confusion, anger); (4) clarification of pathological beliefs that might lead to negative self attributions; and (5) development of skills to prevent future abuse.

Abuse-specific therapy or elements of this therapy may be inappropriate with specific subgroups of victims. For example, some elements of abuse-specific therapy (e.g., encouragement of expression of abuse-related feelings) are inappropriate when sexual abuse remains a question and cannot be substantiated. Additionally, elements of abuse-specific therapy that include exposure to other victims' abuse histories may be inappropriate for preschool children and children who are mentally retarded, diagnosed with pervasive developmental disorder, or have significant mental illness in which perceptions are distorted and thinking processes are disturbed. Finally, abuse-specific therapy, because it is primarily supportive and educational in nature, may be less effective with certain behavioral problems, including sexual behavior problems and externalized problem behaviors that require more targeted and intensive interventions.

TREATMENT APPROACHES: FAMILY, PARENT-CHILD, AND PARENT-FOCUSED INTERVENTIONS

Similar to the literature on child-focused interventions, the clinical literature on family, parent-child, and parent-focused interventions is extensive, primarily developed by individual clinicians, and lacking an adequate research base. Using the criterion-based categorization, the majority of family and parent-child focused treatment approaches reviewed were given a level three or four classification (see National Crime Victims Research and Treatment Center; Saunders et al., 2003). None of the approaches received a level 1 or 2 rating and one approach, Corrective Attachment Therapy (the Evergreen Model), was designated a level 6 classification. Corrective Attachment Therapy lacks treatment outcome research, does not provide an acceptable theoretical basis for the treatment, and constitutes a risk of harm to those receiving it (American Professional Society on the Abuse of Children, 1996).

ETHICS AND GUIDELINES

Because of the potential conflict of interest between the roles of therapist and forensic evaluator (see Greenberg & Shuman, 1997, for a review of this issue more generally), a number of professional organizations have directed that professionals not provide both forensic evaluation and therapeutic services engaging the same case or with the same child. The blurring of roles can be a significant problem when working with sexually abused children. In order to avoid role confusion, the therapist should formally delineate the parameters of his or her role to the child's parent(s). The therapist should make clear to the parent(s) that the therapist's role is to provide treatment to the sexually abused child and is not to provide an evaluation to determine the veracity of a sexual abuse allegation (American Psychological Association, 2002, 2003). A number of organizations have promulgated guidelines relevant to the treatment of sexually abused children and, specifically, to role differentiation (American Academy of Child and Adolescent Psychiatry, 1997; American Professional Society on the Abuse of Children, 1996; American Psychological Association, 1998; National Center for Post-Traumatic Stress Disorder).

SUMMARY

The treatment outcome literature seems to best support the efficiency of behavioral and cognitive-behavioral interventions, but because of the paucity of treatment outcome research, the effectiveness of other treatment models cannot be ruled out. Treatment providers should familiarize themselves with the seminal document *Child Physical and Sexual Abuse: Guidelines for Treatment,* which has been collaboratively prepared by the National Crime Victims Research and Treatment Center and the Center for Sexual Assault and Traumatic Stress (Saunders et al., 2003).

References, Readings, & Internet Sites 

American Academy of Child and Adolescent Psychiatry. (1997). Practice parameters for the forensic evaluation of children and adolescents who may have been physically or sexually abused. *Journal of American Academy of Child and Adolescent Psychiatry, 36,* 423–444. http://www.aacap.org/publications/index.htm

American Professional Society on the Abuse of Children. (1996). *Guidelines for psychosocial evaluation of suspected sexual abuse in young children* (2nd ed.). Chicago, IL: American Professional Society on the Abuse of Children. http://www.apsac.org/

American Psychological Association. (1998). *Guidelines for psychological evaluations in child protection matters.* Washington, DC: American Psychological Association. http://www.apa.org/divisions/div37/child_maltreatment/child.html

American Psychological Association. (2002). Ethics code. Retrieved 2004 from http://www.apa.org/ethics/code2002.html

American Psychological Association. (2003). Professional, ethical, and legal issues concerning interpersonal violence, maltreatment, and related trauma. Retrieved 2004 from http://www.apa.org/pi/pii/professional.html

Beitchman, J. H., Zucker, K. J., Hood, J. E., da Costa, G. A., & Akman, D. (1992). A review of long-term effects of child sexual abuse. *Child Abuse & Neglect, 16,* 101–118.

Browne, A., & Finkelhor, D. (1986). The impact of sexual abuse: A review of the research. *Psychological Bulletin, 99,* 66–77.

Cohen, J. A., Berliner, L., & March, J. S. (2000). Treatment of children and adolescents. In E. B. Foa, T. M. Keane, & M. J. Friedman (Eds.), *Effective treatments for PTSD: Practice guidelines from the International Society for Traumatic Stress Studies* (pp. 106–138). New York: Guilford Press.

Cohen, J. A., Deblinger, E., Mannarino, A. P., & de Arellano, M. A. (2001). The importance of culture in treating abused and neglected children: An empirical review. *Child Maltreatment, 6,* 148–157.

Cohen, J. A., & Mannarino, A. P. (1998a). Factors that mediate the treatment outcome of sexually abused preschool children: 6 and 12 month follow-up. *Journal of the Academy of Child and Adolescent Psychiatry, 37,* 44–51.

Cohen, J. A., & Mannarino, A. P. (1998b). Interventions for sexually abused children: Initial treatment findings. *Child Maltreatment, 3,* 17–26.

Deblinger, E., Lippman, J., & Steer, R. (1996). Sexually abused children suffering post-traumatic stress symptoms: Initial treatment outcome findings. *Child Maltreatment, 1,* 310–321.

Deblinger, E., Steer, R., & Lippman, J. (1999). Two-year follow-up study of cognitive behavior therapy for sexually abused children suffering post-traumatic stress symptoms. *Child Abuse & Neglect, 23,* 1371–1378.

Family Research Laboratory, University of New Hampshire. (n.d.). Home page. Retrieved 2004 from http://www.unh.edu/frl/

Finkelhor, D., & Berliner, L. (1995). Research on the treatment of sexually abused children: A review and recommendations. *Journal of American Academy of Child and Adolescent Psychiatry, 34,* 1408–1423.

Friedrich, W. N. (1993). Sexual victimization and sexual behavior in children: A review of the recent literature. *Child Abuse & Neglect, 17,* 59–66.

Gomes-Schwartz, B., Horowitz, J. M., Cardarelli, A. P., & Sauzier, M. (1990). The aftermath of child sexual abuse: 18 months later. In B. Gomes-Schwartz, J. M. Horowitz, & A. P. Cardarelli (Eds.), *Child sexual abuse: The initial effects* (pp. 132–152). Newbury Park, CA: Sage.

Greenberg, S., & Shuman, D. (1997). Irreconcilable conflict between therapeutic and forensic roles. *Professional Psychology: Research and Practice, 28,* 50–57.

Kendall-Tackett, K. A., Williams, L. M., & Finkelhor, D. (1993). Impact of sexual abuse on children: A review and synthesis of recent empirical studies. *Psychological Bulletin, 113,* 164–180.

Kilpatrick, D. G., Ruggiero, K. J., Acierno, R., Saunders, B. E., Resnick, H. S., & Best, C. L. (2003). Violence and risk of PTSD, major depression, substance abuse/dependence, and comorbidity: Results from the National Survey of Adolescents. *Journal of Consulting and Clinical Psychology, 71,* 692–700.

National Center for Post-Traumatic Stress Disorder. (n.d.). Home page. Retrieved 2004 from http://www.ncptsd.org/

National Clearinghouse on Child Abuse and Neglect. (n.d.). Home page. Retrieved 2004 from http://www.calib.com/nccanch/

National Crime Victims Research and Treatment Center. (n.d.). Home page. Retrieved 2004 from http://www.musc.edu/cvc

Saunders, B. E., Berliner, L., & Hanson, R. F. (Eds.). (2003). *Child physical and sexual abuse: Guidelines for treatment (final report: January 15, 2003).* Charleston, SC: National Crime Victims Research and Treatment Center. http://www.musc.edu/cvc/

Saunders, B. E., & Meinig, M. B. (2000). Immediate issues affecting long term family resolution in cases of parent-child sexual abuse. In R. Reece (Ed.), *Treatment of child abuse: Common ground for mental health, medical, and legal practitioners* (pp. 36–53). Baltimore, MD: Johns Hopkins University Press.

Shipman, K. L., Rossman, B. B. R., & West, J. C. (1999). Co-occurrence of spousal violence and child abuse: Conceptual implications. *Child Maltreatment, 4,* 93–102.

Related Topics

Chapter 86, "The APSAC Study Guides"
Chapter 87, "Interviewing Children When Sexual Abuse Is Suspected"

PART VI
Biology and Pharmacotherapy

89 NORMAL MEDICAL LABORATORY VALUES AND MEASUREMENT CONVERSIONS

Gerald P. Koocher & Samuel Z. Goldhaber

Although conversion data provided here are standard, note that normal biological and chemical values differ across hospitals and laboratories as a function of the methods, reagents, and equipment used. The data presented here represent an overview from several sources and should not be regarded as absolute. When interpreting specific results, contact personnel at the lab in question to ascertain their normal ranges for the test in question.

TABLE 1. Temperature Conversions: Fahrenheit = $\frac{9}{5}$ (Centigrade) + 32; Centigrade = $\frac{5}{9}$ (Fahrenheit − 32)

Fahrenheit	Centigrade
95.0	35.0
96.8	36.0
98.6	37.0
100.0	37.8
100.4	38.0
101.0	38.3
102.0	38.9
102.2	39.0
103.0	39.4
104.0	40.0

TABLE 2. Units of Measurement Conversions

1 kg = 2.204 lb
22 lb = 10 kg
1 lb = 16 oz = 0.454 kg or 454 g
1 oz = 29.57 ml
1 tsp = 5 ml
1 tbsp = 15 ml
1 in = 2.54 cm
1 cm = 0.394 in
1 ft = 30.48 cm
1 yd = 91.44 cm
1 m = 1.093 yd
1 m = 3.28 ft
1 mile = 1669.3 m
1 km = 1093.6 yd

TABLE 3. Prefixes Denoting Decimal Factors

Prefix	Factor	Prefix	Factor
mega	10^{6}	milli	10^{-3}
kilo	10^{3}	micro	10^{-6}
hecto	10^{2}	nano	10^{-9}
deka	10^{1}	pico	10^{-12}
deci	10^{-1}	femto	10^{-15}
centi	10^{-2}		

TABLE 4. Normal Lab Values

Chemistries	Adult Values	Pediatric Values		
Sodium	134–146 mEq/L	Term, 132–142 mEq/L Child, 135–146 mEq/L		
Potassium	3.5–5.1 mEq/L	Term, 3.8–6.1 mEq/L >1 month, 3.5–5.1 mEq/L		
Chloride	92–109 mEq/L	95–108 mEq/L		
Bicarbonate	24–31 mEq/L			
BUN (blood urea nitrogen)	8–25 mg/dl	5–25 mg/dl		
Creatinine	<1.5 mg/dl	0.7–1.7 mg/dl		
Glucose	55–115 mg/dl	Term, 32–100 mg/dl >2 weeks, 60–110 mg/dl		
Calcium	8.0–10.5 mg/dl	Term, 7.2–12.0 mg/dl >1 year, 7.8–11.0 mg/dl		
Phosphorus	2.6–4.6 mg/dl			
Uric acid	2.4–7.5 mg/dl	3.0–7.0 mg/dl		
Total protein	5.6–8.4 g/dl			
Albumin	3.4–5.4 g/dl	3.8–5.6 g/dl		
Total bilirubin	0.2–1.5 mg/dl	Total Bilirubin	Premature	Term
		1 day	< 8–9	<6
		2 days	<12	<9
		1 week	<15	<10
		2–4 weeks	<10–12	<6
Direct bilirubin	0.0–0.3 mg/dl	<0.2 mg/dl		
SGOT, AST (serum glutamic oxaloacetate, aminotransferase)	0–40 U/L	Term, 25–125 U/L Infant, 20–60 U/L Child, 10–40 U/L		
SGPT, ALT (alanine aminotransferase, serum glutamic pyruvate transaminase)	0–40 U/L			
LDH (lactic dehydrogenase)	50–240 U/L	Term, 150–600 U/L <1 year, 140–350 U/L Child, 140–280 U/L		
CK (creatine kinase)	5–200 U/L			
CK MB (CK-myocardial band)	<3–5%			
Cholesterol	<200 mg/dl			
LDL cholesterol (low-density lipoprotein)	<130 mg/dl			
HDL cholesterol (high-density lipoprotein)	>35–40 mg/dl			
Triglycerides	30–135 mg/dl			
Amylase	60–180 U/L			
Lipase	4–25 U/L			
Magnesium	1.6–3.0 mg/dl	1.5–2.1 mg/dl		
GGTP (gamma-glutamyl transpeptidase)	10–50 U/L			

TABLE 4. Normal Lab Values (*continued*)

Chemistries	Adult Values	Pediatric Values
PSA (prostate-specific antigen)	<4.0 ng/ml	
Osmolarity	274–296 mOsm/kg	274–296 mOsm/kg
Iron	50–160 μg/dl	
TIBC (total iron-binding capacity)	240–425 μg/dl	
Iron % sat	20–55%	
Ferritin	30–250 ng/ml	
Anion gap	8–12 mEq/L	10–14 mEq/L
Vitamin B_{12}	200–1,000 pg/ml	
Folate	5–12 ng/ml	
Ammonia	<45 μg/dl	
Lactate	4–16 mg/dl	
Aluminum	4–10 μg/L	
Copper	90–200 μg/dl	
Zinc	50–150 μg/dl	50–160 μg/dl
APF (alpha-fetoprotein)	<25 ng/ml	
CEA (carcinoembryonic antigen)	<2.5 ng/ml	
CEA, smoker	<5.0 ng/ml	
Hematology		
Hgb (hemoglobin)	Males, 14–18 g/dl Females, 12–16 g/dl	Term, 13–20 g/dl 1–4 days, 14–22 g/dl 2 weeks, 13–20 g/dl 1 month, 11–18 g/dl 2 months, 10–15 g/dl 6 months, 10–14 g/dl 1 year, 10–13 g/dl 2–8 years, 11–14 g/dl
Hematocrit	Males, 40–52% Females, 37–47%	Term, 40–58% 1–4 days, 45–60% 2 weeks, 40–58% 1 month, 32–54% 2 months, 28–44% 6 months, 30–42% 1 year, 32–40% 2–8 years, 33–40%
RBC (red blood cell [density])	Males, 4.8–6.0 × 10^6/mm^3 Females, 4.1–5.5 × 10^6/mm^3	
MCV (mean corpuscular volume)	Males, 80–90 fl Females, 80–100 fl	
MCH (mean corpuscular hemoglobin)	27–32 pg	
MCHC (mean corpuscular hemoglobin concentration)	32–36%	
Hgb A_{1c} (hemoglobin A_{1c})	3–5%	
WBC (white blood cells)	5,000–10,000/μl	Term, 8–30 (10^3/mm^3) 1–3 days, 9–32 (10^3/mm^3) 2–4 weeks, 4–20 (10^3/mm^3) 2 months, 5–20 (10^3/mm^3) 6 months, 6–18 (10^3/mm^3)

(*continued*)

TABLE 4. Normal Lab Values (*continued*)

Chemistries	Adult Values	Pediatric Values
		1 year, 5–18 (10^3/mm^3) 2–8 years, 5–15 (10^3/mm^3)
Segs	40–60%	
Bands	0–5%	
Lymph	20–40%	
Mono	4–8%	
Eos	1–3%	
Baso	0–1%	
Platelets	150–400 × 10^3/μl	150–357 × 10^3/μl
Haptoglobin	100–250 mg/dl	
ESR (eosinophil sed rate)	Males, <10 mm/hr Females, <20 mm/hr	
Retic count	0.5–2.0%	Term, 3–8% 2 days, 2–4% 1 month, 0.3–1.6% 6 years, 0.5–1.3%
PT (prothrombin time)	11–13 s	11–14 s
PTT (partial prothrombin time)	25–35 s	21–35 s
Bleeding time	<5–6 min	
Thrombin time	10–14 s	
Fibrinogen	200–400 mg/dl	150–375 mg/dl
Lymphocyte (differential)		
Total T, CD3	60–87%	
Total T/mm^3	630–3,170	
B cell	1–25%	
Suppr, CD8	10–40%	
Suppr/mm^3	240–1,200	
Helper, CD4	30–50%	
Helper/mm^3	390–1,770	
H:S, CD4/CD8	0.8–3.0	
ABGs (Arterial Blood Gases)		
pH	7.35–7.45	Birth, 7.32–7.45 1 day, 7.27–7.44 2 days, 7.36–7.44 1 month, 7.35–7.45
$PaCO_2$	35–45 mmHg	Birth, 25–45 mmHg >2 months, 30–45 mmHg
PaO_2	80–100 mmHg	Birth, 65–80 mmHg Infant, 70–100 mmHg Child, 85–105 mmHg
HCO_3	22–28 mEq/L	
O_2, saturation, artery	95–98%	
O_2, saturation, vein	60–85%	
Endocrinology		
T4 RIA (thyroxine radioiodine uptake)	5.0–12.0 μg/dl	
T3 uptake (thyrotropin)	22–36%	
Free T4 (thyroxine)	0.8–2.2 ng/dl	
T3 (thyrotropin)	75–200 ng/dl	
TSH (thyroid-stimulating hormone)	0.3–5.0 μIU/ml	
Aldosterone, supine	3–12 ng/dl	
Aldosterone, upright	5–25 ng/dl	
Calcitonin	<75 pg/ml	

TABLE 4. Normal Lab Values (*continued*)

Chemistries	Adult Values	Pediatric Values
Cortisol	6–24 μg/dl, A.M. 2–10 μg/dl, P.M.	
Gastrin	0–200 pg/ml	
Growth hormone	1–10 ng/ml	
Pepsinogen	25–100 mg/ml	
Prolactin	Males, 0–5 ng/ml Females, 0–20 ng/ml	
PTH (parathyroid homone)	10–60 pg/ml	
BHCG (beta human chorionic gonadotropin, nonpregnant)	<5 mlU/ml	
0–2 weeks	0–250 mlU/ml	
2–4 weeks	100–5,000 mlU/ml	
1–2 months	4,000–200,000 mlU/ml	
2–3 months	8,000–100,000 mlU/ml	
2nd trimester	4,000–75,000 mlU/ml	
3rd trimester	1,000–50,000 mlU/ml	
Urine		
Albumin	20–100 mg/day	
Amylase	<20 U/hr	
Calcium	<300 mg/day	
Creatinine	0.75–1.5 g/day	
Creatinine clearance	80–140 ml/min	
Glucose	<300 mg/day	
Osmolarity	250–1,000 mOsm/L	
Phosphorous	0.5–1.3 g/day	
Potassium	25–115 mEq/day	
Protein	10–200 mg/day	
Sodium	50–250 mEq/day	
Total volume	720–1,800 ml/day	
Urea nitrogen	10–20 g/day	
Uric acid	50–700 mg/day	
Specific gravity	1.002–1.030	
Cerebral Spinal Fluid		
Protein	10–45 mg/dl	Preterm, 60–150 mg/dl Newborn, 20–170 mg/dl >1 year, 5–45 mg/dl
Glucose	40–80 mg/dl	Preterm, 24–75 mg/dl Newborn, 34–119 mg/dl >1 year, 40–80 mg/dl
Pressure	60–180 mmH_2O	Newborn, 70–120 mmH_2O Child, 70–180 mmH_2O
Leukocytes, total	<5/mm^3	
Leukocites, differential		
Lymph	60–75%	
Mono	25–50%	
Neutro	1–3%	
Cell count	0–5 lymphs/HPF	Preterm, 0–25 WBC/mm^3; <35% polys Newborn, 0–25 WBC/mm^3; <35% polys >2–4 weeks, 0–5 WBC/mm^3; 0% polys

(*continued*)

TABLE 4. Normal Lab Values (*continued*)

Chemistries	Adult Values	Pediatric Values
Toxicology		
Ethanol		
Normal	<0.005% (5 mg/dl)	
Intoxicated	0.1–0.4%	
Stuporous	0.4–0.5%	
Coma	>0.5%	
Mercury, urine	<100 μg/24 hr, normal	
CoHgb (carbon monoxide hemoglobin)		
Nonsmokers	0–2.5%	
Smokers	2–5%	
Toxic	>20%	
Lead	0–40 μg/dl, normal	<10 ug/dl
Lead, urine	<100 μg/24 hr, normal	

TABLE 5. Pediatric Normal Values (Subject to Individual Patient's Circumstances)

Values	Preterm	Term	3 Months	6 Months	9 Months	1 Year	1–1.5 Years	2 Years
Weight in kilograms	< 3	3–4	5–6	7	8–9	10	11	12
Pulse rate	130–160	120–150	120–140	120–140	120–140	120–140	110–135	110–130
Blood pressure (systolic)	45–60	60–70	60–100	65–120	70–120	70–120	70–125	75–125
Respiratory rate	40–60	30–60	30–50	25–35	23–33	20–30	20–30	20–28
Weight in kilograms	14–15	16–17	18	20	24–25	30–32	40	45
Pulse rate	100–120	95–115	90–110	90–110	80–100	75–95	70–90	60–90
Blood pressure (systolic)	75–125	80–125	80–125	85–120	90–120	90–125	95–130	110–130
Respiratory rate	20–28	20–28	20–25	20–25	16–24	16–24	16–24	15–20

References & Readings

Barkin, R. M. (Ed.). (1992). *Pediatric emergency medicine: Concepts and clinical practice*. St. Louis: Mosby.

Bennett, J. C., & Plum, F. (1996). *Cecil textbook of medicine*. Philadelphia: Saunders.

Braunwald, E., Fauci, A. S., Kasper, D. L., Hauser S. L., Longo, D. L., & Jameson, J. L. (Eds.) (2001). *Harrison's principles of internal medicine*. New York: McGraw-Hill.

Henry, J. B. (1991). *Clinical diagnosis and management by laboratory methods*. Philadelphia: Saunders.

Hoekelman, R. A., Friedman, S. B., Nelson, N. M., Seidel, H. M., & Weitzman, M. D. (Eds.) (1997). *Primary pediatric care*. St. Louis: Mosby.

Lee, G. R., Bithell, T. C., Foerster, J., Athens, J. W., & Lukens, J. N. (1993). *Wintrobe's clinical hematology*. Malverne, PA: Lea and Febiger.

Related Topics

Chapter 11, "Medical Evaluation of Children With Behavioral or Developmental Disorders"

Chapter 139, "Common Clinical Abbreviations and Symbols"

90 USE OF HEIGHT AND WEIGHT ASSESSMENT TOOLS

Nancie H. Herbold & Sari Edelstein

In the past, to determine if an individual was over- or underweight, clinicians consulted the Metropolitan Life Insurance Weight for Height Tables. These tables considered sex and frame size to determine desirable weight associated with greater life expectancy. Today, the preferred method for assessing body weight is the use of body mass index (BMI). Body mass index is more closely related to body fat content than the Metropolitan Tables. To determine BMI for either a man or a woman, body weight in kilograms is divided by height in meters squared.

$$\text{BMI} = \frac{\text{Weight (kg)}}{\text{Height (m)}^2}$$

$$\text{BMI} = \frac{\text{Weight (lbs)} \times 703}{\text{Height (inches)}^2}$$

For ease, Table 1 is provided to make the BMI calculation unnecessary. To use the table, find the appropriate height in the left-hand column. Move across to a given weight; pounds have been rounded. The number at the top of the column is the BMI for that height and weight, corresponding designations for normal, overweight, obese, and extremely obese BMI levels.

BMI is a tool for assessing body weight, but it is not without its limitations. For example, BMI does not totally differentiate between weight that is muscle and weight that is fat. Therefore, an athlete in good physical shape may have a high BMI but not high body fat. (Table 2, explained below, can be utilized for athletic individuals.)

INTERPRETATION

Both BMI, shown in Table 1, and waist circumference (WC), shown in Table 2, can be useful measures for determining obesity. According to the National Institutes of Health, a high WC is associated with an increased risk for Type 2 diabetes, hypertension, and cardiovascular disease when BMI is between 25 and 34.9. A BMI greater than 25 is considered overweight, and a BMI greater than 30 is considered obese. Additionally, WC can be useful for those people categorized as normal or overweight in terms of BMI. For example, an athlete with increased muscle mass may have a BMI greater than 25. Changes in WC over time can indicate an increase or decrease in abdominal fat. Increased abdominal fat is associated with an increased risk of heart disease. To use Table 2 for athletic individuals, convert the weight in pounds by dividing by a factor of 2.2 to equal the weight in kilograms (kg).

WAIST CIRCUMFERENCE

To determine your WC, locate your waist and measure the circumference. The tape measure should be snug, but should not cause compressions on the skin. Table 2 should be helpful in determining the possible risks associated with your BMI and WC.

TABLE 1. Body Mass Index Table

	Normal						Overweight					Obese										Extreme Obesity														
BMI	19	20	21	22	23	24	25	26	27	28	29	30	31	32	33	34	35	36	37	38	39	40	41	42	43	44	45	46	47	48	49	50	51	52	53	54
Height (inches)	Body Weight (pounds)																																			
58	91	96	100	105	110	115	119	124	129	134	138	143	148	153	158	162	167	172	177	181	186	191	196	201	205	210	215	220	224	229	234	239	244	248	253	258
59	94	99	104	109	114	119	124	128	133	138	143	148	153	158	163	168	173	178	183	188	193	198	203	208	212	217	222	227	232	237	242	247	252	257	262	267
60	97	102	107	112	118	123	128	133	138	143	148	153	158	163	168	174	179	184	189	194	199	204	209	215	220	225	230	235	240	245	250	255	261	266	271	276
61	100	106	111	116	122	127	132	137	143	148	153	158	164	169	174	180	185	190	195	201	206	211	217	222	227	232	238	243	248	254	259	264	269	275	280	285
62	104	109	115	120	126	131	136	142	147	153	158	164	169	175	180	186	191	196	202	207	213	218	224	229	235	240	246	251	256	262	267	273	278	284	289	295
63	107	113	118	124	130	135	141	146	152	158	164	169	175	180	186	191	197	203	208	214	220	225	231	237	242	248	254	259	265	270	278	282	287	293	299	304
64	110	116	122	128	134	140	145	151	157	163	169	174	180	186	192	197	204	209	215	221	227	232	238	244	250	256	262	267	273	279	285	291	296	302	308	314
65	114	120	126	132	138	144	150	156	162	168	174	180	186	192	198	204	210	216	222	228	234	240	246	252	258	264	270	276	282	288	294	300	306	312	318	324
66	118	124	130	136	142	148	155	161	167	173	179	186	192	198	204	210	216	223	229	235	241	247	253	260	266	272	278	284	291	297	303	309	315	322	328	334
67	121	127	134	140	146	153	159	166	172	178	185	191	198	204	211	217	223	230	236	242	249	255	261	268	274	280	287	293	299	306	312	319	325	331	338	344
68	125	131	138	144	151	158	164	171	177	184	190	197	203	210	216	223	230	236	243	249	256	262	269	276	282	289	295	302	308	315	322	328	335	341	348	354
69	128	135	142	149	155	162	169	176	182	189	196	203	209	216	223	230	236	243	250	257	263	270	277	284	291	297	304	311	318	324	331	338	345	351	358	365
70	132	139	146	153	160	167	174	181	188	195	202	209	216	222	229	236	243	250	257	264	271	278	285	292	299	306	313	320	327	334	341	348	355	362	369	376
71	136	143	150	157	165	172	179	186	193	200	208	215	222	229	236	243	250	257	265	272	279	286	293	301	308	315	322	329	338	343	351	358	365	372	379	386
72	140	147	154	162	169	177	184	191	199	206	213	221	228	235	242	250	258	265	272	279	287	294	302	309	316	324	331	338	346	353	361	368	375	383	390	397
73	144	151	159	166	174	182	189	197	204	212	219	227	235	242	250	257	265	272	280	288	295	302	310	318	325	333	340	348	355	363	371	378	386	393	401	408
74	148	155	163	171	179	186	194	202	210	218	225	233	241	249	256	264	272	280	287	295	303	311	319	326	334	342	350	358	365	373	381	389	396	404	412	420
75	152	160	168	176	184	192	200	208	216	224	232	240	248	256	264	272	279	287	295	303	311	319	327	335	343	351	359	367	375	383	391	399	407	415	423	431
76	156	164	172	180	189	197	205	213	221	230	238	246	254	263	271	279	287	295	304	312	320	328	336	344	353	361	369	377	385	394	402	410	418	426	435	443

Source: National Institute of Health, 2003. Adapted from *Clinical guidelines on identification, evaluation, and treatment of overweight and obesity in adults: The evidence report.*

TABLE 2. Classification of Overweight and Obesity by BMI, Waist Circumference, and Associated Disease Risks

	BMI (kg/m²)	Obesity Class	Disease Risk[a] Relative to Normal Weight and Waist Circumference: Men 102 cm (40 in) or less, Women 88 cm (35 in) or less	Men > 102 cm (40 in), Women > 88 cm (35 in)
Underweight	<18.5		—	—
Normal	18.5–24.9		—	—
Overweight	25.0–29.9		Increased	High
Obesity	30.0–34.9	I	High	Very high
	35.0–39.9	II	Very high	Very high
Extreme obesity	40.0+[b]	III	Extremely high	Extremely high

[a]Disease risk for type 2 diabetes, hypertension, and CVD.
[b]Increased waist circumference can also be a marker for increased risk even in persons of normal weight.
Note: Divide weight in pounds by 2.2 to get kg.
Source: National Institutes of Health, 2003.

References, Readings, & Internet Sources 

National Institutes of Health. National Heart, Lung, and Blood Institute. (2003). *Clinical guidelines on identification, evaluation, and treatment of overweight and obesity in adults: The evidence report:* Retrieved 2004 from http://www.nhlbi.nih.gov/guidelines/obesity/bmi_tbl.htm

National Research Council. (1989). *Diet and health: Implications for reducing chronic disease risk.* Washington, DC: National Academy Press.

United States Department of Health and Human Services. (2003). Center for Disease Control and Prevention. National Center for Chronic Disease Prevention and Health Promotion. Division of Nutrition and Physical Activity. *BMI: Body Mass Index.* See also http://www.cdc.gov/nccdphp/dnpa/bmi/bmi-adult-formula.htm; Web site that calculates BMI: http://www.cdc.gov/nccdphp/dnpa/bmi/calc-bmi.htm

Related Topic

Chapter 95, "Dietary Supplements and Psychological Functioning"

91 MEDICAL CONDITIONS THAT MAY PRESENT AS PSYCHOLOGICAL DISORDERS

William J. Reed

Many medical disorders may present with psychological symptoms or cognitive disturbances. Often the symptoms are the direct result of a disease process, such as the anxiety and mania caused by the overproduction of thyroid hormone or the schizophreniform picture of central nervous system involvement with systemic lupus. What may not be as readily appreciated is how frequently "psychological" disorders present with signs or symptoms of physiological dysfunction, such as the tachycardia and increased blood pressure seen with chronic anxiety. Patient amplification of symptoms frequently produces somatic complaints out of proportion to the objective medical findings as well as occasional diagnostic confusion (Broom, 2000). It is also well documented that the duration of physical complaints and medication side effects may contribute to the presentation of physical disease as well as a psychological illness.

A wide variety of medical conditions can present as psychological disorders in everyday clinical practice. As many as 10% to 20% of all pediatric and adolescent medical complaints may be "psychosomatic" or "somatoform" in origin (Gold & Friedman, 1995); that is, without visible alteration in organic function. Both terms are probably incorrect descriptions since they suggest that disease cannot exist in the absence of recognizable pathological change (Barsky & Burus, 1999). And because of conventional medical training, many clinicians and psychologists frequently struggle with the notion that a "physiologic" cause *must* necessarily exist for every symptom. The dualistic model that created an artificial distinction between organic (medical) illness and psychological (or psychiatric) illness acts an outdated theoretical constraint.

At the present time, there is very little evidence to suggest that the mind (psyche) and the body function (soma) differ psycho-neuroimmunologically, endocrinologically, or psychophysiologically (Ryan, 1998). Clinicians should recognize the contribution of both the mind and the body (psychophysiology) as a continuum, especially when:

- A disease process or disorder persists unexplained (mullerian duct anomalies presenting as enuresis)
- There is poor patient compliance (recurrent abdominal pain with child neglect)
- There is a drop in academic production or school performance (the illicit use of prescribed medications or the abuse of illicit drugs)
- Withdrawal from social or peer activities (avoidant behaviors vs. neurological regression)
- There is clinical evidence of significant mood change and/or disruptive behaviors.

The combination of a complete medical history and physical examination coupled with psychological tests and judicious laboratory testing usually separates the ongoing pathological processes and those conditions that mimic either psychological or physiological disease. The following is an attempt to list those entities seen most often in a pediatric and adolescent medicine practice.

MEDICAL CONDITIONS THAT MAY PRESENT AS ANXIETY (AND PANIC ATTACKS)

- Akathisia from antipsychotic medications
- Cardiovascular
  - Angina
  - Cardiac arrhythmias
  - Congestive heart failure
  - Hypertension
  - Mitral valve prolapse (Barlow's syndrome)
  - Myocardial infarction
  - Pulmonary embolism
  - Subclavian steal syndrome
- Chronic illness
- Deficiencies
  - Calcium
  - Magnesium
  - Potassium
  - Niacin
  - Vitamin B12
- Diet effects, caffeine, nicotine, illicit substance abuse
- Drug use or withdrawal (alcohol, amphetamines)
- Endocrine
  - Carcinoid syndrome

- Cushing's disease
- Hyperthyroidism
- Hypoglycemia
- Pheochromocytoma
- Menopause

- Gastro esophageal reflux
- Hyperhidrosis
- Lack of exercise
- Medications and withdrawal
  - Anticholinergics
  - Antihistamines
  - Barbiturates
  - Bronchodilators
  - Calcium channel blockers
  - Corticosteroids
  - Digitalis
  - Neuroleptics
  - Phenothiazines
  - Theophylline
- Neurological
  - Delirium
  - Labyrinthitis
  - Multiple sclerosis
  - Partial complex seizures
  - Post concussion
  - Vestibular dysfunction
- Nummular eczema (neurodermatitis circumscripta)
- Premenstrual dysphoria syndrome
- Recreational drugs
- Respiratory
  - Asthma
  - Chronic obstructive pulmonary disease (and emphysema)
  - Hyperventilation syndrome
  - Hypoxia
  - Pulmonary embolism
- Urticaria

MEDICAL CONDITIONS THAT MAY PRESENT AS ATTENTION-DEFICIT/ DISRUPTIVE DISORDERS

- Absence seizures
- Complex and simple partial seizures
- Frontal lobe disorders
- Heavy metal toxicity (see above)
- Landau-Kleffner syndrome
- Mania
- Medication side effects (see elsewhere)
- Neurocysticerosis

MEDICAL CONDITIONS THAT MAY PRESENT AS DEPRESSION

- Acne vulgaris
- AIDS
- Cancer-pancreatic
- Collagen diseases
  - Fibromyalgia syndrome
  - Juvenile rheumatoid arthritis
  - Mixed connective tissue disease
  - Sjogren's syndrome
  - Systemic lupus erythematosis
- Cystic fibrosis
- Endocrine disorders
  - Diabetes mellitus
  - Hyperparathyroidism
  - Hyperthyroidism
  - Hypopituitarism
  - Hypothyroidism
- Infections
  - AIDS
  - Encephalitis
  - Hepatitis
  - Influenza
  - Pneumonia
  - Syphilis
- Insulin dependent diabetes mellitus
- Leukemia
- Medications
  - Antihypertensives
  - Barbiturates
  - Benzodiazepines
  - Clonidine
  - Corticosteroids
  - Digitalis
  - Guanfacine
  - Oral contraceptives
- Medication induced personality changes
- Migraine headaches

- Neurologic disorders
  - — Cerebrovascular accidents
  - — Epilepsy
  - — Multiple sclerosis
  - — Subarachnoid hemorrhage
  - — Wilson's disease
- Neurosympathetic dystrophy
- Psoriasis
- Substance related, substance dependent and abusive
- Verrucae vulgaria

MEDICAL CONDITIONS THAT MAY PRESENT AS FATIGUE AND MALAISE (MODIFIED WITH PERMISSION FROM CAVANAUGH, 2002)

- Allergic tension fatigue
- Cardiovascular disease
  - — Arteriovenous fistula
  - — Congenital heart disease
  - — Congestive heart failure
  - — Hypertrophic cardiomyopathy
  - — Persistent pulmonary hypertension
  - — Takayasu's temporal arteritis
- Collagen diseases
  - — Dermatomyositis
  - — Mixed connective tissue disorder
  - — Polymyositis
  - — Rheumatoid arthritis
  - — Sjogren's syndrome
  - — Systemic lupus erythematosus
- Chronic fatigue syndrome
- Chronic renal diseases
- Endocrine disorders
  - — Hyperaldosteronism
  - — Hypercortisolism (Cushing's)
  - — Hyperthyroidism
  - — Hypocortisolism (Addison's)
  - — Hypothyroidism
  - — Pheochromocytoma
- Ehlers Danlos syndrome
- Familial hypokalemic periodic paralysis
- Fibromyalgia
- Gastrointestinal
  - — Chronic liver disease
  - — Inflammatory bowel disease
- Genitourinary
  - — Glomerulonephritis
  - — Pregnancy
  - — Pyelonephritis
- Hematological disorders
  - — Anemia
  - — Leukemia
  - — Lymphoma
  - — Polycythemia
- Infections (common)
  - — AIDS
  - — Epstein-Barr (infectious mononucleosis)
  - — Coccidiomycosis
  - — Cytomegalovirus
  - — Histoplasmosis
  - — Lyme disease (chronic)
  - — Sarcoidosis
  - — Subclinical hepatitides (B, C)
  - — Tuberculosis
  - — Wegener's granulomatosis
- Lymphoid hyperplasia (Down's syndrome)
- Medications
  - — Illicit (e.g., Blue Tuesday from amphetamines)
  - — Over-the-counter
  - — Prescription
- Myasthenia gravis
- Muscular dystrophy
- Narcolepsy
- Orthostatic edema
- Obstructive sleep apnea

MEDICAL CONDITIONS THAT MAY PRESENT AS SLEEP DISORDERS

Hypersomnias

- Chronic fatigue syndrome
- Cranial irradiation
- Depression
- Drug/medication use
- Inadequate sleep
- Intrathecal chemotherapy

- Klein Levin syndrome (with hyperphagia in males)
- Narcolepsy
- Nocturnal hypoventilation
- Poisoning and child abuse
- Postencephalitic sequelae
- Posttraumatic head injury
- Sleep reversals
- Upper airway resistance and sleep apnea

Developmental Dyssomnias/ Parasomnias

- Arousal disorders (non-REM)
  - Bruxism
  - Head banging
  - Night terrors
  - Paroxysmal nocturnal enuresis
  - Somnambulism
- Benign neonatal sleep myoclonus (Lennox Gastaut)
- Bruxism
- Circadian rhythm disorders
  - Primary latency phase disorder
  - Zeitgebers (night shift)
- Enuresis
- Head banging
- Nightmares
- Night terrors
- Nighttime body rocking
- Narcolepsy
- REM disorders
  - Nightmares
  - Seizures
- Obstructive sleep apnea
- Resistance to sleep
- Restless legs syndrome
- Somnambulism
- Somniloquy
- Trained night crying
- Trained night feeding
- Ultradian disorders
  - Seasonal affective disorder
- Vulnerable child

MEDICAL CONDITIONS THAT MAY PRESENT AS CHRONIC PELVIC PAIN IN FEMALES

- Dysmenorrhea (secondary)
- Dyspareunia (painful intercourse)
- Endometriosis
- Functional gastrointestinal disorders
- Mittleschmerz un lust
- Ovarian disorders
- Pregnancy
- Pseudocyesis
- Sexual abuse or sexual assault
- Surgical adhesions, e.g., Ashner's syndrome

MEDICAL CONDITIONS THAT MAY PRESENT AS FAILURE TO THRIVE OR WEIGHT LOSS

- Achalasia (e.g., Trypanosomiasis)
- Aganglionic megacolon (Hirschsprung's)
- Anorexia
- Attachment disorders
- Bartter syndrome
- Celiac disease
- Cerebral damage from hypoxia and hemorrhage
- Child neglect and abuse
- Chronic anemias
- Chronic hypoxemia
- Chronic protein malnutrition
- Congenital anomalies and developmental feeding problems
- Congenital infections
  - AIDS
  - Cytomegalovirus
  - Histoplasmosis
  - Rubella
  - Toxoplasmosis
  - Tuberculosis
- Cystic fibrosis
- Dwarfing syndromes
  - Leprechaunism
  - LeJeune's asphyxiating syndrome
- Diencephalic syndromes
- Endocrine disorders
- Fetal alcohol syndrome

- Hypocalorism
- Idiopathic hypercalcemia
- Inborn errors of metabolism
- Leigh syndrome
- Metabolic storage diseases
- Newborn narcotic withdrawal
- Protein losing enteropathy
- Protein losing nephropathy
- Rumination
- Schwachman-Diamond syndrome (pancreatic achylia)
- Severe gastroesophageal reflux

MEDICAL CONDITIONS THAT MAY PRESENT AS VERTIGO OR DIZZINESS

- Acute labyrinthitis
- Acoustic neuroma
- Benign paroxysmal vertigo
- Benign positional vertigo
- Central vertigo–transient ischemic episodes
- Cerebellar hemorrhage
- Head trauma
- Meniere's disease
- Migraine aura
- Multiple sclerosis
- Perilymph fistula
- Peripheral vertigo (damage/dysfunction of the labyrinth or eighth cranial nerve)
- Orthostatic hypotension
- Postural tachycardia syndrome
- Salicylate, or alcohol toxicity to labyrinth
- Toxic damage to labyrinth
- Vertebrobasilar stroke
- Viral labyrinthitis

MEDICAL CONDITIONS THAT MAY PRESENT AS PSYCHOSIS

- Addison's disease (hypocortisolism)
- Cardiovascular disease strokes
- Cushing's disease (hypercortisolism)
- Central nervous system infections
- CNS neoplasms
- CNS trauma
- Folate deficiency
- HIV and AIDS
- Homocysteinuria
- Hepatic failure/encephalopathy
- Hyperthyroidism
- Hyperparathyroidism
- Hyponatremia
- Hyperparathyroidism
- Hypothyroidism
- Huntington's disease
- Klinefelter's syndrome
- Medication-induced catatonia
- Multiple sclerosis
- Pancreatitis
- Porphyria
- Renal failure
- Systemic lupus erythematosus
- Temporal lobe seizures
- Traumatic brain injury
- Vitamin B deficiencies
- Wilson's disease
- Substance-induced (intoxication or withdrawal)

MEDICAL CONDITIONS THAT MAY PRESENT AS MEMORY LOSS AND DELIRIUM

- Alcohol dependence
- Alzheimer's disease
- Anoxia
- Carbon monoxide poisoning
- Carcinoid syndrome
- Cerebrovascular disorders
- Date rape drugs
  - Gamma hydroxybutyrate (GHB)
  - Rohypnol
- Electroconvulsive therapy
- Head trauma (post-concussion)
- Heavy metal toxicity
- Hypercarbia
- Hypoglycemia
- Infections
  - Herpes encephalitis
  - HIV
  - Koru
  - Malaria
  - Neurocysticerosis
  - Neurosyphilis
  - Rabies encephalitis

- Subacute sclerosing panencephalitis of Dawson

- Keane-Sayres disease
- Kluver-Bucy disease
- Medications
  - Benzodiazepines
  - Diltiazem
  - Thiopental
  - Others

- Multiple sclerosis
- Organic solvents
- Postoperative
- Seizures
- Sheehan's syndrome of postpartum CNS hemorrhage
- Substance abuse
- Metabolic
- Postoperative
- Substance abuse/withdrawal
- Vitamin B12, B6 deficiency

MEDICAL CONDITIONS THAT MAY PRESENT AS DEMENTIA

- AIDS-associated CNS infections
- Alzheimer's disease
- Creuztfeld-Jakob disease
- Head trauma
- Hepatolenticular degeneration (Wilson's disease)
- Huntington's disease
- Hydrocephalus ex vacuo
- Neimann Pick disease
- Neurosyphilis
- Parkinson's disease
- Post anoxia
- SSPE of Dawson (measles)
- Substance abuse
- Vascular thrombosis and embolism

References & Readings

American Psychiatric Association. (2000). *Diagnostic and Statistical Manual* (4th ed., rev.). Arlington, VA: American Psychiatric Press.

Barsky, A. J., & Burus, J. F (1999). Functional somatic syndromes. *Annals of Internal Medicine, 130,* 910–921.

Broom, B. C. (2000). Medicine and story: A novel clinical panorama arising from a unitary mind/body approach to physical illness. *Advances in Mind-Body Medicine, 16,* 161–207.

Cavanaugh, R. M. (2002). Evaluating adolescents with fatigue: Ever get tired of it? *Pediatric Review, 23,* 337–348.

Duchowny, M. (1996). Nonepileptic paroxysmal disorders. In B. O. Berg (Ed.), *Principles of childhood neurology* (p. 285). New York: McGraw Hill.

Gold, M. A., & Friedman, S. B. (1995). Conversion reactions in adolescents. *Pediatric Annals, 24,* 296–306.

Hymel, K. P., & Jenny, C. (1986). Child sexual abuse. *Pediatric Review, 7,* 236–249.

Levine, M. D., Carey, W. B., & Crocker, A. C. (1999). *Developmental behavioral pediatrics* (3rd ed.). Philadelphia, PA: W. B. Saunders.

Levine, R. L. (1995). Eating disorders in adolescents: A comprehensive update. *International Pediatrics, 10,* 327.

Morris, M. (1998). *Pediatric diagnosis: Interpretation of symptoms and signs in children and adolescents* (6th ed.). Philadelphia, PA: W. B. Saunders.

Morrison, J. (1997). *When psychological problems mask medical disorders.* New York: Guilford Press.

Netherton, S. D., Holmes, D., & Walker, C. E. (1999). *Child and adolescent psychological disorders.* New York: Oxford University Press.

Ryan, N. D. (1998). Psychoneuroendocrinology of children and adolescents. *Psychiatry Clinics of North America, 21,* 435–441.

Tasman, A., Kay, J., & Lieberman, J. A. (1997). *Psychiatry* (Vol. 1, chap. 26). Philadelphia, PA: W. B. Saunders.

Wood, B. L. (2001). Biobehavioral continuum of psychologically and physically manifested disease to explain the false dichotomy of organic v. psychological illness. *Child and Adolescent Psychiatric Clinics of North America, 7,* 543–562.

Yaylayan, S., Viesselman, J. O., Weller, E. B., et al. (1992). Depressive mood disorders in adolescents. *Adolescent Medicine: State of the Art Reviews,* 3–41.

Related Topic

Chapter 72, "Psychotherapy With Cognitively Impaired Adults"

92 ADULT PSYCHOPHARMACOLOGY 1
Common Usage

Joseph K. Belanoff, Charles DeBattista, & Alan F. Schatzberg

Make the appropriate diagnosis, but especially identify the target symptoms (see Table 1). Ideally, one would like to see the patient in a drug-free state for 1–2 weeks, although this is not always possible. Target symptoms are critical. Past history of medication response is quite predictive of current response. Family history of drug response is often helpful in making a medication choice.

MAJOR DEPRESSION

Major depression is a common debilitating illness (lifetime prevalence of approximately 16%). Success rates for psychopharmacological interventions are approximately 60–70%.

- *Monoamine oxidase inhibitors (MAOIs):* MAOIs are probably underutilized because of concern about tyramine-induced hypertensive crisis (extreme high blood pressure brought on by eating certain foods, including aged cheese, aged meat, and red wine, while using an MAOI).
- *Tricyclic antidepressants (TCAs):* TCAs have demonstrated proven efficacy in major depression but can produce side effects, ranging from the annoying (dry mouth) to the dangerous (arrhythmia). Least likely to produce sedation, postural hypotension, and anticholinergic side effects are desipramine and nortriptyline.
- *Selective serotonin reuptake inhibitors (SSRIs):* The release of fluoxetine in 1988 greatly expanded the number of patients with major depression treated pharmacologically. The SSRIs (fluoxetine, sertraline, paroxetine, and fluvoxamine) are virtually never lethal in overdose, and their side-effect profiles are relatively benign.
- *Trazodone and nefazodone:* Trazodone is an inhibitor of serotonin reuptake, an agonist at some serotonin receptors, and an antagonist at others. It is also an alpha-adrenergic blocker and an antihistamine, so common side effects include orthostatic hypotension and sedation. Although the primary indication for trazodone is major depression, it is quite effective in low doses (50–100 mg) as a hypnotic.

  Nefazodone has complicated effects on the serotonin system. It, too, is a 5-HT2 antagonist, as well as an inhibitor of serotonin reuptake (this combination may lead to sensitization of 5-HT1A receptors).
- *Venlafaxine:* Like the TCAs, venlafaxine is a nonspecific reuptake inhibitor. Unlike the TCAs, venlafaxine does not block cholinergic, histaminergic, or adrenergic receptors, so its side-effect profile is much more benign.

TABLE 1. Adult Psychopharmacology

Indication	Class	Drug Name	Dosage	Blood Level
Major depression	MAOI	Phenelzine (Nardil)	45–70 mg	
	MAOI	Tranylcypromine (Parnate)	30–50 mg	
	TCA	Imipramine (Tofranil)	150–300 mg	150–300 μg/ml imipramine & desipramine
	TCA	Desipramine (Norpramin)	150–300 mg	150–300 μg/ml
	TCA	Amitriptyline (Elavil)	150–300 mg	100–250 μg/ml amiltriptyline & nortriptyline
	TCA	Nortriptyline (Pamelor)	50–150 mg	50–150 μg/ml
	SSRI	Fluoxetine (Prozac)	20–60 mg	
	SSRI	Sertraline (Zoloft)	50–200 mg	
	SSRI	Paroxetine (Paxil)	20–50 mg	
	SSRI	Fluvoxamine (Luvox)	50–300 mg	
		Trazodone (Desyrel)	300–600 mg	
		Nefazodone (Serzone)	300–600 mg (divided)	
		Venlafaxine (Effexor)	75–375 mg (divided)	
		Bupropion (Wellbutrin)	300–450 mg	
		Mintazapine (Remeron)	15–45 mg	
Antidepressant augmentation		Lithium	600–1,800 mg	0.5–0.8 mEq/L
		L-triodothyramine	25–50 mcg	
Bipolar disorder		Lithium	900–2,000 mg	0.8–1.2 mEq/L*
	Anticonvulsant	Carbamazepine (Tegretol)	400–1,600 mg	6–10 μg/ml
	Anticonvulsant	Divalproex sodium (Depakote)	750–2,250 mg (divided)	50–100 μg/ml
Schizophrenia	Low-potency antipsychotic	Chlorpromazine (Thorazine)	300–800 mg	
	High-potency antipsychotic	Haloperidol (Haldol)	6–20 mg	
	Atypical antipsychotic	Risperidone (Risperdal)	2–8 mg	
	Atypical antipsychotic	Clozapine (Clozaril)	300–900 mg	
	Atypical antipsychotic	Olanzapine (Zyprexa)	5–20 mg	
	Atypical antipsychotic	Quetiapine (Seroquel)	50–400 mg	
	Atypical antipsychotic	Ziprasidone (Zeldox)	40–160 mg	
	Atypical antipsychotic	Aripiprazole (Abilify)	10–15 mg	
Panic disorder	Benzodiazepine	Alprazolam (Xanax)	1–6 mg	
Generalized anxiety disorder		Buspirone (BuSpar)	15–30 mg (divided)	
Obsessive-compulsive disorder	TCA	Clomipramine (Anafranil)	150–250 mg	
	SSRI	Fluvoxamine (Luvox)	100–350 mg	
Insomnia		Trazodone (Desyrel)	50–100 mg (at bedtime)	
	Antihistamine	Diphenhydramine (Benadryl)	25–50 mg (at bedtime)	
Narcolepsy	Psychostimulant	Dextroamphetamine (Dexedrine)	10–40 mg	
	TCA	Protriptyline (Vivactil)	10–40 mg	
Schizotypal personality disorder	Antipsychotic	Haloperidol (Haldol)	3 mg	

(*continued*)

TABLE 1. Adult Psychopharmacology (*continued*)

Indication	Class	Drug Name	Dosage	Blood Level
Borderline personality disorder	Antipsychotic	Loxapine (Loxitane)	5–25 mg	
	SSRI	Fluoxetine (Prozac)	10–40 mg	
Avoidant personality disorder	MAOI	Phenelzine (Nardil)	60 mg	
Alcohol withdrawal	Benzodiazepine	Chlordiazepoxide (Librium)	25–100 mg Q 6 h	
	Benzodiazepine	Lorazepam (Ativan)	1 mg Q 1 hr PRN pulse > 110, BP > 150/100	
	Vitamin	Thiamine	100 mg 1–3 × Q D	
	Vitamin	Folic acid	1 mg Q D	
	Vitamin	Multivitamin	1 tablet Q D	
Alcohol withdrawal	Benzodiazepine	Chlordiazepoxide (Librium)	25–100 mg Q 6 h	
	Benzodiazepine	Lorazepam (Ativan)	1 mg Q 1 hr PRN pulse > 110, BP > 150/100	
	Vitamin	Thiamine	100 mg 1–3 × Q D	
	Vitamin	Folic acid	1 mg Q D	
	Vitamin	Multivitamin	1 tablet Q D	
Heroin withdrawal	Opioid	Methadone	5 mg Q 4 h as needed on first day then decrease by 5 mg Q D until 0	
Relapse prevention		Disulfiram (Antabuse)	500 mg Q D for 2 weeks then 250 Q D (1st dose at least 12 h after last E to H use)	
	Opioid agonist	Naltrexone (ReVia)	25 mg Q D for 1–2 days then 50 mg (1st dose at least 7–10 days after last opioid use)	
Bulimia nervosa	SSRI	Fluoxetine (Prozac)	40–60 mg	
Alzheimer's dementia	Anticholinesterase	Tacrine (Cognex)	Start at 40 mg and raise by 40 mg every 6 weeks up to 110 mg	
	Anticholinesterase	Donezepil (Aricept)	5 mg	

*Levels ≥ 1.5 mEq/L may be toxic, and levels ≥ 2.5 mEq/L may be fatal.

- *Bupropion:* Bupropion was to be introduced in the United States in 1985 but was delayed after the occurrence of seizures in patients with bulimia. It was introduced in 1989 and has proved to be an effective, safe (and underutilized) antidepressant.
- *Mirtazapine:* Mirtazapine enhances both noradrenergic and serotonergic transmission. Side effects include weight gain and sedation but few sexual side effects.
- *Electroconvulsive therapy (ECT):* When depression is very severe or accompanied by delusions, ECT is the treatment of choice.
- *Adjunct therapy:* If a patient's depression has been nonresponsive to a 6-week course of antidepressants at appropriate dosages, adjunct therapy with either lithium or thyroid hormone is an alternative.
- *Atypical depression (hyperphagia, hypersomnia, leaden paralysis, rejection sensitivity, mood reactivity):* MAOIs have demonstrated superior efficacy compared with TCAs in treating this variation of major depression.
- *Psychotic (delusional) depression:* Antidepressant medication alone is usually ineffective. The combination of an antidepressant

and an antipsychotic is effective in many patients. ECT is probably the most effective treatment.

- *Dysthymia:* For many years the prognosis for individuals with dysthymia was poor. There is now increasing evidence that long-term use of antidepressants, particularly SSRIs, is quite effective in improving dysthymia and perhaps in preventing declines into major depression.

BIPOLAR DISORDER

The most effective acute treatment for manic psychotic agitation (virtually always administered in the emergency room) is an antipsychotic medication (i.e., haloperidol) combined with a benzodiazepine (i.e., lorazepam). Shortly thereafter, sometimes following a negative toxicology screen, a mood-stabilizing agent must be started.

- *Lithium:* Lithium remains the gold standard for the treatment of bipolar disorder. Seventy to eighty percent of acutely manic patients respond to lithium, but it often takes 1–3 weeks for a full response.
- *Carbamazepine:* Primarily used as an anticonvulsant, carbamazepine also has been shown to be quite effective in treating bipolar disorder.
- *Valproic acid:* Valproic acid (primarily used now in divalproex sodium form) has been granted FDA approval for the treatment of bipolar disorder. It appears that valproate may be especially effective in the treatment of rapid-cycling bipolar disorder and mixed manic-depressive states. Because there are many drug-drug interactions with valproic acid, the prescribing physician must be made aware of all medication changes (including over-the-counter drugs).
- *Other anticonvulsants:* Lamotrigine is currently being studied for the treatment of bipolar disorder. Other anticonvulsants used for bipolar disorder include tiagabine, oxcarbazepine, gabapentin, and levetiracetam, although none of these are currently approved by the FDA for use in bipolar disorder.

SCHIZOPHRENIA

Antipsychotic medication is often divided into two groups, "typical" and "atypical." All "typical" antipsychotics are dopamine-2 receptor blockers. "Atypical" antipsychotics are less prominent dopamine-2 receptor blockers, and they tend to block many other receptors, particularly serotonin-2 receptors.

- *Dopamine receptor antagonists (D2 receptors):* All traditional antipsychotic medication works essentially the same way and has the same side-effect profile. Medications with a relatively low affinity for D2 receptors ("low potency") require a higher dose, and medications with a relatively high affinity for D2 receptors ("high potency") require a lower dose.
- *Dopamine/serotonin receptor antagonists:* Risperidone, clozapine, olanzapine, quetiapine, ziprasidone, and aripiprasole are all less likely to cause motoric side effects than traditional antipsychotic medication. They may also be more effective in treating the negative symptoms and cognitive deficits of schizophrenia.

ANXIETY DISORDERS

Biological theories of anxiety disorders have pointed to problems in the norepinephrine, serotonin, and gamma-aminobutyric acid neurotransmitter systems. As a consequence, a wide variety of medications has been tried with varying success.

- *Panic disorder:* Antidepressants should be considered the first line of pharmacotherapy for patients with panic disorder. Benzodiazepines have also been shown to be effective in treating panic disorder but have a number of disadvantages over antidepressants. They often produce sedation, increase the effects of alcohol, produce dyscoordination, and are associated with dependence and withdrawal. Patients can have *severe* panic attacks while withdrawing from benzodiazepines.

- *Generalized anxiety disorder (GAD):* Benzodiazepines have been frequently used to treat patients with GAD. They are effective in the short run for symptom relief. However, for all of the reasons listed above, their longer-term use is problematic. Buspirone, a serotonin partial agonist, has been shown to be as effective as benzodiazepines in patients with GAD.
- *Social phobia:* Unfortunately, the pharmacological treatment of social phobia has lagged behind the treatment of other anxiety disorders. Alprazolam and phenelzine have been reported to produce improvement in symptoms of social phobia. Beta-blockers have helped with performance anxiety (in events like public speaking) but not particularly with social phobia.
- *Obsessive-compulsive disorder (OCD):* OCD is both relatively common and quite responsive to pharmacotherapy. Clomipramine, a nonspecific (but very serotonergically potent) reuptake inhibitor, has been best studied and is often effective. All of the SSRIs have been shown to be effective in reducing the symptoms of OCD.

SLEEP DISORDERS

- *Insomnia:* Insomnia is a common symptom in many psychiatric illnesses, particularly major depression. Insomnia often resolves as the depressive episode resolves. However, when insomnia is particularly distressing to the patient, low doses of trazodone or diphenhydramine are often effective in improving sleep.
- *Narcolepsy:* Psychostimulants (i.e., amphetamines) have long been accepted as valuable treatment for the daytime sleepiness seen in narcolepsy. Stimulants do not prevent the cataplexy that some narcoleptic patients experience, but either TCAs or SSRIs in combination with stimulants may be helpful. Modafinil has proven efficacy in maintaining wakefulness in patients with narcolepsy.

PERSONALITY DISORDERS

Despite the fact that pharmacotherapy has increasingly gained acceptance as a treatment option for severe personality disorders, there are few well-controlled studies that document pharmacological efficacy. In addition, many specific personality disorders have not been studied pharmacologically at all. Those that have include the following:

- *Schizotypal personality disorder:* It appears that schizotypal personality disorder has a genetic association with schizophrenia, so it is not surprising that there is some evidence for improvement with low-dose antipsychotic medication.
- *Borderline personality disorder (BPD):* SSRIs seem to help in BPD, particularly with impulsive aggression and affective instability. Low-dose antipsychotic medication is often effective in improving hostility and cognitive perceptual disturbances. Anticonvulsants, particularly valproic acid, seem to improve behavioral dyscontrol; benzodiazepines and noradrenergic antidepressants often seem to make behavioral dyscontrol worse.
- *Avoidant personality disorder:* There are no double-blind placebo-controlled studies, but there is evidence that MAOIs, SSRIs, beta-adrenergic receptor antagonists, and benzodiazepines may be useful in combination with psychotherapy.

PSYCHOACTIVE SUBSTANCE ABUSE AND WITHDRAWAL

- *Intoxication:* Most treatment for serious intoxication is focused on physiological support (controlling blood pressure, heart rate, respiration, etc.). The psychosis seen in amphetamine and cocaine intoxication may be treated with standard antipsychotics, often in combination with benzodiazepines (which help with agitation).
- *Withdrawal:* Withdrawal from alcohol, benzodiazepines, and barbiturates is similar and

is potentially life-threatening. All of these withdrawals are best pharmacologically treated with benzodiazepines. Lorazepam (Ativan) is recommended for patients with significant liver disease because its metabolism is less impaired in advanced liver disease. Methadone and clonidine are used in opiate withdrawal.

- *Relapse prevention:* The prevalence of substance abuse disorders, particularly alcohol abuse and dependence, has sparked interest in pharmacological methods to help prevent relapse. Disulfiram (Antabuse) has been tried for many years, although its popularity has certainly declined. Naltrexone, a synthetic opioid antagonist, is used in the treatment of alcoholism and narcotic dependence. Naltrexone aids abstinence by blocking the "high" caused by narcotics.

SOMATOFORM DISORDERS

Most of the somatoform disorders are ineffectively treated with current medication, and unfortunately psychoactive medication therapies are probably overused significantly. The one exception is body dysmorphic disorder, where the effective use of serotonergic agents (particularly SSRIs) has dramatically improved the prognosis for affected patients.

EATING DISORDERS

- *Anorexia nervosa:* Unfortunately, there is no shining star of pharmacological treatment for this life-threatening illness. Antipsychotic medication has not worked, and cyproheptadine, amitriptyline, and fluoxetine have had limited success.
- *Bulimia nervosa:* Antidepressants work very well in the treatment of bulimia apart from their ability to elevate mood.

IMPULSE-CONTROL DISORDERS

Among the impulse-control disorders, intermittent explosive disorder and trichotillomania are most often treated pharmacologically.

- *Intermittent explosive disorder:* Anticonvulsants are used most often, although the results are mixed. Benzodiazepines often make matters worse, with more behavioral dyscontrol. There is increasing case evidence that buspirone (often in higher doses than used in generalized anxiety disorder) may be effective.
- *Trichotillomania:* New pharmacological studies are taking place with both serotonergic antidepressants and the anticonvulsant valproic acid.

References & Readings

Albani, F, Riva, R., & Baruzzi, A. (1995). Carbamazepine clinical pharmacology: A review. *Pharmacopsychiatry, 28*(6), 235–244.

Andrews, J. M., & Nemeroff, C. B. (1994). Contemporary management of depression. *American Journal of Medicine, 97*, 245–325.

Callahan, A. M., Fava, M., & Rosenbaum, J. F. (1993). Drug interactions in psychopharmacology. *Psychiatric Clinics of North America, 16*, 647–671.

Kunovac, J. L., & Stahl, S. M. (1995). Future direction in anxiolytic pharmacotherapy. *Psychiatric Clinics of North America, 18*, 895–909.

Naranjo, C. A., Herrmann, N., Mittmann, N., & Bremner, K. E. (1995). Recent advances in geriatric psychopharmacology. *Drugs and Aging, 7*(3), 184–202.

Related Topics

Chapter 93, "Adult Psychopharmacology 2: Side Effects and Warnings"

Chapter 94, "Pediatric Psychopharmacology"

93 ADULT PSYCHOPHARMACOLOGY 2

Side Effects and Warnings

Elaine Orabona Mantell

Psychopharmacology is a dynamic field that requires the practitioner to keep up to date on the regularly changing information regarding the pharmacodynamics and pharmacokinetics of psychoactive medications. Given this caveat, several variables do remain constant in the safe and effective practice of pharmacotherapy. The following is not meant to be exhaustive, but rather it highlights information from the average clinical assessment that can affect the interaction between drug and patient.

- *Age:* The elderly metabolize drugs at a slower rate, which is one reason for the axiom, "Start low and go slow." The axiom also holds true for children.
- *Sex:* Psychotropic medications can have physical and behavioral teratogenic effects on the developing fetus and newborn (e.g., lithium has been associated with Ebstein's anomaly, a serious malformation in cardiac development, when taken during the first trimester). Therefore, the rule of thumb is to counsel all women of childbearing age about these risks and to avoid all but essential medications during pregnancy, especially the first trimester. When medication is unavoidable, serotonin-specific reuptake inhibitors (SSRIs) have typically been the first-choice medications, although this is still controversial because tricyclic antidepressants (TCAs) have a longer track record of use in pregnancy and can be measured through blood serum levels. Women also metabolize drugs differently during menstrual cycle phases, pregnancy/lactation, and menopause. For example, Wisner, Perel, and Wheeler (1993) found that by the third trimester, women on average required 1.6 times the nonpregnant dose of TCA.
- *Ethnicity:* Populations differ in their expression of genes that allow them to metabolize various drugs. The cytochrome P450 enzymes responsible for the metabolism of most psychotropic medications are IAD, IID6, and IIIA3/4. IID6, which is the enzyme responsible for the hydroxylation of many psychiatric medications, has been found to be deficient in 5% to 8% of Caucasians. Knowledge of genetic differences can help guide pharmacotherapy when individuals who are "fast" or "slow" metabolizers show either subtherapeutic response or excessive side effects.
- *Symptoms:* An assessment of symptoms will assist with establishing the target symptoms to be treated and monitored. The assessment must include pertinent negatives such as the absence of a history of mania because antidepressants can precipitate a switch into mania for those with a predisposition.
- *Past psychiatric history:* Look for previous psychotropic medication use, including family psychiatric history and use of psychotropic medications (if a drug worked or did not work for the patient's family members before, it is likely to repeat its performance in the future). Suicide history and current profile will suggest whether it is safe to uti-

lize medications with narrow versus broad therapeutic windows.

- *Past medical history:* Medical illness and concomitant drug use—even over-the-counter medication, homeopathic remedies, or folk remedies—can affect the pharmacokinetics and pharmacodynamics of any psychotropic medication. Some combinations can be monitored with relative safety, while others are absolutely contraindicated, such as a monoamine oxidase inhibitor and meperidine or dextromethorphan.
- *Habits:* Regular alcohol use can either speed up or slow down the metabolism of psychotropic medications, depending on the stage of damage to the liver. Also, chronic alcohol withdrawal can lower the seizure threshold, which means drugs that lower the seizure threshold (e.g., bupropion, high doses of tricyclics, and low-potency antipsychotics) should be avoided in individuals with seizure history. Tobacco and caffeine can also induce (speed up) the metabolism of various drugs and should be considered when monitoring for possible subtherapeutic or interaction effects. Illicit drugs can cause a patient to appear depressed, psychotic, and/or anxious. These must always be considered because of their influence on diagnostic and treatment decisions (e.g., whether to withhold, use, or delay the timing of certain psychotropic medications).
- *Laboratory studies:* The most common laboratory studies for psychiatric patients include complete blood count (CBC) with differential; blood chemistries (typically include electrolytes, blood urea nitrogen [BUN], creatinine clearance, liver function tests [LFTs]); thyroid function tests (TFTs); testing for sexually transmitted disease such as syphilis via RPR or VDRL; urinalysis with toxicology screen; blood alcohol level; drug serum levels (for those measurable); and HIV as appropriate. For women of childbearing age, a pregnancy test such as blood or urine HCG should also be included. Some of these studies will assist with differential diagnoses, but they can also provide baselines for the introduction of new medications that can affect various systems. For example, carbamazepine, an anticonvulsant and mood stabilizer, can cause blood dyscrasia and liver disease, and therefore requires periodic monitoring for changes from baseline in CBCs and LFTs. Similarly, lithium is known to cause endocrine effects such as hypothyroidism and renal insufficiency; therefore, BUN, creatinine, and thyroid-stimulating hormone (TSH) should be monitored regularly after baseline levels are obtained.

ANTIDEPRESSANTS

- *TCAs:* All the TCAs cause varying degrees of anticholinergic effects (e.g., dry mouth, urinary retention, constipation, blurred vision); antihistaminic effects such as sedation and weight gain; orthostatic hypotension from alpha-1 blockade; sexual dysfunction; and the potential for cardiotoxicity because of the quinidine-like effects on the heart. In fact, cardiac conduction problems are a significant contraindication to treatment with TCAs.
- *MAOIs:* MAOIs are not used as first-line drugs because of their lethal interaction and overdose effects. A lethal hypertensive crisis can occur when these drugs are mixed with sympathomimetics or foods containing tyramine (a natural by-product of the fermentation process), such as cheeses, wines, beers, chopped liver, fava beans, and chocolate. Besides these agents, L-dopa and TCAs can also cause an excessive elevation in blood pressure, which can result in myocardial infarction and stroke. Other signs and symptoms of hypertensive crisis include severe headache, excessive sweating, dilated pupils, and cardiac conduction problems. MAOIs are also contraindicated with SSRIs, serotonin precursors, and some narcotic analgesics because they can cause central serotonin syndrome, characterized by rapid heart rate, hypertension, neuromuscular irritability, fever, and even coma, convulsions, and death. This is especially important when switching from an SSRI such as fluoxetine, which has a relatively long half-life, to an MAOI because this switch requires a longer waiting period (approximately 4

weeks). All these drugs can cause postural hypotension, sexual dysfunction, weight gain, and symptoms similar to those produced by muscarinic blockage (i.e., anticholinergic side effects). Insomnia and restlessness/activation are more commonly seen with tranylcypromine and not phenelzine.

Of note is the recent introduction of a transdermal form of the MAOI selegiline (eldepryl). This parenteral formulation was designed to eliminate the dietary interactions associated with the oral formulation. To date, the only side effect encountered more often than placebo was skin rash (17% placebo versus 36% with transdermal selegeline). An unexpected but salubrious finding was a more rapid effect on depressive symptoms, as early as the first week of treatment (Bodkin & Amsterdam, 2002).

- *SSRIs:* These drugs tend to show a milder side-effect profile than the older antidepressants. Common side effects include activation (sometimes experienced as anxiety), headache, gastrointestinal distress (e.g., nausea, vomiting, and diarrhea), sexual dysfunction (mainly delayed ejaculation/orgasm), and occasional asthenia. Both activation and sexual dysfunction should be monitored closely as they are the side effects most often associated with early discontinuation and noncompliance with this class of medications. An interesting phenomenon is associated with SSRI side effects. SSRIs may cause either insomnia or sedation with no apparent predictability. Therefore, patients who are given a morning dosing schedule based on the common side effect of activation and insomnia will need to be educated about the freedom to switch to nighttime dosing should they experience sedation.
- *Trazodone (Desyrel) and Nefazodone (Serzone):* Both of these drugs can cause sedation, postural hypotension, nausea, and vomiting. Trazodone has a greater potential for sedation, cardiac arrhythmias, and priapism (a sustained, painful engorgement of the penis or clitoris). Nefazodone's labeling now carries a black box warning concerning hepatoxicity. Patients taking Nefazodone who show symptoms such as anorexia, fatigue , malaise, abdominal pain, discolored stools, dark urine, jaundice, ascites, nausea, vomiting, encephalopathy, and hepatic coma should discontinue the drug immediately. Because of the concern with hepatotoxicity, Nefazodone should no longer be used as a first-line agent, and all patients should be counseled about this risk prior to the initiation of treatment.
- *Venlafaxine (Effexor):* Venlafaxine's side effects are similar to the SSRI side-effect profile plus sweating, constipation, sedation, and dizziness. This drug is associated with a mild to moderate, transient dose-dependent increase in diastolic blood pressure. Therefore, patients with hypertension should be monitored closely upon initiation of treatment and before dose increases.
- *Bupropion (Wellbutrin, Zyban):* Bupropion shows various advantages over the SSRIs in that it does not have anticholinergic, postural hypotension, conduction arrhythmias, sexual dysfunction, or significant drug interaction effects. Side effects include activation and anorexia. In rare cases, bupropion has been associated with psychotic symptoms and seizure in doses over 450 mg per day. Patients with a history of eating disorder, seizure, and alcohol dependence with significant withdrawal symptoms including seizure, should not take this drug.
- *Mirtazapine (Remeron):* A tetracyclic agent that has been associated with inverse, dose-dependent sedation (i.e., sedation is reduced with doses above 15 mg) and significant weight gain. Adverse drug effects include neutropenia (1.5% risk) and agranulocytosis (.1%)—avoid in the immunocompromised, and monitor complete blood counts at baseline, annually and with signs/symptoms of infection. Other side effects include hyperlipidemia and hypercholesterolemia (over 20% above upper normal cholesterol levels).

SELECT MOOD STABILIZERS

- *Lithium (Eskalith, Lithonate, Lithane):* Because of its low therapeutic index, lithium can easily result in toxicity. Toxic effects can be expected at serum levels above 1.5 mmol/L, with severe adverse effects occurring as low as 2.0 mmol/L and above. Signs of toxicity include sluggishness, impaired gait, slurred speech, tinnitus, abdominal distress, tremor, ECG abnormalities, low blood pressure, seizures, shock, delirium, and coma. Aside from toxic effects lithium's side-effect profile includes nausea, vomiting, diarrhea, abdominal pain, sedation, tremor, muscular weakness, increased thirst and urination, swelling due to excessive fluid in body tissues, weight gain, dry mouth, and dermatological reactions. Chronic use can result in leukocytosis, hypothyroidism/goiter, acne, and ECG changes.

- *Carbamazepine (Tegretol):* Carbamazepine is associated with a number of rarely occurring toxicities, which include hepatitis, blood dyscrasias such as agranulocytosis and aplastic anemia, and exfoliative dermatitis (Stevens-Johnson syndrome). Incidents of leukopenia, thrombocytopenia, elevated liver enzymes, and dermatological reactions are typically reversible. Initial signs of toxicity include dizziness, blurred and double vision, sedation, and ataxia. Since carbamazepine is a potent inducer of hepatic enzymes, it speeds up metabolism and therefore can reduce the levels of several other drugs, including antipsychotics, valproate, TCAs, benzodiazepines, and hormonal contraceptives that may result in unintentional pregnancies. Therapeutic drug monitoring is recommended.
- *Valproic acid (Depakote):* Initial common side effects include gastrointestinal effects, sedation, tremor, and incoordination of involuntary muscle movements. With chronic use, there can be mild impairment of cognitive function, alopecia, and weight gain. Hematological effects include those seen commonly (e.g., thrombocytopenia, platelet dysfunction) and uncommonly (bleeding tendency). Hepatic effects include those seen commonly (benign increase of liver enzymes) and uncommonly (hepatitis/hepatic failure).
- *Lamotrigine (Lamictal):* In order of decreasing frequency, the most common side effects are dizziness, tremor, somnolence, headache, rash, nausea, and insomnia. Rash can be a serious adverse event and most commonly leads to drug discontinuation. The lamotrigine-based cutaneous reactions include measle-like rash, hives, and angioedema. But more serious rashes such as Stevens-Johnson syndrome, and toxic epidermal necrolysis can occur. The rate of serious rash requiring hospitalization and discontinuation of treatment is 3 in 1,000 and usually occurs within 1 to 2 months of initiation of treatment. The incidence of rash is higher in patients on more than mood stabilizer, and greater with rapid titration. The consensus of clinical opinion is that, unless an alternative etiology can be clearly identified, the drug should be discontinued when patients present with rash of any kind regardless of severity, since the clinician is unable to predict which rashes will become serious.
- *Topiramate (Topamax):* This medication has few drug interactions based on its predominately renal excretion. Side effects in general order of occurrence include parasthesias, headache, fatigue, somnolence, and weight loss. Because of the weight-loss side effect, this medication is often used for patients who do not comply with treatment on other mood stabilizers because of weight gain. This medication may also decrease the serum concentration of oral contraceptives which can result in pregnancy.
- *Gabapentin (Neurontin):* Side effects are mild with this medication, and include sedation, dizziness, ataxia, and weight gain. Rapid loading is well tolerated up to 4800 mg, with minimal pharmacokinetics interactions based on predominately renal excretion.

ANXIOLYTICS

- *Benzodiazepines:* Predictably, the common side effects are sedation and fatigue. In addition, ataxia, slurred speech, and memory (usually anterograde amnesia) and cognitive function impairment may occur. Behavioral disinhibition can occur in the form of rage, aggression, impulse dyscontrol, and euphoria. All benzodiazepines can cause depression. Although these drugs tend to be safe in overdose, this is not the case when mixed with other CNS depressants, which, in combination, can result in respiratory depression. Patients should be counseled about this risk, particularly those who drink alcohol.

- *Buspirone (Buspar):* This drug does not tend to produce sedation but can be initially activating. Side effects can include headache and gastrointestinal distress (e.g., nausea, diarrhea, heartburn). It is preferable to benzodiazepines in its side-effect profile since it shows virtually no sedation, cognitive and motor impairment, disinhibition, interaction with alcohol, or potential for dependence.
- *First-generation antipsychotics (FGAs):* Four primary side effects include sedation, extrapyramidal symptoms, anticholinergic effects, and weight gain. Extrapyramidal symptoms (mostly associated with high-potency agents) include Parkinsonian symptoms such as rigidity, bradykinesia, and resting tremor, akathisia (internal restlessness), acute dystonias such as muscle contractions or spasms (e.g., ocular gyric crisis), and tardive dyskinesia. Some antipsychotics can also lower the seizure threshold, usually in a dose-dependent fashion. Hyperprolactinemia can cause galactorrhea with all of the conventional agents and with the atypical agent, risperidone. Prolonged elevations of prolactin may reduced bone mineral density and thereby increase the risk of fractures. Thioridazine has been associated with an increased risk of sudden death secondary to torsades de pointes, hypertension, and ischemic heart disease. Its use is contraindicated with the antidepressant sertraline. Drugs that inhibit the cytochrome P450 enzyme IID6 may raise thioridazine levels and therefore the risk for sudden death (Reilly, Auis, Ferrrier, Jones, & Thomas, 2002). A recent study found that patients taking FGAs showed a greater than sevenfold increased risk of venous thromboembolism—more with low-potency than high-potency drugs. The greatest risk was during the first months of treatment (Zornborg & Jick, 2000). Patients on low-potency FGAs should be monitored for symptoms of phlebitis or embolism.
- *Second-generation antipsychotics (SGAs):* Clozapine (Clozaril), Olanzapine (Zyprexa), Risperidone (Risperdal), Quetiapine (Seroquel), Ziprasidone (Geodon)—these agents show similar side effect profiles including dose-dependent extrapyramidal symptoms for olanzapine, risperidone, and ziprasidone. The risk for tardive dyskinesia (TD) is lower with SGAs, and lowest for Clozapine, but with all SGAs, monitoring for TD should occur at baseline and yearly for the duration of treatment. Most SGAs are associated with new onset and impairment of glycemic control (up to 27% with Olanzapine) and hyperlipidemia (with the exception of ziprasidone). Weight gain is also a troublesome side effect of both the FGAs and SGAs and can interfere with treatment compliance. When prescribing SGAs the following should be routinely monitored. Other common side effects for all SGAs include decreased libido, sexual dysfunction, prolactin elevations (dose dependent), temperature dysregulation, photosensitivity, and photoallergic skin reactions. Neuroleptic malignant syndrome may also occur with this class of agents.

OTHER SPECIFIC SIDE EFFECTS

- *Clozapine:* Because of the risk of agranulocytosis, clozapine should only be after treatment failure with two or three other antipsychotics. Weekly blood monitoring is required for the first six months of treatment, and then every other week for the duration of treatment. However, clozapine has the lowest risk of tardive dyskinesia to date and is even used to treat this condition when caused by other antipsychotics. Extrapyramidal symptoms are also minimal. Other significant side effects include agranulocytosis, seizures, orthostatic hypotension, sedation, hypersalivation, tachycardia, constipation, hyperthermia, neutropenia, and eosinophilia. Agranulocytosis mortality is high if the drug is not discontinued and condition immediately treated.
- *Olanzapine:* Initially touted as the "new Clozapine without agranulocytosis." Olanzapine's major side effects include dose-dependent extrapyramidal symptoms, somnolence, agitation, insomnia, nervousness, hostility, constipation, and dry mouth.
- *Risperidone:* Although risperidone has a lower

incidence of extrapyramidal symptoms. At higher doses, its EPS profile approximates the traditional neuroleptics. Other side effects include postural hypotension, sedation, cognitive impairment, asthenia, constipation, nausea, dyspepsia, tachycardia, headache, fatigue, sexual dysfunction, dizziness, galactorrhea, and "burning sensations."

- *Ziprasidone:* This drug tends to prolong the QT interval on an electrocardiogram, which can potentially result in torsades de pointes, a fatal ventricular arrhythmia. The package insert states that it should be prescribed only after other agents have been tried. Postmarketing data have not supported an increased incidence of serious adverse events with regard to cardiac conduction, but conservative treatment would suggest routine EKG monitoring for patients treated with ziprasidone. Holter monitoring is advisable for patients on ziprasidone who complain of dizziness, palpitations, or syncope. This drug should not be used in combination with medications that prolong the QT interval. The most common adverse drug effects are somnolence and nausea; also rash and orthostatic hypotension can occur. It is less likely to cause weight gain than the other SGAs.
- *Quetiapine:* The package insert notes that with chronic use, this drug may result in ocular lens changes. Slit lamp examinations are recommended at baseline and every six months. This warning was based on studies with beagle puppies at four times the recommended human dose. Research on monkeys, at 5.5 times the recommended human dose, did not increase cataract development. Ocular assessments may, therefore, be based more on malpractice concerns than on empirical pharmacological science, especially since individuals with schizophrenia often have other risk factors, such as smoking, and diabetes and therefore greater risk for ocular lens changes. Dose-dependent reductions in total T4 and Free T4 levels have also been observed.

Note: The opinions and assertions contained herein are the private views of the author and are not to be construed as the official policy or position of the U.S. government, the Department of Defense, or the Department of the Air Force.

References, Readings, & Internet Sites

Bezchilibenyk-Butler, K. Z., & Jefferies, J. J. (Eds.). (2002). *Clinical handbook of psychotropic drugs.* Toronto: Hogrefe & Huber.

Bodkin, J. A., & Amsterdam, J. (2002). Transdermal selegiline in major depression: A double-blind, placebo-contolled study in outpatients. *American Journal of Psychiatry, 159,* 1869–1875.

Epocrates. (n.d.). Home page. Retrieved 2004 from http://www.epocrates.com

Hahn, R. K., Albers, L. J., & Reist, C. (1997). *Current clinical strategies: Psychiatry.* Irvine, CA: Current Clinical Strategies Publishing.

Herbmed. (n.d.). Home page. Retrieved 2004 from http://www.herbmed.com

Hyman, S. E, Arana, G. W., & Rosenbaum, J. E. (1995). *Handbook of psychiatric drug therapy.* Boston: Lippincott Williams & Wilkins.

Janicak, G., Davis, J. M., Preskorn, S. H., & Ayd, E. J. (1997). *Principles and practice of psychopharmacotherapy.* Baltimore: Williams & Wilkins.

Jensvold, M. E, Halbreich, U., & Hamilton, J. A. (Eds.). (1996). *Psychopharmacology and women.* Washington, DC: American Psychiatric Press.

Maxmen, J. S., Dubovsky, S. L., & Ward, N. G. (2002). *Psychotropic drugs fast facts.* New York: Norton.

Preston, J., & Johnson, J. (2001). *Clinical psychopharmacology made ridiculously simple.* Miami, FL: MedMaster.

Reilly, J. G., Ayis, S. A., Ferrier, I. N., Jones, S. J., & Thomas, S. L. (2002). Thioridazine and sudden unexplained death in psychiatric inpatients. *British Journal of Psychiatry, 180,* 515–522.

Schatzberg, A. E, & Nemeroff, D. B. (1995). *Textbook of psychopharmacology.* Washington, DC: American Psychiatric Press.

Wisner, K. L., Perel, J. M., & Wheeler, S. M. (1993). Tricyclic dose requirements across pregnancy. *American Journal of Psychiatry, 150,* 1541–542.

Zornberg, G. L., & Jick, H. (2000). Antipsychotic drug use and risk of first-time idiopathic venous thromboembolism: A case-control study. *Lancet, 356,* 1219–1223.

Related Topics

Chapter 92, "Adult Psychopharmacology 1: Common Usage"

Chapter 94, "Pediatric Psychopharmacology"

94 PEDIATRIC PSYCHOPHARMACOLOGY

Timothy E. Wilens, Thomas J. Spencer, & Joseph Biederman

There is a growing awareness of psychiatric disorders in children and adolescents. Many of the children who suffer from psychopathology may benefit from psychopharmacologic treatment. This chapter reviews potential benefits, risks, and treatment guidelines for psychotropic medications used in children and adolescents (see Table 1).

ATTENTION-DEFICIT/ HYPERACTIVITY DISORDER (ADHD)

Attention-deficit/hyperactivity disorder (ADHD) may affect from 5% to 9% of school-age children and persists into adolescence and adulthood in approximately 50% of cases (Barkley, 1998). A child with ADHD is characterized by a degree of inattentiveness, impulsivity, and often hyperactivity that is inappropriate for the developmental stage of the affected child (Barkley, 1998). ADHD symptoms vary between children and may adversely influence all areas of function, including academic performance, overall behavior, and social/interpersonal relationships with adults and peers. ADHD commonly co-occurs with oppositional-defiant, conduct, depressive, and anxiety disorders (Biederman, Newcorn, & Sprich, 1991) and substance-use disorders in adults (Wilens, Biederman, & Mick, 1998). ADHD has a male preponderance and appears to run in families. Approximately half of childhood cases will persist into adulthood, with diminuation of hyperactive/impulsive symptoms relative to the persistence of attentional dysfunction (Biederman, 1998; Biederman, Faraone, & Mick, 2000). The pharmacological management of ADHD relies on agents that affect dopaminergic and noradrenergic neurotransmission—namely the stimulants, antidepressants, and antihypertensives (Spencer, Biederman, & Wilens, 1998).

Stimulants

The most commonly used stimulants are methylphenidate (Ritalin, Ritalin LA, Concerta), amphetamine compounds (Adderall, Adderall XR), dextroamphetamine (Dexedrine), and magnesium pemoline (Cylert). Stimulants have been shown to be effective in approximately 70% of patients and appear to operate in a dose-dependent manner in improving cognition and behavior (Greenhill et al., 2002; Wilens & Spencer, 2000). The beneficial effects of stimulants are of a similar quality and magnitude in patients of both genders and across different ages to adulthood. Whereas there are immediate-release preparations of methylphenidate and amphetamine, the extended-release preparations are preferred and are more frequently prescribed. The extended-release preparations of the stimulants have a duration of action that starts approximately 30 minutes after dosing lasting from 8 (Ritalin LA, Metadate CD) to 12 hours (Concerta, Adderall XR). Dosing starts at the lowest available dose and increases up to 1.5 (amphetamine) to 2 mg/kg/day (methylphenidate products) of medication. The typical starting dose of pemoline is 37.5 mg up to 75 to 150 mg/day. There appears

TABLE 1. Pharmacotherapy of Common Disorders

A. Attention-Deficit and Disruptive Behavioral Disorders

Disorder	Main Characteristics	Pharmacotherapy
Attention-deficit hyperactivity disorder (ADHD)	Inattentiveness, impulsivity, hyperactivity 50% may continue to manifest the disorder into adulthood Associated with mood, conduct, and anxiety disorders	Stimulants (use of extended release preparations; for uncomplicated ADHD; careful in patients with tics) Atomoxetine (nonstimulant, first line for comorbidity?) Tricyclic antidepressants: desipramine, nortriptyline, imipramine (second line for nonresponders) Clonidine (good for preschoolers, severe hyperactivity, aggression, ADHD + tics; nonresponders): guanfacine (Tenex)—generally used if clonidine too sedating Bupropion (second line for nonresponders, useful in mood lability) Venlafaxine (Effexor)—third line Combined pharmacotherapy for treatment resistant or comorbid cases
Conduct disorder (CD)/ Oppositional defiant disorder (ODD)	Persistent and pervasive patterns of aggressive and antisocial behaviors Often associated with other disorders such as ADHD and depression	No specific pharmacotherapy available for core disorder Behavioral Tx For ADHD (see above), complex combinations (i.e., clonidine and stimulants) *For agitation and aggression:* Clonidine or Tenex Beta blockers (i.e., propranolol) Mood stabilizers (i.e., Lithium, Carbamezapine, Valproate) Atypical antipsychotics (e.g., risperidone) Other Axis I disorders (i.e., ADHD, MDD, pyschosis, anxiety): treat the underlying disorder

B. Mood Disorders

Disorder	Main Characteristics	Pharmacotherapy
Major depressive disorder (MDD)	Sad or irritable mood and associated vegetative symptoms occurring together for a period of time Similar to the adult disorders with age-specific associated features	Serotonin-specific reuptake inhibitors (SSRIs): fluoxetine, sertraline, fluvoxamine, paroxetine, (es)citalopram Bupropion, venlafaxine Tricyclic antidepressants Antidepressants and antipsychotics when psychosis develops Adjunct strategies for Tx refractory Antidepressants and low dose mood stabilizers, and BZDs, and thyroid and stimulants
Bipolar disorder depressed	Same as depression	Mood stabilizers (Lithium, Carbamezapine/Oxcarbazepine, Valproate-Depakote) Combined with MDD Tx Use bupropion, short-acting SSRIs
Bipolar disorder manic	Pervasive and/or severely irritable/angry mood Elevated or expansive mood More frequent psychotic symptoms in juvenile mania	Atypical antipsychotics (for acute mania first line; e.g., risperidone, quetiapine, olanzapine, ziprasidone, aripiprasole) Mood stabilizers (first line) Mood stabilizers and antipsychotics if marked mania or mood lability or psychosis For Tx refractory: two mood stabilizers (li and valproic acid) Mood stabilizers and adjunct antipsychotics Mood stabilizers and high potency benzodiazepine Mood stabilizer and clonidine

(*continued*)

TABLE 1. Pharmacotherapy of Common Disorders (*continued*)

B. Mood Disorders		
Disorder	**Main Characteristics**	**Pharmacotherapy**
Bipolar disorder mixed	Mixed depressed and manic symptoms Chronic course Most common presentation of juvenile bipolar disorder Usually very severe clinical picture	Mood stabilizers and atypical antipsychotics Mood stabilizers/antipsychotics and antidepressants (bupropion) Mood stabilizers and benzodiazepines
C. Anxiety Disorders		
Childhood anxiety disorders Overanxious disorder Separation anxiety Panic disorder	Excessive or unrealistic worry about future events Excessive anxiety on separation from caretakers or familial surroundings. Recurrent discrete periods of intense fear (panic attacks) Frequent comorbidity with MDD (50%) and ADHD (30%)	Serotonin reuptake inhibitors (SSRIs) Benzodiazepine (diazepam, clorazepate) Busipirone (Buspar) For panic, use high potency: e.g., lorazepam Tricyclic antidepressants (imipramine, nortriptyline) Combined pharmacotherapy for refractory or comorbid patients
Obsessive compulsive disorder	Recurrent, severe, and distressing obsessions and/or compulsions Often associated with Tourette's disorder, ADHD, mood, anxiety disorders	Serotonin-specific reuptake inhibitors (SSRIs) Clomipramine Venlafaxine Adjunctive: high-potency benzodiazepines, TCAs, Buspirone Combined pharmacotherapy for Tx refractory or comorbid patients (i.e., MDD, ADHD)
D. Other Disorders		
Psychotic disorders	Delusions and hallucinations Loose associations Paranoia often present Often associated with mood disorders	Atypical antipsychotics Traditional antipsychotics (risk for tardive dyskinesia) High potency BZDs for agitation *For treatment-resistant cases:* Antipsychotics and mood stabilizers Antipsychotics and beta blockers Antipsychotics and benzodiazepines Clozaril
Tourette's disorder	Multiple motor and one or more vocal tic Frequently associated with OCD and ADHD	Clonidine or Tenex Tricyclic antidepressants (desipramine, imipramine, nortriptyline) Atomoxetine (?) Beta-blockers Antipsychotics (high potency; Haldol, Orap) or atypical (risperidone) Combined pharmacotherapy for treatment resistant or comorbid cases (+ Klonopin)
Enuresis	Bed wetting	ddAVP (Vasopressin) Tricyclic antidepressants (imipramine)
E. Developmental Disorders		
Pervasive developmental disorders	Qualitative impairment in social interactions, acquisition of, language, and motor skills	For repetitive behaviors, serotonin-specific reuptake inhibitors (SSRIs) Clomipramine (Anafranil)

TABLE 1. Pharmacotherapy of Common Disorders (*continued*)

E. Developmental Disorders

Disorder	Main Characteristics	Pharmacotherapy
Autism	Stereotypies and self-stimulating behaviors often present It can be global, or in specific or multiple areas	Cholinesterase inhibitors (investigational) for cognitive dysfunction (e.g., galantamine, donepezil) No specific pharmacotherapy for the core disorder *Pharmacotherapy of complications:* Aggression and self-abuse: Atypical antipsychotics Beta blockers (i.e., propranolol) Clonidine High potency benzodiazepines Mood stabilizers (i.e., Lithium, Valproate) Mixed Opiate antagonist (Naltraxene) Other Axis I disorders (i.e., ADHD, MDD, psychosis, anxiety): treat the underlying disorder as in individuals

Abbreviations. ADHD = attention-deficit/hyperactivity disorder; OCD = obsessive-compulsive disorder; MDD = major depressive disorder; CD = conduct disorder; MR = mental retardation; TCAs = tricyclic antidepressants; MAOIs = monozmine oxidase inhibitors; SSRIs = serotonin-specific reuptake inhibitors; DDAVP = desmopresin; BZDs = benzodiazepines; Tx = treatment; Dx = diagnosis.

to be a dose response relationship for both behavioral and cognitive effects of the stimulants in ADHD individuals (Rapport et al., 1987). The most commonly reported short-term side effects associated with the stimulants are appetite suppression, sleep disturbances, and abdominal pain (Greenhill et al., 2002; Wilens & Spencer, 2000). Pemoline has also been associated with hepatoxicity, limiting its usefulness. Long-term side effects remain controversial, with mixed literature indicating only a weak association with motor tic development and height/weight decrement (Greenhill et al., 2002; Wilens & Spencer, 2000). Despite concerns of long-term effects of stimulants on later substance abuse, recent work indicates that pharmacotherapy of ADHD reduces the risk for substance abuse in half (Wilens, Faraone, Biederman, & Gunawardene, 2003).

Noradrenergic Agents

Atomoxetine (Straterra) is a recently approved, nonstimulant agent for children and adults with ADHD (Michelson et al., 2002; Michelson et al., 2001). Atomoxetine is a highly specific noradrenergic reuptake inhibitor with efficacy for ADHD (Michelson et al., 2002; Michelson et al., 2001) and perhaps comorbid anxiety, tics, and depression. Atomoxetine demonstrates no abuse liability and is unscheduled. Atomoxetine can be dosed once or twice daily and should be initiated no higher than 0.5 mg/kg/day and increased to 1.2 mg/kg/day in one to two weeks. The peak efficacy of the medication appears to unfold over two to six weeks.

Adverse effects of atomoxetine include sedation, appetite suppression, nausea/vomiting, and headaches. Most short-term adverse effects can be managed by changing the time of administration of the medication. Data are limited on the long-term adverse effects of the stimulants. There do not appear to be drug interactions with the stimulants—a combination that may be very helpful in recalcitrant cases of ADHD.

Antidepressants

Second to the stimulants and atomoxetine, the antidepressants have been the most studied pharmacological treatment for ADHD (Spencer et al., 1998). The tricyclic antidepressants (TCAs) have generally been considered second-line drugs of choice because of a long duration of action, greater flexibility in dosage, and minimal risk of abuse or dependence. Electrocardiographic and serum level monitoring is suggested.

The novel dopaminergic antidepressant bupropion has been reported to be effective and well tolerated in the treatment of ADHD children (Conners et al., 1996). Bupropion should be started at 37.5 mg and slowly titrated upward with beneficial effects for ADHD generally noted at less than 150 mg/day in children. Bupropion may be particularly useful in youth with ADHD and mood lability.

Antihypertensives

The antihypertensive agent clonidine has been used increasingly for the treatment of ADHD, particularly in younger children and those with hyperactivity and aggressivity (Hunt, Minderaa, & Cohen, 1985). Clonidine is short-acting agent with daily dosing ranging 0.05 mg to 0.6 mg given in divided doses up to four times daily. Clonidine is used adjunctly with the stimulants and antidepressants. Short-term adverse effects include sedation (which tends to subside with continued treatment), dry mouth, depression, confusion, ECG changes, and hypertension with abrupt withdrawal. A recent multisite study demonstrated the usefulness of clonidine alone and in combination for the treatment of ADHD in youth with tics (Kurlan, 2002). Abrupt withdrawal of clonidine has been associated with rebound, thus, slow tapering is advised. Guanfacine (Tenex) has also been used for ADHD. Dosing in school-age children generally starts at 0.5 mg/day and gradually increased as necessary to a maximum of 4 mg/day in two or three divided doses. Guanfacine appears to be longer acting, less sedating, and more effective for attentional problems than clonidine (Spencer et al., 1998).

DEPRESSION

Juvenile depression may occur in up to 5% of adolescents. Childhood depression presents with irritability, sad faces, low energy, isolation, withdrawal, negativism, aggression, and suicidality (Birmaher, Ryan, Williamson, Brent, & Kaufman, 1996; Birmaher, Ryan, Williamson, Brent, Kaufman, et al., 1996) Children with subsyndromal chronic depressive disorders may have dysthymic disorder. Childhood depression commonly co-occurs with anxiety, ADHD, conduct, and substance-use disorders. Juvenile mood disorders are chronic and highly recurrent. The antidepressants are the mainstay of treatment.

Serotonin-Specific Reuptake Inhibitors (SSRIs)

The SSRIs, including fluoxetine (Prozac), paroxetine (Paxil), sertraline (Zoloft), fluvoxamine (Luvox), and citalopram (Celexa, Lexapro), are generally considered the first-line drugs of choice for juvenile depression (Ambrosini et al., 1999; Emslie et al., 1997). These agents vary in how long they last and their adverse effects. Whereas fluoxetine has a long half-life of seven to nine days, paroxetine and sertraline have half-lives of approximately 24 hours. Because of its long half-life, missed doses of fluoxetine have less effect on overall clinical stabilization than the other SSRIs. In contrast, for children who are prone to develop mania, the selection of a shorter acting SSRI may be preferable.

The suggested daily doses in pediatric subjects approximate those in adults and varies among SSRIs. Treatment generally begins with 5–10 mg of fluoxetine or paroxetine, or 25 mg of sertraline or fluvoxamine, and may be titrated upward to full adult doses in some cases (i.e., 20–30 mg of fluoxetine or paroxetine; 150–200 mg of sertraline or fluvoxamine). Common adverse effects of SSRIs include agitation, gastrointestinal symptoms, irritability, insomnia, and headaches. Fluvoxamine may cause sedation and is useful in children with comorbid sleep difficulties. Most of the SSRIs, in particular fluoxetine and paroxetine, have been found to inhibit various hepatic (liver) enzymes and thereby increase blood levels of other medications.

Other Antidepressants

Venlafaxine (Effexor) possesses both serotonergic and noradrenergic properties and may prove to be useful in the treatment of juvenile mood disorders with ADHD at typical doses of 50–150 mg daily. Adverse effects of venlafaxine are similar to SSRIs with the addition of nausea, which generally improves within the first week of administration, and increased blood pressure.

Bupropion may be helpful in children with prominent mood lability, dysthymia, or comorbid ADHD. Similar to the management of ADHD (see above), bupropion should be started at 37.5 mg daily and titrated upward as necessary with the major side effects including irritability, insomnia, tic exacerbation, and seizures.

BIPOLAR DISORDER

In children, mania is commonly manifested by an extremely irritable or explosive mood, unmodulated high energy such as over talkativeness, racing thoughts, poor quality of sleep, or increased goal-directed with associated poor functioning (Geller et al., 1995; Geller et al., 2000) Often, youths with bipolar disorder have a relative with bipolar disorder. The clinical course of juvenile mania is frequently chronic and mixed with manic and depressive features co-occurring. Bipolar disorder in youths often onsets with depression with later switching into mania. Juvenile bipolar disorder is highly comorbid with ADHD, anxiety, oppositional and conduct disorders, and in adolescents, substance abuse. For juvenile bipolar disorders, the mood stabilizers and atypical antipsychotics are the treatment of choice.

Mood Stabilizers

Lithium is a salt that is considered one of the initial agents for labile mood disorders (Alessi, Naylor, Ghaziuddin, & Zubieta, 1994) The usual lithium starting dosage ranges from 150 to 300 mg in divided doses once or twice a day and increased based on response, side effects, and serum levels. Suggested serum levels are from 0.6 to 1.5 mEq/l for acute episodes and levels of 0.4 to 0.8 for maintenance therapy. Common short-term side effects include gastrointestinal symptoms, frequent urination and drinking, tremor, somnolence, and rarely memory impairment. The chronic administration of lithium may be associated with weight gain, decreased thyroid functioning, and possible renal impairment. Children should be followed for renal and thyroid function.

Alternative mood-stabilizing agents used in children include the anticonvulsants valproic acid (Depakote, Valproate), carbamazepine (Tegretol, Carbitrol), oxcarbazepine (Trileptal), and others (Kowatch et al., 2000). Valproic acid is an anticonvulsant that is often used as a first-line treatment and is dosed from 250 to 1500 mg daily leading to therapeutic blood levels of 50–100 mcg/ml. Common short-term side effects in children include sedation, nausea, and increased appetite. Carbamazepine is dosed from 200 mg to 1000 mg leading to therapeutic blood levels of between 4 to 12 mcg/ml. Common side effects include dizziness, drowsiness, nausea, blurred vision, white blood cell suppression, and serious rashes. Oxcarbazepine is dosed typically to 1200–1800 mg/daily (no monitoring required). For valproic acid and carbamazepine, monitoring of blood counts and liver function are warranted during treatment.

Atypical Antipsychotics

Because of the adverse effects and paucity of efficacy of the traditional agents for treating robustly the symptoms of bipolar disorder, the atypical antipsychotics have been increasingly used alone or in combination with mood stabilizers, for youth with bipolar disorder. Risperidone (Risperidal), quetiapine (Seroquel), olanzapine (Zyprexa), ziprasidone (Geodon), and aripiprasole (Abilify) are the currently available atypical antipsychotics that are being used for mania. The atypical antipsychotics appear to have both antimanic and antidepressant qualities in youth with bipolar disorder (Frazier et al., 1999; Frazier et al., 2001).

While generally well tolerated, short-term adverse effects of the atypicals include weight gain (olanzapine and risperidone), activation (ziprasidone), and sedation (all). Unlike the traditional antipsychotics, the atypical agents have a low liability to chronic movement disorders. No laboratory monitoring is required.

ANXIETY DISORDERS

The anxiety disorders encompass a wide range of clinical conditions in which anxiety is the predominant feature (Bernstein & Borchardt,

1991; Reiter, Kutcher, & Gardner, 1992). These include childhood disorders such as separation anxiety, generalized anxiety, and social phobia. Also within the umbrella of anxiety disorders of childhood is posttraumatic stress disorder, in which there is an objective stressor outside the usual human experience along with the recurrent experiencing of the event and accompanying hypervigilence or dissociation. Children may also present with panic disorder and agoraphobia—a fear of places with limited escape. Children with anxiety disorders often have other coexisting emotional factors such as depression as well as behavioral problems such as ADHD.

Children and adolescents with anxiety disorders respond to the same pharmacologic approaches as adult patients namely the benzodiazepines and antidepressants (Bernstein & Borchardt, 1991).

Antidepressants

The initial pharmacological treatment of choice for the wide umbrella of anxiety disorders in youth is the serotonin reuptake inhibitors (fluvoxamine and others) (Walkup et al., 2001). As described above, these agents are useful in the chronic management of anxiety and can be combined with other agents for anxiety (benzodiazepines-above) or comorbid conditions (e.g. stimulants). Dosing is similar to that employed for depressive disorders. No laboratory and cardiovascular monitoring is necessary.

Benzodiazepines

The benzodiazepines remain alternative agents for anxiety (Graae, Milner, Rizzotto, & Klein, 1994). Benzodiazepines are chosen based on how long they last and their strength. The more potent agents clonazepam (Klonopin) and lorazepam (Ativan) are often used in children with severe anxiety or panic; whereas the lower potency agents like diazepam (Valium) can be helpful in generalized anxiety. Dosing varies between agents and is usually in divided daily doses. Short-term adverse effects are disinhibition and sedation. Although the benzodiazepines have an abuse liability, there is no evidence that therapeutic use predisposes these children to later abuse.

OBSESSIVE COMPULSIVE DISORDER

Obsessive compulsive disorder (OCD) affects 1% to 2% of the population and is characterized by persistent ideas or impulses (obsessions) that are intrusive and senseless, such as thoughts of becoming contaminated or self-doubting and repetitive, purposeful behaviors (compulsions) such as hand washing, counting, or touching in order to neutralize the obsessive worries (Swedo, Rapoport, Leonard, Lenane, & Cheslow, 1989). Trichotillomania, the compulsive pulling out of one's hair, may be related to OCD. As with other disorders in youth, OCD is often comorbid with other anxiety disorders, depression, and ADHD. The serotonergic antidepressants are the most effective medications for OCD.

Serotonin Reuptake Inhibitors (SRIs)

There is a robust literature and FDA approval of the efficacy and usefulness of the SSRIs for juvenile OCD (Geller et al., 2001; March et al., 1998). Data indicate that relatively higher doses of the SRIs may be necessary for adequate treatment of the condition (i.e., fluoxetine doses of 40–80 mg daily).

Clomipramine has been shown to be efficacious in youth with OCD (Swedo, Leonard, et al., 1989). Clomipramine is dosed from 50 to 200 mg daily and has side effects (e.g., dry mouth, constipation) and monitoring requirements similar to the other tricyclic antidepressants.

TICS AND TOURETTE'S DISORDER

Tourette's disorder is a childhood-onset neuropsychiatric disorder that consists of multiple motor and phonic tics and other behavioral and psychological symptoms (Cohen, Friedhoff, Leckman, & Chase, 1992). Affected patients commonly have spontaneous waxing, waning, and symptomatic fluctuation. Tourette's disorder is commonly associated with OCD, ADHD, and anxiety disorders. The pharmacotherapy of tic disorders has changed in recent years and is influenced by the presence of comorbid conditions.

Clonidine

Clonidine has been increasingly utilized as a first-line drug of choice for tics and Tourette's disorder (Cohen, Detlor, Young, & Shaywitz, 1980). The mechanism of action of clonidine's effectiveness remains unknown. Dosing for tics or Tourette's disorder appears similar to those employed for the management of ADHD (see above). Recent data indicate that clonidine can be used adjunctly with methylphenidate for comorbid ADHD plus tic disorders (Kurlan, 2002).

Antidepressants

The TCAs have been used in youth with this disorder. TCAs may be particularly helpful in reducing tic and ADHD symptoms in children with this comorbidity disorder (Spencer et al., 2002). Patients with commonly comorbid OCD may need additional pharmacotherapy with serotonergic blocking drugs such as clomipramine, or the SRIs.

Antipsychotics

The antipsychotics remain efficacious agents for tics in kids who fail to respond to more conventional treatments (Cohen et al., 1992). The high-potency antipsychotics, including risperidone, pimozide (Orap), and haloperidol (Haldol), are generally used in doses of 0.5 to 2 mg/day. However, antipsychotics have limited effects on the frequently associated comorbid disorders (ADHD and OCD) and carry a risk for substantial adverse effects.

PSYCHOSIS

Psychosis is generally used to describe abnormal behaviors of children with impaired reality testing, such as the presence of delusions, hallucinations, or a thought disorder. Psychosis is present in schizophrenia and related disorders, and in some forms of unipolar or bipolar mood disorders. The antipsychotics (also referred to as neuroleptics) are the major treatment for psychosis.

Atypical Antipsychotics

Because of the efficacy and tolerability, atypical antipsychotics are being increasingly used (Frazier et al., 1997). Risperidone (Risperidal) is a high-potency agent that has fewer extrapyramidal adverse effects than traditional neuroleptics. Quetiapine (Seroquel), Olanzapine (Zyprexa), ziprasidone (Geodon), and aripiprasole (Abilify) are lower potency agents that are also very useful for psychosis and severe mood lability. The atypicals appear useful in treating both positive and negative symptoms of psychotic illness. Weight gain, sedation, and infrequent motor dyskineias and activation are the major adverse effects of the atypical antipsychotics. Clozaril is a low-potency agent that is infrequently used in treatment refractory individuals, particularly those with negative symptoms or in those who develop tardive dyskinesia (Kumra et al., 1996). Clozapine has a relatively high incidence of dose-related seizures and bone marrow suppression, making weekly to biweekly white blood counts mandatory.

Traditional Antipsychotics

There is an extensive array of traditional agents that are classified based on their potency (strength) and, because of long-term adverse effects, are considered second-line agents for the treatment of psychosis. The low-potency agents requiring higher dosages include chlorpromazine (Thorazine) and thioridazine (Mellaril). The intermediate-potency agents include trifluoperazine (Stelezine), thiothixene (Navane), and perphenazine (Trilafon). The high-potency agents requiring lower dosages include haloperidol (Haldol) and fluphenazine (Prolixin). The usual daily doses range between 100 to 400 mg for the low-potency agents, 5 to 40 mg for the intermediate-potency agents, and from 0.5 to 20 mg for the high-potency compounds. Common short-term adverse effects of antipsychotic drugs are motor restlessness or spasms, Parkinsonism, dry mouth, and significant weight gain. However, whereas the low-potency agents are more likely to cause hypotension, tachycardia, and sedation, the high-potency agents may cause muscle spasms. Long-term administration of antipsychotics may be associated with abnormal involuntary motor movements called tardive dyskinesia (Campbell, Adams, Perry, Spencer, & Overall, 1988).

CONCLUSIONS

The field of pediatric psychopharmacology continues to expand as more agents are used and systematically tested for a broad spectrum of child psychopathological conditions. The use of combined pharmacotherapy has proved invaluable for resistant and comorbid conditions. Essential features in treating child psychopathology are a careful diagnostic assessment, the proper sequencing of psychosocial and pharmacological interventions, and the integration of pharmacotherapy as part of a broader treatment plan.

References & Readings

Alessi, N., Naylor, M. W., Ghaziuddin, M., & Zubieta, J. K. (1994). Update on lithium carbonate therapy in children and adolescents. *Journal of the American Academy of Child and Adolescent Psychiatry, 33*, 291–304.

Ambrosini, P. J., Wagner, K. D., Biederman, J., Glick, I., Tan, C., Elia, J., et al. (1999). Multicenter open-label sertraline study in adolescent outpatients with major depression. *Journal of the American Academy of Child and Adolescent Psychiatry, 38*(5), 566–572.

Barkley, R. (1998). *Attention-Deficit/Hyperactivity Disorder: A handbook for diagnosis and treatment* (2nd ed.). New York: Guilford Press.

Bernstein, G., & Borchardt, C. (1991). Anxiety disorders of childhood and adolescence: A critical review. *Journal of the American Academy of Child and Adolescent Psychiatry, 30*(4), 519–532.

Biederman, J. (1998). Attention-deficit/hyperactivity disorder: A life-span perspective. *Journal of Clinical Psychiatry, 59*(Suppl. 7), 4–16.

Biederman, J., Faraone, S., & Mick, E. (2000). Age dependent decline of ADHD symptoms revisited: Impact of remission definition and symptom subtype. *American Journal of Psychiatry, 157*, 816–817.

Biederman, J., Newcorn, J., & Sprich, S. (1991). Comorbidity of attention deficit hyperactivity disorder with conduct, depressive, anxiety, and other disorders. *American Journal of Psychiatry, 148*, 564–577.

Birmaher, B., Ryan, N. D., Williamson, D. E., Brent, D. A., & Kaufman, J. (1996). Childhood and adolescent depression: A review of the past 10 years. Part II. *Journal of the American Academy of Child and Adolescent Psychiatry, 35*(12), 1575–1583.

Birmaher, B., Ryan, N. D., Williamson, D. E., Brent, D. A., Kaufman, J., Dahl, R. E., Perel, J., & Nelson, B. (1996). Childhood and adolescent depression: A review of the past 10 years. Part I. *Journal of the American Academy of Child and Adolescent Psychiatry, 35*(11), 1427–1439.

Campbell, M., Adams, P., Perry, R., Spencer, E. K., & Overall, J. E. (1988). Tardive and withdrawal dyskinesia in autistic children: A prospective study. *Psychopharmacology Bulletin, 24*(2), 251–255.

Cohen, D. J., Detlor, J., Young, J. G., & Shaywitz, B. A. (1980). Clonidine ameliorates Gilles de la Tourettes syndrome. *Archives of General Psychiatry, 37*(12), 1350–1357.

Cohen, D. J., Friedhoff, A. J., Leckman, J. F., & Chase, T. N. (1992). Tourette syndrome: Extending basic research to clinical care. *Advances in Neurology, 58*, 341–362.

Conners, C. K., Casat, C. D., Gualtieri, C. T., Weller, E., Reader, M., Reiss, A., et al. (1996). Bupropion hydrochloride in attention deficit disorder with hyperactivity. *Journal of the American Academy of Child and Adolescent Psychiatry, 35*(10), 1314–1321.

Emslie, G. J., Rush, A. J., Weinberg, W. A., Kowatch, R. A., Hughes, C. W., Carmody, T., et al. (1997). A double-blind, randomized, placebo-controlled trial of fluoxetine in children and adolescents with depression. *Archives of General Psychiatry, 54*(11), 1031–1037.

Frazier, J., Spencer, T., Wilens, T., Wozniak, J., & Biederman, J. (1997). Childhood-onset schizophrenia as the prototypic psychotic disorder of childhood. *Psychiatric Clinics of North America: Annual of Drug Therapy, 4*, 167–194.

Frazier, J. A., Biederman, J., Tohen, M., Feldman, P. D., Jacobs, T. G., Toma, V., et al. (2001). A prospective open-label treatment trial of olanzapine monotherapy in children and adolescents with bipolar disorder. *Journal of Child and Adolescent Psychopharmacology, 11*(3), 239–250.

Frazier, J. A., Meyer, M. C., Biederman, J., Wozniak, J., Wilens, T. E., Spencer, T. J., et al. (1999). Risperidone treatment for juvenile bipolar disorder: A retrospective chart review. *Journal of the American Academy of Child and Adolescent Psychiatry, 38*(8), 960–965.

Geller, B., Sun, K., Zimerman, B., Luby, J., Frazier, J., & Williams, M. (1995). Complex and rapid-cycling in bipolar children and adolescents: A preliminary study. *Journal of Affective Disorders, 34*(4), 259–268.

Geller, B., Zimerman, B., Williams, M., Bolhofner, K., Craney, J. L., Delbello, M. P., et al. (2000). Diagnostic characteristics of 93 cases of a prepubertal and early adolescent bipolar disorder phenotype by gender, puberty and comorbid attention deficit hyperactivity disorder. *Journal of Child and Adolescent Psychopharmacology, 10*(3), 157–164.

Geller, D. A., Hoog, S. L., Heiligenstein, J. H., Ricardi, R. K., Tamura, R., Kluszynski, S., et al. (2001). Fluoxetine treatment for obsessive-compulsive disorder in children and adolescents: A placebo-controlled clinical trial. *Journal of the American Academy of Child and Adolescent Psychiatry, 40,* 773–779.

Graae, F., Milner, J., Rizzotto, L., & Klein, R. G. (1994). Clonazepam in childhood anxiety disorders. *Journal of the American Academy of Child and Adolescent Psychiatry, 33,* 372–376.

Greenhill, L. L., Pliszka, S., Dulcan, M. K., Bernet, W., Arnold, V., Beitchman, J., et al. (2002). Practice parameter for the use of stimulant medications in the treatment of children, adolescents, and adults. *Journal of the American Academy of Child and Adolescent Psychiatry, 41*(2 Suppl.), 26S–49S.

Hunt, R. D., Minderaa, R. B., & Cohen, D. J. (1985). Clonidine benefits children with attention deficit disorder and hyperactivity: Report of a double-blind placebo-crossover therapeutic trial. *Journal of the American Academy of Child and Adolescent Psychiatry, 24,* 617–629.

Kowatch, R. A., Suppes, T., Carmody, T. J., Bucci, J. P., Hume, J. H., Kromelis, M., et al. (2000). Effect size of lithium, divalproex sodium, and carbamazepine in children and adolescents with bipolar disorder. *Journal of the American Academy of Child and Adolescent Psychiatry, 39*(6), 713–720.

Kumra, S., Frazier, J., Jacobsen, L., McKenna, K., Gordon, C., Lenane, M., et al. (1996). Childhood onset schizophrenia: A double blind clozapine-haloperidol comparison. *Archives of General Psychiatry, 53,* 1090–1097.

Kurlan, R. (2002). Treatment of ADHD in children with tics: A randomized controlled trial. *Neurology, 58,* 527–536.

March, J., Biederman, J., Wolkow, R., Safferman, A., Sallee, F., Ambrosini, P., et al. (1998). Sertraline in children and adolescents with obsessive compulsive disorder: A multicenter randomized controlled trial. *Journal of the American Medical Association, 280*(20), 1752–1756.

Michelson, D., Allen, A. J., Busner, J., Casat, C., Dunn, D., Kratochvil, C. J., et al. (2002). Once-daily atomoxetine treatment for children and adolescents with ADHD: A randomized, placebo-controlled study. *American Journal of Psychiatry, 159,* 1896–1901.

Michelson, D., Faries, D., Wernicke, J., Kelsey, D., Kendrick, K., Sallee, F. R., et al. (2001). Atomoxetine in the treatment of children and adolescents with attention-deficit/hyperactivity disorder: A randomized, placebo-controlled, dose-response study. *Pediatrics, 108*(5), E83.

Rapport, M. D., Jones, J. T., DuPaul, G. J., Kelly, K. L., Gardner, M. J., Tucker, S. B., et al. (1987). Attention deficit disorder and methylphenidate: Group and single-subject analyses of dose effects on attention in clinic and classroom settings. *Journal of Clinical Child Psychology, 16,* 329–338.

Reiter, S., Kutcher, S., & Gardner, D. (1992). Anxiety disorders in children and adolescents: Clinical and related issues in pharmacological treatment. *Canadian Journal of Psychiatry, 37,* 432–438.

Spencer, T., Biederman, J., Coffey, B., Geller, D., Crawford, M., Bearman, S. K., et al. (2002). A double-blind comparison of desipramine and placebo in children and adolescents with chronic tic disorder and comorbid attention-deficit/hyperactivity disorder. *Archives of General Psychiatry, 59*(7), 649–656.

Spencer, T., Biederman, J., & Wilens, T. (1998). Pharmacotherapy of attention-deficit/hyperactivity disorder: A life span perspective. In L. Dickstein, M. Riba, & J. Oldham (Eds.), *Review of Psychiatry* (Vol. 16, pp. IV87–IV127). Washington, DC: American Psychiatric Press.

Swedo, S. E., Leonard, H. L., Rapoport, J. L., Lenane, M. C., Goldberger, E. L., & Cheslow, D. L.

(1989). A double-blind comparison of clomipramine and desipramine in the treatment of trichotillomania (hair pulling). *New England Journal of Medicine, 321*(8), 496–501.

Swedo, S. E., Rapoport, J. L., Leonard, H., Lenane, M., & Cheslow, D. (1989). Obsessive-compulsive disorder in children and adolescents. *Archives of General Psychiatry, 46*, 335–341.

Walkup, J., Labellarte, M. J., Riddle, M., Pine, D. S., Greenhill, L., Klein, R., et al. (2001). Fluvoxamine for the treatment of anxiety disorders in children and adolescents. The Research Unit on Pediatric Psychopharmacology Anxiety Study Group. *New England Journal of Medicine, 344*(17), 1279–1285.

Wilens, T., Biederman, J., & Mick, E. (1998). Does ADHD affect the course of substance abuse? Findings from a sample of adults with and without ADHD. *American Journal on Addictions, 7*, 156–163.

Wilens, T., Faraone, S., Biederman, J., & Gunawardene, S. (2003). Does the pharmacotherapy of ADHD beget later substance abuse: A metanalytic review of the literature. *Pediatrics, 11*(1), 179–185.

Wilens, T., & Spencer, T. (2000). The stimulants revisited. In C. Stubbe (Ed.), *Child and adolescent psychiatric clinics of North America* (3rd ed., Vol. 9, pp. 573–603). Philadelphia: Saunders.

Related Topics

Chapter 92, "Adult Psychopharmacology 1: Common Usage"

Chapter 93, "Adult Psychopharmacology 2: Side Effects and Warnings"

95 DIETARY SUPPLEMENTS AND PSYCHOLOGICAL FUNCTIONING

Sari Edelstein and Nancie H. Herbold

Psychological disorders and substance abuse can be associated with nutritional deficiencies. The origin of these nutritional deficiencies can be due to under eating, overeating, abnormal eating patterns (Table 1) or as a side effect of alcohol, drugs (Table 2), and medication use (Table 3). This chapter identifies the criteria for nutrient supplementation, the recommended amount of supplementation, and the signs of both nutrient deficiency and toxicity. The dosage values given in the tables represent the Recommended Dietary Allowance and Adequate Intake levels set by the National Academy of Sciences. These levels were intended to be necessary in the daily diet of healthy adults. Some nutrient supplementation may be contraindicated due to other chronic illness or medications the patient may be sustaining. When the practitioner suspects a deficiency or toxicity, confirmation laboratory values should be made along with consideration of other illness and medication use.

TABLE 1. Dietary Supplements

Diagnosis	Nutrient Deficiency Symptoms	RDA/AI Supplementation and Dosage[a]	Toxicity Symptoms	Food Sources
Eating disorders: Anorexia nervosa Bulimia Bulimia nervosa	Osteomalacia, osteoporosis	Calcium, 1,000 mg/day	Excessive bone calcification	Milk, cheese, turnip, mustard greens, kale, broccoli
	Glossitis; megablastic anemia	Folate, 400 ug/day	None known	Liver, green leafy vegetables, legumes, broccoli, nuts
	Anemia, poor wound healing	Zinc, 12–15 mg/day	None known	Meat, liver, eggs, seafood
Anxiety	Muscle weakness, poor appetite, fatigue, Korsakoff's psychosis	Thiamin Males: 1.2 mg/day Females: 1.1 mg/day	None known	Pork, whole grains
	Skin and mouth lesions	Niacin Males: 16 mg/day Females: 14 mg/day	Flushing, tingling, nausea, dizziness	Lean meats, poultry, peanuts, fish, organ meats
	Oral lesions	Vitamin B6, 1.3 mg/day	Numbness, ataxia, bone pain, muscle weakness	Red meats, liver, whole grains, potatoes, corn, green vegetables
	Pernicious anemia, possible depression, anorexia	Vitamin B12, 2.4 ug/day	None known	Meats, milk products, egg
	Glossitis, megablastic anemia	Folate, 400 ug/day	None known	Liver, green leafy vegetables, legumes, broccoli, nuts
	Anemia, poor wound healing	Zinc, 12–15 mg/day	None known	Meat, liver, eggs, seafood
	Muscle tremors, irritability, tetany, hyperhypoflexia	Magnesium Males: 420 mg/day Females: 320 mg/day	Increased calcium secretion	Whole grains, nuts, dried beans, peas
	Myalgia, muscle tenderness, fragile red blood cells	Selenium Males: 70 ug/day Females: 55 ug/day	Nausea, abdominal pain, diarrhea, fatigue	Meat, eggs, milk, whole grains, seafood, garlic
Depression	Skin and mouth lesions, depessive psychosis	Niacin Males: 16 mg/day Females: 14 mg/day	Flushing, tingling, nausea, dizziness	Lean meats, poultry, peanuts, fish, organ meats
	Oral lessions	Vitamin B6, 1.3 mg/day	Numbness, ataxia bone pain, muscle weakness	Red meats, liver, whole grains, potatoes, corn, green vegetables
	Glossitis, megablastic anemia	Folate, 400 ug/day	None known	Liver, green leafy vegetables, legumes, broccoli, nuts
	Bleeding gums, loose teeth, pinpoint hemorrhages	Vitamin C Males: 90 mg/day Female: 75 mg/day	GI upset, kidney stones, excess iron absorption	Citrus fruit, tomatoes, potatoes, brussel sprouts, broccoli, strawberries
	Muscle tremors, irritability, tetany, hyperhypoflexia	Magnesium Males: 420 mg/day Females: 320 mg/day	Increased calcium secretion	Whole grains, nuts, dried beans, peas
	Poor iron absorption, neutropenia, bone demineralization	Copper, 2.0 mg/day	Wilson's disease, liver cirrhosis, neurological deterioration	Liver, kidney, shellfish, nuts, raisins, chocolate
Schizophrenia	Skin and mouth lesions, depressive psychosis	Niacin Males: 16 mg/day Females: 14 mg/day	Flushing, tingling, nausea, dizziness	Lean meats, poultry, peanuts, fish, organ meats

(continued)

TABLE 1. Dietary Supplements (*continued*)

Diagnosis	Nutrient Deficiency Symptoms	RDA/AI Supplementation and Dosage[a]	Toxicity Symptoms	Food Sources
	Muscle tremors, irritability, tetany, hyperhypoflexia	Magnesium Males: 420 mg/day Females: 320 mg/day	Increased calcium secretion	Whole grains, nuts, dried beans, peas
	Bleeding gums, loose teeth, pin-point hemorrhages	Vitamin C Males: 90 mg/day Females: 75 mg/day	GI upset, kidney stones, excess iron absorption	Citrus fruit, tomatoes, potatoes, brussels sprouts, broccoli, strawberries
Organic brain syndromes	Pernicious anemia, possible depression, anorexia	Vitamin B12, 2.4 ug/day	None known	Meats, milk products, egg
	Osteomalcia	Vitamin D, 5 ug/day	Hypercalcemia nausea, vomiting, polydipsia, polyuria	Fish, liver, eggs, fortified milk
	Myalgia, muscle tenderness, fragile red blood cells	Selenium Males: 70 ug/day Females: 55 ug/day	Nausea, abdominal pain, diarrhea, fatigue	Meat, eggs, milk, whole grains, seafood, garlic
	Anemia, poor wound healing	Zinc, 12–15 mg/day	None known	Meat, liver, eggs, seafood

[a]Food and Nutrition Board, 1989; Food and Nutrition Board, 1998.

TABLE 2. Nutritional Supplementation for Substance Abuse

Diagnosis	Nutrient Deficiency Symptoms	Recommended Dietary Supplementation and Dosage	Toxicity Symptoms
Folic acid deficiency	Glossitis, megablastic anemia	Folate, 400 ug/day	None known
Thiamin deficiency	Muscle weakness, poor appetite, fatigue, depression; Korsakoff's psyhosis	Thiamin Males: 1.2 mg/day Females: 1.1 mg/day	None known
Vitamin B-12 deficiency	Pernicious anemia, possible depression, anorexia	Vitamin B12, 2.4 ug/day	None known
Vitamin B6 deficiency	Oral lesions	Vitamin B6, 1.3 mg/day	Numbness, ataxia, bone pain, muscle weakness
Vitamin A deficiency	Dry eyes, gradual loss of vision, hyperkeratosis of skin	Vitamin A Males: 900 mg/day Females: 700 mg/day	Fatigue, vertigo, night sweats, lesions on lips and skin, abdominal pain, vomiting, jaundice
Zinc deficiency	Anemia, poor wound healing	Zinc, 12–15 mg/day	None known
Copper deficiency	Poor iron absorption, neutropenia, bone demineralization	Copper, 2.0 mg/day	Wilson's disease, liver cirrhosis, neurological deterioration

Source: Food and Nutrition Board, 1989; Food and Nutrition Board, 1998.

TABLE 3. Medications and Their Nutritional Effects

Medication	Nutritional Effect	Recommendation
Alprazolam (Xanax)	Increased or decreased appetite, anorexia, increased or decreased weight, increased salivation, dry mouth, nausea, vomiting, constipation	Take with food or water, limit caffeine, avoid alcohol, caution with some herbal products (kava)
Amantadine HCL (Symmetrel)	Anorexia, dry mouth, nausea, constipation	Avoid alcohol

TABLE 3. Medications and Their Nutritional Effects

Medication	Nutritional Effect	Recommendation
Amitriptyline (Elavil)	Dry mouth, nausea, vomiting, anorexia, taste changes, epigastric distress, diarrhea, constipation, paralytic ileus	Take with food, increase fiber may decrease drug effect. Limit caffeine, avoid alcohol, avoid St. John's Wort, avoid SAM-e, avoid yohimbe.
Bupropion (Wellbutrin)	Anorexia, decreased weight, increased appetite, increased weight, dry mouth, stomatitis, dyspepsia, nausea, diarrhea, vomiting, constipation	Take with food, avoid alcohol, avoid St. John's Wort. Possible anemia.
Benztropine mesylate (Cogentin)	Dry mouth, nausea, vomiting, epigastric distress, constipation	Take with food, avoid alcohol
Carbamazepine (Tegretol)	Anorexia, dry mouth, decreased appetite, stomatitis, glossitis, nausea, vomiting, abdominal pain, constipation, diarrhea	Take with food, avoid alcohol, avoid psyllium seed, aplastic anemia, caution with grapefruit juice
Clonazepam (Klonopin)	Dry/sore mouth, constipation, abdominal cramps, gastritis, changes in appetite, nausea, anorexia, diarrhea, increased salivation	Take with food, limit caffeine, avoid alcohol, caution with some herbal products
Clozapine (Clozaril)	Increased appetite, increased weight, anorexia, dry mouth, increased salivation, nausea, vomiting, dyspepsia, severe constipation, diarrhea	Take with food, limit caffeine, avoid alcohol, avoid St. John's wort. Nutmeg may reduce effectiveness of drug therapy.
Diazepam (Valium)	Occasional nausea and vomiting, diarrhea, constipation	Contraindicated for people with soy protein sensitivity. Take with food, avoid caffeine, avoid alcohol, avoid kava.
Fluoxetine (Prozac)	Anorexia, decreased weight, dry mouth, taste changes, dyspepsia, nausea, vomiting, diarrhea, constipation	Take in A.M. with meals. No tryptophan supplements. Avoid alcohol, avoid St. John's wort. Caution with diabetes—hypoglycemia.
Haloperidol (Haldol)	Increase appetite, increase weight, anorexia, dry mouth, increased salivation, dyspepsia, nausea, vomiting, constipation, diarrhea	Take with food, avoid alcohol
Lorazepam (Ativan)	Occasional dry mouth, nausea, constipation	Take with food, avoid caffeine, avoid alcohol
Levodopa (Dopar, Larodopa)	Dry mouth, bitter taste, nausea, vomiting, anorexia, constipation, diarrhea, abdominal pain, excessive salivation, increased or decreased weight, epigastric distress	May take with low protein food or juice, not with high protein food
Lithium carbonate	Decreased appetite, increased thirst, metallic taste, dry mouth, nausea, vomiting, diarrhea, transient hyperglycemia	Take with foods, avoid caffeine, avoid alcohol, avoid psyllium seed since it may inhibit absorption
Nortriptyline (Pamelor)	Increased or decreased appetite, dry mouth, nausea, vomiting, constipation	Take with food, avoid caffeine, avoid alcohol, avoid St. John's Wort
Paroxetine (Paxil)	Decreased appetite, increased or decreased weight, dry mouth, taste changes, nausea, dyspepsia, constipation, diarrhea	Take with food, avoid St. John's Wort, avoid SAM-e, avoid yohimbe
Phenelzine sulfate (Nardil)	Possible B6 deficiency, increased appetite, increased weight	Avoid foods high in tyramine and tryptophan such as cheese, yogurt, pickled, fermented, and smoked foods. Limit caffeine, avoid tryptophan supplements, may need B6 supplement, avoid St. John's wort, avoid alcohol. Caution with diabetes as it may decrease serum glucose.
Phenobarbital (Phenobarbital)	Nausea, vomiting, constipation	Increase Vitamin D and Calcium intake. Limit xanthine/caffeine, avoid alcohol. May need Vitamin D, Vitamin B12, and Folate supple ment with long-term use.

(continued)

TABLE 3. Medications and Their Nutritional Effects (*continued*)

Medication	Nutritional Effect	Recommendation
Phenytoin (Dilantin)	Taste changes, dysphagia, nausea, vomiting, constipation	Take with food or milk, avoid alcohol, caution with diabetes as it may increase serum glucose. Folate supplement needed. May need Vitamin D supplement.
Risperidone (Risperdal)	Increased appetite, increased weight, increased or decreased salivation, nausea, vomiting, dyspepsia, constipation, diarrhea, abdominal pain	Take with food, avoid alcohol
Sertraline HCL (Zoloft)	Increased or decreased appetite, dry mouth, nausea, vomiting, diarrhea, constipation, dyspepsia	Take with food, avoid alcohol, anemia
Trifluoperazine (Stelazine)	Dry mouth, constipation, nausea, increased weight	Avoid alcohol, avoid kava, avoid St. John's wort, avoid yohimbe
Valproic acid (Depakene)	Anorexia, increased or decreased weight, increased appetite, nausea, vomiting, indigestion, cramps, gastroenteritis, diarrhea, constipation	Take with food, avoid alcohol. Do not take with milk. Do not take syrup in carbonated beverages as it may cause mouth/throat irritation or unpleasant taste.
Venlafaxine (Effexor)	Anorexia, increased or decreased weight, increased appetite, dry mouth, taste changes, nausea, vomiting, constipation, diarrhea, dyspepsia	Take with food, avoid St. John's wort, avoid alcohol

Source: Food and Nutrition Board, 1989; Food and Nutrition Board, 1998.

References & Readings 

Alpert, J. E., Mischoulon, D., Nierenberg, A. A., & Fava, M. (2000). Nutrition and depression: Focus on folate. *Nutrition, 16*, 544–546.

Bottiglieri, T., Laundy, M., Crellin, R., Toone, B. K., Carney, M. W., & Reynolds, E.H. (2000). Homocysteine, folate, methylation, and monoamine metabolism in depression. *Journal of Neurology, Neurosurgery, and Psychiatry, 69*, 228–232.

Food and Nutrition Board. Institute of Medicine–National Academy of Sciences. (1998). *Dietary reference intakes (AI)*. Washington, DC.

Food and Nutrition Board. National Academy of Sciences–National Research Council. (1989). *Recommended dietary allowances (RDA)*. Washington, DC.

Hansen, C. M., Shultz, T. D., Kwak, H., Memon, H. S., & Leklem, J. E. (2001). Assessment of vitamin B-6 status in young women consuming a controlled diet containing four levels of vitamin B-6 provides an estimated average requirement and recommended dietary allowance. *American Journal of Clinical Nutrition, 131*, 1777–1786.

Institute of Medicine, National Academy of Sciences. (1997). *Dietary reference intakes for calcium, phosphorous, magnesium, vitamin D and fluoride*. Washington, DC: National Academy Press.

Institute of Medicine, National Academy of Sciences. (1998). *Dietary reference intakes for thiamin, riboflavin, niacin, vitamin B6, vitamin B12, pantothenic acid, biotin, and choline*. Washington, DC: National Academy Press.

Institute of Medicine, National Academy of Sciences. (2000). *Dietary reference intakes for vitamin C, vitamin E, selenium, and carotenoids*. Washington, DC: National Academy Press.

Institute of Medicine, National Academy of Sciences. (2001). *Dietary reference intakes for vitamin A, vitamin K, arsenic, boron, chromium, copper, iodine, manganese, molybdenum, nickel, silicon, vanadium and zinc*. Washington, DC: National Academy Press.

Penninx, B. W. J. H., Guralnik, J. M., Ferrucci, L., Fried, L. P., Allen, R. H., & Stabler, S. P. (2000). Vitamin B12 deficiency and depression in physically disabled older women: Epidemiologic evidence from the Women's Health and Aging Study. *American Journal of Psychiatry, 157*, 715–721.

Stewart, J. W., Harrison, W., Quitkin, F., & Baker, H. (1984). Low B-6 levels in depressed outpatients. *Biological Psychiatry, 19*, 613–616.

Related Topics

Chapter 93, "Adult Psychopharmacology 2: Side Effects and Warnings"

Chapter 96, "Common Drugs of Abuse"

Chapter 102, "Known and Unproven Herbal Treatments for Psychological Disorders"

96 COMMON DRUGS OF ABUSE

Christopher J. Correia & James G. Murphy

In 2002, the Substance Abuse and Mental Health Services Administration's (SAMHSA, 2001) National Household Survey on Drug Abuse estimated that 28 million Americans aged 12 or older, or 13% of the population, used an illicit drug during the previous year. Approximately 17 million (7%) met the *DSM-IV* diagnostic criteria for substance abuse or dependence, which are among the most common mental disorders (see also Karpiak & Norcross, chap. 1, this volume). Because drug use afflicts individuals from every demographic group, and because drug-related problems are common in clinical settings, it is important for all mental health professionals to understand the common drugs of abuse.

PREVALENCE OF DRUG USE

Table 1 presents SAMHSA prevalence rates for the most common drugs of abuse. The 2001 survey included a representative sample of 68,929 Americans above the age of 12. In Table 1, "binge" alcohol use is defined as drinking five or more drinks on the same occasion on at least one day in the past 30 days. Heavy alcohol use is defined as drinking five or more drinks on the same occasion on five or more days in the past 30 days; all heavy alcohol users are also "binge" alcohol users. Illicit drugs include prescription-type drugs used nonmedically. The table provides information for three age

TABLE 1. Prevalence Rates for Common Drugs of Abuse

	Age 12–17			Age 18–25			Age 26 and older			Serious Mental Illness
Drug	Lifetime	Past year	Past month	Lifetime	Past year	Past month	Lifetime	Past year	Past month	Past year
Alcohol	42.9	33.9	17.3	85.0	75.4	58.8	86.5	65.7	50.8	50.8
Binge alcohol use	—	—	10.6	—	—	38.7	—	—	18.8	27.2
Heavy alcohol use	—	—	2.5	—	—	13.6	—	—	4.8	8.7
Any tobacco	37.0	23.4	15.1	73.6	53.1	43.9	77.5	33.3	29.0	48.1
Any illicit drug	28.4	20.8	10.8	55.6	31.9	18.8	41.2	8.2	4.5	26.5
Marijuana and hashish	19.7	15.2	8.0	50.0	26.7	16.0	37.0	5.6	3.2	18.8
Cocaine	2.3	1.5	0.4	13.0	5.7	1.9	13.6	1.2	0.6	5.2
Heroin	0.3	0.2	0.0	1.6	0.5	0.2	1.5	0.2	0.0	0.7
Hallucinogens	5.7	4.0	1.2	22.1	9.3	2.7	11.9	0.5	0.1	4.3
Inhalants	8.6	3.5	1.0	13.4	2.5	0.6	7.1	0.2	0.1	1.5
Nonmedical use of:										
Pain relievers	9.4	6.4	2.6	18.2	9.6	3.6	8.4	2.3	1.1	10.4
Tranquilizers	2.6	1.7	0.5	8.9	4.2	1.3	6.2	1.2	0.5	6.2
Stimulants	3.7	2.2	0.7	9.5	3.4	1.3	7.1	0.6	0.3	3.5
Sedatives	0.7	0.3	0.1	1.9	0.6	0.2	3.9	0.3	0.1	1.7
Any illicit drug other than marijuana	18.7	12.0	4.9	35.4	18.4	7.8	24.9	4.4	2.0	17.5

Source: SAMHSA, 2002.

groups and for those with a serious mental illness, defined as having a *DSM-IV* disorder that results in functional impairment or interferes with regular life activities.

These data demonstrate that alcohol and marijuana are the most commonly used drugs across all age groups. Individuals under 26 years old and persons with a serious mental illness are much more likely to use all classes of illicit drugs. In fact, only 4% of adults (age 26 or older) without a serious mental illness reported using any drug other than marijuana or alcohol in the past year.

DRUGS OF ABUSE

Table 2 provides an overview of the common drugs abused—specifically, their slang names, routes of administration, acute effects, adverse effects, tolerance potential, and how they interact with other drugs. To avoid redundancy, the adverse effects of drug use on a developing fetus are not mentioned in the table, although all nonmedical drug use should be discontinued during pregnancy. The table provides only general information on drug interactions; it is not an exhaustive list of potentially hazardous drug interactions.

Although prescription medications are generally safe when used as prescribed, when misused their subjective effects and addiction potential are similar to illicit drugs of abuse. For example, medications such as opioid analgesics (e.g., Oxycodone), methylphenidate (Ritalin), and benzodiazepines (e.g., Valium) can produce physiological and subjective effects that are similar to heroin, cocaine, and alcohol, respectively. Prescription drug misuse is especially common among young adults, individuals with other substance-abuse or mental health problems, and individuals who have been treated with prescription analgesics or sedatives for long periods (e.g., chronic pain or anxiety patients).

ASSESSMENT CONSIDERATIONS

Drug-Use Patterns

A drug-use assessment should begin with questions about lifetime and current use of drugs, with consideration of the base rate for the client's demographic group (see Table 1). Individuals are most likely to provide accurate information when they are asked about use of specific substances, including misuse of prescription drugs. In some settings, biological tests (e.g., breath, hair, saliva, urine) can be used to detect recent drug use. The validity of self-reports can be enhanced by asking about drug use in a nonjudgmental manner and by providing assurance of confidentiality. In the absence of legal or other repercussions (e.g., loss of child custody or employment) for reporting drug use, self-reports of drug use are generally consistent with collateral reports and biological tests (Tucker, Vuchinich, & Murphy, 2002).

After gathering information about recent drug use, assess quantity and frequency of use over time. Drug-use patterns are generally quite variable, and information on contextual factors associated with periods of abstinence or increased use can be useful for treatment planning. Changes in substance use are often preceded by changes in other life areas, including employment, relationships, and physical health. Since many abused drugs are not sold in standard quantities, money spent on drugs and hours/days spent under the influence are useful proxies for drug amount. It is also crucial to gather information on route of administration, since this has implications for drug potency, abuse potential, and HIV/hepatitis C risk. In general, snorting, smoking, and injecting drugs are associated with increased potency and abuse potential relative to oral ingestion. For example, prescribed drugs such as Oxycontin or Ritalin are often crushed and either snorted or injected for a more potent and addicting high.

Risks and Negative Consequences

Regular drug use is associated with significant social, interpersonal, legal, health, and occupa-

TABLE 2. Common Drugs of Abuse: Summary of Routes of Administration, Effects, and Interactions

Drugs, Commercial and Slang Name	Routes of Administration	Acute Effects of Intoxication	Possible Adverse Effects	Tolerance and Dependence	Drug Interactions
Cannabinoids—Cannabis products such as marijuana and hashish contain THC, a chemical that produces mild sedative, euphoric, and hallucinogenic effects. Although there is no risk for overdose, regular use can result in tolerance, functional impairment, and mild withdrawal symptoms.					
Hashish boom, hash, hash oil, hemp *Marijuana* Marinol, pot, grass, weed, reefer, blunt	Smoked via cigarette, pipe, or water filtered pipe (i.e., bong). Can also be administered orally.	Increased pulse and appetite, dry mouth, enhanced sensory perception, mild euphoria, relaxation, sedation, and psychomotor impairment. Possible dizziness, illusions, and hallucinations	Some users experience brief paranoid reactions and panic. Chronic use of smoked THC associated with pulmonary damage. Possible deficits in learning, cognition, and motivation. Possible precipitant of psychotic episode among those with latent potential. Possible immunosuppressant.	Tolerance occurs with repeated use. Withdrawal symptoms include restlessness, anxiety, depression, irritability/aggression, insomnia, tremor, and chills. Withdrawal does not pose medical risk.	May interact with heart and blood pressure medication, or with other drugs that suppress the immune system.
CNS depressants—These include alcohol, barbiturates, benzodiazepines, and other drugs that induce behavioral depression, sedation, and relief from anxiety. At high doses these drugs produce motor impairment, amnesia, unconsciousness, and potentially fatal respiratory depression. Chronic use of CNS depressants can produce physical dependence, including severe withdrawal symptoms.					
Alcohol *barbiturates* Amytal, Seconal, Phenobarbital, barbs, reds, yellows *Benzodiazepines* Diazepam (Valium) Lorazepam (Ativan), Clonazepam (Klonopin), Alprazolam (Xanax), candy, downers, sleeping pills	Benzodiazepines and alcohol are orally administered.	Effects of CNS depressants can be context dependent and "biphasic." Euphoria and disinhibition are common at low to moderate doses. High doses produce clouded sensorium, sedation, impaired judgment and motor ability, amnesia/blackouts, affect lability, aggression, delusions, and hallucinations. Benzodiazepines are intended for short-term relief of anxiety and insomnia; higher doses produce lightheadedness, vertigo, and muscle incoordination.	Dangerous levels of respiratory depression. Sedation, impaired judgment and cognitive performance, anmesia, and psychomotor impairment. These effects can increase risk for automobile accidents, falls, and high-risk behavior. High doses of alcohol can lead to asphyxiation from vomiting. Chronic heavy use of alcohol can lead to irreversible liver damage, dementia, pancreatitis, gastritis, peptic ulcers, and cancers.	Tolerance occurs with long-term use. Withdrawal symtoms include agitation and increased anxiety, insomnia, muscle tension, and nausea with vomiting. Severe withdrawal symptoms include tremors and seizures (e.g., deliriums tremens), hallucinations, and psychotic symptoms. These symptoms can be fatal and often require medical attention.	Can produce potentially lethal respiratory depression when taken in combination with other CNS depressants (e.g., alcohol), or with heroin or prescription analgesics.

(*continued*)

TABLE 2. Common Drugs of Abuse: Summary of Routes of Administration, Effects, and Interactions (*continued*)

Drugs, Commercial and Slang Name	Routes of Administration	Acute Effects of Intoxication	Possible Adverse Effects	Tolerance and Dependence	Drug Interactions
Dissociative anesthetics—These drugs are difficult to classify, as they produce a combination of stimulant, depressant, and hallucinogenic effects. They can also cause fatal overdoses resulting from seizures and coma. Ketamine is also referred to as a "club drug" because of its association with all-night dance parties (raves).					
Ketamine cat, K, special K, vitamin K, date rape drug *Phencyclidine* PCP, angel dust, boat, hog, love boat, peace pill, rocket fuel, sherms	Ketamine can be injected, snorted, or smoked. PCP can also be swallowed.	Dream-like disorientation, euphoria, and analgesia. Impaired motor functioning, slurred speech, and detachment from environment. Increased heart rate, blood pressure, and temperature.	PCP can cause potentially lethal seizures and coma. Possible acute and prolonged psychotic states, leading to bizarre or dangerous behaviors. Ketamine produces more extreme CNS depression, numbness, nausea and vomiting, amnesia and dissociation.	Tolerance rises quickly, and chronic users will experience permanent tolerance after several months of use. These drugs do not appear to produce withdrawal symptoms or physical addiction.	Dangerous when used with other drugs that depress respiration. Psychological effects are unpredictable when taken with other drugs.
Entactogens—Drugs from this class produce both stimulant and mild hallucinogenic effects. They are sometimes referred to as "designer drugs," or as "club drugs" because of their association with all-night dance parties (raves).					
Methylenedioxy-amphetamine MDA *Methylenedioxy-ethlylamphetamine* MDEA, Eve *Methylenedioxy-methamphetamine* MDMA, Ecstasy, X, XTC, Adam, lover's speed, peace, STP. Trail mix and sextasy used to denote combination of MDMA and Viagra (sildenafil citrate).	Usually swallowed in the form of a pill, although pure powder forms are sometimes injected, and tablets can be inserted into the anus.	MDMA produced mild hallucinogenic effects, increased tactile sensitivity, empathic feelings, mental alertness, and sympathetic nervous system stimulation. MDEA effects resemble those of MDMA, but without the empathic qualities. MDA produces stronger hallucinogenic effects	MDMA can be fatal when combined with high levels of physical activity, leading to hyperthermia, hypertension, and kidney failure. MDMA appears to lead to long-term changes in the serotonergic system, which may result in residual anxiety, depression, and cognitive impairment. Flashbacks following repeated use have been reported.	Tolerance develops, but there is no evidence of physical withdrawal. After-effects can include fatigue, depression, and anxiety.	Over-the-counter cold remedies and MAO inhibitors. MDMA and Viagra may cause dangerous changes in heart rate and blood pressure, and prolonged erection leading to permanent anatomical changes.

TABLE 2. Common Drugs of Abuse: Summary of Routes of Administration, Effects, and Interactions (*continued*)

Drugs, Commercial and Slang Name	Routes of Administration	Acute Effects of Intoxication	Possible Adverse Effects	Tolerance and Dependence	Drug Interactions
Hallucinogens—Hallucinogens produce altered states of perception and intense emotions that vary widely across individuals and occasions. Hallucinogens do not produce dependence, although use of these drugs can result in negative physical and psychological consequences.					
Dimethyltrypyamine DMT, business man's trip *Lysergic acid diethylamide* LSD, acid, blotter, cubes, microdot *Mescaline* peyote, buttons, cactus *Psilocybin* psychedelic or magic mushrooms, shrooms	Oral administration is typical. LSD can also be absorbed through mouth tissue; DMT and mescaline can be smoked	Altered states of perception and bodily sensations, intense emotions, detachment from self and environment, and, for some users, feelings of insight with mystical or religious significance. Mescaline also has some amphetamine-like effects.	Psychological symptoms such as emotional lability, panic, and paranoia can lead to bizarre or dangerous behavior. Persisting mental disorders, including panic attacks and psychosis, after use in those with latent potential. Hallucinogenic persisting perception disorder (flashbacks).	Tolerance builds up rapidly but fades after a few days. Hallucinogens do not produce withdrawal and are not physically addictive.	Mescaline can be dangerous when used in combination with other stimulants. Effects are more unpredictable when taken with other drugs.
Inhalants—The drugs in this category have little in common in terms of chemical structure, pharmacology, or behavioral effects. They are all taken by inhalation, however, and thus are often considered as a group.					
Anesthetics nitrous oxide *Solvents* paint thinner, glue, correction fluid, marker pens *Gases* butane, propane *Aerosols* paint, hair spray *Nitrites* "poppers" from heart medications	Inhalation	Rapid onset of sedation, euphoria, and disinhibition. Acute effects can include loss of consciousness, blackout, muscle weakness, impaired coordination, and slurred speech. Nitrates dilate blood vessels and produce sensation of heat and excitement believed to enhance sexual pleasure.	Use of inhalants can lead to lack of oxygen, ischemia of heart tissue, life-threatening cardiac arrhythmias, cardiac collapse, peripheral nerve damage, liver or kidney damage, and suffocation. Regular use can produce irreversible brain and peripheral nerve damage.	Tolerance and withdrawal are possible with prolonged use of nitrates. Tolerance to nitrous oxide is possible but unlikely with recreational use. Little is known about the tolerance and withdrawal profile of other inhalants.	Interactions with other drugs with depressant effects, including cold medicines, opiates, alcohol, barbiturates, and benzodiazepines are especially dangerous. Nitrates and Viagra can lead to fatal changes in blood pressure.

TABLE 2. Common Drugs of Abuse: Summary of Routes of Administration, Effects, and Interactions (*continued*)

Drugs, Commercial and Slang Name	Routes of Administration	Acute Effects of Intoxication	Possible Adverse Effects	Tolerance and Dependence	Drug Interactions
Opioid analgesics—These drugs bind to the opioid receptors and block the transmission of pain messages to the brain. They also produce euphoria, drowsiness, and potentially fatal respiratory depression. Chronic use can produce physical dependence, including severe withdrawal symptoms.					
Heroin black tar, smack, junk, dope *Prescription Analgesics* Morphine, Codeine, Demeral, Oxycodone Oxycontin, Percocet, Vicodin	Heroin is injected, smoked, and used intranasally. Oral medications are misused by crushing tablet and snorting or injecting.	Analgesia, euphoria, sedation, reduced anxiety, tranquility, respiratory depression, and cough suppression.	Respiratory depression can be fatal at high doses, or when regular users use in novel environments. Other side effects include nausea, vomiting, constipation and intestinal cramping, severe itching, and asthma-like symptoms. HIV, Hepatitis C, and bacterial infections are spread through injecting.	Tolerance occurs with prolonged use. Withdrawal symptoms include craving, sweating, anxiety, depression, irritability, fever, chills, vomiting, diarrhea, and pain. Compulsive use to avoid withdrawal is common.	Interactions with CNS depressants such as alcohol or benzodiazepines can cause potentially fatal respiratory depression.
Stimulants—These drugs produce sympathetic nervous system stimulation, which leads to increased heart rate and blood pressure, and an increase in purposeful movement. Additional effects include euphoria, increased alertness, and increased energy.					
Amphetamines Adderall, Dexedrine, bennies, speed *Cocaine* coke, blow, crack *Methamphetamine* crank, crystal fire, ice, meth, speed *Methylphenidate* Ritalin, vitamin R *Nicotine* Chew, cigars, cigarettes, smoke-less tobacco, snuff, spit tobacco	Injected, smoked, and snorted. Stimulant medication can be swallowed, or crushed and then snorted or injected.	Feelings of euphoria, increased energy, mental alertness, and rapid speech. Signs of sympathetic nervous system stimulation including increased heart rate, blood pressure, temperature, and both purposeful and compulsive movements.	Rapid or irregular heart beat, heart failure, respiratory failure, strokes, seizures, headaches, abdominal pain, nausea. With prolonged exposure to high doses, a psychotic state of hostility and paranoia can emerge that is similar to acute paranoid schizophrenia. Specific effects of prolonged exposure to nicotine products include chronic lung disease, cardiovascular disease, stroke, and cancer.	Tolerance builds quickly. Users typically experience fatigue and dysphoria after intoxication. Withdrawal symptoms are rarely dangerous but include fatigue, anxiety, sleeplessness, irritability, anhedonia, and depression.	Over-the-counter decongestants, MAO inhibitors, medications that raise heart rate or that increase sensitivity to seizures.

(*continued*)

tional impairment. Substance abusers typically present for treatment because of substance-related impairment, such as marital or health problems, rather than substance use itself. Thus, clinicians need to discuss drug-related negative consequences, and query about the presence of symptoms of drug dependence, such as increasing tolerance, withdrawal symptoms, and compulsive use.

It is especially important to carefully assess risk for immediate harm resulting from drug use. High-risk behaviors such as sharing injection needles, driving while intoxicated, risky sexual behavior, and taking dangerous drug combinations should be an immediate treatment priority.

Comorbidity

Substance-use disorders occur among those with other *DSM-IV* disorders at elevated rates, relative to the general population. In fact, 37% of alcohol abusers and 53% of drug abusers meet criteria for an additional mental disorder (Reiger et al., 1990). Stated differently, 29% of persons with a mental disorder were comorbid for a substance-use disorder. Persons with more severe mental illness are the greatest risk; 47% of persons with schizophrenia and 56% of persons with bipolar disorder have a lifetime diagnosis of substance abuse or dependence. Substance abusers with another psychiatric diagnosis tend to experience more psychosocial and physical health impairment compared to those without a comorbid diagnosis (Johnson et al., 1995).

References, Readings, & Internet Sites

Gavin, D. R., Ross, H. E., & Skinner, H. A. (1989). Diagnostic validity of the drug abuse screening test in the assessment of *DSM-III* drug disorders. *British Journal of Addictions, 84,* 301–307.

Johnson, J. G., Spitzer, R. L., Williams, J. B., Kroenke, K., Linzer, M., Brody, D., et al. (1995). Psychiatric comorbidity, health status, and functional impairment associated with alcohol abuse and dependence in primary care patients: Findings of the PRIME MD-1000 study. *Journal of Consulting & Clinical Psychology, 63,* 133–140.

Julien, R. M. (2001). *A primer of drug action* (9th ed.). New York: Worth.

Kuhn, C., Swartzwelder, S., & Wilson, W. (1998). *Buzzed: The straight facts about the most used and abused drug from alcohol to ecstasy.* New York: Norton.

National Institute on Drug Abuse. (2003). Information on common drugs of abuse. Retrieved 2004 from http://www.drugabuse.gov/drugpages

Reiger, D. A., Farmer, M. E., Rae, D. S., Locke, B. Z., Keith, S. J., Judd, L. L., et al. (1990). Comorbidity of mental disorders with alcohol and other drug abuse: Results from the Epidemiological Catchment Area (ECA) study. *Journal of the American Medical Association, 21,* 2511–2518.

Substance Abuse and Mental Health Services Administration. (2002). Results from the 2001 National Household Survey on Drug Abuse: Volume I. Summary of National Findings (Office of Applied Studies, NHSDA Series H-17, DHHS Publication No. SMA 02-3758). Rockville, MD.

Substance Abuse and Mental Health Services Administration. (2003). National clearinghouse for alcohol and drug information: PREVLINE. Retrieved 2004 from http://www.health.org

Tucker, J. A., Vuchinich, R. E., & Murphy, J. G. (2002). Assessment, treatment planning, and outcome evaluation for substance use disorders. In M. H. Anthony & D. H. Barlow (Eds.), *Handbook of assessment and treatment planning* (pp. 415–452). New York: Guilford Press.

The Vaults of Erowid. (2003). Psychoactive vaults: Plant and chemical library. Retrieved 2004 from http://www.erowid.org/psychoactives

Related Topics

Chapter 93, "Adult Psychopharmacology 2: Side Effects and Warnings"

Chapter 95, "Dietary Supplements and Psychological Functioning"

PART VII
Self-Help Resources

97 TOP INTERNET SITES FOR PSYCHOLOGISTS AND THEIR CLIENTS

John M. Grohol

There are millions of Web sites available today, and tens of thousands available on psychological and mental health concerns. Here you will find a small, select guide to a few of these sites that are some of the most reliable and useful, to satisfy both your professional needs and the needs of your clients. These sites not only offer a balanced perspective on mental health and psychological issues but also provide unique resources and content in a user-friendly format to make them worth the effort.

- About Psychotherapy (http://www.aboutpsychotherapy.com): A down-to-earth information resource that provides detailed descriptions of various types of psychotherapy by psychologist Bennett Pologe, Ph.D. Dozens of pages describe how psychotherapy works, why a person might consider therapy, when to stop, and what legitimate therapy consists of. Like Franklin's Psychology Information Online, About Psychotherapy also provides articles about starting treatment and the differences between types of professionals and their degrees. Case studies help clearly illustrate specific examples of different treatments.
- American Psychological Association (http://www.apa.org/): The American Psychological Association (APA) offers a plethora of resources for all types of psychologists. Updated behavioral healthcare news, research briefings, access to research databases, and journal archives are just a few of the many resources professionals will find at the APA site. Consumers will find the APA HelpCenter at http://helping.apa.org/ more oriented toward their educational needs.
- AtHealth (http://www.athealth.com/): AtHealth provides a wealth of psychoeducational materials for the consumer who is interested in learning more about a particular

disorder or mental health issue. Consumers will also find a practitioner's directory on the site that allows them to find a local therapist in their geographic area. For professionals, AtHealth offers dozens of online continuing education accredited courses.

- DrugDigest (http://www.drugdigest.org/): DrugDigest is a noncommercial consumer health and drug information site that provides a searchable drug and herb database. The results are written in plain English, making it unlike most drug databases available on the Internet today. For each drug, the site provides what the medication is used for, how it works, what a person should know about taking it, common side effects and interactions, how it should be taken, and what to do if the person misses a dose. For more detailed and technical drug information, RxList is recommended (http://www.rxlist.com/).
- The Foundation Center (http://fdncenter.org/): The Foundation Center is an organization that was founded in 1956 to promote philanthropy. Its Web site connects grant seekers with grant makers, but does require a fee for access to its database of grants, fellowships, scholarships, and other financial support. GrantSelect (http://www.grantselect.com/) is another, unrelated fee-based grant research database that provides access to over 10,000 funding opportunities.
- Healthfinder (http://www.healthfinder.gov/): This excellent site, maintained by the U.S. Department of Health and Human Services, is a health and wellness directory of government-backed and other, select Internet resources. It is a good, objective source of sometimes-dated information that provides consumers with a way of orienting themselves to a particular health or mental health topic.
- International Society for Mental Health Online (http://www.ismho.org/): A nonprofit organization founded to promote mental health information and services online, it consists of an international membership of hundreds of professionals and interested consumers. The organization has released a number of white papers about online mental health service provision and a set of suggested ethical principles.
- Mental Health InfoSource (http://www.mhsource.com/): Published by CME, the Mental Health InfoSource has been a strong online resource for years for both professionals and their clients. Offering archives of the *Psychiatric Times* and professional resources such as classified ads, conference listings, and continuing education, the InfoSource also hosts an "Ask the Expert" area and provides educational resources on depression, bipolar disorders, and schizophrenia.
- National Institute of Mental Health (http://www.nimh.nih.gov/): The National Institute of Mental Health offers information and resources on mental health information to consumers, while providing in-depth research and grant information to professionals. The site provides access to clinical trial opportunities, funding opportunities, statistics on mental disorders, fact sheets, consumer-oriented brochures on common mental disorders and their treatments, research reports, national conference and event information, and behavioral science news. It also links to the groundbreaking U.S. Surgeon General's report on mental health.
- National Mental Health Association (http://www.nmha.org/): The National Mental Health Association (NMHA) publishes a consumer-oriented site that provides information on mental health disorders. In addition to updated news headlines, it features information about advocacy, mental health parity, a calendar of events, and links to local community affiliates. The NMHA's online Fact Sheets cover a broad range of mental disorders, including information about mental illness in older adults, children, and families. Much of its information is more consumer-friendly than similar information published by the National Institute of Mental Health.
- Psy Broadcasting Corporation (http://www.psybc.com/): Professionals who are looking to fulfill their continuing education requirements can do so easily online through PsyBC. Offering both real-time seminars and ongoing symposia via online discussion

groups, the site provides a variety of means for obtaining continuing education credits while learning something new.

- Psych Central (http://psychcentral.com/): Focused mainly on consumer's mental health needs, this site (which I founded and maintain) is a great resource that has been around longer than the Web itself. Its offerings include daily-updated behavioral healthcare newsfeeds, a guide containing over 2,000 peer-reviewed Internet resources and support groups, online self-help support community, book reviews, and hundreds of general articles about mental disorders, parenting, mental health, and relationship issues. Psych Central also provides specialized search engines for psychology that integrate Google, MEDLINE, and its own database of mental health Internet resources.
- Psychological Self-Help (http://www.mentalhelp.net/psyhelp/): This online self-help book, one of the first to be published on the Internet in 1996, delves into some practical techniques for individuals to use to try and help themselves with many emotional, relationship, and mental health issues. Offering 15 chapters of insight and handy techniques, psychologist Clay Tucker-Ladd, Ph.D., provides a well-written volume that can be searched online.
- Psychology Information Online (http://www.psychologyinfo.com/): Donald J. Franklin, Ph.D., is a New Jersey psychologist who has put together this resource for consumers looking for more information about psychology. The site has articles that provide symptoms and descriptions for most psychological problems, as well as descriptions of various types of therapies available used to treat them. Articles about selecting a treatment provider and starting therapy are also available, as is a directory of psychologists.
- The Psychology of Cyberspace (http://www.rider.edu/suler/psycyber/psycyber.html): So many professionals operate in an online environment without fully understanding the differences between online and real-world communications. *The Psychology of Cyberspace* is an online book authored by psychologist John Suler of Rider University. A mainstay of the online psychological world, this text is filled with useful articles exploring the psychological underpinnings of virtually every online behavior, from flaming and the use of emoticons (text or small graphics used to denote emotions online) to online personalities and communities.
- PubMed (http://www.ncbi.nlm.nih.gov/entrez/query.fcgi): PubMed is the Internet-based search portal to MEDLINE, the renowned public medical research database. Maintained by the National Library of Medicine under the National Institutes of Health, it covers a vast amount of the social science literature and is a good, free alternative to proprietary, costly research databases. Consumers may find the National Library of Medicine's MEDLINEPlus (http://www.nlm.nih.gov/medlineplus/) a great place to start looking for general health and mental health information online. This information resource provides interactive tutorials, a medical encyclopedia and dictionary, updated health news, and a drug database, among other offerings.
- Social Psychology Network (http://www.socialpsychology.org/): The Social Psychology Network is one of the older psychology resources online. It remains regularly updated by professor Scott Plous, which makes its database of over 5,000 social psychology resources invaluable. Resources are divided into psychology and social psychology subject areas, programs, research groups, journals, textbooks, courses, and teaching resources. The site also features professional discussion forums and makes their whole database searchable.
- WebMD (http://www.webmd.com/): The last remaining large for-profit health portal from the dot.com era, WebMD is a large, relatively well-balanced, and regularly updated resource on all health matters, including mental health concerns. Although broader in context and nature than most resources listed here, it is a critical resource because it reaches millions of people every month who are seeking health information. The site's search engine makes finding some psychological information easier. WebMD also in-

cludes Medscape, a professionally oriented site that has a high-quality section on psychiatry and mental health. Another large commercial site deserves an honorable mention here as well, About's Mental Health Resources (http://mentalhealth.about.com/), overseen by psychologist Leonard Holmes, Ph.D.

References, Readings, & Internet Sites 

Gackenbach, J. (1998). *Psychology and the Internet: Intrapersonal, interpersonal, and transpersonal implications.* New York: Academic Press.

Grohol, J. M. (2002). *The insider's guide to mental health resources online.* New York: Guilford Press.

McGuire, M., Stilborne, L., McAdams, M., & Hyatt, L. (2002). *The Internet handbook for writers, researchers, and journalists.* New York: Guilford Press.

Winkler, M. A., Flanagin, A., Chi-Lum, B., White, J., Andrews, K., Kennett, R. L., et al. (2000). Guidelines for medical and health information sites on the Internet. *Journal of the Americal Medical Association, 283*(12), 1600–1601. Retrieved 2004 from http://jama.ama-assn.org/cgi/content/full/283/12/1600

Wootton, R., Yellowlees, P., & McLaren, P. (Eds.). (2003). *Telepsychiatry and e-mental health.* London: Royal Society of Medicine Press.

Related Topics

Chapter 100, "Facilitating Client Involvement in Self-Help Groups"

Chapter 101, "National Self-Help Groups and Organizations"

98 HIGHLY RATED SELF-HELP BOOKS AND AUTOBIOGRAPHIES

John C. Norcross & Jennifer A. Simansky

Self-help books for mental/behavioral disorders and autobiographies by individuals suffering from such disorders have proliferated in recent years. Bibliotherapy (the use of self-help books with or without formal treatment) and the use of autobiographies as adjuncts to psychotherapy have correspondingly increased. Studies have consistently found that 85% to 88% of practicing psychologists prescribe self-help books to their patients, and 33% of psychologists recommend autobiographies (Clifford, Norcross, & Sommer, 1999; Marx, Royalty, Gyorky, & Stern, 1992; Starker, 1988).

Self-help books and autobiographical accounts promise similar therapeutic benefits. Specifically, they can provide phenomenological accounts of behavioral disorders in everyday terms; enhance identification and empathy; generate hope and insight; offer concrete advice and techniques; explain treatment strategies; and summarize research findings (Pardeck & Pardeck, 1992).

The early research on bibliotherapy is promising. Self-administered treatments are generally cost-effective across a variety of problems with few negative outcomes (Mains & Scogin,

2003; Marrs, 1995; Scogin, Bynum, & Calhoun, 1990). At the same time, caution should be exercised because the vast majority of self-help resources have not been empirically evaluated and because several disorders, such as severe alcohol dependence, do not appear to be amenable to self-help alone (Rosen, 1987; Scogin et al., 1996).

We have conducted a series of national studies over the past 10 years to determine the most highly rated self-help resources. In each study, we mailed a lengthy survey to clinical and counseling psychologists residing throughout the United States. The responding psychologists rated self-help resources with which they were sufficiently familiar on a 5-point scale where +2 was "extremely good or outstanding" and –2 was "extremely bad." Across the eight studies, nearly 3,500 psychologists contributed their expertise to evaluate self-help books, autobiographies, and movies.

Our *Authoritative Guide to Self-Help Resources in Mental Health* (Norcross et al., 2003) features numerical ratings and narrative descriptions on more than 800 self-help books and autobiographies for 36 behavioral disorders and life challenges ranging from abuse to violent youth. Presented below are the top-rated 25 self-help books and 25 autobiographies pertaining to mental/behavioral disorders.

TOP 25 RATED SELF-HELP BOOKS

To be eligible for the top 25 list, a self-help book had to be rated by a minimum of 30 psychologists. Following are the 25 books with the highest average rating in our national studies, beginning with the highest rated.

1. *Skills Training Manual for Treating Borderline Personality Disorder* by Marsha Linehan (borderline personality disorder)
2. *Becoming Orgasmic* by Julia Heiman and Joseph Piccolo (sexual dysfunction)
3. *Why Marriages Succeed or Fail* by John Gottman (marriage)
4. *The Anxiety and Phobia Workbook* by Edmund Bourne (anxiety)
5. *What to Expect When You're Expecting* by Arlene Eisenberg et al. (pregnancy)
6. *Your Defiant Child* by Russell Barkley and Christine Benton (child management)
7. *The 36-Hour Day* by Nancy Mace and Peter Rabins (Alzheimer's)
8. *The New Our Bodies, Ourselves* by Boston Women's Collective (women's health)
9. *The Courage to Heal* by Ellen Bass and Laura Davis (abuse and recovery)
10. *Mastery of Your Anxiety and Panic III* by Michelle Craske and David Barlow (anxiety)
11. *The Relaxation and Stress Reduction Workbook* by Martha Davis et al. (relaxation)
12. *Feeling Good* by David Burns (depression)
13. *The Seven Principles for Making Marriages Work* by John Gottman and Nan Silver (marriage)
14. *What To Expect: The Toddler Years* by Arlene Eisenberg et al. (toddler development and care)
15. *Infants and Mothers* by T. Berry Brazelton (child development and parenting)
16. *Wherever You Go, There You Are* by Jon Kabat-Zinn (meditation and relaxation)
17. *What to Expect the First Year* by Arlene Eisenberg et al. (infant development and care)
18. *What Every Baby Knows* by T. Berry Brazelton (infant development and parenting)
19. *Dr. Spock's Baby and Child Care* by Benjamin Spock and Steven Parker (infant development and parenting)
20. *Mind Over Mood* by Dennis Greenberger and Christine Padesky (depression)
21. *Trauma and Recovery* by Judith Herman (trauma and PTSD)
22. *Reviving Ophelia* by Mary Pipher (female adolescent development)
23. *Dinosaurs Divorce* by Laurene Brown and Marc Brown (for children of divorcing parents)
24. *Taking Charge of ADHD* by Russell Barkley (ADHD)
25. *How to Survive the Loss of a Love* by Melba Colgrove et al. (grief)

TOP 25 RATED AUTOBIOGRAPHIES

To be eligible for this list, the autobiography had to be rated by a minimum of 10 psychologists. Following are the 25 autobiographies with the highest professional ratings in our studies, again beginning with the highest rated.

1. *Letting Go* by Morrie Schwartz (terminal illness and dying)
2. *Breaking Free From Compulsive Eating* by Geneen Roth (compulsive eating)
3. *A Grief Observed* by C. S. Lewis (grieving)
4. *Tuesdays With Morrie* by Mitch Albom (aging and death)
5. *Elegy for Iris* by John Bayley (a spouse's Alzheimer's)
6. *Night Falls Fast* by Kay Jamison (suicide)
7. *Death Be Not Proud* by John Gunther (a parent's loss of an adolescent)
8. *A Man Named Dave* by Dave Pelzer (childhood abuse)
9. *The Lost Boy* by Dave Pelzer (childhood abuse)
10. *Broken Cord* by Michael Dorris (fetal alcohol syndrome)
11. *An Unquiet Mind* by Kay R. Jamison (bipolar disorder)
12. *Heart of a Woman* by Maya Angelou (women's issues)
13. *The Wheel of Life* by Elisabeth Kübler-Ross and Todd Gold (death and dying)
14. *Darkness Visible* by William Styron (depression)
15. *Motherless Daughter* by Hope Edelman (loss of a parent)
16. *Feeding the Hungry Heart* by Geneen Roth (weight management)
17. *I Never Promised You a Rose Garden* by Joanne Greenberg (schizophrenia)
18. *The Noonday Demon* by Andrew Solomon (depression)
19. *After the Death of a Child* by Ann Finkbeiner (grieving the death of a child)
20. *Out of the Depths* by Anton Boisen (schizophrenia)
21. *The Panic Attack Recovery Book* by Shirley Swede and Seymour Jaffe (anxiety disorder)
22. *The Virtues of Aging* by Jimmy Carter (aging)
23. *Girl, Interrupted* by Susanna Kaysen (borderline personality)
24. *ADHD Handbook for Families* by Paul Weingartner (ADHD)
25. *Too Much Anger, Too Many Tears* by Janet Gotkin and Paul Gotkin (schizophrenia)

References, Readings, and Internet Sites

Clifford, J. S., Norcross, J. C., & Sommer, R. (1999). Autobiographies of mental health clients: Psychologists' uses and recommendations. *Professional Psychology: Research & Practice, 30,* 56–59.

Mains, J. A., & Scogin, F. R. (2003). The effectiveness of self-administered treatments: A practice-friendly review of the research. *In Session: Journal of Clinical Psychology, 59*(2), 237–246.

Marrs, R. W. (1995). A meta-analysis of bibliotherapy studies. *American Journal of Community Psychology, 23,* 843–870.

Marx, J. A., Royalty, G. M., Gyorky, Z. K., & Stern, T. E. (1992). Use of self-help books in psychotherapy. *Professional Psychology: Research and Practice, 23,* 300–305.

Neysmith-Roy, J. M., & Kleisinger, C. L. (1997). Using biographies of adults over 65 years of age to understand life-span developmental psychology. *Teaching of Psychology, 24,* 116–118.

Norcross, J. C., Santrock, J. W., Campbell, L. F., Smith, T. P., Sommer, R., & Zuckerman, E .L. (2003). *Authoritative guide to self-help resources in mental health* (2nd ed.). New York: Guilford Press.

Pardeck, J. T., & Pardeck, J. A. (1992). *Bibliotherapy: A guide to using books in clinical practice*. San Francisco: Mellen Research University Press.

Rosen, G. M. (1987). Self-help treatment books and the commercialization of psychotherapy. *American Psychologist, 42,* 46–51.

Scogin, F., Bynum, J., & Calhoun, S. (1990). Efficacy of self-administered treatment programs: Meta-analytic review. *Professional Psychology: Research and Practice, 21,* 42–47.

Scogin, F., Floyd, M., Jamison, C., Ackerson, J., Landreville, P., & Bissonnette, L. (1996). Negative outcomes: What is the evidence on self-administered treatments? *Journal of Consulting and Clinical Psychology, 64,* 1086–1089.

Sommer, R., & Osmond, H. (1983). A bibliography of mental patients' autobiographies, 1969–1982. *American Journal of Psychiatry, 140,* 1051–1054.

Starker, S. (1988). Psychologists and self-help books: Attitudes and prescriptive practices of clinicians. *American Journal of Psychotherapy, 42,* 448–455.

University of California, Davis. Psychology Department. (2002). Autobiographies of mental patients (a compilation of autobiographies). Retrieved 2004 from http://psychology.ucdavis.edu/sommerr/

Related Topics

Chapter 99, "Popular Films Portraying Mental Disorders"

Chapter 100, "Facilitating Client Involvement in Self-Help Groups"

Chapter 101, "National Self-Help Groups and Organizations"

99 POPULAR FILMS PORTRAYING MENTAL DISORDERS

Danny Wedding

Numerous popular films illustrate psychopathology, and any group of mental health professionals can quickly generate a list of films that portray alcoholism, drug addiction, personality disorders, schizophrenia, mood disorders, and sexual and gender identity disorders. The portrayal of psychopathology in the media is a significant factor in shaping and supporting the stigma associated with mental illness, as well as the widespread public belief that mental illness is almost inevitably associated with dangerousness (Wahl, 1995). In addition to shaping the public's perception of people with mental illness, films have a direct effect on the public's image of psychologists, psychiatrists, and other mental health professionals (Gabbard & Gabbard, 1999; Hyler, 1988; Wedding & Boyd, 1999).

CLINICAL BENEFITS OF FILMS

Films can sometimes sensitize the public to mental health issues in a way few other media can. Four examples illustrate this point: *Rain Man* presented a largely sympathetic portrayal of autism and educated many people who were not familiar with the disorder; *As Good As It Gets* provided a vehicle for Jack Nicholson to educate the public about obsessive compulsive disorder; and *Shine* and *A Beautiful Mind* both demonstrated that people with serious mental disorders like schizophrenia could make important societal contributions. In contrast, films like *Me, Myself and Irene* perpetuate myths and misconceptions about mental illness (e.g., that people suffering from schizophrenia have multiple personalities).

Films also provide an efficient way for therapists to introduce clients to different ways of perceiving their situations or problems. Seeing a recommended film is relatively easy given the availability of VHS and DVD rental centers, and compliance with a therapist's recommendation to view a film is both inexpensive and convenient. I have had hundreds of clients who never got around to reading the books I would recommend in therapy, but I have never had a client who would fail to see a film I recommended. Films can serves as powerful metaphors for a client's personal problems, they provide rich opportunities for observational learning, and their discussion can provide grist for the therapeutic mill.

INTRODUCING AND ASSIGNING FILMS IN PSYCHOTHERAPY

The potential applications of film as homework in psychotherapy are limited only by the imagination, creativity, and viewing history of the therapist. A client vacillating about leaving an abusive relationship may benefit from seeing a woman and her son extricate themselves from a pathological environment in *This Boy's Life*; another client concerned about a parent's dementia may find comfort in watching *Iris* or *On Golden Pond*, while someone frustrated with the headaches associated with dealing with a medical bureaucracy might benefit from viewing and discussing the protagonist's experience in *The Doctor*.

Another client suffering from the loss of a child might, at an appropriate time, find it therapeutic to watch and discuss *In the Bedroom*, and a young girl with an eating disorder might learn valuable lessons from *The Karen Carpenter Story*. Clinical judgment and experience will help the therapist decide which clients will benefit from viewing films as homework, and clinical acumen will guide the decision about the optimal time to introduce films in the therapeutic journey.

SPECIFIC MOVIE RECOMMENDATIONS

Anxiety disorders are routinely portrayed in films (especially posttraumatic stress disorder), and some of the images of anxiety disorders in films are almost iconic. Which of us can forget the scene in *Patton* in which George C. Scott slaps a young soldier suffering from "battle fatigue," or the paralysis Jimmy Stewart experiences as he copes with his fear of heights in *Vertigo*? Many of the symptoms of PTSD are evident in Tom Cruise's character (Ron Kovic) in *Born on the Fourth of July*, as well as the alcohol abuse and dependence and the survivor guilt so commonly associated with the disorder. Agoraphobia is illustrated by Elliott Gould's character in the film *Inside Out*, and responses to extreme stress are portrayed in films like *The Pawnbroker, Falling Down, The Deer Hunter, Full Metal Jacket, The Killing Fields, Apocalypse Now*, and *Glengarry Glen Ross*. The particular film(s) recommended for any particular client with an anxiety disorder (such at PTSD) will depend on the client's level of anxiety and his or her comfort levels with in vivo desensitization.

The classic film illustrating a dissociative disorder is Alfred Hitchcock's *Psycho*. Although arguably one of the most important films ever made, *Psycho* unfortunately perpetuates the widespread belief that people with mental disorders are dangerous and unpredictable. The public's fear is underscored by the fact that Norman Bates initially seems harmless and well intentioned, and at most eccentric. Other popular films that address dissociative identity disorder include *Sybil, The Three Faces of Eve*, and *Primal Fear*. This last film presents a scenario in which an altar boy who has murdered an archbishop feigns a dissociative identity disorder in order to avoid prosecution for his crime. Films of this type support the public's misconception that criminals commonly pretend to be mentally ill in order to avoid punishment for their behavior. Films illustrating dissociative amnesia include *Spellbound; Suddenly, Last Summer; Dead Again; Sullivan's Travels; Paris, Texas; The Return of Martin Guerre;* and *Sommersby*. Other films that illustrate some form of dissociation but that have characters who may not meet *DSM-IV* criteria for the dissociative identity disorder diagnosis include *Raising Cain, Persona, Three Women, The Dark Mirror, Sisters, Steppenwolf*, and any of the numerous versions of *Dr. Jekyll and Mr. Hyde.*

Mood disorders are common in movies, and it is not unusual for a character in a film to be suicidal or to actually commit suicide. One of the most compelling recent films to address the linked themes of depression and suicide is *The*

Hours, in which Nicole Kidman reenacts the depression and eventual suicide by drowning of the gifted novelist Virginia Woolf. (This simple synopsis fails to do justice to a film that is rich, complex, and variegated.) Al Pacino plays a depressed and suicidal retired military officer in *Scent of a Woman,* and Pacino's character displays classic risk factors for suicidal (i.e., he is a depressed, older white male, unemployed, familiar with guns, with a chronic medical condition [blindness] and a history of alcohol abuse and probable alcoholism). The same risk factors are present in George C. Scott's character in a slightly older film, *The Hospital.* Some other popular films that address depression and suicide are *Dead Poets Society; 'night Mother; Ordinary People; The Last Picture Show; It's a Wonderful Life; The Deer Hunter; The Field; The Tenant; Mishima; Network; The Last Emperor; Elvira Madigan; The Hairdresser's Husband;* and *Harold and Maude.* The movie *Mr. Jones* stars Richard Gere as a musician with bipolar disorder who presents almost textbook symptoms of the disorder. Unfortunately, the film is marred by his torrid affair with his psychiatrist, perpetuating the myth that sexual misconduct is commonplace among mental health professionals. In *About Schmidt,* Jack Nicholson plays an older man coping with the depression and anxiety associated with his retirement, his wife's death, and his daughter's determination to marry the wrong man. A recent release, *Love Liza,* illustrates the overwhelming pain experienced by someone after a spouse's suicide. I have previously found viewing and discussion of *Ordinary People* to be helpful when working with clients who have lost a child.

Many of the films dealing with mood disorders present dramatic (and almost always negative) demonstrations of electroconvulsive therapy. Three of the many examples of ECT in movies include *An Angel at My Table, One Flew Over the Cuckoo's Nest,* and *Chattahoochee.* McDonald and Walter (2001) reviewed 22 films released between 1948 and 2000 and found that the presentation of ECT in movies was becoming progressively more negative. Films such as these almost inevitably produce considerable anxiety in patients who may possibly benefit from ECT, and it is helpful for clinicians to enquire about negative cinematic portrayals these patients may have encountered.

Any group of psychotherapists (or psychology students) can quickly generate a list of popular films illustrating the entire panoply of personality disorders. The classic example of this genre is the Alex Forrest character in *Fatal Attraction* (Glenn Close is reported to have conducted research on borderline personality disorder in preparation for her role). Among Cluster A disorders, paranoid personality disorder is beautifully illustrated by the title character in *Dr. Strangelove* and by Humphrey Bogart's role as Captain Queeg in *The Caine Mutiny;* the schizoid personality is seen in *Five Easy Pieces, The Accidental Tourist, Taxi Driver,* and *Sex, Lies, and Videotape;* the schizotypal is present in *The Ruling Class* and *Pi.*

Among Cluster B disorders, the antisocial personality is illustrated in any of a hundred films about violence and murder, including *Henry: Portrait of a Serial Killer, Silence of the Lambs, A Clockwork Orange, In Cold Blood, The Boston Strangler, Cape Fear, Reservoir Dogs, Peeping Tom, Strangers on a Train, Helter Skelter, Natural Born Killers, Widows' Peak,* and *Blue Velvet.* In addition to *Fatal Attraction, Who's Afraid of Virginia Woolf* illustrates borderline personality disorder, as does *Mrs. Parker and the Vicious Circle.* The histrionic personality disorder can be seen in the roles played by major characters in *A Streetcar Named Desire, La Cage aux Folles, Long Day's Journey Into Night,* and *Blue Sky.* Narcissistic personality disorder is convincingly portrayed in the movies *Sunset Boulevard, Bugsy,* and *What Ever Happened to Baby Jane.*

Cluster C disorders include avoidant, dependent, and obsessive-compulsive disorders. The avoidant personality is typified in the film adaptation of Tennessee Williams's play *The Glass Menagerie,* and the dependent personality is almost perfectly captured by Bill Murray's character in *What About Bob?* (Interestingly, this film ends with an on-screen note that tells the audience that the neurotic character Bob went back to graduate school, earned a Ph.D. in psychology, and wrote a best-selling self-help book.) The character of Felix Unger in *The Odd Couple* is a vivid example of someone with an obsessive-compulsive personality disorder, as is Major Frank Burns in *M*A*S*H*.

Clinicians will want to be judicious in recommending films to patients with personality disorders to avoid potentially insulting the patient (e.g., a histrionic patient would be unlikely to respond positively to the implicit suggestion that her life parallels Gloria Swanson's portrayal of Norma Desmond in *Sunset Boulevard*).

Substance-use disorders are also staples in popular cinema, and the challenge here is limiting the list of films for consideration. Perhaps the classic film in the genre of films addressing alcoholism is *The Lost Weekend;* other films about alcoholism that are almost as compelling include *Harvey; Come Back, Little Sheba; Days of Wine and Roses; Key Largo; Tender Mercies; Arthur; Ironweed; The Verdict; Under the Volcano;* and *Barfly*. More recent films in which alcoholism is the central theme include *When a Man Loves a Woman, Leaving Las Vegas, 28 Days, Trees Lounge,* and *Drunks*. Any of these recent films would provide a meaningful springboard for a discussion of the effects of alcohol on a client's life and family.

Two classic films dealing with drug addiction are *Long Day's Journey Into Night* and *The Man With the Golden Arm*. Opium addiction is portrayed in *Indochine* and *The Last Emperor*. Drugs also play a central role in Quentin Tarentino's *Pulp Fiction,* and polydrug addiction is portrayed in *Clean and Sober*. Other films that build on drug themes include *The French Connection, Christiane F., Trainspotting, Mona Lisa, Chappaqua, Drugstore Cowboy, Naked Lunch, The Bad Lieutenant, Goodfellas, Scarface,* and *Lady Sings the Blues*.

The most dramatic recent film illustrating sexual and gender identity disorders is unquestionably *Boys Don't Cry,* a movie in which Hilary Swank plays an unforgettable role as Brandon Teena (Teena Brandon), a Nebraska transsexual teen trying to establish her sexual identity in a hostile and ultimately fatal environment. Other films portraying transsexualism include *Myra Breckinridge; Dog Day Afternoon; The World According to Garp; Come Back to the Five and Dime, Jimmy Dean, Jimmy Dean; La Cage aux Folles; To Wong Foo; M. Butterfly; The Ballad of Little Jo; The Crying Game;* and *Hedwig and the Angry Inch*. Fetishes are illustrated by films such as *Claire's Knee* and David Cronenberg's film *Crash*. *Breaking the Waves* is a psychologically powerful Danish film in which a paralyzed man insists that his wife have sex with other men while he watches, and Pedro Almodovar's *Tie Me Up! Tie Me Down!* explores the masochistic relationship between a kidnapper and the woman he kidnaps. Sexual sadism is brilliantly presented in David Lynch's *Blue Velvet;* incest is a central theme in *Angels and Insects,* pedophilia is portrayed by Peter Lorre in *"M"* and by James Mason (and later Jeremy Irons) in *Lolita;* and the sexual obsession of a college professor for a cabaret singer can be seen in a classic film, *The Blue Angel*. Other popular films that address sexual and gender identity disorders include *Cabaret, Chinatown, The Collector, Fellini Satyricon, Female Perversions, The Good Mother, Henry & June, Ju Dou, Jules and Jim, Kiss of the Spider Woman, Matador, Midnight Cowboy, Murmur of the Heart, Peeping Tom, Pretty Baby,* and *The Sergeant*. Clinicians working with clients concerned about homosexuality may find it helpful to assign and discuss both films and TV shows that portray positive gay role models (e.g., the characters of Keith and David on HBO's *Six Feet Under*).

Childhood psychopathology is brilliantly represented in Neil Jordan's *The Butcher Boy*. Some other films that treat childhood disorders include *Forbidden Games,* Bergman's *Fanny and Alexander,* and Francois Truffaut's *The 400 Blows*. Other films addressing mental illness in children include *The Best Little Girl in the World, Lord of the Flies,* and *The Tin Drum*. *The Wild Child* and *Every Man for Himself and God Against All* both explore the effects of deprivation on feral children. The psychological problems associated with childhood poverty are touchingly portrayed in three foreign films: *El Norte, Pixote,* and *Salaam Bombay*. The French film *Ponette* is a remarkable examination of a child's attempt to understanding the meaning of her mother's death in a world in which no one will speak honestly with her about what it really means to be dead. I have previously had good success discussing *Searching for Bobby Fischer* with a demanding, overbearing parent who recognized himself in the figure presented by the father in the film.

Schizophrenia and delusional disorders have been illustrated in a number of successful films including *Angel Baby, Benny and Joon, Birdy, Clean Shaven, The Fisher King, Shine, Sweetie, Taxi Driver*, and, most recently and most successfully, *A Beautiful Mind*. In general, I don't believe films are useful for patients with thought disorders, and they are especially limited with patients with paranoid disorders who may become confused by the purpose and intent of the assignment. However, movies like *A Beautiful Mind* can be very beneficial in helping family members understand what their loved one is experiencing.

References, Readings, & Internet Sites

Berg-Cross, L., Jennings, P., & Baruch, R. (1990). Cinematherapy: Theory and application. *Psychotherapy in Private Practice, 8*, 135–156.

Eight Major Personality Styles. (n.d.). Disability Films home page. Retrieved 2004 from http://www.screenplaysystems.com/reel_people/personalities

Films Involving Disabilities. (n.d.). Web site. Retrieved 2004 from http://www.disabilityfilms.co.uk/index.html

Gabbard, G., & Gabbard, K. (1999). *Psychiatry and the cinema*. Washington, DC: American Psychiatric Press.

Hesley, J. W., & Hesley, J. G. (1998). *Rent two films and let's talk in the morning: Using popular movies in psychotherapy*. New York: Wiley.

Hyler, S. E. (1988). *DSM-III* at the cinema: Madness in the movies. *Comprehensive Psychiatry, 29*, 195–206.

Hyler, S. E., Gabbard, G. O., & Schneider, I. (1991). Homicidal maniacs and narcissistic parasites: Stigmatization of mentally ill persons in the movies. *Hospital and Community Psychiatry, 42*, 1044–1048.

McDonald, A., & Walter, G. (2001). The portrayal of ECT in American movies. *Journal of ECT, 17*, 264–274.

Nicosia, S. Movies and mental illness. (n.d.). Psychology, psychiatry and the movies. Retrieved 2004 from http://faculty.dwc.edu/nicosia/movies andmentalillnessfilmography.htm

Psychiatry in the Cinema. (n.d.). Resource page. Retrieved 2004 from http://www.priory.com/psych/psycinema.htm

Schulenberg, S. E. (2003). Psychotherapy and movies: On using films in clinical practice. *Journal of Contemporary Psychotherapy, 33*, 35–48.

Solomon, G. (1995). *The motion picture prescription: Watch this movie & call me in the morning—200 movies to help you heal life's problems*. Santa Rosa, CA: Aslan.

Solomon, G. (2000). *Reel therapy: How movies inspire you to overcome life's problems*. New York: Lebhar-Friedman Books.

Teague, R. (2000). *Reel spirit: A guide to movies that inspire, explore, and empower*. Unity Village, MO: Unity House.

Vaux, S. (1999). *Finding meaning at the movies*. Nashville, TN: Abingdon.

Wahl, O. F. (1995). *Media madness: Public images of mental illness*. New Brunswick, NJ: Rutgers University Press.

Wedding, D. (2001). The portrayal of alcohol and alcoholism in the western genre. *Journal of Alcohol & Drug Education, 46*, 3–11.

Wedding, D. (n.d.). "Movies and Mental Illness" filmography. Retrieved 2004 from http://www.mimh.edu/Danny_Wedding/

Wedding, D., & Boyd, M. A. (1999). *Movies & mental illness: Using films to understand psychopathology*. Boston: McGraw-Hill.

Wedding, D., & Niemiec, R. (2003). The clinical use of films in psychotherapy. *In Session: Journal of Clinical Psychology, 59*, 207–215.

Related Topic

Chapter 98, "Highly Rated Self-Help Books and Autobiographies"

100 FACILITATING CLIENT INVOLVEMENT IN SELF-HELP GROUPS

Elena Klaw & Keith Humphreys

Self-help groups can be invaluable allies to the work of psychologists. Groups are available for virtually every health and social problem, making them useful referrals for professionals working in a wide range of settings. Further, because self-help groups are free of charge and allow unlimited attendance, they can help psychologists arrange ongoing support for patients in a health care system otherwise cramped by managed care and financial limitations. To help psychologists reap these benefits for themselves and their clients, this chapter describes what self-help groups are available, how they affect members, and how best to interact with them.

SCOPE AND BENEFITS OF SELF-HELP GROUPS

Self-help groups are peer-led organizations of individuals facing a shared health, social, or emotional challenge. Self-help groups are also often called "mutual help groups" to reflect the reality that members provide information and social support as well as receive it; in this respect, self-help groups differ from other activities that are often called self-help, such as reading self-help books. Support groups led by professionals are *not* typically considered self-help groups unless the professional personally shares the focal problem/concern of the group (e.g., a psychologist who has AIDS could lead a self-help group focused on living with AIDS) and relates to group members as a peer.

National data attest to the widespread participation in self-help groups: approximately 7% of American adults (about 11 million people) have participated in a self-help group in the past year, and 18% have done so at some point in their lifetime (Kessler, Mickelson, & Zhao, 1997). Indeed, Americans make more visits to self-help groups for addiction and psychiatric problems than they do to all mental health professionals combined (Kessler et al., 1997).

Figure 1 presents information on the self-help groups most commonly attended in the United States. Substance-related groups constitute the most popular type, the best known of which is Alcoholics Anonymous (AA), which currently has 4 to 6 million members worldwide (Humphreys, 2003). Yet, two-thirds of the 1,000 self-help organizations in the United States developed independently of AA and do not use AA's 12 steps. As inspection of the *Self-Help Sourcebook* of the American Self-Help Clearinghouse will reveal, it is difficult to think of a problem for which no self-help group exists (White & Madara, 2002).

Popularity, of course, does not prove effectiveness, so researchers have made substantial efforts in recent years to evaluate whether self-help group participation benefits members. Many groups have yet to be studied, but thus far evaluation research is encouraging. For example, research supports the conclusions that participation in 12-step addiction-related groups often reduces subsequent use of alcohol and illicit drugs, participation in weight-loss groups

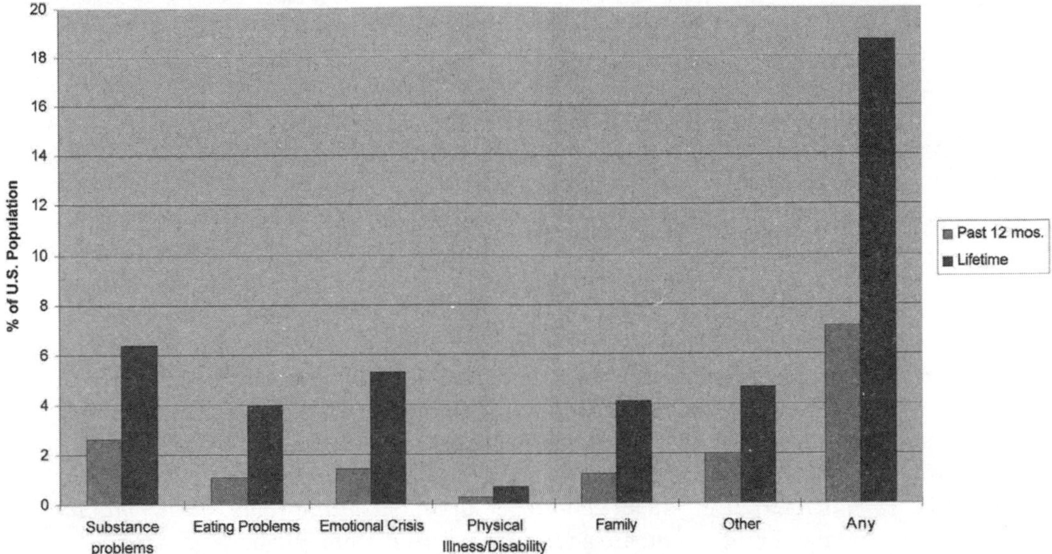

FIGURE 1. Participation in the Most Common Self-Help Groups

promotes healthier weight, joining a group for parents of premature newborns enhances parent-infant connectedness, and referral to a posthospitalization self-help network reduces readmission rates for seriously mentally ill individuals (see Kyrouz, Humphreys, & Loomis, 2002). In addition to helping promote remission of the "presenting problem," self-help groups can produce important quality-of-life benefits such as new friendships, recreational opportunities, and deepened sense of spiritual purpose (Humphreys, 1997). As with all outcome research, practitioners should bear in mind that the above conclusions are based on average results, and self-help groups are thus no more a panacea than is any other psychosocial intervention. With this caution in mind, practitioners can be confident that many of their patients could derive at least some benefit from participating in a self-help group.

Humphreys and colleagues have produced jargon-free, easy-to-read summaries of the main findings of outcome studies of self-help groups for a variety of conditions. This "Review of research on the effectiveness of self-help mutual aid groups" (updated in 2002 with Dr. Colleen Loomis) is included in each edition of the *Self-Help Sourcebook* (White & Madara, 2002) and is also available on dozens of Web sites identifiable through a Web search. The articles are in the public domain and can be printed and given to clients or colleagues free of charge as a way to make a quick assessment of whether self-help groups of a particular type have been studied, and if so, what the outcome results have been. Psychologists interested in more detailed and scholarly reviews of the literature can find them in a number of recent books, including Linda Kurtz's (1997) *Self-Help and Support Groups: A Handbook for Practitioners.*

STRATEGIES TO LINK PROFESSIONAL TREATMENT AND SELF-HELP

The following are suggestions for facilitating professional linkages to self-help groups and fostering client involvement.

1. *Beware of "professional-centris":* That is, be wary of the belief that professional services and expertise are the central components of effective mental health care (Salzer, Rappaport, & Segre, 2001). Negative per-

ceptions about self-help groups include unsubstantiated beliefs that groups are harmful, antiprofessional, foster dependency, and spread misinformation. Such prejudices may lessen appreciation of self-help groups and may be transmitted to clients who might otherwise benefit from group participation.

2. *Incorporate information about self-help methods, principles, and group availability into the curriculum of clinical training programs:* In a study of future providers, students reported that they would be more likely to refer clients to self-help groups if they thought that the faculty perceived them positively (Meissen, Mason, & Gleason, 1991). To enhance training about self-help, training programs might compare and contrast self-help models with professional treatment, simulate self-help meetings, present examples of professional self-help collaborations, and encourage students to join a self-help group (see Salzer et al., 2001).
3. *All professionals should visit at least one self-help meeting:* Professionals can freely attend any "open meetings" of AA and NA, for example. Such visits educate providers about the nature of self-help groups in general and local meetings in particular, which facilitates informed referrals.
4. *Approach self-help groups as respectful collaborators* (Stewart, 1990): Professionals sometimes have the false impression that the best way to assist self-help groups is to take control of them in some respect—for example as a group facilitator—while what groups usually desire is a collaborative relationship.
5. *Provide resources to self-help groups:* Studies suggest that cooperative relationships between self-help groups and treatment providers are characterized by frequent contact, staff membership in self-help groups, and cross-volunteering between members of the self-help organization and the treatment center (Kurtz, 1984). In terms of resource provision, self-help organizations are often in need of assistance with referrals, meeting space, publicity, and Web site development.
5. *Invite self-help groups to demonstrate their potential value to residents of treatment centers:* Many addiction and psychiatric self-help organizations are willing to hold group meetings in hospitals, treatment programs, and correctional facilities that institution residents may attend or observe.
6. *Build relationships with self-help clearinghouses and other organizations that support self-help:* The American Self-help Clearinghouse, for example, is particularly well known for its directory of several thousand self-help organizations, which is available on the World Wide Web as well as in print form (White & Madara, 2002).
7. *In addition to providing self-help brochures in one's waiting room, participate in using nontraditional media to disseminate information about self-help:* Although newspaper announcements are useful in attracting new members, participation in more visible public information campaigns might offer further benefits. For example, one study successfully increased self-help attendance through a psychologist-hosted radio program that featured a live self-help group meeting each week (Jason, LaPointe, & Billingham, 1986).
8. *Provide information about self-help to religious leaders:* Religious leaders are often highly trusted sources of information for disadvantaged groups (e.g., low-income individuals, recent immigrants), and are typically interested in learning about community self-help strategies (Jason, Goodman, Thomas, & Iacono, 1988).

RECOMMENDATIONS TO FACILITATE CLIENT INVOLVEMENT IN SELF-HELP GROUPS

1. Frame self-help participation as a process of experimenting with available alternatives so that the client can find the route best suited to recovery. This generates less resistance than pressuring a client to seek help only from a particular group.
2. Recognize that professional interventions can increase clients' level of affiliation with self-help groups. Belief that professionals

viewed self-help involvement favorably, for example, has been associated with increased goal attainment for individuals with psychiatric disabilities (Hodges & Segal, 2002). Similarly, greater involvement with 12-step groups has been linked to compatibility between treatment beliefs and 12-step ideologies (Mankowski, Humphreys, & Moos, 2001). Research suggests when treatment providers encouraged patients to attend meetings, work the steps, get a sponsor, and engage in other AA/NA-related behaviors, substance-abuse patients were more likely to be involved in self-help groups during and after treatment.

3. Employ the approach termed "Twelve Step Facilitation Therapy" as a powerful intervention for wait-list patients, enabling natural recovery for some individuals and increasing motivation for those in need of professional care. By conducting 12-step facilitation during treatment, providers can increase the likelihood that patients will sustain their recovery after participation in professional services has ended.
4. Consider sending both religious and nonreligious clients to 12-step groups. Evidence suggests that theists and nontheists are equally likely to follow through on and benefit from such referrals (Winzelberg & Humphreys, 1999).
5. Provide significant support when linking clients to self-help groups. One study (Sisson & Mallams, 1981) demonstrated that when clinicians allowed clients to call self-help organizations from their office and connected them with to a sponsor who would take them to a meeting, 100% of clients attended at least one self-help meeting. Conversely, when a self-help meeting was simply suggested in the course of treatment, no clients attended a self-help group.
6. Learn about the specific groups in your community. For example, when referring an atheist to an AA group, one might choose a particular AA meeting that places less emphasis on spirituality. Similarly, a gay or lesbian client may prefer to attend a specialty chapter of a self-help organization that specifically addresses his or her needs.

Note: Thanks to Lynzey Baker Baldwin for her help in preparing this manuscript. Preparation of this manuscript was funded in part by the Department of Veterans Affairs Mental Health Strategic Healthcare Group and The California Wellness Foundation.

References, Readings, & Internet Sites

Hodges, J. Q., & Segal, S. P. (2002). Goal advancement among mental health self-help agency members. *Psychiatric Rehabilitation Journal, 26,* 78–85.

Humphreys, K. (1997). Individual and social benefits of mutual aid/self-help groups. *Social Policy, 27,* 12–19.

Humphreys, K. (2003). *Circles of recovery: Self-help organizations for addictions.* Cambridge, UK: Cambridge University Press.

Jason, L., Goodman, D., Thomas, N., & Iacono, G. (1988) Clergy's knowledge of self-help groups in a large metropolitan area. *Journal of Psychology and Theology, 16,* 34–40.

Jason, L. A., LaPointe, P., & Billingham, S. (1986). The media and self-help: A preventive community intervention. *Journal of Primary Prevention, 3,* 156–167.

Kessler, R. C., Mickelson, K. D., & Zhao, S. (1997). Patterns and correlates of self-help group membership in the United States. *Social Policy, 27,* 27–46.

Kurtz, L. F. (1984). Linking treatment centers with Alcoholics Anonymous. *Social Work in Health Care, 9,* 85–95.

Kurtz, L. F. (1997). *Self-help and support groups: A handbook for practitioners.* Thousand Oaks: Sage.

Kyrouz, E. M., Humphreys, K., & Loomis, C. (2002). A review of research on the effectiveness of self-help mutual aid groups. In B. J. White & E. J. Madara, *The self-help sourcebook: Your guide to community and online support groups* (6th ed., pp. 71–85). Cedar Knolls, NJ: American Self-Help Clearinghouse.

Mankowski, E. S., Humphreys, K., & Moos, R. H. (2001). Individual and contextual predictors of involvement in twelve-step self-help groups after substance abuse treatment. *American Journal of Community Psychology, 29,* 537–563.

Meissen, G. J., Mason, W. C., & Gleason, D. F. (1991). Understanding the attitudes and intentions of future professionals toward self-help. *American Journal of Community Psychology, 19,* 699–715.

Salzer, M. S., Rappaport, J., & Segre, L. (2001). Mental health professionals' support of self-help groups. *Journal of Community & Applied Social Psychology, 11,* 1–10.

Sisson, R. W., & Mallams, J. H. (1981). The use of systematic encouragement and community access procedures to increase attendance at Alcoholics Anonymous and Al-Anon meetings. *American Journal of Drug and Alcohol Abuse, 8,* 371–376.

Stewart, J. (1990). Professional interface with mutual-aid self-help groups: A review. *Social Science and Medicine, 31*(10), 1143–1158.

White, B. J., & Madara, E. J. (2002). *The self-help sourcebook: Your guide to community and online support groups* (6th ed.). Cedar Knolls, NJ: American Self-Help Clearinghouse. http://www.mentalhelp.net/selfhelp/

Winzelberg, A., & Humphreys, K. (1999). Should patients' religious beliefs and practices influence clinicians' referral to 12-step self-help groups? Evidence from a study of 3,018 male substance abuse patients. *Journal of Consulting and Clinical Psychology, 67,* 790–794.

Related Topic

Chapter 97, "Top Internet Sites for Psychologists and Their Clients"

101 NATIONAL SELF-HELP GROUPS AND ORGANIZATIONS

Dennis E. Reidy & John C. Norcross

Self-help groups are supportive, educational mutual-aid groups that address a single life problem or condition shared by their members (Kurtz, 1997). Participation is voluntary, members serve as leaders, and professionals rarely play an active role in the groups' activities. All forms of self-help groups share one thing: promotion of the member's inner strengths. The groups do so by imparting information, emphasizing self-determination, providing mutual support, and by mobilizing the resources of the person, the group, and the community (Reissman & Carroll, 1995).

Millions of Americans have come to rely on self-help or support groups for assistance with virtually every human challenge. The most recognizable of these are the 12-step groups patterned after Alcoholics Anonymous (AA) that address a wide spectrum of addictive disorders, such as those to drugs, food, and sex. But self-help groups encompass much more than addictions; there are self-help groups for practically all mental and physical disorders, as even a casual glance of the blue pages of a telephone directory will confirm. In fact, 5% of American adults attend a self-help group in a given year (Eisenberg et al., 1998).

The following list provides the mailing addresses, telephone numbers, and Web addresses of the national chapters of major self-help groups and organizations in the United States. The national listings appear alphabetically by the title of the organization. Our purpose is to provide the practitioner with quick access to these self-help groups and organizations.

More exhaustive listings of self-help groups may be obtained from two national self-help clearinghouses. The American Self-Help Clearinghouse's *Self-Help Sourcebook* at http://mentalhelp.net/selfhelp/ serves "as your starting point for exploring real-life support groups and networks that are available throughout the world and in your community." The similar National Mental Health Consumers' Self-Help Clearinghouse at http://www.mhselfhelp.org/ (phone: 800-553-4539 or 215-751-1810) is a consumer-run association that connects mental health consumers with peer-run groups and offers technical assistance to self-help groups. We strongly recommend that you visit these sites, particularly if you are searching for a self-help group on a topic or disorder not covered in the following list.

Adult Children of Alcoholics World Services Organization
PO Box 3216
Torrance, CA 90510
Phone: 310-534-1815
E-mail: info@adultchildren.org
http://www.adultchildren.org
A 12-step program for adults raised in alcoholic families.

Agoraphobics in Motion (AIM)
1719 Crooks
Royal Oak, MI 48067
Phone: 248-547-0400
E-mail: anny@ameritech.net
http://www.aim-hq.org
Offers support, publications, and treatment recommendations on anxiety disorders.

Alateen and Al-Anon Family Groups
1600 Corporate Landing Parkway
Virginia Beach, VA 23454
Phone: 800-344-2666
E-mail: wso@al-anon.org
http://www.al-anon.org
A fellowship of young persons whose lives have been affected by someone else's drinking.

Alcoholics Anonymous
Box 459, Grand Central Station
New York, NY 10163
Phone: 212-870-3400
http://www.alcoholics-anonymous.org
A 12-step self-help group for those troubled by alcohol consumption.

Alzheimer's Association
919 North Michigan Avenue, Suite 1100
Chicago, IL 60611-1676
Phone: 800-272-3900, 312-335-8700
E-mail: info@alz.org
http://www.alz.org
Provides information, publications, and support to patients and their caregivers.

Alzheimer's Disease Education and Referral Center (ADEAR)
National Institute on Aging
PO Box 8250
Silver Spring, MD 20907-8250
Phone: 800-438-4380
E-mail: adear@alzheimers.org
http://www.alzheimers.org
Information, referrals, and publications about clinical trials.

Alzheimer's Disease and Related Disorders Association
919 North Michigan Avenue, Suite 1100
Chicago, IL 60611-8700
Phone: 312-335-8700
E-mail: info@alz.org
http://www.alz.org
For caregivers of Alzheimer's patients.

American Association on Mental Retardation
444 North Capitol Street, NW
Washington, DC 20001
Phone: 800-424-3688
http://www.aamr.org
Information on mental retardation.

American Association of Retired Persons (AARP)
601 E Street NW
Washington, DC 20049
Phone: 800-424-3410
E-mail: member@aarp.org

http://www.aarp.org
Multipurpose organization for older adults.

American Cancer Society
Phone: 800-227-2345
http://www.cancer.org
Provides information for cancer sufferers and their family.

American Council of the Blind
1155 15th Street NW, #720
Washington, DC 20005
Phone: 800-424-8666; 202-467-5081
http://www.acb.org
For blind and visually impaired people and their families.

American Diabetes Association
1701 North Beauregard Street
Alexandria, VA 22311
Phone: 800-342-2383
E-mail: AskADA@diabetes.org
http://www.diabetes.org
Provides research, information, and advocacy.

American Foundation for Suicide Prevention
120 Wall St., 22nd floor
New York, NY 10005
Phone: 888-333-AFSP or 212-363-3500
E-mail: inquiry@afsp.org
http://www.afsp.org
Providing information and education about suicide.

American Heart Association
7272 Greenville Avenue
Dallas, TX 75231
Phone: 800-242-8721
http://www.americanheart.org
For cardiac patients and their families.

American Lupus Society
3914 Del Amo Boulevard, Suite 922
Los Angeles, CA 90503
Phone: 310-390-6888
For lupus patients and their families.

American Parkinson's Disease Association
1250 Hylan Boulevard, Suite 4B
Staten Island, NY 10305-1946
Phone: 800-223-APDA or 718-981-8001
E-mail: info@apdaparkinson.org
http://apdaparkinson.com/
Provides information, referrals, and listings of local support groups.

American Sleep Apnea Association
1424 K Street NW, Suite 302
Washington, DC 20005
Phone: 202-293-3650
E-mail: asaa@sleepapnea.org
http://www.sleepapnea.org/
For persons with sleep apnea and their families.

American Social Health Association
PO Box 13827
Research Triangle Park, NC 27709
Phone: 919-361-8400
E-mail: HPVnet@ashastd.org
http://www.ashastd.org
Provides information and education about sexually transmitted diseases.

American Society on Aging
833 Market Street, Suite 511
San Francisco, CA 94103-1824
Phone: 415-974-9600
E-mail: info@asaging.org
http://www.asaging.org/
Offers educational programming, information and training resources.

American Society for Deaf Children
PO Box 3355
Gettysburg, PA 17325
Phone: 717-334-7922
E-mail: asdc@deafchildren.org
http://www.deafchildren.org
For parents and families with children who are deaf or hard of hearing.

American Stroke Association
7272 Greenville Avenue
Dallas TX 75231
Phone: 800-787-8984
http://www.americanheart.org
For stroke victims and their families.

American Suicide Foundation
1045 Park Avenue, Suite 3C

New York, NY 10028
Phone: 800-ASF-4042; 212-210-1111
Provides referrals to national support groups for suicide survivors.

Anxiety Disorders Association of America (ADAA)
8730 Georgia Avenue, Suite 100
Silver Spring, MD 20910
Phone: 240-485-10001
http://www.adaa.org
Promotes the prevention and cure of anxiety disorders.

ARC
1010 Wayne Ave., Suite 650
Silver Spring, MD 20910
Phone: 301-565-3842
Email: Info@thearc.org
http://www.thearc.org
For people with mental retardation or developmental disabilities and their families.

Association for Repetitive Motion Syndromes
PO Box 471973
Aurora, CO 80047-1973
E-mail: arms@lightspeed.net
http://www.certifiedpst.com/arms/index.html
For persons with carpal tunnel syndrome and repetitive motion injuries.

Attention Deficit Disorder Association (ADDA)
1788 Second Street, Suite 200
Highland Park, IL 60035
Phone: 847-432-ADDA
E-mail: mail@add.org
http://www.add.org
For ADHD patients and their families.

Autism Society of America
7910 Woodmont Avenue, Suite 300
Bethesda, Maryland 20814-3067
Phone: 301-657-0881
http://www.autism-society.org
For information, referrals, and networking.

Batterers Anonymous
1041 South Mt. Vernon Avenue
Suite G-306
Colton, CA 92324
Phone: 909-355-1100
For men who wish to control their anger and eliminate their abusive behavior.

Brain Injury Association Family Helpline
Phone: 800-444-6443
http://www.bindependent.com/hompg/interact/com/states.htm
Provides contact information about support groups in each state.

Cancer Care
275 7th Avenue
New York, NY, 10001
Phone: 212-712-8080, 1-800-813-HOPE
E-mail: info@cancercare.org
http://www.cancercare.org/index.asp
For those who have suffered the loss of a loved one to cancer.

Candlelighters Childhood Cancer Foundation
PO Box 498
Kensington MD 20895-0498
Phone: 301-962-3520
E-mail: info@candlelighters.org
http://www.candlelighters.org/
For children with cancer and their families.

CDC National AIDS Clearinghouse
Hotline: 800-458-5231
http://www.cdcnpin.org/hiv/start.htm
Provides educational materials and referrals to support groups.

CFIDS Association
PO Box 220398
Charlotte, NC 28222-0398
Phone: 800-442-3437; 704-365-2343
E-mail: cfids@cfids.org
http://www.cfids.org
For people affected by chronic fatigue and immune dysfunction syndrome.

Child Help USA Hotline
15757 North 78th Street
Scottsdale, AZ 85260
Phone: 480-922-8212
http://www.childhelpusa.org
Referrals and information on child abuse.

Children and Adults with Attention-Deficit/Hyperactivity Disorder (CHADD)
8181 Professional Place, Suite 201
Landover, MD 20785
Phone: 800-233-4050
E-mail: national@chadd.org
http://chadd.org/index.htm
For ADHD patients and their families.

Cocaine Anonymous
3740 Overland Avenue, Suite C
Los Angeles, CA 90034-6337
For local chapters, call 800-347-8998 or 310-559-5833
E-mail:cawso@ca.org
http://www.ca.org
A 12-step program for individuals afflicted with cocaine addiction.

Codependents of Sex Addicts (COSA)
PO Box 14537
Minneapolis, MN 55414
Phone: 763-537-6904
E-mail: cosa@shore.net
A 12-step program for those in relationships with people who have compulsive sexual behavior.

Compassionate Friends
PO Box 3696
Oak Brook, IL 60522-3696
Phone: 630-990-0010
E-mail: Trish@compassionatefriends.org
http://www.compassionatefriends.org/
For families who have lost a child.

Concerned United Birthparents (CUB)
PO Box 230457
Encinitas, CA 92023
Phone: 800-822-2777
E-mail: info@CUBirthparents.org
http://www.cubirthparents.org
For adoption-affected people.

Crohn's & Colitis Foundation of America
386 Park Avenue South, 17th Floor
New York, NY 10016
Phone: 800-932-2423
E-mail: info@ccfa.org
http://ccfa.org
Information, support groups, conferences, and newsletters.

Cult Awareness Network
1680 North Vine Street, Suite 415
Los Angeles, CA 90028
Phone: 800-556-3055
E-mail: can@cultawarenessnetwork.org
http://www.cultawarenessnetwork.org
Public education about destructive mind-control cults.

Debtors Anonymous
PO Box 920888
Needham, MA 02492-0009
Phone: 781-453-2743
E-mail: new@debtorsanonymous.org
http://www.debtorsanonymous.org
A 12-step program for those recovering from compulsive indebtedness.

Domestic Violence Anonymous
DVA, c/o BayLaw
PO Box 29011
San Francisco, CA 94129
Phone: 415-681-4850
E-mail: BayLaw1@ix.netcom.com
http://www.BayLaw.com
A 12-step spiritual support for adults recovering from domestic violence.

Emotions Anonymous
PO Box 4245
St. Paul, MN 55104
Phone: 651-647-9712
http://www.emotionsanonymous.org
Fellowship for people experiencing emotional difficulties.

Epilepsy Foundation
4351 Garden City Drive
Landover, MD 20785
Phone: 800-332-1000
http://www.epilepsyfoundation.org
Information and referral for people with epilepsy and their families.

Family Pride Coalition
PO Box 65327
Washington, DC 200035-5327

Phone: 202-331-5015
E-mail: info@familypride.org
http://www.familypride.org
Provides support for gays, lesbians, bisexuals, and their families.

Food Addicts Anonymous
4623 Forest Hill Boulevard, Suite 109-4
West Palm Beach, FL 33415-9120
Phone: 561-967-3871
E-mail: info@foodaddictsanonymous.org
http://www.foodaddictsanonymous.org
A 12-step organization for individuals with food obsessions.

Friends for Survival
PO Box 214463
Sacramento, CA 95821
Phone: 916-392-0664; 800-646-7322
http://www.friendsforsurvival.org/
For family, friends, and professionals after a suicide death.

Gam-Anon Family Groups
PO Box 157
Whitestone, NY 11357
Phone: 718-352-1671
A 12-step program for relatives and friends of compulsive gamblers.

Gamblers Anonymous
PO Box 17173
Los Angeles, CA 90017
Phone: 213-386-8789
E-mail: isomain@gamblersanonymous.org
http://www.gamblersanonymous.org
A 12-step program for individuals with a gambling problem.

Klinefelter Syndrome and Associates (KSA)
PO Box 119
Roseville, CA 95678-0119
Phone: 916-773-2999
E-mail: ksinfo@genetic.org
http://www.genetic.org/ks
Increasing public awareness and providing support for those suffering.

La Leche League
1400 North Meacham Road
Schaumburg, IL 60173-4808
Phone: (847) 519-7730
http://www.lalecheleague.org/
Support and education for breastfeeding mothers.

Learning Disabilities Association of America
4156 Library Road
Pittsburgh, PA 15234
Phone: 412-341-1515 and 412-341-8077
E-mail: info@ldaamerica.org
http://www.ldanatl.org/
For people with learning disabilities and their families.

Lupus Foundation of America
1300 Piccard Drive, Suite 200
Rockville, MD 20850-3226
Phone: 800-558-0121; 301-670-9292
E-mail: lupusinfo@lupus.org
http://www.lupus.org
For lupus patients and their families.

Marijuana Anonymous (MA)
PO Box 2912
Van Nuys, CA 91404
Phone: 800-766-6779
E-mail: office@marijuana-anonymous.org
http://www.marijuana-anonymous.org
A 12-step program of recovery from marijuana addiction.

Mothers Against Drunk Driving
PO Box 541688
Dallas, TX 75354-1688
Phone: 800-438-6233
http://www.madd.org
Provides education, political activism, and victim assistance.

Multiple Sclerosis Association of America
706 Haddonfield Road
Cherry Hill, NJ 08002
Phone: 800-532-7667
E-mail: msaa@msaa.com
http://www.msaa.com/
For multiple sclerosis patients.

Muscular Dystrophy Association
3300 East Sunrise Drive

Tucson, AZ 85718
Phone: 602-529-2000
E-mail: mda@mdausa.org
http://www.mdausa.org
For fighting 40 neuromuscular diseases.

Nar-Anon World Wide Service
302 West 5th Street, Suite 301
San Pedro, CA 90731
Phone: 310-547-5800
A 12-step program of recovery for families and friends of addicts.

Narcolepsy Network
10921 Reed Hartman Highway
Cincinnati, OH 45242
Phone: 513-891-3522
E-mail: narnet@aol.com
http://www.websciences.org/narnet/default.html
For persons with narcolepsy and other sleep disorders.

Narcotics Anonymous
PO Box 9999
Van Nuys, CA 91409
Phone: 818-773-9999
E-mail: info@na.org
http://www.na.org
12-step association of recovering drug addicts.

National Adoption Center
1500 Walnut Street, Suite 701
Philadelphia, PA 19102
Phone: 800-TO-ADOPT
E-mail: nac@adopt.org
http://www.adopt.org
Information on adoption agencies and support groups.

National AIDS Hotline
Center For Disease Control
PO Box 13827
Research Triangle Park, NC 27709
Phone: 800-342-AIDS (24 hrs.); Spanish: 800-344 7432
Offers telephone support, information, and referrals.

National Alliance for the Mentally Ill
Colonial Place Three
2107 Wilson Boulevard, Suite 300
Arlington, VA 2201
Phone: 703-524-7600 or 800-950-NAMI (Hotline)
http://www.nami.org
For individuals and their relatives affected by mental illness.

National Alliance for Research on Schizophrenia and Depression (NARSAD)
60 Cutter Mill Road, Suite 404
Great Neck, NY 11021
Phone: 516-829-0091
E-mail: info@narsad.org
http://www.narsad.org
Supporting scientific research on brain and behavior disorders.

National Alopecia Areata Foundation
PO Box 150760
San Rafael, CA 94915-0760
Phone: 415-472-3780
http://www.alopeciaareata.com
Support network for people with alopecia areata, totalis, and universalis.

National Association of Anorexia Nervosa and Associated Disorders
PO Box 7
Highland Park, IL 60035
Phone: 847-433-4632
E-mail: anad20@aol.com
http://www.anad.org
For persons with eating disorders.

National Association of the Deaf
814 Thayer Avenue
Silver Springs, MD 20910
Phone: 301-587-1788; 301-587-1789
E-mail: NADinfo@nad.org
http://www.nad.org
For people who are deaf and hard of hearing.

National Center for Men
PO Box 555
Old Bethpage, NY 11804
Phone: 516-942-2020; activism/message line: 503-727-3686
E-mail: ncmen@teleport.com
Men's rights, male choice, fathers' rights.

National Chronic Pain Outreach Association
7979 Old Georgetown Road, #100
Bethesda, MD 20814
Phone: 301-652-4948
For those suffering with chronic pain.

National Clearinghouse for Alcohol and Drug Information
PO Box 2345
Rockville, MD 20847-2345
E-mail: info@health.org
Hotline: 800-788-2800
Information on alcohol and drug abuse, prevention, and treatment.

National Depressive and Manic Depressive Association
730 North Franklin, Suite 501
Chicago, IL 60610
Phone: 800-826-3632
E-mail: questions@ndmda.org
http://www.ndmda.org.
For persons with depressive and manic-depressive illness and their families.

National Domestic Violence Hotline
Phone: 800-799-7233; 800-787-3224
http://www.ndvh.org
Information and referrals for victims of domestic violence.

National Down Syndrome Congress
1605 Chantilly Drive, #250
Atlanta, GA 30324-3269
Phone: 800-232-NDSC; 404-653-1555
http://www.ndsccenter.org
For families affected by Down syndrome.

National Eating Disorders Association
603 Stewart Street, Suite 803
Seattle, WA 98101
Phone: 206-382-3587
E-mail: info@NationalEatingDisorders.org
http://nationaleatingdisorders.org
For persons with eating disorders, their families, and friends.

National Headache Foundation
428 West St. James Place, 2nd Floor
Chicago, IL 60614
Phone: 888-NHF-5552
http://www.headaches.org
Support for chronic headache sufferers and their families.

National Information Center for Children and Youth with Disabilities
PO Box 1492
Washington, DC 20013-1492
Phone: 800-695-0285
E-mail: nichcy@aed.org
http://www.nichcy.org
Provides information on disabilities and disability-related issues.

National Mental Health Association (NMHA)
1021 Prince Street
Alexandria, VA 22314-2971
Phone: 703-684-7722
http://www.nmha.org
Provides advocacy, education, and research on mental illness.

National Multiple Sclerosis Society
733 Third Avenue
New York, NY 10017-3288
Phone: 800-344-4867
http://www.nationalmssociety.org
For MS patients and their families.

National Organization on Fetal Alcohol Syndrome
216 G Street, NE
Washington, DC 20002
Phone: 202-785-4585
E-mail: information@nofas.org
http://www.nofas.org
Provides training workshops, peer education, and referrals.

National Organization for Men
11 Park Place
New York, NY 10007-2801
Phone: 212-686-MALE; 212-766-4030
http://www.tnom.com
For men seeking equal rights divorce, custody, property, and visitation laws.

National Organization for Women (NOW)
733 15th Street NW

Washington, DC 20005
Phone: 202-628-8669
E-mail: now@now.org
http://www.now.org
Provides advocacy on various women's rights issues.

National Stroke Association
9707 East Easter Lane
Englewood, CO 80112
Phone: 303-771-1700 or 800-STROKES
http://www.stroke.org
For stroke victims and their families.

National Parkinson Foundation
1501 NW 9th Avenue
Bob Hope Road
Miami, FL 33136-1494
Phone: 305-547-6666 or 800-327-4545
E-mail: mailbox@parkinson.org
http://www.parkinson.org
For individuals and their families afflicted with Parkinson's disease.

Nicotine Anonymous World Service
419 Main Street, PMB# 370
Huntington Beach, CA 92648
Phone: 415-750-0328
E-mail: info@nicotine-anonymous.org
http:/nicotine-anonymous.org
A 12-step program of recovery from nicotine addiction.

Obsessive-Compulsive Anonymous
PO Box 215
New Hyde Park, NY 11040
Phone: 516-739-0662
http://hometown.aol.com/west24th/index.html
A 12-step group for people with obsessive–compulsive disorders.

Obsessive-Compulsive Foundation
337 Notch Hill Road
North Branford, CT 06471
Phone: 203-878-5669
E-mail: info@ocfoundation.org
http://www.ocfoundation.org
Sponsors a large Internet site with research, newsletters, and conferences.

Overeaters Anonymous (OA)
PO Box 44020
Rio Rancho, NM 87174-4020
Phone: 505-891-2664
E-mail: info@overeatersanonymous.org
http://www.overeatersanonymous.org
A 12-step self-help fellowship for overeaters.

Parents Anonymous
675 West Foothill Boulevard, Suite 220
Claremont, CA 91711-3416
Phone: 909-621-6184
E-mail: parentsanonymous@parentsanonymous.org
http:// www.parentsanonymous.org
For parents who want to learn effective ways of raising their children.

Parents Without Partners
1650 South Dixie Highway, Suite 510
Boca Raton, FL 33432
Phone: 561-391-8833
E-mail: pwppr@parentswithoutpartners.org
http://www.parentswithoutpartners.org
A multiservice organization for single, divorced, or widowed parents.

Planned Parenthood
810 Seventh Avenue
New York, NY 10019
Phone: 800-230-7526
E-mail: communications@ppfa.org
http://www.plannedparenthood.org
Referrals to neighborhood Planned Parenthood clinics nationwide.

Postpartum Support International
927 North Kellogg Avenue
Santa Barbara, CA 93111
Phone: 805-967-736
http://www.postpartum.net/researchpage.htm
For women experiencing emotional changes during and after pregnancy.

PTSD Support Services
PO Box 5574
Woodland Park, CO 80866
Phone: 719-687-4582
http://ptsdsupport.net
Helping persons who have been injured emotionally and physically.

Rape Abuse and Incest National Network (RAINN)
Phone: 800-656-4673
http://www.rainn.org
A national hotline network for victims and survivors of sexual abuse.

Rational Recovery (RR)
PO Box 800
Lotus, CA 95651
Phone: 530-621-2667 or 530-621-4374
http://www.rational.org
For drug and alcohol addictions.

Reflex Sympathetic Dystrophy Syndrome Association
116 Haddon Avenue, Suite D
Haddonfield, NJ 08033-2306
Phone: 215-955-5444; 609-795-8845
http://www.rsds.org
For those suffering from RSD and their families.

RESOLVE: The National Infertility Association
1310 Broadway
Somerville MA 02144
Phone: 888-623-0744
Email: info@resolve.org
Offers support, information, and referrals for the infertile.

SAFE (Self-Abuse Finally Ends) Alternative Information Line
Phone: 800-DONT-CUT
Provides information on self-abuse and treatment options.

Self-Help for Hard of Hearing People (SHHH)
7910 Woodmont Avenue, Suite 1200
Bethesda, MD 20814
Phone: 301-657-2248; 301-657-2249
Email: National@shhh.org
http://www.shhh.org
For hard of hearing people, their families, and friends.

Self Management and Recovery Training (SMART)
7537 Mentor Avenue, Suite 306
Mentor, Ohio 44060
Phone: 440-951-5357
E-mail: srmail1@aol.com
http://www.smartrecovery.org
An abstinence-based, cognitive-behavioral approach.

Sex Addicts Anonymous
PO Box 70949
Houston, TX 77270
Phone: 713-869-4902
E-mail: info@saa-recovery.org
http://www.sexaa.org
A 12-step program of recovery from compulsive sexual behavior.

Sexual Compulsives Anonymous
PO Box 1585, Old Chelsea Station
New York, NY 10011
Phone: 800-977-4325
E-mail: info@sca-recovery.org
http://www.sca-recovery.org
A fellowship for individuals with compulsive sexual behavior.

Shape Up America!
4500 Connecticut Avenue, NW, Suite 414
Washington, DC 20008
E-mail: info@shapeup.org
http://www.shapeup.org
An organization advancing the benefits of maintaining a healthy weight.

Stepfamily Association of America
650 J Street, Suite 205
Lincoln, NE 68508
Phone: 800-735-0329
E-mail: saa@saafamilies.org
http://www.saafamilies.org
Information and advocacy for stepfamilies.

Sudden Infant Death Syndrome Alliance (SIDS Alliance)
1314 Bedford Avenue, Suite 210
Baltimore, MD 21208
Phone: 800-221-SIDS
E-mail: info@sidsalliance.org
http://www.sidsalliance.org/index/default.asp
Provides emotional support for families of SIDS victims.

Survivors of Incest Anonymous (S.I.A.)
PO Box 190
Benson, MD 21018-9998
Phone: 410-282-3400
http://www.siawso.org
A 12-step program for those who have been victims of child sexual abuse.

Tardive Dyskinesia/Tardive Dystonia National Association
PO Box 45732
Seattle, WA 98145-0732
Phone: 206-522-3166
E-mail: skjaer@halcyon.com
For those suffering from TD/TD, their families, and friends.

Tourette's Syndrome Association
42-40 Bell Boulevard, Suite 205
Bayside, NY 11361-2861
Phone: 718-224-2999; 800-237-0717
http://www.tsa-usa.org
Education for patients, professionals, and the public.

United Cerebral Palsy Association
1660 L Street NW, Suite 700
Washington, DC 20036
Phone: 800-872-5827
E-mail: webmaster@ucp.org
http://www.ucpa.org
Provides programs for individuals with cerebral palsy and other disabilities.

Y-ME National Breast Cancer Organization
212 W. Van Buren Street, Suite 500
Chicago, IL 6067
Phone: 312-986-8338
http://www.y-me.org/
Information and support for breast cancer patients and their families.

References, Readings, & Internet Sites 

American Self-Help Clearinghouse. (n.d.). *Self-help sourcebook*. Retrieved 2004 from http://mentalhelp.net/selfhelp

Barlow, S. W., Burlingame, G. M., Nebeker, R. S., & Anderson, E. (2000). Meta-analysis of medical self-help groups. *International Journal of Group Psychotherapy, 50*, 53–69.

Eisenberg, D. M., Davis, R. B., Ettner, S. L., Appel, S., Wilkey, S., Rompay, M. V., et al. (1998). Trends in alternative medicine use in the United States, 1990–1997. *Journal of the American Medical Association, 280*, 1575–1589.

Humphreys, K. (1999). Professional interventions that facilitate a 12-step self-help group involvement. *Alcohol Research and Health, 23*, 93–98.

Kurtz, L. F. (1997). *Self-help and support groups*. Thousand Oaks, CA: Sage.

National Mental Health Consumers. (n.d.). Self-Help Clearinghouse. Retrieved 2004 from http://www.mhselfhelp.org

Norcross, J. C., Santrock, J. W., Campbell, L. F., Smith T. P., Sommer, R., & Zuckerman, E. L. (2003). *Authoritative guide to self-help resources in mental health*. New York: Guilford Press.

Powell, T. J. (1987). *Self-help organizations and professional practice*. Silver Spring, MD: National Association of Social Workers.

Powell, T. J. (1994). *Understanding the self-help organization*. Beverly Hills, CA: Sage.

Reissman, F., & Carroll, D. (1995). *Redefining self-help: Policy and practice*. San Francisco: Jossey-Bass.

Wong, M. M. (1996). *The national directory of bereavement support groups and services*. Forest Hills, NY: ADM Publishing.

Yoder, B. (1990). *The recovery resource book*. New York: Simon & Schuster.

Related Topic

Chapter 97, "Top Internet Sites for Psychologists and Their Clients"

102 KNOWN AND UNPROVEN HERBAL TREATMENTS FOR PSYCHOLOGICAL DISORDERS

Paula J. Biedenharn

Popular in parts of the world for thousands of years (Gardner, 2002), herbal medicines have grown in use dramatically in the United States over the last decade (Hammerness et al., 2003). Herbal medicines are the most commonly used type of complementary and alternative medicines (CAMs). Also known as botanicals or phytomedicines (Fetrow & Avila, 2001), herbal treatments number in the hundreds, with St. John's wort, ginkgo, and ginseng among the most commonly used (Buchanan & Lemberg, 2001). In the United States, these phytomedicines are used by an estimated 16% to 18% of adults. In addition to being used for physical health problems, these herbs are often used by those seeking relief from emotional illnesses. While many tout the efficacy of these herbal treatments for psychological disorders such as depression, there are several concerns about herbal CAMs that warrant a cautious approach.

CAUTIONS FOR HERBAL CAMS

First, many herbal medicines have side effects and the potential for drug interactions, particularly when taken with certain prescription medications (McCabe, 2002). Since consumers can purchase these CAMs at grocery stores and convenience markets, they tend to see herbal medicines as safe, natural substances, not as drugs. Compounding this problematic perception are vague product labels that typically offer little warning or advisory information (Williams, 2003). An added concern is the fact that patients typically do not report the use of CAMs to their physicians (Hammerness et al., 2003); and even when herbal use is reported, it is often not recorded on the patients' medical charts (Cohen, Ek, & Pan, 2002). Given that herbal medicine use has also increased in the older adult population—consumers of nearly half of all prescription and over-the-counter (OTC) medications—their risk for drug interactions may be particularly elevated.

Second, many wonderful medications started as herbal treatments, including: warfarin (sweet clover), capsaicin (red pepper), and Taxol (Pacific yew tree) (Fetrow & Avila, 2001). Therefore it seems plausible that some phytomedicines will be found useful for the treatment of psychological symptoms. However, additional research is needed to confirm both the safety and the effectiveness of these CAMs. Fontanarosa, Rennie, and DeAngelis (2003) suggest we should learn from the recent serious problems discovered about ephedra—a weight-loss and athletic performance enhancer linked to heart attack, stroke, seizure, and death—and require more rigorous regulation by the FDA for these untested CAMs.

Third, there are considerable variations in product strength for herbal medications making accurate, consistent dosages difficult (Gardner, 2002; McCabe, 2002). Because herbal CAMs are considered dietary supplements (1994 Dietary Supplement Health and Education Act), they are not regulated by the U.S. Food and Drug Administration (FDA) and therefore are not standardized. Illustrating this problem, a recent U.S. analysis of St. John's wort products found variations in hyperforin, believed to be the active ingredient in this herb, from 0% to 3.26% in samples from various manufacturers (Gardner, 2002).

Perhaps the most significant problem is the tremendous lack of scientifically rigorous experiments testing the efficacy of CAMs (McCabe, 2002). "Presently, herbal preparations are subject to less stringent safety testing and governmental standards than OTC medications. These medicinal herbs can be marketed without proof of efficacy and are presumed safe until proven harmful" (Buchanan & Lemberg, 2001, p. 439). Fortunately, a clearer picture of herbal medicine efficacy is emerging; randomized controlled trials are becoming more common and more reliable data is appearing in the literature (Gardner, 2002).

A working knowledge of these CAMs is becoming essential for psychologists, as many clients are likely to be using these herbal treatments or may be interested in trying them (Hammerness et al., 2003). The following is a brief review of the known and unproven for the herbal medicines mostly commonly used for psychological disorders.

ST. JOHN'S WORT FOR DEPRESSION

The most commonly used and widely known herb for psychological disorder is St. John's wort (*Hypericum perforatum*). A common roadside weed with yellow flowers, this herb has been used for thousands of years to treat a wide variety of health problems. Today it is most commonly used for the treatment of depression (Hammerness et al., 2003).

There have been more studies of St. John's wort than most other herbal CAMs, and yet solid conclusions remain illusive. In Hammerness and colleagues' (2003) meta-analysis of previous studies, the authors concluded that St. John's wort works better than placebo and equal to selective serotonin reuptake inhibitors (SSRIs) and tricyclic antidepressants (TCAs) for the short-term (1–3 months) management of mild to moderate depression. However, two recent studies found no effect for St. John's wort compared to placebo, thus casting doubt on the herb's efficacy. At this time, St. John's wort is definitely not recommended for people with major or severe depression (Buchanan & Lemberg, 2001). Despite the uncertainty of its efficacy, many people take this herb and report positive benefits (McCabe, 2002). Additionally, St. John's wort has also been examined for effects on anxiety, obsessive-compulsive disorder, and seasonal affective disorder with very limited evidence of support (Hammerness et al., 2003).

While a popular herb worldwide, St. John's wort does have side effects and potentially serious drug interactions, though side effects tend to be lower than those of other antidepressants (Hammerness et al., 2003). Side effects commonly include gastrointestinal upset, restlessness, sedation, dizziness, dry mouth, headaches, and skin reactions. Because photosensitivity is common, people taking St. John's wort should use sunscreen (McCabe, 2002).

Many drug interactions have been identified for this herbal medicine. In particular, St. John's wort interferes with the protease inhibitors used to treat HIV (such as indinavir) and with the most common antirejection drug used after transplant surgery (cyclosporine), causing reduced blood levels of these crucial medications (McCabe, 2002). Acting as a weak monoamine oxidase inhibitor (MAOI), St. John's wort adds to the effect of prescription MAOIs, SSRIs, and TCAs—potentially leading to serotonin syndrome or a hypertensive crisis. St. John's wort can also cause increased anxiety when taken with flagyl. Theoretically, drugs such as warfarin (Coumadin) and oral contraceptives, statin anticholesterol drugs, and anticonvulsant drugs may all have decreased blood levels when St. John's wort is taken (McCabe, 2002).

GINKGO BILOBA FOR MEMORY

Ginkgo biloba is derived from the leaves of a commonly cultivated, ancient tree. In Europe, ginkgo is used to treat vascular disorders and memory problems in older adults and dementia patients (Buchanan & Lemberg, 2001). Five million prescriptions are filled for ginkgo each year in Germany alone (Oken, Storzbach, & Kaye, 1998), and it is commonly prescribed in

France as well (Spinella, 2001). Healthy adults take ginkgo to improve short-term memory, and ginkgo is also used to counteract the sexual dysfunction that often accompanies the use of SSRIs (Buchanan & Lemberg, 2001).

Less is known about ginkgo than about St. John's wort. Oken and colleagues' (1998) meta-analysis of previous studies supports a small but significant effect on cognitive function in Alzheimer's patients when 120 to 240 mg is taken for three to six months. It appears to both improve symptoms and delay further deterioration in these patients (Ernst, 2001). In addition, healthy adults show some improvement in memory and other cognitive functions. Ginkgo is believed to work by increasing cerebral blood flow through small arteries and by inhibiting platelet aggregation (Buchanan & Lemberg, 2001).

Side effects from ginkgo include anxiety, insomnia, headache, and GI distress. More seriously, ginkgo may be a possible teratogen, may cause mania at high dosage, and may cause serious bleeding due to its anticoagulant effect (McCabe, 2002).

GINSENG FOR WELL-BEING

There are several types of ginseng, including Chinese, Korean, Japanese, and American, with the most studied variety being panax ginseng—considered the true ginseng (Spinella, 2001, p. 167). Ginseng may be white or red depending on the preparation of the plant's rhizome (which may alter the pharmacological effect) and is expensive to produce and purchase. Nonetheless, it has been used for several thousand years for numerous illnesses. Spinella (2001) characterizes this CAM as an adaptogenic agent that "increases one's biological and mental resistance to stress." It is also believed to be an aphrodisiac and to increase physical and mental performance (Fetrow & Avila, 2001).

While animal studies suggest that ginseng has great potential for learning and memory, research on the efficacy of ginseng in humans is nearly nonexistent (Spinella, 2001). McCabe (2002) suggests that ginseng may improve appetite, sleep patterns, reaction time, and abstract thinking; however, additional research is needed to confirm this in humans. Ginseng has been found to have vasodilating effects and antioxidant properties that may impact cognitive and sexual performance (Spinella, 2001).

Common side effects for ginseng include insomnia, nervousness, headaches, hypertension, diarrhea, and vaginal bleeding (Fetrow & Avila, 2001). At normal doses, ginseng has little toxicity (Spinella, 2001); however, manic symptoms have been reported at high doses (Ernest, 2001). Drug interactions may occur when ginseng is taken with oral contraceptives, steroids, antidepressants, antipsychotics, and anticoagulants. Also, ginseng is contraindicated for patients with diabetes, hypertension, hypotension, and cardiovascular disease (Ernst, 2001).

KAVA FOR ANXIETY

A native plant of the South Pacific Islands, kava (*Piper methysticum*) is a derivative of the rhizome of a pepper plant (Spinella, 2001). Used ceremonially or recreationally by Micronesian and Polynesian cultures, kava causes a mild euphoria at normal doses and is known for having relaxation, sleep, analgesic, and anticonvulsant effects. In the West, it is most commonly used for anxiety and insomnia.

Again, little research is available on this herbal medicine, but some studies suggest that kava is better than placebo if taken for at least two months for the treatment of anxiety. In addition, kava appears to work as well as benzodiazepines (Ernst, 2001). Data are limited regarding kava's effect on sleep, though it is believed to have potential for sleep induction. Improved coordination, mood, and memory have also been identified (McCabe, 2002).

Numbness of the mouth and tongue is a common side effect of kava use, as are mild gastrointestinal upset, allergic skin reactions, and visual disturbances (McCabe, 2002). Anecdotal reports suggest kava may add to the depressant effect of alcohol and may aggravate underlying depressant states in some individuals. Another problem is that the strength of kava extracts can vary tremendously, as strength is dependent on what part of the plant is processed. The most serious concern about kava is that fact that it is a drug of abuse in the South Pacific and Australia, undoubtedly for its euphoric effects.

VALERIAN FOR SLEEP

Valerian (*Valeriana officinalis*) is a small plant with pink-white flowers. With use dating back at least a thousand years, the plant's roots or rhizomes are the source of this herbal preparation. Used as a muscle relaxant, digestive aid, and anticonvulsant in Europe (Fetrow & Avila, 2001), it is most commonly used for the treatment of anxiety and insomnia (Spinella, 2001).

Empirical research on valerian is limited. Placebo-controlled studies are particularly difficult due to the strong, distinctive, unpleasant odor of this CAM (McCabe, 2002). Although results are mixed, valerian does hold potential as a medication for improving sleep, particularly in poor sleepers. Spinella (2001) also suggests it may have use in treating anxiety or other mood disorders due to its pharmacological mechanisms, but studies have not yet been conducted.

There seems to be little risk of side effects or drug interactions with valerian. Only overdose or chronic use produces symptoms such as nausea, headache, and blurred vision. However, use is contraindicated for those with active liver disease as anecdotal reports suggest hepatotoxicity (Fetrow & Avila, 2001) and for those taking other central nervous system depressants (Ernst, 2001).

OTHER HERBS AND APPLICATIONS

Far less information is available on most of the other herbal CAMs used for psychological concerns. Briefly, rauwolfia has been used as an antipsychotic medication and tranquilizer for thousands of years; however, adverse side effects (primarily depression) and interactions have limited its use (Spinella, 2001). Popular in England, passion flower is a perennial climbing vine whose colorful flowers are dried for a mild sedative and antianxiety agent. Chamomile, lavender, and skullcap are also used for their sedative properties. Spinella (2001) suggests that ginger would probably not work as an antidepressant alone, but could augment other medications and might counteract the negative side effects of other antidepressant medications. Black cohosh is used to ease menopausal symptoms, and its use is likely to increase with growing concerns about pharmaceutical hormone replacement therapy. Evening primose oil has been tested on hyperactive children with mixed results and with the risk of producing temporal lope epilepsy (Fetrow & Avila, 2001). Lastly, one methodologically limited study reported the use of ginseng with ginkgo biloba for the treatment of ADHD in children with some success (Lyon et al., 2001).

References, Readings, & Internet Sites

Buchanan, K., & Lemberg, L. (2001). Herbal or complementary medicine: Fact or fiction? *American Journal of Critical Care, 10*, 438–443.

Cohen, R. J., Ek, K., & Pan, C. X. (2002). Complementary and alternative medicine (CAM) use by older adults: A comparison of self-report and physician chart documentation. *The Journals of Gerontology, 57A*, M223–M227.

Ernest, E. (Ed.). (2001). *The desktop guide to complementary and alternative medicine*. Edinburgh: Mosby.

Fetrow, C. W., & Avila, J. R. (2001). *Professional's handbook of complementary and alternative medicines*. Springhouse, PA: Springhouse.

Fontanarosa, P. B., Rennie, D., & DeAngelis, C. D. (2003). The need for regulation of dietary supplements: Lessons from ephedra. *Journal of the American Medical Association, 289*, 1568–1570.

Gardner, D. M. (2002). Evidence-based decisions about herbal products for treating mental disorders. *Journal of Psychiatry and Neuroscience, 27*, 324–333.

Hammerness, P., Basch, E., Ulbright, C., Barrette, E., Foppa, I., Basch, S., et al. (2003). St. John's wort: A systematic review of adverse effects and drug interactions for the consultation psychiatrist. *Psychosomatics, 44*, 271–282.

Lyon, J. C., Cline, J. C., Totosy de Zepetnek, J., Jie Shan, J., Pang, P., & Benishin, C. (2001). Effect of the herbal extract combination *Panax quinquefolium* and Ginkgo biloba on attention-deficit hyperactivity disorder: A pilot study. *Journal of Psychiatry and Neuroscience, 26,* 221–228.

McCabe, S. (2002). Complementary herbal and alternative drugs in clinical practice. *Perspectives in Psychiatric Care, 38,* 98–107.

National Center for Complementary and Alternative Medicine. (2002). What is complementary and alternative medicine? Retrieved September 9, 2003, from http://www.nccam.nih.gov/health/whatiscam/

Oken, B. S., Storzbach, D. M., & Kaye, D. M. (1998). The efficacy of Ginkgo Biloba on cognitive function in Alzheimer disease. *Archives of Neurology, 55,* 1409–1415.

Reiff, M., O'Connor, B., Kronenberg, F., Balick, M., Fugh-Berman, A., Johnson, K., et al. (2003). Ethnomedicine in the urban environment: Dominican healers in New York City. *Human Organization, 62,* 12–26.

Spinella, M. (2001). *The psychopharmacology of herbal medicine: Plant drugs that alter mind, brain, and behavior.* Cambridge, MA: MIT Press.

Williams, A. (2003). Herbs can cause death or injury. *Journal of the National Medical Association, 95,* 108.

Related Topic

Chapter 95, "Dietary Supplements and Psychological Functioning"

PART VIII
Ethical and Legal Issues

103 ETHICAL PRINCIPLES OF PSYCHOLOGISTS AND CODE OF CONDUCT (2002)

American Psychological Association

CONTENTS

INTRODUCTION

PREAMBLE

GENERAL PRINCIPLES

Principle A: Beneficence and Nonmaleficence
Principle B: Fidelity and Responsibility
Principle C: Integrity
Principle D: Justice
Principle E: Respect for People's Rights and Dignity

ETHICAL STANDARDS

1. Resolving Ethical Issues

1.01 Misuse of Psychologists' Work
1.02 Conflicts Between Ethics and Law, Regulations, or Other Governing Legal Authority
1.03 Conflicts Between Ethics and Organizational Demands
1.04 Informal Resolution of Ethical Violations
1.05 Reporting Ethical Violations
1.06 Cooperating With Ethics Committees
1.07 Improper Complaints
1.08 Unfair Discrimination Against Complainants and Respondents

2. Competence

2.01 Boundaries of Competence
2.02 Providing Services in Emergencies
2.03 Maintaining Competence
2.04 Bases for Scientific and Professional Judgments
2.05 Delegation of Work to Others
2.06 Personal Problems and Conflicts

3. Human Relations

3.01 Unfair Discrimination
3.02 Sexual Harassment
3.03 Other Harassment
3.04 Avoiding Harm
3.05 Multiple Relationships
3.06 Conflict of Interest
3.07 Third-Party Requests for Services
3.08 Exploitative Relationships
3.09 Cooperation With Other Professionals
3.10 Informed Consent
3.11 Psychological Services Delivered To or Through Organizations
3.12 Interruption of Psychological Services

4. *Privacy and Confidentiality*

4.01 Maintaining Confidentiality
4.02 Discussing the Limits of Confidentiality
4.03 Recording
4.04 Minimizing Intrusions on Privacy
4.05 Disclosures
4.06 Consultations
4.07 Use of Confidential Information for Didactic or Other Purposes

5. *Advertising and Other Public Statements*

5.01 Avoidance of False or Deceptive Statements
5.02 Statements by Others
5.03 Descriptions of Workshops and Non-Degree-Granting Educational Programs
5.04 Media Presentations
5.05 Testimonials
5.06 In-Person Solicitation

6. *Record Keeping and Fees*

6.01 Documentation of Professional and Scientific Work and Maintenance of Records
6.02 Maintenance, Dissemination, and Disposal of Confidential Records of Professional and Scientific Work
6.03 Withholding Records for Nonpayment
6.04 Fees and Financial Arrangements
6.05 Barter With Clients/Patients
6.06 Accuracy in Reports to Payors and Funding Sources
6.07 Referrals and Fees

7. *Education and Training*

7.01 Design of Education and Training Programs
7.02 Descriptions of Education and Training Programs
7.03 Accuracy in Teaching
7.04 Student Disclosure of Personal Information
7.05 Mandatory Individual or Group Therapy
7.06 Assessing Student and Supervisee Performance
7.07 Sexual Relationships With Students and Supervisees

8. *Research and Publication*

8.01 Institutional Approval
8.02 Informed Consent to Research
8.03 Informed Consent for Recording Voices and Images in Research
8.04 Client/Patient, Student, and Subordinate Research Participants
8.05 Dispensing With Informed Consent for Research
8.06 Offering Inducements for Research Participation
8.07 Deception in Research
8.08 Debriefing
8.09 Humane Care and Use of Animals in Research
8.10 Reporting Research Results
8.11 Plagiarism
8.12 Publication Credit
8.13 Duplicate Publication of Data
8.14 Sharing Research Data for Verification
8.15 Reviewers

9. *Assessment*

9.01 Bases for Assessments
9.02 Use of Assessments
9.03 Informed Consent in Assessments
9.04 Release of Test Data
9.05 Test Construction
9.06 Interpreting Assessment Results
9.07 Assessment by Unqualified Persons
9.08 Obsolete Tests and Outdated Test Results
9.09 Test Scoring and Interpretation Services
9.10 Explaining Assessment Results
9.11 Maintaining Test Security

10. *Therapy*

10.01 Informed Consent to Therapy
10.02 Therapy Involving Couples or Families
10.03 Group Therapy
10.04 Providing Therapy to Those Served by Others
10.05 Sexual Intimacies With Current Therapy Clients/Patients
10.06 Sexual Intimacies With Relatives or Significant Others of Current Therapy Clients/Patients
10.07 Therapy With Former Sexual Partners
10.08 Sexual Intimacies With Former Therapy Clients/Patients
10.09 Interruption of Therapy
10.10 Terminating Therapy

INTRODUCTION AND APPLICABILITY

The American Psychological Association's (APA's) Ethical Principles of Psychologists and Code of Conduct (hereinafter referred to as the Ethics Code) consists of an Introduction, a Preamble, five General Principles (A–E), and specific Ethical Standards. The Introduction discusses the intent, organization, procedural considerations, and scope of application of the Ethics Code. The Preamble and General Principles are aspirational goals to guide psychologists toward the highest ideals of psychology. Although the Preamble and General Principles are not themselves enforceable rules, they should be considered by psychologists in arriving at an ethical course of action. The Ethical Standards set forth enforceable rules for conduct as psychologists. Most of the Ethical Standards are written broadly, in order to apply to psychologists in varied roles, although the application of an Ethical Standard may vary depending on the context. The Ethical Standards are not exhaustive. The fact that a given conduct is not specifically addressed by an Ethical Standard does not mean that it is necessarily either ethical or unethical.

This Ethics Code applies only to psychologists' activities that are part of their scientific, educational, or professional roles as psychologists. Areas covered include but are not limited to the clinical, counseling, and school practice of psychology; research; teaching; supervision of trainees; public service; policy development; social intervention; development of assessment instruments; conducting assessments; educational counseling; organizational consulting; forensic activities; program design and evaluation; and administration. This Ethics Code applies to these activities across a variety of contexts, such as in person, postal, telephone, Internet, and other electronic transmissions. These activities shall be distinguished from the purely private conduct of psychologists, which is not within the purview of the Ethics Code.

Membership in the APA commits members and student affiliates to comply with the standards of the APA Ethics Code and to the rules and procedures used to enforce them. Lack of awareness or misunderstanding of an Ethical Standard is not itself a defense to a charge of unethical conduct.

The procedures for filing, investigating, and resolving complaints of unethical conduct are described in the current Rules and Procedures of the APA Ethics Committee. APA may impose sanctions on its members for violations of the standards of the Ethics Code, including termination of APA membership, and may notify other bodies and individuals of its actions. Actions that violate the standards of the Ethics Code may also lead to the imposition of sanctions on psychologists or students whether or not they are APA members by bodies other than APA, including state psychological associations, other professional groups, psychology boards, other state or federal agencies, and payors for health services. In addition, APA may take action against a member after his or her conviction of a felony, expulsion or suspension from an affiliated state psychological association, or suspension or loss of licensure. When the sanction to be imposed by APA is less than expulsion, the 2001 Rules and Procedures do not guarantee an opportunity for an in-person hearing, but generally provide that complaints will be resolved only on the basis of a submitted record.

The Ethics Code is intended to provide guidance for psychologists and standards of professional conduct that can be applied by the APA and by other bodies that choose to adopt them. The Ethics Code is not intended to be a basis of civil liability. Whether a psychologist has violated the Ethics Code standards does not by itself determine whether the psychologist is legally liable in a court action, whether a contract is enforceable, or whether other legal consequences occur.

The modifiers used in some of the standards of this Ethics Code (e.g., *reasonably, appropriate, potentially*) are included in the standards when they would (1) allow professional judgment on the part of psychologists, (2) eliminate injustice or inequality that would occur without the modifier, (3) ensure applicability across the broad range of activities conducted by psychologists, or (4) guard against a set of rigid rules that might be quickly outdated. As used in this Ethics Code, the term *reasonable* means the prevailing professional judgment of psychologists engaged in similar activities in similar circumstances, given the knowledge the psychologist had or should have had at the time.

In the process of making decisions regarding their professional behavior, psychologists must consider this Ethics Code in addition to applicable laws and psychology board regulations. In applying the Ethics Code to their professional work, psychologists may consider other materials and guidelines that have been adopted or endorsed by scientific and professional psychological organizations and the dictates of their own conscience, as well as consult with others within the field. If this Ethics Code establishes a higher standard of conduct than is required by law, psychologists must meet the higher ethical standard. If psychologists' ethical responsibilities conflict with law, regulations, or other governing legal authority, psychologists make known their commitment to this Ethics Code and take steps to resolve the conflict in a responsible manner. If the conflict is unresolvable via such means, psychologists may adhere to the requirements of the law, regulations, or other governing authority in keeping with basic principles of human rights.

PREAMBLE

Psychologists are committed to increasing scientific and professional knowledge of behavior and people's understanding of themselves and others and to the use of such knowledge to improve the condition of individuals, organizations, and society. Psychologists respect and protect civil and human rights and the central importance of freedom of inquiry and expression in research, teaching, and publication. They strive to help the public in developing informed judgments and choices concerning human behavior. In doing so, they perform many roles, such as researcher, educator, diagnostician, therapist, supervisor, consultant, administrator, social interventionist, and expert witness. This Ethics Code provides a common set of principles and standards upon which psychologists build their professional and scientific work.

This Ethics Code is intended to provide specific standards to cover most situations encountered by psychologists. It has as its goals the welfare and protection of the individuals and groups with whom psychologists work and the education of members, students, and the public regarding ethical standards of the discipline.

The development of a dynamic set of ethical standards for psychologists' work-related conduct requires a personal commitment and lifelong effort to act ethically; to encourage ethical behavior by students, supervisees, employees, and colleagues; and to consult with others concerning ethical problems.

GENERAL PRINCIPLES

This section consists of General Principles. General Principles, as opposed to Ethical Standards, are aspirational in nature. Their intent is to guide and inspire psychologists toward the very highest ethical ideals of the profession. General Principles, in contrast to Ethical Standards, do not represent obligations and should not form the basis for imposing sanctions. Relying upon General Principles for either of these reasons distorts both their meaning and purpose.

Principle A: Beneficence and Nonmaleficence

Psychologists strive to benefit those with whom they work and take care to do no harm. In their professional actions, psychologists seek to safeguard the welfare and rights of those with whom they interact professionally and other affected persons, and the welfare of animal subjects of research. When conflicts occur among psychologists' obligations or concerns, they attempt to resolve these conflicts in a responsible fashion that avoids or minimizes harm. Because psychologists' scientific and professional judgments and actions may affect the lives of others, they are alert to and guard against personal, financial, social, organizational, or political factors that might lead to misuse of their influence. Psychologists strive to be aware of the possible effect of their own physical and mental health on their ability to help those with whom they work.

Principle B: Fidelity and Responsibility

Psychologists establish relationships of trust with those with whom they work. They are aware of their professional and scientific responsibilities to society and to the specific communities in which they work. Psychologists uphold professional standards of conduct, clarify their professional roles and obligations, accept appropriate responsibility for their behavior, and seek to manage conflicts of interest that could lead to exploitation or harm. Psychologists consult with, refer to, or cooperate with other professionals and institutions to the extent needed to serve the best interests of those with whom they work. They are concerned about the ethical compliance of their colleagues' scientific and professional conduct. Psychologists strive to contribute a portion of their professional time for little or no compensation or personal advantage.

Principle C: Integrity

Psychologists seek to promote accuracy, honesty, and truthfulness in the science, teaching, and practice of psychology. In these activities psychologists do not steal, cheat, or engage in fraud, subterfuge, or intentional misrepresentation of fact. Psychologists strive to keep their promises and to avoid unwise or unclear commitments. In situations in which deception may be ethically justifiable to maximize benefits and minimize harm, psychologists have a serious obligation to consider the need for, the possible consequences of, and their responsibility to correct any resulting mistrust or other harmful effects that arise from the use of such techniques.

Principle D: Justice

Psychologists recognize that fairness and justice entitle all persons to access to and benefit from the contributions of psychology and to equal quality in the processes, procedures, and services being conducted by psychologists. Psychologists exercise reasonable judgment and take precautions to ensure that their potential biases, the boundaries of their competence, and the limitations of their expertise do not lead to or condone unjust practices.

Principle E: Respect for People's Rights and Dignity

Psychologists respect the dignity and worth of all people, and the rights of individuals to privacy, confidentiality, and self-determination. Psychologists are aware that special safeguards may be necessary to protect the rights and welfare of persons or communities whose vulnerabilities impair autonomous decision making. Psychologists are aware of and respect cultural, individual, and role differences, including those based on age, gender, gender identity, race, ethnicity, culture, national origin, religion, sexual orientation, disability, language, and socioeconomic status and consider these factors when working with members of such groups. Psychologists try to eliminate the effect on their work of biases based on those factors, and they do not knowingly participate in or condone activities of others based upon such prejudices.

ETHICAL STANDARDS

1. Resolving Ethical Issues

1.01 Misuse of Psychologists' Work

If psychologists learn of misuse or misrepresentation of their work, they take reasonable steps to correct or minimize the misuse or misrepresentation.

1.02 Conflicts Between Ethics and Law, Regulations, or Other Governing Legal Authority

If psychologists' ethical responsibilities conflict with law, regulations, or other governing legal authority, psychologists make known their commitment to the Ethics Code and take steps to resolve the conflict. If the conflict is unresolvable via such means, psychologists may adhere to the requirements of the law, regulations, or other governing legal authority.

1.03 Conflicts Between Ethics and Organizational Demands

If the demands of an organization with which psychologists are affiliated or for whom they are working conflict with this Ethics Code, psychologists clarify the nature of the conflict, make known their commitment to the Ethics Code, and to the extent feasible, resolve the conflict in a way that permits adherence to the Ethics Code.

1.04 Informal Resolution of Ethical Violations

When psychologists believe that there may have been an ethical violation by another psychologist, they attempt to resolve the issue by bringing it to the attention of that individual, if an informal resolution appears appropriate and the intervention does not violate any confidentiality rights that may be involved. (See also Standards 1.02, Conflicts Between Ethics and Law, Regulations, or Other Governing Legal Authority, and 1.03, Conflicts Between Ethics and Organizational Demands.)

1.05 Reporting Ethical Violations

If an apparent ethical violation has substantially harmed or is likely to substantially harm a person or organization and is not appropriate for informal resolution under Standard 1.04, Informal Resolution of Ethical Violations, or is not resolved properly in that fashion, psychologists take further action appropriate to the situation. Such action might include referral to state or national committees on professional ethics, to state licensing boards, or to the appropriate institutional authorities. This standard does not apply when an intervention would violate confidentiality rights or when psychologists have been retained to review the work of another psychologist whose professional conduct is in question. (See also Standard 1.02, Conflicts Between Ethics and Law, Regulations, or Other Governing Legal Authority.)

1.06 Cooperating With Ethics Committees

Psychologists cooperate in ethics investigations, proceedings, and resulting requirements of the APA or any affiliated state psychological association to which they belong. In doing so, they address any confidentiality issues. Failure to cooperate is itself an ethics violation. However, making a request for deferment of adjudication of an ethics complaint pending the outcome of litigation does not alone constitute noncooperation.

1.07 Improper Complaints

Psychologists do not file or encourage the filing of ethics complaints that are made with reckless disregard for or willful ignorance of facts that would disprove the allegation.

1.08 Unfair Discrimination Against Complainants and Respondents

Psychologists do not deny persons employment, advancement, admissions to academic or other programs, tenure, or promotion, based solely upon their having made or their being the subject of an ethics complaint. This does not preclude taking action based upon the outcome of such proceedings or considering other appropriate information.

2. Competence

2.01 Boundaries of Competence

(a) Psychologists provide services, teach, and conduct research with populations and in areas only within the boundaries of their competence, based on their education, training, supervised experience, consultation, study, or professional experience.

(b) Where scientific or professional knowledge in the discipline of psychology establishes that an understanding of factors associated with age, gender, gender identity, race, ethnicity, culture, national origin, religion, sexual orientation, disability, language, or socioeconomic status is essential for effective implementation of their services or research, psychologists have or obtain the training, experience, consultation, or supervision necessary to ensure the competence of their services, or they make appropriate referrals, except as provided in Standard 2.02, Providing Services in Emergencies.

(c) Psychologists planning to provide services, teach, or conduct research involving populations, areas, techniques, or technologies new to them undertake relevant education, training, supervised experience, consultation, or study.

(d) When psychologists are asked to provide services to individuals for whom appropriate mental health services are not available and for which psychologists have not obtained the competence necessary, psychologists with closely related prior training or experience may provide such services in order to ensure that services are not denied if they make a reasonable effort to obtain the competence required by using relevant research, training, consultation, or study.

(e) In those emerging areas in which generally recognized standards for preparatory training do not yet exist, psychologists nevertheless take reasonable steps to ensure the competence of their work and to protect clients/patients, students, supervisees, research participants, organizational clients, and others from harm.

(f) When assuming forensic roles, psychologists are or become reasonably familiar with the judicial or administrative rules governing their roles.

2.02 *Providing Services in Emergencies*

In emergencies, when psychologists provide services to individuals for whom other mental health services are not available and for which psychologists have not obtained the necessary training, psychologists may provide such services in order to ensure that services are not denied. The services are discontinued as soon as the emergency has ended or appropriate services are available.

2.03 *Maintaining Competence*

Psychologists undertake ongoing efforts to develop and maintain their competence.

2.04 *Bases for Scientific and Professional Judgments*

Psychologists' work is based upon established scientific and professional knowledge of the discipline. (See also Standards 2.01e, Boundaries of Competence, and 10.01b, Informed Consent to Therapy.)

2.05 *Delegation of Work to Others*

Psychologists who delegate work to employees, supervisees, or research or teaching assistants or who use the services of others, such as interpreters, take reasonable steps to (1) avoid delegating such work to persons who have a multiple relationship with those being served that would likely lead to exploitation or loss of objectivity; (2) authorize only those responsibilities that such persons can be expected to perform competently on the basis of their education, training, or experience, either independently or with the level of supervision being provided; and (3) see that such persons perform these services competently. (See also Standards 2.02, Providing Services in Emergencies; 3.05, Multiple Relationships; 4.01, Maintaining Confidentiality; 9.01, Bases for Assessments; 9.02, Use of Assessments; 9.03, Informed Consent in Assessments; and 9.07, Assessment by Unqualified Persons.)

2.06 *Personal Problems and Conflicts*

(a) Psychologists refrain from initiating an activity when they know or should know that there is a substantial likelihood that their personal problems will prevent them from performing their work-related activities in a competent manner.

(b) When psychologists become aware of personal problems that may interfere with their performing work-related duties adequately, they take appropriate measures, such as obtaining professional consultation or assistance, and determine whether they should limit, suspend, or terminate their work-related duties. (See also Standard 10.10, Terminating Therapy.)

3. Human Relations

3.01 Unfair Discrimination

In their work-related activities, psychologists do not engage in unfair discrimination based on age, gender, gender identity, race, ethnicity, culture, national origin, religion, sexual orientation, disability, socioeconomic status, or any basis proscribed by law.

3.02 Sexual Harassment

Psychologists do not engage in sexual harassment. Sexual harassment is sexual solicitation, physical advances, or verbal or nonverbal conduct that is sexual in nature, that occurs in connection with the psychologist's activities or roles as a psychologist, and that either (1) is unwelcome, is offensive, or creates a hostile workplace or educational environment, and the psychologist knows or is told this or (2) is sufficiently severe or intense to be abusive to a reasonable person in the context. Sexual harassment can consist of a single intense or severe act or of multiple persistent or pervasive acts. (See also Standard 1.08, Unfair Discrimination Against Complainants and Respondents.)

3.03 Other Harassment

Psychologists do not knowingly engage in behavior that is harassing or demeaning to persons with whom they interact in their work based on factors such as those persons' age, gender, gender identity, race, ethnicity, culture, national origin, religion, sexual orientation, disability, language, or socioeconomic status.

3.04 Avoiding Harm

Psychologists take reasonable steps to avoid harming their clients/patients, students, supervisees, research participants, organizational clients, and others with whom they work, and to minimize harm where it is foreseeable and unavoidable.

3.05 Multiple Relationships

(a) A multiple relationship occurs when a psychologist is in a professional role with a person and (1) at the same time is in another role with the same person, (2) at the same time is in a relationship with a person closely associated with or related to the person with whom the psychologist has the professional relationship, or (3) promises to enter into another relationship in the future with the person or a person closely associated with or related to the person.

A psychologist refrains from entering into a multiple relationship if the multiple relationship could reasonably be expected to impair the psychologist's objectivity, competence, or effectiveness in performing his or her functions as a psychologist, or otherwise risks exploitation or harm to the person with whom the professional relationship exists.

Multiple relationships that would not reasonably be expected to cause impairment or risk exploitation or harm are not unethical.

(b) If a psychologist finds that, due to unforeseen factors, a potentially harmful multiple relationship has arisen, the psychologist takes reasonable steps to resolve it with due regard for the best interests of the affected person and maximal compliance with the Ethics Code.

(c) When psychologists are required by law, institutional policy, or extraordinary circumstances to serve in more than one role in judicial or administrative proceedings, at the outset they clarify role expectations and the extent of confidentiality and thereafter as changes occur. (See also Standards 3.04, Avoiding Harm, and 3.07, Third-Party Requests for Services.)

3.06 Conflict of Interest

Psychologists refrain from taking on a professional role when personal, scientific, professional, legal, financial, or other interests or relationships could reasonably be expected to (1) impair their objectivity, competence, or effectiveness in performing their functions as psychologists or (2) expose the person or organization with whom the professional relationship exists to harm or exploitation.

3.07 *Third-Party Requests for Services*

When psychologists agree to provide services to a person or entity at the request of a third party, psychologists attempt to clarify at the outset of the service the nature of the relationship with all individuals or organizations involved. This clarification includes the role of the psychologist (e.g., therapist, consultant, diagnostician, or expert witness), an identification of who is the client, the probable uses of the services provided or the information obtained, and the fact that there may be limits to confidentiality. (See also Standards 3.05, Multiple Relationships, and 4.02, Discussing the Limits of Confidentiality.)

3.08 *Exploitative Relationships*

Psychologists do not exploit persons over whom they have supervisory, evaluative, or other authority such as clients/patients, students, supervisees, research participants, and employees. (See also Standards 3.05, Multiple Relationships; 6.04, Fees and Financial Arrangements; 6.05, Barter With Clients/Patients; 7.07, Sexual Relationships With Students and Supervisees; 10.05, Sexual Intimacies With Current Therapy Clients/Patients; 10.06, Sexual Intimacies With Relatives or Significant Others of Current Therapy Clients/Patients; 10.07, Therapy With Former Sexual Partners; and 10.08, Sexual Intimacies With Former Therapy Clients/Patients.)

3.09 *Cooperation With Other Professionals*

When indicated and professionally appropriate, psychologists cooperate with other professionals in order to serve their clients/patients effectively and appropriately. (See also Standard 4.05, Disclosures.)

3.10 *Informed Consent*

(a) When psychologists conduct research or provide assessment, therapy, counseling, or consulting services in person or via electronic transmission or other forms of communication, they obtain the informed consent of the individual or individuals using language that is reasonably understandable to that person or persons except when conducting such activities without consent is mandated by law or governmental regulation or as otherwise provided in this Ethics Code. (See also Standards 8.02, Informed Consent to Research; 9.03, Informed Consent in Assessments; and 10.01, Informed Consent to Therapy.)

(b) For persons who are legally incapable of giving informed consent, psychologists nevertheless (1) provide an appropriate explanation, (2) seek the individual's assent, (3) consider such persons' preferences and best interests, and (4) obtain appropriate permission from a legally authorized person, if such substitute consent is permitted or required by law. When consent by a legally authorized person is not permitted or required by law, psychologists take reasonable steps to protect the individual's rights and welfare.

(c) When psychological services are court ordered or otherwise mandated, psychologists inform the individual of the nature of the anticipated services, including whether the services are court ordered or mandated and any limits of confidentiality, before proceeding.

(d) Psychologists appropriately document written or oral consent, permission, and assent. (See also Standards 8.02, Informed Consent to Research; 9.03, Informed Consent in Assessments; and 10.01, Informed Consent to Therapy.)

3.11 *Psychological Services Delivered To or Through Organizations*

(a) Psychologists delivering services to or through organizations provide information beforehand to clients and when appropriate those directly affected by the services about (1) the nature and objectives of the services, (2) the intended recipients, (3) which of the individuals are clients, (4) the relationship the psychologist will have with each person and the organization, (5) the probable uses of services provided and information obtained, (6) who will have access to the information, and (7) limits of confidentiality. As soon as feasible, they provide information about the results and conclusions of such services to appropriate persons.

(b) If psychologists will be precluded by law or by organizational roles from providing such information to particular individuals or groups, they so inform those individuals or groups at the outset of the service.

3.12 *Interruption of Psychological Services*

Unless otherwise covered by contract, psychologists make reasonable efforts to plan for facilitating services in the event that psychological services are interrupted by factors such as the psychologist's illness, death, unavailability, relocation, or retirement or by the client's/patient's relocation or financial limitations. (See also Standard 6.02c, Maintenance, Dissemination, and Disposal of Confidential Records of Professional and Scientific Work.)

4. Privacy And Confidentiality

4.01 *Maintaining Confidentiality*

Psychologists have a primary obligation and take reasonable precautions to protect confidential information obtained through or stored in any medium, recognizing that the extent and limits of confidentiality may be regulated by law or established by institutional rules or professional or scientific relationship. (See also Standard 2.05, Delegation of Work to Others.)

4.02 *Discussing the Limits of Confidentiality*

(a) Psychologists discuss with persons (including, to the extent feasible, persons who are legally incapable of giving informed consent and their legal representatives) and organizations with whom they establish a scientific or professional relationship (1) the relevant limits of confidentiality and (2) the foreseeable uses of the information generated through their psychological activities. (See also Standard 3.10, Informed Consent.)

(b) Unless it is not feasible or is contraindicated, the discussion of confidentiality occurs at the outset of the relationship and thereafter as new circumstances may warrant.

(c) Psychologists who offer services, products, or information via electronic transmission inform clients/patients of the risks to privacy and limits of confidentiality.

4.03 *Recording*

Before recording the voices or images of individuals to whom they provide services, psychologists obtain permission from all such persons or their legal representatives. (See also Standards 8.03, Informed Consent for Recording Voices and Images in Research; 8.05, Dispensing With Informed Consent for Research; and 8.07, Deception in Research.)

4.04 *Minimizing Intrusions on Privacy*

(a) Psychologists include in written and oral reports and consultations only information germane to the purpose for which the communication is made.

(b) Psychologists discuss confidential information obtained in their work only for appropriate scientific or professional purposes and only with persons clearly concerned with such matters.

4.05 *Disclosures*

(a) Psychologists may disclose confidential information with the appropriate consent of the organizational client, the individual client/patient, or another legally authorized person on behalf of the client/patient unless prohibited by law.

(b) Psychologists disclose confidential information without the consent of the individual only as mandated by law, or where permitted by law for a valid purpose such as to (1) provide needed professional services; (2) obtain appropriate professional consultations; (3) protect the client/patient, psychologist, or others from harm; or (4) obtain payment for services from a client/patient, in which instance disclosure is limited to the minimum that is necessary to achieve the purpose. (See also Standard 6.04e, Fees and Financial Arrangements.)

4.06 *Consultations*

When consulting with colleagues, (1) psychologists do not disclose confidential information that reasonably could lead to the identification of a client/patient, research participant, or other person or organization with whom they have a confidential relationship unless they have obtained the prior consent of the person or organization or the disclosure cannot be avoided, and (2) they disclose information only to the extent necessary to achieve the purposes of the consultation. (See also Standard 4.01, Maintaining Confidentiality.)

4.07 *Use of Confidential Information for Didactic or Other Purposes*

Psychologists do not disclose in their writings, lectures, or other public media, confidential, personally identifiable information concerning their clients/patients, students, research participants, organizational clients, or other recipients of their services that they obtained during the course of their work, unless (1) they take reasonable steps to disguise the person or organization, (2) the person or organization has consented in writing, or (3) there is legal authorization for doing so.

5. Advertising and Other Public Statements

5.01 *Avoidance of False or Deceptive Statements*

(a) Public statements include but are not limited to paid or unpaid advertising, product endorsements, grant applications, licensing applications, other credentialing applications, brochures, printed matter, directory listings, personal resumes or curricula vitae, or comments for use in media such as print or electronic transmission, statements in legal proceedings, lectures and public oral presentations, and published materials. Psychologists do not knowingly make public statements that are false, deceptive, or fraudulent concerning their research, practice, or other work activities or those of persons or organizations with which they are affiliated.

(b) Psychologists do not make false, deceptive, or fraudulent statements concerning (1) their training, experience, or competence; (2) their academic degrees; (3) their credentials; (4) their institutional or association affiliations; (5) their services; (6) the scientific or clinical basis for, or results or degree of success of, their services; (7) their fees; or (8) their publications or research findings.

(c) Psychologists claim degrees as credentials for their health services only if those degrees (1) were earned from a regionally accredited educational institution or (2) were the basis for psychology licensure by the state in which they practice.

5.02 *Statements by Others*

(a) Psychologists who engage others to create or place public statements that promote their professional practice, products, or activities retain professional responsibility for such statements.

(b) Psychologists do not compensate employees of press, radio, television, or other communication media in return for publicity in a news item. (See also Standard 1.01, Misuse of Psychologists' Work.)

(c) A paid advertisement relating to psychologists' activities must be identified or clearly recognizable as such.

5.03 *Descriptions of Workshops and Non-Degree-Granting Educational Programs*

To the degree to which they exercise control, psychologists responsible for announcements, catalogs, brochures, or advertisements describing workshops, seminars, or other non-degree-granting educational programs ensure that they accurately describe the audience for which the program is intended, the educational objectives, the presenters, and the fees involved.

5.04 *Media Presentations*

When psychologists provide public advice or comment via print, internet, or other electronic transmission, they take precautions to ensure that statements (1) are based on their professional knowledge, training, or experience in accord with appropriate psychological literature and practice; (2) are otherwise consistent with this Ethics Code; and (3) do not indicate that a professional relationship has been established with the recipient. (See also Standard 2.04, Bases for Scientific and Professional Judgments.)

5.05 *Testimonials*

Psychologists do not solicit testimonials from current therapy clients/patients or other persons who because of their particular circumstances are vulnerable to undue influence.

5.06 *In-Person Solicitation*

Psychologists do not engage, directly or through agents, in uninvited in-person solicitation of business from actual or potential therapy clients/patients or other persons who because of their particular circumstances are vulnerable to undue influence. However, this prohibition does not preclude (1) attempting to implement appropriate collateral contacts for the purpose of benefiting an already engaged therapy client/patient or (2) providing disaster or community outreach services.

6. Record Keeping and Fees

6.01 *Documentation of Professional and Scientific Work and Maintenance of Records*

Psychologists create, and to the extent the records are under their control, maintain, disseminate, store, retain, and dispose of records and data relating to their professional and scientific work in order to (1) facilitate provision of services later by them or by other professionals, (2) allow for replication of research design and analyses, (3) meet institutional requirements, (4) ensure accuracy of billing and payments, and (5) ensure compliance with law. (See also Standard 4.01, Maintaining Confidentiality.)

6.02 *Maintenance, Dissemination, and Disposal of Confidential Records of Professional and Scientific Work*

(a) Psychologists maintain confidentiality in creating, storing, accessing, transferring, and disposing of records under their control, whether these are written, automated, or in any other medium. (See also Standards 4.01, Maintaining Confidentiality, and 6.01, Documentation of Professional and Scientific Work and Maintenance of Records.)

(b) If confidential information concerning recipients of psychological services is entered into databases or systems of records available to persons whose access has not been consented to by the recipient, psychologists use coding or other techniques to avoid the inclusion of personal identifiers.

(c) Psychologists make plans in advance to facilitate the appropriate transfer and to protect the confidentiality of records and data in the event of psychologists' withdrawal from positions or practice. (See also Standards 3.12, Interruption of Psychological Services, and 10.09, Interruption of Therapy.)

6.03 *Withholding Records for Nonpayment*

Psychologists may not withhold records under their control that are requested and needed for a client's/patient's emergency treatment solely because payment has not been received.

6.04 *Fees and Financial Arrangements*

(a) As early as is feasible in a professional or scientific relationship, psychologists and recipients of psychological services reach an agreement specifying compensation and billing arrangements.

(b) Psychologists' fee practices are consistent with law.

(c) Psychologists do not misrepresent their fees.

(d) If limitations to services can be anticipated because of limitations in financing, this is discussed with the recipient of services as early as is feasible. (See also Standards 10.09, Interruption of Therapy, and 10.10, Terminating Therapy.)

(e) If the recipient of services does not pay for services as agreed, and if psychologists intend to use collection agencies or legal measures to collect the fees, psychologists first inform the person that such measures will be taken and provide that person an opportunity to make prompt payment. (See also Standards 4.05, Disclosures; 6.03, Withholding Records for Nonpayment; and 10.01, Informed Consent to Therapy.)

6.05 *Barter With Clients/Patients*

Barter is the acceptance of goods, services, or other nonmonetary remuneration from clients/patients in return for psychological services. Psychologists may barter only if (1) it is not clinically contraindicated, and (2) the resulting arrangement is not exploitative. (See also Standards 3.05, Multiple Relationships, and 6.04, Fees and Financial Arrangements.)

6.06 *Accuracy in Reports to Payors and Funding Sources*

In their reports to payors for services or sources of research funding, psychologists take reasonable steps to ensure the accurate reporting of the nature of the service provided or research conducted, the fees, charges, or payments, and where applicable, the identity of the provider, the findings, and the diagnosis. (See also Standards 4.01, Maintaining Confidentiality; 4.04, Minimizing Intrusions on Privacy; and 4.05, Disclosures.)

6.07 *Referrals and Fees*

When psychologists pay, receive payment from, or divide fees with another professional, other than in an employer-employee relationship, the payment to each is based on the services provided (clinical, consultative, administrative, or other) and is not based on the referral itself. (See also Standard 3.09, Cooperation With Other Professionals.)

7. Education and Training

7.01 *Design of Education and Training Programs*

Psychologists responsible for education and training programs take reasonable steps to ensure that the programs are designed to provide the appropriate knowledge and proper experiences, and to meet the requirements for licensure, certification, or other goals for which claims are made by the program. (See also Standard 5.03, Descriptions of Workshops and Non-Degree-Granting Educational Programs.)

7.02 *Descriptions of Education and Training Programs*

Psychologists responsible for education and training programs take reasonable steps to ensure that there is a current and accurate description of the program content (including participation in required course- or program-related counseling, psychotherapy, experiential groups, consulting projects, or community service), training goals and objectives, stipends and benefits, and requirements that must be met for satisfactory completion of the program. This information must be made readily available to all interested parties.

7.03 *Accuracy in Teaching*

(a) Psychologists take reasonable steps to ensure that course syllabi are accurate regarding the subject matter to be covered, bases for evaluating progress, and the nature of course experiences. This standard does not preclude an instructor from modifying course content or requirements when the instructor considers it pedagogically necessary or desirable, so long as students are made aware of these modifications in a manner that enables them to fulfill course requirements. (See also Standard 5.01, Avoidance of False or Deceptive Statements.)

(b) When engaged in teaching or training, psychologists present psychological information accurately. (See also Standard 2.03, Maintaining Competence.)

7.04 Student Disclosure of Personal Information

Psychologists do not require students or supervisees to disclose personal information in course- or program-related activities, either orally or in writing, regarding sexual history, history of abuse and neglect, psychological treatment, and relationships with parents, peers, and spouses or significant others except if (1) the program or training facility has clearly identified this requirement in its admissions and program materials or (2) the information is necessary to evaluate or obtain assistance for students whose personal problems could reasonably be judged to be preventing them from performing their training- or professionally related activities in a competent manner or posing a threat to the students or others.

7.05 Mandatory Individual or Group Therapy

(a) When individual or group therapy is a program or course requirement, psychologists responsible for that program allow students in undergraduate and graduate programs the option of selecting such therapy from practitioners unaffiliated with the program. (See also Standard 7.02, Descriptions of Education and Training Programs.)

(b) Faculty who are or are likely to be responsible for evaluating students' academic performance do not themselves provide that therapy. (See also Standard 3.05, Multiple Relationships.)

7.06 Assessing Student and Supervisee Performance

(a) In academic and supervisory relationships, psychologists establish a timely and specific process for providing feedback to students and supervisees. Information regarding the process is provided to the student at the beginning of supervision.

(b) Psychologists evaluate students and supervisees on the basis of their actual performance on relevant and established program requirements.

7.07 Sexual Relationships With Students and Supervisees

Psychologists do not engage in sexual relationships with students or supervisees who are in their department, agency, or training center or over whom psychologists have or are likely to have evaluative authority. (See also Standard 3.05, Multiple Relationships.)

8. Research and Publication

8.01 Institutional Approval

When institutional approval is required, psychologists provide accurate information about their research proposals and obtain approval prior to conducting the research. They conduct the research in accordance with the approved research protocol.

8.02 Informed Consent to Research

(a) When obtaining informed consent as required in Standard 3.10, Informed Consent, psychologists inform participants about (1) the purpose of the research, expected duration, and procedures; (2) their right to decline to participate and to withdraw from the research once participation has begun; (3) the foreseeable consequences of declining or withdrawing; (4) reasonably foreseeable factors that may be expected to influence their willingness to participate such as potential risks, discomfort, or adverse effects; (5) any prospective research benefits; (6) limits of confidentiality; (7) incentives for participation; and (8) whom to contact for questions about the research and research participants' rights. They provide opportunity for the prospective participants to ask questions and receive answers. (See also Standards 8.03, Informed Consent for Recording Voices and Images in Research; 8.05, Dispensing With Informed Consent for Research; and 8.07, Deception in Research.)

(b) Psychologists conducting intervention research involving the use of experimental treatments clarify to participants at the outset of the research (1) the experimental nature of the treatment; (2) the services that will or will not be available to the control group(s) if appropriate; (3) the means by which assignment to treatment and control groups will be made; (4) available treatment alternatives if an individual does not wish to participate in the research or wishes to withdraw once a study has begun; and (5) compensation for or monetary costs of participating including, if appropriate, whether reimbursement from the participant or a third-party payor will be sought. (See also Standard 8.02a, Informed Consent to Research.)

8.03 *Informed Consent for Recording Voices and Images in Research*

Psychologists obtain informed consent from research participants prior to recording their voices or images for data collection unless (1) the research consists solely of naturalistic observations in public places, and it is not anticipated that the recording will be used in a manner that could cause personal identification or harm, or (2) the research design includes deception, and consent for the use of the recording is obtained during debriefing. (See also Standard 8.07, Deception in Research.)

8.04 *Client/Patient, Student, and Subordinate Research Participants*

(a) When psychologists conduct research with clients/patients, students, or subordinates as participants, psychologists take steps to protect the prospective participants from adverse consequences of declining or withdrawing from participation.

(b) When research participation is a course requirement or an opportunity for extra credit, the prospective participant is given the choice of equitable alternative activities.

8.05 *Dispensing With Informed Consent for Research*

Psychologists may dispense with informed consent only (1) where research would not reasonably be assumed to create distress or harm and involves (a) the study of normal educational practices, curricula, or classroom management methods conducted in educational settings; (b) only anonymous questionnaires, naturalistic observations, or archival research for which disclosure of responses would not place participants at risk of criminal or civil liability or damage their financial standing, employability, or reputation, and confidentiality is protected; or (c) the study of factors related to job or organization effectiveness conducted in organizational settings for which there is no risk to participants' employability, and confidentiality is protected or (2) where otherwise permitted by law or federal or institutional regulations.

8.06 *Offering Inducements for Research Participation*

(a) Psychologists make reasonable efforts to avoid offering excessive or inappropriate financial or other inducements for research participation when such inducements are likely to coerce participation.

(b) When offering professional services as an inducement for research participation, psychologists clarify the nature of the services, as well as the risks, obligations, and limitations. (See also Standard 6.05, Barter With Clients/Patients.)

8.07 *Deception in Research*

(a) Psychologists do not conduct a study involving deception unless they have determined that the use of deceptive techniques is justified by the study's significant prospective scientific, educational, or applied value and that effective nondeceptive alternative procedures are not feasible.

(b) Psychologists do not deceive prospective participants about research that is reasonably expected to cause physical pain or severe emotional distress.

(c) Psychologists explain any deception that is an integral feature of the design and conduct of an experiment to participants as early as is feasible, preferably at the conclusion of their participation, but no later than at the conclusion of the data collection, and permit participants to withdraw their data. (See also Standard 8.08, Debriefing.)

8.08 Debriefing

(a) Psychologists provide a prompt opportunity for participants to obtain appropriate information about the nature, results, and conclusions of the research, and they take reasonable steps to correct any misconceptions that participants may have of which the psychologists are aware.

(b) If scientific or humane values justify delaying or withholding this information, psychologists take reasonable measures to reduce the risk of harm.

(c) When psychologists become aware that research procedures have harmed a participant, they take reasonable steps to minimize the harm.

8.09 Humane Care and Use of Animals in Research

(a) Psychologists acquire, care for, use, and dispose of animals in compliance with current federal, state, and local laws and regulations, and with professional standards.

(b) Psychologists trained in research methods and experienced in the care of laboratory animals supervise all procedures involving animals and are responsible for ensuring appropriate consideration of their comfort, health, and humane treatment.

(c) Psychologists ensure that all individuals under their supervision who are using animals have received instruction in research methods and in the care, maintenance, and handling of the species being used, to the extent appropriate to their role. (See also Standard 2.05, Delegation of Work to Others.)

(d) Psychologists make reasonable efforts to minimize the discomfort, infection, illness, and pain of animal subjects.

(e) Psychologists use a procedure subjecting animals to pain, stress, or privation only when an alternative procedure is unavailable and the goal is justified by its prospective scientific, educational, or applied value.

(f) Psychologists perform surgical procedures under appropriate anesthesia and follow techniques to avoid infection and minimize pain during and after surgery.

(g) When it is appropriate that an animal's life be terminated, psychologists proceed rapidly, with an effort to minimize pain and in accordance with accepted procedures.

8.10 Reporting Research Results

(a) Psychologists do not fabricate data. (See also Standard 5.01a, Avoidance of False or Deceptive Statements.)

(b) If psychologists discover significant errors in their published data, they take reasonable steps to correct such errors in a correction, retraction, erratum, or other appropriate publication means.

8.11 Plagiarism

Psychologists do not present portions of another's work or data as their own, even if the other work or data source is cited occasionally.

8.12 Publication Credit

(a) Psychologists take responsibility and credit, including authorship credit, only for work they have actually performed or to which they have substantially contributed. (See also Standard 8.12b, Publication Credit.)

(b) Principal authorship and other publication credits accurately reflect the relative scientific or professional contributions of the individuals involved, regardless of their relative status. Mere possession of an institutional position, such as department chair, does not justify authorship credit. Minor contributions to the research or to the writing for publications are acknowledged appropriately, such as in footnotes or in an introductory statement.

(c) Except under exceptional circumstances, a student is listed as principal author on any multiple-authored article that is substantially based on the student's doctoral dissertation. Faculty advisors discuss publication credit with students as early as feasible and throughout the research and publication process as appropriate. (See also Standard 8.12b, Publication Credit.)

8.13 Duplicate Publication of Data

Psychologists do not publish, as original data, data that have been previously published. This does not preclude republishing data when they are accompanied by proper acknowledgment.

8.14 Sharing Research Data for Verification

(a) After research results are published, psychologists do not withhold the data on which their conclusions are based from other competent professionals who seek to verify the substantive claims through reanalysis and who intend to use such data only for that purpose, provided that the confidentiality of the participants can be protected and unless legal rights concerning proprietary data preclude their release. This does not preclude psychologists from requiring that such individuals or groups be responsible for costs associated with the provision of such information.

(b) Psychologists who request data from other psychologists to verify the substantive claims through reanalysis may use shared data only for the declared purpose. Requesting psychologists obtain prior written agreement for all other uses of the data.

8.15 Reviewers

Psychologists who review material submitted for presentation, publication, grant, or research proposal review respect the confidentiality of and the proprietary rights in such information of those who submitted it.

9. Assessment

9.01 Bases for Assessments

(a) Psychologists base the opinions contained in their recommendations, reports, and diagnostic or evaluative statements, including forensic testimony, on information and techniques sufficient to substantiate their findings. (See also Standard 2.04, Bases for Scientific and Professional Judgments.)

(b) Except as noted in 9.01c, psychologists provide opinions of the psychological characteristics of individuals only after they have conducted an examination of the individuals adequate to support their statements or conclusions. When, despite reasonable efforts, such an examination is not practical, psychologists document the efforts they made and the result of those efforts, clarify the probable impact of their limited information on the reliability and validity of their opinions, and appropriately limit the nature and extent of their conclusions or recommendations. (See also Standards 2.01, Boundaries of Competence, and 9.06, Interpreting Assessment Results.)

(c) When psychologists conduct a record review or provide consultation or supervision and an individual examination is not warranted or necessary for the opinion, psychologists explain this and the sources of information on which they based their conclusions and recommendations.

9.02 Use of Assessments

(a) Psychologists administer, adapt, score, interpret, or use assessment techniques, interviews, tests, or instruments in a manner and for purposes that are appropriate in light of the research on or evidence of the usefulness and proper application of the techniques.

(b) Psychologists use assessment instruments whose validity and reliability have been established for use with members of the population tested. When such validity or reliability has not been established, psychologists describe the strengths and limitations of test results and interpretation.

(c) Psychologists use assessment methods that are appropriate to an individual's language preference and competence, unless the use of an alternative language is relevant to the assessment issues.

9.03 Informed Consent in Assessments

(a) Psychologists obtain informed consent for assessments, evaluations, or diagnostic services, as described in Standard 3.10, Informed Consent, except when (1) testing is mandated by law or governmental regulations; (2) informed consent is implied because testing is conducted as a routine educational, institutional, or organizational activity (e.g., when participants voluntarily agree to assessment when applying for a job); or (3) one purpose of the testing is to evaluate decisional capacity. Informed consent includes an explanation of the nature and purpose of the assessment, fees, involvement of third parties, and limits of confidentiality and sufficient opportunity for the client/patient to ask questions and receive answers.

(b) Psychologists inform persons with questionable capacity to consent or for whom testing is mandated by law or governmental regulations about the nature and purpose of the proposed assessment services, using language that is reasonably understandable to the person being assessed.

(c) Psychologists using the services of an interpreter obtain informed consent from the client/patient to use that interpreter, ensure that confidentiality of test results and test security are maintained, and include in their recommendations, reports, and diagnostic or evaluative statements, including forensic testimony, discussion of any limitations on the data obtained. (See also Standards 2.05, Delegation of Work to Others; 4.01, Maintaining Confidentiality; 9.01, Bases for Assessments; 9.06, Interpreting Assessment Results; and 9.07, Assessment by Unqualified Persons.)

9.04 Release of Test Data

(a) The term *test data* refers to raw and scaled scores, client/patient responses to test questions or stimuli, and psychologists' notes and recordings concerning client/patient statements and behavior during an examination. Those portions of test materials that include client/patient responses are included in the definition of *test data*. Pursuant to a client/patient release, psychologists provide test data to the client/patient or other persons identified in the release. Psychologists may refrain from releasing test data to protect a client/patient or others from substantial harm or misuse or misrepresentation of the data or the test, recognizing that in many instances release of confidential information under these circumstances is regulated by law. (See also Standard 9.11, Maintaining Test Security.)

(b) In the absence of a client/patient release, psychologists provide test data only as required by law or court order.

9.05 Test Construction

Psychologists who develop tests and other assessment techniques use appropriate psychometric procedures and current scientific or professional knowledge for test design, standardization, validation, reduction or elimination of bias, and recommendations for use.

9.06 Interpreting Assessment

Results When interpreting assessment results, including automated interpretations, psychologists take into account the purpose of the assessment as well as the various test factors, test-taking abilities, and other characteristics of the person being assessed, such as situational, personal, linguistic, and cultural differences, that might affect psychologists' judgments or reduce the accuracy of their interpretations. They indicate any significant limitations of their interpretations. (See also Standards 2.01b and c, Boundaries of Competence, and 3.01, Unfair Discrimination.)

9.07 Assessment by Unqualified Persons

Psychologists do not promote the use of psychological assessment techniques by unqualified persons, except when such use is conducted for training purposes with appropriate supervision. (See also Standard 2.05, Delegation of Work to Others.)

9.08 Obsolete Tests and Outdated Test Results

(a) Psychologists do not base their assessment or intervention decisions or recommendations on data or test results that are outdated for the current purpose.

(b) Psychologists do not base such decisions or recommendations on tests and measures that are obsolete and not useful for the current purpose.

9.09 Test Scoring and Interpretation Services

(a) Psychologists who offer assessment or scoring services to other professionals accurately describe the purpose, norms, validity, reliability, and applications of the procedures and any special qualifications applicable to their use.

(b) Psychologists select scoring and interpretation services (including automated services) on the basis of evidence of the validity of the program and procedures as well as on other appropriate considerations. (See also Standard 2.01b and c, Boundaries of Competence.)

(c) Psychologists retain responsibility for the appropriate application, interpretation, and use of assessment instruments, whether they score and interpret such tests themselves or use automated or other services.

9.10 Explaining Assessment Results

Regardless of whether the scoring and interpretation are done by psychologists, by employees or assistants, or by automated or other outside services, psychologists take reasonable steps to ensure that explanations of results are given to the individual or designated representative unless the nature of the relationship precludes provision of an explanation of results (such as in some organizational consulting, preemployment or security screenings, and forensic evaluations), and this fact has been clearly explained to the person being assessed in advance.

9.11. Maintaining Test Security

The term *test materials* refers to manuals, instruments, protocols, and test questions or stimuli and does not include *test data* as defined in Standard 9.04, Release of Test Data. Psychologists make reasonable efforts to maintain the integrity and security of test materials and other assessment techniques consistent with law and contractual obligations, and in a manner that permits adherence to this Ethics Code.

10. Therapy

10.01 Informed Consent to Therapy

(a) When obtaining informed consent to therapy as required in Standard 3.10, Informed Consent, psychologists inform clients/patients as early as is feasible in the therapeutic relationship about the nature and anticipated course of therapy, fees, involvement of third parties, and limits of confidentiality and provide sufficient opportunity for the client/patient to ask questions and receive answers. (See also Standards 4.02, Discussing the Limits of Confidentiality, and 6.04, Fees and Financial Arrangements.)

(b) When obtaining informed consent for treatment for which generally recognized techniques and procedures have not been established, psychologists inform their clients/patients of the developing nature of the treatment, the potential risks involved, alternative treatments that may be available, and the voluntary nature of their participation. (See also Standards 2.01e, Boundaries of Competence, and 3.10, Informed Consent.)

(c) When the therapist is a trainee and the legal responsibility for the treatment provided resides with the supervisor, the client/patient, as part of the informed consent procedure, is informed that the therapist is in training and is being supervised and is given the name of the supervisor.

10.02 Therapy Involving Couples or Families

(a) When psychologists agree to provide services to several persons who have a relationship (such as spouses, significant others, or parents and children), they take reasonable steps to clarify at the outset (1) which of the individuals are clients/patients and (2) the relationship the psychologist will have with each person. This clarification includes the psychologist's role and the probable uses of the services provided or the information obtained. (See also Standard 4.02, Discussing the Limits of Confidentiality.)

(b) If it becomes apparent that psychologists may be called on to perform potentially conflicting roles (such as family therapist and then witness for one party in divorce proceedings), psychologists take reasonable steps to clarify and modify, or withdraw from, roles appropriately. (See also Standard 3.05c, Multiple Relationships.)

10.03 Group Therapy

When psychologists provide services to several persons in a group setting, they describe at the outset the roles and responsibilities of all parties and the limits of confidentiality.

10.04 Providing Therapy to Those Served by Others

In deciding whether to offer or provide services to those already receiving mental health services elsewhere, psychologists carefully consider the treatment issues and the potential client's/patient's welfare. Psychologists discuss these issues with the client/patient or another legally authorized person on behalf of the client/patient in order to minimize the risk of confusion and conflict, consult with the other service providers when appropriate, and proceed with caution and sensitivity to the therapeutic issues.

10.05 Sexual Intimacies

With Current Therapy Clients/Patients Psychologists do not engage in sexual intimacies with current therapy clients/patients.

10.06 Sexual Intimacies With Relatives or Significant Others of Current Therapy Clients/Patients

Psychologists do not engage in sexual intimacies with individuals they know to be close relatives, guardians, or significant others of current clients/patients. Psychologists do not terminate therapy to circumvent this standard.

10.07 Therapy With Former Sexual Partners

Psychologists do not accept as therapy clients/patients persons with whom they have engaged in sexual intimacies.

10.08 Sexual Intimacies With Former Therapy Clients/Patients

(a) Psychologists do not engage in sexual intimacies with former clients/patients for at least two years after cessation or termination of therapy.

(b) Psychologists do not engage in sexual intimacies with former clients/patients even after a two-year interval except in the most unusual circumstances. Psychologists who engage in such activity after the two years following cessation or termination of therapy and of having no sexual contact with the former client/patient bear the burden of demonstrating that there has been no exploitation, in light of all relevant factors, including (1) the amount of time that has passed since therapy terminated; (2) the nature, duration, and intensity of the therapy; (3) the circumstances of termination; (4) the client's/patient's personal history; (5) the client's/patient's current mental status; (6) the likelihood of adverse impact on the client/patient; and (7) any statements or actions made by the therapist during the course of therapy suggesting or inviting the possibility of a posttermination sexual or romantic relationship with the client/patient. (See also Standard 3.05, Multiple Relationships.)

10.09 Interruption of Therapy

When entering into employment or contractual relationships, psychologists make reasonable efforts to provide for orderly and appropriate resolution of responsibility for client/patient care in the event that the employment or contractual relationship ends, with paramount consideration given to the welfare of the client/patient. (See also Standard 3.12, Interruption of Psychological Services.)

10.10 Terminating Therapy

(a) Psychologists terminate therapy when it becomes reasonably clear that the client/patient no longer needs the service, is not likely to benefit, or is being harmed by continued service.

(b) Psychologists may terminate therapy when threatened or otherwise endangered by the client/patient or another person with whom the client/patient has a relationship.

(c) Except where precluded by the actions of clients/patients or third-party payors, prior to termination psychologists provide pretermination counseling and suggest alternative service providers as appropriate.

See accompanying Web site for additional materials.

This version of the APA Ethics Code was adopted by the American Psychological Association's Council of Representatives during its meeting, August 21, 2002, and became effective June 1, 2003. Inquiries concerning the substance or interpretation of the APA Ethics Code should be addressed to the Director, Office of Ethics, American Psychological Association, 750 First Street, NE, Washington, DC 20002-4242. The Ethics Code and information regarding the Code can be found on the APA Web site, http://www.apa.org/ethics. The standards in this Ethics Code will be used to adjudicate complaints brought concerning alleged conduct occurring on or after the effective date. Complaints regarding conduct occurring prior to the effective date will be adjudicated on the basis of the version of the Ethics Code that was in effect at the time the conduct occurred.

The APA has previously published its Ethics Code as follows:

American Psychological Association. (1953). *Ethical standards of psychologists.* Washington, DC: Author.

American Psychological Association. (1959). Ethical standards of psychologists. *American Psychologist, 14,* 279–282.

American Psychological Association. (1963). Ethical standards of psychologists. *American Psychologist, 18,* 56–60.

American Psychological Association. (1968). Ethical standards of psychologists. *American Psychologist, 23,* 357–361.

American Psychological Association. (1977, March). Ethical standards of psychologists. *APA Monitor,* 22–23.

American Psychological Association. (1979). *Ethical standards of psychologists.* Washington, DC: Author.

American Psychological Association. (1981). Ethical principles of psychologists. *American Psychologist, 36,* 633–638.

American Psychological Association. (1990). Ethical principles of psychologists (Amended June 2, 1989). *American Psychologist, 45,* 390–395.

American Psychological Association. (1992). Ethical principles of psychologists and code of conduct. *American Psychologist, 47,* 1597–1611.

Request copies of the APA's Ethical Principles of Psychologists and Code of Conduct from the APA Order Department, 750 First Street, NE, Washington, DC 20002-4242, or phone (202) 336-5510.

104 PRIVACY, CONFIDENTIALITY, AND PRIVILEGE

Gerald P. Koocher

The area of confidentiality-related ethical problems is complicated by common misunderstandings about three frequently used terms: *privacy, confidentiality,* and *privilege.* At least part of the confusion is related to the fact that in particular situations these terms may have narrow legal meanings that are quite distinct from broader traditional meanings attached by psychologists or other mental health practitioners.

- *Privacy* (a constitutional guaranty and personal value addressed in the Fourth, Fifth, and Fourteenth Amendments to the U.S. Constitution) is basically the right of individuals to decide about how much of their thoughts, feelings, or personal data should be shared with others. Privacy has often been considered essential to ensure human dignity and freedom of self-determination and to preclude unreasonable governmental intrusions into individuals' lives.

- *Confidentiality* refers to a general standard of professional conduct that obliges one not to discuss information about a client with anyone else, absent proper authorization. Confidentiality may also be based in statutes (i.e., laws enacted by legislatures such as HIPAA), regulations (i.e., rules promulgated by the executive branch of government), or case law (i.e., interpretations of laws by the courts). When cited as an ethical principle, confidentiality implies an explicit contract or promise not to reveal anything about a client, except under certain circumstances agreed to by both parties.
- *Privilege* and *confidentiality* are oft-confused concepts, and the distinction between them is critical to understanding a variety of ethical problems. *Privilege* (or privileged communication) is a legal term describing certain specific types of relationships that enjoy protection from disclosure in legal proceedings. Privilege is granted by law and belongs to the client in the relationship. Normal court rules provide that anything relative and material to the issue at hand can and should be admitted as evidence. Where privilege exists, however, the client is protected from having the covered communications revealed without explicit permission. If the client waives this privilege, the psychologist may be compelled to testify on the nature and specifics of the material discussed. The client is usually not permitted to waive privilege selectively. In most courts, once a waiver is given, it covers all of the relevant privileged material.
- *Privilege is not automatic.* Traditionally, privilege has been extended to attorney client, husband-wife, physician-patient, and priest-penitent relationships. Some jurisdictions now extend privilege to psychologist-client or psychotherapist-client relationships, but the actual laws vary widely, and it is incumbent on each psychologist to know the statutes in force for his or her practice. (In 1996, the U.S. Supreme Court took up this issue based on conflicting rulings in different federal appellate court districts in the case of *Jaffe v. Redmond* and upheld privilege between a psychotherapist/social worker and her client.)

BREACHING CONFIDENTIALITY

No practitioners can make a convincing case for absolute confidentiality. That is to say, many situations might legally or ethically require disclosure of otherwise confidential material.

- *Waivers:* The most common situation for disclosure of confidential mental health information occurs when a client authorizes the release of information to others.
- *Mandated reporting:* All states and Canadian provinces have laws requiring that certain professionals who might be expected to encounter child abuse (e.g., physicians, nurses, schoolteachers, psychologists, social workers) report their "knowledge" or "reasonable suspicion" to governmental authorities. Some jurisdictions also mandate reporting suspected abuse of handicapped, elderly, or "dependent" individuals. Legislatures have enacted these statutes because protection of otherwise vulnerable individuals is deemed good public policy. Although such mandates preempt professional discretion, they also protect professionals reporting in good faith from suit for defamation. Details of the specific mandates vary by jurisdiction. In some countries there are no reporting mandates.
- *Danger to self:* Clinicians may generally disclose confidential data necessary to hospitalize or otherwise protect clients who are imminently dangerous to themselves (e.g., client status and risk information).
- *Danger to others:* When clients give clinicians reason to believe that they intend to kill or otherwise harm others, disclosure necessary to detain or hospitalize the client may be appropriate. In addition, if the intended targets of violence are identified, the clinician may be obligated to take steps to protect the victims (e.g., by notifying the authorities, the intended victims, or both).
- *Legal or regulatory actions:* If a client sues a clinician or files a licensing board or ethics complaint, the case cannot move forward unless the client releases the practitioner from any confidentiality obligations that might prevent an adequate defense. In addition, a client who has not paid his or her bill may legitimately be taken to court for collection,

even though doing so would make his or her status as a client public information. In all of these circumstances, caution and client notification of the potential consequences should precede any breach of confidence.

- *Other statutory requirements:* In most jurisdictions, courts can compel disclosure of otherwise confidential information under various circumstances. For example, parents' mental health records may be open to the court during child custody disputes in some states, but not in others.

KEY BEHAVIORS FOR AVOIDING PROBLEMS

- Before disclosing information obtained in the course of a professional relationship, check the applicable law in your practice jurisdiction.
- Alert clients to limitations on confidentiality at the outset of the professional relationship, and document delivery of this notice in writing, if possible. If you have initially failed to do so, but realize that the direction a conversation is taking may lead to a disclosure action, interrupt the client and warn about limitations of confidentiality at that point.
- Document any incidence of clear or ambiguous client risk (e.g., abuse or dangerousness), noting whether or not action was taken with rationales.

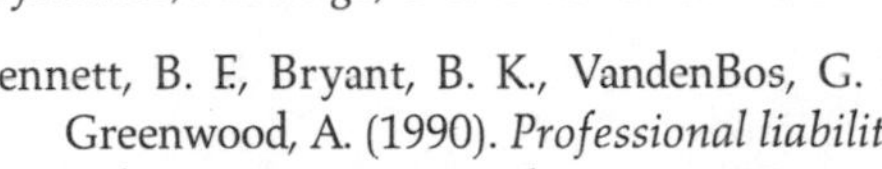

References, Readings, & Internet Sites

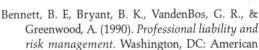

Bennett, B. E, Bryant, B. K., VandenBos, G. R., & Greenwood, A. (1990). *Professional liability and risk management.* Washington, DC: American Psychological Association.

Bersoff, D. N. (Ed.). (2003). *Ethical conflicts in psychology* (3rd ed.). Washington, DC: American Psychological Association.

Boruch, R. E, Dennis, M., & Cecil, J. S. (1996). Fifty years of empirical research on privacy and confidentiality in research settings. In B. H. Stanley, J. E. Sieber, & G. B. Melton (Eds.), *Research ethics: A psychological approach.* Lincoln: University of Nebraska Press.

Burke, C. A. (1995). Until death do us part: An exploration into confidentiality following the death of a client. *Professional Psychology: Research and Practice, 26,* 278–280.

Electronic Privacy Information Center. (n.d.). Home page. Retrieved 2004 from http://www.epic.org

Federal Trade Commission. (n.d.). Privacy page. Retrieved 2004 from http://www.ftc.gov/privacy

Gustafson, K. E., & McNamara, J. R. (1987). Confidentiality with minor clients: Issues and guidelines for therapists. *Professional Psychology, 18,* 503–508.

Jaffe v. Redmond, 116 S. Ct., 64 L.W 4490 (June 13, 1996).

Kalichman, S. C. (1993). *Mandated reporting of suspected child abuse: Ethics, law, and policy.* Washington, DC: American Psychological Association.

Koocher, C. I., & Keith-Spiegel, P C. (1998). *Ethics in psychology: Professional standards and cases* (2nd ed.). New York: Oxford University Press.

Legal Definitions. (n.d.). Online legal dictionary. Retrieved 2004 from http://www.legal-definitions.com

Miller, D. J., & Thelan, M. (1986). Knowledge and beliefs about confidentiality in psychotherapy. *Professional Psychology, 17,* 15–19.

Muehleman, T., Pickens, B. K., & Robinson, E (1985). Informing clients about limits in confidentiality, risks, and their rights: Is self-disclosure inhibited? *Professional Psychology, 16,* 385–397.

National Institutes of Health. (n.d.). Certificate of Confidentiality page. Retrieved 2004 from http://grants1.nih.gov/grants/policy/coc

Pope, K. S. (n.d.). Home page. Retrieved 2004 from http://www.kspope.com

Pope, K. S., & Vasquez, M. J. T. (1998). *Ethics in psychotherapy and counseling: A practical guide for psychologists* (2nd ed.). San Francisco: Jossey-Bass.

Privacy Rights Clearinghouse. (n.d.). Home page. Retrieved 2004 from http://www.privacyrights.org

Smith-Bell, M., & Winslade, W. J. (1994). Privacy, confidentiality, and privilege in psychotherapeutic relationships. *American Journal of Orthopsychiatry, 64,* 180–193.

Taube, D., & Elwork, A. (1990). Researching the effects of confidentiality law on patients' self-disclosures. *Professional Psychology, 21,* 72–75.

Related Topics

Chapter 127, "Basic Elements of Consent"
Chapter 128, "Basic Elements of Release Forms"
Chapter 129, "Prototype Mental Health Records"

105 INVOLUNTARY PSYCHIATRIC HOSPITALIZATION (CIVIL COMMITMENT)

Adult and Child

Stuart A. Anfang & Paul S. Appelbaum

ADULT

History

The state's power to hospitalize involuntarily is based on a combination of two rationales: *parens patriae* (the state caring for those incapable of caring for themselves) and "police power" (the state's obligation to protect the public safety).

In 18th- and early 19th-century America, there was little formal legal regulation of psychiatric hospitalization. As state hospitals developed in the mid-19th century, legislatures began to write statutes that were soon extended to private institutions. The rationale for commitment was treatment oriented, hospitalizing mentally ill persons who were deemed to be in need of care. Procedures by the end of the 19th century often included judicial hearings and occasionally jury trials.

In the early to mid-20th century, several states moved away from judicial procedures, attempting to make initial commitment easier and quicker, and promoting a model primarily of medical decision making. By the 1960s, opponents began to question the legitimacy of psychiatric diagnosis, the effectiveness of long-term hospitalization, and the right of the state to force unwanted treatment. By the late 1960s and early 1970s, states moved to dangerousness-based criteria for civil commitment, permitting the involuntary hospitalization of only those patients who were dangerous to themselves or to others. Several court decisions, led by a 1972 federal district court decision in Wisconsin (*Lessard v. Schmidt*), endorsed dangerousness criteria as the proper model for civil commitment.

A 1977 U.S. Supreme Court decision (*O'Connor v. Donaldson*) appeared to endorse dangerousness-based criteria for commitment, although the Court did not explicitly reject a need-for-treatment model. By the end of the 1970s, every state adopted dangerousness-based criteria for involuntary hospitalization, typically with judicial procedures and protections similar to criminal proceedings.

Criteria

The dangerousness-based criteria vary across states, but they typically require (1) the presence of mental illness (in many states this does not include mental retardation, dementia, or substance abuse, in the absence of other psychiatric illness) and (2) dangerousness.

Dangerousness typically includes (a) danger to self (physical harm); (b) danger to others (physical harm, not usually psychological harm or harm to property); or (c) grave disability (severe inability to care for one's minimal survival needs in the community). There is variability across states regarding the definition of dangerousness—specifically, how imminent or overt the risk of harm must be. Some court decisions and statutes require that involuntary hospitalization be the "least restrictive alternative" before allowing a commitment, raising a question of whether the state is obligated to create less restrictive alternatives, such as community residences. The creation of such alternatives may be required in some circumstances by the U.S. Supreme Court's decision in *Olmstead v. L.C.* (1999), though such requirements may be limited by constraints on financial and programmatic resources.

In recent years, several states have broadened the definition of dangerousness, often expanding the "grave disability" standard to include the prospect of severe deterioration leading to predicted dangerousness. Other states have expanded their commitment criteria to include incompetence, disabling illness, or need for treatment. Future litigation may challenge the constitutionality of these statutes, which appear to move away from strict dangerousness criteria. Clinicians should be familiar with the statutory criteria in their jurisdiction, as well as the relevant regulations and court decisions (case law) regarding civil commitment.

Critiques of the dangerousness standard usually include one or more of three basic arguments: (1) the current system makes it difficult to obtain involuntary treatment for patients who are not overtly dangerous but are desperately in need of care; (2) dangerousness is notoriously difficult for clinicians to predict accurately; and (3) basing commitment on dangerousness, particularly dangerousness to others, alters the character of the mental health system, shifting its mission from providing treatment to a quasi-police function.

Despite considerable and often impassioned debate, the empirical data generally suggest that, in practice, more restrictive commitment criteria appear to have little impact on the qualitative and quantitative characteristics of the civilly committed population as a whole. The system appears to allow involuntary hospitalization for those mentally ill patients in need of treatment, regardless of the precise criteria of the dangerousness-based standards. The "grave disability" standard—or the inability to provide for one's basic survival needs in the community—typically allows for such clinical flexibility.

Procedures

In most states, civil commitment procedures include many of the protections associated with criminal trials. These often encompass such safeguards as timely notice of the allegations that may result in commitment; timely notice of due process rights, including the right to an attorney; the right to a timely judicial hearing, sometimes including the right to jury trial; the right to remain silent when examined by a psychiatrist or at trial; and placing on the state the burden of proving that the patient meets the commitment criteria. Jurisdictions differ in the standard of proof required, ranging from an intermediate "clear and convincing evidence" standard (the minimal constitutionally acceptable standard) to the more stringent "beyond a reasonable doubt" standard required for criminal prosecutions.

Nearly every state allows for emergency commitment based on a physician's or other mental health professional's certification of mental illness and dangerousness; this commitment can typically last from 48 hours to 10–14 days before requiring the scheduling of a judicial hearing for further commitment. Various jurisdictions also allow for emergency commitment based on a judge's order (bench commitment), the certification of a police officer, or approval of another designated official. For roughly 40 years, New York State has had a relatively unique statute allowing for commitment up to 60 days on the certification of two physicians, without a required judicial review; however, on admission every involuntary patient is assigned to a mental health attorney who will inform him or her of the right to an earlier appeal of the commitment and will represent him or her if necessary. A 1982 federal court of appeals decision (*Project Release v. Prevost*) upheld the constitutionality of this procedure, holding that patients' interests may be protected in a variety of acceptable ways.

All mental health clinicians who work with

potentially dangerous patients should be familiar with the commitment procedures and mechanisms within their jurisdictions. Attorneys familiar with mental health law can be an invaluable resource, as can forensically trained clinicians. Clinicians in all jurisdictions should be aware of the need to alert the patient to the limits of confidentiality—that clinical interview information may be disclosed in the judicial commitment hearing. Some states require such a warning and allow the patient the right to refuse to participate further.

In addition to describing the appropriate procedures and criteria, most state commitment statutes provide immunity to mental health clinicians who act in good faith when seeking to hospitalize a patient involuntarily. In all states, if the clinician can document a commitment decision based on appropriate clinical judgment within the professional standard of care, he or she can feel reasonably safe from malpractice liability for improper commitment (although actual verdicts will be based on the particular facts and circumstances of the situation). As with all complex and difficult clinical decisions, consultation with colleagues is often an important tool—both for guidance and for risk-management purposes.

Involuntary Outpatient Commitment

Over the past 20 years, involuntary outpatient commitment (IOC) has gained increasing attention as a possible alternative to inpatient commitment in systems with declining inpatient resources. The majority of states have laws explicitly permitting outpatient commitment, although there is considerable local and regional variation regarding how commonly the option is used.

The latest recommendations from the American Psychiatric Association (see Gerbasi, Bonnie, & Binder, 2000) regarding statutory guidelines for IOC include evidence that a person (1) suffers from a severe mental illness; (2) is likely, without treatment, to suffer a relapse that would render the patient a danger to self or others or unable to care for self in the foreseeable future; (3) is unlikely to seek or comply with needed treatment; and (4) has a reasonable prospect of responding to the proposed treatment. Many state legislatures have included several of these provisions when writing their statutes.

Outpatient commitment laws generally follow one of three basic patterns: (a) conditional release for involuntarily hospitalized patients; (b) "less restrictive" alternative to hospitalization for patients who meet inpatient commitment criteria; or (c) alternative for patients not meeting criteria for inpatient commitment, but at risk for severe decompensation without treatment. This last pattern, often called *preventive commitment* or *predicted deterioration*, has generated considerable debate because it is seen as a move further away from an "imminent dangerousness" standard toward a need-for-treatment approach.

Mental health clinicians should be familiar with the availability of IOC in their jurisdictions and with the range of possible options and resources. Even as state legislatures rush to write IOC statutes, considerable debate continues over the efficacy and utility of these outpatient commitment programs, with a limited but growing number of empirical studies.

CHILD

History

Constitutional due process rights for children in the juvenile justice system were first recognized by the U.S. Supreme Court in 1967 (In re *Gault*). Children were held to be entitled to due process protections similar to those of adults in criminal proceedings, including the right to counsel, the right to written notice of charges, the right to cross-examine witnesses, and the privilege against self-incrimination. At that time, the typical state voluntary psychiatric hospitalization statute allowed a parent or guardian to admit a minor for psychiatric treatment (on a physician's recommendation) without the minor's consent and without further administrative or judicial review. Building on *Gault*, several cases in North Carolina, Georgia, and Pennsylvania challenged the constitutionality of those statutes, contending that unwanted or troublesome children were being "dumped" in mental hospitals.

In 1979, the U.S. Supreme Court (*Parham v. JR*) upheld the right of a parent or guardian to admit a minor to a psychiatric hospital without a judicial hearing. The Court endorsed the need for a "neutral factfinder"—typically the admitting psychiatrist—to review the admission. Absent a finding of parental abuse or neglect, the Court assumed that parents act in their children's best interest and doubted that judges would be able to make better decisions than parents acting in collaboration with objective physicians. Many child-rights advocates viewed the decision as a major defeat, although individual states were free to enact statutes requiring greater protections and judicial oversight. In the 1980s, many commentators pointed to alarmingly high admission rates, especially in private for-profit psychiatric facilities, as evidence of a pattern in which troublesome juveniles without clear psychiatric illnesses were being hospitalized, often as an alternative to the juvenile justice system. As managed care transformed inpatient mental health care in the 1990s, this pattern decreased in frequency. Except in state facilities for severely ill children and adolescents, short-term hospitalization is the rule.

Criteria and Procedures

Given the relatively low constitutional "minimum" required under *Parham*, states have diverse approaches to the issue of child hospitalization. Involuntary civil commitment without the consent of a parent or guardian is extremely rare and typically follows guidelines similar to those for adult civil commitment. More common is the "voluntary" hospitalization by a parent or guardian (including a state social service agency) without the consent of the minor.

States range from the minimum of allowing a parent to admit a child without any administrative or judicial review to requiring a formal judicial hearing for all admissions with specified due process protections. Some states have more rigid regulations covering public psychiatric facilities and minors who are wards of the state. Typically, states require the presence of a mental illness needing treatment, the availability of such treatment through the hospital, and evidence that the hospital is the least restrictive setting available. The American Psychological Association and the American Academy of Child and Adolescent Psychiatry have issued suggested statutory guidelines.

Most states have provisions for the minor to appeal the hospitalization, requesting an adversarial judicial hearing. For adolescents between 13 and 18, states provide varying procedures, allowing minors of a certain age to sign in or out of a hospital voluntarily, without the approval of a parent or guardian. Mental health clinicians should be familiar with the statutory requirements and case law in their jurisdictions. Consultation with an attorney familiar with child mental health issues or a clinician with forensic expertise is helpful.

GENERAL CLINICAL ISSUES

- *Predicting dangerousness:* Clinicians should be familiar with relevant risk factors, base rates, and both external and internal factors that influence the potential for violence. Risks, resources, and benefits must be balanced in a clinically sensitive and sophisticated decision process. Consultation and corroborative clinical data are invaluable.
- *Maintaining a therapeutic alliance with a patient coerced to receive care:* Patients should be involved in the decision process as much as possible. As treatment restores the patient's ability to assess his or her own functioning, the patient and clinician can aim to shape the experience into one that enhances the patient's responsibility, self-respect, and therapeutic rapport.
- *Resolving conflicts between legal mandates and ethical imperatives in the commitment setting:* Whereas legal standards suggest a rigidly defined set of criteria, ethical and clinical imperatives often encourage the clinician to err on the side of caution. Clinicians must be sensitive to both factors and strive for a balanced, thoughtful approach to decision making in cases of involuntary hospitalization.

References & Readings 

American Academy of Child and Adolescent Psychiatry. (1987). *Child and adolescent psychiatric illness: Guidelines for treatment resources, quality assurances, peer review, and reimbursement*. Washington, DC: Author.

American Psychological Association. (1984). *A model act for the mental health treatment of minors*. Washington, DC: Author.

Appelbaum, P. S. (1994). *Almost a revolution: Mental health law and the limits of change*. New York: Oxford University Press.

Appelbaum, P. S., & Anfang, S. A. (1998). Civil commitment. In R. Michels (Ed.), *Psychiatry* (Vol. 3, Chapter 32). Philadelphia: Lippincott-Raven.

Bagby, R. M., & Atkinson, L. (1988). The effects of legislative reform on civil commitment rates: A critical analysis. *Behavioral Sciences and the Law, 6*, 45–62.

Brinich, P. M., Amaya, M., & Burlingame, W. V. (2002). Psychiatric commitment of children and adolescents. In D. H. Schetky & E. P. Benedek (Eds.), *Principles and practice of child and adolescent forensic psychiatry* (pp. 325–338). Washington, DC: American Psychiatric Press.

Gerbasi, J. B., Bonnie, R. J., & Binder, R. L. (2000). Resource document on mandatory outpatient treatment. *Journal of the American Academy of Psychiatry and the Law, 28*, 127–144.

Hiday, V. A. (2003). Outpatient commitment: The state of empirical research on its outcomes. *Psychology, Public Policy, and Law, 9*, 8–32.

Melton, G. B., Petrila, J., Poythress, N. G., & Slobogin, C. (1997). *Psychological evaluations for the courts: A handbook for mental health professionals and lawyers*. New York: Guilford Press.

Monahan, J., & Steadman, H. J. (Eds.). (1994). *Violence and mental disorder: Developments in risk assessment*. Chicago: University of Chicago Press.

Monahan, J., Steadman, H., Silver, E., Appelbaum, P. S., Robbins, P. C., Mulvey, E. P., et al. (2001). *Rethinking risk assessment: The MacArthur Study of Mental Disorder and Violence*. New York: Oxford University Press.

Parry, J. (1994). Survey of standards for extended involuntary commitment. Mental and *Physical Disability Law Reporter, 18*, 329–336.

Stromberg, C. D., & Stone, A. A. (1983). A model state law on civil commitment of the mentally ill. *Harvard Journal on Legislation, 20*, 275–396.

Warren, C. A. B. (1982). *Court of last resort: Mental illness and the law*. Chicago: University of Chicago Press.

Weithorn, L. A. (1988). Mental hospitalization of troublesome youth: An analysis of skyrocketing admission rates. *Stanford Law Review, 40*, 773–838.

Related Topic

Chapter 106, "Physical Restraint and Seclusion: Regulations and Standards"

106 PHYSICAL RESTRAINT AND SECLUSION
Regulations and Standards

Thomas P. Graf

Regulations and practice standards for the use of physical restraint and seclusion have changed since 1998. Federal legislation and standards for hospital and psychiatric facilities have increased patient protection from unnecessary restraint and seclusion, in particular for children and adolescents but also for adults. This chapter will review essential aspects of those regulations, the kinds of restraints that require the order of a licensed independent medical practitioner, and those that do not. These practice standards, as well as the ethical standard to provide effective treatment, should make it important to reduce the need for restraint and the conditions that contribute to it.

RECENT REGULATIONS AND CHANGES OF STANDARDS

Physical restraint and seclusion have been essential parts in reducing safety risks in violent and self-harming patients who are in psychiatric care. Restraints can be human (such as a therapeutic or protective hold), can involve use of mechanical devices (e.g., wrist restraint, jacket vest, or papoose), or can consist of sedating psychoactive drugs. Restraint or seclusion has been used not only for reducing imminent risk for harm to self or others but also for control, convenience, and retaliation. (For an overview of recent changes in laws and regulations in regard to restraint and seclusion, see also Luna, 2001). In 1987, the Nursing Home Reform Act was passed, which applies not only to the elderly but also to all mentally ill or developmentally delayed adults in long-term care that receive Medicare funding. Since then, freedom from unwarranted restraint has been one of the rights monitored in the oversight of care facilities. However, there was no federal or state monitoring of serious injury and death as a result of restraint and seclusion, especially in psychiatric inpatient or residential treatment. In 1998, the Hartford Courant released a five-part investigative report into the alarming number of restraint-related deaths that occurred in psychiatric treatment facilities across the United States (Weiss, Megan, Blint, & Altimari, 1998). The newspaper conducted a 50-state survey in mental health facilities, mental retardation facilities, and group homes, and it documented at least 142 deaths during the preceding decade, mostly through asphyxiation. This contributed to Congress's passing the Children's Health Act in October 1999, which legislated restrictions in the use of restraint and seclusion in residential treatment and all psychiatric facilities that receive federal or state funds like Medicaid (Children's Health Act, 2000). For children and adolescents, only personal restraint and seclusion are permitted and only in emergency situations to ensure the immediate physical safety of the resident or others. The use of both chemical and mechanical restraints is prohibited. Most other provisions in regard to restraint and seclusion have since been incorporated into other regulations, which will be discussed, as this Act was designed to be the minimal floor for further regulations and legislation in this area. Use of restraint and seclusion in correctional and educational settings, including schools, wilderness camps, or prisons, has not been regulated. Nevertheless, many school districts now have a restraint and seclusion policy, which typically stipulates that physical restraint or seclusion be used only if there is imminent danger to self or others, alternative and less restrictive containment has been tried but failed, staff has had training in safe restraint, and there are physician's orders for use of mechanical or chemical restraint while in seclusion. See Cambridge Public Schools (2002) for a sample restraint policy.

The Joint Commission on Accreditation of Healthcare Organizations (JCAHO) issues practice standards for health and psychiatric care facilities. In 1999, JCAHO issued restrictive and protective guidelines in regard to restraint and seclusion of patients of all ages. JCAHO does not investigate individual complaints and its oversight consists mostly of preannounced visits every three years. Nevertheless, implementation and documentation of compliance with JCAHO standards are necessary for all accredited organizations, thus leading to changes in practice.

In 2001, the Centers for Medicare & Medicaid Services (CMS), formerly called the Health Care Financing Administration (HCFA), released its interim final rule regarding restraint and seclusion (Health Care Financing Administration, 2001). This regulation applies to patients under the age of 21 who receive inpatient or residential psychiatric treatment. In contrast, JCAHO standards apply to any accredited medical setting in which emotional or behavioral problems require use of restraint, and the regulations apply to patients of all ages. CMS regulations apply only to psychiatric hospital or residential treatment facilities that receive Medicaid funds.

CMS Standards

What follows is a summary of the CMS standards in regard to restraint and seclusion (Health Care Financing Administration, 2001); exempt conditions of physical containment are also discussed.

- The restraint and seclusion policy of a facility has to be posted. Upon admission to a facility, the patient's guardian has to review the policy and indicate consent by signature.
- Restraint and seclusion can be used only to ensure the patient's safety or the safety of others during an emergency safety situation.
- Restraint and seclusion must end when the emergency safety situation is over.
- The least restrictive intervention should be used. Only a licensed independent practitioner (LIP—i.e., physician, nurse practitioner, or physician assistant, consistent with state law) may give the order for carrying out restraint or seclusion.
- A LIP must perform a face-to-face evaluation of the patient no more than one hour after the restraint or seclusion was initiated.
- Ongoing monitoring of the patient and evaluation of physical and psychological condition are required during seclusion or restraint and has to be documented.
- A LIP must conduct an in-person evaluation immediately after the patient is removed from restraint or seclusion.
- The patient's legal guardian must be notified of the situation that led to the use of restraint or seclusion as soon as possible.
- Two debriefing sessions have to be conducted after the use of restraint or seclusion. One of them is between the patient and the staff involved, and one is only for the staff involved.
- All deaths have to be reported to the regional CMS office.
- All staff must have appropriate training in the use of nonphysical interventions, the safe use of restraint and seclusion, identification of factors that lead to emergency situations, and CPR. Documentation of each staff member's training must be maintained and available for review by a state survey agency.

The following holding situations are not regarded physical restraint or needing a physician order:

- Briefly holding without undue force a patient for the purpose of comforting him or her.
- Holding a patient's hand or arm to safely escort him or her.

JCAHO Definitions and Standards

The JCAHO's regulation regarding restraint or seclusion for behavioral health reasons (furthermore, only called restraint or seclusion) apply whether the patient is in a behavioral health care (psychiatric hospital or residential treatment) or a general hospital setting. For example, if a patient on a postsurgical unit is restrained because he or she assaults another patient, the behavioral health standard applies (TX.7.1–TX.7.4; Joint Commission on Accreditation of Healthcare Organizations [JCAHO], 2002).

A second set of regulations applies to restraint or seclusion used for medical/surgical care reasons. That restraint aims at directly supporting medical healing, such as preventing a patient from trying to walk on an injured leg or preventing the removal of an IV or feeding tube (TX.7.5; JCAHO, 2002). The medical/surgical care standards will not be further discussed here as they are mostly relevant for nurses and physicians. Furthermore, there are more detailed standards regarding the medical assessment of patients during the process of restraint that are also not reviewed. See Orhon (2002) for a review of restraint standards from a nursing perspective. Orhon (2002) also compares JCAHO and CMS standards from a general perspective.

- *Restraint* is defined as the direct application of physical force to a person, with or without the individual's permission, with the purpose of restricting freedom of movement (JCAHO, 2002).
- *Seclusion* is defined as the involuntary confinement of a person in a locked room. It is less restrictive than physical restraints because it allows an individual to move about.
- Patients in restraint and/or seclusion require continuous personal monitoring through observation, and have to be assessed every 15 minutes for injury, health, psychological status, and readiness for the restraint or seclusion to be discontinued. A patient in a physical hold must have a second staff person observe the patient.
- The time limitations for an order for restraint or seclusion are: four hours for patients 18 and older, two hours for children 9 to 17, and one hour for children under 9.
- Prompt notification of the patient's family or guardian when restraint or seclusion is initiated. Extended episodes of restraint or seclusion (more than 12 hours) or multiple episodes (two or more in 24 hours) require notification of the organization's clinical leadership.
- For adults in long-term care and assisted living, the right to a restraint-free environment. Past deaths in long-term care during or after restraint were associated with mechanical and chemical restraints, used for long periods of time and without monitoring of the patient's well-being (U.S. General Accounting Office, 1999). The restraint standards aim at increasing dignity and independence in the long-term care population but are not reviewed here.

The JCAHO standards for restraint and seclusion (2002) do not apply to the following:

- The use of restraint associated with acute and postoperative medical or surgical care.
- Holding or physically redirecting a child, without the child's permission, for 30 minutes or less; staff involved in holding has to be trained in physical restraint and seclusion.
- Time-out, which consists of removing a child from the immediate environment and restricting him or her to an unlocked quiet room for 30 minutes or less in order to regain self-control. The child or adolescent may not be physically prevented from leaving the time-out area. These restrictions have to be consistent with the unit's rules and the patient's treatment plan.
- Physical escorts.
- The use of restraint with patients who are severely developmentally delayed and receive treatment through formal behavior management programs that target intractable, severely self-injurious, or injurious behaviors.
- The use of protective equipment such as helmets.
- Forensic restrictions and restrictions imposed by correction authorities for security pur-

poses. However, restraint or seclusion use related to the clinical care of a patient under forensic or correction restrictions is surveyed under these standards.

COMPARING CMS AND JCAHO STANDARDS

CMS requires continuous in-person monitoring only when patients are concurrently in restraint and seclusion, whereas JCAHO requires continuous monitoring when either restraint or seclusion is used as well. The CMS rule of face-to-face evaluation by an LIP within one hour of initiation of restraint or seclusion is more stringent than the JCAHO rule of evaluation within four hours. However, the JCAHO requires organizations to comply with the CMS rule because organizations must meet federal and state regulations in order to meet JCAHO's requirements.

Compared to the CMS standards, the JCAHO standards are more specific also in defining situations exempt from restraint and seclusion standards. This writer is not qualified to give legal advice about which standards may take precedent, and a qualified lawyer should be consulted if more clarification is needed. Furthermore, the reviewed CMS and JCAHO standards were current as of May 2004, but changes should be monitored as they are announced by CMS and JCAHO.

STAFF TRAINING

The JCAHO Standard TX 7.1.2—Staff Training and Competence (2002)—outlined requirements for competence and training of staff who conduct seclusion or restraint. These standards also comply with CMS standards. Direct care staff should be trained in and understand the following:

- The underlying causes of threatening behaviors exhibited by the patients they serve.
- Aggressive behavior that is related to a patient's medical condition and not related to his or her emotional condition—for example, threatening behavior that may result from delirium in fevers or from hypoglycemia.
- How their own behaviors can affect the behaviors of the patients they serve.
- The use of de-escalation, mediation, self-protection, and techniques, such as time-out.
- Signs of physical distress in patients who are being held, restrained, or secluded.
- Competence in the safe use of restraint, including physical holding techniques, takedown procedures, and the application and removal of mechanical restraints.

Because direct-care staff need to be able to de-escalate potentially aggressive patients, as well as apply physical control strategies safely, both JCAHO and CMS require training documentation. The cumulative training costs are considerable for care institutions—several institutes specialize in training individuals to become trainers in the institution they work in. Information about these institutes can be found on the Internet.

CLINICAL APPLICATION OF RESTRAINT AND SECLUSION

The reviewed seclusion and restraint standards have been mandated to protect patient's physical and mental integrity. However, effective reduction of restraint is also a clinical question about correct diagnosis and treatment of a patient's condition as it contributes to aggression against self or/and others. Luiselli, Bastien, and Putnam (1998) identified contextual variables associated with restraint and seclusion on a child and adolescent psychiatric inpatient unit. They found that staff-initiated physical contact often (34% of instances) precipitated restraint or seclusion and occurred in the context of patients' refusing to leave or enter the quiet room. They recommended, for that specific situation, the use of closed-door seclusion time-out to reduce the avoidance and repeated leaving that precipitated the restraints. Another finding was that mechanical restraints occurred for long periods of time, in the absence of clear release criteria. Luiselli et al. point out that "contingent procedures such as time-out and physical holding are most effective when they are of brief duration and include a differential release criterion. These guidelines ensure that the person who receives time-out learns to end the procedure rapidly by ceasing negative behaviors and achieving a more relaxed state" (p. 153). Luiselli et al. recommended that occurrence of restraint can be reduced through identification of patient-specific triggers. CMS and the JCAHO recommended that this be part of direct-care staff competence. However, Luiselli et al. emphasize linking diagnosis to treatment in a formal treatment plan; to assess the nature, contexts, and consequences of challenging behaviors; and to identify how seclusion or restraint can reduce aggression under specific circumstances. A behavioral assessment is one way to determine a patient's condition as it contributes to injurious behavior, which lends itself well to determine the effectiveness of restraint procedures. The use of restraints in the treatment of retractable, self-injurious behaviors in the developmentally delayed is exempt from JCAHO's restraint and seclusion standards. However, even there, an individualized treatment plan is ethically imperative, in that restraints should be used effectively to reduce the future need for restraints. Fisher, Piazza, Bowman, Hanley, and Adelinis (1997) describe the effective use of restraint fading to control injurious and self-injurious behaviors in such a manner in three profoundly mentally retarded individuals.

References, Readings, & Internet Sites

Cambridge Public Schools. (2002). Cambridge public schools physical restraint policy. Retrieved March 1, 2003, from Cambridge Public Schools Web site: http://www.cps.ci.cambridge.ma.us/pubinfo/PhysicalRestraint062002CSCP.doc

Children's Health Act, Public Law No. 106-310, § 3207, 114 Stat. 1178 (2000). Retrieved March 3, 2003, from http://www.access.gpo.gov

Fisher, W. W., Piazza, C. C., Bowman, L., Hanley, G., et al. (1997). Direct and collateral effects of restraints and restraint fading. *Journal of Applied Behavior Analysis, 30*(1), 105–120.

Health Care Financing Administration. Interim Final Rule, Use of Restraint and Seclusion in Psychiatric Residential Treatment Facilities Providing Inpatient Psychiatric Services to Individuals Under Age 21, 42 C.F.R. § 441 and 483 (2001). Retrieved March 2, 2003, from Federal Register, via GPO access: http://www.access.gpo.gov/su_docs/aces/aces140.html, select year 2001, 05/22/2001.

Joint Commission on Accreditation of Healthcare Organizations. (2002). *Comprehensive accreditation manual for hospitals: The official handbook.* Update 3, Refreshed core on CD-ROM. Oakbrook Terrace, IL: Joint Commission on Accreditation of Healthcare Organizations.

Luiselli, J., Bastien, J., & Putnam, R. (1998). Behavioral assessment and analysis of mechanical restraint utilization on a psychiatric, child and adolescent inpatient setting. *Behavioral Interventions, 13*(3), 147–155.

Luna, J. (2001). Limiting the use of physical restraint and seclusion in psychiatric residential treatment facilities for patients under 21. Retrieved March 1, 2003, from University of Houston Law Center Web site: http://www.law.uh.edu/healthlawperspectives/Mental/010829Limiting.html

Orhon, A. J. (2002). Of human bondage: Alternatives to restraint. Retrieved March 5, 2003, from Nurses Learning Network Web site: http://216.155.28.162/nurse/courses/nurseweek/nw0187/c1/index.htm

U.S. General Accounting Office. (1999, September). Mental health: Improper restraint or seclusion use places people at risk. Retrieved March 9, 2003, from http://www.gao.gov/archive/1999/he99176.pdf

Weiss, E., Megan, K., Blint, D., & Altimari, D. (1998, October 11–15). Deadly restraint: An investigative report. *Hartford Courant.* Retrieved March 1, 2003, from http://courant.ctnow.com/projects/restraint/

Related Topic

Chapter 105, "Involuntary Psychiatric Hospitalization (Civil Commitment): Adult and Child"

107 BASIC PRINCIPLES FOR DEALING WITH LEGAL LIABILITY RISK SITUATIONS

Gerald P. Koocher

What should a mental health practitioner do when an "adverse incident" occurs? If no lawsuit has been threatened or filed, but some significant difficulties or adverse events have occurred (e.g., a client is not benefiting from treatment, is not adhering to key aspects of a treatment program, has become too difficult to work with, commits suicide, or harms a third party), consider the following steps:

1. Obtain a consultation from a colleague experienced with such clients and issues. Consider whether you should initiate termination of the professional relationship. If you decide to do so, follow these steps: (a) Notify the patient both orally and in writing, specifying the effective date for termination; (b) provide a specific professional explanation for terminating the relationship; (c) agree to continue providing interim services for a reasonable period and recommend other care providers or means of locating them; (d) offer to provide records to new providers upon receipt of signed authorization from the client; and (e) document these steps in your case records.
2. Avoid initiating a unilateral termination if: (a) the client is in the midst of a mental health crisis or emergency situation; (b) substitute services will be difficult for the client to obtain (e.g., the client resides in a rural area where other practitioners might not he readily available; or (c) the primary reason for wanting to terminate the client may be regarded as unreasonably discriminatory (e.g., terminating psychotherapy with client after learning of his or her HIV status).
3. Psychologists have the right to unilaterally terminate services when threatened or otherwise endangered by the client/patient or another person with whom the client/patient has a relationship. This includes threats of physical harm or threats of lawsuits. Document any such threats in the clinical record.
4. If a client does not return for a scheduled appointment, follow up by telephone and in writing, documenting these steps in your records. Be especially prompt in doing so if the client seemed depressed or emotionally distressed in the previous session.
5. If a client complains about something, listen carefully and treat the complaint with serious concern. Investigate, if necessary, and respond in as sympathetic and tactful a manner as possible. Apologize, if appropriate. Document all steps taken in your record.
6. In the event of a client's death, express sincere compassion and sympathy to surviving relatives, but do not discuss any personal feelings of guilt you may be experiencing. Save such feelings for your personal psychotherapist.

If a lawsuit is filed or if you become aware of the possibility of a suit against you, follow these steps:

1. Contact your insurance carrier immediately, both orally and in writing. Retain copies of all correspondence and keep notes of phone conversations, including the date and the representative of the insurer you spoke

with. If a suit has actually been filed, your insurance carrier should assign local legal counsel to represent you promptly. If you retain counsel independently, the insurance carrier may not be obligated to pay for those services. Failure to notify the insurer in a timely manner may also compromise the defense of your case.

2. Never interact orally or in writing, "informally" or otherwise, with a client's lawyer once a suit is threatened. Once a lawyer representing your client contacts you in any dispute involving you and that client, get your own attorney involved. Cease all further contact with that client until you have consulted your attorney. Never try to settle matters yourself.
3. Do not discuss the case with anyone other than representatives of the insurance carrier or your lawyer. Do not discuss details of the case with colleagues unless directed to do so by your attorney.
4. Compile and organize all your records, case materials, and chronicles of the event to assist in your defense. Do not throw anything away, and do not show it to anyone except your attorney.
5. When asked to provide information or documents to your insurer or legal counsel, send copies and safeguard the originals.
6. In any malpractice or professional liability action where you are asked to agree to a settlement, consult a personal attorney (in addition to the one assigned by the insurance carrier), especially if sued for damages in excess of the limits of your policy.
7. Take steps to manage your own anxiety and stress level. Such cases can take a severe emotional toll and require several years to resolve, even though there may be no legitimate basis for the suit. Although seeking support from friends and colleagues is a normal reaction, discussions of specific details should occur only in contexts where the discussions are privileged (e.g., with your attorney or psychotherapist).

References, Readings, & Internet Sites 

American Psychological Association Committee on Professional Practice and Standards. (2003). Legal issues in the professional practice of psychology. *Professional Psychology: Research & Practice, 34,* 595–600.

American Psychological Association Insurance Trust. (n.d.). Home page. Retrieved 2004 from http://www.apait.org

Appelbaum, P. S. (1993). Legal liability and managed care. *American Psychologist, 48,* 251–277.

Koocher, G. P., & Keith-Spiegel, P. C. (1998). *Ethics in psychology: Professional standards and cases* (2nd ed.). New York: Oxford University Press.

National Register of Health Service Providers in Psychology. (n.d.). Home page. Retrieved 2004 from http://www.nationalergister.com/NationalRegisterPubs.html

Woody, R. H. (1988). *Protecting your mental health practice: How to minimize legal and financial risk.* San Francisco: Jossey-Bass.

Woody, R. H. (1997). *Legally safe mental health practice: Psycholegal questions and answers.* Madison, CT: Psychosocial Press.

Woody, R. H. (1999). Domestic violations of confidentiality. *Professional Psychology: Research & Practice, 30,* 607–610.

Wright, R. H. (1981a). Psychologists and professional liability (malpractice) insurance: A retrospective review. *American Psychologist, 36,* 1485–1493.

Wright, R. H. (1981b). What to do until the malpractice lawyer comes: A survivor's manual. *American Psychologist, 36,* 1535–1541.

Related Topics

Chapter 108, "Defending Against Legal Complaints"

Chapter 109, "Dealing With Licensing Board and Ethics Complaints"

Chapter 110, "Dealing With Subpoenas"

Chapter 124, "Essential Features of Professional Liability Insurance"

108 DEFENDING AGAINST LEGAL COMPLAINTS

Robert H. Woody

Since the mid-1970s, legal complaints have posed an ominous threat to psychologists. By the early 1980s, the threat of a legal complaint was affecting the profession to the point that terms such as "litigaphobia" and "litigastress" began to appear in professional publications (Brodsky, 1983; Turkington, 1987). Today there is an even greater risk of a lawsuit against a psychologist for alleged malpractice and/or a complaint to the state licensing board. Regrettably, the omnipresence of managed care has created additional liability for psychologists (Appelbaum, 1993).

A PSYCHOLOGIST CAN BE IRREPARABLY DAMAGED BY A LEGAL COMPLAINT

While the majority of complaints are for "nuisance" amounts of money, the negative consequences of a complaint are profound. Even if the malpractice carrier pays the settlement or the licensing board imposes a minor (or no) penalty, merely making a settlement for a civil suit or receiving a finding of probable cause for discipline from a licensing board creates a lifelong blemish on the psychologist's professional record. The reason is simple: Any negative outcome must commonly be reported to any professional association, hospital, or managed care organization. Several psychologists have reported that even minor negative outcomes have sometimes led to rejection from the foregoing types of organizations. Also, whenever the psychologist serves as an expert witness, questions are likely to be asked about any litigation or regulatory action in which he or she has been a party; several psychologists have said that even when a licensing complaint has been dismissed, the mere fact that a complaint had been lodged served to lessen their perceived authority as an expert witness.

Even worse, once a legal action has been resolved, the potential remains for an additional complaint and investigation by, particularly, any other licensing or certification source with which the psychologist is or ever becomes affiliated. Depending on the jurisdiction and the outcome of the initial legal action, an insurance carrier may have to report the matter to a state regulatory agency, which could trigger another investigation. Especially problematic is the possibility that the legal action will be on file in the Disciplinary Data System (DDS), a computerized national registry developed and maintained by the Association of State and Provincial Psychology Boards; this is a new development, but it is expanding (Association of State and Provincial Psychology Boards, 1996).

On another plane, psychologists defending against a legal complaint are prone to suffer emotional stress. Threats to one's professional status cut to the inner core of self-esteem and commonly produce depression, tension, anger, and symptoms of physical illness. Further, marital and familial relations, career motivation, and general satisfaction with life are adversely affected (Charles, Wilbert, & Kennedy, 1984).

In my role as a defense attorney for mental health professionals, I have witnessed complaints lodged against psychologists with the highest of reputations. According to Wright (1981), it appears that "the greater the degree of professionalism one demands of oneself, the more detailed and excruciating is the attendant review and the more intense the accompanying feelings of threat, anxiety, guilt, remorse, and depression" (p. 1535).

Some psychologists bent on preserving their professional reputation question the value of having insurance to cover a malpractice and/or regulatory complaint(s). Often these psychologists believe that the financial benefit (coverage for any judgment or legal fees) is outweighed by the detriment of the insurance carrier's control of settling a legal action. Specifically, an insurance policy can reduce the financial outlay by the psychologist, but the carrier is able to select the attorney. Numerous psychologists have expressed the sentiment that the insurance-selected attorney may be well intentioned and qualified but is under the control of the insurance company, who pressures the attorney to bring about a prompt settlement (so as to lessen the defense costs). Various insurance representatives generally acknowledge that their goal is to minimize expenditures on the defense; although they understand the psychologist's concern about preserving professional reputation, that concern is beyond the scope of the carrier's duty to its investors. Incidentally, this stance is maintained even when the lawsuit is clearly frivolous and without legal merit—it is cheaper to pay the litigious client than to teach the client a lesson. This approach may seem shortsighted, but it is the prevailing viewpoint of insurance carriers. As a result, numerous psychologists find it expeditious and prudent to hire, at their own expense, a personal attorney to deal with the insurance-paid attorney (e.g., to try to persuade against a settlement that unjustly penalizes the psychologist).

A PSYCHOLOGIST FACES A HIGH RISK OF A LEGAL COMPLAINT

It is impossible to know the incidence of legal actions taken against psychologists. Why? Because many, perhaps most, legal actions initially attempt to accomplish an "out-of-court" settlement. That is, the plaintiff's or complainant's attorney contacts the psychologist and offers to accept a financial payment to circumvent the need to file a formal action. Moreover, even if a complaint is filed, be it for alleged malpractice or violation of licensing standards, there are numerous ways in which the record can be closed to public scrutiny (i.e., it will not necessarily be reported). Just as there is considerable variation between states in the amount of risk associated with psychological practice, jurisdictions vary considerably in how complaints are handled prior to a judgment that becomes public record.

A PSYCHOLOGIST IS INADEQUATELY PREPARED TO DEAL WITH LEGAL PROBLEMS

Regardless of the jurisdiction, psychologists need to recognize that they are ill advised to attempt to "theraperize" a disgruntled client (past or present) who threatens a complaint. As Wright (1981, p. 1535) correctly explained, "Our training and our personal philosophies tend to emphasize the importance of the individual and our obligation as a helper/practitioner to evidence humanistic concerns or attempt 'conflict resolution.' We find it hard to believe that our virtue is unappreciated, so we attempt to follow our ethical admonitions to resolve conflict and discover to our subsequent dismay that the plaintiff's attorney made our virtuous and well-meaning efforts appear to be an attempt to 'cover up' or 'cop out'" (p. 1535). Well-intentioned efforts that would be quite proper in a therapeutic context become suspect in the legal context.

In one case, a male psychologist was accused by a female client of sexual misconduct. Without legal counsel, the three partners met with the client and her husband and offered to refund the full amount paid over the years for treatment, contingent on their not filing a lawsuit against the allegedly malpracticing psychologist. The offer was refused, and when a malpractice action was filed, the proposed refund was transformed into a nefarious attempt by the psychologists to subvert the couple's exercising their legal rights.

The foremost problem comes from the fact that the education and training of psychologists are basically antithetical to what leads to excellence in legal defense work. Dedicated to "ivory tower" notions and often divorced from the reality of modern psychological practice, trainers are prone to cling to outdated ideas about practitioners. Specifically, they emphasize altruism and subjugating the rights of practitioners to the preferences and demands of clients. Likewise, the curricula remain rooted in the past, with little or no accommodation to the current practice environment, namely, the "industrialized" marketplace, which is characterized by commercialism and consumer accountability and controlled by nonclinical sources, such as managed care organizations (Cummings, 1996). Some faculty members denounce any proposal to alter the curriculum to provide course work addressing modern practice issues, such as acquiring business skills, dealing with managed care, and being legally safe. As Troy and Schueman (1996) put it: "Among internal obstacles one may note the essential stasis and inflexibility of faculty-owned curricula which particularly resist innovative proposals for instructional design; criteria for faculty promotion and tenure; faculty ignorance of the changing imperatives of the world of work; competency and resources shortfall with programs; and the inappropriate expectations of new trainees" (p. 75). For example, when I proposed adding a "real-world" practice course, my colleagues' prevailing response was that "they can get that kind of learning once they are out in the field." Consequently, few psychologists graduate with a pragmatic understanding of how to succeed in psychological practice, not to mention defending against legal complaints.

A related problem comes from the fact that the psychologist, as a highly intelligent and well-educated individual, is prone to want to serve as "quarterback" in the legal defense. As one attorney told Wright (1981): "Heaven protect me from intelligent, sophisticated clients. While they're 'helping' me win my case, they can find ways I never dreamed of to mess things up. The smarter they are the more ways they can find to botch it" (p. 1535). This same condition has been found with professors who are prone to want to dictate the actions of their attorneys, contrary to legal judgment (LaNoue & Lee, 1987).

The source of the "quarterback" problem is twofold. First, the intelligent, educated professional, whether a psychologist or professor, is equipped with considerable knowledge, including knowledge about human behavior. Unfortunately, the knowledge is not assuredly consonant with the law and certainly not always in accord with the rules that determine what can and should be used in litigation. Second, the knowledge derives from the academy, which has minimal relevance to and is often contradictory to legal reality. Suffice it to say that the legal arena requires expertise foreign to psychological practice. Wright (1981) explains that psychologists facing a legal complaint "enter a whole new dimension of experience" (p. 1535) and that their "training, which tends to emphasize ultimate responsibility of the individual, may be at variance with both the philosophical context of our times and the legal-philosophical context in which we operate" (p. 1539). Wright's comments, which were made in 1981, are even more relevant today.

A PSYCHOLOGIST PRACTICES UNDER LITIGIOUS CONDITIONS

Modern psychological practice is far different from psychological practice in the past, even as recently as the 1980s. A major change has occurred in the tenets of the therapeutic alliance. Prior to psychologists' seeking and gaining admission to the "health care industry" (motivated by the self-serving goal of increased incomes, such as through eligibility for third-party payments), clients tended to treat mental health practitioners differently from other health care providers. There was an unfortunate stigma attached to being the recipient of mental health services, and clients tended to consider the therapeutic relationship to be distinctly different from other caregiving relationships; thus, legal actions against mental health practitioners were relatively few, at least compared with today. The industrialization or commercialization of mental health services led to, among other things, a reformation of the therapeutic alliance; namely, the dyad of the psychologist and client was joined by a third-party payer to create a ménage à trois. With this restructuring, exacerbated by the commanding presence of the third-party payer (dictating the terms for the relationship), the uniqueness of the therapeutic alliance disappeared and litigation increased.

Government regulation has become all-powerful in determining the propriety of psychological practices. When psychologists quested for state licensure (again, motivated by the self-serving goal of increased incomes), they unexpectedly surrendered disciplinary control of professional practice.

Licensing boards, under the watchful eye (some would say "dictates") of state prosecuting attorneys, became the monitors for possible disciplinary action. Relatedly, psychologists have lost their independent determination of clinical matters to the micromanagement of practices by the state house. Many psychologists falsely believe that members of licensing boards are colleagues who will be understanding and prone to forgive. They reason that at least some members of the state board are psychologists; some may have been colleagues known in the past. In point of fact, the members of the licensing board, whether psychologist, consumer representative, or state attorney, are appointed (usually by the governor) to represent politically motivated consumer protection. After dealing with a licensing complaint, numerous respondents have offered comments reflecting their surprise. For example: "The members of the board, especially the psychologists, seemed to take a 'guilty until proven innocent' approach." This is not surprising, since the members are present as protectors of consumers, certainly not as colleagues, and are there by political behest. In fact, some psychologist board members have found their roles to be such a heady experience that unprecedented degrees of egotism, narcissism, and self-aggrandizement are revealed. One psychologist commented, "They seemed to be demanding perfect performance rather than the reasonable standard that I thought determined malpractice." Again, this stance is not surprising, since the degree of proof required for probable cause for discipline is nebulous and usually less strenuous than required for a malpractice action.

Finally, many psychologists find that defending against a licensing complaint is more draining emotionally and financially than defending against a malpractice action. Given that a licensing complaint does involve scrutiny and judgment by members of the same profession (as opposed to a judge or jury), it is easy to think that one's professionalism has been incontrovertibly impugned.

At the time of the first edition of the *Psychologists' Desk Reference* in 1998, it seemed possible that the threat of legal complaints might have reached its peak. Regrettably, the intervening years reveal, to the contrary, there has been an increase in the number of and reasons for complaints. Granted, the financial press on professional associations has led to some ethics committees' being reluctant to enter into adjudication of ethics-based complaints.

In place of collegial reviews and sanctions, the government, through state licensing boards, has expanded its commitment to and resources for regulatory actions against mental health practitioners, including psychologists. Regrettably, there is reason to believe that some licensing boards are, in fact, considering psychologists to be "guilty until proven innocent" (Peterson, 2001) and depriving psychologists' of fair treatment and other legal rights (Williams, 2001).

Also, the courts have, if anything, opened the door of the courthouse further, aided and abetted by additional liability created by managed care (Applebaum, 1993). Now legal actions against mental health professionals in general and psychologists in particular abound.

Historically, the advent of legal complaints became pronounced in the mid-1970s, posing an ominous threat to psychologists. By the early 1980s, the threat of a legal complaint was affecting the profession to the point that terms such as "litigaphobia" and "litagress" began to appear in professional publications (Brodsky, 1983; Turkington, 1987). Today every psychologist, regardless of competency, years of experience, theory advocated, techniques used, or types of clients, is at risk of a legal action from a service user. This chapter explores the issues underlying the threat of legal actions, and offers specific suggestions for the practitioner's maintaining effective risk management.

A PSYCHOLOGIST MUST ACCEPT BEING DEFENSIVE

Clinging to antiquated notions about practices raises legal liability, and lacking legally related knowledge adds to the risk. Since most psychologists do not think like lawyers, it is important to pursue defensive strategies.

Stated simply, there are four essential defensive strategies: (1) the psychologist should have professional liability insurance (including for licensing complaints); (2) the psychologist should rely on a supervisor for protective peer review (albeit potentially creates liability for the supervisor as well); (3) the psychologist should keep detailed records (which are commonly weighted heavily for establishing what was or was not involved in the professional services); and (4) in or out of the practice office, the psychologist should have prudence govern every professional and personal bit of his or her conduct.

Relatedly, Smith (2003) recommends that the psychologist: (1) understand what constitutes a multiple relationship; (2) protect confidentiality; (3) respect people's autonomy; (4) know his or her supervisory responsibilities; (5) identify the respective roles of the client and the psychologist; (6) document professional services carefully; (7) provide only services for which there is expertise; (8) know the difference between abandonment and termination; (9) stick to the evidence; and (10) be accurate in billing.

Elsewhere (Woody, 2000), this author has offered twenty defensive strategies that any mental health practitioner should maintain when faced with a complaint; the twenty strategies are:

1. Maintain a healthy mindset.
2. Accept the adversarial nature of the complaint.
3. Recognize the adversaries.
4. Become defensive.
5. Be a warrior.
6. Adopt a long-range perspective.
7. Obtain legal counsel.
8. Trust and rely on an attorney.
9. Do not allow financial considerations to dominate decision making.
10. Formulate a factual and defensible explanation.
11. Trust no one but your attorney.
12. Avoid creating witnesses for the other side.
13. Learn to respond properly to discovery methods and during testimony.
14. Be modest in professional representations.
15. Implement a risk management system.
16. Define an appropriate standard of care.
17. Buttress your professional credentials.
18. Screen clients to eliminate undue risks.
19. Guard against a copy-cat complainant.
20. Develop a healthy personal-professional life.

The foregoing can be reduced to the following eight detailed recommendations.

1. A psychologist should acquire training to view practice operations and client communications with a defensive eye. Since this need is commonly unfilled by graduate training programs, the psychologist should arrange for self-study and seminars.
2. When a potentially litigious client waves a "red flag," the psychologist should set aside any illogical idea that services must be continued. Some clients have actually filed legal actions against their psychologists and then objected when services to them were terminated! If a client threatens or takes legal action against the psychologist, the client has sacrificed any logical claim to the title of "client" and has justified the new title "party opponent."
3. A psychologist should have a personal attorney readily "on call." As described earlier, an attorney appointed by a malpractice insurance carrier enters the conflict after the fact and primarily serves the insurance carrier.
4. The psychologist should rely on preventive legal counsel at the first possible "red flag" of litigation. Obtaining the advice of counsel proactively can reduce the possibility of a complaint.
5. If a client demonstrates negativism toward the psychologist that goes beyond "therapeutic resistance" or "reasonable transference," the psychologist should acknowledge the possibility of a legal complaint. If resistance or transference moves to the client's mentioning a complaint, the psychologist

should not persevere. In the clinical interests of the client, a psychologist cannot be expected to function effectively under the threat of litigation, and thus it would be a disservice to the client to continue.

6. A psychologist should not wait until a complaint seems inevitable or even probable before shifting into a defensive posture. The mere possibility of a complaint justifies action to safeguard the rights of the psychologist, as well as being a service to the client.
7. When legal safeguards are necessary, the psychologist should assume a defensive posture in all communications with the client or client's attorney; implement a tactful and reasonable termination of the clinical service (such as making a referral to another practitioner); and immediately turn the matter over to his or her personal attorney.
8. When an attorney has become involved, the psychologist should accept that the matter is outside of psychological competence and personal control. The fundamental assumption must be that the matter will best be handled by legal strategies. Consequently, the psychologist must avoid trying to be a "quarterback" to the legal situation.

These eight recommendations pose ideas that may seem foreign to traditional psychological practice. Some psychologists are reluctant to pass clinical conditions through a legal filter and object to the added expense (such as paying for a personal attorney). Nonetheless, modern psychological practice requires a defensive posture and legal protection (with the expense being the "cost of doing business" in this litigious era). To do otherwise is to jeopardize professional survival and practice success.

References & Readings 

Appelbaum, P. S. (1993). Legal liability and managed care. *American Psychologist, 48,* 251–277.

Association of State and Provincial Psychology Boards (1996). Disciplinary data system pilot project kicks off. *ASPPD Newsletter, 17*(1), 1, 4.

Brodsky, S. L. (1983). Litigaphobia: The professionals' disease [Review of B. Schutz, *Legal liability in psychotherapy*]. *Contemporary Psychology, 28,* 204–205.

Charles, S. C., Wilbert, J. R., & Kennedy, E. C. (1984). Physicians' self-reports of reactions to malpractice litigation. *American Journal of Psychiatry, 141,* 563–565.

Cummings, N. A. (1996). The resocialization of behavioral healthcare practice. In N. A. Cummings, M. S. Pallak, & J. L. Cummings (Eds.), *Surviving the demise of solo practice: Mental health practitioners prospering in the era of managed care* (pp. 3–10). Madison, CT: Psychosocial Press (International Universities Press).

LaNoue, G. R., & Lee, B. A. (1987). *Academics in court: The consequences of faculty discrimination litigation.* Ann Arbor: University of Michigan Press.

Peterson, M. D. (2001). Recognizing concerns about how some licensing boards are treating psychologists. *Professional Psychology, 32*(4), 339–340.

Smith, D. (2003). 10 ways practitioners can avoid frequent ethical pitfalls. *APA Monitor, 34*(1), 50–55.

Troy, W. G., & Shueman, S. A. (1996). Program redesign for graduate training in professional psychology: The road to accountability in a changing professional world. In N. A. Cummings, M. S. Pallak, & J. L. Cummings (Eds.), *Surviving the demise of solo practice: Mental health practitioners prospering in the era of managed care* (pp. 55–79). Madison, CT: Psychosocial Press (International Universities Press).

Turkington, C. (1987). Litigaphobia. *Monitor, 17*(11), 1, 8.

Williams, M. H. (2001). The question of psychologists' maltreatment by state licensing boards: Overcoming denial and seeking remedies. *Professional Psychology, 32*(4), 341–344.

Woody, R. H. (1988a). *Fifty ways to avoid malpractice: A guidebook for the mental health practitioner.* Sarasota, FL: Professional Resource Exchange.

Woody, R. H. (1988b). *Protecting your mental health practice: How to minimize legal and financial risk.* San Francisco: Jossey-Bass.

Woody, R. H. (1989). *Business success in mental health practice: Modern marketing, management, and legal strategies.* San Francisco: Jossey-Bass.

Woody, R. H. (1991). *Quality care in mental health services: Assuring the best clinical services.* San Francisco: Jossey-Bass.

Woody, R. H. (1997). *Legally safe mental health practice: Psycholegal questions and answers.* Madison, CT: Psychosocial Press (International Universities Press).

Woody, R. H. (2000). What to do upon receiving a complaint. In L. VandeCreek & T. L. Jackson (Eds.), *Innovations in clinical practice: A source book* (Vol. 18, pp. 213–229). Sarasota, FL: Professional Resource Press.

Wright, R. H. (1981). What to do until the malpractice lawyer comes: A survivor's manual. *American Psychologist, 36,* 1535–1541.

Related Topics

Chapter 107, "Basic Principles for Dealing With Legal Liability Risk Situations"

Chapter 109, "Dealing With Licensing Board and Ethics Complaints"

Chapter 110, "Dealing With Subpoenas"

109 DEALING WITH LICENSING BOARD AND ETHICS COMPLAINTS

Gerald P. Koocher & Patricia Keith-Spiegel

Receiving a formal inquiry or complaint letter from a licensing board or professional association's ethics committee invariably becomes one of the most stressful events in a psychologist's career. The actual incidence of actionable complaints against psychologists is relatively low. In 2002, for example, the APA Ethics Committee received 321 inquiries, but opened only 34 cases, and only 16 members were expelled or forced to resign of approximately 85,000 members (APA, 2003). Nonetheless, receiving a notification letter often feels like an attack or a personal affront from one's colleagues. In such situations it is important to understand the system, know one's rights, and assure oneself of fair treatment. Keep in mind that "beating the system" is not the appropriate goal. Psychologists have previously agreed—voluntarily and with full informed consent—to enter a profession that has obligated itself to formal peer monitoring. All of us, as well as the public, gain advantage from this system. Psychologists initiated the legislation that created our licensing boards and professional association ethics committees. If the profession abandoned an active role in self-regulation, it would ultimately fall under regulation by outsiders with inadequate understanding of the history, practices, and scientific foundations of the profession.

We have seen a wide range of reactions from respondents to official inquiries and complaints. Some psychologists become so stressed that they appear to jeopardize their own health. Others become hostile or avoidant in ways that only serve to antagonize those charged with evaluating the complaint. Many seem able to retain a dignified approach to the charge, but all become anxious to get to the matter as soon as possible and gain a favorable resolution. Receiving an inquiry or formal notice of charges from any professional monitoring agent will not, of course, improve anyone's day. However, we offer some advice to consider in the event you ever find yourself in such a situation.

First and foremost, know who you are dealing with and understand the nature of the complaint and the potential consequences before responding.

- Are you dealing with a statutory licensing authority or a voluntary professional association? A professional association's most severe sanction is likely to be expulsion, but a licensing board has the authority to suspend or revoke a professional license.
- Are you dealing with nonclinician investigators or professional colleagues? In some smaller states or provinces, the staff of the licensing board may consist of a nonpsychologist who lacks a fully professional understanding of the applicable ethics codes and regulations. Even when the investigator for a licensing board or ethics committee has training as a psychologist, the degree of experience and expertise can vary widely. In many cases additional clarification from others in authority may be warranted.
- Is the contact you received an informal inquiry or a formal charge? Sometimes licensing boards and ethics committees approach less serious allegations by asking the psychologist to respond before they decide to whether to open a formal complaint. In such instances, however, "informal" does not mean "casual." Rather, such inquiries may be a sign that the panel has not yet concluded that the alleged conduct was serious enough to warrant drastic action or meets their definition of issuing a formal charge. The correct response should always be thoughtful and cautious.
- Have you been given a detailed and comprehensible rendition of the complaint made against you? You should not respond substantively to any complaint without a clear written explanation of the allegations. In many jurisdictions you may also be entitled to a written copy of the actual complaint made against you.
- Have you been provided with copies of the rules, procedures, or policies under which the panel operates? If you do not have this information, request it and review it care fully to determine where you fall in the time line of the investigatory process and what rights, options, and inquiries you have available before responding.

Second, do not respond impulsively. Kneejerk actions will more likely than not be counterproductive and complicate the process unnecessarily.

- Do not contact the complainant directly or indirectly. The matter is no longer subject to informal resolution. Any contact initiated by you may be viewed as an attempt at coercion or harassment.
- If the complaint involves a current or former client, be sure that the authorities have obtained and provided you with a waiver signed by the client authorizing you to disclose confidential information before responding to the charges. We know of instances where licensing boards initiated complaints based on third party inquiries without such waivers and then asked the psychologists complained about to obtain release of information consent from their own clients. Such requests are inappropriate, because they put the psychologist in the uncomfortable and awkward position of asking someone to surrender confidentiality to serve the needs of another. The Federal HIPAA (Health Insurance Portability and Accountability Act) regulations prohibit the release of protected health information without such a signed release.
- Obtain consultation before responding. A colleague with prior experience serving on ethics panels or licensing boards is an ideal choice. Pay for an hour or two of professional time. Doing so establishes a confidential and possibly privileged relationship (depending on state law) with the consultant. Consultation with an attorney is also advised, especially if the matter involves an alleged legal offense, if the ethics committee does not appear to be following the rules and procedures, or if the case might result in any public disciplinary action. Some professional liability insurance policies provide coverage for legal consultation in the event of a licensing

board complaint. This insurance does not generally apply to professional association ethics complaints and may not be allowed in some jurisdictions. We recommend that you check your liability policy and secure such coverage if you do not already have it.

- If asked to provide unusual materials during the investigatory process, do not comply without first seeking legal consultation. We know of one state licensing authority that claimed the right to examine "samples of reports" from a psychologist's work with clients other than the ones involved in the complaint—a clear violation of the privacy rights of the affected clients. In another case, a licensing board insisted that a psychologist provide typed transcripts of substantial files of handwritten notes at his own expense.
- If offered a settlement, "consent decree," or any resolution short of full dismissal of the case against you, obtain additional professional and legal consultation. Even an apparently mild "reprimand" may result in difficulty in renewing liability insurance policies, gaining access to insurance provider panels, qualifying for hospital staff privileges, or being hired for some jobs. Any formal disciplinary action, even as mild as a reprimand, may result in reports to interstate monitoring agencies or professional associations. Agreeing to accept an ethics or licensing sanction may also compromise your legal defense, should the client file suit. If you have done something wrong, a penalty may be appropriate. However, you should be fully aware of the potential consequences before simply agreeing to the sanction.

Third, organize your defense and response to the charges carefully and thoughtfully.

- Assess the credibility of the charge. Compile and organize your records and the relevant chronology of events. Respond respectfully and fully to the questions or charges within the allotted time frame. Failure to cooperate with a duly constituted inquiry is, itself, an ethical violation.
- Psychologists are expected to respond personally to the inquiry. It is appropriate to consult with colleagues or an attorney before responding, but a letter from your attorney alone (i.e., without a response over your signature) is often not sufficient and may also be regarded as inappropriate or evasive.
- Limit the scope of your response to focus on the content areas and issues that directly relate to the content of the official complaint letter. Do not ramble or introduce tangential issues.
- If you need more time to gather materials and respond, ask for it. Be sure to retain copies of everything you send in response to the inquiry.
- Do not take the position that the best defense is a thundering offense. This will polarize the proceedings and reduce the chances for a collegial solution.
- If you believe that you have been wrongly or erroneously charged, state your case clearly and provide any appropriate documentation.
- If the complaint accurately represents the events, but does not accurately interpret them, provide your own account and interpretation with as much documentation as you can.
- If you have committed the offense charged, document the events and start appropriate remediation actions immediately (e.g., seek professional supervision to deal with any areas of professional weakness, enter psychotherapy for any personal problems, or take other steps to demonstrate that you do not intend to allow the error to recur). Present information regarding any mitigating circumstances. It would probably also be wise to seek legal counsel at this point, if you have not already done so.
- If a charge or complaint is sustained and you are asked to accept disciplinary measures without a formal hearing, you may want to consider reviewing the potential consequences of the measures with an attorney before making a decision.
- Know your rights of appeal.

Fourth, take steps to support yourself emotionally over what is likely to be a stressful process extending over several months.

- Be patient. It is likely that you will have to wait for what will seem like a long while before the matter is resolved. It is perfectly acceptable to respectfully inquire regarding the status of the matter from time to time.
- If appropriate, confide in a colleague or therapist who will be emotionally supportive through the process. Your relationship with your therapist may be protected by privilege. We strongly suggest, however, that you refrain from discussing the charges against you with many others. Doing so may increase your own tension and likely produce an adverse impact as more and more individuals become aware of your situation and may possibly raise additional problems regarding confidentiality issues. In no instance should you identify the complainant to others, aside from the board or committee making the inquiry (after they produce a signed release) and your attorney.
- Take active, constructive steps to minimize your own anxiety and stress levels. If this matter is interfering with your ability to function, you might benefit from a professional counseling relationship in a privileged context.

References, Readings, & Internet Sites

American Psychological Association. (2001). *Rules and procedures.* Washington, DC: Author. http://www.apa.org/ethics

American Psychological Association. (2003). Report of the Ethics Committee, 2002. *American Psychologist, 58,* 650–657.

Association of State and Provincial Psychology Boards. (n.d.). Home page. Retrieved 2004 from http://www.asppb.org

Bass, L. J., DeMers, S. T., Ogloff, J. R., Peterson, C., Pettifor, J. L., Reaves, R. I., et al. (1996). *Professional conduct and discipline in psychology.* Washington, DC: American Psychological Association.

Bersoff, D. N. (Ed.). (2003). *Ethical conflicts in psychology* (3rd ed.). Washington, DC: American Psychological Association.

Canter, M. B., Bennett, B. E., Jones, S. E., & Nagy, T. F. (1994). *Ethics for psychologists: A commentary on the APA ethics code.* Washington, DC: American Psychological Association.

Fisher, C. (2003) *Decoding the ethics code: A practical guide for psychologists.* Thousand Oaks, CA: Sage.

Koocher, G. F., & Keith-Spiegel, P. C. (1998). *Ethics in psychology: Professional standards and cases* (2nd ed.). New York: Oxford University Press.

Pope, K. S. (n.d.). Licensing information site. Retrieved 2004 from http://www.kspope.com/licensing/index.php

Related Topics

Chapter 103, "Ethical Principles of Psychologists and Code of Conduct (2002)"

Chapter 107, "Basic Principles for Dealing With Legal Liability Risk Situations"

Chapter 108, "Defending Against Legal Complaints"

110 DEALING WITH SUBPOENAS

Gerald P. Koocher

Receipt of a legal document commanding that you appear at a legal proceeding or turn over your records to attorneys, especially when unexpected, can be a very stressful experience. This brief guide can help you understand the nature of a subpoena and how to respond. However, law and procedures vary from jurisdiction to jurisdiction; when in doubt, consult with an attorney who is knowledgeable about your local jurisdiction.

QUESTIONS ABOUT SUBPOENAS

What Is a Subpoena?

A subpoena is a document served in a legally prescribed manner on a person who is not a party to a case (i.e., not the plaintiff or defendant) requiring that person to produce documents, appear and give testimony at a deposition or trial, or both. In the case of depositions, seven days' notice is often required.

What Is a Subpoena *Duces Tecum*?

From the Latin meaning "bring it with you," a subpoena *duces tecum* requires the person to bring specified records, reports, tapes, documents, or other tangible evidence to court or a deposition. For deposition testimony, 30 days' notice is often required.

Who Issues the Subpoena, and What Is in It?

Depending on the jurisdiction, the issuing authority may be a clerk of the court, notary public, or justice of the peace. The document must state the name of the court and issuing authority, the title of the legal action, and the time and place of testimony or production of documents.

How Is a Subpoena Served?

A subpoena may generally be served by any adult person who is not a party to the litigation. Usually service is done by a constable or sheriff, who delivers a copy in person or leaves it at the intended recipient's residence or place of business.

Must I Comply With the Subpoena?

Failure to obey a subpoena may lead to being held in contempt of court. However, simply because you have been served does not mean that the subpoena is valid or that you must produce all materials requested.

What Is the Difference Between a Subpoena and a Court Order?

It is important to understand the differences between a subpoena and a court order. A subpoena simply compels a response and in some jurisdictions can be issued routinely by an attorney's request to a clerk of courts. A psychologist's response to the subpoena need not be what is demanded in the actual subpoena document. If the papers seek records, documents, or testimony that may be privileged, the psychologist should seek clarification from the client's attorney or the court. A court order, on the other hand, generally issues only after a hearing before a judge; it compels a disclosure, unless the order is appealed to a higher court. In the end, the court must decide what information or records are protected and what are not.

Consult your own attorney or the relevant client's attorney to assess matters of privilege, overbroad requests for documents or materials, and other specific questions regarding the validity of the documents.

What If I Cannot Attend on the Specified Date?

Contact the lawyer who issued the subpoena to discuss the matter. If the attorney is intransigent, states that the date cannot be rescheduled, and the time line is unreasonable (e.g., if you are given only 24 hours' notice and do not have time to cancel appointments or provide patient coverage), tell the attorney that you plan to contact the judge in the case in order to complain about the inadequate notice. This approach often stimulates increased flexibility by the attorney. If necessary, do contact the judge and explain your scheduling problem. Except in unusual or urgent circumstances, the judge is likely to be accommodating.

DEALING WITH SUBPOENAS FOR PRODUCTION OF DOCUMENTS

When a subpoena demanding production of documents is served, the psychologist should not provide anything immediately. That is to say, nothing should be surrendered to the person serving the subpoena, no matter how aggressive the request. The subpoena document should be accepted, and the psychologist should then consult legal counsel regarding applicable law and resulting obligations. If it is ultimately determined that the call for the records has been appropriately issued by a court of competent authority, a psychologist may be placed in a very awkward position, especially if the client does not wish to have the material disclosed.

Consider the following actions:

- If a subpoena arrives from a client's attorney and no release form is included, check with your client, not the attorney, before releasing the documents. In a technical sense, a request from a client's attorney is legally the same as a request from the client himself or herself; however, it is not unreasonable for the clinician to personally confirm the client's wishes, especially if the content of the records is sensitive.
- If a signed release form is included, but the clinician believes that the material may be clinically or legally damaging, discuss these issues with the client.
- Psychologists concerned about releasing actual notes should offer to prepare a prompt report or summary, but they ultimately may have to produce the full record. The original record or notes need not be provided. A notarized or authenticated copy of the records will generally suffice.
- On rare occasion, a subpoena generated by an attorney opposing the psychologist's client or representing another person may arrive at a clinician's office in the hands of a person seeking immediate access to records. Under such circumstances it is reasonable to inform the person: "I cannot disclose whether or not the person noted in the subpoena is now or ever was my client. If the person were my client, I could not provide any information without a signed release from that individual or a valid court order." Next, contact your client, explain the situation, and ask for permission to talk with his or her attorney. Ask the patient's attorney to work out privilege issues with the opposing attorney or move to quash the subpoena. These steps will ensure that the person to whom you owe prime obligations (i.e., your client) is protected to the full extent allowed by law.
- If a valid subpoena seeks raw test data or test materials sold only to professionals (e.g., certain psychological test kits or record forms), one should generally respond by offering to provide the raw data to a qualified professional, explaining that laypersons are not qualified to interpret the raw data. Test kits whose purchase is restricted by the publisher to "qualified users" should also generally be withheld. However, both raw data and test kit materials would have to be produced in response to a court order. These issues are discussed in the 2002 version of the American Psychological Association's Ethical Principles of Psychologists and Code of Conduct,

reprinted in this volume and available online.

GENERAL ADVICE

When in doubt, consult your own attorney for advice, but never ignore a subpoena.

References, Readings, & Internet Sites 

American Psychological Association. (1993). Record keeping guidelines. *American Psychologist, 48,* 984–986.

American Psychological Association. (1996). Strategies for private practitioners coping with subpoenas or compelled testimony for client records or test data. *Professional Psychology: Research and Practice, 27,* 245–251.

Boruch, R. P., Dennis, M., & Cecil, I. S. (1996). Fifty years of empirical research on privacy and confidentiality in research settings. In B. H. Stanley, J. E. Sieber, & C. B. Melton (Eds.), *Research ethics: A psychological approach* (pp. 129–173). Lincoln: University of Nebraska Press.

Burke, C. A. (1995). Until death do us part: An exploration into confidentiality following the death of a client. *Professional Psychology: Research and Practice, 26,* 278–280.

Committee on Legal Issues, American Psychological Association. (1996). Strategies for private practitioners coping with subpoenas or compelled testimony for client records of test data. *Professional Psychology: Research and Practice, 27,* 245–251.

Committee on Psychological Tests and Assessment. (1996). Statement on disclosure of test data. *American Psychologist, 51,* 644–668.

Koocher, G. P., & Keith-Spiegel, P. C. (1998). *Ethics in psychology: Professional standards and cases* (2nd ed.). New York: Oxford University Press.

Koocher, G. P., & Rey-Casserly, C. M. (2002). Ethical issues in psychological assessment. In J. R. Graham & J. A. Naglieri (Eds.), *Handbook of assessment psychology*. New York: Wiley.

'Lectric Law Library. (n.d.). Lexicon on subpoena. Retrieved 2004 from http://www.lectlaw.com/def2/s083.htm

Legal Definitions. (n.d.). Online legal dictionary. Retrieved 2004 from http://www.legal-definitions.com

United States Department of Justice. (n.d.). Kid's page glossary. Retrieved 2004 from http://www.usdoj.gov/usao/eousa/kidspage/glossary.html

Related Topics

Chapter 104, "Privacy, Confidentiality, and Privilege"

Chapter 107, "Basic Principles for Dealing With Legal Liability Risk Situations"

Chapter 128, "Basic Elements of Release Forms"

111 GLOSSARY OF LEGAL TERMS OF SPECIAL INTEREST IN MENTAL HEALTH PRACTICE

Gerald P. Koocher

Abandonment: Unilateral termination of a psychotherapist-patient relationship by the psychotherapist without the patient's consent at a time when the patient requires continuing mental health care and without the psychologist's making arrangements for appropriate continuation and follow-up care.

Affidavit: Sworn statement that is usually written.

Agency: Relationship between persons in which one party authorizes the other to act for or represent that party.

Allegation: Statement that a party expects to be able to prove.

Answer: A defendant's written response to a complaint.

Appeal: The process by which a decision of a lower court is brought for review before a court of higher jurisdiction. The party bringing the appeal is the *appellant*. The party against whom the appeal is taken is the *appellee*.

Assault: Intentional and unauthorized act of placing another in apprehension of immediate bodily harm.

Battery: Intentional and unauthorized touching of a person, directly or indirectly, without consent. For example, a surgical procedure performed upon a person without express or implied consent constitutes a battery.

Causation: Existence of a connection between the act or omission of the defendant and the injury suffered by the plaintiff. In a suit for negligence, the issue of causation usually requires proof that the plaintiff's harm resulted proximately from the negligence of the defendant.

Cause of action: Set of facts that give rise to a legal right to redress at law.

Civil action: Action invoking a judicial trial either at law or in equity, which is not criminal in nature.

Common law: Body of rules and principles based on Anglo-Saxon law, derived from usage and customs, and developed from court decisions based on such law. It is distinguished from statutes enacted by legislatures and all other types of law.

Complaint: The initiatory pleading on the part of the plaintiff in filing a civil lawsuit. Its purpose is to give the defendant notice of the general alleged fact constituting the cause of action.

Consent: Voluntary act by which one person agrees to allow another person to do something. *Express consent* is that directly and unequivocally given, either orally or in writing. *Implied consent* is that manifested by signs, actions, or facts or by inaction and silence, which raises a presumption that the consent has been given. It may be implied from conduct (implied-in-fact), for example, when someone rolls up his or her sleeve and extends an arm for vein puncture, or by the circumstances (implied-in-law), for example, in the case of an unconscious person in an emergency situation.

Contributory negligence or comparative negligence: Affirmative defense to a successful action against a defendant where the plaintiff's concurrent negligence contributed to his or her own injury, even though the defendant's actions may also have been responsible for the injury.

Damages: Money receivable through judicial order by a plaintiff sustaining harm, impairment, or loss to his or her person or property as the result of the accidental, intentional, or negligent act of another. *Compensatory* damages are intended to compensate the injured party for the injury sustained and nothing more. *Special damages* are the actual out-of-pocket losses incurred by the plaintiff, such as psychotherapy expenses and lost earnings, and are a part of the *compensatory damages*. *Nominal damages* are awarded to demonstrate that a legally cognizable wrong has been committed. *Punitive damages* are awarded to punish a defendant who has acted maliciously or in reckless disregard of the plaintiff's rights. (Some states do not allow punitive damages except in actions for wrongful death of the plaintiff's decedent.)

Defamation: Willful and malicious communication, either written (libel) or spoken (slander), that is false; injures the reputation or character of another.

Defendant: The person against whom a civil or criminal action is brought.

Deposition: The testimony of a witness or party taken before trial, consisting of an oral, sworn, out-of-court statement.

Directed verdict: A verdict for the defendant that a jury returns as directed by the judge, usually based on the inadequacy of the evidence presented by the plaintiff as a matter of law.

Discovery: Pretrial activities of the parties to litigation to learn of evidence known to the opposing party or various witnesses and therefore to minimize surprises at the time of trial.

Due process: Course of legal proceedings according to those rules and principles that have been established in systems of jurisprudence for the enforcement and protection of private rights. It often means simply a fair hearing.

Expert witness: Person who has special training, knowledge, skill, or experience in an area relevant to resolution of the legal dispute and who is allowed to offer an opinion as testimony in court.

Fraud: Intentionally misleading another person in a manner that causes legal injury to that person.

Guardian: Person appointed by a court to manage the affairs and protect the interests of another who is adjudged incompetent by reason of age, physical status, or mental status and is thereby unable to manage his or her own affairs.

Guardian ad litem: Person appointed as a guardian for a particular purpose, interval, or matter. Functioning in this role may involve undertaking investigations and issuing reports to the court (e.g., as in child custody matters). The court order appointing the guardian ad litem should specify the nature of the role and duties.

Hypothetical question: A form of question put to a witness, usually an expert witness, in which things which counsel claims are or will be proved are stated as a factual supposition and the witness is asked to respond, state, or explain the conclusion based on the assumptions and questions.

Immunity: In civil law, protection given certain individuals (personal immunity) or groups (institutional immunity) that may shield them from liability for certain acts or legal relationships. Ordinarily, the individual may still be sued, because immunity can be raised only as an affirmative defense to the complaint, that is, after a lawsuit has been filed.

Incompetency: Inability of a person to manage his or her own affairs because of mental or physical infirmities. If this status or condition is legally determined, a guardian will usually be appointed to manage the person's affairs.

Indemnity: Agreement whereby a party guarantees reimbursement for possible losses.

Independent contractor: Person who agrees with a party to undertake the performance of a task for which the person is not expected to be under the direct supervision or control of the party. Ordinarily this arrangement and relationship shield the party from liability for negligent acts of the independent contractor that occurred during the performance of the work. For example, a psychological consultant is an independent contractor for whose negligent acts the attending psychologist is not liable.

Informed consent: Patient's voluntary agreement to accept treatment based on an awareness of the nature of his or her disease, the material risks and benefits of the proposed treatment, the alternative treatments and risks, and the choice of no treatment at all.

Injunction: Court order commanding a person or entity to perform or to refrain from performing a certain act or otherwise be found in contempt of court.

Interrogatories: Written questions propounded by one party to another before trial as part of the pretrial discovery procedures.

Intestate: One who dies leaving no valid will.

Invasion of privacy: Violation of a person's right to be left alone and free from unwarranted publicity and intrusions.

Joint and several liability: Several persons who share the liability for the plaintiff's injury can be found liable individually or together.

Libel: Defamation of a person's reputation or character by any type of publication, including pictures or written word.

Malice: The performance of a wrongful act without just cause or excuse, with an intent to inflict an injury or under such circumstances that the law will imply an evil intent.

Malicious prosecution: Countersuit by the original defendant to collect damages that have resulted to the original defendant from a civil suit filed maliciously and without probable cause. Ordinarily, it may not be brought until the initial suit against the original defendant has been judicially decided in favor of the defendant.

Malpractice: Professional negligence. Failure to meet a professional standard or care resulting in harm to another. Failure to provide generally acceptable psychological care and treatment.

Negligence: Legal cause of action involving the failure to exercise the degree of diligence and care that a reasonably and ordinarily prudent person would exercise under the same or similar circumstances; the result is the breach of a legal duty, which proximately causes an injury which the law recognizes as deserving of compensation. The standard of care of a defendant doctor in a malpractice case is not that of the reasonable and ordinarily prudent person (such as an automobile operator) but that of the average qualified psychologist practicing in the same area of specialization or general practice as that of the defendant psychologist.

Opinion evidence: Type of evidence that a witness gives based on his or her special training or background rather than on his or her personal knowledge of the facts in issue. Generally, if the issue involves specialized knowledge, only the opinions of experts are admissible as evidence.

Pain and suffering: Element of "compensatory" nonpecuniary damages that allows recovery for the mental anguish and/or physical pain endured by the plaintiff as a result of injury for which the plaintiff seeks redress.

Perjury: Willful giving of false testimony under oath.

Plaintiff: Party who files or initiates a civil lawsuit seeking relief or compensation for damages or other legal relief.

Pleadings: The technical means by which parties to a dispute frame the issue for the court. The plaintiff's complaint is followed by the defendant's answer, and subsequent papers are filed as needed.

Prima facie case: A complaint that apparently contains all the necessary legal elements for a recognized cause of action and will suffice until contradicted and overcome by other evidence.

Prima facie evidence: Such evidence as is sufficient to establish the fact; if not rebutted, it becomes conclusive of the fact.

Probate court: Court having jurisdiction over the estates of deceased persons and persons under guardianship.

Proximate causation: Essential element in a legal cause of action for negligence; that is, it must be shown that the alleged negligent act proximately caused the injury for which legal damages are sought. The dominant and responsible cause necessarily sets other causes in operation. It represents a natural and continuous sequence, unbroken by any intervening cause.

Proximate cause: Act of commission or omission that through an uninterrupted sequence of events directly results in an injury that otherwise would not have occurred or else becomes a substantial factor in causing an injury.

Publication: Oral or written act that makes defamatory material available to persons other than the person defamed.

Reasonable medical certainty (or reasonable psychological certainty): As used in personal injury lawsuits, a term implying more than mere conjecture, possibility, consistency with, or speculation; similar to a probability, more likely than not 50.1%, but an overwhelming likelihood or scientific certainty is not required.

Release: Statement signed by a person relinquishing a right or claim against another person or persons usually for a payment or other valuable consideration.

Respondeat superior: "Let the master answer." A doctrine of vicarious or derivative liability in which the employer (master) is liable for the legal consequences of the breach of duties by an employee (servant) that the master owes to others, if the breach of duty occurs while the servant is engaged in work within the scope of his or her employment. For example, a hospital is liable for the negligent acts of a psychologist it employs if the acts occurred while the psychologist was working within his or her job description.

Settlement: Agreement made between the parties to a lawsuit, which resolves their legal dispute.

Slander: Method of oral defamation in which the false and malicious words are published by speaking or uttering in the presence of another person, other than the person slandered, which prejudices another person's reputation and character.

Standard of care: Measure against which a defendant's conduct is compared. The required standard in a professional negligence or psychological malpractice case is the standard of the average qualified practitioner in the same area of specialization.

Statute of limitations: Statutes that specify the permissible time interval between the occurrence giving rise to a civil cause of action and the actual filing of the lawsuit. Thus failure to file the suit within the prescribed time limits may become an affirmative defense to the action. In malpractice actions, a typical statute of limitations might be 3 years from the date the cause of action accrues, but the measuring time for bringing the suit does not begin to run until the party claiming injury first discovers or should reasonably have discovered that he or she was injured and that the defendant was the one who caused the injury. Further, if the injured party is a minor, additional extensions may be provided. Practitioners should check their own state laws for applicable details.

Stipulations: An agreement entered into between opposing counsel in a pending action.

Subpoena: Court document requiring a person to appear to give testimony at a deposition or in court.

Subpoena duces tecum: Subpoena that requires a person to personally bring to the court proceeding a specified document or property in his or her possession or under his or her control.

Summary judgment: Preverdict judgment rendered by the court in response to a motion by a plaintiff or a defendant, who claims that the absence of factual dispute on one or more issues eliminates those issues from further considerations.

Summons: A process served on a defendant in a civil action to secure his or her appearance in the action.

Tort: Civil wrong in which a person has breached a duty to another, which requires proof of the following: that a legal duty was owed to the plaintiff by the defendant; that the defendant breached the duty; and that the plaintiff was injured as a proximate cause of action, such as negligence.

Vicarious liability: Derivative or secondary liability predicated not upon direct fault but by virtue of the defendant's relationship to the actual wrongdoer, in which the former is presumed to hold a position of responsibility and control over the latter.

Waiver: Intentional and volitional renunciation of a known claim or right or a failure to avail oneself of a possible advantage to be derived from another's act. For example, a waiver might allow a person to testify to information that would ordinarily be protected as a privileged communication.

Wanton: Conduct that by its grossly negligent, malicious, or reckless nature evinces a disregard for the consequences or for the rights or safety of others.

Willful: Term descriptive of conduct that encompasses the continuum from intentional to reckless.

Internet Sites 

Legal Definitions. (n.d.). Online legal dictionary. Retrieved 2004 from http://www.legal-definitions.com

'Lectric Law Library. (n.d.). Legal Lexicon's Lyceum. Retrieved 2004 from http://www.lectlaw.com/def.htm

Related Topics

Chapter 110, "Dealing With Subpoenas"

Chapter 139, "Common Clinical Abbreviations and Symbols"

112 FIFTEEN HINTS ON MONEY MATTERS AND RELATED ETHICAL ISSUES

Gerald P. Koocher & Sam S. Hill III

Money matters raise myriad complex issues in a psychologist's practice. One must consider the effect of money from the perspectives of business, ethics, and professional relationships with one's clients. The following items address essential principles to keep in mind when dealing in money matters.

1. Inform clients about fees, billing and collection practices, and other financial contingencies as a routine part of initiating the professional relationship. Repeat this information later, if necessary. From the outset of a relationship with a new client, the psychologist should take care to explain the nature of services to be offered, the fees to be charged, the mode of payment to be used, and other financial arrangements that might reasonably be expected to influence the potential client's decisions. Many practitioners find it useful to put such information in a pamphlet or handout for clients along with other basic information, such as confidentiality and emergency coverage notices.

2. What to charge? Many factors contribute to this decision. Determining the customary charges for one's services is a complicated task that mixes issues of economics, the competitive business environment, the practitioner's self-esteem, and a variety of cultural and professional taboos. When it comes to mental health services, the task is complicated by a host of both subtle and obvious psychological and ethical values. Fees generally vary as a function of training and activity. As reported in the summary of the current *Psychotherapy Finances* fee survey (see chapter 133), fees vary by region, with psychiatrists generally charging more than psychologists, who charge more than social workers and other master's-degree-level providers. Some practitioners charge premium fees for services of a forensic nature that run considerably higher than their fees for psychotherapy. One psychiatrist from the Northeast who testifies in high-profile litigation, for example, recently reported charging $150 per 45-minute psychotherapy session and $400 for 60 minutes of forensic time.

3. Offering sliding fee scales for clients who cannot afford their customary charges provides an important public service. Some practitioners prefer to maintain a high "usual and customary rate" while providing an assortment of discounts. For example, a client who has been in treatment for an extended period may be paying a lower rate than a new client. Or an individual who is being seen three hours per week may be offered a lower hourly rate than a person seen only once per week. The American Psychological Association (APA) ethics code specifies the aspirational expectation that psychologists render at least some *pro bono* services (i.e., professional activity undertaken at no charge in the public interest).

4. Honoring an estimate is very important. Clients may well ask for an estimate regarding the likely cost of services for a neuropsychological evaluation, a child-custody assessment, or a course of treatment. If an estimate of charges is given, it should be honored unless unforeseen circumstances arise. In the latter situation, any changes should be discussed with and agreed to by the client. If it seems that financial difficulties may be an issue, they should be dealt with directly at the very outset of the professional relationship.

5. Some practitioners whose clients delay in paying bills occasionally add interest or "billing charges" to unpaid invoices. This practice may run afoul of the law because state and federal laws generally require special disclosure statements informing clients about such fees in advance and agreed to in writing by the client.

6. The ethical practitioner will attempt to avoid financially triggered abandonment of clients with two specific strategies. The first is to never contract for services without first explaining the costs to the client and mutually determining that the costs are affordable. The second is to not mislead the client into thinking that insurance or other third-party coverage will bear the full cost of services when it seems reasonably clear that benefits may expire before the need for service ends. When treatment is in progress and a client becomes unemployed or otherwise can no longer pay for continued services, the practitioner should be especially sensitive to the client's needs. If a psychologist cannot realistically help a client under existing reimbursement restrictions, and the resulting process might be too disruptive, it may be best to simply explain the problem and not take on the prospective client. At times it may become necessary to terminate care or transfer the client elsewhere over the long term, but this should not be done abruptly or in the midst of a crisis period in the client's life.

7. Increasing fees in the course of service delivery poses ethical dilemmas. If a commitment is made to provide consultation or conduct an assessment for a set fee, it should be honored. Likewise, a client who enters psychotherapy at an agreed-upon rate has a reasonable expectation that the charges will not be raised excessively. Once service has begun, the provider has an obligation to the client that must be considered. Aside from financial hardship issues, the psychologist may have acquired special influence with the client that should makes it difficult for the person to object.

8. Some practitioners require clients to pay certain fees in advance of rendering services as a kind of retainer (e.g., in forensic cases or other complex assessments). This is an unusual practice in psychology, but not unethical so long as the contingencies are mutually agreed upon. The most common use of such advance payments involves relationships in which the practitioner is asked to hold time available on short notice for some reasons (as in certain types of corporate consulting) or when certain types of litigation are involved. For example, practitioners conducting evaluations for the courts have a right to be paid for their time, even if the clients do not like the recommendations that result. In such situations, it is not unusual for the practitioner to request a retainer or escrow payment prior to commencing work.

9. Payment for missed appointments occasionally becomes another source of problems. It is not unethical to charge a client for an appointment that is not kept or that is canceled on short notice, so long as this policy is explained and agreed to by the client in advance. Insurance companies and other third-party payers generally do not pay for missed appointments.

10. Relationships involving kickbacks, fee splitting, or payment of commissions for client referrals may be illegal and unethical. Careful attention to the particular circumstances and state laws is important before agreeing to such arrangements. Clients should be told of any aspects of the arrangement that might reasonably be expected to influence their decision about whether to use the practitioner's services.

11. It is important for psychologists to pay careful attention to all contractual obligations, to understand them, and to abide by them. Similarly, psychologists should not sign contracts with stipulations that might subsequently place them in ethical jeopardy. When in doubt, obtaining a legal review of the contract may help.

12. Psychologists should not profit unfairly at the expense of clients. Psychologists must exercise great care, and at times suffer potential economic disadvantage, so as not to abuse the relative position of power and influence they have over the clients they serve.

13. Psychologists may be held responsible for financial misrepresentations effected in their name by an employee or agent they have designated (including billing and collection agents). They must, therefore, choose their employees and representatives with care and supervise them closely.

14. In all debt collection situations, psychologists must be aware of the laws that apply in their jurisdiction and make every effort to behave in a cautious, businesslike fashion. They must avoid using their special position or information gained through their professional role to collect debts.

15. In dealing with managed-care organizations, psychologists should adhere to the same standards of competence, professionalism, and integrity as in other contexts. Heightened sensitivity should be focused on the potential ethical problems inherent in such service delivery systems.

References & Readings

DiBella, C. A. W. (1980). Mastering money issues that complicate treatment: The last taboo. *American Journal of Psychotherapy, 24,* 510–522.

Faustman, W. O. (1982). Legal and ethical issues in debt collection strategies of professional psychologists. *Professional Psychology: Research and Practice, 13,* 208–214.

Grossman, M. (1971). Insurance reports as a threat to confidentiality. *American Journal of Psychiatry, 128,* 96–100.

Karon, B. P. (1995). Provision of psychotherapy under managed care: A growing crisis and national nightmare. *Professional Psychology: Research and Practice, 26,* 5–9.

Lovinger, R. J. (1978). Obstacles in psychotherapy: Setting a fee in the initial contact. *Professional Psychology: Research and Practice, 9,* 350–352.

Myers, W., & Brezlei, M. (1992). Selling or buying a practice. *Independent Practitioner, 12,* 521.

Pope, K. S. (1988). Fee policies and procedures: Causes of malpractice suits and ethics complaints. *Independent Practitioner, 7,* 24–29.

Pope, K. S., & Keith-Spiegel, P. (1986, May). Is selling a practice malpractice? *APA Monitor, 4,* 40.

Rodwin, M. (1993). *Medicine, money and morals: Physicians' conflicts of interest.* New York: Oxford University Press.

Related Topics

Chapter 107, "Basic Principles for Dealing With Legal Liability Risk Situations"

Chapter 125, "Sample Psychotherapist-Patient Contract"

Chapter 133, "Psychologists' Fees and Incomes"

113 HOW TO CONFRONT AN UNETHICAL COLLEAGUE

Patricia Keith-Spiegel

What action should be taken upon learning of an alleged unethical act by a colleague? Either rationalizing away the colleague's behavior as a minor or a onetime mistake or assuming that others who know of the behavior will take care of it is an inadequate excuse for shirking professional responsibility. Yet too many practitioners decide not to get involved. Conflicting feelings over perceiving a duty to take some action toward unethical colleagues and yet maintaining a loyal and protective stance toward them are common sources of reticence to get involved. One of the very attractive features of informal peer monitoring, however, is that both goals can be met simultaneously. When you success fully intervene, you will have solved a problem and possibly protected a colleague from having to interact with a more formal (and onerous) correctional forum.

The American Psychological Association (APA) ethics code (2002) actively deputizes psychologists to monitor peer conduct, although in a somewhat cautious and protective manner. Earlier versions of the ethics code mandated that psychologists deal directly with ethics violations committed by colleagues as the first line of action. Only if an informal attempt proved unsuccessful should an ethics committee be contacted. Currently, and partly because of reported incidents of harassment and intimidation, and the potential for violations of confidentiality, the 2002 code gives psychologists the option of deciding the appropriateness of dealing with the matter directly. If an informal solution seems unlikely (for reasons left unspecified in the code), psychologists are mandated to take formal action—such as contacting a licensing board or ethics committee—so long as any confidentiality rights or conflicts can be resolved (Ethical Principles of Psychologists and Code of Conduct, Sections 1.04 and 1.05). The level of seriousness of the alleged behavior is not a stated consideration in the 2002 code, although Canter, Bennett, Jones, and Nagy (1994) advise against attempting informal resolutions in cases of complex violations, such as when serious sexual misconduct has occurred.

Peer monitoring often may involve colleagues whose conduct and professional judgment are affected by stress, addiction, or physical or mental disability. According to a survey undertaken by the APA Task Force on Distressed Psychologists, almost 70% of the sample personally knew of psychologists who were experiencing serious emotional difficulties. Moreover, only about a third made substantive attempts to help (reported in VandenBos & Duthie, 1986). From our own experience on ethics committees, we estimate that almost half of those psychologists for whom complaints were made appear to have some personal problem that contributed to the alleged ethical violation.

It is not uncommon to be told of an ethics violation by parties who then request assistance to deal with the alleged violator, but who insist that their identities not be revealed. Often these people are fearful of reprisal or feel inadequate to defend themselves.

Occasionally, the problem is that yet another person, critical to the case, is unavailable or unwilling to get involved or to be identified. These situations pose extremely frustrating predicaments. Approaching colleagues with charges issued by "unseen accusers" violates the essence of due process. Further, alleged violators often know (or think they know) their accusers' identities anyway. When the alleged unethical behaviors are extremely serious, possibly putting yet others in harm's way, and when the fearful but otherwise credible individuals making the charges are adamant about remaining anonymous, psychologists may not feel comfortable ignoring the situation altogether. However, there may be nothing else that can be done. Sometimes the option to do nothing may not exist, as with state mandatory reporting laws. However, for other nonlegally required reporting situations, the current APA code does not leave psychologists any options if confidentiality issues cannot be resolved.

The following list provides guidelines for how to confront a colleague suspected of engaging in unethical conduct.

1. The relevant ethical principle that applies to the suspected breach of professional ethics should first be identified. This may involve an overarching moral principle, or it may involve a specific prohibition in an ethics code or policy. If nothing can be linked to the action, and no law, relevant policy, or ethics code has been violated, then the matter may not be an ethical one. This conclusion is reached most often when a colleague has an offensive personal style or holds personal views that are generally unpopular or widely divergent from your own. You have the right, of course, to express your personal feelings to your colleague, but this should not be construed as engaging in a professional duty.

2. Assess the strength of the evidence that a violation has been committed. Ethical infractions, particularly those that are more serious, are seldom committed openly before a host of dispassionate witnesses. With few exceptions, such as plagiarism or inappropriate advertising of services, no tangible exhibits corroborate that an unethical event ever occurred. A starting point involves categorizing the source of your information into one of five types: (a) clear, direct observation of a colleague engaging in unethical behavior; (b) knowing or unknowing disclosure by a colleague that he or she has committed an ethical violation; (c) direct observation of a colleague's suspicious but not clearly interpretable behavior; (d) receipt of a credible secondhand report of unethical conduct from someone seeking out your assistance as a consultant or intervening party; or (e) casual gossip about a colleague's unethical behavior.

If you did not observe the actions directly, how credible is the source of information? Can you imagine a reason that would not be unethical that would explain why the person might have engaged in this action? That is, can you think of more than one reason the person might have acted that way? If the information came by casual gossip, proceed with considerable caution. If there is no way to obtain any substantial, verifiable facts, you may choose to ignore the information or, as a professional courtesy to the colleague, inform your colleague of the "scuttlebutt." If the colleague is guilty of what the idle hearsay suggests, you may have had a salutary effect. However, we recognize that this is risky business and may be effective only if the colleague is one whose reaction you can reasonably anticipate in advance.

If the information is secondhand, and you are approached by a credible person who claims firsthand knowledge and is seeking assistance, we advise being as helpful as you can. Because we often advise consulting with colleagues before taking any action, it is only fitting that you should be receptive when others approach you for assistance in working through ethical issues. Often you will be able to assist the person with a plan of action that will not include your direct involvement or else offer a referral if the dilemma is not one about which you can confidently comment. If you do agree to be come actively engaged, be sure that you have proper permission to reveal any relevant identities and that you have available all possible information.

3. Get in close touch with your own motivations to engage in (or to avoid) a confrontation with a colleague. Psychologists who are (or see themselves as being) directly victimized by the conduct of a colleague are probably more willing to get involved. In addition to any fears, anger, biases, or other emotional reactions, do you perceive that the colleague's alleged conduct—either as it stands or if it continues—may undermine the integrity of the profession or harm one or more of the consumers served by the colleague? If your answer is affirmative, then some form of proactive stance is warranted. However, if you recognize that your emotional involvement or vulnerability (e.g., the colleague is your supervisor) creates an extreme hazard that will likely preclude a satisfactory outcome, you may wish to consider passing the intervention task on to another party. In such cases, any confidentiality issues must first be settled.

4. Consultation with a trusted and experienced colleague who has demonstrated sensitivity to ethical issues is strongly recommended at this point, even if only to assure yourself that you are on the right track. Identities should not be shared if confidentiality issues pertain.

5. Make your final decision about confronting the colleague and how to best do it. Even though you are not responsible for rectifying the unethical behavior of another person, the application of a decision-making model may facilitate a positive educative function. You might well find yourself, at this point, tempted to engage in one of two covert activities as alternatives to confronting a colleague directly. The first is to pass the information along to other colleagues in an effort to warn them. Although informing others may provide a sense that duty has been fulfilled, it is far more likely that responsibility has only been diffused. Idle talk certainly cannot guarantee that an offending colleague or the public has been affected in any constructive way. Moreover, as noted earlier, to the extent that the conduct was misjudged, you could be responsible for an injustice to a colleague that is, in itself, unethical. The second temptation is to engage in more direct but anonymous action, such as sending an unsigned note or relevant document (e.g., a copy of an ethics code with one or more sections circled in red). Constructive results, however, are hardly guaranteed. The recipient may not understand the intended message. Even if the information is absorbed, the reaction to an anonymous charge may be counterproductive. Also, the warning may instill a certain amount of paranoia that could result in additional negative consequences, such as adding suspiciousness to the colleague's character. Thus, although both of these covert actions seem proactive, we strongly recommend neither.

6. If you decide to go ahead with a direct meeting, schedule it in advance, although not in a menacing manner. For example, do not say, "Something has come to my attention about you that causes me grave concern. What are you doing a week from next Thursday?" Rather, indicate to your colleague that you would like to speak privately and schedule a face-to-face meeting at his or her earliest convenience. A business setting would normally be more appropriate than a home or restaurant, even if the colleague is a friend. Handling such matters on the phone is not recommended unless geographic barriers preclude a direct meeting. Letters create a record, but they do not allow for back-and-forth interaction, which we believe to be conducive to a constructive exchange in matters of this sort. We do not recommend e-mail for the same reason, as well as the additional concern that electronic communications can be accessed by unauthorized others.

7. When entering into the confrontation phase, remain calm and self-confident. The colleague is likely to display considerable emotion. Remain as nonthreatening as possible. Even though it may feel like a safe shield, avoid adopting a rigidly moralistic demeanor. Most people find righteous indignation obnoxious. We suggest noninflammatory language such as expressing confusion and seeking clarification. It might go some thing like this: "The data reported in your article is not quite the same as what you showed me earlier. I am confused about that and wonder if you could help mc understand it. Is there a problem here?" Or, "I met a young woman who, upon learning that I was a psychologist, told me that she was your client and that the two of you were going to start dating. I thought we should talk about it." Things are not always as they seem, and it would be wise at the onset to allow for an explanation rather than provoke anxiety. For example, it is at least possible that the colleague might learn that the young woman was briefly a client years earlier. Such responses may not render the matters moot, but the discussion would likely proceed far differently than with a more strident opening.

8. Set the tone for a constructive and educative session. Your role is not that of accuser, judge, jury, and penance dispenser. The session will probably progress best if you see yourself as having an alliance with the colleague—not in the usual sense of consensus and loyalty, but as facing a problem together.

9. Describe your ethical obligations, noting the relevant moral or ethics code principles that prompted your intervention. Rather than equivocating, state your concerns directly and present the evidence on which they are based. Do not attempt to play detective by trying to trap your colleague through asking leading questions or by withholding any relevant information that you are authorized to share. Such tactics lead only to defensiveness and resentment and diminish the possibility of a favorable outcome.

10. Allow the colleague ample time to explain and defend in as much detail as required. The colleague may be flustered and repetitive; be patient.

11. What is your relationship with the suspected colleague? This will affect both the approach taken and how you interpret the situation. Those who observe or learn of possible unethical actions by other psychologists often know the alleged offenders personally. They could be good friends or disliked antagonists. They could be subordinates or supervisors. Reactions, depending on the relationships with those suspected of ethics violations, affect both the approach taken to deal with them and the attributes assigned to colleagues. Fear of reprisal can stifle action and enhance the rationalization of inaction. If the colleague is disliked, courage to act may come more from the thrill of revenge rather than from genuine courage and conviction. If the colleague is a friend or acquaintance with whom there have been no previous problematic interactions, the meeting usually goes easier. You can express to your friend that your interest and involvement are based on caring and concern for his or her professional standing. The danger, of course, is that you may feel that you are risking an established, positive relationship. If your friend can be educated effectively by you, however, you may well have protected him or her from embarrassment or more public forms of censure. Moreover, if you have lost respect for your friend after observing or learning of possible ethical misconduct, the relationship has been altered anyway. Discomfort, to the extent that it ensues, may be temporary.

If the colleague is someone you do not know personally, the confrontation will be, by definition, more formal. An expression of concern and a willingness to work through the problem cooperatively may still be quite effective. If the colleague is someone you do know but dislike, your dilemma is more pronounced. If the information is known to others (or can be appropriately shared with others), you might consider asking someone who has a better relationship with this person to intercede or to accompany you. If that is not feasible and a careful assessment of your own motivations reveals a conclusion that the possible misconduct clearly requires intervention on its own merits, then you should take some form of action. It may still be possible to approach this individual yourself, and if you maintain a professional attitude, it may work out. If you are intervening on behalf of another, you will first have to disclose why you are there and offer any other caveats. You might say something like, "I, myself, have no direct knowledge of what I want to discuss, but I have agreed to speak with you on behalf of two students." Your role in such instances may be to arrange another meeting with all the parties present and possibly serve as mediator during such a meeting.

12. If the colleague becomes abusive or threatening, attempt to steer him or her to a more constructive state. Although many people need a chance to vent feelings, they often settle down if the confronting person remains steady and refrains from becoming abusive in return. If the negative reaction continues, it may be appropriate to say something calming, such as, "I see you are very upset right now, and I regret that we cannot explore this matter together in a way that would be satisfactory to both of us. I would like you to think about what I have presented, and if you would reconsider talking more about it, please contact me within a week." If a return call is not forthcoming, other forms of action must be considered. This could involve including another appropriate person or pressing formal charges to some duly constituted monitoring body. It is probably wise to have another consultation with a trusted colleague at this point. The suspected offender should be informed (in person or in a formal note) of your next step. If you are ever the recipient of a colleague's inquiry, be grateful for the warning about how you have been perceived and try to openly and honestly work for the goal of settling the matter in a way that satisfies all those involved without necessitating a review by outside evaluators.

References & Readings 

American Psychological Association. (2002). *Ethical principles of psychologists and code of conduct.* Washington, DC: Author.

Bennett, B. E., Bryant, B. K., VandenBos, G. R., & Greenwood, A. (1990). *Professional liability and risk management.* Washington, DC: American Psychological Association.

Canter, M. B., Bennett, B. E., Jones, S. E., & Nagy, T. F. (1994). *Ethics for psychologists: A commentary on the APA ethics code.* Washington, DC: American Psychological Association.

Koocher, G. P., & Keith-Spiegel, P. C. (1998). *Ethics in psychology: Professional standards and cases* (2nd ed.). New York: Oxford University Press.

VandenBos, G. R., & Duthie, R. F. (1986). Confronting and supporting colleagues in distress. In R. R. Kilburg, P. E. Nathan, & R. W. Thorenson (Eds.), *Professionals in distress.* Washington, DC: American Psychological Association.

Related Topics

Chapter 103, "Ethical Principles of Psychologists and Code of Conduct (2002)"

Chapter 109, "Dealing With Licensing Board and Ethics Complaints"

Chapter 136, "Therapist Self-Care Checklist"

114 CONFIDENTIALITY AND THE DUTY TO PROTECT

Tiffany Chenneville

It is generally agreed that information shared within the context of a psychotherapy relationship should be kept confidential. However, the delicate balance between clinicians' duty to their clients, on the one hand, and their duty to protect others, on the other hand, is highlighted when threats of violence are made. The complexity of such matters is discussed in this chapter, along with recommendations for addressing this dilemma.

CONFIDENTIALITY

Confidentiality refers to a standard of professional conduct between mental health professionals and their clients. It represents an ethical principle that can be distinguished from privacy and privilege (see Koocher, chap. 104 in this volume). *Privacy* is a constitutional right, the importance of and limits to which are outlined thoroughly by Gates and Fitzgerald (2000). *Privilege* is a legal term that refers to the right for communication between individuals within special relationships to remain private. Special relationships include those between attorneys and their clients, husbands and wives, doctors and patients, and priests and penitents. In a Supreme Court ruling, the attorney-client privilege was upheld even after the client's death (*Swidler & Berlin and James Hamilton v. United States*, 1997), thus exemplifying the legal system's acknowledgement of the importance of confidentiality. The values underlying confidentiality, which include stigma, trust, privacy, and autonomy (Petrila, 2000a) are particularly important within the mental health domain. Confidentiality is considered critical to the development and maintenance of therapeutic relationships. For this reason, and because breaches of confidentiality have the potential to cause harm to clients, the ethical standard of confidentiality often is upheld through state laws and regulations.

In an effort to protect the public, provisions for confidentiality and the disclosure of confidential information are outlined by the American Psychological Association (APA) in its ethical codes and standards (2002). Ethical Standard 4.01, which addresses maintaining confidentiality, states: "Psychologists have a primary obligation and take reasonable cautions to protect confidential information obtained through or stored in any medium, recognizing that the extent and limits of confidentiality may be regulated by law or established by institutional rules or professional or scientific relationship" (APA, 2002, p. 1066).

Confidentiality is one of the most frequent complaints made to regulatory bodies by members of the general public (Josefowitz, 1997). Decisions regarding when it is acceptable to breach client confidentiality weigh heavily on the minds of clinicians. The ethical and legal principles of confidentiality often compete with other equally important principles, sometimes resulting in the division of loyalties for clinicians between clients and third parties.

DUTY TO PROTECT

Duty to protect represents one of the most important principles competing with confidentiality. The potentially disastrous consequences of this dilemma are exemplified by the landmark court case *Tarasoff v. Regents of the University of California* (1974, 1976). This case involved a university counseling center psychologist who was informed by his client of intent to harm Tatiana Tarasoff. The psychologist reported the situation to campus police, who briefly detained the client. However, the client subsequently was released based on the campus police's conclusion that he did not pose a threat to Tarasoff. Tarasoff, who had been vacationing out of the county at the time the threat was made, was killed by the client upon her return to the country two months later. The psychologist, among other defendants, was sued by Tarasoff's parents for failing to protect their daughter from harm, either by way of warning or through civil commitment of the client.

This case commenced in a ruling by the Supreme Court of California, in which a duty to warn potential victims of imminent danger was imposed on psychologists. However, upon appeal, the "duty to warn" was replaced with a more general "duty to protect." Based on this ruling, a duty to protect exists when it is determined, or should have been determined, that a client poses a serious risk of violence to others.

Pre-*Tarasoff*, public protection of a client's potential for violence primarily was limited to civil commitment (Felthous, 2001), while psychological malpractice associated with dangerousness was associated with negligent hospital release (Walcott, Cerundolo, & Beck, 2001). Post-*Tarasoff*, courts initially expanded the role of psychologists to protect third parties. Such expansions included broad interpretations of violence, as evidenced by case law wherein transmission of HIV was considered a violent act under *Tarasoff* principles (Chenneville, 2000). However, the more recent trend has been to limit the situations in which the duty to protect applies and toward permissive or protective disclosure laws. These laws legally protect clinicians who decide that breaching confidentiality is warranted to protect a third party. When a duty does exist, public protection involves "reasonable actions," which include, but may not be limited to, an actual warning, notifying law enforcement, or civil commitment. Parenthetically, in the absence of a special relationship (e.g., parent-child, doctor-client, priest-penitent), no duty to protect exists. In most states, mental health professionals fall under the special relationship of doctor-client.

From a legal perspective, rules governing third-party liability have become increasingly diverse. However, it generally is accepted that in order for a duty to protect to exist, there must be a serious and imminent risk of harm directed toward an identifiable person (Simon, 2001). It is important to note that the "naming" of a victim is not a necessary component of identification (Walcott et al., 2001). Rather, the onus is on the mental health professional to identify, within reason, potential victims. For example, if a client makes a threat against his "wife," without providing his wife's name, it would not be unreasonable to assume the clinician could gain access to the wife's identification.

The practitioner's legal obligations potentially compete with two ethical principles regarding avoiding harm and disclosures. Ethical Standard 3.04 states that "psychologists take reasonable steps to avoid harming their clients/patients, students, supervisees, research participants, organizational clients, and others with whom they work, and to minimize harm where it is foreseeable and unavoidable" (APA, 2002, p. 1065). With regard to disclosures, Ethical Standard 4.05b states: "Psychologists disclose confidential information without the consent of the individual only as mandated by law, or where permitted by law for a valid purpose such as to (1) provide needed professional services; (2) obtain appropriate professional consultations; (3) protect the client/patient, psychologist, or others from harm; or (4) obtain payment for services from a client/patient, in which instance disclosure is limited to the minimum that is necessary to achieve the purpose" (APA, 2002, p. 1066). These professional standards clearly invoke conflicting duties for clinicians. Absent of applicable statutory or case law, these standards establish an ethical duty not only to prevent harm to clients but also to prevent others from harm.

Beyond competing ethical standards, moral issues on the duty to protect are also operating (Gutheil, 2001). Among these, the Hippocratic Oath has been referenced in support of maintaining confidentiality. In support of disclosure, it has been argued that clinicians acting as the "agents" of their clients should breach confidentiality when doing so would be in their clients' best interest. Similarly, it has been argued that mental health professionals have a fiduciary duty. Trusted to put their clients' best interest before their own, it has been argued that warning may be justified in an attempt to spare clients from the potential emotional, social, and legal consequences associated with harming others, even if doing so causes the clinician distress (Gutheil, 2001). The shift in the way society views the "victim paradigm" is unclear and further complicates matters. Historically, the client was viewed as the victim, but society frequently now views the potential target of the client as the victim. Finally, it has been posited that warning is morally justified to save a life within the context of an emergency (Gutheil, 2001).

CLINICAL RECOMMENDATIONS

When confronted with the confidentiality versus duty to protect dilemma, the psychologist must take several factors into consideration. These factors include professional ethical standards, the best interest of the client, the major premises of *Tarasoff*, and applicable statutory and case law. The following recommendations take into account these factors and represent the adaptation of a decision-making model for clients whose threat of violence is the transmission of HIV (Chenneville, 2000).

1. *Determine whether disclosure is warranted.* Foreseeability of harm and identifiability of the victim are the two major issues that must be addressed when making a determination whether disclosure is warranted. In terms of foreseeability, the extent to which the threat of harm is serious and the danger imminent need to be considered. It has been argued that risk appraisal should be "fact based and deductive" as opposed to the "more inductive risk assessment approach for general violence recidivism" (Borum & Reddy, 2001, p. 377). This would include an assessment of the following: (a) attitudes that support or facilitate violence, (b) the capacity to carry out the threat, (c) whether or not certain thresholds of violence have been crossed, (d) intent, (e) others' reactions and responses to threats (i.e., the extent to which others are supporting violent behavior in the client and/or the extent to which others are threatened by the client), and (f) compliance with attempts to reduce risk of violence. Although tools are available to assist clinicians in assessing the risk of violence, it generally is agreed that clinicians' ability to accurately predict violence is limited (Walcott et al., 2001). However, a thorough assessment of violence risk is expected, even if the accuracy of predictions is not. Following are questions to consider when assessing the foreseeability of harm:

- Has the client made a specific threat?
- Has the client specified a plan including a date, time, or place?
- Does the client have the means to carry out the threat?
- Does the client have access to weapons?
- Does the client possess the physical capabilities required to carry out the threat?
- Does the client possess the intellectual capabilities to carry out the threat?
- Does the client have access to the intended victim(s)?
- Does the client believe violence is justified?
- Does the client believe violence will result in positive outcomes?
- Does the client believe his/her needs can be met without violence?
- Is the client being encouraged or supported by others to engage in violent behavior?
- What personality characteristics exist that increase the risk for violence?
- Does the client have a history of violence?
- Does the client have a history of antisocial or illegal behavior?
- Does the client have a history of substance abuse?
- Does the client perceive others as hostile?
- Is the client impulsive?
- Does the client typically use good judgment?
- Has the client been diagnosed with an

Axis I or Axis II disorder? If so, what symptoms are likely to increase the risk of danger to others?

- Does the client adhere to prescribed treatment?
- Has the client been prescribed medication and is s/he compliant?
- Does the client possess motivation to prevent or avoid violence?

Once the foreseeability of harm has been established, the clinician next must determine whether or not the intended violence is directed toward a specific victim or victims. The following questions can help determine whether an identifiable victim exists:

- Has the client named a specific victim?
- Has the client made reference to an identifiable victim whose name was unspecified, but who could be identified via association with the client?
- Has the client made reference to a general class of victims (e.g., colleagues at work)?

2. *Refer to the ethical code.* An examination of relevant professional ethical guidelines is the second step of this decision-making model. Members of the American Psychological Association should refer to Ethical Standards relating to confidentiality (4.01), avoiding harm (3.04), and disclosures (4.05b). Members of the APA also should refer to Ethical Standard 1.02, which addresses conflicts between ethics and law, regulations, or other governing legal authority and states: "If psychologists' ethical responsibilities conflict with law, regulations, or other governing legal authority, psychologists make known their commitment to the Ethics Code and take steps to resolve the conflict. If the conflict is unresolvable via such means, psychologists may adhere to the requirements of the law, regulations, or other governing legal authority" (APA, 2002, p. 1063).

3. *Refer to state guidelines.* The third step involves referring to statutory and case law, which typically specifies either mandatory confidentiality, required disclosure, or protective (i.e., permissive) disclosure whereby clinicians are allowed, but not legally obligated, to disclose confidential information. Legal mandates governing confidentiality and third-party disclosures vary by state, so it is important for clinicians to investigate the laws and rules set forth by the states in which they practice. The ever-changing legal climate with regard to *Tarasoff* has been well documented (Felthous, 2001; Glancy, Regehr, & Bryant, 1998), and it is the responsibility of clinicians to keep informed of these changes. State laws and rules often can be obtained from individual state boards of psychology or by accessing the state statutes and legislation on the Internet (http://www.prairienet.org/~scruffy/f.htm). Readers also are referred to an appendix compiled by Petrila (2000b) that includes the key provisions of state laws pertaining to confidentiality and mental health.

4. *Implement the least invasive alternative.* After carefully assessing the situation, the least invasive alternative should be chosen with priority given to clinical and moral reasoning (Felthous & Kachigian, 2001). Indeed, prediction of dangerousness ultimately is a clinical decision, not a legal one. In cases where threats are not deemed serious or imminent, or where victims are not and cannot be identified, maintaining confidentiality may be the best course of action. This may help to preserve the therapeutic alliance, which can then be used to modify the client's thoughts, feelings, and behavior in an attempt to prevent future violence.

In situations where warning is not appropriate or feasible, protective action may include notifying law enforcement or civil commitment. If disclosure is warranted, it is important to disclose only the information necessary to protect potential victims. For example, it probably would not be necessary to include diagnoses or personal information shared in psychotherapy. Rather, the victims or appropriate others (e.g., family members or law enforcement) need only be informed of the potential danger of harm by the client. It also is recommended that clients not only be informed but also be included, to the extent feasible, in the protective action. For example, in some situations, assuming no clinical contraindications exist, it may be appropriate to make disclosures in the presence, or with the assistance, of the client. Finally, given that the best safeguard against malpractice is documentation, it is crucial for clinicians to document not only their actions but also the reasons behind their actions.

In summary, the confidentiality versus duty to protect dilemma entails a clinical assessment of dangerousness, as opposed to its being a legal issue. In many cases, ethical standards are more stringent than legal standards in terms of protecting the client. It is the clinician's responsibility, as outlined in the APA ethical codes, to make known their commitment to the ethical standards and to attempt to resolve the ethical-legal conflict in the most appropriate manner possible. Clinicians may be able to minimize these difficulties by making clear at the onset of the therapeutic relationship the limits of confidentiality and possible procedures to be taken should a breach be deemed necessary.

References, Readings, & Internet Sites 

American Psychological Association. (2002). Ethical principles of psychologists and code of conduct. *American Psychologist, 57,* 1060–1073.

Borum, R., & Reddy, M. (2001). Assessing violence risk in Tarasoff situations: A fact-based model of inquiry. *Behavioral Sciences and the Law, 19,* 375–385.

Chenneville, T. (2000). HIV, confidentiality, and duty to protect: A decision-making model. *Professional Psychology: Research and Practice, 31,* 661–670.

Felthous, A. R. (2001). Introduction to this issue: The clinician's duty to warn or protect. *Behavioral Sciences and the Law, 19,* 321–324.

Felthous, A. R., & Kachigian, C. (2001). To warn and to control: Two distinct legal obligations or variations of a single duty to protect? *Behavioral Sciences and the Law, 19,* 355–373.

Gates, J. J., & Fitzgerald, J. (2000). The importance of privacy and limits to privacy. In J. J. Gates & B. S. Arons (Eds.), *Privacy and confidentiality in mental health care* (pp. 193–218). Baltimore: Paul H. Brookes.

Glancy, G. D., Regehr, C., & Bryant, A. G. (1998). Confidentiality in crisis: Part I—The duty to inform. *Canadian Journal of Psychiatry, 43,* 1001–1005.

Gutheil, T. G. (2001). Moral justification for Tarasoff-type warnings and breach of confidentiality: A clinician's perspective. *Behavioral Sciences and the Law, 19,* 345–353.

Josefowitz, N. (1997). Confidentiality. In D. R. Evans (Ed.), *The law, standards of practice, and ethics in the practice of psychology* (pp. 111–134). Toronto: Emond Montgomery Publications.

Petrila, J. (2000a). Legal and ethical issues in protecting the privacy of behavioral health care information. In J. J. Gates & B. S. Arons (Eds.), *Privacy and confidentiality in mental health care* (pp. 91–126). Baltimore: Paul H. Brookes.

Petrila, J. (2000b). State mental health confidentiality law provisions. In J. J. Gates & B. S. Arons (Eds.), *Privacy and confidentiality in mental health care* (pp. 219–232). Baltimore: Paul H. Brookes.

Prairienet. (n.d.). Link to full-text state statutes and legislation. Retrieved 2004 from http.//www.prairienet.org/~scruffy/f.htm

Simon, R. I. (2001). Duty to foresee, forewarn, and protect against violent behavior: A psychiatric perspective. In S. Mohammad & S. Lee (Eds.), *School violence: Assessment, management, and prevention* (pp. 201–215). Washington, DC: American Psychiatric Press.

Swidler & Berlin and James Hamilton v. United States, No. 97-1192 (1997).

Tarasoff v. Regents of the University of California, 118 Cal. Rptr. 129, 529 P.2d 533 (1974).

Tarasoff v. Regents of the University of California, 17 Cal.3d 425, 551 P.2d 334 (1976).

Walcott, D. M., Cerundolo, P., & Beck, J. C. (2001). Current analysis of the Tarasoff duty: An evolution towards the limitation of the duty to protect. *Behavioral Sciences and the Law, 19,* 325–343.

Related Topic

Chapter 121, "A Model for Clinical Decision Making With Dangerous Patients"

PART IX
Forensic Matters

115 FORENSIC EVALUATIONS AND TESTIMONY

Stanley L. Brodsky

1. *Introducing forensic evaluations:* Forensic clients should be notified that any of their statements or findings of the evaluation may become part of a public record. Rather than assuring the privilege of confidentiality, forensic evaluators fully inform the person that no psychologist-client privilege exists. Caution individuals against saying anything they prefer not to be reported (Greenberg & Moreland, 1993).

2. *Detailed reporting and documentation:* Record and maintain detailed information regarding times, dates, and durations of appointments, phone calls, interviews, reviews of records, consultations, and examination of possible corroborating information. Vagueness about such information may become a source of vulnerability on the witness stand.

3. *Never change records:* Some evaluators revise their notes when further information is received. Avoid this practice. Add and date any supplementary information to notes and records, but do not change already recorded observations or notes.

4. *Keep only one set of records:* The occasional practice of securely filing away a second set of "secret and private" notes for one's own use is wrong. All written notes, observations, corroborative information, and reports should be considered to be on the record.

5. *Prepare responsibly:* Before testifying, ensure that your knowledge is current in psychological conceptualizations, assessment practices, and relevant professional issues (Brodsky, 1994).

6. *Depositions:* Besides the stated purpose of discovery by opposing counsel of facts and findings, depositions serve two additional and sometimes nonobvious purposes. They inform both sides so that evidence may be weighed that would influence settlement discussions. Depositions also allow witnesses to learn the lines of inquiry that may be pursued in the trial. The following is a piece of specific advice for depositions: If you don't know, don't discuss. Much more than in live trials, witnesses in depositions sometimes babble on and speculate far beyond their knowledge, competence, and findings.

7. *Meet before the direct examination:* Some attorneys are unavailable or reluctant to meet with their witnesses before trials. It is worthwhile to pursue such meetings so you will know what questions will be asked (Brodsky, 1991). Attorneys who have not met with their experts often miss essential parts of psychological findings during direct examinations.

8. *Understand the legal context:* The legal rules of evidence and procedure profoundly affect acceptability of testimony (Committee on Ethical Guidelines for Forensic Psychologists, 1991). Read one of the psychology and law texts on this subject. I recommend the book by Melton, Petrila, Poythress, and Slobogin (1987).

9. *Testify only within the scope of reasonable and accepted scientific knowledge:* Experts are bound to this standard by the U.S. Supreme Court *Daubert* decision. These research results should be used in an impartial manner in the face of adversarial pulls of attorneys. It is not unethical to disagree with other experts about readings or applications of knowledge. It is unethical to relinquish the role of neutral expert in favor of highly selective gleaning of knowledge (Sales & Shuman, 1993; Sales & Simon, 1993).

10. *Stay clearly within the boundaries of your own professional expertise:* This mandate from the APA Code of Ethics (American Psychological Association, 1992) means that practitioners with expertise only in psychology of adults do not assess children or testify about child psychology. In the same sense, one should not consider observation of other witnesses' behavior on the stand to be remotely equivalent to findings from conventional psychological assessments.

11. *Credentials:* Skilled opposing counsel can always find something you have not accomplished, written, or mastered. Admit all nonaccomplishments in a matter-of-fact way.

12. *Experience:* The legal system uses breadth, depth, and duration of experience as part of credentialing expert witnesses. Clinicians should be aware that, by itself, clinical experience is unrelated to accuracy of diagnostic judgments (Faust, 1994; Garb, 1989, 1992).

13. *Credibility:* An implicit goal of witnesses is to be credible and believed. People believe witnesses who are likable and confident. To the extent possible, given the nature of the setting, allow the likable aspects of who you are to be visible, and confidently present your findings and conclusions.

14. *Data that do not support your conclusions:* Excessively partisan witnesses attempt to deny existing information they have gathered that contradicts their conclusions. Conscientious and responsible witnesses freely and without defensiveness acknowledge and discuss contradicting information.

15. *Admitting ignorance:* Some expert witnesses present themselves as omniscient and infallible in their fields. Don't. Instead, state "I don't know" in response to queries when you truly do not know the answer.

16. *Use evaluations and testimony as stimuli to learn:* Evaluators and witnesses are typically so caught up in "doing" that they are not open to conceptualizing cases and testimony as learning experiences. I suggest asking, "What additional validated measures might I administer that are directly related to these forensic issues? What else should I read or what short courses should I take to be better prepared? What have I learned about my own needs for professional and scholarly growth?"

References & Readings 

American Psychological Association. (1992). Ethical principles of psychologists and code of conduct. *American Psychologist, 47,* 1597–1611.

Brodsky, S. L. (1991). *Testifying in court: Guidelines and maxims for the expert witness.* Washington, DC: American Psychological Association.

Brodsky, S. L. (1994). Are there sufficient foundations for mental health experts to testify in court? Yes. In S. A. Kirk & S. D. Einbinder (Eds.), *Controversial issues in mental health* (pp. 189–196). Needham Heights, MA: Allyn and Bacon.

Committee on Ethical Guidelines for Forensic Psychologists. (1991). Speciality guidelines for forensic psychologists. *Law and Human Behavior, 15,* 655–665.

Faust, D. (1994). Are there sufficient foundations for mental health experts to testify in court? No. In

S. A. Kirk & S. D. Einbinder (Eds.), *Controversial issues in mental health*. Needham Heights, MA: Allyn and Bacon.

Garb, H. N. (1989). Clinical judgment, clinical training, and professional experience. *Psychological Bulletin, 105*, 387–396.

Garb, H. N. (1992). The *trained* psychologist as expert witness. *Clinical Psychology Review, 12*, 451–467.

Greenberg, S. A., & Moreland, K. L. (1993, October 16–17). Forensic evaluations and forensic applications of the MMPI and MMPI-2. Paper presented at continuing education workshop sponsored by the University of Minnesota in cooperation with the Alabama Psychological Association, Montgomery, AL.

Melton, G., Petrila, J., Poythress, N. G., & Slobogin, C. (1987). *Psychological evaluation for the courts: A handbook for mental health professionals and lawyers.* New York: Guilford Press.

Sales, B. D., & Shuman, D. W. (1993). Reclaiming the integrity of science in expert witnessing. *Ethics and Behavior, 3*, 223–229.

Sales, B. D., & Simon, L. (1993). Institutional constraints on the ethics of expert testimony. *Ethics and Behavior, 3*, 231–249.

Related Topics

Chapter 116, "Forensic Evaluation Outline"
Chapter 117, "Forensic Referrals Checklist"
Chapter 119, "Forensic Assessment Instruments"
Chapter 120, "Evaluation of Competency to Stand Trial"

116 FORENSIC EVALUATION OUTLINE

David L. Shapiro

I. Identifying data (include name, date of birth, age, place of birth, birth order, religious background, present living arrangement, marital status, occupation, race)
II. Charges against defendant
III. Documents reviewed and people interviewed
IV. Confidentiality waiver (state understanding in client's own words)
V. Statement of facts (obtain from police reports, witnesses' statements, interviews of police officers and witnesses, results of drug and alcohol screening if available)
VI. Patient's version of offense (include patient's perceptions, drug or alcohol usage at time, symptoms indicative of mental disorder, behavior at time of offense as related by family or friends, relevant history leading to offense)
VII. Behavior in jail (include patient's statements and interviews of correctional personnel)
VIII. Jail psychiatric records (include discussions of consultations, medications, diagnoses, consistency or inconsistency with above self-described behavior)
IX. Mental status examination (include appearance, behavior, orientation, attention, perception, memory, affect, speech, delusions, hallucinations, suicidal ideation, judgment, indications of toxicity, estimated intelligence and insight)
X. Social history (obtain from patient and include history obtained from family and/or friends)

A. Early childhood (include family composition, nature of interactions, family intactness, major events, illnesses or injuries)
B. Latency age (include school performance, attitude toward studies, outside interests, nature of peer interaction)
C. Adolescence (include sexual development, identity issues, drugs, alcohol, nature of peer interaction, occupations)
D. Young adulthood (include nature of interpersonal relationships, quality of job history)
E. Adulthood
F. Sexual and marital (include dating, number of marriages, personality of spouse, reasons for separation if any)
G. Education (include types of schools, grades, extracurricular activities)
H. Vocational (include number of jobs, length of jobs)
I. Military (include branch, dates, rank obtained, disciplinary actions if any)
J. Religious history
K. Drug and alcohol abuse (include history, kinds, extent, effects on behavior)
L. History of physical or sexual abuse

XI. Criminal history (include for each charge, date of charge, place, and disposition)

XII. Psychiatric history (include nature of admissions, whether voluntary or involuntary, willingness to sign releases, type of treatment rendered)
A. Family psychiatric history
B. Patient's psychiatric history

XIII. Neurological history
A. Head injuries and sequelae (include hospitals, where treatment rendered)
B. Blackouts (unrelated to drugs or alcohol)
C. Dizzy spells
D. Seizures
E. Stupor or staring
F. Repetitive stereotype movements
G. Perceptual distortions
H. Pathological intoxication
I. Spatial disorientation
J. Learning disabilities
K. Explosive behavioral outbursts with minimal provocation (note especially amnesia, aura, peculiar tastes or smells)
L. Confusional episodes and/or slurred speech unrelated to drugs or alcohol
M. Hallucinations unrelated to functional mental disorder
N. Fugue states
O. Déjà vu phenomena
P. Jamais vu phenomena
Q. Depersonalization or derealization
R. Double vision or blurriness
S. History of delirium tremens
T. Memory disturbances
U. Difficulty understanding what is read
V. Difficulty following conversations
W. Contact with chemicals
X. History of venereal disease (syphilis)

XIV. Chronological review of psychiatric records

XV. Interview with treating therapists

XVI. Review of general medical records (check especially for head trauma, antianxiety or antidepressant medication)

XVII. Review of school records

XVIII. Review of occupational records

XIX. Review and critique of prior evaluations in current case

XX. Referrals to other consultants and results of their examinations

XXI. Test results (include test-taking attitude, behavior, degree of defensiveness, validity, motivation, reaction time, evidence of perseveration)
A. WAIS-III or WISC-III
B. Projectives
C. Objective personality tests
D. Neuropsychological screening
E. Neuropsychological battery
F. Assessment of malingering
G. Summary of testing

XXII. Opinion on criminal responsibility (or competence) (specify how mental disorder may affect each functional capacity)
A. Competence
1. Factual understanding
2. Rational understanding
3. Relation to attorney
4. Knowledge of roles of various people
5. Knowledge of pleas and outcomes
B. Criminal responsibility
1. Mental disorder: In what way does it affect
a. Ability to appreciate wrongfulness of behavior
b. Ability to conform to law (if applicable)

c. Other forensic issues (e.g., ability to waive Miranda rights, competence to confess, whether or not the mental disorder resulted in an inability to form specific intent) (for each issue, how does mental disorder relate to each of the functional capacities?)

XXIII. Recommendations for disposition

References & Readings 

Curran, W., McGarry, A. L., Shah, S. (1986). *Forensic psychiatry and psychology*. Philadelphia: F. A. Davis.

Melton, G., Petrila, J., Poythress, N., Slobogin, C. (1997). *Psychological evaluations for the courts* (2nd ed.). New York: Guilford Press.

Shapiro, D. L. (1990). *Forensic psychological assessment: An integrated approach*. Boston: Allyn and Bacon.

Shapiro, D. L. (2000). *Criminal responsibility evaluations*. Sarasota, FL: Professional Resource Press.

Smith, S., & Meyer, R. (1987). *Law, behavior, and mental health: Policy and practice*. New York: New York University Press.

Weiner, I., & Hess, A. (1998). *Handbook of forensic psychology* (2nd ed.). New York: Wiley.

Related Topics

Chapter 115, "Forensic Evaluations and Testimony"
Chapter 117, "Forensic Referrals Checklist"
Chapter 119, "Forensic Assessment Instruments"
Chapter 122, "Principles for Conducting a Comprehensive Child Custody Evaluation"

117 FORENSIC REFERRALS CHECKLIST

Geoffrey R. McKee

Forensic psychology is the application of the theories, methods, and research of psychology to questions of law. Attorneys seek the assistance of psychologists to develop expert opinion to support their arguments before or during trials or hearings involving clients they represent. The purpose of this chapter is to highlight questions you can employ to decide whether to accept such cases and to specify the scope and content of your consultation to the attorney. The competent attorney always anticipates that the case will go to trial. Thus he or she seeks a psychologist who will qualify as an expert witness to provide either "opinion testimony" based on direct contact with the attorney's client or "dissertation testimony" (Myers, 1992) based on the psychologist's research, which the jury then applies to the facts of the case. This chapter also offers questions you should ask to help you decide whether the attorney is seeking professional consultation or a "hired gun."

1. *What is (are) the legal issue(s) in the case?* This question clarifies the type of case (civil, criminal, domestic, administrative) being referred, the issues the attorney considers to be most important, and what general area(s) of expertise are being sought. Any legal case may have a host of issues to be litigated (e.g., competence to confess, competence to stand trial, criminal responsibility, and capital mitigation in a murder case). An early stage in the legal process is negotiation of the issues to be argued. For example, in a personal injury case, the plaintiff files a *complaint* of facts or allegations to which the defendant agrees or denies in an *answer*. The resulting items of disagreement, some of which may require the expertise of a psychologist, become the issues for litigation.

2. *What case facts support your side? The adverse side?* A competent attorney will present the case succinctly and understand both sides of the litigation. This question identifies ill-prepared lawyers seeking only a "hired gun" and also illuminates potential biases or prejudices the attorney may have (e.g., that all plaintiffs malinger illness for disability). For example, an attorney representing a documented alcoholic and domestically abusive husband might request consultation regarding child custody. Knowing these facts, you might decline the case, despite the attorney's protestations that the client's problems are "irrelevant" to his capacity as a parent.

3. *What specific questions would you like me to answer?* This inquiry identifies the parameters of your "contract" with the attorney, affirms the basis for his or her client's informed consent to your services, clarifies the foundation (sources of data) necessary for the formation of your professional opinion(s), and delimits the scope of your expert testimony, if subpoenaed. For example, if you have completed an evaluation only of a client's competence to stand trial, it would be unethical, beyond the scope of your agreement with the attorney, and beyond the client's consent to employ the same set of data to testify about the client's parenting capacity or his or her mental state at the time of the alleged offense.

Once you have a basic understanding of the facts and issues of the case, you should ask Questions 4 and 5 of yourself. Because public testimony might occur in any legal case, thus placing the attorney's client in jeopardy, you should be conservative when answering these questions and realize the adverse side may have retained a psychologist to assist with cross-examination of your credentials to impeach your testimony.

4. *Can the attorney's questions be answered by current psychological knowledge and research?* While psychology can be of great assistance to the court's and/or jury's decision making by providing information about the parties in litigation, many issues may exceed the competence of our methods and practice. The admissibility requirements of *Daubert v. Merrell Dow Pharmaceuticals, Inc.* (1993; see especially Marlowe, 1995) now mandate methods with higher reliability and validity than the "general acceptance" standards of *Frye v. United States* (1923). The current American Psychological Association's "Ethical Principles of Psychologists and Code of Conduct" (2002) specify that psychologists have an ethical responsibility to base their work on "established scientific and professional knowledge of the discipline" (2.04), including diagnostic statements and forensic testimony (9.01a). In certain jurisdictions, it is now not uncommon for the clinician to testify in a pretrial "Daubert hearing" about the scientific validity and reliability of his or her proposed evaluation procedures to assist the judge's admissibility of evidence decisions.

5. *Am I competent on the basis of my training, experience, and licensure to qualify as an expert witness in court to answer the referral questions?* Numerous legal decisions (e.g., *Ibn-Tamas v. United States*, 1979) have affirmed that a judge's determination of a witness's qualification as an expert is not dependent solely on professional title (e.g., psychologist, psychiatrist). Rather, the relevance of the witness's training and work experience to the issues litigated is of paramount importance. Both the American Psychological Association's "Ethical Principles of Psychologists and Code of Conduct" (2.01; 2002) and the "Specialty Guidelines for Forensic Psychologists" (III; 1991) suggest the parameters for competence when engaging in clinical or forensic practice. The clinician should also be familiar with the professional discussions and controversies in the current professional literature relevant to the case's psycholegal issues, such as psychometric "profiles" (Murphy & Peters, 1992), forensic use of projective measures (Grove, Barden, Garb, & Lilienfield, 2002), violence prediction (Monahan et al., 2001), or battered woman syndrome (Follingstad, 2003). Beyond clinical competence, in forensic cases, psychologists have an ethical responsibility to "become reasonably familiar with the judicial or administrative rules governing their roles" and ensure that those to whom the psychologist delegates services have relevant competence (American Psychological Association Standards 2.01(f) and 2.05.2, 2002).

If you answered "Yes" to Questions 4 and 5, proceed to the items below.

6. *Will my consultation (evaluation, etc.) be privileged as your work product?* Work product is any evidence a lawyer develops that is prohibited from disclosure under attorney-client privilege, a more protective standard than professional confidentiality. This question clarifies the conditions under which your service to the attorney (and his or her client) might be shared with the adverse attorney or the court and the client's informed consent regarding release of information (including your courtroom testimony). Each state has its own set of criminal procedure and civil procedure rules governing discovery. This question addresses a fundamental legal issue that requires an answer from the referring attorney.

7. *When is this case likely to go to trial or hearing?* The well-prepared attorney anticipates the use of experts well in advance of trial and realizes that thorough psychological consultation requires time to review documents, evaluate the client over more than one session, conduct collateral interviews, and suggest additional consultations beyond the expertise of the retained psychologist. Accepting last-minute consultations may leave you vulnerable to cross-examination questions of practicing "curbside psychology," the accusation of superficial preparation of expert opinions. In cases where notice is short, you may wish to accept the case on the condition that the attorney will seek a continuance for time to complete a full examination. Midtrial consultations should be avoided unless your testimony will be of "dissertation" form, explaining published research for the court's consideration of a particular issue (e.g., eyewitness memory, relationship violence; see generally Goldstein, 2003).

8. *What documents do you have pertinent to your client? What records does the other side have, and when will they be disclosed?* Because of the high rates of malingering and distortion by clients in criminal, civil, domestic, and administrative litigation, the psychologist cannot rely solely on the statements of the plaintiff or defendant. The "Guidelines" (VI.B) mandate corroboration by other sources as fundamental to the formation of your expert opinions. Ask what records the attorney has for your review; at this point, the attorney's description of the case should suggest other documents needed to complete your consultation. Place the burden of obtaining the documents on the lawyer—subpoenas short-circuit institutional resistance to disclosure of records and also allow the attorney to overcome any discovery rules that you, as a nonlawyer, would not necessarily know.

9. *Who will be responsible for payment of my time? How shall we arrange my retainer?* Financial matters need to be resolved prior to your acceptance of the case. You should clearly describe your fee structure (per hour, per day, etc.) and what will constitute billable hours of your work (e.g., travel time, different fees for records review or courtroom testimony). Early confirmation of fee arrangements is an ethical obligation (American Psychological Association Standards 6.04(a), 2002). Many experienced forensic psychologists have clearly written contracts that are signed by all relevant parties prior to formal case acceptance (for examples, see Pope, Butcher, & Seelen, 2000). Agreements for retainers, if requested, should also be made at this point and precede actual work on the case. Avoid cases where contingency fees are offered, since this practice is patently unethical ("Guidelines," IV.B). If courtroom testimony or deposition is anticipated, request that payment for your time be held in the attorney's escrow account prior to your court appearance so that the content of your testimony will not be influenced by the anticipation of fee payment.

10. *In what form would you like my report?* The task of the forensic psychologist is to form expert opinion(s), using professionally accepted methods, about case-relevant psycholegal issue(s) as defined by legal standards from statutory or case law. When retained by counsel, the forensic psychologist is not necessarily required to prepare a written report; indeed, the psychologist is encouraged to limit unnecessary disclosure of material about the client ("Guidelines," V.C: APA Standards 4.04(a), 4.06, 2002). Elsewhere (McKee, 1995), I have suggested ways to avoid misuse of reports in legal contexts. Report content may be influenced by discovery rules, which may vary among criminal, civil, domestic, and administrative procedures, as well as from jurisdiction to jurisdiction. Excellent examples of forensic report formats for a variety of psycholegal issues may be found in Heilbrun, Marczyk, and DeMatteo (2002). Because the attorney is your client, he or she has the right to decide the format of your report and is also more familiar with the discovery rules governing work product (see Question 6). Although the attorney may govern the form of report, he or she does not control the content; thus, when a report is drafted, the attorney should be forewarned that both supportive and adverse data will be included. Avoid attorneys who wish to control the content of your opinions or want you to alter your opinions to support their argument.

11. *What if my opinion does not support your side?* This is the acid test for the attorney's integrity in seeking your consultation. Lawyers have a duty to explore mental health issues, if such facts are known or available, in the course of case preparation. Attorneys have been cited for ineffective assistance of counsel for failing to explore mental health issues. Resolution of this issue at this point will minimize conflict later if your data suggest an opinion other than what the attorney wished. Remember that when you are retained, you have a duty to advocate your opinion, not the attorney's position. If an attorney decides not to retain you after this question, that is the attorney's choice and may likely increase his or her estimation of you. Having a reputation as a psychologist who "calls 'em as you see 'em" will significantly enhance your credibility during testimony and also deflect cross-examination aspersions that you are a "hired gun." Indeed, balanced opinions are not reflected in the number of times you testify for one side or the other but rather in the percentage of cases in which you do not testify because your opinion is adverse to the attorney who retained you.

References & Readings 

American Psychological Association. (2002). Ethical principles of psychologists and code of conduct. *American Psychologist, 57,* 1060–1073.

Committee on Ethical Guidelines for Forensic Psychologists. (1991). Specialty guidelines for forensic psychologists. *Law and Human Behavior, 15,* 655–665.

Daubert v. Merrell Dow Pharmaceuticals, Inc., 727 F. Supp. 570 (S.D. Cal. 1989), remanded 113 S.Ct. 2786 (1993).

Follingstad, D. R. (2003). Battered woman syndrome in the courts. In A. M. Goldstein (Ed.), *Handbook of psychology. Forensic psychology* (Vol. 11, pp. 485–507). Hoboken, NJ: Wiley.

Frye v. United States, 293 F. 1013 (D.C. Cir. 1923).

Goldstein, A. M. (Ed.). (2003). *Handbook of psychology. Forensic psychology* (Vol. 11). Hoboken, NJ: Wiley.

Grove, W. M., Barden, C., Garb, W. N. & Lilienfield, S. O. (2002). Failure of Rorschach-Comprehensive-System-based testimony to be admissible under the Daubert-Joiner-Kumho standard. *Psychology, Public Policy, and Law, 8*(2), 216–234.

Heilbrun, K., Marczyk, G. R., & DeMatteo, D. (Eds.). (2002). *Forensic mental health assessment: A casebook.* New York: Oxford University Press.

Ibn-Tamas v. United States, 407 A.2d 606 (1979).

Marlowe, D. B. (1995). A hybrid decision framework for evaluating psychometric evidence. *Behavioral Sciences and the Law, 13,* 207–228.

McKee, G. R. (1995). Insanity and adultery: Forensic implications of a divorce case. *Psychological Reports, 76,* 427–434.

Monahan, J., et al. (2001). *Rethinking risk assessment.* New York: Oxford University Press.

Murphy, W. D., & Peters, J. M. (1992). Profiling child sexual abusers. *Criminal Justice and Behavior, 19,* 24–37.

Myers, J. E. B. (1992). *Legal issues in child abuse and neglect.* Newbury Park, CA: Sage.

Pope, K. S., Butcher, J. N., & Seelen, J. (2000). *The MMPI, MMPI-2, and MMPI-A in court* (2nd ed.). Washington, DC: American Psychological Association.

Related Topics

Chapter 111, "Glossary of Legal Terms of Special Interest in Mental Health Practice"

Chapter 115, "Forensic Evaluations and Testimony"

Chapter 116, "Forensic Evaluation Outline"

Chapter 118, "Expert Testimony in Depositions"

Chapter 134, "Establishing a Consultation Agreement"

118 EXPERT TESTIMONY IN DEPOSITIONS

Geoffrey R. McKee

The psychologist as expert witness has received considerable attention and discussion over the past 20 years (Blau, 1984; Brodsky, this volume, chap. 115; Brodsky & Robey, 1973; Pope, Butcher, & Seelen, 2000; Ziskin, 1981). Most of the literature focuses on courtroom testimony during criminal trials or domestic court hearings. Little, however, has been written about the psychologist giving depositions, the most common form of expert testimony in civil proceedings. Depositions are considered by many experts to be the "most grueling, intense, and anxiety-producing aspect of litigation" (Sacks, 1995, p. 18). The purpose of this chapter is to highlight the differences between expert testimony during depositions versus courtroom (Table 1) to facilitate psychologists' effective participation in this stage of litigation.

The Federal Rules of Civil Procedure Rule 26(b)(4)(A) (1995) and Federal Rules of Criminal Procedure Rule 15 (1995) provide that any party (plaintiff or defendant; prosecution or defense) may take the deposition of any expert who will testify at trial regarding his or her already disclosed report. A deposition is a statement from a witness (deponent) under oath taken in question-and-answer form (Blau, 1984). Depositions are one of several methods of pretrial discovery in which an attorney attempts to uncover evidence from the opposing attorney. Depositions may be given orally in face-to-face contact with the attorneys, or they may be given in written form through interrogatories (Horowitz & Willging, 1984). Such procedures are governed by specific rules, which may vary from jurisdiction to jurisdiction; however, many states have simply adopted the Federal Rules of Civil Procedure (1995) and/or the Federal Rules of Criminal Procedure (1995). The remainder of this chapter discusses depositions in terms of context and issues relevant to the deposing (adverse) attorney and nondeposing (retaining) attorney.

CONTEXT

The purpose of a deposition is to discover (and preserve for future use at trial) evidence possessed by competing parties in litigation. In a case involving mental health issues, both attorneys will often depose the other side's experts in an attempt to find out the expert's credentials and the foundation (database), methods, content, and reasoning of the expert's opinions. Because depositions are a pretrial procedure, the deposition typically occurs in a private setting, such as the psychologist's office or, for strategic purposes (e.g., to unsettle the expert), in the office of the deposing attorney. Neither a judge nor a jury is present; however, the questions and answers are preserved by a court stenographer and, increasingly, by videotape. Prior to the deponent psychologist's testimony, the attorneys will resolve any variations from the "usual stipulations" governing depositions such as the method of taking the deposition, the use of the deposition (e.g., for impeachment of the expert's testimony at trial), the waiver of the nondeposing attorney's objections to his or her psychologist being deposed, and the documentation of either attorney's objections to deposi-

TABLE 1. Differences Between Expert Testimony in Deposition and Courtroom

Issue	Deposition	Courtroom
Context		
Purpose	Discover evidence	Resolve dispute
Setting	Private office	Public courtroom
Scope of inquiry	Extensive (civil)	Limited (prejudice to jury)
Authority	Deposition rules	Rules of court; statutes
Procedure	Deposing attorney first	Retaining attorney first
Fees	Paid by deposing attorney	Paid by retaining attorney
Objections' resolution	Delayed until trial	Immediate by judge
Posttestimony issues	*Never* waive reading/signing transcript	Leave; credibility decreases if you stay at attorneys' table and consult through trial
Deposing (Adverse) Attorney		
Intent	Investigative	Adversarial
Demeanor	Deliberate	Theatrical
Pace	Leisurely	Expedited
General questions	Highly technical	Laymanlike for jury
Vita questions	Extensive	Limited; stipulated if better than adverse attorney's expert
Opinion questions	Extensive	Selective to minimize impact
Error questions	Delayed until trial	Immediate: embarrassment
Nondeposing (Retaining) Attorney		
Intent	Resistance to disclosure	Instructive to judge, jury
Demeanor	Passive to minimize exposure of strategy	Active to influence juror decision making
Questions	None or limited to selected issues	Extensive on direct; active on redirect as necessary
Consultation with expert	Limited or prohibited during testimony	Collaborative prior/during trial (though not during testimony)

tion questions that will be reserved for the judge's ruling. In contrast to courtroom testimony, wherein the retaining attorney begins the questioning of his or her expert, followed by cross-examination by the adverse attorney, in a deposition the deposing (adverse) attorney initiates questioning of the deponent. Typically the deposing attorney's scope of inquiry is extensive because a deposition is a discovery procedure and concerns regarding prejudice of the jury are minimal. Similar to the sequences in courtroom testimony, the deponent psychologist is first questioned regarding his or her qualifications (credentials), followed by investigation of the content of his or her opinions relevant to the case's psycholegal issues. If, during questioning, the retaining attorney objects to the deposing attorney's question, resolution of the objection is delayed until a hearing before the judge; despite the objection, the expert is typically requested to answer the question. After testifying, but before the deposition is formally concluded, the psychologist should *always* request his or her right to read and sign the transcript of the deposition to correct any typographical, form, or substance mistakes made by the stenographer (Sacks, 1995). The transcript will be the document against which the psychologist's trial testimony will be compared; any differences may be employed by the deposing attorney to discredit the psychologist's conclusions and opinions. If the psychologist and retaining attorney have not discussed the review and signing of the transcript, the attorney may unwittingly agree to waive this "usual stipulation," with disastrous results for the psychologist at trial.

DEPOSING (ADVERSE) ATTORNEY

Because the deposing attorney has requested the deposition and is paying the deponent psychologist's fees, he or she is the central figure of the proceedings. The deposing attorney's intent is to be investigative and, at times, confrontational. He or she hopes to learn as much as possible about the expert's credentials, foundation, methods, and content of opinion(s), as well as the psychologist's demeanor, persuasiveness, and credibility as a witness. In contrast to courtroom theatrics to influence jury perceptions, the deposing attorney will likely be subdued, deliberate, and methodical in questioning to ensure that he or she has a full understanding of the basis for the expert's opinions. The deposing attorney will likely have retained a psychologist to review the deponent psychologist's report prior to deposition and to assist in his or her questioning. Without the judge's implied pressure to avoid wasting the court's time with exploratory inquiries of dubious relevance, the attorney's pace can be leisurely during a deposition, with frequent consultations with the attorney's colleagues and long pauses between questions—delays that are rarely tolerated by trial judges.

In general, the deposing attorney's questions will be highly technical rather than simplistic for juror influence because he or she wishes to obtain a full and complete exposition of the expert's qualifications, methods, and reasoning in forming his or her opinions. Many of the deposition questions may have been developed by the deposing attorney's retained psychologist, who will subsequently review the deponent psychologist's testimony for errors of foundation, method, and/or reasoning and may suggest further inquiries during trial. The deposing attorney's retained psychologist may also provide an opinion about the overall competence of the deponent psychologist's opinions to assist the attorney in deciding whether to proceed to trial or seek settlement. The quality of the expert's consultation is dependent on the quality of the attorney's questions; thus, the deponent psychologist is likely to face very specific, highly technical inquiries.

The extensiveness of inquiry may begin with the expert's qualifications. Rather than a few superficial questions or stipulations at trial (especially with highly qualified experts), the deposing attorney may spend hours in a case-by-case review of the psychologist's experience, course-by-course review of the psychologist's training, article-by-article review of the psychologist's publications, and/or transcript-by-transcript review of the psychologist's prior testimony. The intent is part factual and part strategic: The attorney wants to find anything that might be used to impeach the expert's credibility while also exhausting the psychologist so that he or she might make errors during direct questioning that could subsequently be used at trial to diminish the influence of his or her testimony. For example, suppose that the psychologist inadvertently scored the MMPI results for the male plaintiff using the female norms. If the attorney (or his or her retained psychologist) detects the error, he or she may wish to highlight the error immediately to challenge the competence of the deponent psychologist's opinions as a prelude to settlement or wait until trial to embarrass the expert in front of the jury. Error detection might also force the retaining attorney to "rehabilitate" the psychologist's testimony through additional questioning, causing unexpected disclosure of that attorney's case strategy and further inquiry by the deposing attorney in response to the deponent's additional testimony.

Typically, the majority of the deposing attorney's questions will focus on the deponent psychologist's opinions of the psycholegal issues of the case. During trial, the deposing (adverse) attorney would be seeking to minimize the impact of the expert's testimony on the judge and/or jury by often dramatic, theatrical, and/or dismissive interrogation. During deposition, the attorney's inquiry will be broad and deep, patiently probing for any weaknesses in the psychologist's foundation, methods, or reasoning. The attorney may use a variety of methods, including the "learned treatise" (Poythress, 1980) or "hypothetical question" (Myers, 1992); descriptions and responses to such gambits may be found in Brodsky (this volume, chap. 115) and other sources (Appelbaum & Gutheil, 1991; Brodsky & Robey, 1973; Pope et al., 2000). The more deliberate, unhurried climate of the deposition allows for extensive inquiry of the psychologist's methods based on *Daubert v. Merrell Dow Pharmaceuticals, Inc.* (1993; see especially the *Daubert* questions proposed by Marlowe, 1995). If the psychologist is unable to rebut such challenges to the testimony, his or her opinions may be deemed inadmissible at trial, negating the psychologist's contribution to the retaining attorney's case and forcing the attorney into either dropping the case or reaching a significantly diminished settlement (or, if a criminal defense attorney, an unfavorable conviction).

NONDEPOSING (RETAINING) ATTORNEY

Generally, the intent of the nondeposing attorney during the deposition of his or her expert is to minimize discovery of his or her case facts and strategy by the opposing attorney. In contrast to active, instructive, persuasive direct inquiry of his or her psychologist at trial to maximize the impact of the expert's testimony on the jury's decision making, during deposition the nondeposing attorney is frequently very passive, objecting only when absolutely necessary. Often, following the psychologist's deposition testimony, the attorney will not ask questions. The nondeposing attorney may ask the deponent psychologist to reiterate the opinions of his or her report "for the record," especially if the deposing attorney has avoided the psychologist's conclusions and focused only on the expert's suspected weaknesses. Finally, the retaining attorney is typically prohibited from conferring with his or her psychologist during deposition testimony to allow the deposing attorney to question the witness without obstruction or coaching (*Hall v. Clifton Precision,* 1993).

The purpose of this chapter has been to describe the basic elements and issues pertaining to the psychologist's participation in pretrial depositions. Brodsky's (this volume, chap. 115) outline is an excellent guide for preparation of forensic psychological consultation services and expert testimony. The reader is referred to Pope et al. (1993) for specific questions attorneys might employ during qualification, direct examination, or cross-examination: To be forewarned is to be forearmed.

References & Readings 

Appelbaum, P. S., & Gutheil, T. G. (1991). *Clinical handbook of psychiatry and the law* (2nd ed.). Baltimore: Williams & Wilkins.

Blau, T. H. (1984). *The psychologist as expert witness.* New York: Wiley.

Brodsky, S. L. (2000). *The expert expert witness.* Washington, DC: American Psychological Association.

Brodsky, S. L., & Robey, A. (1973). On becoming an expert witness: Issues of orientation and effectiveness. *Professional Psychology, 3,* 173–176.

Daubert v. Merrell Dow Pharmaceuticals, Inc., 727 F. Supp. 570 (S.D. Cal. 1989), remanded 113 S.Ct. 2786 (1993).

Federal Rules of Civil Procedure, Fed. R. Civ. P. Rule 26(b)(4)(A) (1995).

Federal Rules of Criminal Procedure, Fed. R. Crim. P. Rule 15 (1995).

Hall v. Clifton Precision, Civ. A. No. 92-5947 (E.D. Pa., 1993).

Horowitz, I. A., & Willging, T. E. (1984). *The psychology of law: Integrations and applications.* Boston: Little, Brown.

Marlowe, D. B. (1995). A hybrid decision framework for evaluating psychometric evidence. *Behavioral Sciences and the Law, 13,* 207–228.

Myers, J. E. B. (1992). *Legal issues in child abuse and neglect.* Newbury Park, CA: Sage.

Pope, K. S., Butcher, J. N., & Seelen, J. (2000). *The MMPI, MMPI-2, & MMPI-A in court* (2nd ed.). Washington, DC: American Psychological Association.

Poythress, N. G. (1980). Coping on the witness stand: Learned responses to "learned treatises." *Professional Psychology, 11,* 169–179.

Sacks, M. E. (1995). *An overview of the law: A guide for testifying and consulting experts.* Horsham, PA: LRP Publications.

Ziskin, J. (1981). *Coping with psychiatric and psychological testimony* (3rd ed.). Venice, CA: Law and Psychology Press.

Related Topics

Chapter 115, "Forensic Evaluations and Testimony"
Chapter 117, "Forensic Referrals Checklist"

119 FORENSIC ASSESSMENT INSTRUMENTS

Randy Borum

Psychologists often rely on standardized tests and measures for assistance in diagnosis and treatment planning. Most of these instruments are designed to assess the presence, nature, and degree of mental disorders and their symptoms—issues that are the focus of most clinical psychological assessments. However, in a forensic evaluation, information concerning one's mental disorder is only one component of the answer to a psycholegal question. Typically, the psychologist must also assess and address some *specific* functional ability such as competence to stand trial or capacity to function as a parent. Provided below are brief descriptions of several forensic assessment instruments (FAIs) designed to assess functional capacities relevant to a given forensic issue. For a comprehensive review of FAIs, Thomas Grisso's *Evaluating Competencies: Forensic Assessments and Instruments* (1986) is an excellent reference. A second edition of this text is currently being written. Topic-specific review articles are listed beneath the appropriate topic heading.

CRIMINAL FORENSIC EVALUATIONS
(Review articles: Grisso, 1986; Rogers & Ewing, 1992)

The two most frequent evaluation issues for forensic psychologists in the criminal justice system relate to competency to stand trial and insanity/criminal responsibility. In chapter 120, Paul D. Lipsitt has reviewed the primary FAIs used for assessing competency to stand trial (the Competency Screening Test, the Competence to Stand Trial Assessment Inventory, and the Interdisciplinary Fitness Interview; Borum & Grisso, 1995). An FAI developed for assessments of legal insanity/criminal responsibility is described below.

Rogers Criminal Responsibility Assessment Scales (R-CRAS; Rogers, 1984): The R-CRAS is designed to structure and quantify the decision-making process in clinical-forensic assessments of insanity. After the examiner conducts a thorough evaluation, including relevant interviews and reviews of pertinent records, the R-CRAS presents 30 items, called Psychological and Situational Variables, which must be assigned a numerical rating. The Psychological and Situational Variables cover the following domains: Patient's Reliability; Organicity; Psychopathology; Cognitive Control; and Behavioral Control. The examiner uses these ratings and the assessment information in a decision tree analysis, which leads to a conclusion that the defendant is either "sane" or "insane," according to the relevant legal standard. Interrater reliability coefficients for the R-CRAS averaged .58 for the clinical variables and .81 for the decision variables (malingering and components of the legal insanity standard). In a sample of 93 defendants, the R-CRAS decision concurred with the court's decision in 88% of the cases where the court was not given information concerning R-CRAS results.

CHILD CUSTODY AND PARENTAL CAPACITY
(Review article: Heinze & Grisso, 1996)

Ackerman-Schoendorf Scales for Parent Evaluation of Custody (ASPECT; Ackerman & Schoendorf, 1992): "The ASPECT is not a test but rather a system combining the results of psychological testing, interviews, and observations of each parent and child to provide data regarding the suitability of the parent for custody" (Heinze & Grisso, 1996). Each parent must complete an extensive Parent Questionnaire, and each parent as well as each child must complete a specified battery of psychological tests. The clinician uses these data to complete a series of 56 dichotomous questions (yes/no) for each parent. The results of this form yield three subscale scores (Observational, Social, and Cognitive-Emotional) and a Parenting Custody Index (PCI). The PCI is considered to be the global measure of parenting effectiveness. The scores for each parent are presented in color graphs, with suggestions concerning the comparative parenting effectiveness and identification of the "preferred parent." The ASPECT was normed on a sample of 200 parents. When two independent raters reviewed a sample of 88 records, the interrater reliability coefficient for the PCI was .96, with other subscales falling in the low to mid-.90s. The primary validity study shows that ASPECT results agreed with the judges' custody decision in 75% of 118 cases. However, it appears that the ASPECT results were presented as part of the evidence in these cases.

Bricklin Perceptual Scales (BPS; Bricklin, 1984): The BPS is a 64-item instrument designed for children over 6 years of age; 32 items relate to each parent. The BPS is administered by presenting the child with an item and asking him or her to indicate how well the item describes the parent. For each question, the child is given an 8-inch card with a black line labeled with "not so well" at one end and "very well" at the other. The child responds to the item by punching a hole at the appropriate point along the line. On the back of the card the line is divided evenly into 60 segments, each of which has a corresponding point value. The parent who has the highest score for a given item "wins" that item. According to the BPS, the "parent of choice" is indicated by the parent who "wins" the greatest number of items. There are currently no normative data available for this instrument. A preliminary study of test-retest showed coefficients for individual items ranging from .61 to .94, with the scores of older children (aged 15–17) generally being more consistent than those of younger children (aged 12–14). Concerning potential validity, Bricklin reports a high level of concurrence between the BPS and other instruments he has developed, but it is unclear if any other validity data exist for the measure at this time.

Parenting Stress Index (PSI; Abidin, 1990): The PSI is a 101-item self-report inventory designed to assess the type and severity of stresses associated with the child-rearing role. A 36-item short form also exists. Parent-respondents rate their agreement with an item using a 5-point Likert-type scale. Response style is assessed with a Defensive Responding Scale. In the Child Domain, the PSI measures child characteristics associated with stress in parenting (subscales relating to child adaptability, acceptability, demandingness, mood, hyperactivity/distractibility, and reinforcing of parent); in the Parent Domain, it assesses stress resulting from the parenting role (subscales relating to depression, attachment, restriction of role, sense of competence, social isolation, relationship with spouse, and parental health). A Total Stress Score is derived by summing the two Domain scores. The normative sample is composed of 2,633 parents. Alpha coefficients for domain scores, subscales, and total scores range between .70 and .95. Test-retest coefficients across numerous studies with varying time frames have yielded estimates from .55 to .96. The PSI has shown significant correlations, in the expected directions, with other similar measures and with abusive parental behaviors, parental roles, marital satisfaction, and social support. To date, there have been approximately 200 studies involving the PSI.

Parent-Child Relationship Inventory (PCRI; Gerard, 1994): The PCRI is a 78-item self-report inventory comprising seven content scales: Parental Support; Satisfaction with Parenting; Involvement; Communication; Limit Setting; Autonomy; and Role Orientation. There are also two validity scales to measure social desirability and inconsistent responding. Parent-respondents rate their agreement with an item using a 4-point Likert-type scale. Normative data are provided for a sample of 1,139 parents.

Alpha coefficients for the subscales range from .70 to .88, with 1-week test-retest reliabilities from .68 to .93. Concurrent validation studies have shown significant correlations between the PCRI and the Personality Inventory for Children; parental discipline style; and parents' sense of social support, competence, and self-esteem.

GUARDIANSHIP
(Review article: Grisso, 1994)

Independent Living Scales (ILS; Loeb, 1996): The ILS is a 70-item instrument designed to evaluate an individual's capacity to care for himself or herself and manage his or her own affairs. The ILS is administered as a performance-based structured interview with items that relate to a range of situations and tasks encountered in daily living. It takes approximately 45 minutes to administer and 10 minutes to score. The administration can be adapted to accommodate an examinee's physical/visual/literacy limitations. Extra materials (e.g., telephone, telephone book, envelope, pencil and paper, and money) are required to administer some tasks. The ILS yields five subscale scores (Memory/Orientation; Managing Money; Managing Home and Transportation; Health and Safety; and Social Adjustment); two factor scores (Performance/Information and Problem Solving); and a Full Scale standard score, which provides a global index of the examinee's level of functioning (low, moderate, or high). Internal consistency for the ILS scores ranges from .72 to .92, with test-retest coefficients between .81 and .94. Interrater reliabilities range between .95 and .99. Although the ILS was designed primarily for use with older adults (65+), normative data are also available for adults with dementia, severe mental illness, mild mental retardation, and mild brain injury. In validation studies, the ILS has shown appropriate correlations with measures of intellectual and cognitive functioning and with other instruments measuring Activities of Daily Living (ADLs).

Direct Assessment of Functional Status (DAFS; Lowenstein et al., 1989): The DAFS is an 85-item instrument with seven sections (time orientation, communication, transportation, financial, shopping, grooming, and eating) and a total administration time of approximately 30 minutes. Each item requires the examinee to demonstrate knowledge or perform a task relevant to daily independent living—for example, using a telephone, identifying and counting currency, working with a grocery list, and using eating utensils. Interrater reliabilities for composite and subscale scores are in the .90s. Test-retest coefficients over several weeks ranged between .55 and .92 in a sample of impaired patients and were even higher in normal controls. The DAFS also correlated significantly with an independent dementia rating scale and with independent chart reports of specific functional impairments.

VIOLENCE RISK ASSESSMENT
(Review article: Borum, 1996)

Violence Prediction Scheme (VPS; Webster, Harris, Rice, Cormier, & Quinsey, 1994): The VPS combines clinical and actuarial factors in a comprehensive scheme for assessing dangerousness and risk. The actuarial component is based on the Violence Risk Assessment Guide (VRAG), a 12-item tool that showed a classification accuracy rate of about 75% in a sample of patients from a maximum security psychiatric hospital. Preliminary efforts at cross-validation with sex offenders in the community and maximum security inmates in prison have been promising. In the VPS scheme, the actuarial and VRAG data are combined with an assessment of current status and clinical information, including a 10-item clinical scheme called the ASSESS-LIST, an acronym that stands for *A*ntecedent history, *S*elf-presentation, *S*ocial and psychosocial adjustment, *E*xpectations and plans, *S*ymptoms, *S*upervision, *L*ife factors, *I*nstitutional management, *S*exual adjustment, and *T*reatment progress. The examiner scores each of these items as either "favorable" or "unfavorable." Currently no psychometric data are available for the ASSESS-LIST items.

HCR-20 (Webster, Douglas, Eaves, & Hart, 1997): The HCR-20 is an instrument/guide "designed for use in the assessment of risk for future violent behavior in criminal and psychiatric populations. Briefly, the first 10 items of the HCR-20 pertain to the *historical*, or static, variables of the individual being assessed (H Scale), the next five items reflect the current *clinical* status and personality characteristics of the individual (C Scale), and the remaining five pertain to future *risk* of violent behavior (R Scale)" (Webster et al., 1997, emphasis added). The historical and risk variables can primarily be coded from records or secondary information sources, although the clinical factors need to be evaluated and rated by a qualified mental health professional based on interviews, progress notes, psychological assessments, or similar sources. The HCR-20 has a defined three-level scoring system for each item, similar to that of the Psychopathy Checklist-Revised (PCL-R). Preliminary data have shown significant correlations between the H Scale and C Scale and scores on the VRAG (see above), PCL-R, and number of previous charges for violent offenses. It also appears likely that the items can be reliably coded with average interrater reliability coefficients of about .80. The HCR-20 cannot currently be considered a test in the formal sense, but it may be useful as a checklist to prompt the examiner to cover or consider the major relevant areas of inquiry. Several new studies involving the HCR-20 are currently under way.

Spousal Assault Risk Assessment Guide (SARA; Kropp, Hart, Webster, and Eaves, 1995): The SARA is a 20-item clinical checklist of risk factors for spousal assault. It has an operationally defined three-level scoring scheme but is constructed to be used as a clinical guide —rather than a test—for assessing the risk of future violence in men arrested for spousal assault. The SARA has four main sections: the Criminal History section; Psychosocial Adjustment section; Spousal Assault History section; and a final section relating to the Alleged (Current) Offense. After all four sections are completed, the clinician makes a "summary risk rating" (low, moderate, or high) of imminent risk of violence toward a partner and imminent risk of violence toward others. Preliminary data from one retrospective study showed that interrater reliability for the sum of items was .92, and reliability for the SARA-informed risk rating was .80. The SARA-informed summary risk ratings were also strongly related to reoffending, with those rated as "high" risk being 5.5 times more likely to reoffend than those with ratings of "low" or "moderate" risk.

References & Readings 

Abidin, R. (1990). *Parenting Stress Index* (3rd ed.). Odessa, FL: Psychological Assessment Resources.

Ackerman, M., & Schoendorf, K. (1992). *ASPECT: Ackerman-Schoendorf Scales for Parent Evaluation of Custody*. Los Angeles: Western Psychological Services.

Borum, R. (1996). Improving the clinical practice of violence risk assessment: Technology, guidelines, and training. *American Psychologist, 51,* 945–956.

Borum, R., & Grisso, T. (1995). A survey of psychological test use in criminal forensic evaluations. *Professional Psychology: Research and Practice, 26,* 465–473.

Bricklin, B. (1984). *The Bricklin Perceptual Scales: Child-perception-of-parents-series*. Furlong, PA: Village.

Gerard, A. (1994). *Parent-Child Relationship Inventory (PCRI): Manual*. Los Angeles: Western Psychological Services.

Grisso, T. (1986). *Evaluating competencies: Forensic assessments and instruments*. New York: Plenum Press.

Grisso, T. (1994). Clinical assessments of legal competence of older adults. In M. Storandt & G. VandenBos (Eds.), *Neuropsychological assessment of dementia and depression in older adults: A clinician's guide* (pp. 119–139). Washington, DC: American Psychological Association.

Heinze, M., & Grisso, T. (1996). Review of instruments assessing parenting competencies used in child custody evaluations. *Behavioral Sciences and the Law, 14,* 293–313.

Kropp, P. R., Hart, S. D., Webster, C. D., & Eaves, D. (1995). *Manual for the Spousal Assault Risk Assessment Guide* (2nd ed.). Vancouver: British Columbia Institute on Family Violence.

Loeb, P. (1996). *Independent Living Scales*. San Antonio, TX: Psychological Corporation.

Lowenstein, D., Amigo, E., Duara, R., Guterman, A., Hurwitz, D., Berkowitz, N., et al. (1989). A new scale for the assessment of functional status in Alzheimer's disease and related disorders. *Journal of Gerontology: Psychological Sciences, 44,* 114–121.

Rogers, R. (1984). *Rogers Criminal Responsibility Assessment Scales.* Odessa, FL: Psychological Assessment Resources.

Rogers, R., & Ewing, C. (1992). The measurement of insanity: Debating the merits of the R-CRAS and its alternatives. *International Journal of Law and Psychiatry, 15,* 113–123.

Webster, C. D., Douglas, K. S., Eaves, D., & Hart, S. D. (1997). *HCR-20: Assessing risk for violence, Version 2.* Burnaby: Mental Health Law and Policy Institute, Simon Fraser University.

Webster, C. D., Harris, G. T., Rice, M. E., Cormier, C., & Quinsey, V. L. (1994). *The Violence Prediction Scheme: Assessing dangerousness in high risk men.* Toronto, Ontario: Centre of Criminology, University of Toronto.

Related Topics

Chapter 86, "The APSAC Study Guides"
Chapter 87, "Interviewing Children When Sexual Abuse Is Suspected"
Chapter 120, "Evaluation of Competency to Stand Trial"
Chapter 122, "Principles for Conducting a Comprehensive Child Custody Evaluation"

120 EVALUATION OF COMPETENCY TO STAND TRIAL

Paul D. Lipsitt

Competency for trial evaluation has been the object of psychological research for several decades. Forensic psychologists and other mental health professionals have aided the courts in developing objective measures to determine whether defendants meet the criteria for the legal standard for competency. An individual who suffers from impairment due to mental illness or mental defect may not possess sufficient psychological presence to contribute to an adequate defense to the charges and, therefore, may be deprived of a fair trial. The basic assumption enunciated in Kinloch's Case (1764) is that one accused of a crime is entitled to psychological as well as physical presence in court to defend oneself against one's accuser. Derived from English Common Law, competency for trial is a necessity in order to meet the Constitutional requirement of due process.

The defendant who has permanent incapacity may not be tried. The temporarily incapable defendant is entitled to a postponement of trial until competency has been restored. Any person charged with a criminal offense must be able to muster a sufficient level of cognitive and affective resources to effect an adequate defense to the charges with the aid of an attorney. To avoid indefinite commitment, the U.S. Supreme Court has held that those unlikely to ever gain competency may be detained for only a reasonable period for competency observation and treatment (*Jackson v. Indiana,* 1972). Long-term hospitalization must meet the same standards required for a civil involuntary commitment (Lipsitt, 1970).

The issue of competency is usually raised prior to trial but may be raised at any time during the procedures. While usually initiated as a request for evaluation by the defense, the prosecution or the judge may raise the question of competency.

Competency for trial is based on legal criteria rather than psychological diagnosis of mental illness or mental defect. Defendants who are mentally disabled, even to a serious degree, such as those with psychosis or moderate mental retardation, may be functionally competent for trial. However, psychological factors may impact on the ability to perform the task of adequately participating in one's criminal trial. If the results of an initial evaluation indicate that the requirements for competency are sufficiently compromised, the court would order treatment with the goal of restoration of competency, to be followed by proceedings in court to face the criminal charges. In the event that the incompetency is determined to be permanent or unlikely to be restored in the foreseeable future, other steps are taken to protect the rights of a defendant who has been charged but has yet to be adjudicated.

The general criteria that determine competency for trial include (a) an ability to communicate and cooperate with one's attorney in defending oneself in court, (b) an awareness of the nature and object of the legal proceedings, and (c) an understanding of the possible consequences of a trial. These elements provide a framework for the psychologist to assess the defendant's ability to function on a task that will require some level of understanding and active participation. The assessment and evaluation data are generated by the psychologist or other forensic mental health professional, but the conclusion of competency or incompetency is the prerogative of the judge.

In 1960, the U.S. Supreme Court stated that competency should be determined by assessing whether the defendant has "sufficient present ability to consult with his attorney with a reasonable degree of rational understanding and a rational as well as a factual understanding of the proceedings against him" (*Dusky v. United States*, p. 402). In 1993, the United States Supreme Court held that a defendant's decision to plead guilty or waive the right to counsel need not be measured by a higher or different standard than *Dusky* (*Godinez v. Moran*, 1993). The forensic examiner may take into consideration impaired reasoning or other psychological aberrations that may prevent a defendant from serving as his own counsel, but legal skills are not a relevant issue.

Most state statutes do not define competency, nor do they offer guidelines for its assessment. In order to mitigate the subjectivity of the competency assessment and to provide a guide for its determination, various tests and procedures have been developed by research social scientists.

During the 1960s, in conjunction with an increasing concern for the civil rights and liberties of the mentally ill, involuntary commitment procedures were challenged through the legal system, many reaching the U.S. Supreme Court. Persons charged with offenses, but never found guilty, were frequently hospitalized involuntarily, often for life. A federally funded study at Harvard Medical School (Laboratory of Community Psychiatry, 1973) was initiated to address the absence of standards for assessing competency in the criminal justice system. The Competency Screening Test (CST) and the Competency Assessment Instrument (CAI) were developed as a part of this project. About 10 years after the first use of the CAI, the Interdisciplinary Fitness Interview (IFI) was developed (Golding, Roesch, & Schreiber, 1984). Later revised (Golding, 1993), the IFI-R focuses on 11 competence categories, such as "appreciation of the charges" and "relationship to counsel," and 9 clinical symptom categories, such as "impaired reasoning" and "thought disorder." More recently, as part of research funded by the MacArthur Foundation, John Monahan and colleagues have developed a test of competency, based on three parameters: understanding, reasoning and appreciation (Hoge, Bonnie, Poythress, & Monahan, 1999; Otto et al., 1998). These three parameters have been incorporated into a 22-item instrument.

The CST was developed as a screening instrument to reduce the need for pretrial commitment of those who can be declared clearly competent. Using the CST, many individuals for whom the competency issue has been raised can be tested in the court or place of detention. Those receiving a score within the competent

TABLE 1. The Competency Screening Test

1. The lawyer told Bill that . . .
2. When I go to court the lawyer will . . .
3. Jack felt that the judge . . .
4. When Phil was accused of the crime, he . . .
5. When I prepare to go to court with my lawyer . . .
6. If the jury finds me guilty, I . . .
7. The way a court trial is decided . . .
8. When the evidence in George's case was presented to the jury . . .
9. When the lawyer questioned his client in court, the client said . . .
10. If Jack has to try his own case, he . . .
11. Each time the D.A. asked me a question, I . . .
12. While listening to the witnesses testify against me, I . . .
13. When the witness testifying against Harry gave incorrect evidence, he . . .
14. When Bob disagreed with his lawyer on his defense, he . . .
15. When I was formally accused of the crime, I thought to myself . . .
16. If Ed's lawyer suggests that he plead guilty, he . . .
17. What concerns Fred most about his lawyer . . .
18. When they say a man is innocent until proven guilty . . .
19. When I think of being sent to prison, I . . .
20. When Phil thinks of what he is accused of, he . . .
21. When the jury hears my case, they will . . .
22. If I had a chance to speak to the judge, I . . .

range can proceed directly to trial, avoiding unnecessary hospitalized observation for competency evaluation.

The CST, which has been the subject of several validation studies (Nicholson, Robertson, Johnson, & Jensen, 1988; Nottingham, & Matson, 1981; Randolph, Hicks, Mason, & Cuneo, 1982), consists of 22 sentence-completion stems, each of which focuses on a legal as well as a psychological aspect of competency for trial (Table 1). A factor analysis of the CST reveals six factors, all closely related to the established legal criteria for competency for trial. These are (a) relationship of the defendant to his or her attorney in developing a defense; (b) defendant's understanding and awareness of the nature of the court proceedings; (c) defendant's affective response to the court process in dealing with accusations and feelings of guilt; (d) judgmental qualities in engaging in the strategy and evaluation of the trial; (e) defendant's trust and confidence in his or her attorney; and (f) defendant's recognition of the seriousness of his or her position.

The CST is administered as a paper-and-pencil test, with a brief instruction regarding the completion of each sentence as it relates to the law and going to court. Although typically self-administered, for individuals with inadequate reading skills the stems may be read and responses recorded by the administrator. On average, the CST can be administered in about 25 minutes and scored in 15 to 20 minutes with the aid of the scoring manual.

The scoring system uses a 3-point scale from 0 to 2. The scoring manual serves as a guide, with examples of prototypical responses at the three levels of scoring. In general, characteristics that would merit a score of 0 involve substantial disorganization in content, inability to relate or to trust, defining the lawyer's role as punitive or rejecting, extreme concreteness, or self-defeating behavior. A 1-point score is given when the response can be characterized as passive, acquiescent, avoidant, or impoverished, though not clearly inappropriate. Reference to the scoring manual provides specific guidelines for each item. For example, a 2-point response to Item 2, "When I go to court, the lawyer will . . . ," is "defend me." In contrast, a sentence completion of "put me away" would merit a 0. The legal criterion relates to the defendant's understanding of the lawyer's role in aiding in his or her defense. The psychological referent is the ability to trust and accept the attorney.

The CST can be used when the competency

issue is raised before the trial or at any time during the trial proceedings. Defendants who score in the competent range on the CST are unlikely to present as false negatives, that is, incompetent after further assessment (Lipsitt, Lelos, & McGarry, 1971). A low score on the CST places the defendant in the questionable category for competency and in need of more extensive assessment. The semistructured format of the CAI or the IFI can elicit more detailed clinical information for evaluating competency when the CST score is in the questionable range.

The CAI designates the parameters for inquiry into competency in language familiar to lawyers and judges. The guidelines aid the mental health professional in translating psychological factors into an assessment of ability to function and cope with a trial. Thirteen variables guide the interviewer in conducting the competency assessment (Table 2). The 13 items are rated from a grade of 0 (least competent) to 5 (most competent). A clinical opinion based on each function offers information to help the court determine the ultimate issue of competency in the case. The weight the court assigns to one function may differ from another, since each function is considered independently, and the various ratings are not cumulative. The judge must assess the various scales to determine whether the defendant's overall competency is at an adequate level to proceed to trial. While there are no objective standards for making the ratings, sample interview questions and responses are provided in the manual to aid in assessing the level of competency. If a substantial number of

TABLE 2. Competency to Stand Trial Assessment Instrument

	Degree of Incapacity					
	Total	Severe	Moderate	Mild	None	Unratable
1. Appraisal of available legal defenses	1	2	3	4	5	6
2. Unmanageable behavior	1	2	3	4	5	6
3. Quality of relating to attorney	1	2	3	4	5	6
4. Planning of legal strategy, including guilty plea to lesser charges where pertinent	1	2	3	4	5	6
5. Appraisal of role of:						
a. Defense counsel	1	2	3	4	5	6
b. Prosecuting attorney	1	2	3	4	5	6
c. Judge	1	2	3	4	5	6
d. Jury	1	2	3	4	5	6
e. Defendant	1	2	3	4	5	6
f. Witnesses	1	2	3	4	5	6
6. Understanding of court procedure	1	2	3	4	5	6
7. Appreciation of charges	1	2	3	4	5	6
8. Appreciation of range and nature of possible penalties	1	2	3	4	5	6
9. Appraisal of likely outcome	1	2	3	4	5	6
10. Capacity to disclose to attorney available pertinent facts surrounding the offense including the defendant's movements, timing, mental state, actions at the time of the offense	1	2	3	4	5	6
11. Capacity to realistically challenge prosecution witnesses	1	2	3	4	5	6
12. Capacity to testify relevantly	1	2	3	4	5	6
13. Self-defeating vs. self-serving motivation (legal sense)	1	2	3	4	5	6

Examinee_______ Examiner_______

Date_______

ratings are 3 or lower, the assumption of competency should be strongly questioned.

When ordering a competency evaluation, the judge often includes a request for an evaluation to determine criminal responsibility. The examiner must clearly separate the issues of competency for trial from criminal responsibility and develop separate reports. Competency for trial is a description of current status, whereas criminal responsibility refers to "legal sanity" at the time of the offense.

In cases in which a finding of legal incompetency may be likely, it is generally recommended that information regarding remediation be provided to the court (Lipsitt, 1986). Courts usually rely on the forensic examiner's information and judgment with regard to the defendant's deficits and on the opinion regarding treatment options and recommendations relating to appropriate interventions for the restoration of competency within a reasonable period of time.

SUMMARY

Competency is a legal concept, not a psychological diagnosis. It refers to the capacity or ability to perform the task of adequately participating in one's criminal trial. Criteria have been established to evaluate the affective and cognitive factors that contribute to defending oneself in court with the aid of an attorney. The competency issue usually arises at the pretrial stage when a defendant is charged or indicted, but it may be raised at any time during the trial procedures. The issue may be raised by the defense attorney, the prosecutor, or the judge. Competency is an evaluation of current functioning and is clearly distinguished in concept and focus of evaluation from criminal responsibility or the insanity defense. Instruments described here have been developed as aids for the forensic mental health professional in assisting the court in the determination of competency for trial.

References & Readings

Dusky v. U.S., 362 U.S. 402 (1960).

Godinez v. Moran, 509 U.S. 389; 113 S. Ct. 268 (1993).

Golding, S., Roesch, R., & Schreiber, J. (1984). Assessment and conceptualization of competency to stand trial: Preliminary data on the Interdisciplinary Fitness Interview. *Law and Human Behavior, 9,* 321–334.

Golding, S. L. (1993). Interdisciplinary Fitness Interview-Revised: Training manual. Unpublished manuscript.

Hoge, S. K., Bonnie, R. J., Poythress, N. G., & Monahan, J. (1999). The MacArthur Competence Assessment Tool—Criminal Adjudication (MacCAT-CA). Odessa, FL: Psychological Assessment Resources.

Jackson v. Indiana, 406 U.S. 715 (1972).

Kinloch's Case, 18 How. St. Tr. (Eng.) 395 (1746).

Laboratory of Community Psychiatry, Harvard Medical School. (1973). *Competency to stand trial and mental illness* (DHEW Publication No. HSM 73-9105).

Lipsitt, P. D. (1970). The dilemma of competency for trial and mental illness. *New England Journal of Medicine, 228,* 797–798.

Lipsitt, P. D. (1986). Beyond competency to stand trial. In L. Everstine & D. S. Everstine (Eds.), *Psychotherapy and the law* (pp. 131–141). Orlando: Grune & Stratton.

Lipsitt, P. D., Lelos, D., & McGarry, A. L. (1971). Competency for trial: A screening instrument. *American Journal of Psychiatry, 128*(1), 105–109.

Nicholson, R. A., Robertson, H. C., Johnson, W. G., & Jensen, G. (1988). A comparison of instruments for assessing competency to stand trial. *Law and Human Behavior, 12,* 313–322.

Nottingham, E. J., IV, & Mattson, R. E. (1981). A validation study of the Competency Screening Test. *Law and Human Behavior, 5,* 329–335.

Otto, R. K, Poythress, N. G., Nicholson, R. A., Edens, J. F, Monahan, J., Bonnie, R. J., et al. (1998). Psychometric properties of the MacArthur Competence Tool—Criminal Adjudication. *Psychological Assessment 10,* 435–443.

Randolph, J. J., Hicks, T., Mason, D., & Cuneo, D. J. (1982). The Competency Screening Test: A validation study in Cook County, Illinois. *Criminal Justice and Behavior, 9,* 495–500.

Related Topics

Chapter 115, "Forensic Evaluations and Testimony"
Chapter 116, "Forensic Evaluation Outline"
Chapter 117, "Forensic Referrals Checklist"
Chapter 119, "Forensic Assessment Instruments"

121 A MODEL FOR CLINICAL DECISION MAKING WITH DANGEROUS PATIENTS

Leon VandeCreek

Dangerous patients pose a special challenge to psychotherapists. If, on the one hand, the therapist underestimates the patient's threats and harm comes to a third party, the therapist may feel that more should have been done to protect the innocent victim, and the victim, or survivors, may initiate a lawsuit. On the other hand, if the therapist incorrectly believes that harm is imminent and acts to warn a potential victim, the patient may feel betrayed and the therapeutic relationship may be threatened. Even worse, the patient may drop out of therapy and lose faith in therapists, thereby ending any preventive role that therapy may have had in preventing violence.

The American Psychological Association's (APA) "Ethical Principles of Psychologists and Code of Conduct" (2002) permits psychologists to breach confidentiality if it is necessary to protect the patient or others from harm. The option of breaching confidentiality, permitted by the ethics code, may protect the psychologist from charges of ethical violations, but the psychologist must still exercise judgment about when to breach confidentiality or when to engage in other strategies that may reduce the potential for violence.

Decision making with dangerous patients is made more precarious by the increased possibility of legal liability. Prior to the 1976 California Supreme Court decision of *Tarasoff v. Regents of the University of California*, psychotherapists did not have to contend with legal repercussions surrounding confidentiality in their management of dangerous patients. The *Tarasoff* ruling, and that of other courts and legislation that followed the lead of *Tarasoff*, however, has created a "duty to protect" doctrine that therapists are often advised to follow even if their states have not formally endorsed the doctrine through legislation or court decisions (VandeCreek & Knapp, 1993). Consequently, therapists must now consider clinical issues in the context of both ethical and legal constraints. Fortunately, courts recognize that psychotherapists cannot predict dangerousness with complete accuracy. Instead, the courts consider whether the psychotherapist used acceptable professional judgment in completing an assessment of dangerousness and in developing and implementing the treatment plan (VandeCreek & Knapp, 2000).

One of the difficulties that therapists face, however, when managing dangerous patients is that no standard of care has been established. The recent practice of specifying empirically supported treatments for a variety of mental health conditions has not yet been applied to the diagnosis and treatment of patients who pose a danger to others (VandeCreek & Knapp, 2000). Botkin and Nietzel (1987) surveyed psychologists about their use of interventions with dangerous patients. They found that hospitalizing, strengthening the therapeutic alliance, managing the patient's environment, and breaking confidentiality were the most frequently employed interventions. Similarly, Monahan (1993) recommended three broad areas of intervention for patients who pose a high risk of violence: hospitalizing patients, intensifying treatment, and warning potential victims. More recently, Truscott, Evans, and Mansell (1995)

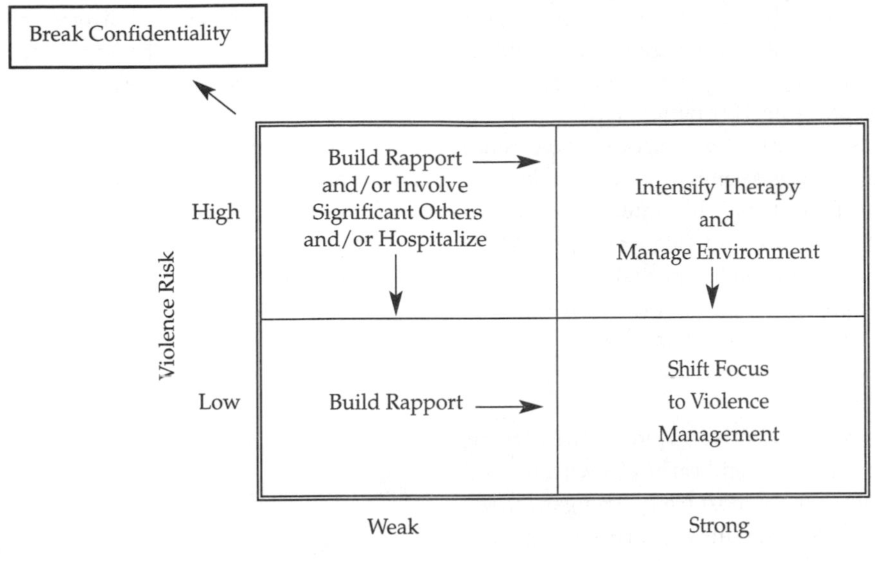

FIGURE 1. Model for Decision Making with Dangerous Clients (reprinted with permission from Truscott, Evans, & Mansell, 1995)

presented a model for decision making when working with dangerous patients. Their model is presented here.

The model proposes that patients who pose a threat of violence be thought of as occupying one of four cells in a 2 × 2, Violence Risk × Therapeutic Alliance Strength table. Interventions can be selected to strengthen the alliance and reduce the violence risk as suggested by Botkin and Nietzel (1987) and Monahan (1993). The model is presented in Figure 1.

The authors suggest that whenever possible, psychologists should work to strengthen and maintain the therapeutic alliance because the alliance is the backbone of most interventions. If the alliance is weak, the psychologist has a reduced chance of effectiveness with the patient, especially when risk of violence is high. The model suggests that when the alliance is strong, the psychologist can focus on violence management, and if the risk of violence increases, therapy should be intensified and the patient's environment more carefully managed. On the other hand, if the alliance is weak and the risk of violence is high, the psychologist should attempt to strengthen the alliance and/or involve significant others in treatment and consider hospitalization. Breaking confidentiality, then, should occur only in the context of a weak alliance and high violence potential.

To implement this model, or any other decision making model, when working with potentially dangerous patients, psychologists must make assessments of violence potential. The legal test in predicting violence is one of "reasonable foreseeability." That is, would other psychologists with a similar patient make a similar assessment and draw a similar conclusion? Liability is more likely to be imposed if the psychologist failed to follow appropriate procedures in reaching a decision and in implementing the decision than if an incorrect prediction was made. Thorough records are imperative to document decision making about dangerous patients.

The following variables should be considered when reviewing a patient's potential for violence (Borum, 1996; Litwack, Kirschner, & Wack, 1993; Meloy, 1987; Monahan & Steadman, 1994; Otto, 2000). Truscott et al. (1995) provide several case examples that use these risk factors within the context of the decision-making model. Individual characteristics include the following:

- *History of violence:* This is the single best predictor of violent behavior. The age at which the first offense occurred is also an important variable. Individuals who commit their first violent offense prior to adolescence are more likely to engage in violent behaviors throughout their lifetime.
- *Clinical risk factors:* A diagnosis of substance abuse or dependence is probably the second most important factor. Persons with mental illness who believe that they are being threatened by others are also more likely to resort to violence.
- *Demographic variables:* Non-White persons in their late teens and early 20s with low IQ and education are most likely to engage in violent behaviors. Unstable residential and work histories increase the risk. Until recently, men were believed to pose more risks of violence than women, but research now suggests that clinicians, at least those working with more disturbed patient populations, should not consider patient sex to be a baseline risk factor (Otto, 2000).

Situational characteristics include the following:

- *Availability of potential victim(s):* Most violent crimes occur between people who know each other.
- *Access to weapons:* Persons with martial arts training or combat experience, and those who possess great physical strength are capable of inflicting greater harm.
- *Stressors:* Daily stressors such as relationship and financial problems can reduce a person's frustration tolerance.

Psychotherapists can assess the quality of their management of dangerous patients by asking the following questions:

1. Am I aware of state and federal laws and agency policies?
2. Have I done a thorough evaluation of the dangerousness of the patient and have I updated it recently?
3. When patients have presented a threat of harm, have I modified my treatment plan to address the increased risk, such as by increasing the frequency of sessions, addressing anger in psychotherapy, incorporating other parties into treatment, asking the patient to release weapons, and reviewing requirements of relevant duty-to-protect statutes?
4. Have I consulted with a knowledgeable colleague?
5. Have I carefully documented my clinical judgment and treatment and my consultations?

References & Readings 

American Psychological Association. (2002). Ethical principles of psychologists and code of conduct. *American Psychologist, 57,* 1060–1073.

Borum, R. (1996). Improving the clinical practice of violence risk assessment. *American Psychologist, 51,* 945–956.

Botkin, D. J., & Nietzel, M. T. (1987). How therapists manage potentially dangerous clients: Toward a standard of care for psychotherapists. *Professional Psychology: Research and Practice, 18,* 84–86.

Lidz, C., Mulvey, E., & Gardner, W. (1993). The accuracy of predictions of violence to others. *Journal of the American Medical Association, 269,* 1007–1011.

Litwack, T. R., Kirschner, S. M., & Wack, R. C. (1993). The assessment of dangerousness and predictions of violence: Recent research and future prospects. *Psychiatric Quarterly, 64,* 245–273.

Meloy, J. R. (1987). The prediction of violence in outpatient psychotherapy. *American Journal of Psychotherapy, 41,* 38–45.

Monahan, J. (1993). Limiting therapist exposure to Tarasoff liability: Guidelines for risk containment. *American Psychologist, 48,* 242–250.

Monahan, J., & Steadman, H. J. (Eds.). (1994). *Violence and mental disorder: Developments in risk assessment.* Chicago: University of Chicago Press.

Mossman, D. (1994). Assessing predictions of violence: Being accurate about accuracy. *Journal of Consulting and Clinical Psychology, 62,* 783–792.

Otto, R. K. (2000). Assessing and managing violence risk in outpatient settings. *Journal of Clinical Psychology, 56,* 1239–1262.

Stromberg, C., Schneider, J., & Joondeph, B. (1993). *Dealing with potentially dangerous patients: The psychologist's legal update.* Washington,

DC: National Register of Health Service Providers in Psychology.

Tarasoff v. Regents of the University of California, 17 Cal. 3d 425, 551 P.2d 334 (1976).

Truscott, D. (1993). The psychotherapist's duty to protect: An annotated bibliography. *Journal of Psychiatry & Law, 21,* 221–244.

Truscott, D., Evans, J., & Mansell, S. (1995). Outpatient psychotherapy with dangerous clients: A model for clinical decision making. *Professional Psychology: Research and Practice, 26,* 484–490.

VandeCreek, L., & Knapp, S. (1993). *Tarasoff and beyond: Legal and clinical considerations in the treatment of life-endangering patients.* Sarasota, FL: Professional Resource Press.

VandeCreek, L., & Knapp, S. (2000). Risk management and life-threatening patient behavior. *Journal of Clinical Psychology, 56,* 1335–1351.

Related Topics

Chapter 114, "Confidentiality and the Duty to Protect"
Chapter 115, "Forensic Evaluations and Testimony"
Chapter 116, "Forensic Evaluation Outline"
Chapter 117, "Forensic Referrals Checklist"
Chapter 119, "Forensic Assessment Instruments"

122 PRINCIPLES FOR CONDUCTING A COMPREHENSIVE CHILD CUSTODY EVALUATION

Barry Bricklin

STEPS IN STRUCTURING AND CONDUCTING A COMPREHENSIVE CUSTODY EVALUATION

1. Seek to be a neutral, bilateral evaluator, appointed to this role by a court order that details the participants. If you cannot obtain a court order, seek a stipulation signed by both sides. If you lack access to both sides, inspect any existing divorce and/or custody order to make certain the person seeking your services has a legal right to waive confidentiality and give consent that the evaluation take place for the child in the possible absence of agreement by the other parent. Prior to a written order, either parent can seek the services of a psychologist, albeit the issue of whether an evaluator should or should not notify the other parent may arise. Following a written court order, one must be aware of the controversies and widespread misunderstandings about the implications of what different legal custody dispositions allow a parent to do on behalf of a child should the other parent not be asked to share in the decision-making and/or object. For example, some psycholegal experts interpret shared legal custody as indicating that *either* parent can seek psychological services, and others as indicating the agreement of *both* parents is required. The latter is a safer position. (Members of the legal community are also divided on the implications of shared legal custody.) The main arguments *against* notifying and/or inviting the other

parent to participate, is that it may result in either alienation pressures directed at a child, or physical intimidation of the person seeking the services. If the written order is unclear, which is often the case, request that the judge who wrote it clarify the matter.

2. When you cannot secure the cooperation of all critical participants, document efforts to do so. Remember to limit conclusions to those made possible by available clinical and/or published databases and to detail in any written report and/or courtroom testimony what remains to be done to bring the evaluation to the level of a bilateral, comprehensive one.
3. Make certain there is an explicit (or implicit) database in terms of which the referral question can be addressed. Many parents want custody evaluators to help overturn an existing plan on the basis of some highly subjective complaint (e.g., "He lets them go to bed dirty"). There are no databases available by means of which an evaluator can address such issues.
4. Have the involved attorneys clarify whether the change-of-circumstances issue must be addressed; that is, if there is an existing custody order, it can be modified only under certain conditions.
5. Have the attorneys clarify all the legal issues involved. This would include the "must assess" aspects demanded in a given jurisdiction (e.g., whether joint custody is presumed to be the best choice unless proven not to be). Make sure you understand both statutory and case-law legal criteria. See Bricklin and Elliot (1995) for a sample model contract that covers many of the points mentioned here.
6. Obtain signed consent forms to waive confidentiality requirements (to reveal as well as seek relevant information, as when you need to obtain parent B's reactions to allegations made by parent A) and to administer tests and gather interview, observation, and document data in regard to all participants.
7. Mail out requests for pertinent documents from schools, pediatricians, and so forth. Have the main participants send appropriate consent-to-share information forms to relevant parties.
8. Mail out self-report questionnaire forms or use them as in-person interview guides with all main participants. (See Bricklin & Elliot, 1995, and Bricklin, 1995, for the tremendously extensive data needed for a comprehensive evaluation.)
9. Arrange to have both parents bring in the child for any initial psychological testing. Arrange for the current noncustodial parent to spend several hours with the child on the two days prior to the initial visit. If you choose to interview the child at this initial session, be aware that each parent may subtly or openly question the child regarding what he or she said, and alienating pressures on the child may needlessly increase. Conduct an observation session involving the child and both parents together on this initial day. Make sure the parents put aside expressing their hostilities during this session.
10. Arrange observation schedules that are fair and balanced. Make sure the child spends an equal amount of time with each parent prior to one-on-one observation sessions. (The existing visitation schedule may have to be modified.) Each child should be seen with both parents together and with each alone. One may desire to observe other family subsystems (e.g., all the children together with each parent). It is exceedingly important to see the parents together if you are considering true joint (physical as well as legal) custody; one should document their capacity for cooperative communication. Set up scenarios in which you can observe how a parent guides, sets limits, teaches, and so forth. In regard to all observations, pay special attention to how a child utilizes parental communications, not simply to what parents are doing and/or saying. A formal, quantified observation format designed to measure a caretaker's impact on a child is presented in Bricklin and Elliot (2002a, 2002b) and Bricklin and Halbert (2004).
11. Test and further interview the parents.

12. Test and interview significant others (e.g., grandparents, live-in companions).
13. Distinguish collateral sources of information (e.g., neighbors, pediatricians) that require in-person contact from those that do not.
14. Interview the child.
15. Use the gathered data to address the critical assessment targets listed later.
16. While various legal criteria of custody dispute resolution detail what to evaluate (e.g., the Uniform Marriage and Divorce Act, Section 402, 1979), none specify how to prioritize the huge amount of information collected, especially in terms of what it means to an involved child. As of the time this was written (February 2003), there were only two published systems offering formal models to aggregate the data gathered. Our model, A Comprehensive Custody Evaluation Standard System (ACCESS; Bricklin & Elliot, 1995), uses data-based tests designed to illuminate the range of impacts each parent is having on an involved child to prioritize the information gathered and a modified Bayesian decision model to consider evidence for which no "relevance" databases exist (e.g., a parent's health, finances, time availability). Reliability, validity and normative data now exist on 3,880 cases (Bricklin & Elliot, 2002a). Another model is by Ackerman and Schoendorf (1992).

    Without a database, the evaluator must seek convergent and independent lines of information.

    There is controversy as to whether a psychologist in the role of an expert witness in a courtroom setting should address an "ultimate issue," which in a custody case might be who should be the primary custodial parent. If in doubt, seek clarification from the presiding judge.

CRITICAL ASSESSMENT AREAS

Orientational Targets

A comprehensive custody evaluation seeks to generate information relevant to legal custody (the right and responsibility to make educational, interpersonal and elective medical/psychological decisions for a child) and physical custody (a time-share plan). Either parent can make emergency decisions. There is controversy regarding what constitutes a psychological emergency. Judges usually prefer to award shared rather than sole legal custody (it keeps both parents involved) unless there are blatant reasons not to (bad logistics, serious psychopathology, the parents never agree about anything).

An orientational target is one of such major importance that it must be addressed immediately and/or kept in mind at all times. For example, a severe physical impairment on the part of a child may make parental time availability a controlling factor in a given case.

1. The probability that the parents can reach an agreement on their own. (If high, one might recommend mediation instead of evaluation.)
2. Information gleaned from prior legal proceedings: isolate what has already been established and what remains to be done.
3. Pertinent legal issues: jurisdictional criteria of dispute resolution (e.g., joint custody presumption); need to address potential change of circumstances; and so forth.
4. Child's psychological, physical, developmental, educational, and cultural status. Seek to identify a child's unique needs so that the visitation plan suggested addresses them.

Assessment Targets

Assessment targets are custody-relevant areas that are assessed by a wide variety of clinical techniques, generating data from psychological tests, observations, interviews, medical and educational documents, and home visits.

Specific assessment targets are the degree to which

1. The child seems really "wanted" by each disputant (e.g., does a parent pick up a child only to drop him or her off immediately at a grandparent's home?).
2. Each parent congruently offers (and mod-

els) communications to the child so as to engender signs of positive affective responses in the child (e.g., happiness, good self-feeling).

3. Each parent congruently offers (and models) communications to the child so as to engender signs of behavioral self-sufficiency (e.g., responses mirroring competency, independence in thought and action).
4. Each parent has demonstrated caretaking skills in prior relationships.
5. Each parent can avoid episodes of neglect and physical or sexual abuse; the degree to which each parent and person to whom the child might be exposed under competing visitation arrangements can avoid episodes of *any* criminal behavior.
6. Each parent can avoid episodes of alcohol or drug use that could impair child care responsibilities.
7. Each parent can avoid episodes of distractibility and/or irritability that could impair child care responsibilities.
8. Each parent is aware of the child's daily routine, interpersonal relationships, health needs, developmental history, school history, fears, personal hygiene, communication patterns.
9. Each parent is able to recognize the critical issues involved in child care situations; the necessity of selecting adequate solutions in child care situations; the importance of communicating to the child in words and actions understandable to the child; the desirability of acknowledging the feelings aroused in a child by various situations; the desirability of considering a child's unique past history in deciding how to respond to child care situations; the importance of considering feedback data in responding to a child.
10. Each parent is aware of his or her own weak spots and vulnerabilities in dealing with children, and the degree to which each parent has developed strategies to cope with these weaknesses.
11. Each parent shows flexibility, honesty, and supportiveness in dealing with the child's other parent and members of his or her family and takes care introducing new parent-companions into a child's life.
12. Each parent can provide continuity in all important phases of a child's life (e.g., extended family, school, friendships, religious affiliations).
13. Each parent can enhance the child's relationship with each sibling.
14. Each parent is available to be with the child.
15. Each parent can provide adequate babysitting, day care, and so forth.
16. Each parent can provide for the child's material needs, including on-time meals, appropriate sleeping arrangements and homework space, and so forth.
17. Each parent is able to maintain good physical health.
18. A child's consciously stated wishes (if verbalized) may be taken into account. Our data indicate that children's consciously sourced opinions about custody, even those of older children, have only a 50% agreement rate with those of mental health experts.

Data-Based Assessment Targets

A data-based assessment target refers to a target that can be addressed by tests or procedures in which the interpretations of the information yielded by the latter have been developed from a population representative of the cases to which this target is to be applied. The degree to which

1. Each parent teaches and models the skills of competency.
2. Each parent offers and models warmth, empathy, and support.
3. Each parent appropriately insists on (and models) consistency.
4. Each parent teaches and models admirable traits (e.g., trustworthiness, altruism).
5. Each parent is a source of psychological assets and/or liabilities.
6. Each child seeks to be psychologically "close" to each parent (Bricklin & Elliot, 1995).

Note: A more comprehensive version of these materials can be found in Barry Bricklin, *The Custody Evaluation Handbook: Research-Based Solutions and Applications* (New York: Brunner/

Mazel, 1995) and a summary of normative, reliability, and validity data can be found in Bricklin and Elliot (2002a and 2002b).

References & Readings 

Ackerman, M. J., & Schoendorf, K. (1992). *Ackerman-Schoendorf scales for parent evaluation of custody.* Los Angeles: Western Psychological Services.

Bricklin, B. (1995). *The custody evaluation handbook: Research-based solutions and applications.* New York: Brunner/Mazel.

Bricklin, B., & Elliot, G. (1995). *ACCESS: A comprehensive custody evaluation standard system.* Furlong, PA: Village Publishing.

Bricklin, B., & Elliot, G. (2000). Qualifications of and techniques to be used by judges, attorneys and mental health professionals who deal with children in high conflict divorce cases. *University of Arkansas at Little Rock Law Review, 122*(3), 501–528.

Bricklin, B., & Elliot, G. (2002a, April). *What can empirical data on 4,500 child custody cases tell us?* Paper presented at the American College of Forensic Psychology, San Francisco, CA.

Bricklin, B., & Elliot, G. (2002b). *The Perception-of-Relationships Test (PORT) and Bricklin Perceptual Scales (BPS): Current and new empirical data on 3,880 cases, 1961–2002.* Furlong, PA: Village Publishing.

Bricklin, B., & Halbert, M. (2004). Can child custody data be generated scientifically? Part I. *American Journal of Family Therapy, 32,* 189–203.

Brodzinsky, D. (1993). On the use and misuse of psychological testing in child custody evaluations. *Professional Psychology: Research and Practice, 24,* 213–219.

Gordon, R., & Peek, L. A. (1988). *The custody quotient.* Dallas, TX: Wilmington Institute.

Halon, R. L. (1990). The comprehensive child custody evaluation. *American Journal of Forensic Psychology, 8*(3), 19–46.

Sales, B., Manber, R., & Rohman, L. (1992). Social science research and child-custody decision making. *Applied and Preventive Psychology, 1,* 23–40.

Schutz, B. M., Dixon, E. B., Lindenberger, J. C., & Ruther, N. J. (1989). *Solomon's sword: A practical guide to conducting child custody evaluations.* San Francisco: Jossey-Bass.

Stahl, P. M. (1994). *Conducting child custody evaluations: A comprehensive guide.* Thousand Oaks, CA: Sage.

Uniform Marriage and Divorce Act. (1979). In *Uniform Laws Annotated,* 9A.

Related Topics

Chapter 12, "Interviewing Parents"
Chapter 115, "Forensic Evaluations and Testimony"
Chapter 116, "Forensic Evaluation Outline"
Chapter 119, "Forensic Assessment Instruments"

123 RECOGNIZING, ASSISTING, AND REPORTING THE IMPAIRED PSYCHOLOGIST

Gary R. Schoener

DEFINITIONS AND HISTORY

The term *impaired,* when applied to a psychologist or other health care professional, has historically been considered almost synonymous with the notions of alcoholism or substance abuse. This reflects the fact that one of the most common sources of impairment in health professionals is drug or alcohol addiction. Most "impaired practitioner" programs in health professions, and even in the legal profession, focus on alcoholism and other substance abuse. Each of these programs also deals with other problems—for example, depression, marital difficulties, anxiety disorders, and sexual compulsivity—but today the focus remains on chemical abuse or dependency problems.

As defined in psychology,

> impairment refers to objective change in a person's professional functioning. An impaired psychologist is one whose work-related performance has diminished in quality. This may be manifested in one or more of the following ways: work assignments are typically late or incomplete; conflict with colleagues has noticeably increased; clients, students, or families have registered complaints; or the amount of absenteeism and tardiness has markedly increased. (Schwebel, Skorina, & Schoener, 1994, p. 2)

Organized psychology's first major thrust at identifying and dealing with impairment involved a task force and then a book, *Professionals in Distress: Issues, Syndromes, and Solutions in Psychology* (Kilburn, Nathan, & Thoreson, 1986). This was followed by the Advisory Committee on the Distressed Psychologist, which reported to the Board of Professional Affairs of the American Psychological Association (APA), which soon changed the name to the Advisory Committee on Impaired Psychologists and then produced the book *Assisting Impaired Psychologists: Program Development for State Psychological Associations* (Schwebel, Skorina, & Schoener, 1988). A revised edition was published in 1994. The committee's current name uses "Colleague Assistance" in place of "Impaired Psychologists" in order to underline a broader focus, including prevention, and to stress the need to help colleagues who are distressed or impaired.

The topic of sexual misconduct by professionals has generated literally thousands of books and articles (e.g., Lerman, 1990), with some focused on prevention (e.g., Pope, Sonne, & Holroyd, 1993) and others examining treatment of the offending professional (e.g., Gabbard, 1995; Gonsiorek, 1995; Schoener, Milgrom, Gonsiorek, Luepker, & Conroe, 1989). For psychology, sexual misconduct is probably the most visible outcome of impairment, as well as the most expensive in terms of the generation of ethics complaints and licensure board actions, and it accounted for at least half of the cost of defense and awards to plaintiffs in malpractice actions. Sexual misconduct has typically not been dealt with by committees on impaired practitioners in other professions, and in psychology there has been debate over whether it should be dealt with differently. Some have questioned whether rehabilitation should be attempted in such cases (e.g., Pope et al., 1993), whereas others provide assessment and/or rehabilitation (e.g., Abel, Osborn, & Warberg, 1995; Gabbard, 1995; Gonsiorek, 1995; Schoener, 1995).

A relatively new factor in the handling of impairment is the Americans With Disabilities Act (cf. Bruyere & O'Keeffe, 1994). While prohibiting discrimination against individuals with disabilities, both mental and physical, the act requires employers to "make reasonable accommodation" to employees' disabilities. This affects the handling of the impaired professional in two ways. First, it provides an incentive to acknowledge disability rather than hide it; second, it directs the psychologist in the role of employer to make reasonable efforts to help someone dealing with a disability function on the job. Thus, the impaired or potentially impaired psychologist has reason to present his or her difficulties to an employer or supervisor in hopes of negotiating a helpful accommodation.

RESPONSIBILITY TO REPORT

Psychologists often have professional responsibilities with regard to clients, students, and others who may be affected by the practitioner's impairment. Where such individuals are at risk, there may be a duty to act quickly. In addition, reporting duties need to be carried out if you learn of possible child abuse or neglect or of anything that must be reported to a state board or other regulatory authority.

First and foremost, never agree to keep something confidential until you know what the impaired professional has to say and whether you can keep it confidential. As with clients, anyone with whom you consult about impairment needs to know the limits of the privacy of your discussions with them. All of the following reporting duties would be based on state laws or guidelines:

1. Reporting of abuse or neglect of a minor or of a vulnerable adult
2. Any reporting to a state board required by licensure statutes (e.g., Minnesota requires reporting of certain offenses unless they are communicated by the psychologist who is seeking help)
3. Any reporting duties based on your knowledge of dangers to others, such as potential dangers to clients
4. Duties to report impaired functioning of a staff member who works in the same facility as you do

In some states, colleague assistance or impaired practitioner programs have selected exemptions from reporting duties. It is important that you determine whether such an exemption might apply to your activities. They are typically limited to work by professional review committees or impaired practitioner programs. Those involved in subsequent treatment or rehabilitation should also note their responsibilities (cf. Jorgenson, 1995).

GUIDELINES FOR INTERVENTION

The APA Code of Ethics and general standards in professional practice, education, and research require that psychologists consult with colleagues who are at risk to engage in unethical practice. The practical issue of how and when to intervene depends on the following factors:

1. Your relationship with the colleague who is, or may be, impaired
2. Your professional status vis-à-vis the colleague—for example, a supervisor, professor, administrator
3. Whether or not the colleague has come to you for assistance
4. The organizational or institutional setting in which you work and what policies, procedures, and departments exist to help with the situation

The 2002 revision of APA Ethical Principles of Psychologists and Code of Conduct contains a new section relating to students that cautions those who might begin inquiring about a student's personal adjustment. Section 7.04 reads:

Student Disclosure of Personal Information. Psychologists do not require students or supervisees to disclose personal information in course- or program-related activities, either orally or in writing, regarding sexual history, history of abuse and neglect, psychological treatment, and relationships with parents, peers, and spouses or significant others except if (1) the program or training facility has clearly identified this requirement in its admissions and program materials or (2) the information is necessary to evaluate or obtain assistance for students whose personal problems could reasonably be judged to be preventing them from performing their training- or professionally related activities in a competent manner or posing a threat to the students or others.

Before acting, examine any organizational policies or guidelines concerning impaired staff. In larger organizations, human resources departments often play a role in such intervention. They may be consulted for advice or for direct assistance. Employee assistance programs also provide guidance that may be of help.

There also may be experts in your local community who can be of assistance. A number of state psychological associations have colleague assistance committees. The Practice Directorate at the APA has such information through staff for the Advisory Committee on Colleague Assistance. The APA effort, in fact, is focused on the creation of state committees to provide assistance to those seeking to intervene or obtain help for colleagues. If there are no readily identifiable local experts and there is no state committee, it is also possible to arrange for help with substance-abusing or alcoholic colleagues through Psychologists Helping Psychologists (PHP), a national organization founded in 1980. It can be contacted through Ann Stone at 703-578-1644 (e-mail: AnnS@Erols.com). Its Web site can also be contacted for referrals.

Another possible resource is the colleague assistance committee of another health profession, such as medicine. These committees can be most easily located by contacting the state professional organization. In addition, PHP is connected to International Doctors in Alcoholics Anonymous, which consists of professionals in many fields who are involved in Alcoholics Anonymous. This 53-year-old organization, which has a yearly convention, can be contacted for resources through its Web site.

Several videotapes that focus on practitioner impairments may be quite useful for staff orientation in an organization for assisting an individual professional. *The Journey Back*, produced by a public television station in Los Angeles, is available from Video Finder (800-343-4727). Michael F. Myers, M.D., has produced two films. *Physicians Living With Depression*, done under the auspices of the Committee on Physician Health, Illness, and Impairment, is part of the American Psychiatric Association Videotape Series and can be purchased from American Psychiatric Press. Another tape consists of Dr. Myers interviewing a physician who became impaired and had sexual contact with a patient. *Crossing the Boundary: Sexual Issues in the Doctor-Patient Relationship* can be ordered from Dr. Michael Myers (604-732-8013 or 604-631-5498).

One of the fundamental questions in this area is the manner of intervention. Some circumstances permit a private talk with an impaired practitioner to start things moving, whereas in other cases a more active intervention is necessary. Whenever several professionals confront an impaired psychologist jointly, or involve others, such as family members, there is the potential for greater anger and defensiveness. However, in some circumstances, little else works. Four intervention options (Schwebel et al., 1994) are presented below.

Voluntary Intervention

In some situations, an impaired psychologist calls for help or approaches a colleague. It is essential to remember the importance of follow-through. The fact that a colleague comes in for help does not mean that he or she will take the next step. Sometimes receiving support reduces the person's motivation. Furthermore, it is important to have a competent diagnostician determine what sort of treatment is needed. Professionals often look healthier than they are, and as a result inadequate treatment may be planned. In the case of professional misconduct, such as sex with clients, it is critical that someone with specialized experience do the assessment and treatment planning to avoid common pitfalls in such cases (Gabbard, 1995).

The "12-Step" Intervention

The 12-step intervention is aimed at someone who appears to be alcoholic or to have a substance abuse problem. Psychologists or other health professionals who are in recovery from substance abuse and who have experience in this type of intervention arrange a meeting with the impaired psychologist; they share their own experiences and encourage the person to join Alcoholics Anonymous or Psychologists Helping Psychologists or to seek help in another way. Although such an intervention is intrusive, it is not intended to be confrontive. The goal is to provide a model for recovery and to convey the relief that a psychologist can be alcoholic and benefit from help.

Confrontive Intervention

In confrontive intervention, an employer or a colleague assistance committee receives a report that a psychologist has a significant problem and has not responded to suggestions that he or she seek help. An investigation is conducted to determine if such a problem can be documented behaviorally, and then a small team of professionals (or, in some instances, a work supervisor) confronts the psychologist with the evidence that has been gathered. A treatment referral has previously been identified, the psychologist is offered a plan of action, and peer pressure is used to try to bring about an agreement to receive help and follow through. This approach is more confrontive than the 12-step intervention in that considerable peer pressure is applied.

Comprehensive Intervention

Comprehensive intervention is reserved for situations in which the psychologist's problem is severe, or at least getting worse, and he or she has not responded to input or suggestions that he or she seek help. It goes beyond the confrontive intervention in that the information-gathering process usually involves discussions with the psychologist's spouse or significant other, and an intervention team is organized that includes a number of key people in the psychologist's life. Prior to the intervention, this group meets and plans the intervention, including some role playing of possible scenarios. The eventual intervention is thus scripted beforehand. The psychologist is then told that if he or she does not enter and complete treatment, specific negative consequences will occur. This can involve job suspension, a report to a licensing body, or a spouse filing for divorce. This approach is coercive and intrusive, and it may bring about an angry response from the psychologist. It should be done with the aid of persons experienced in such work.

SUPPORT AND MONITORING

A major factor in the success of colleague assistance is the degree to which you can help the psychologist start the treatment process. Helping to arrange for work coverage, an appropriate medical leave, and identification of affordable treatment covered by insurance is very important. Many such practical problems can sabotage treatment efforts. When someone is in treatment for impairment, maintaining contact in a supportive fashion can be quite helpful. It is also important to monitor compliance, to the degree possible, in order to be able to confront those who attempt to quit before completion.

WORK REENTRY

The main goal of any intervention should be to facilitate a professional assessment and treatment planning of the psychologist. After that, it is important to consult with the assessor concerning job or practice limitations. When it seems that the treatment is completed, there should be an assessment of the situation, including a "return to work" assessment, which specifies things that would help prevent a recurrence and also reduce the risk of any misconduct or relapse.

With alcoholism there may be a requirement that the psychologist attend support groups and also a warning that the smell of alcohol on his or her breath may be sufficient cause for suspension. In the case of substance abuse, random urine testing may be required. It is also likely that more frequent supervisory meetings will be required at first in order to ensure that workload and duties are realistic given the recovery process.

REDUCING LEGAL RISKS

Some of the legal risks connected with various types of intervention are discussed in Schwebel et al. (1994). The more confrontive the intervention, the riskier it is. However, despite fears of retaliation for invasion of privacy, such cases appear to be quite rare. The most common mistakes with legal consequences are failures: to consult with human resources personnel; to plan the intervention within the personnel guidelines of a facility; and to review the Americans With Disabilities Act for its applicability to the situation. Psychologists need to be aware that when disputes arise within the family, especially in cases of family dissolution or divorce, well-intentioned helpers can find themselves pawns in intrafamilial power struggles. Thus, it is important to carefully gather background data and to be clear on what basis you believe the psychologist has a problem.

References, Readings, & Internet Sites

Abel, G., Osborn, C., & Warberg, B. (1995). Cognitive-behavioral treatment for professional sexual misconduct. *Psychiatric Annals, 25,* 106–112.

Bruyere, S., & O'Keeffe, J. (1994). *Implications of the Americans With Disabilities Act for psychology.* Washington, DC: American Psychological Association.

Gabbard, G. (1995). Transference and countertransference in the psychotherapy of therapists charged with sexual misconduct. *Psychiatric Annals, 25,* 100–105.

Gonsiorek, J. (1995). Assessment and treatment of health care professionals and clergy who sexually exploit patients. In J. Gonsiorek (Ed.), *Breach of trust: Sexual exploitation by health care professionals and clergy* (pp. 225–234). Thousand Oaks, CA: Sage.

Health, S. (1991). *Dealing with the therapist's vulnerability to depression.* Northvale, NJ: Jason Aronson.

International Doctors in Alcoholics Anonymous. (n.d.). Home page. Retrieved 2004 from http://www.ida.org

Jorgenson, L. (1995). Rehabilitating sexually exploitative therapists: A risk management perspective. *Psychiatric Annals, 25,* 118–122.

Kilburn, R., Nathan, P., & Thoreson, R. (1986). *Professionals in distress: Issues, syndromes, and solutions in psychology.* Washington, DC: American Psychological Association.

Koocher, G. P., & Keith-Spiegel, P. (1998). *Ethics in psychology: Professional standards and cases* (2nd ed.). New York: Oxford University Press.

Lerman, H. (1990). *Sexual intimacies between psychotherapists and patients: An annotated bibliography of mental health, legal, and public media literature and relevent legal cases* (2nd ed.). Washington, DC: Division of Psychotherapy, American Psychological Association.

Pope, K. S., Sonne, J. L., & Holroyd, J. (1993). *Sexual feelings in psychotherapy: Explorations for therapists and therapists-in-training.* Washington, DC: American Psychological Association.

Psychologists Helping Psychologists. (n.d.). http://www.crml.uab.edu/~jah/php.html

Schoener, G. R. (1995). Assessment of professionals who have engaged in boundary violations. *Psychiatric Annals, 25,* 95–99.

Schoener, G. R., Milgrom, J. H., Gonsiorek, J. C., Luepker, E. T., & Conroe, R. (1989). *Psychotherapists' sexual involvement with clients: Intervention and prevention.* Minneapolis, MN: Walk-In Counseling Center.

Schwebel, M., Skorina, J., & Schoener, G. (1994). *Assisting impaired psychologists: Program development for state psychological associations* (Rev. ed.). Washington, DC: American Psychological Association.

Skorina, J. K., Bissell, L. C., & De Soto, C. B. (1990). The alcoholic psychologist: Routes to recovery. *Professional Psychology: Research and Practice, 21,* 248–251.

Related Topics

Chapter 65, "Refusal Skills Training"

Chapter 66, "Sexual Feelings, Actions, and Dilemmas in Psychotherapy"

Chapter 113, "How to Confront an Unethical Colleague"

Chapter 136, "Therapist Self-Care Checklist"

124 ESSENTIAL FEATURES OF PROFESSIONAL LIABILITY INSURANCE

Bruce E. Bennett

THE RELATIONSHIP BETWEEN RISK AND INSURANCE

Risk management essentially involves the transfer of financial obligations from one party to another.

- A significant feature of managed care arrangements is that some of the risk for payment of claims is shifted from the payer to the provider.
- In clinical practice, a missed diagnosis or improper treatment that damages a patient may result in a malpractice suit against the practitioner.
- Fortunately, the psychologist can shift the risk for the potential financial loss to another party by purchasing professional liability insurance.

WHO NEEDS PROFESSIONAL LIABILITY COVERAGE?

Ideally, risk management would lead to the total elimination or avoidance of activities that could lead to harm, damage, or other negative consequences. In practice the risk of damage or harm to a client or other entity receiving professional services can only be minimized. Even the most ethical and skilled practitioners have been subject to malpractice suits. It is important that psychologists recognize there is always the possibility of a negative outcome associated with the delivery of professional services.

- The risk of real or perceived damage or harm is not limited to psychologists who deliver health care services.
- Psychologists working for or consulting with business or governmental agencies, industrial organizational psychologists, academic and research psychologists, and school psychologists also are vulnerable to litigation for any harm or injury that may result from their services. For example, a psychologist who uses psychological tests for employee selection, retention, or promotion may be sued for any negative outcome based on the evaluation. A student who feels harassed or is dissatisfied with a grade or evaluation may sue his or her psychology professor or supervisor.
- The delivery of psychological services is never without risk.
- Any psychologist who provides professional services without adequate professional liability insurance has assumed the entire risk for any financial losses, including legal expenses to defend the practitioner and any damages awarded.

POLICY TYPE

Insurance is a written contract between the insured and the insurance carrier. For the premium received, the insurance carrier agrees to both defend the psychologist (i.e., pay the legal expenses associated with defending a claim) and indemnify the psychologist (i.e., pay for any cash settlements or damages awarded by a jury, subject to any policy limitations). Two basic types of professional liability coverage are available: occurrence coverage and claims-made coverage.

- *Occurrence coverage:* An occurrence policy covers any incident that happens while the policy is in force—regardless of when the claim is filed. In an occurrence policy, the claim will be covered according to the terms and conditions of the policy in force at the time the alleged malpractice occurred. A psychologist who terminates an occurrence policy (e.g., due to retirement, leave of absence, or changing to another policy type or another carrier) would be covered for any claim filed in the future based on any alleged malpractice during the policy period. There would be no need to purchase additional insurance.
- *Claims-made coverage:* A claims-made policy covers any incident that happens after the policy is in force. The claim, however, must be reported while the policy is in force. All claims-made policies have a *retroactive date*—the day that continuous coverage under the claims-made policy begins. In order to be covered under a claims-made policy, the incident must have occurred after the *retroactive date* and the claim filed before the policy is terminated. Claims filed after coverage ends will be covered only if the practitioner has purchased an *extended reporting period,* commonly referred to as "tail coverage." In a claims-made policy, the claim will be covered according to the terms and conditions of the policy in force at the time the claim is filed.

FACTORS AFFECTING POLICY PRICE

The majority of psychologists today purchase claims-made insurance with coverage levels at \$1 million/\$3 million (i.e., a maximum of \$1 million in coverage for a single incident and up to \$3 million aggregate coverage for all claims filed in the year). The range of coverage available extends from \$200,000/\$200,000 up to \$2 million/\$4 million.

- The premium for an occurrence policy is higher than the premium for a claims-made policy because coverage in an occurrence policy is provided for all future claims that resulted from alleged malpractice during the policy period. Occurrence premiums remain relatively stable over time, changing primarily as a function of losses in the program, increases in legal expenses, and general inflation.
- Premiums for a claims-made policy are lower during the first few years because coverage is provided only for claims filed during the coverage period. For example, first-year premiums need only cover the claims filed during the first year. As the policy matures, however, the premiums will increase.
- The differential in cost between an occurrence and a claims-made policy will generally exceed the price of the tail coverage necessary to terminate the claims-made policy. The psychologist can save considerable money by purchasing claims-made coverage.
- Independent of policy type, premiums will increase as the policy limits increase, as the scope of coverage increases, and as benefits and enhancements are added to the policy.
- Premiums for practitioners are higher in some states than in others.
- Premiums are generally lower in policies that exclude certain types of activities, services, or service settings (e.g., custody evaluations, certain types of forensic activities, and working in a correctional setting).
- Some policies include the cost of defending a malpractice suit within the policy limits, thus reducing the amount available for payment of damages by the amount of the legal expenses. When the policy limits are reduced by defense cost, the policy price should be lower. Because of the high cost of defense, however, psychologists are encouraged to avoid this restriction.

READ YOUR POLICY AND UNDERSTAND HOW IT WORKS

It is important that psychologists be familiar with the terms, conditions, and exclusions in their professional liability policy.

Policy Conditions

Insurance policies contain a number of conditions that the insured must meet in order to keep the policy in force.

- The policy may require that the insured cooperate with the carrier in the defense of a claim against the insured and that the insured immediately report a suit or threat of suit to the carrier.
- The policy may prohibit the insured from assuming any obligations, incurring any costs, or settling any claims without the company's written consent. These and other conditions are included in the policy to protect the carrier from additional unnecessary losses that may result from the practitioner's inappropriate actions.
- If the psychologist violates policy provisions, the insurance company may attempt to restrict or deny coverage for a specific claim. In the extreme, the carrier may sue the psychologist to rescind the policy, thus avoiding all coverage for any claim.
- If the carrier determines that the psychologist is a bad risk for coverage, the policy may be terminated or not renewed.

Policy Limitations or Exclusions

In addition to specific conditions regarding coverage, professional liability insurance policies place limitations on, or exclude, coverage for specific activities.

- Psychologists' professional liability insurance generally will not cover claims against the insured for business relationships with current or former clients or as an owner or operator of a hospital or other overnight facility. These functions involve business and managerial decisions rather than the delivery of professional services. Facilities such as hospitals will need "directors and officers" and "errors and omissions" coverage.
- The policy may exclude claims of dishonest, criminal, or fraudulent acts by the psychologist. Insurance is not sold to protect dishonest or criminal behavior.
- A malpractice suit may allege that the psychologist's services and conduct were intended to injure the plaintiff. Intentional and willful acts are generally excluded from coverage.
- If a claim alleges acts or services that are excluded from coverage, the carrier will issue a "reservation of rights" letter to the defendant. This letter generally provides that the carrier will defend the case but may not have responsibility to pay for any damages awarded for the noncovered acts.

Special Provisions Related to Sexual Misconduct Claims

Approximately half of the losses in the psychologists' professional liability program are due to sexual misconduct claims. Small wonder, then, that many insurance carriers have imposed specific limitations on such claims. The carriers, noting that sexual misconduct is unethical and that an increasing number of states have criminalized sexual relations between therapist and patient, are not willing to assume the liability for associated losses. Put differently, the company shifts the risks associated with such behaviors to the practitioner, keeping the premiums charged to ethical practitioners lower.

- Some carriers cap the amount the policy will pay for damages.
- Other carriers will fully defend a sexual misconduct claim but exclude any payments for damages.

An insurance carrier may control for potential future losses by terminating or not renewing the policy of a psychologist who has been found guilty of sexual misconduct by a licensing board or ethics committee, even if no malpractice suit has been filed. Psychologists dropped by one carrier will have difficulty finding another carrier willing to offer coverage.

Ethical practitioners should be concerned with how the policy will respond to a frivolous claim alleging sexual misconduct.

- A policy that contains a blanket exclusion for therapist-patient sex may not even provide a legal defense. It is important that the policy defend claims alleging malpractice, regardless of the claim's merit.

- Some policies cap the carrier's liability for damages in sexual misconduct cases at a fixed dollar amount. Under these terms, if a frivolous case is settled, the psychologist may be required to pay that part of the settlement that is in excess of the capped amount.
- A policy that will not pay damages but will defend multiple claims for sexual misconduct may, in fact, provide the best protection for a frivolous claim. The legal costs of going to trial can be very high, for both plaintiff and defendant. If the case is frivolous or weak, the plaintiff, or plaintiff's attorney, may wish to negotiate a settlement. Generally, insurance carriers will attempt to settle a case for an amount that is less than the cost of defense. If such a settlement is reached, the carrier will make the payment.

CHANGING POLICY TYPES OR INSURANCE CARRIERS

When changing policy types or changing carriers, be careful to avoid gaps in coverage.

- *Occurrence coverage to claims-made coverage:* In order to avoid any gap in coverage when moving from an occurrence policy to a claims-made policy, the retroactive date of the claims-made policy must be the same as or earlier than the termination date of the occurrence policy.
- *Claims-made coverage to occurrence coverage:* In order to avoid any gap in coverage when moving from a claims-made policy to an occurrence policy, the psychologist must (a) purchase the *extended reporting period* or the "tail coverage" for the terminated claims-made policy and (b) purchase occurrence coverage with a date that is the same or earlier than the termination date of the claims-made policy. If the tail coverage is not purchased, any claims filed after the claims-made policy is terminated will not be covered. Because of the general long reporting period for psychological malpractice claims, the insured is advised to purchase the longest tail coverage possible. The cost for indefinite tail coverage is usually 175% of the final year's premium.
- *Occurrence coverage to occurrence coverage by a different carrier:* In order to avoid any gap in coverage when moving from an occurrence policy to an occurrence policy from another carrier, the policy date of the new coverage should be the same as or earlier than the termination date of the terminated policy.
- *Claims-made coverage to claims-made coverage by a different carrier:* The psychologist who desires to change claims-made carriers has two choices. (a) Purchase the tail coverage on the old claims-made policy and purchase the first-year step rates on the new claims-made policy using the same renewal date as the old policy. If tail coverage is purchased on the old policy, the previous carrier will cover all claims generated under the terminated policy. The new carrier will cover claims resulting from alleged malpractice occurring after the effective date of the new policy. (b) Drop the old claims-made policy and purchase the new claims-made policy using the same retroactive date as the old policy. If the practitioner drops the old policy and purchases the new policy at the next step rate (e.g., if the current policy is at the fourth-year step rate, the new policy will be at the fifth-year step rate), all claims will then be covered by the new carrier. Purchasing the new claims-made policy at the next step rate will generally be more cost-effective in the short run. In addition, if the new carrier has a better reputation for handling claims, the practitioner should follow this latter strategy.

COVERAGE FOR PSYCHOLOGISTS EMPLOYED IN GROUP SETTINGS

Psychologists employed in group or corporate practices, in schools or academic settings, or in agency settings (e.g., mental health centers, hospitals, or other government agencies) need to determine if they are adequately covered for the services they perform in that setting. If not, they should purchase their own personal liability insurance. The following issues should be considered:

- Does the employer/group (e.g., group or corporate practice, mental health center, hospital, corporation, government agency, school, academic institution) have professional liability insurance?
- Does the insurance list both the group and the employee as a named insured under the policy?
- Are the levels of coverage adequate to cover any losses against the group and its employees?
- Do all members in the group share the aggregate limit of coverage, or does each member have his or her own aggregate limit? Although managed care companies may prefer to contract with group practices, many are hesitant to deal with groups in which all members share the aggregate limit of coverage.
- Does the policy require the carrier to defend and indemnify an employee who is sued for malpractice if the employee is not a named insured under the policy?
- Will the group policy cover an employee for services rendered outside the group setting?
- Do local, state, or federal statutes provide good-faith immunity for employees working in certain government settings? If a jury determines that the psychologist actually acted in bad faith (e.g., acted in a way to intentionally harm the plaintiff), the immunity statute may be voided, and the psychologist would then be responsible for payment of the damages.
- Regardless of the workplace setting, psychologists should avoid an uninsured risk. If the practitioner renders professional services outside the group setting (e.g., part-time consulting, supervision, teaching, or private practice), it is always recommended that individual coverage be in place.
- Psychologists serving as independent contractors for a group should have individual coverage. Group policies will cover a suit brought against the group as a result of the wrongdoing of an independent contractor, but they will not cover the independent contractor.
- If a group is uninsured, it is possible that the group may refuse to defend or indemnify a psychologist-employee named in a malpractice suit. The group may attempt to defend itself by asserting that the psychologist-employee acted outside the scope of the employment contract and that the group has no duty to defend the alleged wrongdoing. In effect, the group might join the plaintiff against the psychologist-employee.
- Whereas an uninsured agency or organization may have resources to defend a claim, it may be unable to pay damages. Uninsured psychologists employed by such agencies who are named as codefendants in the case may have to contribute to any damages awarded.
- If a group or agency does not have professional liability coverage, or if a psychologist-employee determines that the coverage available is not adequate, serious consideration should be given to purchasing individual coverage.

SETTLEMENT VERSUS TRIAL

Very few malpractice suits go to trial. Insurance carriers know that the most cost-effective resolution of this type of litigation is to settle the case. On the other hand, psychologists who do not believe they are guilty of malpractice usually want to go to trial, even if an appeal to the U.S. Supreme Court is necessary.

- Regardless of the "innocence" of the practitioner, there is always the possibility that a jury will award large damages. The psychologist would be personally responsible for any damages that exceed the policy limits.
- No one can predict how a jury will respond, even to a claim that has no merit.
- The plaintiff may want to settle the case if the allegations of malpractice will be difficult to prove, if the evidence indicates that the case is not clear-cut, or if the damages are not significant.
- The defendant may wish to settle to avoid

painful depositions, prolonged litigation, potential embarrassment in the public arena, and the loss of income due to time away from the practice.

- The net effect is that both the plaintiff and the defendant may have strong incentives to seek a settlement rather than go to trial.
- Most frivolous cases are dismissed or settled for small amounts. Fortunately, frivolous cases are generally transparent; if so, they may not have a significant impact on the psychologist's insurability.
- On the other hand, a large settlement is often interpreted as an indication of the seriousness of the charges and resulting damages.

PSYCHOLOGIST'S ROLE IN CASE SETTLEMENT

Most insurance policies (e.g., auto or homeowner's insurance) permit the insurance company to settle a claim without the consent of the insured. One professional liability policy contained a provision that required the written consent of the insured to settle a claim; if an insured refused to settle, the carrier was forced to take the case to trial. Although this provision may seem beneficial to the insured individual, the result is that almost all cases go to trial, at great expense to all practitioners insured under the program.

The major psychologists' professional liability policies provide a compromise between these two extreme positions. In the course of litigation, the attorneys for the plaintiff and defendant may discuss settlement as an option to trial. Even if the attorneys representing the plaintiff and defendant reach agreement on a proposed settlement, the carrier cannot settle the case without the written consent of the insured. However, if the insured refuses to accept the settlement proposal, the carrier's ultimate liability will be capped at the amount of the proposed settlement. If a jury awards damages in excess of the capped amount, the psychologist, not the carrier, will have to pay the difference.

PROFESSIONAL LIABILITY INSURANCE IS FOR THE LONG TERM

Over time, the insurance industry tends to go through market cycles, fluctuating between "soft" and "hard" markets. Competition is a key factor in a soft market: the return on investments is high, and insurance carriers attempt to increase their cash flow by offering new products or by decreasing premiums on current products to capture competitors' business. In a hard market, when the economy is not doing well, rates usually increase dramatically, and some companies may go out of business.

Malpractice suits against psychologists tend to be filed long after the alleged negligence or misconduct occurred. The premiums collected today must provide coverage for a possible claim against the psychologist in the future, sometimes years later. If current rates are too low, the carrier may not be able to provide the protection when needed. Moving from a soft to a hard market when premiums have been artificially low could result in large rate increases, modifications in the scope of coverage, or a decision by the carrier to drop this line of coverage. Psychologists are advised to view the purchase of professional liability insurance as an investment in the future. Put differently, a cheap policy may come with a high price.

ADMITTED VERSUS SURPLUS LINES CARRIERS

Most insurance carriers are "admitted," that is, approved by the state insurance commissioner to do business in that state. Admitted carriers are required to participate in consumer protection programs in the state. If an admitted carrier cannot meet its obligations to cover losses, state insurance funds may be available to protect the insureds. Some carriers, however, offer policies on a *nonadmitted* basis, commonly referred to as "surplus lines coverage." Such policies will clearly state that insured psychologists are not protected by state-authorized consumer protection programs.

- Surplus lines coverage may be available for practitioners who are otherwise uninsurable because of a history of previous claims. Such policies are usually very expensive and may restrict available limits of liability.
- Other carriers may offer surplus lines coverage in markets where coverage is not readily available (e.g., in hard markets when carriers fail or stop offering this type of coverage).

WHERE TO PURCHASE PROFESSIONAL LIABILITY INSURANCE

The diligent psychologist will approach the subject of professional liability insurance as an important business decision, both to protect the psychologist's assets and to provide the comfort and security needed to function in a professional capacity.

Policy features, strength and stability of the carrier, price, special enhancements, and representation of the psychologist's interests with the carrier are important aspects of any purchasing decision. The majority of practitioners purchase professional liability insurance from programs endorsed or sponsored by their national professional association. The American Psychological Association Insurance Trust has endorsed or sponsored comprehensive and cost-effective professional liability insurance for more than 30 years, during both soft and hard markets, including times when some carriers dropped psychology as a line of coverage. The Trust-sponsored professional liability insurance program was developed by psychologists for psychologists. The Trust serves as an ombudsperson for practitioners, representing their interests on all aspects of coverage and price.

References & Readings

Koocher, G. P., & Keith-Spiegel, P. C. (1998). *Ethics in psychology: Professional standards and cases* (2nd ed.). New York: Oxford University Press.

Woody, R. H. (1988). *Protecting your mental health practice: How to minimize legal and financial risk.* San Francisco: Jossey-Bass.

Wright, R. H. (1981). Psychologists and professional liability (malpractice) insurance: A retrospective review. *American Psychologist, 36,* 1485–1493.

Related Topics

Chapter 107, "Basic Principles for Dealing With Legal Liability Risk Situations"

Chapter 108, "Defending Against Legal Complaints"

PART X
Practice Management

125 SAMPLE PSYCHOTHERAPIST-PATIENT CONTRACT

Eric A. Harris & Bruce E. Bennett

This draft psychotherapist-patient contract has been prepared for two reasons. First, it allows one to comply with the requirement that practitioners have the informed consent of their patients (American Psychological Association, 2002, Standards 3.01 and 10.01). Second, it allows a therapist to establish a legally enforceable business relationship with the patient and avoids risks that such business issues will become the basis of a malpractice suit or an ethics or licensing board complaint. Most commentators suggest that full informed consent is both ethically necessary and a good risk management strategy.

This draft was designed for psychotherapy practices. It can and should be modified to include other practice areas such as psychological evaluations, testing, neuropsychological assessment, family therapy, and group psychotherapy if these are part of a practitioner's work.

There is a great variety of business practices among psychologists. You should redraft the contract to fit your business practices, rather than adjusting your practices to fit the contract. More importantly, you should make sure that the provisions of this contract are in compliance with the requirements of the HIPAA Privacy Rule (Standards for Privacy of Individually Identifiable Health Information). In addition, since regulations and laws governing certain institutions are somewhat different than those governing private practitioners, these forms may also need to be modified before they can be used in hospitals, clinics, or other institutional settings.

This document includes some basic, general language about the risks and benefits of psychotherapy; these should be supplemented, either in writing or orally, by the therapist on a case-by-case basis. This approach was selected because the risks and benefits of therapy can vary considerably from case to case. Therefore, it is hard to design a single draft that is appropriate for all situations. For example, it is probably important to have a much more thorough discussion of risks and benefits with those patients considered to be either most difficult or most risky. If one is a group or family therapist, additional issues may need to be included. The psychologist may orally provide whatever additional information is required and make a note in the record about what was said. Of course, this will not be as protective as a signed agreement, but in most cases it makes the most sense clinically.

Although this model contract was originally developed for Massachusetts psychologists, most of it can be used anywhere. There are two exceptions: (a) patients' access to their own records and (b) the laws and regulations governing therapeutic confidentiality and testimonial privilege, as well as exceptions to these protections of the psychotherapist-patient relationship. The model provides sufficient alternative sections to cover almost all variations regarding record access. However, there is much variation from state to state in laws governing privilege, confidentiality, and exceptions to both, so an adaptation should be made for each state in which a psychologist practices.

The reader is strongly advised to have his or her personal attorney review the informed consent document prior to implementation. The document should be in compliance with local and state statutes regulating the practice of psychology. It should also avoid language that could be interpreted as a guarantee or implied warranty regarding the services rendered.

This consent form is the property of the American Psychological Association Insurance Trust (APAIT), and copyright to the form is owned by the APAIT, © 1997 American Psychological Association Insurance Trust. This form is used with permission.

What follows is a specific draft text that you may adapt for your practice or agency. Sections of the draft where you should insert numbers are designated *XX*, and sections you may want to specially modify are bracketed [thus].

Outpatient Services Contract

Welcome to my practice. This document contains important information about my professional services and business policies. Please read it carefully and jot down any questions that you might have so that we can discuss them at our next meeting. Once you sign this, it will constitute a binding agreement between us.

Psychological Services

Psychotherapy is not easily described in general statements. It varies depending on the personality of both the therapist and the patient and the particular problems which the patient brings. There are a number of different approaches which can be utilized to deal with the problems you hope to address. It is not like visiting a medical doctor, in that psychotherapy requires a very active effort on your part. In order to be most successful, you will have to work on things we talk about both during our sessions and at home.

Psychotherapy has both benefits and risks. Risks sometimes include experiencing uncomfortable feelings such as sadness, guilt, anxiety, anger and frustration, loneliness, and helplessness. Psychotherapy often requires discussing unpleasant aspects of your life. Psychotherapy has also been shown to have benefits for people who undertake it. Therapy often leads to a significant reduction in feelings of distress, better relationships, and resolutions of specific problems. But there are no guarantees about what will happen.

Our first few sessions will involve an evaluation of your needs. By the end of the evaluation, I will be able to offer you some initial impressions of what our work will include and an initial treatment plan to follow, if you decide to continue. You should evaluate this information along with your own assessment about whether you feel comfortable working with me. Therapy involves a large commitment of time, money, and energy, so you should be very careful about the therapist you select. If you have questions about my procedures, we should discuss them whenever they arise. If your doubts persist, I will be happy to help you to secure an appropriate consultation with another mental health professional.

Meetings

My normal practice is to conduct an evaluation which will last from two to four sessions. During this time, we can both decide whether I am the best person to provide the services that you need in order to meet your treatment objectives. If psychotherapy is initiated, I will usually schedule one 50-minute session (one appointment hour of 50 minutes' duration) per week at a mutually agreed time, although sometimes sessions will be longer or more frequent. Once this appointment hour is scheduled, you will be expected to pay for it unless you provide *XXX* hours/days advance notice of cancellation [or unless we both agree that you were unable to attend due to circumstances which were beyond your control]. [If it is possible, I will try to find another time to reschedule the appointment.]

Professional Fees

My hourly fee is *$XXX*. In addition to weekly appointments, it is my practice to charge this amount on a prorated basis for other professional services you may require such as report writing, telephone conversations that last longer than *XX* minutes, attendance at meetings or consultations with other professionals that you have authorized, preparation of records or treatment summaries, or the time required to perform any other service that you may request of me. If you become involved in litigation that requires my participation, you will be expected to pay for the professional time required even if I am compelled to testify by another party. [Because of the complexity and difficulty of legal involvement, I charge *$XXX* per hour for preparation for and attendance at any legal proceeding.]

Billing and Payments

You will be expected to pay for each session at the time it is held, unless we agree otherwise or unless you have insurance coverage that requires another arrangement. Payment schedules for other professional services will be agreed to at the time these services are requested. [In circumstances of unusual financial hardship, I may be willing to negotiate a fee adjustment or installment payment plan.]

If your account is more than 60 days in arrears and suitable arrangements for payment have not been agreed to, I have the option of using legal means to secure payment, including collection agencies or small claims court. [If such legal action is necessary, the costs of bringing that proceeding will be included in the claim.] In most cases, the only information I release about a client's treatment would be the client's name, the nature of the services provided, and the amount due.

Insurance Reimbursement

In order for us to set realistic treatment goals and priorities, it is important to evaluate what resources are available to pay for your treatment. If you have a health insurance policy, it will usually provide some coverage for mental health treatment. I will provide you with whatever assistance I can in facilitating your receipt of the benefits to which you are entitled including filling out forms as appropriate. However, you, and not your insurance company, are responsible for full payment of the fee that we have agreed to. Therefore, it is very important that you find out exactly what mental health services your insurance policy covers.

You should carefully read the section in your insurance coverage booklet that describes mental health services. If you have questions, you should call your plan administrator and inquire. Of course, I will provide you with whatever information I can based on my experience and will be happy to try to assist you in deciphering the information you receive from your carrier. If necessary to resolve confusion, I am willing to call the carrier on your behalf.

The escalation of the cost of health care has resulted in an increasing level of complexity about insurance benefits which sometimes makes it difficult to determine exactly how much mental health coverage is available. "Managed Health Care Plans" such as HMOs and PPOs often require advance authorization before they will provide reimbursement for mental health services. These plans are often oriented toward a short-term treatment approach designed to resolve specific problems that are interfering with one's usual level of functioning. It may be necessary to seek additional approval after a certain number of sessions. In my experience, while quite a lot can be accomplished in short-term therapy, many clients feel that more services are necessary after insurance benefits expire. [Some managed care plans will not allow me to provide services to you once your benefits are no longer available. If this is the case, I will do my best to find you another provider who will help you continue your psychotherapy.]

You should also be aware that most insurance agreements require you to authorize me to provide a clinical diagnosis and sometimes additional clinical information such as a treatment plan or summary or in rare cases a copy of the entire record. This information will become part of the insurance company files, and, in all probability, some of it will be computerized. All insurance companies claim to keep such information confidential, but once it is in their hands, I have no control over what they do with it. In some cases they may share the information with a national medical information data bank. If you request it, I will provide you with a copy of any report I submit.

Once we have all of the information about your insurance coverage, we will discuss what we can expect to accomplish with the benefits that are available and what will happen if the insurance benefits run out before you feel ready to end our sessions. It is important to remember that you always have the right to pay for my services yourself and avoid the complexities described above.

Contacting Me

I am often not immediately available by telephone. While I am usually in my office between 9 A.M. and 5 P.M., I usually will not answer the phone when I am with a client. I do have call-in hours at *XXXXX* on *XXXXX*. When I am unavailable, my telephone is answered by an automatic [answering machine] that I monitor frequently [is answered by my secretary, or answering service who usually knows where to reach me, or voice mail that I monitor frequently]. I will make every effort to return your call on the same day you make it with the exception of weekends and holidays. If you are difficult to reach, please leave some times when you will be available. [In emergencies, you can try me at my home number.] If you cannot reach me, and you feel that you cannot wait for me to return your call, you should call your family physician or the emergency room at the nearest hospital and ask for the [psychologist or psychiatrist] on call. If I am unavailable for an extended time, I will provide you with the name of a trusted colleague whom you can contact if necessary.

Professional Records

Both law and the standards of my profession require that I keep appropriate treatment records. You are entitled to receive a copy of the records, but if you wish, I can prepare an appropriate summary. Because these are professional records, they can be misinterpreted and/or can be upsetting to lay readers. If you wish to see your records, I recommend that you review them in my presence so that we can discuss the contents. [I am sometimes willing to conduct such a meeting without charge.] Clients will be charged an appropriate fee for any preparation time that is required to comply with an information request.

Professional Records

[This section is for psychologists who practice in states that do not require that psychologists provide clients with access to their records.]

As I am sure you are aware, I am required to keep appropriate records of [the professional services I provide] [your treatment] [our work together]. Because these records contain information that can be misinterpreted by someone who is not a mental health professional, it is my general policy that clients may not review them. However, if you request, I will provide you with a treatment summary unless I believe that to do so would be emotionally damaging. If that is the case, I will be happy to forward the summary to another appropriate mental health professional who is working with you. [This service will be provided without any additional charge.] [You should be aware that this will be treated in the same manner as any other professional (clinical) service and you will be billed accordingly.] [There will be an additional charge for this service.]

Professional Records

[This section is for psychologists who practice in states that require psychologists to provide clients with access to their records unless to do so would cause emotional damage, upset, etc.]

Both law and the standards of my profession require that I keep appropriate treatment records. You are entitled to receive a copy of the records, unless I believe that seeing them would be emotionally damaging, in which case, I will be happy to provide them to an appropriate mental health professional of your choice. Because these are professional records, they can be misinterpreted and/or can be upsetting, so I recommend that we review them together so that we can discuss what they contain. [I am sometimes willing to conduct such a meeting without charge.] Clients will be charged an appropriate fee for any preparation time that is required to comply with an information request.

Minors

If you are under 18 years of age, please be aware that the law may provide your parents with the right to examine your treatment records. It is my policy to request an agreement from parents that they consent to give up access to your records. If they agree, I will provide them only with general information about our work together unless I feel that there is a high risk that you will seriously harm yourself or another, in which case I will notify them of my concern. I will also provide them with a summary of your treatment when it is complete. Before giving them any information I will discuss the matter with you, if possible, and will do the best I can to resolve any objections you may have about what I am prepared to discuss.

Confidentiality

In general, the confidentiality of all communications between a client and a psychologist is protected by law, and I can only release information about our work to others with your written permission. However, there are a number of exceptions.

In most judicial proceedings, you have the right to prevent me from providing any information about your treatment. However, in some circumstances such as child custody proceedings and proceedings in which your emotional condition is an important element, a judge may require my testimony if he or she determines that resolution of the issues before him or her demands it.

There are some situations in which I am legally required to take action to protect others from harm, even though that requires revealing some information about a client's treatment. For example, if I believe that a child, an elderly person, or a disabled person is being abused, I must [may be required to] file a report with the appropriate state agency.

If I believe that a client is threatening serious bodily harm to another, I am [may be] required to take protective actions, which may include notifying the potential victim, notifying the police, or seeking appropriate hospitalization. If a client threatens to harm himself or herself, I may be required to seek hospitalization for the client or to contact family members or others who can help provide protection.

These situations have rarely arisen in my practice. Should such a situation occur, I will make every effort to fully discuss it with you before taking any action.

I may occasionally find it helpful to consult about a case with other professionals. In these consultations, I make every effort to avoid revealing the identity of my client. The consultant is, of course, also legally bound to keep the information confidential. Unless you object, I will not tell you about these consultations unless I feel that it is important to our work together.

While this written summary of exceptions to confidentiality should prove helpful in informing you about potential problems, it is important that we discuss any questions or concerns that you may have at our next meeting. The laws governing these issues are quite complex, and I am not an attorney. While I am happy to discuss these issues with you, should you need specific advice, formal legal consultation may be desirable. If you request, I will provide you with relevant portions or summaries of the applicable state laws governing these issues.

Your signature below indicates that you have read the information in this document and agree to abide by its terms during our professional relationship.

References & Readings 

American Psychological Association. (2002). Ethical principles of psychologists and code of conduct. *American Psychologist, 57,* 1060–1073.

Bennett, B. E., Bryant, B. K., VandenBos, G. R., & Greenwood, A. (1990). *Professional liability and risk management.* Washington, DC: American Psychological Association.

Berglas, S., & Levendusky, P. G. (1985). The Therapeutic Contract Program: An individual-oriented psychological treatment community. *Psychotherapy, 22,* 36–45.

Greene, G. L. (1989). Using the written contract for evaluating and enhancing practice effectiveness. *Journal of Independent Social Work, 4,* 135–155.

Koocher, G. P., & Keith-Spiegel, P. C. (1998). *Ethics in psychology: Professional standards and cases* (2nd ed.). New York: Oxford University Press.

Miller, L. J. (1990). The formal treatment contract in the inpatient management of borderline personality disorder. *Hospital and Community Psychiatry, 41,* 985–987.

Selzer, M. A., Koenigsberg, H. W., & Kernberg, O. F. (1987). The initial contract in the treatment of borderline patients. *American Journal of Psychiatry, 144,* 927–930.

Standards for Privacy of Individually Identifiable Health Information (2000 as amended). U.S. Department of Health and Human Services, Office of Civil Rights (45 CFR Parts 160 and 164).

Yoemans, F. E., Selzer, M. A., & Clarkin, J. F. (1992). *Treating the borderline patient: A contract-based approach.* New York: Basic Books.

Related Topics

Chapter 38 "Patients' Rights in Psychotherapy"
Chapter 127, "Basic Elements of Consent"
Chapter 132, "Billing Issues"

126 FUNDAMENTALS OF THE HIPAA PRIVACY RULE

Jason M. Bennett

This chapter summarizes the fundamentals of the Standards for Privacy of Individually Identifiable Health Information, otherwise known as the "Privacy Rule." The Privacy Rule, promulgated by the Department of Health and Human Services (HHS), is the most comprehensive federal regulation related to the privacy of patient health information. The Privacy Rule compliance date was April 14, 2003. Of course, no part of this chapter is intended as a substitute for specific legal or consulting advice. This chapter does not create an attorney-client relationship.

BACKGROUND

The Health Insurance Portability and Accountability Act of 1996, or HIPAA, as it is commonly known among mental health practitioners, is an expansive and complex law. The general purpose of the HIPAA statute is to require portability, nondiscrimination, and renewability of health benefits provided by group health plans and group health insurance issuers. The HIPAA statute includes "administrative simplification" provisions that require the adoption of national standards related to electronic transactions, security, and privacy of health information. A specific privacy regulation, the Privacy Rule, was drafted in order to ensure that a patient's health information is protected and kept confidential when maintained or transmitted electronically. This chapter does not specifically address any other rule or standard under HIPAA other than the Privacy Rule.

According to HHS, there are three major purposes for the Privacy Rule: (1) to protect and enhance the rights of consumers by providing them access to their health information and controlling the inappropriate use of that information; (2) to improve the quality of health care by restoring trust in the health care system among consumers, health care professionals, and the multitude of organizations committed to the delivery of care; and (3) to improve the efficiency and effectiveness of health care delivery by creating a national framework for health privacy protection that builds on efforts by states, health systems, and individual organizations.

The Privacy Rule has many concepts with specific definitions. An important term for this chapter is *individual,* which generally includes patients, research participants, and any other person who is the subject of the health information. For the purposes of this chapter, however, the term *patient* will be used instead of *individual* because the focus is on the delivery of services to patients.

COVERED ENTITIES

Mental health practitioners will need to ascertain whether they are considered "covered entities" under the Privacy Rule. The Privacy Rule applies to all covered entities including health plans, health care clearinghouses, and health care providers who transmit any health information in electronic form in connection with "covered transactions." *Covered transactions* are those transmissions of information between two parties to carry out financial or administrative activities related to health care. Such transactions include, but are not limited to, payment of health care claims, benefit eligibility inquiries, referral authorization requests, or other transactions the federal government may establish by regulation.

Many mental health practitioners have had difficulty in determining if they are covered entities. The confusion primarily stems from attempting to understand what is and is not an "electronic transmission." The mere utilization of electronic technology such as personal use of the Internet or e-mail does not constitute an electronic transmission. The following are two examples of covered electronic transmissions under the Privacy Rule: (1) practitioners who transmit patient information by e-mail or over the Internet (using a Web application or software product) when determining eligibility of benefits; and (2) practitioners who use billing services to transmit patient information electronically. Mental health practitioners making these types of transmissions are considered covered entities.

The following are not examples of covered electronic transmissions under the Privacy Rule: (1) practitioners who share patient information during telephone calls when determining eligibility of benefits; (2) practitioners who seek reimbursement from third-party payers by sending a paper claim through the mail and the third-party payer converts the paper claim into an electronic format; and (3) practitioners who transmit patient information using a computer-generated fax program to a plain-paper fax machine. Mental health practitioners making these types of transmissions will not be considered covered entities. (Note that practitioners are considered to be covered entities if health information is transmitted from a computer by a computer fax.)

Many mental health practitioners have questioned whether the Privacy Rule applies to them. A better question for almost all practitioners may be, "When will HIPAA apply?" Many insurance companies are moving toward handling health claims through electronic submission in order to reduce transactional costs. The health care industry will probably soon require electronic submission of claims for the reimbursement of treatment. Additionally, those practitioners who continue to deal solely with paper claims may face barriers in seeking reimbursement for treatment from third-party payers. One such barrier is part of HIPAA's new administrative simplification provision, which requires all Medicare claims to be submitted electronically after October 16, 2003, with the exception of certain small providers (defined as either a provider of services with fewer than 25 full-time equivalent employees or a practitioner with fewer than 10 full-time equivalent employees). In addition, practitioners who deal solely with paper claims will face delays in receiving payment because Medicare is required by law not to pay paper claims until 28 days after receipt of the claim; electronic claims will be processed in 14 days.

PREEMPTION ANALYSIS—STATE SPECIFIC INFORMATION

The Privacy Rule establishes a national floor of privacy protection for patients. In order to be compliant, the physician must conduct an analysis in each state to determine if the Privacy Rule preempts the state laws. This is a complicated process that oftentimes requires a legal background. The results of the preemption analysis for each jurisdiction will almost always be different.

Generally, state laws that are contrary to the Privacy Rule are preempted and the federal standards or requirements apply. "Contrary" means that a practitioner would find it impossible to comply with both the state and federal requirements, or a provision of state law stands as an obstacle to the "accomplishment and execution of the full purposes and objectives" of the Privacy Rule and other relevant HIPAA standards and rules. The Privacy Rule will not preempt those state laws that provide higher levels of privacy protections to patients. Additionally, those state laws that allow patients greater access to or amendment of their individually identifiable health information will not be preempted.

Most important, the Privacy Rule requires that all privacy forms presented to patients must include the results of the preemption analysis between the Privacy Rule and state law. Additionally, all internal written policies and procedures must include this state-specific analysis.

ADMINISTRATIVE REQUIREMENTS

The privacy of patient information is not a new concept to psychologists. Many jurisdictions already have fairly strong confidentiality laws related to mental health care. Practitioners should view the Privacy Rule as a formalization of many of the current practices and administrative issues that are part of practitioners' daily practice.

There are, however, several labor-intensive administrative requirements that practitioners must meet that are expressly required by the Privacy Rule. Several of these activities include: (1) designating a "privacy official" within the practice responsible for developing, implementing, and overseeing written privacy policies and procedures (a contact person should also be designated for receiving and documenting complaints from patients); (2) training employees (if any) in the practice's written privacy policies and procedures so that each member may carry out his or her respective functions; (3) safeguarding all patient information from those who do not need or are not permitted access; and (4) providing patients with information about their privacy rights and explaining how their personal information may be used (within the practice) or disclosed (to others outside of the practice).

NOTICE OF PRIVACY PRACTICES

The Privacy Rule requires mental health practitioners in direct treatment relationships with patients to give a Notice of Privacy Practices to each patient no later than the date of first service delivery and to make a good-faith effort to obtain each patient's written acknowledgment of receipt of the notice. The notice must contain specific core elements including, but not limited to, each patient's rights in relation to his or her health information and the practitioner's duties to each patient. Practitioners are required to abide by the terms of their current privacy notice. Additionally, practitioners who maintain an office must also post the notice in the office in a clear and prominent location. The posted notice must contain the same information that is distributed directly to patients.

CONSENT

The Privacy Rule permits mental health practitioners to obtain consent to use or disclose patient information for treatment, payment, and health care operations. Mental health practitioners generally must comply with stronger laws and ethical standards regarding confidentiality than other non–mental-health care providers. Many jurisdictions require that mental health practitioners obtain "consent to release information" and "informed consent" on the first date of treatment. In almost all instances, mental health practitioners should continue to obtain consent from their patients as they always have for these purposes.

Practitioners are required by the Privacy Rule to make "reasonable efforts" to limit the amount of patient information they disclose to the "minimum necessary" to accomplish the intended purpose of a use, disclosure, or request. The "minimum necessary" standard does not apply to: (1) disclosures made to other health care providers for treatment purposes; (2) uses or disclosures permitted by a written authorization (see below); and (3) uses or disclosures that are required by law.

AUTHORIZATION

The Privacy Rule requires mental health practitioners to obtain written authorization for any use or disclosure of patient information that is not for treatment, payment, or health care operations. There are specific "core elements" and "required statements" to be included in written authorizations that are outlined in the Privacy Rule. Practitioners should not release patient information after receiving a written authorization if the authorization does not contain the necessary core elements and required statements. Therefore, it will be important for practitioners to become familiar with, and likely develop, written authorization forms.

PSYCHOTHERAPY NOTES

The Privacy Rule allows mental health practitioners to maintain certain types of sensitive private information in psychotherapy notes. The rule requires that psychotherapy notes be kept separate from the rest of the patient's record. Psychotherapy notes are "notes recorded (in any medium) by a [. . .] mental health professional documenting or analyzing the contents of conversation during a private counseling session or a group, joint, or family counseling session." Such notes exclude medication prescription and monitoring; counseling session start and stop times; the modalities and frequencies of treatment furnished; results of clinical tests; and any summary of the following items including diagnosis, functional status, the treatment plan, symptoms, prognosis, and progress to date.

Psychotherapy notes are afforded an extra layer of privacy protection due to the sensitive nature of this type of information. Except in limited circumstances, practitioners must obtain a written authorization for any use or disclosure of psychotherapy notes. For instance, practitioners may share a patient's psychotherapy notes for treatment purposes with another practitioner only if the latter is within the same practice. Generally, however, practitioners must obtain a written authorization from the patient in order to disclose psychotherapy notes to practitioners outside of their practice, third-party payers, or others. Health plans and third-party payers may not condition treatment, payment, enrollment, or eligibility for benefits on obtaining information in psychotherapy notes. Each written authorization for psychotherapy notes must contain only the request for the psychotherapy notes and not for any of the information kept in the patient's separate "clinical record."

Obviously, psychologists maintaining psychotherapy notes will face some additional complexities when attempting to achieve compliance with the Privacy Rule. Therefore, practitioners should make an informed decision before electing to maintain psychotherapy notes. This will include weighing the additional complexities of maintaining psychotherapy notes against providing specific patient information an extra layer of privacy protection.

INCIDENTAL DISCLOSURES

Mental health practitioners will be happy to know that they are not required to eliminate all risks of "incidental uses and disclosures" of their patients' information. Any use or disclosure of patient information that is "incident to" another permitted use or disclosure is permitted so long as "reasonable safeguards" to protect patient information have been adopted by the practitioner. An example of a permitted incidental disclosure is when an individual in the practitioner's waiting room accidentally overhears a confidential conversation between another patient and the doctor.

SCALABILITY OF THE PRIVACY RULE

In order to ease the burden of becoming compliant, the Privacy Rule requirements are "scalable" to apply to the various types and sizes of practices. The scalability of the Privacy Rule allows for flexibility when a practice creates its own privacy information that is disseminated to patients, as well as the practice's internal written policies and procedures. For instance, the privacy official in a solo practitioner's practice will, in most instances, be the solo practitioner; the privacy official in a large group practice may be a receptionist, the office manager, a practitioner, or if the practice is large enough, a full-time employee solely dedicated to the position of privacy official. The scalability of the Privacy Rule does not remove the requirement for each practice, whether large or small, to implement written policies and procedures that reflect the results of the state specific preemption analysis.

BUSINESS ASSOCIATES

A business associate is an individual or entity that carries out specific services or activities related to the use or disclosure of patient information on behalf of a practitioner. The Privacy Rule requires that practitioners enter into business-associate contracts with such individuals or entities. Business-associate contracts must obligate business associates to safeguard patient information and preclude any use or disclosure of patient information that would violate the Privacy Rule.

COMPLIANCE AND ENFORCEMENT

The Office for Civil Rights of HHS has responsibility for enforcement of the Privacy Rule. HHS has stated it will take an educative position for the initial period after the Privacy Rule compliance date. During this initial period, HHS will follow a complaint-driven model for enforcing compliance with the Privacy Rule. The Office for Civil Rights will investigate all properly submitted complaints. One of the foremost reasons for the incredible amount of attention to the Privacy Rule is the possibility that civil monetary and/or criminal penalties can be levied against practitioners.

Investigations may include a review of the pertinent policies, procedures, or practices of the covered entity and of the circumstances regarding any alleged acts or omissions concerning compliance. Psychologists should be aware that site visits are possible during investigations.

The following are likely to be considered some of the least invasive measures taken by

HHS during an investigation: (1) a request for the notice of privacy practices the practitioner has disseminated to patients; (2) a request for the written policies and procedures maintained by the practitioner; (3) a request for any documentation required by the Privacy Rule (including the documentation of training of all individuals working within the practice); and (4) [a showing] that the practitioner has in place appropriate administrative, technical, and physical safeguards to protect the privacy of patient information.

References, Readings, & Internet Sites 

American Psychological Association Insurance Trust. (n.d.). Health Insurance Portability and Accountability Act site. Retrieved 2004 from http://www.apait.org/hipaa

American Psychological Association Practice Organization. (n.d.). Home page. Retrieved 2004 from http://www.apapractice.org

U.S. Department of Health and Human Services. (2000). Standards for privacy of individually identifiable health information (amended). Office of Civil Rights (45 CFR Parts 160 and 164). Washington, DC: Government Printing Office.

U.S. Department of Health and Human Services. (n.d.). HHS resources on complying with the Privacy Rule. Retrieved 2004 from http://www.hhs.gov/ocr/hipaa

Related Topics

Chapter 104, "Privacy, Confidentiality, and Privilege"
Chapter 127, "Basic Elements of Consent"
Chapter 128, "Basic Elements of Release Forms"

127 BASIC ELEMENTS OF CONSENT

Gerald P. Koocher

Competence is a prerequisite for informed consent. An offer to provide a person with informed consent is not meaningful unless the individual in question is fully competent to make use of it. Consent is a voluntary act by which one competent person agrees to allow another person to do something, such as provide treatment to them, study them in research, or release their confidential records to another.

- Competence to grant consent is generally categorized as either de facto or de jure. De jure refers to competence under law, while de facto competence refers to the actual or practical capacities of the individual to render a competent decision.
- In most jurisdictions, persons over the age of 18 years are presumed to be competent unless proved otherwise before a court. When a determination of incompetence is made for such adults, it is usually quite precise. That is to say, under law a person's competence is conceptualized as a specific functional ability. In legal parlance, the noun *competence* is usually followed by the preposition *to* rather than presented as a general attribute of the person. An adult who is deemed incompetent to stand trial for a particular offense is still presumed competent to function as a custodial parent or manage his or her financial affairs. For the adult, incompetence must be proved on a case-by-case basis.

- Conversely, minor children are presumed incompetent for most purposes without any concern for whether or not the child has the cognitive and emotional capacity to make the requisite decision(s). Children who are deemed legally competent for one purpose are likewise still considered generally incompetent in other decision-making contexts. For example, juvenile offenders who have been transferred to adult court for trial and found competent to stand trial are still considered generally incompetent to consent to their own medical treatment or enter into legal contracts.

Assessment of specific competence (in the case of children) or incompetence (in the case of adults) revolves around four basic elements:

1. The person's access to and ability to understand all relevant information about the nature and potential future consequences of the decision to be made (i.e., informed consent).
2. The ability to manifest or express a decision.
3. The manner in which the decision is made (e.g., whether it is rational or reasonably considered).
4. The nature of the resulting decision (e.g., whether it is a lawful decision).

Psychological factors in competence assessment include the following:

1. Comprehension
2. Assertiveness and autonomy
3. Rational reasoning
4. Anticipation of future events
5. Judgments in the face of uncertainty or contingencies

MAKING DECISIONS FOR OTHERS: PROXY CONSENT, PERMISSION, AND ASSENT

Consent is defined as a decision that one can make only for oneself. Thus, the term *proxy consent* is decreasingly used in favor of the term *permission*. Parents or guardians are usually those from whom permission must be sought as both a legal and an ethical requirement prior to intervening in the lives of their minor children or adults adjudged incompetent.

Assent, a relatively new concept in this context, recognizes that minors or incompetent adults may not, as a function of their developmental level or mental state, be capable of giving fully reasoned consent but may still be capable of reaching and expressing a preference. Assent recognizes the involvement of the child or incompetent adult in the decision-making process, while also indicating that the child's level of participation is less than fully competent. Granting assent power is essentially the same as providing a veto.

References, Readings, & Internet Sites 

Appelbaum, P. S., Lidz, C. W., & Meisel, A. (1987). *Informed consent: Legal theory and clinical practice*. New York: Oxford University Press.

Koocher, G. P., & Keith-Spiegel, P. C. (1990). *Children, ethics, and the law*. Lincoln: University of Nebraska Press.

Koocher, G. P., & Keith-Spiegel, P. C. (1998). *Ethics in psychology: Professional standards and cases* (2nd ed.). New York: Oxford University Press.

Malcolm, J. G. (1988). *Treatment choices and informed consent: Current controversies in psychiatric malpractice litigation*. Springfield, IL: Charles C. Thomas.

Office for Protection from Research Risks. (n.d.). Tips on informed consent. Retrieved 2004 from http://www.ohrp.osophs.dhhs.gov/humansubjects/guidance/ictips

Pope, K. S., & Vasquez, M. J. T. (1991). *Ethics in psychotherapy and counseling: A practical guide for psychologists*. San Francisco: Jossey-Bass.

Public Responsibility in Medicine and Research. (n.d.). Home page. Retrieved 2004 from http://www.primr.org

Stanley, B. H., Sieber, J. E., & Melton, G. B. (Eds.). (1996). *Research ethics: A psychological approach*. Lincoln: University of Nebraska Press.

University of Washington. (n.d.). Ethics in medicine, informed consent. Retrieved 2004 from http://eduserv.hscer.washington.edu/bioethics/topics/consent

White, B. C. (1994). *Competence to consent*. Washington, DC: Georgetown University Press.

Related Topics

Chapter 104, "Privacy, Confidentiality, and Privilege"
Chapter 128, "Basic Elements of Release Forms"

128 BASIC ELEMENTS OF RELEASE FORMS

Gerald P. Koocher

What is a "release form" anyway? As used by mental health professionals, this term refers to a legally appropriate authorization that releases the clinician from some particular duty to a client or research participant. Most often the release permits the sharing of otherwise confidential information or records with other professionals or agencies. Other types of releases may authorize the recording of voice or images by any means (e.g., photographic, magnetic tape, or digital) of otherwise confidential content, the storage of data or recorded material in databases, or the use of such material for teaching purposes. Releases are sometimes sought prior to application of certain treatment procedures that may have potential adverse consequences (e.g., electroconvulsive therapy); however, no release can legally absolve a practitioner from the negligent infliction of damages.

Releases should be drafted for highly specific purposes, addressing each of the key elements cited below. In addition to these basic elements, releases should be used only in the context of informed consent (see chapter 127). Use the following guidelines in preparing a release form.

- Identify the person(s) to whom the release applies. Ideally this will include a name, address, telephone number, birth date, and any known record-identifying numbers. This will minimize risk of improper releases when names are similar, as well as permitting confirmation that the release is valid should a question arise.
- Indicate what is being authorized (e.g., transfer of oral information, transfer of records, audio or video recording, or other disclosure of protected data).
- Indicate the purpose of releasing the duty of confidentiality (e.g., assisting in treatment, educational planning, teaching, research, or other purpose to be specified).
- State who is granting authority (e.g., is a competent person granting informed consent, is a legally responsible party granting permission, or is a person who is not deemed legally competent granting assent?). Note that at least one signer of the release form must be legally authorized to do so.
- Explain the grantor's relationship to the parties to whom a duty is owed (e.g., is the grantor of the authorization the focal party himself or herself, a parent, or some other person having legal guardianship?).
- Indicate for what duration the release is granted. Each release should have a specific time limit. For example, the release may authorize a onetime issuance of records, an ongoing communication between two professionals for a specified period, or open-ended access to archival data in a research database.
- Include a valid signature. The name of the person signing the release form should be printed as well as signed, in the event that the signature is difficult to read. Although not strictly necessary in most situations, it is ideal to have the release signed by a third party who witnessed the grantor's signing.

SAMPLE RELEASE FORMS

Copies of the sample forms outlined below and suitable for editing with a word processing program are included on the Web site accompanying this book.

Authorization for Release of Information

Patient's name:

Date of birth:

Address:

Telephone number:

Record number:

I hereby authorize the release of information records on: [the psychological assessment of, psychotherapeutic treatment of, etc.]

Name:

Address:

For the purposes of: [assisting in treatment planning, preparing an educational plan, use in court-ordered evaluation, etc.]

This release shall be valid for [90 days] from the date signed, unless withdrawn sooner and shall [include all professional records; be limited to the psychological testing data; be limited to services provided between September 1996 and March 1998; etc.].

Signed: [printed name, date]

Relationship to patient: [parent, legal guardian]

Witnessed by: [printed name, date]

Sample Release for Recording and Subsequent Teaching

This release form would be similar to the record release form in terms of the client information and signature sections. The statements of "authorization" (i.e., what type of recording or disclosure is being allowed) and the statement of "purpose" (i.e., how the material will be used). Sonic examples follow: "I authorize Mr. Jones to make videotape recordings of my therapy sessions at the University Counseling Center for purposes of supervision. I understand that these will be viewed only by Mr. Jones and his clinical supervisor, Dr. Smith. I also understand that the tapes will be destroyed following the supervisory session."

Suppose one of the sessions seems particularly useful or exemplary for teaching purposes and that Dr. Smith would like to use it in the future. An additional release with the following text might be sought: "I authorize Dr. Smith and his successors as director of the University Counseling Center to use previously authorized video recordings of my psychotherapy sessions with Mr. Jones between January 1996 and May 1996 for teaching purposes with future classes of doctoral students. I understand that although my likeness will be visible, my name will not be used and all observers will have a professional obligation to treat the mate-

(*continued*)

rial confidentially. I also understand that I may revoke this authorization at any time in the future by notifying Dr. Smith or any subsequent director of the clinic."

Similar elements should be included in release forms developed for other confidential material that may be stored and used by others in the future, such as longitudinal research data archives. In the case of institutional clinical records that are routinely collected as a function of clinical care (i.e., medical records or clinic case files) or that were collected years earlier from clients who are no longer easily located, the agency's official institutional review board (sometimes called a clinical investigations committee) should be consulted and that group's procedures followed.

Readings & Internet Sites 

American Psychological Association. (2002). *Ethical principles of psychologists and code of conduct.* Washington, DC: Author.

Keith-Spiegel, P., Wittig, A. F., Perkins, D. V., Balogh, D. W., & Whitley, B. E. (1993). *The ethics of teaching: A casebook.* Muncie, IN: Ball State University Office of Academic Research and Sponsored Projects.

Koocher, G. P., & Keith-Spiegel, P. C. (1998). *Ethics in psychology: Professional standards and cases* (2nd ed.). New York: Oxford University Press.

Lawson, C. (1995). Research participation as a contract. *Ethics & Behavior,* 5, 205–215.

National Institutes of Health. (n.d.). HIPAA Privacy Rule. Retrieved 2004 from http://privacyruleandresearch.nih.gov/pr_02.asp

Sieber, J. E., & Stanley, B. (1988). Sharing scientific data I: New problems for IRBs. *IRB: A Review of Human Subjects Research, 11,* 4–7.

Stanley, B. H., Sieber, J. E., & Melton, G. B. (Eds.). (1996). *Research ethics.* Lincoln: University of Nebraska Press.

United States Department of Health and Human Services, Office for Civil Rights. (n.d.). Office for Civil Rights Web site. Retrieved 2004 from http://www.hhs.gov/ocr/hipaa/

United States Department of Health and Human Services, Administrative Simplification. (n.d.). Administrative simplification in the health care industry. Retrieved 2004 from http://aspe.hhs.gov/admnsimp/

129 PROTOTYPE MENTAL HEALTH RECORDS

Gerald P. Koocher

This article describes a recommended style and content for mental health practitioners' clinical case records covering 15 specific content domains and 4 other important issues in record keeping aside from content. Not all of the content information described here will be necessary for every record, nor would one expect to complete a full record as described here during the first few sessions with a new client. By the end of several sessions, however, a good-quality clinical record will reflect all of the relevant points summarized below.

CONTENT ISSUES

- *Identifying information:* Name, record or file number (if any), address, telephone number, sex, birth date, marital status, next of kin (or parent/guardian), school or employment status, billing and financial information.
- *First contact:* Date of initial client contact and referral source.
- *Legal notifications:* The Health Insurance Portability and Accountability Act (HIPAA) requires that clients be given specific notifications regarding privacy and other matters (discussed elsewhere in this volume) at the initiation of the professional relationship. Some states have parallel or more extensive requirements, and the APA Code of Conduct specifically requires psychologists to notify clients about the limits of confidentiality at the outset of the professional relationship. Provision of this notice, ideally by means of a signed notice form, should be noted in the record.
- *Relevant history and risk factors:* Take a detailed social, medical, educational, and vocational history. This need not necessarily be done in the very first session and need not be exhaustive. The more serious the problem, the more history you should take. Get enough information to formulate a diagnosis and an initial treatment plan. Be sure to ask: "What is the most impulsive or violent thing you have ever done?" and "Have you thought of hurting yourself or anyone else recently?" Seek records of prior treatment based on the nature of the client (e.g., the more complex the case, the more completely one should review prior data). Always ask for permission to contact prior therapists, and consider refusing to treat clients who decline such permission without giving good reason (e.g., sexual abuse by former therapist).
- *Medical or health status:* Collect information on the client's medical status (i.e., When was his or her last physical exam? Does the client have a personal physician? Are there any pending medical problems or conditions?). This is especially important if the client has physical complaints or psychological problems that might be attributable to organic pathology.
- *Medication profile:* Collect information on all medications or drugs used, past and present, including licit (e.g., prescribed medications, alcohol, tobacco, and over-the-counter drugs) and illicit substances. Also note any consideration, recommendation, or referral for medication made by you or others over the course of your work with the client.
- *Why is the client in your office?* Include a full description of the nature of the client's condition, including the reason(s) for referral and presenting symptoms or problems. Be sure to ask clients what brought them for help at this point in time, and record the reasons.
- *Current status:* Include a comprehensive functional assessment (including a mental status examination), and note any changes or alterations that occur over the course of treatment.
- *Diagnostic impression:* Include a clinical impression and diagnostic formulation using the most current *DSM* or *ICD* model. Do not underdiagnose to protect the patient. If you believe it is absolutely necessary to use a "nonstigmatizing" diagnosis as opposed to some other diagnostic label, use the R/O (rule-out) model by listing diagnoses with the notation "R/O," indicating that you will rule each "in" or "out" based on data that emerge over the subsequent sessions. Your diagnosis must also be consistent with the case history and facts (e.g., do not use "adjustment reaction" to describe a paranoid hallucinating client with a history of prior psychiatric hospital admissions).
- *Treatment plan:* Develop a treatment plan with long- and short-term goals and a proposed schedule of therapeutic activities. The plan should be updated every 4 to 6 months and modified as needed.
- *Progress notes:* Note progress toward achievement of therapeutic goals. Use clear, precise, observable facts (e.g., I observed; patient re-

ported; patient agreed that . . .). As you write, imagine the patient and his or her attorney looking over your shoulder as they review the record with litigation in mind. Avoid theoretical speculation or reports of unconscious content. Do not include humorous or sarcastic personal reflections or observations. Your record should always demonstrate that you are a serious, concerned, dedicated professional. If you must keep theoretical or speculative notes (e.g., impressionistic narratives for review with a supervisor), use a separate "working notes" format, but recognize that these records may be subject to subpoena in legal proceedings.

- *Service documentation:* Include documentation of each visit, noting the client's response to treatment. In hospitals or large agencies, each entry should be dated and signed or initialed by the therapist, with the service provider's name printed or typed in legible form. It is not necessary to sign each entry in one's private (i.e., noninstitutional) case files, since it is reasonable to assume that you wrote what is in your own private practice files.
- *Document follow-up:* Include documentation of follow-up for referrals or missed appointment, especially with clients who may be dangerous or seriously ill. Retain copies of all reminders, notices, or correspondence sent to clients, and note substantive telephone conversations in the record.
- *Obtain consent:* Include copies of consent forms for any information released to other parties, or for other forms of recording (e.g., consent to record interviews).
- *Termination:* Include a discharge or termination summary note for all clients. In cases of planned termination, be certain that case notes prior to the end of care reflect planning and progress toward this end.

NONCONTENT ISSUES

- *Control of records:* Psychologists should maintain (in their own practice) or support (in institutional practice) a system that protects the adequate control over and confidentiality of records. Clear procedures should be in place to preserve client confidentiality and to release records only with proper consent. The medium used (e.g., paper, magnetic, optical) is not especially important, so long as utility, confidentiality, and durability are assured.

  In multiple-client therapies (e.g., family or group treatment), records should be kept in a manner that allows for the preservation of each individual's confidentiality should the records of one party be released. Psychologists are responsible for construction and control of their records and those of people they supervise.
- *Retention of records:* Psychologists must be aware of and observe all federal and state laws that govern record retention. In the absence of clear regulatory guidance under law, the American Psychological Association (1993) recommends maintaining complete records for 3 years after the last client contact and summaries for an additional 12 years.

  If the client is a child, some records should be maintained until at least 3 to 5 years beyond the date at which the child attains the age of majority. All records, active or inactive, should be stored in a safe manner, with limited access appropriate to the practice or institution.
- *Outdated records:* Outdated, obsolete, or invalid data should be managed in a way that assures no adverse effects will result from its release. Records may be culled regularly so long as this is consistent with legal obligations. Records to be disposed of should be handled in a confidential and appropriate manner. Never remove items from a record that has been subpoenaed or is otherwise subject to legal proceedings.
- *Death or incapacity:* Psychologists need to make arrangements for proper management or disposal of clinical records in the event of their death or incapacity.

References, Readings, & Internet Sites

American Psychological Association. (1993). Record keeping guidelines. *American Psychologist, 48,* 308–310.

Koocher, C. P., & Keith-Spiegel, P. C. (1998). *Ethics*

in psychology: Professional standards and cases (2nd ed.). New York: Oxford University Press.

National Guideline Clearinghouse. (n.d.). Home page. Retrieved 2004 from http://www.guideline.gov

U.S. Department of Health and Human Services. (n.d.). Privacy issues in mental health and substance abuse treatment. Retrieved 2004 from http://aspe.hhs.gov/datacncl/reports/MHPrivacy

Related Topic

Chapter 25, "Assessing the Quality of a Psychological Testing Report"

130 UTILIZATION REVIEW CHECKLIST

Gerald P. Koocher

This chapter is intended to assist clinicians in conducting internal utilization review of mental health records. The purpose of utilization review is to focus on the client's progress in a systematic course of treatment and to monitor the adequacy of clinical records. The goal is to audit records in order to assure that effective treatment is taking place using clinical documentation. For purposes of internal utilization review, create a checklist using the points listed below and review the case record to determine whether sufficient content appears in the record to address each category. Ascertain whether the clinical record has been updated with reasonable frequency. Records should be updated at least quarterly, unless data are routinely updated as they change on a session-by-session basis.

- *Vital statistics:* Are the following noted: full name, record or file number (if any), address, telephone number, sex, birth date, marital status, employment or educational status, family structure, next of kin, ethnicity, primary language, name of primary care physician (if any)?
- *First contact:* Are the date of initial contact and referral source recorded?
- *Presenting problem:* Are the client's complaints and symptoms at the time of the initial visit clearly described? Is notation made of thought disorder, delusions/hallucinations, paranoia, obsessive-compulsive behavior, isolation, inappropriate affect, depression, anxiety, eating or sleeping disturbance, peer relationship difficulties, bizarre behavior, violent/aggressive behavior, appositional/defiant behavior, manic behavior, sexual inappropriateness, substance abuse, physical abuse, or suicidal ideation? Is a history of present illness and prior treatment noted? Are specific focal problems requiring attention listed, such as affective, attitudinal, family, school or work, social, medical conditions, and others? Are recent environmental stressors such as marital changes, death, illness, financial losses, or employment changes noted?
- *Diagnosis:* Has a problem list or a complete diagnosis been formulated, preferably using all 5 *DSM* axes, with R/O (rule-out) diagnoses specified, as needed? Is the diagnosis consistent with symptoms reported in the record? For example, if hallucinations and delusions are described in the record, schizophrenia should be a confirmed or rule-out di-

agnosis. Similarly, if depression is a diagnosis, the record should reflect an inquiry about suicidal ideation.

Axis I: Clinical disorders and other conditions that may be a focus of treatment.

Axis II: Personality disorders and mental retardation.

Axis III: General medical conditions.

Axis IV: Psychosocial and environmental problems, with notation of severity.

Axis V: Global Assessment of Functioning (GAF) with numerical score.

- *Current status:* Is a comprehensive functional assessment (including a mental status examination) provided? Are any changes since intake and last treatment plan noted? Is the status of presenting and diagnostic symptoms reported periodically, documenting progress or lack of same?
- *Consultations obtained:* Is a summary of any consultations (e.g., medication or psychological testing) obtained since last update included?
- *Long- and short-range goals:* Are therapeutic goals mentioned and discussed over the course of treatment? Are modalities of treatment reported and any referrals noted? Goals should reference initial symptoms and the client's presenting complaints. Notes should address any movement toward or away from prior goals since the last plan. Progress should be documented with test data, diary entries, behavior records, school reports, or other data.
- *Authentication:* Are the record notes dated and signed, including the degree and institutional title (if any) of the writer? If the writer is unlicensed or a trainee, are the notes countersigned by someone with legal responsibility?

References & Readings

American Psychiatric Association. (1994). *Diagnostic and statistical manual of mental disorders* (4th ed.). Washington, DC: Author.

American Psychological Association. (1993). Record keeping guidelines. *American Psychologist, 48,* 984–986.

Koocher, G. P., & Keith-Spiegel, P. C. (1998). *Ethics in psychology: Professional standards and cases* (2nd ed.). New York: Oxford University Press.

Related Topics

Chapter 47, "Psychotherapy Treatment Plan Writing"

Chapter 129, "Prototype Mental Health Records"

131 CONTRACTING WITH MANAGED CARE ORGANIZATIONS

Stuart L. Koman & Eric A. Harris

Managed care is the general term used to describe organizations and practices of organizations whose primary raison d'être and motivation is controlling the cost of health care. Typically, a managed care organization (MCO) receives a standard monthly fee from a payer, usually an employer or government entity, to purchase a defined set of health care services (benefit plan) for each individual (covered life) utilizing the plan. Mental health or behavioral health services can be included as part of a comprehensive package of medical services or *carved-in*, as is the case with health maintenance organizations (HMOs) like Kaiser-Permanente Health Plan or Harvard Community Health Plan, or contracted for separately, or *carved-out*, to a managed behavioral health provider such as Value Options Behavioral Health or Magellan Behavioral Health. Regardless of type, most MCOs seek maximum cost efficiency and utilize some variation of the following techniques to manage cost and quality of care.

- *Utilization management and utilization review:* This is the general practice of closely scrutinizing the manner in which decisions are made about when, where, and how many of each type of service is used in responding to the needs presented by a participant in the health plan. Decisions for care are judged against an organizationally defined standard known as *medical necessity*. Many MCOs require that services be *preauthorized* and periodically reviewed (*concurrent review*) by company-employed *case managers* who are clinicians specially trained in the company's criteria for medical necessity and treatment preferences.
- *Selective contracting:* This is the practice of defining a group of providers to perform required services. The *provider network*, as it is often called, is chosen from a pool of potential providers by an application process that weighs various company preferences in making selections. These preferences may include the type of degree and specialization, sex, age, geographic location, availability in the evenings and on weekends, and other characteristics about the manner in which the provider practices, especially as they may relate to the cost of care.
- *Favorable payment structure:* This is the practice of negotiating price discounts and/or passing along *financial risk* to providers in return for directing referrals to them. Risk-based contracting comes in many forms but always provides incentives for the clinician to complete the treatment in the fewest sessions or the least costly manner.

KEY ISSUES IN DECIDING TO JOIN A MANAGED CARE PANEL

The following questions and issues should be reviewed when considering potential relationships with MCOs.

Business Issues

- Is the company financially stable?
- What is the proposal for payment of professional services, and how long will it take to be paid? What has been the experience of other clinicians in terms of the reliability of the MCO's claims payment system?
- What is the company's volume of business in your geographic area, and what level of referrals are you likely to receive? What types of patients will be referred?

Professional Practice Issues

- What is the philosophy or general approach to providing care, and does it fit your clinical model?
- How is care managed, and what are the credentials of the individuals employed by the company to make decisions about the treatment?
- What has been the experience of other providers in the area in terms of satisfaction with the care management process?

Legal Issues

- Is the provider contract fair to both parties or seemingly one-sided?
- Does the contract contain any provisions that are particularly problematic?

Administrative Issues

- What are the requirements for authorizing treatment both at the outset and as treatment proceeds? What medical records documentation is required?
- What billing documentation is required?
- Are there any special requirements such as outcome evaluations?
- Are the case managers and claims personnel available in a reasonable time frame to discuss clinical or administrative problems? What has been the experience of other providers in dealing with problems?
- What is the process for appealing decisions regarding authorization and/or payment of care?

REVIEWING MCO CONTRACTS

Many MCOs would have providers believe that the contract document sent for review is inviolate, immutable, and unchangeable. Resist the temptation to go quietly along, and be sure to review the contract carefully. Be especially careful if the contract seems one-sided; look for sections that clearly spell out the obligations of the company to pay promptly, to notify you of changes in the benefit plan, to authorize treatment in a timely manner, to publish criteria for treatment decisions, and to process appeals and grievances. Managed care contracts are written by company attorneys who are paid to look out for the company's interest. The following is a list of potentially problematic clauses to watch out for.

- *Indemnification:* In one form or another, indemnification agreements state that if the managed care company is sued because of the provider's activities, the practitioner agrees to reimburse the company for its expenses and for any damages assessed against it. This clause can be drafted in many ways, but in any case, since the responsibility is created by the provider's agreement to the contract, not by the provider's professional activities, malpractice insurance companies can refuse to provide coverage of any expenses that result from this provision. Check with your insurance carrier before signing these agreements, and attempt to have the provision removed if the insurance company indicates that it will not cover actions resulting from this clause. Providers should also insist that indemnification responsibility is mutual and that the managed care company agrees to indemnify the practitioner in the same manner that the managed care company is proposing to be indemnified.
- *No legal action:* This provision eliminates your right to bring action against the managed care company for any reason.
- *Exclusive dealing:* This provision restricts you from working with patients who have a different insurance plan. You should consider agreeing to this only if the managed care company has guaranteed very high volume and payment, and then only if you can cancel the contract on short notice should serious problems arise.
- *Most favored nation:* This provision guarantees that the managed care company will always have charges equal to or lower than any other company you contract with now or in the future. You can consider an arrangement like this if the volume is high, the administration relatively moderate, and the payment history good, but only if you have the right to cancel should circumstances change.
- *No-cause terminations:* This provision allows the managed care company to eliminate you from its provider panel for no reason. It is fairly standard language at this point and is currently being challenged in court by a group of practitioners with support from the American Psychological Association. Their argument is that the managed care companies are using this clause to eliminate practitioners who do not conform to their rules or have publicly spoken out against the company and that this is really a "for-cause" termination, which the practitioner has the right to appeal. By using the "no-cause" provision, the providers argue, the company eliminates the individual's right to due process.
- *Nondisparagement:* This "gag" clause prohibits you from publicly speaking out directly against the company in any way.

- *Agreement not to bill for covered services except for copayments and deductibles:* This provision prohibits you from collecting reimbursement from patients to augment the managed care company's payment; it also prohibits you from billing for services that you and the client agree are indicated but which the managed care company has not authorized.
- *Agreement not to provide services when benefits are exhausted:* In some cases, this provision may put you at risk for client abandonment and leave you vulnerable to both legal and ethical challenge.
- *Agreement to abide by utilization review processes and decisions:* This provision binds you contractually to the company's decisions regarding the treatment of your patients regardless of your professional evaluation of the patient and situation at any given time. In fact, you are legally and ethically required to act in the best interest of the patient at all times and would be at severe risk if you followed the company's decision despite your own assessment and some tragic consequence ensued.
- *Agreement to abide by contract provisions which have not yet been developed or published:* This practice is common in situations where the managed care company is under pressure to put a network together.

As always, the best advice is to consult an attorney, preferably one who specializes in health care, if you are uncomfortable with any contract provisions you encounter. Other sources of support can often be found through your professional liability insurance carrier, your state professional association, and the legal and regulatory office of the Practice Directorate of the American Psychological Association.

ATTRACTING MANAGED CARE CONTRACTS

MCOs seek contracts with competent clinicians who will work within their management systems with little complaint and will price or accept reimbursement for clinical services at a low rate. In many instances, however, reimbursement is fixed by the MCO in accordance with the clinician's training and the type of service being delivered. When this is the case, network selection is based on a variety of other factors that are important to the MCO and/or the consumer. Generally, MCOs look for the following attributes:

- Use of short-term and group treatment modalities because this helps to contain cost by limiting the length of the treatment episode or by utilizing less expensive units of service
- Ease of access as demonstrated by 24-hour availability, night and weekend services, reliable phone answering, and responsive emergency coverage
- Wide range of clinical expertise often found in multidisciplinary groups so that consumers and the MCO itself can conveniently access different services that are required for treatment of an individual or his or her family
- Professional affiliations with other health care providers, especially primary care physicians who are responsible for medical management of individuals in HMOs
- Unambiguous professional credentials, including clinical licensure at the independent practice level, absence of professional liability claims, listing in a national practitioner data bank, and a well-organized clinical record-keeping system
- Demonstrated expertise in a specific clinical specialty area
- Demonstrated value of services provided by outcome evaluation data
- Location in an underserved area or area of high need

NEGOTIATING WITH MCOS

In general, negotiating leverage and the ability to achieve a successful outcome for your practice revolve around the perception of "who needs who more." Factors that enhance your negotiating position are often related to simple supply and demand. For instance, a practice in a rural community where few clinicians are available is in a good negotiating position. This is especially true if the MCO operates under a contract with the primary payer, a governmental or business entity, which specifies performance standards for geographic access to care. Similarly, a practice known for its highly specialized services is in a good position whether or not it is in an area where there is an abundance of practitioners because it offers a unique service that specifically addresses the needs of a particular group of consumers. Most MCOs will not want to be viewed as denying legitimate specialized care to their subscribers. These kinds of complaints often find their way back to the payer or, even worse, to the media. Professional and political affiliations can also enhance your negotiating leverage. If you are the preferred provider of mental health services for an important group of physicians in the area, the MCO will probably want to make sure that you are in the network. If you find yourself in a less than ideal position, you can do a number of things to improve your contract possibilities: lower your price, increase the value of your offer by providing more service, and provide evidence of superior performance through outcome data or case example.

References & Readings

Feldman, J., & Fitzpatrick, R. (1992). *Managed mental health care.* Washington, DC: American Psychiatric Press.

Giles, T. R. (1993). *Managed mental health care.* Boston: Allyn and Bacon.

Minkoff, K., & Pollack, D. (1997). *Managed mental health care in the public sector.* Amsterdam: Harwood Academic Publishers.

Oss, M., & Smith, A. (1994). *Behavioral health practice management audit workbook.* Gettysburg, PA: Behavioral Health Industry News.

Psychotherapy Finances. (1993). *Managed care handbook.* Hawthorne, NJ: Ridgewood Financial Institute.

Related Topics

Chapter 124, "Essential Features of Professional Liability Insurance"

Chapter 125, "Sample Psychotherapist-Patient Contract"

Chapter 130, "Utilization Review Checklist"

132 BILLING ISSUES

Gerald P. Koocher

This section is intended as a summary guide to the most common practice questions involving billing for mental health services, along with a discussion of related ethical issues.

BASIC PRINCIPLES

- Psychologists ideally perform some services at little or no fee as a pro bono service to the public as a routine part of their practice.
- Providing information and good communication is more important than the actual amount charged. Clients should be informed about fees, billing and collection practices, and other financial contingencies as a routine part of initiating the professional relationship whether or not they ask. This information should also be repeated later in the relationship if necessary. Ascertain the client's ability to pay for services as agreed. Be sure to include the following:

1. Amount of fee or "hourly rate," including the duration of the "hour"
2. When fees are payable (i.e., weekly, monthly)
3. Other services for which you will charge a fee (e.g., telephone contacts, preparation of documents, completing insurance forms)
4. Your policy for missed or canceled sessions
5. What happens if the client cannot or does not pay the bill

- Do not permit clients to accumulate an inordinately large bill. Practitioners should carefully consider the client's overall ability to afford services early in the relationship and should help the client to make a plan for obtaining services that will be both clinically appropriate and financially feasible. Encouraging clients to incur significant debt is not psychotherapeutic. In that regard, psychologists should be aware of referral sources in the community. Offering excessive credit, when a reduced fee cannot be offered, may create an unreasonable burden on the client.
- Consider the realities of client finances in future fee increases. In some cases it may be most appropriate to apply rate increases to new, rather than continuing, clients.
- Honor all posted or advertised fees.
- Be prepared to justify fees that deviate significantly from comparable services in the community.
- Never agree to a contingency fee arrangement based on the outcome of a case when testifying as an expert in forensic matters.

COLLECTION PRACTICES

- *Ethical obligations:* The professional is obligated to develop a respectful contractual relationship with the client and follow it. This involves all of the points listed above. In the event that a client cannot pay for services, it is desirable to work out an appropriate plan. If the practitioner must decline to continue services for nonpayment, care must be taken not to abandon a dependent client. Referral to community agencies or some limited continuation of services may be an option when abrupt termination would cause harm to a client.
- *Legal obligations:* The professional must obey all laws governing debtor-creditor relations in his or her jurisdiction. Such laws may include prohibitions against adding surcharges to unpaid bills, making threatening telephone calls, and certain other collection practices. See the discussion regarding use of collection agencies below.

THIRD-PARTY RELATIONSHIPS

Relationships with insurance companies and managed care organizations (known collectively as third-party payers) can be strained at times. It is important to clarify with all clients that you will assist them in obtaining all benefits to which they are entitled; however, clients must also be informed of their responsibilities in the event third-party payment is not made. Some third parties seek to sign a contract with providers before agreeing to pay for their services; Blue Shield is an example of such a provider in many states. In the typical contract, a provider is asked to agree to accept the company's payment as specified in full for the service rendered to the subscriber or client. The provider also promises not to charge a policyholder more for any given service than would be charged to another client. In other words, the provider agrees to accept certain set fees determined by the company and agrees not to treat policyholders differently from nonpolicyholders. In this way, the company attempts to provide good, inexpensive coverage, while attempting to prevent its policyholders from being overcharged or treated in a discriminatory manner. Ideally, the psychologist gains access to a client population, timely payment for services, and the ability to treat covered clients at less expense to them. The precise nature of these financial obligations will vary as a function of the particular company, specific policy coverage, and any contractual relationships between the provider and payer. Some particular issues of concern include the following:

- It is important for psychologists to pay careful attention to all contractual obligations, understand them, and abide by them. Similarly, psychologists should not sign contracts with stipulations that might subsequently place them in ethical jeopardy.
- *Balance billing:* Some contracts between insurers and practitioners require that the clinician accept a specific fee schedule. Such contracts may prohibit billing a client for more than the specified payment.
- *Burying the deductible or ignoring the copayment:* At times a clinician may be asked to issue a false invoice inflating actual charges to cover a required deductible amount. In other circumstances a client may ask the practitioner to waive a copayment required under his or her policy without informing the insurer. Agreeing to either practice is unethical and may constitute fraud.
- *Musical chairs (in family therapy):* "Musical chairs" refers to a practice of switching billing from the name of one family member to another in order to extend reimbursement benefits as the limit for an individual is reached. This practice may be acceptable to some payers but not to others. The best strategy is to check with the claims department of the third-party payer, explain the services being provided, and bill as directed. Keep a record of the call, including the date, person consulted, and instructions you were given.
- *Services not covered:* Another common problem relates to billing for services that are not covered under the third party's obligations. Most third parties are health insurance companies and as a result limit their coverage to treatment for illness or health-related problems, usually defined in terms of medical necessity. One must invariably assign a diagnosis to the client to secure payment. Some services provided by psychologists are not, strictly speaking, health or mental health services. For example, marriage counseling, educational testing, school consultation, vocational guidance, child custody evaluations, and a whole variety of forensic functions may not be considered health services and as such would not be covered by health insurance. Some insurance carriers also specify certain types of diagnostic or therapeutic procedures that are not "covered services." Such treatments or services might be considered ancillary, experimental, unproven, or simply health-promoting (e.g., weight control and smoking cessation) but not treatment for a specific illness. Attempts to conceal the actual nature of the service rendered or otherwise attempt to obtain compensation in the face of such restrictions may constitute fraud. Some third-party payers will not pay for services that are not clearly tied to the treatment of a psychological disorder. Examples include divorce mediation, child custody evaluations, smoking cessation programs, or weight loss consultations. If in doubt, consult with the third party's representative (as described above) and do not misrepresent the service provided.
- *Fraud:* As a legal concept, fraud refers to an act of intentional deception resulting in harm or injury to another. There are four basic elements to a fraudulent act:

  1. False representation is made by one party who either knows it to be false or is knowingly ignorant of its truth. This may be done by misrepresentation, deception, concealment, or simply nondisclosure of some key fact.
  2. The maker's intent is that false representation will be relied on by another.
  3. The recipient of the information is unaware of the intended deception.
  4. The recipient of the information is justified in relying on or expecting the truth from the communicator. The resulting injury may be financial, physical, or emotional.

IMPORTANT DON'TS

- Never bill for services you have not actually rendered. If you are billing for services provided by a supervisee, this should be made clear on all bills and claim forms.
- Never give anyone a blank insurance claim form with your signature on it. This is an invitation to fraud.

- Never change diagnoses to fit reimbursement criteria.
- Never bill insurance companies for missed or late canceled sessions. You may have an agreement with clients to pay for such missed appointments; however, third-party payers may be billed only for services rendered.
- Never change the date when you first saw the client in order to fit reimbursement criteria.
- Never bill for multiple client therapy sessions (i.e., couple, family, or group) as though they were individual treatment sessions. When in doubt about who to bill, contact a claims representative at the company. Note the name of the claims representative, follow instructions, and keep a record of the conversation.
- Do not forgive or waive copayments or deductibles without informing the third-party carrier.

AREAS OF CONTROVERSY

- *Bill collecting:* Creditor and debtor relationships are just as much a part of the psychologist-client relationship as in most other purchases of service. Inevitably, some clients will fall behind in paying for services or fail to pay for them at all. Because of the nature of clients' reasons for consulting psychologists and the nature of the relationships that are established, however, psychologists have some special obligations to consider in formulating debt collection strategies. When a client remains in active treatment while incurring a debt, the matter should be dealt with frankly, including a discussion of the impact of the debt on treatment. In most cases, however, the problems that arise occur after formal service delivery has terminated.
- *Collection agencies:* As a general concept, it is not inappropriate for a psychologist to use a professional collection agency. Ideally, a client should be cautioned that this may happen and should be given the opportunity to resolve the matter without involving a collection agency. Practitioners who employ such agencies are responsible for any misconduct by the agency.

   1. Psychologists may be held responsible for financial misrepresentations effected in their name by an employee or agent they have designated (including billing and collection agents). They must, therefore, choose their employees and representatives with care and supervise them closely.
   2. In all debt collection situations, psychologists must be aware of the laws that apply in their jurisdiction and make every effort to behave in a cautious, businesslike fashion. They must avoid using their special position or information gained through their professional role to collect debts from clients.
   3. In dealing with debt collection, whether through an agency or small claims court, the clinician should remember that only pertinent elements (e.g., client status, number of sessions, and amount owed) can be disclosed without violating the confidentiality of the client. Disclosure of client status in such situations is generally allowed because the client has violated his or her contract to pay the agreed-upon fees.

- *Caution:* Fee disputes are a frequent basis of legal complaints against psychologists (Bennett, Bryant, VandenBos, & Greenwood, 1990; Woody, 1988), and this is also true in instances of client-initiated ethical complaints.
- *Bartering:* Although permitted under limited provisions of the APA's Code of Conduct (Section 1.18), this should be undertaken thoughtfully and only as a last resort to assist a client who might otherwise be unable to afford services.
- *Missed appointments and last-minute cancellations:* These may represent a significant economic loss to a practitioner; however, not all practitioners charge for occasional events of this sort. The key point is not to surprise the client with such a charge. Either discuss such charges at the outset of treatment or caution clients that repeated incidents will result in such charges. Such charges are not payed for services rendered and hence may not be billed to third parties.

- *Fee splitting:* Relationships involving kickbacks, fee splitting, or payment of commissions for client referrals may be illegal and unethical. Careful attention to the particular circumstances and state laws is important before agreeing to such arrangements. Fee splitting refers to a general practice, often called a "kickback," in that part of a sum received for a product or service is returned or paid out because of a prearranged agreement or coercion. As it is practiced in medicine or the mental health professions, the client is usually unaware of the arrangement. Traditionally there was nearly universal agreement among mental health professionals that such practices are unethical, chiefly because they may preclude a truly appropriate referral in the client's best interests, result in delivery of unneeded services, lead to increased costs of services, and generally exploit the relative ignorance of the client. Unfortunately, fee splitting may exist in rather complex and subtle forms that tend to mask the fact that it is occurring. There is a continuum of types of agreements that range from reasonable and ethical to clearly inappropriate. At the two extremes are employer-employee relationships (clearly appropriate) and arrangements wherein the person making the referral gets money solely for making the referral.

References & Readings

Balch, P., Ireland, J. F., & Lewis, S. B. (1977). Fees and therapy: Relation of source of payment to course of therapy at a community mental health center. *Journal of Consulting and Clinical Psychology, 45,* 504.

Bennett, B. E., Bryant, B. K., VandenBos, G. R., & Greenwood, A. (1990). *Professional liability and risk management.* Washington, DC: American Psychological Association.

Dightman, C. R. (1970). Fees and mental health services: Attitudes of the professional. *Mental Hygiene, 54,* 401–406.

Koocher, G. P., & Keith-Spiegel, P. C. (1998). *Ethics in psychology: Professional standards and cases* (2nd ed.). New York: Oxford University Press.

Kovacs, A. L. (1987). Insurance billing: The growing risk of lawsuits. *Independent Practitioner, 7,* 21–24.

Pope, K. S. (1988). Fee policies and procedures: Causes of malpractice suits and ethics complaints. *Independent Practitioner, 8,* 24–29.

Pope, K. S., Geller, J. D., & Wilkinson, L. (1975). Fee assessment and out-patient psychotherapy. *Journal of Consulting and Clinical Psychology, 43,* 835–841.

Pope, K. S., Tabachnik, B. T., & Keith-Spiegel, P. C. (1987). Ethics of practice: The beliefs and behaviors of psychologists as therapists. *American Psychologist, 42,* 993–1006.

Woody, R. H. (1988). *Protecting your mental health practice: How to minimize legal and financial risk.* San Francisco: Jossey-Bass.

Related Topics

Chapter 112, "Fifteen Hints on Money Matters and Ethical Issues"

Chapter 125, "Sample Psychotherapist-Patient Contract"

133 PSYCHOLOGISTS' FEES AND INCOMES

John C. Norcross

This brief chapter extracts the highlights of recent studies on the psychotherapy fees, psychological testing fees, and professional incomes of psychologists across the United States.

PSYCHOTHERAPY FEES

Probably the most systematic study of psychotherapy fees is that undertaken by the Ridgewood Financial Institute every two or three years and published in *Psychotherapy Finances*. Since 1979, this nationwide survey of private practice mental health clinicians has covered individual and group therapy fees, psychological testing fees, regional variations in fees, managed-care allowances, practice expenses, and total professional income, among other elements of the financial profile of psychotherapy practice. (Subscriptions for monthly issues of *Psychotherapy Finances* can be directed to 1-800-869-8450 or purchased through its Web site; see References.) The most recent survey, conducted in early 2000, encompassed 1,565 psychotherapists, principally psychologists (n = 621) and social workers (n = 434). Slightly more than half of the respondents were women, and 99% were licensed in their respective states. Solo practice was still king of the private practice sample with 57%, followed by 23% of psychotherapists in solo practice with expense sharing and 17% in group practice.

Table 1 presents the median individual and group psychotherapy fees for the national sample of psychologists. Three types of fees are provided: direct pay; managed care; and indemnity insurance.

These fees are quite similar to those reported in a separate study conducted of 480 doctoral-level psychologists belonging to the APA Division of Psychotherapy (Norcross, Orlinsky, & Beutler, 1999). Their mean and median fees for three types of patients are summarized in Table 2.

From 1979, when the first *Psychotherapy Finances* survey was conducted, median fees had constantly risen for private practitioners. Starting in the mid-1990s, however, there was a definite downward pressure on fees. Most psychotherapists reported that their usual and customary fees had either remained the same (thus actually decreasing when adjusted for inflation) or eroded by an average of $5. In fact,

TABLE 1. Psychologists' Median Fees for Individual and Group Therapy Sessions

	Direct Pay Fee	Managed Care Fee	Indemnity Insurance Fee
Individual therapy	$95	$75	$90
Group therapy	$50	$37	$45

Source: October 2000 *Psychotherapy Finances*, extracted with permission of the publisher.

TABLE 2. Psychologists' Mean and Median Fees for Three Types of Patients

	Direct Pay Patients	Managed Care Patients	Third-Party Patients
Mean fee	$94	$70	$93
Median fee	$100	$75	$90
Inter-quartile range	$80–110	$65–$85	$80–$110

Source: October 2000 *Psychotherapy Finances*, extracted with permission of the publisher.

the consumer price index (CPI) is climbing faster than psychotherapy fees are rising.

In several respects, the results substantiate the obvious economics: providing psychotherapy to managed-care patients yields lower hourly reimbursements. Managed care exacts significant "costs" from the practitioner: a 25% fee reduction on average and the additional paperwork and administrative duties that such programs typically entail. Heavy reliance on managed-care fees concretely translates into decreasing annual incomes for full-time clinical practitioners.

PSYCHOLOGICAL TESTING FEES

The *Psychotherapy Finances* study also collects data on psychologists' fees for administering various psychological tests. The mean fees charged for psychological testing are presented in Table 3 for four types of patients: managed care, indemnity insurance, self-pay, and Medicare. As seen there, there are large discrepancies in testing fees between self-pay and managed-care patients.

PSYCHOLOGIST INCOMES

The American Psychological Association (APA) Research Office collects salary data every other year from psychologists across the United States. The 2001 Salaries in Psychology report (Singleton, Tate, & Randall, 2003) represents the twelfth in the series and is based on the current salaries or net incomes of APA members who are working full time in a variety of positions. A total of 10,082 psychologists (50% response) responded to the latest survey. The data are divided by employment setting, experience level, and geographic region, and they are published in reports available for purchase at a modest cost from the APA or for perusal on APA's home page (see References).

Table 4 presents the 2001 median and mean salaries for doctoral-level psychologists in academic positions by rank. These are the salaries for individuals employed full time in 9- or 10-month positions. Because many psychologists in academic settings have additional sources of income from multiple work settings, these figures may not represent total income.

Table 5 presents the salaries for doctoral-level clinical psychologists employed in institutional settings for at least 35 hours per week, as well as the net incomes for doctoral-level clinical psychologists employed at least 32 hours per week in private practice. Because many psychologists will work in more than one position or setting, these figures may not represent total income.

The 2000 *Psychotherapy Finances* survey reports comparable incomes for psychologists

TABLE 3. Mean Fees Charged by Psychologists for Psychological Tests

Test	Insurance Self-Pay	Medicare	Managed Care	Indemnity
Wechsler Adult Intelligence Scale III	$134	$211	$209	$151
Wechsler Intelligence Scale for Children III	$134	$214	$209	$157
Leiter International Performance Scale—Revised	$145	$160	$168	$132
Wechsler Memory Scale III	$129	$176	$182	$139
Minnesota Multiphasic Personality Inventory II (or MMPI-A)	$ 89	$121	$131	$106
Millon Clinical Multiaxial Inventory III (or MACI)	$ 97	$133	$127	$ 98
NEO Personality Inventory	$ 99	$140	$141	$100
Rorschach (Exner system)	$117	$194	$219	$118
Wechsler Individual Achievement Test	$101	$160	$159	$100
Wide Range Achievement Test III	$ 78	$ 96	$ 99	$ 67
Peabody Individual Achievement Test	$ 92	$119	$128	$ 75
Child Behavior Checklist	$ 55	$ 78	$ 82	$ 84
Dementia Rating Scale	$ 97	$107	$123	$ 96

Source: October 2000 *Psychotherapy Finances,* extracted with permission of the publisher.

TABLE 4. Salaries for Doctoral-Level Psychologists in Academic Settings

Setting and Rank	Median	Mean	SD
University, psychology department			
Full professor	$ 78,000	$ 81,887	$24,024
Associate professor	$ 53,000	$ 54,796	$12,330
Assistant professor	$ 44,000	$ 46,408	$25,392
University, education department			
Full professor	$ 75,000	$ 76,672	$16,750
Associate professor	$ 52,500	$ 54,734	$ 9,986
Assistant professor	$ 45,000	$ 45,431	$ 6,133
University, business department			
Full professor	$115,000	$124,385	$45,875
Associate professor	$ 78,000	$ 83,867	$25,292
Assistant professor	$ 73,000	$ 73,148	$19,382
Four-year college, psychology department			
Full professor	$ 54,500	$ 59,074	$17,966
Associate professor	$ 48,000	$ 48,960	$10,687
Assistant professor	$ 39,000	$ 38,733	$ 6,478
Medical school, psychiatry department			
Full professor	$ 96,500	$112,222	$46,545
Associate professor	$ 73,500	$ 71,083	$19,233
Assistant professor	$ 47,000	$ 47,537	$ 9,484

Source: 2001 Salaries in Psychology, American Psychological Association (2003).

TABLE 5. 2001 Salaries for Doctoral-Level Clinical Psychologists in Practice Settings

Setting and Experience	Median	Mean	SD
Public psychiatric hospital			
10–14 years	$ 61,000	$ 59,500	$12,422
20–24 years	$ 60,000	$ 56,667	$12,340
25–29 years	$ 62,000	$ 62,800	$ 2,775
VA hospital			
5–9 years	$ 71,000	$ 70,200	$ 7,208
10–14 years	$ 77,000	$ 59,200	$ 5,848
15–19 years	$ 78,500	$ 76,200	$ 8,728
20–24 years	$ 78,000	$ 75,333	$ 6,593
25–29 years	$ 80,500	$ 76,875	$11,154
Individual private practice			
5–9 years	$ 66,000	$ 70,355	$28,711
10–14 years	$ 76,500	$ 91,767	$69,828
15–19 years	$ 87,000	$ 92,752	$43,555
20–24 years	$ 90,500	$100,019	$46,766
25–29 years	$ 75,000	$ 85,127	$41,225
Group private practice			
5–9 years	$ 52,000	$ 59,154	$21,969
10–14 years	$ 70,000	$ 83,100	$68,988
15–19 years	$ 95,000	$ 94,174	$39,093
20–24 years	$ 80,000	$ 93,676	$41,763
25–29 years	$110,000	$ 99,733	$28,679

Source: 2001 Salaries in Psychology, American Psychological Association (2003).

TABLE 6. Private-Practice Psychologists' Income

	Private Practice Income	Total Professional Income
$140,000+	9%	12%
$130,000–$139,999	3%	4%
$120,000–$129,999	3%	5%
$110,000–$119,999	2%	4%
$100,000–$109,000	9%	9%
$90,000–$99,999	6%	7%
$80,000–$89,999	9%	9%
$70,000–$79,999	10%	11%
$60,000–$69,999	11%	11%
$50,000–$59,999	11%	11%
$40,000–$49,999	11%	8%
$30,000–$39,999	8%	6%
$29,999 or less	7%	3%

Source: October 2000 *Psychotherapy Finances*, extracted with permission of the publisher.

in full-time private practice. The median private practice income was $71,856 and the total professional income was $80,000. Psychologists were more likely than other mental health professionals to draw professional income from organizations other than insurance companies and managed care. That is, they are likely to consult, teach, supervise, or contract with entities such as school systems or health services in addition to their private practice.

More detailed data on psychologists' incomes are presented in Table 6 in terms of the percentage of full-time practitioners falling into discrete income ranges.

The APA Salaries in Psychology report also provides salaries for psychologists employed in a multitude of positions. Doctoral-level psychologists in educational administration, for example, reported a median 11- or 12-month salary of $90,000 in 2001. Doctoral psychologists employed in full-time research positions reported a median salary of $65,000. The median 11- or 12-month salary for master-level school psychologists was $61,000. And the median 11- or 12-month salary for doctoral-level industrial/organizational psychologists was $96,000 in 2001.

Although the incomes of psychologists in academia, administration, and hospitals have steadily increased of late, such is not the case for psychologists employed full time in private practice. Starting in the mid-1990s, the research studies consistently document the negative impact of managed care on clinicians' incomes, especially for more experienced independent practitioners (see also Phelps, Eisman, & Kohout, 1998; Rothbaum, Bernstein, Haller, Phelps, & Kohout, 1998; Williams, Kohout, & Wicherski, 2000). Practice income is down in real dollars. In the 2000 *Psychotherapy Finances* survey, for example, private-practice psychologists' incomes decreased by 1.7% since 1997. In the 2001 APA study, for another example, 46% of private practitioners reported decreased income. For those reporting a decrease, the mean and median reduction in net income was 15% over the years.

References, Readings, & Internet Sites

American Association of University Professors (AAUP). (n.d.). Annual Report on the Economic Status of the Profession. Retrieved 2004 from http://www.aaup.org/research/Index.htm

American Psychological Association Research Office. (n.d.). Home page. Retrieved 2004 from www.research.apa.org/

Norcross, J. C., Orlinsky, D., & Beutler, L. E. (1999). Managed care involvement and psychotherapy fees among APA Division 29 members. *Psychotherapy Bulletin, 34*(4), 40–43.

Phelps, R., Eisman, E. J., & Kohout, J. (1998). Psychological practice and managed care: Results of the CAPP Practitioner Survey. *Professional Psychology: Research and Practice, 29,* 31–36.

Pingitore, D., Scheffler, R., Sentell, T., Haley, M., & Schwalm, D. (2001). Psychologist supply, managed care, and effects on income: Fault lines beneath California psychologists. *Professional Psychology: Research and Practice, 32,* 597–606.

Psychotherapy Finances. (n.d.). Home page. Retrieved 2004 from http://www.psyfin.com/

Rothbaum, P. A., Bernstein, D. M., Haller, O., Phelps, R., & Kohout, J. (1998). New Jersey psychologists' report on managed mental health care. *Professional Psychology: Research and Practice, 29,* 37–42.

Singleton, D., Tate, A., & Randall, G. (2003). *Salaries*

in psychology 2001: Report of the 2001 APA Salary Survey. Washington, DC: American Psychological Association Research Office.

Williams, S., Kohout, J. L., & Wicherski, M. (2000). Salary changes among independent psychologists by gender and experience. *Psychiatric Services, 51,* 1111.

Williams, S., Wicherski, M., & Kohout, J. L. (2000). *1999 salaries in psychology.* Washington, DC: American Psychological Association.

Related Topics

Chapter 112, "Fifteen Hints on Money Matters and Related Ethical Issues"

Chapter 132, "Billing Issues"

134 ESTABLISHING A CONSULTATION AGREEMENT

Len Sperry

As health care delivery continues to evolve, mental health clinicians are likely to become more involved as consultants to various organizations and agencies. This chapter overviews considerations the clinician may face in establishing an agreement for consultation services. As a backdrop for this overview, the focus and types of consultation are briefly discussed.

1. *The focus of consultation:* Caplan (1970) describes a classification system based on the focus of consultation. Consultation can be focused in four ways:

- *Client-centered consultation:* The goal is to aid the client, such as executive coaching.
- *Consultee-centered case consultation:* The goal is to enhance the consultee's skills; for example, a psychologist meets with a group of line supervisors to study their understanding of and recognition of substance dependence in the workplace.
- *Program-centered administrative consultation:* The goal is to diagnose and resolve the consultee's difficulty in dealing with administrative problems. A common example is assisting EAP personnel to develop a corporation-wide depression awareness program.
- *Consultee-centered administrative consultation:* The goal is to diagnose and resolve the consultee's difficulty in dealing with administrative problems, such as functioning as a consultation-liaison psychologist to a weight management program at a community hospital.

2. *The types of intervention:* It is useful to distinguish two types of consultant interventions: organizational interventions and clinical-organizational interventions (in contrast to clinical interventions). Traditionally, clinicians were thought to provide clinical interventions such as individual, family, marital, or group therapy, whereas organizational consultants were more likely to provide individual, team, and organizational interventions such as executive coaching, team building, and reengineering. Whereas traditional forms of organizational consultation require considerable skill and experience, there are a number of clinical-organizational interventions that mental health clinicians can competently provide corporations, schools, health care agencies and organizations, community groups, and government agencies. *Corporate Therapy and Consulting* (Sperry, 1996) provides a detailed description of 10 common organizational interventions and 14 clinical-organizational interventions. The following is a listing of the clinical-organizational interventions:

- Hiring, discipline, and termination consultation
- Work-focused psychotherapy
- Outplacement counseling and consultation
- Stress-disability and fitness-for-duty consultation
- Dual-career couples counseling and consultation
- Conflict resolution consultation with work teams
- Conflict resolution in a family business
- Crisis intervention consultation
- Consulting on resistance to planned change efforts
- Merger syndrome consultation
- Downsizing syndrome consultation
- Treatment outcomes consultation
- Mental health policy consultation
- Violence prevention consultation

3. *Assessing the request for consultation:* Irrespective of the type of consultation offered, the process begins with a request from a prospective client. These requests can include a workshop on stress management, a violence prevention policy, team conflict resolution, stress-disability evaluation, or strategic planning, to name a few. The request is usually made by phone or face-to-face. How the clinician-consultant handles the request can greatly impact not only whether a consultation contract is offered but also the outcome of the intervention itself. Just as in psychotherapy, the first five minutes of the prospective consultant and client relationship is critical.

Backer (1982) argues that an accurate assessment of client need must occur very early in the consultation process. This assessment will probably address the following questions:

- *What is the context of the consultation request?* Specifically, what is the client requesting? For example, if a hospital administrator phones a clinician asking if he or she can "do something about employee morale," what is the administrator really asking for help with? As in psychotherapy, the initial presenting problem is often not the client's reason for seeking consultation. Consultation requests may be disguised because of lack of understanding of the consultation request, embarrassment, misperception of the basic problem, or even deceit. So, the consultant would inquire about what is meant by "morale" and, specifically, by whom, where in the organization, and how it is being manifested and what effects it is having on productivity and communication between management and employees.
- *Why now?* As in psychotherapy, the answer to this question can be extremely revealing. Consultations are often requested only after the agency or organization has attempted to deal with its difficulty for a period of time without requesting outside help. What efforts were tried, and to what extent were they successful? In the "morale" example, it is critical to know what efforts the administrator has made and why these efforts have not worked as well as expected.
- *What is the client's readiness to change?* The likelihood that the client is willing to make changes to resolve the problem must also be assessed. Because the client and personnel resources are involved, it is essential that the clinician-consultant determine the client's willingness to allocate such resources. If it emerges that the hospital's problem is widespread and the administrator will authorize only two or three workshops on "team building," it may well be that the client's readiness is insufficient. Extended inquiry and discussion may be required before an appropriate level of readiness is achieved.
- *Can I competently provide the requested consultation?* The prospective consultant needs to ask himself or herself whether he or she has sufficient content knowledge, technical and interpersonal skills, and experience to undertake this consultation.

For fairly straightforward requests, such as presenting a lecture on stress management or providing a disability evaluation, both of which require specific technical expertise, the question may be easily answered. When process *plus* technical expertise is required, the question of competence is more complex.

- *Can I ethically perform this consultation?* Potential conflict of interest and dual roles must be considered by the consultant. Obviously, if the clinician is providing or has provided marital therapy to the hospital administrator, he or she probably should not be directly involved in consultation.

4. *Responding to the consultation request:* The clinician-consultant now is in a position to respond to the service request. As in psychotherapy, the clinician-consultant first responds to the manifest content of the request by expressing awareness of the need and/or discomfort of the client organization. Next, the clinician-consultant proposes a plan for meeting the request. This may involve a face-to-face meeting—or a series of meetings—to discuss a plan of action for more complex consultations, or it may require only a brief phone meeting for straightforward consultations such as a workshop presentation.

5. *Drafting a consultation agreement or contract:* Usually, a letter of agreement or a formal consulting contract will finalize these discussions. Although most consultants routinely draft a written contract, some do not (Lippitt & Lippitt, 1978). The written document of agreement becomes a contract if a consideration is stated (i.e., the provision of specified consultation for a given fee), and both parties sign the document. Typically, the document should contain the specified service to be performed, the time frame, travel and lodging expenses, cost of assessment and/or intervention materials, and the consulting fee, which may include preparation time.

6. *Establishing a consulting fee:* The fee a clinician-consultant charges a client can be established either on a project or a fixed-fee basis or on a time basis, in which the increments can be hours or days. Circumscribed activities or projects, such as presenting a stress management workshop or conducting a fitness-for-duty evaluation, are usually billed as a fixed fee, whereas facilitating team development or organizational restructuring is usually billed as day rate, called a *per diem*. Some consulting activities, such as critical incident stress debriefing (CISD) or facilitating a strategic planning retreat, may be charged on a project or a per diem basis depending on local or regional customs. Generally speaking, government contracts require fixed-fee agreement. For complex consulting activities, consultants tend not to use fixed-fee rates for projects with which they have little experience (see Metzger, 1993, for further discussion of this point).

- *Calculating utilization rate: Billable hours* refers to the number of working hours the consultant bills the client. Experienced, full-time consultants do not actually consult full-time. They have down time in which they may devote up to 20% of their time marketing their services to secure new consulting arrangements. Obviously, this time is nonbillable. *Utilization rate* refers to the percentage of total working hours the client can be billed. According to Kelley (1981), the utilization rate is the number of billable hours divided by the number of total working hours available. For instance, if a clinician-consultant plans to consult 12 hours per week and actually bills for 6 hours per week, the utilization rate is 50%. Obviously, the higher the utilization rate, the greater one's compensation. Utilization rate indicates how much consulting time clients are directly paying for, as compared with the time the consultant must absorb as overhead.
- *Calculating billable rate:* The "rule of three" is widely used by consultants to calculate their billing rate (Kelley, 1981). The rule assumes that a consultant should generate overhead and benefits that should equal base salary, while also producing a profit equal to base salary. For example, suppose a clinician-consultant works half-time as a clinician at a college counseling

center and develops a half-time consulting practice. If he or she specifies a half-time base consulting salary as $50,000 a year, the total revenues of $150,000 should be estimated. This is derived from $50,000 for base salary, plus $50,000 for overhead plus benefits and $50,000 for profit. The billing rate is estimated by dividing total revenue by yearly billable hours. For example, $150,000 is divided by 1,000 hours (based on 2,000 hours/year as full-time work). The minimum hourly billing rate is thus $150 per hour, and the minimum billing rate would be $1200 per day. A corollary of the rule of three is that the more hours billed, the less one needs to charge to maintain profit levels, whereas the fewer the hours billed, the more that must be charged to maintain profit level.

- *Other ways of establishing a billing rate:* A second way of setting a billing rate is based on the usual and customary fees in a geographic region. Usually, there is a typical daily rate for psychologists in particular metropolitan areas. For example, while $1,200 per day is considered the norm in some midwestern cities, the rate in large northeastern cities may be $2,000–$2,500 per day. Finding out the billing rates of three or four clinician-consultants should reveal the usual and customary rate for a given community. A third way of establishing fee arrangements is to consider the client's circumstances. Schools and community organizations may have limited funds for consultation, whereas defense attorneys may have unlimited funds for expert testimony. The beginning clinician-consultant also may be willing to offer a low-cost consultation fee to one or more clients in return for gaining experience and receiving a positive reference from that client.

7. *Completion of consultation services rendered:* Following completion of the consultation services rendered, it is customary to send or deliver the bill for payment. If a report of the consultation was specified in the agreement, the report is also sent. Following payment, it is customary to send a follow-up thank-you note.

8. *Marketing/soliciting future consultations:* Experienced consultants usually do not view termination of consultation services rendered as termination of the consultation relationship. Successful consultations often result in other consultation requests from the same client. These clients tend to communicate their satisfaction with a consultant to their professional colleagues and friends. Since word-of-mouth advertising is the consultant's most effective marketing strategy, it behooves the consultant to make his or her initial consultations as successful as possible. Consultants may also seek written permission to mention the names of clients of their most successful consultations in written materials—such as brochures—or in verbal conversation with prospective clients.

References & Readings

Backer, T. E. (1982). Psychological consultation. In J. R. McNamara & A. G. Barclay (Eds.), *Critical issues in professional psychology* (pp. 227–269). New York: Praeger.

Biech, E. (1999). *The business of consulting: The basics and beyond.* San Francisco: Jossey-Bass.

Caplan, G. (1970). *The theory and practice of mental health consultation.* New York: Basic Books.

Kelley, R. E. (1981). *Consulting: The complete guide to a profitable career.* New York: Scribner's.

Lippitt, G., & Lippitt, R. (1978). *The consulting process in action.* San Diego, CA: University Associates.

Metzger, R. (1993). *Developing a consulting practice.* Newbury Park, CA: Sage.

Sperry, L. (1996). *Corporate therapy and consulting.* New York: Bruner/Mazel.

Related Topics

Chapter 117, "Forensic Referrals Checklist"

Chapter 125, "Sample Psychotherapist-Patient Contract"

Chapter 131, "Contracting With Managed Care Organizations"

135 COMPUTERIZED BILLING AND OFFICE MANAGEMENT PROGRAMS

Edward L. Zuckerman

Computerization of clinical practice is not only almost unavoidable but also quite beneficial. Typing on a computer is easier than handwriting, computers rarely lose anything and can find it anywhere in a few seconds, and the Internet holds great riches. Commonly available programs allow you to cope with billing and managed-care needs, assist in psychological assessment, construct reports, survey the research, administer treatments, and put you in instant touch with colleagues around the world.

However, for many, the most pressing need is a program that can ensure accurate and timely billing and that can handle routine office tasks like appointment scheduling and recording progress notes. Most of the software described below will do these tasks, and many programs offer additional functions. This list is not exhaustive. It omits programs for the larger systems like clinics. Small programs for billing are listed at the end. I estimate that this list is 98% complete and certainly contains all the major developers of these programs for mental health offices. This listing is current as of April 2003.

Since developers are constantly improving and modifying their products, confirm important aspects of a program before you make a purchase. Because the Health Insurance Privacy and Accountability Act (HIPAA) will substitute a new electronic billing form—the ANSI 827-P for the familiar HCFA-1500—ask each developer how he or she is handling this. All computers, software, and other product names listed herein are property of their respective copyright and trademark holders.

SELECTING A PROGRAM

You probably turned to this section to find out which program to buy. I wish I could tell you the answer, but I can't know your situation or needs, so here is a general strategy. First, look at the available features and decide which are most important. As you explore, add more features or more explanation of them to your checklists. Get the demos and experiment with them. Do not decide on the basis of price. Your income and stress level will depend on this program for many years, and a program that is confusing or unnecessarily complex will be a continuing source of distress. If you have an office manager, he or she should make the final decision even though you have the advanced degree.

FORMAT OF THE ENTRIES

- *The developer's name, address, phone, and Web site.* The list is alphabetical. The size of the description is not related to the size of the program.
- *The name of the program.* I have put this second because many programs have similar names.
- *A description of the program.* Since all these programs do billing, only unusual aspects are listed. Where they do additional functions, they are called "office management" programs and may include schedulers, mailing list handling, treatment plan writing, recording of medications, and the like. *ECS*

means *electronic claims submission*—the ability to send a claim for payment to the insurance company over the phone line using your modem and specialized software. This makes the insurance company's work easier, it may speed up your payment, and it certainly speeds up their denying your claim.

- *The computer hardware or "platforms" the program is designed to run on.* All of these programs work under Microsoft's operating system, Windows, and they are not so identified. There are fewer that work on Apple's Macintosh computers (but you only need one program); these are indicated with the word *Macintosh.*
- *The current costs of the program, where advertised or available.* These may change or your needs may not fit the configuration of the program listed, so call to confirm prices.
- *The availability of downloads or cost of demonstration disks.* Some of these contain only a "guided tour" that describes and illustrates the program's major features. Others contain a limited version of the whole program or limit you to a small number of clients or a fixed period of time. You can enter data and see how the program works, but you cannot use the demo to run your practice. These "fully functional" demos will take a lot of your time to enter client information, but you will then really understand their strengths and limitations.

THE PROGRAMS

Accurate Assessments
1823 Harney Street, Suite 101
Omaha, NE 68102
http://www.accurateassessments.com/software.htm
AccuCare is a suite of integrated programs for billing, ECS, assessment, and monitoring of progress and outcomes that offers specialized modules for addictions, criminal justice, and Native Americans. Free demos by download. No prices on Web site.

Affinity Software Corporation
Walpole, MA 02175
800-437-4307
http://www.internexsys.com/main/htm/infomanager.asp
Medical InfoManager is an integrated collection of modules for accounting and billing, word processing, reports, scheduling, treatment plans, and ECS. Highly medical but adaptable to psychology. No prices on the Web site. Macintosh and Windows.

Applied Computing Services
212 Fair View Road
Elk, WA 99009
800-553-4055
http://www.pma2000.com/
PMA-2000 does billing, insurance, scheduling, and progress notes, especially for mental health. ECS through a clearinghouse and directly is $195. Full-featured demo for 20 patients is $20 on CD or a free download. Solo version is $295, three providers is $495, each with a year's support but additional years are $100 to $180.

Beaver Creek Software
525 SW 6th Street
Corvallis, OR 97333-4324
800-895-3344
http://www.beaverlog.com
The *Therapist for Windows* is a full-scale billing program; its features are as follows: fills in forms, all diagnostic codes (*DSM-IV, CPT, ICD-*9), prints on letterhead or HCFA 1500, makes mailing labels, deposit slips; tracks referrals and pre-authorizations, simple clinical notes; password protection, backup and restoration of data, pre-authorizations and insurance maximums, dunning messages, form letters, and so on. Program cost is $499 with more for added clinicians and networks. Demo on CD ($20) or free download, includes 60 days tech support. Options: Appointment scheduler ($150), case manager ($200) with treatment plans, progress notes, histories, managed-care data, group therapy note, medications.

Blumenthal Software
528 Palmer Farm Drive
Yardley, PA 19067
215-702-9550
http://www.blumenthalsoftware.com

PBS: The Psychologist's Billing System. This mature, full-featured billing program does it all—accounting, forms generation and printing, management reports; transfers data into spreadsheets, sliding scale and Medicare fee generation, handles managed-care limitations, etc. Solo or groups $595. Inherently networkable. $100 more for version with encryption.

Cornucopia Software
626 San Carlos Avenue
Albany, CA 94706
510-528-7000
http://www.practicemagic.com
Practice Magic is a very complete billing and office management system at a low price; it runs on Macintoshes as well. It prints to HCFA 1500, uses an appointment book format (and prints Daytimer inserts); exports to Quicken; does progress notes, managed-care functions, bank deposit slips, and more. ECS billing through a clearinghouse. The standard version is $130 with manual. After three years updates are $40 per year. For $180, the yearly updates cost is eliminated. Multiusers are 50% more. Demo free download or $10 on CD.

DocuTrac
20140 Scholar Drive, Suite 218
Hagerstown, MD 21742-6575
800-850-8510
http://www.quicdoc.com
Office Therapy is a fully featured insurance and billing program with ECS through clearinghouses. Managed-care information is well integrated, data can be easily exported to other databases, and much of the program can be user-modified. Free fully functional demo by download or by request. $499. Now available for the Palm OS. *QuickDoc* is a fully featured records program with documentation for intakes, progress and discharge notes, scheduling, treatment goals and plans, patient satisfaction, practice forms, letters, mail merge, etc. QuicForms fit all managed-care formats. QuicWord allows easy creation and integration of records with other programs. $549 or both programs for $863.

PC Consulting Group
800-847-8446
http://www.delphipbs.com/index.htm
Delphi/PBS. This very complete package has been around for many years and includes all billing functions, scheduling, ECS through a clearinghouse, passwords, mailing labels, online help, payroll calculation, finance charges, networkable, backups, and more. No demos are listed at the Web site. Toll-free phone support. Free annual updates. $895 for solo and $100 more for each additional provider.

Practice Management Software
285 Engle Street
Englewood, NJ 07631
800-874-2159
http://www.pm2.com
PM/2 is a longstanding and complete billing program with dozens of features including insurance billing, scheduling, managed-care tracking, and security. PM/2 Clinical Planner generates treatment plans and OTRs from checklists. Solo practitioner is $600, additional providers are $300. ECS, $300. Clinical Planner, $395.

Pragmatic
PO Box 33551
Reno, NV 89533
877-773-4481
http://www.centerdigital.com/software/
Center Psych. This is a combination of a billing program and, with options, additional services. It can serve 1–99 providers, a single office or multiple locations, and makes good use of the Macintosh interface. There are no prices or downloads at the Web site, but a slideshow is available.

Psychotherapy Practice Manager
800-895-1618
http://www.anacapa.net/~jhmullin/#toc13
The *Psychotherapy Practice Manager* is a quite comprehensive and mature office management set of programs for basic client records (client registration, intake assessment, progress notes), billing, appointments (intake form, scheduler, reminders, "To Do" lists), Rolodex (sorting codes, address books, labels), accounting (revenues, expenses, profit and loss, IRS 1040 Schedule C summary), management reports (accounts receivable, aging, detailed and summary activity), *DSM-IV/CPT* codes, and generic forms (con-

sent to treat, release of information). 90-day free tech support. Single therapist version for Windows and Macintosh $395; multiple-therapist practices are $100 more. Options: managed-care module $195, ECS $195. Full-featured demo $20, credited toward purchase.

Psyquel
12758 Cimarron Path, Suite 127
San Antonio, TX 78249
877-779-7835
http://www.psyquel.com
Scheduling, billing, and insurance for mental health providers with a twist. It is a subscription based Internet service. They pursue unpaid claims, track authorizations, backup records, and provide free support training, upgrades, and more. The program also supports progress notes and other patient records.

Saner Software
253, 2460 W. Main Street D
St. Charles, IL 60175
630-513-5599
http://www.sanersoftware.com
ShrinkRapt is a very complete billing and insurance program with some records features like clinical notes and treatment plans. It is available for the Macintosh and technical support is free. A walk-through demo on a CD is free and includes sample reports and manual. Modules for scheduling and ECS are an additional $49 each. Solo practitioner $585, $985 for multiple users of one machine.

SOS Software
352-242-9100
http://www.sosoft.com
SOS Office Manager is a fully featured mature product based on the familiar daysheet/ledger card model. Simplified data entry, managed-care tracking, useful management reports, and much more. Prices start at $1,999 for single computer and more for networks. A very functional scheduler is $150 solo and $300 networked. ECS is $395. SOS Case Manager for Windows offers very flexible clinical records including intake, history, problem/goal/asset/obstacle-oriented treatment plans and progress notes, group therapy progress notes, medication, a glossary for reusable text, templates for most used information. $495 for solo, more for networks.

SumTime
995 Vintage Avenue, Suite 102
St. Helena, CA 94574
888-821-0771
http://www.sumtime.com
SumTime is a very complete and full featured billing and practice management software package including ECS and scheduler, billing and managed-care functions, 10 pages of password protected notes per session, customized form letters, etc. Free demo by download or on CD for $10. Windows or Macintosh, $499 single user, $599 for group practice. 90-day support included, additional tech support by the year.

VantageMed
600 West Cummings Park, Suite 3450
Woburn, MA 01801
800- 3-HELPER/ 800-343-5737
http://www.helper.com
Therapist Helper. A very comprehensive multifunctional program that, besides billing, includes scheduling, managed-care and meds tracking, many reports, progress notes. Options include ECS, credit card processing, Palm Organizer version, and QuicDoc (see DocuTrac, above). No prices on the Web site. Downloadable fully functional demo.

Related Topics

Chapter 112, "Fifteen Hints on Money Matters and Related Ethical Issues"
Chapter 132, "Billing Issues"

PART XI
Professional Resources

136 THERAPIST SELF-CARE CHECKLIST

John C. Norcross & James D. Guy, Jr.

Mental health professionals, by definition, study and modify human behavior. That is, we study and modify other humans. Psychological principles, methods, and research are rarely brought to bear on psychotherapists ourselves, with the probable exception of our unsolicited attempts to diagnose one another (Norcross, 2000). Although understandable and explicable on many levels, this paucity of systematic study on psychotherapists' self-care is unsettling indeed.

Our aims in this brief chapter are threefold: first, to remind busy practitioners of the personal and professional need to tend to their own psychological health; second, to provide evidence-based methods to nourish themselves; and third, to generate a positive message of self-renewal and growth.

The following list summarizes practitioner-recommended and research-informed methods of alleviating the distress of clinical work, or more optimistically, of replenishing the practitioner. Unfortunately, the research on psychotherapist self-care has not progressed to the point where controlled studies have been conducted. Nonetheless, the list presents a practical synthesis of clinical wisdom, research literature, and therapist experience on self-care methods from disparate theoretical traditions. The list is adapted from a more extensive catalogue of self-care activities published in our book *Leaving It at the Office* (Norcross & Guy, in press), and is divided into 11 broad strategies of self-care.

MIND THE BODY

- We occasionally become so intent and focused on sophisticated self-care methods that we overlook the basics. What is the quality of your nutrition, your body? Do you obtain sufficient exercise and healthy food during the day, or, as one of us discovered himself doing a few years ago, are you subsisting throughout the day without exercise and with only diet soda and hard pretzels?
- How many hours of sleep do you average per evening? How many hours do you need?
- Increase your sensory awareness: beholding your surroundings using vision, hearing, touch, and olfaction can be a powerful elixir and can counterbalance the primarily cognitive and affective work of psychotherapy.
- Take your own advice: exercise and relax regularly.
- Take minibreaks between sessions to self-massage your face and neck muscles; perhaps schedule regular massages to nourish yourself and relieve muscle tension.
- Monitor your use of substances. Are you self-medicating with alcohol, tobacco, food, or drugs?

REFOCUS ON THE REWARDS OF CLINICAL WORK

- Attend to the rewards associated with clinical work. For example, recall the life-transforming psychotherapies in which you were privileged to participate.
- Satisfaction from helping others is crucial, so be sure to include at least some clinical activities that demonstrate you are actually helping someone!
- Enjoy maintaining relationships with clients spanning years, even decades, that include intermittent courses of treatment.
- Your work will ideally capitalize on both your natural and acquired abilities. Do what you do well.
- Be careful when applying your expertise to your family of origin (fools rush in where angels fear to tread).
- Remember: you are actually self-employed, regardless of whom you work for. Look for ways to create a greater sense of freedom and independence in your work.
- Clinical practice may not make you rich, but if it is your calling, it is a wonderful way to make a living.
- There are typically many more benefits than hazards associated with the practice of psychotherapy. If you've forgotten this, find methods to help you remember.

RECOGNIZE THE HAZARDS OF THE "IMPOSSIBLE PROFESSION"

- All accounts indicate that clinical practice exacts a negative toll on the practitioner, particularly in the form of problematic anxiety, moderate depression, and emotional underinvolvement with family members. Have you identified the impact of clinical practice on you and your loved ones?
- Reading about and reflecting on the stresses of psychotherapy commonly leads to the realization that similar strains are experienced by virtually all mental health professionals. Can you affirm the universality of these stresses?
- Consider the amount of physical isolation that you experience each day. What steps can you take to create more opportunities for contact with other clinicians?
- Invite family and friends to point out when you become too interpretive and "objective" when it would be healthier to be spontaneous and genuine.
- The possibility of patient violence is disturbing but important to consider. How can you act now to enhance your personal safety at the office?
- Do you frequently hear stories of abuse and cruelty in your work with clients? Limit your exposure to traumatic images outside the therapy room by choosing movies, literature, and other entertainment carefully.
- How much confidential client material do you share with your significant others? Have you thought out all of the implications of what you do share?
- Consider how you have managed the delicate balance between empathic connection and self-preserving distance in your work with distressed patients. Do you find yourself on one end of the pendulum more often than you would like? How might you intentionally pursue balance here?
- Reflect on the number of clients that you've said good-bye to over the years. What has been the cumulative impact of these terminations?
- Therapists tend to minimize their own limitations and needs, particularly when talking with colleagues. With which colleague can you be vulnerable and honest?
- Periodically reevaluate why you became a psychotherapist and why you continue to practice. Look for ways to work through those unhealthy motivations.
- You can't always keep your personal life from influencing your practice. Accept some spillover as an inevitable cost of being human.
- Marital and relationship difficulties related to the practice of psychotherapy are frequently reported by clinicians. Discuss with your spouse the topics covered in this chapter. How does he or she perceive their impact on your relationship?
- Burnout among therapists is a real but rela-

tively rare phenomenon. What steps are you taking to reduce the possibility of burnout?

NURTURE RELATIONSHIPS

- In one study of well-functioning psychologists (Coster & Schwebel, 1997), peer support emerged as the highest priority. How does your peer support fare?
- Are you getting enough alone time? Do you know what to do with it when it's available?
- Identify the three most nurturing people in your life. What can you do to increase the amount of support you receive from them?
- Ongoing peer supervision or consultation is highly valued by experienced clinicians throughout their careers. Do you have such arrangements in your own life? Under what circumstances do you seek supervision or consultation?
- Try to include phone calls, lunches, and breaks in your workday several times each week to provide contact with family and friends.
- What have you learned about yourself as a result of experiencing loss following completion of treatment with a favorite patient? Specifically, what interpersonal gratifications did you receive?
- Name your most significant mentor during your career. What made this relationship so important? How are your needs for mentoring being met today?
- A spouse/significant other is an important source of nurturance for many clinicians. How important is this in your life?
- Have your friendships become fewer in number and diminished in significance over the years of professional practice? What does this tell you, if anything?
- Support groups and peer supervision groups offer multiple advantages. Consider joining or creating one.
- Something may be askew if you are habitually giving out more nurturance than you are receiving. Consider corrective actions.

SET BOUNDARIES

- Setting boundaries emerges in our research as the most frequent self-care strategy of mental health professionals. Be clear with your clients about professional expectations and limitations.
- Clearly delineate your policies regarding extra sessions, late appointments, telephone contacts, payment for services, and the like.
- Your work expresses a combination of personal style, theoretical orientation, and individual preferences. Caring professionals customize their work to individual patients, but there is a limit to bending.
- Clarify your expectations of your clients early in your work. What are the ground rules for treatment?
- Understand what your client needs most, and don't allow that goal to be compromised by conflicting roles and agendas.
- Your clients are not there to meet your needs; treatment relationships are not reciprocal.
- Define your relationships with colleagues with care. Transference influences these relationships, too.
- Establishing an identity apart from your role as a clinician will enrich your private life with variety and meaning. Don't get stale!

RESTRUCTURE COGNITIONS

- Self-monitor your internal dialogue, particularly in regard to countertransference feelings.
- Attend to what Ellis calls "stinking thinking" through introspection, reflection, using triple column logs, or sharing concerns with others.
- Think through your reactions to transferential feelings directed to you. To whom are they aimed and to whom do they belong?
- Beware of absolutistic thinking: musturbation and the tyranny of the shoulds. They can affect you as much as your patients.
- Dispute the common fallacy that "good psychotherapy is equivalent to having all patients like us." It is not!

- Yes, you are an expert on human behavior—but you're still nutty at times!
- Recall that the other side of caring consists of confrontation. Caring about others includes being tough at times.
- Take Coach John Wooden's advice and refuse to believe either your most idealizing or your most demeaning client—you are neither God nor the devil.
- Remind yourself that you cannot cure every patient.
- Balance the amount of time you devote to thinking about your successful cases and your frustrating cases. Dwell on your successes as well as your failures.
- Assertively lessen unrealistic demands made on you: don't take on more work than you need to or wrongly believe you're expected to do more.
- Consider alternate explanations that may cause events. Psychotherapy is not the only causal event in clients' lives. Nor are you the sole or primary causal agent!
- Calculate real probabilities. The worst does not always happen—to you or to your patients.
- Evaluate events on a continuum to avoid dichotomous thinking; psychotherapy outcomes are rarely on either extreme of a continuum.

SUSTAIN HEALTHY ESCAPES

- A sense of humor is one of your most important stress relievers. Practice!
- In one study (Mahoney, 1997), over 80% of therapists routinely engage in reading or a hobby, take pleasure trips or vacations, and attend artistic events and movies as part of their self-care patterns. Is your life balanced?
- Monitor your vacation and down time. Is it less than you, as a psychotherapist would recommend to patients in similarly stressful occupations?
- Variety and intellectual stimulation are indispensable. What can you do to increase their impact on your schedule and professional duties?
- Pace your day, space appointments, and take a break or two.
- How much adventure and other diversions do you have away from the office? Is play a steady staple for your emotional diet?
- Consider taking steps to create variety in your day, such as intermingling psychotherapy sessions with supervision, consultations, study breaks, a trip to the gym, and so on.
- Involvement in other professional activities balances your workload and expresses a full array of your skills. Psychotherapy, teaching, supervision, administration, consultation, assessment, and writing are all part of the mental health professional landscape.

UNDERGO PERSONAL THERAPY

- Freud (1964) recommended that every therapist should periodically—at intervals of five years or so—reenter or initiate psychotherapy without shame as a form of continued education. Do you heed his sage advice? Do you struggle with the shame?
- Between 52% and 65% of psychotherapists enter personal treatment following completion of formal training. Do you subscribe to the illusion, or perhaps the delusion, that mental health professionals do not experience a need for personal therapy once they are in practice?
- Can you give yourself 50 minutes of time every few weeks in a holding environment? Are you practicing what you preach about the value of psychotherapy?
- If you do not participate in formal psychotherapy, consider an annual satisfaction checkup with a valued mentor, trusted colleague, or former therapist.

CREATE A FLOURISHING ENVIRONMENT

- Do you fall prey to American individualism and neglect systemic forces in and outside of your office? Employ stimulus control: structure your environment to help, not hinder, your clinical effectiveness.
- Are your clinical talents and interpersonal interests poorly invested in paperwork? If so,

consider a computer, a clerical assistant, or other alternatives.

- Search for ways to create a greater sense of freedom and independence in your work.
- Enhance your work environment: comfort in your furniture, aesthetics in your decor, replenishment in your refrigerator, and nourishment in your peers.

CULTIVATE SPIRITUALITY AND MISSION

- We emphasize the personal experience of spirituality or what Maslow called *mission*. Can you identify and resonate to an abiding mission or spirituality?
- Embrace your sense of calling to be a clinician. What are the spiritual antecedents to your career choice?
- Your work grows out of a legacy of socially sanctioned healers that extends back for many centuries. Try to feel connected to the heritage and to the privilege of practicing psychotherapy.
- A sense of personal mission can fruitfully incorporate larger societal concerns, such as enhancing women's rights, promoting social justice, teaching conflict resolution, eradicating poverty, and abolishing sexual abuse. What are the sympathies that renew you?
- Optimism and belief in the potential for personality change are prerequisites for good clinical practice. Assess yourself and then ask a friend to assess you.
- How does your belief in a mission, God, or a transcendent force influence your work? How does this serve as a resource for you? Are you squarely confronting your own yearnings for a sense of transcendence and meaning?
- Try to invoke and augment your client's spirituality worldview to enrich their experience of psychotherapy.
- Since the practice of psychotherapy is not to provide ultimate meaning for your life, what does? What should?

FOSTER CREATIVITY AND GROWTH

- Opportunities for dedicated reflection and discernment are a professional obligation, not a luxury. How often do you engage in spiritual exercises, journaling, meditation, or other forms of renewal?
- Are you finding ways of nurturing your creativity? Are staleness and repetition starting to get you down?
- Diversify, diversify, diversify.
- Attending clinical conferences, reading literature, and continuing your education are the life springs of a committed professional. Do you feel you are just getting CE hours or truly refining and building your skills?
- Everything comes together for a therapist in the creative process (Kottler, 1999). How are you coming together, nourishing yourself, and growing as a psychotherapist?

References & Readings 

Baker, E. K. (2003). *Caring for ourselves: A therapist's guide to personal and professional well-being*. Washington, DC: American Psychological Association.

Brady, J. L., Norcross, J. C., & Guy, J. D. (1995). Managing your own distress: Lessons from psychotherapists healing themselves. In L. VandeCreek, S. Knapp, & T. L. Jackson (Eds.), *Innovations in clinical practice* (pp. 293–306). Sarasota, FL: Professional Resource Press.

Coster, J. S., & Schwebel, M. (1997). Well-functioning in professional psychologists. *Professional Psychology: Research and Practice, 28*, 5–13.

Dryden, W. (Ed.). (1995). *The stresses of counselling in action*. Thousand Oaks, CA: Sage.

Freud, S. (1937/1964). Analysis terminable and interminable. In J. Strachey (Ed.), *Complete psychological works of Sigmund Freud*. London: Hogarth.

Geller, D. D., Norcross, J. C., & Orlinsky, D. E. (Eds.). (2005). *The psychotherapist's own psychotherapy: Patient and clinician perspectives*. New York: Oxford University Press.

Guy, J. D. (1987). *The personal life of the therapist*. New York: Wiley.

Kottler, J. A. (1999). *The therapist's workbook: Self-assessment, self-care, and self-improvement exercises for mental health professionals*. San Francisco: Jossey-Bass.

Mahoney, M. J. (1997). Psychotherapists' personal problems and self-care patterns. *Professional Psychology: Research and Practice, 28,* 14–16.

Norcross, J. C. (2000). Psychotherapist self-care: Practitioner-tested, research-informed strategies. *Professional Psychology: Research and Practice, 31,* 710–713.

Norcross, J. C., & Aboyoun, D. C. (1994). Self-change experiences of psychotherapists. In T. M. Brinthaupt & R. P. Lipka (Eds.), *Changing the self* (pp. 253–278). Albany: State University of New York Press.

Norcross, J. C., & Guy, J. D. (in press). *Leaving it at the office: Psychotherapist self-care.* New York: Guilford Press.

Rippere, V., & Williams, R. (Eds.). (1985). *Wounded healers.* New York: Wiley.

Schaufeli, W. B., Maslach, C., & Marek, T. (Eds.). (1993). *Professional burnout: Recent developments in theory and research.* Washington, DC: Taylor & Francis.

Scott, C. D., & Hawk, J. (1986). *Heal thyself: The health of health care professionals.* New York: Brunner/Mazel.

137 CONDUCTING EFFECTIVE CLINICAL SUPERVISION

Nicholas Ladany

Supervision is the primary means of imparting psychotherapy knowledge and skills to supervisees. Yet, relative to the psychotherapy literature, the supervision literature is in an earlier phase of development in terms of generating evidence-based advice for performing supervision. The following pantheoretical recommendations for conducting effective clinical supervision are derived from the extant theoretical and empirical literature, and are grounded in clinical experience.

1. *Emphasize and readily attend to the supervisory relationship.* The supervisory working alliance is the likely foundation for the effectiveness of all supervisor interventions. Bordin (1983) conceptualized the working alliance as consisting of a mutual agreement on the (a) goals and (b) tasks of supervision, and (c) an emotional bond between the supervisor and supervisee. The strength of the supervisory alliance has been empirically shown to relate to supervision process and outcome.

2. *Apply models of supervision, as opposed to generalizing models of psychotherapy to supervision.* Supervision-based models, albeit only moderately comprehensive, have been in place for decades. Two general types have been identified: developmental models (e.g., Stoltenberg, McNeill, & Delworth, 1998) and general skill-based or competency models (e.g., Holloway, 1995). Most of the empirical work has focused on the developmental models; however, this preference seems more heuristically useful than empirically supported. It seems supervisors like to think developmentally, but act from a skills-based approach. Although multiple models have been expounded, only one technique has demonstrated efficacy in supervision: Interpersonal Process Recall (Watkins, 1997).

3. *Attend to supervision's own unique dynamics.* The art and science of conducting supervision is different from the art and science of conducting psychotherapy in at least three primary ways. First, it is intended to be primarily educative. Supervision occurs with the inherent assumption that the supervisee is there to become more adept at psychotherapy-related skills. Second, supervision is evaluative. A critical role for the supervisor is to evaluate the supervisee on these predefined skills. Third, supervision is typically (especially pre-licensure and outside the United States) involuntary for the supervisee. In many instances, the supervisee has little choice in whether, or from whom, he or she receives supervision. These three conditions create different dynamics than does psychotherapy, and as such, supervision should be viewed through a supervision, rather than a psychotherapy, lens.

4. *Engage in role induction and contracting with all supervisees.* In role induction and contracting, supervisors provide supervisees with explicit and understandable parameters of supervision work. Although it may be reasonably assumed that more advanced supervisees are aware of what transpires in supervision, it is frequently the case that supervisees' experiences do not consist of typical experiences. Therefore, supervisors should engage in role induction and contracting that includes supervisor disclosures about educational, training, and clinical experience; theoretical approach to supervision and therapy, and confidentiality limits; supervision parameters that include meeting time, length of time, place, fee arrangements, contact and crisis information, and use of taping; and supervisee expectations such as informed consent, who is primarily responsible for initiating the supervisory discourse, supervisee disclosure, note taking, supervisee's use of self in supervision, supervisory goals, and supervisor evaluation.

5. *Tend to administrative responsibilities.* Supervisors must fulfill a variety of administrative responsibilities that include keeping records of supervision, keeping abreast of all clients supervised, ensuring clients are aware of the supervisee's and supervisor's status, signing off on supervisee notes, using due diligence in selecting supervisees, and ensuring that supervisees with rigid interpersonal difficulties are prevented from continuing to work with clients. In addition, the supervisory work has a legal dimension that varies by jurisdiction and supervisors are reminded to familiarize themselves with those laws and rules.

6. *Supervision should not be psychotherapy for the supervisee.* Although it can be legitimately argued that part of supervision is to help the supervisee explore how her or his reactions may influence the therapy work, supervision is not a place solely for therapeutic change in the supervisee. Supervision should focus on supervisee interpersonal dynamics inasmuch as they relate to work with the client. More thorough attention should be provided by a therapist outside of supervision.

7. *Balance the 16 general supervisor tasks.* In pursuit of achieving positive supervision outcomes, supervisors essentially engage in 16 tasks (Ladany, Nelson, & Friedlander, in press). These are focusing on the supervisory alliance, normalizing the supervisee's experience, focusing on countertransference, focusing on multicultural awareness, focusing on evaluation, attending to parallel process, focusing on conceptual skill, focusing on technical skill, focusing on interpersonal skill, focusing on the therapeutic process, focusing on self-efficacy, exploration of feelings, focusing on the supervisee's interpersonal dynamics, assessing ethical awareness, assessing theoretical knowledge, assessing research knowledge, and case discussion. The supervisor must decide when and how much, each of these competing demands must be attended.

8. *Supervisors should attend to both supervisee-focused and client-focused outcomes.* Client outcome, while always alluded to as important, has been examined in only a handful of mostly case study empirical investigations, and a clear link between supervision and client outcome has not been established. Conversely, supervisee-based outcomes have been identified in the literature and include strengthening the supervisory relationship; enhancing supervisee conceptualization skills, therapy knowledge, multicultural awareness, self-efficacy, tolerance of ambiguity, awareness of countertransference, awareness of parallel process, and therapy skills; decreasing supervisee anxiety; and facilitating the development of supervisee self-evaluation. Supervisors should flexibly approach the supervisee with a mix of collegial, interpersonally sensitive, and task-oriented styles in order facilitate these positive outcomes.

9. *Recognize the importance of covert processes.* Although supervisee self-disclosure and, at least to some extent, supervisor self-disclosure are implicit assumptions in most models of supervision, it is likely that what they leave unsaid is critical to the supervisor work. Some typical supervisee nondisclosures include negative reactions to the supervisor, clinical mistakes, sexual attraction toward a client, and negative reactions to a client. Some typical supervisor nondisclosures include negative reactions to the supervisees' therapy and supervision work, supervisor self-efficacy, and sexual issues in supervision. Hence, it behooves supervisors to consider what may not be said in supervision, as well as ways of conducting supervision to minimize important nondisclosures.

10. *Keep abreast of ethical and legal issues that influence the practice of supervision.* Supervisors accept two types of liability: first, direct liability when supervisors are found responsible for specific actions in which they engage causes harm to a client; and second, vicarious liability when supervisors are found responsible for actions of supervisees. Along with liability for supervisees' clients, supervisors also need to be concerned with malpractice where the supervisee is harmed.

11. *Evaluate supervisees consistently and objectively.* Bernard and Goodyear (1998), not completely facetiously, postulate that there may be as many evaluation instruments as there are training sites. With this lack of consistency, supervisor evaluation has been a problematic enterprise. Supervisors should consider, and communicate to the supervisee, the components of supervisee work that are under scrutiny. These components will frequently entail: mode of therapy (e.g., individual, group, family), domain of supervisee behaviors (e.g., therapy, supervision, professional), competence area (e.g., therapy techniques, theoretical conceptualization, assessment), method (supervisee self-report, case notes, audiotape, videotape, live supervision), proportion of caseload (all clients, subgroup of clients), segment of experience (e.g., a specific session, or a segment of a session), time period (early, middle, or late in client treatment as well as early, middle, or late in training experience), evaluator (e.g., supervisor, clients), level of expected proficiency (e.g., demonstrated skill, comparison to cohort group) and feedback (e.g., quantitative vs. qualitative). No single evaluation can account for all of these components, however, having a clear set of parameters, will enhance the effectiveness of supervisor's evaluation.

12. *Set clear goals and provide both summative and formative feedback.* Supervisor evaluation consists of two components: goal-setting and feedback (summative and formative). Effective goal-setting consists of goals that are explicit, specific, feasibly reached, related to identified tasks, clarified early, and mutually agreed upon. To be effective in giving feedback, the supervisor should provide it in a way that is systematic, timely, clearly understood, positively and negatively balanced, and reciprocal.

13. *Enhance your own multicultural competence in order to enhance supervisee multicultural therapy competence.* As multicultural training has become an integral part of many psychotherapy training programs, so too has the situation in which supervisees are more knowledgeable about multicultural issues than are supervisors. In order to avoid becoming part of these "regressive" relationships, supervisors need to keep current on the evolving content of multicultural therapy. Multicultural (i.e., gender, race, ethnicity, sexual orientation, disability, socioeconomic status) competence can be assessed along six dimensions for the supervisee: self-awareness, general knowledge about multicultural issues, multicultural therapy self-efficacy, understanding of unique client variables, an effective therapy working alliance, and multicultural therapy skills (Constantine & Ladany, 2001). Hence, supervisors need to develop these skills in themselves in order to be adept in assessing supervisees along these dimensions.

14. *Consider group supervision and peer supervision as adjuncts to individual supervision.* Group supervision, consisting of a leader and typically three to six supervisees, offers an educative experience whereby supervisees can experience the benefit of group work (e.g., universality) along with skill development. Additionally, peer supervision is one avenue through which supervisees may disclose more readily their challenges and receive supplemental guidance.

15. *Secure training in clinical supervision.* The majority of psychotherapy supervisors did not complete formal training in supervision themselves (Bernard & Goodyear, 1998) nor does any mental health organization currently require supervisor training. It seems likely that the lack of supervisor training may be responsible for many of the unmet challenges that supervisors face. Hence, systematic and comprehensive supervisor training is recommended for those who engage in supervision.

References, Readings, & Internet Sites 

American Association of State and Provincial Psychology Boards. (2003). Supervision guidelines. Retrieved 2004 from http://www.asppb.org/pubs/Supervision%20Guidelines.asp

American Psychological Association, Division 17, Society of Counseling Psychology, Supervision and Training Special Interest Group. (2003). Supervision and training resources. http://www.lehigh.edu/~nil3/stsig/

Bernard, J. M., & Goodyear, R. K. (1998). *Fundamentals of clinical supervision* (2nd ed.). Boston: Allyn & Bacon.

Bordin, E. S. (1983). A working alliance based model of supervision. *The Counseling Psychologist, 11,* 35–41.

Bradley, L. J., & Ladany, N. (Eds.). (2001). *Counselor supervision: Principles, process, & practice* (3rd ed.). Philadelphia: Brunner-Routledge.

Constantine, M. G., & Ladany, N. (2001). New visions for assessing multicultural counseling competence. In J. G. Ponterotto, J. M. Casas, L. A. Suzuki, & C. M. Alexander (Eds.), *Handbook of multicultural counseling* (2nd ed., pp. 215–236). Thousand Oaks, CA: Sage.

Ekstein, R., & Wallerstein, R. (1972). *The teaching and learning of psychotherapy* (2nd ed.). Madison, WI: International Universities Press.

Ellis, M. V., Ladany, N., Krengel, M., & Schult, D. (1996). Clinical supervision research from 1981 to 1993: A methodological critique. *Journal of Counseling Psychology, 43,* 35–50.

Falvey, J. E. (2002). *Managing clinical supervision: Ethical practices and legal risk management.* Pacific Grove, CA: Brooks/Cole.

Forrest, L., Elman, N., Gizara, S., & Vacha-Haase, T. (1999). Supervisee impairment: A review of identification, remediation, dismissal, and legal issues. *The Counseling Psychologist, 27,* 627–686.

Holloway, E. L. (1995). *Clinical supervision: A systems approach.* Thousand Oaks, CA: Sage.

Ladany, N., Hill, C. E., Corbett, M., & Nutt, L. (1996). Nature, extent, and importance of what therapy supervisees do not disclose to their supervisors. *Journal of Counseling Psychology, 43,* 10–24.

Ladany, N., Lehrman-Waterman, D. E., Molinaro, M., & Wolgast, B. (1999). Psychotherapy supervisor ethical practices: Adherence to guidelines, the supervisory working alliance, and supervisee satisfaction. *The Counseling Psychologist, 27,* 443–475.

Ladany, N., Nelson, M. L., & Friedlander, M. L. (in press). *Critical incidents in supervision.* Washington, DC: American Psychological Association.

Ladany, N., & Walker, J. A. (2003). Supervisor self-disclosure. *In Session: Journal of Clinical Psychology, 59,* 611–621.

Stoltenberg, C., McNeill, B., & Delworth, U. (1998). *IDM supervision: An integrated developmental model for supervising counselors and therapists.* San Francisco: Jossey-Bass.

Watkins, C. E., Jr. (Ed.). (1997). *Handbook of psychotherapy supervision.* New York: Wiley.

138 GUIDE TO INTERACTING WITH THE MEDIA

Lilli Friedland & Florence W. Kaslow

Psychologists interact with the media both directly and indirectly. This article will cover the traditional media of radio, television, magazines, and newsprint, as well as the new technologies, given that these have become a major venue of psychologists' interactions and contributions, and they are the avenue that much of the public we serve turns to for information. Initially, media psychology developed as a formal field to address the ethical and professional concerns of "on air" psychologists. Currently, media psychology encompasses a much broader array of activities (Luskin & Friedland, 1998). New, increasingly complicated opportunities exist for psychologists to interact with the media and new technologies. Though it is clear that professional standards and ethics are the same when psychologists use the new technologies as when they use traditional processes, prudent professionals need to be vigilant as they participate in these cutting-edge areas.

PUBLICITY BY AND ABOUT PSYCHOLOGISTS

Public statements encompass but are not limited to paid or unpaid advertising, product endorsements, grant applications, licensing applications, other credentialing applications, brochures, printed materials, directory listings, personal resumes or curricula vitae, or comments for use in the media for print or electronic transmission, statements in legal proceedings, lectures and public oral presentations, published materials, or online chat or open forums. When the psychologist pays for the development of a marketing brochure or public relations release, the psychologist is responsible for the content and should critique it carefully before it goes to press. Frequently, the psychologist cannot exercise the same power over what is released by media personnel. It is important to be aware that public relations, publishing, marketing and media personnel are not familiar with psychologists' ethical or professional standards, and therefore may be accustomed to exaggerating the claims of the individuals with whom they work. It is recommended that psychologists give a printed document describing their training and expertise to media personnel and publicists to minimize error. This printed copy should include one's degree, training, and a list of publications and speaking engagements on the given subject.

ON-AIR MEDIA PSYCHOLOGY

There are constructive steps psychologists can take when receiving a call from a program director of a show or someone involved with electronic media asking for an interview or information regarding a particular topic. If one is not an expert on the requested subject matter and the time allocated is insufficient to acquire the requisite information, then the psychologist should decline the interview and recommend someone else who has expertise in the given area. Because the period to provide the information or interview is often immediate to a few hours; there may not be sufficient time to locate an available expert. If this request does not fall within the psychologist's areas of expertise, the psychologist who is approached can offer to rapidly conduct a literature search. To minimize inaccuracies, it is recommended that the most significant findings and conclusions be written, including citations, and submitted to the interviewer. Experienced media psychologists have noted that electronic and print editors rarely refer to or cite the researchers. Nonetheless, these efforts can be viewed as an opportunity to educate media personnel.

Frequently, media psychologists are asked to comment on a particular individual's psychotherapist or mode of therapy. Usually the personal information provided by the individual posing the question is brief. Psychologists should indicate that they are commenting about the general psychological issues or processes posed rather than on the type of treatment given for a particular individual's symptoms or behaviors, or about the specific therapy itself. If another professional's competence or treatment is questioned, the psychologist should encourage the questioner to discuss the concerns with the therapist directly.

Psychologists who work with the media need to be aware of the possible myriad ramifications of their participation. It is not appropriate to compensate any member of the media in return for publicity or for being showcased. The psychologist must realize that, to the consumer or viewer, he or she is seen as representing the profession; therefore, the information imparted must be accurate and current. Further, the psychologist needs to be aware of the real and potential effects on viewers of the media activities in which he or she participates. Is the psychologist seen as endorsing or condemning a behavior? Is the psychologist's stance a subjective one (based upon personal values or opinions) or an objective one (based upon research and prevailing community practice standards)? Clearly, the positions stated need to be based upon the current state of research and treatment.

Every effort should be made by psychologists to determine the media person's sources, integrity, and previous history of type of guests and experts. To do this, one can try to become familiar with the media staff and program format prior to agreeing to participate. For example:

- Observe if the host habitually interrupts the guest experts.
- Determine the source for the story idea (a current headline or a standing topic).
- Determine if the host has a particular viewpoint that the show wants to substantiate, although current psychological knowledge does not confirm the particular position.

If the program or media personnel have a history of seeking sensationalism or of demeaning their guests, it is wise to refuse to be involved, no matter how tempting the invitation. When psychologists do participate, they should alert media personnel as to potential harm, stress, or need for referrals for program guests, audience, or staff if they become aware that psychotherapeutic help seems warranted.

When approached by TV and radio program personnel, psychologists are sometimes requested to bring along guests, preferably past or present clients. If a client is asked to participate, the reason for this can be questioned: For whose benefit the client is participating—for his/hers, the show's ratings, or the psychologist's? Even if the client gives informed consent to submitting his or her name, and the potential emotional effects of participating have been discussed, it is urged (in accordance with American Psychological Association [APA] ethical guidelines; APA, 2002) that psychologists not participate in this manner, especially with current clients. Some patients are apt to say yes to please their therapist, and this seeming inducement should be avoided. Psychologists should attempt to educate members of the media to the possible dual relationships entailed and the negative long-term effects on guests when brought in by their treating professional. There are additional issues that need to be considered if a minor is the client. The effects on clients of being on TV shows and "telling all" before scores of viewers sometimes do not surface for a long time (McCall, 1990).

When psychologists are being paid for their services, this should be made clear, if relevant. They can be paid as actors if their professional identity is not known or the presentation cannot be seen as an endorsement. In working with the media, there is a distinction that can be made between advertisements (i.e., using an actor to speak about a product or service) and an infomercial (i.e., the professional endorses and gives a testimonial about the particular service or product). Some infomercials are camouflaged as news programs. Psychologists should be sure that the infomercials and programs in which they participate do not mislead the public. As in all media communications, any information provided by the psychologist must be based on current research, practice, and ethical standards.

Remember, while working with media personnel, that nothing is "off the record" or "confidential" for them; informal comments and expressions have been known to be used in the final product. Sometimes psychologists are asked to agree a statement or give an example of a public figure whose behavior is illustrative of a particular psychological problem; the circumspect professional does not do so, for this comment may well be taken out of context and also this does not fall within the realm of psychologists' capabilities and ethics. It is essential to maintain one's professional stance and composure until one is out of range of all microphones, cameras, and telephones (Koocher, Norcross, & Hill, 2001).

When being interviewed, it is important to use language at the level of the general public and not use jargon, technical terms, or acronyms. Try to find out characteristics of the usual audience (e.g., age, gender, education). Successful strategies for presenting "on air" are:

- Smiling
- Leaning toward the interviewer
- Keeping legs together with feet flat on the floor (not crossed)
- Using relaxed, slow, deep breathing
- Engaging in casual (though not "off the record") conversation with media personnel

Certain visual factors influence the appearance of the psychologist:

- Clothing and overall appearance can affect the presentation, so solid colors should be worn (many types of stripes or designs are problematic).
- Wear conservative professional clothing, without accessories that may distract from what is being said.
- Wear clothing, makeup, and hairstyles that are in fashion but not too trendy.

When interacting with the media, prudent psychologists ask themselves: What is the message I want to send about this topic? It is recommended that psychologists prepare three to five clearly stated points to facilitate their clarity and succinctness about the subject matter. They should also rehearse their "talking points" in order to become more comfortable and eloquent in their delivery, as this is the customary practice of media professionals.

Experienced media psychologists know the key to the successful media interview is to make the points, and not necessarily to answer the questions posed (American Psychological Association, 2003). Therefore, if psychologists are asked questions that do not speak to particular information they deem necessary to present on this subject, they can bring up their "talking points" by using bridges such as "the real issue . . . " or "the three issues involved are . . . " (personal communications in APA Media Psychology Division Board dialogues; Friedland & Kaslow, 1995–2003).

"Talking points" can be printed on the psychologist's letterhead and given to the interviewer after the taping, as a technique for affirming the importance of these points and reducing the possibility that the psychologist's information is unclear or misquoted.

The information presented by psychologists should be based upon current psychological research and practice. Be consistent with the APA's current ethical code (American Psychological Association, 2002). Don't lead the audience to infer that the psychologist has a personal relationship with the individual asking the questions, or with a personal particular product.

In sum, psychologists can follow the following steps when called upon by the media for expertise:

1. *Clarify the objectives of the caller.* Does he or she want support for a particular position? Does he or she want a thoughtful psychological perspective on a topic or individual? For example, frequently the caller asks about a personality type, and then asks if the information given would apply to a particular public figure. What is the type of information requested? What is the context in which the information will be used? What type of psychological expertise is necessary to provide the interview or information necessary? Does the psychologist have this type of expertise? If not, is there an appropriate psychologist with the requisite knowledge to recommend? If not, can a literature search on the topic suffice? Also, what is the time frame for the interview or information? Is this time frame sufficient for the psychologist to develop a cogent presentation?

2. *Know the medium.* Psychologists should familiarize themselves with the format of the magazine, newspaper, radio or TV program, or other media forum prior to giving the interview to be both better prepared with the type of information that could be useful and also to determine how the interviewer uses experts. For example, (a) if it will be an on-air program, become acquainted with the type of questions asked to anticipate the questions and research answers prior to the show.

Be aware of the audience and gear your presentation to their level of interest and understanding. For example, if it is a woman's television show, use examples aimed at the type of women who watch that program (i.e., educational level, socioeconomic status, ethnic/cultural level).

Note the manner that the host uses to bring in experts and question them. Does the host try to get experts to give definitive opinions or one word answers to complex issues? Does the expert have an opportunity to explain multiple viewpoints or factors about particular issues?

3. *Develop three to five "talking points" on the subject.* Rehearse the "talking points." Give a brief outline of these points printed on professional letterhead to the host following the interview to further clarify the position. A brief biographical sketch can be attached. Media personnel usually want simple, definitive answers and clear 30-second sound bites. Psychologists typically need to be trained or practice giving brief, yet accurate information.

The format of on-air programs is such that the hosts control the focus. It is common for inexperienced guest experts to feel they did not state important points. Experienced media psychologists find that planning and rehearsing the three or five of the most salient facts on the subject yield a successful presentation.

4. *Recognize that the appearance of on-air psychologists contributes to the message.* Therefore, professional dress is recommended. This generally means a solid-colored outfit.

PRINT MEDIA

All of the principles cited above also apply when one is contacted by a newspaper reporter or writer for a magazine. These principles will be reiterated here briefly, interspersed with some additional points.

- Only give an interview if you are knowledgeable about and up to date on a topic/breaking story.
- If the media staff stress the immediacy of their deadline, try to be cooperative, but do not participate in the interview if you are not well prepared or they are placing you under duress. Remember, it is their deadline, not yours (and you cannot interrupt a therapy hour, cancel a class, stop while conducting research, or disrupt a consultation) for what will be a one- or two-line or paragraph quote.
- Whenever possible, if accepting their request, ask for a minimum of half an hour to organize your thoughts and for them to call you back at a mutually agreed upon time. While preparing, check the accuracy of any statements you plan to make about which you are dubious.
- Keep comments short, straightforward, succinct, pithy, and free of jargon.
- Ask any newspaper reporter to e-mail or fax you the article before it is submitted to go to press to review for accuracy. When there is sufficient time, we have found many reporters will do so.
- Most magazines have fact checkers who call before the article goes to press. When they call, listen carefully and suggest needed corrections.
- Ask the author to see that a complimentary

copy of the magazine is sent to you with the particular article checked in the table of contents.

- Thank the individual for calling. If a local newspaper reporter approaches you more than once, see if you can arrange to meet the individual in person. If so, this can lead to more frequent usage by this person and perhaps additional recommendations that other colleagues will call also.

THE NEW TECHNOLOGIES: GENERAL CONSIDERATIONS

To participate in the new media technologies, the psychologist may be working outside the customary benchmark practices of the profession. The wise professional will substantiate the underlying scientific bases or assumptions when going into new areas, and obtain supervision or consultation from respected colleagues. The new technologies enable interactions between individuals and groups throughout the world; therefore psychologists need to consider a specific client's language, ethnicity and culture, and the licensing and credentialing requirements in the geographic locale. It is important to ensure that the psychologist's malpractice insurance coverage extends to the new modalities of practice. It is recommended that before psychologists employ the new technologies, they consult with respected peers and/or ethics committees, and document the process, safeguards, and procedures used (APA, 2002; Kutner, 1997).

THERAPY ON THE AIR AND ONLINE

In an effort to educate the public, some professionals have conducted "live" therapy sessions on television or other types of media technology. Because psychologists cannot work ethically with current patients in such a manner, it is advised that actors be used. Personality characteristics and typical responses for a character can be discussed beforehand and actors can ad lib the situations. This kind of media broadcast of therapist-patient interaction portrayal usually is not harmful, but one should be cautious about ensuring that characters do not resemble specific patients.

The definition of the "therapeutic relationship" has been undergoing reexamination, in part due to the impact of new media technologies. Using the new technologies raises issues of substantiating the identity of the clients, location of clients (crossing geographic borders where there may be licensing and training differences), being sensitive to different ethnic or cultural populations, authentication of informed consent and fee arrangements, and risks to privacy and limits to confidentiality. Because these issues remain unclear, psychologists are urged to inform potential clients/patients about these concerns and take all reasonable precautions to protect the clients. Whenever there is a question, consultation with peers is advised, as well as documenting the process with careful notes.

"Virtual communities" such as chat groups and forums are ongoing entities on the Internet. These modalities serve as sources of support and information to their members: studies substantiate that these modalities reach clients in rural areas, as well as disabled or challenged individuals who might not otherwise receive service. However, there are ethical implications to be considered when a psychologist establishes or participates as the professional in a "group therapy" online with individuals he or she has not met. For example, if the psychologist has never met the patient, he or she has no idea whom he or she is "treating," and if that individual is participating using his or her real identity. Currently, the knowledgeable media psychologist refrains from involvement in such endeavors, as consumer protection parameters have not yet been developed (e.g., to whom would the consumer make a complaint given that the licensing boards and the various mental health professions may not yet have promulgated standards for these modalities, and where these standards exist, they may differ across states?). As issues get resolved, it is likely that online therapy groups will become permissible and professionally acceptable.

IN RETROSPECT

Despite all of the possible pitfalls, being a media psychologist is challenging, expands the person's knowledge and horizons, and enables the individual to share the benefits of psychological research and practice with the public.

References, Readings, & Internet Sites 

American Psychological Association. (2002). *Ethical principles of psychologists and code of conduct.* Washington, DC: Author.

American Psychological Association. (2003). How to work with the media: Interview preparation for the psychologist. http://www.apa.org/journals/media/index.html#identifying

American Psychological Association, Division of Media Psychology. (n.d.). Home page. Retrieved 2004 from http://www.apadiv46.org/

American Psychological Association, Public Affairs Office. (n.d.). Home page. Retrieved 2004 from http://www.apa.org/publicinfo

Friedland, L. & Kaslow, F. (1995–2003). Personal conferences with APA Division of Media Psychology Board.

Kutner, L. (1997). New roles for psychologists in the mass media. In D. Kirschner & S. Kirschner. (Eds.), *Perspectives on psychology and the media.* Washington, DC: American Psychological Association.

Luskin, B. J., & Friedland, L. (1998). Task Force Report: Media Psychology and the New Technologies, Division of Media Psychology, American Psychological Association. Retrieved 2004 from http://www.apadiv46.org/arttaskforcereport.html

McCall, R. (1990). Ethical considerations of psychologists working in the media. In C. B. Fisher & W. W. Tryon, *Ethics in applied developmental psychology: Emerging issues in an emerging field* (pp. 163–185). Norwood, NJ: Ablex Publishing.

Related Topics

Chapter 127, "Basic Elements of Consent"
Chapter 128, "Basic Elements of Release Forms"

139 COMMON CLINICAL ABBREVIATIONS AND SYMBOLS

John C. Norcross

a	before
AA	Alcoholics Anonymous
A&B	apnea and bradycardia
AAV	AIDS-associated virus
abd	abduction; abdomen
ABG	arterial blood gas
a.c.	before meals
ADHD	attention-deficit/hyperactivity disorder
ad lib	as desired
AFL	activities of daily living
adm	admission
ADTP	alcohol and drug treatment program

aero, aero Rx	aerosol inhalation equipment, treatment
AF	auricular fibrillation
A/G	albumin-globulin ratio
AIDS	acquired immune deficiency/ immunodeficiency syndrome
AK	above knee
A&O	alert and oriented
alb	albumin
alks, p'tase	alkaline phosphatase
ALL	allergy
AMA	against medical advice
amb	ambulatory
anes	anesthesia
angio	angiogram
ANS	anesthesia
AODM	adult-onset diabetes mellitus
Ao DT	descending aorta
AP	anteroposterior
AP & Lat	anteroposterior and lateral
≈	approximate
AQ	achievement quotient
ARC	AIDS-related complex
art mon	arterial pressure monitor
ARV	AIDS-related virus
AS	aortic stenosis; left ear
ASA	aspirin
AsAo	ascending aorta
ASD	atrial septal defect
@	at
A2	aortic second sound
AU	both ears
AV	arteriovenous
AVC	atrioventricular canal
AVVR	atrioventricular valve regurgitation
AWOL	away without official leave
AX	angle jerk
b	born
Bab	Babinski
bact	bacteria
BBS	bilateral breath sounds
BC/BS	Blue Cross/Blue Shield
BD	birth defect
BDD	body dysmorphic disorder
BDI	Beck Depression Inventory
BE	barium enema
b.i.d.	twice a day
BJM	bones, joints, muscles
BK	below knee
BM	bowel movement
BMT	bone marrow transplant
BP	blood pressure
BPD	borderline personality disorder
BS	bowel sound
B/S	breath sounds
BUN	blood urea nitrogen
c̄	with
C	centigrade
ca	calcium; chronological age
CA	cancer, carcinoma
CAM	cardiac medical
C&S	culture and sensitivity
cap	capsule
CAS	cardiac surgery
CAVC	complete atrioventricular canal
CBC	complete blood count
CBG	capillary blood gas
CBT	cognitive-behavior therapy
cc	cubic centimeter
CC	chief complaint
CDC	Centers for Disease Control and Prevention
CDI	Children's Depression Inventory
CF	cystic fibrosis
Δ	change
CHD	congenital heart disease
□	check
chol	cholesterol
Cl	chloride
cldy	cloudy
cm	centimeter
c. monitor	cardiac monitor
CNS	central nervous system
c/o, CO	complaint of
coarc	coarctation
conj	conjunctive
conv	convergence
CO_2	carbon dioxide
CP	cerebral palsy
CPAP	continuous positive airway pressure
CPC	clinicopathological conference
CPR	cardiopulmonary resuscitation
CPT	chest physiotherapy
CRC	clinical research
C/S	cesarean section
CSF	cerebrospinal fluid
CT	chest tube
CT, CT scan, CAT	computerized tomography
CVA	cerebrovascular accident
CVL	central venous line
CVP	central venous pressure
CVS	clean-voided specimen
CXR	chest X-ray
CYS	cystic fibrosis
D&C	dilation and curettage
DAT	diet as tolerated

d/c	discontinue
D/C	discharge
↓	decrease
DID	dissociative identity disorder
dil	dilute
DOA	dead on arrival
DOB	date of birth
DOC	doctor on call
DOE	dyspnea on exertion; date of evaluation
DOPP	duration of positive pressure
DP	dorsalis pedis
DPT	diphtheria, pertussis, tetanus
DS	Down Syndrome
D/S	dextrose and saline
DSM-IV	*Diagnostic and Statistical Manual of Mental Disorders*, fourth edition
DTR	deep tendon reflex
DTV	due to void
D/W	dextrose and water
DX, Dx, dx	diagnosis
EAP	employee assistance program
ECG, EKG	electrocardiogram
ECHO	enterocytopathogenic human orphan viruses
ECMO	extracorporeal membrane oxygenation
ECT	electroconvulsive treatment
EDC	endocrine
EEG	electroencephalogram
e.g.	for example
EMDR	eye movement desensitization and reprocessing
EMV	expired minute volume
ENT	ears, nose, throat; otolaryngology
EOM	extraocular movement
eos	eosinophils
ER	emergency room
ERG	electroretinogram
ESR	erythrocyte sedimentation rate
ETOH	alcohol
ETT	endotracheal tube
eve	evening
ext	extension
extrem	extremities
EYE	ophthalmology
f	frequency
F	fahrenheit; father
FAS	fetal alcohol syndrome
FBS	fasting blood sugar
♀	female
FFP	fresh frozen plasma
FH	family history
FIO_2	fractional inspired oxygen
flex	flexion
FOO	family of origin
for. bend	forward bending
FP	family physician
FTT	failure to thrive
f/u	follow up
FUO	fever of unknown origin
g, gm	gram
GAD	generalized anxiety disorder
GB series	gallbladder series
GC	gonorrhea
g/dl	grams per hundred millimeters
GF&R	grunting, flaring, and retracting
GI	gastrointestinal
GIS	gastroenterology
GNS	general surgery
gr	grain
gtt	drops
GTT	glucose tolerance test
gyn	gynecology
h	hour
H	husband
HA	headache
HC	head circumference
HCT	hematocrit
HEENT	head, eyes, ears, nose, throat
HEM	hematology
Hgb	hemoglobin
HI	homicidal ideation
HIV	human immunodeficiency virus
HLHS	hypoplastic left heart syndrome
HMO	health maintenance organization
HO_2	humidified oxygen
HPF	high-power field
HR	heart rate
HRT	hormone replacement therapy
h.s.	at bedtime
ht	height
HTN	hypertension
Hx	history
IA	intra-arterial
I&D	incision and drainage
I&O	intake and output
ICP	intracranial pressure
ICU	intensive care unit
IDS	infectious diseases
i.e.	that is, namely
IJ	internal jugular vein
IL	intralipid

IM	intramuscular
imp	impression
↑	increase (elevated)
in rot	in rotation
inv	inversion
IOFB	intraocular foreign body
IP	inpatient
IQ	intelligence quotient
IT	intrathecal
IV	intravenous
IVC	inferior vena cava
IVH	intraventricular hemorrhage
IVP	intravenous push
JT	jejunostomy tube
K	potassium
kg	kilogram
KJ	knee jerk
KUB	kidney, ureter, bladder
kV	kilovolt
L	left
LA	left atrium
lab	laboratory
L&A	light and accommodation
LAO	left anterior oblique
LAP	left atrial pressure
lat. bend	lateral bending
LBP	low back pain
LFT	liver function test
LL	lower lid
LLE	left lower extremity
LLL	left lower lobe
LLQ	left lower quadrant
L/min	liters per minute
LMP	last menstrual period
LOA	leave of absence
LP	lumbar puncture
LPA	left pulmonary artery
LTM	long-term memory
LUE	left upper extremity
LUL	left upper lobe
LUQ	left upper quadrant
LV	left ventricular
lymphs	lymphocytes
lytes	electrolytes
m	meter
M	mother
♂	male
M&T	myringotomy and tubes
MAP	mean arterial pressure
MAPI	Millon Adolescent Personality Inventory
MCL	midclavicular line
MCMI-III	Millon Clinical Multiaxial Inventory-III
med	medicine
mEq	milliequivalent (per liter, mEq/L)
mets	metastasis
mg	milligram
Mg	magnesium
mg/dl	milligrams per hundred milliliters
MHC	mental health center
MI	myocardial infarction
ml	milliliter (preferred over cc)
ML	middle lobe
M&M	morbidity and mortality
MMPI	Minnesota Multiphasic Personality Inventory
Mn	manganese
mod	moderate
mono	monocyte infectious; mononucleosis
MR	mental retardation
MS	multiple sclerosis
MSE	mental status examination
MVA	motor vehicle accident
Na	sodium
NAD	no apparent distress
neb, htd neb	nebulizer, heated nebulizer
NEC	necrotizing enterocolitis
NEO	neonatology
neph	nephrotomy
NG	nasogastric
NICU	newborn ICU
NIH	National Institutes of Health
NIMH	National Institute of Mental Health
NKA	no known allergies
NKDA	no known drug allergies
nl	normal
NLS	neurology
NMJ	neuromuscular joint
NOS	not otherwise specified
NP	nasopharyngeal
NPO	nothing by mouth
NRC	normal retinal correspondence
N/S	normal saline
NSS	neurosurgery
NT	nasotracheal
NTA	nothing to add
N_2	nitrogen
N_2O	nitrous oxide
N/V	nausea and vomiting
NVD	normal vaginal delivery
N/V/D	nausea, vomiting, diarrhea

O&P ova and parasites, stool
obs obstetrics or obstetrical
OBS organic brain syndrome
occ occasionally
OCD obsessive-compulsive disorder
OD right eye
ODD oppositional defiant disorder
odont odontectomies
OHID oxygen tent
OM otitis media
1:1 one to one
OOB out of breath; out of bed
OOP out on pass
op operation
OP oropharyngeal
OPD outpatient department
OR operating room
ORL otorhinolaryngology (ENT)
orth, ORT orthopedics
OS left eye
OT occupational therapy
O_2 oxygen
O_2sat oxygen saturation
OU both eyes

p after
P phosphorous
PA posteroanterior; pulmonary artery
PA cath pulmonary artery catheter
P&A percussion and auscultation
P&V percussion and vibration
PAP pulmonary artery pressure
p.c. after meals
PCA patient-controlled analgesia
PCO_2 partial carbon dioxide pressure
PDD pervasive developmental disorder
PE physical examination
ped, pedi, peds pediatrics
PEEP positive end-expiratory pressure
PERLA pupils equal, reactive to light and accommodation
PF plantar flexion
PFC persistent fetal circulation
PFO patent foramen ovale
PFT pulmonary function test
pg per gastric
pH hydrogen ion concentration
PH past history
PHP posthospital plans
PI present illness
PIE pulmonary interstitial emphysema
PIV peripheral intravenous
PKU phenylketonuria
PLS plastics
plts platelets
PMH past medical history
p.o. by mouth
PO_2 partial pressure oxygen
PPH persistent pulmonary hypertension
p.r. per rectum
PRBC packed red blood cells
premie premature
prep preparation
p.r.n. as needed
prot protein (total protein preferred)
PS pulmonic stenosis; pulmonary stenosis
psi pounds per square inch
PSP phenolsulfonphthalein
psy; psych psychiatry; psychology
pt patient
PT physical therapy; prothrombin time
PTMDF pupils, tension, media, disk, fundus
PTSD posttraumatic stress disorder
PUL pulmonary
PVC premature ventricular contraction
PWS Prader-Willi syndrome

q every
q.a.m. every morning
q.d. every day
q4h every 4 hours
q.h. every hour
q.h.s. every night
q.i.d. four times a day
q.n.s. quantity not sufficient
q.o.d. every other day
QR Quiet Room
qs quantity sufficient
q3h every 3 hours
q2h every 2 hours

R right
RA right atrium
RAO right anterior oblique
RBC red blood cell; red blood count
RD radial deviation
RDS respiratory distress syndrome
re regarding
REBT rational-emotive behavior therapy
REN renal/dialysis
Rh+, Rh– rhesus blood factor
RHD rheumatic heart disease
RLE right lower extremity
RLL right lower lobe
RLQ right lower quadrant

RML	right middle lobe
R/O	rule out
RPA	right pulmonary artery
RR	respiratory rate
RRE	round, regular, and equal
RT	respiratory therapy; reaction time
RTC	return to clinic
RTH	radiation therapy
RTO	return to office
RUE	right upper extremity
RUL	right upper lobe
RUQ	right upper quadrant
RV	right ventricle or ventricular
Rx	treatment; treatment with medication
s̄	without
S	suction
SAD	seasonal affective disorder
SC	subcutaneous
SCA	subclavian artery
sed. rate	erythrocyte sedimentation rate
SG	specific gravity
SH	social history; serum hepatitis
SI	suicidal ideation
SIDS	sudden infant death syndrome
SLR	straight leg raising
SOB	shortness of breath
sol	solution
SP	special precautions
S/P	status post
SPA	serum protein analysis
SS	signs and symptoms
SSRI	selective serotonin reuptake inhibitor
STAT	immediately and only once
stm	short-term memory
strep	streptococcus
sub AS	subaortic stenosis
surg	surgery or surgical
SV	single ventricle
SVC	superior vena cava
SW	social worker
Sz	seizure
TA	tricuspid atresia
tab	tablet
T&A	tonsillectomy and adenoidectomy
T&C	type and crossmatch
T&H	type and hold
TAT	Thematic Apperception Test
TB	tuberculosis
TBA	to be announced
tbsp	tablespoon
TCA	tricyclic antidepressant
TCO_2	total (calculated) carbon dioxide
TENS	transcutaneous electrical nerve stimulator
TF, TOF	tetralogy of Fallot
TGA	transposition of great arteries
TGV	transposition of great vessels
t.i.d.	three times a day
TLC	tender loving care
TM	tympanic membrane
TP	total protein
TPR	temperature, pulse, and respiration
Tq	tourniquet
TSH	thyroid stimulating hormone
tsp	teaspoon
TT	tracheostomy tube
TTX	tumor therapy
TV	tidal volume
2	secondary to
TX, Tx	treatment
U	unit
UA	urinalysis
UDT	undescended testicles
UGI	upper gastrointestinal series
umb(i)	umbilical
UO	urinary output
ureth	urethral
URI	upper respiratory infection
uro, urol	urology or urological
US	ultrasound
V, VA	volt; vision or visual acuity
vag	vagina or vaginal
VAMC	Veterans Administration Medical Center
VC	vital capacity
VCO_2	carbon dioxide production
VD	venereal disease
VDRL	Venereal Disease Research Laboratory
vert	vertebrae (D. vert: dorsal; L. vert: lumbar)
VF	volar flexion; vocal fremitus
vit	vitamin when followed by specific letter (e.g., vit A)
VO_2	oxygen consumption
VS	vital signs
Vx	vertex
W	wife
WAIS-III	Wechsler Adult Intelligence Scale-Third Edition

WB	whole blood
WBC	white blood cell; white blood count
WD	well developed
WDWN	well developed, well nourished
WISC-III	Wechsler Intelligence Scale for Children-III
wk	week
WMS	Wechsler Memory Scale
WN	well nourished
WNL	within normal limits
WRAT	Wide Range Achievement Test
wt	weight
w/u	work-up
y.o.	years old

See accompanying Web site for additional materials. 

Related Topics

Chapter 89, "Normal Medical Laboratory Values and Measurement Conversions"
Chapter 111, "Glossary of Legal Terms of Special Interest in Mental Health Practice"

140 MAJOR PROFESSIONAL ASSOCIATIONS

John C. Norcross

The following list provides the mailing addresses, telephone numbers, and Web sites of the major professional associations of interest to psychologists and other mental health professionals. The compilation is divided into three sections:

1. *Core mental health disciplines in the United States.* Psychology, psychiatry, clinical social work, mental health nursing, and marital and family therapy. For each discipline, we feature the largest professional organizations, certification/diplomate providers, and national registers.
2. *Interdisciplinary mental health organizations*
3. *Regional psychological associations in the United States*

CORE MENTAL HEALTH DISCIPLINES IN THE UNITED STATES

Psychology

American Board of Professional Psychology (ABPP)
514 East Capitol Avenue
Jefferson City, MO 65101
Phone: 573-634-7157
Web site: http://www.abpp.org

American Psychological Association (APA)
750 First Street, NE
Washington, DC 20002-4242
Phone: 800-374-2721
Web site: http://www.apa.org

American Psychological Society (APS)
1010 Vermont Avenue, NW, Suite 1100
Washington, DC 20005-4907
Phone: 202-783-2077
Web site: http://www.psychologicalscience.org

Association for the Advancement of Psychology
PO Box 38120
Colorado Springs, CO 80937
Phone: 800-869-6595
Web site: http://www.aapnet.org

National Register of Health Service Providers in Psychology
1120 G. Street, NW, Suite 330
Washington, DC 20005
Phone: 202-783-7663
Web site: http://www.nationalregister.com

Psychiatry

American Board of Psychiatry and Neurology
500 Lake Cook Road, Suite 335
Deerfield, IL 60015
Phone: 847-945-7900
Web site: http://www.abpn.com

American Psychiatric Association (ApA)
1000 Wilson Boulevard, Suite 1825
Arlington, VA 22209
Phone: 703-907-7300
Web site: http://www.psych.org

Clinical Social Work

Academy of Certified Social Workers (ACSW)
750 First Street, NE, Suite 700
Washington, DC 20002-4241
Phone: 800-742-4089, ext. 367
Web site: http://www.socialworkers.org/credentials.acsw.asp

Diplomate in Clinical Social Work
750 First Street, NE, Suite 700
Washington, DC 20002-4241
Phone: 800-742-4089
Web site: http://www.naswdc.org

National Association of Social Workers (NASW)
750 First Street, NE, Suite 700
Washington, DC 20002-4241
Phone: 202-408-8600
Web site: http://www.naswdc.org

NASW Register of Clinical Social Workers
750 First Street, NE, Suite 700
Washington, DC 20002-4241
Phone: 800-742-4089, ext. 298
Web site: http://www.naswdc.org

Mental Health Nursing

American Nurses Association (ANA)
600 Maryland Avenue, SW, Suite 100 W
Washington, DC 20024-2571
Phone: 800-274-4ANA
Web site: http://www.nursingworld.org

American Nurses Credentialing Center
600 Maryland Avenue, SW, Suite 100 W
Washington, DC 20024-2571
Phone: 202-651-7000
Web site: http://www.nursingworld.org/ancc/ancc

American Psychiatric Nurses Association
1555 Wilson Boulevard, Suite 515
Arlington, VA 22209
Phone: 703-243-2443
Web site: http://www.apna.org

Marital and Family Therapy

American Association for Marriage & Family Therapy (AAMFT)
112 South Alfred Street
Alexandria, VA 22314
Phone: 703-838-9808
Web site: http://www.aamft.org

American Family Therapy Academy
1608 20th Street, NW, 4th Floor
Washington, DC 20009
Phone: 202-333-3692
Web site: http://www.afta.org

INTERDISCIPLINARY MENTAL HEALTH ORGANIZATIONS

American Association of Sex Educators, Counselors and Therapists
PO Box 5488
Richmond, VA 23220
Phone: 315-895-8407
Web site: http://www.aasect.org/home

American Counseling Association (ACA)
5999 Stevenson Avenue
Alexandria, VA 22304
Phone: 800-347-6647
Web site: http://www.counseling.org

American Group Psychotherapy Association
25 East 21st Street, 6th Floor
New York, NY 10010
Phone: 212-477-2677
Web site: http://www.groupsinc.org

American Psychoanalytic Association
309 East 49th Street
New York, NY 10017
Phone: 212-752-0450
Web site: http://www.apsa.org/

Association for Advancement of Behavior Therapy (AABT)
305 Seventh Avenue, 16th Floor
New York, NY 10001
Phone: 212-647-1890
Web site: http://www.aabt.org

Association for Humanistic Psychology (AHP)
1516 Oak Street, 320A
Alameda, CA 94501
Phone: 510-769-6495
Web site: http://www.ahpweb.org

International Psychoanalytical Association
Broomhills, Woodside Lane
London N12 8UD
United Kingdom
Phone: 44-20-8446-8324
Web site: http://www.ipa.org.uk

Society of Behavioral Medicine (SBM)
7600 Terrace Avenue, Suite 203
Middleton, WI 53562
Phone: 608-826-7267
Web site: http://www.sbm.org

Society for the Exploration of Psychotherapy Integration (SEPI)
The Derner Institute
Adelphi University
Garden City, NY 11530
Phone: 516-877-4803
Web site: http://www.cyberpsych.org/sepi

REGIONAL PSYCHOLOGICAL ASSOCIATIONS IN THE UNITED STATES

Eastern Psychological Association
Department of Psychology
Rowan University
Glassboro, NJ 08028
Phone: 856-256-4500, ext. 3783
Web site: http://www.easternpsychological.org

Midwestern Psychological Association
Department of Psychology
DePaul University
2219 North Kenmore
Chicago, IL 60614
Phone: 773-325-4243
Web site: http://www.condor.depaul.edu/~psych/mpa/

New England Psychological Association
Department of Psychology
Johnson & Wales University
8 Abbott Place
Providence, RI 02903
Phone: 609-895-5437
Web site: http://www1.rider.edu/~brosvic/frame.html

Rocky Mountain Psychological Association
Department of Psychology
McKee 14
University of Northern Colorado
Greeley, CO 80639
Phone: 308-234-8235
Web site: http://www.rockymountainpsych.org/

Southeastern Psychological Association
Department of Psychology
University of West Florida
Pensacola, FL 32514
Phone: 850-474-2070
Web site: http://www.cas.ucf.edu/sepa/

Southwestern Psychological Association
Department of Psychology
Bethany College
421 North First Street
Lindsborg, KS 67456
Phone: 785-827-5541, ext. 1280
Web site: http://www.swpsych.org/

Western Psychological Association
5929 Westgate Boulevard, Suite C
Tacoma, WA 98406
Phone: 253-752-9829
Web site: http://www.westernpsych.org

See accompanying Web site for additional materials. 

Related Topic

Chapter 101, "National Self-Help Groups and Organizations"

INDEX

AABT (Association for Advancement of Behavior Therapy), 699
AAMD Adaptive Behavior Scale, 127–128
AAMFT (American Association for Marriage & Family Therapy), 698
Aamiry, Arwa, 401–405
AARP (American Association of Retired Persons), 507–508
Abandonment, definition, 572–573
Abbreviations, 691–697
Abdomen, examination, 52
Abdominal trauma, child abuse, 419
Abnormal physical traits, in MSE, 8
About Psychotherapy, Internet site, 491
ABPP (American Board of Professional Psychology), 697
Abrasive clients, 259
Abstinence violation effects (AVE), 352–353
Abuse. *See also* Alcohol abuse/dependence; Child abuse; Drug abuse/dependence; Sexual abuse/assault; Substance abuse/dependence
  abuse-focused therapy, 433
  common drugs, 481–487
  couples and families, 376
  multiple forms of child mistreatment, 430–431
ACA (American Counseling Association), 699
Academy of Certified Social Workers (ACSW), 698
Acceptance and Commitment Therapy (ACT), 213
ACCESS (A Comprehensive Custody Evaluation Standard System), 615–619
Accountability, patients' rights, 183
AccuCare, 671
Acculturation
  definition, 77
  ethnic minority child, 48
  linguistic measures, 77–78
  measures of, 77–79
  negative effects of acculturative stress, 77
  self-report, 78
  standardized measures, 78–79
Acculturation Rating Scale for Mexican Americans-II (ARSMA-II), 78
Accuracy, clinical judgment, 23–27
Accurate Assessments, 671
Ackerman-Schoendorf Scales for Parent Evaluation of Custody (ASPECT), 603–604
Acquired immunodeficiency syndrome. *See* AIDS
ACSW (Academy of Certified Social Workers), 698
ACT (Acceptance and Commitment Therapy), 213
ACT (American College Testing Program), 108
Action stage, 227
Activity, in MSE, 8–9
Acute stress disorder, *DSM-IV*, 42
ADAA (Anxiety Disorders Association of American), 509
Adaptation, childhood chronic illness, 406–407

Adaptive functioning tests, 127–128
ADDA (Attention Deficit Disorder Association), 509
Addition Potential Scale (APS), MMPI-2, 139
ADEAR (Alzheimer's Disease Education and Referral Center), 507
Adequate Intake (AI), 476–478
Adherence
  adult disease management, 275
  childhood chronic illness, 407–408
  enhancement, 208–211
  motivational interviewing, 270
Adjustment disorders
  DSM-IV, 42
  DSM-IV-TR classification, 89
  prevalence of, 3
Admitted carriers, professional liability insurance, 630–631
Adolescent diagnosis, *DSM-IV*, 41–44
Adolescents
  assessment, 411
  confidentiality, 412
  countertransference, 414
  empirically supported therapies, 189–190
  empowerment, 413–414
  group therapy, 413
  involving parents, 412–413
  methods to engage reluctant, 410–415
  psychological testing, 411–412
  recovery after disasters, 253
Adoption, self-help groups, 510, 512
Adult Children of Alcoholics World Services Organization, 507
Adults. *See also* Older adults
  attention-deficit/hyperactivity disorder, 62
  cognitively impaired, 342–346
  disease management, 274–278
  empirically supported therapies, 184–188
  involuntary psychiatric hospitalization, 548–550
  moderate to severe traumatic brain injury, 342–343
  neuropsychological assessment, 33–37
  older, 305–307
  recovery after disasters, 253–254
  Rorschach assessment, 174
  self-help groups, 507-508, 510, 514
  Values in Action Inventory of Strengths, 97
Advertising, ethical standards, 535–536
Aerosols, administration, effects, and interactions, 485
Affect, in MSE, 9
Affective disorders, treatment manuals, 194–195
Affidavit, definition, 573
Affinity Software Corporation, 671
African American Acculturation Scale (AAAS), 78
Age. *See also* Older adults
  pharmacotherapy, 460
  recovery after disasters, 253–254
  self-help groups, 507–508
  suicide risk, 64–65
Age equivalents, 115–116
Agency, definition, 573
Aggression, disasters, 252
Agoraphobia
  DSM-IV, 43
  empirically supported therapies, 184
Agoraphobia without panic disorder, prevalence of, 3
Agoraphobics in Motion (AIM), 507
AGS (American Guidance Service), 108
AHP (Association for Humanistic Psychology), 699
AI (Adequate Intake), 476–478
AIDS (acquired immunodeficiency syndrome), 291–292
  assessment of risk, 292–294
  burden of denial, 293
  CDC National AIDS Clearinghouse, 509
  HIV transmission, 292
  infection with HIV, 291–295
  National AIDS hotline, 295, 512
  questions for assessment, 293–294
  risk reduction counseling, 294–295
AIM (Agoraphobics in Motion), 507
Alateen and Al-Anon Family Groups, 507
Alcohol abuse/dependence. *See also* Drug abuse/dependence; Substance abuse/dependence
  administration, effects, and interactions, 483
  empirically supported therapies, 185
  identification and assessment, 71–75
  intoxication and suicidal risk, 64
  MMPI-2 scales, 138–139
  prevalence of, 3
  prevalence rates, 481
  relapse prevention, 456, 459
  self-help groups, 507, 513, 515
  treatment matching, 263–267
  withdrawal, 456, 458–459
Alcoholics Anonymous, 507
Alcohol scales, MMPI-2, 138–139
Alcohol use disorders, *DSM-IV-TR* classification, 82–83
Alcohol Use Disorders Identification Test (AUDIT), 73
Alexithymia, normative male, 278–281
Allegation, definition, 573
Alliance
  emphasis on building, 374

repairing ruptures, 216–219
ruptures, 204–205
therapeutic, 203
Alopecia areata, self-help, 512
Alternative medicines. *See* Complementary and alternative medicines (CAMs)
Alzheimer's
accuracy of clinical judgment, 24
DSM-IV-TR classification, 81
prevalence of, 3
Alzheimer's Association, 507
Alzheimer's Disease and Related Disorders Association, 507
Alzheimer's Disease Education and Referral Center (ADEAR), 507
American Association for Marriage & Family Therapy (AAMFT), 698
American Association of Retired Persons (AARP), 507–508
American Association of Sex Educators, Counselors and Therapists, 699
American Association on Mental Retardation, 507
American Board of Professional Psychology (ABPP), 697
American Board of Psychiatry and Neurology, 698
American Cancer Society, 508
American College Testing Program (ACT), 108, 115
American Council of the Blind, 508
American Counseling Association (ACA), 699
American Diabetes Association, 508
American Family Therapy Academy, 698
American Foundation for Suicide Prevention, 508
American Group Psychotherapy Association, 699
American Guidance Service (AGS), 108
American Heart Association, 508
American Lupus Society, 508
American Nurses Association (ANA), 698
American Nurses Credentialing Center, 698
American Parkinson's Disease Association, 508
American Professional Society on the Abuse of Children (APSAC) Study Guides, 416–422
American Psychiatric Association (ApA), 698
DSM-IV-TR classification, 80–90
use of Global Adaptive Functioning (GAF) scale of *DSM-IV-TR*, 91–92
American Psychiatric Nurses Association, 698
American Psychoanalytic Association, 699
American Psychological Association (APA), 697
APA Salaries in Psychology report, 665
Committee on Lesbian and Gay Concerns, 299
competence, 346–347
confronting an unethical colleague, 580
"Ethical Principles of Psychologists and Code of Conduct (2002)," 525–545, 612
guidelines for treating women, 296–297
Internet site, 491
American Psychological Society (APS), 698
American Red Cross (ARC), 249, 251
American Sleep Apnea Association, 508
American Social Health Association, 508
American Society for Deaf Children, 508
American Society on Aging, 508
American Stroke Association, 508
American Suicide Foundation, 508–509
Americans with Disability Act (ADA), 345
Amnestic disorders
DSM-IV, 44
DSM-IV-TR classification, 82
Amphetamine abuse/dependence
administration, effects, and interactions, 486
DSM-IV-TR classification, 83
prevalence of, 4
AMT (Anxiety Management Training), 271–273
ANA (American Nurses Association), 698
Anamnestic interviews, 16
Anatomically detailed dolls, 425–426
Androgyny, 303
Anesthetics, administration, effects, and interactions, 485
Anfang, Stuart A., 548–552
Anger. *See also* Violence
adult disease management, 276
Anxiety Management Training (AMT), 271–273
conflict resolution, 381, 382
disasters, 252
high-conflict couples, 379–380
Anonymous testing, human immunodeficiency virus (HIV), 294
Anorexia nervosa. *See also* Bulimia nervosa; Eating disorders
dietary supplements, 477
DSM-IV, 43
empirically supported therapies, 186
prevalence of, 4
psychopharmacology, 459
self-help group, 512, 513
Answer, definition, 573
Anticonvulsants, 457
Antidepressants, pharmacotherapy, 461–462, 469–471, 472, 473
Antihypertensives, 470
Antipsychotics, 457, 464, 471, 473, 473–474
Antisocial disorders, movie recommendations, 499
Antisocial personality disorder, prevalence of, 4
Anus, examination, 53
Anxiety
conflict resolution, 381

Anxiety (*continued*)
dietary supplements, 477
kava, 519–520
medical conditions that may present as, 448–449
Anxiety disorders
Anxiety Management Training (AMT), 271–273
disasters, 252
DSM-IV, 43
DSM-IV-TR classification, 86–87
empirically supported therapies, 184–185, 189
MACI, 164
movie recommendations, 498
pediatric pharmacotherapy, 468, 471–472
prevalence of, 4
psychopharmacology, 457–458
self-help group, 509
treatment manuals, 193–194
Anxiety Disorders Association of American (ADAA), 509
Anxiety Management Training (AMT), 271–273
Anxiolytic-related disorders, *DSM-IV-TR* classification, 84–85
Anxiolytics, 463–464
APA, 697. *See* American Psychological Association (APA)
ApA (American Psychiatric Association), 80–90, 91–92, 698
Appeal, definition, 573
Appearance, in MSE, 8
Appelbaum, Paul S., 548–552
Applied Computing Services, 671
APSAC (American Professional Society on the Abuse of Children) Study Guides, 416–422
APS (Addition Potential Scale), MMPI-2, 139
APS (American Psychological Society), 698
ARC, 509
ARSMA-II (Acculturation Rating Scale for Mexican Americans-II), 78
Arterial blood gas values, 442
ASGW (Association of Specialists in Group Work), 393
ASPECT (Ackerman-Schoendorf Scales for Parent Evaluation of Custody), 603–604
Asperger's syndrome, *DSM-IV*, 44
Assault. *See* Sexual abuse/assault
Assault, definition, 573
Assent, definition, 646
ASSESS-LIST, 605
Assessment. *See also* Interviewing; Neuropsychological (NP) assessment
adherence, 209
alcohol abuse, 71–75
behaviorally disordered children, 403
bisexuals, 299–301
borderline personality disorder, 255–256
character strengths, 93–97
child custody evaluation, 617–619
client's stage of change, 227–228
consultation, 667–668
couple and family therapy, 374
drug-use patterns, 482
drug use risks and negative consequences, 482, 487
ethical standards, 541–543
ethnic minority children using *DSM-IV-TR*, 45–49
executive dysfunction, 39–40
feigned cognitive impairment, 69–70
feigned mental disorders, 68–69
gay men, 299–301
genograms, 366–372
global, of functioning (GAF) scale, 92
height and weight, 445–447
human immunodeficiency virus (HIV), 291–295
individual functioning, 369–370
infant, 124–125
journal, 168
lesbians, 299–301
male sexual dysfunction, 282–286
malingering, 67–70
MMPI-2 profile validity, 128–132
normative male alexithymia, 279
older adults, 306
play, for children, 122–123
psychotherapy outcome, 236–239
quality of psychological testing report, 117–118
Rorschach questions and reservations, 169–172
sex offenders, 416–417
suicidal patient, 243
suicidal risk, 63–65
suicide lethality, 247
systematic, 220–222
teleassessment, 120–121
tools for relapse prevention, 351
Values in Action (VIA) strengths, 94–97
Assimilation, problematic experiences, 207
Association for Advancement of Behavior Therapy (AABT), 699
Association for Humanistic Psychology (AHP), 699
Association for Repetitive Motion Syndromes, 509
Association for the Advancement of Psychology, 698
Association of Specialists in Group Work (ASGW), 393
Association of State and Provincial Psychology Boards, 108
AtHealth, Internet site, 491–492
Attachment behavior, children, 121

Attention
in MSE, 11
neuropsychological assessment, 35
Attention-deficit disorder (ADD), children, 121–122
Attention Deficit Disorder Association (ADDA), 509
Attention-deficit/hyperactivity disorder (ADHD)
adults, 62
bibliotherapy, 62
children, 62
DSM-IV, 42, 61
empirically supported therapies, 189
evaluation, 61–62
ginseng and ginkgo biloba, 520
medical conditions that may present as, 449
parent management training, 328
pediatric psychopharmacology, 466, 467, 469–470
prenatal factors, 50
prevalence of, 4
self-help groups, 509, 510
through life span, 60–62
treatment, 62, 401–405
Attire/grooming, in MSE, 8
Attitude, in MSE, 8
Attribute by treatment interaction (ATI), 264–265
Atypical presentations, malingering, 70
AUDIT (Alcohol Use Disorders Identification Test), 73
Authorization, release forms, 647–649
Autism
Autism Society of America, 509
children, 122
DSM-IV, 44
pediatric pharmacotherapy, 469
prevalence of, 4
Autobiographies, 351, 496
Automatic movements, in MSE, 8–9
AVE (abstinence violation effects), 352–353
Aversion to sex, 290–291
Avoidant personality disorder
empirically supported therapies, 188
prevalence of, 4
psychopharmacology, 456, 458

Back F ($F_{(B)}$) Scale, MMPI-2, 130, 131
BADS (Behavioral Assessment of the Dysexecutive Syndrome), 40
Baker, Jeannie, 416–422
Baker, Robert W., 7–12
Bartering, 660
Base rates of behaviors, 14–15
Batterers Anonymous, 509
Battery, definition, 573
Beaver Creek Software, 671
Beck System, 166
Behavioral Assessment of the Dysexecutive Syndrome (BADS), 40
Behavioral disorders. *See also* Developmental disorders
DSM-IV, 42
laboratory tests and indications, 53
medical evaluation of children with, 50–54
parent management training for childhood, 327–331
treatment, 401–405
Behavioral indicators, sexually abused children, 424
Behavioral observation, neuropsychological assessment, 34
Behavioral referents, interviewing, 14
Behaviors, Multimodal Life History Inventory, 19, 22
Belanoff, Joseph K., 454–459
Bender Visual Motor Gestalt Test-Second Edition, 126
Beneficence, 528–529
Bennett, Bruce E.
professional liability insurance, 625–631
psychotherapist-patient contract, 635–640
Bennett, Jason M., 640–645
Benzodiazepines, 463–464, 472, 482, 483
Bereavement, suicide risk, 65
Bernstein, Jane Holmes, 28–32
Beutler, Larry E., 220–225
Biases in interviewing, 15
Bibliotherapy, 62, 387, 494–496
Bicultural Involvement Scale, 78
Biedenharn, Paula J., 517–521
Biederman, Joseph, 466–476
Bilateral listening, 383
Billable hours, 668
Billing
basic principles, 657–658
collection, 658, 660
consultation, 668–669
controversy, 660–661
important don'ts, 659–660
issues, 657–661
managed care organizations, 656
psychotherapist-patient contract, 637
third-party relationships, 658–659
utilization rate, 668
Binge-eating disorder, empirically supported therapies, 186. *See also* Eating disorders
Biological factors, Multimodal Life History Inventory, 22, 23

Bipolar disorders
  DSM-IV-TR classification, 86
  empirically supported therapies, 186
  pediatric pharmacotherapy, 467–468, 471
  prevalence of, 4
  psychopharmacology, 455, 457
  treatment manuals, 194
Bisexuals, 299–303, 510–511
Bishop, Matthew, 192–202
Black cohosh, 520
Blind, self-help group, 508
Blood injury phobia, empirically supported therapies, 184
Blumenthal Software, 671–672
BMI (body mass index), 52, 445–447
Body disapproval, MACI, 163
Body mass index (BMI), 52, 445–447
Body part or function disorders, *DSM-IV*, 43–44
Bongar, Bruce, 240–245
Bootzin, Richard R., 325–327
Borderline character of childhood Axis II, *DSM-IV*, 44
Borderline personality disorder
  assessment, 255–256
  empirically supported therapies, 188
  MACI, 163
  prevalence of, 4
  psychopharmacology, 456, 458
  treatment, 255–257
Borum, Randy, 603–607
Boundaries, clients' rights, 181–182
BPD. *See* Borderline personality disorder
BPS (Bricklin Perceptual Scales), 604
Brain injury. *See* Traumatic brain injury (TBI)
Brain Injury Association Family Helpline, 509
Brazelton Neonatal Behavioral Scale (NBAS), 124
Breast cancer, self-help group, 516
Breastfeeding mothers, La Leche League, 511
Bricklin, Barry, 615–619
Bricklin Perceptual Scales (BPS), 604
Brief Acculturation Scale for Hispanics, 78
Brief Situational Confidence Questionnaire (BSCQ), 73
Brodsky, Stanley L.
  forensic evaluations and testimony, 591–593
  psychotherapy with reluctant and involuntary clients, 257–262
Brown, Laura S., 295–298
BSCQ (Brief Situational Confidence Questionnaire), 73
Buhrke, Robin A., 299–304
Bulimia nervosa. *See also* Anorexia nervosa; Eating disorders
  dietary supplements, 477
  DSM-IV, 43
  empirically supported therapies, 186
  pharmacotherapy, 456, 459
  prevalence of, 4
  self-help group, 512, 513
Bupropion, 456, 462, 479
Burden of denial, AIDS, 293
Burlingame, Gary M., 393–398
Burns, child abuse, 420
Burying deductible, 659
Buspirone, 464
Butcher, James N.
assessing MMPI-2 profile validity, 128–132
empirical interpretation of MMPI-2 codetypes, 149–153
Bybee, Taige, 192–202

Caffeine-related disorders, *DSM-IV-TR* classification, 83
CAI (Competency Assessment Instrument), 608, 610–611
Calzada, Esther J., 401–405
Cancer
  children, 51
  self-help groups, 508, 509, 516
Cancer Care, 509
Candlelighters Childhood Cancer Foundation, 509
Cannabis-related disorders, *DSM-IV-TR* classification, 83
Cannot Say Score, MMPI-2, 128–129, 131
Cantor, Dorothy W., 181–183
CAPS (Clinician-Administered PTSD Scale), 14
Carbamazepine, 457, 463, 479
Carey, Michael P., 291–295
Carpal tunnel syndrome, self-help, 509
Causation, definition, 573
Cause of action, definition, 573
CDC National AIDS Clearinghouse, 509
Center Psych, 672
Centers for Medicare & Medicaid Services (CMS), standards for restraint and seclusion, 554, 556
Central nervous system (CNS), 29
Cerebral palsy, self-help group, 516
Cerebral spinal fluid lab values, 443
CFIDS Association, 509
CHADD (Children and Adults with Attention-Deficit/Hyperactivity Disorder), 510
Chambless, Dianne L., 183–192
Chamomile, 520
Change
  client motivation, 270
  concrete changes, 261
  mechanisms of, for female sex therapy, 287–291
  mechanisms of, for male sex therapy, 283–286

motivational interviewing, 269
prescriptive guidelines, 227–231
readiness in alcohol abusers, 73, 75
stages of, 206, 226–231
substance abuse, 266
Character strengths, assessment, 93–97
Chemical abuse/dependence, empirically supported therapies, 185
Chemical vasodilators, 285
Chemotherapy side effects, empirically supported therapies, 186
Chenneville, Tiffany, 584–588
Chest examination, 52
Chest injuries, child abuse, 420
Child abuse. *See also* Sexual abuse/assault
MACI, 163
physical, 419–421
questioning children, 428
self-help groups, 509, 515, 516
sexual, 417–422
treatment of sexual abuse, 430–435
Child behavior observations, 119–123, 376–377
Child custody, 603–605, 615–619
Child diagnosis, *DSM-IV*, 41–44
Child-directed interaction (CDI), 330–331
Child Help USA Hotline, 509
Child heritage, 30
Childhood adolescent disorders, treatment manuals, 195
Childhood behavioral disorders, parent management training, 327–331
Childhood disorders, movie recommendations, 500–501
Childhood schizophrenia, *DSM-IV*, 44
Children. *See also* Ethnic minorities; Neuropsychological (NP) assessment
assessment of sexual offenders, 416–417
assumptions of neuropsychological assessment, 28
attention-deficit/hyperactivity disorder (ADHD), 60–62
childhood behavior disorders, 330
disclosure of abuse, 425
empirically supported therapies, 189–190
interviewing sexually abused, 423–430
interview outline, 427–429
involuntary psychiatric hospitalization, 550–551
medical evaluation of, with behavioral or developmental disorders, 50–54
medical lab values, 444
memories, 424–425
pain management for chronic illness, 408
parent management training, 327–331
pediatric psychopharmacology, 466–474
physical abuse, 419–421
recovery after disasters, 253
reliability of information, 424
Rorschach assessment, 174
self-help groups, 507, 508, 509, 510, 513, 516
sexual abuse, 417–422
sexually transmitted diseases (STDs), 422
suggestibility, 426
treatment of behavioral disorders, 401–405
treatment of sexual abuse, 430–435
Children and Adults with Attention-Deficit/Hyperactivity Disorder (CHADD), 510
Children's Health Act, restraint and seclusion, 553–554
Child therapy, termination, 358–359
Chromosome determination, children, 54
Chronic fatigue and immune dysfunction syndrome (CFIDS), 509
Chronic illness, psychological interventions in childhood, 406–409
Chronic pain
empirically supported therapies, 186, 189
medical conditions that may present as pelvic, 451
self-help group, 513
Chronic renal disease, children, 51
Chronic severe illnesses, children, 51
CIDI (Composite International Diagnostic Interview), 14
Civil action, definition, 573
Civil commitment, 548–551
Clarkin, John F.
borderline personality disorder, 255–257
choice of treatment format, 363–365
Clients
clinical supervision, 682–685
early termination and referral, 346–349
inviting hypnosis and relaxation, 333–337
litigious, 260
Privacy Rule, 640–645
problem members in psychoeducational groups, 396
psychotherapy with reluctant and involuntary, 257–262
reactions to termination, 355–357
religiously committed, 338–341
reluctant, 257–262
right to refuse treatment, 258
self-help groups, 502–506
sexual involvement between therapist and, 532, 533, 538, 544
signs for relapse prevention, 352
top Internet sites, 491–494
Clinical abbreviations and symbols, 691–697

Clinical geropsychology, 307
Clinical interviewing, 13–15. *See also* Interviewing
Clinical issues, commitment, 551
Clinical judgment, accuracy, 23–27
Clinical method, neuropsychological assessment, 34–37
Clinical psychologists, widely used tests, 101–102
Clinical scales
  high and low scores on MMPI-2, 141–148
  MMPI-2, 132–136
Clinical social work, 698
Clinical supervision, 682–685
Clinical syndromes, MACI, 160, 164
Clinical utility, Rorschach assessment, 176–177
Clinician-Administered PTSD Scale (CAPS), 14
Clonidine, 473
Clozapine, 464, 479
Club drugs, administration, effects, and interactions, 484
CNS (central nervous system), 29
CNS depressants, administration, effects, and interactions, 483
Cocaine
  administration, effects, and interactions, 486
  Cocaine Anonymous, 510
  empirically supported therapies, 185
  prevalence rates, 481
Cocaine-related disorders, *DSM-IV-TR* classification, 83
Code of conduct, 525–545
Codependents of Sex Addicts (COSA), 510
Codetypes of MMPI-2, 149–152
Cognition, in MSE, 11–12
Cognitions, restructuring, 679
Cognitive-behavioral treatment, substance abuse, 263
Cognitive behavior therapy (CBT), 212
Cognitive processes, executive dysfunction, 38
Cognitive therapy, substance abuse, 263
Colitis, self-help group, 510
Collaboration
  psychotherapy, 204
  psychotherapy homework compliance, 323
Collaborative interview style, 13
Collection, bill, 658, 660
The College Board, 108
Coming out process, 301–303
Commitment, clinical issues, 551
Commitment, involuntary outpatient, 550
Common Alcohol Logistic (CAL) scale, MMPI-2, 139
Common law, definition, 573
Communicating findings, neuropsychological assessment, 31–32
Communication
  high-conflict couples, 382–383
  neuropsychological assessment, 31–32
Communication disorders, *DSM-IV-TR* classification, 81
Community reinforcement approach, substance abuse, 264
Community resources, suicidal patient, 244
Comorbidity
  alcohol abuse, 73, 74
  drug problems, 74–75
  substance use disorders, 487
Comparative negligence, definition, 573
Compassionate Friends, 510
Compassion fatigue, 349
Compensatory damages, definition, 573
Competence
  clinical supervision, 684
  ethical standard, 530–531
  informed consent, 645
Competency Assessment Instrument (CAI), 608, 610–611
Competency Screening Test (CST), 608–610
Competency to stand trial, evaluation, 607–611
Competing behaviors, 328
Complaint, definition, 573
Complementary and alternative medicines (CAMs)
  cautions for herbal CAMs, 517–518
  ginkgo biloba for memory, 518–519
  ginseng for well–being, 519
  kava for anxiety, 519–520
  St. John's wort for depression, 518
  valerian for sleep, 520
Complexity
  assessment, 221
  treatment matching, 223–224
Compliance, 208. *See also* Adherence
  Privacy Rule, 644–645
  psychotherapy homework, 319–324
Composite International Diagnostic Interview (CIDI), 14
Comprehension
  in MSE, 10
  questions in interview, 14
Comprehensive Assessment-to-Intervention System (CAIS), 55, 57–59
A Comprehensive Custody Evaluation Standard System (ACCESS), 615–619
Comprehensive intervention, impaired psychologist, 623
Comprehensive System (CS) norms, caution, 169–170
Compulsions, in MSE, 9

Computed tomography (CT), children, 54
Computerized billing, 670–671
Concentration
  in MSE, 11
  neuropsychological assessment, 35
Concerned United Birthparents (CUB), 510
Conduct disorder
  DSM-IV, 42
  empirically supported therapies, 189
  family therapy, 377
  parent management training, 328
  pharmacotherapy, 467
  prevalence of, 4
  treatment, 401–405
Confidentiality
  adolescents, 412
  breaching, 546–547, 612, 613
  clinical recommendations, 586–588
  couple and family therapy, 374
  definition, 546, 584
  duty to protect and, 584–588
  ethical standards, 534–535
  HIV testing, 294
  marital infidelity, 385–386
  media, 688
  patient right, 181
  peer monitoring, 580
  psychotherapist-patient contract, 639–640
  sexually abused children, 423–424
Confidential testing, human immunodeficiency virus (HIV), 294
Conflict of interest, ethics, 532
Conflict resolution, couples, 381, 382
Conflicts and personal problems, 531
Conforming, MACI, 163
Confrontation of unethical colleague, 579–583
Confrontive intervention, impaired psychologist, 623
Congenital heart disease, children, 51
Congruence, psychotherapy, 204
Connectedness, in MSE, 10
Consciousness level, in MSE, 8
Consciousness raising, 229
Consent. *See also* Informed consent
  basic elements, 645–646
  definition, 573, 646
  Privacy Rule, 643
Consultation
  agreement, 666–669
  suicidal patient, 243
Consulting Psychologists Press, 108
Contemplation stage, 226–227
Contempt, divorce risk, 376
Contingency management, 229
Contract, psychotherapist-patient, 635–640
Contracting managed care organizations, 653–657
Contraindications, couple therapy, 380
Contributory negligence, definition, 573
Control and inhibition, MMPI-2, 138
Cooperation, crisis intervention, 248
Cooperativeness, in MSE, 8
Co-payment, ignoring, 659
Coping skills
  adult disease management, 275
  relapse prevention, 351–352
Coping styles, assessment, 222
Core concerns, high-conflict couples, 382
Cornucopia Software, 672
Correia, Christopher J., 481–487
COSA (Codependents of Sex Addicts), 510
Counseling, risk reduction for human immunodeficiency virus (HIV), 294–295
Counseling psychologists, widely used tests, 101–102
Counterconditioning, 229
Countertransference, 205, 347–348, 414
Couples therapy
  bibliotherapy, 387
  communication, 382–383
  confidentiality, 374
  conflict levels, 379–380
  conjoint, 376
  contraindications, 380
  ethical standards, 543–545
  guidelines for conducting, 373–378
  marital infidelity, 384–387
  selection criteria, 364
  substance abuse, 264
  termination, 383
  treating high-conflict couples, 378–383
Courage, Values in Action (VIA) classification, 96
Court-mandated treatment, substance abuse, 264
Court order and subpoena, 570–571
Courtroom, expert testimony in deposition vs., 599–602
Covered transactions, Privacy Rule, 641–642
Creativity, therapist self-care checklist, 681
Criminals. *See* Forensic matters; Reluctant and involuntary clients; Sex offenders
Crisis characteristics, 246
Crisis intervention
  adult disease management, 275–276
  disasters, 251
  guidelines, 245–249
Crisis reduction counseling, 251
Criticism, divorce risk, 376
Crohn's & Colitis Foundation of America, 510
CST (Competency Screening Test), 608–610

CTB/McGraw-Hill, 108–109
CUB (Concerned United Birthparents), 510
Cult Awareness Network, 510
Cultural history, family, 369
Culture, definition, 46. *See also* Ethnic minorities
Curtis, Rebecca C., 354–359
Customizing therapy, 206–207
Cyclothymia, *DSM-IV*, 43
Cyclothymic disorder, prevalence of, 4
Cytomegalovirus (CMV), 50–51

DAFS (Direct Assessment of Functional Status), 605
Damages, definition, 573
Dangerousness, crisis intervention, 248
Dangerousness criteria
  breaching confidentiality, 546
  involuntary psychiatric hospitalization, 548–549, 551
Dangerous patients, 612–614
Daubert v. Merrell Dow Pharmaceuticals, Inc., 602
Deaf, self-help groups, 508, 512
DeBattista, Charles, 454–459
Debiasing strategies, 15
Debriefing, disasters, 251
Debt collection, 658, 660
Debtors Anonymous, 510
Decisional Balance Exercise, 73
Deductible, burying, 659
Defamation, definition, 573
Defendant, definition, 573
Defense mechanism, in MSE, 12
Defensiveness, divorce risk, 376
Defusing, disasters, 251
Delinquent predisposition, MACI, 164
Delirium
  DSM-IV-TR classification, 81
  medical conditions that may present as, 452–453
  prevalence of, 4
Delphi/PBS, 672
Delusional disorders
  movie recommendations, 501
  prevalence of, 4
Delusions, in MSE, 10
Dementia
  DSM-IV-TR classification, 81–82
  empirically supported therapies, 188
  medical conditions that may present as, 453
  prevalence of, 4
  psychopharmacology, 456
Department of Health and Human Services (HHS), Privacy Rule, 644–645
Depersonalization disorder, *DSM-IV*, 44
Deposition, definition, 573
Depositions, 591–592, 599–602
Depression
  Anxiety Management Training (AMT), 272
  atypical, 456
  conflict resolution, 381
  dietary supplements, 477
  disasters, 252
  DSM-IV, 43
  empirically supported therapies, 186, 189
  interpretation of high scores, 143
  MACI, 164
  medical conditions that may present as, 449–450
  MMPI-2 codetype, 151–152
  movie recommendations, 498–499
  pediatric pharmacotherapy, 467, 470–471
  psychotic, 456–457
  St. John's wort, 518
  Scale 2 of MMPI-2, 133
  screen, 210–211
  self-help groups, 512, 513
  suicide risk, 64
  treatment manuals, 194–195
Depressive disorders, *DSM-IV-TR* classification, 86
Designer drugs, administration, effects, and interactions, 484
Developmental disorders. *See also* Behavioral disorders
  laboratory tests and indications, 53
  medical evaluation of children with, 50–54
  pediatric pharmacotherapy, 468–469
Developmental neuropsychological assessment, 28–32
Diabetes
  Anxiety Management Training (AMT), 272
  self-help group, 508
Diagnosis
  DSM-IV, 41–44
  high-conflict couples, 379
  mental health records, 650
  neuropsychological assessment, 36–37
  older adults, 305
  treatment plan writing, 235
  utilization review checklist, 652–653
Diagnostic and Statistical Manual of Mental Disorders, 4th edition. See *DSM-IV*
Diagnostic and clinical interviewing, 13–15. *See also* Interviewing
Diagnostic strategy, neuropsychological assessment, 29–30
DiClemente, Carlo C.
  stages of change, 226–231
  treatment matching in substance abuse, 263–267
Dietary supplements, 476–478

Digestive listening, 383
Dignity, 529
DiMatteo, M. Robin, 208–212
Dimethyltrypyamine, administration, effects, and interactions, 485
Diplomate in Clinical Social Work, 698
Direct Assessment of Functional Status (DAFS), 605
Directed verdict, definition, 573–574
Direct observation, children, 119–120
Directory of Unpublished Experimental Mental Measures, 106
Disabilities, self-help groups, 511, 513
Disaster Response Network, 249–250
Disasters
  age-related issues, 253–254
  common mental health problems after, 252
  context of evaluation and intervention, 250
  crisis intervention, 251
  crisis reduction counseling, 251
  debriefing and defusing, 251
  elements of traumatic exposure, 250
  factors influencing recovery, 252–253
  impact, 249–254
  impact and short-term adaptation phases, 250–251
  long-term adaptation phase, 251–254
  predisaster planning, 249–250
  psychological first aid, 250–251
Disclosure, patients' rights, 182–183
Disconfirmation strategy, 15
Disconnection disorders, *DSM-IV*, 44
Discovery
  definition, 574
  extramarital involvement, 385–387
Discrepancy, motivational interviewing, 268
Dissociative anesthetics, administration, effects, and interactions, 484
Dissociative disorders, *DSM-IV-TR* classification, 87
Dissociative fugue, prevalence of, 4
Dissociative identity disorders
  DSM-IV, 44
  movie recommendations, 498
  prevalence of, 4
  treatment manuals, 196
Distress
  assessment, 221
  treatment matching, 223–225
Diversity, therapist self-care checklist, 681
Divorce, couples therapy, 376
Dizziness, medical conditions that may present as, 452
DNA testing, children, 54
Documentation
  suicidal patient, 243
  treatment planning, 232, 233
Document production, subpoena, 571–572
DocuTrac, 672
Dolefulness, MACI, 162
Dolls, anatomically detailed, 425–426
Domestic violence, self-help, 509, 510, 513
Dopamine receptor antagonists, 457
Dopamine/serotonoin receptor antagonists, 457
Dorado, Joyce S., 423–430
Down syndrome, self-help group, 513
Dramatic relief, 229
Dramatizing, MACI, 162
Drug abuse/dependence
  administration, effects, and interactions, 483–486
  assessment considerations, 482, 487
  common drugs of abuse, 481–487
  comorbidity, 74–75, 487
  drugs of abuse, 481, 482
  drug-use patterns, 482
  prevalence of, 4
  prevalence of drug use, 481–482
  risks and negative consequences, 482, 487
  self-help groups, 510, 512, 513, 515
  treatment matching, 263–267
Drug Abuse Screening Test (DAST–10), 73
DrugDigest, Internet site, 492
Drug scales, MMPI-2, 138–139
Drug use, prevalence, 481–482
Drug Use History Questionnaire (DUHQ), 73
DSM-IV (Diagnostic and Statistical Manual of Mental Disorders, 4th edition)
  child and adolescent diagnosis, 41–44
  lifetime prevalence of mental disorders, 3–6
  multiaxial system, 80–90, 90
  Structured Clinical Interview, 14
Due process, definition, 574
DUHQ (Drug Use History Questionnaire), 73
Dusky v. United States, 608
Duty to protect, confidentiality and, 584–588
Dyscontrol and dysinhibition scales, MMPI-2, 138
Dysmenorrhea, Anxiety Management Training (AMT), 272
Dyspareunia, 290
Dysthymia, 457
Dysthymic disorder
  DSM-IV, 43
  prevalence of, 4

Ear examination, 52
Eastern Psychological Association, 699

Eating disorders. *See also* Anorexia nervosa; Bulimina nervosa
dietary supplements, 477
DSM-IV-TR classification, 81, 88
Food Addicts Anonymous, 511
MACI, 164
pharmacotherapy, 459
self-help groups, 511, 512, 513, 514
treatment manuals, 196
ECA (Epidemiological Catchment Area), 3–6
Ecstasy, 484
ECT (electroconvulsive therapy), 456
Edelstein, Sari
dietary supplements and psychological functioning, 476–480
height and weight assessment, 445–447
EdITS (Educational & Industrial Testing Service), 109
Education
ethical standards, 537–538
neuropsychological assessment, 32
Educational & Industrial Testing Service (EdITS), 109
Educational Testing Service (ETS), 109
Education and training programs
Anxiety Management Training (AMT), 271–273
parent management training (PMT), 327–328
refusal skills training (RST), 308–311
EEG (electroencephalography), children, 54
Efficacy, motivational interviewing, 270
Egocentricity Index, 174
Egotism, MACI, 162
Electroconvulsive therapy (ECT), 456
Electroencephalography (EEG), children, 54
Electronic listings, psychological tests, 105
Elimination disorders, *DSM-IV-TR* classification, 81
Ellis, Albert, 212–215
Emergencies, older adults, 306
Emergency mental health intervention, 245–246
EMI (extramarital involvement), 384–385
Emotion, neuropsychological assessment, 36
Emotional arousal, 229
Emotions, normative male alexithymia, 278–281
Emotions Anonymous, 510
Empathy
interviewing alcohol abusers, 72
motivational interviewing, 268
psychotherapy, 204
Empirically supported therapies
adults, 184–188
children and adolescents, 189–190
comparison, 190
reactions, 190–191
Empowerment, adolescents, 413–414
EMS (extramarital sex), 384
Encopresis
DSM-IV, 43
empirically supported therapies, 189
prevalence of, 4
Endocrinology lab values, 442–443
Enforcement, Privacy Rule, 644–645
Entactogens, administration, effects, and interactions, 484
Enuresis
DSM-IV, 43
empirically supported therapies, 189
pediatric pharmacotherapy, 468
prevalence of, 4
Epidemiological Catchment Area (ECA), 3–6
Epilepsy Foundation, 510
Erectile failure, 284–285
Ethical issues
advertising and public statements, 535–536
APA "Ethical Principles of Psychologists and Code of Conduct (2002)," 525–545, 612
assessment, 541–543
bill collection, 658
breaching confidentiality, 546–547
child sexual abuse, 434
clinical supervision, 684
competence, 530–531
confronting an unethical colleague, 579–583
education and training, 537–538
fees, 536–537
human relations, 532–534
money matters and, 577–579
physical restraint and seclusion, 553–557
privacy, confidentiality, and privilege, 545–547
privacy and confidentiality, 534–535
psychoeducational groups, 396
record keeping, 536–537
research and publication, 538–541
resolution, 529–530
sexual involvement between therapist and client, 532, 533, 538, 544, 620–621, 627–628
therapy, 543–545
Ethics issues, dealing with ethics complaints, 566–569
Ethnic history, family, 369
Ethnicity, pharmacotherapy, 460
Ethnic minorities
acculturation, 48
assessment of minority children using *DSM-IV-TR*, 45–49
treatment planning for children, 47–49
ETS (Educational Testing Service), 109
Evaluation
attention-deficit/hyperactivity disorder (ADHD), 61–62

disasters, 250
suicidal patient, 243
Exclusive dealing, managed care organizations, 655
Executive dysfunction
assessment, 39–40
cognitive processes, 38
common disorders, 39
intervention, 40
Executive functions
description, 38
in MSE, 12
neuropsychological assessment, 36
Expectations, customizing therapy, 206–207
Experience, witnesses, 592
Expert testimony, 591–593, 599–602
Expert witness, definition, 574
Express consent, definition, 573
Expressed concerns, MACI, 160, 163
Externalization
coping style, 222
treatment matching, 224–225
Externally induced disorders, *DSM-IV*, 44
Extramarital involvement (EMI), 384–385
Extramarital sex (EMS), 384
Extremities, examination, 53
Eyberg, Sheila M.
behaviorally disordered children, 401–405
parent management training for childhood behavior disorders, 327–332
Eye contact, in MSE, 8
Eye examination, 52
Eye injuries, child abuse, 421

Facial injuries, child abuse, 420
Factitious disorders, *DSM-IV-TR* classification, 87
Failure to thrive, medical conditions that may present as, 451–452
FAIs (forensic assessment instruments), 603–607
False allegations, sexual abuse, 418–419, 426
Family
resistance to doing genogram, 369
social context of older adults, 306
Family discord, MACI, 163
Family history, children, 51–52
Family information, genograms, 366–369, 372
Family interaction patterns, genogram format, 372
Family involvement, adult disease management, 276
Family Pride Coalition, 510–511
Family therapy
billing, 659
confidentiality, 374
ethical standards, 543–545
guidelines for conducting, 373–378
musical chairs, 659
play genograms, 371
professional associations, 698
selection criteria, 364
self-help groups, 510–516
substance abuse, 264
Fatigue, chronic, 509
Fatigue, medical conditions that may present as, 450
Faust, David, 23–27
$F_{(B)}$ or Back F Scale, MMPI-2, 130, 131
Fears
death, 276
psychotherapy, 338
Feedback
clinical supervision, 684
neuropsychological assessment, 37
psychotherapy, 204
Feeding disorders, *DSM-IV-TR* classification, 81
Feelings, Multimodal Life History Inventory, 19–20, 22
Fees. *See also* Billing
consultation, 668–669
debt collection situations, 579, 658, 660
ethical standards, 536–537
forensic testimony, 597
missed appointments, 578, 660
pro bono services, 577
psychotherapist-patient contract, 637
psychotherapy, 662–663
therapy, 577–579
Fee splitting, 578, 661
Feigned cognitive impairment, assessment, 69–70
Feigned mental disorders, assessment, 68–69
Females. *See also* Gender issues
guidelines for treating, 295–298
guidelines for treating women, 295–298
National Organization for Women, 513–514
medical conditions that may present as chronic pelvic pain, 451
sexual dysfunction, 286–291
Fetal alcohol syndrome, self-help, 513
Fetal causes, intrauterine growth retardation, 51
Fidelity, 529
Films, clinical benefits, 497–498
First-generation antipsychotics (FGAs), 464
F-K Index of MMPI, 130–131
Flemons, Douglas, 332–337
Flexibility, executive dysfunction, 40
Floor effect, malingering, 69
Fluency, in MSE, 9–10
Fluoxetine, 454, 455, 479
Foelsch, Pamela A., 255–257
Food Addicts Anonymous, 511
Forcefulness, MACI, 163
Forensic assessment instruments (FAIs), 603–607

Forensic examination, sexually assaulted child, 422
Forensic matters. *See also* Legal issues
  child custody and parental capacity, 603–605, 615–619
  clinical decision making with dangerous patients, 612–614
  competency to stand trial evaluation, 607–611
  criminal forensic evaluations, 603
  expert testimony in depositions, 599–602
  forensic assessment instruments, 603–607
  forensic evaluation outline, 593–595
  forensic evaluations and testimony, 591–593
  forensic referrals checklist, 595–598
  guardianship, 605
  professional liability insurance, 625–631
  recognizing, assisting, and reporting impaired psychologist, 620–624
  treatment manuals, 196
  violence risk assessment, 605–606
Forensic psychologists, widely used tests, 101–102
Foundation Center, Internet site, 492
$F_{(P)}$ (Psychopathology Infrequency Scale), MMPI-2, 130, 131
Fractures, child abuse, 420
France, Kenneth, 245–249
Fraud, billing, 659
Fraud, definition, 574
Friedland, Lilli, 686–691
Friends for Survival, 511
F Scale, MMPI-2, 129–130, 131
Functional impairment, psychotherapy, 206
Future editions, 701

GAD. *See* Generalized anxiety disorder
Gabapentin, 463
Gam-Anon Family Groups, 511
Gamblers Anonymous, 511
Garb, Howard N., 169–172
Gases, administration, effects, and interactions, 485
Gatz, Margaret, 305–307
Gault, In re, 550
Gay men, 299–303, 510–511
Gender identity disorders
  DSM-IV-TR classification, 88
  movie recommendations, 500
  prevalence of, 4
Gender issues. *See also* Females; Males
  guidelines for treating women, 295–298
  normative male alexithymia, 278–281
  psychotherapy models, 297
  suicide risk, 64
Generalized anxiety disorder
  Anxiety Management Training (AMT), 272
  empirically supported therapies, 184
  prevalence of, 4
  psychopharmacology, 455, 458
Generalized emotional distress scales, MMPI-2, 137
Genitalia and anus, examination, 53
Genograms
  assessment tool, 366, 372, 375
  dealing with family resistance to, 369
  difficult questions about individual functioning, 369–370
  ethnic and cultural history, 369
  family information net, 366–369
  format, 372
  index person (IP), 366
  mapping, for those in multiple settings, 370–371
  Ortiz-Brown family, 367
  play, for individual child and family therapy, 371
  setting priorities for organizing, 370
  standard symbols, 368
Geriatric anxiety, empirically supported therapies, 185
Geriatric depression, empirically supported therapies, 186
Geropsychology, 307
Ginger, 520
Ginkgo biloba
  ginseng and, for ADHD children, 520
  memory, 518–519
Ginseng
  ginkgo biloba and, for ADHD children, 520
  well-being, 519
Gioia, Gerard A., 38–41
Global, lifelong inorgasmia, 287–288
Global assessment of functioning (GAF) scale, *DSM-IV-TR*, 91–92
Glossary of legal terms, 572–576
Goal consensus, psychotherapy, 204
Goal development, treatment plan writing, 234
Goal-setting, executive dysfunction, 40
Godinez v. Moran, 608
Goldhaber, Samuel Z., 439–444
Goldman, Stuart M., 41–45
Gonzalez, Juan Carlos, 77–80
Goodheart, Carol D., 274–278
Goodman Lock Box, 122
Gordon, Betty N., 55–60
Grade equivalents (GE), 115–116
Graf, Thomas P., 553–557
Graham, John R.
  clinical scales of MMPI-2, 132–136
  high and low scores on MMPI-2 clinical scales, 141–149
Greene, Roger L.,137–141
GRE scores, 112, 114

Grohol, John M., 491–494
Grooming/attire, in MSE, 8
Grossman, Seth D.
  Millon Adolescent Clinical Inventory (MACI), 159–165
  Millon Clinical Multiaxial Inventory (MCMI–III), 153–159
Group conversation method, 261
Group dynamics, psychoeducational groups, 395–396
Group psychotherapy. *See also* Psychoeducational groups (PEGs); Psychotherapy
  applications, 388
  cohesion, 203–204
  common errors, 390–391
  issue-focused groups, 392
  mandatory, 538
  obstacles to forming and starting groups, 391–392
  refusal skills training (RST), 311
  selection criteria, 364
  self-help groups, 502–506
  substance abuse, 263
  tasks of therapist, 389–390
  theory, 388–389
Growth, therapist self-care checklist, 681
Guardian, definition, 574
Guardian ad litem, definition, 574
Guardianship, 605
Guidelines for Psychological Practice with Girls and Women, 296
Gustafson, Kathryn E., 406–409
Guy, James D., Jr., 677–682

Habits, 461
Haldeman, Douglas C., 299–304
Hallucinations, in MSE, 11
Hallucinogen-related disorders
DSM-IV-TR classification, 83–84
Hallucinogens
  administration, effects, and interactions, 485
  prevalence rates, 481
Hall v. Clifton Precision, 602
Harassment, 532
Harcourt Educational Measurement, 109
Hard of hearing people, self-help group, 515
Harris, Eric A.
  managed care organizations, 653–657
  psychotherapist-patient contract, 635–640
Harvard University Press, 109
Hashish
  administration, effects, and interactions, 483
  prevalence rates, 481
HCR–20, 605–606
Headaches
  empirically supported therapies, 186, 190
  self-help group, 513
Head circumference, 52
Head injuries, child abuse, 421
HEADSSS Psychosocial Interview, 52
Healthfinder, Internet site, 492
Health insurance, right to know, 182–183
Health Insurance Portability and Accountability Act of 1996 (HIPAA)
  computerized billing, 670
  legal notifications, 650
  Privacy Rule, 640–645
Health problems, empirically supported therapies, 186–187
Health status, suicide risk, 65
Hearing testing, children, 53
Heart, self-help, 508
Height, assessment tools, 445–446
Heitler, Susan, 378–384
Hematology lab values, 441–442
Herbal treatments, 517–521
Herbold, Nancie H.
  dietary supplements and psychological functioning, 476–480
  height and weight assessment, 445–447
Heritage, child, 30
Heroin
  administration, effects, and interactions, 486
  prevalence rates, 481
HHS (Department of Health and Human Services), Privacy Rule, 644–645
High-conflict couples, 378–383
Hill, Clara E., 202–208
Hill, Sam S., III
  APSAC Study Guides, 416–422
  children's psychological development, 124–128
  future editions, 701
  money matters and ethical issues, 577–579
Hill-Briggs, Felicia, 342–346
HIPAA (Health Insurance Portability and Accountability Act of 1996), Privacy Rule, 640–645
Hippocratic Oath, confidentiality, 585–586
The Hiskey-Nebraska Test of Learning Aptitude, 127
History
  medical history of children with behavioral or developmental disorders, 50–52
  neuropsychological assessment, 30, 34
  pharmacology and psychiatric history, 460–461
Histrionic personality disorder, prevalence of, 4
HIV. *See* Human immunodeficiency virus (HIV)
Hogan, Thomas P.
  psychological tests, widely used, 101–104

Hogan, Thomas P. (*continued*)
publishers of psychological tests, 108–111
sources of information about psychological tests, 105–107
test scores and percentile equivalents, 111–116
Home Observation for Measurement of the Environment Inventory (HOME), 120
Home visit observation, children, 120
Homework compliance, 319–324
Homosexuality. *See* Bisexuals; Gay men; Lesbians
Hopelessness, suicide risk, 64
Hospitalization
crisis, 247
involuntary psychiatric, 548–551
suicide risk upon release, 65
Houston, Ryan, 192–202
Human immunodeficiency virus (HIV)
assessing and reducing risk of infection, 291–295
assessment of risk, 292–294
HIV transmission, 292
risk reduction counseling, 294–295
Humanity, Values in Action (VIA) classification, 96
Human relations, ethical standards, 532–534
Humphreys, Keith, 502–506
Hyperbilirubinemia, 51
Hypertension, Anxiety Management Training (AMT), 272
Hypnosis, 332–337
Hypnotic-related disorders, *DSM-IV-TR* classification, 84–85
Hypochondriasis
DSM-IV, 43
empirically supported therapies, 188
interpretation of high scores, 142–143
Scale 1 of MMPI-2, 133
Hypomania
interpretation of high scores, 147–148
Scale 9 of MMPI-2, 136
Hypothetical question, definition, 574
Hysteria
interpretation of high scores, 143–144
Scale 3 of MMPI-2, 133–134

ICD-10 (International Classification of Diseases, 10th edition), 7, 47
ICPE (International Consortium in Psychiatric Epidemiology), 3–6
Identification, alcohol abuse, 71–75
Identity diffusion, MACI, 163
Idiopathic pain, empirically supported therapies, 186
IDU (injection drug users), 294
IFI (Interdisciplinary Fitness Interview), 608, 610
Illicit drugs, prevalence rates, 481
Illness
adult disease management, 274–278
empirically supported therapies, 186–187
sexual dysfunction, 282
ILS (Independent Living Scales), 605
Images, Multimodal Life History Inventory, 20, 22
Imaging procedures, children with behavioral or developmental disorders, 53–54
Immunity, definition, 574
Impaired psychologist, 620–624
Implied consent, definition, 573
Impossible profession, 678–679
Impulse-control disorders
DSM-IV-TR classification, 89
pharmacotherapy, 459
treatment manuals, 196
Impulsiveness, MACI, 164
Incest, self-help group, 516
Incomes, psychotherapists, 663, 665
Incompetency, definition, 574
Inconsistent presentations, malingering, 70
The Incredible Years, 330
Indemnification, managed care organizations, 655
Indemnity, definition, 574
Independent contractor, definition, 574
Independent Living Scales (ILS), 605
Indications, neuropsychological assessment, 29
Individual, definition, 641
Individual therapy
mandatory, 538
play genograms for child, 371
selection criteria, 364
Infant development, measures, 124–125
Infertility, self-help group, 515
Infidelity, 384. *See also* Marital infidelity
Influence, refusal skills training (RST), 308
Informed consent. *See also* Consent
assessments, 541–542
clients' rights, 182
competence, 645
definition, 574
research, 538–539
therapy, 533, 543
Infrequency F Scale, MMPI-2, 129–130, 131
Inhalant-related disorders, *DSM-IV-TR* classification, 84
Inhalants, prevalence rates, 481
Inhibition, MACI, 162
Injection drug users (IDUs), 294
Injunction, definition, 574
Inorgasmia, global lifelong, 287–288
Insight
in MSE, 12
sex therapy, 290

Insight-action crossover, 228
Insomnia, 455, 458
stimulus control instructions, 325–326
Institute for Personality and Ability Testing (IPAT), 109
Insurance
adolescent, 410
health insurance coverage, 182–183
professional liability, 625–631
reimbursement, psychotherapist-patient contract, 637–638
third-party relationships, 658–659
Integrity, 529
Intelligence, neuropsychological assessment, 35
Intelligence tests
preschool, 125
school-age, 126
Intercoder agreement, Rorschach assessment, 173–174
Interdisciplinary Fitness Interview (IFI), 608, 610
Intermittent explosive disorder, 459
Internalization
coping style, 222
treatment matching, 224–225
International Classification of Diseases, 10th edition (ICD-10), 7, 47
International Consortium in Psychiatric Epidemiology (ICPE), 3–6
International Psychoanalytical Association, 699
International Society for Mental Health Online, Internet site, 492
Internet sites, psychologists and clients, 491–494
Interpersonal relationships, Multimodal Life History Inventory, 21–22, 23
Interpretations, psychotherapy, 205
Interrogatories, definition, 574
Interruption, therapy, 544
Intervention
adult disease management, 275–276
Anxiety Management Training (AMT), 272
child-focused, 433
childhood chronic illness, 406–409
comprehensive, 623
confrontive, 623
consultation, 666–667
couple and family therapy, 374, 375
creation, treatment plan writing, 235
crisis, 245–249
disasters, 250
executive dysfunction, 40
family, parent-child, and parent-focused, 433
female sex dysfunction, 290–291
guidelines, 621–623
motivational interviewing, 269
older adults, 306
refusal skills training (RST), 308–309, 310
sexual dysfunction, 283–284
twelve-step, 623
voluntary, 622–623
Interviewing
anamnestic interviews, 16
collaborative style, 13
Comprehensive Assessment-to-Intervention System (CAIS), 55, 57–59
delaying decision reaching during, 15
diagnostic and clinical, 13–15
HEADSSS Psychosocial Interview Technique, 52
listening, 13–14
motivational, 72, 74, 267–271
parents, 55–60
purpose, 13
sexually abused children, 417, 418, 423–430
Structured Interview of Reported Symptoms (SIRS), 68–69
structured interviews, 14
termination, 15
testing with, 14
Values in Action Structured Interview (VIA-SI), 97
Intestate, definition, 574
Intoxication, 458. *See also* Alcohol abuse/dependence; Drug abuse/dependence
Intrauterine growth retardation (IUGR), 50, 51
Introversion, MACI, 162
Invasion of privacy, definition, 574
Involuntary clients. *See* Reluctant and involuntary clients
Involuntary movements, in MSE, 8
Involuntary outpatient commitment, 550
Involuntary psychiatric hospitalization, 548–551
IPAT (Institute for Personality and Ability Testing), 109
IQ scores, 112–114
Irritable bowel syndrome, empirically supported therapies, 187
Isquith, Peter K., 38–41
Item response theory (IRT), 116
IUGR (Intrauterine growth retardation), 50, 51

Jackson v. Indiana, 607
Jasper, Bruce W., 236–239
Johnson, Ronn, 45–50
Joint and several liability, definition, 574
Joint Commission on Accreditation of Healthcare Organizations (JCAHO), 232, 233
standards for restraint and seclusion, 555–556
Jongsma, Arthur E., Jr., 232–236
Journal for Personality Assessment, 168

Judgment, in MSE, 12
Justice, 96, 529

Kammerer, Betsy, 28–32
Karg, Rhonda S., 13–16
Karpiak, Christie P., 3–7
Kaslow, Florence W., 686–691
Kaufman Assessment Battery for Children–II, 125
Kava for anxiety, 519–520
Keith-Spiegel, Patricia
  confronting an unethical colleague, 579–583
  dealing with licensing boards and ethics complaints, 566–569
Ketamine, administration, effects, and interactions, 484
Klaw, Elena, 502–506
Klinefelter Syndrome and Associates (KSA), 511
Klopfer System, 166
Knight, Bob G., 305–307
Knowledge, Values in Action (VIA) classification, 96
Koch, Manferd D., 346–349
Koman, Stuart L., 653–657
Koocher, Gerald P.
  billing issues, 657–661
  consent, 645–646
  dealing with licensing boards and ethics complaints, 566–569
  future editions, 701
  glossary of legal terms, 572–576
  legal liability risk situations, 558–559
  mental health records, 649–652
  money matters and ethical issues, 577–579
  normal medical laboratory values and measurement conversions, 439–444
  privacy, confidentiality, and privilege, 545–547
  quality of psychological testing report, 117–118
  release forms, 647–649
  subpoenas, 570–572
  utilization review checklist, 652–653
Kortte, Kathleen B., 342–346
KSA (Klinefelter Syndrome and Associates), 511
K Scale, MMPI-2, 129, 131
Kuehnle, Kathryn, 430–435

Labeling, interviewing alcohol abusers, 74
Laboratory studies, pharmacotherapy, 461
Laboratory tests, children with behavioral or developmental disorders, 53–54
Ladany, Nicholas, 682–685
Lafayette Instrument Company, 109
La Leche League, 511
Lambert, Michael J.
  psychotherapy outcome, 236–239
  psychotherapy treatment manuals, 192–202
Lamotrigine, 463
Language
  in MSE, 9–10
  neuropsychological assessment, 36
Language trouble, *DSM-IV*, 43
Lapse, 351
Lavender, 520
Lazarus, Arnold A., 16–23
Lazarus, Clifford N., 16–23
Learning, neuropsychological assessment, 35–36
Learning Disabilities Association of America, 511
Learning disorders
  DSM-IV-TR classification, 81
  executive dysfunction, 39
  prevalence of, 5
Learning trouble, *DSM-IV*, 43
Lebow, Jay L., 373–378
Legal issues. *See also* Forensic matters
  bill collection, 658
  clinical supervision, 684
  dealing with licensing boards and ethics complaints, 566–569
  defending against legal complaints, 560–565
  forensic referrals checklist, 595–598
  glossary of terms, 572–576
  liability risk situations, 558–559
  managed care organizations, 654
  subpoenas, 570–572
Legal liability risk situations, 558–559
Legal risks, intervention with impaired psychologist, 624
Leiter International Performance Scale-Revised (Leiter-R), 127
Lesbians, 299–303, 510–511
Lessard v. Schmidt, 548
Levant, Ronald F., 278–281
Liability and risk situations, 558–559
Liability insurance, 625–631
Libel, definition, 574
Licensing boards, 563, 566–569
Life skills enhancement, 260
Lifestyle balance, 353
Lilienfeld, Scott O., 169–172
Lipsitt, Paul D., 607–611
Listening
  diagnostic and clinical interviewing, 13–14
  high-conflict couples, 383
Lithium, 457, 462–463
Litigaphobia, 560, 563
Litigastress, 560, 563
Litigious clients, 260
Long-term memory, in MSE, 12
LoPiccolo, Joseph

femalc sexual dysfunction, 286–291
male sexual dysfunction, 282–286
L Scale, MMPI-2, 129, 131
Lukefahr, James L., 50–54
Lupus Foundation of America, 511
Lupus, self-help groups, 508, 511
Lusterman, Don-David, 384–388
Lysergic acid diethylamide, 485

McCarthy Scales of Children's Abilities–Second Edition, 125
McGoldrick, Monica, 366–373
MACI. *See* Millon Adolescent Clinical Inventory
McKee, Geoffrey R.
expert testimony in depositions, 599–602
forensic referrals checklist, 595–598
Magnetic resonance imaging (MRI), children, 54
Magnitude of error, malingering, 70
MAI (Millon Adolescent Inventory), 160
Maintenance, refusal skills training (RST), 310
Maintenance stage, 227
Major depressive disorder
DSM-IV, 43, 44
pediatric pharmacotherapy, 467, 470–471
pharmacotherapy, 454–457
prevalence of, 5
Malaise, medical conditions that may present as, 450
Male orgasmic disorder, 285–286
Males. *See also* Gender issues
normative male alexithymia, 278–281
sexual dysfunction, 282–286
self-help group, 512, 513
Malice, definition, 574
Malicious prosecution, definition, 574–575
Malingering, assessment, 67–70
Malpractice, 559, 630. *See also* Legal issues
Malpractice, definition, 575
Malpractice action, suicidal patients, 240, 243
MA (Marijuana Anonymous), 511
Managed care organizations, 653–657
Management, suicidal patient, 241–243
Management plan, neuropsychological assessment, 32
Manic-depressive disorder
DSM-IV, 43, 44
prevalence of episode, 5
self-help group, 513
Mantell, Elaine Orabona, 460–465
Manuals, psychotherapy treatment, 192–199
MAPI (Millon Adolescent Personality Inventory), 160
Marijuana
administration, effects, and interactions, 483
Marijuana Anonymous (MA), 511
prevalence rates, 481
Marital discord, empirically supported therapies, 187
Marital infidelity, treatment, 384–387
Marital relationship, sexual problem, 283
Marital therapy, professional associations, 698
Marketing, consultation, 669
Marlatt, G. Alan, 350–353
Masculinity/femininity
interpretation of high scores, 145
Scale 5 of MMPI-2, 134–135
Maternal causes, intrauterine growth retardation, 51
Mathematics anxiety, Anxiety Management Training (AMT), 272
MCMI–III. *See* Millon Clinical Multiaxial Inventory
MCOs (managed care organizations), 653–657
Measurement conversions, 439
Mechanisms, change, 228–229
Media
guide to interaction with media, 686–691
on-air psychology, 686–689
print, 689–690
Medical conditions, presenting as psychological disorders, 447–453
Medical evaluation
children with behavioral or developmental disorders, 50–54
physically and sexually abused children, 419–422
Medical history, 461
children with behavioral or developmental disorders, 50–54
genogram format, 372
Medical InfoManager, 671
Medical issues, suicidal patient, 243–244
Medical laboratory values, 440–444
Medication. *See also* Complementary and alternative medicines (CAMs)
DSM-IV-TR classification of induced movement disorders, 89
mental health records, 650
nutritional effects, 478–480
Medicine. *See* Complementary and alternative medicines (CAMs)
Meetings, psychotherapist-patient contract, 636–637
Memory
children, 424–425
ginkgo biloba, 518–519
neuropsychological assessment, 35–36
Memory loss, medical conditions that may present as, 452–453

Menstrual history, Multimodal Life History Inventory, 22
Mental disorders
  assessment of feigned, 68–69
  childhood and adolescence in *DSM-IV-TR*, 47
  data sources, 6–7
  popular films portraying, 497–501
  prevalence of, 3–6
Mental health
  glossary of legal terms, 572–576
  intervention, 245–246
  professional associations, 697–700
  self-help group, 512, 513
Mental health-crime false syllogism, 258
Mental Health InfoSource, Internet site, 492
Mental health nursing, professional associations, 698
Mental health records, 649–652
Mental Measurements Yearbooks (MMY), 105–106
Mental retardation
  children, 122
  DSM-IV-TR classification, 80
  prevalence of, 5
  self-help group, 507, 509
Mental status examination (MSE), 7–12
Merck Manual of Diagnosis and Therapy, 274
Merrill-Palmer Scale of Mental Tests, 127
Mescaline, 485
Methamphetamine, 486
Methylenedioxyamphetamine, 484
Methylenedioxyethlylamphetamine, 484
Methylenedioxymethamphetamine, 484
MET (Motivational Enhancement Therapy), 269–270
MHS (Multi-Health Systems), 109
Midwestern Psychological Association, 699
Migraine, empirically supported therapies, 187
Mild traumatic brain injury, 342
Miller, William R., 267–271
Millon, Theodore
  Millon Adolescent Clinical Inventory (MACI), 159–165
  Millon Clinical Multiaxial Inventory (MCMI-III), 153–159
Millon Adolescent Clinical Inventory (MACI)
  administration and scoring, 161–162
  clinical syndromes, 164
  comparison of MACI and MAPI scales, 160
  expressed concerns, 163
  historical development, 160–161
  interpretation and computer–generated reports, 164–165
  personality patterns, 162–163
  scale descriptions, 162–164
Millon Adolescent Inventory (MAI), 160
Millon Adolescent Personality Inventory (MAPI), 160
Millon Clinical Multiaxial Inventory (MCMI–III)
  administration and scoring, 156
  description, 153–155
  interpretation, 156–158
  uses, settings, and limitations, 155–156
Mind Garden, 109
Minnesota Multiphasic Personality Inventory-2. *See* MMPI; MMPI-2
Minorities. *See* Ethnic minorities
Minority-Majority Relations Survey, 78–79
Minors, psychotherapist-patient contract, 639
Mirtazapine, 456, 462
Mission, 681
MMPI (Minnesota Multiphasic Personality Inventory)
  comparison with MMPI-2, 149–150
  F-K Index, 130–131
  subtle-obvious items, 131
MMPI-2 (Minnesota Multiphasic Personality Inventory-2)
  alcohol and drug scales, 138–139
  assessing profile validity, 128–132
  cannot say score, 128–129
  clinical scales, 132–136
  codetypes, 149–152
  control/inhibition and dyscontrol/dysinhibition scales, 138
  $F_{(B)}$ or Back F Scale, 130
  F-K Index, 130–131
  F Scale, 129–130
  generalized emotional distress scales, 137
  high and low scores on clinical scales, 141–148
  K Scale, 129
  personality psychopathology five (PSY–5) scales, 140
  Psychopathology Infrequency Scale $F_{(P)}$, 130
  Scale 0 (social introversion), 136, 148
  Scale 1 (hypochondriasis), 133, 142–143
  Scale 2 (depression), 133, 143
  Scale 3 (hysteria), 133–134, 143–144
  Scale 4 (psychopathic deviate), 134, 144–145
  Scale 5 (masculinity-femininity), 134–135, 145
  Scale 6 (paranoia), 135, 145–146
  Scale 7 (psychasthenia), 135, 146
  Scale 8 (schizophrenia), 135–136, 146–147
  Scale 9 (hypomania), 136, 147–148
  subtle-obvious items, 131
  Superlative Self-Description (S) Scale, 129
  supplementary scales, 137–141
  TRIN (True Response Inconsistency), 130

validity assessment guidelines, 131
VRIN (Variable Response Inconsistency), 130
MMY (*Mental Measurements Yearbooks*), 105–106
Mobility, in MSE, 9
Modality analysis of problems, Multimodal Life History Inventory, 19–22
Model, decision making with dangerous clients, 613
Money matters. *See* Fees
Monitoring, executive dysfunction, 40
Monoamine oxidase inhibitors (MAOIs), 454, 455, 461–462
Mood, in MSE, 9
Mood disorders
DSM-IV, 42–43
DSM-IV-TR classification, 86–87
movie recommendations, 498–499
pediatric pharmacotherapy, 467–468, 470–471
prevalence of, 5
Mood stabilizers, 462–463, 471
Mothers Against Drunk Driving, 511
Mothers, self-help groups, 511
Motivational Enhancement Therapy (MET), 269–270
Motivational interventions, substance abuse, 264
Motivational interviewing, 72, 74, 267–271
Motivation for change. *See* Change
Motor functions, neuropsychological assessment, 35
Motor skills disorder, *DSM-IV-TR* classification, 81
Movie recommendations, 498–501
Moyers, Theresa B., 267–271
Mueller, Felicia A., 295–298
Multiaxial system, *DSM-IV-TR* classification, 90
Multi-Health Systems (MHS), 109
Multimodal Life History Inventory, 16–23
Multiple relationships, 532
Multiple sclerosis, self-help groups, 511, 513
Multiple settings, mapping genograms, 370–371
Multiple treatments, adolescents, 413
Murphy, James G., 481–487
Muscular Dystrophy Association, 511–512
Musical chairs, family therapy, 659

Naming, in MSE, 10
Nar-Anon World Wide Service, 512
Narcissistic personality disorder
domain descriptors, 157
prevalence of, 5
Narcolepsy, 455, 458
prevalence of, 5
self-help, 512
Narcolepsy Network, 512
Narcotics Anonymous, 512
NARSAD (National Alliance for Research on Schizophrenia and Depression), 512
NASW (National Association of Social Workers), 698
NASW Register of Clinical Social Workers, 698
National Adoption Center, 512
National AIDS Hotline, 512
National Alliance for Research on Schizophrenia and Depression (NARSAD), 512
National Alliance for the Mentally Ill, 512
National Alopecia Areata Foundation, 512
National Association for the Deaf, 512
National Association of Anorexia Nervosa and Associated Disorders, 512
National Association of Social Workers (NASW), 698
National Career Assessment Services, 109
National Center for Men, 512
National Child Traumatic Stress Network, 249
National Chronic Pain Outreach Association, 513
National Clearinghouse for Alcohol and Drug Information, 513
National Depressive and Manic Depressive Association, 513
National Domestic Violence Hotline, 513
National Down Syndrome Congress, 513
National Eating Disorders Association, 513
National Headache Foundation, 513
National Information Center for Children and Youth with Disabilities, 513
National Institute of Mental Health, Internet site, 492
National Mental Health Association, Internet site, 492
National Mental Health Association (NMHA), 513
National Multiple Sclerosis Society, 513
National Organization for Men, 513
National Organization for Women (NOW), 513–514
National Organization on Fetal Alcohol Syndrome, 513
National Parkinson Association, 514
National Register of Health Service Providers in Psychology, 698
National Stroke Association, 514
NBAS (Brazelton Neonatal Behavioral Scale), 124
NCAST (Nursing Childhood Assessment Tool), 122
NCS (National Comorbidity Study), 3–6
NCS Pearson, 109–110
Neck examination, 52
Nefazodone, 454, 455, 462
Negligence, definition, 575
Negotiating, managed care organizations, 656–657

Nelson, Aaron P., 33–37
Neonatal jaundice, 51
Neurological examination, 53
Neuropsychological (NP) assessment
  adults, 33–37
  assumptions of developmental analysis, 28–29
  behavioral domains, 30
  clinical method, 34–37
  communication of findings, 31–32
  developmental, 28–32
  diagnostic formulation, 36–37
  diagnostic strategy, 29–30
  domains of neuropsychological function, 35–36
  education, 32
  fundamental assumptions of, of children, 28
  fundamental assumptions of clinical, 33
  indications, 29
  management plan, 32
  recommendations, 32
  recommendations and feedback, 37
  sources of data, 30–31
  use of psychological tests, 31
  uses, 33–34
Neuropsychologists, widely used tests, 101–102
New England Psychological Association, 699
Nicotine, 486
Nicotine Anonymous World Service, 514
Nicotine-related disorders, *DSM-IV-TR* classification, 84
Nightmares, *DSM-IV*, 43
Night terrors, *DSM-IV*, 43
NIMH Epidemiological Catchment Area (ECA) study, 3–6
NIMH Treatment of Depression Collaborative Research Program (TDCRP), 216
Nitrites, 485
NMHA (National Mental Health Association), 513
Nominal damages, definition, 573
Nonadherence, 210–211
Nonaffective psychosis, prevalence of, 5
Nondiscrimination, patients' rights, 183
Nondisparagement, managed care organizations, 655
Nonmaleficence, 528–529
Noradrenergic agents, 469
Norcross, John C.
  abbreviations and symbols, 691–697
  empirically supported therapy relationships, 202–208
  future editions, 701
  national self-help groups and organizations, 506–516
  prevalence of mental disorders, 3–7
  psychologists' fees and incomes, 662–666
  self-help books and autobiographies, 494–497
  stages of change, 226–231
  therapist self–care checklist, 677–682
Normal curve equivalents (NCEs), 113–114, 115
Nose examination, 52
NOW (National Organization for Women), 513–514
Nursing Childhood Assessment Tool (NCAST), 122
Nutritional effects, medications, 478–480

OA (Overeaters Anonymous), 514
Obesity, 445–447
empirically supported therapies, 187, 189
Objective construction, treatment plan writing, 234–235
Objective self-awareness, 260
Observations, child behavior, 119–123
Obsessions, in MSE, 10–11
Obsessive-Compulsive Anonymous, 514
Obsessive-compulsive disorder
  DSM-IV, 43
  empirically supported therapies, 185, 189
  movie recommendations, 499–500
  pediatric pharmacotherapy, 468, 472
  prevalence of, 5
  psychopharmacology, 455, 458
  self-help groups, 514
Obsessive-Compulsive Foundation, 514
OCD. *See* Obsessive-compulsive disorder
O'Connor, Margaret, 33–37
O'Connor v. Donaldson, 548
Office for Civil Rights of HHS, Privacy Rule, 644–655
Office management programs, 671–673
Office Therapy, 672
"Off the record," media, 688
O'Grady, Kari A., 338–341
Olanzapine, 464
Older adults
  AARP, 507–508
  assessment, 306
  cognitively impaired, 343–344
  differential diagnosis, 305
  family, 306
  psychotherapy, 305–307
  referrals, 307
  relationship issues, 306–307
  self-help groups, 507–508, 514
  suicide, 306
Olmstead v. L.C., 549
Online therapy, 690
Opiate dependence, empirically supported therapies, 185

Opinion evidence, definition, 575
Opioid-related disorders, *DSM-IV-TR* classification, 84
Oppositional defiant disorder
 DSM-IV, 42
 empirically supported therapies, 189
 family therapy, 377
 parent management training, 328
 pharmacotherapy, 467
 prevalence of, 5
 treatment, 401–405
Oppositional pattern, MACI, 163
Organic brain syndromes, dietary supplements, 478
Ortiz-Brown family genogram, 367
Outcome of psychotherapy, 236–239
Outpatient commitment, involuntary, 550
Outpatient services contract, 636–640
Outpatient therapy, crisis, 247
Outpatient treatments, manuals, 196–197
Overeaters Anonymous (OA), 514
Overtesting, neuropsychological assessment, 29
Overvalued ideas, in MSE, 10

Pain and suffering, definition, 575
Pain management, childhood chronic illness, 408
Pain reduction, adult disease management, 275
Pain relievers, prevalence rates, 481
Panic attacks
 DSM-IV, 43
 medical conditions that may present as, 448–449
Panic disorder
 empirically supported therapies, 184, 185
 pediatric pharmacotherapy, 468
 prevalence of, 5
 psychopharmacology, 455, 457
Paranoia
 interpretation of high scores, 145–146
 Scale 6 of MMPI-2, 135
Paranoid personality disorder, prevalence of, 5
Parens patriae, involuntary hospitalization, 548
Parental capacity assessment, 603–605
Parent-child interactions, 122, 330–331
Parent-child interaction therapy, 330–331
Parent-Child Relationship Inventory (PCRI), 604–605
Parent-directed interaction (PDI), 330–331
Parenting Custody Index (PCI), 604
Parenting Stress Index (PSI), 604
Parent management training
 childhood behavior disorders, 327–331
 The Incredible Years, 330
 long-term effectiveness, 328–329
 parent-child interaction therapy, 330–331
 parents at risk, 329
 problem-solving skills training and, 329–330
 The Incredible Years, 330
Parent psychopathology, 403
Parents
 characteristics, 58
 Comprehensive Assessment-to-Intervention System, 55, 57–59
 interviewing, 55–60
 rating scales and questionnaires,, 55–56
 reluctant adolescents, 410–411, 412–413
 social context of family, 57
Parents Anonymous, 514
Parents Without Partners, 514
Parham v. JR, 551
Park, Nansook, 93–98
Parkinson's disease, self-help, 508, 514
PAR (Psychological Assessment Resources), 110
Partner relational problems, treatment manuals, 197
Passion flower, 520
Pathological gambling, prevalence of, 5
Payments, 637. *See also* Billing; Fees
PBS: The Psychologist's Billing System, 672
PC Consulting Group, 672
PCI (Parenting Custody Index), 604
PCL-R (Psychopathy Checklist-Revised), 606
PCRI (Parent-Child Relationship Inventory), 604–605
PDI (parent-directed interaction), 330–331
Peabody Picture Vocabulary Test-Revised, 126
Pediatrics. *See* Children
Peer insecurity, MACI, 163
Peer monitoring, 580
Penile prostheses, 284
People's rights, 529
Percentile equivalents of test scores, 111–116
Percentile ranks, 115
Percentiles, 115
Perception, neuropsychological assessment, 35
Perceptual abnormalities, in MSE, 11
Performance anxiety, 282, 283
Performance curve, malingering, 69
Perinatal factors, 51
Perjury, definition, 575
Permission, definition, 646
Personal and social history, Multimodal Life History Inventory, 18
Personality disorders
 DSM-IV-TR classification, 89
 movie recommendations, 499–500
 treatment manuals, 197
Personality patterns, MACI, 160, 162–163
Personality psychopathology five (PSY-5) Scales, MMPI-2, 140

Pervasive developmental disorders, *DSM-IV-TR* classification, 81
Peterson, Christopher, 93–98
Petry, Sueli S., 366–373
Pharmacotherapy
  adult psychopharmacology, 454–465
  anorexia nervosa, 459
  anxiety disorders, 455, 457–458, 468, 471–472
  avoidant personality disorder, 456, 458
  bipolar disorder, 455, 457, 467–468, 471
  borderline personality disorder (BPD), 455, 458
  bulimia nervosa, 456, 459
  common drugs of abuse, 481–487
  depression, 454–457, 470–471
  dietary supplements and psychological functioning, 476–480
  eating disorders, 459
  impulse-control disorders, 459
  intermittent explosive disorder, 459
  major depression, 454–457
  obsessive-compulsive disorder (OCD), 455, 458, 468, 472
  panic disorder, 455, 457, 468, 472
  pediatric, 466–474
  personality disorders, 455–456, 458
  psychiatric history, 460–461
  psychosis, 473–474
  schizophrenia, 455, 457
  schizotypal personality disorder, 455, 458
  side effects and warnings, 460–465
  sleep disorders, 455, 458
  social phobia, 458
  somatoform disorders, 459
  substance abuse and withdrawal, 456, 458–459
  tics, 472–473
  Tourette's disorder, 472–473
  trichotillomania, 459
Phencyclidine, 484
Phencyclidine use disorders, *DSM-IV-TR* classification, 84
Philosophy, crisis intervention, 246
Phobias
  empirically supported therapies, 189
  in MSE, 11
  prevalence of, 5
Physical abuse, children, 419–421
Physical examination, children with behavioral or developmental disorders, 52–53
Physical restraint and seclusion, 553–557
Physical sensations, Multimodal Life History Inventory, 20, 22
Pictorial Test of Intelligence-Second Edition, 127
Placental causes, intrauterine growth retardation, 51
Plaintiff, definition, 575
Planned Parenthood, 514
Planning of treatment. *See* Treatment planning
Play assessments, children, 122–123
Play therapy
  disruptive children, 401
  genograms, 366, 371
Pleadings, definition, 575
PM/2, 672
PMA-2000, 671
PMT. *See* Parent management training
Police power, involuntary hospitalization, 548
Pope, Kenneth S.
  assessment of suicidal risk, 63–66
  sexual feelings, actions, and dilemmas in psychotherapy, 313–319
Portland Digit Recognition Test (PDRT), malingering, 69
Position/posture, in MSE, 8
Postmodern sex therapy, 282–283, 287
Postpartum Support International, 514
Post-traumatic stress disorder
  DSM-IV, 42
  empirically supported therapies, 185
  prevalence of, 5
Practice Magic, 672
Practice management
  billing issues, 657–661
  computerized billing and office management programs, 670–673
  consent, 645–646
  consultation agreement, 666–669
  managed care organizations, 653–657
  mental health records, 649–652
  Privacy Rule, 640–645
  psychologists' fees and incomes, 662–666
  psychotherapist-patient contract, 635–640
  release forms, 647–649
  utilization review checklist, 652–653
Practice Management Software, 672
Pragmatic, 672
Prather, Penny A., 28–32
Precontemplation stage, 226
Preemption analysis, Privacy Rule, 642
Premature ejaculation, 285
Premature terminations, therapy, 358
Prenatal factors, 50–51
Preoccupation, in MSE, 11
Preparation stage, 227
Preschool intelligence tests, 125
Prescription analgesics
  abuse, 482
  administration, effects, and interactions, 486
Prescriptive guidelines, stages of change, 227–231

Prevalence, adherence, 209
Preventative preparation, suicidal patient, 244
Pride skills, 330–331
Prima facie case, definition, 575
Prima facie evidence, definition, 575
Print media, 689–690
Privacy, 584
  ethical standards, 534–535
  ethics, 545–546
Privacy Rule, 640–645
Private-practice psychologists' income, 665
Privilege, 546, 584
Probate court, definition, 575
Problem definition, treatment plan writing, 234
Problem selection, treatment plan writing, 234
Problem solving, crisis intervention, 246
Problem-solving skills training, 329–330
Processes of change, 228–229
Prochaska, James O., 226–231
Product of documents, subpoena, 571–572
PRO-ED, 110
Professional associations, 697–700
Professional fees, psychotherapist-patient contract, 637
Professional liability insurance, 625–631
Professional records, psychotherapist-patient contract, 638–639
Professional resources
  clinical abbreviations and symbols, 691–697
  clinical supervision, 682–685
  interacting with media, 686–691
  major professional associations, 697–700
  therapist self–care checklist, 677–682
Proficiency levels, 116
Programs, computerized billing, 671–673
Project MATCH, substance abuse, 265
Project Release v. Prevost, 549
Prolapse, 351
Prosody, in MSE, 10
Proximate causation, definition, 575
Proximate cause, definition, 575
Proxy consent, definition, 646
Psilocybin, 485
PSI (Parenting Stress Index), 604
PSST (Problem-solving skills training), 329–330
Psy Broadcasting Corporation, Internet site, 492–493
Psychasthenia
  interpretation of high scores, 146
  MMPI-2 codetype, 151–152
  Scale 7 of MMPI-2, 135
Psych Central, Internet site, 493
Psychiatric comorbidity, alcohol abusers, 73, 74
Psychiatric Diagnostic Screening Questionnaire, 14
Psychiatric history, 460–461
Psychiatric hospitalization, involuntary, 548–551
Psychiatry, professional associations, 698
Psychoeducational groups (PEGs)
  application and effectiveness, 393–394
  distinctive characteristics, 394–395
  ethical issues, 396
  group climate, 396
  group dynamics, 395–396
  leader competencies and training, 396
  problem members, 396
  shared characteristics with other group treatments, 395–396
  steps in forming and running PEG, 397
  treatment, 393–398
Psychoeducational tests, publishers, 108–111
Psychological Assessment, journal, 168
Psychological Assessment Resources (PAR), 110
The Psychological Corporation, 110
Psychological disorders, medical conditions that may present as, 447–453
Psychological factors, neuropsychological assessment, 36
Psychological factors affecting medical condition, *DSM-IV-TR* classification, 89
Psychological first aid, disasters, 250–251
Psychological resources, recovery after disasters, 252
Psychological self-help, Internet site, 493
Psychological sequelae, malingering, 70
Psychological services, psychotherapist-patient contract, 636
Psychological tests. *See also* Testing
  50 widely used, 101–104
  assessing quality of report, 117–118
  publishers, 108–111
  sources of information about, 105–107
Psychologists. *See also* Psychotherapists
  rated autobiographies, 496
  rated self-help books, 495
  top Internet sites, 491–494
The Psychologist's Billing System (PBS), 672
Psychology
  choice of treatment format, 363–365
  professional associations, 697–698
Psychology Information Online, Internet site, 493
Psychology of Cyberspace, Internet site, 493
Psychopathic deviate
  interpretation of high scores, 144–145
  Scale 4 of MMPI-2, 134
Psychopathology, parent, 403
Psychopathology Infrequency Scale ($F_{(P)}$), MMPI-2, 130, 131
Psychopathy Checklist-Revised (PCL-R), 606

Psychopharmacology. *See* Pharmacotherapy
Psychophysiological disorder, empirically supported therapies, 190
Psychosis
medical conditions that may present as, 452
pediatric psychopharmacology, 473–474
Psychosomatic, pediatric and adolescent medical complaints, 448
Psychotherapist-patient contract, 635–640
Psychotherapists
APA "Ethical Principles of Psychologists and Code of Conduct (2002)," 525–545
case settlement role, 630
chronically ill adults, 276–277
confronting an unethical colleague, 579–583
dealing with licensing boards and ethics complaints, 566–569
defending against legal complaints, 560–565
early termination and referral of clients, 346–349
expert witness, 599
fees and incomes, 662–666
general principles, 528–529
informed consent to therapy, 543
inviting hypnosis and relaxation, 333–337
metatherapeutic issues, 344–345
motivational interviewing, 267–271
outcome assessment, 236–237
recognizing, assisting, and reporting impaired psychologist, 620–624
salaries for doctoral-level, in academic settings, 664
salaries for doctoral-level, in practice settings, 664
self-care checklist, 677–682
sexual involvement with client, 181–182, 313–319, 620–621, 627–628
tasks of group psychotherapist, 389–390
terminating therapy, 354–359
therapeutic meta-communication, 217–219
Psychotherapy
abuse-focused therapy, 433
brain functioning, 344
chronically ill adults, 274–278
clients' rights, 181–183
cognitively impaired adults, 342–346
customizing relationship to individual patient, 205–207
early termination and referral of clients, 346–349
empirically supported therapies, 183–191
empirically supported therapy relationships, 202–207
ethical standards, 543–545
general elements of therapy relationship, 203–205
genograms, 366–372
group therapy, 203–204
guidelines for terminating, 354–359
high-conflict couples, 378–383
homework compliance, 319–324
introducing and assigning films, 498
methods to reduce and counter resistance, 212–215
older adults, 305–307
outcome, 236–239
Privacy Rule, 643–644
religiously committed clients, 338–341
reluctant and involuntary clients, 257–262
repairing ruptures in therapeutic alliance, 216–219
sexual feelings, actions, and dilemmas, 313–319
stages of change, 226–231
systematic assessment, 220–222
therapeutic alliance, 203
therapy on air and online, 690
treatment manuals, 192–199
treatment matching, 222–225
treatment plan writing, 232–236
treatment women, 295–298
Psychotherapy Practice Manager, 672–673
Psychotic disorders
DSM-IV-TR classification, 85–86
pediatric pharmacotherapy, 468, 473–474
Psyquel, 673
PTSD Support Services, 514
Publication
definition, 575
ethical standards, 538–541
Publicity, psychologists, 686
Public speaking anxiety, empirically supported therapies, 185
Public statements, ethical standards, 535–536
Publishers, psychological and psychoeducational tests, 108–111
PubMed, Internet site, 493
Punitive damages, definition, 573

Quality of speech, in MSE, 10
Quetiapine, 465
QuickDoc, 672

Race. *See also* Ethnic minorities
suicide risk, 65
RAINN (Rape Abuse and Incest National Network), 515
Rapaport System, 166
Rape Abuse and Incest National Network (RAINN), 515

Rational emotive behavior therapy (REBT), 212, 213
Rational Recovery (RR), 515
Rauwolfia, antipsychotic and tranquilizer, 520
RCIs (Reliable Change Indices), 238–239
R-CRAS (Rogers Criminal Responsibility Assessment Scales), 603
RDA (Recommended Dietary Allowance), 476–478
Reactive attachment disorder, *DSM-IV-TR* classification, 81
Reactivity, in MSE, 9
Readiness to Change Ruler, 73
Reading, in MSE, 10
Reasonable medical/psychological certainty, definition, 575
Recommendations, neuropsychological assessment, 32, 37
Recommended Dietary Allowance (RDA), 476–478
Record keeping
  ethical standards, 536–537
  mental health records, 651
Recovery, disasters, 252–253
Recurrent illnesses, children, 51
Recycling treatment, 228
  substance abuse, 264
Reed, William J., 447–453
Referrals
  early termination and referral of clients, 346–349
  forensic referrals checklist, 595–598
  reluctant and involuntary clients, 258
Reflex Sympathetic Dystrophy Syndrome Association, 515
Refusal skills training, 308–311
Registration, in MSE, 11
Reidy, Dennis E., 506–516
Reinforcement, 408
Relapse, term, 351
Relapse prevention, 264, 350–353
Relational problems, *DSM-IV-TR* classification, 89–90
Relationship issues
  older adults, 306–307
  restructuring, 679–680
Relaxation, 332–337
Release, definition, 575
Release forms, 647–649
Reliability
  children's reports, 424
  quality of psychological testing report, 117
  Rorschach assessment, 174
Reliable Change Indices (RCIs), 238–239
Religion, suicide risk, 65
Religiously committed client, 338–341
Reluctant and involuntary clients
  abrasive clients, 259
  coping skills, 261
  errors in technique, 260
  group conversation method, 261
  guidelines for working with, 257–261
  life skills enhancement, 260
  litigious clients, 260
  low trust-high control dilemmas, 259
  mental health-crime false syllogism, 258
  methods to engage adolescent, 410–415
  objective self-awareness, 260
  psychotherapists' reactions to, 258
  referral clarification, 258
  resistance, 260
  right to refuse treatment, 258
  therapy as aversive contingency for inappropriate behavior, 259
  time and therapy, 261
Remarriage, couples therapy, 376
Repetition, in MSE, 10
Repetitive motion, self-help, 509
Repression scale, MMPI-2, 138
Research, ethical standards, 538–541
Residential treatment, substance abuse, 264
Resistance. *See also* Reluctant and involuntary clients
  assessing level, 221–222
  family's, to genogram, 369
  motivational interviewing, 268
  in MSE, 8
  psychotherapy, 205
  reducing and countering, in psychotherapy, 212–215
  reluctant and involuntary clients, 260
  transference, 348–349
Resnick, Robert J., 60–63
Resolution, ethical issues, 529–530
RESOLVE: The National Infertility Association, 515
Respect for people's rights and dignity, 529
Respondeat superior, definition, 575
Responsibility
  psychologist's, 529
  reporting impaired psychologist, 621
Restraint, definition, 555
Restraint and seclusion, 553–557
Retention, motivational interviewing, 270
Retinal hemorrhages, child abuse, 421
Rey-Casserly, Celiane, 28–32
Rey-Osterrieth Complex Figures Test, 126
Rheumatic disease pain, empirically supported therapies, 187
Rice, Sara, 192–202

Richards, P. Scott, 338–341
Ridge, Nathanael W., 393–398
Right to know, health insurance coverage, 182–183
Right to refuse treatment, 258
Risk
  diagnostic strategy, 30
  parents, 329
  psychotherapy, 635–636
  reduction, 26
  relationship with insurance, 625
Risk assessment, suicidal patient, 241–243
Risk factors
  dangerous patients, 614
  mental health records, 650
  nonadherence, 211
Risk reduction, human immunodeficiency virus (HIV), 294–295
Risperidone, 464–465, 480
Ritzler, Barry A., 166–168
Riverside Publishing, 110
Rocky Mountain Psychological Association, 699
Rogers, Richard, 67–71
Rogers Criminal Responsibility Assessment Scales (R-CRAS), 603
Rorschach Comprehensive System, 166, 169–172, 175–176
Rorschachiana, yearbook, 168
Rorschach Method
  administration procedures, 166–167
  applications, 168
  clinical utility, 176–177
  coding (scoring), 167
  frequently used systems, 166
  information sources, 168
  intercoder agreement, 173–174
  interpretation, 167
  normative reference base, 175–176
  questions and reservations for assessment, 169–172
  reliability, 174
  scientific status, 173–176
  training, 167–168
  validity, 174–175
Roth, Robert M., 38–41
RR (Rational Recovery), 515
RSD (reflex sympathetic dystrophy syndrome), 515
Rubenstein, Alice K., 410–415
Rumination
  DSM-IV, 43
  in MSE, 11

SADS (Schedule for Affective Disorders and Schizophrenia), 14
SAFE (Self-Abuse Finally Ends) Alternative Information Line, 515
Safety
  high-conflict couples, 380
  time-out routines, 381
Safran, Jeremy D., 216–219
St. John's wort for depression, 518
Sanders, A. Danielle, 192–202
Saner software, 673
SARA (Spousal Assault Risk Assessment Guide), 606
SAT scores, 112–114
Saywitz, Karen J., 423–430
SBM (Society of Behavioral Medicine), 699
Schatzberg, Alan F, 454–459
Schedule for Affective Disorders and Schizophrenia (SADS), 14
Schizophrenia
  debiasing strategies, 15
  dietary supplements, 477–478
  DSM-IV-TR classification, 85–86
  empirically supported therapies, 188
  interpretation of high scores, 146–147
  movie recommendations, 501
  prevalence of, 5
  psychopharmacology, 457
  Rorschach assessment, 175
  Scale 8 of MMPI-2, 135–136
  self-help group, 512
  structured interview, 14
  treatment manuals, 198
Schizotypal personality disorder
  prevalence of, 5
  psychopharmacology, 455, 458
Schoener, Gary R., 620–624
Schoenfield, Laura J., 327–332
School-age intelligence tests, 126
School psychologists, widely used tests, 101–102
Schroeder, Carolyn S., 55–60
SCID-I and SCID-II (Structured Clinical Interview for the *DSM-IV*), 14
SCID Screen Patient Questionnaire, 14
Scientific status, Rorschach assessment, 173–176
Seclusion, definition, 555
Seclusion and physical restraint, 553–557
Second-generation antipsychotics (SGAs), 464
Sedative-related disorders
  DSM-IV-TR classification, 84–85
Sedatives, prevalence rates, 481
Seizure disorders, children, 51
Selective mutism, prevalence of, 5
Selective serotonin reuptake inhibitors (SSRIs), 454, 455, 456, 460, 462, 472
Self-Abuse Finally Ends (SAFE) Alternative Information Line, 515

Self-awareness of strengths/weaknesses, executive dysfunction, 40
Self-care checklist, therapist, 677–682
Self-control
  Anxiety Management Training (AMT), 272
  childhood chronic illness, 408
Self-demeaning, MACI, 163
Self-devaluation, MACI, 163
Self-disclosure, psychotherapy, 205
Self-efficacy, motivational interviewing, 268
Self-expression, communication, 383
Self-harm ideation, in MSE, 11
Self-help books, 494–495
Self-Help for Hard of Hearing People (SHHH), 515
Self-help groups, 502–506, 506–516
Self-Help Sourcebook, 507
Self-liberation, 229
Self Management and Recovery Training (SMART), 515
Self-monitoring, relapse prevention, 351
Self-Monitoring (SM), 73
Self-reevaluation, 229
Self-report measures, aculturation, 78
Seligman, Martin E. P., 93–98
Sensation, neuropsychological assessment, 35
Sensitivity to medical issues, suicidal patient, 243–244
Separation anxiety disorder
  DSM-IV, 43
  pediatric pharmacotherapy, 468
  prevalence of, 6
SEPI (Society for the Exploration of Psychotherapy Integration), 699
Serotonic reuptake inhibitors (SRIs), 472
Services, disasters, 251
Settlement, definition, 576
Settlement vs. trial, professional liability coverage, 629–630
Severity
  assessment, 220–221
  treatment matching, 222–225
Sex, pharmacotherapy, 460
Sex Addicts Anonymous, 515
Sex offenders, assessment, 416–417
Sex therapy
  female sexual dysfunction, 286–291
  male sexual dysfunction, 282–286
  postmodern, 282–283, 287
  therapist-client sexual involvement, 313, 314
Sexual abuse/assault. *See also* Abuse; Child abuse
  anatomically detailed dolls, 425–426
  APSAC Study Guides, 416–422
  behavioral indicators of children, 424
  children, 417–422
  false allegations, 418–419
  interviewing children, 423–430
  interview outline, 427–429
  self-help groups, 510, 515
  treatment of child, 430–435
Sexual attraction to patients, 315–316
Sexual Compulsives Anonymous, 515
Sexual desire, 290–291
Sexual discomfort, MACI, 163
Sexual disorders
  DSM-IV-TR classification, 87–88
  movie recommendations, 500
  treatment manuals, 198
Sexual dysfunction
  dyspareunia, 290
  empirically supported therapies, 187
  female, 286–291
  female arousal and orgasm dysfunctions, 287–289
  global lifelong inorgasmia, 287–288
  low sexual desire and aversion to sex, 290–291
  male, 282–286
  patient problem/diagnosis, 364
  situational orgasmic dysfunction, 288–289
  vaginismus, 289
Sexual harassment, 532
Sexual involvement, ethical standards for therapists, 532, 533, 538, 544, 620–621
Sexually transmitted diseases (STDs), children, 422
Sexual orientation. *See* Bisexuals; Gay men; Lesbians
Sexual victimization, 287
Shape Up America!, 515
Shapiro, David L., 593–595
Shefet, Oren M., 354–359
SHHH (Self-Help for Hard of Hearing People), 515
Short-term memory, in MSE, 11–12
ShrinkRapt, 673
S.I.A. (Survivors of Incest Anonymous), 516
Sickle cell disease pain, empirically supported therapies, 187
Side effects in psychopharmacology, 460–465
SIDS Alliance (Sudden Infant Death Syndrome Alliance), 515
Sigma Assessment Systems, 110
Simansky, Jennifer A., 494–497
Simple phobia, *DSM-IV*, 43
Situational orgasmic dysfunction, 288–289
Skill and motivation, interviews, 14
Skin evaluation, 53
Skin injuries, child abuse, 421
Skull and extremity X-rays, children, 54
Skullcap, 520
Slander, definition, 576

Sleep, valerian for, 520
Sleep disorders
  DSM-IV-TR classification, 88–89
  empirically supported therapies, 188
  insomnia treatment, 325–326
  medical conditions that may present as, 450–451
  self-help groups, 508, 512
  treatment manuals, 198
Sleep terror disorder, prevalence of, 6
Sleepwalking disorder, prevalence of, 6
Slosson Educational Publications, 110
SMART (Self Management and Recovery Training), 515
Sobell, Linda Carter, 71–76
Sobell, Mark B., 71–76
Social health, self-help, 508
Social history, 52
Social insensitivity, MACI, 163
Social introversion
  interpretation of scores, 148
  Scale O of MMPI-2, 136
Social liberation, 229
Social network therapy, substance abuse, 264
Social phobia, 458
  empirically supported therapies, 185
  prevalence of, 6
Social Psychology Network, Internet site, 493
Social support, recovery after disasters, 252
Society for the Exploration of Psychotherapy Integration (SEPI), 699
Society of Behavioral Medicine (SBM), 699
Socioeconomic status, recovery after disasters, 252–253
Solicitation, consultation, 669
Solvents, administration, effects, and interactions, 485
Somatic complaints, disasters, 252
Somatic disorders, treatment manuals, 198
Somatization disorder, prevalence of, 6
Somatoform, pediatric and adolescent medical complaints, 448
Somatoform disorders
  DSM-IV, 43
  DSM-IV-TR classification, 87
  pharmacotherapy, 459
Somatoform pain disorders, empirically supported therapies, 187
SOS Office Manager, 673
SOS Software, 673
Southeastern Psychological Association, 700
Southwestern Psychological Association, 700
Special damages, definition, 573
Specific/simple phobia
  empirically supported therapies, 185
  prevalence of, 6
Speech, in MSE, 9–10
Spencer, Thomas J., 466–476
Sperry, Len, 666–669
Spiral pattern, 227
Spirituality, 339, 681
Spousal Assault Risk Assessment Guide (SARA), 606
Stage-based methods, substance abuse, 264
Stages of change, 226–231
Standard of care, definition, 576
Standard scores, 111–115
Stanford-Binet, Fifth Edition (SB5), 114–115
Stanford-Binet Intelligence Scale-Fifth Edition, 125
Stanines, 113–114, 115
State laws, Privacy Rule, 642
Statute of limitations, definition, 576
Stens, 115
Stepfamily Association of America, 515
Stimulants, prevalence rates, 481
Stimulus control, 229, 408
Stimulus control instructions, insomnia, 325–326
Stipulations, definition, 576
Stoelting Company, 110
Stonewalling, divorce risk, 376
Stressful events, suicide risk, 65
Stress reduction, adult disease management, 275
Stroke, 343, 508, 514
Structural profile, Multimodal Life History Inventory, 22–23
Structured Clinical Interview for the *DSM-IV* (SCID-I and SCID-II), 14
Structured Interview of Reported Symptoms (SIRS), 68–69
Structured interviews. *See* Interviewing
Stuttering, prevalence of, 6
Submissiveness, MACI, 162
Subpoena, definition, 576
Subpoena duces tecum, definition, 576
Subpoenas, 570–572
Substance Abuse and Mental Health Services Administration, 481
Substance abuse/dependence. *See also* Alcohol abuse/dependence; Drug abuse/dependence
  DSM-IV, 44
  DSM-IV-TR classification, 82–85
  family therapy, 377
  MACI, 164
  movie recommendations, 500
  nutritional supplementation, 478
  prevalence of, 6
  sexual dysfunction, 282
  treatment manuals, 198–199
  treatment matching, 263–267

Sudden Infant Death Syndrome Alliance (SIDS Alliance), 515
Suggestibility
precautions to minimize, 428–429
sexually abused children, 426
Suicidal ideation, in MSE, 11
Suicide
age and risk, 64–65
bereavement, 65
depression, 64
gender, 64
health status, 65
hopelessness, 64
intervention, 247
intoxication, 64
lethality assessment, 247
MACI, 164
malpractice action, 240, 243
movie recommendations, 498–499
older adults, 306
past attempts, 64
race, 65
release from hospital, 65
religion, 65
risk assessment, 63–65
self-help groups, 508–509, 511
treatment and management of suicidal patient, 240–245
unemployment, 65
verbal warning, 64
Suinn, Richard M., 271–273
Suinn-Lew Asian Self-Identity Acculturation Scale, 79
Sullivan, Glenn R., 240–245
Summary judgment, definition, 576
Summons, definition, 576
SumTime, 673
Superlative Self-Description (S) Scale, MMPI-2, 129, 131
Supervision, conducting effective clinical, 682–685
Supplements, dietary, 476–478
Support, crisis intervention, 248
Surplus lines carriers, professional liability insurance, 630–631
Survivors of Incest Anonymous (S.I.A.), 516
Swidler & Berlin and James Hamilton v. United States, 584
Symbols, 691–697
genogram format, 368, 372
Symptom Checklist 90-R (SCL-90-R), 73, 237
Symptoms, pharmacotherapy, 460
Symptom validity testing (SVT), malingering, 69
Systematic assessment, psychotherapy, 220–222
Systematic assessment and treatment matching, 220–225
Systematic reviews, psychological tests, 105–106
Systematic Treatment Selection (STS), 220

Talking points, media, 688, 689
Tarasoff v. Regents of the University of California, 584–585, 586, 587, 612
Tardive Dyskinesia/Tardive Dystonia National Association, 516
TC (*Test Critiques*), 105–106
TEA (Test of Everyday Attention), 40
Teachers, childhood behavior disorders, 330
Teleassessment, 120–121
Temperance, Values in Action (VIA) classification, 96
Temperature conversions, 439
Termination
assessing and avoiding premature, 358
child therapy, 358–359
couples therapy, 387
early termination, 346–349
guidelines, 354–359
high-conflict couples therapy, 383
interview, 15
managed care organizations, 655
mental health records, 651
tasks, 357–358
therapy, 544–545
timing, 354
Terrorism and Disaster Branch (TDB), 249–250
Test Critiques (TC), 105–106
Testimony. *See* Expert testimony
Testing
adaptive functioning, 127–128
adolescents, 411–412
children with behavioral or developmental disorders, 53–54
ethical standards, 541–543
executive dysfunction, 40
fees by psychologists for, 663
interviewing with, 14
neuropsychological assessment, 31
psychological tests, 101–104
scores and percentile equivalents, 111–116
vision and hearing for children with disorders, 53
Test Locator, 105, 107
Test of Everyday Attention (TEA), 40
Tests: A Comprehensive Reference for Assessments in Psychology, Education, and Business, 5th edition, 106
Tests in Print (TIP), 103, 106

Therapeutic alliance
  failure to form, 348
  maintaining, with coerced patient, 551
  psychotherapy, 203
  repairing ruptures, 216–219
Therapeutic impasse, resistance and, 348–349
Therapist for Windows, 671
Therapist Helper, 673
Therapy. *See* Psychotherapy
Theta scores, 116
Third-party relationships, billing, 658–659
Thompson, Robert J., Jr., 406–409
Thought content, in MSE, 10–11
Thought process, in MSE, 10
Thoughts, Multimodal Life History Inventory, 20–21, 23
Throat examination, 52
Thyroid function tests, children, 52, 54
Tic disorders
  DSM-IV, 43
  DSM-IV-TR classification, 81
  in MSE, 9
  pediatric pharmacotherapy, 472–473
Time, therapy, 261
Timeline Followback (TLFB), 73
Time-out routines, emotional safety at home, 381
Timing, therapy termination, 354
TIP (*Tests in Print*), 103, 106
Tobacco, prevalence rates, 481
Tobacco use, stages of change, 228
Tompkins, Michael A., 319–324
Topiramate, 463
Tort, definition, 576
Tourette's disorder
  DSM-IV, 43
  pediatric pharmacotherapy, 468, 472–473
  prevalence of, 6
Tourette's Syndrome Association, 516
Toxicology lab values, 444
Training. *See also* Education and training programs
  ethical standards, 537–538
  restraint and seclusion, 556
Tranquilizers, prevalence rates, 481
Transcendence, Values in Action (VIA) classification, 96
Transference, 347, 389
Transmission, human immunodeficiency virus (HIV), 292
Traumatic brain injury (TBI)
  mild, 342
  moderate to severe, 342–343
Traumatic exposure, 250
Trazodone, 454, 455, 462
Treatment
  accuracy of clinical judgment, 24
  approaches, 222–225
  attention-deficit/hyperactivity disorder (ADHD), 62
  behaviorally disordered children, 401–405
  bisexuals, 301–303
  borderline personality disorder, 255–257
  child sexual abuse, 430–435
  choice of format, 363–365
  clients' rights, 181, 182, 183
  erectile failure, 284–285
  female sexual dysfunction, 286–291
  gay men, 301–303
  guidelines for treating women, 295–298
  herbal for psychological disorders, 517–521
  high-conflict couples, 378–383
  insomnia, 325–327
  lesbians, 301–303
  male sexual dysfunction, 282–286
  marital infidelity, 384–387
  normative male alexithymia, 280
  psychoeducational groups (PEGs), 393–398
  psychotherapy manuals, 192–199
  self-help groups, 502–506
  substance abuse, 263–266
  suicidal patient, 240–245
  vaginismus, 289
Treatment matching
  psychotherapy, 222–225
  substance abuse, 264–265
Treatment of Depression Collaborative Research Program (TDCRP), 216
Treatment planning
  benefits, 23–233
  development, 233–236
  diagnosis determination, 235
  ethnic minority children, 47–49
  goal development, 234
  historical background, 232
  individuality, 235–236
  intervention creation, 235
  mental health records, 650
  objective construction, 234–235
  problem definition, 234
  problem selection, 234
Treatment populations, cognitively impaired adults, 342–344
Trial vs. settlement, professional liability coverage, 629–630
Trichotillomania, prevalence of, 6
Tricyclic antidepressants (TCAs), 454, 455, 460, 461
TRIN (True Response Inconsistency), MMPI-2, 130, 131

True Response Inconsistency (TRIN), MMPI-2, 130, 131
Trzepacz, Paula T., 7–12
T scores, 112–114
Twelve-step approach
  intervention, impaired psychologist, 623
  self-help, 505
  substance abuse, 264, 265
Type A characteristics, Anxiety Management Training (AMT), 272

ULA (unconditional life-acceptance), 215
Unconditional life-acceptance (ULA), 215
Unconditional other-acceptance (UOA), 213, 215
Unconditional self-acceptance (USA), 212–213, 215
Unemployment, suicide risk, 65
Unethical colleague, confronting, 579–583
Unipolar major depression, *DSM-IV*, 43
United Cerebral Palsy Association, 516
University of Minnesota Press, 110
Unruliness, MACI, 163
UOA (unconditional other-acceptance), 213, 215
Urge-surfing, 352
Urine lab values, 443
USA (unconditional self-acceptance), 212–213, 215
Utilization rate, 668
Utilization review checklist, 652–653

Vacuum erection device (VED), 285
Vaginismus, treatment, 289
Valerian, sleep, 520
Validation, Rorschach scores, 171
Validity
  psychological testing report, 117
  Rorschach assessment, 174–175
Validity assessment guidelines, MMPI-2, 131
Valproic acid, 457, 463, 480
Values in Action (VIA) Classification of Strengths, 93–97
VandeCreek, Leon, 612–615
Van Male, Lynn M.
  female sexual dysfunction, 286–291
  male sexual dysfunction, 282–286
VantageMed, 673
Varela, R. Enrique, 249–254
Variable Response Inconsistency (VRIN), MMPI-2, 130, 131
Vasquez, Melba J. T., 63–66
Venlafaxine, 454, 455, 462, 470–471, 480
Vernberg, Eric M., 249–254
Vertigo, medical conditions that may present as, 452
Vicarious liability, definition, 576
Victimhood, marital infidelity, 386
Victimization, sexual, 287
Vineland Adaptive Behavior Scale–Third Edition, 127
Violence. *See also* Anger
  aggression after disasters, 252
  decision making with dangerous clients, 612–614
  family, 376
  high-conflict couples, 379–380
  relapse prevention, 350–353
  risk assessment, 605–606
  self-help groups, 509, 510, 513
  women survivors, 298
Violence Prediction Scheme (VPS), 605
Violence Risk Assessment Guide (VRAG), 605–606
Violent ideas, in MSE, 11
Vision testing, children, 53
Visuoconstructional ability, in MSE, 12
Visuospatial functions, neuropsychological assessment, 36
Vital signs, 52
Voluntary intervention, impaired psychologist, 622–623
Voluntary movement, in MSE, 8
VRAG (Violence Risk Assessment Guide), 605–606
VRIN (Variable Response Inconsistency), MMPI-2, 130, 131

Waist circumference (WC), 445, 447
Waiver, definition, 576
Wanton, definition, 576
Ware, Janice, 119–123
Warnings in psychopharmacology, 460–465
Weapons, dangerous patients, 614
WebMD, Internet site, 493–494
Wechsler Intelligence Scale for Children-IV, 126
Wechsler Preschool and Primary Scale of Intelligence-III, 125
Wechsler subtests, 112–114
Wedding, Danny, 497–501
Wegener, Stephen T., 342–346
Weight
  assessment tools, 445–447
  Shape Up America!, 515
Weight loss, medical conditions that may present as, 451–452
Weight management, treatment manuals, 196
Weiner, Irving B., 173–177
Well-being, ginseng for, 519
Western Psychological Association, 700
Western Psychological Services, 110
White, Joanne, 236–239
Wide Range, 111

Wide Range Assessment of Memory and Learning-II (WRAML-2), 126
Wiens, Arthur N., 13–16
Wilens, Timothy E., 466–476
Wilkinson, Ron, 192–202
Willful, definition, 576
Williams, Oliver B., 220–225
Wisdom, Values in Action (VIA) classification, 96
Withdrawal, substance abuse, 458–459
Witkiewitz, Katie, 350–353
Witnesses, children, 418
Women. *See* Females; Gender issues
Wood, James M., 169–172
Woodcock-Johnson Psychoeducational Battery III, 126
Woody, Jennifer K. H., 308–312
Woody, Robert H.
  defending against legal complaints, 560–566
  refusal skills training (RST), 308–312
Work reentry, impaired psychologist, 623–624
WRAML-2 (Wide Range Assessment of Memory and Learning-II), 126
Writing, in MSE, 10

Yalom, Victor J., 388–393
Yanick, Kathryn, 220–225
Yearbook of American and Canadian Churches, 338
Y-ME National Breast Cancer Organization, 516
Youth, Values in Action Inventory of Strength (VIA–Youth), 97

Ziprasidone, 465
Zuckerman, Edward, 670–673

WHAT DO YOU WANT IN THE NEXT EDITION?

The second edition of the *Psychologists' Desk Reference* has attempted to organize and present the most frequently requested materials for practicing psychologists. We conducted considerable research to secure a consensus on what information practitioners desire to have at their desks. In all, we spent several years determining the optimal content and proper mix of the *Psychologists' Desk Reference.*

At the same time, we realize that individual clinicians hold different preferences and that practice requirements evolve rapidly. For these reasons, we cordially invite you, the reader, to inform us of what you would like to be included in future editions. Kindly send us an e-mail message (koocher@simmons.edu and norcross@scranton.edu) containing your suggestions. If you are the first to suggest a new chapter that makes it into the next edition, we shall send you a complimentary copy—as we did to nine colleagues who recommended new chapters that appeared in this edition.

In the meantime, we wish you and your patients the very best of health and happiness.

Gerry P. Koocher, Ph.D.
John C. Norcross, Ph.D.
Sam S. Hill III, Psy.D